benedicat dōmi

be de bita sunt tibi dan da

cia sunt re so nan da.

t referanda. Organa ꝯ Hec quoq; splen

randa. Organa ꝯ Tam pia tam bona

EVROPA MVNDI PARS QVARTA

Iulio cesare imperante · a theodoto dimensa · nominatur pars tercia ·
Sed uere est quarta · na asia etiam partes diuisa affrica tercia · europa
habet europa maria XI · insulas XL · prouincias XX · ojontes XXVI · habet
aute opida CXX · flumina XXI · Gentesq; diuersas numero XXIIII ·
Regna uq ue si colore rubeo circuscripta ad romano frocoq pertine m iu
Evropa dicta e ab europa filia agenoris regis lybie · uxoris iouis ·

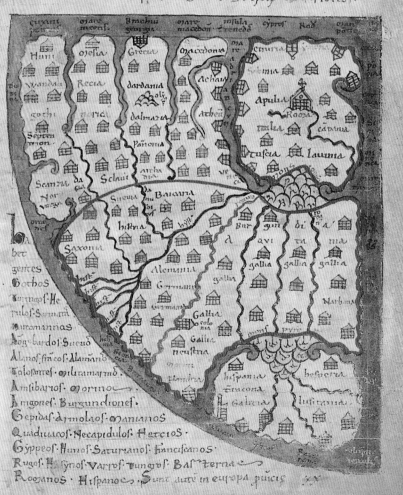

ba
bet
gentes
Gothos
Turnos · He
rulos · Sarmata
Marcomannas
Longobardos · Sueuo
Alanos · fracos · Alamano
Tolosentes · militamay mo
Amsibarios · Morinos
Ingones · Burgundiones ·
Gepidas · armolaos · Marianos
Quadiuacos · Necapidulos · Hercios ·
Gyppeos · Hunos · Saturianos · franciscanos ·
Rugos · H iynos · Varros · tungros · Basiterna
Rocanos · Hispanos · Sunt aute in europa pricis

The Christian West and its Singers

THE FIRST THOUSAND YEARS

Christopher Page

Yale University Press   New Haven and London

Designed by Gillian Malpass

Printed in China

Library of Congress Cataloging-in-Publication Data

Page, Christopher, 1952–
The Christian west and its singers : the first thousand years /
Christopher Page.
p. cm.
Includes bibliographical references and index.
ISBN 978-0-300-11257-3 (cl : alk. paper)
1. Church music–To 500. 2. Church music–500–1400. I. Title.
ML2902.P34 2010
782.3209–dc22

2009035843

A catalogue record for this book is available from
The British Library

Page i
Two young men with scrolls, possibly liturgical readers.
Gold-glass image of the fourth or fifth century

Frontispiece
The earliest map of western Europe as a geopolitical entity.
A map of 'Europe, the fourth part of the world' in the autograph manuscript of
the *Liber Floridus* of Lambert of St-Omer, completed in 1120.
The red line, drawn by Lambert and corresponding to no 'natural' frontier,
circumscribes the '*imperium* of the Romans and the Franks'.
Ghent, Bibliotheek van de Universiteit, MS 92, fol. 241ʳ.

For Anne

Non, tu n'as pas mené la charrue et tu n'as pas frappé avec le fléau. Mais le premier grain de blé, c'était toi.

Marcel Pagnol, *Regain.* After Jean Giono

The toil which stole from thee so many an hour
Is ended . . .

Shelley, *The Revolt of Islam*

Athalongus prbr p illatam sibi cecitate ammonitus querere corpa ciliani sociorq; eu. inuentis scorum corporib; uisu recepit. ea q; re scs Bonefatius moguntie epc ab athalongo ad se relata castrum wirziburch ad honore Ciliani mris qui ad p dicandum ibi a papa Conone epc ordinatus fuerat. ibiq; mortis & quietis locu a do acceptat. epalis sedis priuilegio insigniri decreuit. primumq; ibi epm scm burghardum inuenit. Maruan principatur sarracenis annis xi. Karolomann fr pippini regis rome a zacharia papa in monachu attonsus. primo inserapti mon te incenobio quod ipse fundatur. deinde apud castrum cassinu laudabili uita enituit

Pippinus Griphone frem suu contra se rebellantem. insaxoniam psequitur. Sarraceni intestino bello colliduntur.

Pippinus Grifone insaxonia & eius complices Tassilonem. Landfridu & suidi ger bello uictos capit. & Tassilonem quide Baioarie duce facit. Griphoni uero inneustria xii. comitatus concedit. qd illi n sufficit. s; ad watfariu in aquitania fugit. In Calabria & sitilia fit pestilentia & mortalitas hominu nimia. Inuestib; hominu & inuelis eccliaru apparent crucicule quasi oleo designate.

Rachis langobardoru rex dum rupto federe romam inquietare nititur. a zacharia papa non solum a malo reprimitur. sed etiam eius instinctu cu uxore & filiis romam ueniens. monachus efficitur. cui haistulfus frater eius substitutus regnat annis. vii.

Baldricus rex francoru in monachu tonsoratur. pippinus uero princeps auctoritate aplica & francoru electione a sco Bonefacio moguntie archiepo in regem ungitur. & consecratur. & regnat annis. xviii. post annos circiter. lxxxviii. p qua maiores domi cepunt principari sup reges francorum.

Pippinus rex contra saxones pugnat. Gripho frater pippini pimitur. & Re migi eiusde pipini regis fr rodomensis archiepc ingallia claret. Pippin rex galliarum ecclias cantib; romane auctoritatis studio meliorauit.

Stephanus. lxxxvii. romane ecctie psidet. Maruia amira pempto. muhamad principatur. sarracenis annis. v. Haistulpho langobardoru rege contra roma nos adeo grardescente ut tributum exigeret ab uniuscuiq; capite. stephs papa ad expetendu pippini regis auxiliu cogitur infranciam uenire. Qui inueniendo

CONTENTS

facing page   The revised edition of Sigebert's chronicle (detail of Pl. 62)

PREFACE AND ACKNOWLEDGEMENTS

WHEN SOME MATERIAL FROM THIS BOOK was presented at a seminar in the University of London, Professor Michael Clanchy remarked that previous books of mine 'were written for professionals but also considered the needs and interests of common readers *like myself*'. Long after the event, it still strikes me as remarkable that the author of *From Memory to Written Record* (1979), surely one of the most influential works of medieval scholarship written in recent times, should consider himself a common reader of books on any medieval matter. Nonetheless, I have encountered similar sentiments from distinguished medievalists in other fields time and again when they speak of musicology. It is a frequent and well-founded claim of musicologists, and especially of those working on the Middle Ages, that other scholars (to say nothing of Common Readers in the more familiar sense) generally regard musicology as an esoteric study with little of the valency necessary for combinations with other subjects and disciplines to form. Even a great master of the musicological art like Kenneth Levy finds himself reminded, in a review of his collected papers by a distinguished early-medieval historian, that 'those preoccupied with the books containing music from [the Carolingian] period must necessarily engage . . . with Carolingian and Ottonian culture as a whole'.

I have no ambition to engage with the Carolingian or any other cultural period *as a whole*, but I have endeavoured to place the history of singers, in so far as it can be reconstructed, in the context of social, political and economic developments. Thus Chris Wickham's monumental *Framing the Early Middle Ages: Europe and the Mediterranean 400–800*, or Michael McCormick's equally magisterial *Origins of the European Economy AD 300–900* have been by my side as often as the indispensable works of musicologists in the medieval field. The evidence relating to Christian ritual singers in the first millennium is intelligible only in relation to a wide panorama of social, political, economic and linguistic contexts, in addition to the many liturgical issues that have been much studied in the past where I must bow to the experts. I have tried to adjust the contextual frame and the central picture of singers so that they are in proportion to one another, but such questions of balance are largely a matter of personal judgement and I doubt if the result here will be to the satisfaction of every reader. On the other hand, I have sometimes deliberately risked such opinion by attempting to expand the corpus of evidence and the scope of the issues deemed relevant to the stated subject. Thus the silencing of the layman's voice in liturgical singing, for example, except in simple responses and litanies, is treated here as a fundamentally linguistic issue in the history of Latin, which was the language (but not always necessarily the exclusive language) of the Western liturgies.

In some other books written long before this one, I bore in mind the needs and interests of the Common Reader in the more familiar sense: the layman with a non-specialist interest in the history of Western music. I have tried to write this one also with a readership in mind extending somewhat beyond the confines of the musicological guild where, despite having been trained in medieval literature and philology, I have long been accorded a better welcome than I deserved. My colleagues among musicologists will, I hope, find some emphases, ideas and (especially) some new literary and epigraphic sources in these pages that they can build, here and there, into their own work. I would not presume to hope for more.

Although contemplated long before, this book developed from the Royal Holloway–British Library Lectures in Musicology that I gave in 2004–5 under the title 'Music and the Making of Europe'. I am most grateful to Professor Jim Samson for the invitation to give those talks. I have incurred many other obligations, reaching back nearly a decade. Mary and Richard Rouse provided hospitality in Los Angeles when parts of Chapter 21 were presented as the History of the Book Lecture for 2005 at UCLA, and they discussed many points with me. Professor Stephen Jaeger's invitation to give a lecture at the University of Illinois gave me the chance to discuss a number of matters with two experts on late antique Gaul, Danuta Shanzer and Ralph Mathisen, as well as the chance to benefit from the advice of Margot Fassler. Miri Rubin has been a constant source of encouragement and kindly translated for me some modern scholarly material from the Hebrew. It was also a piece of very good fortune when Rosamond McKitterick accepted a Fellowship in my College. During the last year of the work, she has been a fund of advice and good humour at every turn. She kindly agreed to read the chapter on Pippin, and a trespasser in the field of Carolingian studies could not hope for more. It was a similar stroke of good fortune when John Smith joined the College for a term as a Visiting Fellow; anyone who knows his fine series of meticulous articles on the earliest Christian psalmody, and on the psalmody of the Temple, will appreciate what an advantage it was to be able to discuss matters with him on a daily basis. He kindly read much of the earlier part of the book. For specialist advice on particular chapters, I profited much from the Revd Dr Peter Waddell's reading of Chapters 2 and 3, from Jim Adams's comments on substantial parts of Chapter 5. Greg Woolf did excellent service reading Chapter 1 on Roman communications (what will we do when all the classicists are gone?). David Hiley read an early draft of the material on *Gregorius presul* and called my attention to Tom Kelly's useful checklist of composers (see

Appendix to Chapter 19). Professor Jonathan Conant read the material on Vandal Africa and shared with me chapters from his forthcoming book on late antique and early medieval Africa. Susan Rankin offered me hospitality several times in her home, where she hosts seminars on plainsong, and I am most grateful to her and to the members of the seminar, especially Jessie Billett, Sam Barrett and the late David Chadd. Alejandro Planchart gave advice about the liturgy for Saint Martin and Michel Huglo, through Barbara Haagh, kindly sent me his (then) unpublished work on the León antiphoner. Peregrine Horden, prince of polymaths and yet so clubbable with it, gave me invaluable advice on medieval hospitals for Chapter 22. Alice Rio generously allowed me to read material from her forthcoming book on Frankish formularies 500–1000. For help and advice of various kinds I am also very grateful to Charles Brittain, Andreas Bucher, Sylvain Destephen, Nancy van Deusen, Eamon Duffy, David Dumville, Robin Flower, Emma Hornby, Sarah James, Jochen Johrendt, Tom Kelly, Michael Lapidge, Thomas F. X. Noble, Hérold Pettiau, Joyce Reynolds, Nicholas Rogers, Sebastian Sobecki, the late John Stevens, Andrew Wallace-Hadrill, Roger Wright and Neil Wright.

I owe a unique debt of gratitude to Joseph Dyer, who read the entire book, and to Leofranc Holford-Strevens, who read Parts I and II. They detected many errors and infelicities. I am responsible for those that remain. I am also much indebted to Gillian Malpass, at Yale University Press, who believed in this book from the beginning. One of the blessings of publishing with Yale was Gillian's readiness to grant me the copy-editor of my choice – indeed, of my dreams: Bonnie J. Blackburn. Never was an author's assurance that he is responsible for any mistakes which remain in his work better justified. I owe her an inestimable debt. I would also like to thank Jacquie Meredith for her meticulous work on the proofs, and Alistair Warwick for preparing the musical examples.

During the last nine months of work, Professor Richard Penty took over my duties as Vice-Master of my College in Cambridge at a time when the burden of administration was high. I owe an immense debt to him. I am also very grateful to my colleagues in the Faculty of English in the University of Cambridge, especially to Professor Helen Cooper, for shouldering various burdens during that same period. The staff of the University Library in Cambridge, especially Morag Law, Colin Clarkson, Lucas Elkin, Michael Fuller, Neil Hudson, Paul Hudson and Godfrey Waller, have helped me on a daily basis more than I can say. A project like this one necessarily draws upon many resources abroad, but I would like to make special mention of the prompt assistance received from the staff of the Hessische Landes- und Hochschulbibliothek in Darmstadt, the Sint-Adalbertabdij (Egmond-Binnen); the Pastoraal Centrum of the Grootseminarie in Mechelen, the Stiftsbibliothek in Sankt Gallen, the Bibliothèque de la Faculté de Médecine in Montpellier, the Bibliothèque de la Société Archéologique (Musée des Arts Anciens du Namurois) in Namur, the Stadtbibliothek/Stadtarchiv in Trier, the Bibliothèque municipale in Valenciennes, the Bibliotheek der Rijksuniversiteit in Utrecht, the Herzog August Bibliothek in Wolfenbüttel and the Zentralbiliothek in Zürich.

Friends have made a great contribution. Claire Preston and Kevin Jackson have offered their hospitality at Moosebank many times. Clive Wilmer, who read an early draft of the introduction, Richard Humphreys, Martin Wallen and Stephen Romer have been ready to lend a sympathetic ear. I owe a special debt to David, Christine and Rachel Skinner. David has always been prepared to take time off from his duties and give me help, especially with the images. He and his family have been loyal friends all the way through. It has also been one of the blessings of my life to spend many days with professional singers, sharing with them the slings and arrows of outrageous accommodation on the road. It was hard to leave them so that work on this book could continue uninterrupted, and I thank Catherine King, Charles Daniels, Rogers Covey-Crump, Leigh Nixon, Margaret Philpot, Emma Kirkby, Paul Agnew, Larry Charlesworth, Don Grieg, Stephen Harrold and Julian Podger. They were ever the best of singers and friends.

To Marie-Claude Thomas, her husband, Williams, and Mamie, Dédée Salva, I owe a debt beyond all repayment. It is thanks to them that I was able to draft much of this book near the ancient Roman city of Nîmes, going into the garden to hear the *Angelus* at noon and leaving their house in the village of Courbessac only to lunch within yards of the Roman amphitheatre. That Marie-Claude is also the mother of my wife, Anne, *une Nîmoise*, to whom this book is dedicated, is also decidedly in her favour.

Christopher Page
Cambridge
Michaelmas 2009

Preface to the Second Printing

Some misprints and slips have been rectified in this printing. I am especially grateful to Professor David Hiley and to Clifford Bartlett for bringing a number of these to my attention.

Cambridge
Easter 2012

PLATES

FIGURES

MAPS

MUSIC EXAMPLES

Music engraved by The Art of Music, Dunblane, Scotland

ABBREVIATIONS

AMS	*Antiphonale Missarum Sextuplex*, ed. Dom R.-J. Hesbert (Brussels, 1935)
AH	*Analecta hymnica Medii Aevi*, 55 vols (Leipzig, 1886–1922)
AS	*Acta Sanctorum*, 68 vols (Brussels and Antwerp, 1643–1940)
Bauer–Danker	W. Bauer and R. W. Danker, *A Greek–English Lexicon of the New Testament and Other Early Christian Literature*, 3rd edn (Chicago, 2000)
BHL	*Bibliotheca Hagiographica Latina Antiquae et Mediae Aetatis*, 3 vols (Brussels, 1900–1). *Novum Supplementum*, ed. H. Fros (Brussels, 1986)
BNF	Bibliothèque nationale de France
CCCM	Corpus Christianorum Continuatio Mediaevalis
CCM	Corpus Consuetudinum Monasticarum (Sieburg, 1963–83)
CCSA	Corpus Christianorum Series Apocryphorum
CCSL	Corpus Christianorum Series Latina
ChLA	Chartae Latinae Antiquiores (Olten, 1954–)
CIL	*Corpus Inscriptionum Latinarum* (Berlin, 1863–)
CLA	*Codices Latini Antiquiores: A Palaeographical Guide to Latin Manuscripts Prior to the Ninth Century*, ed. E.A. Lowe, 11 vols (Oxford, 1934–66)
CSEL	Corpus Scriptorum Ecclesiasticorum Latinorum
CSM	Corpus Scriptorum de Musica
C.Th.	*Theodosian Code. Codex Theodosianus. Theodosiani libri XVI cum Constitutionibus Sirmondianis et leges novellae ad Theodosianum Pertinentes*, ed. Th. Mommsen, 2 vols (Berlin, 1905)
DACL	*Dictionnaire d'archéologie chrétienne et de liturgie* (Paris, 1907–53)
DMA	Divitiae Musicae Artis Schola Palaeographica Amstelodamensi Conspirante Collectae, ed. J. Smits van Waesberghe (Buren, 1975–)
EH	Eusebius, *Ecclesiastical History*, ed. and trans. K. Lake, 2 vols (Loeb Classical Library; London and New York, 1926 and 1932)

GELS	*A Greek–English Lexicon of the Septuagint*, ed. J. Lust, E. Eynikel and K. Hauspie, 2 vols (Stuttgart, 1992–6).
GS	*Scriptores Ecclesiastici de Musica Sacra Potissimum ex Variis . . . Codicibus Manuscriptis Collecti*, ed. M. Gerbert, 3 vols (St. Blasien, 1784; repr. Milan, 1931)
HMT	*Handwörterbuch der musikalischen Terminologie*, ed. H.H. Eggebrecht (Wiesbaden, 1972–2007)
ICUR	*Inscriptiones Christianae Urbis Romae*, ed. J.-B. de Rossi, 2 vols (Rome, 1857–61 and 1888); revised and expanded as *Inscriptiones Christianae Urbis Romae Septimo Saeculo Antiquior Nova Series*, ed. A. Ferrua, 10 vols (Rome, 1935–)
ILCV	*Inscriptiones Latinae Christianae Veteres*, ed. E. Diehl, 3 vols (Berlin, 1924–31); vol. 4, *Supplementum* (Dublin, 1967); and *Nuove correzioni alla silloge de Diehl*, ed. A. Ferrua (Vatican City, 1981)
JAMS	*Journal of the American Musicological Society*
JECS	*Journal of Early Christian Studies*
LHD	*Gregorii Turonensis Libri Historiarum decem*, ed. B. Krusch and W. Levison (MGH SSRM, i (Editio Altera); Hannover, 1951)
LP I, II, III	*Le Liber pontificalis: Texte, introduction et commentaire*, ed. L. Duchesne, 2 vols (Paris, 1866); vol. 3 ed. C. Vogel (Paris, 1955)
LS	*A Greek–English Lexicon*, 9th edn with Supplement, ed. H.G. Liddell and R. Scott (Oxford, 1996)
LRE	A.M. Jones, *The Later Roman Empire*, 2 vols (Oxford, 1964)
MAMA	*Monumenta Asiae Minoris Antiqua*, ed. W.M. Calder, 8 vols (London, 1928–62)
MECL	J. McKinnon, *Music in Early Christian Literature* (Cambridge, 1987)
MGG	*Die Musik in Geschichte und Gegenwart*, 2nd edn, ed. L. Finscher (Kassel and Stuttgart, 1994–2007)
MGH	Monumenta Germaniae Historica
——AA	Auctores antiquissimi
——BdK	Briefe der deutschen Kaiserzeit
——C	Capitularia
——Co	Concilia
——Con	Constitutiones
——CRF	Capitularia regum francorum
——DK	Diplomata Karolinorum
——DRF	Diplomata regum francorum
——DRIG	Diplomata regum et imperatorum Germaniae

——E	Epistolae
——EKA	Epistolae Karolini aevi
——EMA	Epistolae Merowingici aevi
——EMKA	Epistolae Merowingici et Karolini aevi
——L	Legum
——LMN	Libri memoriales et necrologia
——LNG	Leges nationum Germanicarum
——OCC	Ordines de celebrando concilio
——PAK	Poetae Latini aevi Karolini
——SS	Scriptores
——SSRG	Scriptores rerum Germanicarum
——SSRL	Scriptores rerum Langobardicarum et Italicarum
——SSRM	Scriptores rerum Merovingicarum
MLLM	*Mediae Latinitatis Lexicon Minus*, ed. J. F. Niermeyer and C. Van der Kieft, rev. J. W. J. Burgers, 2 vols (Leiden, 2002)
New Grove Online	*New Grove Dictionary of Music and Musicians*, online edn, ed. Laura Macy
OLD	*Oxford Latin Dictionary*, ed. P. G. W. Glare (Oxford, 1968–82)
PG	Patrologiae Cursus Completus Series Graeca, ed. J. P. Migne, 165 vols (Paris, 1857–66)
PL	Patrologiae Cursus Completus Series Latina, ed. J. P. Migne, 217 vols (Paris, 1844–5) with 4 vols of indexes (Paris, 1862–4)
PLRE	*The Prosopography of the Later Roman Empire*, ed. A. H. M. Jones, J. R. Martindale and J. Morris (Cambridge, 1971–)
PM	Paléographie musicale (Saint-Pierre de Solesmes, 1889–)
PMM	*Plainsong and Medieval Music*
RICG	*Recueil des inscriptions chrétiennes de la Gaule antérieures à la . . . Renaissance carolingienne* (Paris, 1975–)
SC	Sources chrétiennes
SEECO	Series Episcoporum Ecclesiae Catholicae Occidentalis (Stuttgart, 1982–)
SSCISAM	Settimane di studio del Centro italiano di studi sull'alto medioevo

V DCLXXXV zenon · ann · xxii · acebalox he
repir opta ħt : -   ⌐pre dicatur : ~
V DCCXII · Anaftarz · ann · xxiii · fulgentur ħt
V DCCXX · lufanz · ann · viii · azebalox hęireg abdicat.
V DCCLVIII luzqniarz · ann · xxxviiii · uudndæ
li cæpit fęqnzuntur .   ⌐cęapiunt .
V DCCLXX · lufanz · ann · xi · apmfni fide xp̄i sus
V DCCLXXVII · Tibfiurz · ann · vii · Aanzubaqidi tca
liam Cæpiunt .   ⌐effecti runt .
V DCCXCVIII · Mumciuf · ann · xci · zothi catholici
V DCCCVI · pocar · ann · viii · nomæni cedunt apr.
V DCCC xxiii · hęiacliuf · ann · xxiii · huiuf
          quinto · & quatto pelezio rirrime .
          prinicipir rire buq In hirpaniu
          ludħ bupta zantur .
          Rericduum rętæie ætatif æn pur
          dõ roli ħt cognitum : - ~

EXPLICIT LIBER QVINVS ·

INCIPIVNT CAPL LIB SEXTI ·

- I·   De nono & uetfu tħcta mento ·
- II·   De feripcoribur & uocæbulr ſcōrū libroum ·
- III· De bibliotecir ·
- IIII· De cæptur · & pħiza menir ·
- V·   De canonibur euanzelioum ·
- VI·   De canonibur Concilioum ·

Annals and chapter headings from the *Etymologies* by Isidore of Seville. Cambridge, Trinity College, MS 368, fol. 25ʳ. Anglo-Saxon, 10th c. The tenth line down refers to the end of Arianism amongst the Visigoths.

INTRODUCTION

W HEN A STRING QUARTET GIVES A RECITAL, perhaps featuring works
that many in the audience regard as masterpieces of Western musical art,
the sounds are produced with a basic raw material of the Asian nomad. Bows
strung with horsehair momentarily bring the world of skin-tents and fermented
mare's milk into a surprisingly happy conjunction with Beethoven's late quartets.
When the four players read the music from staff-notation they use a device of
the twelfth-century song-school, for in its most familiar form, with five parallel
lines, the musical staff records the octave that medieval singers of plainsong were
required to supply, with a few extra notes on either side that might also be
expected of them. These two inventions may have far-flung sources. For all we
know, the musical bow may have come westwards as early as the fifth century –
long before there is any record of it – with the horsemen of Attila, while the staff
may owe something to the scholars of tenth-century Italy who first learned to
move counters marked with Hindu-Arabic numerals on the abacus. The tradition of Western classical music, in the widest sense of the term 'classical', bears
the marks of its long evolution in the curious assembly of peninsulas, islands and
creeks at the Western end of Eurasia commonly called Europe.[1]

To emphasize the importance of Christian worship to the development of
Western music, as I do in the title of this book, is not to narrow this field of
vision or to commandeer the musical tradition of the Western world for any particular group. Nor is it to suggest that Western music developed in some kind
of ethnic or cultural enclosure. By recognizing the importance of the Christian
heritage we trace the roots of European music down to eastern Mediterranean
levels in antiquity where singers in the service of many different Christian groups
are taking their place in the soundscape beside the psalmists of the Jewish gatherings and the hymnodists that sang for the many different cults of the Romans.
All these singers may have shared a commonwealth of musical techniques, to
judge by the want of any suggestion in the first three centuries of the churches
that it was considered essential to define a distinctively Christian musical idiom.
As the new faith spread in the western Roman Empire, first to Greek-speaking
communities and then to Latins, the end of imperial power and the rise of
separate kingdoms created a situation in which singers serving churches or

inhabiting monasteries, inheritors of a Mediterranean musical legacy, became the only constituency of musicians in the Occident whose duties were made easier by the use of written texts and eventually by the creation of forms of notation. This is the principal source of literate music-making in the West.

Despite the abundant evidence that Christians between the first century and the fourth were rethinking some fundamental categories of social and political life in the eastern Mediterranean, they did not wander so far from the heritage of Jewish psalmody in the home, or in the Temple, as to suppose that their gatherings should be without song. They could not. Christians hoped that the righteous would eventually stand, in some form of bodily life, before the throne of God, where the only imaginable alternative to ecstatic praise was the disobedience of Satan and the rebel angels. Christians were therefore making a pilgrimage through a temporary world, which was not their true home, to an eternal liturgy. The kingdom of God was at hand and the work had already begun; they should begin their liturgy now in preparation for the future time when the righteous would join the angels, imagined in the Jewish manner as eternal hymnodists. Allusions to the psalmody of Christian groups already appear in the New Testament, and continue with references by writers such as Tertullian to the practices of families and households convened for worship in private homes. For anything beyond community singing it must have already mattered who the appointed singers were, just as it mattered what they sang, and by the fourth century some wealthier cathedrals in eastern Asia Minor already acknowledged a ministry of ritual song, although the bishops of the churches were not inclined to give the singers too much status, and certainly not as much as they desired. (The long history of the Church's ambivalent relationship with its singers had begun.) Information for the later centuries of the Western Empire is in many places thin, but by approximately the year 500 singers with a title of office begin to be traceable in cathedral churches of the West.

Even when the records of Western singers in the first millennium are fragmentary, as they generally are, their history can rarely be made to accord with the familiar model of a Roman Empire experiencing a catastrophe. There are still some echoes of Gibbon's famous *Decline and Fall of the Roman Empire*, notably in *The Fall of Rome and the End of Civilization* (2005) by Bryan Ward-Perkins, whose purpose is to address what the author regards as a modern policy of appeasement towards the barbarians. Ward-Perkins argues that the Vandals, Goths and others are often presented today as pacific incomers who oversaw a mutation of late Roman government, rather than as invaders and despoilers. He certainly has a point. The dissolution awaiting every polity that conquers widely in the interests of a core territory – every empire – was especially violent in the case of Western Rome. The central power, keeping its networks of patronage and mutual advantage in place by the blessings of high culture and the offer of lucrative careers, backed by the threat of violence, gradually lost the ability to convince provincials that it was worth paying tax to keep its equally violent competitors in check. Nonetheless, there is much to be said for viewing the kings in Spain, Gaul and Italy as indigenous populations must often have seen them, namely as Romano-barbarians of the kind that the Empire had long been accustomed to employ but who were now largely autonomous and in that sense magnified, not diminished. Thus a king like Clovis (d. 511) no longer seems the scarcely tamed figure of some nineteenth-century art, entering the baptismal font with his axe and with the long hair of his dynasty flowing. He emerges from some recent accounts as a general who reviewed his troops in the Roman manner on a parade ground, although his army was very small by Roman standards, and who inherited the *administratio* of a Roman province, but with a greatly impoverished system of taxation and a considerably greater dependence upon the bishops. This is the kind of Roman-barbarian context where much of the evidence for singers and their activities between 450 and 900 belongs. There is a measure of continuity with the Roman language, religion and imperial ideals, but the consequences of narrowed communications, impoverished taxation and government by household rather than by imperial bureaucracy are very apparent.

The music at the fountainhead of the Western musical experience, Gregorian chant, arose in the late eighth century from complex adjustments in the long-term geopolitics of east and west involving Franks, Romans and Byzantines. The work seems to have begun when the first Carolingian kings of the Franks resolved to import Roman plainsong into certain churches ruled by their kindred, or by their closest *fideles*, and into their royal chapels. The question of the Carolingians' motive for turning to the liturgy and chant of Rome has often been settled with a brief allusion to their politics or their piety. Nonetheless, Charlemagne did not think like Jean-Jacques Rousseau, distinguishing the political domain from the religious, and the familiar view that the Carolingians disseminated Gregorian chant by acting as a central power, sending out court-trained singers to the provinces, is precisely the kind of judgement one might now wish to refine. We shall find the music flowing outwards along lines of blood, loyalty and prayer-brotherhood in a kingdom-wide and cooperative enterprise that continued when the Carolingians were gone. The forces involved were more pervasive, and less sharply associated with a single vested interest, than anything suggested by the notion of a central power at work. Viewed in the long term, as it is here, the Carolingian realm that produced Gregorian chant appears as the largest in a series of Romano-barbarian kingdoms with a certain understanding of their place in Christian history.

Who was a Singer?

According to Venantius Fortunatus, the citizens of sixth-century Poitiers sang and danced outside the walls of their city on feast days of the liturgical year. If there were only more information surviving about them, and about their fellow townspeople elsewhere, then it would perhaps have been possible for a history of singers in the first millennium AD to be written as a history of all who sang. Today, when so much attention is paid to voices formerly silenced or occluded, and when Matthew Arnold's sea of faith continues to recede (at least in Europe) with its 'melancholy, long withdrawing roar', some would no doubt prefer to read a history of such singers rather than of clerics and monks. One day it may be possible to write one; for the present, however, the high road through the most extensive material in literary texts and inscriptions lies with the clerical and monastic singers whose importance for the literate tradition of Western music is considerable.[2]

Often these singers were monks who became abbots of their houses – for talented singers were sometimes gifted in other ways – and yet the question of who was a monk and who was not runs through much of the first millennium and is by no means clarified by the appearance of monastic Rules, most famously the Rule of Saint Benedict, that appear to give an answer. At present, the earliest known individual recorded with the title *monachos* was not a solitary in the desert but a fourth-century villager in Egypt. Monks lived in many different kinds of environment, including some that probably evolved from the urban and domestic asceticism that was already well known to Tertullian in Carthage around the year 200, together with its traditions of house-psalmody. Generally speaking, however, the monks of late antiquity were distinct from the cathedral clergy, with whom they nonetheless had much interaction, notably as singers providing psalmody as a kind of liturgical entr'acte in the urban cathedrals, especially at the extremes of night and day, that gave an ascetic tone to their labours. By the seventh century, however, the distinction had become much less clear, suggesting how little the various Rules, by now in existence, had accomplished to clarify the situation in the general mind. A great basilica or a baptismal church staffed by clergy could be called a *monasterium* in the West for many centuries if the clerics were living some form of common life. Thus the Frankish *monachi* who studied chant with a Roman teacher in the 760s prove to be cathedral clergy of Rouen, members of a secular chapter. As that example suggests, beside the great monasteries of the West that were unmistakably monastic, 'there was a wide, blurred borderland where monks under mixed and various Rules overlapped with the clergy, or were distinguishable but lived in the same establishment'. This reference to 'mixed and various Rules' may reveal the modern historian's desire for a tidy formulation somewhat better than it captures a situation in which acceptance of a Rule, both for monks and clergy, could mark an inclination to a particular form of Christian life and discipline but nonetheless leave a great deal to the workings of conscience and local custom. It is therefore a delicate question what the various monastic Rules and Customaries reveal about the actual practice of monastic life and the place of singers within it, as opposed to what they plainly declare about the many different ideals of monasticism.[3]

A letter in which Charlemagne's father asks a pope whether it is acceptable for women to sing the responsorial psalm in public services suggests that much information about the activity of women singers has been lost. So does the story of Wiborada, the female solitary who astonished a congregation at the abbey of Sankt Gallen by showing that she had learned the elaborate Lenten Tract *Qui habitat* during years of attending Mass. Women will sometimes come into view during the following chapters as teachers of their own or of others' offspring, as house ascetics, as literate wives accepting (perhaps demanding) to live in continent marriages with their clerical husbands, as the founders of monasteries and as patrons in many other ways. Nonetheless, there seems to be no sure sign that the early Church, sometimes visualized today as a paradise of lost equalities, evolved a musical equivalent of the deaconess, and material from later ages is not extensive. For the most part, the chance simply does not arise to turn from male lectors and cantors to a female counterpart with a suitably elegiac line from John Keats: *Think not of them, thou hast thy music too.*

This book is principally based upon literary sources such as chronicles, Lives of saints, letters and charters, with a particular emphasis (where possible) upon the curiously neglected evidence of epigraphy. This allows regions of the Romano-barbarian West to come into prominence that have almost no profile in received histories of Western music and musicians. One could read many recent books and articles, for example, without hearing very much about Vandal Africa or the sixth-century Sueves. There is also something to be learned from archaeologists, who alone have the power to enlarge the base of source material. It may seem unlikely that the rim of an amphora dredged from the mud of Carthage harbour can have much to reveal about the singers of Vandal Africa, and in precise terms, of course, it does not. Yet the question of how extensively the lands of old Roman Africa remained in touch with the north in the centuries before Islam took them out of the Latin-Christian system is a vital part of the context in which these Latin singers, active in what is now Tunisia, pursued their art. A hitherto unexpected amphora or two, suggesting the continuing health of trade routes thought to be moribund, can make a difference.

This book is not about what singers actually sang, and I should explain why. Firstly, and to put the matter with a trenchancy not out of place here, there are no systematic or consolidated records of Western musical notation for about nine-tenths of the period announced in the title of this book. There are Greek materials from the ancient world through to the celebrated Oxyrhyncus Hymn and beyond, but I suspect that only a lifetime's expertise in Greek musical remains will suffice to interpret them correctly. Secondly, I am not a liturgist.

Some scholars who *are* historians of chant and liturgy have concluded that certain configurations of words, melodies and readings are likely to be very archaic, perhaps testifying to liturgical states that are hundreds of years older than the earliest manuscript sources with music. Such arguments are based upon considerations of musical style, upon similar or identical liturgical assignments in different rites, and upon other criteria that are too complex to summarize. Do the three chants of the Paschal Vigil, which share the same melody and have non-psalmic texts drawn from the Old Testament, carry us back 'aux origines du chant liturgique de l'antiquité tardive'? I wish I knew the answer or were qualified to make a guess. The field of chant study is a highly specialized one that novices stray into at their peril. What is more, even novices may suspect that there is no way of finally discovering what relation there may be, if any, between music preserved in sources from *c.*900 onwards and the practices of Christian singers at a very much earlier date. There are many other gaps in the musical record, all of them familiar to those who work in this field. It remains a mystery just how much of the Franks' indigenous Gallican chant was absorbed into the Gregorian repertory, or how extensively Roman chant of the eighth century was absorbed into the same Gregorian alchemy. The Visigothic repertory is mostly indecipherable. Until the notated records begin – and to a large extent even then – we stand on a slender shore facing an ocean of uncertainty that requires the courage of Odysseus from any who would venture upon it.[4]

A final word is necessary about annotation and bibliographical coverage. One reader of this book in typescript asked that more of the original texts be given. In an ideal world that would be done, but while many may wish this book were better, none will wish it longer. The days of A. H. M. Jones's two-volume study *The Later Roman Empire 284–602*, with its massive citations of textual sources in the original, are long gone. I hope the two appendices attached to Chapters 3 and 19 will suffice in addition to what the notes provide. For annotation, I have decided to follow the practice of ending a paragraph, where necessary, with a note giving a bibliographical conspectus of the material there discussed. This avoids littering the page with numbers, so unlovely to the eye (and one of the most transparent forms of academic defensiveness) in favour of a system that is good enough for Brown's survey of the late Roman Empire in the east, *Gentlemen and Officers*, and therefore seems good enough for me. On the question of coverage, every month scholars in Europe and America publish astonishing amounts of research relevant to the various concerns of this book. The material on the first three hundred years of Christianity alone is colossal. The pile of material on plainsong and liturgy is nearly as large. Only at the last moment, for example, did I finally get to see Andreas Pfisterer's *Cantilena Romana* (still, as I write this, not available in any Cambridge library). There I discovered some important parallel lines of research, notably in the matter of the Roman *schola cantorum* and the importance of certain inscriptions for assessing when that 'institution' began. Joseph Dyer's fine article on the boy singers of the Roman *schola cantorum* came to me after the book was submitted – a gift from the author – but not too late to be included. No doubt I have missed a great deal, as readers who specialize in various fiefs of the great domain surveyed here will soon discover. Some of the omissions are surely egregious, and for those I must apologize. To compare great things with small, I can only repeat the words Chaucer uses when he apologizes for his work. Like him, 'I wold ful fain have seid bettre if I hadde had konninge'.

PART I

MEDITERRANEAN BEGINNINGS:
LECTOR AND CANTOR

D URING THE BRIEF PERIOD THAT Pliny the Younger was governor of
Bithynia and Pontus, in 111–12, he interrogated a group of Christian
prisoners to satisfy himself that they had not offended against his recent edict
banning clubs and associations that might acquire a political slant. Reporting
subsequently to Trajan, Pliny recorded that the Christian prisoners brought
before him had given an account of their meetings. They said that they convened
before dawn on Sundays, when they were accustomed to sing a hymn of praise
(*carmen*), and that they met subsequently to share a common meal. Perhaps to
confute the rumour that Christians indulged in cannibalism at these gatherings,
and certainly to emphasize that they were blameless in their collegiate dining, the
prisoners insisted that they ate perfectly innocent food when they gathered for
this second assembly of the day. Like many others in the first and second centuries, Pliny thought the Christians very strange. So they were in many respects,
but they were not so strange that they repudiated the use of ritual song. Like
Roman polytheists with their processional hymns as they paraded to cultic
centres, or the Jews with their Temple psalmody, Christians knew the power of
the singing voice to lift the mind above the quotidian to the heights of joy, or to
carry it far below to the depths of lamentation. 'Jesus Christ is sung in your
harmony and symphonic love', wrote Pliny's contemporary Saint Ignatius to the
Church of Ephesus, 'and each of you should join the chorus.'

During the second half of the twentieth century it became ever more apparent that terms such as 'Christianity', 'the Church', 'orthodoxy' and 'the
Eucharistic meal' are problematic and to some extent retrospective constructions
imposed upon a diversified landscape of cults and practices. Something similar
may be said for the issue of 'Jewish' as opposed to 'Gentile' identity, or for
'Gnostic' as opposed to 'mainstream' Christians. Texts reflecting forms of
Christian belief once regarded as plainly heretical or marginal, such as the various apocryphal Gospels and Acts, have attracted fresh attention in recent years
and have begun to appear in modern critical editions, notably in the Corpus

1 (*facing page*)   The ruins of Lepcis Magna, Libya.

Christianorum Series Apocryphorum. Some, such as the *Acts of John* or the *Acts of Paul*, are important documents for ritual singing amongst those who regarded themselves as Christians, and while the history of the former text is a distinctly chequered one, the latter was received by Tertullian around 200 and circulated as part of an influential pseudo-Pauline dossier until the fourth century. There can be no return now to the days of 1924 when a great scholar like M. R. James could condemn the 'loose talk' of those inclined to speak up for the importance of apocryphal writings on the grounds that the New Testament canon represents a set of choices that could have been different. Even the days of the late 1980s, when James McKinnon (perhaps echoing M. R. James) repudiated the 'loose speculation' of those seeking to extend the significance of Christ's dance in the *Acts of John*, now seem very far away. It is a sign of how far things have moved, and how fast, that such a master of these arts as McKinnon finds very little space for apocryphal material in his indispensable collection *Music in Early Christian Literature* of 1987 (*MECL*). Today, questions about Christian ritual singers and singing necessarily raise issues of identity. Whose practices are being explored? Why are these practices commanding attention rather than others? In short, there is no 'early Christian' background against which the history of liturgical singers can be written. There is only foreground with singers occupying various positions from the blurred margin to the sharply focused centre.

To find the individuals most directly concerned with singing in the early church we must look to the readers, the lectors. Since the earliest lectors were entrusted with the task of reading the Scriptures, or other works deemed worthy of public declamation, the rise of their ministry owed much to the gradual coalescence of a biblical canon, including the fourfold gospel, towards the end of the second century. Indeed, the office of lector is first traceable in Western (specifically African) sources around 200, approximately the time when the four-fold gospel canon can first be traced, through papyrus fragments, as a coherent scribal project. For further material about singers, the substantial remains of Christian epigraphy, much of it from Rome, prove to be of considerable importance. The common and early Greek term for a Christian liturgical singer, *psaltes*, does not appear in the Latin inscriptions, and *cantor* does not appear until the sixth century in these sources. Readers, however, are abundantly commemorated under the name *lector* in the epigraphic record. As late as the Second Council of Braga, convened in 572 and so towards the end of the period covered in Part 1, bishops were still legislating for lectors whose task was to 'sing or read'.

I

A PROSPECT OF THE SEA:
THE ROMAN CIRCUIT

Prologue: Communications and the Cantor

The singers of the Christian West in the first millennium served an Asian religion spread by traders, artisans and itinerant evangelists using the roads and sea-lanes of the Roman Empire. Like an aerial photograph of fields where a Roman villa once stood, the lowly but important place of singers in Christian worship, during the period covered by this book, reveals the trace of a Christian-Roman polity that had formerly existed on a Eurasian scale, gathering tax revenue from the entire circuit of the Mediterranean and beyond. When the earliest singers called *cantor* as a title of office finally appear, around 500, they are mostly to be found in wealthy port cities of the littoral such as Naples and Marseille, which still counted in what remained of trans-Mediterranean exchange and the Roman maritime system. When power in the West finally passed into the hands of barbarian generals and warlords, many of whom had known periods of Roman military service, the kings had mostly either converted to Christianity (but not necessarily to Catholicism) or were soon to receive baptism, and the most exalted model they knew for the exercise of power was Roman, Christian and imperial, reconfigured on a local scale as a territorial kingship. To be a Constantine writ small, a king needed to know that his bishops were staffing the major churches in the cities of his kingdom, and his own royal chapels, with singers apt for the performance of liturgical song. As early as the 520s, a bishop in Gaul will be found hauling a young man with a fine voice out of his monastery and putting him into royal service.

There was no barbarian wave here to sweep away a Roman order. The general preference today for evoking the 'transformation of the Roman world' where an earlier generation would speak of 'decline and fall' seems quite justified in the domain of liturgical singing. Within the new kingdoms, the regulation of worship lay in the hands of the prelates, and they were often men of Roman lineage in the sense that they could claim descent from indigenous speakers of Latin, perhaps even from ancestors within the curial class of city councillors. Liturgical singers, in other words, were principally answerable to men whom the kings valued precisely because in many respects they still seemed so Roman. For our purposes, therefore, the contrast between Western conditions in 300 and 500 is less to be measured in terms of a catastrophic rupture of the Roman social order – for here there was none – and more in relation to narrowed communications, for that was the inevitable consequence of a vast tributary Empire ceasing to exist in the West. The imperial capital of Rome had grown in symbiosis with conquest; as new lands were subjugated and made subject to taxation, a capital city whose population had long passed the point where it could be nourished from its hinterlands using antique methods of agriculture in conditions of Mediterranean ecology, grew still further. The Roman population is widely assumed to have reached a million by the time of Augustus; only by the conquest of other peoples, and by the exaction of tax in cash or kind, could the imperial authorities guarantee the public doles of bread and grain that were the principal insurance against rioting in the streets. (As the Roman authorities sometimes found to their cost, starving people can sometimes discover remarkable reserves of energy.) The need for extra supplies was partly met by state provision in the form of the *annona*, a term whose narrower sense includes the free or low-priced distribution of grain, olive oil, wine and pork to Romans who were the emperor's clients by virtue of this dole. Massive ships carried grain to Rome from various sources at different times, including Carthage, Alexandria and Sicily, across waters which were apparently safe enough for the transporters in convoy to dispense with a military escort. Shippers contracted to the state, selling their cargo at a fixed price, brought in more, supplemented by others working on their own initiative. The members of the Roman elite came to regard themselves as masters and arbiters of the world's plenty and luxury: consumers who could import from afar what they could not exact within their own borders.[1]

With the gradual passage of imperial power into the hands of the Western warlords on whom Rome had once relied, the state apparatus for moving legions, auxiliaries, kit and supplies in theatres of war from the Atlantic to the Levant faded away. Kings remained with small armies – sometimes barely greater in manpower than a single Roman legion – who might regard a campaign covering 100 miles as a great undertaking and a foray southwards across the Alps as a breach into a zone of dangerously hot weather and pestilence. The consequences of this contraction for the higher refinements of material existence in the West were especially marked in the developing contrast between liturgical opulence and many aspects of daily life as it was generally lived. From the sixth century onwards, clergy and singers performed their liturgical tasks on ecclesiastical islands of luxury, with precious metals for liturgical vessels (even rural priests were not supposed to use ceramic or wooden chalices), dyed textiles for vestments and the costly spice of incense, which liturgy sacrificed in large quantities. Such things were necessary for the celebration of rites whose material culture reached back through imperial Roman ceremony to the cedar forests and spice-fairs of Jews and Gentiles in the Middle East. The costly materials of worship registered the deepening disparity between liturgical appurtenances and the penury of fine goods beyond cathedral, monastery and royal court once the imperial armies and tax revenue had gone, for luxury goods had often travelled with these, like birds on the back of an elephant. A Frankish queen of the early sixth century believed that an impressive show of hangings in the streets might help induce her pagan husband to convert to Christianity; liturgy and worship spelled Roman material culture and insignia of power as surely as the dyed silken cloaks and other costly garments that the Eastern Romans used as diplomatic bargaining counters in their dealings with the Western kings.[2]

The consequences of these contrasts, measured in terms of horizons for movement or the narrowed supply of fine goods, contributed to a north–south dynamic in the recruitment of singers, and in the formation of their repertories, that is traceable throughout the period 500–900. A king might be proud that he was a new breed of Roman governor, no longer answerable to a distant emperor as his predecessors in the governor's palace had been; he might also glory in his command of an ethnicized army of Franks, Vandals or Goths. Nonetheless, his triumphalism rarely eclipsed his sense of being an epigone: a latecomer who had missed the Roman experience and needed to refer back constantly in order to understand the world in which he wielded power and in which his royal office had been created. In the domain of liturgy, this did not mean he expected his bishops or any other influential person in his realm to recruit singers from Rome itself, although there are signs of that being done as early as the seventh century; the point is rather that many liturgical reforms involving the movement or retraining of singers show the subjects of northern kings (and eventually the kings themselves) connecting and reconnecting with regions to the south where the imprint of a Roman, imperial and Christian civilization was believed, rightly or wrongly, to be deeper and more durable. The case cited above from sixth-century Gaul, showing a monk pressed into royal service, reveals a singer from Clermont in the Auvergne going to serve in Reims, Trier and Cologne, considerably further north than the land of his birth. A singer at the cathedral of Metz, a generation later, was probably from Languedoc or Spain, given his Gothic name, and therefore a southern visitor to the Moselle. Another Messine singer at the same time was probably a Greek (see below, p. 231). The Roman singer dispatched around 760 to teach the Frankish cantors at Rouen may have been a Greek-speaking Syrian, suggesting that even in Rome there was a sense that liturgical practice best considered in relation to usages and personnel that reached – as far as one could – towards the eastern Mediterranean where the Christian faith began. The history of singers in the West during the first millennium AD is in many respects the history of communications.

Roman Communications

The *Res gestae* of Augustus, the emperor's account of his achievements intended for public display, is as magnificent in its arrogance as the inscriptions of a Darius or Xerxes. It proclaims the success of Augustus in pacifying territory 'from Cadiz to the mouth of the Elbe', and for imposing an administration that allowed his officials to mount three great enrolments for taxation. In these and many other declarations, Augustus gave passers-by in Rome and other cities much to ponder, but few would have suspected that one of his imperial enrolments would soon figure, albeit unadvisedly, in the history of a very different ruler:

> And it came to pass in those days, that there went out a decree from Caesar Augustus, that all the world should be taxed. And this taxing was first made when Cyrenius was governor of Syria. And all went to be taxed, everyone into his own city. (Luke 2: 1–3)

The impression of historical precision in this passage – the dating of events by reference to an imperial census and the governorship of Cyrenius – is characteristic of Luke's writing in his two-volume history of early Christianity, comprising the third gospel and the Acts of the Apostles. In both, but especially in Acts, Luke conveys a vivid sense of the eastern Mediterranean under Roman governance. He locates events in terms of urban amenities such as a forum, theatre or agora, and populates the cities, ports and ships with fiscal administrators, judges, soldiers, artisans united in proud and defensive corporations, Athenian philosophers, magicians and sailors. The gazetteer of cities, ports and provinces dispersed through Acts is even more extensive than the one Augustus evokes in the *Res gestae*. Not counting roads and other locations in Rome, there are some fifty toponyms in the Augustan proclamation, but Luke uses significantly more. He mentions Roman provinces such as Asia, Bithynia and Galatia; great cities appear including Alexandria, Athens and Damascus, together with the ports of Antioch, Ephesus, Caesarea Maritima, Corinth, Sidon and Tyre. The appearance of a eunuch from the royal court of Ethiopia (meaning the kingdom of Axum) even extends Luke's maritime horizon southwards to the African littoral of the Red Sea.[3]

Christianity did not arise in an obscure corner of the Empire but in a region with many long-distance connections that carried an Asian religion, and an Asian material culture of worship, deep into Europe. The sea currents in the eastern Mediterranean demanded that the essential supplies of grain, brought to Rome from Alexandria, should be taken around the Levantine coast to their final destination. Paul came to Rome, under guard, on a grain ship as it tramped around the eastern Mediterranean on this route, from Alexandria to Rome (Acts 27). The Levantine coast offered an extended series of ports for the onward distribution of luxury commerce arriving from the east. Ebony and Gangetic cotton came in from India, silk from China, white marble from southern Arabia, tortoise shell

2   Stretch of Roman street at Ambrussum (Hérault). In the *Acts of Peter*, the captain who brings Peter to Rome on his ship expresses concern that the apostle 'may be hurt by the shaking' when he takes the paved road from Puteoli to Rome. Given the way Roman roads are often imagined today, as marvels of engineering for the entire Empire, it is surprising to find a paved highway in the very heart of the imperial space presented as a test of endurance to a visitor from the provinces like Peter. Nonetheless, surviving stretches of paved road and street, sometimes with their large stones still showing the ruts created by wheeled traffic, as here, leave no doubt what is meant. It seems that a civilian from a rural province needed time to become accustomed to the rigours of travel on a Roman road.

from ports of trade reaching as far as southern India, frankincense from Arabia and pearls from Arabia or Persis (but also Britain). Behind the Holy Land lay two vast lock gates, the Red Sea and Persian Gulf, where Roman ships were lifted from the Mediterranean into the Indian Ocean, with its immense horizon of maritime opportunities, and then brought back into the Great Sea.[4]

The importance of maritime communications to the Roman polity is thrown into relief by the sidelight of Christianity's success as a missionary religion. Most of the literary sources that show Christianity spreading around the Roman Empire reveal patterns of communication by sea. Some associate it with ships bringing commodities from an eastern port, like the *Acts of Peter*, where the apostle comes from Caesarea Maritima to Puteoli on what seems to be a trading ship. Others associate the spread of the new faith with merchantmen passing out of the Mediterranean down the coast of western Africa, perhaps towards India. Archaeology also suggests the importance of bulk transport to Rome, notably African grain or Spanish oil (see below, Maps 1 and 2). From the composition of the canonical Acts of the Apostles, in the last decades of the first century, to the time of Saint Jerome in the late decades of the fourth, Christian communities were rarely very far from the sight of masts against the skyline or the sounds of a busy wharf. Christianity was the faith of port cities and their immediate hinterlands, or of cities on major rivers.

Rome appears here as the indispensable maritime hub. Acts of the Apostles 28: 13–15 and Paul's Epistle to the Romans both reveal the presence of Christian communities in Rome's harbour of Puteoli and in Rome itself, even before Paul's letter to the communities there. The Trastevere district of Rome, with its wharves and transients, Jewish and Gentile, seems to have been one of the earliest areas of the city where Christians were to be found in some number. Many of them were probably traders and artisans who could travel far to seek work. (Of the twenty-six Christians of Rome named by Saint Paul, at least twelve had visited the East.) The unique position that Rome eventually achieved in Christendom owes much to the provisioning of the city through state-funded transportation moving around the Roman circuit, bringing such people in and sending them out. The capital, anomalously well supplied, was able to extend a duty of care to churches elsewhere. A letter preserved by Eusebius credits Soter (*c.*166–75), an early official in the Roman Church eventually listed as a pope, with the work of 'sending support to many communities in all cities', presumably by supervising the dispatch of food and other material aid to other Christian groups. By this date, the third quarter of the second century, a surplus in cash and kind from virtually the entire Mediterranean circuit passed to Rome as tax, and it was probably quite possible for Christian groups in the city to establish a common fund of generous proportions. No doubt it was enhanced by donations from prosperous members, both within Rome and without, that could include a substantial amount of new money. When Marcion, a shipowner from Pontus, joined the Roman Church in the middle of the second century, he donated 200,000 sesterces to the common fund, implying a yearly income to place him among the upper reaches of the decurions and even the members of the equestrian order. With funds on this scale – but Marcion's donation had to be returned when he was deemed a heretic – the Romans could reserve space with a *navicularius* and ship grain, oil or wine to communities that did not share Rome's measure of security from the consequences of unpredictable variations of climate in the crucial months leading up to the various harvests.[5]

To look beyond Rome, within the western Mediterranean, is to see Carthage, the great city at the other end of the tax spine that gave the western seas their distinctively Roman character. For at least half of the period covered by this book, certain sections of the Mediterranean littoral of Africa are still part of the Roman and post-Roman West. However damaged and worn it became, the great circuit of the Roman shoreline is more visible in the centuries from 200 to 700 than anything one might choose to regard as a proto-Europe ending in the south at the Pillars of Hercules. Carthage and its hinterlands will appear repeatedly in the following chapters, and there are grounds for regarding that city as the cradle of a Latin-speaking Christianity in the West rather than Rome, where Christians

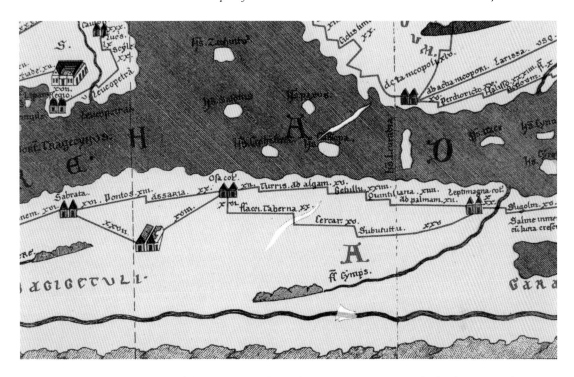

3 Part of the interprovincial coastal highway in Tripolitania between Lepcis Magna and Sabratha, via Tripoli (Oea) as shown in the Peutinger Table, a medieval copy of a 4th-c. original. Elsewhere on the map, a number of the place names on the roads towards Carthage reveal sites where travellers could obtain water (such as *Putea nigrorum*, the 'Well of the Blacks'), some of which probably reflect Roman attempts to build on pre-existing hydrographic works (as in *Ad Cisternas*, 'At the Cisterns'). Leaving the fertile region of Cyrenaica, going west, the stretch shown here runs through the Libyan Desert and looks exceptionally dry. There is only one site labelled *taberna*. The place called *Ad palmam*, twelve Roman miles out of Lepcis, is probably an oasis at what is now Al-Qasabat.

worshipped in Greek until at least the third century (see below, pp. 125–9). The first trace of any New Testament books being read in Latin rather than Greek appears around 180 in Numidia; the earliest reference to the chant later known, in Roman tradition, as the gradual appears some twenty years later in what is now Tunisia, specifically in Carthage. No account of singers being trained to serve a great church in a kingdom is earlier than the one that appears in later fifth-century (and therefore Vandal) Carthage. Contacts between that city and Rome were predominantly maritime of necessity, for between Egypt and Tunisia the traveller is committed to a long tramp along coastal roads that became especially arduous past the fertile margin of Cyrenaica, a trek between the cities of the semi-arid coastal plain, relieved by the intermittent appearance of oases, estates, *tabernae* and the occasional cistern (Pl. 3). The sea-routes were another matter, however, notably the summertime voyages carrying grain, wine and later olive oil from Carthage's port to Rome.

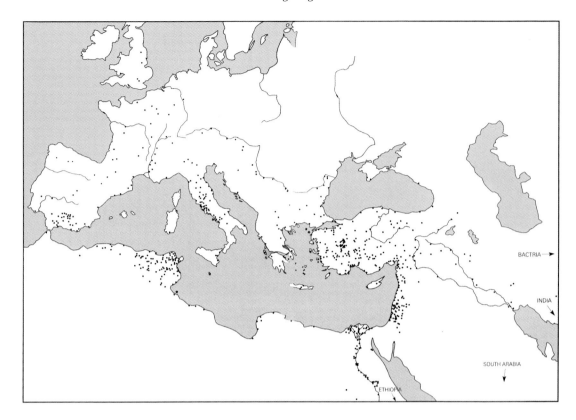

Map 1   Distribution of Christian sites to 325 AD. Adapted from Mullen, *The Expansion of Christianity.*

Map 1 plots the Christian sites currently traceable from literary, epigraphic and other archaeological sources before AD 325. The result is an imperfect picture of conversion by the first quarter of the fourth century, but one that is enough to reveal some notable configurations. The importance of Carthage and its deep hinterland leaps to the eye.[6]

In terms of archaeology, early Christian Africa is difficult to bring into focus. Most of the archaeological work undertaken in North Africa has taken place in Tunisia (first accomplished by the French and then by French-trained Tunisians) and there has been little archaeology, or none at all, in either Algeria or Morocco for some time. Hence it is fortunate that the literary material, including the epigraphy, is relatively abundant. A survey of the seventy-five sites in the relevant Roman province, Africa Proconsularis, reveals that virtually all these locations are more or less satisfactorily established by references in written sources, such as the Acts of martyrs or the Proceedings of the Council of Carthage in 256. Among the various reasons for this remarkable density of martyrs, episcopal sees and other testimonies to Christianity in this part of Roman Africa, the trans-Mediterranean contacts arising from Carthage's position as the redistribution point for grain

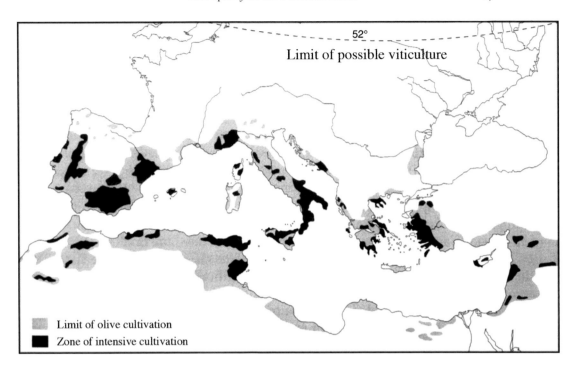

Map 2   The zone of olive cultivation under the Empire, with areas of maximum intensity marked. Adapted from Brun, *Le Vin et l'huile*, 9.

gathered in her hinterlands for annual shipping to Rome must rank fairly high. This was a trade involving many small producers, including makers of transport amphorae for the oil, porters, shippers and smallholders, perhaps offering considerable scope for contact between Roman and African Christians, or between them and potential converts at the kind of social level from which many (but by no means all) early Christians came: dockworkers, drovers, the skippers of river-boats reaching inland to collection centres, local producers, their agents and fieldworkers.

Map 1 may have something more to reveal, and again it lies in the West. There is a marked concentration of sites in southern Spain, mostly contained within the oil-rich province of Baetica Felix. A comparison with Map 2 shows a good match within the necessary limitations and approximations of such charts. The leaders of Christian communities in the Spanish province of Baetica may already have received letters in Greek from their counterparts in Rome as early as the time of Pope Anteros (235–6); if these letters are genuine, they were perhaps carried to their destination by ships passing between Baetica and Rome for the transport of oil. The earliest synod of Western bishops whose proceedings survive, the Council of Elvira (?300–6), took place in the heartland of Baetica's olive-oil industry, still significant at the time of the council although the long-distance market had by now largely collapsed, or at least it has become archaeologically illegible. The kilns for producing the transport amphorae which contained the oil, the collection points for the transit into the Mediterranean then on to Rome, and the Christian churches and cemeteries of Seville, Éjica, Almodóvar del Rio, Cordoba and Cortijos de S. Eufimia, among others, were all strung out together along the navigable reaches of the Guadalquivir and the Genil that provided essential fluvial routes for the oil. The bishops of the Elvira council ruled that prelates, presbyters and deacons should not forsake their churches 'for reasons of trade' (*negotiandi causa*) nor seek 'profitable markets by going round from province to province'. Some of these were perhaps among the small dealers in Baetican oil whose amphorae are widely found.[7]

The movement of military provisions and equipment was also an important stimulus to longer-distance communications. There was some incentive for skippers, the *magistri navium*, to diversify what they carried when they bore essential supplies to the legionary encampments. At times when soldiers were remunerated with coin, the flow of pay and donatives could turn a military fortress into an important source of spending power. Many costly goods such as silk, plain or dyed, and prized foodstuffs such as pepper, probably travelled to the northern regions, even as far as the northern British forts, with bulk movements of materials that agents of the State and subsidized carriers transported along the military routes; this is probably one of the ways in which silk and pepper, for example, reached the end of the run for any Roman trader in northern Britannia. More came with merchants working on their own initiative, like the Syrian Julianos Euteknios who is commemorated in a verse epitaph of the third or fourth century from Lyon. This trader, probably moving on an axis between Lyon and his home city of Laodicea in Syria, is praised in his epitaph for committing himself 'continually to the waves, carrying to the Celts and the lands of the West all the gifts which God instructed the bountiful east to bear'. It is impossible to establish from the inscription whether Julianos was a Christian or a pagan; one can only say that if he were indeed a Christian he could have made many contacts with his coreligionists at major cities along this route by the third or fourth century. The presence of Christian communities at Lyon and Vienne by the late decades of the second century unmistakably shows Christianity passing along the first stages of the Rhône–Rhine system. There was already a bishopric at Cologne by the time of Constantine, and what is perhaps more surprising, there were already Roman military leaders of Frankish descent by the 350s who worshipped in the city's chapels. The Rhône district of this arterial line will also be the heartland of synodal activity in the West between the fourth century and the seventh.[8]

The *Acts of Peter* mentioned above, probably of the second century, shows the apostle travelling to Rome from Caesarea on a merchantman whose cargo is not specified, but since the port of embarkation is Caesarea, the range of possible freight is considerable, including amphorae of oil as a bulk cargo but also textiles,

4   The divine and the hazards of sea travel. A Roman citizen from Beirut, Gaius Julius Tiberinus, a centurion of the first rank (*primipilaris*), pays his vow to Jupiter-Ba'al and to Nemausus, the tutelary deity of Nîmes, with a votive tablet. Having come safely to Nîmes, Gaius Julius Tiberinus was perhaps anxious to thank the presiding deities at either end of the journey in accordance with a promise made before he left Beirut, or during a difficult moment during his travels when there was a danger of shipwreck. Juvenal (*Satires*, 16) mentions painted tablets, in honour of Isis, commissioned by sailors who survived storms at sea. This inscription was discovered in the summer of 1752 near the Jardin de la Fontaine, the principal cult-centre of Nemausus and probably the original location of the tablet. *CIL, Inscriptiones Galliae Narbonensis Latinae*, 3072; 2nd c. The tablet is now in the Musée archéologique de Nîmes.

ivory, spices and exotic woods. When the ship docks at Puteoli, the captain sells off the cargo at the best price he can obtain, suggesting he carried nothing for the state that would be sold for a fixed price. The non-canonical status of the *Acts of Peter* does not diminish the interest or significance of this second-century account of Christian mission, which can perhaps stand for many other voyages carrying Christians aboard floating shops, in effect, that included many light but costly commodities, before reaching a major port and selling off the remaining contents of the hold.[9]

Another apocryphal source, the *Acts of Thomas*, shows an apostle sailing with a merchant named Habban on a return voyage to India from the Levantine coast. Perhaps originally composed in Syriac in the early years of the third century, but surviving complete only in Greek, this account of an apostolic journey can surely be trusted in its report of the faith passing out of the Mediterranean through the channel of the Red Sea. In the early years of the fourth century a stoic philosopher named Pantaenus, a Christian teacher in Alexandria, followed a similar route, travelling as far as India, according to Eusebius (*EH*, v. 10), and it is surely right to suspect he journeyed by sea 'to make contact with Christian groups among the trading communities established in the Persian Gulf and along the Malabar coast'. The Red Sea route appears in the story of Frumentius, a philosopher from Tyre. He set sail to evangelize in 'India' but was attacked as he passed down the Red Sea and then enslaved in the kingdom of Axum, where he rose to become a civil administrator and eventually bishop in the region of the year 330. He even converted the crown prince of Ethiopia. Rufinus, who claims to have derived his account from an eyewitness, reveals how readily an influential Christian's concern for the welfare of his co-religionists could merge with the kind of protectionism liable to enhance the importance of commercial activity to the spread of the faith yet further. According to Rufinus, Frumentius was always careful to ascertain 'whether there were any *Christiani* among the Roman merchants' who came within his territory of jurisdiction; when he found some, he gave them unlimited scope of action (*plenam potestatem*), which must have provided them with a considerable advantage over their competitors vowed to the older faiths.[10]

Frumentius also encouraged these traders to form *conventicula* in various places. The term means 'places of assembly', but is recorded with the sense 'meeting place of Christians' by the middle of the fourth century. The nature of the conventicles that Frumentius encouraged remains undefined, although they were not exactly churches since Rufinus does not use the term *ecclesia*. They sound like a means to make the most of transient contacts, perhaps with a trading-station, a *collegium* (albeit with an abnormally broad membership) and a church all in one. They were certainly places for some kind of worship, because the merchants gathered there 'to pray according to the Roman custom' (*Romano ritu orationis*), but it is hard to believe traders so far from home, plying the same routes and perhaps carrying some of the same wares, would have ended their prayers and then simply dispersed to their ships or lodgings. Something altogether more organized is suggested by the way Frumentius attempted to win converts with marks of favour and various benefits, perhaps including exemption from tolls and privileged use of warehousing facilities in the ports where he had authority. This is a relatively late source, but it is reasonable to suppose the spread of Christianity owed much of its impetus to such protectionism, with believers offering hospitality and favourable terms to co-religionists (especially to those practising the same craft or trade) that potential converts, making their living in the same way, might find alluring. In the first years of the fourth century, Eusebius had good reason to choose a metaphor derived from long-distance commerce when he wished to convey what the apostle Peter had taken to Rome, 'carrying the costly merchandise of the light of understanding from the East to those who dwelled in the West'.

Communications into the Early Middle Ages

With the decline of European colonialism in the second half of the twentieth century, historians became increasingly inclined to doubt the validity of using the distinctions ancient writers make between Roman insiders and barbarian out-siders, the latter resting upon ethnic distinctions that filtered mobile and change-able groupings into *gentes* such as the Franks, the Goths or the Vandals. Imperial powers need simple categorizations of those whom they conquer as a rough guide to what makes a particular group useful, dangerous or useless (as in the British-imperial notion of 'the African' and distinction between the 'martial races' of India and others). In recent years, archaeologists have added to the debate by increasingly emphasizing that Franks, Vandals, Goths and Romans are easier to distinguish with a pen than with a spade. Although a classicist could evoke the 'racial hatred of a Gothic garrison' among Romans or their mistrust of a 'half-Vandal generalissimo' as recently as 1975, such language now looks decidedly old-fashioned.[11]

Nonetheless, the end of the Roman Empire in Gaul, as elsewhere in the West, was in some measure the consequence of an ethnicized hatred on a massive scale. In the 370s, a new force in Roman politics began moving across the Steppe lands that run above the Black Sea and lead to the door that lies eternally unfastened at the back of the European house. These were the Huns, equestrian archers who remained a major force in Roman affairs until the 450s and the death of their most famous leader, Attila, and throughout this time they were determined to be players in imperial politics. Highly mobile and militarily effective, the Huns moved rapidly between different theatres of war, and the proof of their success lies in their many periods of Roman service. Theodosius I (379–95) drove the Huns from the northern Balkans but also used them to make a swift cavalry vic-tory against the usurper Maximus in 388. In 409, Honorius employed 10,000 Huns against Alaric. Most of the Roman high commanders such as Stilicho (d. 408) and Aetius (d. 454) can be found employing Hunnic troops. Thus 'the Huns were not only the foes of the Romans towards the close of the fourth century and in the opening years of the fifth; also to some extent they were their friends, and served not without effect as mercenaries in the imperial armies'.[12]

Roman writers, however, refused to assimilate the Hunnic warriors to any-thing admirable, or even intelligible. Ammianus Marcellinus places their home-land near 'the ice-bound Ocean', so unlike the sustaining warmth of the Roman Mediterranean, and declares that they belonged nowhere in the sedentary world of cities and fertile estates; the Huns had 'not so much as a hut thatched with reed'. Claudian locates their core territories across the frozen Don, a traditional frontier of *Europa* in the east, and reports that their faces are 'hideous to look upon', their bodies loathsome. According to the sixth-century historian Jordanes, writing long after the event but probably recording old calumnies, the Huns emerged when Scythian witches mated with unclean spirits in the wilderness, producing 'a stunted, foul and puny tribe, scarcely human'. The Romans saw the Huns as the kind of fearful enemy described by Clausewitz (*On War*, i. 3): 'a wild, warlike race' where the martial spirit 'is much more common than amongst civilized people' because they have so few other employments. Roman writers simply could not understand what the Huns' other employments might be. The second circumstance was that the Hunnic movements westward created a tsunami of fear and rumour, causing a large-scale flight involving many thousands of human beings who negotiated or forced their way across imperial frontiers onto taxable land.

The movements of the Huns produced a series of connected crises whose chain reaction has only recently become clear. Some of the refugees sought asylum within imperial territory during protracted negotiations, notably two large but separate groups of Goths in 376; others took matters into their own hands, like the Vandals, Alans and Sueves (the terms, once again, are those of Roman writers) who ventured with their horses and wagons across the frozen Rhine and entered Gaul on the last day of the year 406. The Roman authorities now had to cope with large confederations either seeking asylum within imperial frontiers, including two groups of Goths, or crossing unbidden in large numbers. Others were raiding across weak points and settling in captured cities, like the Franks in the Lower Rhine. The Empire's financial base shrank as occupied or wasted lands in the West became impossible to tax at previous levels or to tax at all. When the Vandals left the province of Numidia they took so much of the livestock and other movables with them that the Roman government wrote off 13,000 centuriae as desert; losses of lands owned by the *res privata* in the first quarter of the fifth century were estimated by the Emperor Honorius at about a third to a half, levels that may be called catastrophic. Elsewhere in the West, no more revenues came to Rome from Britannia by 410, and about the same time Spanish income was lost through Vandal settlement. In Gaul, where the military situation in the 410s and 430s seriously reduced the revenue from the land tax in many regions, the corporation of shippers at Arles had ceased to function by the early fifth century, to judge by the want of any constitution for it in the Theodosian Code, promulgated in the West in 438. If this is true, then no imperial freight or *onus fiscale* was now leaving this major port of the western Mediterranean. A turning point was reached in 439 when the Vandals captured Carthage and broke the tax spine running across to Rome. In former times, Roman commanders in periods of civil strife had sometimes used the expedient of blocking the African ports to turn Rome into the famished virago of Claudian's poetry, her shield unpolished and her spear a mass of rust; now, with the coming of the Vandals, a de facto blockade was in place that was to last a hundred years.[13]

A passing reference shows that merchants found it almost impossible to carry olive oil to the major settlements in the province of Noricum, encompassing territories now in Slovenia, Austria, Germany and Italy, in the wake of the depredations of Attila. Yet even if the oil supply to Noricum must remain an isolated case, this kind of disturbance is unlikely to have been quickly remedied, if remedied at all, and may have had many parallels elsewhere. The cumulative result was not just the want of a culinary delicacy or a base for unguents, but a systematic collapse of the means to create, to earn or to steal the food necessary to keep body and soul together. The chronicles of the fourth to sixth centuries, though sometimes very sparse, often find room to mention hungry barbarians. Writers such as Ammianus, Procopius, Hydatius and Olympiodorus show warlords and their bands on the verge of starvation in central Europe and northern Italy. In Italy, almost every Roman villa excavated has shown signs of degradation and abandonment in the fifth and sixth centuries, a sure sign of traumtic disturbance in the food supply, among other things. The urban centres also suffered, although in any modern assessment of the fate of the towns a great deal will inevitably rest upon the chosen definition of key concepts like 'degradation'. What seems certain is that lines of supply to many cities were cut in the fourth and fifth centuries, sometimes never to be remade.[14]

These are all isolated details, and conditions must have varied from one region to another, or even from one city to another, creating micro-environments of

5   The accoutrements of a 5th-c. warlord, probably Frankish. The 'treasure of Pouan', discovered in 1842 at Pouan-les-Vallées (Aube). The equipment may have belonged to a chieftain killed in the battle of the Catalaunian fields against Attila (451). Troyes, Musée archéologique, Musée Saint-Loup.

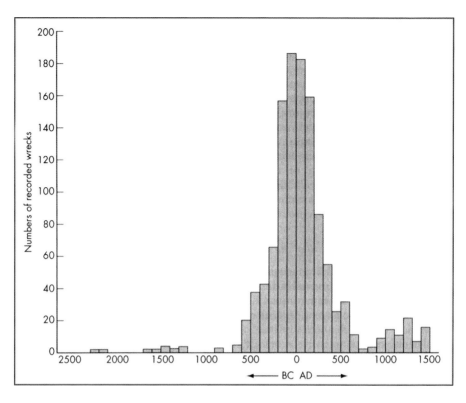

Fig. 1 Mediterranean shipwrecks by period. After Parker, *Ancient Shipwrecks of the Mediterranean and the Roman Provinces.* The chart reveals a peak in the time of the emperor Augustus (d. AD 14) but towards the period AD 600–800 there is a sharp decline. This chart is suspect for the way it shapes fragmentary data around the year zero, since many of the shipwrecks were discovered by chance in the western Mediterranean by amateur divers. It includes no deep-sea wrecks, and it does not distinguish military from merchant vessels; no allowance is made for the fact that ships whose cargo was carried in perishable wooden barrels (rather than ceramic amphorae) are much harder to detect on the sea bed because they are not advertised by a scatter of imperishable jars. And yet, the chart is curiously plausible in certain respects. It rises when the Roman Empire was at its height and had recently come to include the Near Eastern territories that gave the Romans exceptional access to slaves, salt, dried foods, dyed purple cloth, perfumes, silk, jade, muslin, spices and ebony. (This is a list of items traded through Palmyra by AD 137.) These goods could be shipped westwards into the Mediterranean from the Levantine ports and bridgeheads. The equally dramatic decline coincides with the transmutation of Roman government in the western Empire, producing a cluster of barbarian kingdoms that were often engaged in war – an acute form of competition – and could not sustain the 'ecumenical' structures of Roman exchange.

surplus and want in the Early Middle Ages that were no doubt as complex as the ecological and biological diversity that may be found in some parts of the Mediterranean shoreline within five kilometres or less. Yet in recent years the accumulation of archaeological material, including the dramatic expansion of maritime archaeology, has given fresh substance to the account of the early medieval depression in Henri Pirenne's celebrated *Mahomet et Charlemagne* of 1937. In this remarkably brief study, left in manuscript at Pirenne's death, the shift of power in early medieval Europe from the Roman Mediterranean across the Alps to the Frankish north is interpreted as a comparatively late development produced by the rise of Islam, turning the Mediterranean into an Islamic lake and ending a Roman world that had survived more or less intact into the seventh century. The spread of Islam, Pirenne maintained, severed Western European links with Byzantium and the Near Eastern ports, concentrating the political and economic affairs of occidental Europe on the western reaches of the plain. It blocked the routes that had hitherto brought papyrus and such luxuries as silks and spices from Asia or Africa. This theory of a relatively rapid rupture has often served as a point of reference, if only for dissent, since Pirenne's book was published. Some have suggested that he erred in seeking a predominant cause – the rise of Islam – for the end of Roman power in the West and its shift across the Alps. Others have argued that Pirenne's concern with long-distance trade in goods like spices or papyrus carries him away from the late antique economy, something better studied in terms of cheaper products conveyed in bulk, often but by no means always over relatively small distances, for modest profits. Nonetheless, the evidence of marine archaeology, although its value may be questioned, is almost disconcertingly clear in its support for Pirenne's belief in a general collapse of Mediterranean exchange in the seventh and eighth centuries (Fig. 1). 'The archaeology of the last few decades', writes Chris Wickham, drawing upon a much wider range of material than marine archaeology alone, 'invites us to reinstate one of the major planks of Pirenne's theory, the substantial cutback in Mediterranean-wide exchange around 700.' The best surveys of political and cultural history in late antiquity have already begun to engage afresh with the issue of the early medieval depression: a collapse of the Roman circuit.[15]

A trajectory for the history of liturgical singers in the first six hundred years AD has begun to emerge. In the new political order of kingship, singers were answerable to bishops whom the kings valued for their *romanitas*: the mastery of a good Latin, including perhaps the ability to write a fine letter or poem; a long family history in the region where the king had come to rule, and at least a residual knowledge of Roman administration in terms of daily legal practice and provincial organization. The liturgy that the singers served, in an island of material opulence, was a link with the Roman social order that the kings inherited and valued as miniature Constantines who knew no more exalted model for power than imperial dominion, and whose access to the aulic and religious material culture of Rome, both old and new, was much reduced.

6   The sarcophagus of a married couple, surrounded by scenes from both Testaments. Unlike some counter-churches of the 2nd c., notably the movement associated with Marcion, the mainstream was committed to understanding the ministry of Jesus *secundum scripturas*, according to Old Testament prophecy. Dating from the first or second generation of Christianity as a cult with the imperial sponsorship (and allegiance) of Constantine, this tomb is a witness to the retention of the synagogue books by the form of Christianity that Constantine chose to accept. First half of the 4th c., found in the lateral channel of the road between Arles and Les Saintes-Maries-de-la-Mer, with the skeletons of the two deceased still inside. Musée de l'Arles antique.

2

THE GOD OF THE HOUSEHOLD
AND HIS MUSIC

The Making of the Mainstream

The history of liturgical singers in the first millennium is predominantly the story of musicians in the service of the Church that constructed the New Testament canon. It is by no means a random collection of documents. The New Testament comprises the only corpus of Christian writing commonly dated to the first century or the early second with some confidence, apart from a handful of early texts including *I Clement* and perhaps the *Didache*. In other words, the finalized canon contained books believed to date from the time of the apostles or their immediate successors. To a degree that cannot be attributed to a later phase of disingenuous redaction, they record how a community of named individuals experienced something they interpreted as a series of encounters with their former teacher, quite soon after his crucifixion and death, which made everything in their lives new. Paul makes a comparable claim for himself. It is immaterial here whether Peter, Mary, Thomas and the others were mistaken about what happened to them. What matters is their belief in a seminal Easter experience and in the post-Resurrection appearances. In the words of Larry Hurtado:

> The earliest traditions attribute [the beginnings of Christianity] to powerful experiences taken by the recipients as appearances of the risen Christ. We have no historical basis for attributing the[ir] innovative convictions to some other source . . . Whether one chooses to consider these particular experiences as hallucinatory, projections of mental processes of the recipients, or the acts of God, there is every reason to see them as the ignition points for the Christological convictions linked to them.[1]

As Jesus appeared to his disciples after his crucifixion so 'Patroklos appeared to Achilles, Samuel to Saul, the elder Scipio to his grandsons, as did numerous others to their survivors'; but although communication with the dead could occur whenever a soul in the otherworld chose to push the veil between living and dead aside, in Matthew 28: 8 the women depart from the empty tomb 'with fear and great joy', and their reports are treated as 'idle tales' in Luke 24: 11 then bluntly denied by Thomas in John 20: 24–9. The difference between the resurrection narratives and accounts of such revenants as Hector or Patroklos is the claim in all the first-century documents destined for canonical status (save Mark's gospel as originally composed) that Jesus returned in some form of bodily life that was not illusory. He did not appear in one of three or four different forms he could have chosen, as in the Gnostic *Apocalypse of Peter*, or come like an intangible angel of light, as in *The Sophia of Jesus Christ*. By the end of the second century, a mainstream Church can be discerned that was committed to the doctrine of a fully human and yet also fully divine Christ. Hurtado is right to imply that the rise of this church cannot be entirely explained as the work of a vociferous and increasingly empowered faction of believers among many others, all initially equal and in competition. That picture does not accord with the encounters, reported in the earliest sources, that show men and women convinced they are speaking with a man who had passed through the valley of the Shadow of Death, emerging the other side with the marks of an arduous journey upon his living body.[2]

Dance and Dissent

This does not mean that those who had looked Jesus in the face were agreed about his humanity, his divinity or the relationship between the two. By the second century, such issues of Christology already had certain musical consequences. As the Last Supper comes to a close, Jesus rises from the table and asks the apostles to stand around him in a circle. He wishes to sing a hymn with them, but it is not the *Hallel*, the corpus of Psalms with an Alleluia refrain that may be implied in Matthew 26: 30 and Mark 14: 26. This is to be a different song, and he begins to sing it as the apostles, holding one another by the hand, dance around him in a circle (*gyron*), responding *Amen* to each verse in the manner of these:

Σωθῆναι θέλω
Καὶ σῶσαι θέλω   Ἀμήν.

Λυθῆναι θέλω
Καὶ λῦσαι θέλω   Ἀμήν.

I wish to be saved and I wish to save. Amen. I wish to be delivered and I wish to deliver. Amen.

This account of the Last Supper derives from the second-century *Acts of John*, 'a lengthy, romantic and at crucial points highly unorthodox portrayal of the son of Zebedee's ministry in and around Ephesus' which is available only in modern reconstructions. These *Acts* may be addressing readers who were drawn to a cult of Jesus – and here is a founding element of the forms of faith now commonly called 'Gnostic' – but who were also spiritually and intellectually repelled by the notion of a god swathed in the corruption of flesh and submitting to a base execution. In this text, Christ appears to John *during* the Crucifixion and claims he is not the one hanging on the cross; and in a reversal of the tradition received into the gospel canon, Jesus mocks the onlookers at Golgotha. He neither suffers nor dances in the flesh because he only appears to be corporeal; John is able to pass his hand through him. (For a conspectus of the texts on which this and the next chapter are based, see the Appendix to Chapter 3.)[3]

There is no reason to doubt that some kind of rite is being described in the *Acts of John*. The compiler calls it one of Christ's *mystēria*, a term for cultic activities that could encompass 'sacrifice, communal meals, reenactment of the myths of the gods, sacred processions and hymn singing . . .'. There may be further echoes of such rites in *The Banquet* by Methodius, probably from the second half of the third century and describing a ring-dance of virgins on the day of general resurrection, the first day of the Millennium. They sing a long hymn in Greek with a refrain repeated between each verse. To claim that the scene Methodius describes is pure allegory (whatever *pure* allegory may be), and that Christian women would not have developed some equivalent to the Bacchic and other cultic dances of polytheism, would be to go well beyond any generalization the fragmentary materials for early Christian music license us to make. To claim that such rites were widespread, however, would be unwise in a different way. Until quite recently, most forms of mainstream Christianity have maintained an ambivalent attitude to dance, which dramatizes the body and often evokes sexuality, while the most energetic forms can induce distracted states of mind that Christian worship has regarded with some mistrust since Paul counselled the Corinthians to make judicious use of speaking in tongues. It is no coincidence that the dancing scene in the reconstructed *Acts of John* appears in a text with a highly unorthodox Christology so that a form of worship not widely practised (one assumes) is associated there with a doctrine not eventually accepted. These *Acts* therefore suggest how the members of a Christian community might compound their beliefs and any performance routines they employed for hymnody together, creating a matrix of belief and cultic action that competing groups might regard as comprehensively heretical. The *Acts* also show that a musical practice could become the accepted complement of a community's doctrines in ways that now seem distinctly counter-intuitive. The fourfold gospel emphasizes the physicality of Jesus, both before and after the Crucifixion, but it contains nothing to associate that physicality with dance, which is the art of displaying the human form. The *Acts of John*, in contrast, denies the physical humanity of Christ, but shows his body in motion.[4]

The various attempts by the canonical evangelists to broach the nature of Christ's body after the Resurrection show how unwise it may be to interpret the

earliest centuries of the Church as if subsequent developments in orthodox doctrine and worship were already assured. For as an apostle in the apocryphal *Acts
of John* can pass his hands through the body of Christ, so Christ in the canonical Gospel of John can pass through a bolted door. It would be just as mistaken
to interpret the range of the earliest Christian music in terms of what the mainstream Church eventually found acceptable. One of the charges laid against
Christians by Celsus, perhaps in the 170s, is that the officials of the communities
caused a drum and the reed pipe or aulos to be played before worship, like priests
of Cybele, to induce a state of orgiastic frenzy. A biting insult loses its teeth if it
has no basis. The writings of the Church Fathers condemning instruments at
banquets and theatrical shows, a stream of denunciation that gathers force in the
third and fourth centuries (and therefore mostly long after Celsus), are sometimes open to the interpretation that rank-and-file Christians did not view the
use of instruments in worship in the same way as the bishops and other polemicists who harangued them on the subject. Celsus believed that nobody in their
senses could accept the Christians' claim about the death and resurrection of
Jesus so it was necessary for the priests to rob the congregation of their sanity and
put them into a distracted state. Celsus may also have given some credence to
rumours that Christians held orgiastic and even cannibalistic rites, a charge often
levelled against cultic groups that met in secret. Yet even though the text of
Celsus's book is known only from the passages that Origen chose to quote in
order to confute them, he emerges from what survives as a well-informed observer in most matters that can be verified. He had taken the trouble to read the
Scriptures, and his description of how believers gathered in shops, or sought
converts among the artisans of private houses, is no less convincing for being
partial and contemptuous. When Origen quotes the passage about the aulos and
drum in his rebuttal of Celsus, he does not deny the charge. Perhaps he thought
the comparison between Christian presbyters and the priests of Cybele so wide
of the mark that it was beneath contempt; it is impossible to say, but there were
probably as many varieties of Christian music and performance in the first two
centuries as there were competing groups who claimed the name of 'Christian',
and it would be unwise to rule anything out of nascent mainstream practice on
the grounds that it seems anomalous when judged in terms of later traditions.[5]

The Household Church

Between the period of the New Testament and later sources such as the *Apostolic
Tradition* of the third century, some Christian writings suggest a community
markedly at variance with the norms and ideals of Graeco-Roman society. The
public pleasures of the arena and amphitheatre, with all their ancillary importance as opportunities for civic generosity and patronage, were to be foregone.
The honours due to the tutelary gods of the cities were no longer to be paid,

meaning that some Christians (but by no means all) opted out of festivals and rites that their pagan neighbours regarded as fundamental to the well-being of their *polis*. Some Christians went further still. When Celsus accuses Christians of forming secret associations contrary to the law, Origen replies that Christians are compelled to live among pagans like civilized men among the Scythians, 'whose laws are unholy'. Civilized individuals who found themselves among such barbarians, having no opportunity of escape, would naturally enter into associations contrary to the Scythian laws 'for the sake of the law of truth'. The Scythians, for their part, would regard those associations as illegal. In the same way, Origen argues, Christians, 'suffering the tyranny of him who is called the devil, form associations contrary to the laws of the devil, working against his power and hoping to ensure the safety of those whom they may succeed in persuading to revolt from a government which is, as it were, Scythian, and despotic'.[6]

For a passage so passionate in its defence of the churches this is curiously revealing about the reasons why Christians were often attacked. Origen implies a sharply dissident view of the society in which Christians must dwell while in exile from their true home. The Roman value of *humanitas*, a civilized and liberal equity, seems to mean little or nothing to the Christians for whom a Roman is no better than a Scythian from the frozen reaches beyond the Don. It is almost as if the senate and the traditions of Roman oratory and poetry count for nothing. Even the traditions of law are judged to be wicked and contrary to 'the law of truth'. It is not difficult to understand how such language could land Christians in serious trouble with their neighbours and with the public authorities. What kind of friendship and coexistence could polytheists expect from residents in the same city who were known to disavow the tutelary deities responsible for the prosperity of the *polis*? How could the authorities trust men and women to be law-abiding when they regarded the imperial government, in Origen's phrase, as 'Scythian, and despotic'?

Many more questions of this kind might be asked, and yet in a sense they would be posed in vain. Despite the defiant speeches sometimes put into the mouths of martyrs by Christian apologists, showing contempt for both physical suffering and the Roman state, Origen's response to Celsus cannot represent the kind of language that Christians used openly. Passages such as Revelation 2: 14 with its reference to Christians eating food formerly sacrificed to idols, show that some were accustomed to take meals with polytheists, perhaps in the banquets of trade guilds. From the end of the first century onwards, Christians generally seem to have lived in relative harmony with neighbouring polytheists. In 111–12, Pliny thought the Christians innocuous enough, and since he could find no existing law concerning them it would seem that no relevant cases had yet been brought to trial. This is quickly said, and yet in some respects it is all quite extraordinary. A form of monotheism with its beginnings in the rural radicalism of a distant province, eventually so welcoming to Gentiles that it could no longer claim the concessions from the Roman state due to a Jewish sect, nonetheless became a faith that urbanites could espouse amongst polytheists and remain, for the most part, tolerably respectable save when the winds of circumstances fanned any latent resentments into a blaze.

The question of how this was achieved can have no simple answer, but it probably had much to do with a widespread recognition that the new faith was integrated into the fundamental social unit of the eastern Mediterranean in antiquity. This was the biological household of the family with an extended *familia* that might comprise artisans working in the domestic space and serving as dependents and slaves. In the Greek of both Jews and Gentiles, the word *ekklesia* possessed a political sense ('a regularly summoned legislative body, an assembly') and a broader, more relaxed meaning ('a gathering of people', an 'assembled throng'). As far as can be determined, any place could temporarily become an *ekklesia* if Christians met there, even a rented room, but before the third century a church was usually convened in part of a private house, perhaps reverting to daily use when the assembly dispersed. Given this focus on the household in the most material but also in the broadest social sense, the social hierarchy of a city quarter could probably exert a strong influence over the process of conversion and the establishment of such officialdom as the community possessed, for networks of families had always been of importance to the implantation of cults. The household conversions recorded in Acts and in Paul's letters, or the references in the *Apostolic Tradition* to those who hosted meetings in their homes, suggest how a patriarchal leadership with juridical powers over slaves and family members could have developed from the elders or presbyters of the more notable families in an urban quarter, without the period of itinerant apostles and charismatic teachers necessarily coming to an end.[7]

The evolution of proto-clerical offices was certainly very uneven in different churches. The *Didache*, possibly one of the oldest Christian documents in existence outside the letters of Paul, enjoins its community of Gentiles and Torah-observant Jews to elect 'bishops and deacons who are worthy of the Lord, gentle men who are not fond of money, who are true and approved' (15. 1–2). This sounds very much like the language of 1 Timothy 3: 1–13, where the qualities of bishop and deacon are described in terms of public morality that any Roman censor could approve. The *Didache*, however, speaks of bishops in the plural and knows nothing of presbyters. Soon after 100, Ignatius insists that the churches of Asia Minor addressed in his letters should each have a bishop, whereas his contemporary Hermas, author of *The Shepherd*, seems to know of no such institution in Rome. By the third century, however, there were probably many Christian communities governed by elders who were sometimes fit by birth, wealth and attainments to be city councillors, to judge by some remarks of Origen in his critique of Celsus. According to Origen, these men nonetheless declined to accept public office in order that they could better devote themselves to the spiritual and social well-being of their members, especially widows,

7   A family group of father, mother, son and daughter. antique cast, 1st c. AD. Musée de l'Arles.

orphans and other poor. The result was something that a potential convert could recognize as a *collegium* led by respectable men of the quarter, in some ways resembling a Graeco-Roman burial society and based around a cult in the usual way but quite distinct from some cults, such as Mithraism, in its admission of slaves, women and freedmen.[8]

These esteemed family groups did not necessarily dominate the nascent offices of the churches. They may sometimes have resembled 'the great men of the generation' mentioned in later rabbinic sources: the wealthy leaders of the community who were not necessarily *archisynagogoi* themselves and might rank above them. In many places, the wealthiest householders in the Christian community were perhaps more conspicuous as hosts and as benefactors than as officers. The *Acts of Peter* shows a senator named Marcellus hosting meetings for worship in his Roman house and dispensing charity there. He sounds like a deacon, but there is no indication that he is a minister and he is definitely not a presbyter because he is obliged to summon one before the service can begin in his *triclinium* or dining room. Nonetheless, 'all the widows who trusted in Christ had recourse to him . . . all the fatherless were fed by him . . . and the poor called Marcellus their patron; his house was called the house of the strangers and the poor'. Marcellus seems to be acting as the Gentile *patronus* for a Christian community in the city that still encompasses Jews like his guest Peter. This section of the *Acts of Peter* is perhaps an attempt to reconstruct events at the beginning of the apostolic ministry in Rome, and its principal purpose here is to show how a household-based Christianity developed in Rome in direct contact with the first apostolic generation, indeed with Saint Peter himself. It also shows how decisively the memory of a wandering Messiah who required a man to 'hate his father and mother, wife and children' had yielded to a mitigated understanding of that message in the interests of Christian families who had no wish to appear subversive to their fellow citizens.[9]

Householders were early targets of the Pauline missions, and archaeology suggests some of the reasons why. The members of such households, whether Jewish or Gentile, often lived together in cellular environments of remarkable complexity. Jewish sites at Meiron, Khirbet Shema and Sepphoris in Palestine have revealed houses above shops, with all manner of work being undertaken in different spaces below, including the preparation of food, the manufacture of textiles and carpentry. The conversion narratives in Acts show how an apostle's success with the head of a household could net the entire catch of souls dwelling within such a complex and layered *oikos*. The account of Cornelius the centurion reveals he accepted baptism 'with his complete household', described in Acts 10: 24 as his 'kinsmen and near friends'. Crispus, the leader of the synagogue at Corinth, also believed 'with all his household', while Acts 16: 14–15 describes the baptism of Lydia 'and her household'. The second generation of converts among the Gentiles included Claudius Ephebus and Valerius Biton, mentioned in *I Clement* and both revealed by their *gentilicia* as imperial freedmen of the Claudian and Valerian clans. Men and women of this class could own considerable wealth and possess large households, despite their slave origin.[10]

The New Testament narratives of conversion are all in some measure literary constructions designed to show the Holy Spirit inducing a complete change of religious allegiance. They cannot be allowed to establish 'the household' as the means whereby an infant orthodoxy was sheltered indoors and protected from heresies ranging wide like thieves in the common streets. No doubt conversions of the kind that Luke reports did occur, but progress must often have been made in different ways that did not involve complete households or indeed complete conversions of the kind that he is naturally eager to emphasize. The biography of the Emperor Severus Alexander (222–35) in the *Historia Augusta* records that Alexander had an image of Christ together with Abraham, Orpheus 'and others of this sort' in his private shrine or *lararium*. This was where polytheists kept the assemblage of small statues and other cherished materials, by no means necessarily costly, which focused their minds for their devotions (in the Latin phrase, *quando rem divinam faciebant*). The detail may well be spurious in this particular case, given the amount of fabricated material in the *Historia Augusta*, but it may represent the kind of direction that polytheists, accustomed to perceive gods in fluid combinations rather than in isolation, were inclined to take when they heard some form of gospel. The eclectic forms of Christianity commonly called 'Gnostic' now may often have arisen like this, when educated persons assimilated a cult of Jesus to their existing philosophical and cultic commitments, compounding it with an esoteric polytheism. To view the same issue from below, there can be little doubt that Christianity sometimes made headway amongst the slaves of a household but not the biological family, to judge by Tacitus's complaint that slaves and free artisans working within household spaces were often receptive to new cults, especially those coming from the east, that they did not hold in common with their masters. This was one of the Christian constituencies that proved especially offensive to Celsus: the 'workers in wool and leather, and fullers, and persons of the most uninstructed and rustic character in private houses, not venturing to utter a word in the presence of their elders and wiser masters'.[11]

In this, as in many things, Celsus was an astute critic, although he was wrong if he supposed that all Christians were secretly ashamed of such coreligionists. In the second half of the second century, Athenagoras was proud to admit that the Christian communities he endorsed included 'uneducated persons, artisans and old women' (*Legatio pro Christianis*, 11). It is possible to see how the household, viewed as a complex amalgam of spaces and lives, could nurture a form of the faith at least nominally indifferent, in the matter of admission, to boundaries of gender, juridical status, education and social position, which is essentially the faith that Paul and subsequent champions of orthodoxy like Justin and Athenagoras preach. The household of biological family with dependents, free artisans and slaves was the place where that broad church found its full range of addressees assembled and involved in cooperative lives already organized into forms of leadership and dependence. A single house could encompass those who were lowly enough to recognize that the teachings of a carpenter Messiah gave them a unique dignity just as it accommodated those who were elevated enough to recognize that those same teachings called them to a humility and service that could become the core of a new cultic identity as patrons, hosts and community elders.

A Christian Music

Two of the earliest references to hymnody in Christian worship, the 'spiritual songs' of Ephesians 5: 19 and Colossians 3: 16 both appear in the context of advice to householders for maintaining an unimpeachable standard of conduct. Within three verses of counselling these spiritual songs the author of Ephesians is advising women to be obedient to their husbands, and having elaborated that theme he turns to the duties of children who should obey their parents, fathers who should be mild to their offspring and slaves who should be obedient to their masters. Often quoted out of context, the reference to hymnody in Ephesians is actually embedded in one of the so-called household codes.

Why did such Christians have ritual song? The search for an answer can best begin with the earliest information about the forms household worship could take, all contained in Paul's First Letter to the Church of Corinth. On one hand, Paul found the meals of the Corinthians too strict because they tended to preserve the social hierarchies of Hellenistic dining: the guests brought their own food during the Lord's Supper whence the poorer members were thinly supplied and shamed. On some occasions they might even go hungry (11: 21–2). On the other hand, however, Paul believed some aspects of Corinthian worship were disturbingly informal. The meals were sometimes eaten without due recollection of the words of institution, painstakingly repeated by Paul at 11: 23–5, and men attended the gatherings with their heads covered, women with their hair loose (11: 4–7). Any member might bring something to worship so that a service was gathered from individual contributions like the food brought for the Lord's Supper. The contributions could include a psalm, some perhaps new compositions, others the Davidic poems so vital to the effort of Jesus-believing Jews and Gentiles to understand the life and death of Jesus *secundum scripturas* and to debate with detractors or potential converts. The general context of this worship, when all the elements were assembled (one might say tabled), was seemingly fervent. It welcomed spontaneous interventions from those moved by the Spirit to prophesy or to speak in tongues, sometimes with results that were not always interpreted for the edification of the community. 'Yet in the church', says Paul, 'I had rather speak five words with my understanding, that by my voice I might teach others also, than ten thousand words in an unknown tongue' (14: 19).[12]

Paul is not exactly describing a *ritual* here. There is no developed sense of worship organized into a fixed sequence of words, gestures and events. Yet it is fundamental to most forms of religious ritual that predictability and repetition carry the principal burden of meaning, not surprise and innovation. Ritual often requires 'an accepted conventional procedure having a certain conventional effect, the procedure to include the uttering of certain words by certain persons in certain circumstances'. In contrast, the worship at Corinth included interventions that were valued (but not by Paul) because they arose from motions of the Holy Spirit beyond the control of any present. The results could be formalized in a ceremony of interpretation when the language of tongues was translated into intelligible speech, but the Corinthian believers were not always minded to take that step, or so Paul's account suggests. Fervent commitment was still more important at their meetings than a show of *acceptance*. Religious ritual often provides a formalized sequence of words and gestures that everyone present accepts as authoritative and beyond disruption; formalization is vital for the worshippers to sense that quotidian experience has been momentarily suspended, that time is

8   The ritual activity of a mystery cult. There are abundant but enigmatic signs of fixed tasks to be performed. The chief
figures are Qodvoldeus and Feloxsomedix. He receives a (? sacrificed) chicken from Qodvoldeus, who appears to be about
to place it in a bag or basket. The egg in the bowl held by the kneeling figure presumably has some ritual significance.
Trier, Mosaic of the Mysteries.

passing in a sanctified way, and that they may be approaching (as they are certainly invoking) the presence of the divine. Those who participate in ritual can
momentarily transcend their doubts, or come to terms with their own want of
fervency, by simply being present during the event and by accepting what is
going forward. Participation 'in liturgical performance may be highly visible,
[yet] it is not very profound, for it neither indicates nor does it necessarily produce an inward state conforming to it'. The Christians of Corinth were much
concerned with belief-producing or belief-confirming events such as prophecy
and speaking in tongues, but there was not much place for a formalized liturgy
as yet that marked a simple acceptance.[13]

Yet no matter how much worship may seek to establish a connection with
divine power(s) too terrible or magnificent to be met with mere diligence and
custom, hymnody contains the seed of a ritualizing process. Music is one of
the most widespread ways in which communities at worship create sequences of

formalized actions and words. Song can be used to distinguish ministers with the right to sing certain interventions from those who are sanctioned to use their voice only somewhere else in the service, perhaps in a much less prominent way. Music is therefore a prime source of the roles, and the proprietary rights to use certain forms of words, that are fundamental to many forms of ritual. At the same time, however, song allows these roles to be established in a way that bonds the community, and the authority of those with special ritual tasks to perform is therefore confirmed precisely because it helps to establish a commonwealth of worship.

This is because song has the power to abolish the familiar distinction between speaker and interlocutor established by speech. The reasons for this are poorly understood, and are ultimately a matter for psycho-acousticians to explain, but they are clearly registered in a simple and familiar contrast: singing to oneself is commonly regarded as a sign of insouciance whereas talking to oneself is popularly construed as the first mark of madness. It is arguably the presence of musical pitch that makes the cardinal difference, the organized and stabilized frequencies somehow working against the analytical categories of *you* and *me* established in speech:

> People sing to make sure, through direct experience, of their existence in a layer of reality different from the one in which they encounter each other and things as speakers, as facing one another and separate from one another – in order to be aware of their existence in a place where distinction and separation of man and man, man and thing, thing and thing, gives way to unity, to authentic togetherness.[14]

This manages to be both perplexing and persuasive. Music can weaken the listener's default sense of language as an altercation demanding a calculated response. Its scalar patterns efface the swooping flight of intonation in speech so effectively that the transient impressions of daily existence associated with the pitch cues of speech patterns disappear; thus song can offer a release from evanescent associations and even from the fundamental structures of speaking self and listening other. This sense of unity can be fervent, but it does not have to be so. To sing in company with others is to participate in ways that may range from near vacuity of mind, the lips barely moving, to a state where music may seem to carry the singer beyond words altogether. Christian writings of the first millennium are thinly strewn with attempts to explain these things. 'In melodies', wrote Isidore of Seville soon after 600, 'the divine words more readily and ardently stir our minds to piety when they are sung than when they are not.' Why should this be so? Even a scholar whose principal work remained in use for a thousand years did not care to answer that question.[15]

There is very little here that can be described as a distinctively Christian experience, and Christians probably valued the spiritual songs of Ephesians and Colossians for some of the reasons that inspired their polytheistic neighbours to prize their own ritual hymnody. Thus one of the earliest discussions of music by a Christian contains little that either a contemporary pagan or a modern historian of ritual song would find unusual since the emphasis is so firmly placed upon song as harmonious togetherness. In a series of letters, widely received as authentic today and addressing Churches in the eastern Mediterranean soon after 100, Ignatius summons believers to unity and harmony in the face of dissent and false teaching. Writing to the Church in Ephesus, he develops this theme with an extended musical comparison:

> It is fitting for you to run together in harmony with the mind of the bishop, which is exactly what you are doing. For your presbytery, which is both worthy of the name and worthy of God, is attuned to the bishop as strings to the lyre. Therefore Jesus Christ is sung in your harmony and symphonic love (*sumphōnōi agapēi*). And each of you should join the chorus, that by being symphonic in your harmony, taking up the divine inflection (*chrōma*) together, you may sing in one voice through Jesus Christ to the Father, that he may both hear and recognize you through the things you do well, since you are members [*melē*, perhaps punning on *melē* meaning 'melodies', or words to that effect] of his Son. Therefore it is useful for you to be in a flawless unison, that you may partake of God at all times as well.

There is little here to surprise an educated Gentile like Plutarch or a learned Jew like Philo. The belief that participation in hymnody draws the attention of a god to his devotees ('sing . . . so that he may both hear and recognize you') would be confirmed by any Roman hymnodist, and the metaphor of the chorus is a common coin of antique learning, used to invoke many kinds of ordered motion from the dances of maidens to the circuit of the planets. The image of the lyre, whose strings were often numbered at seven in imitation of the Pleiades, is just as familiar (Pl. 9). Even the phrase 'in symphonic love', *sumphōnōi agapēi*, which

9 Orpheus with his lyre. Arcosolium in the Christian cemetery of SS. Pietro e Marcellino, Rome, end of the 4th c.

sounds as though it might be a crucial concept for early Christian hymnody, would be at home in the writings of Plutarch, who refers to the affection between brothers, for example, as a *sumphonia*. If there is a distinctively Christian understanding of music here it is one that emphasizes the characteristically Ignatian theme of cooperative hierarchy and obedience from the rank-and-file believers to the deacons, presbyters and bishops on 'through Jesus Christ to the Father'. Yet even that fits perfectly well with the notion of ritual music as a source of roles that consolidate the worshipping community as a body sharing an experience of the divine.[16]

The musical legacy of the synagogue, whatever it may have been, should be assessed with the mounting evidence that Jews and Christians in many Mediterranean cities maintained some forms of festive and cultic contact into at least the fourth century. It is very important here, in other words, not to allow our sense of the early Church to slide back into the older view of an *ekklesia* that became overwhelmingly gentile with great rapidity leading to an early parting of the ways. That is precisely the position that much recent work seeks to combat. The history of Christian negotiations with any music used when Jews assembled as Jews in their gatherings or 'synagogues' is not necessarily a story of influence followed by independent Christian development; we should be looking instead for an evolving relationship in the matter of ritual singing between sibling commitments during some four hundred years. Hence it may be unwise to place too much emphasis upon the earliest Jewish materials from the Common Era as if the question of the Jewish imprint on Christian ritual singing rapidly loses importance as the first century passes to the second. The use of the Mishnah, redacted in the region of AD 200, offers a prime example, for there is no mention of synagogue music in that compilation, and the pressure to find early testimony in Jewish sources has impelled some to construe its silence as significant. Yet the Mishnah is in many respects an enigmatic compilation that poses as many questions about Jewish identities between the first and third centuries as it answers. The book seems designed to exercise minds with the task of debating how Israelites would live in a profoundly Torah-observant community under the guidance of teachers in a venerable tradition of erudite reflection. The prominence and influence of the Mishnah redactors in their own day is difficult to assess, especially because they do not always seem attentive to the practical consequence of their decrees. These are some of the reasons why their silence on any matter, whether it be the ritual singing of the synagogue or some other, can be difficult to interpret.[17]

In this particular case the silence may mean little, for the Mishnah was compiled at a time when an office of psalmist probably did exist in some synagogues. A famous inscription from Aphrodisias, in what is now western Turkey about 140 km east of Ephesus, records an individual with the Hebrew name of Benjamin called ψαλμο⁵, probably to be expanded as ψαλμολόγος, 'one who voices psalms'. There has been much debate about the period to which this inscription should be assigned, but the most recent discussion places it in the late second or early third century, and it may date from before the universal grant of Roman citizenship in AD 212. A second item of early testimony is the epitaph found in the Jewish catacomb of the Via Nomentana in Rome, commemorating 'Gaianos, secretary, psalm singer (*grammateus*/*psalmōdos*), lover of the Law; may he sleep in peace'. The duties of the *grammateus*, a term found in more than twenty Roman epitaphs of Jews, are not well established, but this Gaianos was probably the secretary to the synagogue congregation and perhaps a psalmist.[18]

There is no reason to suppose the advent of a Jesus-believing sect of Judaism revolutionized the cultic practices of Jews who belonged to it, and this could be where the true interest of the dance episode in the reconstructed *Acts of John*, quoted at the beginning of this chapter, actually lies. A tradition of Jewish dancing on Shabbat is recorded in sources both Gentile and Christian from the late second century AD onwards, but may be much older since the biblical models for choreographic hymnody include Exodus 15: 20 (the dance of Miriam) and 2 Samuel 6: 14 (The dance of David). The Mishnah is probably alluding to Sabbath dance when it lists the clapping of hands and stamping of the feet as violations of the command to rest on the Sabbath (*Beitzah* 5. 2:D), and it is certainly doing so when it quotes the second-century sage Simeon b. Gamaliel on the 'Jerusalemite girls' who dance in the vineyards on 15 Ab and Yom Kippur (*Ta'anit* 4. 8). Even the traditions of Jewish asceticism could accommodate a choreographic element, to judge by the famous passage where Philo Judaeus describes an ascetic Jewish community of men and women to the south of Alexandria, the *Therapeutai*, who gathered for the 'wheeling and counter-wheeling of a choric dance'. Philo, who died perhaps soon after AD 40, describes this cultic group of celibates with such respect for their common life, and for their asceticism, that Eusebius at the beginning of the fourth century took them to be the first Alexandrian Christians under another name.[19]

The *Therapeutai* were an enclosed community, but the main traditions of Jewish festive dance included elements that were public, for 'much of ancient Jewish religious festival (dancing, singing, communal eating, processing) occurred out of doors, inviting and accommodating the participation of interested outsiders'. There are continuing signs that Gentiles were drawn to these public Jewish festivals and held them in respect. As late as the 380s, John Chrysostom can be found denouncing Christians who regard Lent as a preparation for the Pasch, who celebrate Easter as a Passover and who participate in Jewish festivals that include Sabbath dancing. 'They dance with bare feet in the agora; effeminates in a chorus drag the theatre into the synagogue with its actors and the rest.' His contemporary Augustine had encountered the same Sabbath dances, especially as performed by young women. He exhorted his congregation at Hippo Regius to plough rather than to dance in the manner of the Jews for 'it would be better for their women to card their wool than to spend the whole day in shameless dancing'. At the beginning of the seventh century, Licinianus of

Cartagena is still warning Christians of the danger they face 'if they keep the Sabbath in the Jewish manner, with dances and song'.[20]

This leads to a surprising conclusion. If Christian music means hymnody in praise of Jesus-Messiah, then it may first have been sung openly, and not in a clandestine manner, in public places. The choreographic hymnody in the *Acts of John* may reveal one of the earliest forms that the shared worship of Jesus-believing Jews and Gentiles assumed as a continuation of the tradition of dancing on Shabbat. Some Gentile converts, indeed, may have supposed choreographic hymnody was exactly what an oriental cult should provide. 'There is not a single ancient mystery cult without dancing', claims the second-century satirist Lucian. No matter how much polemicists like Augustine and Chrysostom may have wished things otherwise, Christian music during the first four centuries, and even beyond, probably showed Jewish, Christian and polytheist currents continuously mingling and forming different configurations in the cosmopolitan context of the Diaspora cities.[21]

Amongst the polytheists, colleges of hymnodists sang paeans of praise that accompanied the processions celebrating the cities' tutelary gods or the sacrifices made in the temple forecourts. In Asia Minor, where such colleges were especially common, there were 'functionaries associated with the composition and per-formance of hymns' for the mysteries of Demeter and Dionysius at Pergamum. In the ceremonies of many other mystery religions hymnody took its place among sacrifices, communal meals and re-enactments of the myths of the gods. In Pergamum, as in other cities of the East, the singing of hymnodists also adorned the festivities of the imperial cult. 'Since it is appropriate to offer a visible expression of piety', runs an inscription from the city set up by the provin-cial council of Asia,

> the hymn-singers coming together . . . for the most sacred birthday of the god *Sebastos* Tiberius Caesar accomplish a magnificent work for the glory of the association. They sing hymns to the revered household, accomplishing sacri-fices to the revered gods, leading festivals and banquets.

Songs were also performed, often to instrumental accompaniment, in the formal meals or *convivia* of colleges and associations that were usually cultic occasions and would often involve libations and sacrifice.[22]

Benjamin the Jewish psalmist from Aphrodisias, Gaianos the secretary and psalm singer from Rome, and now the polytheistic hymn-singers of Pergamum: with these individuals, named or anonymous, the sense of shared traditions for cultic music in the eastern Mediterranean registers more strongly than any clear division between Jewish, polytheistic and Christian customs. Hence it remains very uncertain whether Christians would have wished to create a tradition of rit-ual music whose musical idioms, style and sonorities consistently set them apart from the Jews and other cultic groups. (Divisions within themselves were an-other matter.) The compiler of the main body of the *Letter to Diognetus*, perhaps writing around 200 in Alexandria, insists on the need for Christians to put away old habits and ways of thought, but he has no difficulty reconciling that aim with deep integration into Roman society. 'Christians are no different from other people in terms of their country, language or customs, for nowhere do they inhabit cities of their own [as the Jews once did in Jerusalem], use a strange dialect [like Hebrew or Aramaic] or live life out of the ordinary [like the Jews with their food laws, circumcision and celebration of the new moon]'. What mattered, one suspects, is that Christians be associated with musical practices consistent with the Roman social morality of respectable families.[23]

It may now be possible to sense how swiftly the churches found their equivalent to men such as Benjamin the Jewish psalmist or the hymnodists of Pergamum. The earliest named individual on record identifiable as a Christian singer appears in an epitaph of the third century, or perhaps of the fourth, but in a damaged state so that only a textual emendation allows him to be named as Gaios. The epitaph, from Dinek Serai in southern central Turkey, was carved to commemorate a deacon named Nestor. The inscription, in Greek verse, reveals that Gaios was a presbyter and 'far the best in hymns . . . beautiful hymns from which others hereafter will tell even posterity to learn':

> Stranger (I address him who comes forward), a welcome to you that are fond of listening. Who is interred here? It is one who for a long time planted the earth of this land. So I pray you to linger here and, in approaching, to be kind to me. Delighting in what you read, clearly learn that Nestor Telephides was a mighty helper of modest widows, a deacon of virginal temperance, faithful servant of Christ, chosen treasure of the whole province, teacher of heavenly doctrine to the young and wise and trustworthy judge among men; and that he sat in council with governors, [as] many local communities know. Remembering my dear friendship and wisdom, pour me a libation while lamenting, rejoicing once more in your wailing and remaining ever mindful of our affection. Presbyter Gaios, far the best in hymns and the one who officiated the funeral rites, rewarded the reverend, sisterly wife of mine Mammeis (born of a line of priests, a faithful stewardess of temperance and now a servant of Christ for the same memory and honour) by means of his own art, beautiful hymns which others hereafter will tell even posterity to learn.[24]

The epitaph commemorates a deacon named Nestor Telephides, apparently of city-council rank and the holder of a high but undisclosed position in his ecclesiastical province. Remembered for the traditional virtues of a dutiful and pious deacon, notably his charity to widows, he is also praised for his desire to meet the strictest standards of the higher clerical life by living in continence as 'a deacon of virginal temperance'. His wife is named as Mammeis, 'born of a line of priests' and therefore descended from a clerical family that did generally not embrace the continence that this married coupled evidently regarded as a defining choice of their Christian lives together. The epitaph assures the reader that this woman was a 'sisterly wife' and a faithful 'stewardess of temperance'. Both expressions are perhaps intended to imply that the couple lived in continence. The last lines describe the service that 'Gaios' the presbyter offered this respected and ascetic couple. 'Far the best in hymns', he officiated at the funeral service for the husband and somehow rewarded the wife with hymns 'which others hereafter will tell even posterity to learn'. This implies that the hymns were new and the work of Gaios, who was evidently held in high regard by a prestigious local family with a tradition of clerical service, city-councillorship and asceticism.

The Singing Body of Christians

For signs of a distinctively Christian attitude to ritual singing among such men as 'Gaios' one should to look to the distant future, indeed to the end of time. The agonies of the Israelites in captivity, and the constant lacerations of their conscience by the prophets, fill the Old Testament with the imagery of final reconciliation with Yahweh and of plenty, imagined in terms of a peaceable Levantine landscape of houses, villages, vineyards and crops. Isaiah offers many examples, for he describes feasts and overflowing harvests in the fields or vineyards; even the harshness of Mediterranean ecology in summer recedes in the final reconciliation with Yahweh when 'the parched ground shall become a pool, and the thirsty land springs of water' (35: 7). Yet Isaiah, like Saint John the Divine in Revelation, also envisages the place where the nations will be gathered as a paradisiacal urban temple where 'burnt offerings and their sacrifices shall be accepted upon mine altar, for mine house shall be called a house of prayer for all people' (56: 7). The traditions of the Jews found many ways to envisage living the end-time in the presence of God, often returning to a mental map of the Jerusalem region before the destruction of the Temple: a hinterland of villages around an urban core with a magnificent temple at its heart, and therefore a liturgy of song and prayer. 'Behold, my servants shall sing for joy of heart' (Isaiah 65: 14).

Christians who received the books of the synagogue were therefore engaged in a pilgrimage through a transitory world, where they were strangers, to the eternal liturgy foretold by the prophets and awaiting the righteous. This is the praise of Isaiah 35: 10: 'And the ransomed of the Lord shall return, and come to Zion with songs and everlasting joy upon their heads', just as it is the service of the blessed as priests in the paradisiacal temple prophesied in Revelation 21. Yet there was more to the hymnody of Christians than an anticipation of the eternal worship where they hoped to find a place. There was also a particular relationship to time and eschatology. Christians lived in the world; some of them no doubt thrived there. Psalmody in the common assembly, or at the shared Sunday meal, was a way for them to celebrate and rediscover the true cosmic order, and their true home, amidst the distractions of life in the cities of the eastern Mediterranean that might gradually induce them to forget they were in exile.

In Revelation, often assumed to be a work from the time of the emperor
Domitian (81–96), Saint John urges his coreligionists to think upon this true cosmic order, described by him in the visionary language of Daniel and Isaiah. John
presents a narrative of Rome's destruction, the coming of the millennium and the
perpetual harvest of plenty, to be followed by the definitive victory over Satan,
the final judgement and the creation of the New Jerusalem. Christians who have
become settled amongst polytheists must recognize anew that Rome, symbolized
by Babylon, is destined for the destruction that overtook Jerusalem in AD 70,
whereas the Holy City will be rebuilt during the Last Things as a paradisiacal
end-time Temple. This is a sequence of events, or it seems to be, but any attempt
to read John's vision as a narrative of the Last Things, unfolding in time, crum-
bles away before the 'already-and-not-yet' view of God's final glory that dominates Revelation. In John's text, things that will happen are evoked as if they are
already in the process of occurring. In the words of a recent commentator, an
'end-time new creation . . . has irrupted into the present old world through the
death and Resurrection of Christ', and therefore Christians are urged 'to see their
own situation in this world in the light of the eternal perspective in the new
world which is now their true home'. This perspective (if perspective it can be
called that seeks to dismantle terrestrial categories of perception) encompasses
the various descriptions of celestial hymnody in the text, notably chapter 14,
where John hears 'the voice of harpers harping with their harps' as the 144,000
surround the Lamb. They sing 'as it were a new song . . . and no man could learn
that song but the hundred and forty four thousand which were redeemed from
the earth'. Rome (Babylon) has been destroyed and the persecuted righteous
receive their due reward. This is a vision of hymnody in the 'already-and-not-yet'
final glorification of God.[25]

The desire to sing together in this life so that the categories of present and
future momentarily dissolve, and so that one may be mystically present in a life
still to come and yet already available to be lived, was not simply a concern of
Revelation, a markedly Jewish text long destined for a liminal position in the
Christian scriptural canon; it was also shared by those Christians who accepted
a general resurrection in some form of bodily existence. What is more, this view
of hymnody was enhanced by a doctrine that pagan critics like Celsus deemed to
be absurd and which even some wings of Christian opinion repudiated, namely
that a general and bodily resurrection would occur in preparation for the final
judgement. Many Christians therefore believed that the bodily activity of vocal
praise they knew in the present would continue after death, albeit in some mode
of being beyond full human comprehension. For Christians who received the
gospels destined for canonical status, there was only one way to understand what
this bodily life might be, and that was to ponder the final chapters of the evangelists.[26]

The answer these books give to the question of *how* Jesus was in the body after
his death is far from clear. Matthew and Mark (including the redacted verses

16: 9–20) say little about the nature of Christ's body after the Resurrection, while the gospels of Luke and John shimmer with different understandings of his physical state after the Crucifixion. In the redacted ending to Mark 16, at verse 12, Jesus appears 'in a different form' to disciples having already appeared to Mary. In Luke 24: 31 he becomes invisible or *aphantos* ('not apparent') at Emmaus. He suddenly appears among the community in Jerusalem in 24: 36 yet insists in verse 39 of the same chapter that he is made of flesh and blood and is not a spirit or *pneuma*. He even asks for food in verse 41. In John's gospel, Christ forbids Mary to touch him (20: 17) then twice appears in the midst of his disciples even though the door of the room where they are gathered is locked and barred (20: 19 and 26). On the second of these two occasions, Thomas is present and assuages his doubts by touching Christ's body. At 21: 1–14 there is another post-Resurrection meal, convened by Christ, who apparently partakes of the grilled fish and bread with his followers.

The gospels leave little doubt that there was considerable debate in the first and second century, as we would expect, about the nature of Christ's body, not only after the Resurrection but also throughout his ministry. The docetism of the *Acts of John*, or the moderated teachings of the *Acts of Peter*, where Jesus only appears to eat for the sake of his disciples, had their adherents. It is no accident these two texts were not received into the New Testament canon; their doctrines do not allow for the bodily sufferings of Christ and therefore deny the teaching, perhaps originating with Jesus himself, that the agonies of the Crucifixion were necessary to fulfil the prophecy of the Suffering Servant in Isaiah 53 (including the famous fifth verse: 'But he was wounded for our transgressions, he was bruised for our iniquities, the chastisement of our peace was upon him, and with his stripes we are healed'). Despite the necessarily imperfect attempts of the evangelists to broach the mystery of the Saviour's resurrected body, various passages in the writings of the Apostolic Fathers show that many Christians of the second and third generations believed that Jesus had risen in the flesh and hoped to follow him. To this end, *I Clement* confidently quotes Job 19: 26: 'And though after my skin worms destroy this body, yet in my flesh shall I see God.' According to Ignatius, writing to the Church of the Trallians, 'Christ was truly raised from the dead, his Father having raised him: in the same way, his Father will also raise us in Jesus Christ', while *II Clement* is equally explicit: 'For just as you were called in the flesh [to be born], so also you will come in the flesh [into eternal life]'. Justin, in a fragmentary treatise that is probably his, insists that 'the flesh shall rise perfect and entire'; he also ponders the question of whether the members will discharge the same functions in the heavenly state as they do now (*On the Resurrection*, 2 and 3). His contemporary Athenagoras, a more stringent author than Justin, reveals that many Christians believed a general resurrection in the body was essential for the final judgement. What justice could there be for the soul if the body, responsible for so many temptations to vice, was not also called to account before the heavenly tribunal?[27]

By the end of the second century, reflection on these matters had become more elaborate and systematic, notably in the earliest sustained discussion of bodily resurrection by an Occidental Father, Tertullian. It is no part of Tertullian's purpose in *De Resurrectione Carnis* to correct those who hoped the dead would one day 'rise up from the earth possessing the same bodies as before' (in the words of Celsus, who held that belief in contempt). Tertullian, whatever his reputation as a philosopher amongst his fellow Carthaginians, is quite prepared to endorse this and other positions that Celsus regards as irredeemably feeble, including the belief that the risen dead will be able to know God through their five senses, all restored to their formerly corrupted bodies. Tertullian argues that flesh is not the servant or handmaid of the soul, as commonly supposed, but its consort. It must be so, since all things are mediated to the soul, the seat of intellection, through the senses, and 'if this is true in things temporal, it is also true in things eternal'. If Christians are to rise after the example of Christ, who rose in the flesh, then they must ascend in the body themselves. In response to questions from pagans, Tertullian replies that the various members of the human body will be 'delivered from their lower functions' in the blessed state. Neither troubled by the reference to Christ's post-Resurrection hunger nor anticipating John Milton's conviction that even angels devour their food 'with keen dispatch', Tertullian argues that eating, drinking, coitus and the need for labour will pass away in heaven. Are there not even now, he asks, some who use those functions sparingly by fasting and living celibate lives? These ascetics are already drifting towards the bodily state of Paradise.[28]

Now we reach the heart of the matter. Tertullian insists that while the baser functions of the body will pass away in the blessed state, the higher ones will remain. Addressing both his fellow Christians and pagan doubters, he poses a simple question: 'You have been given a mouth for eating and for drinking; why not rather for speaking and praising God?' One would give much to know how many other Christian teachers had followed this line of thought, for it offers a profound way of viewing a Christian purpose for hymnody. In the blessed state, whether it be the millennial paradise envisaged by Saint Irenaeus with abundant grapes and corn, or the paradisiacal end-time temple of Revelation envisioned by Saint John, vocal praise of God is a higher faculty of the resurrected and restored body that will persist in Paradise when other, lower functions have become unnecessary and are therefore forgone. In contrast to labour with the hands, eating, drinking and the exertions of coitus, the use of the voice is one of the principal continuities between the states of bodily life on either side of the grave. Viewed in retrospect, this looks like a relatively narrow and imperilled stream of belief since it rested upon one among many understandings of Christ's post-Resurrection state. Yet the thinness of the stream is precisely the point. The view of hymnody suggested here would have served to distinguish the worship and Christology of those who advocated it from a great many other commitments, including those of many Gnostics who could not accept that the highest divine being either genuinely suffered in the body or ever took flesh, let alone that he was garbed in it after death. It is the combination of eschatological hope and diligent domesticity – the desire to stand *sub specie aeternitatis* and yet to walk in the common street as a respected householder with a body not in itself a source of disgrace – that gives the first two centuries of evidence for Christian psalmody their especially moving quality.[29]

Some Performers: The Apostolic Tradition

The breadth of occasions for the performance of Christian ritual singing, and indeed the scope of the recruitment for suitable singers within the household groups, emerges with striking clarity from the church order commonly known as the *Apostolic Tradition*, whose core materials are usually dated to the first decades of the third century. Long believed to be a work of the third-century scholar Hippolytus, the *Apostolic Tradition* is now widely regarded as a composite text whose history begins as early as the middle years of the second century, and continues (as far as the core of the Greek text is concerned) well into the third or fourth. Only fragments of the Greek original survive, but there are partial translations and adaptations of its material in Latin, Sahidic (southern Coptic), Bohairic (the Coptic of the more cosmopolitan Nile Delta), Arabic and Ethiopic. There are also versions of its material in three other church orders: the *Apostolic Constitutions* (probably Syrian, 375–80), the so-called *Canons of Hippolytus* (extant only in Arabic), and the *Testamentum Domini* (surviving only in Syriac). The rubble of Babel's tower lies thick and disordered here.[30]

Three fragments contain material describing a common meal of the Christian community, held in the evening and beginning with a lamp-lighting ceremony. Taken together, the three accounts of this supper demonstrate the need to keep an open mind about the diversity of Christian meals in the first three centuries of the Common Era and the scope of musical provision before the coalescence of a named minister of ritual song. The redaction in the *Canons of Hippolytus* calls the meal '[a supper] of the Lord' in which the members of the assembly take wine and bread in that order, while the version surviving in Ethiopian plainly states the meal 'is not the Eucharist'. Perhaps the meal is a love-feast supper or *agape*, yet one can never be sure where, in the many different redactions, a stratum is reached so archaic that no clear distinction is yet made between the common meals of the community and the Eucharist. The evening gathering begins as the deacon enters with the lamp and greets the assembled congregation with 'The Lord be with you', receiving the response: 'And with thy spirit'. He rejoins: 'Let us give thanks unto God' and they reply: 'It is right and just; greatness and exaltedness with glory are fitting for him.' The deacon then says a prayer for illumination, literal and metaphorical, which ends with a doxology. The people reply 'Amen'. All these details are given in the Ethiopian version, which continues:

10   The literate child in the household. Detail from a household shrine or *aedicule*, with the portrait of a curiously epicene boy (his sex is indicated by the bare chest and absence of jewellery). Beside him are a slate and stylus. From an unidentified site in the Fayyum. First half of the 3rd c. Cairo, Egyptian Museum

[1.] And when they have then risen after the supper and have prayed, the children and the virgins are to say the psalms.

[2.] After this a deacon, holding the mixed cup of the oblation, is to say a psalm from the ones over which 'Hallelujah' is written.

[3.] And after this a presbyter, if he has commanded, [is also to read] in this way from those psalms.

[4.] After this, the bishop, when he has offered the cup, is to say the psalm that is appropriate for the cup, with all of them saying ever Hallelujah. When they read the psalms they are all to say Hallelujah, that is to say 'We praise the one who is God glorified and praised, who established the entire world with one word'.

[5.] And in this way, when the psalm has been completed, he is to give thanks [for] the cup and he is to give some of the crumbs to all the faithful.

In the first of these suspiciously detailed instructions, there is a call for psalms to be rendered by 'the children and the virgins'. The word for 'children' in the Ethiopian (*däqaweqt*) is gender neutral, the compiler using neither of the forms available to indicate male children or females. The word for 'virgins', *dänagel*, is also gender neutral; they are probably urban house-ascetics, both male and female, vowed to a life of continence and either residing in the dwellings of their parents or sharing a common lodging in what was in effect a proto-monastery, though it might be no more than rented accommodation or rooms in a bishop's residence.

Only this first instruction, calling for 'children and virgins' to sing psalms, has any counterpart in another redaction of the *Apostolic Tradition* dossier. The parallel passage appears in the *Testamentum Domini*, a short tract that 'incorporates the *Apostolic Tradition* within a much enlarged context of instructions given by Jesus himself to his disciples before his ascension, and beginning with an apocalyptic discourse'. Originally composed in Greek, the *Testamentum* survives only in Syriac and may date to the late decades of the fourth century or to the fifth: 'And let the little boys say spiritual psalms and hymns of praise by the light of the lamp. Let all the people respond "Hallelujah" to the psalm and to the chant together, with one accord, with voices in harmony.'[31] This reference to the performance of psalms by 'little boys' is not a precise match for the allusion to 'the children' in the Ethiopian, where the original makes no distinction of gender, and 'the virgins' of the Ethiopian redaction (again gender neutral) now seem to have disappeared. Yet the correspondence is close enough to suggest that some regulation involving the psalmody of children was present in an ancient layer of the lost *Apostolic Tradition* dossier in Greek. The implicit social context for this psalmody lies once more in the houses of those who designated rooms for the worship of the community and who might pay for much of the food that was consumed. This is the host who is evoked several times in the *Apostolic Tradition* and who invites people under his or her roof.[32]

The children and virgins mentioned together in the Ethiopian version of the *Apostolic Tradition* were all in a state of sexual innocence. The virgins, as house-ascetics, if that is what they were, would no doubt have enhanced their discipline of continence with fasting and vigils. Whether by nature or by choice, the chosen singers were already advancing towards their post-Resurrection state of flesh purged of some lower functions that would vanish in Paradise. Among later sources from the fifth and sixth centuries, epitaphs of liturgical readers and reader-singers, the lectors, will sometimes explicitly commemorate the sexual innocence of the departed. In the *Apostolic Tradition*, the context of the children's performance is convivial in the strict sense, centred upon evening meals that commemorate and continue the table-fellowship of Jesus. This is where much of the early evidence for Christian music-making will be found.

11   A goblet in a mosaic of the 3rd c. AD, found in 1951 in the Rue de Gambetta, Nîmes. Nîmes, Musée archéologique.

3

ECHOES OF CHRISTIAN MUSIC AT COMMUNITY MEALS AND ELSEWHERE

Food and the Faith

By 200, many Christians had come to accept a fourfold gospel canon with two similar redactions of an extraordinary episode. In Mark 11: 12–14 as in Matthew 21: 18–22, Jesus curses a fig tree out of season for failing to provide any fruit. This is a most unexpected intrusion of hunger into the life of a teacher who rarely went without food unless he chose to fast, a discipline he did not comprehensively enjoin upon his disciples. Jesus is often presented in the fourfold gospel as a miraculous bringer of plenty: one who makes wine from water and can feed five thousand persons with stores barely adequate for half a dozen. These were blessings unlikely to be forgotten in the eastern Mediterranean where cities such as Jerusalem and Damascus could endure up to four months of summer drought, to judge by modern figures, and where the farmer of James 5: 7, anxiously waiting for the rains, must have been a familiar sight. Jesus was dubbed 'a glutton and a drunkard' by his enemies because of his willingness to share meals with fiscal officers of the Roman state and with other sinners (Matthew 11: 19), and his meals in the houses of influential Jews seem to place him somewhere between the rabbi and the Hellenistic dinner sage, issuing an invitation to a heavenly banquet where the blessed 'shall eat bread in the kingdom of God'. In its earthly guise, table fellowship to share a common store of food was a means to celebrate a temporary escape from the endemic curses of poor harvest, parched soil and dried riverbeds that every Mediterranean community knew. Unpredictable shortages, sometimes sharply localized, made the followers of Jesus in the countryside well able to understand what it meant to 'hunger and thirst' after righteousness.[1]

The history of Christianity during its first three centuries is in many respects the story of who was prepared to sit down at table with whom to enjoy Nature's bounty in a good year and give thanks for it. The ritual meals of the Jews, with their prayers and blessings of cup and bread, were an expression of Israelite identity in the common language of social dining in the eastern Mediterranean that often possessed a cultic dimension among Gentiles as well. Christians became a presence to be reckoned with in the cities because some very early and influential Jewish groups who accepted Jesus as the Messiah also believed that the eschatological age had begun; the work for the salvation of the Gentiles could commence and the new converts could be invited to the table for votive meals of a kind they recognized, in general terms, from the polytheistic cults they had forsaken. Other Jewish groups, including the original Jerusalem community, proved more resistant to table fellowship with Gentiles. In Acts of the Apostles, Luke builds a picture of slow but successful persuasion on many fronts as this Aramaic-speaking community is gradually induced to accept Greek-speaking Gentiles, easing the requirement that males should accept circumcision and that all should observe the food laws. The factors involved seem to be many and various. An influx of Greek-speaking Jews into Jerusalem from the Diaspora gives rise to food-related disturbance very early on, perhaps because the Diaspora Jews were accustomed to much lower barriers between themselves and Gentiles than their coreligionists in the holy city, and had been expecting to receive a dole of food from the Jerusalem Church that they could eat with Gentile guests (6: 1). In Acts 10, Yahweh spectacularly makes Saint Peter his spokesman for a repeal of the food laws and for a mission to the Gentiles; Luke shows the Jerusalem community greeting the news with anger and incomprehension when Peter returns from Joppa, where the vision occurred. Luke then abbreviates a protracted process by having Peter recount his vision at length, and for a second time, so that the members of the Jerusalem community 'held their peace and glorified God' (11: 18). Acts then moves swiftly to an account of a persecution that scatters members of the nascent churches, some going to Antioch, where the term 'Christians' was first employed, according to 11: 26. There are many signs of unease in the relationship between the Antioch community and the Jerusalem Church, given the speed with which the former was embracing table fellowship with Gentiles. The Antiochenes could even be addressed from Jerusalem as 'the brethren of the Gentiles'. Luke determinedly shows a Messianic summons to dine together in the already and not yet kingdom of God continually broadening the commitments of Jews who accepted Jesus as the Messiah and associated with Gentile converts.[2]

In some respects, these Gentiles would have found nothing so very puzzling about the ceremony of sharing food after giving thanks to a divinity (hence 'Eucharist', from the verb that appears in the Last Supper narratives of Matthew, Mark and Luke in the form *eucharistēsas*, 'giving thanks'). The belief that full participation in a ritual meal could be secured by eating a token sample is expressed around 200 in the Mishnah regulations for the Passover; Jews can fulfil their obligation if the herbs they consume, for example, equal the mass of a single olive when joined together (*Pesahim*, 2. 6:E). In the moments of votive prayer over bread and wine, converted polytheists would perhaps have recognized a form of the practice whereby certain token portions of food in a meal might be set aside as the god's share. Even the notion that the god was mystically present at the table could perhaps be perceived as hospitality for the deity of a kind familiar to

12 A 3rd-c. scene of a meal from the Catacomb of Callistus, Appian Way. Scenes such as this, with a semicircular or 'sigma' table, implying a similarly shaped dining couch or *stibadium*, are not rare in either the Christian or the non-Christian catacombs of Rome. There are often seven figures, as here. The shared meals of the Christians do not seem to have inspired any major departures in the catacomb iconography of dining, and it is an open question what departures of *practice* from common Jewish and Gentile custom there were to illustrate. Such images of convivial pleasure amidst the tunnels of the catacombs that give the senses of sight, smell and touch so many reminders of death, cannot fail to impress. Some of these images have been interpreted as both Eucharist and *agape* (the 'love-feast' or community supper) by modern commentators, plainly uncertain when the distinction between the two becomes valid and deciding the matter on the basis of details such as the food shown, the aspect of the diners or the absence of wine that rarely carry complete conviction. From Wilpert, *Roma Sotteranea: Le pitture delle catacombe romane*, Tav. 41.

pagans, while the language used by Ignatius soon after 100, describing the bread and wine as 'the medicine of immortality' or 'the antidote preventing death', would not have surprised any polytheist or Jew who had used magical papyri and amulets.[3]

The question of what else converts encountered when they joined the common meal of a Christian community can have no single answer. Much presumably depended upon the location and constituency of the church they joined. Before the compilation of any gospels now known, if the current mainstream datings are correct, Paul gives the words of institution ('This is my body . . .') in 1 Corinthians 11: 23–7, declaring that he had 'received [them] of the Lord'. (Not all manuscripts have this, though some read 'from God'.) Despite the suggestion of divine intervention, the language of 'receiving' is technical and implies the transmission of a school tradition. If Paul did not devise these words himself he presumably derived them from the same source as his information about the Resurrection appearances, namely his encounters with the original Jerusalem community. In other words, Paul may have had the words of institution from men who had been with Jesus in his last hours of freedom. The four canonical evangelists, however, do not seem to have received anything as well defined as the tradition passed to Paul, even though some of them may be dependent upon him. Matthew, Mark and Luke all give words of institution in their accounts of the Last Supper, while John 6 has Jesus pronounce a discourse about salvation through eating his flesh which he places after the Feeding of the Five Thousand. Matthew and Mark, whose accounts are essentially the same, have the words of institution but no injunction to institute a rite. The words 'do this in re-membrance of me', the foundation of the Eucharistic meal, appear only in 1 Corinthians 11: 24 (the earliest attested appearance) and in Luke 22: 19, perhaps following Paul. Thus the heart of the mystery is indeed veiled. Nonetheless, these passages suggest that there were some trajectories for the shared meals of Christian communities where the ingestion of bread and wine, hallowed by prayer and thanksgiving, was already crystallizing during the first century into the crucial phase of a meal in which the conviviality of table fellowship gave way to a more sombre remembrance of the Passion, perhaps through especially charged portions of the food provided. This ceremony eventually became impos-sible to reconcile with the pleasure and bodily satisfaction of genuine dining, with the result that it was separated from the supper or love feast and become a Eucharistic meal for the refection of the soul only.[4]

The chronology of this development is very uncertain. According to McGowan

> none of [the primary sources for the love feast or *agape*] provides the sort of dichotomy of two meals, a substantial one called *agape* and a purely symbolic one called Eucharist . . . we should probably stop speaking of 'the *agape*' as though there were an ancient consensus about it that we could use in the clear absence of a modern one.[5]

Broadly speaking, this is wise advice. The history of early Christian worship, including its ritual singing, has sometimes been distorted by a certain eagerness to establish the Eucharist in a tolerably recognizable form as early as possible by distinguishing it from the love feast or *agape*. The signs of different traditions and practice can be discerned as soon as the documents begin. Paul gives the words of institution because he believes the Corinthians are in danger of celebrating the Lord's Supper in a way that came easily to converts from polytheism, namely as a banquet to honour a deity with none of the fretting about idolatry that wor-ried Paul the Jew and with no close connection to the Palestinian trajectory for the Lord's Supper, known to Paul, where the bread and wine are a remembrance of the Passion. In Paul's view, the Corinthians did not draw a sufficiently sharp distinction between the Supper and other meals, or perhaps between domestic space and special *ekklesia* space within the house. Several documents commonly placed in the second century still describe forms of meal with an element of thanksgiving but with no words of institution, no commemoration of the Passion and seemingly no eschatological dimension. The second-century *Acts of*

13   The memorial to a certain Saturninus, showing transport amphorae that are probably intended to represent the oil, water and wine for his funeral repast or *refrigerium*, presumably named from
the cold food eaten by the dead in shadow and by the living in their memory. The evolution of an
ascetic Eucharist among Christians, the ingestion of small portions of food detached from the sat-
isfactions of real dining, owes something to the gravity and meaning of the Graeco-Roman funeral meal with its portions of lighter foods (notably fish) eaten in commemoration of the dead. From
the catacomb of Callistus, 3rd or 4th c. (De Rossi, *La Roma sotterranea*, pl. XLI, 39).

Paul knows no common meal except a shared feast, while the *Acts of Peter*
describes a Eucharist celebrated on shipboard by the apostle himself with an
impromptu prayer over the food apparently provided as the main meal. There is
no sense in this latter text that Peter is giving thanks for elements of bread and
wine to be sampled rather than eaten as a repast for the nourishment of the body.
Whether this is a description of the kind of Eucharist known to the compiler
of the *Acts of Peter* in the late second century, or his attempt to reconstruct a
primordial service of the apostolic period, it urges the importance of emphasizing the diversity of early Christian meals and of any musical practices associated
with them.[6]

The Literary Sources for Singing at Early Christian Meals and Elsewhere: A Rapid Conspectus

'One of the rules to be most strictly observed in studying early Christian worship
is to abstain from any kind of generalisation [except this one]. Every piece of evidence is only of value for the time and place to which it refers.' Maurice Goguel's
warning, though issued long ago, has lost none of its force. The evidence for
a Fore-Mass service with readings *and* psalmody, for example, is stronger in

Carthage around 200 than it is in Rome two centuries later. Hence it is essential to take four crucial steps that guard against the tendency to generalize. The first is to keep the diversity of early Christian meals at the front of the mind, as mentioned above. The second is to relax the distinction between sources identified only in a later period as canonical or as apocryphal writings. (One of the most important texts soon to be examined is a non-canonical book, the *Acts of Paul*). The third step is to recognize the diversity of doctrine that could exist even within the mainstream Church, so that a valuable witness like Tertullian is not unduly marginalized or even discounted on the grounds that he was a 'Montanist'. The fourth and final step is to investigate all the source material again in case anything of potential value has escaped.[7]

The sources gathered in the Appendix to this chapter burn like candles thinly dispersed at different hours through the vastness of a cathedral in the dead of night. Some fade long before others have begun to give light; rarely do two sources combine to shed a radiance greater than one alone. For the most part, only the material by known authors can be approximately dated and localized. Some of the anonymous texts, including some of outstanding importance such as the *Apostolic Tradition* or the pseudo-Clementine letter on virginity, may have come from almost anywhere in the eastern Mediterranean. The earliest Western materials are virtually all African, and in the first three centuries of the faith it would be surprising if they came from anywhere else since the evidence of a Latin-speaking Church outside Africa is sparse until the fourth century. Apart from Pliny, Justin Martyr is the only relevant author writing elsewhere in the West before 300, and he uses Greek.

The quality of the information is often difficult to assess. Pliny the Younger, the earliest independent witness to Christian ritual singing, gathered his information from men and women under threat of torture; some of his other informants admitted to being Christians and then changed their story by claiming they had lapsed in their faith some twenty years earlier. (See no. 4 in the Appendix, to which all subsequent numbers refer.) The apocryphal *Acts of Paul*, with its reference to 'psalms and songs' at a shared meal in the Church of Corinth, is the work of a later second-century polemicist, unique among the authors of our documents for the energy with which he tries to build alternative traditions about the apostle at a time when there were competing claims to his legacy (no. 5). If the *Acts of John*, with its account of choral dance at the last meal of Jesus with his disciples, records the cultic practices of a Christian group (no. 6), the *Acts of Paul*, better than any other text, shows how hazardous it may be to distinguish canonical from apocryphal sources without due circumspection. Those *Acts* originally formed part of a comprehensive dossier that included three other writings that

14 (*facing page*)   A shroud or funerary hanging of *c.*125–50, tempera on linen, from Saqqara. A young man, modelled by the artist in a Greek manner, stands at the entrance to an Egyptian temple in the company of the jackal-headed god Anubis modelled in the Egyptian fashion. To the left stands Osiris in mummy form. The young man holds a scroll, and Anubis what appears to be a key. The image evokes the deepest longing of the mystery cults: to be initiated into the mysteries of the Oriental gods in their most secret inner sanctum. Justin Martyr labours hard to disassociate the Christians from such cults. Moscow, Pushkin Museum.

became detached and circulated independently: the *Acts of Paul and Thecla*, the *Correspondence of Paul with the Corinthians* (or *III Corinthians*) and the *Martyrdom of Paul*. The collection was widely read and admired in various forms and was especially well known in Egypt, to judge by the numerous papyrus fragments found there.

By no means all of the sources establish beyond doubt that a sung performance is involved rather than a spoken recitation. A passage in *Ad Donatum* by Cyprian of Carthage, alluding to the suppers of wealthy Christians in Carthage and calling for a psalm from the melodious voice of Donatus, is one of the more secure examples (no. 18). Each instance has to be argued case by case; the result is a corpus of material suggesting contexts for psalmody that are both diverse and often convivial. There are early morning gatherings of Christians for worship in Pontus, described to Pliny at the beginning of the second century but separate as yet from the evening supper (no. 4). The supper of a community, with a lighting of lamps, is described in several witnesses to a Syrian dossier of the earlier third century, the *Apostolic Tradition*, probably incorporating substantially older material; the singers in this instance are children and house-ascetics (no. 19). There is the Sunday liturgy (nos 7 [a Jewish domestic meal] and 11, perhaps also 17), psalmody in the home both Jewish and Christian (nos 1, 12, 14 and 15) and the psalmody of itinerant ascetics, a most intriguing group, residing with Christian or even pagan hosts for the night and singing during or after meals (no. 20). The arrangements for ritual song, where they can be detected, seem to be decidedly informal to the point where one might well begin to question the applicability of the term *ritual* song. Tertullian, describing a shared meal, says in unmistakable terms that 'anyone who has anything to offer from the divine Scriptures, or from his own devising, is called into the centre [of the assembly] to *canere* before God', where the versatile term *canere* may encompass the singing of hymns, be they biblical or newly composed, and the recitation of Scripture from memory or a text (no. 13). There is no explicit sense anywhere that singing is associated with any kind of ministry. The singers mentioned include members of the Corinthian house-churches in Paul's first letter to that Church (no. 2 (iii) and (iv)), the members of churches addressed in Ephesians and Colossians (no. 2 (v) and (vi)), members of the primordial Jerusalem community (no. 2 (vii), if the *Epistle of James* is authentic), husband and wife at home (no. 15), a householder at home freed from the distractions of marriage and childrearing (no. 12), a member of the higher society of Carthage, perhaps a lawyer (no. 18), children and virgins of both sexes (no. 19) and itinerant ascetics (no. 20). There are traces of many different occasions of meals and worship here, and many kinds of singing may be audible from the minimal-ability chanting perhaps implied by Pliny's early morning *carmen* to the singing of Cyprian's gifted friend Donatus in the cool of evening in a garden of ancient Carthage. In every explicit case the setting appears to be domestic in the strict sense that the location is a house, but some suggest a foregathering of families whereas others evoke husband and wife at home.

15 An aristocratic woman of Africa Proconsularis grooms herself with attendants. Floor mosaic from a large private bath discovered in 1975 at Sidi Ghrib, south of Carthage. Although made long after the time of Tertullian, the image suggests the kind of high-status convert the Church of Carthage had already attracted by *c*.200, and whom Tertullian addresses in many of his treatises in Latin. Tertullian gives no clue as to the status of the woman who received the gift of prophecy during the Fore-Mass psalmody at Carthage. Late 4th or early 5th c. Carthage Museum.‾

Four Crucial Texts

At some time in the second century, an anonymous author commented most unfavourably upon the household-based mainstream Church by constructing a competing claim to Paul's legacy. His work provides an outstanding chance to witness a counter church or tradition in the making, complete with its psalmody. The *Acts of Paul* (no. 5) has sometimes been read as a Greek romance or as an eccentric relative of the Acts of the Apostles (which has its own debts to the Greek novels), and has only recently begun to acquire a better reputation for its sympathetic presentation of Thecla, Paul's female devotee and ascetic companion. The compiler uses most of the Pauline documents, including Ephesians and Colossians, and his account of the Corinthian gathering owes something to them. He knows the passages in 1 Corinthians concerning the use of startling and pneumatic gifts in the community's worship.

Thus armed, the compiler enters the battle between different interpreters of Paul's legacy at a time when there was perhaps still some oral record of his ministry to place beside the letters. The opponents in view are principally the authors of the Pastoral Epistles (1–2 Timothy and Titus) together with the Pauline letters to the Ephesians and the Colossians, precisely because they exalt the family life of Christian parents in the household. In contrast to those documents, perhaps received into the proto-New Testament on a wave of approval from the married householder-presbyters whose Christian commitment they endorse, the *Acts of Paul* advocates strict forms of sexual renunciation and champions various initiatives (such as the ministry of women) that run counter to teachings associated with Paul's name in the New Testament. As so often with the books not received into the canon, the original Greek text of this one survives in a fragmentary state, so it is especially fortunate that a reference to liturgical practice during Paul's stay in Corinth is relatively complete and survives in the original Greek rather than in a later translation. The apostle attends a communal meal where 'each one took of the bread and feasted according to custom, with a psalm of David and a song (*psalmōn te David kai ōdōn*)'. The meaning of *psalmōn* is not in doubt, given the reference to David, while *ōdē* was commonly used in second-century Jewish Greek for the songs attributed to Moses and others in the books of the Synagogue. They are both sung (if they are *sung*, there is no pertinent verb) during a repast that provides sustenance for the body as well as the soul. It is not in any sense an ascetic Eucharist. Since the meal is interrupted when a woman suddenly receives the gift of prophecy from the Holy Spirit, the diners seem to be gathered in the presence of the sacred as they say or sing the hymnody, and the compiler envisages this gathering as the customary convocation of the Corinthian Church for worship.[8]

The *First Apology* of Justin Martyr (no. 7) is designed to throw the doors of a house-church open during a Sunday service and to let the imperial family look in. Born into a pagan family in what is now the West Bank town of Nablus, Justin converted sometime before 135 and had by that time received a philosophical education in the East, first as the student of a Stoic, then of a Peripatetic, and finally as the pupil of 'a very famous Pythagorean'. This background gives him an assured place among the first generation of Christian intellectuals that was gradually taking shape in the late second century. After his conversion, he moved to Rome and took lodgings above an unidentifiable bathhouse. He was therefore one of the innumerable Greek-speaking immigrants in the imperial capital and the information he gives cannot be regarded as Roman in any exclusive sense; if he emigrated by land (to say nothing of travels that are unrecorded) he may have attended services in an immense circuit of house-churches from Antioch, Tarsus and Ephesus through the Balkans to Italy.[9]

Justin presents his account of Christians and their worship as if he wishes to defend the liberties and explain the customs of his co-religionists to the Roman imperial powers. Aiming high, he offers what appears to be an imperial petition with an opening address to the Emperor Antoninus Pius and his sons, Marcus Aurelius and Lucius, together with 'the sacred senate and the whole Roman people'. Impelled to write by the recent persecutions of Christians in the East, Justin speaks for those 'who are unjustly hated and mistreated' and who may be 'men of every race' (that is to say not simply Jews). This seems clear enough, but much remains mysterious about Justin's *First Apology*. He calls it a petition, as if he intends it to join the many thousands of documents creating what Seneca calls 'a crush of matters coming together from the whole world' in a torrent across the emperor's desk; yet it seems highly unlikely that the *First Apology* was ever truly intended to pass under the eyes of an emperor or indeed of anyone wielding power in Rome. A local magistrate, to say nothing of an emperor, would have needed all the resources of his philosophical training to tolerate the vigorous effrontery with which Justin champions Christian beliefs and ceremonies, to say nothing of his refusal to offer the flattery that was required if such a petition were to be deemed acceptable at the highest level. In short, it remains a mystery why Justin wrote and for whom. Nonetheless, the realities of being a Christian in the second-century Empire do seem to underlie the passage where he exonerates his coreligionists from the charge that their weekly assembly is a closed and potentially treasonable gathering:

> For all the food that we receive we bless the creator of the universe through his Son Jesus Christ and through the Holy Spirit. On the day that is generally called the Day of the Sun, all of us, whether they live in the city or in the countryside, gather together in the same place. There we read the memoirs of the Apostles or the writings of the prophets, for as long as time allows. Then, when the reader has finished, the president of the assembly addresses us with teachings and injunctions that we should heed these fair mandates. Then we all rise together and pray aloud. Then, as I have said, when the prayer is finished bread, wine and water are brought in; the one presiding says aloud the prayers and thanksgiving, with all the fervour of which he is capable, and the people reply with *Amen*. Then the eucharistic food is distributed to that it may be shared between all present, and those who are absent receive their portion through the ministering of the deacons. (*First Apology*, 67)

This sounds like a Eucharist with a sampling of hallowed elements, not a shared meal. Yet even here it may be necessary to tread carefully. The service seems to have involved sitting or reclining at some stage, since there was at least one moment when the congregation was required to rise to its feet, and the shared bread, wine and water should not be too quickly taken to imply that there is no meal. The other elements of the ritual include a gospel reading and a homily, but there is no apparent reference to hymnody. This has sometimes been regarded as a strong argument that psalmody was added much later to the Eucharistic service, indeed in the fourth century; yet it is possible that Justin regarded chanted psalms and other texts as a form of reading, just as Augustine and some other later Fathers will do. If this was indeed the view in Justin's church, then the moment when 'the reader . . . finished' might refer to the end of the phase when those present expected to hear both readings and psalmody. The performance would have been entrusted to the reader, or at least led by him, just as we shall find it given to the reader or *lector* at a later date in Western churches. Above all, however, Justin's *First Apology* is not a liturgical ordinal designed to give a definitive account of liturgical actions. It is an attempt to record how he wishes the Roman authorities to be addressed on the matter of Christians who were neither atheists nor members of a secret society trying to gain knowledge of the future that might make them a political threat. The picture he gives is undoubtedly selective, possibly describing forms of worship that retained something of the Pauline churches where ceremonies were 'a blend of the familiar and the novel . . . the spontaneous and the customary'. Thus the president of the assembly in Justin's church pronounced words of thanksgiving *according to his ability*, presumably producing a different result each time, while the reader delivered a passage from the gospels *or* the prophets *for as long as time allows*. This is more of a meeting with a flexible agenda than a Mass in the later sense of the term.[10]

This brings us to the core of what Justin has to offer. Sometimes, it seems, there was indeed vocal music as a ritual item in Justin's church, for he describes the performance of 'hymns' (*hymnous*) in a Eucharistic context elsewhere in the *First Apology*. The material appears in the thirteenth section, where he vaunts the superiority of Christian worship over the traditional Roman religions because it does not require any of the things provided for the sustenance of Mankind to be destroyed by fire upon an altar, as in the sacrifices of Jews before the destruction of the Temple and in the continuing rites of polytheists:

> No we are not godless; we worship the creator of the universe, and according to the doctrine that we have received we proclaim that He has no need of bloody sacrifices, nor of libations, nor of incense; we praise Him, as far as lies within our power, *through the word of prayer* and by giving thanks for all the food that we eat, for we have learned that the only manner of worship worthy of him is not to burn, and therefore to lose, the good things that he has made for our subsistence, but rather to employ them for themselves and to give them to the needy; it is to hold festivities for Him and to address hymns (*hymnous*) to Him with words that express our gratitude . . . (*First Apology*, 13; emphasis mine)

The hymns that Justin heard in the assemblies evoked here were probably sung, since he contrasts them with words (*logou*) of thanksgiving. The context of their performance is Eucharistic, for the italicized expression 'through the word of prayer' appears elsewhere in the *First Apology*, where it denotes the blessing of the Eucharistic elements. In the passage quoted above, Justin seems to be describing a common meal where the faithful gather to consume the things that God 'has brought into being for our sustenance', rather than to destroy them on the altar during a sacrifice in a temple forecourt. The presbyter offers prayers of thanksgiving on the community's behalf over a portion of bread and wine that the members of the assembly then share, together with other foods. At some stage in the proceedings there were hymns.[11]

By approximately 200, significant traces of psalm-singing appear along the Mediterranean littoral of Africa, from Alexandria to Carthage; here the psalmody just about discernible in Justin's reports of the Church in Rome had become an established ritual item. The context, as in Justin, is the service of reading(s) before the sharing of Eucharistic food. The earliest appears in the anonymous *Letter to Diognetus*, xi. 6, a curiously neglected source for early Christian singing, possibly compiled *c.*200 in Alexandria (no. 17). The letter is addressed to a pagan currently making 'an exacting and careful enquiry' about Christians, perhaps in Alexandria. Chapter II in this masterly piece of apologetic turns to the life of the Church in the world and the conduct of catechumens undergoing instruction prior to baptism. In a mode of exhortation, the anonymous author praises the Church, imbued with a plenitude of grace in its worship: 'Then the fear of the law is sung, the grace of the prophets is made known, the faith of the gospels is established, the tradition of the apostles is guarded, and the grace of the church leaps for joy.'

There is some doubt about the authenticity of the chapter whence this passage comes. Some recent editors and commentators have accepted it as genuine, although a recent summary is probably right to say that 'virtually all scholars acknowledge' chapters II–12 of the letter to come from a different work by a different author. Certainly the Greek style is different, and the text seems to address Christians rather than the inquiring pagan Diognetus. If it is indeed a document of about 200, or at least of the third century, then the section quoted above gains considerably in importance, for it seems to be describing a Liturgy of the Word. The assembled worshippers can expect to hear reading(s) from the Old Testament ('the grace of the prophets is made known') and from the gospels ('the faith of the gospels is established'). There is psalmody ('the fear of the law is sung') and a homily (if that is what is meant by 'the tradition of the apostles is guarded'). The reference to 'singing the fear of the law' has no exact parallel in either the New Testament or the Apostolic Fathers, but unless 'fear of the law' is a synonym for the much more common 'fear of god', then 'the law' must be the Torah, set in rhetorical parallelism against the Prophets, the Gospels and the Apostles. 'Fear of the Law' will refer to the Commandments. In the context of advice for catechumens, this passage can be read as a list of elements in the pre-Eucharistic ceremony to which they were admitted, and the elements include psalmody.[12]

There is some support for this interpretation in a contemporary document of seminal importance for the history of music in Christian worship: the treatise *De Anima* composed around 206–7 by Tertullian, the first theologian of the Latin Occident and a Christian intellectual of Carthage (no. 11). At one point in this characteristically dense treatise on the soul, Tertullian turns to the recent experience of prophets and visionaries, especially liable to be women, who have been granted insight into mysteries while in an intense spiritual state. Pursuing the nature of the soul in the most physical sense, Tertullian records what he has learned from a female visionary in Carthage who recently had a pneumatic experience during the Sunday Eucharist. She was often favoured with 'such gifts of revelation' and conversed with angels, even with Christ himself, during states of ecstasy (*per ecstasin*) that came upon her during the pre-Eucharistic service. Tertullian's references to her healing powers place her in a familiar and somewhat contentious category of the third-century Church that was even in some places an order, namely the charismatic healer. The material for these visions, Tertullian explains, comes directly from the materials of the Sunday service:

> There is among us today a sister favoured with the gifts of revelation that she experiences through an ecstasy of the spirit during the Sunday liturgy. She converses with angels, sometimes even with the Lord; she sees and hears mysteries, reads some people's hearts and applies remedies to those who need them. The material for her visions is supplied as the Scriptures are read (*leguntur*), psalms are sung (*canuntur*), the homily delivered and prayers offered.[13]

With its reference to psalms, this passage seems to be as clear an inventory of elements in a Liturgy of the Word as one is entitled to expect from an author who passed the greater part of his life in the second century. The distinction between *legere* for the Scriptures and *canere* for the psalms shows that the latter are sung, not recited. The *Letter to Diognetus* and the *De Anima* of Tertullian both lead to the same conclusion: one of the most important of the chants in the various rites of both Western and Eastern rites, as they are known from later sources, the psalm before the Eucharistic meal, was in place by 200 in at least two African Churches. Justin Martyr may be referring to the same practice. This is the second-century origin of the gradual.[14]

Tertullian has been described as 'a representative of the Montanist heresy' at the time he composed the *De Anima*, whose favoured form of worship would therefore have been a Montanist gathering, perhaps including 'heretical hymns'. Is he a reliable guide to worship in the mainstream Church of Carthage? When Tertullian compiled the *De Anima* in 206–7 his faith had acquired a character that does indeed complicate the matter of what it means to call him a Catholic. He counted himself among the Christians who believed in the value of spirit-inspired visions, tongues and prophecies, as in the days of the apostles when the nascent Church witnessed the miracle of Pentecost in Jerusalem and the pneumatic worship of the believers addressed by Saint Paul in Corinth. The elderly Tertullian was plainly confident that material received in visions and prophecies, once it was judged to be authentic, could reveal mysteries not disclosed in the Scriptures. That is why he repeats what a woman of Carthage had learned about the soul and passed to on the members of her congregation.[15]

Tertullian knew the apostolic experience of pneumatic events from the Pauline letters (especially 1 Corinthians), from the canonical Acts of the Apostles and from texts still widely received in his day, such as the *Acts of Paul*. In the late second century, this spirit-centred Christianity was increasingly associated with a figure from western Asia Minor named Montanus. Tertullian's commitment to Montanism, or what Tertullian himself calls 'the word of the New Prophecy', explains why his writings are divided into *Opera Catholica* and *Opera Montanistica* (the latter including the *De Anima*) in the modern edition of his works. Yet it is one thing to emphasize the pneumatic aspect of Tertullian's later theology and another to regard him as the representative of a *heresy* whose account of a liturgical service with psalmody is a doubtful source for worship in the mainstream and proto-Catholic Church. Recent work on the first three centuries of the Church has tended to emphasize the pluralism and diversity of Christian assemblies, resisting the tendency to envisage the nascent mainstream Church of the second century in relatively consolidated and fourth-century terms.[16]

This is not to minimize the somewhat anomalous nature of Tertullian's position. In later life, his opinions may have diverged from those of many other Christians in his city when he began to emphasize the importance of prophets 'in ecstacy of the spirit' or when he expressed his belief that the authority of the bishops was inferior to the workings of the Holy Spirit in a layman. Nonetheless, one should not underestimate the extent to which Tertullian could migrate within the Catholic Church of Carthage without passing beyond its borders. The *Passio Perpetuae*, of the early third century and long ascribed to Tertullian, describes the martyrdom of a young Carthaginian woman named Perpetua who corresponds very closely to the kind of female visionary that he evokes in our episode of *De Anima*. She receives visions, and in all aspects of her life inspires her biographer to ask the 'Montanist' question of why new witnesses to the work of the Holy Spirit should not be put in writing like those of the first days. Does it not say in Acts 2: 17 that 'I will pour out of my spirit upon all flesh: and your sons and your daughters shall prophesy'? There is no suggestion in the *Passio Perpetuae* that Perpetua belongs to any other Christian community than the mainstream Church of Carthage. Indeed, one of her visions shows her meeting Bishop Optatus and Aspasius the presbyter, officials of the Catholic Church in the city that Perpetua calls 'our Father and our priest'. It is significant that she was accepted as an authentic Christian martyr whereas the defiant Cataphrygians or Montanists were not.[17]

As the acceptance of Perpetua suggests, the African form of Montanism in the second and third centuries was assimilated by the official Church without undue difficulty. It has been said that 'the Montanism of North Africa (especially Carthage) was a second phase of the movement and it is not easy to determine whether and to what extent it resembled the more original Asian kind . . . Far from being driven out, as had happened in Asia . . . New Prophets seem to have remained integrated into congregations in Carthage.' A recent survey of inscriptions and other primary materials supposedly relating to Montanism rejects the view that Tertullian 'left the official church in Carthage to join a dissident or sectarian group in that city'. As far as the evidence of inscriptions is concerned, the corpus of assuredly Montanist epitaphs is not a large one, precisely because a commitment to Montanist ideals did not generally draw the form or wording of an epitaph away from the common language of Christian memorials. Indeed 'there is nothing to suggest that a separate Montanist congregation existed in Carthage during the early third century' for Tertullian to join. Thus there is good reason to view Tertullian's commitment to the New Prophecy as a migration within his Catholicism, leading him to place more emphasis than some of his coreligionists upon the authority of duly authenticated visions inspired by the Holy Spirit but not putting him outside the mainstream Church. The woman who passed into an ecstatic condition during the service described in *De Anima* was inspired by the regular Sunday liturgy.[18]

Tertullian's account comes from a metropolitan region of the Roman world. The *annona* run from Carthage to Rome, bringing the autumn supply of grain in the great transporters, still in his day sustained the tax spine that gave the Mediterranean to the west of the Italy its coherence as a governed space with dense maritime connections. In the archaeological record African exports, notably the tableware known as African Red Slip Ware (ARS), still predominated around the coasts of the western sea, often extending deep into the hinterlands as the choice of elite customers who repudiated locally made ceramics for more ceremonial or formal occasions in their homes. Communications between Italy and Tunisia were good in the second and third centuries, whether measured in terms of the state-funded transport of men and materials (the *onus fiscale*) or the movement of merchants and chartered ships carrying the surplus of the African grain fields and oil-growing estates. There were many and varied opportunities for presbyters, pilgrims and couriers to move between the Christian communities of the two great cities at either end of the tax spine in Rome and Carthage. Of Tertullian and the psalmody of his Church in Carthage one may fairly say, in the words of Saint Paul, that those things were not done in a corner.

In his extensive writings, Tertullian never uses the Latin word *cantor* as a title of office. The only term for a ministry of the voice that he uses is *lector*, or 'reader', and he regards the stability of that office, among others, as a characteristic of the mainstream Church to which he belonged. Who were the singers who performed the *psalmodia* when Tertullian and his fellow Christians met in one another's houses? Perhaps one should look to men like Cyprian's friend Donatus in third-century Carthage, who might agree to sing at the evening supper of Afro-Roman Christians, but he was very well born and one cannot be certain that his Christian faith would have entirely dissolved his reluctance to perform in public. For the first signs of Christian ritual song being configured into a ministry, or at least into one of the duties associated with a ministry, one should look to the readers, the *lectores*.

APPENDIX TO CHAPTER 3

A NUCLEUS OF SOURCES FOR MUSICAL PRACTICE IN CHRISTIAN ASSEMBLIES BEFORE THE CONVERSION OF CONSTANTINE

The task of isolating a 'practical' kernel of material relating to Christian worship among the literary sources of the first three centuries is a hazardous one. Every reference to music in early Christian writing is of potential value for practice, however tenuous the link may appear, and assessments of what constitutes 'practical' information in the sources will vary from one interpreter to another. Yet certain texts stand out for their concern to commend or condemn certain aspects of worship, including the use of music. Many of these are available in James McKinnon's *Music in Early Christian Literature* (*MECL*) of 1987, but eight and perhaps nine further sources are added here for the first centuries (nos 2, 5, 8, 12, 16, 17, 20, 21 and possibly 22, depending upon date). Most of the relevant extracts are given in the original and in translation, the exceptions usually being cases (1) where a passage of interest is too extensive for quotation and recourse to the original edition is essential for even the most preliminary purposes, or (2) I have no professional competence in the relevant languages (Syriac, Ethiopic and Arabic). For the Syriac text of item 20, see Fig. 2. The orthography of the extracts is that of the editions used, and no attempt has been made to impose a consistent policy upon them.

The meaning of the texts is sometimes unclear in precisely the respect that matters most in the present context, namely whether the action at issue is speaking or singing (I use the term 'singing' to encompass any means of voicing a text that requires the fluid intonation patterns of speech to be resolved into the steps of a musical scale). Much depends upon the degree of musical sense one assigns, text by text, to verbs such as the Greek ᾄδω, λέγω, λαλέω, μελῳδέω, ὑμνήῳ, ψαλλω and to nouns like ψαλμὸς or ὕμνους; the same case-by-case interpretation is required for the Latin expressions *carmen dicere, psalmi canuntur, Deo canere, uox canora* and in the Syriac verb *mᵉzamrīnan*. The standard lexical records of these languages can do no more than offer general guidance based upon the compilers' attempts to grapple with the very problems the user consults the dictionaries to elucidate.

Dates for Tertullian are those proposed by Barnes, *Tertullian*.

List of texts	MECL number(s)
1. 4 Maccabees	—
2. New Testament	3, 6, 10, 11, 13, 14 and 17
3. *I Clement*, 34. 6–8	—
4. Pliny the Younger, *Letters*, x. 96	41
5. *Acts of Paul*	—
6. *Acts of John*	38
7. Justin Martyr, *First Apology*	24 and 25
8. Celsus, *The True Doctrine*	—
9. Clement of Alexandria, *Paedagogos*	51–6
10. Clement of Alexandria, *Stromateis*	57–62
11. Tertullian, *De Anima*	82
12. Tertullian, *De Exhortatione Castitatis*	—
13. Tertullian, *Apologeticum*	74
14. Tertullian, *De Oratione*	78 and 79
15. Tertullian, *Ad Uxorem*	80
16. Inscription from *Aphrodisias*	—
17. *Letter to Diognetus*, xi. 6	—
18. Cyprian of Carthage, *Ad Donatum*	94
19. *Apostolic Tradition*	89
20. Pseudo-Clement, *Epistolae de virginitate*	—
21. The Martyrs of Abitina	—
22. Epitaph of 'Gaios'	—

1 4 Maccabees 18: 9–18

AD 19–54? Edition and English translation in M. Hadas, *The Third and Fourth Book of Maccabees* (New York, 1953), 240–1.

ὑπεμίμνησκεν δὲ ὑμᾶς καὶ τὴν Ησαιου γραφὴν τὴν λέγουσαν Κᾶν διὰ πυρὸς διέλθῃς φλὸξ οὐ κατακαύσει σε. τὸν ὑμνογράφον ἐμελῴδει ὑμῖν Δαυιδ λέγοντα Πολλαὶ αἱ θλίψεις τῶν δικαίων.

He admonished you of the Scripture of Isaiah, which declares, 'When thou walkest through fire the flame shall not burn thee'. He chanted to you the psalm of David which says, 'Many are the ills of the righteous'.

This passage, an outstanding source for Jewish domestic psalmody in the first century AD (if that dating can be relied upon), is part of the reminiscence of the mother of the martyrs in the form of an address to her children, placed at the very end of 4 Maccabees. The predominant theme is fortitude in suffering and righteousness, based upon an understanding of the law and the prophets that the paterfamilias passes on to his family. The mother recalls how the Father 'sang' the psalms of David to the family. The use of the verb μελῳδέω indicates melody or intonation of some kind (LS, s.v. μελῳδέω 'to chant, sing'; GELS, s.v. μελῳδέω).

2 New Testament
   Eastern and central Mediterranean. Text cited from *Novum Testamentum Graece*, ed.
   E. Nestle et al., 7th rev. edn (Stuttgart, 1979).

Within the New Testament books eventually received as canonical, evidence for the musical practice of Christian assemblies is very sparse, and is thinly spread over as much as three generations. The reference to Christ and the apostles ὑμνήσαντες at the end of the 'Last Supper' (i) was written long after the event by Mark, perhaps soon after AD 70, whence the account passed into Matthew's gospel. There is nothing corresponding to this hymnodic reference in either Luke or John, although the 'lacuna' in John's gospel at this point is spectacularly filled by the dancing sequence in the non-canonical *Acts of John* (no. 6). The narrative from Acts of the Apostles (ii) was written closer to the events described. The remaining material reflects pastoral, ecclesiological and doctrinal concerns that were sharply contemporary at the time when the letters were written, but not necessarily at the time when the letters were redacted into their canonical forms. These are the concerns of Paul in his mission (iii and iv), the matters of moment to one who was perhaps closely associated with Paul, if not Paul himself (v), the concerns of those evoking Pauline authority to consolidate established churches in the generation after the death of the Apostle (v and vi), and the need to redact material presented as the teaching of James, brother of the Lord (vii).

(i) Matthew 26: 30; Mark 14: 26 (*MECL* 3)
      ? Hallel at the Last Supper

If the meal is indeed a Passover Supper, then ὑμνήσαντες is presumably a reference to the *Hallel* sung to some form of melody or intonation. The verb ὑμνήω in unmistakably musical senses is common in the Septuagint, as 1 Chronicles 16: 9 (David's orders to Asaph and his brethren) and 2 Chronicles 23: 13 (with trumpets and singers). See *GELS*, s.v. ὑμνήω; Bauer–Danker, s.v. ὑμνήω ('to sing a song in a cultic setting'). The sense of the term in first-century writings has often been discussed. It is not possible to establish what combination of Alleluia psalms constituted the *Hallel* in first-century Palestine.

(ii) Acts 16: 25–6 (*MECL* 6)
       Paul and Silas sing in prison

'Praying, they praised God in a hymn' ὕμνουν τὸν Θεόν. Possibly a reference to singing, to judge by ὕμνουν.

(iii) 1 Corinthians 14: 15 (*MECL* 10)
        Singing with spirit and mind

The context of this passage is Paul's concern for the conduct of what is presumably house-church worship in Corinth 'when the whole *ekklesia* comes together' (14: 23). He expresses concern about the charism of speaking in tongues because it engages the spirit but not the mind. In insisting that he will sing with the mind as well as the spirit Paul may be censuring a custom of hearing impromptu psalms in tongues in the assemblies of the Corinthian community. The term used (twice) is ψαλλω, originally 'to pluck', thence 'to play a stringed instrument by plucking' and thence by transference 'to sing, to voice a psalm' (LS, s.v. ψαλλω; Bauer–Danker, s.v. ψαλλω, 'to sing a song of praise, with or without instrumental accompaniment'). In the Septuagint, the term often means 'sing' (*GELS*, s.v. ψαλλω, with abundant references).

(iv)   1 Corinthians 14: 26–7 (*MECL* 11)
       Psalm(s) in the liturgy of Corinth

In a rapid conspectus of the materials that believers bring to their assemblies, apparently on their own initiative, Paul mentions that each one has a psalm (ψαλμὸν), a teaching, a revelation, a tongue and an interpretation. There is a sense here of fervent worship, animated by pneumatic acts of speaking (and singing?) in tongues, and of prophecy; Paul believes that Corinthian house-church worship is not properly cautious in the members' display of charisms, is not sufficiently egalitarian in terms of rich–poor and free–servile distinctions, but is too egalitarian in terms of gender roles. There is perhaps an implication that the Corinthians bring the various elements of the service, according to their own impulse and choice, much as they might bring various foodstuffs to the common meal as their contribution. It is impossible to tell from this passage whether the psalms were sung, intoned or spoken.

(v)   Colossians 3: 16–17 (*MECL* 14)
       Psalms, hymns and spiritual songs

Neither Colossians nor Ephesians is now commonly accepted as an authentic work of Paul, although his authorship of both is still stoutly defended by some. Colossians 3 addresses the *ekklesia*, advocating a radical abandonment of things belonging to one's earthly nature (3: 5) and a rejection of the distinction between the circumcised and the uncircumcised to envisage a new identity in Christ ('Here there is no Jew nor Greek . . .'). The chapter closes with a household code. Developing the Pauline theme of Christ's mystical body, the author counsels the Colossians to let the word of Christ dwell among them as they teach and counsel one another with all wisdom 'singing psalms, hymns and spiritual songs' (ψαλμοις ὕμνοις ῷδαις πνευματκαις). The verb ἄδω has a considerable breadth of meaning (LS, s.v. ἀείδω, 'all kind of vocal sounds'; Bauer–Danker, s.v. ἄδω, 'to sing' ('in praise'); *GELS*, s.v. ἄδω, 'to sing (a song), to sing of, to chant') but the sense is assuredly musical here. As a noun, ἄδοντες is the standard term in the Septuagint for the Temple singers (Ezra 2: 41, 65, 70, etc.). As for the three terms for songs, the surprising wealth of terminology is probably rhetorical, the 'psalms', 'hymns' and 'spiritual songs' being more or less synonymous. The term πνευματκαις may refer to all three and not indicate a special kind of song (perhaps in tongues), although that has been proposed. The sense is perhaps 'songs sung in Christ'.

(vi)   Ephesians 5: 19 (*MECL* 13)
        Psalms, hymns and spiritual songs

Based upon Colossians (no. v), Ephesians may be an encyclical letter addressed to several churches; the words 'to the Ephesians' in 1: 1 are omitted in some manuscripts. Ephesians 5 counsels the avoidance of foolish and coarse talk, among other vices, and closes, like the corresponding chapter of Colossians, with a household code (5: 22–33). In what is presumably a reference to suppers ('Do not get drunk on wine . . .') the compiler advises the Ephesians that they should be engaged λαλουντες ἑαυτοις [ἐν] ψαλμοις καὶ ὕμνοις καὶ ᾠδαις πνευματκαις, ᾄδοντες καὶ ψαλλοντες ('speaking to yourselves in psalms and hymns and spiritual songs, singing and psalming . . .'). For ᾄδοντες, see (no. v) above. The term ψαλλοντες reinforces the musical sense here. The root sense of λαλέω is 'to prattle', and the word was therefore sometimes used for inarticulate speech (including the chirping of locusts or the twittering of swallows). Bauer–Danker, s.v. λαλέω, 1 (including musical sense) and *GELS*, s.v. λαλέω, with no musical senses.

(vii) James 5: 13 (*MECL* 17)
        Commending psalmody when cheerful

The view that this epistle may be a genuine work of James, the brother of the Lord, or at least a later redaction of teaching that is authentically his, is developed in the commentary by Davids, which reviews the evidence for authorship and characterizes the book as perhaps 'the last picture of the Palestinian church before the storms of war closed over it' (*The Epistle of James*, 34). James enjoins those who are joyful to sing (ψαλλέτω) songs of praise.

(viii) Revelation, chs. 4, 5, 15, 18 *et passim* (*MECL* 18–19)
        The psalmody of the elders in the already and not yet vision of the end-time glory of God.

3 *I Clement*, 34. 6–8
      90s of the first century. Rome. Edition and English translation in Erhman, *Apostolic Fathers*, i. 95–7.

      λέγει γὰρ ἡ γραφή· μύριαι μυριάδες παρειστήκεισαν αὐτῷ, καὶ χίλιαι χιλιάδες ἐλειτούργουν αὐτῷ, καὶ ἐκέραγον· ἅγιος, ἅγιος, ἅγιος κύριος σαβαώθ, πλήρης πᾶσα ἡ κτίσις τῆς δόξης αὐτοῦ. καὶ ἡμεῖς οὖν ἐν ὁμονοίᾳ ἐπὶ τὸ αὐτὸ συναχθέντες τῇ συνειδήσει, ὡς ἐξ ἑνὸς στόματος βοήσωμεν πρὸς αὐτὸν ἐκτενῶς εἰς τὸ μετόχους ἡμᾶς γενέσθαι τῶν μεγάλων καὶ ἐνδόξων ἐπαγγελιῶν αὐτοῦ.

For the Scripture says, 'Myriads upon myriads stood before him, and thousands upon thousands were ministering to him; and they cried out, "Holy, holy, holy, Lord Sabaoth, all of creation is full of his glory"'. So too we should gather together in harmony, conscientiously, as we fervently cry out to him with one voice, that we may have a share in his great and glorious promises.

In this letter to the Church of Corinth, Clement quotes the seraphic praise of Isaiah 6: 3 ('Holy, holy, holy is the Lord of hosts; the whole earth is full of his glory'), then exhorts the Corinthians, whose Church has recently been troubled by dissent, that all Christians should join in this hymnody.

4 Pliny the Younger, *Letters*, x. 96, to Trajan (*MECL* 41)
      111–12. Bithynia-Pontus. Text and English translation in Pliny, *Letters and Panegyrics*, ed. Radice, ii. 285–93 (with Trajan's reply), translating the text in *C. Plinii Caecili Secundi Epistolarum Libri Decem*, ed. R. A. B. Mynors (Oxford, 1963), 338–40.

Adfirmabant autem hanc fuisse summam vel culpae suae vel erroris, quod essent soli-
ti stato die ante lucem convenire carmenque Christo quasi deo dicere secum invicem
seque sacramento non in scelus aliquod obstringere, sed ne furta ne latrocinia ne adul-
teria committerent, ne fidem fallerent, ne depositum adpellati abnegarent. Quibus
peractis morem sibi discedendi fuisse rursusque coeundi ad capiendum cibum,
promiscuum tamen et innoxium; quod ipsum facere desisse post edictum meum, quo
secundum mandata tua hetaerias esse vetueram. Quo magis necessarium credidi ex
duabus ancillis, quae ministrae dicebantur, quid esset veri, et per tormenta quaerere.
Nihil aliud inveni quam superstitionem pravam et immodicam.

They also declared that the sum total of their guilt or error amounted to no more than
this: they had met regularly before dawn on a fixed day to chant verses amongst themselves in honour of Christ as if to a god, and also to bind themselves by oath, not for
any criminal purpose, but to abstain from theft, robbery and adultery, to commit no
breach of trust and not to deny a deposit when called upon to restore it. After this ceremony it had been their custom to disperse and reassemble later to take food of an
ordinary, harmless kind; but they had in fact given up this practice since my edict,
issued on your instructions, which banned all political societies. This made me decide
it was all the more necessary to extract the truth by torture from two slave women
whom they call 'deaconesses' (*ministrae*). I found nothing but a degenerate sort of cult
carried to extravagant lengths.

When Pliny the Younger was Trajan's special representative in the Black Sea province of
Bithynia-Pontus in AD 111–12 he interrogated a group of Christians to satisfy himself that
they had not offended against the emperor's recent edict banning clubs and associations
that might acquire a political slant. These persons included people of every age and social
class (*omnis aetatis, omnis ordinis*). Pliny derived the information that he records from
somewhat unpromising sources, namely (1) persons who first admitted to being
Christians but then denied it under threat of punishment, claiming that they had actually abandoned their faith two years (or as much as twenty years) previously, and (2) two
slave women (*ancillae*) whom Pliny submitted to torture. He calls them *ministrae*; they
may have been deaconesses. These informants told Pliny that the *Christiani* convened
before dawn on 'a fixed day', presumably Sunday, when they were accustomed to sing a
hymn of praise (*carmenque dicere*), and that they met subsequently on that day (the time
is not specified) to share a common meal. Perhaps to confute the rumours that Christians
were members of a secret mystery cult, or even that they indulged in cannibalism, the
prisoners insisted that they ate perfectly innocent food, *cibum promiscuum et innoxium,*
when they gathered for this second assembly of the day. Pliny's idiom *carmen dicere* is the
'ordinary Latin for to sing a song or to intone verses' (Sherwin-White, *The Letters of
Pliny,* 702–10, esp. 705).

5 *Acts of Paul*

 *c.*140–200? Asia Minor. Edition and facsimile of Hamburg, Staats- und Universitäts-
bibliothek Pap. Bil. 1 (van Haelst, *Catalogue,* 605) in *Acta Pauli,* ed. Schubart and
Schmidt. English translation of the various fragments in *New Testament Apocrypha,* ed.
Schneemelcher, ii. 322–90.

μεταυ[τί-]
[κα δὲ οὕτ]ως κατασταλέντος τοῦ πνεύματος τοῦ ἐν Μύρτῃ μεταλαβῖν [ἔκα-]
[στον το]ῦ [ἄ]ρτου καὶ εὐωχεῖσθαι αὐτοὺς κατὰ τὴν συνήδια[ν τῆς]
νη[. . .νη]στίας ὑπὸ αὐτῶν ψαλμῶν τε Δαουὶδ καὶ ᾠδῶν

Paul attends a communal meal at Corinth where 'each one took of the bread and feasted according to custom, with a psalm of David and a song (ψαλμῶν τε Δαυὶδ καὶ
ᾠδῶν)'. The terms 'psalm' and 'song', appearing together in this way, would seem to
imply music. The *Acts of Paul* was widely read, especially in Egypt, to judge by the
numerous papyrus fragments that have been found there (see van Haelst). It was used by
Tertullian in Africa (who attributes it to an unnamed presbyter from Asia), by
Hippolytus in Rome and by Origen, none of whom considered it to be apocryphal or
heretical. Modern scholars have sometimes regarded the book as a Greek novel and an
eccentric relative of the canonical Pauline letters and Acts of the Apostles. The *Acts of Paul*
has only recently begun to acquire a better reputation for its sympathetic presentation of
Thecla, Paul's female devotee and ascetic companion.

6 *Acts of John* 94–6 ('Gnostic addition') (*MECL* 38)
2nd c. Egypt? The hymn perhaps Syrian, and partly non-Christian in origin? Text and
French translation in *Acta Iohannis*, ed. Junod and Kaestli, i. 198–205; English from *the
Apocryphal New Testament*, trans. James, 253.

Πρὶν δὲ συλληφθῆναι αὐτὸν ὑπὸ τῶν ἀνόμων καὶ ὑπὸ ἀνόμου ὄφεως
νομοθετουμένων Ἰουδαίων συναγαγὼν πάντας ἡμᾶς ἔφη· Πρίν με ἐκείνοις
παραδοθῆναι ὑμνήσωμεν τὸν πατέρα καὶ οὕτως ἐξέλθωμεν ἐπὶ τὸ προκείμενον.
Κελεύσας οὖν ἡμῖν γῦρον ποιῆσαι, ἀποκρατούντων τὰς ἀλλήλων χεῖρας, ἐν μέσῳ
δὲ αὐτὸς γενόμενος ἔλεγεν· Τὸ ἀμὴν ὑπακούετέ μοι. Ἤρξατο οὖν ὑμνεῖν καὶ λέγειν

Δόξα σοι πάτερ.

Καὶ ἡμεῖς κυκλεύοντες ὑπηκούομεν αὐτῷ τὸ ἀμήν.

Δόξα σοι λόγε,
δόξα σοι χάρις. Ἀμήν.

Δόξα σοι τὸ πνεῦμα,
δόξα σοι ἅγιε,
δόξα σου τῇ δόξῃ. Ἀμήν.

Now before he was taken by the lawless Jews, who also were governed by the lawless
serpent, he gathered all of us together and said: Before I am delivered up unto them
let us sing an hymn to the Father, and so go forth to that which lieth before us. He
bade us therefore make as it were a ring, holding one another's hands, and himself
standing in the midst he said: Answer Amen unto me. He began, then, to sing an
hymn and to say:

Glory to be thee, Father.
And we, going about in a ring, answered him: Amen.

Glory be to thee, Word:
Glory be to thee, Grace. Amen.

Glory be to thee, Spirit:
Glory be to thee, Holy One:
Glory be to thee glory. Amen.

The most recent editors of the *Acts of John* propose that the author belonged to a cultivated class that was committed to a Jesus-cult of some kind (in their phrase, 'qui s'est ralliée au christianisme') but had not abandoned the spiritual ideals of its paganism (i. 687). The body of the text is customarily dated to the late second century, with the hymn (chs. 94–6) forming part of a 'Gnostic' addition and itself already layered and in part, perhaps, of non-Christian origin (i. 198–205).

These chapters of the *Acts* tell how, at the close of the Last Supper, Christ and his disciples perform a ring-dance with Christ in the middle; he 'sings and enunciates' (ὕμνειν καὶ λέγειν) the verses of a hymn, capable of being arranged in quatrains, with the apostles answering with an Amen refrain. For parallels to such choreographic hymnody in a ring, see Junod and Kaestli, i. 644, who conclude, surely correctly, that 'la disposition adoptée pour l'execution de l'hymne reflète certainement une pratique liturgique de l'Église ancienne'. Augustine knew at least part of this hymn (ibid. 647), and he associated it with Manichees, Marcionites, Montanists, Cataphyrygians and Priscillianists (PL 33: 1034–8).

7 Justin Martyr, *First Apology*, 13. 1–2 and 67. 2–5 (*MECL* 24–5)
Mid-2nd c. Rome. Text and French translation in *Apologies*, ed. Wartelle, 112–13 and 191–3.

13. 1–2. Ἄθεοι μὲν οὖν ὡς οὔκ ἐσμεν, τὸν δημιουργὸν τοῦδε τοῦ παντὸς σεβόμενοι, ἀνενδεῆ αἱμάτων καὶ σπονδῶν καὶ θυμιαμάτων, ὡς ἐδιδάχθημεν, λέγοντες, λόγῳ εὐχῆς καὶ εὐχαριστίας ἐφ᾽ οἷς προσφερόμεθα πᾶσιν, ὅση δύναμις, αἰνοῦντες, μόνην ἀξίαν αὐτοῦ τιμὴν ταύτην παραλαβόντες, τὸ τὰ ὑπ᾽ ἐκείνου εἰς διατροφὴν γενόμενα οὐ πυρὶ δαπανᾶν, ἀλλ᾽ ἑαυτοῖς καὶ τοῖς δεομένοις προσφέρειν, ἐκείνῳ δὲ εὐχαρίστους ὄντας διὰ λόγου πομπὰς καὶ ὕμνους πέμπειν

For the translation, see above, p. 64.

67. 2–5. Ἡμεῖς δὲ μετὰ ταῦτα λοιπὸν ἀεὶ τούτων ἀλλήλους ἀναμιμνήσκομεν· καὶ οἱ ἔχοντες τοῖς λειπομένοις πᾶσιν ἐπικουροῦμεν, καὶ σύνεσμεν ἀλλήλοις ἀεί. Ἐπὶ πᾶσί τε οἷς προσφερόμεθα εὐλογοῦμεν τὸν Ποιητὴν τῶν πάντων διὰ τοῦ Υἱοῦ αὐτοῦ Ἰησοῦ Χριστοῦ καὶ διὰ Πνεύματος τοῦ Ἁγίου. Καὶ τῇ τοῦ ἡλίου λεγομένῃ ἡμέρᾳ πάντων κατὰ πόλεις ἢ ἀγροὺς μενόντων ἐπὶ τὸ αὐτὸ συνέλευσις γίνεται, καὶ τὰ ἀπομνημονεύματα τῶν ἀποστόλων ἢ τὰ συγγράμματα τῶν προφητῶν ἀναγινώσκεται, μέχρις ἐγχωρεῖ. Εἶτα παυσαμένου τοῦ ἀναγινώσκοντος ὁ προεστὼς διὰ λόγου τὴν νουθεσίαν καὶ πρόκλησιν τῆς τῶν καλῶν τούτων μιμήσεως ποιεῖται. Ἔπειτα ἀνιστάμεθα κοινῇ πάντες καὶ εὐχὰς πέμπομεν· καί, ὡς προέφημεν, παυσαμένων ἡμῶν τῆς εὐχῆς ἄρτος προσφέρεται καὶ οἶνος καὶ ὕδωρ, καὶ ὁ προεστὼς εὐχὰς ὁμοίως καὶ εὐχαριστίας, ὅση δύναμις αὐτῷ, ἀναπέμπει, καὶ ὁ λαὸς ἐπευφημεῖ λέγων τὸ Ἀμήν, καὶ ἡ διάδοσις καὶ ἡ μετάληψις ἀπὸ τῶν εὐχαριστηθέντων ἑκάστῳ γίνεται, καὶ τοῖς οὐ παροῦσι διὰ τῶν διακόνον πέμπεται.

For a partial translation, see above, p. 65.

8 Celsus (fl. *c.*170?), *The True Doctrine*, iii. 16; see Origen, *Contra Celsum*, ed. Borret. Translation adapted from Chadwick.

> Ἀλλὰ καὶ ἐπὰν λέγῃ ὅτι τὰ τοῦ παλαιοῦ λόγον παρακούσματα συμπλάττοντες τούτοις προκαταυλοῦμεν καὶ προκατηχοῦμεν τοὺς ἀνθρώπους ὡς οἱ τοὺς κορυβαντιζομένους περιβομβοῦντες, φήσομεν πρὸς αὐτόν· ποίου παλαιοῦ λόγου παρακούσματα;

> Furthermore he says that *with these we combine misunderstandings of the ancient tradition, and we overwhelm men beforehand by playing auloi and cymbals like the priests of Cybele who with their clamour stupefy the people whom they wish to incite into a frenzy.* We reply to him: 'What sort of tradition is it of which we have misunderstandings?'

Celsus claims that Christian leaders cause the reed pipe or aulos to be played before worship, together with a drum, like priests of Cybele to induce a state of orgiastic frenzy. See above, p. 32.

9 Clement of Alexandria (d. *c.*215), *Paedagogos*, ii. 4 (*MECL* 51–6)
Text and French translation in *Le Pédagogue, Livre II* and *Livre III*, ed. Marrou, trans. Harl et al. Text in *Clemens Alexandrinus*, ed. O. Stählin et al., 4 vols (Die Griechischen Christlichen Schriftsteller der ersten Jahrhunderte; Berlin, 1960–80).

This is the celebrated chapter on banquets in Clement's wide-ranging book on the Christian life, much concerned with moral education and addressed to converts who have already received baptism.

ii. 4. §43. 1–3. Keenly aware, throughout *Paedagogos*, ii. 4 (a chapter too extensive to be quoted here), of the many enticements to the five senses that a port-city like Alexandria could offer, Clement here warns against the indulgences of non-Christian banquets, including their instrumental music. Comprehensively rejecting these, and allegorizing the activities associated with them, he reminds the Alexandrians that when they are drinking there should be graces (εὐχαριϛτίας, perhaps not 'eucharist' in the technical sense) and psalm singing (καὶ ψαλμῳδίας).

> ii. 4. §44. 1. Ὡς δὲ ἁρμόδιον πρὶν ἡμᾶς μεταλαβεῖν τροφῆς τῶν συμπάντων εὐλογεῖν τὸν ποιητήν, οὕτως καὶ παρὰ πότον καθήκει ψάλλειν αὐτῷ τῶν αὐτοῦ μεταλαμβάνοντας κτισμάτων· καὶ γὰρ ὁ ψαλμὸς ἐμμελής ἐστιν εὐλογία καὶ σώφρων· "ᾠδὴν πνευματικὴν" ὁ ἀπόστολος εἴρηκε τὸν ψαλμόν.

> Since it is appropriate, before taking our food, to bless the Creator for all things, so too, when one drinks, it is fitting to sing a psalm, since one is part of his creation; and in effect the psalm is a harmonious and healthful praise; the apostle says that it is a "spiritual song" (Ephesians 5: 19; Colossians 3: 16).

> ii. 4. §44. 5. Καὶ γαρ ἁρμονίας παραδεκτέον τὰς σώφρονας, ἀπωτάτω ὅτι μάλιστα ἐλαύνοντας τῆς ἐρρωμένης ἡμῶν διανοίας τὰς ὑγρὰς ὄντως ἁρμονίας, αἳ περὶ τὰς καμπὰς τῶν φθόγγων κακοτεχνοῦσαι εἰς θρύψιν καὶ βωμολοχίαν ἐκδιαιτῶνται· τὰ δὲ αὐτηρὰ καὶ σωφρονικὰ μέλη ἀποτάσσεται ταῖς τῆς μέθης ἀγερωχίαις. Καταλειπτέον οὖν τὰς χρωματικὰς ἁρμονίας ταῖς ἀχρώμοις παροινίαις καὶ ἀνθοφορούσῃ καὶ ἑταιρούσῃ μουσικῇ.

One should select only from musical idioms those that are healthful, and for the sake of sparing our moral health we should cast away as far as possible those that are genuinely lascivious, those that by their inflections corrupt and give rise to softness and foolishness; we should also cast aside crude and excessively vigorous melodies for the sake of drunken ravings. Let chromatic music be left to the shameless excess of winebibbers and to music crowned with the garlands of whores.

In this passage, which concludes the chapter on banquets, Clement counsels the use of certain types of melodies for Christian meals, and therefore presumably for psalmody. In accordance with Clement's asceticism, they are to be σώφρονας, presumably something like 'wisely judged' or 'sage' in the French sense of *sage*.

iii. 11. §80. 4. καὶ τὸν περὶ θεοῦ λόγον σεβασάμενοι καταλελοίπασιν ἔνδον οὗ ἤκουσαν, ἔξωθεν δὲ ἄρα μετὰ τῶν ἀθέων ἀλύουσι, κρουμάτων καὶ τερετισμάτων ἐρωτικῶν αὐλῳδίας τε καὶ κρότου καὶ μέθης καὶ παντὸς ἀναπιμπλάμενοι συρφετοῦ· τοῦτο δὴ ἄδοντες καὶ ἀντάδοντες αὐτοὶ οἱ πρόσθεν ἐξυμνοῦντες ἀποθανασίαν, ἐπὶ τέλει τὴν ἐξωλεστάτην κακοὶ κακῶς ψάλλοντες παλινῳδίαν· "Φάγωμεν καὶ πίωμεν, αὔριον γὰρ ἀποθνήσκομεν".

Having respectfully paid attention to what has been preached about God, they have left what they have heard inside [the church] and, once outside, they go off seeking a good time in the company of atheists, allowing themselves to be taken over by the sounds and harmonies of erotic music, by the sounds of auloi and the rhythmic beating of dance, by drunkenness and by all the riot of the populace. Singing and singing back again, the unfortunates who were previously celebrating immortality finish by singing the most detestable of songs: 'Let us eat and drink, for tomorrow we die.'

Referring to the conduct of the faithful after they have heard preaching in the *ekklesia*, Clement accuses them of joining their pagan friends with instrumental music and dancing. Hence they who are now engaged outdoors in 'singing and singing back again' (ἄδοντες καὶ ἀντάδοντε) are those who were formerly celebrating eternal life indoors. The term ἀντάδοντες may indicate a structure of verse and response to the dance-songs, and is interpreted that way by McKinnon (*MECL*, 34), which may in turn (but this is clearly very weak) imply a responsorial psalmody for the gathering.

10 Clement of Alexandria (d. *c*.215), *Stromateis*, Books 6 and 7 (*MECL* 57–62)
Reign of Severus (193–211). Text and French translation of Book 6 in *Clément d'Alexandrie: Les Stromates: Stromate VI*, ed. P. Descourtieux (SC 446; Paris, 1999). Text of both books in *Clemens Alexandrinus*, ed. Stählin, ii (Book 6, pp. 422–518) and iii (Book 7, pp. 3–79).

Stromateis, or 'miscellanies', is aptly described by Eusebius as 'a tapestry combining Holy Writ with anything [Clement] considered helpful in secular literature. He includes any view generally accepted, expounding those of Greeks and non-Greeks alike, and even correcting the false doctrines of the heresiarchs, and explains a great deal of history, providing us with a work of immense erudition' (*EH*, 63. 4–8).

6. 11. §90. 1. Ἀμέλει καὶ παρὰ πότον ψάλλειν ἀλλήλοις προπίνομεν, κατεπᾴδοντες ἡμῶν τὸ ἐπιθυμητικὸν καὶ τὸν θεὸν δοξάζοντες ἐπὶ τῇ ἀφθόνῳ τῶν ἀνθρωπείων

ἀπολαύσεων δωρεᾷ τῶν τε εἰς τὴν τοῦ σώματος τῶν τε εἰς τὴν τῆς ψυχῆς αὔξησιν τροφῶν ἀϊδίως ἐπιχορηγηθεισῶν.

During a meal, we drink to one another's health while singing psalms, calming the las-civious part of ourselves with the music and glorifying God for the generous gift of his beneficences to Mankind, food lavishly provided for all eternity for the growth of the body and soul.

MECL 59 translates *Stromateis* 6. 11, §89 but unaccountably stops before §90 and what can be plausibly rendered (and is so rendered by Descourtieux) as a reference to psalm singing at Christian suppers. In a brief section concerning the right music for Christians to use, Clement says 'during a meal we drink to one another's health while singing psalms'. This is presumably a reference to table psalmody.

7. 7. §49. 1. Part of Clement's discussion of the true Gnostic, that is the ascetic Christian philosopher who has learned to master his passions. The devotions of the true Gnostic are 'converse with the Scriptures before the banquet, psalms and hymns (ψαλμοὶ δέ καὶ ὕμνοι) at the banquet and before bed, and again during the night'. Nothing pos-itively indicates singing here, unless it is implied by ὕμνοι.

11 Tertullian, *De Anima*, ix. 4 (*MECL* 82)

　　206–7. Carthage. Text in *Opera omnia*, ii. 792. Text and commentary in *De Anima*, 　　ed. Waszink.

Est hodie soror apud nos reuelationum charismata sortita, quas in ecclesia inter dominica sollemnia per ecstasin in spiritu patitur; conuersatur cum angelis, aliquando etiam cum domino, et uidet et audit sacramenta et quorundam corda dinoscit et med-icinas desiderantibus sumit. Iamuero prout scripturae leguntur aut psalmi canuntur aut allocutiones proferuntur aut petitiones delegantur, ita inde materiae uisionibus subministrantur.

There is among us today a sister favoured with the gifts of revelation that she experi-ences through an ecstacy of the spirit, during the Sunday liturgy. She converses with angels, sometimes even with the Lord; she sees and hears mysteries, reads some peoples' hearts and applies remedies to those who need them. The material for her visions is supplied as the Scriptures are read, psalms are sung, the homily delivered and prayers offered.

This passage of the *De Anima* offers the first reference in early Christian literature, either East or West, to Eucharistic psalmody.

12 Tertullian, *De Exhortatione Castitatis*, x. 2

　　208–9. Carthage. Text in *Opera omnia*, ii. 1029–30.

Recogitemus enim ipsam conscientiam nostram, quam alium so homo sentiat, cum forte a sua femina cessat. Spiritaliter sapit; si orationem facit ad dominum, prope est caelo; si scripturis incumbit, totus illic est; si psalmum canit, placet sibi; si daemonem adiurat, confidit sibi.

Let us ponder our conscience itself, to see how different a man feels when, by chance, he is deprived of his wife. He savours things spiritually; if he prays to the Lord, he is near heaven; if he is bent over the Scriptures, he is wholly in them; if he is singing a psalm, he satisfies himself; if he is adjuring a demon, he is confident in himself.

This treatise, an important document for the early history of Christian asceticism among the house-owning and slave-owning classes, concerns the spiritual benefits of continence and of abstaining from the responsibilities brought by marriage and parenting. One has the time to pray, read the Scriptures and to voice psalms.

13 Tertullian, *Apologeticum*, 39. 16–18 (*MECL* 74)

Autumn 197 or later 198. Carthage. Text in *Opera omnia*, i. 152–3.

> Post aquam manualem et lumina, ut quisque de scripturis diuinis uel de proprio inge-nio potest, prouocatur in medium Deo canere: hinc probatur quomodo biberit.

> After the water for the hands and the lighting of the lamps, anyone who has anything to offer from the divine Scriptures, or from their own devising, is called into the cen-tre [of the assembly] to recite before God: thus a test is made of his drinking.

This part of the *Apologeticum* is a defence of Christian suppers and banquets. There is an implied contrast throughout between Christian practice and aspects of dining among the devotees of the mystery cults and dining in any cultic context that the Roman authori-ties might construe as a threat to public order. Tertullian implies that the supper is called *agape* ('it is called by that which means *dilectio* among the Greeks'). Held in the evening, there is hand-washing and a lighting of the lamps. Thereafter 'anyone who has anything to offer from the divine Scriptures, or from their own devising, is called into the centre [of the assembly] to recite before God . . .', revealing thereby whether they have been temperate in their drinking of wine. The material from the Scriptures is perhaps some passage that one of the brethren had learned by heart, or the reflections that he or she wished to offer upon a passage they had recently been reading. *Canere* here may have the sense of 'to sing'; this would therefore be a reference to musical settings of scriptural pas-sages or hymns of the believers' own devising offered as devout party-pieces, in effect. Since Cyprian envisages something very similar for affluent Carthaginian society (see no. 18 below), it is tempting to conclude that this is what Tertullian has in mind. This reference is valuable for what it reveals about the breadth of the constituency whence an *ekklesia* might draw the singers for its meals.

14 Tertullian, *De Oratione*, xxvii (*MECL* 78 and 79)

198–203. Carthage. Text in *Opera omnia*, i. 273. Text and English translation in *Tertullian's Tract on the Prayer*, ed. and trans. Evans.

> Diligentiores in orando subiungere in orationibus alleluia solent et hoc genus psalmos, quorum clausulis respondeant qui simul sunt. Et est optimum utique institutum omni quod praeponendo et honorando Deo competit saturatam orationem uelut optimam hostiam admouere.

> The more conscientious in prayer are accustomed to append to their prayers Alleluia and such manner of psalms, so that those who are present may respond with the end-ings of them. And it is certainly an excellent custom to present, like a rich oblation, a prayer fattened with all that conduces to setting forth the dignity and honour of God.

Citing scriptural sources for each hour (ch. 25), Tertullian advocates an horarium of prayer at the third, sixth and ninth hours of the day, before meals and before using the baths. Plainly referring to contexts in which a number of the faithful are gathered together (in the family home?), he observes that some of the more diligent believers (*diligentiores*) append 'Alleluia' to their prayers 'and such manner of psalms' so that 'those who are present may respond with the endings of them'. Presumably Tertullian is thinking primarily of the biblical psalms that already have 'Alleluia' as a refrain – but not exclusively of those – and a manner of voicing in which someone leads the prayer of those assembled by giving the verses of the psalms, followed by an 'Alleluia' response from the company at the end of each verse. There is nothing definitively to indicate whether this procedure, identical (as interpreted here) to the manner of liturgical performance more securely documented from the fourth century onwards, involves singing.

15 Tertullian *Ad Uxorem*, ii. 8 (*MECL* 80)
     ?198–203. Carthage. Text in *Opera omnia*, i. 394.

> In ecclesia Dei pariter utrique, pariter in conuiuio Dei, pariter in angustiis, in persecutionibus, in refrigeriis. Neuter alterum celat, neuter alterum uitat, neuter alteri grauis est. Libere aeger uisitatur, indigens sustentatur. Elemosinae sine tormento, sacrificia sine scrupulo, quotidiana diligentia sine impedimento; non furtiua signatio, non trepida gratulatio, non muta benedictio. Sonant inter duos psalmi et hymni, et mutuo prouocant, quis melius Domino suo cantet. Talia Christus uidens et audiens gaudet. His pacem suam mittit. Vbi duo, ibi et ipse; ubi et ipse, ibi et malus non est.

> Equally (are they) both (found) in the Church of God; equally at the banquet of God; equally in straits, in persecutions, in refreshments. Neither hides from the other; neither shuns the other; neither is troublesome to the other. The sick is man visited, the indigent man relieved, with freedom. They give alms without torment; attend sacrifices without scruple; are diligent without impediment. There is no stealthy signing, no trembling greeting, no mute benediction. Psalms and hymns echo between the two, and they mutually challenge each other which shall better chant to their Lord. Christ rejoices when he sees and hears such things. To these He sends His own peace. Where there are two, there he is Himself, and where He is, there the Evil One is not.

This is another document of considerable importance for psalmody in the Christian household. The meaning of *canto* remains uncertain here, since it could denote either speaking or singing. Much may have depended upon the talents that the members of each family could bring to the routines of private worship on days when no assembly was convened.

16 Inscription from Aphrodisias
     Before 212? About 140 km east of Ephesus. Face a, column 1: 15. Text and commentary in Reynolds and Tannenbaum, *Jews and God-Fearers at Aphrodisias*, 5 and 46.

Face a of this stone, probably dating from before the grant of a virtually universal Roman citizenship in the Antonine Constitution of AD 212, records a Βενιαμιν ψαλμος. The abbreviation might be expanded to ψαλμολόγος (Reynolds and Tannenbaum read ψαλμο(λόγος?), and seem reasonably sure that a psalmodist is at issue here) but presumably cannot be expanded to the much more familiar ψαλμῳδός unless there is a mis-spelling.

17 *Letter to Diognetus*, xi. 6
   ? *c.*200. Text and translation in *The Apostolic Fathers*, ed. and trans. Ehrman, ii. 156–7.

εἶτα φόβος νόμου ᾄδεται, καὶ προφητῶν χάρις γινώσκεται, καὶ εὐαγγελίων πίστις ἵδρυται, καὶ ἀποστόλων παράδοσις φυλάσσεται, καὶ ἐκκλησίας χάρις σκιρτᾷ.

Then the fear of the law is sung, the grace of the prophets is made known, the faith of the gospels is established, the tradition of the apostles is guarded, and the grace of the church leaps for joy.

There is a question about the authenticity of the relevant chapters, 11 and 12. Marrou (*A Diognète*, 219–40, *et passim*) makes a case for their authenticity (and for a date in the region of 200 and an Alexandrian provenance). Rizzi, *La questione dell'unità*, also accepts them as genuine. In a mode of exhortation, the anonymous author praises the Church where 'The fear of the law is sung'.

18 Cyprian of Carthage (d. 258), *Ad Donatum*, xvi (*MECL* 94)
   ? 246. Text and French translation in *Cyprien de Carthage: A Donat et La Vertu de Patience*, ed. and trans. J. Molager (SC 291; Paris, 1982), 114–17.

et quoniam feriata nunc quies ac tempus est otiosum, quicquid inclinante iam sole in uesperam dies superest, ducamus hunc diem laeti nec sit uel hora conuiuii gratiae cae-lestis immunis. Sonet psalmus conuiuium sobrium; ut tibi tenax memoria est, uox canora, adgredere hoc munus ex more. Magis carissimos pascis, si sit nobis spiritalis auditio, prolectet aures religiosa mulcedo.

and since now is a time of holiday quiet and leisure, and the sun begins to go down leaving some light remaining into the evening, let us pass the end of this day in delight so that even the hour of the evening meal is not devoid of heavenly grace. Let a psalm sound at our frugal meal; since you have a good memory and a melodious voice, take on this charge as is your custom. You will the better nourish your dearest friends if you charm our ears with a devout sweetness.

Ad Donatum, written before Cyprian became bishop, is a brief exhortation to a friend who had already been baptized and may have been a lawyer or a rhetorician. The text is presented as an address to Donatus delivered in a beautiful garden in autumn. The dis-course closes as the evening comes on, and in a highly mannered passage Cyprian calls upon his friend to sing 'so that the hour of the evening meal (*hora conuiuii*) will not be devoid of heavenly grace.'

19 *Apostolic Tradition*, 29c (*MECL* 89)
   Greek original, early 3rd c.? Reconstructions in (1) 'Hippolytus', *La Tradition apos-tolique*, ed. Botte; (2) Bradshaw et al., *The Apostolic Tradition* and (3) *The Treatise on the Apostolic Tradition of St. Hippolytus of Rome*, ed. Dix, rev. Chadwick.

The *Apostolic Tradition* is now widely regarded as a composite text whose history begins as early as the middle years of the second century, and continues (as far as the core of the

Greek text is concerned) well into the third or fourth. Only fragments of the Greek original survive, but there are partial translations, redactions and adaptations of its material in several other compilations in Latin, Sahidic, Arabic, Ge'ez and Greek. Three fragments contain material describing a common meal of the Christian community, held in the evening and beginning with a lamp-lighting ceremony (Bradshaw et al., *The Apostolic Tradition*, 156–7). The evening gathering begins as the deacon enters with the lamp and greets the assembly. Eventually, according to the Ethiopic version, 'when they have then risen after the supper and have prayed, the children and the virgins are to say the psalms'. Only this first instruction, calling for 'children and virgins' to sing psalms, has any counterpart in another redaction of the Apostolic Tradition dossier. The parallel passage appears in the *Testamentum Domini*: 'And let the little boys say spiritual psalms and hymns of praise by the light of the lamp. Let all the people respond "Hallelujah" to the psalm and to the chant together, with one accord, with voices in harmony.'

20   Pseudo-Clement, *Epistolae duae de virginitate*, Letter II, ch. 6
     ?Early 3rd c. Greek original, relevant material only in Syriac version. Text with two Latin translations in (pseudo-)Clement, *Epistolae binae de Virginitate*, ed. Beelen.

These two letters, originally perhaps only a single document, were written in Greek, arguably as early as the first decade of the third century, and are of fundamental importance for the psalmody of ascetics, who in this text are plainly not 'desert' monks (and could not be if the text does indeed date from soon after 200). For the text, see Fig. 2 and above, Ch. 6.

Fig. 2   The passage from the Syriac translation of the '*Second' Letter concerning Virginity* originally written in Greek and falsely attributed to Clement of Rome. The text concerns the restrictions that men and women vowed to lifelong continence should place upon their activities when compelled to lodge in places where there are no Christian converts. They are not to read the Scriptures to them and not to 'sing', lest they seem like pipers or secular singers.

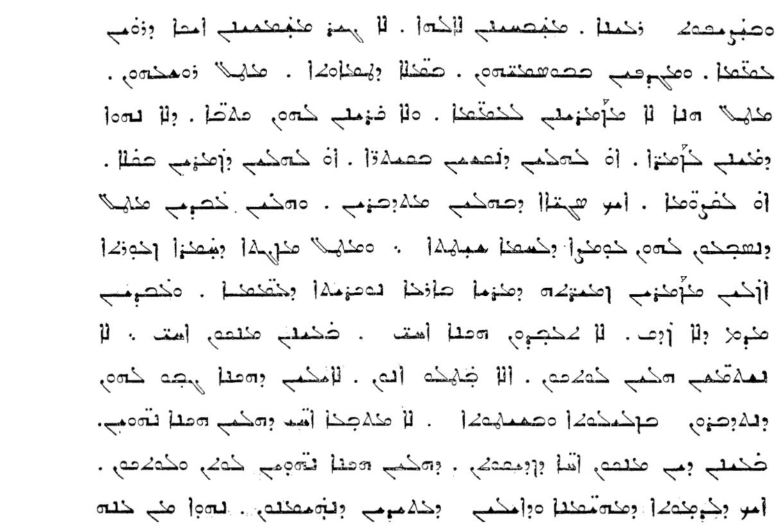

21 Anonymous

The record of the inquisition of the martyrs of Abitina, probably modern Chahoud el-Batin, in Africa Proconsularis. Events of February 304. Text in *Passio SS. Dativi*, ed. De' Cavalieri.

This remarkable text discloses an African house-church where a Eucharistic assembly has gathered, and then refers to the psalmody of its members as they are led away for interrogation in Carthage, then to torture and death. The events took place in February 304. The context is provided by the Great Persecution, launched by Diocletian and Galerius in February 303, requiring churches to be demolished, holy vessels to be confiscated, and liturgical books to be given up for burning. A group of Christians was arrested during their Sunday service at the house of Octavius Felix in Abitina, probably to be identified with Chahoud el-Batin, west of Membressa. If there was psalmody here of any kind, it was provided by the *lectores* and the community. There is no mention of a minister of song.

22 Epitaph of 'Gaios'

3rd or 4th c., Dineksarai.

. . . Γάϊ]ος, ὅχ' ἄριστος ἐν ὕμνοις, τεῖσεν ἀπὸ σφετέ-
[ρης τέχνης, ἧς ἄλλοι ἔπειτα ᾄσ]ματα καλὰ φράσουσι καὶ ἐσσομέ-
νοισ[ι πυθέσθαι].

At present, 'Gaios' (the name is the result of an emendation), mentioned in an epitaph from Dineksarai in southern central Turkey, is the earliest named Christian singer or composer of hymns, which may come down to the same thing ('far the best in hymns, honoured [her] from his art, from which others hereafter will utter beautiful hymns for even posterity to learn'). For bibliography and sources, see Destephen, *Prosopographie chrétienne du Bas-Empire*, s.v. Gaios[2].

16 The ruins of Laodicea.

4

PSALTES AND *LECTOR*:
TOWARDS A MINISTRY OF SINGING

A Ministry of Music Appears in the East

At some time in the fourth century the bishops of various sees in western Asia Minor gathered for a synod in Laodicea, the metropolitan Church of their province, Phrygia Pacatiana. Today, the site retains little of the grandeur that made it an appropriate choice for such a gathering; there are only broken walls in a coarsened landscape to recall the colonnades and forum of the ancient city with its basilicas, some of which have only recently been unearthed. There is no record of the bishops who attended the synod there, but the province was one of considerable size, extending some 230 km from the northernmost see to its southern extreme, and eventually numbering thirty-eight bishoprics. In their deliberations, as represented by fifty-nine extant chapters, the prelates strove to keep the doctrine, worship and discipline of the mainstream Church pure. Outside the fragile fold of that Church there were Montanists and followers of Photinos, luring orthodox Christians to the shrines of their heretical martyrs or marrying their children to the offspring of orthodox parents. There were Jews inviting Christians to celebrate the Israelite festivals, offering them gifts on Jewish holidays and issuing invitations to observe the Saturday Sabbath. There were women, even in the mainstream Church, called 'female elders' or female priests. As for the faithful themselves, they would not be ruled. They celebrated birthdays and marriages in Lent, a time of mandatory fasting, and they worshipped angels, perhaps an allusion to forms of Gnosticism. Some sought magical amulets from the clergy. In short, the prelates at Laodicea saw a Church infiltrated by heretics, weakened by fraternization with Jews and enervated by the laxity of clergy. Their response is necessarily censorious, with most chapters addressing something the prelates consider unwise, improper or downright destructive to the Christian community gathered around the sacraments.[1]

It was therefore judged essential to have capable and scrupulous clerics, and in the course of legislating for them the bishops at Laodicea had cause to mention liturgical singers. Under the title of *psaltes*, which is by no means a distinctively Christian term, ministers named after a charge of ritual singing make their first appearance here in any surviving Christian document. All told, there are six chapters touching upon singers, psalmody and the related issue of liturgical reading:

Chapter xv. Only 'regularly appointed' [or orthodox?] singers, *kanonikōn psaltōn*, capable of reading from parchment, should be allowed to ascend the pulpit from now on and sing in churches.

Chapter xvi. The gospels should be read publicly on Saturdays with other scriptures.

Chapter xvii. Psalms should not be performed one after another but always interspersed with a reading after each psalm.

Chapter xxiii. Singers and readers must not wear the *orarion* when they read or sing.

Chapter xxiv. Clerics with a ministry of the altar, presbyters and deacons must not attend taverns, nor must the others in orders of subdeacon, reader, singer, exorcist, doorkeeper and ascetic.

Chapter lix. There should be no delivery of non-canonical or 'home-made' psalms (*idiōtikous psalmous legesthai*) in Church, but only of canonical books.

These chapters are succinct in the original and may be no more than the headings for chapters now lost. They nonetheless suggest how these bishops regarded their singers, how the singers regarded themselves, and how they were to be recruited henceforth from literate men who had passed through some form of induction. The picture that emerges is not very reminiscent of 'Gaios', the hymnodist holding the rank of presbyter with connections to good clerical families and also from Asia Minor (see above, p. 45). This is partly a matter of sources, for it was rarely the purpose of an epitaph to minimize the status of anyone there was cause to mention and never the purpose of an ecclesiastical synod to congratulate anyone there was reason to address. Yet this cannot entirely account for the contrast. For the first time in Christian history, the Laodicea chapters sound the note that becomes so familiar as the centuries pass: singers are necessary for the celebration of the liturgy but are constantly to be kept under surveillance. In that regard, the singers evoked at Laodicea do not sound like a pagan college of hymnodists from Pergamum or Smyrna simply redirected to the service of a different god. The prelates at the council were much concerned with their singers' sense of professional identity and conviction of their own importance, but to look beyond the chapters they issued is soon to discover that Christian singers did not give monumental expression to any sense of forming a college like their pagan counterparts. A hymnodist in the service of a pagan cult might belong to a proud *collegium* on the urban scene, still committed to the traditions of public epigraphy; the Christian *psaltes*, in contrast, was a junior functionary in the miniature palatine ministry that surrounded his bishop.[2]

A glance at the paraphrase of the Laodicea rulings given above is enough to show that the prelates were not concerned with the *music* of their singers. At first sight, this may seem very curious. Long before, in the time of the house-churches, a letter of Ignatius addressed to a Church in western Asia Minor suggests that some Christians of the early second century valued ritual song as a means to express the concord of a hierarchy extending upwards from the individual believer through the ranks of the clerical ministries to Christ and then the Father himself. Yet even as early as this, Ignatius is characteristically concerned as much with obedience as with harmonious accord (*To the Ephesians*, 4). Theologians of the late fourth century, such as Augustine, show great concern for the spiritual powers and benefits of psalmody, at least for a disciplined soul, but as evoked at Laodicea the day-to-day commerce between singers and bishops in the cathedrals of western Asia Minor places the emphasis firmly upon episcopal oversight rather than the musical character or spiritual import of the singers' contribution. The latter is a question the bishops found no reason to address, for they say nothing about any aspect of the ritual music their singers performed. The fervent sense of ritual singing suggested by Ignatius at the beginning of the second century does not seem to have survived the process whereby the offices of the first householder-patrons and others developed into clerical ministries eventually ruled by a monarchical episcopate.

Although the *psaltes* mentioned at Laodicea ranks with the clerical orders (there is no sign that any of the singers at issue were monks) the prelates conceded clerical rank to them with some dissatisfaction. Chapter XXIII reveals that the singers and readers had ambitions to wear the long stole or *orarion* widely associated with the deacons and explicitly forbidden to subdeacons in Chapter XXII. This desire for the vesture of a higher order may owe something to rivalry with the colleges of pagan hymnodists, and it is precisely the concern to be expected in a fourth-century context when many offices, insignia and titles in the army and the bureaucracy were being elaborated and redefined in response to a massive increase in recruitment (see below, pp. 162–5). The liturgy, like the imperial court, was acquiring its own sumptuary laws, and violations were regarded with severity, just as in secular life. The prelates regarded the psalmists' desire to wear an item of diaconal vesture as wholly reprehensible and they legislated to suppress it.

Chapter XV, concerning 'regular' singers, intercepts the Catholic Church at a crucial moment in its extension of jurisdiction over ritual singing, progressively thinning the diversity of practice and personnel inherited from the era of the house-churches. The prelates at Laodicea were concerned that candidates for every order should meet the highest standards and should be subject to episcopal control. Henceforth, only 'canonical singers' or *kanonikoi psaltai* were to be inducted into the office of psalmist. This suggests that singers had sometimes been admitted hitherto on an ad hoc basis without any regularized process of induction, and even perhaps without sufficient vetting of their abilities. There is nothing in later ordination rituals to suggest that singers were inducted in some form of ceremony, least of all one involving the bishop, and the only explicit criterion mentioned at Laodicea is that candidates should be able to read from parchment (*diphthera*). There is no hint of an investigation into their reputation for piety or probity, and no apparent scrutiny of their musical abilities. Previously, it seems, singers were selected from a broader constituency that either included illiterates or those accustomed to use cheaper and ephemeral copies of texts on papyrus. From now on, only candidates who had received substantial parts of a traditional Roman education, beginning and perhaps ending with a grammarian, were to be inducted.[3]

This implies a considerable range of skills combined with the necessary musical talents and a willingness to accept the commitments of service for what must have been a modest stipend. There are cases of readers traceable as episcopal secretaries (in 431 a reader was notary for his bishop in Rhodus) but there are no traces of singers serving in a similar capacity. Nonetheless, Chapter xv of the Laodicea proceedings implies that psalmists henceforth should be able to construe a written text, divide the words written in the *scripta continua* of the surviving scriptural codices and add any punctuation or diacritics that might help them point the text intelligibly when they sang. The texts on parchment, to which the proceedings refer, sound like expensive copies of the Scriptures, perhaps to be inspected by the bishops for their textual accuracy, canonicity and orthodoxy. They may even be counterparts to the large and handsome manuscripts of the fourfold gospel and other texts that emerge into view during the fourth century, too costly to be kept anywhere save *in domo ecclesiae*, the episcopal quarters of the church. It may seem unlikely that singers enjoyed access to magnificent manuscripts like the famous Codex Sinaiticus, but such books would not have been beyond the resources of cathedral churches in wealthy cities of Asia Minor such as Laodicea itself.[4]

By insisting upon singers who could read from parchment, the bishops at Laodicea may also be implicitly forbidding the use of texts on papyrus booklets. Much cheaper to produce than codices made of parchment, it is perhaps just possible that these were documents some literate candidates for the post of *psaltes* might possess since they formed a continuum, despite their sacred content, with papyrus amulets, prayers, hymns, financial accounts and other administrative documents that create the background noise of literacy in the eastern Mediterranean during the fourth century. At this date, when it is very uncertain who singers were, it might be unwise to suppose that the much later situation (whereby the church controlled all materials used for worship through the bishops) was already firmly established in the fourth century, and that there was therefore no overlap between the materials literate laymen might own and those commandeered for use in a service. It was difficult for a bishop or his presbyters to control the accuracy of the texts recorded in any such booklets, or even to ensure they were canonical and orthodox, except by the laborious process of having each candidate for induction present his books for inspection and run through any hymnody he had memorized and intended to offer for use in a context of ad hoc recruitment. Such auditions may have taken place during the kind of trial period that Cyprian of Carthage imposed on readers in the first half of the third century, but the bishops' duty to extend their oversight of worship would plainly have been facilitated if the *psaltes* were required to consult an authorized library copy of the Scriptures, or even sing from one during the service.[5]

The Laodicea chapters concerning singers are therefore shaped as much by a concern for episcopal authority, orthodoxy and the biblical canon as for the regulation of the *psaltes*. Towards 400, the scriptural canon was rapidly closing around the books received as the work of apostles or of those whom they had taught. The last chapter of the Laodicea council raises this matter explicitly by insisting that nothing should be sung or read during a service save material drawn from the canonical books of the two Testaments. The biblical canon was still sufficiently fluid at this date for some copyists to see the wisdom of supplementing this final provision of the council with a list of canonical books to clarify the bishops' ruling. This list probably reflects one form of the biblical canon during essentially the same generation as Athanasius's famous Easter Letter of 367, giving the earliest dateable inventory of the Christian canonical Scriptures. The council of Hippo (393) requiring *scripturae canonicae* to be used for public readings, and no others, falls within the same thirty-year band. Like most forms of legislation, all these injunctions are designed to redress a situation judged to be both fluid and imperfect. The gates of the canon had a tendency to creak open, and as late as 397 certain bishops in Africa still thought it necessary to verify their list of canonical books by consulting their fellow prelates overseas.[6]

Hence the bishops gathered at Laodicea could not possibly regard the canonicity and textual authority of materials used by their singers with indifference. The time had come to make a decisive intervention. There was a danger that any *psaltes* without due oversight might sing from a canonical book whose text was poor or even inadvertently heretical. Perhaps he might even use a text still widely admired but not received as Scripture, such as *The Shepherd* of Hermas, 'used in public churches' according to Eusebius and regarded as especially useful for instruction, 'even though it is rejected by some and for their sake should not be placed among the accepted books' (*EH*, iii. 3. 6). Worst of all, perhaps, a *psaltes* might sing non-scriptural hymns from ephemeral and unchecked papyrus copies. There must have been a great deal of vagrant hymnody in circulation in the fourth century, some of it left over from the losing (or not yet entirely vanquished) sides in various theological controversies, notably Arianism and perhaps even the counter-church of Marcion. The Muratorian Fragment, commonly regarded as the earliest list of canonical books though it cannot be precisely dated, picks up some of this heretical material when it censures 'the psalms of the book of Marcion', and the Laodicea proceedings net some more when they ban the performance of *idiōtikoi psalmoi*, presumably hymnody of recent origin and somewhat 'home-made', which is one possible translation for *idiōtikoi*. Other hymns in circulation were probably Gnostic productions, hymning the angelic entities that the proceedings of the council forbid the faithful to worship (xxv) or invoking protection with dubious invocations or centos of scriptural texts, like some of the amulets the prelates of Laodicea probably had in mind when they emphatically banned them (xxxvi).[7]

As mentioned above, the musical procedures used by the *psaltes* seem to give the prelates no cause for concern. The singers are not charged with introducing the sounds of the theatres, mimes or pagan processions into the churches, nor are they accused of singing in a manner deemed effeminate, a cardinal sin in later periods. The ban on *idiōtikous psalmous* is perhaps an attempt to constrain the musical style of new compositions or even to ban them altogether, but the unbroken silence of the proceedings on musical matters suggests that the prelates believed their singers had made a satisfactory accommodation with the musical soundscape of the eastern Mediterranean. At first this may seem somewhat surprising, since it is so much easier to form a general impression from explicit sources such as the writings of Jerome, quite prepared to castigate singers for 'daubing the mouth and throat with some sweet medicine after the manner of tragedians, so that theatrical melodies and songs are heard in the church' (*MECL* 333). Yet the silence of the Laodicea chapters on these matters is a reminder that the issues of musical style and sonority in Christian ritual singing belong with the broader question of when Christians sought their own ways of doing things and when the cultural forms they intuitively and perhaps unquestioningly endorsed were those of the Graeco-Roman world. Augustine was taunted by one of his opponents, Faustus the Manichean, with the charge that the rituals of Christians were not so very distinctive from those of either Jews or polytheists:

> you change their sacrifices into love feasts, the idols into martyrs, whom you worship with similar rites. You appease the shades of the departed with wine and food. You keep the same holidays as the Gentile [polytheists], for example the calends and the solstices. In your way of living you have made no change. Plainly you are a mere schism, showing no difference from the original [that is to say pagan polytheism] save that you meet separately. Your predecessors the Jews, moreover, separated from the Gentiles and you differ from them only in not having images. For they used temples, sacrifices, altars, a priesthood and the whole round of ceremonies the same as those of the polytheists, only much more superstitiously than the Gentiles.[8]

This is obviously intended to provoke, and Augustine duly rose to the challenge; yet despite the polemical edge in this passage, it may reveal something about Christian ritual singing in the late fourth century. By now, 'very little separated a Christian from his pagan counterpart in Roman society. Dancing, rowdy celebrations, especially those connected with cemeteries, the theatre, games, resorting to baths, a variety of magical practices and the like, often aroused suspicions and provoked denunciation by bishops; but they were part of that "vast shared territory" which Christians inherited from the pagan past.' The prelates at Laodicea condemn the singers' desire to appear in a part of the deacons' vesture (they level the same charge against subdeacons), and implicitly disapprove of recruiting illiterate men or those unable to use expensive library copies of Scripture, but they express no other criticism. If the style and sonority of ritual singing were significant issues, the prelates assembled on this occasion passed over it.[9]

That is remarkable enough, but there is something more. Chapter xvii marks a vital stage in the evolution of Christian ritual singing by revealing, seemingly for the first time in any known document, *that there were churches where psalmody was no longer regarded as a form of reading*. The custom of considering psalmody before the Eucharist as form of lesson reaches deep into the terminology of late antique authors, whence (to anticipate) the widespread use of the term reader or 'lector' in Western sources for those who sang in churches. Chapter xviii of the Laodicea council, however, forbids the performance of psalms in sequence so that readings (*anagnōsin*) may always be interspersed between them. This implies that the psalmody of the Eucharistic service was no longer regarded as a form of lesson but rather as a separate form of intervention that threatened to unsettle the decorum of liturgies and perhaps even redirect their spirituality if used to excess.[10]

The Apostolic Constitutions and Some Epigraphy

Towards 400, another document began to circulate containing references to liturgical singers and demanding the greatest reverence from anyone who accepted its contents as authentic. Now commonly called the *Apostolic Constitutions*, it purports to offer a large body of legislation for worship and discipline assembled by the Jerusalem apostles in council with Paul. To create this dossier, the compiler (if there was only one) assembled an impressive collection of older writings, probably from collections in Syrian Antioch, to produce a stratified manual that weaves its sources together with the doctrine, discipline and worship of an unknown church in the city. Three books of the *Apostolic Constitutions* mention the singer, but not in any passage that can be securely traced to one of the compiler's known sources. As at Laodicea, the psalmist is firmly distinguished from the reader, who here declaims his lesson and then steps down from the tribune so that another may perform the psalmody (ii. 57. 5). This time, however, there are some welcome details of the singer's musical tasks. He performs responsorial psalmody after the readings of the pre-Eucharistic service, the congregation replying to him with the refrains (ii. 57. 5), and he sings Psalm 33 as a communion hymn (viii. 14. 1). This is one of the earliest indications that psalmody was used after the dismissal of the catechumens, carrying vocal music from the narthex of the service, so to speak, into the inner regions of the mystery. In several respects, psalmists and readers seem to possess much the same status in *The Apostolic Tradition*, as one might expect for the practitioners of separate skills that were perhaps still sometimes combined in a single individual. They are both permitted to take a wife *after* ordination, which marks them out as minor clergy: candidates could be ordained to higher orders only if they were lifelong celibates or already married at the time of their induction. Both resemble higher clergy, however, in the sense that they must be chosen from candidates who have shown a discipline of continence by not seeking a second wife in the event of widowhood. They must both take communion after the deacons. Yet despite these marks of parity between the two ministries of the voice, the psalmist is consistently listed after the reader and therefore as his inferior, and while there is a rite of ordination in the text for a reader there is no such rite for the singer. The proceedings of Laodicea reveal much about the psalmist's presumption, and the *Apostolic Constitutions* are just as ready to remind him of his place.[11]

All the earliest evidence for a named ministry of Christian ritual song therefore comes perhaps from Antioch in Syria or certainly from Asia Minor. The search for a broader range of material leads sooner or later to the abundant remains of epigraphy, mostly in the form of inscribed epitaphs, and to the various modern prosopographies, some achieving a very extensive coverage. A recent inventory of Christian persons from the diocese of Asia for 325 to 641, for example, encompasses some 1,400 individuals in 330 episcopal sees, and therefore covers approximately two-fifths of all the dioceses in the Eastern Roman Empire. Repertories such as the eight volumes of *MAMA*, the *Monumenta Asiae Minoris Antiqua*, add more material. Yet in the event, the traces of individuals holding a named ministry of ritual song are remarkably thin. Published repertories reveal little save three examples that all come, bizarrely enough, from the same coastal city of Corycus in southern Turkey, close to the modern Silifke. Each inscription announces itself as the tomb of a psalmist and then gives the name(s) of the singer. The first two examples are assuredly Christian, since they are marked with a cross or crosses, and the third does not appear in any recent survey of Jewish inscriptions from Corycus:

	MAMA
+Sōmatothēkē H(e)rakli(ou) psaltou	373
Sōmatothēkē Petrou k(ai) Mēna ps(altou) + +	451b
Sōmatothiki Iōannou psaltou Louka	472

Corycus was the saffron capital of the ancient world, and the main port of Seleucia. Yet if the wealth of the city explains why Corycus was so well provided with ministers of song then it is hard to explain why the Christian inscriptions of some greater and more populous cities offer no comparable material.[12]

Why are singers so rarely named in inscriptions and other literary sources? Many a *psaltes* may be concealed in the inscriptions and other documents because he passed from this minor order to become deacon or presbyter, perhaps on occasion even a bishop, and was duly commemorated under that title of office. The case of Gaios the hymnodist, mentioned in his epitaph as a presbyter, may be one such instance (see above, p. 45). Another explanation is that a *psaltes* did not often spring from the social classes with money to spare for the initiatives that have preserved so many names of deacons, presbyters and bishops. The prosopographical records of Christians in late antique Italy and Africa, for example, reveal only one individual endowing a stretch of mosaic pavement and holding a ministry of ritual song at the time. (He was a Westerner, a *cantor* in the cathedral of Trento; see below, p. 216.) Such pavements are a valuable source of names, titles and affiliations for all existing inventories of late antique clergy since it was the custom for each benefactor's section to be duly attributed. More than a modest social level is implied by the insistence on literacy in the Laodicea chapters, given the expense of lessons with a grammarian, but the chapter implies that many singers in the past had been recruited from a constituency with rudimentary literacy, or none at all. Many of those in minor clerical orders, like the singers and readers, were perhaps artisans or local traders of a higher kind, unlikely to travel so far week by week that they became unavailable to serve, and either illiterate or possessing only the functional literacy necessary for keeping papyrus accounts. A reader or lector in the capital of Numidia in 304 was a *sarsor*, presumably a tailor, and it is conceivable that singers and readers were often recruited from the social levels richly documented in Asia Minor as Christian armourers, 'dealers in general merchandise', woodcarvers, bakers, goldsmiths, orchard-keepers and craftsmen in stone, examples all chosen from Anatolian inscriptions. Even some presbyters and deacons in the diocese of Asia (but not many) were compelled to be professional men, in higher callings like medicine and the law, because their stipends did not amount to a married man's livelihood. One deacon of the third or fourth century, Tabeis, appears to have been a maker of mosaics or a mason. The stipend for a *psaltes* would have been lower than for a deacon or presbyter, and the incidence of men necessarily pursuing some other occupation, in addition to their clerical duties, higher in consequence. Some were perhaps barely clergy at all, but laymen with the necessary gifts who had been enrolled as singers without ever intending (or being eligible) to ascend the clerical *cursus*; the Church received the services it needed and the individual maintained a special contact with his Church. A *psaltes* of this kind would have generally been too insignificant a figure to be engaged in activities liable to be noticed in chronicles and other documents. He did not carry letters for his bishop, deputize for him at synods, correspond with influential men or become notorious for expounding contentious doctrines.[13]

A *psaltes* of possibly higher rank appears in an inscription from Seleucia Sydera (province of Pisidia), seemingly unique for the way it shows a singer as the member of a local association and holding a place of some prestige within it. The inscription survives because it was re-employed for the mosque at Bayad near the ancient site, and is dated either to 365 or 419, depending on the initial point of reckoning (the latter date, reckoning from Actium, is probably the more reliable). According to the text, the seventy members of a *synodia* or pious guild wished to record their dedication of a church to Saint George. Such associations were very common among the polytheists of the ancient world, and there is nothing remarkable about the commitment of this one to a Christianized form of civic benefaction in the form of a church. Two municipal magistrates, men of considerable status, head the list, but in first place after them comes a certain 'Porphyrios the singer of antiphons'. There is no indication that he was a monk or cleric, and he was presumably therefore a layman. Whether the correct date of the inscription be 365 or 419, the duties of this 'singer of antiphons' were probably quite varied and extensive. While the term antiphon, in this early period of its use, 'does not exclude refrains, it seems to imply something larger, encompassing both invariant and variable elements – the whole form, in other words, along with its popular, non-scriptural texts and various schemes for group participation'. Porphyrios provides a valuable example of a singer holding a ministry of ritual song and apparently occupying an esteemed position in the pious guild of a city in Asia Minor. He is perhaps just the kind of man the bishops at Loadicea would have been keen to employ.[14]

The emergence of the psalmist as a titled minister of song in western Asia Minor reveals much about developments in the fourth-century Church, especially those that produced a change in the weight of its coffers. The accession of Ambrose to the episcopal throne of Milan shows that it was already possible in the earlier 300s for the Church to attract men of exalted status, education and wealth who recognized there was a clerical alternative to careers in the civil and military bureaucracy. As bishops, the most successful of these men were being transformed into major civic figures. Their responsibilities were too emphatically charitable in a Christian sense for them to be regarded as a new class of civic administrators or governors, but they often controlled greater wealth in land and buildings than the local count or any other landowner, and as Roman public power declined so their duty of care became more onerous. The effects of this wealth upon the size of the clerical staff in the cathedrals of the eastern Mediterranean was probably much the same as it was for provision of lavish textiles or highly wrought lamps: there was money to have more stipendiary clergy, including singers. Although there is no list of the bishops present at the Laodicea council discussed above, a synod for its province could have drawn representatives from Aizanoi, Appia, Eumeneia, Colossae, Hierapolis (modern Pamukkale), Sanaos, Sebaste and Traianoupolis, all with bishops recorded for the fourth century and some with epigraphic evidence of Christianity that reaches back into the third or further still, as in the case of Colossae. In legislating for these and other churches, the prelates at the council assume a descending hierarchy of bishop, presbyter, deacon, subdeacon, reader, singer, exorcist, doorkeeper and ascetic. This implies rich and well-staffed churches, but the difference between a major urban centre like Laodicea and smaller cities, in terms of material culture and ceremonial, was probably quite marked. Ephesus, Antioch, Corinth and Aphrodisias (to look more widely in Asia Minor) 'retained their classical monu-mentality into the mid-sixth century and beyond, but ordinary cities lost their classical monumentality much more rapidly'.[15]

Ministers of Song in the West

Did ministers of ritual music appear earlier in the East than in the West? It is widely held that many devotional and liturgical innovations travelled in an east–west direction, albeit with transit times that could be remarkably short if some recent assessments are correct. If the custom of appointing a *psaltes* in many Eastern sees did indeed antedate the same development in the West, then it would join monasticism, the use of antiphons (whatever that term means in a fourth-century context) and perhaps the 'psalmodic movement' as initiatives of the *ecclesia orientalis* taken up in the Occident. At first sight this may seem to be a justifiable view, for no instance of the term *cantor* as a title of office has been found in any Western source dating from earlier than *c.*475 (see below, pp. 214–18). Nonetheless, it may be possible to push the use of this word as a term of office back to the late 300s and therefore to within the century of the Laodicea council. In Jerome's translation of the Bible, commissioned by Pope Damasus (366–84), there are signs that Jerome regarded *cantor* as the best term for trans-lating words denoting musicians of the Temple, whereas the compiler(s) of the Old Latin that preceded him were content with much less consistency. To take *II Paralipomenon* as an example (Vulgate from *Biblia Sacra iuxta Latinam Vulgatam*; Old Latin from *Les Anciennes Versions*, ed. Weber):

	Jerome	*Old Latin*
5: 12	tam Levitae quam cantores	Levitae qui psallebunt
9: 11	cantoribus	cantatoribus
20: 21	cantores	psalmorum canentes
29: 28	cantores	tuba canentes
35: 15	cantores	psalmos cantantes
35: 25	cantores	cantores

Jerome almost always prefers the noun *cantor* to the considerably more varied choices of the Old Latin versions, which suggests he regarded it as an established term of office for Christian ritual singers, here strongly identified with their Jewish predecessors, the Levites. Indeed, there is a passage in Jerome's commen-tary upon Ephesians 5: 19 which suggests that he knew an established office of ritual song in the churches. Here Jerome counsels adolescents and others charged to sing in church that they should sing to God and not to an audience whom they wish to impress; true singing is done with the heart, not with the voice, and certainly not 'in daubing the mouth and throat with some sweet medicine after the manner of tragedians, so that theatrical melodies and songs are heard in the church'. Jerome's language here, as he knows full well, is loud with echoes of Cicero and other Classical writers who inveighed against histrionic or 'theatrical' styles of oratory; nonetheless, it reveals the existence of singers, many of them youths, who were keen to make an impression when they sang in church with musical materials and idioms that were all too familiar to Jerome from the world of Roman art-song and who used professional tricks like the application of 'sweet medicine' to strengthen the voice. 'The office of the cantor is implicit in th[is] text', wrote James McKinnon in 1987. One might add that Jerome's letter LII clearly identifies the singer or *psaltes* as a minor order together with the lector and acolyte. If the churches of the western Empire were behind those of the eastern in having a named ministry of song, the distance was not very great.[16]

If there were indeed ministers of music known as cantors in some Occidental churches of the fourth century, they were by no means the only men with a charge of singing. There was another trajectory for a ministry of music in the Western churches, and it leads from the *psaltes* of the Laodicea canons to the reader or lector of many Western texts and epitaphs. Consider a brief conspectus of some principal sources. At Augustine's church in Hippo Regius, a reader or lector delivered the responsorial psalm of the Fore-Mass. A later source from Africa, the *Historia Persecutionis Wandalicae* by Victor of Vita, describes an Epiphany service at Arbal where a Catholic lector mounted the pulpit to sing the 'Alleluia melody' or *alleluiaticum melos*, during events datable to 455–77. He sang from the raised dais or *pulpitum* and held a book, which suggests a form of responsorial psalmody (the people are singing as well) for which he requires a Psalter to find his place in the text after being interrupted, so to speak, by the congregation. In fifth-century Gaul, Bishop Gennadius of Marseille reports that his predecessor, Venerius (428–52), commissioned a book with the scriptural readings for the festive days of the liturgical year, interleaved with psalms specially chosen for their appropriateness to both the readings and the day; this book presumably contained all the texts needed by those who read and sang, but Gennadius says its usefulness was proved by the daily experience of lectors. At Milan, it was well understood that 'some [persons] are more apt for giving readings and some others for psalmody', in the words of Saint Ambrose, but Ambrose never uses the terms *cantor* or *psalmista* as titles of office in his extensive writings. The singers were presumably called readers or lectors, which explains why the funeral oration Ambrose gave for his brother, perhaps in 378, reminds the members of the congregation that they heard the voice of a lector delivering Psalm 23: 4 earlier that day, *Innocens manibus, et mundo corde*. 'He that hath clean hands and a pure heart'. This was presumably the responsorial psalm at Mass, not the reading, for Ambrose reveals that the lesson for the day had been *Fundamenta ejus in montibus sanctis* (Psalm 87). Many lectors, it seems, were also required to be singers from at least the fourth century.[17]

The use of *lector* to mean a lector-singer, or sometimes perhaps simply a singer, proved remarkably durable in some of the Western churches. The proceedings of the Second Council of Braga, convened in 572, rule that no person should 'sing or read' (*psallere aut legere*) from the *pulpitum* unless they have been 'ordained a lector by a priest'. There may also be echoes of the lector's musical duties in some of the oldest treatises on the grades of clerical office, already ossified compilations of material by the time they come to light in the late seventh century. *De officiis vii graduum*, in existence by 700, requires the reader 'to read for him who preaches and to sing the lections' (*lectiones cantare*) where the intended meaning of *cantare* may be musical and *lectiones*, in accord with the late antique custom of regarding psalmody as a form of reading, may mean the Fore-Mass psalm(s). There may also be traces of musical duties in several of the earliest sacramentaries, multilayered books for the celebrant with rites of ordination for various degrees of clergy, including the reader. Here again, the sense of strata forming deep but unfathomable chronological layers is insistent, especially in the textual variants, where transmission has reduced some readings to a meaningless state. In the so-called *Missale Francorum*, probably of the eighth century in its surviving form, the lector's rite of ordination calls upon God to make the Church resound with *curis modulis*, presumably '*moduli* executed with due care', although *curis* does not construe. The intended sense of *moduli* is assuredly musical. The Gellone Sacramentary, attesting to a Frankish–Roman model of the 760s, describes the reader as one 'whose *moduli*' may make the church resonate (*cuius modolis*). Finally, the Angoulême Sacramentary goes one better, summoning the lector to perform *puris modulis* ('with pure *moduli*'). The musical term *modulus*, applied to the voice of the lector, is the only stable element in a text otherwise beyond reconstruction. At some stage in the gestation of these documents, it seems that the induction of a reader might also be the admission of a minister, albeit a very lowly one, with a charge of singing.[18]

Reading is Believing

In Rome around 150, Justin Martyr mentions 'the person reading' (*anaginōs-kontos*) who declaims from 'the memoirs of the apostles or the works of the prophets, as long as time allows', followed by a homily from the president of the assembly (see above, p. 65). In the same century, and again referring to a Roman milieu, the *Acts of Peter* describes a gospel reading when the senator Marcellus invites the members of the Christian community accustomed to receive his charity, mostly widows and elderly women, to his house for worship. He tells Peter that 'all is now prepared for the service (*ministerium*)', and when the apostle enters the *triclinium* or dining room of the house he hears an account of the

Transfiguration being read to the assembly. Peter takes the scroll and begins to deliver a homily in the manner of many synagogues or indeed of Christ's own synagogue reading in Luke 4: 16–20. Justin is describing the services he knew, possibly in a selective manner, while the compiler of the *Acts of Peter* is presumably projecting the services of his day back to the first generation of apostles. The two texts could scarcely be more different; nonetheless, they both assume that worship in a house-church includes a reading from a canonical account of Christ's life and a subsequent homily. Neither gives any clear sign that the readers hold a *ministry* of reading; Justin Martyr's 'person reading' may be no more a minister than a Jew in a synagogue called up to read the Torah as an honour.[19]

An order of Christian reader was slow to form. The churches inherited no firm sense from the synagogue that it was necessary to have a titled office of reading, and Christian practice for much of the second century in regard to the prophets, psalms and other Jewish books was perhaps just as fluid. It may have been the same for the Epistles of Paul and other letters, such as those attributed to Clement, not retained in the long term. With reports of the life and sayings of Christ, however, the situation was more complex. Until the late decades of the second century, the bishops and presbyters were the principal trustees of the relationship between the written records of Christ's sayings made in the apostolic generation (if any were made) and the continuing oral tradition in which those sayings were continuously repeated and refashioned in homilies. The sermons in which the president of the assembly passed on the sayings of Christ conveyed the sense of a tradition that was still being made and remade in the community's presence. Everything that one heard was believed to derive, in a sequence of face-to-face exchanges, from the voices of the apostolic generation and ultimately from the voice of Christ himself. This would not have encouraged anyone to suppose that the way in which a homilist configured Christ's sayings was a version of something in a text, if text there was. The president's voice provided an independent channel of information and arguably the most authoritative. Why should anyone replace the urgent and perhaps pneumatic reconstitution of Christ's words in each new presidential homily with an inert textual deposit that late antique minds might regard as considerably more tenuous? Many Christians in the second century would probably have agreed with the remark by Papias, as reported by Eusebius: 'For I did not imagine things out of books would help me as much as the utterance of a living and abiding voice' (*EH*, iii. 39).[20]

For much of the second century, the situation was probably still fluid. Justin Martyr refers explicitly to readings from the prophets and from gospels believed to be of apostolic authorship in Rome around 150, but his 'memoirs of the apostles' cannot simply be equated with the fourfold gospel to the exclusion of everything subsequently deemed to be apocryphal. Justin cites one non-canonical episode, the appearance of fire in the Jordan during Christ's baptism, which he could have derived from the *Gospel of the Ebionites*. (He also received the *Acts of Pilate*.) What is more, the gospels plainly did not exist for Justin as inviolable

17   Fragment from a papyrus codex, originally written with two columns per page and containing, as connected fragments show, all four of the canonical gospels (this one shows part of Matthew 26). Commonly dated to the late 2nd c. Attempts to substantiate earlier datings remain controversial. Oxford, Magdalen College, P[64].

texts giving the canonical form to the sayings of Christ. In a manner that may reveal much about the nature of presidential homilies before the written gospel tradition was established, Justin approaches all his gospel material with some freedom. His citations combine passages that are now in different gospels and often expand them with clarifications in the manner of a Targum. Comparison of Justin's quotations with the received texts of the Synoptic Gospels shows that ten of them are exact, twenty-five are slightly varied and thirty-two are appreciably different. This is in contrast to Justin's quotations from the Septuagint translation of the Psalms, where his citations are much more consistently exact. It seems he almost always turned to the Septuagint text when quoting from the Psalter, but consulted a more fluid and perhaps still partly oral tradition when citing the 'memoirs of the apostles'.[21]

By the end of the second century it becomes possible to discern the nucleus of the New Testament canon. Papyrus fragments begin to reveal that the fourfold gospel was recognized as a comprehensive scribal project (Pl. 17), while the famous gospel harmony of Tatian, entitled *Diatessaron* and perhaps composed in the third quarter of the second century, plainly implies a fourfold canon. These texts connected a community's worship, preaching and sacraments to an external world of scribes and stationers, just as they began to restructure duties within the community to accommodate some version of the librarianship and textual skills that had flourished in the Mediterranean for so long among Jews and polytheists. The effect upon the position of those who read in the Christian assemblies cannot be traced in any detail, but it may be no coincidence that the earliest known Occidental reference to an order of readers appears just after 200, and therefore at the end of the half century when the fourfold gospel canon first comes into view. The emergence of canonical readers, discharging a ministry on a weekly basis, may therefore be connected with the consolidation by 200 of a fourfold gospel canon for them to read as the preparation for a homily by presbyters or bishops who, once the canon became widespread, were no longer remaking both the word of Christ and its meaning in the assembly but only its meaning. It was for other ministers, the readers, to declare the word first.

The key text for the Occident is Tertullian's *De Praescriptione Haereticorum*, written to deny heretics any access to the Scriptures as if by an imperial *praescriptio*, hence the title of the work. Tertullian proclaims the transmission of Christ's teaching to the apostles who founded churches and deposited their teaching directly or indirectly in the Scriptures. He claims that heretics, in contrast, are not schooled in any secure doctrine so it is no surprise to find they are very lax in their preparations for baptism. One cannot tell who is a catechumen among them and who is baptized. These heretics are even inconsistent in their 'ordinations' or *ordinationes*, a term that already seems to possess the familiar technical sense. Their churches have 'one bishop today, but tomorrow another. That man is a *diaconus* today who will be a *lector* tomorrow. Today he is a *presbyter* who will tomorrow be a layman.' We have only Tertullian's word for this indifference to continuity of office in the churches he condemns, although a certain weakness in the institutions of those communities would help to explain how the Great Church became Great and no other did. Be that as it may, his polemic reveals that the office of reader already existed in some African churches by the year 200 under a Latin not a Greek name, *lector*, and that Tertullian in Carthage regarded it as an established ministry of the mainstream Church. Tertullian has probably simplified matters somewhat, for that is ever the fault of the polemicist, but his claims may not be greatly exaggerated. A letter in Greek, preserved by Eusebius, reveals that the Roman Church some fifty years after Tertullian possessed 'fifty two exorcists, readers (*anagnōstas*) and doorkeepers' (see Pl. 18). Rome cannot have been far behind Carthage in the development of the reader's office as a minor order (*EH*, vi. 43,11).[22]

Certain developments were taking place throughout the Mediterranean that encouraged the rise of the lectors. By the third century, Christians can be found seeking public places of worship, claiming parity with Jews and polytheists. The process is difficult to trace, for there are very few relics of Christian monumental architecture before the fourth century, either in terms of archaeological sites or of inscriptions and literary references. Even in the lifetime of Paul, however, the house-churches were not the only places where meetings might be held. The hall or *scholē* where Paul preached in Ephesus represents one kind of interior that a city could offer to a cultic group, and so does the warehouse or *horreum* on the outskirts of Rome, mentioned in the second-century *Acts of Paul* as a place where Christians gathered. Bathhouses, both public and private, also make a sporadic but significant appearance as places adaptable for meetings. These were often spacious buildings, and even when they were private baths or small buildings for local use, these *thermae* had the great advantage of being plumbed in for use as baptisteries, at least in cases where the pipes and the water source were still viable when Christians began to use them. The Roman titular Church of Pudenziana, recorded as early as the first decades of the fourth century, began as an insertion into the large bath-hall of a private house of the second century, and one of the earliest Roman lectors on record (between 360 and 384) was commemorated as a reader there. There may be some substance in the claim of the *Vita Sancti Cyriaci* that the Roman titular Church of Saint Cyriac *in thermis* developed from a house next to the baths occupied by Cyriac at the beginning of the fourth century. It may be no coincidence that Justin Martyr lodged above a bathhouse in Rome. On a broader front, great cities such as Carthage (probably) and Alexandria (certainly) possessed churches that were public in a relaxed sense of the word by the third century; there was even a church, albeit newly built, facing Diocletian's imperial palace in Nicomedia, for the city prefect and his men demolished it to signal the beginning of the Great Persecution in February 303. Long before Constantine put an end to such harassment, the Christians of some cities met in large spaces apt to encourage a considerably more structured approach to the liturgical readings.[23]

By the middle of the third century – still in Carthage – the readers had a ritual space allotted to them. In two letters written to inform the presbyters and deacons of Carthage of recent appointments to the lectorate, Bishop Cyprian (d. 258) twice mentions the reader's *pulpitum*, a platform or dais akin to the *tribunal*, the raised platform for magistrates, orators or judges. 'There', writes Cyprian, 'the reader is easily seen by the brethren.' In the letter concerning the appointment of Celerinus, a Carthaginian who had recently suffered during the Decian persecution in Rome, Cyprian compares his new reader to a light which will be placed high on a candelabrum, readily seen by all and illuminating the room. 'Through the conspicuous radiance of his glory he may read the commandments and Gospel of the Lord to all the people.' Since Celerinus was technically a confessor, one who had not renounced his faith under interrogation but had not suffered martyrdom, Cyprian is able to develop an exalted conception of the reader's voice in this instance: 'A confessor can do nothing greater for his brothers than that whoever hears the gospels from his mouth should imitate the lector's faith.' Well before Cyprian's death in 258, therefore, the Christians of Carthage gathered for worship in a place with a (moveable?) fixture for the reader, the *pulpitum*, which was presumably placed at one end of a space being used as a proto-nave.[24]

The Youthful Reader

Cyprian's letters concerning the appointment of two readers both mention the lector's duty to read the fundamental texts of the faith (*Evangelica lectio, Evangelium Domini, Evangelium Christi*). They also disclose that the two

18 A cubiculum showing the epitaph of Favor, *lector*, from the primitive and probably mid-3rd-c. nucleus of the catacomb of S. Agnese (Regio 1), Via Nomentana, Rome. When first discovered, this inscription was dated to a very early period and regarded by some as proof that the order of lector had existed in apostolic times. It is nonetheless one of the earliest known memorials to a lector, and may be approximately contemporary with the report by Pope Cornelius, preserved by Eusebius, that the Church of Rome had fifty-two exorcists, lectors and doorkeepers.

individuals in question, Aurelius and Celerinus, were young men. Aurelius is described as an *adolescens*; epitaphs from Gaul and Spain show this term being used in commemorative inscriptions for those still under their parents' guardianship and aged somewhere between 2 and 26 at the time of death. Cyprian's meaning lies in the earlier part of the range for Aurelius is 'new in years as yet', *in annis adhuc novellis*. Celerinus was also appointed while a young man; Cyprian assures his clergy that both he and Aurelius will 'sit with us hereafter in their advanced and strengthened years'. When the epigraphic record of lectors begins, perhaps in the late 200s (Pl. 18), it reveals that many who began the *cursus* of clerical promotion became lectors while still in boyhood or in early adolescence. An eastern example, from Laodicea in Pisidia, records a fourth-century reader named Appas, commemorated for being 'young (*neoterōs*) and of fine appearance'. Epitaphs from Italy, Spain, Gaul and Africa confirm that many acquired the title of *lector* within the age range implied by *adolescens*. A census of the Roman inscriptions naming lectors, surveyed below in Chapter 5, shows the average age of the

Roman lectors who died before their twenty-fifth birthday to be just 15. One was only 5, and therefore perhaps too young even to have begun his studies with a grammarian, but not necessarily too young to have learned to read, especially if he had been set to learn the passage more or less by heart beforehand. A similar picture emerges from a poem by Commodian, probably writing in Rome during the third century and perhaps as early as 220–40, although there is much uncertainty about his dates. He gives advice to lectors and addresses them as 'little sons' (*filioli*). This might be read as an affectionate form of address, implying more about the paternalistic authority Commodian is taking to himself, with certain New Testament letters in mind, than about the youth of the lectors for whom he writes. Nonetheless, the evolution of *filiolus* in Christian Latin shows that the sense of 'tender years' remained strong. Thus FILIOLUS > Spanish *hijuelo*, 'little child', French *filleul* and Occitan *filhòla*, 'a child received from the baptismal font'.[25]

Why was the task of declaiming the most exalted documents of the faith entrusted to boys or young men holding one of the lowest clerical positions? The grade of lector was so low that it could perhaps be conferred as a kind of viaticum upon those who expired in early childhood (which may explain the epitaphs for lectors aged 5) or upon laymen who wished to maintain an association with the clergy of a church, like the purchasing agent known to Sidonius Apollinaris in the fifth century and enrolled in his church as a lector. Nonetheless, there is perhaps a very simple answer to the question of why the ministry of reading was associated with adolescents and boys. Soon after 250, Cyprian of Carthage already assumes that clergy begin at the lowest rung of the clerical *cursus* and then ascend as high as their abilities and patrons can take them. In theory, if not always in practice, this was eventually required throughout the Christian West,

19   The precocious Latin-Christian literacy of Roman Africa, the earliest documented in the West, was grounded in the early victory of Latin over indigenous Punic and Libyan. As the language of Carthage and therefore of the Phoenicians (the terms 'Punic' and 'Phoenician' have the same root) Punic yielded nothing to Latin in terms of an ancient literacy. Yet on this plaque from the north-west access corridor to the theatre in Lepcis Magna (Libya), commemorating the creation of a theatre in 1–2 AD by Annobal Himilcho, the Latin text comes first and the Punic name of the donor is inflected with Latin morphology, in the usual way, as Himilchonis.

and there were obvious advantages to ensuring that the lowest grade of clergy should impose exacting duties of scriptural reading and study upon new entrants. There was no better way to train receptive minds, still of an age to be schooled, than with the weekly task of working through a biblical passage with a teacher, looking to the sense, grammar and meaning in preparation for giving a reading.[26]

Yet if this were the *only* motive for making the lectorate a neophyte's grade one would expect clergy in later centuries to have continued the practice, and yet they did not. The youthful lectorate was not destined to survive, and by the fifth century the tasks of reading the gospels and the Old Testament had been promoted in many Western churches to the deacons and the celebrant. With the end of the house-church period, it seems the domestic context of worship was replaced by a more hieratic conviction that the Word and the ministers of the altar belonged together in the public institution of the Church. Recent work on the social environment of early Christianity, and especially on the household matrix discussed above in Chapter 2, provides one way to illuminate the second-century developments that contributed to the formation of a youthful lectorate. There are few areas of early Christian life where the continuities between pagan and Christian social attitudes are clearer than they are in matters touching family life in a context of marriage, parenting and the household. The education of children provides one example, despite the fraught negotiations between Christians and the Classical literary heritage that formed the basis for a traditional education in grammar and oratory, the latter with a view to the public office. Epitaphs often reveal the fondness with which Roman parents would exaggerate the intellectual accomplishments of their offspring, praising a 'conspicuously educated young man', honouring a boy who was 'remarkably clever and able in his studies' or commemorating a youth who was 'outstanding in learning and wise beyond his years'. The mid-second century sarcophagus of M. Cornelius Statius vividly suggests the investment of time parents might make in the education of their children, especially of the males who alone could achieve public office (Pl. 20). At the far left, Cornelius is breast-fed while the father looks on, holding in his left hand a *volumen* to suggest the intellectual contribution he will later make to the child's development. The father is then shown again, holding his son, followed by a representation of the boy, now much older, driving a small chariot pulled by a goat. In the last scene, the boy declaims his lesson before his seated father.[27]

It was perhaps a matter of pride for Christian householders to see a young son, perhaps barely emerged from boyhood, inducted into the order of reader, a ceremony already regulated in the third-century dossier of liturgical material the *Apostolic Tradition*. Pictorial sources show that Christian parents, with the means to secure an education for their offspring, placed a high value on reading and study. The catacomb paintings commemorating a young man named Trebius Iustus, for example, provide an outstanding illustration of what the literate skills of a son could mean to a wealthy Christian family in the imperial capital towards

20   Detail of the sarcophagus of M. Cornelius Statius. 2nd c. Paris, Musée du Louvre.

the end of the third century or the beginning of the fourth. Discovered under the Via Latina in Rome, these accomplished pictures adorn the hypogeum of a young man who died at the age of 21 (Pl. 21A). At the summit of the picture, Trebius appears seated between his parents as they hold a cloth displaying items of plate, perhaps their offerings to a local church. The lowest stage of the painting emphasizes the family's prosperity by showing Trebius again, or perhaps the steward of the estate, inspecting baskets of produce that may be intended for charitable donation to a widow, Asella, or to a deaconess serving as the clearing agent for such donations somewhat like the woman named Grapte mentioned much earlier in the Roman *I Clement*. The superscription *Asellae piae* might then be rendered '[This basket] to the devout Asella'. In the middle range Trebius appears with an open codex (Pl. 21B). Other materials for reading and writing float in the air around him and another book drifts to his right, its pages open; there is also a large rectangular chest for books, two pen-cases, a round basket for scrolls and two wax tablets with the ligatures holding the plates together clearly visible. The painting gives early expression to an influential wing of opinion in late antique Rome that did not expect rich Christians to pursue their own salvation at the cost of their dependents and clients by abandoning their wealth, lands and traditions for a life of voluntary poverty. The duty of the wealthy was to discharge their obligations in full and if possible to extend them beyond the circle of their household slaves and clients to the Church's dependents. These images also show what literate studies meant to wealthy converts, whose studies in grammar and rhetoric were as important as precious tableware, a large complement of slaves or a fertile estate in the making of their identity.[28]

Was it also the *sound* of youthful voices that mattered to the Christian communities? Conciliar material from fourth-century Africa contains several canons insisting lectors should read until the age of puberty but no further, at which time they should either marry or be induced to live in perpetual continence. The

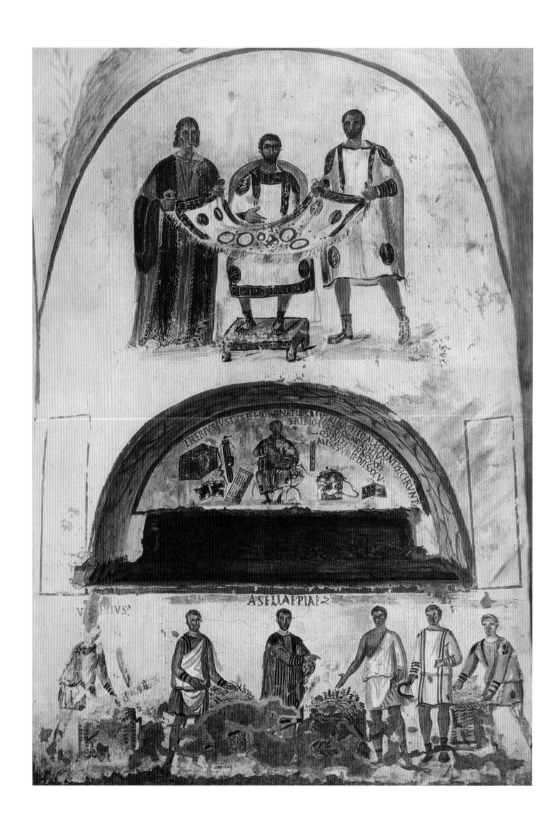

21a and b (*facing page and above*)   Trebius Iustus and his parents. From a catacomb discovered in the early years of the 20th c. under the Via Latina. Late 3rd or early 4th c.

epigraphic record, although very scattered and mostly late, is sometimes explicit about the sexual innocence of lectors who died young (Table 4.1). A recent historian of childhood and early Christianity may be right to suggest that 'the extreme youth of certain lectors suggests that it was the child's voice rather than any reading skills that may have been valued in this context'. The same might be said for the proposal that 'in the early Church, the holy innocence which Christians nowadays ascribe to choirboys rested on boys who were reading God's word aloud to their audience'. It was perhaps considered especially appropriate to hear the canonical gospels voiced by a candid and even artless voice that was neither darkened by the beginnings of a sexual identity with the onset of

TABLE 4.1. *'Innocent lectors' in the epigraphic record*

Location	Name	Title and place	Date	Age	Inscription
Rome	LEOPARDUS	Lector de Pudentiana	360–84	24	*mirae innocentiae*
Viennensis	TIGRIDIUS	[l]ector; Autun	–	–	*castus puer*
	SEVERUS	lectur	–	13	*lectur ennocens*
Byzantine Africa	CASTALINUS ('little chaste one')	lector; Ammaedara	–	6	

Note: in epigraphy, the term 'puer' is widely used for the age range 7–14, but there are cases of males as old as 35 given this title.

puberty nor yet equipped to gild the reading very much with the skills of the Classical orator. Indeed, a Christian commitment perhaps allowed many parents to hear the voices of their male children, as they read aloud, in a new way. Slowly ceasing to hear these pre-pubescent voices as a promise of what might be won (parents hoped) in a later life of public office for which rhetorical skills were essential, many Christians perhaps began to hear those sounds as an expressive testimony to what was already possessed and might (parents feared) be all too readily lost: a simplicity and innocence expressing the truth of the Church, the *ecclesiastica simplicitas*.[29]

The founding texts for this childish innocence are both in Matthew's gospel, where Christ tells his disciples they shall not enter the kingdom of heaven unless they 'become as little children' (18: 3), and quotes Psalm 8: 2 to the priests of the Temple: 'Out of the mouths of babes and sucklings thou hast perfected praise' (21: 16). The theme of juvenile innocence reaches well beyond the New Testament canon into the earliest layers of patristic commentary and even to texts not received as canonical by the mainstream Church. The childishness they advocate is not the vulnerable infancy of Ephesians 4: 14, 'tossed to and fro, and carried about with every wind of doctrine by the sleight of men', but a strength that guides the trusting heart to the truth of the gospel. In some of the earliest layers of Christian writing outside the New Testament corpus the sexual innocence and sinless quality of the child is the nature of Christ himself, who was 'like a child, like a root in the dry land' (*I Clement*, 16. 20). More broadly, the purity of the child is associated with faith in the plain word of Scripture, which many teachers in the Great Church vaunted against the sophistry of late antique philosophy, with its luxuriance and associations with worldly fame. The *Epistle of Barnabas*, of the second century, gives thanks to Christ for having 'made us into a new type of person, that we might have the soul of children, as if he were indeed forming us all over again' (6. 11). The same note is sounded, this time in Rome but again in the early years of the second century, by Hermas. The teaching of this freedman in *The Shepherd* is that the faithful should be innocent 'like little children who do not know the evil that ruins human life'.[30]

For the commentators of the third and fourth centuries, this was the heart of the issue. Clement of Alexandria longs for the single-hearted believer of 'virgin speech, tender and free of fraud', qualities he associates with the quality of *nēpiotēs*, 'the state of being as a child'. Among the Western Fathers there are many who join in this rhapsody to childish innocence. In the judgement of Ambrose, a boy trusts all whom he meets and believes what he is told. He seeks to emulate his father and loves his mother; he does not wear vain clothing and does not persist in anger. (One can tell that the Church Fathers were fathers in a metaphorical sense only.) The innocence and candour of a boy, studious in his lessons, might even be regarded as a guarantee he would not wish or presume to falsify his texts in the vain belief he knew better than his copy. The verse epitaph of Pope Liberius (352–66) records how he was appointed a lector in Rome while still

22 A woman with her child. From the Priscilla Catacomb in Rome (cubiculum in the south-west corner, first level), dating from the second half of the 3rd c. The image faces a painting widely regarded as the scene of her marriage. From Wilpert, *Pitture*, ii, Tavola 81.

a boy, with a 'simple childishness', an *infantia simplex*, which ensured he would never read in a perverse or negligent way. In short, it was better to have readers who were young, for puberty was what Peter Brown has called 'the first, pre-monitary symptom of the world of adult cunning, of self-interest and of adult hypocrisy'.[31]

Perhaps the youthful lectorate was also a means for married householders of the mainstream Church faith to celebrate Christian marriage and childbearing (Pl. 22). As early as the end of the first century, parent-householders of the nascent mainstream faced a markedly ascetic strain of opinion that placed continence and especially virginity above the married state. For the most part, the documents received into the New Testament corpus are vociferously opposed to this view. Ephesians 5: 25–30 exhorts husbands to love their wives as Christ loved the Church and gave his life for her. 1 Timothy expresses with particular clarity how Christian parents might resent the charge they had adopted a lower form of life because they declined to remain in a virginal or continent state. The Epistle forcefully associates leadership of the Church with parenting, and even proclaims childbearing as the deed that absolves all women from the sin of Eve: 'For Adam was not deceived, but the woman being deceived was in the transgression.

Notwithstanding she shall be saved in childbearing' (2: 14–15). Advocates of
celibacy are 'those speaking lies in hypocrisy . . . forbidding to marry' in
1 Timothy 4: 2–3. The beauty of the youthful lectorate was its ability to gratify
different shades of opinion on these matters. For some, to have a son's name
placed on the register of readers might express the piety of parent-householders
who had done their childrearing but sought an ascetic life in their later years. For
other families among the householders of the cities, a child lector was perhaps a
public avowal of Christian parenthood and the married state in which they
intended to pass the rest of their lives.[32]

   If this reconstruction is justified, then one would expect to find a phenomenon that might be called the nuclear-family clerisy: a prominent Christian household in a particular city where the paterfamilias was one of the elders of the
community, even perhaps its leader, while some of his offspring held lower positions in the clerical hierarchy, including the position of reader. By a remarkable
piece of good fortune, the only pre-Constantinian text that inventories the
persons present at a Christian assembly by name reveals essentially this kind of
domestic clerisy. This is the detailed cross-section of a community that assembled
for a Eucharistic service near Carthage in 304, only to be captured by soldiers and
hauled off to Carthage for interrogation, torture and death (Table 4.2). A
Donatist hagiographer, who apparently worked from a copy of the interrogation
records, or a later compiler soon after 411, compiled the document on which we
rely for these details. Just before the arrest, the community had gathered for its
Sunday service at the house of Octavius Felix in Abitina, possibly Chahoud
el-Batin, west of Membressa in modern Tunisia. The president of the assembly
was a presbyter named Saturninus who was present with two of his sons whose

TABLE 4.2. *The composition of a Christian community gathered for the Sunday Eucharist
in the house of Octavius Felix at Abitina, possibly modern Chahoud el-Batin, in Africa
Proconsularis, in February 304*

	Saturninus *presbyter*		
Saturninus junior *lector adolescens*	Felix *lector*	Hilarianus *infans . . . puer*	Maria *sanctimonialis*

Female congregation

Telica (= Tazelita?), Restituta, Prima, Eva, Pomponia, Secunda, Ianuaria, Saturnina,
Margarita, Honorata, Regiola, Matrona, Caecilia, Berectina, Secunda, Matrona,
Ianuaria, Victoria (*flos virginum*)

Male congregation

Dativus *qui et senator*, Felix, Felix, Rogatianus, Quintus, Maximianus, Rogatianus,
Rogatus, Januarius, Cassianus, Victorianus, Vincentius, Caecilianus, Rogatianus,
Givalius, Rogatus, Martinus, Clautus, Felix, Maior, Victorianus, Pelusius, Faustus,
Dacianus, Emeritus *lector*, Ampelius (librarian?)

ages are not specified, but one is called *adolescens*. Both of these sons are listed as readers or lectors. The presbyter's daughter Maria, also taken by the soldiers, was an ascetic or a *sanctimonialis*. There was at least one other lector present, named Emeritus, who was not from the family of Saturninus. Another individual present at this Eucharist, named Ampelius, was a 'most faithful keeper of the divine Scriptures', perhaps the community's librarian. So while Saturninus and his family did not entirely dominate the gathering at Abitina, there is a strong sense that he and his children (there is no mention of his wife) form the core of its ministry, including his sons the lectors, followed onto the 'field of martyrdom' by his congregation.[33]

Although the term *cantor* may have been used as a title of office as early as the last quarter of the fourth century, musical interventions at Mass are principally traceable in the West as the task assigned to the lector. The material comes from Milan, Africa and Gaul (on which, see below). Jerome's reference to the *adolescentuli* who must not groom their voices dates from 388, three years after he left Rome, where he had served as secretary to Pope Damasus from 382 to 385. Amidst the great diversity of persons who can be found singing psalmody between 200 and 400, either in the home or in assemblies, the youthful lector comes into view as a performer of the Fore-Mass psalm in all parts of the West save Spain and Britain, which have left no relevant material. The lector in Augustine's church at Hippo Regius was usually 'an adolescent boy, presumably of the pre-clerical state', and when his contemporary Saint Jerome cautions psalmists not to refine their voices with special medicines or 'theatrical' techniques he addresses *adolescentuli* and 'those who have the charge of psalmody'. At Milan, Ambrose calls the singer of the responsorial psalm a *parvulus*, a term widely used for boys who were still in the period of their primary schooling. For Gaul, there is the material of uncertain age and provenance in the seventh-century compilation commonly called the *Expositio antiquae Liturgiae Gallicanae*, for there the *Responsurium*, the Gallican equivalent of the Roman gradual, is assigned to boys (*a paruolis canitur*), recalling Ambrose's reference to the *parvulus* whom his congregation heard deliver the psalm at Mass.[34]

The widespread retention of the term *lector* in this context, still current in some Western churches as late as the sixth century, as at Braga, suggests that the duty of reading was historically primary, and that a charge of singing was extended to lectors who had the necessary talents. There is no telling how early the duties of singing were conferred upon those readers able to perform them. To judge by the dossier of material in *The Apostolic Tradition*, with its hymnody of children so redolent of processions in the Roman cults, it could have been as early as the third century, in which case the youthful lector-singer may also have roots in the family structures of the house-churches.

23 A young man with a codex, the Christians' preferred medium for their texts. From a catacomb, near the Via Latina, that came to light in 1955. The bulk of the burials appear to date from before the year 360.

5

LECTORS IN ROME AND ELSEWHERE

Roman Lectors

Christian archaeology knows of few greater events than the sighting of a previously unknown catacomb. In 1955, an important discovery was made when a sequence of painted chambers came to light near the Via Latina in Rome. Well into the catacomb there is a sequence of chambers commandeered by a single Roman family of the fourth century. Like many other catacombs, this one proved to be a gallery of ancient art within a hidden necropolis. One of the spaces is a painted hall with many human figures, including a young man (Pl. 23). Dressed in the toga of a patrician or a magistrate, he ostentatiously holds aloft an open codex, the Christians' preferred form for keeping a record of their Scriptures, directing his gaze and our own to where the artist has suggested the writing on the leaves. This elegant and literate young man, certainly of good family, wears no distinctive vestment to suggest that he is a presbyter or a deacon. Like some other figures with books or scrolls in this gallery of the catacomb, both young and old, he may have been a reader or lector in the Roman church, occupying a minor order in the *cursus* of clerical promotion that would perhaps have carried him much higher, had he not died young.[1]

This can be only guesswork, yet even if the guess is incorrect this image without a name nonetheless provides a valuable complement to the abundant records of Roman lectors, mostly in the form of inscribed epitaphs, which give a name and a title. The dust of the catacomb or cemetery lies very heavily on most of them. Yet these inscriptions are nonetheless impressive, for no other city in Christendom can offer such an extensive record of the lectors in its churches. No trace has ever been found of anyone called *cantor* as a title of office in a Roman source prior to the seventh century; if the singers of the many different Roman churches between 400 and 600 are to be found anywhere – and given the amount of material that survives they must surely be *somewhere* – then many of them are presumably to be sought among the lectors, salaried members of the Roman clergy since at least the mid-third century when Pope Cornelius included fifty-two exorcists, readers and doorkeepers among those 'whom the grace and bounty of the Lord feeds', according to Eusebius (*EH*, vi. 43. 11).

The materials for the Roman lectorate open in the mid-third century with that report of Pope Cornelius, in Greek, about the readers receiving some form of stipend or caritative dole in Rome. They begin to become plentiful from approximately 318–38 with the inscribed epitaph of Claudius Atticianus. This is so early that it is far from clear what any singers among these *lectores* were actually required to do. Indeed, the register of papal biographies, the *Liber pontificalis*, appears to claim that the Fore-Mass psalm was not introduced into the Roman service until the time of Pope Celestine I (422–32).[2]

Roman Psalmody and Celestine I

After the doctrine of a Christ, both human and divine, who suffered in the body, consubstantial and coeternal with the Father, no belief has been dearer to the Church of Rome throughout its long history than faith in the continuity and stability of its own institutions under the guidance of the Holy Spirit. Yet the clergy of late antique Rome also possessed a deep sense of their Church's painful progress towards freedom from persecution and the material opulence that expressed its dignity and exalted purpose. That sense of a long history in the world, inspired by the memory of Roman martyrs in the past and by the constant accumulation of precious goods and lands in the present through benefactions and alms, was too acute for the clergy to suppose that their liturgy had remained untouched since the apostles, for that would mean it had remained without enrichment. Even as the urban fabric of Rome declined in the fourth and fifth centuries, and even as the scale of new ecclesiastical buildings shrank to a size that may surprise the modern visitor to Italian cities like Ravenna with a rich late antique heritage, the Roman clergy belonged to an increasingly wealthy corporation that constantly received lands and lavish gifts from Christians encouraged to believed that the clergy were paupers in juridical terms, possessing nothing of their own. It was the Church, a great common enterprise in the cause of salvation, that was wealthy, and which possessed in the great basilicas of Constantine, for example, some of the most impressive public buildings created anywhere in the Western Empire of the fourth century. In respect of this wealth and embellishment, a liturgy was not so very different from the stock of chandeliers that gave light in the churches, or from the array of cloths and hangings that might adorn the altars; all belonged to the same patrimony that was continuously being enhanced with piety and prudence.

A prime source for many aspects of the church in Rome between 300 and 500 is the compilation of papal biographies, from Saint Peter onwards, now known as the *Liber pontificalis*. According to the reconstruction of its history commonly accepted as authoritative, the *Liber pontificalis* survives in a second edition begun under Pope Vigilius (537–55), the first edition being not much older. Read in some quantity, the biographies in the book reveal a general uniformity of tone and approach that suggests (as it was surely intended to) the work of dutiful annalists keeping an accurate and sober record from one pontificate to the next; yet in many places the book is a hazardous source for the development of Roman liturgy and worship between the first century and the middle of the sixth. Liturgical innovations required no written instrument that could be deposited in an archive. The compilers of the *Liber pontificalis* make a brave attempt to show how the Roman liturgy developed from the first century onwards as successive popes made felicitous additions to the rite they had inherited, but the biographies had to be drafted (or for much of the pre-fifth century period, invented) with almost no support from the kinds of material on stone, papyrus or parchment that the compilers used to chronicle such matters as papal struggles with heresy, gifts of plate and other valuables, or dealings with the emperors in Constantinople.[3]

In a somewhat ad hoc manner, the biographies make of each early pontificate what they can, variously listing each pope's contributions to the Roman Church, his writings if there were any, his decrees, the great synods he convened or attended, his combats against heresy, his benefactions and building works (including the restoration of existing fabric), the ordinations he performed, the place of his burial, and any other matters that the compilers could draw from such written sources as they could find, from oral tradition or from their own pious reconstructions. The development of the Roman liturgy naturally holds an important place in these entries. Always a story of bounty rather than of economy, the history of papal ritual that unfolds in the *Liber pontificalis* shows individual popes taking wise steps so that the liturgy accumulates through the centuries like a network of estates or a collection of church plate: part of the common endowment entrusted to the care of the bishop and his clergy on the understanding that they will watch over it and accumulate more when it is judicious to do so. These references to liturgy form a thin but important stream, beginning so early that the narrative of liturgical enhancement opens at a date when the Roman Church probably had no monarchical bishop at all and looked to a college of presbyters for governance. Thus Alexander (*c*.110) is said to have 'inserted the Lord's passion into what *sacerdotes* recite when Mass is celebrated', while in some sources of the *Liber pontificalis* Xystus (*c*.120) is said to have decreed that the people should sing 'Holy, Holy, Holy' at Mass. Telesphorus (*c*.130) ruled that 'Glory be to God on High' should be sung before the Eucharist. One would need considerable confidence in oral tradition to accept these entries as more than pious inventions, for even Alexander and Xystus themselves are probably fabrications; only Telesphorus figures in a recent prosopography of Roman Christians prior to 200, where he is firmly called an elder (that is to say a presbyter) rather than a pope or a bishop.[4]

For the duties performed by the singers of Rome, the most important of the early entries in the *Liber pontificalis* concerns a reform attributed to Pope Celestine (422–32). Arranged according to the prevailing testimony of the three principal classes of manuscripts, it runs:

> (*I, II and III*) Hic multa constituta fecit et constituit ut psalmi David CL ante sacrificium psalli antephanatim ex omnibus, quod ante non fiebat, nisi tantum epistula

I–II	*III*
beati	–
Pauli	Pauli
–	apostoli
recitabatur et sanctum evangelium	–
–	et sic missas fiebant.

> He issued many constitutions and ruled that the 150 psalms of David be sung before the Eucharist antiphon-wise by all, which was not done before, but only the Epistle of *blessed* Paul *the apostle* was read and the holy gospel *and thus they celebrated Masses.*[5]

The reference to the Epistle and Gospel establish that the subject of this passage is the Liturgy of the Word 'before the sacrifice' (meaning the Eucharist proper rather than the complete service of Mass). Mindful of the difficulties that attend any attempt to draw such material from the *Liber pontificalis* into a historical argument, Joseph Jungmann long ago dealt briskly with this entry in his classic study of the Roman Mass ('unfortunately the account cannot be relied upon as an historical report'), and there are indeed grounds for treating it with caution. In its present form, the biography of Celestine was probably composed approximately a century after the death of its subject and was subsequently enlarged several times to include, among other layers, the curiously unnecessary assurance in one branch of the tradition that Celestine's reform concerned the liturgy of the Mass ('and thus they celebrated Masses'). There are also some curious gaps. The entry makes no reference to Celestine's part in the Christological controversy between Nestorius and Cyril of Alexandria, which means that the compiler deliberately or inadvertently overlooked the Roman synod that Celestine convened in 430 together with certain letters and documents from Cyril, among others, that were presumably still kept in the Roman archives to which the compiler alludes elsewhere in this very entry, and with the implied assurance that he knows what is in them. A few pages further on, indeed, the compiler claims that it was Leo I (440–61) and not Celestine who discovered the heresy of Nestorianism, probably because nobody in the compiler's orbit could be ignorant of the Ecumenical Synod of Chalcedon in 451 which produced a settlement, or of Pope Leo's *Tome* that was of such importance in the work of finding a resolution. In all this, Celestine has been forgotten. The compiler may have known relatively little about his pontificate beyond what he learned from the auditors' records of the Julian basilica, listing the pope's gifts to that Church after the destruction caused by Alaric's sack of Rome.[6]

Yet if the passage is to be approached, however tentatively, as a witness to a liturgical change in early fifth-century Rome, then the most persuasive interpretation may be a version of one pondered but not finally endorsed by Peter Jeffery, namely that Celestine began (and perhaps completed) the work of assigning proper psalms (not psalms *per se*) to the feasts of the year:

> The statement [in the *Liber pontificalis* that Celestine introduced psalms] 'which had not been done before – only the Epistle and Gospel were read', carries an implication that the psalms were viewed in much the same way as the scriptural lections, *as if Celestine added liturgical pericopes from the psalms alongside those already in use of the Epistles and Gospels'* (emphasis mine).[7]

This does not have to mean that Celestine created a *book* (a meaning Jeffery certainly does not intend), least of all a proto-missal with the choice of psalms added to the readings; yet if Celestine did fix the choice of psalm for the major feasts of the year then he was doing the work at a time when it was also being accomplished elsewhere. In Jerusalem, a complete cycle of readings, *prokeimena* (corresponding to the Western graduals in function, if not exactly in position), and Alleluias were written into a lectionary between 417 and 439, preserved in an Armenian translation. In Gaul, Bishop Venerius of Marseille (428–52) commissioned one of his clergy, Musaeus, to produce a book with 'responses apt to the liturgical season and the readings' according to the testimony of Gennadius, a later bishop of Marseille in the fifth century who may well have used the book in question. So the datelines for the work of fixing at least the texts of responsorial psalms run like this, and are very close:[8]

Pontificate of Celestine I	422–32
Jerusalem lectionary	417–39
Lectionary of Venerius	428–52

Perhaps Celestine, or some other pope not too long before or after him, began the work of choosing responsorial psalms for the feasts of the liturgical year, replacing an older practice, of unknown antiquity, whereby lectors sang what was chosen for them on an ad hoc basis.

The reason for these initiatives can perhaps be found in the Church's continuing creation of its own festive calendar, notably in the feasts of the martyrs. The annual cycle of celebrations was not only a means for the Church to create its own sacred round of time as distinct from the festivals of the polytheists so deeply dyed into the fabric of society; it was also a way for the legalized Church, at peace with the imperial government, to assert its continuity with the heroic age of persecution. The sermons of Pope Leo the Great (440–61) show how much value the Roman Church of the fifth century placed upon the cycle of feasts, the 'return of duly appointed time' or *legitimi temporis recursus*. Leo constantly emphasizes the meaning and significance of the feast of the day: the *solemnitas* or *festivitas hodierna*. By constantly calling the congregation to recognize where they are in the annual cycle, he attempts to build a rampart of piety and orthodoxy around a lay congregation that is still vulnerable to the seductions of heretical Christologies presented as philosophical schools, is still at risk from strange doctrines brought by Egyptian merchants, and is still eager to reverence the sun from the top of the staircase leading to Saint Peter's basilica. It would not be surprising, in a context such as this, if the Roman church had joined others in creating a determinate assignment of psalms for the cycle of Eucharistic services, specially chosen to bring out the meaning of each festivity in the best possible way and to fix that choice so that it did not have to be made again, perhaps with less felicitous results.

The Roman Lectors

Table 5.1 shows the recorded Roman lectorate to approximately 400, almost exclusively based upon published epitaphs. In accord with the important theme of the lectors' youthfulness, Table 5.2 shows lectors in Rome and elsewhere who died under the age of 25. It was not rare for individuals in the late Roman world to prepare the texts of their own commemorations, and those who had known the deceased customarily oversaw the work when someone else drafted the inscription. This is therefore tolerably dependable evidence for the names of the lectors, their title of office and ancillary details, here and there, concerning the churches they served. Some of the information is remarkably ancient considered in relation to other materials of fourth-century Christianity in Rome. The memorial to Cinnamius Opas (Pl. 24) was found in the great church of S. Paolo fuori le mura, which may be its original site, but since he was buried on 20

24   The epitaph of the lector Cinnamius Opas, *lector tituli Fasciole*, who was buried on 20 February 377. *ILCV* 1269. *Prosopographie* (Italy) 1554.

February 377, it must have been set up in the *predecessor* of the famous late antique basilica that was begun under Theodosius after 384, and which still stands, albeit much restored after the nineteenth-century fire. The inscription that commemorates Leopardus, dated between 360 and 384, provides the earliest evidence for the existence of the church in which he served, the *titulus* of Pudentiana, supposedly built on the site of the house of Pudens, the host of Saint Peter, and his daughters Pudentiana and Praxedes. A bath was eventually built over the site and its large hall at least minimally adapted to serve as a church by the time of Leopardus; he gave his readings in this modified bathhouse before the major work of conversion during the late fourth century that transformed the building into something more obviously shaped for worship.[9]

Some of these lectors are associated with a *titulus*, meaning a church within the urban district as opposed to the suburban district with *parochiae* and *coemeteria*. Two of the lectors served the *titulus Fasciolae*, which stood near (but not on) the site of a church near the baths of Caracalla, later dedicated to SS. Nereo ed Achilleo. The style *de Pallacine* in the fragmentary inscription for the reader named '[ ]antius' commemorates the ancient *vicus Pallacinae* joining the northern end of the Circus Flaminius with the beginning of the Via Lata. This leaves the mysterious *de Fullonices*, where a lector named Alexius served at some time in the fourth century. This probably has some connection with the trade of the Roman fullers, *fullonica*, suggesting a site for this long-vanished church somewhere in the district of Trastevere, where many tanners worked close to the river. Fullers and tanners sometimes used the same noxious materials, accounting for the infamy of both trades in Roman antiquity, and both needed ready access to water. The lingering presence of pools and ponds used by the fullers, some of them eventually built into baptisteries, may explain some of the much later church dedications in Trastevere such as S. Andreae, S. Benedicti and S. Laurentii, all 'in Piscinula', where the sense of *piscinula* is presumably 'pond' or 'cistern'. The origin and nature of the titular churches remains a matter of some dispute, with implications for the status of those who served them. Some were probably founded by lay members of the senatorial aristocracy who made sure to ring-fence their church's endowment and keep it out of the bishop's control; foundations like these were perhaps sometimes governed by a college of presbyters in a client relationship to the lay patron. Or perhaps the term *titulus* implied 'a church that the bishop of Rome wanted to be understood, whenever it was legally questioned, as the property of the Roman Church'. Yet however one chooses to assess the balance of power and influence between the bishops and wealthy members of the laity, it seems likely that the lectors who are associated with *tituli* in their epitaphs were sometimes members of a family with a special interest in that church.[10]

There is almost no trace among the readers of a distinctively Christian nomenclature or reluctance to use pagan names. Semitic names such as JOHANNES (to give the Latin form) and other scriptural names made slow progress and the lectorate shows no trace of them. Established Roman names *de bon augure* such as VICTOR, were capable of acquiring a Christian inflection, hence also a FAVOR and a LEOPARDUS. There is also a SIMPLICIUS, well known in pagan Rome but rapidly becoming a Christian favourite for reasons that are not very difficult to

TABLE 5.1. *Roman lectors to c. 400*

Name	Catacomb	Title	Date	Source
Claudius Atticianus	Maius	lector	3rd/4th c.?	*ILCV* 1265b; *Prosopographie* (Italy) 216
Favor	S. Agnese	lector	end 3rd/beg. 4th c.	*ILCV* 1265a; *Prosopographie* (Italy) 745
Eq[uitius] Heraclius	Domitilla	lector r[egionis] sec[undae]	318–38	*ILCV* 1266; *ICUR* NS iii. 8719; *Prosopographie* (Italy) 977
Cinammius Opas	S. Paolo fuori le mura (the pre-Theodosian church)	lector tituli Fasciole	330–77	*ILCV* 1269; *Prosopographie* (Italy) 1554
Leopardus	unspecified	lector de Pudentiana	360–84	*ILCV* 1270; *Prosopographie* (Italy) 1293
Alexius	Marcus and Marcellianus	lector de Fullonices	4th c.	*Prosopographie* (Italy) 90
Megalus	unspecified	lector	4th c.	*Prosopographie* (Italy) 1479
Proficius	ad Decimum (Via Latina)	lec[tor] et exorc[ista]	4th c.	*Prosopographie* (Italy) 1850
Victor	Callixtus	lector	4th c.	*Prosopographie* (Italy) 2273
[Si]mplicius	Marcus et Marcellianus	lector	4th c.	*Prosopographie* (Italy) 2080
Rufinus	Basilica S Hermes	lector	371–402	*ILCV* 1274A; *Prosopographie* (Italy) 1925
Navigius	known from epitaph of his granddaughter	lector	4th or 5th c.	*Prosopographie* (Italy) 1532; son of Cresimus (probably bishop of Subaugusta and father of Primigenius, lector, later bishop). See next.

Table 5.1. (*Continued*)

Name	Catacomb	Title	Date	Source
Primigenius	known from epitaph of his daughter	lector? episcopus	4th or 5th c.	*Prosopographie* (Italy) 1821; son of Navigius, q.v
[ ]antius	Priscilla	lector de Pallacine	d. after 348	*Prosopographie* (Italy) 2386
[ ]theus	unspecified	lector	4th c.?	*ICUR* NS i. 284; *Prosopographie* (Italy) 2397
Iul[ ] [ ]tius	Domitilla	lec[tor] ecles[ie c] atolice	289–362	*ILCV* 1268; *ICUR* NS iii. 8143; *Prosopographie* (Italy) 2398
Pascentius	Domitilla	lector de Fasc[iola]	386–422	*ICUR* NS 3 8165; *Prosopographie* (Italy) 1609
Eusebius		Lector urbis romanae, 'natione Sardus'	d. 370	Jerome, *De Viribus illustribus* (PL 23: 697); later bishop of Vercelli (from *c.*340)

discern. None of the Roman lectors bears names designed to set them apart as Christians, or as worshippers with some historic affiliation to Judaism, from their fellow Romans practising other religions. They are the sons of Roman families amidst many tens of thousands of others of comparable and no doubt very varied social standing.[11]

The Lectors and the Language of Roman Psalmody

The Roman lectors give every sign of being native speakers of Latin who read and sang in that tongue, the public and official language of the Roman State. In the time of Hermas, author of *The Shepherd* and usually placed in Rome around 100, the principal language of Christians in Rome was Greek, and so it long remained. Yet with the beginnings of the Peace of the Church under Constantine, when Christian epitaphs of many kinds begin to appear in appreciable quantities, including those of the lectors, it becomes possible to re-examine the equilibrium

TABLE 5.2. *Lectors below 25 years of age named in Latin funerary inscriptions from Rome, with other Western examples extending the date-range to the sixth century*

Cities and towns listed according to the Diocletianic dioceses				
Name	Title and place	Date	Age	Source
1 Rome				
EQ[UITIUS] HERACLIUS	lector r[egionis] sec[undae]	318–38	19	*ILCV* 1266; *ICUR* NS iii. 8719; *Prosopographie* (Italy) 977
LEOPARDUS	Lector de Pudentiana	360–84	24	*ILCV*, 1270; *ICUR* NS i. 3200; *Prosopographie* (Italy) 1293; 'mirae innocentiae'
VICTOR	lector	4th c.	24	*Prosopographie* (Italy) 2273
GEMMULUS	lictor t[i]t[uli] s[an]c[t]ae marturis Caecil[i]ae	6th or 7th c.	16	*ILCV* 1273; *Prosopographie* (Italy) 909
PASCENTIUS	lector de Fasc[iola]	386–422	21	*ICUR* NS 3 8165; *Prosopographie* (Italy) 1609
[ ]NIO	lector de Saui[?ne]	unknown	16–19	*ILCV* 1274; *ICUR* NS iv. 11746; *Prosopographie* (Italy) 2393
[ ]US	lec[tor]	4th or 5th c.	20	*ICUR* NS ii. 6098; *Prosopographie* (Italy) 2399
2 Italia (other than Rome)				
POMPEIUS LUPICINUS	lector, Florence	5th or 6th c.	5	*ILCV* 1277A; *CIL* XI 1709; *Prosopographie* (Italy) 1340
FUNDANIU[s] [I]OVIANUS	lec[to]r, Florence	unknown	17	*ILCV* 1277; *CIL* XI 1704; *Prosopographie* (Italy) 1148
ATTIUS PROCULUS	lector, Brescia	4th c.	18	*ILCV* 1279; *CIL* V 4847; *Prosopographie* (Italy) 1848

TABLE 5.2. (*Continued*)

Cities and towns listed according to the Diocletianic dioceses				
Name	Title and place	Date	Age	Source
[. . .]NUS LECTOR	lictor, Avellino (found in the monastery of S. Pietro)	d. 558	13	*ILCV* 3869; *CIL* X 1193; *Prosopographie* (Italy) 2394
Name destroyed	[le]cto[r] huius ecc[lesiae] Marsala (found in the nunnery of S. Pietro)	unknown	20	*CIL* X 7252
3 Viennensis				
TIGRIDIUS	[l]ector, Autun		*castus puer*	*ILCV* 1281; *CIL* XIII 2799
SEVERUS	lectur ennocens	unknown	13	*ILCV* 1280; *CIL* XII 2701
4 Hispaniae				
TYBERIUS	[l]ictor, Mértola	d. 566	14	*ILCV* 1283; Hübner, *Inscriptiones, Supplementum,* 314
5 Africa proconsularis				
VITALIS	LECTOR, Haidra	probably of Byzantine date	5	*ILCV* 1285; *CIL* VIII 453; *Recherches,* ed. Duval, 404
CRESCONIUS	lector regionis primae, Carthage	Byzantine period	11	*Inscriptions latines de Tunisie,* ed. Merlin, 1122
QUINTUS	lector, Uppenna (Henchir Chigarnia, Tunisia)	6th c.	22	*ILCV* 1286A; *CIL* VIII 23045; *Prosopographie* (Africa) 944
PASSIBUS	lector, Cape Bon (Tunisia)	4th/5th c.	14	*Prosopographie* (Africa) 830
IOHANNES	lector, Haidra	Byzantine period	6	*Recherches,* ed. Duval, 63
CASTALINUS	lector, Haidra	Byzantine period	6	*Recherches,* ed. Duval 108

between Christian Greek and Latin in Rome. Taking the Roman-Christian epitaphs as a whole, a corpus comprising many thousands of items, a significant number record the names of parents in Greek script and in their Greek form, while the names of their children appear in Latin script and in a Latin form. These inscriptions suggest a first generation of immigrants that sought to be remembered as native speakers of Greek, followed by a second generation that wished to be identified with Latin and had probably acquired a good deal more of that language than their parents. The epitaphs reveal other ways in which an inscription could mix the Greek language, the Greek script, the Latin language and the Latin script to establish various markers of identity. A Latin inscription might be written in Greek letters but in the Latin language. Hence the epitaph Ἀρτουριαε ιν πακε idus Iunias' gives the name of the deceased in Greek script, followed by the Latin words *in pace* transliterated into Greek letters, and then the date of the subject's death in Latin, using the Roman alphabet. This epitaph was perhaps designed to mark the deceased as a first-generation immigrant from a region where Greek was the first language – presumably a matter of some pride – but who nonetheless wished to be commemorated in the language of official-dom and public record. Epitaphs of that kind unmistakably register a sense of Greek (or at least of Greek-speaking) identity.[12]

The question of 'the language of the liturgy in fourth-century Rome' therefore raises socio-linguistic questions that will admit no single answer or confident reconstruction. There were simply too many different levels of identification with the Greek on one hand and with the public language of Rome on the other, both at the level of the individual congregations and at the more exalted level of the bishops, where a centralized policy was easier to devise than to impose. During the third century, the fortunes of Latin as the language chosen for some parts of the liturgy probably varied from one regional church to another depending upon patterns of settlement by Greek-speaking immigrants in the relevant quarter and the nature of the ritual texts at issue. The epitaphs of the Roman lectors, however, almost universally suggest a strong identification with Latin. There are no epitaphs of Roman lectors couched in the Latin language but using Greek script, whether it be for an entire epitaph, for a key phrase or even for a single word such as a personal name. The lector inscriptions are written throughout in Latin and its alphabet. If it is correct to interpret the use of Greek letters in a Latin-language epitaph as the sign of a first-language speaker of Greek, then there are no such tokens in the lector epitaphs. There is also nothing to indicate that the Roman readers held an office that was especially associated with the Greek language or with Greek terminology; the official title of each reader is always given in its Roman form as *lector*. Finally, no name of Greek etymology is given in the appropriate script or spelled in its Greek form (*Megalus*, for example, is not written *Megalos*). This is not to say that these lectors were all native-born Romans, or that they were first-language speakers of Latin. It is conceivable that some of these individuals were bilingual in Latin and Greek to some extent, but that need not cloud the issue. All of the lector inscriptions from Rome associate the lectors' office with the public language of the Empire. They suggest that these lectors read their lessons and sang their responses in Latin, save on exceptional occasions, or when performing certain ritual items, and that they did so from the time of the earliest inscriptions, reaching back to the end of third century.[13]

In broad terms, the Peace of the Church in the fourth century can be said to open the history of the institutional and public *ecclesia* in fourth-century Rome, just as it marks the decline of the old house-churches. But the tensions between the bishops of Rome and the lay patrons of churches, including some of the parish churches or *tituli*, were not quickly resolved. Until the time of the Gothic Wars of 535–54, aristocratic Christian donors often founded private churches on their rural estates, and may have done the same in the city or the suburbs; in Rome, this was the kind of work that a rich man or woman with many slaves or clients was expected to perform, reconciling any ascetic inclinations they felt with the domestic and caritative responsibilities of wealth they were not encouraged to relinquish. As late as the pontificate of Gelasius I (492–6), or even of Pelagius I (556–61), such lay patrons could expect to appoint the clerical staff for their foundations, often without the supervision of the bishop, and many of the clergy who served these churches, including the lectors, were probably drawn from the founders' own kindred. Careful sifting of Roman epigraphy has already begun to reveal a 'fluid model of social and political organization in which clergy, laypeople and monks were often members of the same households, interconnected through ties of blood and/or bonds of friendship'. The paterfamilias, in other words, was still a key figure in late antique Rome, and so was the materfamilias, as the so-called 'papal legends' written between the fourth century and the seventh continually emphasize by showing wealthy Roman householders being converted and baptized, often with vast numbers of slaves and clients, in a milieu that looks very much like the world of the second-century *Acts of Peter*, a text not forgotten in Rome (see above, pp. 101–2). The *Passio SS. Alexandri, Eventii et Theodoli martyrum*, for example, adorns an account of 'Pope' Alexander (*c*.110) with the conversion and baptism of a Roman prefect together with his wife and 1,250 slaves, while the *Passio S. Marcelli* has a Roman *matrona* named Lucina asking Pope Marcellus (306–7) to consecrate a church in her house. Even as late as 500, it is far from certain that the days of the Roman house-church, or of the Christian singer's deep and ancient roots in domestic liturgy, were as yet entirely over.[14]

The necessary reminder that even the wealthiest and most hieratically organized Church of the West had not lost all contact with significantly older forms of structure and patronage provides a fitting introduction to a class of psalmist not mentioned hitherto: the urban ascetics who chose a life of enclosure in their own family homes, in parts of the *domus ecclesiae*, in purpose-built houses or even in rented rooms. This is an important constituency, and in no sense a creation of the late third century, which is so often associated with the emergence of monasticism. Instead, a long-standing tradition of urban ascetics with forms of devotion encompassing psalmody gave rise to a migration; towards 300, for reasons that are not entirely clear, many ascetics chose to live either alone in the 'desert' or in remote communities so that they could dwell (as they could not in the cities) in places where all around them had made the same choices as themselves. The roots of these urban ascetics may extend as far back as the first century, when the New Testament documents give clear signs of an ascetic wing of opinion opposed to marriage and childbearing. (Needless to say, the pagan traditions of such asceticism, as a means to show a philosophical commitment, go further back still.) In some respects, these urban solitaries may carry aspects of the house-churches into the fourth century and far beyond, including their psalmody, for there is no sudden break that turns these urban ascetics into recognizable 'monks' of a familiar and later medieval kind. There is only a seamless process of development to which the marked fluidity of the term *monachus* in pre-ninth-century Latin bears abundant witness.

6

THE PSALMODY OF URBAN
HOUSE-ASCETICS

The Fourth Century and the 'Psalmodic Movement'

Slowly at first, but with a quickening pace, a polytheist of the fourth century would have noticed some unsettling changes. Within the first two decades of the century the emperor Constantine became the devotee of an imported Oriental and Messianic religion that many still regarded as an exotic novelty. Worse still, Constantine revered a god that had never watched over the fortunes of the Roman Empire, had never served as the tutelary spirit for one of its great cities, and had never ensured (in contrast to Isis) that the sailing season would begin on time. Pagan observers who enjoyed long lives would also have witnessed the beginnings of the slow transformation that eventually saw the Roman emperors in Constantinople becoming delegates of Christ who were not entitled to wear their crowns in the churches lest they appeared to usurp his kingship. Within several generations of Constantine, the advocates of the traditional religions even lost the reassurance that their cults were the only ones with the right to be regarded as truly Roman in a profound and historical sense; towards the close of the fourth century the emperor Theodosius I (379–95) completed what Constantine had begun by making Christianity the official cult of the Empire and therefore the one in which its fortunes were invested. Polytheists with fine houses were now left with statues and mosaics of the old deities, images that often exerted a profound influence upon the nascent art of Christians (Pl. 25), but were increasingly regarded by many as the abodes of demons that might emerge from the image and (as experience showed) bite any man who wished to replace them. These malicious spirits, appearing from the stones like poisonous insects from the stump of a tree, were once the marbled gods of Rome. Apollo had begun his long descent into the monstrous Apollyon of *The Pilgrim's Progress*.

There were other developments in the fourth century that many polytheists probably regarded as beneath their notice. The first Roman epitaphs appeared referring to the bishop of the city as *papa*, or 'father' (Pl. 26, there applied to Marcellinus, 295–303); the Church found its greatest early historian, after Luke,

25 Hermes presents the infant Dionysius to a group of nymphs; all personages are named. Floor
mosaic from Paphos in Cyprus, first half of the 4th c. The scene is 'a striking pagan version of the
theme of the epiphany of a divine child which would become one of Christianity's most significant
iconographic forms' (Elsner, *Imperial Rome*, 220).

in Constantine's biographer Eusebius (d. 339), who could look westwards to bishoprics founded deep in the hinterland of the Mediterranean, as at Córdoba, or
far along the river systems of the European interior, as at Cologne. The first reliable traces of the bishops of those and many other sees appear in the late decades
of the third century and in the fourth; so do the earliest proceedings that survive
from Western synods of bishops in a reasonably complete state. (These two
developments are obviously related, because the lists of witnesses that accompany the proceedings of synods provide the names of many bishops and their sees.)
Late in the fourth century, Saint Athanasius wrote his seminal biography of Saint
Antony, casting him as a founding father of Christian monasticism, an opponent
of Arianism, but also as an illiterate Copt of the previous generation who left his
home for the Egyptian desert to live an ascetic life of prayer. Christian history
seems to have many niches where the lamps remain unlit until the 300s, when
they begin to flare.[1]

At first sight, the history of Christian worship and its music might seem to be
one of the corners most suddenly illuminated in the fourth century. After all,
that is when the initiatives of Constantine and the bishops of Rome produced
the first great basilicas of the city, the earliest public buildings of the Christian

26   The epitaph of the deacon Severus (Catacomb of Callistus), which refers to Bishop Marcellinus (295–303) as P[A]P[A] in line 2. This is the first known instance of this term being used of a bishop of Rome. It is well known that the name *papa* was commonly applied to any Western bishop (especially in inscriptions), until approximately the 6th c. *ICUR* IV, 10183.

cult to be built on such a scale. For the first time, epigraphic evidence now brings the names of Christian ministers to light in bulk and from many parts of the Western Empire, but especially from Rome, including the lectors discussed in the previous chapter. Among the clerical orders there is a growing sense of parity with the proliferating grades of the salaried and militarized bureaucracy of the imperial government, revealed to excess in the story of a profoundly incautious deacon who commissioned a purple-dyed dalmatic from a Tyrian workshop in the 340s so that he could have some enviable insignia of office (see below, pp. 164–5). What is more, a considerable amount of information concerning the musical practices of Christians now begins to appear in the voluminous writings of Western Fathers from the generations that emerged between approximately 350 and 425, including Augustine, Hilary, Jerome and Ambrose, to mention only the greatest among the Westerners. The references to singers and Christian music in the homilies, letters and commentaries of these loquacious men is of such unprecedented scope that the materials from the first three centuries appear very scattered by comparison.[2]

These Fathers variously mention the psalmody of the Mass and such cathedral Hours as they knew, but most of them are especially interested in the psalmody of the new fourth-century monks in the 'desert'. Among much else, the writings of these and other fourth-century churchmen reveal a wave of enthusiasm for reciting, intoning or chanting the psalms at various times during the course of the day and night as a spiritual exercise for ascetic Christians, or other exceptionally devout spirits, with the example of the monks in mind. The key figures in their references to this psalmody are sometimes the men and women leading lives of continence and withdrawal in the houses of cities and villages, but more often the determined ascetics who left the cities and villages of Egypt, Asia Minor, Palestine and Syria to live alone or to seek a life as part of an ascetic community. With various degrees of commitment and emphasis, most of the Fathers writing between approximately 350 and 425 hold such forms of renunciation before the eyes of their readers as a model for men and women who had not (or not yet) chosen such lives themselves but had much to gain, in the opinion of the Fathers, by imitating certain aspects of a desert experience that included psalmody at various hours of the day and, for sterner spirits, at night. For this advocacy of desert monasticism and psalmody, these Fathers have been credited with identifying a 'psalmodic movement' in the late fourth century.[3]

The term 'psalmodic' here does not necessarily imply a musical manner of performance in the sense of replacing the fluid intonation of the speaking voice with the steps of a musical scale; it may not even imply something between the two. Some solitaries, both in urban houses and in a rural or village context, may have only murmured the psalms in a low undertone, a kind of constant respiration for the spirit, low in expenditure of energy so that it could be accomplished for much of the day. This is the technique that some Latin texts indicate by the verb *meditare*, often translated 'to meditate' but conspicuously used in Psalm 1: 2, where it corresponds to a Hebrew word meaning the growling of a lion, the cooing of a dove or the rumbling of thunder rather than to singing or intoning. As Joseph Dyer has remarked, whatever psalmody meant 'to the semi-anchoritic monks of Nitria, Kellia, Scetis, or to the cenobites of the Thebaid, it never reached a musical level that attracted notice or provoked condemnation from the severe defenders of monastic discipline'. The chanting of urban ascetics, however, both in their household-monasteries and in the cathedrals to which they were admitted between clerical services, appears to have been more dependably musical, just as it was more public. Many of these urban ascetics lived a concentrated form of the household-based Christianity that is already appearing in the New Testament documents, residing in their private houses, devoting their lives to virginity (or to continence if they were married), to prayer, reading and psalmody. Other ascetics joined small communities that were still based in houses (including sometimes the bishop's house) but forming groups where the lines of

27   Oil lamp of the 1st or 2nd c. AD. The lamp-lighting ceremonies at eventide amongst Christians often seem to have preceded some form of psalmody, whether as an adornment to a communal supper or, at a later date, to a formalized *lucernarium* ceremony as part of the evening office. These ceremonies concentrated an imagery of light and dark, sleep and wakefulness, prayer and vigil upon the perishable and vulnerable flame of lamps that must often have been simple, ceramic examples akin to this one in addition to more elaborate chandeliers. The lamp-lighting ceremony among Christians created a gallery of glimmering discs of terracotta showing winged victories, masks of Zeus, scenes from the *Iliad* or even the heads of satyrs. Nîmes, Musée archéologique.

family and kindred were less clearly defined. Some of these men and women offered a psalmody that the laity would come to hear, and perhaps to join, before the beginning of the working day and morning prayer on at least the greater feasts of the year and on Sundays, depending upon local custom. During the fourth century, such ascetics became ever more important in the liturgical life of their local cathedrals, singing and leading psalmody between the appointed services of the clergy as a kind of liturgical entr'acte. As the famous pilgrimage diary of Egeria reveals for Jerusalem in Holy Week at the end of the fourth century, there might be only a token clerical presence on such occasions when the doors were unlocked in the darkness and the lamps were lit (see below, and Pl. 27).[4]

    The place of these and other ascetics in a fourth-century 'psalmodic movement' raises fundamental questions about tradition versus innovation in fourth-century Christianity. With the exception of an imperial conversion, most of the fourth-century innovations evoked at the beginning of this chapter were to some extent more apparent than real. The development of monasticism provides a pertinent example. Athanasius famously reports that Saint Antony left Alexandria about 285 to live in desert solitude, and that he formed a loosely knit community some twenty years later. 'At that moment', a modern historian of liturgy declares, 'the institution of Christian monasticism was born.' Yet Antony lived as an urban house-ascetic before he migrated to the desert, and the earliest known document referring to a *monachos* by that name identifies an individual who lived in the Egyptian village of Karanis; he was well known in his community and held the title of *monachos* in something like the way that the person named with him on the papyrus bore the title of *diakonos*. This was in the year 324. Stable ascetics, as opposed to evangelising wanderers had long been urban creatures, in other words, and were long to remain so. As late as 526 it was possible for a member of the senatorial aristocracy in Rome to have a reputation for asceticism while holding high public office as *comes rerum privatarum*. Rome was no doubt a special case, but the principle remains that an inclination to prayer, fasting, psalmody and sexual continence did not necessarily require an individual to forsake the company of those who had made less stringent choices for the course of their own Christian lives. For some it did, and the rise of a desert monasticism towards 300 was in some measure a migration of the old house-asceticism into the countryside, where lives of withdrawal were no longer inserted into an existing and potentially indifferent milieu but became the centre of settlement, drawing in whatever subsidiary resources were necessary for survival. If this is an accurate picture of at least some communities, then only a disproportionate (but characteristically patristic) emphasis upon the desert monks would lead one to suppose that the institution of Christian monasticism was born when Antony formed his community.[5]

This suggests that the psalmodic movement was not necessarily a new wave of enthusiasm for psalmody, but rather a movement that took ascetics long accustomed to make psalmody part of their domestic round into a new and predominantly rural environment. Once there, their lives attracted an unprecedented amount of comment from two generations of writers including Athanasius (d. 373), Basil (d. 379), Gregory of Nyssa (d. 395), Ambrose (d. 397), John Chrysostom (d. 407), Jerome (d. 420) and Augustine (d. 430). All were writing within a period of some seventy-five years, perhaps a century at the outside, and some were bound by ties of blood, correspondence or personal acquaintance. Augustine wrote letters of the most civilized acrimony to Jerome and knew Ambrose at Milan; Gregory of Nyssa was the brother of Basil. The enthusiasm of this group for psalmody reveals the desire to extol the ascetic life of desert monks, which developed among a remarkable group of intellectuals who were mostly so inspired by the monastic life of the desert that they chose to experience it for a time themselves and regarded it as an ideal which all Christians could use to measure their weaknesses and sharpen their aspirations. Placed in this context, the psalmodic movement is apt to appear as an abnormally well-documented phase in a long and perhaps continuous history of psalmody among those considerably more dedicated to the disciplines of fasting, prayer and continence than the majority of their co-religionists. It is a history that may reach back beyond the rise of desert monasticism to older traditions of psalmody among urban house-ascetics in the 200s and perhaps earlier still.

Psalmody 'in House'

At the end of 4 Maccabees, perhaps composed between AD 20 and 54, the mother of the martyrs remembers her contented family where the father taught his sons the Law and the Scriptures. He also 'sang (*emelōdei*) the psalms of the psalmist David where it says *Many are the troubles of a just man* (Psalm 33: 20)'. The use of the Greek verb *melōdeō* here leaves little doubt that singing is meant, while the citation of a psalm verse in a sharply personal context reaches deep into the long history of the Psalter in its canonical form, probably assembled from various earlier configurations to make a book with at least some of its materials intended for private devotion (see above, p. 73).

Deeply graven into the common experience of the Israelites, and rich in materials for the rites of the Jewish home and for private prayer, the Psalter could not fail to become a major text for Christians. The New Testament reveals that Jesus-believing Jews and Gentiles looked to it for prophecies of the life and sufferings of Christ, thus ensuring that the Psalms were among the principal texts at issue between Jews, Jewish-Christians and converted Gentiles. Paul assumes that members of the Christian community at Corinth will contribute a 'psalm', among other things, to the community's worship and so does the compiler of the apocryphal *Acts of Paul* (see above, pp. 77–8). Paul may imply in his letter to Corinth that psalms and other holy texts of the synagogue were accompanied by an 'interpretation' (*hermēneia*), perhaps identifying the process of intense discussion that must have taken place in many assemblies of the first century and beyond. The nature of these interpretations may be revealed here and there in passages of the canonical gospels that embody the results, notably the climax of the passion narratives presented as a cento of lines from Psalm 22 with the casting of lots for clothes, the piercing of hands and feet and Christ's anguished quotation of the first verse. One of the earliest Christian commentaries upon a psalm in existence, written in the middle decade of the second century by Justin Martyr, is devoted to precisely this psalm and is addressed to a Jewish-Christian interlocutor.[6]

There seems no obvious reason why the domestic psalmody of Jewish households should have been rapidly abandoned in the first and second centuries by Jesus-believing Jews or the Gentiles, and the latter may have added or substituted other musical idioms or procedures of Gentile origin. Soon after AD 200, Tertullian provides a glimpse of such Christian household psalmody in his *De Exhortatione Castitatis* ('An Exhortation to Chastity'), addressed to a widower and probably composed after 207. A product of Tertullian's later years, when the tone of his writing became more narrowly ascetic, this book is sharply critical of marriage, especially second marriage, which he regards as a form of lewdness or *stuprum*. He warns Christians against childrearing, which subjects them to the distraction of children's demands and weakens any singleness of heart they might hope to sustain. Pursuing this theme, he celebrates various kinds of sexual abstinence among virginal children, married couples who make a pact to abstain from sexual relations, widows, widowers and divorcees who renounce sexual activity henceforth and refuse to make a second marriage. Tertullian is seeking to defend a kind of house-based (but not a house-confined) asceticism, broadly understood, that a man or woman may begin to practise at any time of life, once they have made the decision to do so, and which is here commended to householders with slaves. He has a firm idea of the devotions that such domestic celibates will have time to pursue once they are liberated from the ties of marriage and the distractions of desire. A man can engage in prayer any moment of the day and study the Scriptures; he will also have freedom for psalmody 'if he is singing a psalm'.[7]

In the early 200s, therefore, Tertullian can already urge an horarium of prayer upon his readers, most intense at morning and night but also including the third, sixth and ninth hours. He takes pains to defend the apostolic status of these hours, citing Acts of the Apostles 2: 15 (the miracle of Pentecost at the third hour of the day), 10: 9 (Peter praying at the sixth hour in Joppa) and 3: 1 (Peter and John go up the Temple to pray at the ninth hour) to justify his position. In an especially revealing passage of another treatise, *De Oratione*, Tertullian contemplates a responsorial element in such psalmody (no. 14). He mentions prayer before meals and before going to the bath, then proceeds to explain a practice of the more conscientious Christians, presumably encompassing the sexually continent householders for whom he has such praise, but not confined to them. They append *Alleluia* to their prayers 'and such manner of psalms, so that those who are present may respond with the versicles'. No doubt there is a figurative element to this description of Christian householders who are both literally and metaphorically in harmony, but that does not necessarily limit the importance of the passage. It seems that shortly after AD 200 it is possible to isolate, at least in the Christian communities of Carthage, a prosperous kind of ascetic householder, still regulating the affairs of the *domus* with its slaves and menial tasks to be supervised, but now living a life of sexual continence, seeking a singleness of purpose without distractions, and following an horarium of prayer, scriptural study and psalmody, quite possibly sung, that was sometimes responsorial (Pl. 28). There was an horarium of domestic psalmody amongst house-ascetics a hundred years or more before anyone thought of going into the desert as a monk.[8]

This domestic psalmody should be seen against the background of Jewish and Christian customs of education, revealed with especial vividness by Egyptian papyri that provide a vivid and sometimes an affecting glimpse of masters and pupils at work. Among the papyri interpreted as fragments of books once used by teachers and students, the Psalter is better represented than any other volume of Jewish or Christian canonical Scripture, strongly suggesting that the Davidic

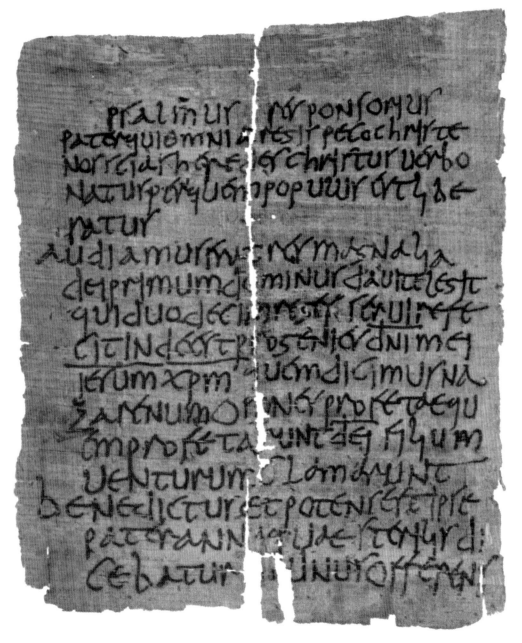

28 A *psalmus responsorius*. This Latin and Christian poem, non-biblical and of unknown date but surviving in a 4th-c. copy, appears to be the earliest text of Western Christianity explicitly labelled a 'responsorial psalm'. The opening four lines, set off from the rest (*Pater qui omnia Regis / Peto Christi nos scias heredes / Christus, verbo natus / Per quem populus est liberatus*) are metrically distinct from the remainder of the verses and form a refrain that is presumably to be recited or sung between each stanza. The poem is an abecedarius, each stanza (not including the refrain) beginning with a separate letter. Twelve more or less complete stanzas remain, giving the verses for A–M and fragments of N and O. Pap. Barc. Inv. 149b–153. Van Haelst, *Catalogue*, 121. 4th c. Provenance unknown.

Psalter was more used and read 'than any book of the Old Testament, perhaps more than any book of the Bible, throughout the Christian centuries in Egypt'. A recent inventory of papyrus notebooks lists eleven items for the period between the third century and the seventh inclusive, of which eight give primarily or exclusively the texts of psalms. Narrowing the period from the third century to the fifth gives seven papyrus items of which five contain copies of psalms. These notebooks are the best guide to what the literate slaves of larger households, grammar masters and attentive parents were teaching their infants in Egypt, both Jewish and Christian, and they suggest that the psalms were a fundamental teaching text in the social circles where men and women used writing, or aspired to it for their children. That is hardly surprising, since the psalms were ideal for teaching the young in households wealthy enough to afford the luxury of an education for an offspring. An almanac of prayer and counsel for times of good and adverse fortune, the poems of the Psalter are arranged in sense-units of moderate length by virtue of the poetic form. This makes them amenable to study, including the slow process of acquiring the skills of penmanship (Pl. 29).[9]

Where papyrus documents have not survived, one must seek out other traces of the Psalter as a teaching text. In the year 304, during the Great Persecution, a certain Babylas was executed in the city of Nicomedia, now Izmit in northern Turkey, where he was a schoolmaster with ninety-two pupils in his charge. The great majority of his pupils shared both their master's Christianity and his fate, for Babylas was charged with teaching them 'sacred hymns and psalms' in place of the traditional Greek syllabus. When Babylas was denounced he was already an old man, so his classes presumably reached back into the late decades of the third century and perhaps to the 250s; some of his pupils, however, were of such tender years that they could not be brought before the Roman authorities in Bithynia to be questioned. As it stands, this story is probably a fabrication, for the large number of pupils who died with Babylas seems suspiciously high and a modern catalogue of late antique grammarians duly places him among the doubtful cases; yet the same catalogue reveals that the story of his death is not entirely without foundation. Priscillianus, the *praeses Bithyniae* who presides over the executions in the narrative account, was a historical figure involved in the persecution of Christians at Nicomedia in 304, and that imperial city is exactly the kind of centre that attracted grammarians to leave the provincial towns, where their careers often began, to seek pupils and a modest fortune. What is more, Nicomedia was not an inherently dangerous place to be a Christian, to judge by the existence of a church in full view of Diocletian's palace until the Great Persecution began. So while the story of Babylas may be only partly true it is more than partly true to life, at least in its depiction of a Christian grammarian using the psalms and biblical lyrics in the primary education of urban schoolchildren.[10]

In a purely domestic context – which should not be contrasted too strongly with the grammarian's school, since lessons were often given in the home – a sig-

29 Lessons in penmanship with the Psalter had their *longueurs*, to judge by the wandering attention of a schoolchild from Fayyum, probably of the 4th or perhaps of the 5th c., who drew a human
figure when practising a verse of Psalm 32. He or she was learning to form Greek letters by copying a verse, but lost interest and turned the page over (and upside down) to draw a stick figure.
From a complete notebook of four double papyrus sheets of inferior quality. Arsinoite, 4th or 5th
c. P. Rainer 4. 24 (P. Vindob. G. 29274). Van Haelst, *Catalogue*, 136. Cribiore, *Writing, Teachers and
Students*, catalogue 403.

nificant proportion of the sources relating to the use of psalms in domestic and
private devotion concern young women. An education in letters based upon the
Psalter, leading perhaps to a life of sexual renunciation and house-enclosure,
flourished especially amongst relatively well-born and leisured women in the late
Roman world. Their importance to the fourth-century overflow of asceticism
into the first desert monasteries must have been appreciable. Indeed, some of
these women were active at a sufficiently early date to be regarded as contemporaries of the first or second generation of desert monks. One of them makes a distressing appearance in an encyclical letter of Bishop Athanasius, datable to 339
and describing events in Alexandria where Athanasius's rival, the Arian bishop of
the city, had seized a number of Catholics during worship. They included an
unmarried woman who was still clutching her Psalter when the bishop's men
publicly whipped her. Athanasius describes her as 'a virgin fond of learning and
literature' or 'fond of philosophical argument'. The book that the young woman
refused to relinquish – but which was soon snatched from her hands – was perhaps her own copy of the Psalter and a portable codex of papyrus or parchment
leaves; the traces of such pocket books among Christians emerge in the third

century, well before the event described by Athanasius, when they were often the work of professional scribes, even the productions of a local book trade. This woman had presumably obtained one that she was accustomed to take to the assemblies.[11]

It was also in the 330s that a young woman was educated with the Psalter and the Proverbs of Solomon as her basic textbooks, the latter beginning some sixteen centuries of history as a schoolbook and primer of morality and wisdom for the young. This was Macrina, the sister of Basil, who is commonly regarded as the founder of desert monasticism in Asia Minor. Macrina's mother did not wish her to learn her letters with books of pagan verse or prose; according to her biographer and brother Gregory of Nyssa, writing a generation after the events he describes, Macrina studied the Psalter and 'recited each of its parts at a predetermined moment of the day'. At her meals, and her rising from bed, 'she always had psalmody'. Towards the end of the fourth century, Saint Jerome proposed an almost identical programme of reading and prayer for a young woman named Paula in Rome. 'Let her be ignorant of the songs of the world', he urged her mother in a letter; 'instead, let her tender tongue be imbued with sweet psalms'. Instead of jewels and silk, Paula was to develop a love for books, studying the Psalter before any other volume so that she could rise up during the night to recite the psalms, perhaps indeed to chant them, since Jerome hoped they would keep her mind off worldly *cantica*.[12]

Macrina's syllabus of education, reading and observance sounds very similar to the usages of desert monks. The same could be said of Jerome's requirement that Paula rise in the night to say part of her Psalter. There is certainly an attempt here to bend the devotions of two female protagonists into the shape of desert monasticism, yet this may be to put the matter back to front. The education and devotion of fourth-century solitaries, both in the cities and the desert, owed something to antecedent traditions within the Christian households of the cities and villages, as much among boys and girls in their schooling as among men and women of ascetic inclination in their maturity, first securely documented some two hundred years before Jerome by Tertullian. There is a sense in which male and female solitaries of the fourth century who went into the desert, and who have been associated by some modern historians with a psalmodic movement, 'were simply continuing to do what ordinary Christians of earlier centuries had done'.[13]

The Forgotten Monasticism

Ascetics who sought a rural abode were entering the desert in several different senses. For some, it meant crossing an ecological frontier and living in a place not yet brought under systematic human control. For others, and perhaps for the majority, it meant an emblematic migration away from a place where they were outnumbered by those with less exacting standards, where they were caught within the net of the Roman fiscal system (although their relief was only temporary) and where they were directly subject to the authority of local officials such as the *praefectus alae* or head of a military unit. Patristic writers of the fourth century often emphasize the isolation of such monks in order to stimulate the conscience of men and women who, for the most part, remained in their urban or village households or sought no more than a brief period of cohabitation with rural monks during a pilgrimage. That is one of the reasons why Saint Jerome draws a sharp distinction between the desert monks and those whom he will not even dignify with a Latin name: the *remnuoth* who had chosen to retain some close connection with the cities, towns and villages. To praise such ascetics was to set the bar much too low. Yet monks of this kind were perhaps a familiar sight in some parts of Egypt, to look no further for the moment, where slender but unmistakable evidence shows them in a more positive light than any Saint Jerome chose to shed.[14]

This is the forgotten monasticism of the fourth century, involving 'withdrawal from certain social patterns of human behaviour (family and sex) but not a physical separation from the community'. It is best understood as the organic development of a house-asceticism reaching back at least to the time of Tertullian, a monasticism practised in *urbs*, *vicus* or *castellum*, where ascetics were not necessarily detached from the social or economic concerns of their communities. As late as the end of the fourth century, these individuals were associated with no single name; *monazontes*, *parthenae*, *aputactitae*, *ascetes*, *monachos*, *anachoretes* and *remnuoth* are all found in fourth-century writings, the first three in the famous passages where the pilgrimage diary of Egeria describes the chanting of urban ascetics in late fourth-century Jerusalem. Nor, it seems, were these ascetics associated with any sharply distinguished forms of life. In its variety, their withdrawal could be considered as a profound way to live the gospel that could be an example to all, even to the clergy; it is a remarkable moment in the diary of Egeria (383–4) when the bishop in the Jerusalem liturgy completes his pre-dawn tasks and returns to his nearby residence, his obligations over, his conscience presumably clear, while the ascetics whom Egeria calls *monazontes*, *parthenae* and *aputactitae* remain in the church and continue their vigil with psalmody, in the company of the populace, until daybreak.[15]

Who were these urban ascetics and in what sense were they urban? An urban solitary was a man or woman whose place of habitation was essentially domestic, adapted to provide shelter or used as it stood. The lodging could encompass rooms rented in a house or even a lavish residence that a family might own for generations. As far as one may discern, these lodgings were rarely built for the specific purpose of sheltering ascetics, and therefore they marked no symbolic act of *displacement* to a location where new accommodation had to be built to meet the demands of a new departure in the religious life. A papyrus of 400 from Oxyrhyncus (P. Oxy. 3203), for example, reveals a ground-floor room and a basement leased to two sisters, Theodora and Tauris, described as *monachai apotak-tikai*, the latter term not rare in the papyri and used in much of the eastern Mediterranean. It may have its origin in Luke 14: 33, where Christ declares that only those who 'say goodbye' (*apotassetai*) to their possessions may then become his disciples.[16]

Secondly, urban ascetics were not necessarily sedentary but often moved in the ambience of a bishop. Their existence was bounded as much by the hierarchy and congregation of their local *ekklesia* as by the presence of other ascetics. A papyrus of 349 records a transaction between a 'deacon of the Catholic Church' and a village presbyter that was copied by an *apot[aktikos]* named Agathon. The lodging of many an ascetic around 300, both east and west, was often a chamber in the cellular complex of the *domus ecclesiae*, comprising the residential and public spaces outside the episcopal church itself. In this way, these ascetics may be said to have carried forward the early Church's conception of lay orders such as the order of widows. Such orders were designed to integrate those who held no sacred ministry, or who were ineligible for one, but who might nonetheless be notable in the community for living an exemplary form of life, in the widows' case, by refusing a second marriage. Already in 324, an Egyptian villager regarded the term *monachos* as akin to *diakonos* and therefore as the name for a defined, respected and named form of life within the local church hierarchy.[17]

There is one remarkable and generally overlooked document that may reveal traditions of psalmody amongst such urban ascetics. Two letters, originally forming a single treatise, were attributed in antiquity to Clement, the author of the non-canonical Epistle to the Corinthians known as *I Clement* and commonly located in Rome (at the site of San Clemente?) during the decades around AD 100, serving as the corresponding secretary of the church there. Both are addressed to male and female virgins. The Greek text of the letters survives only in a few fragments, embedded in a work by the seventh-century Palestinian monk Antiochus, but there are translations into the Sahidic dialect of Coptic and Syriac, the latter being the only one that is complete. This suggests a broad dissemination for the letters in Upper Egypt, Syria and Palestine, though their original home cannot be traced. Despite the confusing implications of this complex pedigree, it is certain that these letters are genuine late antique documents. Epiphanius mentions them in his *Panarion* of *c.*374–6, and Saint Jerome knew them in the early 390s as Clementine *epistolas . . . de virginitate*. These two references establish the latest possible date for the composition of the letters, which may be significantly older since they reflect a stage of evolution when exorcism was still practised by itinerant ascetics and had not yet become the preserve of bishops or presbyters, nor in any way drawn into the structures of a Church becoming increasingly institutionalized. A dating as early as *c.*200 has received influential support, but not recently.[18]

The letters are addressed to both male and female virgins who build their lives upon Christ's praise for those who become eunuchs for the kingdom of heaven, repudiating the command that married Christian householders must often have used in their own defence: 'go forth and multiply' (I, ii and iv). The compiler anticipates that these virgins will be surprisingly mobile, travelling into many different kinds of social context where they will need to guard their virginity, including places where there may be no Christians at all (II, iii, iv and v). These travels encompass both rural and urban settings, and the ascetics may have to face oppression and opprobrium when away from home (II, i). Little is said in detail about their own dwellings, although the compiler expects that some of those whom he addresses live together in houses of males or females (I, x), and they are accordingly warned against houses where men reside with the virgins 'on the pretext of piety'. The ascetics are also warned against others who visit the houses of solitaries, apparently under the guise of being ascetics themselves and read the Scriptures to their hosts, perform exorcisms for them or presume to teach, all of which emerge elsewhere in the letters as the standard responsibilities of these ascetics towards the wider Christian community (I, x). The compiler places special emphasis upon the duty to visit others, including orphans, widows, indigent families with many children and persons 'afflicted with demons' (I, xii). This last injunction plainly concerns the duty to perform exorcisms, and the ascetics are advised to prepare for this work of cleansing with fasts and vigils; they are also advised not to perform exorcisms 'with multiform words luxuriously arranged', but with simpler texts (I, xii).

There are two references to worship in the letters, one of which mentions their duty of psalmody. When the ascetics find themselves far from their dwellings at eventide they are advised to seek hospitality from fellow Christians, repaying them by participating in vigils with them, by preaching and by reading the Scriptures. After this, they receive bread and water in a common meal that may be an *agape*, a Eucharist or both (II, ii). Another reference to worship occurs in the second letter where the compiler gives advice for ascetics who must lodge overnight with non-Christians. He advises them to occupy themselves with praise but not to 'minister' where there are pagans revelling in their banquets with impure words. Furthermore

> on account of their impiety, we do not chant among the pagans, nor read the Holy Scriptures to them, so that we do not appear to resemble pipers, singers or soothsayers, like many who go to such places and do so in order that they may dunk their mouthful of bread for themselves, and for a small portion of wine go and sing the Lord's song in a strange land of the pagans, and do what is forbidden.

The key word in the Syriac text, translated here as 'we . . . chant', is undoubtedly a musical term. It appears in the third line of Fig. 3 as the fourth word from the right, *mᶜzamrīnan*, a participial form with plural ending (*īn*) and a first person suffix *-an*. The result is a virtual present tense 'we [do not] *zmr*'. This root appears throughout much of the Islamic world and Asia, developed into various names for musical instruments, including the double-reed pipe or *zummara* of North Africa (recalling the compiler's statement that the ascetics whom he addresses should not sing at pagan gatherings lest they resemble pipers). The compiler of this letter leaves no doubt that some of these Christian ascetics, albeit the irresponsible ones, did sing the hymns of their religion at pagan gatherings where there was feasting and music, presumably implying that all responsible ascetics capable of doing so would think it appropriate to chant among their coreligionists. On this count he makes a repeated and emphatic appeal: 'Do not do so, brothers; we beseech you, brothers, let these things not be done among you, but disown those who thus wish to conduct themselves in this filthy and abject manner. These things must not be done, brothers. We beseech you . . .'.

The identity of these ascetics, both male and female, is difficult to determine. They are by no means confined to their places of residence, for they frequently seek lodgings with other Christians and may sometimes venture where there are no Christians at all. Since they include men and women, they cannot be all be itinerant presbyters or teachers. Their ministrations to their coreligionists, and the scope of the authority those ministrations imply, are quite extensive; they encompass chanting, preaching, declamation of the Scriptures, joining evening vigils with the hosts who lodge them on their travels and the performance of exorcisms. Wherever they go, these ascetics seem to be recognized by their co-religionists as men and women leading a superior but quite familiar form of Christian life, founded upon virginity and spiritual chrisms such as the gift of healing.

The letters of pseudo-Clement appear to carry us far eastwards, but that may be an illusion created by a necessary dependence upon the Syriac translation. The original was written in Greek and Saint Jerome, among others, believed it to be an authentic work of Saint Peter's successor Clement. The text could have been written in any city or community where Christians understood Greek, and depending upon the date one assigns to the letters that could mean anywhere from Lyon in southern Gaul to parts of Tunisia across to Egypt and Syria or beyond.

Amulets

The performance of exorcisms by these ascetics may provide a means to clarify what 'singing the Lord's song' meant when they were present at Christian and indeed pagan gatherings. A great many papyri and some other early fragments on wood and parchment from late antiquity reveal how often the psalms were used for apotropaic purposes in late antique Egypt, and no doubt widely elsewhere in Christendom. These are the psalm-amulets that survive from approximately the fourth century AD (although some may date from as early as the second) to the eighth, with a concentration of material in the fifth and sixth. Much of this material is uncomfortably late, but the traditions here are ancient, and often assuredly pre-Christian; Jews did not have to wait until the fourth century AD, for example, to realize that Psalm 90 (*Qui habitat*) guarantees the Lord's protection against the noontide demon, but there are no surviving amulet sources with extracts from this psalm earlier than the 300s (see Appendix, nos 184–202). Boxes containing scriptural verses and worn on the body, the *phylactēria*, were common enough among certain first-century Jews for Christ to speak out against them in Matthew 23: 5, and the largest corpus of surviving texts in Hebrew and Aramaic from the third to ninth century AD comprises magical incantations on amulets. Most of the surviving examples are from Upper or Lower Egypt with texts in Greek, Coptic or both, sometimes with mystical letters and designs, including the cross, which may often be the only detail that identifies an amulet as Christian if the material is drawn from a book of the Old Testament. Augustine inveighs against those who wear such amulets around the neck, while John Chrysostom complains that members of his flock sought healing charms from rabbis in the synagogues. Jerome insisted that none in the monastic or clerical life should use amulets, while Augustine makes a contemptuous reference to the *phylactēria* that devout Catholics refused to employ.[19]

The category of 'amulet' is a broad one and open to challenge at any time. What is more, many of the surviving amulets are of uncertain date, and of unknown provenance, because antiquarians or museums purchased them from private dealers who kept no records. The finds that can be definitively identified as amulets include inscriptions on wooden plaques or ceramic objects drilled with holes for the supporting cord that once allowed the text to be placed in a house, hung in a tomb, or placed around the neck as a talisman. At the other end of the spectrum, in more uncertain territory, are the isolated fragments of parchment or papyrus that might be scraps of liturgical books, rather than amulets, or the remains of stray pages from books for the private prayer of Jews or Christians. The makers of those that are certainly amulets plundered the Psalter for material more often than any other biblical book, whence the standard catalogue of Christian and Jewish papyri includes some forty documents on papyrus, but also some on parchment and pottery that display material drawn from psalms. For Jews and Christians, the psalms brought the apotropaic power of an ancient priestly language into the home, together with an unrivalled store of prayer, petition and prophecy. With such riches to exploit, few amulets present a complete psalm but rather seek to draw a charge from many different psalms by touching them momentarily. Some of the larger amulets offer a tight cento of versicles – or merely fragments of versicles – from different psalms, sometimes as many as seven.

The appearance of so many detached psalm verses on these amulets raises the question of whether some of them were chosen because they were used in liturgical psalmody as refrains. Attention is naturally drawn to the amulets that employ material from one of the psalms with an *Alleluia* refrain written into the title (see Table 6.1). One amulet, number 5 from Hermopolis Magna, actually gives the response *Alleluia* (together with the sign of the cross) after the last of the verses used there from Psalm 118. This is verse 160, so the psalm in its full biblical text extends for another sixteen verses beyond the end of the extract used for the amulet. The addition of *Alleluia* might indicate that the scribe had heard a responsorial performance verse by verse.

TABLE 6.1. *Excerpts from* Alleluia *psalms in documents identified as amulets, all from Egyptian sites*

No.	Type	Provenance	Date	Psalm excerpt	Source[a]
1	Amulet or perhaps from a liturgical compilation	Fayyum	4th c.?	111: 1 (and 73: 2)	22
2	Amulet or perhaps from a liturgical compilation	?	5th–6th c.	114: 5–8	221
3	Bilingual ostrakon-amulet, Greek and Coptic	Deir el-Bahri	4th c.	117: 19–20	222
4	Amulet	Dîmeh (Fayyum)	6th c.	118: 122–3, 130–2	225
5	Amulet	Hermopolis Magna	5th–6th c.	118: 155–60[b] (and 3: 2–4)	222

[a] Page number in Van Haelst, *Catalogue*.
[b] Has *alilouia* + at the end of verse 160, but no other.

In some instances, the material excerpted for an amulet can be connected with liturgical psalmody, as in this fifth- or sixth-century amulet discovered at Hermopolis Magna:

		XP
Line	1–2	Psalm 2: 7 (first versicle)
		'The Lord said to me, you are my son'.
	3	ηδε υδε προσκυνω
		'And behold I worship you' (untraced)
	4	Psalm 109: 3 (part of first versicle)
		'You the first cause'
	5	Psalm 86: 2 (part of first versicle)
		'The Lord loves the gates of Sion . . .'

6   Psalm 86: 5 (part of first versicle)
     'Shall not Sion say: 'Man [and a man is born . . .]'
7   Psalm 64: 2 (part of first versicle)
     'A hymn beseems you . . .'

The lines in bold make an unmistakable allusion to an early stratum of liturgical celebration connected with the birth of Christ and Epiphany. This amulet shows Psalms 2 and 109 in the correct order for three services of the Jerusalem liturgy as it was in the fifth century, for the Epiphany feasts. Between 417 and 439, a complete cycle of readings with *prokeimena* (the counterpart to the Roman gradual) and Alleluia psalms was written down in Jerusalem, and although the original Greek is lost there is a translation into Armenian 'in the oldest manuscript lectionaries of the Armenian Orthodox Church, which adopted the rite of Jerusalem as the basis of its own'. This translation gives Psalm 2 for three services on the fifth, sixth and seventh of January, each one commemorating the birth of Christ, and specifies the seventh verse, the one whose beginning is given in the amulet, as the refrain. The lectionary also specifies Psalm 109 as the Alleluia psalm, but gives verse 1 as the refrain, rather than the third verse given in the amulet. The earliest documents that give the assigned texts for the Frankish–Roman rite correspond yet more closely to the amulet, since Psalm 2: 7 supplies the Introit text (with Ps. *Quare fremuerunt*) for the First Mass of Christmas while 109: 3 forms the text of the Gradual (with Ps. *Dixit Dominus*). Psalm 2: 7 (also with verses 8–10) is the text of the Christmas *prokeimenon* in the Byzantine rite. Gallican usage from as early as the sixth century is witnessed in the Psalter of St-Germain, where Psalm 2 has verse 7 marked with the letter *R* for *R*[*esponsurium*], to use the non-Classical and Gallican form of the term.[20]

The commerce between amulets and the first five centuries of Christian worship is one of the least-investigated sources for early Christian liturgy, and yet this amulet strongly suggests a compiler exploiting the apotropaic powers of liturgy and specifically of responsorial psalmody. Another striking correspondence reaches forward to the earliest records of the texts assigned for chanting in the Frankish–Roman rite and concerns Psalm 90, by far the best-represented psalm on the surviving apotropaic amulets. Beginning *Qui habitat* in the Vulgate version, this psalm guarantees the Lord's protection against nocturnal fears, the danger that walks by night and most famously the noontide demon in verses 5–6. In the Frankish–Roman rite, *Qui habitat* is the Tract assigned to the First Sunday in Lent, but in the earliest sources for that rite which give the full text to be chanted, rather than simply an incipit, verses 8–10 are missing. On the face of things, this is not so difficult to explain, since *Qui habitat* is not the only Tract of the Frankish–Roman repertory to omit verses. But the issue of the 'missing' verses from this Tract gains an extra dimension from one of the amulet sources for this psalm. This is a beech plaque, perhaps of the sixth century, which contains the greater part of this psalm text after the Septuagint version. Within the body of the psalm, there is a striking omission: the text ends in the middle of verse 7 and omits verses 8 and 9. There seems to be no obvious reason in the amulet text, or indeed in the sources of the Septuagint, for this pattern of disturbance that overlaps in large part with the omissions in the Frankish–Roman Tract.[21]

It is possible that both the amulet and the Tract independently attest to the use of this psalm as a chanted exorcism whose roots may reach back as far as the Jews and the Jewish-Christians of the 300s. As late as the second half of the fourth century, Saint John Chrysostom was still trying to persuade his congregation that they should not attend synagogues or seek out sages there to be healed, which may well have encompassed a brisk trade in the apotropaic (and therefore therapeutic) amulets which were apparently of some importance to the status of many rabbis. There is some support for the adventurous suggestion of a common origin for the omission of verses in this psalm in the Jerusalem Talmud, probably redacted in the last quarter of the fourth century AD, which envisages the use of Psalm 90 as an invocation for divine protection against a future accident, including recitations by someone specially brought in so that they may voice the psalm to protect a child from nightmares or help him sleep (*Shabbat*, VI, 2). The recitation is to extend no further than the end of verse 9. So the three sources give the following pattern of verses included or omitted from Psalm 90:[22]

Jerusalem Talmud	1 2 3 4 5 6 7 8 9 . . . .
Amulet	1 2 3 4 5 6 7a 10 11 12 13
Frankish–Roman Tract	1 2 3 4 5 6 7 . . . . 11 12 13–16

This is far from being a neat pattern of correspondences, and the inclusion of other amulets showing material from Psalm 90 would do nothing to make it any tidier. Yet the correspondence is perhaps as neat as we have any right to expect, given that the sources are a late fourth-century Jewish Talmud, a sixth-century amulet found in Egypt and a chant text of the Frankish–Roman rite not documented until the ninth century in what is now northern France. The Jewish evidence explicitly links a break in this region of the psalm with the legitimate incantations of outsiders – presumably sages – that a family may bring in to administer, somewhat in the manner of the itinerant ascetics who may perform exorcisms for their hosts in the Pseudo-Clementine letters on virginity.

Firm conclusions are clearly impossible here, but the apotropaic amulets suggest that the ascetics in the Clementine letters who 'sang the Lord's song' to both Christians and (in some cases) to pagan gatherings probably had a repertory showing many points of contact with the psalmody, including the responsorial psalmody, of the liturgy. Indeed, the simplest hypothesis is that these ascetics used texts, musical techniques and sequences of psalmic material directly derived from the liturgical services.

These urban solitaries of the fourth and fifth centuries bring one close to the threshold of the Middle Ages: to the coming of kingdoms in the West. The preceding chapters have introduced three categories of singer: the lector, the urban solitary and (in the east) the *psaltes*. They can all be described as creations of late antique Christianity. Yet there is one more category of psalmist that the centuries between the second and the fifth bequeathed to the new political order of the Occident: the deacon. Contrary to all expectations, there was a phase of Christian music in the West where the task of making some sustained musical interventions at Mass was entrusted to ministers of the altar.

APPENDIX TO CHAPTER 6

AMULET PSALMS

This table has been compiled from Van Haelst, *Catalogue des papyrus littéraires juifs et chrétiens*, items 84–240. It incorporates all items definitively or tentatively classified as amulets either there or elsewhere in the literature it cites from any date. Items marked with an asterisk are those that Van Haelst does not confidently identify as amulets.

IPL = Isolated papyrus leaf

IPaL = Isolated parchment leaf

C = fragment of a parchment codex (reused as amulet)

Catalogue	Psalm	Description	Date	Provenance
84	1: 1	IPL	II/V	unknown
85	1: 1–2	IPL	V–VI	unknown
88*	1: 3	IPL	VII	unknown
93	2: 7	IPL	VI	Hermopolis
	31: 11			
	64: 2			
	86: 2			
	86: 5			
	96: 12			
94*	3: 4–5,7–8, 9, 6	IPL	VI	unknown
105	9: 22–5	IPL	V	Hermopolis
121	19: 7–8	IPL	III/IV/V	unknown
122	20: 1–5	ostrakon	VI–VII	Medinet-Habu
124*	21: 19	IPL	VI	unknown
129	28: 3	IPL	VI–VII	Upper/Middle Egypt
132	30: 2–8			Medinet-Habu
	1–7 Coptic	ostrakon	VI–VII	
152	49: 1–7	IPL	VI	unknown
160	62: 2–3			Fayyum
	3: 5–6	IPL	VI–VI	
169	70: 20	C	X	Qarara (tomb)
	71: 5, 10, 16, 19			
	72: 7			

Catalogue	Psalm	Description	Date	Provenance
183	90 (complete)	IPL	VI/VI	Oxyrhyncus
184	90: 1	bracelet	VI–VII	Saqqarah
185	90: 1	bracelet	VI–VII	Saqqarah ?
186	90: 1	bracelet	VI–VII	Saqqarah ?
187	90: 1	bracelet	VI–VII	Saqqarah ?
188	90: 1	bracelet	VI–VII	unknown
189	90: 1	bracelet	VI–VII	Syria
190	90: 1–4?	bronze band	VI-VII	Syria
191	90: 1	silver band	VI-VII	Syria
192*	90: 1	plaque	VII-IX	unknown
193	90: 1	plaque	Unknown	unknown
194	90 : 1	wooden plaque	unknown	unknown
195	90: 1–2	IPL	IV/VI/VII	Fayyum
	Romans 12: 12			
	John 2: 1–2			
196	90: 1–4	IPL	V	unknown
197	90: 1–6	IPL	VI–VII	unknown
198	90: 1–7, 10–13	beech plaque	VI	unknown
199	90: 1–13	IPaL	VII–VIII	unknown
200*	90: 5–10	IPaL	VI–VI	Oxyrhyncus
201*	90: 5–16	IPL	V–VI	Oxyrhyncus
202*	90: 13–16	IPL	V–VI	unknown
220*	11: 1			Fayyum
	73: 2	IPL	IV	
221*	114: 5–8	IPL	V–VI	Unknown
222	117: 10–20	ostrakon	IV	Deir el-Bahri
	118: 10–11 Coptic			
225	118: 122–3	C	VI	Soknopaoiu-Nesos ?
	130–2			
227	118: 155–60	Parchment bifolium	V–VI	Hermopolis
	3: 2–4			
228	135: 1–18, 21, 26	wooden plaque	VII–VIII	Qarara
232	140: 1–6,8,10	IPL	VII	unknown

INDEX BY PSALM

Psalm	Catalogue number	Psalm	Catalogue number
86: 5	93	90: 1–6	197
90 (complete)	183	90: 1–7, 10–13	198
90: 1	184	90: 1–13	199
90: 1	185	90: 5–10	200*
90: 1	186	90: 5–16	201*
90: 1	187	90: 13–16	202*
90: 1	188	96: 12	93
90: 1	189	114: 5–8	221*
90: 1–4?	190	117: 10–20	222
90: 1	191	118: 10–11 Coptic	222
90: 1	192*	118: 122–3, 130–2	225
90: 1	193	118: 155–60	227
90: 1	194	135: 1–18, 21, 26	228
90: 1–2	195	140: 1–6, 8, 10	232
with Romans 12: 12 and John 2: 1–2			
90: 1–4	196		

7

DEACONS AS READERS AND PSALMISTS IN THE FOURTH AND FIFTH CENTURIES

To a soldier and pagan like Ammianus Marcellinus in the fourth century, the Christians' use of the term *diakonos* or 'deacon' seemed so specialized that he was reluctant to employ the word in their sense. When he found that he had a story about a deacon to tell, and therefore no choice, he called the individual in question 'a deacon, *as the Christians say*' (xiv. 9, 7). For Ammianus, a native speaker of Greek, *diakonos* principally meant a minister or one who performs various kinds of service, especially at table. There was nothing rare or strange about the word, and Ammianus knew that many cults had their ministers or *diakonoi*. Three hundred years after the ministry of Paul, however, he also knew that there was something distinctive about the usage of Christians which good prose could not readily accommodate. Some of the earliest sources, such as *Didache* XV, do not distinguish the *diakonos* at all sharply from the *episkopos*, and whatever was distinctive to the deacon must lie with the complex inflections that Christ's teaching, as represented by the gospel canon, gave to the concept of service that the term implies. In Mark's gospel, Christ calls those who would be first in the Kingdom to make themselves the servant or *diakonos* of all (9: 35), a teaching that evokes his imminent fulfilment of the prophecy in Isaiah 53 concerning the redemptive trials of the suffering servant. Paul calls himself a *diakonos* (1 Corinthians 3: 5), meaning the herald or messenger who brings others to believe in the gospel. The compiler of Ephesians associates Paul's becoming a *diakonos* with the power to preach the mystery of Christ's death and Resurrection (3: 7). Like the apostles in Acts 6: 4, the Christian deacons had the power of the Word.[1]

When the delay of the Parousia caused the flame of the *diakonoi* to burn with the more enduring fire of an ordained ministry, the deacons still retained the power of the voice when the communities gathered for their rituals. That was a privilege indeed, and it is perhaps explicable only in terms of what the *diakonoi* had been in the earliest days of the churches. In an act of worship, silence may form like a film on water; anyone who breaks it is liable to be accused of gross irreverence, even a kind of cultic treason, unless the sound and the moment are all anticipated as part or an established ritual. By the third century, the deacons were associated with various kinds of licensed intervention during the Eucharistic assembly. They might speak to correct members of the congregation when they or their children proved disorderly; they might read a commemoration or give a summons to prayer, attentiveness or piety. All the tasks that deacons performed, both within the liturgy and without, are intelligible only in terms of a long-standing relation to the gospel as servants and messengers. The charge of the servant explains why they ranked below the presbyters and were obliged to remain standing during convocations of clergy (Pl. 30). The position of herald clarifies the charge of reading Scripture in the Fore-Mass that was so often assigned to the deacons after *c.*400 rather than to lectors.

These tasks help to explain why deacons appear as psalmodists in the liturgies of Jerusalem and Rome. The famous travel diary of the Spanish 'nun' Egeria (?383–4) reveals at least three levels of psalmody in Jerusalem for the Easter liturgies, with deacons involved as psalmists in the first two. For the most exalted, the bishop was present throughout, and on these occasions, presbyters, deacons and other clergy were principally responsible for the chanting, with the congregation supplying the refrain in the responsorial psalmody. Thus on Easter Day, a service that may be Sunday lauds or a preceding vigil was attended by the bishop in the Anastasis; one of the priests sang a psalm and all responded; then one of the deacons sang another psalm and yet another was given out by certain clergy. The bishop then read a gospel narrative of the Resurrection, after which he processed with hymns to the cross. In the next layer of services, the bishop was not continuously present and there was chanting by presbyters, deacons and other clergy; there might also be some processional movement with chanting involving urban ascetics, the *monazontes* and *parthenae*. In the third and final layer of services, the bishop was not present at any time; a skeleton staff of priests and deacons said prayers, their chanting (if there were any) being accompanied or led by *monazontes* and *parthenae*.[2]

The first traces of deacon psalmists in the West appear in Rome, and at much the same time as in Jerusalem; towards 400, funerary inscriptions from Rome begin to commemorate deacons prized for their skill in psalmody during unspecified services. These epitaphs are often quite extensive compositions and are sometimes in verse, two marks of social status (or of social pretension) that draw them away from the laconic IN PACE memorials of those in minor orders such as the lectors and gravediggers. The musical terminology is explicit and diverse, as we shall see, suggesting more than the occasional brief intervention or succinct response by a cleric blessed with a good voice. Some of these inscriptions may refer to the years when the deceased was a lector (such retrospective glances at the course of a career, be it temporal or spiritual, are common enough in funeral epigraphy) but examples where musical excellence is mentioned in the same breath, so to speak, as characteristic duties of the Roman deacon around 400, including the supervision of caritative work, suggest that this cannot be so in all

30   Front of a 4th-c. marble sarcophagus showing Christ enthroned among apostles. Ravenna, Church of S. Francesco.

cases. What is more, deacons as psalmodists, in the developed sense that they bore responsibility for the Fore-Mass psalm or gradual, can be traced in various parts of the West in the sixth century, notably Africa and Gaul, suggesting a late antique practice that passed without a break into many churches within the new political order of the kingdoms (see Ch. 10).

It is unlikely that the diaconate was ever regarded as a long-term means to phase out singers altogether, replacing very junior members of the clerical staff (if they were judged to be clergy at all) with more senior ministers. That would represent a means for promoting psalmody, in effect, such as few late antique or medieval churches are positively known to have made. Viewed in the long term, therefore, the assignment of psalmody to clerics so senior would have been anomalous if it were consistently broadened to make a *ministry* of music into one of the deacons' charges. It was the fate of most singers in late antiquity and the early Middle Ages to move on the periphery of the clerical communities they served. On the very few occasions when singers were asked to witness charters or other juridical instruments, they invariably came very near the end of the descending order of subscriptions, as if about to fall off the document into the oblivion from which they have been so briefly and unexpectedly drawn. Deacons, however, often attest the charters of their bishops and of any others whose business they were called upon to witness as distinguished members of their clerical hierarchy. They could even witness the proceedings of synods if they were serving as their bishop's delegate. A deacon was therefore a trusted episcopal agent and counsellor who often stood closer to the bishop's throne, both in a literal and a figurative sense, than the presbyters who technically ranked above him, whence the various Roman deacons who vaulted over the order of presbyter to become bishop.

The Deacon as Man of Letters

Ammianus Marcellinus may often have encountered deacons 'as the Christians call them' when he found them carrying letters sent by their bishops to distant correspondents. By his lifetime, the stream of reports from governors and military commanders no longer flowed so plentifully into the public archives, and only a few exceptional individuals in civil or military life, like Ammianus himself, decided to write their memoirs. In contrast, the genre of the fraternal or pastoral letter between churchmen, a literary form as old as Christianity itself, survived and continued to flourish within an essentially clerical and monastic network of communications. Deacons, so often the right-hand men of their bishops, were often chosen to be couriers for letters sent many hundreds of miles. The Italian cases include a certain Heraclius, traceable in 397–8, who visited Saint Jerome in the East and carried back a letter to a Pannonian correspondent; he also undertook a second journey, bearing letters to Jerome from a priest and a bishop. Deacons also appear as the bearers of papal communications. A deacon named Hilarius, recorded between the mid-350s and the late 370s, carried a letter from Pope Liberius to the Emperor Constantius II at Milan announcing a synod, and a second missive, on the same journey, to Bishop Eusebius of Vercelli. The African material is almost equally rich. In 431 a deacon of Carthage named Bessula carried a letter to Ephesus to explain why his bishop could not send a delegation to a synod, while in 426/7 Saint Augustine chose a deacon named Paulus to carry a communication to a *comes*.[3]

Paulus had the ear of the count that Augustine wished to address. Like many of his contemporaries, Augustine wrote some letters with words so carefully chosen in relation to a fraught situation that he probably wished the courier to deposit the letter and depart, adding nothing by way of explanation. Yet there were other occasions when the carrier's responsibilities did not end when he placed a letter in the hands of the recipient's servants, for that was the moment when he ceased to be postman and became an envoy. A deacon might then be required to supplement the text of the letter he bore with additional information that the sender had entrusted to him. In that case, the letter he carried was not so much a communication as a certificate that gave him licence to speak on a superior's behalf. When Saint Basil chose a deacon named Strategios to be his courier he assured the recipient of the letter that 'whatever escapes the words in this letter will be supplied by the bearer'; in another epistle, he reminds Italian and Gallic bishops that the bearer of the letter, a deacon named Sabinus, 'can fully inform you of things which the text passes over'. Examples could easily be multiplied, notably from the letters of Augustine.[4]

Deacons were sometimes chosen to extend the task of expanding upon the contents of a letter by declaiming written documents at synods and convocations of clergy. When Pope Felix III called a council in 487–8 to judge whether two bishops were guilty of bribery, the deacon Anastasius read the opening address.

In 502 Pope Symmachus convened a council in Saint Peter's basilica that called for a document to be read and solemnly revoked; it was passed to the deacon Hormisda, who read the text aloud, pausing only when a member of the council wished to comment. (This trusted adviser and envoy became bishop of Rome in 514; the route between the higher echelons of the Roman diaconate and the throne of Saint Peter could be short. The Seven Deacons of Rome regarded it as a great affront if a mere priest were made pope, instead of one of themselves.) A homily that Saint Augustine delivered to his clergy in 426 began with an introduction by Augustine and continued when a deacon named Lazarus read from the account of Pentecost in Acts 4: 31–5.[5]

The Deacon as a Liturgical Reader: A View from Toledo

In the middle of the Iberian Peninsula, where the Roman road from Mérida to Zaragoza meets the Tagus, the river curves to enclose a mound of granite on three sides (Pl. 31). This is the site of Toledo, reinforced by the Romans with a wall on the northern face, an aqueduct and a monumental circus, among other amenities of which traces still remain. Within this cityscape, probably degraded in

31   View of Toledo, showing the granite outcrop on which the city stands. Its natural defences and central position made it an ideal choice of situation for the Visigothic royal capital.

many places by the end of the fourth century, nineteen bishops gathered in the year 400 for a synod that is commonly counted as the First Council of Toledo. It was an extraordinary moment in the fortunes of Spain. The Gothic confederations destined to shape Spanish history for three centuries had recently been granted leave to enter the Roman Empire (on condition they accept Christianity), where they hoped they would be safe against the raids of the Huns. To the north, the Vandals were about to cross the frozen Rhine and eventually force the Roman government to abandon the hope of maintaining any military presence in Spain beyond the province of Tarraconensis.

The assembled prelates at Toledo had other problems to address. Recent years had produced persistent rumours that Antichrist had already been born, 'no superhuman or demonic figure but a man within history'. The bishops had also striven with the devout and cultivated layman Priscillian of Avila, whose summons to his fellow Christians had been markedly ascetic, a dangerous challenge to any community of cathedral clergy if its members were not known for their monastic inclinations. The prelates at the council therefore attached considerable importance to the way different duties and standards of discipline defined the various clerical grades, for only by following canonical procedures with great scrupulosity could the clergy command respect and illuminate their ministries with the Holy Spirit. Among many other questions of administration and discipline, the bishops at Toledo I considered whether penitents should be ordained to any ministry of the Church. This was partly an issue of ritual purity, concerning what a man doing public penance, perhaps with blood on his hands, could be allowed to do in the sanctuary and whether he should be allowed to enter it at all. The prelates decided that no penitent should be admitted to a clerical order unless custom allowed, or necessity required, that he be appointed a doorkeeper or lector.

The somewhat surprising reason for this decision is that penitents who enter these orders will therefore be barred from declaiming the gospel or the Epistle. The reader, in other words, no longer read from the New Testament in the Spanish dioceses represented at the Council. A comparable ruling appears in the fourth canon and requires that subdeacons making a second marriage should be demoted to the level of doorkeeper or lector, and for the same reason. It is no surprise that the bishops wished to place the Scriptures beyond the reach of the doorkeepers, who had no more right to a liturgical ministry of reading than the *fossores* who are depicted on their epitaphs with shovels not sheets of papyrus; yet the readers present a very different case. If the bishops could be confident that it was safe to make penitents into lectors without the New Testament documents being sullied, then the honour of reading from those Scriptures must have been promoted beyond the lector's reach.[6]

This had already happened at the opposite end of the Christian world. In fourth-century Antioch, the compiler of the dossier commonly known today as the *Apostolic Constitutions* assumed that the reader would declaim from the Old

Testament while a presbyter or deacon would be entrusted with the gospel. This seems to be exactly what the compiler's contemporaries among the Hispano-Roman bishops of Toledo took for granted some 2,500 miles away. The New Testament canon of Scripture, whose gates were only now finally beginning to close, had passed upwards through the hierarchy of clerical orders from the lectors to the deacons: to the men who had long been prominent in the Eucharistic services for their spoken interventions, breaking the film of silence, and indeed in the wider world as envoys and couriers. In making this journey, the books of the New Law traversed an important frontier, for deacons were universally agreed to be clergy. The lower orders of reader, doorkeeper, exorcist and gravedigger were divided from the clerical ministries of the altar by a veil of legislation that was constantly being rewoven in synod just as it was being daily rent in practice. Abundant legislation from the Church in Council reveals the pressure for deacons to have no dealings with excommunicates and never to celebrate Israelite festivals with Jews; they were forbidden to desert their church for service in another and were never to engage in commercial enterprises. Many of the other rulings concerning deacons in the conciliar tradition of the early Church raise questions of ritual and specifically of sexual purity. A canon from the Council of Elvira in Spain, issued soon after 300, forbids bishops, presbyters and deacons to have sexual relations with their wives or to become fathers (XXXIII), while another canon of the same Council prohibits those who fornicated in their adolescence from becoming deacons (XXX). To judge by a number of remarkable epitaphs, mostly perhaps of women, the demand to have a chaste marriage was widely heeded by deacons and their spouses (Pl. 32).[7]

Inscriptions record enough young lectors to suggest that many Christian communities thought it especially appropriate to hear scriptural readings delivered by pre-pubescent voices that were not yet darkened by a sexual identity (see above, p. 161). The proceedings of fourth-century African councils confirm this impression with their unusually explicit rulings that lectors should read 'up to the age of puberty' and no further unless they are prepared to make a chaste marriage

32 The epitaph of Aurelia, wife of Felix the Deacon, with whom she lived in lifelong chastity. From Perret, *Catacombes*, v, tab. 36, n. 112.

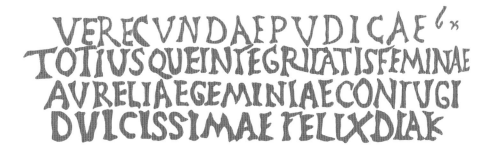

and continue. An alternative was to have the Scriptures voiced by young or indeed mature men who showed the restraint of the clerical ministries to which they aspired or had already been ordained. This could result in severe and perhaps impossibly ambitious demands upon some lectors. The *Testamentum Domini*, perhaps of the late fourth or fifth century, requires that a candidate for the office of reader should be 'pure, quiet, meek, wise, with much experience, learned and of much learning, with a good memory, vigilant, so that he may deserve a higher degree'. That was a great deal to ask of those at a low level of the clerical *cursus*, to say nothing of those who had scarcely emerged from boyhood or early adolescence. One solution is succinctly adumbrated in the so-called *Canons of Hippolytus*: 'When one chooses a reader, he is to have the virtues of a deacon.' The best way to ensure that result was to have the deacons read.[8]

The Deacon as Reader in a New 'Departmental Empire'

Liturgy is never the pure and disinterested domain of activity that its devotees seek, rising above the contingencies of social forms and politics like incense floating into the highest reaches of a vault. The enlargement of the deacons' duties to include scriptural reading and forms of psalmody reflected widespread social and political changes in the late Roman Empire. Both in the churches and in the bureaux of imperial government, the fourth century brought a markedly enhanced emphasis upon departmental enclaves, titles of office and insignia. In response to the political and military disasters of the third century, Diocletian (285–305) restructured the imperial administration to create 'a Fortress Empire in which each person was assigned his place and secured to it by new bonds'. The result was a proliferating series of departments and a wellspring of what many European languages today mean by the term 'Byzantine' in a pejorative sense. Since imperial administrators and bishops were often recruited from similar social groups, it is not surprising that many churches in the fourth century were seeking to extend and refine the differences between the various clerical orders in terms of the rights and obligations associated with each one, just as the imperial bureaucracy was refining its structure of salaries and titles. The assignment of New Testament readings to the deacons meant putting rolls and books into the hands of deacons, enhancing the insignia of their office in a very familiar way, for the written materials that an imperial official was entitled to compile and use were among the most potent emblems of his office in late antiquity.[9]

The illustrated copies of the *Notitia Dignitatum* make the point with literally emblematic force. In its surviving form, this famous document from the end of the fourth century lists military units with the offices of the army and the administrative bureaux. Plate 33 shows the material relating to the Western Masters of the Palace Bureaux of Memorials, Correspondence and Records, the *magistri scriniorum memoriae, epistolarum et libellorum*. The upper section shows the

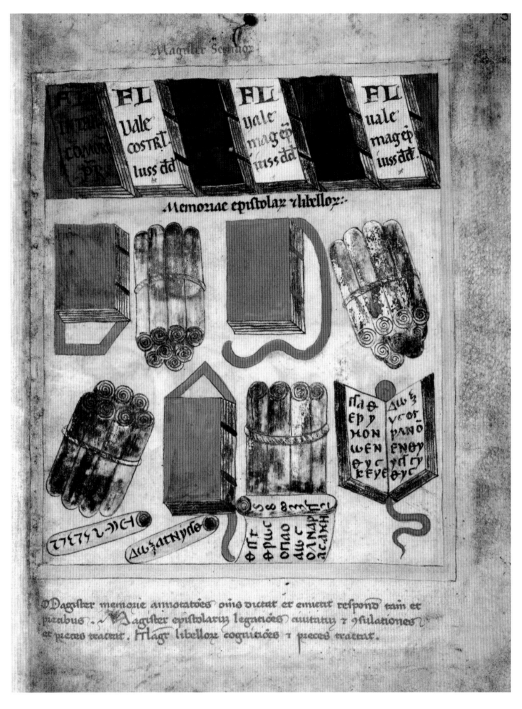

33 Fragment of the *Notitia Dignitatum*. Cambridge, Fitzwilliam Museum, MS 86–1972. Italian, perhaps Neapolitan. Copied by Antonius Angeli in 1427, from a manuscript at Speyer. The *Notitia Dignitatum* was originally compiled *c*.400.

34 A 4th-c. dalmatic of undyed linen found at Akhmim, in Middle Egypt. Recovered from a Christian burial, and now mounted on modern cloth. The strips for the shoulders and sleeves are made of purple-dyed wool, probably imported from the Levant and possibly from Tyre. London, Victoria and Albert Museum, T. 361–1887.

appointment documents or *codicilli* pertaining to one of the masters named below. Below are books and scrolls from the masters' offices. Liturgical celebrations provided extraordinary opportunities for the dramatization of the book, taken from its place of safekeeping, paraded through the church to the point of use and then carried back again. Like a Master of the Palace Bureau of Memorials, a deacon newly entrusted with lessons in the fourth century had a book for his insignia.

Similar forces were at work in the evolution of the deacons' vesture. Like other clerical vestments, the deacon's distinctive clothing began as a means to distinguish one grade of the clerical hierarchy from the others and then to separate them all from the garb of laymen whose repertory of clothing, free from the ossifying effect of liturgical practice, gradually evolved away from the universal late antique forms that the clergy retained, and still do. With special and poignant reference to deacons, the process can be detected in the story that compelled Ammianus Marcellinus, writing in his second language of Latin, to use the word *diaconus*. He had heard of a deacon who ordered a special garment from Tyre, the city famous for the expensive shade of purple manufactured from the shellfish *murex*, the imperial hue. It was indeed rumoured that a royal robe had been commissioned on this occasion. Suspicion fell upon a certain Maras, 'a deacon, as the Christians say', who had ordered 'a short, sleeveless tunic to cover the chest'. Maras was tortured to within an inch of his life, but he was neither seeking purple dress as an imperial pretender nor as a plotter in someone else's bid for power; he was a churchman who unwisely tried to purchase a particularly lavish dalmatic, still a widespread garment in less elaborate forms at this date and destined to become the distinctive vesture of the deacons' order. (The dalmatic was worn with sleeves so short that it might indeed be called sleeveless.) The *Liber pontificalis* records that Pope Sylvester (314–35) made the use of the dalmatic mandatory for Roman deacons, and although that testimony carries little weight it accords in date with the order Maras the deacon placed with the Tyrians in 354 (Pl. 34).[10]

The Deacon as Psalmist

In Rome, by the end of the fourth century, some deacons were beginning to follow the path that has already been traced for some lectors: they exploited their musical gifts to become reader and psalmist combined, if only on an ad hoc basis. In the West, the traces of these men can be found in the outstandingly rich legacy of Christian epigraphy in Rome, the greatest single hoard of Christian inscriptions from any late antique city. They are all elaborate and sometimes ostentatious epitaphs in which the dead are by no means envisaged as revenants that have momentarily left the cold and shadowed banquets of the afterlife to address the living. 'I am he who sang psalms with voice and art; I sang holy words with varied notes', claims the archdeacon Sabinus, interred during the fifth century beneath the porch of S. Lorenzo fuori le mura. 'Scorning wealth', says another, 'it was my duty to clothe naked petitioners, to pour out for the needy whatever harvest the year conceded, and I wished to chant among the people, the prophet's music going forth . . .' (for details, see below).[11]

The evidence for the activities of these deacons reaches beyond the inscribed epitaphs to texts in which members of their order are given the title of *levita*, or Levite. In Nehemiah 11: 16 the Levites are charged to minister to the sons of Aaron, and the priests, to maintain the Temple and to perform other tasks appointed for the 'outward business of the house of God'. In all these respects, the Levites might be compared to the deacons conceived as servants of the bishops and presbyters, both in the liturgy and in the wider administration of the Church. Yet the Old Testament Levites were also the Temple musicians, instituted in 1 Chronicles and especially in 15: 16: 'David spake to the chief of the Levites to appoint their brethren to be the singers with instruments of music, psalteries and harps and cymbals, sounding, by lifting up the voice with joy.' Silenced by the Romans in AD 70, the Levites continue to resonate through the mystical *heikhalot* writings of post-Temple Judaism that so often envisage celestial liturgies with a plenitude of music and instruments.[12]

Hence the many references in late antique sources to deacons as Levites can perhaps be read as indirect evidence for their musical responsibilities during the Mass, less explicit in character than the epitaphs but nonetheless suggestive. There are also signs that the title of Levite was regarded as distinctly prestigious, for it was anything but _prosaic_ in the strict sense of that word. The epitaphs of the Roman deacons generally commemorate a _diaconus_ when they are in prose but a _levita_ when in verse. Why should this be? There were still careful poets in the workshops of the Roman masons in the fourth and fifth centuries, but the reasons for their choice in this case cannot lie with the niceties of versification. The word _diacŏnŭs_ (<διάκονος, where the alpha is naturally long) fits just as well as _lēvītă_ into the dactylic hexameters that the poets of the epitaphs so often employ. An alternative explanation for the consistent use of _levita_ in verse might be based upon the word itself, for it turned the deacons into the only clerical order with a title referring back to the ministries of the Jewish Temple. _Levita_ is one of the very few Hebraisms in either ecclesiastical Greek or Latin.[13]

The enemies of change are often better guides to what took place in the past than its advocates. Towards 400, an anonymous writer now known as Ambrosiaster became a trenchant critic of the Roman deacons, whom he found arrogant and contumacious. 'What audacity it is for the deacons to make themselves equal to presbyters', he exclaims; 'it is a vain presumption, showing great temerity, to compare the bearers of the canopy and of all its vessels . . . to those who exercise a priesthood.' At first sight, this looks like a local squabble that sets Ambrosiaster against the seven regional deacons of Rome, who did indeed form an elite entrusted with high charges, notably poor-relief and the management of funds. As mentioned above, these men were often tempted to regard themselves as superior to the presbyters who served the basilicas, to say nothing of the presbyters in the titular churches and in the dioceses beyond the walls of Rome. Yet the records of the Latin Church in council show that the presumptuousness of deacons caused widespread concern throughout the West during the late fourth and fifth centuries. The pervasive sense in the synods and canonical collections before 500 is that subdeacons and deacons are being viewed through the eyes of presbyters and bishops who wish to check the ambitions of men eager to move away from their position on the threshold where those who were indisputably clergy gave way to those in minor orders who were not. Hence the deacons were variously forbidden to take communion before the presbyters, to bless the chalice, to sit in the company of presbyters or to dispense the Eucharistic elements save in time of necessity, and then only when presbyters were present. They were to sit only when and where the presbyters instructed them, for a deacon was endowed at ordination with a _ministerium_, a duty of service, not a _sacerdotium_. As late as the seventh century, Braulio of Saragossa still finds that he must condemn the presumption of deacons for daring to anoint.[14]

The number of Roman deacons commemorated as _levita_ rather than _diaconus_ in verse suggests the title was regarded as honorific by the deacons themselves and indeed as a poetic one in the strict sense that it was the preferred usage in epitaphs composed in verse. It identified the deacons as the descendants of officials in the Jewish Temple hierarchy and asserted the antiquity of their office. One begins to appreciate why the possession of the title _levita_ seems so important in

35   A deacon, vested in a dalmatic of remarkably antique design (compare Pl. 34), and mounted on an ambo, sings (or prepares to sing) the *Exultet* while touching the Paschal candle that the bishop is lighting. His other hand is held aloft. Vatican City, Biblioteca Apostolica Vaticana, MS 9820 (detail). Beneventan, 10th c.

the one ancient trace of deacons' psalmody that survives: the rite for the blessing of the Paschal candle in the Easter Vigil (Pl. 35) and in its most widespread hymn, the *Exultet*.[15]

Quapropter, astantibus vobis fratres karissimi,
ad tam miram sancti huius luminis claritatem
una mecum queso dei omnipotentis misericordiam invocate,
Ut qui me, non meis meritis,
In Levitarum numero dignatus est aggregare,
Luminis sui gratiam infundens,
Cerei huius laudem implere precipiat.

Wherefore, with you my dearest brothers standing by, I ask you to invoke with me the mercy of almighty God before the wondrous radiance of this holy light, *so that he who has deigned to include me among the Levites,* not for my merits, infuses the grace of his light, may command me to fulfil the praise of this candle [emphasis mine].

Epitaphs reveal that deacons of the local Roman Church might also be charged with the psalmody that sounds like the performance of the responsorial psalm in the Fore-Mass, the future gradual:

1. **Leo** (*ILCV*, 997; *ICUR*, NS 7 19004; Pietri and Pietri, *Prosopographie*, s.v. Leo[4]). The metrical epitaph of Leo, a Roman bishop (of a church in a *suburbium* of Rome?) at the end of the fourth century, but plainly referring here to his time as a deacon. He was a convert from paganism, and married to a woman named Laurentia:

   CONTEMPTIS OPIBVS MALVI COGNOSCERE CHRISTVM,
   HAEC MIHI CVRA FVIT NVDOS VESTIRE PETENTES
   FVNDERE PAVPERIBVS QVIDQVID CONCESSERAT ANNVS
   PSALLERE ET IN POPVLIS VOLVI MODOLANTE PROPHETA . . .

   (Scorning wealth, I desired to know Christ; it was my duty to clothe naked petitioners and to pour out for the needy whatever [harvest] the year conceded, and I wished to chant among the people, the prophet's music going forth . . .)

2. **Redemptus** (*ICUR*, NS 4, 10129; Pietri and Pietri, *Prosopographie*, s.v. Redemptus[1]). The metrical epitaph of a Roman deacon (*levita*) named Redemptus, interred in the fourth or fifth century in the cemetery of Callistus (*coemeterium inferius*) between the Via Appia and the Via Ardeatina. The text calls upon the Christian community of Rome, who must be wondering why Redemptus has vanished from their midst; it is because 'the kingdom of heaven has suddenly snatched him away'. Redemptus performed well as a musician, 'with nectared singing' that certainly included psalms since he celebrated the 'ancient prophet with serene music' (Pl. 36):

STRINGE DOLOR LACRIMAS; QVAERIS PLEBS SANCTA REDEMPTVM
LEVITAM? SVBITO RAPVIT SIBI REGIA CAELI.
DVLCIA NECTARIO PROMEBAT MELLA CANENDO
PROPHETAM CELEBRANS PLACIDO MODVLAMINE SENEM.

(Grief, hold back tears! People of Holy Church, do you seek Redemptus the Levite? The kingdom of heaven has suddenly snatched him away. He put forth sweet honey with nectared singing, celebrating the ancient prophet with serene music.)

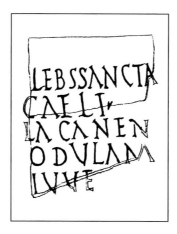

36 Fragments of the epitaph for Redemptus the deacon, showing the words *canen[do]* and *[m]odulam[ine]*. From De Rossi, *Roma sotterranea,* iii. 244 (2).

3. **Sabinus** (*ILCV*, 1194; *ICUR*, NS 7, 18017; Pietri and Pietri, *Prosopographie*, s.v. Sabinus[5]). The metrical epitaph of Sabinus *levita*, a Roman archdeacon, interred at some time during the fifth century beneath the porch (*in limine*) of the basilica of S. Lorenzo fuori le mura. The inscription entreats Saint Lawrence that he may conduct Sabinus to the angelic choir. Like many epitaphs, this drifts in and out of the first and third person, and includes an elegiac couplet decisively revealing that Sabinus was an accomplished psalmodist. The figure of zeugma in the claim that Sabinus 'sang with voice and art' is as subtly ostentatious as the blaze of musical vocabulary that the poet has compressed into two lines (VOCE . . . MODVLATVS . . . CECINI . . . [DIVE]RSIS SONIS). The assurance that this deacon's melodies were 'varied' proclaims that the quality of his singing was more than functional, and he was certainly responsible for psalmody (PSALMOS).

[AST EG]O QVI VOCE PSALMOS MODVLATVS ET ARTE
[DIVE]RSIS CECINI VERBA SACRATA SONIS

(but I who sang psalms with voice and art; I sang holy words with varied notes . . .)

4. **Deusdedit** (*ILCV*, 1195; *ICUR*, NS 4, 12601; Pietri and Pietri, *Prosopographie*, s.v. Deusdedit[1]). The metrical epitaph of the Roman archdeacon Deusdedit, interred at some time during the fifth century in an uncertain region of the cemetery of Callistus between the Via Appia and the Via Ardeatina:

+ HIC LEVITARVM PRIMVS IN ORDINE VIVENS
DAVITICI CANTOR CARMINIS ISTE FVIT.

(The first among the order of levites (= archdeacon) he was a singer of Davidic song.)

The deacons of Rome formed concentric rings of clergy with an inner circle occupied by the seven regional deacons (*regionarii*) and successive rings inhabited by those of the basilicas, the titular churches and the suburbicarian dioceses. While there may be no reason to suppose that any of the deacons commemorated in these inscriptions were *regionarii*, two of them were certainly archdeacons, including Sabinus. These were men of considerable prestige, hence the use of verse, which meets the better standards of prosody in fifth-century Rome (such metrical epitaphs are virtually unknown for the lower orders of lector, acolyte, doorkeeper or *fossor*; they are less common than one might suppose for presbyters). These epitaphs belong in the superior layers of Roman commemorative epigraphy using the public language of the state, and were seen by eyes familiar with roadways lined with the funerary plaques of wealthy pagan families, with bridges bearing dedicatory verses and with cult centres adorned with votive altars. Indeed, that is where the literary congeners of these epitaphs are to be found, tending to confirm once more that these deacon-psalmists were men of considerable stature and education, the equivalent in the clerical *cursus* to those who achieved high position in the army or the bureaux.

Here and there, the epitaphs reveal traces of a literary classicism in their diction as well as in their form, which may point in the same direction. There are a few metrical errors, but in the allusions there is nothing either slavish or ostentatious; Virgil and other Classical poets were still well assimilated in the minds of the educated Romans who composed these inscriptions. When the epitaph for Bishop Leo evokes his years *manens in vita*, the possible allusion to one of Virgil's more common expressions (*dum vita manebit*) is light and effortlessly redistributed within the line. Adapted from pagan epigraphy, and seemingly without strain, is the sense of having occupied a senior clerical grade in the manner of a Roman public office, entitling the deceased to the admiration and respect of grateful fellow citizens. Bishop Leo, while a deacon, 'wished to chant among the people', *in populis*; the epitaph of Redemptus imagines the Christians of Rome, the *plebs sancta*, searching anxiously for one whom 'the kingdom of heaven has suddenly snatched away'. A charge to perform liturgies in the old sense—the duty to spend personal wealth on civic projects as a member of the city council—had been replaced by the obligation to perform liturgy in the new and Christian sense. It seems that no small part of the public reputation these men enjoyed can be traced to their skill as singers, which explains why the language used to convey it is rich and indisputably musical, encompassing CANTOR, CARMINIS, CANENDO, MODOLANTE and PSALLERE. Their skills were applied to the PSALMOS of David, who is mentioned by name (DAVITICI CANTOR CARMINIS) or by his conventional title 'the prophet' (PROPHETAM CELEBRANS . . . MODOLANTE PROPHETA). This is in many ways a compact group of men. The epitaphs of Leo and Redemptus even share a line of verse (SIC MERVI PLEBEM CHRISTI RETINERE SACERDOS), a circumstance that is perhaps not entirely explained by the inscriber(s) having recourse to the same model book or to one inscriber copying another.[16]

In musical terms, there is no sense here of limited horizons. Redemptus 'put forth sweet honey with nectared singing, celebrating the ancient prophet with serene music', which could scarcely go further in ten Latin words to praise the sublime quality of his voice. His sound was *nectareus*, used for sensations as sweet as balm, as honey or as the odour of nard. Sabinus claims that he sang 'varied notes with voice and art'. The invocation of art or skill (*ars*) is plainly unashamed. These were not men dutifully performing a modest function with indifferent results.

In Rome, the psalmody of deacons was eventually condemned by the synod that Gregory I convened on 5 July 595 in Saint Peter's basilica, partly concerned with the practice of assigning deacons the duties of a psalmist. Gregory told his clergy there that this was a reprehensible usage of recent origin (it was actually some two hundred years old, possibly more), and he ruled that henceforth the deacons should only read (*legere*) the gospel. The time had come for them to give their full attention to their ministry of the altar, to their administration of alms and (somewhat surprisingly) to their preaching. No longer were the deacons' probity and manner of life to be compromised by the vices that so readily followed when a singer seeks a pleasing voice, in Gregory's phrase a *blanda vox*. The task of singing psalms and intoning or reading other lections must therefore be left to subdeacons, or if necessary to 'the minor orders' of the ecclesiastical hierarchy, whom Gregory does not trouble himself to name. 'If anyone be tempted to go against this my decree', he declared, 'let him be anathema.' In Rome, at least, the experiment with deacon-psalmodists was mostly over. In the next chapter their traces will appear again in sixth-century Gaul and Vandal Africa: in the kingdoms of a new political order.[17]

37 Anton Pitloo, *The Temples at Paestum* (detail), beginning of the 19th c. Naples, Galeria Nazionale de Capodimonte. This elegiac painting of the ruined temples at Paestum inadvertently captures the generally unhealthy aspect that many Italian and other sites may have assumed in late antiquity as population levels sank and malarial wetlands began to reclaim the areas near even the major public buildings. Much of the work clearing and cleaning drains had formerly been done by *corvées* imposed on the craftsmen and shopkeepers of the cities.

PART II

THE KINGDOMS COME

THE KINGDOMS AROSE WHEN BARBARIAN COMMANDERS won or drifted into a de facto independence from an Empire that could no longer pay them as soldiers, contain them as settlers or suppress them as insurgents. By 500, many of the kings were Christians, but not necessarily Catholics. The liturgies of their churches, and the men who sang them, were regulated by royal appointees who were often important landowners and trusted advisers of the king, namely the bishops. Well into the sixth century, these prelates or their delegates selected the readings and psalms to be chanted for the Eucharistic service in their church; everything read during the course of the year, and the choice of texts assigned to the singers, expressed the depth of a prelate's scriptural knowledge and his conscientiousness in office. The liturgy a cantor knew was the usage of his Church duly modified by any customs that the bishops of a province, or even of an entire kingdom, had agreed to share when they met in synod at the king's command, with his permission or (in rare cases) in spite of his wishes. These matters reflected the bishop's position within a local sphere of influence where he was an arbitrator and the overseer of such public services as remained. Increasingly responsible for the schooling of his clergy, he also assumed some of the responsibilities of both the local Roman administrators and of the city councillors, whose numbers were much depleted, where they existed at all. We shall see that Western musical history owes much to the bishops' willingness to be the envoys of their cities and to care for the poor in hospitals modelled on Byzantine institutions like the Great Orphanage of Constantinople.

During the early Middle Ages, the Christian West that can be discerned beyond the relatively narrow circuits in which men and women traded the essentials of their lives does not find expression in widespread cooperation between polities or in large networks of treaties. Instead, the sense of an emerging Christian West will be found among those equipped to recuperate a sense of the Ecclesia Occidentalis, no longer conceived as a set of Western-imperial provinces, as in the days of the first ecumenical councils, but as a group of kingdoms within an Ecclesia larger than any single cell of spiritual or temporal jurisdiction such as a see or a realm. Obedience to the see of Rome, however, was sometimes of small consequence; it meant little to Clovis, the first Christian king of the Franks, less to the Catholic monarch of Visigothic Spain in 589 and nothing at all, one might guess, to the Arian Vandals of Carthage. Yet the theme of Rome as the patriarchate for a recuperated Western Church of barbarian 'national' churches dominates the core chapters of this Part, concerned in various ways with the efforts of some churches to realize their place in this Ecclesia Occidentalis by importing elements of the liturgy of the Eternal City, including the materials of its plainsong. For the most part, this work was highly localized, done by men and women committed to a church in which they had a special place. At first, these efforts will be made on various peripheries of the Latin Christian world: in Ireland, Northumbria, Gallaecia, Bavaria and the see of Naples. Finally, they will appear in the Frankish heartlands between the Seine and the Rhine. Then, at last, they will be definitively royal.

8

A NEW POLITICAL ORDER,
AND TWO SINGERS FROM GAUL

In one of the most famous passages ever written about music and musicians, composed not very long before 500, Anicius Manlius Severinus Boethius takes the patrician view of practical musicians one would expect a Roman gentleman from an ancient and illustrious clan to adopt. Repeatedly using a metaphor drawn from the Roman household, Boethius declares that 'physical skill serves as a slave, while reason rules like a mistress'. Hence 'the study of music as a rational art is much nobler than composition or performance' because those who sing and play instruments have no knowledge of musical theory; since they have not explored the art of music with the power of reason they remain in a state of servitude. This is more than a figure of speech, for many of the instrumentalists and singers whom Boethius heard in Ostrogothic Italy must have been slaves in the legal sense, ranking no higher than domestic chattels. In this scheme, power-fully shaped by the juridical conceptions of freedom and servility, there can be no such thing as an accomplished performer who understands the rational basis of music, for only those belonging to a class contemptuous of the public display that performance requires receive the necessary education in the appropriate terms and concepts. The true musician confines his involvement with practical music to criticism, for he knows what performers do without actually doing it himself, just as performers do what he knows without actually knowing it them-selves. Ultimately, the true musician is not concerned with audible sound at all, for he knows with John Keats that 'Heard melodies are sweet but those unheard are sweeter'.[1]

Long before Boethius, the young Augustine had exalted musical judgement above practical expertise in his treatise *De Musica*, giving a Latin dress to well-established conceptions of the Greeks. Both authors accept that one is more liable to be deceived by something one senses than by something one under-stands. Boethius is nonetheless considerably more insistent upon the servility of the performer and the free status of the true musician or critic. With Greek mod-els before him, and unable to imagine a world without the vast number of tasks that public and private slaves performed, Boethius advocates a form of musical study that cultivates the rational mind and seeks to define the means whereby knowledge can be attained. Despite its appeal to the desire for music lifted above the contingencies and imperfections of performance to a higher sphere, this is plainly a political position as well as a philosophical one, for minds educated in such liberal studies as music theory promote the *humanitas* of those in power. By no means a simple term to translate, *humanitas* encompassed the shared ideals of those who judged themselves fit to rule by their self-mastery, their liberal equity and their acumen schooled by engagement with demanding liberal disciplines. Boethius leaves no doubt that musical discernment is unique for the intimacy of its engagement with this quality, for 'nothing is more characteristic of *humanitas* than to be soothed by pleasant modes or disturbed by their opposite'.[2]

At Ravenna, Boethius must have heard the liturgies of the Catholics, and perhaps of the Arians, in some of the finest churches of the Christian West. Nonetheless, the transformations that Christianity brought to Graeco-Roman conceptions of musical ability make no impression upon his book. The chapters of Book 1, the most anecdotal and the least technical, give no indication that the literate elites of the West had become extensively clericalized in the fifth century, or that many sons of senatorial families in the provinces were now becoming bishops and presbyters charged with services for which trained singers were essential. To be sure, the *De Institutione musica* is concerned with immutable aspects of nature, and to a lesser extent with the mutable judgements of the ear, not with contemporary musicians, but this does not mean it lacks all connection with the musical life of Ostrogothic Italy. One passage mentions the vocal techniques used for the recitation of heroic poems, citing the authority of the Roman music theorist Albinus (whose writings do not survive) but quite possibly reflecting Boethius's own experience of public recitations and singing competitions (i. 12). There is also a sharp sense, mentioned above, of musical life conceived in terms of a slave society, by no means simply a dutiful imitation of Greek literary models. Nonetheless, there is no trace of Christian liturgical musicianship in contemporary Italy unless it be the disparaging reference to the 'harsher modes of the Goths', which are perhaps to be identified with the chants of Ostrogothic singers in the Arian Church of St Anastasia at Ravenna.

This is not to suggest that the *De Institutione musica* is unaccountably silent on a matter of moment to its principal concerns, but rather to establish an important contrast. In 500, there were men all over the West of senatorial family; none was precisely like Boethius, but many resembled him. They took unfreedom for granted, and their outlook was profoundly conservative at a time when accommodation to barbarian regimes was essential, as it was in Italy. In some regions, notably in central and southern Gaul, surviving letters show these men keeping in close contact with one another to sustain their sense of belonging to a privileged and cultured elite, and many of them shared Boethius's fondness (rarely his ability) for literary studies that might include writings of the Greeks

38   Isidore of Seville (d. 636) explains the difference between liturgical readers and singers (*Etymologies*, vii. 12). Bishop Isidore, who saw the singers and lectors of the Visigothic church ascend the pulpitum of his cathedral almost every day when he was in residence, maintains that readers should 'announce' (*praedicant*) scriptural teaching to the people and that singers should 'excite the minds of their hearers to compunction'. Isidore believed that readers could also achieve an affective result; indeed, they could move their listeners to tears when they delivered the text assigned to them 'with such pathos' (*ita miseranter*) that those present were overwhelmed. Cambridge, Trinity College, MS 368, fol. 92ʳ (detail). Anglo-Saxon, 10th c.

in Latin translation. They also shared Boethius's commitment to bringing the skills and culture of educated Romans to the service of barbarian monarchs, albeit at a less exalted level, and like him they gravitated to the royal palaces that had replaced the courts of emperors, Roman provincial governors and urban prefects as centres of political importance by the late fifth century. The contrast between these provincial figures and Boethius, however, lies in the way their reflection of his pedigree, learning and royal service, especially as it was cast upon the silken screen of clerical life in southern Gaul, encouraged them to view musical skill of a practical kind in a wholly different light from the great but ill-fated senator. In some parts of the West around 500, and notably between the Massif Central and the Mediterranean littoral of France, studious and spiritual young men of long-established family, who entered monastic or clerical life, could be highly valued if they were gifted singers of ritual music, notably when they passed to higher clerical grades without relinquishing their involvement in performance or teaching.

Two outstanding cases can be documented in the axial period between 450 and 530 that produced a new political order of kingship. The material comes from central and southern Gaul, which means that it reveals a particular social and political bias. The senatorial elites in central and southern France during the fifth and sixth centuries faced the hard political realities of political accommodation to barbarian rule as their counterparts did in Spain and Italy, but men of distinguished family among the Gallo-Romans were generally more inclined than their contemporaries elsewhere to seek clerical careers leading to bishoprics. Prelates in other parts of the West were often of less exalted stock, and the relationship between aristocracy and higher clerical office was correspondingly less clear. For the history of singers in the late antique West, no sources can compare with the letters of Bishop Sidonius Apollinaris or the writings of Bishop Gregory of Tours, the former from the highest rank of Gallo-Roman society and the latter proud of a lineage reaching back to late imperial Gaul. Sidonius, bishop of Clermont and brother-in-law of a Roman emperor, had no peer anywhere in the non-Italian West as a writer of letters during the late fifth century, while Gregory, a Clermontois who became bishop of Tours, compiled the largest body of historical and associated work in praise of saints prepared anywhere in the Occident during the sixth. Both of the two singers documented in their writings, by name and career, were men of good family themselves (the one praised by Gregory was his uncle, and therefore of the same distinguished lineage) and both were of high clerical rank, being either presbyter or bishop. What is more, they were decidedly not men of the Frankish hills and grasslands; the horizon of their lives, as recorded by Sidonius and Gregory, runs from the luminous city of Vienne by the banks of the Rhône, proud of its Roman past, up to the volcanic and mountainous landscape of Clermont with its somber churches cut from blocks of lava. In one case the story extends to Trier, even to Cologne, but that is precisely because a Frankish king and plainsman wanted clergy from the Auvergne to staff churches set by the Moselle and the Rhine.

An epitaph, a few letters, a sketch of an ancestor's career and a treatise on the nature of the soul: this is a small body of material with which to illuminate the lives of two singers whose combined activity spans the decades on either side of the year 500. Yet the authors upon whom we depend for it were not men of narrow horizon. Sidonius had known high office in Rome, and while Gregory of Tours has a more provincial mind, the career of the singer he praises had reached from Clermont to the lower Rhine, while the Merovingian kings who chose northern cities like Trier, Cologne or Rheims for their residences extended their power southwards during Gregory's lifetime in ways that did not leave him deprived of news from distant parts. The accounts that Sidonius and Gregory give of two singers in episcopal and royal service have much to reveal if they are read in terms of the major themes in the history of the late antique West that give

them a broader relevance. These two cases therefore welcome a historical prologue tracing the late Roman context, for while the singers these two writers
mention lived and worked in a post-Roman political order, they were valued precisely because they represented a form of continuity with the Roman past secured
by the traditions of their homeland, where the symbiosis between aristocracy and
higher clerical office was especially strong. They show the figure of the musical-
ly gifted and respected churchman, last seen in Chapter 7 among the deacons of
Rome, emerging into view for the first time in the Western provinces, enhanced
by the necessary accommodation between provincial elites of Roman background and the barbarian regimes as many urban sites shrank to a cathedral complex with new interstitial housing and public buildings slowly decayed for want
of interest in their original functions.

Cathedral Culture and the Cities

By the sixth century, when the city councils had mostly vanished, the number of
individuals capable of making an intervention in the Western cityscapes was
dramatically reduced from imperial levels and for secular public monuments was
virtually restricted to kings and prelates. Rulers that came into an especially rich
heritage of late Roman urbanism, as in northern Italy and parts of Africa, could
still nurse ambitions to create public monuments of a recognizably Roman kind.
A number of poems survive to commemorate the baths 'with glinting marble'
built by the Vandal king Thrasamund (496–523), while his contemporary
Theoderic the Great undertook major building works in Ravenna, Verona, Pavia,
Monza and Galeata. Theoderic also built 'an amphitheatre at Pavia, baths at
Pavia, Verona, Spoleto and Abano, and aqueducts in Ravenna and Verona'. As
late as the first half of the eighth century, a Lombard king could still speak of his
desire to plan 'royal baths with beautiful columns and marbles' until he decided
it would be better to build a great church instead. Yet in many areas of the West,
including most of those between the Loire and the Rhine destined to become so
powerful in Western geopolitics, the situation could be quite different. In Paris,
Rheims or Trier, a Frankish king might adapt a bathhouse, a governor's palace or
even an imperial audience hall for his own use, but he had no intention of building one, not least because the marble trade, or what remained of it by the sixth
century, was conducted very far from his heartlands.[3]

Some Western regions knew only *oppida* and villages before the Roman conquest, and they received the Mediterranean city too early for the roots to take
permanently in a new soil. These regions tend to be precisely the ones where
imperial power flickered and then failed in the first half of the fifth century. They
include Britannia, extensive parts of northern Gaul and much of northern and
central Spain with no Carthaginian heritage. In these regions, the history of
many Roman cities between 400 and 600, insofar as it can be reconstructed from

archaeological finds and literary sources, often shows progressive contraction around a fortified nucleus, material impoverishment and sometimes temporary or permanent abandonment of areas *intra muros*. The layers of waste and rubbish in the forums and theatres of Roman Britain are archaeologically legible by the fourth century; by the late 300s, market waste was being tipped into the forum at St Albans and the temple precinct at Bath was flooded, 'washing silt and mud into the courtyard, effectively marking the end of Roman use'. Metz, at least according to one recent (and contested) assessment, was virtually derelict by the seventh century and Toledo unable to fill all the seats in its massive Roman amphitheatre. The dispute over the fortunes of Metz provides a salutary reminder that the evidence is often sparse and liable to be interpreted in markedly different ways; overall, the picture is very diverse across the Western Empire and needs to be presented on a city-by-city basis; yet the general picture north of a line connecting Valencia, Lyon and Metz is generally one of slow transformation marked by the continued spread of houses and other structures that were no worse in material terms, perhaps, than those in which the general run of humanity had lived under the Empire; the difference by 500 was that such buildings were now encroaching into spaces that the Roman sense of a monumental cityscape required to be both clear and relatively uncluttered. When the fiscal and military system that sustained this sense of urban space decayed, many a Western city evolved like a garden left untended, gradually losing its planned vistas and *allées* as new growth sprang up as unplanned infill, or as corners no longer needed for habitation died for want of care.[4]

As many Western cities contracted, the bishops began to emerge as important figures in urban life and politics, ever more so as the city councils folded and the urban prefects vanished. To some extent, this picture of episcpal ascendancy is probably deceptive, despite the large quantity of sources conspiring to present it, for the bishops of the fifth and even the sixth centuries were engaged in a struggle to extend their influence over a great many private ecclesiastical foundations that have generally left a limited trace in the literary or archaeological evidence. The relatively abundant records of singers who served episcopal churches during the period 450–550, including all the earliest known with the title *cantor* as a term of office, reflect this struggle to establish the influence and prestige of the diocesan churches over a great many others, both in the episcopal cities and in their rural hinterlands. More systematic provision for the music of liturgical services was part of a complex process whereby the creation of a new and public religious institution 'carried with it new ideas of public justice, increasingly centralized control over ritual and doctrine, and new expectations of personal [Christian] virtue as a criterion for public office'. The general state of musical provision in the private foundations is much less clear and may have been decidedly variable. Contemporaries may often have judged that a team of trained singers in attendance for the Eucharistic service was a decidedly urban, public and episcopal entity.[5]

A late antique bishop had the right in Roman law to judge clergy and any lay-man who wished to be tried before him. He could be an emissary for his city and its representative, especially when a parley might avert some imminent danger; Pope Leo's journey to negotiate with Attila is only one example, albeit the most famous. To a king, who might have limited ability with the higher forms of self-expression in Latin, a bishop could be a valuable source of expertise in the Latin language and Roman vulgar law (see below, pp. 200–2). Holding his office for life, he inherited what could still be maintained of Roman public charges, some of them stable and routine, such as control of weights and measures, and others requiring ad hoc reaction to such emergencies as a famine or an outbreak of disease. Once in his seat, a bishop of any background might control more finan-cial resources in his city than the count or any other notable, and although his church generally dated from a time when the relatively good state of temples, theatres and other public buildings in the urban core meant that space was avail-able only near the walls (as at Geneva), and so in a peripheral position, the cathe-drals tended to gain in importance at the expense of the old forum area so that there are some Western cities today where the forum area is scarcely detectable. (At Brescia, for example, 'the forum is now in a quiet residential quarter of the old town'.)[6]

39 The city of Arles in the 7th c. The figure 2 marks what is almost certainly the original site of the city's bishopric, traceable from the middle of the 4th c. onwards, set in a corner of the Augustan walls. The figure 1 marks the site to which the cathedral was transferred some time before 500, in the heart of the city, facing the forum.

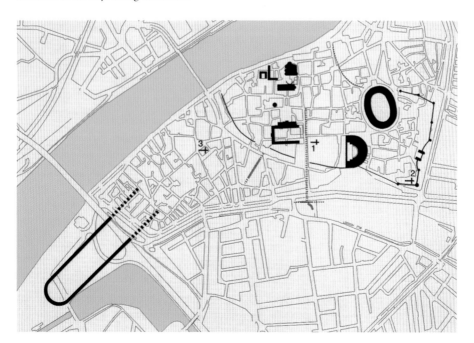

Only in the late fourth century could Christian communities and their leaders begin to raise the money, and secure the benefactions, necessary for the creation of an episcopal church, and while many Western cities must have acquired a cathedral by 500 the evidence for these buildings is for the most part extremely fragmentary and uncertain; it is often buried (if anything remains at all) beneath later structures, or must be recovered from texts that are often late. Many episcopal churches were built *intra muros*, but usually very close to the walls since, as mentioned above, they were generally the last public buildings added to the cityscape. Where any traces of a structure remain, the building suggested is often comparatively small (at Vienne perhaps no more than 23 m × 16 m), occupying a very modest proportion of the later medieval site. The bishop's church and its ancillary buildings (the *domus ecclesiae*) were often the only public structures by 400 that were still being maintained to a relatively high standard of craftsmanship, save when kings decided to intervene in the cities chosen as their capitals. Moreover, the cathedral complex was liable to be expanded and developed at a time when many of the older public buildings were receiving an infill of poor-quality domestic building, or what French archaeologists call *l'habitat parasitaire*. At Geneva, where excavations in the cathedral and *domus ecclesiae* have yielded especially important results, the cathedral grew in a corner of the third-century walls, acquiring many ancillary buildings which included an impressive audience hall of the fifth century, supplied with a heating system with floor mosaics (a reminder that a bishop exercised what amounted to a magistrature in the service of God, receiving his clients in a ceremony akin to the Roman *salutatio*). Beyond such a hall, a site like this might acquire chapels, reception rooms, dining rooms served by a kitchen, a baptistery, residences for senior clergy, lodgings for urban ascetics dwelling *in domo ecclesiae*, quarters for the bishop's wife (clerical celibacy was not yet the law: a married man could become a bishop), and a lodging house for guests or paupers, a *xenodochium*.[7]

By the first half of the sixth century, and in some cities earlier still, cathedral singers therefore worked in surroundings of some opulence relative to the degradation of older and originally secular (or pagan) public buildings, and the often indifferent quality of new constructions in the form of interstitial housing. The bishops and kings of the early Middle Ages espoused an Asian religion whose ceremonies, in their most exalted form, were associated with the luxurious material culture of sixth-century Italy under Theoderic or with Byzantine Rome and the continuing tradition of imperial gifts. The favoured materials of that bounty, like the silken and purple-dyed cloak offered to the Frankish king Clovis by the Emperor Anastasius I (491–518), and proudly worn by him at Tours, reflected the vast geographical scope of the Roman Empire's trading links across to India and even to China through nomadic intermediaries. Kings, bishops and abbots inherited from the Roman achievement a sense that liturgical and aristocratic culture at an exalted level should be defined by expensive materials sourced in different climates and brought over long distances, not simply obtained in the local markets where artisans, peasants and domestic staff obtained their farming tools, their cooking pots and their ceramic jars.

Claudianus of Vienne (d. 470–1)

Among the inland cities of the western Mediterranean, those on the banks of the Rhône below Lyon were still relatively well connected during the fifth century. As mentioned above (p. 24), the shipping college at Arles may already have been disbanded by as early as *c.*400, and the ports of Narbonne and Fos were going into eclipse, but the harbour at Marseille was still a crucial gateway from the Mediterranean into the Rhône valley route. Bulk goods such as the oil, papyrus 'and other wares' mentioned by Gregory of Tours were brought up from Marseille, together with more luxurious commodities that included the many kinds of spices sought by the Frankish kings at Metz, Reims or Trier. There were wealthy churches in southern Gaul, notably at Marseille, Vienne, Narbonne and Arles, proud of their deep Roman past and already possessing (or in the process of acquiring) cathedrals enriched by the abundant spoils of Roman public buildings left over from a rich tradition of imperial monumentality.

In the time of Claudianus, the city of Vienne was still a major late Roman site with an imposingly monumentalized centre and a continuing tradition of rhetors. The cathedral was of modest size, occupying only a small proportion of the later medieval site, and yet Vienne had every reason to maintain an exemplary clerical establishment. It was locked in competition with Arles, 'the Rome of Gaul', in a way that shows how easily the kind of rivalry between competing *civitates*, so well known in earlier phases of Roman history, could be translated into fifth-century terms as a rivalry of prelates and their churches. Vienne was a civil metropolis facing the challenge of a metropolitan *ecclesia* that claimed a continuous history reaching back to the apostolic period. Claudianus, the brother of the bishop of Vienne, held a secure place in the network of friendships and epistolary connections that kept the higher clergy of Gaul in contact. He corresponded with Sidonius Apollinaris, who commemorated his death in a long and revealing letter that includes an epitaph in verse. In addition, two of Claudianus's own letters survive, together with an extensive theological treatise, *De Statu Animae*, which places him in the front rank of contemporary minds.[8]

Claudianus was a presbyter and seemingly the member of a clerical dynasty since his brother was the bishop of the church in which he served. There is a clear case here of land and the highest clerical offices lying in the same hands. In central and southern Gaul, where the Roman tradition of using at least two personal names was still common among the presbyterate (Claudianus is really Mamertus Claudianus), an exceptional symbiosis between the landed aristocracy and the clergy gave special lustre to the highest grades of the clerical *cursus*. This had gradually been configured in the fourth century and was widely regarded as

40   Antique columns
reused for the first cathedral
of Narbonne. Narbonne,
Jardin de l'Horreum, rue
Rouget de Lisle.

the equal of the secular course in prestige. A southern Gallic prelate like Sidonius
Apollinaris, bishop of Clermont, could consider all grades of the clerical hierarchy, even the lowest, as superior to all secular offices *tout court*. The prestige of
the late antique bishop, as the leader of his clergy in what was liable to be the
most opulent building of the city, could scarcely go further than in Sidonius's
remark that 'the humblest ecclesiastic ranks above the most exalted secular dignitary'.[9]

Sidonius revered the presbyter Claudianus as a teacher:

> Gracious heaven! What an experience it was when we gathered to him for the
> sole purpose of having discussions! How he would straightaway expound
> everything to us all without hesitation and without arrogance, deeming it a
> great delight if some questions presented a labyrinthine intricacy which
> required him to ransack the treasure-houses of his wisdom![10]

The principal source for the life of Claudianus is the letter and epitaph that Sidonius wrote to a certain Petreius, otherwise unknown. Sidonius describes Claudianus as everything a bishop could reasonably expect from one of his presbyters, and more. He was 'a deputy (*vicarius*) in the bishop's churches', serving as celebrant in the cathedral when the bishop was absent, and at times in the episcopal foundations *intra muros*. He was also an agent (*procurator*) for the bishop as landlord, and an accountant or *tabularius*, supervising the records of rents and other revenues. He was also a 'counsellor in the bishop's court'. Sidonius also describes him as the bishop's companion in his private reading and his adviser on matters of scriptural interpretation. Fortunately, the epitaph Sidonius composed for him says more about the musical aspects of Claudianus's liturgical duties and skills:

> psalmorum hic modulator et phonascus
> ante altaria fratre gratulante
> instructas docuit sonare classes.
> Hic sollemnibus annuis paravit
> Quae quo tempore lecta convenirent.[11]

a singer of psalms and choir director; admired by his brother, he taught the trained companies to sing before the altar. He selected readings appropriate for each season for the yearly festivals.

Claudianus was an orator, a philosopher, a poet, a geometer and a musician or *musicus*. All these accomplishments imply the greatness of sentiment that prompts Sidonius to call a learned and fellow Gallo-Roman 'magnificent', *magnificus*, the term he applies to the scholar and lawyer Leo of Narbonne. But the term also implies greatness of action, and on this count it would be easy to miss what Sidonius admires in Claudianus. The last lines of the passage quoted above imply that Claudianus was involved in the compilation of a lectionary some time in the 450s and 460s. In retrospect, this may seem humble work, but it was not in the context of the fifth-century churches both East and West. The Jerusalem lectionary, with a choice of psalmody for each reading and surviving only in an Armenian translation, dates from 417–39, while the liturgical work of Pope Celestine I, which may have been comparable, dates from 422–32. More pertinent still is the lectionary with psalmodic responses prepared by a presbyter during the episcopate of Venerius at Marseille (428–52). Since Sidonius mentions Claudianus's work immediately after his proficiency as a singer and teacher of psalmody, it seems likely that he was engaged in the work of choosing a schedule of psalmodic responses to the lessons. During the fifth century this work of consolidation, so important to the development of the various liturgies, seems to have been proceeding across Christendom, presumably as one of the various ways in which bishops sought to extend their authority as prelates over the liturgical usages of private foundations whose rituals and endowments often escaped their jurisdiction. A prelate of the fifth century had much to gain from setting his liturgy, like his church, in stone.[12]

Sidonius does not call Claudianus a *cantor* in the epitaph. As a term of clerical (or quasi-clerical) office, *cantor* does indeed make its first recorded appearance during the generation of Sidonius, and in southern Gaul, but Claudianus had ascended too far in the clerical *cursus* to be called by the name of a minor order he had long since relinquished, if indeed he had ever held it. Instead, Sidonius gives him by the more grandiose and periphrastic title *psalmorum modulator*. The 'ranks' or *classes* whom Claudianus teaches 'before the altar' are perhaps best interpreted as the other clerics of Vienne, for the expression *ante altaria* was generally used to mean the area of ministry, the sanctuary; the meaning here is probably comparable to the sense implied in the pre-Christian Latin of Juvenal, who refers to making an oath before a votive altar in *Satires* 10. 268, or in the text of Deuteronomy 26:4, which describes the offering of first fruits to the priest. There seems to be no question of any lay presence in the part of the cathedral to which Sidonius alludes. Instead, the work of psalmody is somehow divided between the different ranks of clergy. *Classis* is often used in later Latin to denote a throng ordered into subgroups or files, whence the 'distinct classes' of musicians that Niceta of Remesiana attributes to Moses in his fourth-century treatise *De psalmodio bono*, or pseudo-Augustine's reference to the *classes* of string-players and singers among the Levites. Two centuries later, Aldhelm of Sherborne refers to psalmody *classibus . . . geminis*, 'with twinned companies'. In all these instances there is a sense of assigned musical functions in worship that involve a division into teams or some kind of subgrouping, comparable to the divisions of a military company. (Isidore defines *classes* as maniples, the small subdivisions of a Roman legion, in *Etymologies*, ix. 3. 60.) Sidonius's epitaph for Claudianus probably refers to some kind of divided labour in chanting, either antiphonal or responsorial psalmody, apparently among the clergy alone.[13]

In calling Claudianus a *phonascus*, Sidonius uses a rare and grandiose Graecism that has no doubt been carefully chosen both for its meaning and for its implied compliment to the Greek learning (mostly in Latin translation?) for which Claudianus was known. In Ancient Greek, *phōnaskos* meant 'one who exercises the voice, a singing-master, a declamation master', and Sidonius could have quarried the word in its Latin guise from Quintilian or Suetonius, two authors whom he names in his letters and evidently admired. Both of them use the word in senses close to the Greek, for it was evidently a specialized term. Suetonius mentions a *phonascus* who taught declamation at the highest level since he was one before whom an emperor might rehearse his speeches; another is a master given the unenviable task of training Nero for the competitions where he sang, declaimed and played the lyre. For Quintilian, the *phonascus* was a more exclusively musical figure and certainly more of a Greek: a singing-teacher who could 'tune his voice at leisure from the lowest to the highest notes', who looked after his body with great care; he could 'soften all sounds, even the highest, by a certain modulation of the voice', in contrast to the orator, who must often 'speak with roughness and vehemence, frequently watch whole nights, imbibe the smoke of the lamp by which he studies, and must remain long, during the course of the day, in garments moistened with perspiration'. In the epitaph for Claudianus, the word beautifully suggests both a precentor who would hear his singers rehearse and a singer in his own right who took such care of his voice as was consistent with his ascetic inclinations.[14]

In part, the interest of the Claudianus dossier lies in the way it shows how a kind of *musicus* who is entirely absent from Boethius's scheme in the *De Institutione musica* could nonetheless emerge in those ecclesiastical milieux where the bishops and presbyters were often reduced and provincial versions of Boethius himself. Claudianus and his brother, the bishop of Vienne, were Gallo-Roman aristocrats and members of a local clerical dynasty with impressive connections, not least because they were friends of Sidonius Apollinaris, who had known high civil office in Rome. Boethius had a vocation to translate the riches of Greek philosophy and liberal studies for the Latins, and by the standards of any age had the skills to fulfil it; Claudianus's reputation for expertise 'in three literatures, namely the Latin, Greek and Christian', was exceptional for southern Gaul in his time, and nothing else from there in the late fifth century rivals the ambition of his treatise on the soul, *De Statu Animae*.[15]

What of Claudianus's musical learning? How much does Sidonius imply by calling him a *musicus*? Educated Gallo-Romans in the late fifth century knew, with their contemporary Boethius, that the formal study of music was largely a Greek matter to be conducted with a great wealth of technical terminology. Claudianus certainly knew it. One of his two surviving letters addressed to a rhetor of Vienne named Sapaudus offers an appropriately rhetorical lament that the liberal studies of music, geometry and arithmetic (*musicen vero et geometricam atque arithmeticam*) 'are now cast out as if they were thieves'; the unexpected Graecism in the form *musicen* suggests that Claudianus had not forgotten where the fount of wisdom in musical matters lay. He also refers to 'Greece the teacher of all studies and arts' and elsewhere in his writings mentions Aristoxenus on music, geometry and arithmetic (materials he almost certainly did not know first hand) and Varro for writings on the same three subjects.[16]

It is difficult to assess what this means for the musical learning of a choirmaster in late fifth-century Gaul, although it is important to avoid the implication that if Claudianus and his friends did not pursue Greek learning in music then they *should have done* for the sake of their craft and its development as a literate and rational art. As far as we may discern, the musical art of the liturgical singer in the time of Claudianus was essentially oral. Only in the sense that there were records of the texts to be sung in psalters and other books was it a literate practice. There is no trace of musical notation in the Occident at this date, with the result that we do not know, and almost certainly never will, what actually happened when Claudianus sang a psalm in response to a liturgical reading, for example, at Mass. He and his contemporaries may have been the masters of an extemporized practice, compiling music on the spot from elements, learned during their apprenticeship, that provided them with melodic formulas, with ways to mark a pause in the sense of the text with a musical figure of the appropriate weight, and so on. In that case, the principal constraints were presumably that a singer should voice the appointed text in the expected way and bring his chanting to a satisfactory close. Simply speaking, it is possible for liturgical singing in this manner to contain no melodies if the term 'melody' means a contour of pitches judged more appropriate to its ritual purpose than anything likely to be achieved by improvising something on the spot or by making significant changes to the memorized material. The fact that Claudianus was involved in the compilation of a lectionary suggests that important elements in the liturgy of his cathedral of Vienne were still largely unproperized for much of his lifetime, and that the choice of psalm texts for any feast still lay with the bishop, who could no doubt delegate it to men such as Claudianus, where they were to be found. It would not be surprising, in such a context, if the musical materials of the psalmodic response(s) were not fully properized either, and that the liturgical meaning of the music used did not inhere in it being perceived as a fixed, canonical melody in the sense defined above. There is no sure sign in the Claudianus dossier that singers in a wealthy and prestigious see of later fifth-century Gaul felt either the practical need or the intellectual impetus to codify their materials and practice for the sake of teaching or memorization. If anyone could be expected to reveal that such work had begun, it would be Claudianus, but it seems he does not.

The musical terminology of the Greeks may have done little to commend musical studies to the Gallo-Roman elite of the late 400s, which produced no equivalent to Martianus Capella. Sidonius believed that 'the most stony teachings of philosophy' were those that required the student to master words like *diastemata*, a Greek musical term, and he supposed that the only option for a man who did not care for such things was to abandon the study of music altogether:

> music . . . cannot be made intelligible without these terms; and if anyone look down on them, as being Greek and foreign expressions (which they are), let him be assured that he must forever renounce all mention of this sort of science or else that he cannot treat the subject at all, or at least that he cannot treat it completely, in the Latin tongue.[17]

Despite the attention Sidonius draws to the Greek learning of Claudianus, fifth-century Gaul was probably not a place where anything more than a shadow of Boethius's competence could be found. The tone of what survives from the period is mostly Latinate, theological and literary, not Greek, secular and technical.

Theuderic and Gallus

In the first decades of the sixth century, a Frankish king who ruled in Reims, Cologne and Trier reached southwards to connect one of the great churches of his realm with what remained of the world Claudianus and Sidonius had known with its 'trained companies' of singers. This was Theuderic, king in what are now parts of north-eastern France, Belgium and the Netherlands. He and his line had come an immense distance in just some forty years. In 482, his grandfather Childeric had been buried near the Roman *castrum* of Tournai with costly regalia and a seal ring marked *Childirici Regis*, giving him his Frankish title but using the language of the Roman army (in which he had served) and of the Gallo-Roman population. The mourners also slew twenty-one horses, perhaps the entire stock of the royal stable, and placed the corpses in pits near the mound where the massive and entangled skeletons, eventually discovered and photographed, provide an unnerving reminder of what being a pagan could entail in northern Europe towards 500. Childeric was succeeded by his son Clovis, whose conversion to Catholicism provides a fine illustration of how personal inclination and shrewd political calculation could lead a pagan king to the font. A king could secure the loyalty and counsel of his bishops even if he remained a pagan, but baptism recast his cooperation with them as communion, a Christian fellowship with men who might wield considerable influence in their cities, and whose synods could give a distinctly sub-imperial tone to a king's instruments of Christian government. There was no independent source of prestige to compare with what Clovis could derive from being regarded by Gallo-Romans as a kind of Roman governor writ large by an autonomy that did not prevent him from receiving imperial gifts like the purple cloak he proudly wore at Tours, and which was not diminished by accepting the title of king and an honoured place in a version of the Roman political order that he had done so much to preserve. To put it another way, there was very little reason to continue resisting allegiance to the Roman religion, and around 500 (the precise date is disputed) he was baptized a Catholic.[18]

Clovis divided his realm amongst his sons, one of whom was Theuderic (Map 3). The most important cities in his heartlands were Cologne, Reims and Trier, but only the last of these had the lustre of being a former imperial capital. The emperor Valentinian had established his court at Trier in 347 to be near major theatres of war, bringing the imperial administration from Rome and inspiring a strain of pastoral verse, including the *Mosella* of Ausonius. (One could not have an imperial capital set by a watercourse that did not figure among 'the rivers made famous by the songs of the poets', in the words of Sidonius Apollinaris.) Yet because the Moselle valley was prosperous, home to both administrators and military officers serving the court, the villas built almost up to the frontiers proved too tempting to Theuderic's ancestors, the Franks and others who lived beyond the last Roman trading posts, and there were many violent incursions.

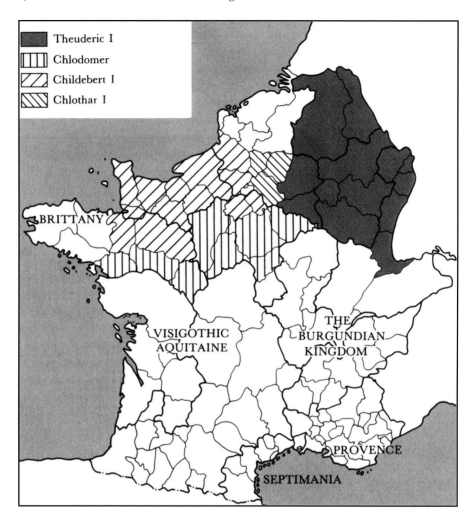

Map 3   Reconstruction of the Merovingian kingdoms in the generation after Clovis by Ian Wood.
The zone in grey marks the kingdom of Theuderic. After Ian Wood, *The Merovingian Kingdoms*,
Pearson Education Limited, © Longman Group UK Limited, 1994.

Confident that their strength would enable them to strike at the imperial court,
the Franks overran Trier in a series of attacks, leaving parts of the city severely
damaged. The citizens, eager for some sense of continuity, could perhaps have
convinced themselves that the reign of king Theuderic, when it finally came, was
another instance of public order being entrusted to a Germanic officer, creating
a regime that was only different from its antecedents in the sense that its chances
of survival in the medium to longer term were unusually good.[19]

Theuderic probably exercised his royal power in Trier by using the imperial
basilica as the heart of his royal manor, ruling from the hall where the emperors

had once received reports from provincial governors and listened to the pane-gyrics of the poets. Theuderic also expected, as all the later Merovingians did, to receive such prestige luxuries as could still be brought in the thin stream of sup-ply that came up along the Rhône–Saône corridor from Marseille. He is proba-bly the Theuderic addressed in a culinary manual by a certain Anthimus, possi-bly a Greek or 'Syrian', a book which shows how well merchants who served as dealers in luxuries to assured markets, such as a royal courts, could still help a king in the most northerly of the Frankish kingdoms sustain a Mediterranean *romanitas* at his table as if he were a late antique senator of the Auvergne like Sidonius, with olive oil, pepper, ginger and cloves. Theuderic also recognized the responsibilities a Christian king bore to the Roman religion. Without usurping the charge of the bishop in Trier, he decided that he should ensure that the cathe-dral be staffed with able clergy, including gifted singers, in what ranks as the first recorded act of its kind in the annals of the new political order in the West.[20]

To accomplish this, he looked to the regions of Gaul further south, in the Auvergne. Theuderic's father Clovis had given his son extensive responsibilities in this region after the battle against the Visigoths of Alaric in 507, and Theu-deric led some raids described as very destructive by Gregory of Tours. Yet not all the king's involvement with the city was so damaging, although it involved another kind of plunder. According to Gregory of Tours, Theuderic 'brought many clerics from Clermont, whom he ordered to serve in the church at Trier'. Quintianus, the bishop of Clermont, was so vigilant on the king's behalf that he succeeded in recruiting a young man of excellent Gallo-Roman family, named Gallus. It is very fortunate that this man was Gregory's uncle, for the chronicler often speaks of his family in the *Libri Historiarum decem* and his collection of biographies, the *Liber Vitae Patrum*, devoted to distinguished Gallic churchmen of recent decades. Gallus, however, is one of the numerous individuals whom Gregory, with an appealing modesty, does *not* explicitly identify as a member of his kindred, but his account nonetheless provides a valuable and fairly detailed case history of a talented singer: a Claudianus for a northern king.[21]

With understandable warmth, Gregory describes Gallus as 'a man of the Auvergne whom neither the greatness of his birth nor the elevation of the sena-torial order nor his immense riches were able to turn away from the worship of God'. At this date in Gaul the term 'senatorial' probably indicates descent from distinguished members of the curial class in Roman Clermont, the *civitas Arvenorum*, and there is no doubt that Gallus, like Gregory, came from illustri-ous stock. Gallus could trace his descent from Vettius Apagatus, one of the Lyon martyrs of 177, through to the senator Leocadius of Bourges, whose house (so Gregory claims) became the first church of that city in the third century. Gregory celebrates the wealth and illustriousness of Gallus's background to glorify yet further his decision to abandon secular life and to enter a monastery. Refusing the marriage envisaged for him by his father, Gallus entered the monastery of Cournon near Clermont. At this time he was still a *puer*, an adolescent of marriageable age, but only just. Once the abbot of the house learned from Gallus's father that he was (reluctantly) prepared to see his first-born son enter a monastic community, he accepted him and conferred an unspecified clerical order upon him.

Gallus had 'a voice of wonderful sweetness with a sweet melodiousness', according to Gregory. When Bishop Quintianus of Clermont heard him sing at the abbey of Cournon, he recognized at once that he should be nurtured and taught in the *domus ecclesiae* of the church in Clermont, not left in a rural monastery. The bishop acted a 'spiritual father' to Gallus, and eventually King Theuderic took a hand in events, for it was evident to all that Gallus's 'voice was becoming more and more perfect with each day'. The king's policy of drafting clergy from Clermont to Trier was supposed to gather Gallus up and transplant him a second time, but in the event neither Theuderic nor his queen could let him go from their court. The queen especially loved him 'not only because of his beautiful voice but also because of his chastity'. Gallus was therefore kept with the royal family at Cologne. The bishop of Clermont had recruited Gallus from a monastery where he heard him sing, making this whole story a revealing instance of a talented singer who was plucked (perhaps against his will) from the monastic life by a bishop who was scouting, in effect, for musical talent with a cathedral in mind that was also a well-established channel to royal service. These were probably events of the 520s, and despite the scarcity of the sources at this date they may not be unparalleled. Within some forty years, and further down the Moselle, the cathedral of Metz had recruited at least one psalmist from the Visigothic territory of the Languedoc or perhaps from Spain, to judge by the presence within the Messine chapter of a singer with the Gothic name of Sinderic (see below, pp. 230–3). So in the Frankish heartlands between the Seine and the Rhine, and in only the second generation of Christian Frankish kings, there were those who believed that the best singers were those from the central and southerly parts of Gaul, such as the Auvergne, where aristocrats like Sidonius Apollinaris had enjoyed the twilight of the Gallic senators.

Although Theuderic's activities are unusually well documented, there is no reason to suppose they were exceptional; Gregory of Tours mentions them only because they involved one of his own ancestors and his native city of Clermont. When the kings assumed what remained of public power they also acquired the churches and took a proprietary (and by no means entirely spiritual) interest in their lands and governance. The changes that took place in the forty years between Childeric and Theuderic mark the emergence of a new political order whose triumph, should one wish to call it so, seems substantially qualified by the commitment of its royal masters to the state-cult of the old order and by the history of accommodation between indigenous Romans and incomers necessary to prepare the days of Theuderic's majesty at Trier. The kings offered a sub-Roman court to the bishops, to members of the residual senatorial class and to any others who did not wish to gamble on leaving their estates and making for

Rome or for Constantinople. To judge by Theuderic's actions, capable singers in the great churches of the realm, or in the travelling contingents that formed their private chapels, were a valued part of this sub-Roman continuation. For their political strength and their salvation, the kings needed liturgies on a lavish scale with gifted singers, supported by textiles, precious metals and imported glassware that raised the interiors of at least the cathedral churches to something meeting the western and royal conception of aulic art of the eastern Roman Empire. Such things gave an imperial profile to a reign as surely as any coins they struck in imitation of Byzantine originals.

Seeking an 'Ordo psallendi'

At Vienne and Trier, Claudianus and Gallus were responsible for what other contemporary sources call an *ordo psallendi*, or 'order of chanting', the term generally used throughout the period 450–800 to denote a schedule of sung interventions at Mass or Office. Between 461 and 491, the Council of Vannes ruled for a single *ordo psallendi* within the province of Tours to mark the shared Trinitarian commitment of its bishops. At the Council of Gerona in 517, the assembled prelates required a single order of Mass and *ordo psallendi* in the arch-diocese to follow the usage of the metropolitan church. Here, as so often, the issue of unity in the *ordo psallendi* is inseparable from the matter of the metro-politan's authority. At the First Council of Braga in 561, the work was still being done at the metropolitan level; the bishops ruled that there was to be one *ordo sallendi* and that monastic practices were not to be mixed with the morning and evening offices; they also legislated for the lectionary, requiring the same readings to be used at vigils and Masses on feast-days (*sollemnium dierum*). From being a local or at most a diocesan matter at Marseille in 428–52, the issue of liturgical uniformity, including uniformity of psalmody, had gradually become archi-episcopal and provincial. With the Fourth Council of Toledo in 633, it became kingdom-wide when the bishops called for one *ordo psallendi* in a Visigoth realm that was now Catholic: another posthumous victory for the Roman Empire.[22]

The question of what these sources mean by the imposition of a single *ordo psallendi*, or sometimes *psallendi consuetudo*, is considerably complicated (or per-haps it is simplified) by the likelihood that metropolitans were sometimes satis-fied with the removal of major anomalies between the usages of cathedrals in their archdioceses and were content to leave much of the rest to the judgement of the bishops, to local custom and to whatever orders of psalmody for the hours they judged to be appropriately 'monastic' in the sense of night and day obser-vance with an ascetic tone. The metropolitans, in other words, probably had a realistic sense of what could be achieved in the way of unification. When Caesarius of Arles commended a *psallendi consuetudo* to his clergy in the early sixth century he was asking them to adopt a quasi-monastic round of liturgical offices and used the term to cover the entire schedule of psalms, canticles and prayers for each Office. The *ordo psallendi* advocated by the Council of Tours in 567 comprised a detailed regulation for the psalmody of Matins, defining the number of psalms and antiphons to be sung in the different seasons.[23]

There is nothing here, at this date, to encourage the view that any *ordo psallendi* for either Mass or Office yet comprised a repertory of fixed melodies for particular feasts. For want of notated records, the problem of when such melodies began to arise is one of the most exasperating mysteries of the singer's art in late antiquity and the early Middle Ages, not least because it rests upon a history which may have a different profile for each cathedral church as it acquired its first Mass lectionary and its first stabilized choice of psalmodic responses to those readings for at least the principal feasts of the liturgical year. There are also many ways in which a text can be sung in a manner acknowledged to be the right one for a text at a particular liturgical moment without the appropriateness of the music to its ritual purpose necessarily being deemed to lie in repeatable musical events. If the key factor in the emergence of such a repertory is the existence of a *schola cantorum*, or at least a foundation of singers supported in the difficult task of developing and learning such a repertory, then there is no reason why such stabilized liturgical melodies should not have existed in some considerable quantities by 500 in such coastal cities as Naples, Carthage or Ravenna, where hints (but no more than that) of collegiate organization appear by that date, or soon after.

There may be some clue to the mystery in the many somewhat puzzling but enthusiastic references to 'antiphons' in Eastern and Western texts from the late fourth century onwards, suggesting that many churches in Christendom gradually acquired forms of cultic song after *c.*400 that were regarded as new and markedly appealing. Called 'antiphons', they were often sung in connection with psalms but were distinct from them, and were perhaps more closely connected to forms of secular song than the psalmody in use hitherto which had perhaps employed (and perhaps continued to employ) forms of intonation practice more remote from the idioms of Mediterranean lyric. This can be only speculation, although it is one way to read a curiously large and intriguing body of source material relating to the 'antiphon' phenomenon. What is clear, however, is that the meaning of *ordo psallendi* was progressively expanded between 450 and 650 from a schedule of psalms and canticles assigned for monastic or quasi-monastic offices to encompass a fixed schedule of texts to be sung, and eventually of fixed melodies, against a background which shows the concern for an *ordo psallendi* moving upwards from the level of the individual diocese to the ecclesiastical province and finally becoming part of much wider schemes in what would now be called the political affairs of realms and their national churches. The history of what singers were charged to learn and accomplish in the early Middle Ages is the history of the Western kingdoms becoming consolidated theocracies.[24]

9

SCHOOLING TO SILENCE THE LAYMAN'S VOICE

The Beginnings of 'Chant' in the Kingdoms

The Africans who gathered in the Church of Saint Augustine at Hippo Regius for the Sunday Eucharist knew they could look forward to some supervised community singing. A lector sang the psalm of the Fore-Mass while the congregation and the clergy together replied with a verse, or part of a verse, chosen to serve as the recurring refrain. Augustine's reference in one of his homilies to something he heard 'from the mouth of the singing congregation' during the performance of a psalm probably alludes to this form of musical interchange between lector and people. In Milan, Ambrose had cause to comment on the way a congregation might make a distracting noise during a liturgical reading when their attention wandered, but not in the performance of responsorial psalmody because they were occupied in singing. In the Catholic Church of Vandal Carthage, the people both sang and listened as the lector sang the 'Alleluia chant' or *alleluiaticum melos*, a ritual item that cannot be precisely identified but certainly seems to have involved lay participation, perhaps with an Alleluia refrain. By the fourth century these practices had already inspired Western poets to produce responsorial psalms of their own, explicitly entitled *psalmus responsorius* in one case because of the recurring refrain between each stanza (see above, Pl. 28). In the Eucharistic service, the Christians of late antiquity raised their voices in responsorial psalmody with the permission of their bishops and clergy.[1]

Why should it have been otherwise? Many bishops presumably discerned the same kind of profit in the psalmody of the Fore-Mass as in the cathedral vigils when the populace gathered to join the chanting of psalms, often led by urban house-ascetics. To praise the benefits of these vigils, as many fourth-century writers do, was necessarily to extol the virtues of having the laity join their voices in psalmody. No prelate speaks of these benefits with more enthusiasm than Niceta, bishop of Remesiana in what is now Serbia and the author of the outstanding late antique apologia for Christian music, the *De Psalmodiae Bono*. According to Niceta, Christians had rejected the sounds of the pagan tradition in its coarsest manifestations, associated with professional mimes and actors; in its place, they had chosen musical styles with a *christiana simplicitas*. Yet there was also a beauty in this musical simplicity for which Niceta makes no apology: psalmody is spiritually profitable because of its sweetness, and not in spite of it. A psalm 'penetrates the heart when it gives pleasure, is easily remembered when it is sung, and what the sternness of the Law cannot dispel from human minds, the psalms expel through the sweetness of music'. Niceta does not share Augustine's anxiety that the beauty of musical sound may be a distraction, even a seduction, although his claim that music rinses evil from the hearts of those more susceptible to the pleasures of sense than to the precepts of Scripture certainly provides scope for Isidore's view, expressed some two centuries later, that music was first introduced into Christian rites *propter carnales*: for the sake of those who worship more in the flesh than in the spirit. Nonetheless, Niceta and Augustine both assume that the outstanding value of adding music to a psalm lies in the way the beauty of musical sound can often affect the human person more deeply than purely verbal persuasion, partly because it involves participation. Much more dependably than a sermon or a psalm recited under the breath, a melody performed by a solo psalmist may induce *compunctio*, a sudden and sharp awareness of sinfulness, perhaps with a tearful dissolution of hard-heartedness. Singing in a group created a chanting brotherhood, what Niceta calls a *psallens fraternitas*. The surrender of the individual voice to the common chorus testified to the unity of the Church.[2]

Hence it seems all the more surprising that the voices of the laity were eventually silenced, for the most part. The history of Western music as a literate art is essentially the story of professionals, the cantors, performing liturgies that gave very limited scope to the singing voices of the congregation except in chants that were essentially litanies, both the *Kyrie eleison* and litanies in the familiar sense of invocations to saints. The more one ponders Niceta's enthusiasm for psalmody (and he was by no means alone in his opinions) the more counter-intuitive it seems that this silencing of the laity in most chants of the Eucharistic liturgy should ever have occurred. Were the reasons primarily musical? It is certainly possible to imagine how lector-singers might have evolved increasingly elaborate melodies for the solo sections of psalmody, with results that many bishops valued (despite the concession to sensuality) for the attention the psalmists commanded and for the affective reaction their music might produce. The psalmody of the Roman deacons, including the 'nectared singing' of Redemptus or the 'varied notes with voice and art' of Sabinus, suggests that the standards of musical proficiency were already high among the clergy in Rome by the end of the fourth century, as perhaps elsewhere. When Victor of Vita describes an Easter Sunday service at Regia in modern Algeria, held sometime between 455 and 477, he places the lector in the *pulpitum* to sing the *alleluiaticum melos* mentioned above; the people both sing and listen, yet the Greek term *melos* ('melody', 'song'), a poeticism for writers such as Ausonius, Sidonius and Prudentius, may

have been chosen to suggest musical qualities in this chanting that could eventually leave the laity just listening, their eyes and ears fixed upon a singer who
was raised above them in more senses than one. A point could have been reached
in many churches where clergy and laity alike accepted that psalmody was from
now on to be a specialized domain 'with voice and art', in the words of Sabinus's
epitaph. The custom of regarding psalmody as a form of reading, well attested in
the writings of Augustine and elsewhere, and of placing the singer in the same
pulpitum, might have facilitated the transition to a practice in which the singer
was heeded in much the same passive manner as the reader, with no more than
a concluding response, if indeed there were any.

No doubt other musical explanations for the general silencing of the laity
might be found, but the fundamental difficulty with them all will be the same:
there are no musical documents to substantiate them until a period when everything relevant had long since taken place. Comparative study of chants in the
Spanish, Milanese and Gregorian manuscripts has shed some light on pre-
notational phases of Western psalmody, but it cannot illuminate musical practices very much before the period when the melodies on which such studies necessarily depend first appear in decipherable form. The texts used for psalmody,
however, are another matter. Indeed, it may be possible to sketch another explanation for the silencing of the laity by recognizing that the history of ritual song
in Latin before the beginning of the notational record is as much an issue of
linguistic as of musical history. What matters is the structure of syllables.

The idea to be explored in this chapter is that the silencing of the congregational voice in liturgical chanting may be connected with the deepening differences between the conservative enunciation of liturgical Latin and the common
Latin speech in its most rapidly evolving forms. The reason for this is that the
difference between the two varieties was not just linguistic but *social*: the monks
and clergy, forming literate groups apart, were for the most part the only ones
trained to wield the liturgical variety. In other words, one way to understand why
the lay voices were generally silenced may lie in the liturgical consequences of the
linguistic situation that is commonly known today as diglossia.

Simply speaking, a diglossic situation arises when the common speech learned
at the mother's knee coexists with a heightened and often archaizing form of the
same language that is nobody's native tongue; instead, it is controlled by a literate and essentially conservative elite trained to wield it and inclined to associate
it with their privileges and status. They shift from their version of the common
speech into the higher register as circumstance demands. This was the position,
I suggest, to which the liturgical Latin of some Western kingdoms moved inex-
orably as the common Latin speech evolved, and as repertories of chant developed with canonical melodies, or with closely defined formulae and musical
idioms, that rested upon a learned and conservative, even a bookish, syllabifica-
tion of the Latin text to be sung. As many linguists have observed, in situations
where the higher register of the language in a diglossic situation is required,

speakers who cannot wield it cannot simply use their colloquial idiom and get by. *The expectation is that they will remain silent.* In most chants of the Eucharistic liturgy, it seems, that is exactly what happened.[3]

Cassiodorus and the Art of Being Careful

Given the care with which Saint Augustine weighs each concession to uneducated speech in his many writings, it is not surprising to find that the Fathers of the fourth century were generally emphatic that liturgical readings should be delivered in a careful and educated pronunciation. Ambrose of Milan forbids any kind of ill-tutored reading with *subrusticum . . . sonum*, an expression meaning clownish or coarse enunciation that he borrows, like other terms he employs in this context, from Cicero. The ease with which Ambrose places the delivery of liturgical lessons in the tradition of Cicero's oratory says much about the ethos of reading among the lectors, many of good family, who were gathered round him in fourth-century Milan. Saint Jerome, for his part, insists that young Christian women should enunciate with a studied elocution, and he would surely have expected the same from liturgical readers. As one would expect, the surviving grammars by Consentius, Pompeius, 'Servius', Priscian and Donatus, the mainstays of grammatical teaching in the early Middle Ages, are by no means permissive towards contemporary pronunciation in the common speech. Consentius, for example, probably writing in fifth-century Narbonne, strongly opposes the syncope that was developing widely, as Romance derivatives show, for he objects to *socru(m)* instead of *soceru(m)* and *salmentu(m)* for *salsamentu(m)*, both of which he had noticed 'in day-to-day converse'.[4]

The influence of such grammatical teaching depended in large measure upon the continuance of the grammarian's profession into the early Middle Ages. Here we should look first to Italy. Among the many letters that Cassiodorus drafted in the service of the Ostrogothic regime in the peninsula, duly collected and embellished in his *Variae*, there is one of *c.*533 in which king Athalaric asks the Roman senate to pay the stipends, by now overdue, owed to the grammar masters of the city. Few other documents of the sixth century, and few places other than Italy, can show such an apparently seamless transition from imperial governance to a barbarian kingdom with the system of state-funded positions for grammarians and rhetors apparently still intact. Nor indeed can anywhere outside Italy show a sixth-century king studying with a grammarian in the manner recorded of Athalaric. He was a minor when he took the throne, and his mother Amalasuintha wished him to be educated like a Roman gentleman; by now, the royal line of the Amals had considerable experience presenting itself as the guardian of *civilitas*, implying a quality of discernment in matters of ethics and social order akin to the exercise of an educated literary taste. Despite the resistance of a powerful Gothic faction at courts, Amalasuintha believed that the king-

41   A milestone (this one *does* carry marks of distance) set up on the Roman road from Toulouse to Narbonne, between 306 and 308. 'To the Emperor Caesarius Flavius Valerius Constantinus, most noble Caesar, son of the divine Constantius, *pius* and *augustus*, nineteen miles'. Toulouse, Musée Saint-Raymond, Inv. 31017.

dom had found in her son a ruler who could be the embodiment of a Romano-Gothic Italy. In the time of Athalaric, Italy could still show tight social networks of grammarians and pupils who might be the wards or the nephews of important men, and there were still professional judges for the literary competitions that were being held.[5]

The prospect of a distinguished career in one's home city, with service on the city council, an occasional speech in some good cause and a display of munificence meant little by the sixth century except as the kind of history that families celebrated wherever it was considered the best pedigree for a bishop, as it was in central and southern Gaul. The accompanying contraction of literacy is very apparent in the preponderance of epitaphs for bishops, deacons and presbyters – that is to say for literate clergy – in the Western epigraphic record for 450–600, and in the absence of any royal equivalent to the imperial 'milestones', those billboards of stone that the emperors placed along the axial roads of their dominions (Pl. 41). Often lacking indications of distance, these pillars reminded travellers of an emperor's names and titles, part of the Empire's rich tradition of wayside literacy that was also carried forward with statues set upon inscribed bases, with tombs and with votive altars. The barbarian kings' indifference to such public inscriptions reflects the virtual disappearance of a vast and literate constituency on the move that the Western imperial government had once sought to impress and persuade.[6]

As the literacy of government contracted in most of the kingdoms, so the literacy of cultic activity increased beyond anything a Greek or Roman polytheist could have anticipated from his experience of domestic or temple religion. The members of a pagan cultic group might have curses to engrave on plaques of lead, votive inscriptions to commission or registers of members to maintain, but their worship did not form a glimmer of devotion around holy writings declaimed and then interpreted in public assemblies. For Christians, it was a different matter. The salvation of the immortal soul from eternal punishment, an unintelligible concern to the Roman polytheist, had nonetheless become what Romans could recognize as an essentially grammatical concern. Salvation rested upon certain canonical texts, the Holy Scriptures, that were to be copied, emended, studied and interpreted by those qualified to do the work. Since the biblical commentator could perform his task proficiently only if he had a good knowledge of secular arts such as dialectic, the skilled commentator upon Scripture gradually moved into the space vacated by the vanishing secular grammarian and could even claim to be keeper of the biblical and Mosaic wellsprings whence (Christians often claimed) the arts of the pagan secular teachers had sprung. Despite the importance of these labours, however, the schooling of future clergy was bound to remain essentially private, familial and even paternalistic in a West where most cities were shrinking, where careers on a pan-European scale were becoming increasingly rare and where the flow of fiscal income was often much reduced from early imperial levels. Teaching could take place wherever those who possessed the requisite skills were in regular contact with those who did not, often because they were living with them in some form of familial cohabitation. This might be a 'monastery' within the house of a bishop, the house where a group of urban ascetics lived together, the dwelling of a rural priest and no doubt many other kinds of place and context.

The task of giving an authoritative example of proficient Latin speech, as of accomplished Latin writing, principally fell to the bishops and the higher clergy. The bishops in synod became the closest equivalent to the old trans-imperial class of administrators, legists and senators responsible for maintaining an educated norm in Latin enunciation. Some lines of continuity between the two groups can be identified. The bishops, and indeed the Western clergy as a whole, were generally drawn from the same social classes as the secular administrators in the fourth and fifth centuries, and the prelates often formed a hereditary class, inheriting their offices in the manner common enough with the Praetorian Prefecture. Putting aside for a moment the question of how the educated Latin of different periods and churches might be characterized, it seems very likely that the use of a schooled Latin was the mark of bishops who recognized the gravity

42   Mosaic showing the abduction of Europa, reconstructed from fragments found in the 4th-c. Roman villa at Lullingstone in Kent. The image carries an elegiac couplet INVIDA SI TA[VRI] VIDISSET IVNO NATATVS / IVSTIVS AEOLIAS ISSET ADVSQVE DOMOS ('Had jealous Juno seen the swimming of the bull / she would have had yet more reason to go to the hall of Aeolus'), alluding to Virgil's *Aeneid*, i. 50, where Juno persuades Aeolus, god of the winds, to destroy the ships of Aeneas by stirring up a storm. Allusions to Virgil's poem, or direct quotations from it, have been found in many different contexts (some of them little more than graffiti) from many parts of the Empire, attesting to the trans-imperial Latin literary culture of the educated.

of their responsibilities and the illustriousness of the Christian imperial past that the traditions of their office brought into the present. The treatise on Latin spelling addressed by one Agroecius to Bishop Eucherius of Lyon (434–50) revealingly praises the bishop for taking the Latinity of his clergy in hand; just as he seeks to correct their lives, so he corrects their Latin orthography. When bishops were conscientious, especially in areas like southern Gaul where prelates were often drawn from the landed aristocracy, such episcopal care for the Latinity of the cathedral clergy was probably common. There is no mistaking the disgust that Bishop Gregory of Tours felt when he heard a slave in flight pretending to be a priest and saying his prayers 'in a rustic and filthy' speech.[7]

Political changes had produced some major reversals in the more familiar kinds of relationship between language and temporal power. In a manner that reverses the most fundamental relationship of all, whereby the language of the powerful is the tongue that principally commandeers written record, the native

Germanic languages of the incoming warrior elites in Gaul, Spain and Italy were rarely committed to writing. Until the eighth century, the Frankish tongue was banished to the exile where languages that the Romans judged too coarse for grooming with the alphabet lay unwritten, while the Gothic version of the Scriptures composed in the fourth century was a resolutely literal rendition of the Greek into a Gothic corresponding to nobody's speech in either Italy or Spain. Latin, in contrast, continued to be used for liturgy, for the issuing of law codes, for charters, for all other administrative documents and for the proceedings of ecclesiastical councils. However proud the kings became, the juridical and conciliar documents they directly or indirectly issued were written in a language that showed who they were *de jure* if not *de facto*. They were incomers ruling in the West as delegates of a surviving Roman imperial power.

Hence a bishop's Latin speech could be a powerful tool. When Bishop Remigius of Reims addressed a letter to the Frankish king Clovis around 486, congratulating him on his accession to the throne, he deliberately irradiated the king with the exalted Latin idiom that it was his privilege as a Gallo-Roman bishop to wield. (According to Sidonius, the experience of reading Latin poetry by Bishop Remigius was like passing one's finger 'over plaques of crystal or onyx', the language was so smooth.) In his letter to the king, Remigius makes a judicious concession to the new political order by evoking the kingdom or *regnum* that Clovis must govern with justice, but he defines the king's scope of royal action as *administratio*, a term of art from Roman law whose tone is far from suggesting the kind of kingship, with murderous dynastic competition, that came naturally to Clovis and indeed to many a late Roman emperor. In language that owes much to the tradition of panegyrics in praise of emperors and consuls, but also to the pastoral letters of bishops, Remigius requests and requires the king to care for the afflicted, to nourish orphans and to provide for widows. He discreetly refers to the king's *populus* in the Roman manner, not to his *gens* or 'tribe', and calls the subjects of the kingdom 'citizens', but he takes care in addressing Clovis to describe them as 'your fellow citizens', *tui cives*. The Latin language could not give a more succinct and shrewd expression of the new political order than the expression *tui cives*, giving Clovis an aura of *romanitas* that subtly implies he is the citizens' magistrate.[8]

For some indication of what a schooled and ecclesiastical Latin enunciation meant in the sixth century we can return to Cassiodorus and his *Institutiones*. In this short book, Cassiodorus emphasizes the need to have correct and pure texts of the Scriptures. Scribes must exercise the greatest care in copying from good and preferably venerable exemplars; readers must always be alert to mistakes and the need to correct them. In contrast to the labours of the secular grammarians with their copies of Virgil, however, there were certain respects in which the transactions of a Christian scholar with Scripture were not like those of his secular counterpart. Virgil might be 'divine Virgil' to some, but his text was not holy. Thus while a secular grammarian might expect to emend his texts of the poet on the basis of good Latin usage in lexis and grammar, Cassiodorus warned his readers that the Latin Scriptures contain many passages where the eloquence of its divine author does not accord with the merely human rules of grammar, and where some figurative expressions may seem distinctly odd. In the less contentious cases, Cassiodorus advises that scribes should be careful about adding or subtracting the letter *m* (which can mark a difference of case, as in *causa* and *causam*) and should correct any cases of *b* written for *v*, of *v* written for *b*, and of *o* written for *u*. In part, these errors reflect phonetic changes in the common Latin speech that caused scribes to become careless or indifferent in the way they used traditional Latin spelling. When Cassiodorus declares that scribes must avoid putting *o* where *u* is needed, for example, he is referring to confusion arising from the normal Romance evolution of Latin *ō* and *ŭ* into a single sound, whence vōcem > Italian *voce* and crŭcem > Italian *croce*. Latin manuscripts of the period 500–900 abound in misspellings (if one wishes to call them that) which confuse *u* and *o* of any origin, such as such as *negutia, matrimunium* and *volontas*.[9]

To ensure that the scriptural texts he placed in the library at Vivarium were duly corrected, Cassiodorus collated them with ancient manuscripts by having others read aloud from the exemplars as he scanned the copies to be corrected. Consider this process as it might have worked in relation to words from Genesis 28: 17: *non est hic aliud nisi domŭs dei*, 'this is none other but the house of God'. If confusion of *o* for *u*, mentioned above, intervened *in pronunciation* then Cassiodorus would have heard his reader say *domos* rather than *domus*, the latter being grammatically correct. But how was Cassiodorus, as he listened, to determine whether the incorrect accusative plural *domos* he had just heard was an example of the way divine eloquence, as manifest in Scripture, often ignores the merely human doctrine of cases, and of grammatical agreement, with results that are not to be emended away? The problem would not have arisen if the pronunciation used by Cassiodorus's readers followed the spelling of the old copies on an essentially sound-per-letter manner so that the sounds of *domōs* and *domŭs* were still distinct (but not necessarily retaining the old quantities). To judge by other remarks Cassiodorus makes, he required a Latin elocution in which initial or intervocalic *v* would not be voiced as *b* (compare verbena with Tuscan dialect *berbena* and French *verveine*), and in which *quod* and *quot* would be kept distinct. His method needed what he calls a 'diligent reading' or *sedula lectio*.[10]

Perhaps it is not to be expected that the enunciation of Latin in the liturgy, both in reading and singing, would be as exacting as the elocution used when attempting to correct faulty books by reading aloud from venerable ones with a superior claim to accuracy. Yet Cassiodorus insists that readings of a purified scriptural text should themselves be pure and intelligible. In his separate treatise on spelling, *De Orthographia*, he envisages one reader saying, with justice, that 'we cannot render with our voices what we are not able to understand when we see it written'. The purpose of purifying a text by careful emendation of spelling and grammatical errors was not just designed to achieve a lucid understanding; it was also to produce a correct reading in the context of the liturgy, or what Cassiodorus calls an *inoffensa pronuntiatio*. This presumably means that most (and perhaps all) of the faults regarded as errors of spelling were also errors of speaking and for the same reason, namely that they obscured or changed the sense. If it was important to write *bibere* and not *vivere* in a particular passage of Scripture then it was just as important to distinguish their pronunciation.[11]

The pronunciation used by Cassiodorus's readers probably reflected the elocution of the best readers in the Roman Church of the sixth century, and what was required of lectors in this domain was probably required of singers who were also charged to enunciate Holy Scripture in the Eucharistic service. (Some of the singers in fifth-century Rome, perhaps most of them, were probably both readers and singers, as argued above in Chapter 5.) The act of singing vowels and consonants may introduce or require many departures from the phonology of the spoken language, as every singing teacher knows, but there is no obvious reason to assume that the standards of elocution maintained by the most accomplished and conscientious singers were any different from those of the readers, especially since by a long tradition in both the Eastern and the Western churches they were often one and the same.

Augustine and the Art of Letting Things Pass

No author of late antiquity speaks with more fervour or articulacy about matters of communication in Latin than Augustine, a professor of rhetoric turned bishop for whom the language of the Latin Bible, whether it be the *Vetus Latina* or Jerome's new version destined to become 'the widespread Bible', *biblia vulgata*, was a stabilized and written variety of the African vernacular that supervened over Punic and Libyan. Augustine was sharply aware of the different varieties of speech he heard around him; his congregation included young men with an ambition to become judges, literate men who would be advanced students of grammar and rhetoric; there must also have been well-educated slaves, some perhaps tutors in letters and grammar to their masters' children, together with traders and merchants with at least the rudiments of a functional literacy. At a lower point on the social scale were the simple artisans: the potters, weavers, midwives and others whose preponderance in the Christian communities of the second century had seemed so scandalous to Celsus.

Referring to the Latin speech of Africa, Augustine distinguishes between *latinum*, meaning the usage of the educated when speaking amongst themselves, and verbal exchanges conducted *vulgi more*, 'in the common manner', and he recognizes that it is sometimes necessary to permit vulgarisms of speech in homilies, readings and psalmody. In one case, he heard a grammatical mistake 'in the mouth of the singing congregation' and pondered what should be done. This occurred as the people sang the last verse of Psalm 131 (132) – presumably the congregational response – using the words *Super ipsum autem floriet sanctificatio mea*, where *floriet* is a grammatical error for *florebit* or *efflorebit*. Augustine is quite explicit that he heard this mistake as the congregation sang (*de ore cantantium populorum*). There is nothing mysterious about this mistake, which probably arose because many illiterate members of Augustine's congregation spoke a Latin in a state of rapid evolution; their speech, not generally constrained by the conservative influences of written grammar and spelling, was beginning to lose distinctions that they intuitively deemed to be redundant, or which they were encouraged to ignore by the erosion of final syllables that had once served as inflectional markers but no longer did so. In Augustine's example from the psalmody of Hippo Regius, the second-conjugation verb *floreo* has shifted into the fourth conjugation, the kind of category mistake that may often occur as a form of speech evolves by levelling forms into parts of the system, where they do not belong by analogy. There are other indications in Augustine's writings of changes in the common speech. His uncertainty whether it was best to write and say *inter homines* or *inter hominibus* probably reflects a hypercorrection by those who were using accusatives when they knew they should have been employing ablatives, but it may also may reflect a weakening of the termination *-ibus* in the common speech of Africa. Augustine's willingness to defend the form *fenerat* for *feneratur* suggests he was prepared to see deponent verbs abandoned if that were necessary for effective communication. These verbs, passive in form but active in meaning, were prime candidates for the kind of systemic regularization that is often found as a speech evolves without the restraints of a literate norm. All three of Augustine's linguistic examples, *floriet/floreBIT, inter homines/inter hominiBUS* and *fenerat/feneratUR*, suggest the erosion of final syllables in certain contexts, and at different rates, according to the education and pretensions of the speaker.[12]

The broad outlines of the picture coming into view here are not difficult to trace. In much of the West, the common Latin speech was the basic means of communication, although it existed in many different varieties and registers: some closely influenced by the conservatism that literacy inspires, others entirely free to evolve. There was a body of texts in Latin, the Holy Scriptures, which had to be preserved in a written form and protected from the encroachment of any radical linguistic changes taking place in the common speech, even though these texts were in some measure a transcription (using standard Latin spelling) of a raised version of the common vulgar tongue, whence the 'Vulgate'. A small elite of monks and clergy now exercised a long-term (but not wholly exclusive) monopoly over the tradition of literacy, and therefore over the crucial documents that expressed the community's Christian values. To view this situation in theoretical rather than in historical terms is to recognize that all the essential conditions were present for the rise of diglossia: a state when 'two or more . . . varieties of the same language are used by some speakers under different conditions'.[13]

Augustine, confronted by the necessity of allowing some carefully sifted elements of substandard Latinity into his church, seems never to have reached the limits of his patience. He was nonetheless one among many, in the fourth century, who felt that communication with untutored Christians posed many problems. 'Between the oral usage of the people and the system of the written tradition, even when written Latin was read out, there were differences which were of a systemic nature, even if they were apparently peripheral.' How long would the clergy wish, or feel themselves able, to maintain the humane pastoral care of Augustine in this respect? The alternative, perhaps in many ways an attractive one, was to identify clerical and especially sacerdotal authority ever more closely with the mastery of a schooled Latin for readings, psalmody, prayers, blessings and homilies. It is vital to recognize that this development would not necessarily have hindered communication with the unschooled or illiterate members of the congregations; as late as the eighth century, clerical writers in Gaul and elsewhere still took it for granted that untutored Christians could follow the meaning of texts which prove (when they can be inspected today) to be written in more or less traditional Latin. Lay congregations retained their *passive* competence in a schooled, conservative Latin for some four hundred years after the creation of the Vulgate Bible by Jerome. Their *active* competence, however, was becoming progressively weaker.[14]

There is a linguistic basis here for explaining the silencing of lay participation in the responsorial psalm of the Fore-Mass and in chants more generally. In addition to any musical factors that can no longer be traced, but can perhaps be faintly glimpsed in some literary testimony, the practice of lay participation in psalmody may have been hastened to its end as the literate administrators, scribes, senators and military commanders of the Roman Empire surrounding Augustine on every side gave way to a situation in which literacy, and the public use of a schooled Latin, was increasingly restricted to monks and clergy. This Latin became one of the ways in which the clerisy was configured as cultic group, other means being the abundant legislation of synods and councils governing sacerdotal authority and identity, both social and sexual. In regions where the educational traditions of the Empire had survived best, including much of Italy, southern Gaul and seventh-century Spain, this was a continuation of the high standards demanded by Ambrose or Jerome; for others, less well supported, it may simply have meant a conscientious effort to lift liturgical elocution above the stream of the *sermo vulgaris*. This was something that the sheer density of scriptural words with no living counterparts in the common speech (like *equus*, *vir* or *ignis*) probably encouraged many clergy to do.

None of this requires one to assume that Latin was always pronounced in the same way or was always enunciated well; the quality of the vowels must have varied very greatly – spelling variations give ample evidence of that, especially in Gaul – and so must the manner of articulating or not articulating the written consonants. But the issue here is not only pronunciation in this sense *but also the syllabic integrity of words*, a matter of much concern to later grammarians like Consentius. Brief congregational responses by the laity, like *et cum spiritu tuo*, were probably frozen into a correctly syllabified form by the brief melodic formulae used to chant them, just as they still are today wherever Catholics celebrate a Latin Mass, regardless of their native tongue. Yet the more varied and elaborate responses the congregations were required to make during responsorial psalmody were another matter, for it is possible to imagine how the kinds of licence tolerated by Augustine were multiplied by time beyond anything the bishops would accept. (See below, p. 372, for the case of *Tu illum adjuva* licensed to be sung in an eighth-century public litany as *Tu lo juva*.)

If this is correct, then the silencing of the laity belongs in the political and social context of the late Empire. Both East and West, the voice of the common citizen was increasingly weak or occluded from the fourth century onwards. In the imperial administration, the decline and eventual disappearance of the rescripts meant the end of the practice whereby emperors dictated a reply to be written at the bottom of a petitioner's letter, communicating directly with private individuals anywhere in the Empire and creating law in the process. The level of rescripts fell sharply under Diocletian (284–305) and they disappeared not long afterwards. The number of recorded embassies to the emperors from cities and provincial councils also fell considerably. The palace administration, much enlarged, gathered around an increasingly hieratic and proto-Byzantine notion of the imperial presence like clergy around an episcopal celebrant at the altar.

The final words, in more senses than one, belong with the musical sources: the antiphoners, cantatoria, sequentiaries and missals that begin to appear around 900. These offer material from much of Latin Christian Europe, giving the text and the music, according to region and date, of the Frankish–Roman, Roman, Ambrosian, Mozarabic and Beneventan repertories. No manuscript of chant has yet been found which provides substantial evidence for the liturgy being sung in anything other than a hypercorrect Latin with most developments in the common speech or *sermo vulgaris* diligently suppressed. For a precise example one might turn to the responsory *Justus ut palma florebit*, published in facsimile in substantially over a hundred versions. There is no trace anywhere in this material of the mistake made by the members of Augustine's congregation who sang *floriet* instead of *florebit* in another text as the conjugation system of the fourth century began to drift in their common speech. One would not necessarily expect a fourth-century African error to be represented in a book from twelfth-century Milan or Tours, yet Augustine is describing a systemic error of major importance for the evolution of spoken Latin, not some passing slip of the tongue. A wider search shows that with the exception of a few forms like *domnus* for *dominus*, one would never know from thousands of pages of notated Latin in the plainchant manuscripts of 900–1100 that syncope of short medial vowels had ever occurred in Latin speech to produce a form like Old Occitan *dons* (<DOMI-NUS). As far as one can tell when complex neume figurations cluster over the

words of a text, the notation articulates every written syllable whether it be initial, medial or final. Configurations with yod like 'iu' in *consilium* are dutifully syllabified (*con-si-li-um*), staunchly resisting the development to *konseljo that had probably already taken place by the fifth century in Gaul, for example. Words beginning with s + consonant are notated, with remarkable regularity, in ways that show the same resistance to spoken developments and the same insistence upon the indications of traditional Latin spelling. Thus the prosthetic 'e' that developed in this context throughout many parts of the Romance area is very rarely acknowledged by the musical notation; confronted with STELLA or SPERARE, singers of the tenth century onwards did not sing an ancestor of French *étoile* or Spanish *esperar*. The Latin in these plainsong manuscripts is so familiar that one may readily forget how extraordinary it is. The noted chantbooks reveal a long tradition of highly conservative Latin elocution in liturgical psalmody that eventually left no place for the layman's voice.[15]

10

MINISTERS OF MUSIC IN THE SIXTH-CENTURY KINGDOMS: DEACONS AND CANTORS

Deacon Psalmists in the Kingdoms: Vandal Africa and Southern Gaul

An impressive sequence of Latin poets can be traced in Vandal Africa around 500. Their verses are as sensuous, in a somewhat studied way, as one would expect from authors living in a great port-city like Carthage whose hinterlands formed a grain basket for Rome. They speak of mosaics, richly dressed tables and precious textiles, a décor that seems as thoroughly Roman as anything described a generation earlier by Sidonius Apollinaris in southern Gaul. The African poets praise the culture of a city that 'abounds in teachers', maintaining the distinguished African tradition of schooling in Latin grammar, and in some poems they heap praises upon the Vandal king Thrasamund (496–523) for building public baths of rich marble like an emperor or a Roman civic dignitary (see below, Pl. 45). In pursuit of royal favour, and perhaps of a continuing political accommodation between Afro-Romans and Vandals, these poets generally pass in silence over the confessional divide between Catholics and Arians, just as they ignore the phases of persecution, chronicled by Victor of Vita, when Vandal kings imitated Byzantine methods for dealing with heretics but turned them against the Catholic population. The churches and clergy of Africa rarely make an appearance in their work.

A notable exception appears in four lines by Luxorius, one of the most prolific of these Afro-Roman authors. They form an epigram that mocks a cleric for indulging too deeply in the metropolitan pleasures of Carthage:

> Quid festinus abis gula impellente, sacerdos?
> an tibi pro psalmis pocula corde sedent?
> pulpita templorum, ne pulpita quaere tabernae,
> almina quo caeli, non phialas referas.

Wherefore, O priest, do you hasten away, driven by gluttony? Surely your mind is fixed on goblets rather than psalms? Seek not the benches of taverns but the lecterns of churches, the food of heaven, not drinking vessels.

This poem carries a title that identifies the *sacerdos* in line 1 as a deacon 'hastening to an inkeeper's dinner'. That may well be the intended meaning conveyed by *sacerdos* here, for these verses survive in a collection traceable to a lost original of 532–4 where several other poems by Luxorius bear titles that provide information not found in the lines themselves; they may be his own. (It is technically incorrect to call a deacon a *sacerdos*, but Luxorius is using the word as a classicizing substitute for the specialized Christian term *diaconus*.) He associates his victim's clerical duties with the Psalter ('Surely your mind is fixed on goblets rather than psalms?'), and while this might be read as a fling at the deacon's general want of devotion, epigrams usually seek more precise targets so that they can display a better mastery of their weapons. Line 3 provides the necessary clarification by mentioning the raised tribune or *pulpitum* that was used by lectors and psalmists and which also appears in a slightly earlier text from Vandal Africa (see above, p. 196). Since the congregations would most often have heard psalms from the *pulpitum* delivered as the psalmody of the Fore-Mass, it seems that this deacon sometimes served as a psalmist when he exchanged the church for the tavern.[1]

Deacon psalmists have already appeared in Rome (see Ch. 7), and with this poem by Luxorius they make an appearance in Vandal Carthage. Perhaps it would be too zealous to consider the deacon psalmist as a trans-Mediterranean figure, but the archaeology and communications of the late Roman world abundantly suggest how such a custom might have become established. The maritime route from Carthage to Rome created the tax spine finally broken by the Vandal conquest of 439 when African grain ceased to cross the Mediterranean in the great transporters. The movement of grain and oil to Rome, the extensive African properties of Roman senators prior to the Vandal incursion, and the wide dissemination of African products (notably the famous red tableware known as African Red Slip or ARS) all suggest that a wide and busy corridor of communication had long been open between Rome and Carthage where the transporters docked to collect their cargo. The custom of entrusting psalmody to deacons in Carthage, and perhaps beyond in the African churches, may therefore be much older than Luxorius's poem, and indeed older than the late 430s when the tax spine was shattered. The Roman evidence, all in the form of inscriptions, begins in the late 300s, but that is only the estimated date of the oldest material that happens to survive. Some of the Roman deacons may have been prominent psalmists earlier still.

Deacon Psalmody and a Gallo-Romanitas in Gaul

There are traces of deacons who were psalmists in sixth-century Gaul, a tradition perhaps associated there with a late *romanitas*. This is a broader issue than the question of Rome's ritual influence in Gaul, for it is as much social as liturgical.

The prelates of late antique Gaul, notably those installed in sees to the south of the Loire, were often men of Roman ancestry. This means that they claimed descent through a line of indigenous Latin speakers, often of considerable local prestige, to the point where they identified ancestors who held Roman citizenship (which was not claiming very much) and who were senators qualified by their wealth and probity to serve on the city councils (which was claiming a good deal more). Many such bishops, Gregory of Tours included, regarded their senatorial lineage as a necessary qualification for their spiritual authority and their powerful position within the *civitas*, while the kings valued such men, when they were pliant, for their local influence and good counsel. Equally important to the kings was the knowledge of Roman law such men could acquire in certain cities where elements of a higher schooling remained. Plate 43 shows a sixth-century copy of the Theodosian Code, the collection of Roman law issued between Constantine and Theodosius II (408–50), in one of two sixth-century manuscripts produced in Lyon or its region. This code formed the basis for legal compilations throughout Gaul, and men like Bonitus of Clermont, with a good knowledge of it, were much sought after in the heartlands of Frankish and Visigothic royal power. Bonitus was adviser to king Sigebert III of Austrasia and later became bishop of Clermont, a city abounding in 'senators of noble Roman stock' according to its native son Gregory of Tours.[2]

A few surviving epitaphs from the sixth and seventh centuries show deacons of Gaul commemorated in metrical verse, and on the basis of what survives this seems a distinctly Roman touch in the strict sense of imitating what was customary in the imperial capital. We have already encountered some highly prestigious Roman examples. To be more precise, these epitaphs from Gaul are not so much metrical as written in the best approximation to metre that local

43 A 6th-c. copy of the collection of Roman law (essentially a collection of imperial judgements giving responses, in the form of letters, to specific enquiries), called the Theodosian Code. Biblioteca Apostolica Vaticana, MS Reg. Lat. 886, perhaps from Lyon or its environs. The passage shown is from ix. 45. 5 and concerns the rights of those who flee for sanctuary to churches. *CLA* 110.

men could manage, and their work suggests that Gregory of Tours had good reason to lament the decline of literature and learning in his lifetime. The schools that trained pupils to write metrical poetry had long since begun to collapse, and phonetic changes in Latin had turned the art of writing metre into a highly demanding intellectual puzzle. The poet was now compelled to assemble fragments of what he could *gather* from grammars, epitaphs and poems about vowel quantities that had once been audible but had not survived as an integrated system:

1. Clermont-Ferrand, Church of Saint Laurence. The epitaph of Æmilius, deacon, d. 28 July 621. A tissue of phrases from traditional funerary epigraphy. They scan here and there but are impossible to interpret throughout as correct metrical verse. *RICG*, viii. 23.
2. Clermont-Ferrand, Church of Saint Venerandus. The epitaph of Innocenius, deacon, seventh century. Rhythmic (syllable-counting) imitation of quantitative hexameters, with the correct accentual pattern for the end of the line in all lines but one, and with a semiquinaria caesura. *RICG*, viii. 16.
3. Andance (Ardèche). The epitaph of Æmilius (to be distinguished from 1 above), deacon, sixth century. This begins with two hexameters that are correct save for the insertion of *diac[onum]* in line 1. Presumably the word was simply inserted into a pre-existing pair of lines taken from a model. *RICG*, xv. 35.

These epitaphs, rescued from the detritus to which time has reduced much of the surviving Gallo-Roman epigraphy, may reveal a level of schooling well below the requirements for producing correct metrical hexameters in the best of the late Roman epigraphic tradition, but the results of a poet's struggle with these problems can be revealing in many ways. An ideal is often more vividly expressed in a failed attempt than in an assured success, and the poor poetry of these inscriptions says much about the strength of determination in parts of central and southern Gaul to imitate the traditions of Roman funerary verse, often chosen by Roman deacons for their own memorials in preference to the laconic prose usually associated, for example, with the humble lectors.

A search beyond the inscriptions produces much more explicit traces of deacons as liturgical singers in Gaul, all in the writings of Gregory, bishop of Tours from 573 until his death in 594. By a curious coincidence, one of Gregory's stories concerns a deacon from Clermont, whence two of the epitaphs considered above. Throughout his ministry, Gregory was deeply involved in the liturgical and political life of central Gaul, presented in his writings as the Merovingian chapter of a salvation history in which the peace of Christ on earth is the true desire of all just kings and pious clergy. Gregory's account of his uncle Gallus, a gifted singer, has already been considered above in Chapter 8, but Gregory also has something to say about a deacon who served in the Church of Clermont once Gallus became its bishop. Long after his period as the court favourite of

King Theuderic and his queen, Gallus attended the Fifth Council of Orléans (549) and took with him a deacon whom Gregory calls *vocalis*. The implication that this deacon served as a singer is soon confirmed. Custom required that the deacon of the bishop acting as celebrant should sing the responsorial psalm during the Masses celebrated as part of the Council. On one occasion when Bishop Gallus was *not* the celebrant his deacon was incensed to find himself eclipsed by another. Indeed, he was determined to sing at the Mass 'through vanity rather than fear of God'. Gallus reminded him that it was the right of the celebrant's deacon to sing, and that he would have that right himself, in due course, when it fell to the bishop of Clermont to celebrate. The deacon persisted nonetheless, elbowing his way forward, and he sang so disagreeably that he was held to ridicule by all who were present. Some time later, when the Council had disbanded and Gallus was celebrating Mass in his cathedral at Clermont, he gave the same deacon leave to sing, and 'this he did, with such a fine voice that everyone praised him'. A gathering of prelates for a Mass in Council was not the kind of occasion likely to favour a liturgical anomaly, so it is significant that the psalmist chosen held the order of deacon. The proceedings of the Council survive, complete with Gallus's subscription, and they show that more than seventy bishops were present from sees throughout Gaul including Tongres, Chartres, Meaux, Verdun and Paris in the north, through Auxerre, Clermont, Trier and Bourges in the central lands to the southern sees of Vienne and Arles. Presumably it was acceptable in all these churches for the psalm in the Gallican Liturgy of the Word to be performed by a deacon.[3]

A fuller account of deacon psalmody, now explicitly concerning the responsorial psalm, appears in Book VIII where Gregory explains how King Guntram (561–92) came to Orléans for a council with his bishops. Gregory was one of the prelates who attended, so this is an eyewitness account. The second day of the royal sojourn in the city began with the king visiting Gregory in his lodgings, at the Church of St Avitus, where Gregory offered him 'Saint Martin's holy bread' and a cup of wine. The same day ended with a banquet to which all the bishops were invited, and during the course of the evening the king made a request with few parallels in early medieval accounts of music at royal or episcopal courts, for he ordered Gregory to tell his deacon to sing. 'This was the man', says Gregory, 'who had chanted the responsorial psalm (*responsurium*) at Mass the previous day.' While the deacon was giving his performance of the psalm, the king commanded that

> each of the other bishops in turn should provide a single cleric from his retinue to sing before the king. I communicated this order to the prelates. Each one sang a responsorial psalm [or: the responsorial psalm], to the best of his ability, in the presence of the king.[4]

This is a more potent story than it appears. The scene is probably to be imagined as a large hall with a high table, where the king sits, and lower tables where the prelates have been placed as a group, Gregory included. Gregory is summoned to the king's table and given the command that he duly passes to his own deacon and to the assembled prelates. Now the stage is set for the king to pay a compliment to Gregory, one of the few prominent bishops present who had not recently given him cause to question their loyalty. King Guntram had arrived in Orléans on 4 July, the Feast of the Translation of the Relics of Saint Martin to the Church of Tours. This evening banquet is taking place on the next day, 5 July, and the king wishes to hear the deacon who had sung the responsorial psalm at the dawn Mass, celebrated by Gregory. As a further compliment to Gregory, clerics (not explicitly said to be deacons) in the retinues of the other bishops are commanded to sing what is presumably the same responsorial psalm, but after Gregory's man, therefore giving him precedence. This was a most unusual kind of royal reward for a prelate's loyalty, but it was surely one that Gregory appreciated, especially since it was so conspicuously given.[5]

The First Cantors

The landscape of churches in southern Gaul was lavish by 450. New sees had recently emerged at Nîmes (396), at Avignon and Carpentras (both 439), at Toulon (441) and in the hilltop citadel of Uzès (442), to look no further. The lands of cypress and olive were fertile territory for the study of ecclesiastical legislation with its roots in the Greek-speaking churches of the eastern Mediterranean and its natural appeal to erudite and conservative spirits. A bishop of Marseille, named Gennadius, is probably responsible for the primordial compilation of legislation that is now commonly called the *Statuta Ecclesiae antiqua*, and dated to approximately 475. The document is aptly named, for these 'ancient statutes of the Church' stand near the fountainhead of ecclesiastical legislation in Latin. The general plan of the collection follows the *Apostolic Constitutions*, the Syrian compilation of the late fourth century that Gennadius probably knew in Latin translation. It nonetheless reveals the profound influence of eastern models upon his thought and more broadly upon the high-ecclesiastical culture of Provence, notably in this passage concerning the appointment of a psalmist:[6]

> Psalmista, idest cantor, potest absque scientia episcopi, sola iussione presbyteri, officium suscipere cantandi, dicente sibi presbytero: *Vide ut quod ore cantas, corde credas; et quod corde credis operibus probes.*

The *psalmist*, that is to say the *cantor*, can assume the charge of singing solely at the bidding of a presbyter without the knowledge of the bishop, the presbyter saying to him: 'See that you believe in your heart what you sing with your mouth, and that you prove in your works the things that you believe in your heart'.

The *Apostolic Constitutions* has no rite of ordination for a psalmist, even one as simple as this, conducted by a single presbyter (see above, p. 96). Nonetheless, the reference to 'canonical singers' in the canons of the Laodicea Council proves that some form of induction rite, however rudimentary, must have existed in certain churches of eastern Asia Minor during the fourth century. Some such source in Greek, perhaps through a Latin intermediary, probably lies behind this passage, although the words assigned to the priest here seem curiously autonomous in the way they make balanced members of ostentatiously alliterative Latin. Does the term *cantor* serve no other purpose than to supply the standard Latin word for 'singer' as a gloss for *psalmista*, perhaps retained from a Greek original? Elsewhere in his writings, Gennadius implies that the standard term for a singer in the Church of Marseille was *lector*, as many other sources would lead one to expect, and not *cantor* (see above, p. 100). The question is impossible to resolve. Nonetheless, it is clear that within a few decades of Gennadius *cantor* can be traced as an established term for a ministry of song very widely in the southern and mainly coastal reaches of the Christian West. (For the evidence that *cantor* as a term of office was known to Jerome around 400, see above, pp. 99–100.) Between the 470s and the 550s, a span of little more than two generations, *cantor* can be found as a term of clerical (or semi-clerical) office at Trento, Ravenna, Rome and Naples across to Mértola and Tours:[7]

1. 'psalmista, id est cantor'
   From the *Statuta Ecclesiae antiqua*, c.475; southern Gaul, probably Marseille. As mentioned above, this set of canons is usually placed late in the period 442–506, probably from c.475 in their surviving form and often attributed today to Gennadius of Marseille.
2. 'Marinus quoque primicerius cantorum sanctae ecclesiae Neapolitanae'
   Eugippius, *Vita Sancti Severini*, c.510, on a miraculous cure experienced by Marinus, *primicerius* of the cantors of the cathedral of Naples. This would have been a team serving the cathedral, and one that followed the late antique custom of treating any command structure as essentially military or bureaucratic if it governed a matter of importance to imperial affairs. Thus any man who rose to become the director of an imperial arms' factory, for example, was given the title *primicerius fabricae*. The term *primicerius* is found abundantly at Rome in the schools of notaries and defensors.
3. 'Moderatu[s] cantor ecclesiae'
   Also from Eugippius, *Vita Sancti Severini*. Moderatus was cantor of the Church of Ioviacus in Batavia.
4. 'cantores' (rendering Greek *psalton*)
   Dionysius Exiguus (d. 540), *Dionysiana*, c.520, Rome (PL 67: 70 (rendering Laodicea Canon xv), 72, *et passim*), a canonical collection, often rendering forms of Greek *psaltes*. Dionysius is the direct source of some later references to *cantores* among the canonists, notably Cresconius.

5. ANDREAS FAMVLV[S] DEI PRINCEPS CANTORVM SACROSANCTE AECLISIAE MER-
   TILLIANE . . .

   Funerary inscription, 525; Mértola (southern Lusitania). *Inscripciones Cristianas de la España Romana y Visigoda*, ed. Vives, no. 93.[8]

6. 'Honorius cantor, Tranquillus cantor, Antonius cantor, Melitus cantor'

   Papal letter of Pope Felix IV (526–30) (*Regesta Pontificum*, ed. Jaffé et al., 877) arbitrating a dispute between Bishop Ecclesius of Ravenna (d. 532) and his clergy, many of whom travelled to Rome with their bishop and witnessed the document. The four cantors, together with numerous lectors, are among the signatories. Quoted by Agnellus of Ravenna in his ninth-century history of the bishops of Ravenna, the *Liber Pontificalis Ecclesiae Ravennatis* (MGH SSRL 319–22), possibly not directly from the original. The only complete manuscript of this history dates from the fifteenth century. Since the letter survives only in a ninth-century history of the bishops of Ravenna by Agnellus, the text and its subscriptions may have been doctored in various ways to accord with much later usage or polemical intent, but as far as the cantors are concerned there is no strong reason to suppose that the text is suspect.

7. DE DONIS DEI ET S[AN]C[TORVM CVSME ET DAMMIANI TEMPOR[IBVS] DO[MI]NI
   EVGYPI EP[ISCOP]I LAVRENTIVS CANT[OR].

   Inscription in a mosaic pavement 530–5, discovered in 1900 in Trento *(CIL Supplementa Italica*, vi. 173–5).

8. 'post tertiam uero lectionem qui cantat dicat gloriam. Quam dum incipit cantor dicere . . .'

   Rule of Saint Benedict, ix. 7 (?540–60); Roman ambience. *La Règle de Saint Benoît*, ed. de Vogüé, ix. 6–7.

9. 'Valentinianus cantor'

   Gregory of Tours (d. 594) *Liber vitae patrum*, MGH SSRM I, 686.

There are many gaps in this listing, some no doubt partly explained by the destruction of material. There is nothing African, which may seem surprising, but it is possible that *cantor* was not used as a term of office in Vandal times, the liturgical singer retaining the title of *lector*, as in Victor of Vita (see above, p. 196). There is nothing from Spain (as opposed to what is now Portugal), but the evidence of other sources suggests once more that *lector* was still the chosen term for those who sang the liturgy in some northerly dioceses of Iberia, notably Braga, as late as the sixth century. The examples nonetheless provide a miniature prosopography that is curiously focused in some respects and gratifyingly wide-ranging in others. The chronological span is relatively compact, extending from *c*.475 to sometime not long before 553. Italian material predominates, but the geographical spread reaches across the western Mediterranean from Trento (7), Ravenna (6), Rome (8) and Naples (2 and 3) to Mértola in Lusitania (5), and extends northwards into Noricum (2, if this is not simply a projection of

Neapolitan usage onto a distant church) and central Gaul (9). Some of the material that does survive was impelled into existence by the peculiarities of local circumstances, perhaps without parallel elsewhere. A survey of Iberian epigraphy, for example, reveals that the wealthier and more influential citizens of Mértola were exceptionally concerned with the epigraphic commemoration of social status in the first decades of the sixth century, for reasons that remain unknown. This probably explains the presence of Andreas 'princeps cantorum' (5). In the *Rule* of Saint Benedict (8), *cantor* probably means 'the brother delegated to sing at that time', or what John Cassian calls 'one who rises to sing a psalm in the midst of the community'. Nonetheless, Benedict is emphatic that only those capable of edifying the brothers by their singing should be appointed to do so. Otherwise *cantor* can be regarded with some confidence as a term of office, reinforced in one case (2) by a title indicating primacy within a group of singers (*primicerius cantorum*) and in another (5) by a term that may be its equivalent (*princeps cantorum*). There are nine named individuals, all of whom can be placed within a specific church.[9]

44   The River Guadiana at Mértola.

The examples also show that *cantor* as the term for a minister of ritual song was already well placed around 500 to enter further into the bloodstream of the Occidental Church. Cathedrals of the fifth and sixth centuries were rarely to be found in isolated corners, or with no antecedent history in the network of Roman government. A late antique bishop was 'an official of a second Empire-wide administration', and often the controller of greater financial resources than any but the wealthiest members of his city. Even in remote sees, such as Rouen at the northern extreme of Gallia Lugdunensis, there was generally a maritime or fluvial route nearby, or a network of arterial roads. Most of the cities represented on the list were either located on the coast, or were near to harbours and riverine routes. Two sources are from Naples (2 and 3) and two from Rome or its environs (4 and 8). Trento (7) lies in the Adige river valley. Marseille, the probable home of the *Statuta Ecclesiae antiqua* (1), was one of the great ports of the ancient and late Roman world, the gateway for Mediterranean goods passing northwards and the head of a fundamental north–south artery. As for Ravenna, an active sea-route can be traced between Rome and the docks at Classe, the point of embarkation for ships carrying envoys – including a number of popes – to the Byzantine emperors in Constantinople. The vitality of Classe is revealed with especial clarity by the wrecks of ships that set out to carry marble to Ravenna for the intense building activity there in the sixth century, including the construction of S. Vitale and S. Apollinare. Mértola, on the River Guadiana (Pl. 44), was already sufficiently renowned in the time of Pliny for him to call it (with more suggestiveness than geographical accuracy) 'a notable town on the coast'.[10]

11

SCHOOLING SINGERS IN THE CATHEDRALS
450–650

A singer in a church of 450–650 was generally appointed in much the same way as a gravedigger, or so the surviving rules for induction suggest. Both of these offices were too lowly for a new appointment to demand the bishop's attention. Whereas the task of ordaining a reader required the prelate to hear reports of the candidate's reputation for honest living, and then to present him with a codex in a public ceremony, a *psalmista* who was often charged to voice the same divine words, but in song, could be admitted without taking up references or undergoing any codified rite of induction. These ad hoc arrangements were apparently no barrier to the creation of sophisticated musical procedures that bishops might value highly for their effect upon the congregation, but without feeling the need to take recruitment in hand themselves or to solemnize the admission of a new psalmist with an episcopal ceremony. In the early 600s, Bishop Isidore of Seville still assumes that the performers of Visigothic chant, 'which moves our souls ardently and devoutly to the flame of devotion', will be appointed by priests alone 'from those whose skill in singing has been noticed'. The account of Gallus given by Gregory of Tours shows how a star might be 'noticed' by chance and recruited by a vigilant bishop. No doubt prelates and their clergy kept an ear open for reports of promising boys and young men lodged in a wide variety of contexts: in monasteries, in such schools as were still being maintained from the cathedrals down to the rural parishes, among the *nutriti* in the royal courts, if they had connections there, and even in hospitals or orphanages, the latter apparently vital in Rome. We shall soon find indications that singers themselves, at least in Visigothic Spain and perhaps elsewhere, were expected to be vigilant for new recruits.[1]

In Classical Latin the senses of *schola* included 'leisure given to learning' and by transference 'a school' in the familiar sense. Other meanings in the period 300–600 encompassed various kinds of association such as a guild, where men who had received the same training pursued a common end. One of the most prominent senses was military: 'a company of soldiers'. When Constantine disbanded the old Praetorian Guard of the Roman emperors, for example, he created new contingents of cavalry known as the *scholae*. In direct imitation of Byzantine usage, the Latin adjective *scholaris* also began to be employed from the fourth century in the sense 'a member of the imperial guard', the guiding sense of *schola* in this context being 'a corps, guild or college' but especially 'a military detachment'.[2]

Any search for schools where liturgical singers were configured into a corps and trained between 450 and 650 is liable to involve a somewhat arbitrary definition of what constitutes a 'school'. Any monastery that mounted some form of choral liturgy made provision for nurturing singers who were living some form of common life and studying their chant at certain points in a more or less well-regulated day of work, prayer and worship. It would be a challenging task to frame any definition of a *schola cantorum* that could positively exclude the provision such monastic houses made, or indeed the instruction offered in many other contexts such as a presbyter's house or one of the larger orphanages. The picture is complicated still further by the difficulty of determining what pre-ninth-century writers mean by the terms *monachus* and *monasterium*, widely used for persons and for houses that would not satisfy the criteria for monasticism accepted later. The Frankish reforms of plainsong that began under the first Carolingian king began with *monachi* who prove to be members of the cathedral chapter of Rouen (Ch. 15). Examples could easily be multiplied.

The confusion is to some extent ours alone, for if there was one kind of church that Christians in the period 450–650 could not fail to recognize it was a cathedral. In pursuing schools of singers we are principally searching for cathedral teams responsible for singing the music of the Mass and such offices as their bishops had induced their clergy to celebrate. As we shall see, their titles of office, together with their structures of command, alluded to the palatine ministries of the late Empire rather than the customs of the monasteries. The bishop's church was liable to be the largest in the city, either standing in a quarter once associated with Roman public power and civic amenities, such as a forum area, or perhaps transferred there if the bishopric had been founded somewhere else when no central space was available or permitted to Christians. (For the striking case of Arles, see Pl. 39.) The cathedral's status as the principal public church of the city, as the keeper of relics the urban laity had most chance to venerate, and as the place for the ceremonial ordination of clergy, made it a recognizable entity to all.

Schooling Singers in Vandal Africa

The kingdom of Vandal Africa is by any measure one of the most intriguing of the barbarian realms. Here was a Germanic and household-based kingdom established in one of the richest areas of the western Roman Empire, a distended margin looking southwards to the Sahara. The zone of Vandal civilization was still connected to the circuit of the Roman and Christian littoral – the future shape of Christian Europe has not yet appeared – but arguably only just. The question of what Vandal occupation meant to the continuity of trade and communications in the western Mediterranean is a delicate one in the sense that seemingly minor archaeological finds can sometimes falsify existing answers. The issue of ethnic identity among Romans and barbarians, as expressed through clothing, language and confessional difference, is also especially intricate in this kingdom, partly because the sources often seem content to remain mute about many important issues but are then inclined to flare up with lurid accounts of persecutions led by Arians against Catholics in a manner scarcely paralleled in the barbarian West. In some respects, notably in the resolutely Germanic names of their kings and possibly in the Arian faith, the Vandals maintained a vigorous native and warrior pride; in others, they embraced Roman insignia of power, domestic luxury and (amongst the kings, at least) the tradition of public building in a remarkably conservative fashion.[3]

  This impression owes much to the predominance of a single narrative source of sharply polemical intent. The *Historia Persecutionis Wandalicae*, compiled in the late fifth century by Victor of Vita, is a Catholic's account of the persecutions his coreligionists suffered in Carthage at royal behest, with few details of the violence spared. Both the matter and the manner are often lurid, but in passing Victor reveals some aspects of worship and liturgy that are by now quite familiar and place the Catholic singers of the kingdom in a pan-Mediterranean as much as a Vandalic context. Thus Victor shows that liturgical singers in the Catholic churches, and perhaps in the Arian basilicas also, were called *lector* and were appointed at a relatively tender age. When he describes the exile of Catholic clergy from Carthage in 484 with the loss of 500 clerics, he records that there were many lectors among them 'who were mere children' (*infantuli*). In another passage, Victor shows that lectors were assigned important duties as singers. At an Easter Sunday service in Regia, perhaps modern Arbal in Algeria, a lector mounted the pulpit to sing the 'Alleluia chant', only to be slain by the arrow of an Arian soldier. He was killed in the very act of singing, so that the book fell from his hands. Victor has no doubt shaped this episode so that a Catholic martyr suffers at the hand of an Arian heretic while singing a ritual item with special prominence in the Easter Sunday liturgy, delivered from a conspicuous (and a fatally exposed) place. Nonetheless, this exceptional event took place within an established liturgical routine. The chant is clearly something quite specific, both in its text and music. Although it is impossible to assess the sophistication of the music, or its stability from one performance to another, Victor's use of the Greek term *melos* (always something of a poeticism in Latin) has already suggested to us that the musical demands of this *alleluiaticum melos* should not be under-estimated, at least in the sections that fell to the lector as soloist. Since the lector used a book, and the people in the congregation were both listening and singing (see above, p. 100), the chant at issue was perhaps one of the psalms already supplied with an Alleluia refrain in the Psalter, in which case the performance probably unfolded with the congregation singing *Alleluia* between the verses of the lector soloist.[4]

Elsewhere, Victor of Vita provides a valuable insight into the way these African lectors might be schooled. During the exile of Catholic clergy mentioned above, the task of supervising the expulsion of clerics from Carthage was entrusted to both Arians and apostate Catholics. Among the latter was a lector named Theucarius, once a Catholic but now a convert to the Arian faith who was perhaps seeking preferment in royal service. Huniric, the king whose edict led to the expulsion, had also ruled that only Arians should serve in the royal administration, based in the *palatium*. Theucarius the lector, in his days as a Catholic, had taught twelve boys whom he now saw leaving Carthage to begin their banishment. He knew that they were 'hardy singers and fit for the melodies of chant'. He was able to keep them in Carthage, apparently on his own authority since he had prospered so far in the service of Arian kings that he was helping to supervise the exile of Catholics. These twelve boys (the number is biblical and cannot be pressed) subsequently lived some form of common life when the persecution subsided, for Victor observes that 'they eat at the same time, they sing the psalms as a group and they glorify the Lord at the same time'. These boys were not living a monastic life in any simple sense, for Victor calls them 'clerics of the Church of Carthage', which seems to rule out the possibility of them being a monastic team drafted in for the offices and living, perhaps, *in domo ecclesiae* or in an urban house monastery. Victor also reports that the Catholics of the city held the boys in great affection, once the persecutions were over. Perhaps they were lodged in the bishop's palace as a caritative gesture, since they were effectively orphans. One might compare the contemporary children in the great orphanage of Byzantium, the Orphanotropheion, who in the 470s used to sing hymns, specially composed for them by the brother of the rector, to the delight of the people of the city of Constantinople, 'who flocked in crowds to hear them'. We shall encounter more boys like these, seemingly rootless and going spare, in the history of schooling singers. They were the loose copper coin of the human fund that careful churches could save against a future shortfall of clergy.[5]

Like most of the literary material pertaining to the Vandals after Augustine, the story of these boys is embedded in a work of anti-Arian polemic. Yet it may nonetheless reveal something about the training of singers in at least one major city of a kingdom extending from eastern Algeria to Tunisia, and a realm that was in many ways (despite the subsequent reputation of the Vandal name) markedly Roman in character. 'Imperial models are indeed the only visible sources for nearly every aspect of the Vandal state', and imperial example would have encouraged the Vandal kings and their elites, like the Catholics, to have sumptuous liturgies, just as it encouraged them to organize persecutions that were closely based upon imperial precedent. The Vandal kings and their higher

45   A silver issue of the Vandal king Thrasamund (496–523), the value marked within the wreath as D.NL (50 *denarii*). The Vandal kings do not appear to have issued a gold coinage; their need for gold was met by large stocks already in Africa when they arrived as conquerors, by plunder (notably Genseric's sack of Rome) and by the corn and oil trade with Italy that continued after the conquest in the old Carthage–Rome tax corridor, but no longer at previous levels. The liturgies sponsored by the wealthy Vandal kings (several of whom are praised in Afro-Roman poetry for building baths, in the Roman manner, as a civic amenity) were probably lavish, with a luxurious material culture. Cambridge, Fitzwilliam Museum.

servants were certainly rich enough to sponsor elaborate forms of liturgical ceremonial with abundant lamps, vessels of precious metal and textiles. The sale of grain that grew so abundantly in parts of their kingdom, the rewards of plunder (notably in Rome) and the gold reserves they found when they conquered Roman territory in Africa all made them rich enough to dispense with striking either a royal or a municipal gold coinage (Pl. 45). Theucarius the lector presumably taught potential psalmists for the Catholic liturgies and then, after his apostasy, for their Arian equivalents. That explains how he knew that his twelve former pupils were proficient singers.[6]

In his Catholic days, Theucarius taught for the Church of Carthage. A cathedral context seems assured, for it is hard to imagine where else a lector might find himself schooling a large class of boys, filtered perhaps from a yet greater number because they were gifted singers. He eventually embraced Arianism, but it is uncertain whether this would have greatly changed the nature of his duties or the content of his teaching when he schooled future singers. Martin of Braga, a missionary from Pannonia who converted the Arian elite of the Suevic kingdom to Catholicism during the 550s, explains in his *De correctione rusticorum* that Arians celebrate with a Psalm, an Epistle, a Gospel 'and many other things just as Catholics do'. The *psalmus* at issue is clearly the Fore-Mass psalm, embedded in a Liturgy of the Word that Martin presents as the common property of Arians and Catholics. Despite these very significant points of contact, however, it remains a distinct possibility that some Arians in Vandal Africa used a liturgy, and an accompanying repertory of chants, that were at least partly in the Vandalic tongue or in Gothic. (The latter was perhaps the primordial ritual language of Germanic Arianism, nurtured from the fourth century under a Byzantine tutelage that encouraged worship in the native tongues of the converted.) A source of exceptional importance in this regard is the anonymous *Altercatio Sancti Augustini cum Pascentio Arriano*, probably of the late fifth century, which purports to be the transcript of a public debate between Saint Augustine, as bishop of Hippo, and Pascentius, an Arian count of the Vandal royal household and a fiscal official. The issue of worship in a barbarian tongue arises on several occasions in this debate, plainly the work of a Catholic polemicist in the Vandal kingdom. At one point, Augustine is made to observe that the words *Amen* and *Alleluia* are always declaimed or sung (*decantare*) in Hebrew, for neither 'the Roman nor the barbarian' translates them into his own speech. This implies an Arian liturgy that was at least partially in Vandalic or Gothic, making use of some translated material (presumably from Greek) but not translating these two Hebrew terms. The next pertinent reference to a liturgy in barbarian speech cites a specific case of translation from Greek, for here the compiler quotes the words *Sihora armen*, long recognized as a Gothic translation of *Kyrie eleison*, 'Lord have mercy'; compare the Modern German cognates *Sieger*, 'victor', and *arm* 'poor' (corresponding to Old English *earm*, 'poor' but *earmheort*, 'merciful').[7]

Singers studying a repertory of chants in Gothic would have required schools of their own, whatever the nature of the music they employed, for it was one thing to sing

> *Pater noster qui es in caelis,*
> *sanctificetur nomen tuum,*
> *adveniat regnum tuum . . .*

and quite another to be assigned

> *Atta unsar þu in himinam,*
> *weihnái namō þein;*
> *qimái þiudinassus þeins . . .*

A liturgy all or partly in Gothic could well have arisen in the 340s and 350s when the emperor Constantius sponsored missionary activity among the Goths north of the Danube frontier and ordained Ulfilas (d. 383), creator of the Gothic Bible, to be bishop for his people. The chanted texts would have been translations into Gothic of Greek models, using adapted versions of the Greek melodies or musical practices (by no means an exotic phenomenon in the lands of the Eastern churches). If there were indeed singers in the Vandal kingdom required to learn a repertory in Gothic as the special liturgical language of the Vandal kings, their high officials like Pascentius and their state, then the Vandal cantor was the representative on African soil of an Arian Church which spanned much of the western Mediterranean and was not subject to Rome. The 'Latin West' at this date, the late fifth century, is merely a convenient turn of phrase. The sounds of these Gothic chants, if they ever existed, have perished forever, but there may be an echo of them in the *De Institutione musica* of Boethius, written in Ostrogothic Italy. In the preface to this book, Boethius refers disparagingly to those who have a liking for the harsher melodies of the Goths, the *Getarum durioribus . . . modis*, perhaps (as already suggested) an allusion to the chants of the Arian Church of Saint Anastasius in Ravenna. Whatever the music was, Boethius believed he could hear in it the sounds of a civilization that was not in his eyes truly Roman, and never could be so, despite its many achievements and sub-imperial pretensions under Theoderic.[8]

Boethius can be allowed this fling at the regime that eventually had him murdered without us having to conclude that acceptance of Arian doctrine and chants in Vandalic or Gothic distinguished Arian vandals from Catholic Afro-Romans in a quasi-ethnic manner. Even to put the matter in such terms may be false to contemporary perceptions. The biographer of Augustine, Possidius, refers to a Bishop Maxentius in Africa whose name suggests he was a Roman and a Catholic, but he actually came with the Vandal invaders and was an Arian. What is more, Possidius does not describe those incomers as Vandals at all, but rather as Goths. The *Altercatio Sancti Augustini cum Pascentio Arriano* does not even refer to a Vandal kingdom, but rather to a *respublica*. This is a political commonwealth brought into existence by Roman political thought and jurisprudence; the Vandal kingdom was simply the current actualization of it at the level of military defence and tax. The ethnic dimension of the division between Arians and Catholics in the Vandal kingdom can rarely be demonstrated from fifth-century sources, save in relation to moments of unusually sharp conflict between the two where the confessional divide appears to run alongside an Afro-Roman/Vandal split. The accounts we possess, notably Victor of Vita's chronicle of the persecutions, are mostly written with a polemical intent, and it remains uncertain whether Catholic and Arian liturgies were generally perceived as any more Roman and Vandalic respectively than such extra-liturgical matters as forms of civil dress. The evidence of clothing, as represented in mosaics or preserved in tombs, provides little ground for assuming that a Roman and a Vandal were easy to distinguish in the streets of Carthage, while in the royal *palatium* men of different ancestry served together indifferently wearing 'Roman' or 'Vandal ' costume, according to Victor of Vita. This means that the costumes were different – that they were styles of dress – but that they were not in themselves ethnic markers (Pl. 46). The liturgy of choice for many educated members of the Vandal higher administration and fluent in Latin – men such as Pascentius himself – was probably couched in the Latin tongue like the rite used by the Catholics, except in such crucial details as the content of the Trinitarian doxology and the baptismal blessings.[9]

46   Fragment of a late 5th- or 6th-c. mosaic showing a man, often supposed to be a member of
the Vandal nobility, riding out from a walled city. London, British Museum, Department of
Prehistory and Europe, Mosaic 1857, 0405.18.

Southern Gaul

Below Lyon, late antique Gaul by 650 possessed many rich cathedrals whose
bishoprics and endowments lay principally in the hands of powerful Gallo-
Roman families. They should not necessarily be thought a conservative influence. An appreciable number of southern Gallic bishops in the late fifth and sixth
centuries had been radicalized by a period of monastic experience on the island
of Lérins in the bay of Cannes, and they sometimes sought to introduce into
their cathedral the monastic practice of an horarium with multiple sequences of
psalms, especially at the extremes of the day, associated with ascetic and penitential deprivation of food and sleep. Broadly speaking, Gallo-Roman prelates in
southern Gaul between 450 and 550 were often more scrupulous and energetic as
bishops than their frequently lustrous lineages, and their complacently Classical
names, might lead one to expect.

Some of the earliest signs that singers were being organized and schooled
comes from the Church of Marseille. We have already seen that Bishop
Gennadius relates how one of his predecessors, Bishop Venerius (428–52), commissioned a member of his clergy to produce a book with 'responses apt to the

liturgical season and the readings'. The result was presumably a systematic record of the psalms and readings used by custom or decreed by the bishops, week by week. In other words, and to use Roman terminology, the Church of Marseille had embarked on an annual cycle of Proper graduals. Such initiatives presuppose a well-organized foundation with recruitment and training that progressively dispelled the ad hoc arrangements of the past. For the Church of Vienne, in the Rhône valley, there is Sidonius's account of Claudianus (d. 472), a *psalmorum modulator* who taught the other clergy the psalmody they were required to sing. Claudianus also prepared a lectionary for the year in a manner reminiscent of the work at Marseille and perhaps the fragmentary Wolfenbüttel lectionary with occasional notes of the responsorial psalms to be used.

Broadly speaking, this is Rhône-valley material that marks the exit from the Mediterranean at Marseille and follows the course of the Rhône up to Vienne. These accounts therefore derive from the heartland of ecclesiastical deliberation and organization in late antique Gaul. A map of cities where ecclesiastical councils were held between the fourth century and the sixth reveals the commanding position of *civitates* that bishops could reach by taking the Rhône-valley route (Map 4). The context for this conciliar activity lies in part with the continuing commercial and military use of the river system, albeit reduced from second-century levels, that led from the Mediterranean to Lyon and if necessary pushed further still into increasingly disturbed and uncertain territory up to Cologne. Marseille was still a thriving port in the 400s and one of many southern Gallic centres where the aristocracy, source of the principal episcopal families, lived in what was essentially a late and provincial western Roman Empire. Vienne was an important and ancient see of the Rhône system whose late *romanitas* is apparent in the highly accomplished verse epitaphs composed for some of its bishops and extending as far in date as the seventh century. The work done at both Churches suggests organized cells of singers who were able to provide the kind of consistency, under the direction of the bishop or his delegate, which could be severely damaged by a want of able recruits or by discontinuities of the pupil–master lineages when teachers left or died. It may be no coincidence that Gennadius of Marseille is the first Western author known to have used the term *cantor* as a title of office.[10]

After the account of Gallus by Gregory of Tours, considered above in Chapter 8, there is no solid information from southern Gaul before the Life of Saint Praiectus, the *Passio Praiecti*, where the scene is once again the cathedral of Clermont. This document appears to be unique for the way it discloses a scene in a Merovingian choir school. Praiectus was bishop of Clermont during the reign of Childeric II (662–75) where an anonymous author composed his biography around 680. Born to parents of middling station in the Auvergne, Praiectus learned his letters with a master at the Church of Issoire. The Council of Vaison (529) had required the priests of the rural churches to teach young and unmarried lectors their psalms and readings, so that they might have competent

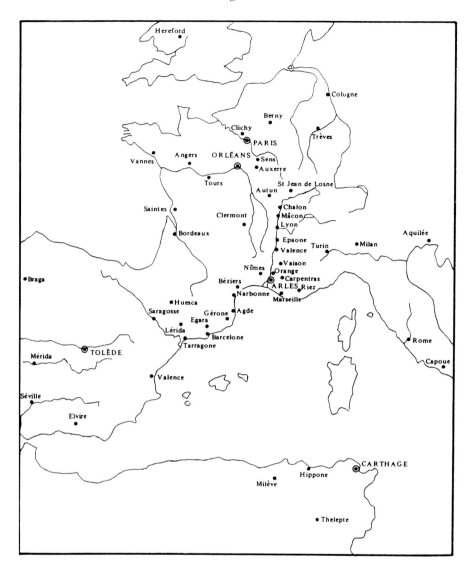

Map 4   The cities of the western Empire where the earliest recorded councils of the Latin Church
were held. Cities associated with at least five councils are shown in capitals. From Gaudemet, *Les
Sources du droit de l'église.*

successors. The bishops assembled for the council regarded this as an Italian practice well worth imitating, and Praiectus was fortunate enough to find a master at
Issoire, probably the presbyter, who did his duty. Under his guidance, Praiectus
showed himself more talented than his contemporaries 'in *soni* and antiphons'.
The term *sonus* might be a general one, meaning little more than 'chants'. Yet
there is an intriguing possibility that it is technical, since the Offertory chant of

the Gallican rite was called *Sonus.* Having already come to notice for the musical proficiency he showed in boyhood during his schooling at Issoire, Praiectus was placed by his parents in the household or *aula* of archdeacon Genesius of Clermont (this was probably part of the *domus ecclesiae,* the essentially residential part of the cathedral complex). There were other pupils there, for the *Passio* describes Praiectus as 'a boy amongst the others'. His relation with his classmates provides the context for an important episode in chapter 4 where he is challenged to sing a *sonus.* According to the account given by the biographer, the saint's fellow pupils were stung by their jealousy and persuaded a competent singer of chant, Martinus, to shame Praiectus by demanding that he a perform a *sonus* he had yet to learn. With the aid of a prayer to Saint Julian of Brioude, a favoured saint of the Auvergne aristocracy and the patron of a rich collegiate church, Praiectus was able to sing the plainsong like a master of the singer's art:[11]

> concitat clericorum venena in Preiecti invidiam, prefundunt in aure, ut fatiat puerum inter ceteros modulum cuiusdam soni, unde ipse inscius erat, vix tandem, ut ita dicam, puncto ore ineditum [*ed.:* meditum] personasse, quem sui aemuli longo iam evo sonitum vocibus decantabant.

> The clergy, jealous of Praiectus, poured their venom against him, urging that he should sing, in the presence of the others, the *modulus* of a certain *Sonus* at length, though it was unknown to him, with difficulty and with a mouth stung into action (if I may put it so); it was a *Sonus* that his schoolfellows had sung long ago.

Although there can be no very secure translation of this passage, which shows Merovingian Latin at very nearly its worst, it raises a fundamental question about the chant of late Merovingian Francia. Was the chant of the seventh-century Franks generally extemporized by soloists as 'lector chant' in the manner that some have proposed for period of Gregory of Tours, or were there stabilized melodies that required singers to spend many hours memorizing them? Here it is valuable to collate the Praiectus episode with the results of Kenneth Levy's independent findings about the layers of Gallican chant that may lie in the Gregorian, Mozarabic and Milanese repertories, the musical deposits of movement and human contact during centuries of post-Roman experience in the West. Levy has succeeded in isolating a body of Offertory chants that reveal different networks of textual and musical connection across the Latin West, with a central place for the traditions of Gaul. 'Offertory' or *offertorium* is the Roman name for the chant that performs the same function as the Gallican *Sonus,* the kind of plainsong that Praiectus was challenged to sing. The chants Levy considers do not use psalms but material from other biblical books instead, arranged into a kind of libretto seemingly designed for musical setting from the first. There are traces of these chants in the Gregorian, Mozarabic and Milanese chant

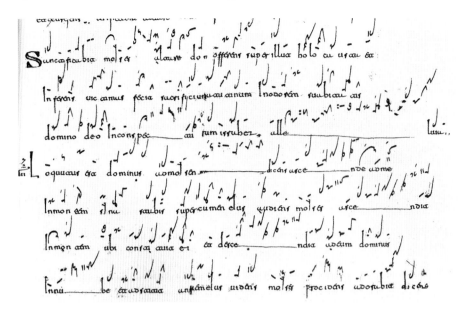

47   Part of the Mozarabic Sacrificium, *Sanctificabit* (= *Sanctificavit*) *Moyses*, from the 10th-c. León antiphoner (León, Archivo Capitular, Codex 8, fol. 305ʳ).

repertories when they eventually appear in sources of the tenth to twelfth centuries. Their music is often elaborate and melismatic, which makes excellent
sense of the Praiectus story. A plainsong drawn into the heart of Levy's argument
like the Mozarabic *Sacrificium* (= *Offertorium* = *Sonus*) beginning *Sanctificabit
Moyses* vividly suggests the kind of elaborate *Sonus* that it now seems the young
Praiectus may have been provoked to sing in the choir school at Clermont
(Pl. 47). The account given there confirms that the music of a *Sonus* was stabilized and singers therefore had to learn it as part of an unfolding syllabus that
could give the older boys an advantage over the younger.[12]

Metz

The city of Metz is the only other northern see of the sixth century where it is
possible to document a cantor as part of a clerical establishment. For a singer, he
seems to have ranked relatively high in the community, suggesting that he was
perhaps the prior or precentor in the cathedral of St Stephen that he served. His
name appears in the *Epistulae Austrasicae*, a collection of letters assembled in eastern Francia and containing items with extreme dates of *c*.460 and *c*.590. Four of
these letters were sent around 568 by Gogon, a high-ranking royal servant of
King Sigebert I, whose territories included the eastern Frankish zone together

with large parts of the Auvergne and Provence. Gogon, to judge by his four surviving letters and the praise lavished upon him by Venantius Fortunatus, was a
notably well-educated and impressive figure who was entrusted with the care of
the king's son, sent on important royal embassies, and was given grants of land
in the customary display of royal favour and patronage. One of his letters concerns a grant that he wishes to place under the spiritual protection of the bishop
and clergy of Metz, a major city in King Sigebert's realm. After a brief announce-
ment of his wishes, Gogon proceeds to salute various abbots of the diocese and
members of the cathedral clergy. The last two on the list, after the archdeacon
and the *notarius*, are 'Sinderic, in his duly ordained place, singing chants of
psalms at dawn' ('Sindericum psalmorum carmina in positionis ordine diluculo
concinnentem') and Theodosius, 'easing the ears of all with serene chants' ('uni-
versorum auribus serenis cantibus lenientem'). The list is strictly hierarchical, and
in descending order, with these two singers in the final position but with Sinderic
ranking higher than Theodosius.[13]

Theodosius, to judge by his name, was perhaps a Greek or Syrian who may
have come to Francia with one of the various delegations known to have carried
letters between the royal court of Austrasia and the Byzantine emperors. Yet
Greek names were not rare among the Gallo-Roman episcopal families of the
600s (although they were sometimes assumed on election) so the point cannot
be pressed. Sinderic, however, may be another matter. His name is not Frankish,
as one might expect at Metz, nor even Gallo-Roman, but Gothic, incorporating
the Gothic word *sinps* meaning 'journey' or 'going'. Hence the name Sinderic
means something like 'mighty journey' or 'great undertaking'. Names with the
element *Sind-* are not well attested in the sixth century, and when they are the
bearers are almost invariably Goths, like the Sinderith who briefly appears in 535
as the military leader of the Ostrogothic garrison in Syracuse, the Sindila who
served in the Arian basilica of Ostrogothic Ravenna in 551, or the Sinderedus who
was archbishop of Toledo in the time of Gregory II (715–31). The psalmist at
Metz may therefore have been a Goth from southern Gaul who came to Metz
from the southern possessions of King Sigebert, bordering on Visigothic
Languedoc. Marseille, which was in the king's hands, and which had known the
office of cantor since at least *c.*475, is a plausible candidate for Sinderic's original
church, for Metz and Marseille were linked by the Rhône–Saône–Moselle river
system that had brought a cult of Saint Victor of Marseille to Metz by the time
of Sinderic. Alternatively, Sinderic may have come from a great church in
Septimania such as the cathedral of Narbonne.[14]

Perhaps the most intriguing possibility, however, is that Sinderic was a Visigoth from Spain who had come to eastern Francia in the court retinue of the
Visigothic princess Brunechild. King Sigebert married her at Metz in 565, some
three years before Gogon's letter to the clergy there. There is a link, for Gogon
was one of the Frankish royal officials sent to Spain to conduct Brunechild to the
territory of the eastern Franks for her dynastic wedding; Venantius Fortunatus

48   The Maison Quarrée at Metz as it was in the late 18th c. From François and Tabouillot, *Histoire générale de Metz* (1787–90). This large Roman building, just to the south of the cathedral, was probably the site chosen by King Sigebert of Austrasia in the 560s for his royal residence in Metz.

addressed a poem to Gogon soon after this venture, praising him for 'recently returning from Spanish lands after so many perils'. Perhaps Sinderic was a cantor in royal service, possibly in Princess Brunechild's household chapel in Visigothic Spain; he might then have travelled to Metz with her and converted, as she did, from Arianism to Catholicism so that he was able to serve as a psalmist in the cathedral church of a city chosen as the principal urban residence of the Austrasian kings and their queens in the 560s, exactly when Sinderic comes to light. Newly resident in Metz in the late 560s, Brunechild was well capable of such patronage, and more besides. The kings probably used the old Roman Maison Quarrée for a royal palace (Pl. 48), providing them with an immense audience hall; Queen Brunechild and her former chaplain, if that is indeed what he was, would have dwelled less than 500 m apart when they were both in the city.[15]

  Until quite recently, the archaeological context for this clerical establishment in mid-sixth-century Metz looked distinctly unpromising. The preceding 400s seemed severely impoverished, with scarcely more than half a dozen shards of pottery to give signs of occupation and 'the bulk of the walled city abandoned . . . fallen into disrepair'. In effect, the city destined to become the heart of the

Carolingians' chant reforms in the eighth and ninth centuries was sometimes supposed to have been a ghost town by 500. Recently, however, a more promising and plausible picture has emerged with Metz envisaged as 'a flourishing late Roman-Christian *urbs*' that acquired a stone cathedral by 451, and one so well built that it served the Carolingians through to the eighth century and beyond. (This building will be the church inherited by Archbishop Chrodegang and the capital of the Carolingians' *cantus romanus*.) The work of creating such a cathedral, and the other Messine churches of fifth- or sixth-century date, required skilled workers such as glaziers and sculptors, together with a local workforce of unskilled labourers; a broad range of materials would have to be brought into the city using supply systems by land and water, carting, woodcutting and charcoal burning. Without such resources as these, it is impossible to explain why the kings of Austrasia chose Metz for their royal residence, beginning in the 560s, and perhaps why Sinderic the psalmist came to the city's cathedral.[16]

As reconstructed here, the career of Sinderic casts a momentary shaft of light upon the movements of singers from Visigothic Spain into Francia. Once again, Kenneth Levy's studies of Offertory chants with shared textual and musical material (between the Mozarabic, Ambrosian and Gregorian repertories) come to the fore. The Mozarabic Offertory *Sanctificabit Moyses* (see Pl. 47) has parallels in the Milanese and Gregorian repertories, with the Mozarabic and the Gregorian showing clear signs of a musical connection. This pattern of shared material suggests that the Gregorian may have used or adapted a Merovingian melody with important trans-Pyrenean affiliations. In Visigothic Spain, stabilized chants to be sung at the offering were already in existence by the time of Sinderic in the late 560s; we know this because Isidore of Seville praises his brother Leander, bishop of Seville from 579, for composing *Sacrificia*, which means the Old Spanish equivalent of the Roman Offertory chants (see below). There must have been extensive contacts between singers on either side of the Pyrenees, moving from Visigothic territory in Spain or Septimania into Frankish territory, but it has not been possible hitherto to identify a specific case history of such a singer, let alone one from this unexpectedly early date. With Sinderic it may be possible to follow a singer's trajectory from the heart of the Mozarabic rite in Visigothic Spain to one of the major churches of the Gallican liturgy in Francia.[17]

Italy and Iberia

Apart from Rome, considered in the next chapter, the literary evidence from Italy in the period 450–650 is disappointingly thin, largely due to the want of extended narrative sources. The musical history of the Lombard kingdom and dukedoms, whose history is so interwoven with Beneventan chant, is a complete blank for this period. The chronological range also embraces the creation and destruction of the Ostrogothic kingdom, but a recent prosopography of Goths in Italy finds no individual recorded as a *cantor* or *psalmista*, and if an equivalent title in Gothic was employed in the Arian churches there is no record of it unless it be *liupareis,* known only from the fourth-century fragments of the Gothic Bible. For the Catholics, as one might expect since they eventually prevailed, the material is a little better. We have seen that the *Life of Saint Severinus* by Eugippius of Naples mentions a certain Marinus who was 'the *primicerius* of the cantors of the Church of Naples', a precious and very early indication of a command structure. For Ravenna, there is the letter of Pope Felix IV (526–30) to the clergy of that city naming four individuals of the cathedral called cantor. These four cantors of the Catholic basilica in the Ostrogothic capital, soon to be the base of the Byzantine Exarch, suggest a consolidated establishment of singers in the cathedral of a wealthy royal capital served by a flourishing Mediterranean port. The attenuated process that has brought this sixth-century document in its ninth-century redaction to a fifteenth-century manuscript issues a reminder of how much information has probably perished.

Contemporary traces of another school appear far to the west in Visigothic Spain, where an impressive funerary monument from the city of Mértola, in southern Lusitania, commemorates the death in 525 of a certain ANDREAS FAMVLV[S] DEI PRINCEPS CANTORVM. Mértola lay within one of the richest and most cosmopolitan regions of Iberia. Mérida, capital of Roman Spain and the richest city of Iberia, was close by; so too were the Baetican heartlands of a Spanish oil trade, now in abeyance from first- or second-century levels but still helping to make the south one of the richest areas of Spain and probably one of the few still maintaining long-distance maritime connections through the ports of the Spanish Levant. If there was a cell of singers at Mértola under the direction of Andreas, then it was active well before the creation of the kingdom of Toledo by Leovigild in the 560s and 570s. It may reveal an ecclesiastical hierarchy in a part of south-western Iberia, now Portugal, that the coercive and centralizing kingdom of Toledo swept away: a regional identity in which the evidently proud Church of Mértola had its place.

These are among the first traceable cells of singers in the Western cathedral churches and they are widely spread, encompassing Vandal Africa, southern Gaul, Spain in the time of the Ostrogothic regency and Ostrogothic Italy. The individuals concerned were not urban ascetics who sang during psalmodic vigils or other liturgical entr'actes in the great urban churches; for the most part, they were probably minor or otherwise peripheral members of a salaried clerical staff in cathedrals such as those of Clermont, Metz, Vienne, Marseille, Naples, Ravenna, Carthage and Mértola. The wealthiest of all these churches was surely Ravenna, a metropolitan see enriched by many gifts from the emperors and high-ranking government officials. Here no fewer than four cantors, selected from what was presumably a significantly larger staff, could be spared for a mission to Rome; they went as part of a delegation concerning the revenue of the see (probably meaning the bishop's stipend), which was set at a staggering 160 pounds of

49 The cathedral of Marseille in the (?)1890s. As the tangle of masts and rigging reveals, the city's cathedral stands (where it has always stood) within sight of the sea that supported this gateway port of late antiquity.

gold. The Ravenna papyri survive to show how that church also profited from 'countless small bequests from humble folk'. These cantors were no doubt relatively prestigious and well-remunerated individuals by the standards of many other churches.[18]

The traces of these groups also begin to appear remarkably early, spanning the period from some time in the middle years of the fifth century to approximately 530. This is scarcely more than one or at most two generations after the creation of a new political order in Gaul, Spain, Africa and Italy (the last two monarchies were destined to be swept away in Justinian's wars). In many respects, this network of churches reveals a West that is still recognizably Roman in the scope of its long-distance contacts and concentrations of wealth. The extent to which the cities involved were still part of an active trade network in the period covered by this chapter remains uncertain and was doubtless very variable, but it is not difficult to find distribution maps for bulk goods that have a very similar appearance to the chart of cathedrals slowly forming here. Map 5 shows the distribution of the amphora type Keay LII, possibly of eastern Mediterranean origin and used to carry wine. Once more, Marseille, Ravenna, Naples and Carthage all make an appearance, but there are also contacts with south-western Spain and the Rhône valley. Naples and Marseille, together with Rome, were among the old

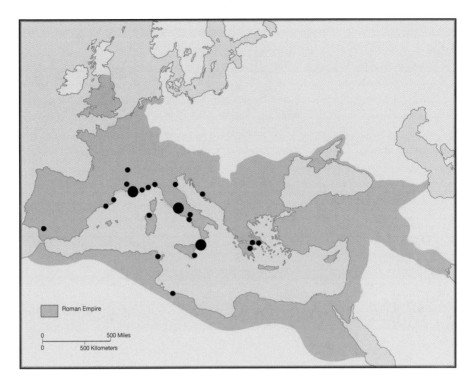

Map 5   Distribution pattern for Keay LII amphorae. Adapted from P. Reynolds, *Trade in the Western Mediterranean.*

Roman political centres still receiving ARS, the African Red-Slip Ware that was once traded very widely in the western Mediterranean and in 530 still had a century and a half to go. It is tempting to use this map as a guide to other cities where cathedrals may have possessed relatively well-organized cells of singers at this date but which have left no trace in the literary sources, such as Lyon, Arles, Seville and Narbonne.

Schooling Singers in the Last Century of Visigothic Spain

Like the Vandals in Africa, the Visigoths who had settled in Spain by the middle of the fifth century were often Arians committed to the doctrine that the Son was the Father's creation and therefore not coeternal with him, contrary to what Catholics proclaimed with the familiar doxology including the words *Sicut erat in principio.* The eventual creation of a national and Catholic Spanish Church in 589 had important consequences for the schooling and professional self-esteem of the Visigothic singers. Within a generation of 589, the Spanish bishops believed that the liturgical reforms they wished to make were among the most important of their new initiatives. There was to be one order of psalmody for their entire kingdom (including its trans-Pyrenean reaches). At the same time, new chants for the liturgy emerged from a tight circle of bishops bound by ties of *amicitia* and sometimes of blood. The work of the Visigothic singer was at the centre of a new kingdom, the united Catholic realm of Toledo, and the singer's opinion of himself, as we shall soon see, was appropriately high, just as his schooling, to judge by the writings of Visigothic scholars like Isidore, was the best any cantors had yet received outside of Italy.

In 580, King Leovigild convened a council at Toledo to devise a Trinitarian compromise that would be acceptable to both Arians and Catholics in his king-dom. Soon afterwards, around 582, his son Hermengild repudiated his father's authority over Baetica and southern Lusitania, then converted to Catholicism. In retrospect, this looks like an attempt to remedy a situation that appears decid-edly anomalous in a barbarian kingdom at this date, namely a confessional divide between the king and the bishops upon whom he relied for counsel and repre-sentation in the localities. At the time, however, Hermengild's move was widely regarded as divisive by Arians and Catholics alike. Leovigild died in 586, leaving the kingdom of Toledo he had built during years of campaigning to his other son, Reccared, who immediately summoned a council. Perhaps the new king did not wish to leave his realm open to a holy war waged against him by Nicaean Christians, be they Franks or Byzantines; he may also have seen that a confes-sional division between kings and prelates in a country that Nature had already made difficult to govern was unwise. Reccared had some liberty of action, for he ruled alone and in large part uncontested. In the year 587, he became a Catholic.[19]

Reccared proclaimed his conversion at the Third Council of Toledo in 589, and so far from being weakened by his choice, like his brother Hermengild a few years before, he succeeded by careful preparation in taking many eminent Arians of the kingdom with him, both from the clergy and the nobility. The Arian con-verts were commanded to abjure their former liturgy (*officia*) and to yield up their books. Eternal anathema was pronounced against anyone who kept the document issued by Leovigild's synod of 580, with its attempt to find a Trinitarian compromise and now branded a *libellum detestabilem*. As for other Arian remains, Toledo III makes no explicit mention of a liturgy in Gothic; if such a rite was still in use anywhere in Spain it was presumably suppressed forth-with and the singers set to learn the Latin liturgy that the prelates now modified in one predictable respect (Pl. 50). The Catholic Creed was to be said in every Mass before communion throughout the kingdom, 'in the manner of the Oriental regions', once the people and the clergy had said the Lord's Prayer. These reforms were taken further in the Fourth Council of Toledo (633), con-vened just one year after the death of Muhammad and under the guidance of Isidore of Seville. Steps were now taken to ensure that Easter would henceforth be celebrated on the same day throughout Spain and Septimania (the Visigothic

50   In Septimania, which was the trans-Pyrenean extension of the Visigothic Spanish kingdom reaching as far as Toulouse, the foundation of an oratory *c.*600 by a female ascetic with the Gothic name of Rinilo was commemorated with this damaged inscription in Latin, the Catholic language and formerly the public language of the Roman state. It begins + FVNDABIT HOC TEMPLVM RINILO DEO DICATA VIRGO SACRATVM. There may never have been a very substantial tradition of functional literacy in Gothic in Spain. The use of the Visigothic language in the liturgy seems just as doubtful. This is a cast of the original, found near Agde on the site of the Church of Notre-Dame du Grau. This cast is now in the Musée archéologique at Agde.

possessions in southern France); single immersion, as opposed to triple, was made mandatory for baptism; churches, hitherto closed on Good Fridays and their pulpits silent, were now to be opened with regular preaching of the Lord's passion; all priests were to repeat the Lord's Prayer every day, not just on Sundays.[20]

To judge by the sequence in which the chapters of Toledo IV were issued, the prelates considered the canons concerning the order of services, and the chants that accompanied them, to be of special importance. Henceforth the *Laudes*, with its multiple Alleluias, was no longer to be sung between the Epistle and Gospel, but after the Gospel. Furthermore there was to be 'one *ordo* of praying and of psalmody'. In making that ruling, the bishops were performing the normal task of a synod and affirming the provisions of previous councils such as Gerona (517), Braga I (561) and Narbonne (569), where the term *ordo psallendi* generally meant the arrangement of psalms at morning and evening services. Yet the bishops at Toledo IV were greatly enhancing the traditional scope of such regulations, for their synod was not provincial but national. For the first time, a comprehensive regulation for the ordonnance of liturgical plainsong was being issued on the scale of an entire kingdom, from Seville and Granada in the south to Toulouse and Carcassonne in the north, from a southern coastline facing Africa to the northern limits of the olive.[21]

In some respects, to be sure, nothing much had altered. The concentration of ceremony and royal power in Toledo did not halt a continuing drift to regionalism. 'Spain was becoming, in economic terms, even more localized in the seventh century, as archaeology is making increasingly clear; aristocrats may have clustered in Toledo, but at home their environments were becoming more and more isolated from each other.' Yet if localism in liturgical practice continued, and even intensified in the 600s, one should still reckon with the consequences of aristocrats 'clustering' in Toledo, for many of them were bishops forming a tight network of both *amicitia* and blood. It is precisely among these men, and only among them, that the impulse to create new chants can be traced.[22]

The earliest of these chant-makers was the prelate who closed Toledo III with a triumphant homily: Leander, bishop of Seville from 579 to 599. He composed 'many a sweet *sonus* for *Sacrificia* and *Laudes*', according to his brother Isidore, a precise remark which names two genres of Old Spanish Mass chant and shows that Isidore has specific compositions in mind. In the next generation, Bishop Ildefonsus of Toledo was able to praise four bishops whose chants had enriched the Old Spanish liturgy. John of Saragossa, a *nobilis* from the region of the Ebro valley, 'composed certain things for liturgical celebrations, both words and music, in an elegant manner', while Conantius of Palentia 'put forth many musical melodies in a distinguished fashion'. Braulio of Saragossa was 'illustrious for his songs and writings', while Bishop Eugenius of Toledo took pains to 'correct chants damaged by long use'. Ildefonsus never gives a textual incipit for these chants, yet his admiration for the way these eminent men composed in a 'refined' or 'elegant' manner leaves no doubt that each one had 'put together' (*composuit*) or had 'put forth' (*edidit*) both words and music in a sufficiently stabilized form that the results could be praised in writing. This does not have to imply composition in the Romantic or post-Romantic sense of original creation; *composuit* and *edidit* are both consistent with the suggestion that these prelates sometimes redacted material drawn from other traditions, perhaps from southern Gaul. Yet however these prelates produced the plainsongs associated with their names, it mattered to know who had issued these chants because the episcopal status of the maker assured the orthodoxy of their texts while a more diversified palette of human and intellectual qualities associated with the episcopal order gave an assurance that the music emanated from a benign and cultivated nature. Thus John of Saragossa was 'bountiful' and 'jovial'; Conantius of Palentia was 'eloquent' and 'pleasing in his conversation'. These chants these men composed remained the property of their makers in a sense that could never be finally usurped by singers, whatever the freedom conceded to them in performance.[23]

These composers were an elite indeed. Sixty-four bishops signed the proceedings of Toledo III, with another five represented by delegates chosen from their higher clergy; of the sixty-nine bishops directly or indirectly represented, only Leander of Seville was subsequently praised for his skill as a maker of chant. This is under 2 per cent of the episcopate at the council of 589. Toledo IV has sixty-two signatories, with seven more delegates, but only two were later praised as musicians, namely Braulio of Saragossa and Conantius of Palentia. These numbers are so low that one begins to suspect the bishop-composers shared more than an interest in composition. Braulio was the brother of John and was his immediate successor as bishop of Saragossa; he was also the literary executor of Isidore, who was the brother of Leander, whom he followed as bishop of Seville; Eugenius of Toledo wrote the epitaph of John and was a close friend of Braulio; Leander signed the proceedings of Toledo III, and delivered the closing homily; Conantius and Braulio were both present at Toledo IV, where Isidore presided. These links are relatively tight, and in places they are familial, revealing brief episcopal dynasties of blood at Saragossa and Seville.

An exceptional insight into the schooling of Visigothic singers who sang these chants, together with the *ordo psallendi* of the new Catholic kingdom in Spain, is provided by a Latin poem, the 'Admonition to a Cantor', surviving among the prefatory material to the tenth-century antiphoner of León. There are four prologues there, of which ours is number III. From the very beginning the poem communicates a clear sense of the cantor as a supported and highly trained professional, but it also expresses a remarkably developed sense of the ethical demands of the cantor's calling. The poet addresses the reader as *doctor* in the first line, implying advanced literate and even theological skills; if these verses were originally conceived as the prologue to an antiphoner then they present a flattering (and so perhaps an insider's) view of the singers who might have a use for such a book. Nonetheless, the cantor must learn the 'gift of humility' (2) and understand the difference between pleasing human as opposed to divine ears. Cantors should not be carried away with the 'vain human plaudits' that the poet mercilessly calls 'poisonous human praise, drawing the soul into the terrible fires of hell' (4, 9–10). Yet despite the necessary appeal to the ear of God, there is a strong sense in the poem of a listening congregation, indeed of an audience. Its members are placed 'at a distance' (*eminus*, 16), while other expressions chosen by the poet seem to bring them closer. They are 'those standing by' and even 'the listeners' (14, 18). Most dangerous for the cantor, they may also be 'admirers' (21). The cantor should sing with a contrite heart and with a voice that accords with his inner disposition, for that is how he will inspire compunction in others. (In this poem, as in the writings of Isidore, it is the affective power of music that makes it an art to fear and to admire in equal measure). As for the praise that the cantor is offered, he should regard it as a bag full of wind, but without ever lapsing into indifference so that he neglects his art. He must always strive to augment the *talentum* entrusted to him because the heavenly King may come at any time to see how he has used it (Matthew 25: 14–30).[24]

The process of schooling singers comes into view with the poet's requirement that the cantor, now envisaged as the leader of a group or at least as a teacher, has an obligation to teach promising pupils (48). In an explicit reference to scouting for recruits, the cantor is told to seek among his friends and colleagues for those who can sing well (49–50), an instruction that would make little sense in an enclosed monastic context and which therefore implies a cathedral community or at least a church of substance. The suggestion that there is some kind of infrastructure in the background becomes more pronounced when the poet warns the cantor against the rare but nonetheless attested career path that might carry him to a higher order of the clergy and even to a bishopric. No matter how well he succeeds in recruiting pupils or in teaching, these successes are not to become the basis for seeking higher office in the Church. The cantor should follow Paul's counsel and remain in the state to which he has been called (1 Corinthians 7: 20). The reserve that a good cantor should possess – the sense of liturgical decorum, in effect – reaches outwards in this poem to a comprehensive ethic for those who follow the psalmist's calling. Indeed, it reaches to a philosophy as defined by Isidore, 'a knowledge of human and divine things, joined to the study of how to live well'. Cantors should be benign, peaceable and modest; they must be without guile and men of good reputation, always behaving with rectitude and measure. This is an unexpectedly ambitious combination of Christian humility with Senecan ideals of moderation.

There are several reasons for supposing that this poem is significantly older than the unique copy in the antiphoner of León, where the four prologues show many signs of interdependence. A gathering of the antiphoner (fols 20–7) with astronomical and other tables contains a note recording that the manuscript was copied after an exemplar from the time of King Wamba in 672; these leaves were not part of the original compilation, and are in a later hand, but they naturally excite a curiosity that mounts when lines 57–62 of Prologue IV in the set prove to come from a poem by Eugenius of Toledo (d. 657). Prologue III begins with what appears to be a note carried over from an approved exemplar ('This prologue should always be put in the beginning of a book'). Three of the prologues are insistent that the chant in the antiphoner contains no teaching contrary to pure Catholic doctrine, consistent with the concerns of Toledo IV (633) when it was recognized that much new liturgical material, not all of it universally accepted, had been created in the context of victory over the long-standing heresy of Arianism. Hence there is 'nothing deviant' (Prologue I); the antiphoner contains 'splendid doctrine' (Prologue II); and it 'illuminates many [episcopal] seats with ancient teaching' (Prologue III). The third prologue also mentions the doxology in a prominent way, which was naturally a matter of great concern at Toledo IV in 633, where three chapters of the proceedings mention the Trinitarian doxology *Gloria et honor patri.* Yet perhaps the most suggestive lines in Prologue III, concerning cantors, are these which are addressed to the antiphoner itself:

> Tempore te prisco per choros canebant antiqui,
> Conexi nunc psallunt exules a docmata.

In the primordial period the ancients sang you in choirs, now those exiled from the doctrines sing psalmody joined.

Who are these exiles 'from the doctrines' that have joined their voices to psalmody? The most likely answer is that they are the Arians who accepted conversion with the king in 589 and therefore joined the Catholic faith. The reference to 'those who are joined', *conexi,* may even be an allusion to the homily preached by Leander, at the close of Toledo III, when he celebrated the *conexio gentium,* the 'joining of peoples', that marked the emergence of Catholic Spain.[25]

12

SCHOOLING SINGERS IN ROME

A manuscript that was lost for many years gives unexpected prominence to the cantors of Rome. Now in the library of the Abdij van Egmond in the Netherlands, the book reproduces a reference collection compiled sometime before 750 by the notaries of the papal *scrinium* or secretariat. In order to standardize the records they issued, and to expedite the task of drafting them under pressure, the notaries compiled a set of form documents to normalize the wording for salutations, grants of land and transfers of property, among many other matters. The result was a daybook or *Liber diurnus.* The third formulary in this collection concerns the due process to be observed when the clerics of a suburbicarian diocese request the pope to ordain a new bishop for their church. The formula gives the authorized text of the request, and at the end the members of the cathedral clergy are required to subscribe in the usual descending order of seniority, beginning with the archipresbyter then passing through the grades of presbyter, deacon and subdeacon. There is nothing exceptional in this arrangement, but it is quite another matter for the list of subscribers to extend so far down that it reaches the level of the lector and then, in final position, the 'cantor and others'. Singers were rarely asked to witness juridical instruments in this way at any time in the Middle Ages, and even if the cantor's place here is so low that only unspecified 'others' can come below him, this is still an exceptional document for including a category of person whose clerical status was by no means always agreed and whose position was perhaps regarded as ephemeral (Pl. 51).[1]

The *Liber diurnus* offers an apt introduction to the exceptional richness of the sources liable to illuminate the singers of early medieval Rome. Just as no formulary of the early Middle Ages concerns a more exalted Western church than this collection, so no episcopal records of the sixth century compare with the Register of Gregory I (d. 604) for scale and comprehensiveness. After 500, no series of episcopal letters has survived so extensively as the correspondence of the Roman bishops, while the corpus of Roman and Christian epigraphy is much larger than the material remaining from anywhere else in the West. The sequence of papal biographies in the *Liber pontificalis,* continuous from Saint Peter onwards (thanks to the learning and pious inventiveness of the Roman clergy)

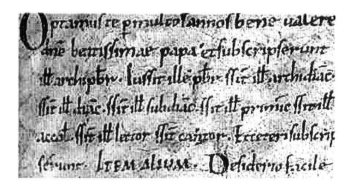

51   Formula III of the *Liber diurnus*, cueing a subscription by a cantor in the fifth line down (s[ub]s[crips]it cantor). The original is badly faded and has here been digitally enhanced. From the Clarmontanus source of the *Liber diurnus*, now in the library of the Abdij van Egmond, Egmond-Binnen. Reproduced by permission.

has no rival from any other Western see, despite imitations at Ravenna and Metz, begun much later.

Yet in some respects the copy of the *Liber diurnus* shown in Plate 51 gives inadvertent testimony to the difficulties that beset any attempt to trace the singers of a city whose ecclesiastical organization was complex and distended, despite the appearance of centralization conveyed by the continuing rise of the Roman bishops from the fifth century onwards at the expense of lay patrons and their private foundations. There are three copies of the *Liber diurnus*, but the example shown here is the only one that has a legible (though much faded) form of the document requiring the signature of a cantor; in another the text is fragmentary and largely indecipherable, while in the third it is missing altogether. Despite the unrivalled scope and prestige of the many Roman documents that survive on stone, parchment and papyri, they are not enough to reconstruct with certainty the different ways in which singers were recruited, trained and deployed in a city that remained, despite demographic decline and the decay of certain regions *intra muros*, one of the larger urban agglomerations of the Christian Occident during the first millennium. Thus the distinction between pontifical services, where the pope acted as the celebrant, and services conducted by presbyters within the titular churches of the city does not necessarily have clear implications for the recruitment and duties of the singers who served in each. The presbyters had some duty of oversight in the patriarchal basilicas that were also served, in some cases as early as the fifth century, by urban monks whose responsibilities eventually developed well beyond the duty to sing night and morning offices with an evolving set of interleaved canonical hours for the daytime. By the early 700s, there were abbots in some of these communities who were long remembered, both in Rome and elsewhere, as masters of the annual cycle of chant, presumably meaning that they knew the Proper chants for the entire liturgical year, at both Mass and Office, by heart. In early medieval Rome, the boundaries between different ministries of ritual song were doubtless very fluid.[2]

By 700 the singers of Rome nonetheless included a seemingly coherent body known as the *schola cantorum*. A relaxed notion of coherence is required here, for this *schola* cannot have been a closed college. The supply of trained singers may never have been enough, and never sufficiently dependable, for the *schola* to function continuously at papal Masses without co-opting members from elsewhere as the need arose. One of the institutions that provided the *schola* with its supply of young boys and adolescents, a Roman orphanage, first comes to light precisely because its endowment was under threat; steps had to be taken 'lest the order of cantors should be imperilled'. Cantors like those required to sign the form document in Plate 51, serving a suburbicarian cathedral, would perhaps on occasions have joined other companies of singers whose terms of reference for their sphere of competence, so to speak, may never have been sharply defined in relation to pontifical or presbyteral services, monastic or secular status, and public or private churches. Behind the impressive colonnade of Roman documents like *Ordo Romanus 1* with its quasi-imperial cavalcade of clergy and its choreographed liturgy of the Mass, there probably lay a fragile network of ad hoc arrangements and connections, reaching across the city, largely impossible to reconstruct in any detail today but possible to glimpse in the document which shows the supply of recruits to the *schola cantorum* endangered for want of resources to support one of the foundations that fed it. One would give much to know more about the singers who served in the chapels of hospitals and charitable institutions, to say nothing of the chapels, monasteries and hospitals in the suburbicarian dioceses or the churches founded on private lands.[3]

The duties of the *schola* are described for the first time, and at a relatively late date, in *Ordo Romanus 1,* an account of the Pontifical Mass on Easter Day. This seminal document for the history of Western liturgy survives in numerous copies made north of the Alps but was undoubtedly produced in Rome, probably around 700, although that is little more than an informed guess. Richly embroidered with many terms borrowed from the Byzantine Greek of Constantinople and Greek-speaking clergy in Rome, *Ordo Romanus 1* is distinctly imperial in tone. The pope processes in a cavalcade from the Lateran palace to the appointed church for the Mass he is to celebrate amidst the columns and mosaics of S. Maria Maggiore. In response to a sign, the *schola* sings an Introit that gives the pope and his clergy their cue to enter the church from the sacristy with lights and incense. When the pontiff gives the signal, the singers bring the Introit to a close; the *Kyrie eleison* follows, unravelling in performance like a roll of silk to be cut or extended as required, for the leader of the *schola* is charged to keep his eyes on the pontiff 'so that the pope may sign to him if he wishes to change the number of Kyries'. The celebrant then begins the *Gloria in excelsis* when it is the appropriate season. A subdeacon reads the epistle from a raised platform, then a cantor holding his *cantatorium* as a sign of his office mounts to the same place and sings the Gradual; another sings the Alleluia or a Tract according to the liturgical season. A deacon reads the gospel and then the elaborate ceremonies for collecting the offerings begins with passing and wrapping of loaves as the pontiff receives offerings from the noblemen present and then from the noblewomen. The *schola* sings the Offertory the while, until the pope signals that they should cease. The next task is to sing the Sanctus, whose close is the celebrant's signal to begin the Canon of the Mass. This elaborate process of internal telegraphy between the participants continues as the archdeacon signals to the *schola* that they should begin the *Agnus dei* to accompany the breaking of the bread. Next, the singers perform the communion chant 'until all the people have communicated' and the pope gestures to show that the doxology should begin. On feast-days, twelve of the singers take communion at the papal throne, but on other days they communicate in the presbytery.[4]

   With so many interventions to make, the singers bore such a heavy responsibility for the ordered performance of the service that one of them faced a grave penalty if something went amiss. The fourth-in-command of the *schola* faced excommunication if the assignment of chants to individual singers, announced beforehand, was changed in any way during the course of the service so that the pope was left vainly signalling to the wrong cantor. Yet although the decorum of the rite owed much to the professionalism of the *schola*, the members did not enjoy much prestige, at least in their own city, and they possessed even less ceremonial dignity. The importance of installing them in any stational church before the pope's arrival made them more or less equivalent in status to the *provisores*, the agents who went ahead of the pope on his travels to prepare a residence, just as it denied them any place in the cavalcade to the stational church with its impressive display of liturgical books, textiles and precious plate. Whereas the subdeacon and archdeacon processed to the appointed church with the books from which they were assigned to read, the ceremonial book of the cantor was borne by someone who is not important enough for *Ordo Romanus I* to identify. It may also be revealing that the leader of the *schola* bore the title of *Prior* at Rome rather than *Primicerius*, granted to the heads of the much more prestigious schools of Notaries and Defensors. The most one can say for the singers of the *schola* around 700 is that their corporate identity had been consolidated to the point where they are expected to answer a summons in the singular, replying 'I am here' (*adsum*) when the regional subdeacon called them at the beginning of the service.[5]

   If *Ordo Romanus I* does indeed date from *c*.700 then the Roman *schola cantorum* was certainly in existence by the beginning of the eighth century and integrated into a rite of Mass whose earlier forms, one might suppose, must have been very different if the Roman Church were able to celebrate them *without* organizing the singers into some kind of collegiate body for recruitment and training. Nonetheless, the antecedents of the *schola cantorum* are mysterious.

One recent survey dates this institution (if that is the right word) to the late seventh century and populates the new school with singers stirred to endeavours of such scope by the advantages of their newly corporate organization that they created, in a relatively short period, the Proper chants of the Roman Mass for the entire liturgical year. This is James McKinnon's 'Advent Project', named after the place in the liturgical cycle where he argues that the work of the Roman singers began. The theory virtually requires one to accept a seventh-century date for the *schola cantorum* if it was the impetus of a *new* structure that impelled the work of creating the Mass Proper. Rome, on this understanding, had mostly known extempore forms of psalmody hitherto; a Roman cantor sang a gradual psalm, for example, by compiling music on the spot from elements, learned during his apprenticeship, that provided him with pre-shaped melodic ideas, with ways to mark a pause in the sense of the text with a melodic turn of the appropriate weight, and so on. The principal constraints would be that he should sing the appointed text in the expected way and bring his chanting to a satisfactory close. Simply speaking, this extemporized art would then have given way to liturgical melody during the Advent Project, where 'melody' means a contour of pitches judged more appropriate to its ritual purpose than anything likely to be achieved by improvising something on the spot or by making significant changes to the memorized material. If this development ever took place as described, then the singers of the *schola* engaged in the Advent Project chose texts, or used texts chosen by others, then repeatedly experimented with certain musical ideas within each ritual category to evolve and then memorize musical settings for them, functioning as 'an established group of quasi-professional musicians'.[6]

The suggestion that a new form of organization for the Roman singers produced a comprehensive revision of musical materials for the entire liturgical year in Rome is an inspired one, and yet a veil of uncertainty soon descends. As Joseph Dyer has observed, with the exception of a very few sources from northern Italy, the early sacramentaries and lectionaries all place Advent 'at the end of the liturgical year, not at its beginning'. Advent would therefore have been a peculiar place to begin the project McKinnon associates with its season. One might add that the senior clergy of Western churches in the first millennium were not generally indulgent or charitable towards the singers who served them, but that does not mean they were indifferent to the music and texts that the singers performed. Liturgical celebration is an inherently conservative activity that principally invests meaning in what is believed to be venerable and traditional (but may be neither). Prelates might be willing to see new feasts enhanced with new observances, but it was another matter to remake the words and music of chants for the established feasts of an entire liturgical year. It seems doubtful whether singers could have revolutionized their musical interventions in the manner implied by the Advent Project without extensively involving the entire clerical hierarchy of the city. It required considerable expertise to choose ritual texts that did not create improper or even unorthodox associations relative to the feasts for which they were employed, and that is not a skill that clergy of the early Middle Ages commonly associated with cantors. (As late as the thirteenth century, and in a city full of scholars, Johannes de Grocheio urged composers to seek the text for a new conductus from a theologian, not to write one themselves.) There seems to be no independent record of such collaboration on a major scale between singers and higher Roman clergy in the seventh century. Ritual singing was simply too important to be left to ritual singers.[7]

The theory that the *schola cantorum* was established in the late seventh century nonetheless produces an obliging and perhaps slightly suspicious coincidence between the period when the *schola* is assumed to have emerged and the decades when it is first (but somewhat indirectly) mentioned. If a new form of collegiate organization inspired the Advent Project during the late decades of the seventh century then the beginnings of the *schola* can presumably be pushed no further back than the period 650–70, when it would have been new enough to provide the stimulus required for fashioning the liturgy already in place in *Ordo Romanus I* of *c.*700. This accords with the first traces of future popes being entrusted for their education to a *Prior cantorum*, an official whose title probably indicates that the *schola cantorum* was already functioning (that is why the earliest reference to the school is indirect). The first of the pontiffs to be mentioned in this context is Sergius I (687–701), entrusted to the head of the singers 'because he was studious and competent in the task of chanting' when he first came to Rome as a boy during the pontificate of Adeodatus (672–6). The coincidence of dates is close (foundation of the *schola* perhaps 650–70, first likely traces in 672–6) and seems to offer a welcome reassurance that there is no need for an argument from silence: if the *schola* cannot be identified in documents referring to any period before the 670s it is because there was no institution in existence, and not because relevant documents have been lost or because the materials that survive find no cause to mention it at an earlier date.

Unfortunately, however, there is simply no way of knowing whether the *schola cantorum* was in existence, under that name or some other, and functioning as 'an established group of quasi-professional musicians', long before the surviving sources find cause to mention it. The scope for arguments from silence is in fact very wide, and there are distinguished historians of early medieval Rome, not themselves musicologists, who seem quite prepared to accept that the *schola cantorum* existed in the time of Gregory the Great (d. 604).[8]

Traces of a college unambiguously called *schola cantorum* are admittedly hard to find anywhere in the Latin West before *c.*700 and *Ordo Romanus I*. There seems to be nothing pertinent in the voluminous Register of Gregory I (590–604) and there is only silence in the *Liber pontificalis* before the entry, mentioned above, referring to the youth of Sergius I in the time of Adeodatus (672–6), which does not actually mention the school by name. Even here, however, it is necessary to tread warily. Gregory's Register covers only thirteen and a half years, from September 590 to March 604, and gives only a selection of letters from the fourteen volumes that were still in the papal archive as late as the 880s when they were used by Gregory's Roman biographer, John the Deacon. The number of letters attributed to Gregory and currently regarded as authentic runs to about 850, but one modern estimate suggests that papal notaries possessed the capacity to produce some 20,000 letters during the years of Gregory's pontificate. This seems far too high, but if it were to be accepted for the purposes of argument, then the survival rate for Gregory's documents can be put at approximately one in twenty-four. If the figure were nearer 3,000, which seems more plausible, then it is approximately one in four. The silences in the *Liber pontificalis* are equally problematic. Many layers of information in the book may be generally trustworthy, especially perhaps the lists derived from the property inventories of churches to which the popes made gifts; but other reliable material is not always easy to identify amidst the pious inventions or brief narratives that introduce anachronisms, omit important information known from elsewhere or transfer important initiatives from the biographies of lesser popes to greater ones. The silences of the *Liber pontificalis* are another element of its selectivity, often perhaps of its partiality.[9]

Rome was a larger city than Naples, but the Neapolitan church had a corps of singers led by a *primicerius* soon after 500. Mértola had its *princeps cantorum* at about the same time. If Naples and Mértola had already organized their singers by the sixth century into some form of corps with a title of command then perhaps the Romans had done the same. Here once more it is the sheer size of the Roman establishment that weighs heavily. The patriarchal basilicas, titular churches, monasteries, private foundations and churches without the walls of Rome formed a complex and cellular structure reaching across the city, with each cell in the body of the Church energized by its own endowments, rights and privileges. Despite the serene and cultivated appearance of imperial order given by *Ordo Romanus I*, arrangements made at any time for the training and provision of singers were perhaps liable to be scattered and difficult to centralize. From a vantage point in the eighth century, when the *schola cantorum* certainly did exist, one looks back to an obscure prehistory which is all the more mysterious for lacking a central thread.

There is one theme, however, that may help to assemble the fragments into a tolerably coherent picture. This is the debt of the Roman *schola cantorum* to various forms of charitable provision. By the sixth century, the term *schola* when adapted to ecclesiastical use often implied some form of familial cohabitation, especially in a monastic context. 'I would not have the monks living in their own cells', wrote Caesarius of Arles (d. 542) in his monastic Rule, 'but let them all remain in one *schola*.' Any attempt to envisage the forms that an 'established group of quasi-professional musicians' could take in early medieval Rome should look to the many ways in which men and women might live in some form of supported and familial coexistence. At one extreme, this could encompass singers who received a stipend from the endowment of the church they served, and who sometimes shared certain facilities such as a lodging or common chapel. More developed forms of cohabitation encompassed those who sang as part of a celibate common life. In the case of urban ascetics, their lodging might be a bishop's house, or somewhere else *in domo ecclesiae*, supported by charitable provision. To judge by the Roman document mentioned above, which shows an orphanage feeding the *schola cantorum*, familial cohabitation could also include education within various kinds of caritative foundation. When a 'professional' body of singers is defined in these various ways, the notion of the *schola cantorum* possessing some form of collegiate organization does not so strongly imply a new initiative, or indeed a new foundation. Instead, it places the history of the *schola* back where it probably belongs: with many different and yet overlapping forms of familial cohabitation for the purposes of education, piety, and charitable care in hospitals and liturgy.[10]

Hostel and Hospital

The period 350–500 has been associated with 'the birth of the hospital' in the eastern Roman Empire, marked by the rise of public and private foundations bearing specialized names such as *orphanotropheion*. These institutions reflected a change in perception, fundamental to the emergence of a Christian Byzantium from the eastern Roman Empire, whereby the weak and disadvantaged gradually ceased to be citizens whose juridical status entitled them to aid, in the form of doles, and became instead the poor of Christ. These *pauperes* were persons from any social level who were powerless to help themselves in this present life, but who were able to ease the path towards salvation in the next life for those who helped them with charitable works. In the Roman imperial system of public duties, enforceable by law, the obligation to care for the weak, the elderly or the infirm was never as highly regulated as the duty to provide temporary lodging for soldiers and imperial administrators, or the charge to spend part of one's personal fortune on public works. The Peace of the Church brought new obligations to accommodate a new kind of *pauper*. When bishops, presbyters and deacons rose to positions of public eminence in the fourth century they became the directors of small corporations, in effect, that were continuously being enriched by alms and gifts; by a paradox that only a legal mind can fathom, Roman lawyers began to regard the clergy as destitutes, or what a law of Constantine issued in 326 calls *pauperes ecclesiarum*, paupers of the churches. Juridically speaking, the clergy were dependents of the Christian community and their status rested, in part, upon their willingness to recognize their pastoral obligations towards impoverished laymen and laywomen who shared that same state of dependency. The clergy gradually began to view the Christian populations of the cities in a manner that combined imperial traditions of paternalistic care, such as the public dole, with the emphasis upon charitable care for all the weak, regardless of juridical status, that characterizes the ministry of Christ. By the end of the fourth century, various forms of hospital for *pauperes* appear around the Mediterranean in Italy (Ostia and Rome) and in North Africa (Hippo, in the time of Augustine).[11]

The *Liber pontificalis* makes no mention of provision for paupers until the entry for Symmachus (498–514), 'who constructed dwellings for the poor', but other traces reach further back and indeed to the very end of the fourth century and connect with late Roman tradition. The senator Pammachius (d. *c*.409) devoted himself to works of charity from 397; after his wife's death, he joined Saint Fabiola in building a hospice for poor strangers at Portus by the mouth of the Tiber, with results that have been excavated. After the sack of Rome in 410, the Valerii turned their derelict house on the Mons Caelius into a hospital. A letter of Pope Celestine I (422–32) praises Anicia Faltonia Proba for setting aside income from her estates for the care of the poor. In the *Liber pontificalis*, the specialized terminology of the Byzantine hospitals makes its first appearance with the *xenodochium* founded by the Byzantine general Belisarius with the profits of the Vandal War. This was during the pontificate of Vigilius (537–55). The reign of Pelagius II (579–90) brings another Latinized word from the technical terminology of Byzantine hospitals with the *ptochium* or 'hostel for the poor' that Pelagius founded in his own house for the benefit of aged men. Such hospitals as these were often relatively small, taking their place in the early medieval cityscape of Rome where the characteristic new foundations within the built-up area 'comprised a church (or chapel) associated generally with a small private monastery or with a charitable institution . . .'. The result may have produced a general appearance not far removed from the scenes recorded in the sixteenth century before the demolition of Old Saint Peter's, showing files of buildings that appear to be little more than small private houses in scale (Pl. 52).[12]

There are various ways in which charitable provision could cross with the need to train and stabilize a body of singers. The model was obvious and already ancient: a form of familial cohabitation *in domo ecclesiae*, or somewhere nearby, either configuring the group as a cell within the resident clergy, as monks, or as the recipients of episcopal or private charity. For private founders one might look to the Roman deacons, who included more than one distinguished psalmist and who had duties of care that were sometimes institutionalized in their governance of hospitals. In 598 a deacon named Antonius was provost of the *xenodochium Valerii* in Rome; in the same year the deacon Florentius administered the *xenodochium Anichiorum*, a foundation by one of Rome's most powerful families (this was the kindred of Boethius). In Sicily, where so many Roman foundations had much of their patrimony, a certain Cresciturus was deacon and abbot of the *xenodochium* of Saint John in Catania, traceable in 559. No such hostels or hospitals administered by deacons are known to have provided education, so these foundations can illustrate only one kind of caritative institution with the potential to metamorphose into elements of a *schola cantorum* still in solution.[13]

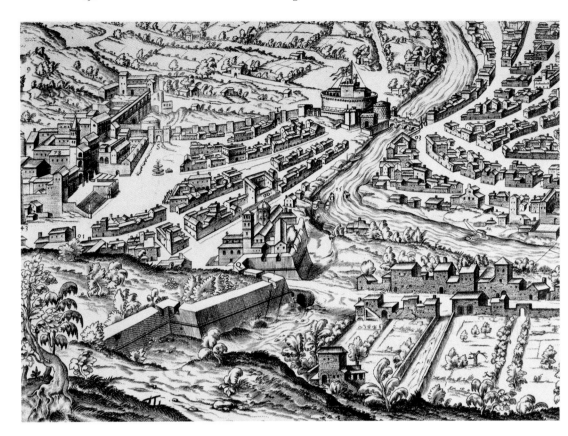

52   Detail of the plan of Rome by U. Pinard (1555), showing the region of Old Saint Peter's. From F. Ehrle and H. Egger, *Piante e vedute di Roma e del Vaticano dal 1300 al 1676* (Città del Vaticano, 1956), Tav. XXI.

A more secure path probably lies through the charitable provision made for children, partly inspired by Byzantine example. Boys, many of them probably orphans or children vowed to the monastic life by their parents, often appear in Roman documents from the sixth century onwards as a form of property, subject to the *jus* and *dominium* of an owner and moved from place to place as the resources or needs of their master dictated. The Register of Gregory I shows the pontiff requesting one churchman to transmit 'one hundred *solidi* and an orphan boy' to the bishop of Nepi, while the *Liber diurnus* contains a formula for the document to be drafted when a boy lodged in a Roman hospital or *xenodochium* is dedicated to the special service of a sick individual. Another formula in the same book concerns transactions when a boy is 'conceded' by one owner to another. Girls are rarely mentioned in this context, which suggests that these boys passing from hand to hand were regarded as potential clergy that would eventually emerge from the many different contexts, scattered across Rome, where ad hoc arrangements had deposited them to receive some form of training. As one would expect, given the long history of monasticism's involvement with education, there are documented cases of monks and abbots in deacon's orders who accepted boys, including orphans, into their charge for nurture and training, either in an associated hospital or simply within the walls of the monastery. For the latter, one need look no further than Gregory the Great's own house-monastery of Saint Andrew. When Gregory was still a deacon, his monastery sheltered a boy who had followed his brother into the house 'more for necessity than choice', suggesting that he was an orphan.[14]

'A place for bringing up orphans' is one of the earliest names for the Roman *schola cantorum*, or at least for one of the foundations that fed into it. As mentioned above, the *Liber diurnus* contains a document recording the diversion of funds to an *orphanotrophium* 'lest the order of singers be wanting'. The text is undated, as the materials in formularies so often are, leaving the question of when this orphanage was founded wide open. Presumably the same institution is meant when the *Liber pontificalis* credits Sergius II (844–7) with repairing 'the *schola cantorum*, once called *orphanotrophium*'. The name is a Latinized version of Greek, the model for both the institution and the name being the Great Orphanage or *orphanotropheion* of Constantinople. This imperial hospital was certainly in existence by 472, when it received public funds and was so closely identified with the higher levels of the imperial church that one of its governors, Akakios, known in the West as Acacius, became patriarch of Constantinople.

By this date, the Great Orphanage in the Byzantine capital was also a kind of song-school, in a relaxed sense of that term, making it one of the earliest Christian institutions to figure in the long and curious history of musical and dramatic performances in charitable foundations for foundlings and other disadvantaged children. The ecclesiastical history written by Zachariah of Mitylene for the years 450–91, surviving only in a multilayered Syriac redaction, records that a certain Timokletos composed hymns for children in the Great Orphanage to sing, apparently to the great pleasure of the people of Constantinople. 'Timokletos . . . set verses to music, and [the orphans] used to sing them. The people were delighted with them, and they flocked in crowds to the Orphan Hospital.' In some form, this tradition of public performance at the Great Orphanage may have passed to its Roman imitation, the *orphanotrophium*. In the last decades of the ninth century a Roman deacon named John, best known today as a biographer of Gregory the Great, composed a satirical poem entitled the *Cena Cypriani* with a description of the Roman festival known from a later and unique source of 1140–3 as the Cornomania. Celebrated on the first Saturday after Easter, the festival is described in John's ninth-century version as a public celebration in the presence of the pope which requires the *scolae prior* to wear horns and ride on an ass like Silenus, the son of Pan, while mocking songs are sung on every side. *Prior scolae* is the title borne by the leader of the *schola cantorum* in both *Ordo Romanus 1* of *c*.700 and the *Liber pontificalis*. The later, twelfth-century

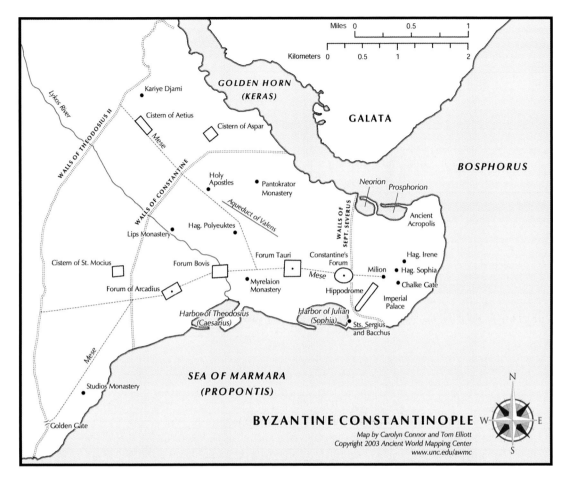

Map 6   Byzantine Constantinople. The *orphanotropheion* stood on the site of the ancient acropolis on the easternmost hill of the city. Hagia Sophia is to the south. © 2009, Ancient World Mapping Center, www.unc.edu/awmc.

account of these Roman revels even includes the texts of Greek songs, mangled and transliterated into Latin letters, which were sung at the festival and are of unknown age.[15]

These curious details may shed some light on the beginnings of the Roman orphanage or *orphanotrophium* that was one of the institutions feeding the *schola cantorum* to the point where it was identified with it in the ninth century. If the Roman name *orphanotrophium* implies a debt to a specific model, namely the Great Orphanage of Constantinople, then the Roman house may have been conceived from the beginning (whenever that was) as a place to educate the inmates in song of some kind, as well as other studies. The Great Orphanage in Constantinople was able to offer a model for such arrangements from at least the 470s.

This is a decidedly early date for the foundation of the Roman orphanage as a nascent *schola cantorum*, but it is not an impossible one, for there may be other signs that the *schola* is considerably older than the seventh century.

When the *schola* finally emerges into the light of written record it has a four-fold direction of *Primus* (or *Prior*) *scholae*, *Secundus*, *Tertius* and *Quartus*. The same kind of fourfold command structure appears in some of the palatine min-istries as early as the fourth century, including the four senior grades of inferior judicial clerks or *exceptores* (called *Primicerius*, *Secundicerius*, *Tertioserius* and *Quartoserius*). These were the four seniors of the *mittendarii*, the couriers of the *comites sacrarum largitionum*, and the notaries, who formed a corps or *schola* that can be traced as far back as 565. The *schola cantorum* preserved the late Roman custom of promotion by seniority within these grades, as revealed by the letter where Pope Paul I explains to Pippin, king of the Franks (751–68), why he has been compelled to recall the *Secundus scholae* from Rouen; the *Prior scholae* had recently died and Paul had no choice but to appoint his immediate junior, a step that the pope was evidently prepared to take, for the sake of due form, despite the risk of causing offence to the Frankish royal family (see below, p. 305). There is an argument to be made that the resemblances between the structure of the *schola cantorum* and certain palatine ministries of the late Empire reflect a late antique origin for the school of singers. Once more, we remember that Naples possessed a corps of singers led by a *primicerius* soon after 500, while Mértola has its *princeps cantorum*, perhaps a title of office, before 520.[16]

The sixth century is certainly the period when Italian evidence for charitable foundations of Byzantine type, and using the appropriate Greek names, begins to gather strength. The ninth-century chronicler Agnellus records that Bishop Ursicinus of Ravenna, traceable from 532 to 536, founded a monastic house dedicated to Saint Peter 'which is called *orfanum trofium*'. The value of this late report has its limits, but the great Church of Sant'Apollinare in Classe still stands to prove that Bishop Ursicinus was indeed a builder, and Roman evidence from almost exactly the same years shows the Byzantine commander Belisarius found-ing a house called *xenodochium* in Rome with riches gained by his destruction of the Vandal kingdom in the wars of 533–4. The end of Justinian's wars in Africa and Italy brought a large-scale immigration of Greek-speaking and bilingual Byzantine functionaries into Rome. The foundation of a hospital for aged poor, or *ptochium*, by Pope Pelagius II (579–90) fits easily into the context of the post-conquest Byzantine presence in the city. The foundation of the Church of Santa Maria *in Cosmedin*, Latinizing the Greek *kosmidion*, and the creation of a place on the Aventine called *ad Balcernas* after a district of the same name in the north-western part of Constantinople, may both belong to this period. Perhaps the beginnings of the Roman *orphanotrophium*, later associated with the name *schola cantorum*, lie in the same chronological layer.[17]

Gregory the Great and the Schola: A Local Habitation and a Name

Some of the greatest of all the nineteenth-century experts on Christian-Roman antiquities, including Louis Duchesne and De Rossi, supposed that the *schola cantorum* existed in the time of Gregory the Great (d. 604). Modern historians are not wanting who hold the same opinion (see above, p. 248). Gregory does indeed appear as a benefactor in the most detailed and controversial document for the history of the Roman *schola cantorum*, namely the biography completed by John the Deacon between 875 and 882 in Rome. By John's day, and indeed long before, Gregory was regarded as the fountainhead of liturgical song in the Roman tradition. In contrast, the contemporary and near-contemporary assessments of Gregory's achievements from Visigothic Spain, Anglo-Saxon England (the Whitby *Life*) and Italy, including the Roman *Liber pontificalis*, make no mention of chant. Even Bishop Taio of Saragossa (d. 651), who scoured the libraries of Rome for the best copies of Gregory's choice writings in the decades after his death, and who claimed to have seen a vision of the pontiff at work in all his different domains of activity, says nothing about plainsong. Nonetheless, Gregory's musical reputation was firmly established in the tradition that John the Deacon received in the 880s:[18]

> in the House of the Lord, in the manner of the most wise Solomon, and because of the spur to devotion that the sweetness of music affords, he assembled an extremely useful antiphoner for cantors in a most studious manner; he also created the *schola cantorum* which sings in the Holy Roman Church to this day on the same bases; he also used the revenue of certain estates to construct two small dwellings, that is to say one at the bottom of the stairs of the basilica of Saint Peter the Apostle, the other below the residential buildings of the Lateran palace, where, to this day, the bed in which he used to compose while reclining is kept together with his rod, with fitting veneration, the one he used to chastise the boys, and the authentic antiphoner. With a *praeceptum*, on pain of anathema, he divided the daily grace of divine service between these places.[19]

John was incensed by the presumption that Frankish singers had shown long before in the days of Charlemagne, equipped with a 'Roman' chant of their own and proud to claim – even when in Rome – that their version of Gregory's chant was more authentic than the Roman. John assimilates these presumptuous Franks to the ancient Gauls and scorns their 'bibulous throats' that cannot render the subtleties of the Roman music. This is the kind of writing that makes John the Deacon easy to discount, on first reading. He has already appeared in this chapter as a satirist and (unlikely as it may seem) as a humourist. Yet John was also a scholar with access to the papal archives that included the full collection of Gregory's correspondence. John also knew papal Rome intimately. One hostel for singers (or potential singers) did indeed exist at one of the two places that he specifies in the passage quoted above, and that is the *orphanotrophium.* The second 'little dwelling' that he mentions, by the great staircase of Saint Peter's, may be traceable in some form to at least the pontificate of Hadrian I (772–97), who founded a centre of poor-relief at a place 'close to Saint Gregory's *hospitale*' or hostel in front of the staircase to the basilica. This site was long associated with a charitable foundation and with Gregory's name, for in the twelfth century Mallius still believed Gregory had founded a *xenodochium* there. The Church of S. Gregorio in Cortina survived on the site, together with an attendant hostel, until the demolitions of the sixteenth century. Even after that, Alfarano still mapped on this site a 'church of Saint Gregory in the piazza for the dwelling of the singers'.[20]

Now, perhaps, one may begin to close in upon the quarry. John mentions three relics of Gregory: his bed (for Gregory was rarely in good health), his rod for correcting the boys and the antiphoner that he compiled. There is no indication in John's text how these relics were distributed between the two *habitacula* where they were kept in his day. Strange as it may seem, Gregory's couch may prove to be the most important relic in this story. The earliest reference to it appears in a pilgrim guide to Rome, the *Notitia Ecclesiarum Urbis Romae,* commonly dated to the pontificate of Honorius I (625–38), or perhaps shortly afterwards, and therefore reaching to within a generation of Gregory. The compiler advises pilgrims who reach Saint Peter's basilica to 'ascend to the bed of the holy father Gregory in which he gave up the ghost, and there you have eleven altars'. The second reference to the bed, of much later date, appears in the Life of Pope Stephen V (885–91) written for the *Liber pontificalis.* Now it seems that the bed lies in an oratory of Saint Gregory that is not *within* Saint Peter's basilica but *near* it. This means that some time between approximately 623–38 and 885–91 Gregory's bed was moved from a site in Saint Peter's basilica into an oratory near that same church. This oratory is surely to be identified with the *habitaculum* at the foot of the great staircase leading up to the basilica, mentioned by John the Deacon.[21]

This intimate relic of Saint Gregory can have been moved to the *habitaculum* near Saint Peter's basilica only because the site had a precise association with him. What was the nature of that association? One possibility is that Gregory did indeed found something on this site, perhaps a small oratory or hospital remembered for centuries in the name of San Gregorio de Cortina, the church that survived on this spot, together with an attendant hostel, until the sixteenth century. If this is the case then John the Deacon was right to say that Gregory diverted funds to create a new *habitaculum* by the staircase up to Saint Peter's basilica, and was not necessarily trying to mislead his readers when he alluded to a surviving juridical instrument or *praeceptum* from Gregory's time that specified the endowments for these two institutions and detailed the liturgical duties of the inhabitants. Perhaps he was also right to say that the *habitaculum* was intended for singers. It may have been for the training or even lodging of them

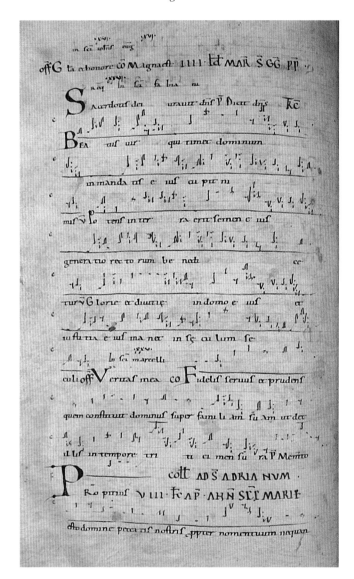

53   The Tract *Beatus
vir*, for the feast of
Saint Gregory, in the
Roman (or 'Old
Roman') version of
Bodmer 74, fol. 32ᵛ.
Cologny-Genève,
Fondation Martin
Bodmer.

as a caritative institution or hospital. Mallius's description of Saint Peter's basilica as it was in the time of Alexander III (1159–81) refers to our building, or more
likely another on the same site, as a *xenodochium* in which Gregory installed three
cantors and a superior, a Primicerius.

One might also add that the Roman clergy in the eleventh century, and perhaps long before that, celebrated Gregory's feast-day with a Tract using part of
Psalm 111 that has now, perhaps, acquired a special significance (see Pl. 53). One
of the verses runs *Gloria et divitie in domo eius*: 'Let there be glory and riches in
his house'.[22]

The syllabus in the Roman *schola cantorum* of the eighth century can perhaps be glimpsed in the biography of another Gregory, sometime bishop of Girgenti in Sicily. Gregory died in 638, but his biographer was a Roman priest named Leontius who was active (and writing in Greek) in the decades around 800. Leontius relates that Gregory was placed in the charge of Girgenti's bishop, who then supervised the boy's education at the request of his parents. At the age of 8, he joined a school (*didaskaleion*) within the city where he learned his letters, basic arithmetic (probably for the computation of Easter), the rudiments of astronomy, and the cycle of liturgical days and feasts. He also surpassed the other boys in his singing of the chants for both night and day. When he was 12, his parents requested that he be made a cleric, and the bishop ordained him a lector. Then the bishop's archdeacon and librarian took charge of Gregory's education, showing him many books and setting him to study their contents. By now, Gregory had learned to sing so well that all wondered at him.[23]

Although Gregory's biographer is describing an education for service in the Byzantine church, the elements of study that he describes were probably much the same throughout Christendom, at least when young men were being trained for the clergy in the orbit of a bishop and his cathedral. Viewed in this light, there seems nothing very unusual about the Roman *schola cantorum*. It was a way to coordinate the training of young men who were ultimately in the bishop's care, and whose number included some who showed the right gifts and aptitude for some position within the Church. This was a formalized and delegated version of the charge that many bishops were undertaking in their episcopal palaces far and wide. The principal tasks of the Roman pupils was presumably to learn how they should participate in the papal liturgies with their almost soldierly chain of command from the pope down to the lowest acolyte, transforming ritual actions and signals into a relay of ceremonious gestures. Once the pupils had learned to read and write Latin they were surely required, like Gregory of Girgenti, to study the liturgical calendar, to acquire the rudiments of arithmetic required for the determination of Easter, and to memorize the Psalter. They were probably expected to learn the musical language of the Roman liturgy by their repeated presence at services, and by constant imitation of what they heard, until some became so fluent that the clergy espied some future lectors or cantors in the cohort currently passing through the *schola*. Some of these singers passed into the papal choir, while others served as acolytes in one of the Roman *tituli* (effectively parish churches) as assistants to the priest or as cantor. Other 'graduates' of the school joined the papal administration based in the Lateran.

54   Detail of a late 4th-c. sarcophagus showing Christ giving the law to Peter. From the antique cemetery of Alyscamps, Arles. Arles, Musée de l'Arles antique.

13

STEERING IN DISTANT WATERS
BY THE ROMAN LIGHTHOUSE

Ecclesiastical Rome

In the Early Middle Ages it was impossible to deny that Rome was the western-most city reached by the first wave of apostolic mission. Christ's commission to Peter, the record of Paul's travels to the city and his extensive letter to the Christians there left little room for an alternative account (Pl. 54). Rome, approx-imately in the middle of the Italian peninsula that divides the Mediterranean into two maritime zones, was a bridgehead for the advance of the faith into the west-ern Empire. New writings tended to confirm the picture. Just as the canonical Acts of the Apostles places 'visitors from Rome' amongst those in Jerusalem at the time of Pentecost, so the apocryphal *Acts of Peter*, probably of the late second century, describes how the prince of the apostles travelled to Portus on a trading ship, then preached in the city until he suffered martyrdom there. The popes of the Roman world in transformation were rarely inclined to neglect the central place of their city in the developing geopolitics of the Christian faith. Thus in a famous letter of 411, Innocent I presents a sweeping vision of the West as an apos-tolic colony established under the direction of Peter:

> It is plain that in all Italy, the Gauls, the Spains, Africa and Sicily, and the islands lying between, no churches have been founded save those where the venerable Apostle Peter or his successors established bishops. Let them seek in their records whether any other Apostle can be found for these provinces, or is said in a book to have taught there. If they do not read that (for it can in no place be read), it behoves them to follow the faith of which the Roman Church is the guardian, and from which their churches undoubtedly take their origins . . .[1]

This is a Roman story in several senses. The apostolic missions of the first cen-tury, undertaken by Palestinian Jews and probably looking no further westwards than a line drawn between Rome and Carthage, have here become a Roman proj-ect reaching an Atlantic horizon. Just over thirty years before Innocent wrote his letter, an imperial edict had imposed the orthodoxy of the Roman and Alexandrian bishops upon the entire Empire. In the wake of that legislation, Innocent writes as arbiter of the true faith for his Western patriarchate, and with due confidence that many churches had good reason to accept his account for the sake of their own assured place in the genealogy of apostolic missions. In many ways he was right to be so self-assured. The Church of Arles, for example, claimed a founder of the apostolic period in Saint Trophimus, while the Church of Clermont, according to Gregory of Tours, traced its origins to a papal initiative during the reign of the emperor Decius (249–51).[2]

The surviving papal letters to the West from the time of Innocent to approximately 550 show the pontiffs variously reacting to news of heresies, conferring blessings, supplying collections of canons and answering questions about clerical discipline in language so crisp it could no doubt stimulate the conscience of bishops in distant churches. Relative to most other Western prelates, the popes of late antiquity and beyond maintained a high level of correspondence with consistently far horizons. To read these letters in bulk – for an appreciable number survive – is to discover how determinedly the bishops of Rome used their correspondence to fashion a Roman obedience in the Western churches, supported by eloquent additions from couriers, who may often have been deacons of the Roman Church (see above, pp. 157–8). An early but foundational example from 404 shows Innocent I once more, this time writing to Bishop Victricius of Rouen in a region that had only just ceased to be an important collecting point for military supplies to Britannia. Before 386, Victricius had already obtained relics of Gervasius, Protasius, John the Baptist, Saint Andrew and Saint Thomas from Italy, apparently with the help of Saint Ambrose, and to house them in a more glorious manner he built the church that still stood in the 750s to serve the first Carolingians as a cathedral and atelier to begin work on Frankish-Roman chant (Ch. 15). The letter Victricius received from Innocent lays out various matters of clerical and monastic discipline in a manner plainly designed to enhance the distant bishop's store of Roman canonical documents. Indeed, this communication is not so much a letter as a dossier incorporating an important canonical collection. The matters discussed in the document include sexual continence, criteria for admission to the clergy and advice for dealing with clerics who seek public office, including (somewhat surprisingly) service on the surviving Roman city councils or *curiae*. One provision in the letter requires that the apostolic see should be consulted in all weighty matters, especially including disputed questions of doctrine. For Innocent, the fundamental strictures laid out in this papal letter for the governance of clergy and laity are quite simply *Romae disciplina*: the teaching of Rome.[3]

When Innocent wrote his letter to Victricius, the imperial capital was still receiving the grain-ships from Tunisia. The pope speaks there, as in much of his correspondence, with an assurance based upon the continuing and by now long-established centrality of Rome in the maritime system of the western Mediterranean. In many respects, however, the breadth of communications and flow of wealth that underwrote the narrative of Rome's primacy in the western lands was soon to be narrowed with long-term effects reaching forwards some three hundred years. The Vandal seizure of Carthage in 439 put an end to the Tunisian supply-line with consequences that can be measured in the fortunes of the granaries and storerooms at Portus. Some were abandoned or used as cemeteries. The Roman population, which had perhaps already sunk by the time of Constantine to a third of its Augustan levels, cannot have been enhanced by the losses that followed this fracture of the tax spine between Rome and Carthage. Although Rome never ceased to be a place of architectural vistas that could humble most Western pilgrims in the first millennium (Arabs who had come for the textile markets were another matter) the city contracted in the sixth and seventh centuries around a densely impacted coop of tombs and hollowed altars where innumerable relics of the Roman saints and martyrs were kept. Men and women with less money to spare than Constantine, or than some of the popes, now founded monasteries and hostels for travellers on the reduced scale that can still surprise the modern visitor to certain late antique churches of Ravenna. The new Roman foundations included the various kinds of hospital that Romans began to adopt on the Greek model after the Byzantine conquest of Italy in 552, including those built for strangers and visitors (*xenodochia*), together with other foundations that included orphanages (*orphanotrophia*) and hostels for the sick and aged, not always clearly distinguishable from private monastic foundations.[4]

The range of Roman commercial contacts had contracted sharply by the 650s, to judge by the archaeological evidence of ceramics with its mounting preponderance of local ware. Nonetheless, recent archaeological finds in levels from around 700 have 'decisively changed all preceding knowledge of economic life' in early medieval Rome. Near the monastery of S. Lorenzo in Pallacinis traces of workshops have been found that once manufactured luxury goods, apparently for an elite clientele, and used recently made transport amphorae from Africa, the Aegean, Syria and Palestine. When envoys from the Frankish king Pippin arrived in Rome in 753 they would probably have seen signs of recovery. Their pilgrimages around the churches showed them new statues of the Apostles in silver 'weighing 180 pounds', and in the Church of Santa Croce in Gerusalemme new roof beams, a marble ambo 'and various linens'. Saint Agatha had acquired 'a canopy of silver weighing 720 pounds, and six silver arches, all weighing fifteen pounds'. These were among the works of Pope Gregory II (715–31) and by no means the only ones that pontiff undertook. Early medieval Rome was a city where many different forms of clerical and monastic life flowed among the great basilicas, titular churches and baths. The markets in luxury goods were still fed by maritime contacts with the Levantine ports and Byzantium that cities in many Western kingdoms would have been glad to possess.[5]

The brief document known as *Ordo Romanus I*, commonly dated to *c.*700, gives the earliest sustained picture of Roman liturgical celebrations and one that must have seemed profoundly impressive to many. The opening account of the city's ecclesiastical districts in the text has a quintessentially Roman and legalistic tone, being much concerned with duties, rights and cases in passages that may be brief, but which nonetheless sound the purest of Roman accents: the voice of statute. The account of the papal Mass that comes next in *Ordo Romanus I* evokes a late Roman and Mediterranean world where gold, silver and incense need not be spared, and where many officials of the Church appear with imperial titles of office like *primicerius notariorum* ('chief of the notaries'), which possessed an impressively Byzantine and military flavour. The nobles whom the pope approaches in person for their offerings at Mass are even located in a part of the church called 'the senate' or *senatorium*. All this gave readers of the document a unique insight into the ceremonial of a city whose name was still associated with the most exalted formalities, the most established laws, and the most venerable ecclesiastical traditions in the Latin world.[6]

The stimulus of Rome's reputation for liturgies conducted in material conditions of imperial splendour emerges with especial clarity in writings from Anglo-Saxon England, a remote corner of the old western Empire. The surviving Roman buildings there were apt to be called *enta geweorc*, or the 'work of giants', by the poets of a people accustomed to build in wood, but there was also fervent and well-informed devotion to Rome in gratitude for the Gregorian mission of the late 590s. The Life of Saint Wilfrid, commemorating the saint who led a second and northern wave of Romanizing conversion after the Gregorian mission, shows its hero building a church at Ripon in 671–8 with blocks of dressed stone in the Roman manner, probably taken from ruinous buildings nearby. Wilfrid set up columns, which were undoubtedly spoils, to create an interior adorned 'with gold and silver and varied purples', perhaps provided by textiles obtained in the markets of Rome during one of his several recorded journeys there. He ordered a copy of the gospels to be made for Ripon with golden letters on purple parchment, imitating models he had seen in Rome in 'the oratory of Saint Andrew the Apostle', that is to say in the house-monastery of Gregory the Great (a building no Anglo-Saxon pilgrim could visit without the deepest reverence). On his next visit to Rome in 679–80 Wilfrid obtained relics 'for the building up of the churches of Britain' together with many other valuables that he purchased, and he returned from his third visit in 704 with 'vestments of purple and silk to ornament the churches'. For Wilfrid and most other Occidentals, the shops and markets of Rome at this time provided the best access available anywhere west of Asia to the materials of Byzantine aulic and liturgical art.[7]

In remote parts of the Latin world, like Northumbria or the see of Kildare in Ireland, it could be especially difficult to sustain the rich materialism of Christian rites. Westerners had only to question travellers – or read *Ordo Romanus I* – to become convinced that those rites were celebrated with greater luxury and ceremoniousness in Rome than anywhere else in the lands of the Western churches. Much depended upon what especially adventurous individuals could obtain. The

Mass vestments of Kildare's first bishop, Saint Conlaed (d. ?*c*.520), were report-ed in the seventh century to have been *vestimenta transmarina et peregrina*, 'over-seas vestments of foreign origin', and may have been purchased in Rome; some Old Irish glosses reveal that Saint Conlaed tried three times to get there and eventually died on his third attempt. Others of his party may have succeeded. Benedict Biscop travelled to Rome on merchant ships to fetch what Bede calls the riches 'of spiritual commodities', *spiritualium mercium*. That is a potent expression, and much might be made of it. A given state of liturgy in an early medieval monastery or church expressed a particular state of long-distance com-munications and trade – or rather the strength of the determination to triumph over any impoverishments the decline of such communications were felt to be imposing upon rites intended to express the glory of the divine and the author-ity of the bishop. This gave some Christians north of the Alps yet another reason to look to Rome.[8]

In sources from the eighth century onwards, various individuals appear who were impressed by Rome's reputation for an imperial liturgy, for a pure faith, for a rigorous clerical discipline and for an ecclesiology refined with the subtlety of Roman legalism. These scattered reformers make a varied group. There is a soldier who became an abbot and brought a singer across the Alps from Rome; a female ascetic who was a major figure in her cathedral community and twice sent delegates to the papal city in search of liturgical material; a duke who became a bishop of Naples and sent three singers to study in the Roman *schola cantorum*; a Bavarian duke who was minded to adopt the Roman rite after a visit to the city and a synod of Iberian bishops. The middle years of the eighth cen-tury also bring the first efforts of the Frankish church to introduce what the Franks invariably call 'Roman' chant, requiring the passage of singers across the Alps in both directions. With various degrees of support, this mixed set of reformers sought elements of the Roman liturgy by visiting the papal city on pilgrimage or by sending their delegates to gather books, relics, singers and the materials of aulic ceremonial in the long tradition of using Rome as a warehouse of resources. In the context of this work, singers appear once more as a kind of imported luxury, part of a stream that could include many costly material goods for liturgical and other use. Now, however, the scale of displacement is longer than anything recorded for the sixth century, and the symbolic geography is quite different. Soon after 500, King Theuderic's reach for a singer extended from northern Gaul to Clermont in the Auvergne where the layers of late Roman Christianity lay thick in Gallo-Roman levels (see above, pp. 189–93). The initia-tives of the later reformers show the same need to reach towards a more author-itative tradition, but now they are not content with a local tributary. They seek the source.

Taken together, the recorded cases of liturgical reform on a Roman model give little sign of anything one might wish to call a *phase* of Romanization. The work was done during some two hundred years and the results achieved were no doubt as varied as the methods employed. Yet there are certain common patterns that can be called geopolitical, if that term will bear an extension beyond the mundane in the strict sense of the word. Most of the reformers came from places on the very edge of Christendom, such as Kildare in Ireland and Braga in Western Iberia. Others were situated uncomfortably close to large and potentially hostile pagan polities, including the dukes of Bavaria, in the old legionary fort of Regensburg, where Latin Christianity faced the Slavs and the Avar Khanate. In some other cases, the reformers had inherited quite enough geographical literacy from Classical writings, or from the reports of merchants and pilgrims, to appreciate just how remote they were from the Roman capital of Catholic Christianity, and how close to pagans across an unhelpfully narrow sea. So it was, for example, in Anglo-Saxon Northumbria. In another instance, three singers were sent to the Roman *schola cantorum* by a Neapolitan bishop at a crucial period in that city's emancipation from Byzantine control as an isolated outpost of imperial dominance in Italy. Time and again singers and their masters with a pronounced interest in the liturgies of Rome can be found with their backs against some kind of frontier, looking inwards.

Braga and Toledo

Conscious of meeting 'in this extremity of the world', eight bishops of Tarraconensis convened in 561 within the metropolitan church of Braga. For a number of years, the Arian kings of the Sueves had prevented them from meeting in synod, and now that their king was the Catholic Ariamir the time had come to restate the ancient canons and cleanse their churches of heresy. The prelates who assembled at Braga wished to do this with continual and scrupulous reference to writings received from Rome. These included a text from Pope Leo I (440–61) concerning the Iberian heretic Priscillian of Avila, and a set of canons embodying a rule of faith that former bishops of Iberia had composed under the guidance of Leo's materials. These canons were read in the assembly, for although Priscillian had long been dead the bishops associated his name with many serious faults of faith and discipline to which their province had fallen victim. With him in mind, the council pronounced anathema on those who deny that the Son is consubstantial with the Father, who believe that Christ had no physical body, who read apocryphal gospels and who teach that the stars exert an influence upon human affairs, 'as Priscillian said'. Other names appearing in this brief but rich conspectus of late antique heresy are Marcion (dead for some three hundred years) and Mani. This is a major piece of housekeeping by a far-flung Church.

To recover their unity in the rule of faith, and to share the peace of Christ, the prelates sought to establish a measure of consistency in the liturgies of their diocesan churches. Here, as so often in sources of the first millennium, consistency of liturgical practice is designed not only to express the peace and the orthodox faith of a Church but also to promote them. The prelates therefore decided that there should be one way of arranging the psalms for morning and evening worship (as usual, the term for this is *ordo psallendi*) and warned their singers not to confound the usage of cathedral churches with those of the monasteries. In two canons that recall the provisions of Laodicea, the psalmists of the Braga archdiocese, called lectors, are forbidden to perform their psalmody in secular clothes or to employ anything other than scriptural texts. On major feast-days, the bishops require that the same readings should be used in all churches of the archdiocese at Mass and the nocturnal services. When the prelates turn to the order of Mass, the presence of 'those materials we have from the apostolic see for the purposes of instruction' become especially telling. In addition to those mentioned above, they include a letter from Pope Vigilius to Profuturus, a former metropolitan of Braga, dated 29 June 538 and sent in response to a series of questions from the Iberian bishops addressing Priscillianism, baptism, Arianism, the dedication of churches and the correct date of the celebration of Easter. In his reply, Pope Vigilius had referred to a series of headings or chapters, appended to his letter, explaining how the feasts of Easter, the Ascension, Pentecost, Epiphany and unspecified saints should be celebrated. This is the earliest case on record of a church on a periphery of Christendom seeking liturgical material from Rome. Like their Suevic king, the Catholic bishops of Braga shared the Iberian Peninsula with the much larger and potentially threatening kingdom of the Visigoths, still ruled by Arian monarchs and destined to obliterate the Suevic kingdom altogether within a few decades of the council. By their liturgical reform on the Roman model, the bishops of the Sueves probably hoped to mark their independence from an uncomfortably close temporal power by enhancing their subjection to an uncomfortably distant spiritual one.[9]

A foreign visitor to other parts of Spain might well have assumed that the Visigothic Church would follow the Romanizing example of the Suevic kingdom. A blaze of filial affection for Rome and its bishops illuminates many of the writings produced by Visigothic bishops in the decades around 600. The prelate whose homily closed the proceedings of the Third Council of Toledo in 589, Leander of Seville, formed a friendship with Gregory the Great in Constantinople before the latter's accession to the papacy, and Gregory offered him the dedication of his *Moralia in Job*, a book so widely read in later centuries that the gesture was never forgotten or undervalued. Leander's brother Isidore regarded himself as head of the Church in Seville 'as long as I show due obedience reverently, humbly and devotedly in everything to the Roman pontiff'. Romanism of another kind was manifest around 600 when a bishop of Ibiza brandished a letter before his astonished congregation and claimed that Saint Peter had simply dropped this new addition to Scripture through the clouds for anyone to find. In 642, Taio of Saragossa reported to Eugenius of Toledo that he had received a vision of Pope Gregory I while seeking out copies of that pontiff's writings in Rome. 'I saw, I saw our Gregory at Rome', he writes excitedly, 'not with the eyes

55 *Romanitas* in Braga. The 7th-c. funerary chapel of São Frutuoso de Montelios, built from large blocks of dressed stone in the Roman manner and to a strikingly late Roman design. The plan and proportions are strongly reminiscent of late antique buildings in Ravenna.

of the body but of the mind.' These Spanish prelates were even more Gregorian in their sympathies than the Anglo-Saxons and Franks a hundred years later. To them, he was 'our Gregory'.[10]

Yet in contrast to what happened in the Suevic kingdom, or indeed in Anglo-Saxon England and Francia, the Visigothic Church did not seek to train its singers in customs borrowed from the liturgy of Rome. The reasons probably have much to do with the attitude of the kings in a realm that was in many respects politically and materially self-sufficient. When the kingdom of Toledo was established under Leovigild in the late sixth century, the scope for military adventurism beyond the limits of the realm was small. Westwards lay the wastes of the Atlantic. To the south, the Byzantines had to be dislodged from the enclave they had established, which was eventually done; further south lay the straits of Gibraltar and Africa, where the Visigoths maintained some commercial and other connections (to judge by Isidore's report that the Goths believed themselves related to the inhabitants of Mauretania) but they had no reason to suspect the Islamic apocalypse that would soon sweep in across the southern straits. To the north beyond Toulouse the Franks blocked the way, but the Spanish kings did not venture major campaigns there, despite some notable victories. Those monarchs possessed a large belt of territory in Gaul that reached to the northern limits of the olive and ensured that some 85 per cent of the Visigothic kingdom lay within the olive-line at this date (for the Franks the figure was more like 5 per cent). Kings who already ruled in Baetica, Lusitania and much of Languedoc had little reason to risk campaigns in the Auvergne or Aquitaine. At home, they financed an elaborate palace administration from taxation and could count on bishops who by the 580s wrote the best Latin in the West. When king Reccared proclaimed himself a Catholic in that year, he barely communicated with Rome on his own account except to report that a first relay of messengers to the Holy See had been shipwrecked on the way.

Ireland and Anglo-Saxon England

As a marker of Christendom's westernmost reach, Kildare in Ireland yields to Braga in Iberia by only a few miles. The greatest early saint of Kildare, Saint Brigid, died some time in the 520s, and her life inspired several layered biographies that purport to describe the primordial years of the Christian faith in Ireland and the rivalry between the sees of Kildare and Armagh. Some of the oldest material is contained in the Life known as *Vita I*, widely believed to contain a stratum of seventh-century material. This Life reveals how Brigid often heard the sound of Masses being celebrated in other lands, and on one occasion her supernatural hearing, scanning the airwaves for Masses celebrated in distant stations, chanced upon the wavelength for Rome. Better still, she heard Masses being celebrated over the tombs of Saint Peter and Saint Paul. From that moment on, she conceived a passionate desire to obtain 'the order of the Mass and the universal rule' from the pontifical city. Brigid sent several experts, perhaps trained singers from the clergy of Kildare, who duly obtained what she sought. But after some time, she summoned these same envoys again and said: 'I discern that certain things have been changed in the Mass in Rome since your return from there. Go back again.'

The primordial and semi-legendary figure of Saint Patrick stands only a generation back from the events reported in this first Life of Brigid. The question of what the narrator is remembering in this passage therefore seems wide open, for there may be little or no authentic information about the decades around 500 in his account. He is probably engaging with the liturgical customs of Kildare as he knew them in the seventh or even in the eighth centuries, and constructing a history for them by tracing them to Rome and to the most famous saint of his own diocese. Perhaps the clergy of Kildare did indeed seek elements of the Roman Mass *ordo* at some stage in the seventh century to rival, or even to surpass, the see of Armagh. If so, the story of Brigid's two embassies to Rome is perhaps the foundation narrative they chose for the rite they had introduced.[11]

From the last quarter of the seventh century onwards, signs of interest in the Roman liturgy pick up sharply, beginning with the Anglo-Saxon soldier turned abbot, Benedict Biscop. In 674, when many churches among the Angelcynn were still essentially long houses constructed of wood and roofed with thatch, Benedict built a monastery of stone 'after the Roman fashion' at Wearmouth, near the modern city of Newcastle upon Tyne in Northumbria. Whatever else it may imply, the expression 'Roman fashion' certainly means large blocks of dressed stone similar to those cut for the seventh-century funerary chapel of São Frutuoso de Montelios (Pl. 55 above), or seen in the remains of the legionary fortress at Regensburg (Pl. 57 below). The house was dedicated to Saint Peter, and in 681 Benedict established a second branch at nearby Jarrow, dedicated to Saint Paul and completing his invitation that the greatest saints of Rome should direct their gaze to one of the most isolated corners of the Christian world. More than a thousand miles, and a bleak expanse of the North Sea, separated Wearmouth and Jarrow from Rome. Benedict nonetheless worked hard to establish a spiritual canal between the Tiber and the Tyne, where his twin houses were among the most exposed stations of the Catholic faith in the north. They were not at the limit of Christendom, for the Picts had determined to follow the customs of the Roman Church in Bede's lifetime ('remote though they were from the Roman people and from their language', says Bede) yet the monks of Wearmouth-Jarrow faced a belt of pagan lands across the North Sea running down from northern Scandinavia to at least the modern Franco-Belgian border. It would be an exaggeration to suggest that Bede continuously sensed an ominous presence across the expanse of the waves, for he shows more awareness in his writings of great churches like Tours in Francia than of pagan settlements like Birka in Sweden. Nonetheless, Bede and Benedict Biscop knew what a missionary would find if he sailed round the north and eastern coast of Britain, and that was 'Frisians, Rugians, Danes, Huns [!] and Old Saxons . . . practising heathen rites'.[12]

Benedict Biscop repeatedly overcame the great distance that separated his monastic foundation from the papal city, undertaking six pilgrimages to assemble a library at Wearmouth-Jarrow with few parallels in the West outside parts of Italy or Seville. According to Bede, who spent his life at Jarrow reading these volumes and supplementing them with books of his own, Benedict also wanted the 'yearly *cursus* of chanting' together with 'its *ordo* of rite, chanting and reading aloud'. To accomplish this, Benedict returned from his fifth pilgrimage with John, an *archicantator* of Saint Peter's basilica and abbot of Saint Martin's, one of four monasteries serving the basilica in the services of the Hours but also, by this date, at Mass. So that John might 'teach the monks . . . the mode of chanting throughout the year', Bede explains, John 'committed to writing all things necessary for the celebration of festal days' (see Pl. 56). It would be unwise to insist that John, as a monk, did not serve with the Roman *schola cantorum*, given how little is known about the constitution and recruitment of that body or its overlap with other teams in the city; all that seems certain is that Benedict Biscop was more than fortunate in the choice of adviser assigned to him, especially in the matter of the musical tradition to which John the arch-chanter belonged. John's

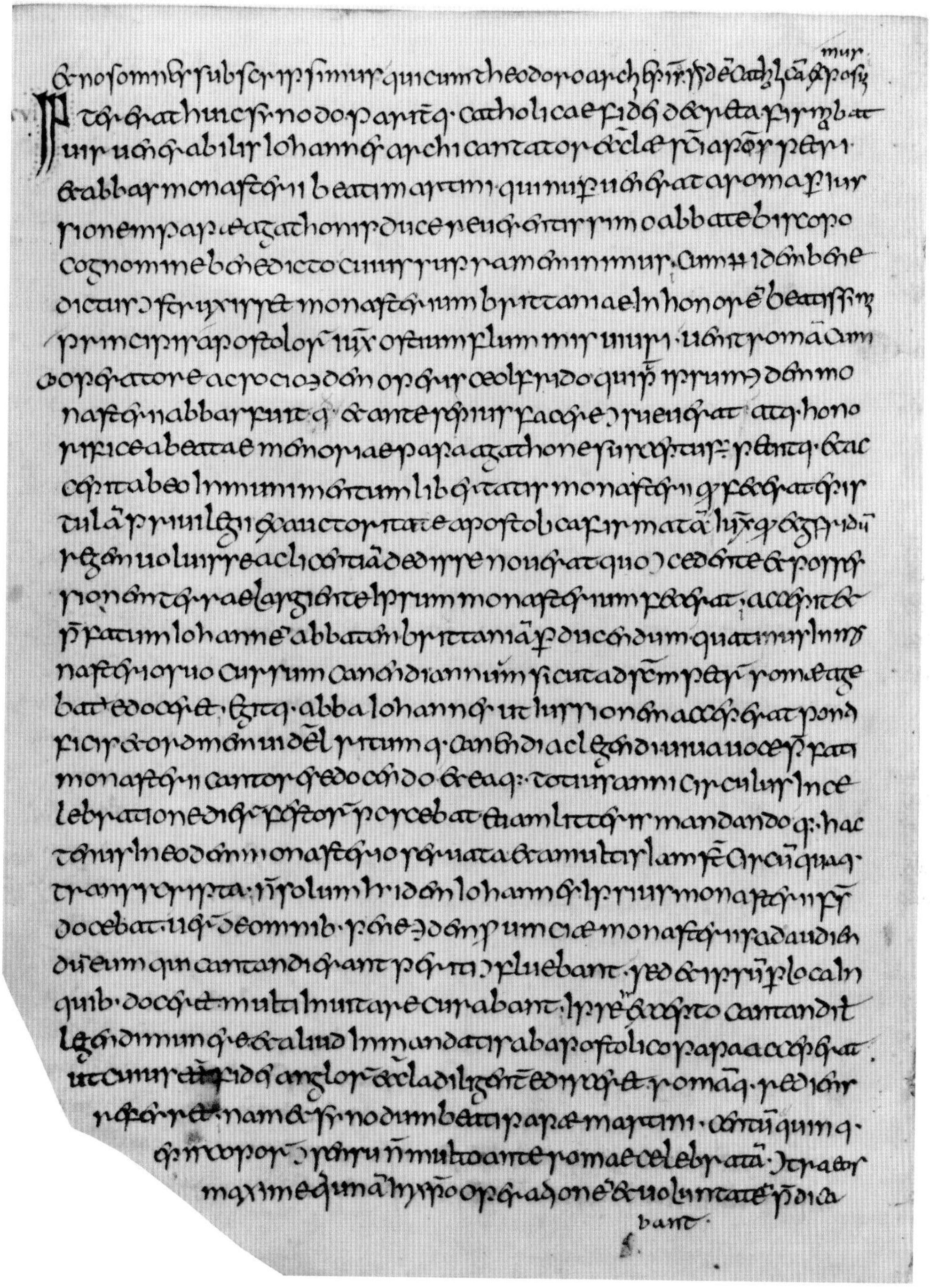

56 Bede explains how Benedict Biscop brought John the 'archicantator' of St Peter's basilica, and abbot of St Martin's, to his foundation of Wearmouth-Jarrow in Northumbria. Cambridge University Library, MS Kk.5.16, fol. 84v (the Moore Bede). Northumbrian, written in or soon after 737.

recent predecessors as monastic singers in the patriarchal basilica of Saint Peter's included the three abbots Catalenus, Maurianus and Virbonus, known to the curiously excitable compiler of *Ordo Romanus XIX* around 750 as men skilled 'in the chant for the course of the year', the *cantus anni circuli*.[13]

This is the earliest securely documented case in the early Middle Ages of one centre lending a singer to another (even if the real interest of the visit, when viewed from Rome, did not lie in the lessons John was to give Anglo-Saxon singers but rather in the report he was commissioned to give on the state of the English Church). Such loans were fundamental to the life and work of singers in churches and monasteries but are rarely mentioned in the surviving documents. During the first millennium, ways to sing a text generally travelled by foot or horse along channels of communication that were carrying other traffic at the same time, much of it probably regarded as more important. John the arch-chanter was one stream of information, so to speak, in the complex message that Benedict Biscop was bringing back from Rome with manuscripts, images and other materials. Whether it was the pupils who moved from place to place or the teachers, a long period of displacement might be necessary to imprint the contents of one memory upon others; death or other accidents might intervene to interrupt the work or to erode its results; vast distances might be travelled carrying pupils or teachers into different polities, cultures and ecological zones. These studies were as so many leaves borne forward on the streams of loyalty or obligation that flowed between communities or individuals, and which invariably gave the work the character of a favour or an alliance. The transfer of a singer in this Northumbrian context shows that Benedict wanted more than Roman prayers from the priest at the altar; for that he could simply have obtained a good sacramentary. He wanted Roman ways to intone the psalms, for he would scarcely have needed a senior official in a major basilica for that. He needed a singer whose many years of experience had carried him to the leadership of his community: one from the heart of the Roman and specifically the pontifical tradition who could single-handedly Romanize the rite and the calendar of Benedict's monastery. Even this was not the end of John's compendious ability as a Roman churchman, for Pope Agatho (678–81) entrusted him with the tasks of verifying that the English Church was free from heresy and of giving the report mentioned above.

The value that subsequent generations in Anglo-Saxon England placed upon the *romanitas* of their chant emerges from the poem *Gregorius presul meritis et nomine dignus* ('Gregory the prelate, worthy in merits and in name'), which survives in an extended version in a unique and poor copy of the late eighth century. The poet begins by associating Pope Gregory the Great with the Roman *schola cantorum* and the compilation of a book for their use:

> Gregory the prelate, worthy in merits and in name, ascends from where he has his birth to the highest honour and, one of the moderns, he renewed the mon-

uments of the ancient fathers; the wise man, trusting to heavenly reward, prepared and then gathered together for the *schola cantorum* this booklet. (1–5)

These same lines, with minor variants, appear in several sources of the late eighth or ninth century, including the magnificent Monza cantatorium, where they are copied in silver uncials on purple parchment (see below, Pl. 63). But in the Lucca manuscript they are extended with another thirty lines as the poet exhorts all singers to divine praise in the manner of the psalmist:

Let the rational voice of the singer resound repeatedly so that it may strike the lofty summit of heaven with sonorous chant. Let us praise God with harmonious voice, and let the throng of those who are His burst forth in continual chants! On these feast-days we shall chant hymns, psalms and the appropriate responds beneath the roof of the church, intoning the melody with the continuous music of the Psalter, and let us strive to tune the harp with its ten strings, just as the psalmist urges us to 'praise with twice-five strings . . .'. (10–18)

The poet also admires Gregory the theologian, praising him for filling 'the meadows of Mankind with various fruits of flowers to light weak minds with books'.[14]

Gregorius presul was seemingly designed for a luxurious form of presentation. 'Here it shines', says the poet in line 19, 'brightly made from radiant silver', suggesting that the poem was originally composed to preface a chant book with the poem – perhaps with the entire manuscript – written in silver letters. The reasons for supposing that the poem was written in England, or in an Anglo-Saxon foundation on the Continent, lies in verses 8–18, which prove to have been taken from a poem by Aldhelm, the Anglo-Saxon scholar who was consecrated bishop of Sherborne in 705 or 706. The compiler of *Gregorius presul* found the lines he has borrowed in a poem that Aldhelm composed between 689 and 726 for an unidentified Minster of Saint Mary. What is more, this poet had access to other poems by Aldhelm, perhaps even to a manuscript of his collected works. Indeed, he is so deeply imbued with the diction and the metrical practice of Aldhelm that he probably belongs to the period before 750 rather than later, for after the middle of the century the style of Bede – the metre more limpid, the diction less esoteric – began to exert its influence. If the compiler of the Lucca *Gregorius presul* was indeed working in England before *c.*750, then his poem may be connected with a particular Romanizing initiative in the chanting of Anglo-Saxon singers during the first half of the eighth century, and one closely associated with the materials for the Roman *schola cantorum*.[15]

There may be other traces of it. In 747, Archbishop Cuthbert of Canterbury convened a reforming council at an unidentified place in Southumbria called *Clofesho*. Several of the canons are designed to secure liturgical unity throughout the metropolitan province of Canterbury, with particular attention to the man-

ner of chanting. The twelfth chapter insists that priests should not imitate 'secular poets' when they sing but should keep to the 'plain and holy melody according to the manner of the Church', which probably means the manner which the
Anglo-Saxons regarded as Roman. The next chapter confirms this ruling and
expands it, requiring that for the 'holy festivals of the Lord's incarnation' the
manner of chanting to be used by the singers at Mass should everywhere be
'according to the exemplar that we have in writing (*scriptum*) from the Roman
church'. It also requires an annual cycle of saint's days 'according to the martyro-
logy of the same Roman Church, with the psalmody or chant that goes with it'.
This sounds like a Roman cursus of chant for the Temporale and Sanctorale of
the entire liturgical year, using material that was intended – however well
or poorly the intention was carried out – to follow the usage of the *schola cantorum* in Rome.[16]

Nivelles, Regensburg and Naples

Saint Gertrude of Nivelles (d. 659) belonged to the Austrasian clan that eventually produced the Carolingians. Her life was shaped by the common practice of
installing widows, daughters or both as the heads of small family nunneries,
often purpose-built and perhaps enclosing as few as a dozen religious in a space
scarcely larger than a house. Foundations on this scale may rarely have mounted
anything other than a spoken service, but there is every reason to form a lofty
impression of the liturgical life that the largest might enjoy and of the *romanitas*
they could cultivate in Mass and Office. The Life of Gertrude, composed not
long after her death, provides the earliest evidence there is for a Pippinid interest
in the liturgy of Rome, and it places that interest firmly in the context of
Gertrude's activity in her nunnery at Nivelles.[17]

    After the death of her father, Gertrude was placed in this nunnery built by her
mother Itta, the first abbess of the house. Upon Itta's death, Gertrude followed
her as abbess. At some stage she sent reliable and trustworthy men to Rome so
that they might gather relics and books, while from unspecified regions overseas
they obtained experienced men who were capable of teaching 'the *carmina* of
divine law'. The books may have included papal letters, collections of conciliar
proceedings, books by Gregory the Great and much else that Westerners were
accustomed to seek in Rome or to have copied and dispatched. They may also
have included some of the brief manuals of liturgical practice that were perhaps
already being collected and copied north of the Alps, the *ordines romani*. But
what were 'the *carmina* of divine law' that the 'experienced men' brought from
overseas? The expression is disconcertingly vague and could mean a great deal
including Lives of Saints in verse, poems on the calculation of days when Easter
would fall year by year, or major works of Christian-Latin literature such as the
Psychomachia of Prudentius. The common use of *carmen* for metrical Latin poet-

ry suggests that they might also be hymns in a quantitative metre, by no means lacking in early medieval sources, and while that can only be a guess the qualifier 'of divine law' suggests that if the author intends anything precise then he is thinking of liturgical material. The question of whether they might also be chants for Frankish singers to perform is delicate. The belief that liturgical chants were a source of instruction in true faith ran deep in seventh-century Spain, for example, as emphasized above in Chapter 10, and will appear again in Francia during the 760s when Pope Zacharias will commend 'chants of ecclesiastical doctrine' to King Pippin in a context which establishes beyond any doubt that he means psalmody sung at Rome by the *schola cantorum*. To be sure, the teachers whom Gertrude obtained were not Roman, or rather they came from unspecified regions overseas that might be Anglo-Saxon England or Ireland, but that does not rule out the possibility that the *carmina* were Roman chants of some description carried by 'experienced men' who were trained singers.

A generation after Gertrude, plans were laid to bring Roman psalmody to the dukedom of Bavaria. The dukes resided within the old imperial fort at Regensburg described in the eighth century as a *civitas* with lofty towers and squared stones, a reference once more to Roman masonry and military architecture that can still be seen in the city (Pl. 57). There were Christian communities in old Roman settlements such as Augsburg, Salzburg and indeed Regensburg, but the Christian infrastructure in the east was still rudimentary and the dukes

57   Roman squared masonry from the legionary fortress of Regensburg.

had much to gain from sponsoring the work of missionaries ready to preach, arrange clearances in wooded areas and supervise the building of churches. Soon after 700, the first duke from the Agilolfing kindred, a line destined to hold the dukedom with considerable resilience into the time of Charlemagne, obtained the help of Rupert, who had recently fled or been expelled from the bishopric of Worms. The duke, named Theoto, saw the spiritual and temporal benefits of making himself the centre of a Bavarian Church allied with Rome well before any Carolingian unless one counts Gertrude of Nivelles. Theoto allowed Rupert to restore existing churches and to build new ones on the modest scale suggested by the term *habitacula*, or 'small dwellings'. The motif of the saint who clears wooded land to build churches, destroy pagan shrines and bring converts to baptism is one of the most familiar in medieval hagiography, and even the biographer of Saint Rupert (as he became) felt compelled to admit that there were impressive remains of Roman structures in parts of Theoto's dominion which compromised any attempt to describe them as wilderness. Yet much of the duke's territory had seen frontier conflict in the late Roman period, its communities shifting from fort to fort as the tide of military emergency flowed, and there may be some truth in the Life of Rupert when it describes the hero clearing land granted to him by the duke for the foundation of new churches. There was good reason for the duke to encourage work that organized and populated his territories, and those of his dependents, with tenants attracted to a cleared area with a place of worship. At least one of the churches that Rupert created (supposedly in a cleared area) was given a clerical staff, of undisclosed size, for a liturgical *cursus*, but Rupert's greatest initiative within the dukedom was the creation of a major church dedicated to Saint Peter, which marks the beginning of Salzburg as an ecclesiastical centre, indeed as a city. In a striking example of how missionary and a magnate might collaborate to enhance the infrastructure of Christian government, Rupert and Theoto established the first Bavarian bishopric there.[18]

Perhaps inspired by Corbinian, the first bishop of the new see of Salzburg, Theoto determined that the Church in his dukedom should henceforth show a more diligent and comprehensive respect for the norms of doctrine, organization and liturgy that he, like most Westerners by now, associated with the Church in Rome. Here was a form of spiritual fealty that could reset the frontier of the Roman obedience so that it ran around the edges of the dukedom and conferred Saint Peter's protection against political predators, notably the Franks that pressed on Theoto's western and northern borders. (Sixty years later, the Frankish king Pippin will still be battling against this Rome–Regensburg axis in Bavaria; see below, pp. 295–6). Having prepared the ground with Gregory II (715–31), Theoto went to Rome, where his arrival on such business was considered so worthy of note that the biographer of Gregory in the *Liber pontificalis* selects it as one of the significant events of his papacy. For his part, Gregory no doubt saw an opportunity to establish a Bavarian province that would acknowledge the primacy of the Holy See. Subsequently, in 716, Theoto joined the long list of

Christian kings and magnates in the Occident who received a collection of papal decretals direct from Rome. These survive, and if they embody the results of preliminary discussions in Rome, which seems likely, then the duke was contemplating a major reform of the Church in his lands, including its liturgy. One canon in the set requires all clergy to adopt the manner of celebrating Mass, of ministering and of psalmodizing (*psallendi*) after the manner of the Roman Church.[19]

This may simply mean that churches were to adopt a Roman (perhaps a Benedictine) practice of psalmody at the morning and evening services, a practical agenda for reform since it could be carried through in all churches, from the merest rural *habitaculum* with a single priest and acolyte, up to the new cathedral church in Salzburg. If something more elaborate was meant by the Roman manner of psalmody, then it was perhaps an adapted Roman *ordo* of Mass for the cathedrals, for churches on lands in the duke's possession equipped to mount such a liturgy and for churches where the local magnate wished to show himself a *fidelis* of Theoto by following the ducal example in foundations on his own estates. There is no way of establishing what was attempted or indeed what was achieved in this early wave of ecclesiastical reform in Bavaria; Theoto's initiative nonetheless provides one of the clearest examples from the first millennium of a collaborative project between a pope and a temporal lord to establish a Romanized liturgical frontier in a highly exposed situation. The sees of Regensburg, Freising, Würzburg, Buraburg, Erfurt and Eichstätt did not yet exist to exert the controlling influence of parochial organization in Bavaria or to provide the soft but cumulatively dragging resistance that agricultural estates, churches and other buildings might offer to an invader on his intrusive progress. On his eastern flank Theoto faced the pagan Slavs, whose territory went down as far as the southern coasts of Greece. More dangerous still, perhaps, was the Khanate of the Avars; only the river Inn stood between them and the dukedom of Bavaria, together with a belt of townships and settlements whose inhabitants had fled. Theoto ruled in borderlands of Latin Christendom where the sedentary world contemplated the nomadic Avar and where the Catholic world looked across to the pagan Slav. Like any physical frontier of walls and forts, a liturgical frontier could have stretches of greater and lesser strength. A simple *habitaculum* with one priest and an acolyte, both of them possibly slaves, could fall away through neglect or the seizure of its modest endowments as easily as a wooden palisade could become useless for want of maintenance. To retain the comparison a moment longer, a major church like the cathedral of Salzburg was a nodal fort, perhaps built of stone from the beginning, and even if singers were only minor foot-soldiers in its garrison, their contribution to the festive liturgy that could bring divine aid to a vulnerable frontier was out of all proportion to their often humble status.

The dukedom of Naples was another polity on a borderland, albeit of a very different kind, for it was an outpost of Byzantine imperial power in the Italian peninsula. In 766 the city was smitten with a grievous attack of bubonic plague. When scarcely anyone was left to bury the dead, the remaining people of the city turned to Duke Stephen and asked him to become their bishop. Stephen 'granted their request', says his biographer, duly sensitive to any charge of overweening ambition on the part of his aristocratic subject. Once Stephen had been consecrated at Rome, he founded a dynasty that was to last for seventy-seven years by promptly conferring the title of duke upon his son, even though the dukedom was not a hereditary title. He also took decisive action in the matter of Naples's obedience to the see of Rome. For many decades, the tide of Neapolitan loyalty had been shifting between Rome and Constantinople. Naples was a Byzantine city in Stephen's day, and could be viewed as a legitimate possession of the Emperor; at the opposite extreme of opinion, there were some who regarded Naples as a valuable maritime possession that the Byzantine Greeks cynically maintained in a country they had long ceased to administer, defend or provision in an effective manner, despite their legal obligation to do so. For those with pro-Roman sympathies, this was in sharp contrast to what the popes had done for their people by acting as civic officials charged with public welfare, and as pastors in the lands of the Roman Church within Italy. The situation upon Stephen's accession was delicate and he surely remembered recent tensions in Naples between pro-Byzantine and pro-Roman factions that had prevented his predecessor, Paul, from remaining within the walls of the city, at least for a time, after his appointment to the see. Stephen showed his preferred allegiance to old Rome by sending three clerics to study in the Roman *schola cantorum*. His envoys presumably studied the Roman rite, the manner of singing the texts assigned to be sung throughout the liturgical year, and the intricacies of the Roman calendar in what was essentially a college of singers. The three clerics from Naples eventually left the *schola* and returned 'excellently trained and imbued with the sacred rites of the Romans', apparently to Stephen's satisfaction. He made one into a cardinal priest and placed two more in the Benedictine monastery of Saint Paul.

Once again, a psalmodic reform on the Roman model leads to the rim of the Latin world, this time almost to its southern extreme. By now the Moslems dominated the sea-lanes of the Mediterranean with the Abbasid Caliphate and the Umayyad Emirate in Spain controlling about two-thirds of the Mediterranean coastline between them. Naples was a Byzantine outpost in the 760s. Gold coins were minted there in the Emperor's name until the ninth century, Greek continued to be used for inscriptions and many officials bore Byzantine titles, including Bishop Stephen himself, for the duke of Naples was always an imperial *spatharius*. Yet one of Stephen's charters reveals him taking an oath upon the life of the Emperor Constantine Copronymus but also upon the 'life and pallium of our most blessed and angelic Paul, supreme pontiff and universal father'. Stephen's biographer, a clerical official in the episcopal household of Naples, openly attacks the Byzantine Emperor for wishing to wield authority in Rome, and while Stephen himself might not have wished to venture so far, the epitaph of his son Caesarius (788) pointedly calls a later emperor 'king of New Rome', denying him his imperial title. Stephen was essentially the first autonomous duke of Naples, and his wish to seek the chant of Rome from the *schola cantorum* is a minor but important chapter in the history of Neapolitan independence from imperial control. The years of his episcopate lie on a rising curve of Neapolitan separatism that peaked in the early 800s when his descendant in office, duke Anthemius of Naples, refused an imperial request for ships to send against the Arabs. Viewed more broadly still, Stephen's despatch of singers to the *schola cantorum* reveals the shifting equilibrium between Latin and Byzantine power in Italy that the popes and Carolingians were doing so much to readjust at exactly the same time, and with musical consequences (Chs. 14–16). Indeed, it may be no coincidence that Stephen sent his singers to the *schola cantorum* only a few years after arrangements were made for a Carolingian bishop of royal blood to send some of his singers to the same Roman *schola*. The two delegations may even have met there.[20]

By the time of Stephen, however, and indeed by the time of the Carolingian Franks, who beat his men to the Roman *schola* by just a few years, something far-reaching may have happened recently in the repertory of the Roman singers, pontifical and presbyteral. Kildare preserved a seventh-century tradition about clerics from the see who were sent to Rome and then sent back again on a second journey because it was rumoured that something had changed in the Roman manner of celebrating the liturgy. It is striking how quickly the signs of a new or renewed interest in Roman chanting accelerate as the seventh century comes to an end. Gertrude's interest in Roman *carmina*, whatever they were, is probably too vague a testimony to be much use and is perhaps too early, since she died in 659. Within less than thirty years, however, the evidence begins to accumulate. In 674, Benedict Biscop builds his Northumbrian Church in the Roman manner and eventually imports a Roman singer to teach his monks; in 716, Theoto of Bavaria receives his injunction to introduce Roman psalmody, impossible to achieve without the transalpine movement of singers if an annual *cursus* of liturgical melody is meant. The year 747 brings the Council of *Clofesho* requiring the liturgy of both Temporale and Sanctorale to be celebrated 'according to the exemplar that we have in writing (*scriptum*) from the Roman church'. This may also be the period of the long version of *Gregorius presul*, probably composed as the prefatory poem to an Anglo-Saxon copy of a liturgical book 'of the *schola cantorum*'. The 760s reveal singers from Naples and Rouen taking lessons at Rome in the *schola*.

In sending three singers to the Roman *schola cantorum*, Stephen of Naples was entrusting their education to the resources of a city that used long-standing forms of schooling and charitable provision, both with late antique roots, to supply its incomparably prestigious churches with boys and men brought to a preparatory stage of literacy and acquaintance with the Roman liturgy. Hence while it is perfectly possible that the singers of the *schola* were reorganized, at various times, by receiving new premises supported by new endowments, it is probably misleading to suppose that there was a particular period when the *schola cantorum* was founded or somehow brought into focus as an institution, not least because one thereby tends to lose touch with the true context for the *schola*: the rich history of charitable provision in late antique and early medieval Rome. The true source of the Romanizing reforms traced in the later part of this chapter probably lies elsewhere than in a new repertory or a newly organized *schola*. In most of the cases discussed here, a powerful conception is already beginning to shape the imagination and enterprise of influential men and women, but it is not one that is easily accommodated to modern habits of thought, for while it spans territories and polities it was neither geographical nor social but (to coin a term) geo-ecclesiastical. These reforms show how keenly men and women in liminal places that were somehow vulnerable or potentially unstable could value the notion of a Latin West where all cells of spiritual and temporal authority acknowledged the bishop of Rome as sole patriarch and Roman liturgy – whatever they took it to be – as the supreme rite. Sheer distance from Rome played its part, and could be very candidly acknowledged, as at Braga, but political dangers, including a clash of civilizations, mattered just as much. Where the members of a polity believed themselves strong and sternly purposeful, as in the kingdom of Visigothic Spain, Rome could count for remarkably little to most of the kings and their temporal magnates, however much it mattered to influential bishops. But where extensive pagan territories lay nearby, or where, as in Naples, the Byzantine Empire was perceived to be tenaciously holding on to a dominion in a West that had long ago been parcelled out to kings, the sense of a Latin Church with a single patriarch at Rome could be compelling. To share the liturgical forms and observances of another Church in the Middle Ages was to achieve a communion that cancelled the separations imposed by space and time so that one stood with others, wherever or whenever they might be, in the eternal and universal presence of the *ekklesia* as the mystical body of Christ. 'I listen daily to the sounds of spiritual melodies . . . I hear the Masses of holy men in distant lands as if they were close by' is the rapturous claim of Saint Brigid of Kildare in *Vita I*. Rarely has the power of trained singers to evoke a universal Church, knowing neither boundaries of space nor time, been more succinctly expressed.

14

PIPPIN AND HIS SINGERS, I:
THRONES, DOMINATIONS, POWERS

During the lifetime of the magnate who gave his name to the Carolingian kings of the Franks, Charles Martel, a cantor in the cathedral of Auxerre suffered total paralysis. His name was Aidulfus and he had passed directly from the position of cantor to bishop, or as the ninth-century *Deeds of the Bishops of Auxerre* records, with censorious brevity, *Aidulfus ex cantore episcopus.* The cause of the malaise which left Aidulfus unable to perform his duties as bishop was a deep sense of shame, but not because he had become a prelate without passing through the intermediary grades of subdeacon, deacon and presbyter. Instead, he felt profoundly humiliated because his cathedral had lost so much of its landed property to the Mayor of the Palace, Charles Martel. According to the house chronicle, many *villae* and *mansiones* had been given to Bavarian princes whom Charles wished to reward as he extended his landed following. It is not difficult to understand why Aidulfus was distressed; a former cantor, he knew that the quality of the chanting in any great church rested upon stable arrangements for schooling and equipping the necessary personnel. The music gave audible form to the dutifulness of the clergy and their prudence in husbanding the resources of their foundation. Loss of *villae* and *mansiones* at Auxerre would have reduced the cathedral's income from rents or any census the bishop and chapter levied on *precariae*, the lands a donor could give to a church but receive back in usufruct, perhaps with other lands, not part of his or her original donation, so that he or she continued to receive the profit from them for an agreed term, perhaps for life, on payment of a rent. Such rents were an important source of the money that paid for oil and wax, for vestments and for the copying of liturgical books.[1]

Did Aidulfus see the musical provision of his church at Auxerre severely diminished, perhaps with a reduction of choral forces? He may have done, but the long-standing reputation of Charles Martel for being an inveterate thief of ecclesiastical property has been questioned in recent years. It now seems that single cases of abuse were sometimes polemicized in a general context of monastic sensitivity to lay interference or depredation of any kind, to say nothing of resentment amongst those who found the rise of the Carolingians a bruising experience. All that seems certain is that we cannot assess the general health of musical provision in the late Merovingian Church, long regarded as the nadir of ecclesiastical organization in the early Middle Ages, for want of sufficient case histories. The examples we possess, such as they are, point in different directions. In Aquitaine, the clerical staff of St-Julien at Brioude, a rich collegiate church, had withered so far by the first decades of the ninth century that the work of foundation had to be done all over again. St-Julien was surely not alone among the churches of this region, for by the time the college was founded anew the Franks had been continuously plundering Aquitaine for the better part of a century. Much further north at St Goar, near Koblenz, it was a different story. Here in the heartlands Pippin was able to take a long-established church in hand during the 750s and find the clerics there singing the liturgy to a large congregation.[2]

Less precise in its implications, but in many ways more suggestive, is a question that Pippin put to Pope Zacharias in 746–7 when the future king of the Franks was still Mayor of the Palace. Amongst other matters of ecclesiastical discipline, Pippin asked whether nuns were 'permitted to read the lessons publicly (*pubplice*) at Mass or on Holy Saturday, and to chant either *Alleluia* or the Response at Mass'. The news that nuns were chanting the Fore-Mass psalm at public services in Frankish churches probably came as a shock to Pope Zacharias, who replied with a stern reproach drawn from a decretal of Gelasius I: 'It is forbidden for women to minister at holy altars or to presume to perform any of those offices which men are required to discharge.' The performance of all the chants and readings mentioned in Pippin's question can be understood as public in a tolerably familiar sense of that word, for *pubplice* in his Latin original presumably refers to what is done openly or before the people, just as *publicus* does in contemporary documents insisting upon public marriages or distinguishing public baptisteries from those on private estates. What is more, the Mayor's willingness to seek papal advice, and to frame his question in general terms (to judge by the pontiff's reply), shows that the Franks regarded this as a matter of general concern and not as a minor or local issue arising from one or two cases that had become notorious but were nonetheless delicate because they involved aristocratic women in royal or noble foundations. Everything here suggests that some nunneries in the late Merovingian church were well supplied with well-trained singers and that Pippin, as Mayor of the Palace in 746–7, had more good psalmists to hand than his sharpened sense of the church's canonical tradition allowed him readily to approve. There seems no obvious reason why the secular churches and monasteries should have been less well supplied with trained men.[3]

The best guide to the state of musical provision in the Frankish kingdom on the eve of Carolingian kingship is probably the work that singers trained in the late Merovingian church were asked to accomplish during the reign of Pippin as king (751–68) and his infinitely more famous son, Charlemagne. The first sure

58 Pippin's 'mark'. Paris, Archives nationales, K 4, 6.[1] *ChLA*, 595. Pippin, if it was indeed he who made the mark, signs as Mayor of the Palace (*Signum + industri uiro pippino maior domus*).

signs of these labours appear in the 760s when a member of the Roman *schola cantorum* (the second-in-command no less) resided at Rouen to teach the cantors of the cathedral. This residency is established beyond doubt by a letter in which Pope Paul I explains to Pippin why the Roman teacher was recalled to Rome before his work was complete, and undertakes to ensure the lessons will be continued in Rome. Paul says twice in the letter that the Rouen Franks had been learning the Roman *psalmodii modulatio* or 'music of psalmody'. Although it is uncertain what the work at Rouen came to in the end (see Ch. 15), Charlemagne always presented his father as the one who reformed the Gallican liturgy of the Frankish Church and imposed the Roman. To be sure, this cannot be an entirely justified claim, for a liturgy cannot be quickly and decisively routed like an army of Bavarians or Avars; yet the evidence from Rouen shows that Pippin certainly did begin the work of setting Frankish singers to study with a Roman, labours which his descendants continued with results that begin to appear by 900 in the first relatively systematic and consolidated records of Frankish-Roman chant. No matter how ephemeral the effects of the work at Rouen proved to be in the longer term, or how little consistency of practice an eighth-century king would genuinely expect to accomplish in this domain, there is no doubt that Pippin can have sought to introduce Roman chant at Rouen and elsewhere only because he knew there were talented singers in some centres to pursue it. To a very large extent, that must mean singers trained in the late Merovingian Church. Viewed in those terms, the Carolingian achievement in liturgical music, however one chooses to assess it, begins to look like the foliate capital on a sturdy Merovingian column.[4]

Pippin found singers to pursue this work in the context of some sweeping geopolitical events, including the rise of the Carolingian dynasty in Francia and the final acceptance by the popes that Rome was situated on the eastern extreme of the Latin West and not on the western edge of the Byzantine East. The realignment of Rome helps to explain an event of immediate moment for the singers of the Frankish kingdom under Pippin, namely the journey that brought the first pope ever to cross the Alps, Stephen II (752–7), onto the grasslands and forest-lands of Francia with an entourage of Roman clergy. The records of that event, and of subsequent developments both Roman and Frankish, are pitifully sparse, but they have nonetheless often been scrutinized for traces of the changing balance of power in the West, and even for signs of the beginning of the Middle Ages. The Occident, it has been said, 'turned medieval' when Pope Stephen anointed Pippin and his family at the abbey of St-Denis, near Paris, in 754. That may seem excessively sweeping, indeed somewhat Romantic, but the work of Frankish singers in the 760s and beyond is indeed impossible to understand without reference to transalpine geopolitics and to the need, felt at the time by both Romans and Franks, for significant gestures and contacts, including contacts between singers, to mark what was taking place.[5]

Ponthion 754

Pippin took the throne of Francia in 751 on a wave of military success reaching back a decade. In his youth, the wider Frankish kingdom in Aquitaine, Alemannia and Bavaria owed its coherence to his redoubtable father, Charles Martel. The subject territories around the Seine–Rhine core of the Frankish kingdom were always in danger of turning from temporarily pacified dependencies into what the compiler of the *Annales Mettenses priores* calls 'enemies in the circuit of the Franks'. When Charles died in 741, Aquitaine, Alemannia and Bavaria began to separate from the core in a series of moves that the pro-Carolingian chronicles (by far the loudest and most insistent voices) naturally present as rebellions. The dukes and other magnates there had sacrificed much of their independence to keep peace with Charles, so a change of leadership at the Frankish political centre was the time to expect bids for autonomy, or at least for a more advantageous settlement. The two sons of Charles Martel who dominate the chronicles for the next few years, Pippin and Karloman, had no choice but to respond. In some further reaches of the kingdom beyond the heartlands, notably in Aquitaine, the strife never ceased throughout Pippin's lifetime, but such insurrections were the making of him in what was still essentially an age of raiding by the king and his followers to capture booty, arrange for annual tribute and take captives to serve as *mancipia* or bonded labourers. The entries in most of the Frankish chronicles for the 740s show magnates in the subject territories rebelling, surrendering then giving oaths, tribute and hostages, only for their solemn undertakings to be thrown to the winds and the whole process to begin again within two years or less. For Pippin this was all to the good, for he had no real interest in obliterating the leaders of the Saxons, Aquitanians and Bavarians. By departing homeward with the rebellious leaders pardoned and still in place, he allowed a subject polity to generate wealth for its treasury, to accumulate cattle and stores on its farms and to maintain a demographic level whose surplus could be seized in a spring campaign then supplemented with annual tribute. The flames of the 740s helped forge the Carolingians, and were arguably the making of King Pippin from a highly successful Mayor.[6]

Military success weighed heavily with Frankish lords inclined to judge a leader by his victories, but Pippin was more than an effective commander. He was able to take the throne in 751 because the members of an extensive and powerful following believed it was in their interests that he should. To put it another way, Pippin became king through the workings of the consensus politics he had always encouraged. As far back as 744, he called a synod 'with the consent of the bishops, priests and servants of God and with the council of the counts and the great men of the Franks'. In part, Pippin and his brother Karloman convened such councils because the proceedings of the Church in council were vital instruments of Christian government. Rulers of the early Middle Ages can often be found turning to their bishops and to the conciliar tradition in this way, especially in the first years of their power. Yet the 740s in Francia do seem to reveal something new: a cooperative form of government in which the tradition of synods, the Germanic royal custom of convening councils and a Benedictine emphasis upon a community ordered according 'to the demands of justice . . . for the purpose of amending vices or preserving charity' (to use words from Benedict's *Rule*) came together. It is no surprise that Karloman eventually joined Benedict's former monastery of Montecassino, probably in 746/7, or that a divine miracle during Pippin's reign prevented the translation of Benedict's relics from Fleury to Italy. Benedict, it seems, was happier in Francia than in his native land.[7]

The importance of such consensus in the 740s, before Pippin took the throne, shows that it may be somewhat excessive to associate his emphasis upon consultation with a need to overcome 'the problem of Carolingian legitimacy'. To be sure, the position of any early medieval king was more or less precarious, and once Pippin became king by deposing a monarch of the old royal bloodline he sometimes had reason to seize *castella* and crush potential insurgents, more than once in places very close to home. Yet he never seems to have faced any serious military challenge in his heartlands and certainly no opposition from a rival Frankish *army*. As mentioned above, his brother Karloman retired to a monastery in 747, and his brother Grifo was killed or assassinated in 753 while on his way to collude with the Lombard king Aistulph at an acutely sensitive time in Pippin's Lombard politics. As a result, it could certainly be said of Pippin (as it was of Charlemagne, and with keen admiration), that he gloried in having survived the plots of his brother and in coming to the throne with the minimum of bloodshed.[8]

During the first three years of Pippin's reign, 751–3, Italian events moved swiftly. In Lombardy, King Aistulph pursued the long-standing ambitions of the Lombard rulers in the peninsula with renewed vigour, capturing lands and cities from the patrimony of Saint Peter, always with an eye to dangerous alliances that might be formed against him. The papal city had lain in the Byzantine duchy of Rome since the wars of the emperor Justinian (527–65) took Italy from the Ostrogoths, but by the 750s the Byzantines were engaged in conflict with Arabs, Slavs, Avars or Persians and therefore increasingly unable or unwilling to ensure the welfare and security of their imperial subjects in Rome. The emperor's commands were often defied in Italy during the decades around 700, and his officials were more than once driven out of Rome or sent away empty-handed. Yet imperial authority had not ceased to be legal in Italy simply because it could be flouted. When the situation with the Lombards seemed especially threatening, in 752–3, Pope Stephen II was still an imperial subject, but his see was located at the exposed western edge of an increasingly Asiatic and Byzantine Empire that was losing the military reach necessary to fight in the Italian peninsula. Earlier popes had showed themselves ready to patch up alliances and to make friends wherever they could find them: in Constantinople, perhaps in the dukedom of Bavaria, in one or both of the southern Lombard duchies, and even in the Lombard kingdom itself. In 753, however, Stephen II decided to follow a policy that had been in the minds of the popes since at least the time when Pelagius II (579–90) assured a bishop of Auxerre the Romans might one day look north for help. Stephen would turn for military aid to Pippin and the Franks.[9]

Pippin's envoys duly conducted the pope to Pavia but the council there failed, and on 6 January 754, the Feast of Epiphany, Pope Stephen II came to the *villa* of Ponthion in Champagne and implored Pippin to put pressure on Aistulph, whose ambitions threatened to reduce Rome to a tributary city and even to turn the papacy into a Lombard bishopric, an ancient fear. The *Fourth Life of Boniface* envisages the initial meeting, which took place in the chapel of the *villa* by the river Saulx, as an intimate one by early medieval standards, Stephen being accompanied by only two deacons and two presbyters, no more. This is probably accurate, at least in general terms, for the first encounter was probably reserved for the relatives and the most trusted *fideles* of the king, including Bishop Remedius of Rouen, Bishop Chrodegang of Metz and Abbot Fulrad of St-Denis, men with whom Pippin could have a candid discussion before matters were put to larger assemblies of the Franks at Berny and Quierzy, held within a few months of Ponthion and no doubt already envisaged. Pippin was accompanied by his sons (making Charlemagne, now aged 6 or 7, an eyewitness to these events) and probably by his wife, Bertrada, who had come down to Ponthion with him from Thionville. From a vantage point some two generations later, the compiler of the first layer of the *Annales Mettenses priores* has Stephen and his clergy lie prostrate upon the ground, the pope placing ash upon his head and donning a penitential hair-shirt. The chronicler maintains that Stephen would not rise until Pippin and several other Franks helped him from the ground. It is a delicate question whether this staunchly pro-Carolingian version of events can be trusted in any of its several intriguing details, since neither the Continuator of Fredegar IV (closer to the events) nor the near-contemporary account in the

59   A reused capital, now in the parish church of Ponthion, probably from the riverside oratory
in Pippin's villa.

Liber pontificalis says anything about this ritual. The latter source, however,
would not be expected to abase the pope in any sense, and the most widely disseminated of the early medieval *ordines* for synods and councils, composed in
seventh-century Spain, does indeed begin with ritual prostration. The penitential shift and ash would not look so strange to Roman eyes familiar with the crisis litanies when, as during the pontificate of Stephen II, 'ash was placed on the
heads of all the people, and they made their way with great wailing and besought
the most merciful Lord our God'. If something like the ritual and pre-conciliar
abasement of the *Annales Mettenses priores* did take place then Pippin took Saint
Peter's representative on earth literally in hand and raised him up in a gesture
whose significance could not be mistaken. The naive artistry of the face that
probably looked down upon these events (Pl. 59), and the fact this was all taking
place in a rural oratory on a royal palace-farm, should not obscure the extraordinary character of what was going forward: something between a national synod
of the Frankish Church, a council of the king with his most intimate followers
and papal-imperial diplomacy at the highest level.[10]

   If Pope Stephen rose from his prostration to address Pippin and his family in
the style of his letters to both the king and his Franks, then the royal family and
selected *optimates* heard an exalted rhetoric ranging from the abjection of Israel
in Egypt to the anger of Christ in judgement. At times, the Franks may even have
noticed the sharp smell of the pit, for Stephen was not reluctant to predict the
consequences should they fail to act on Saint Peter's behalf:

Do not harden your ears against us, nor turn your face away from us, lest we be confounded in our petition and lest we be tested to the end. So may the Lord also not harden his ear to your entreaties and turn not away his face away from you in that day of judgement to come when, with Saint Peter and his other apostles, he will sit to judge every rank, both sexes and every human power and the world through fire, so that it be not said to you . . . 'I do not know you, because you did not come to the aid of the Church of God and did not seek to take charge of his chosen people when sorely tried'.[11]

Coming from Saint Peter's representative on earth, this exalted righteousness, with its explicit warning, may have given a fearfully transcendental character to the meeting in the *villa*. Stephen was quite prepared to make the Franks feel the Apostle's presence with some intensity, to judge by a letter he sent the next year. This extraordinary document, presented as a communication from Saint Peter himself, is unparalleled anywhere in materials of the period 600–800 save in writings denounced as forgeries by the most influential voices. Where epistolary convention directed the Franks to look for the name of the sender, they read the words *Petrus vocatus apostolus.*[12]

Pippin became the pope's protector during his meeting with Pope Stephen, and while the pontiff wintered at St-Denis Pippin held a council with his nobles. It was decided the Franks would go to Italy and do battle with Aistulph if he could not be induced, by a handsome bribe, to withdraw. By Easter, Pippin had met with Pope Stephen again and issued a written promise to restore territories the Lombards had taken. By the summer, Pippin had reason to look back on his work with as much triumph as trepidation. He had entertained a pope (the first ever to cross the Alps) in a great abbey of his kingdom, together with important members of the higher Roman clergy; he had been anointed by a pope in person and on his home territory, something no Western king had ever experienced before, and he had entered into a mutually protective alliance with Saint Peter, the Prince of the Apostles. This was good work for just six months, extending from January to June 754.[13]

The Singers of 754

At first sight, the signs that Pope Stephen II brought Roman singers with him to Francia in 753–4 seem very sparse. Stephen's biography in the *Liber pontificalis* is the only source for the membership of the papal party that made the journey to Ponthion with him, and it gives no indication that he travelled with a contingent of singers, still less that 'the chief musical instructors of the Roman *Schola Cantorum*, the *Primicerius* and the *Secundicerius* were present', as one distinguished historian of music has maintained. The Roman narrative does indeed mention 'the *Primicerius* Ambrose and the *Secundicerius* Boniface', but these were officials of the much more prestigious school of notaries, not of the *schola canto-rum*. The truth, less enticing but more revealing, is that the compiler of the *Liber pontificalis* does not consider any member of the papal delegation worth men-tioning below the '*sacerdotes*, dignitaries and other ordained clerics, together with the military chiefs'. Much later, under the Ottonians, a long list of the laymen and bishops gathered in Saint Peter's basilica from all over the Frankish Empire will place 'Leo, the *Primicerius* of the *schola cantorum*' near the end of the inven-tory, after the papal clerks (*scrinarii*) and just before the acolytes and laymen.[14]

Nonetheless, one would certainly expect the supreme pontiff to have been accompanied by members of the *schola*, for there were many Masses to be cele-brated on a journey expected to run for at least 500 kilometres through the Advent season to Christmas, perhaps beyond. Although the *Liber pontificalis* omits to mention any singers in Pope Stephen's entourage, some later sources retain a curiously vivid (but not always accurate) recollection that they were there. In the 880s, the Lombard chronicler Andreas of Bergamo was not only convinced that singers had travelled with the pope to Ponthion, he also believed they were part of something very grand:

> At this time the Roman Church was governed by Pope Leo, who suffered much oppression from the Lombards; leaving his own see, he sought Francia with many who were most learned in the art of letters, especially singers . . . who, remaining there [at Metz] for three years, did work of such refinement that to this day, throughout Francia and Italy, one may say throughout many cities, they resound as an ornament of the Church.

This is an account of Stephen's journey to Francia in which almost every verifi-able detail is false. Pope Leo III (795–816) has supplanted Stephen II and Charlemagne has replaced Pippin, mistakes that may be lamentable but are not so very surprising. Charlemagne left a much deeper mark on common memory than his father. Yet while there is nothing very striking about the details that have certainly been lost in the tradition Andreas of Bergamo received, there is some reason to pause over the details that have perhaps been retained. Andreas believed the meetings of 754 were of great significance for the liturgical chant of Francia and Italy because the pope came with a team of Roman singers who began con-certed work destined for transalpine influence. Far from being imagined as invis-ible minor clergy, these singers are placed in a party that included 'many most learned in the art of letters' whose work was concentrated at Metz. (This was indeed one of the principal centres for the development of Frankish-Roman or Gregorian chant; Ch. 16.) More than a century after the event, the significance of the papal visit in 754 seems to be credited with something like Andreas of Bergamo's sense of a Carolingian renaissance, and singers are part of it.[15]

Andreas of Bergamo's account receives confirmation of a kind from the writ-ings of his contemporary Notker Balbulus of Sankt Gallen, a superb source of gossip about Charlemagne accumulating in cathedral close and cloister for some hundred and fifty years. Notker reports in his *Gesta Karoli Magni Imperatoris* of 886–7 that Charlemagne once noticed how the chant of different 'provinces, and even regions and *civitates*' in his kingdom did not agree. He therefore asked Pope Stephen to send two singers. This pope was 'Stephen, of blessed memory, who, after the most wretched king of the Franks, Childeric, had been deposed and tonsured, anointed [Charlemagne] in accordance with the custom of the ancients to the governance of the kingdom . . .'. This refers to events of 751–4 and is correct in every verifiable detail save that Charlemagne has once more ousted his less famous father. In response to a request from Charlemagne, Notker relates, Stephen sent twelve clerics from Rome, all gifted singers of liturgical chant, but because they were jealous of the 'glory of the Franks' each one decided to teach a different and false version so Charlemagne would never achieve the uniformity he desired. Once more, the chronology of events is mangled and here infected with long-standing Frankish–Roman rivalries, but the tradition that there were singers in Pope Stephen's entourage of 754 remains intact.[16]

A considerably more reliable source for the singers of that retinue appears in Walafrid Strabo's *Libellus de Exordiis*, composed in 842–4. According to Strabo,

> the more perfect knowledge of chanting, which now virtually all Francia loves, was brought by Pope Stephen, at Pippin's request, through his clergy (*per suos clericos*) when he came to Francia in the first place to Pippin, the father of Charlemagne, to seek justice for Saint Peter against the Lombards, whence the use of it has grown strong far and wide.

This has a good claim to represent the Carolingian family's own version of events, for Strabo became tutor to Charlemagne's grandson Charles the Bald in 829. Taken together, these very different sources tend to confirm what one has good reason to suspect: the Vicar of Saint Peter making a long journey towards a new protector required a staff of singers and clergy to sing Masses at the various points of repose along the journey. These singers would have been especially serviceable when the combined entourages of Pippin and Stephen travelled the last three miles to Ponthion, the stage where Pippin is supposed to have performed the service of a groom by leading Stephen's horse. According to the *Liber pontificalis*, the two retinues made their way to the *villa* 'rendering in a loud voice glory and unceasing praise to Almighty God, and with hymns and spiritual chants'. The phrase *hymnis et canticis spiritualibus* is a common formula of medieval prose and never came more easily to writers than when describing some form of festive cavalcade or progress into a city; yet there is nothing implausible in such a scene, and if the chants involved the members of the Roman *schola* then they had very appropriate material in their repertory for that very feast-day. Having completed an arduous journey across the Alps from Rome, and forming part of a retinue bringing gifts for Pippin and his Franks, they might well sing the appointed gradual *Omnes de Saba*: 'They will all come from Sheba bringing gold and incense and giving praises to the Lord', or indeed the communion: 'In the East we have seen his star and we have come with gifts to adore the Lord.' Better still, as they contemplated their potential protector, or indeed if they were able to watch him lead the papal horse in the manner of the emperor Constantine, was the Roman introit for the feast of the day in all of the six earliest graduals: 'Behold, the Lord comes; and the kingdom is in his hand, and power and *imperium*.' In three of the early graduals, even the appointed psalm verse was ideal for the appeal Stephen II was about to make: 'O God, endow your king with judgement.'[17]

Questions of Motive

The Frankish chronicles are universally reticent concerning Pippin's liturgical initiatives. Only in later documents such as the tenth-century *Vita Beregisi*, composed in Carolingian heartland at the monastery of St-Hubert, in the Belgian Ardennes, and much concerned with the ascendancy of the Pippinids, do Frankish writers emerge who are ready to mention liturgical chant in a brief conspectus of Pippin's achievements (Pl. 60). Even the most loyal and forthcoming writers, such as the Continuator of the Fourth Book of Fredegar's chronicle, or the compilers of the *Annales Mettenses priores*, say nothing about a liturgical reform. Yet the silence of the Frankish chronicles offers one way to understand Pippin's work in contemporary terms, for whatever Pippin sought to accomplish in liturgical matters there seems no doubt his contemporaries were able to assimilate it without strain to familiar concepts of royal responsibility. Chief among these was the duty to convene and even to set the agenda for assemblies of bishops at the provincial or inter-provincial level. Any assembly of prelates *pro ecclesiarum restauratione* had a responsibility in the Frankish Church, as in every national *ecclesia*, to ensure the standardization of worship, often with a view to borrowing whatever seemed good in the practice of other churches, and always conducted under the ultimate juridical authority of the king.

In 754, Pippin and Pope Stephen formed what the *Liber pontificalis* calls 'treaties of peace', *pacis foedera*. This was the standard expression for a negotiated settlement with the plural ('treaties') drawing the sense away from the written document that one might now associate with a treaty and moving it towards the undertakings given by word of mouth and with good faith (*fides*) that mattered most to contemporaries. It was also a common way to perceive bonds that were not quite the affective ties now associated with the idea of friendship but instead marked an *amicitia* with a contractual dimension. Many years after Pippin formed these 'treaties of peace' with Stephen II, binding upon his descendants, Charlemagne's great capitulary the *Admonitio generalis* (789) refers back to Pippin's liturgical initiatives and gives the sonorous explanation that he undertook them 'for the sake of unanimity with the Apostolic See and the peaceful harmony of God's Holy Church'. The *Admonitio* is a substantial document but only two chapters in the entire collection mention Pippin by name, and this is one of them. It is canon number 80 and the other immediately follows it as canon 81. These back-to-back references to Pippin suggest that these two chapters may form a discrete layer within the *Admonitio*. Canon 81 forbids all labour on Sundays unless it serves the needs of the army, helps to move provisions or is necessary to carry a corpse to the grave; men are accordingly forbidden 'to cultivate the vines, plough the fields, reap or cut the hay' on the Lord's day while women must not 'engage in cloth working, sew, embroider, card wool, break flax, launder in public or shear sheep'. This ban is so detailed in its provisions that it surely restates the terms of a lost capitulary issued by Pippin a generation earlier. There is at least a possibility that the adjacent canon concerning Pippin's reform of liturgy also quotes from a lost act of conciliar legislation issued during his reign. If so, it is the only document in existence presenting the motives for the reform in language sponsored by Pippin himself, and it is the language of unanimity and peace.[18]

For an early medieval king, the task of preserving peace meant securing freedom from external threat and from internal disturbance by armed action in times of crisis, and more generally by the routine workings of justice in the localities. This was not peace in the modern sense of a highly desirable condition of freedom from armed conflicts regarded as political and humanitarian disasters for both militia and people. It was peace in the early medieval sense of a *pax* extending from good social order to the loyal collaboration of the *fideles* in whatever undertakings the king conceived, in a manner that revealed his greatness of station, and which his loyal followers endorsed in a manner that revealed the greatness of theirs. The treaties between Pippin and Stephen show that Pippin regarded the peace of Stephen and of Saint Peter as henceforth his own; he would therefore move against those who threatened it, with violence if necessary, trusting that enough of his *fideles* would regard this as a kingly act for him to win the necessary support.

Peace also meant the communion of those bound by the same doctrine, and existing in the state described by Augustine where 'they do not ponder schismatic thoughts for there is peace between them'. To share a doctrine, however, was not necessarily to share a *rite*, as the example of Visigothic Spain plainly shows, for there a great many liturgical initiatives were taken in a new Catholic kingdom after 589 with minimal reference to Roman custom. This does not mean that divergent liturgies were generally viewed with indifference in the churches of the seventh and eighth centuries; they were sometimes regarded as cracks in the surface of ecclesiastical life that either allowed the weeds of heresy and schism to grow or gave enemies and malcontents a reason to think that they might spring forth. At the Council of Vannes, convened between 461 and 491 to regulate clerical discipline and other matters in the north-western dioceses of France and Brittany (although the only signatory from there was the bishop of Quimper), the assembled prelates ruled for a single *ordo psallendi* within the province of

60 Part of the Prologue to the *Vita Beregisi*, by a monk of the monastery of St-Hubert in the Belgian Ardennes, composed in the 930s. The monk praises Pippin for overthrowing the last Merovingian 'from the line of Clovis' and for bringing chants from Rome (*ecclesiasticis cantibus a Roma delatis*). From a collection of Saints' Lives, Namur, Musée provincial des Arts anciens du Namurois, fonds de la ville de Namur, MS 15, fol. 21ʳ, 12th c.

Tours as an anti-Arian move; they judged it appropriate that those who held one Trinitarian faith should use one liturgy. The majority of fifth- and sixth-century councils with chapters concerning liturgy or psalmody were held in areas ruled by Arian kings and sought to consolidate the Catholic liturgy of a metropolitan diocese around the usages of the mother church. So it was at Agde (506), convened during the reign of the Arian Alaric II, and at Gerona in 517, when Visigothic Spain was under the regency of the Arian Theoderic. Caesarius of Arles convened the councils at Epaone (517) and Vaison (529) during the Ostrogothic (and therefore Arian) peace, while the Council of Valencia (529) was convened under the Arian Visigothic kings. The councils of Braga I (561) and II (572) were both impelled by the energy of a newly Catholic Suevic kingdom at the end of its Arian period. Sharing a rite was the daily emblem of a shared doctrine.[19]

This is the conciliar tradition that speaks through Charlemagne's most sustained attempt to construct an account of his father's reforming work, part of the *Opus Caroli Regis contra Synodum* that he issued in 792 to counter what the Franks wrongly supposed to be the decision of a recent Byzantine synod concerning the devotion due to images. The early chapters of this book seek to establish the right of a Frankish king to intervene in such theological questions, and one of the grounds Charlemagne cites is Pippin's introduction of the Roman *ordo psallendi* 'so that there should be no disparity in the order of psalmody between churches with an equal ardour of faith':

> The Church in our parts has never retreated from the holy and worshipful communion of Rome during the passage of the years . . . Since this Church has stood with Rome in the unity of holy faith, and has been sundered from it only slightly – and in a matter which is not deleterious to true belief – in the celebration of the liturgy, by the solicitude and labour of our father King Pippin of honourable memory, a man most *inlustris* and *excellens*, and the coming into Gaul of the most reverend and holy man Stephen, prelate of the city of Rome, it has also been joined to it in *ordo psallendi*, so that there should be no discrepancy in that *ordo* between churches sharing an identity of belief, and so that churches united in the study of one holy law should also be united in one worshipful tradition of chant (*modulamen*) and that a dissimilar manner of celebrating the liturgy should not sunder churches joined by devotion to one holy faith.[20]

This is duly qualified, for Charlemagne is certainly not prepared to say that his ancestors had been guilty of anything 'against faith' by singing a non-Roman liturgy, and indeed one should be wary of the claims, often made, that the liturgical reforms of Pippin and Charlemagne were intended to *break* rather than consolidate the continuity of Carolingian kingship with the Merovingian past. Cyrill Vogel's belief that the Carolingians made 'a very clean break' in the liturgical and political life of Francia does not accord with the kings' own eagerness to speak of their Merovingian predecessors as 'our forebears', *antecessores nostri*, and it is easy to forget that two of Charlemagne's sons, Louis and Lothar, were given Merovingian dynastic names. What matters to Charlemagne in the passage quoted above is not a change, or even a reform in the familiar sense, but a means of showing exceptional *amicitia* between the rulers of the Franks and the popes by taking great trouble to go far beyond the call of duty, as friendship will often require. Those liable to construe a dissimilar manner of celebrating the liturgy as a mark of dissent in matters of doctrine will now be confounded. In 754, Pippin and Stephen may well have considered that sharing 'one worshipful tradition of chant' was a natural complement to their treaties of peace and their friendship alliance: the gesture was all the more telling because *it was not strictly necessary.*[21]

The question of Bavaria may also have been in Pippin's mind when he and his advisers considered having the Roman *ordo psallendi* taught to Frankish singers. The Bavarian ducal house, the Agilolfing kindred, proved very troublesome. Duke Odilo of Bavaria married Pippin's sister Hildtrude, contrary to his wishes, creating a Carolingian–Agilolfing alliance Pippin never condoned because it was never securely under his tutelage. In 743, Odilo became one of the magnates in 'rebellion' around the Frankish core, maintaining links with others including Hunaldus of Aquitaine and Pippin's brother Grifo, who was half Agilolfing himself. Pippin rode out against Odilo and defeated him in Bavaria, but during the days he spent making a circuit of the dukedom he encountered a Roman presbyter named Sergius with news to give him pause for thought. Sergius claimed that Pope Zacharias (741–52) had charged him to prevent the Franks joining battle with the Bavarians and to persuade the Franks to withdraw their claim to Bavaria altogether. The first of these commissions was dangerously close to being a command from Saint Peter that the Franks should not re-establish dominance in Bavaria by force, while the second threatened the very basis of Frankish hegemony there on the strength of their previous conquests and the oaths the Bavarian dukes had given them. The compiler of the *Annales Mettenses priores*, writing *c*.805 and highly sensitive on the question of Pippin's standing with Saint Peter, gives the Mayor a short speech at this point, delivered after his victory against the Bavarians. It is an unusually leisurely affair introduced by a dactylic hexameter (*Cui Pippinus princeps sedato pectore dixit*, 'to whom Pippin the Mayor said in a measured manner'). In tones that are indeed serene, Pippin refutes the presbyter's claims to be acting on apostolic authority:

> O Sergius, now we know that you do not bear a charge from Saint Peter [*or*: 'from the Pope'] nor are you truly his envoy. For you said to us yesterday that the pope, on the authority of Saint Peter and on his own, denied our right to do justice in Bavaria. Therefore you must now know that if Saint Peter were indeed opposed to our doing justice here he would not have given us aid in

this battle today. Now indeed it is certain that Bavaria and the Bavarians are subject to the *imperium* of the Franks through the intercession of Saint Peter, the prince of the apostles, and through the judgement of God that none can escape.[22]

Despite the confidence Pippin expresses here, Sergius almost certainly was a *bona fide* envoy from Pope Zacharias to Duke Odilo of Bavaria and to the senior churchmen of his kingdom. It says a good deal that Sergius was brought before Pippin in company with Gauzebaldus, bishop in the ducal capital of Regensburg. This episode suggests that Duke Odilo was a favoured son of Rome in 743, and that the Agilolfings figured in papal policies being pursued from Rome quite independently of Frankish interests. Perhaps those policies even included an alliance with the Bavarians rather than with the Franks.

This is where Pippin's history as a reformer of liturgy crosses with the work initiated by Duke Odilo's father, Theoto of Bavaria, when Pippin was only 3 years old (see above, pp. 276–7). In 716, Theoto went to Rome to consult with Gregory II and returned with various canonical documents and reforms in mind that included the introduction of a Roman order of psalmody, or *ordo psallendi*. For Theoto, this initiative was probably part of an attempt to connect his dukedom across the Alps with the canonical discipline and authority of the Roman Church, strengthening the instruments of Christian government in a frontier polity compressed between domineering Franks on one side and the Avar Khanate on the other. The Romans had every reason to welcome Theoto's overture, and he is duly mentioned in the *Liber pontificalis* with enthusiastic hyperbole as 'the first of the Bavarian people to come and pray at the home of Saint Peter'. The reasons for the compilers' enthusiasm on this count are not far to seek; Theoto was well placed to put diplomatic and even military pressure on the Lombard kingdom to the south, so the Romans had good reason to enlarge his sphere of autonomous political action by every possible means available to their diplomacy, which would have to encompass at some stage the thorny issue of Frankish claims in the Bavarian duchy. When Pippin came to Bavaria in 743, twenty-six years later, to put down the rebellion of Theoto's son Odilo, the encounter with Sergius the presbyter strongly suggests Rome was still working at this policy and was prepared, in consequence, to meddle in Frankish–Bavarian politics at the highest level.

This provides some further context for Pippin's motives in seeking both an alliance with Pope Stephen II and the liturgy of Rome. Throughout the 740s, Pippin had led spring campaigns to prevent new political configurations forming in western Europe to the disadvantage of the Franks, and had often done so under the shadow of a possible alliance between Bavaria and one or more of the rebels. With the papal alliance of 754, and the subsequent work to bring a Roman *ordo psallendi* to certain chapels and churches in the heartlands, Pippin and his Franks definitively supervened over Bavaria's liturgical and diplomatic relations with the papal city. The speech assigned to Pippin in the *Annales Mettenses priores*, although plainly a rhetorical exercise and of minimal authority for the Bavarian campaign of 743, is valuable precisely for the insight it gives into the language possible later in the century. After Ponthion, there was a potent and supernatural participant, Saint Peter, in Pippin's councils and military retinues. Pippin had rights over subject territories, established by oaths of loyalty the most powerful families there had given him after defeat; when those oaths were broken he had a right to restore the situation, by force if necessary, and to 'do justice'. Henceforth it was not just Pippin's justice but also Saint Peter's that would be done. That is Pippin's claim in the speech invented for him by the compiler of the *Annales Mettenses priores*, using terms that may not be so far from the manner of his political negotiations in the 760s: 'Now indeed it is certain that Bavaria and the Bavarians are subject to the *imperium* of the Franks through the intercession of Saint Peter.'

Pippin surely also hoped that the liturgical reform undertaken by his singers would consolidate a *Frankish* Church. The immediate and harshly political context for that motive lies in the work of his father, Charles Martel, whose reputation as a despoiler of Church property owes much to exaggerated reports of one particular case where Charles's purpose was to wrest control of the region around Orléans from Bishop Eucharius, whose family, of Gallo-Roman ancestry, treated the bishopric as a family property. Yet there is also a longer perspective to be seen. When the Franks settled in Gaul, they formed something between a Germanic warrior-elite and a sub-Roman garrison in what had formerly been part of the Roman Empire. The episcopate, strongest in the south after the disturbances of the fifth century, was dominated by Gallo-Roman aristocrats such as Bishop Remigius of Reims, often men with aromatic personal names of Greek or Roman ancestry like Sidonius Apollinaris, Rusticius or Desiderius. The conciliar activity of the Gallic bishops was mostly concentrated in the Rhône valley and to the south of Autun, a pattern decisively changed by the Carolingians, and the Frankish Church in the north owed much of its conversion in rural areas to the missionary work of Aquitanians like Saint Amand and Saint Eligius. The latter, consecrated to the see of Noyon-Tournai in 641, could still be called a 'Roman' with some contempt by the villagers of his diocese, and as late as the time of Pippin a Frankish noble could still nurse a loathing for 'all those of the Roman nation and tongue', meaning speakers of the common Latin speech.[23]

From the very beginning of the Frankish evidence, the art of liturgical singing also seems to possess a markedly southern cast. At the beginning of the sixth century king Theuderic went to Clermont to find clerical staff for the cathedral of Trier, including the gifted singer Gallus, while the chapter of Metz recruited a psalmist who was probably a Visigoth brought from Languedoc or Spain, where a *princeps cantorum* can be traced in an epitaph of 525 (see above, p. 216). There is no Frankish equivalent to that inscription, and none of the material allowing an office of cantor to be traced under that name in the Western churches from *c.*475 into the sixth century comes from any further north than Tours. Most of it is concentrated around the great churches of the Mediterranean littoral. The only glimpse of the Merovingian choir school afforded by any literary source, in the *Passio* of Saint Praiectus, concerns work to the south of the Carolingian heartlands, once more at Clermont. If there is any substance in the suggestion that Pippin knew of this episode and chose Praiectus as the patron of his liturgical work then he had gone in search of a southerner like King Theuderic two and a half centuries before him. With Pippin's reform, the authoritative liturgy and its traditions of liturgical song passed definitively into safe Frankish hands in good Frankish churches north of the Loire. The two earliest centres of work, Rouen on the Seine and Metz on the Moselle, could scarcely map the frontiers of the Frankish core with more clarity.

This liturgy or *ordo psallendi* was presumably a yearly liturgical cycle of appointed texts and melodies for Mass and Office, perhaps already established in seventh-century Rome and in Visigothic Spain. This is surely the scope of change Charlemagne means to imply when he maintains that Pippin 'bore away the Gallican rite', *Gallicanum tulit*, for the context does not invite very much conjuration with the meanings of *tulit*. The sense is presumably 'he bore away [the Gallican rite]' as in the expression *tulit peccatum mundi*, 'He took away the sins of the world', common from the patristic period onwards and only gradually replaced by the more familiar *tollis peccata mundi* at a later date. A less committed translation might say that Pippin 'took [the Gallican rite] in hand', as in the idiom *tulere in manu*, although this version may miss the more decisive sense, perhaps intended by Charlemagne, that his father's accomplishment showed a kingly and essentially martial competence, as if the Gallican rite were the remains of a broken bridge Pippin commanded his men to cart away during an episode in a spring campaign.[24]

There will always be scope for doubting whether Pippin's liturgical reform was even remotely as decisive as this. It has even been suggested that Charlemagne and his advisers deliberately constructed a narrative in which their own attempts to impose a Roman liturgy were traced back to the time of Pippin, and duly exaggerated, so that they could receive the sanction of a papal visit to Francia, somewhat as eighth-century scholars and singers evolved the legend of Saint Gregory the Great:

> Perhaps Charlemagne and his followers, wishing to legitimize their own efforts to impose a standard Roman ritual, simply harked back to this favorable but brief coming together of the pope and king as authority. Certainly their motives were political; they wanted to demonstrate both the political unity of Gaul and their close ties with Rome.

This is cautiously phrased, but a legend that developed around the memory of Pope Gregory I some 150 years after his death cannot easily be compared with Charlemagne's claims about the importance of a meeting that he witnessed as a boy aged 6 or perhaps 7 in 754. The encounter at Ponthion may have impressed his young mind in much the same way as the discovery of Saint Germanus's relics did in that very same year when, or so a later author claims, the 7-year-old Charles 'wondered at the things he saw and retained them deeply in his memory'. Some who had been present at the Ponthion meeting lived on into the 770s and therefore not so very far short of the period when documents sponsored or commissioned by Charlemagne trace the Romanizing reforms to the time of Pippin. His half-brother Bishop Remedius of Rouen, who entertained a Roman singer from the *schola cantorum* in his cathedral, probably lived on until 771/2, while Pippin's widow, Bertrada, survived until 783.[25]

The heart of the issue here is that 'the political unity of Gaul' cannot have been the motive impelling either Pippin or Charlemagne to charge the singers of certain churches to follow Roman usage. This is the major mistake that a great many commentators on these matters have made. Pippin would never have supposed that it lay within his power to impose a uniformity of rite in his kingdom, even in the empirical sense of agreement on essentials that would have come more easily to eighth-century minds more disposed to conceive agreement, *unanimitas*, as an experience than as a particular kind of textual deposit assessed by comparing books. Pippin's greatest asset was his sharp sense of the forces at play as his royal heartland of support led outwards to a much less secure periphery; he would have been poorly informed to suppose that a design to impose the Roman rite could succeed against the grain of so many local interests, or in spite of the practical difficulties it would encounter. Romanized liturgical books and calendars would be required in vast numbers, monks and clergy would have to be persuaded, perhaps against the interests of local cults, to learn a new ritual during years of upheaval when their liturgy was neither the old Gallican nor the new Roman; the laity would need to accommodate new chants, ceremonies and saints; Roman singers (taken away from a Roman Church not necessarily overstocked with trained personnel) would be required to spend years in Francia teaching their Frankish pupils. It was one thing for the monarch to revise the liturgy in the royal chapels, and Pippin could probably hope to accomplish much with the presbyters and chaplains who celebrated Masses for him and carried his most precious relics when he travelled; he could also look to the churches governed by his relatives or especially trusted servants. The kingdom, however, even in the narrowed sense of the heartland, was another matter. The liturgies there might prove too heavy to bear away, even upon the shoulders of a king.

Consider a comparison with Visigothic Spain. In 589, the Spanish kings and bishops consolidated a Catholic kingship for the first time, but they did not endorse the project of a single *ordo psallendi* for the entire realm until 633, a generation later, despite the fact that they were in a better position than Pippin to pursue the work. The Spanish kingdom was a tax-raising polity with a ceremonial core in the royal city of Toledo, and the court housed a complex palace organization, the *palatinum officium*. The Spanish prelates and nobles had eventually shown themselves willing to sustain a consensus by attending the king at Toledo, creating a political entity above regional interests. The situation in Pippin's Francia was quite different. His royal ceremonial was dispersed between St-Denis, Metz and Soissons, to look no further, and he did not raise the land-tax that probably helped to support the Toledan court. It is hard to imagine why such a king would attempt something so contentious as a major liturgical reform throughout all the lands he sought to dominate. Pippin might hope to persuade some powerful men and women to adapt the liturgies they were accustomed to hear in their proprietary churches (although they would surely be mindful that rites good enough for their ancestors should not be thoughtlessly changed); he could also hope to carry many bishops of the heartland sees with him. Where prelates or abbots proved unwilling or obstinate, he could bide his time until the opportunity arose to nominate a pliant candidate of his choice to a vacancy. None of this, however, would be an easy task, not least because a great many churches of the kingdom were not his to rule. The synods of the late Merovingian Church often had cause to criticize Frankish nobles who regarded the churches on their lands as private property with endowments to be kept clear from the control of the bishops, let alone the king. Those nobles had not vanished with the deposition of the last Merovingian in 751. Once Pippin's wishes for liturgical change were explained to them, some of the Frankish *optimates* might well have replied with the words a recent historian has envisaged as the response of lords confronted by episcopal claims to authority over their proprietary churches: 'these churches are ours, why should anyone else control them?'[26]

Perhaps there is no need to reconstruct such a reply because a late eighth-century author has already done so in the document commonly called *Ordo Romanus XIX*. This is the work of anonymous polemicist possibly writing in the time of Pippin, for his Latin grammar (if well represented by the single surviving copy of his work now at Sankt Gallen) shows little trace of the progress associated with Charlemagne's later years. The author sets out to explain how the Roman liturgy and its chant embody the wisdom of the Roman Church in a manner comparable to the canonical tradition whose core of papal decretals and other Roman documents developed at the same time, or so he maintains, and in the same way. Both bodies of material grew together as the popes exercised their duty of vigilance over the liturgical and canonical discipline of the Church in their care and ruled for improvements and refinements. The compiler duly lists the great tradition of popes who built up the Roman liturgy by a series of judicious and pious interventions from Damasus I (366–84) to Martin I (649–55), followed by several Roman abbots of a time much nearer his own, the heads of Roman monastic communities serving the great basilica of Saint Peter's. Thus Damasus 'decreed psalms should be sung by day and by night', while Gelasius I (492–6) 'produced hymns in the metre of Saint Ambrose'. Leo the Great 'instituted chant for the liturgical year and produced a most resplendent collection of canonical institutions; let anyone be anathema who does not accept it and venerate it down to the last iota'. When he reaches Gregory the Great, the compiler joins the great tradition that begins with Isidore of Seville, and then flows through Bede, offering his readers an enthusiastic inventory of Gregory's works but departing from them by including the significant final note: 'And he issued noble chant for the liturgical year.'[27]

Mounting a broader attack, the compiler anathematizes partisans of the indigenous Gallican rite of the Franks and reveals their spirited defence of Gallican tradition. Having the means to accept the Roman liturgy, but refusing it, 'they are submerged in a mist of error'. They cite saints of the Gallican Church like Martin in their defence of the old rite, but they forget that Roman doctrine was always the point of reference for those saints who maintained contact with the popes or with the Christian emperors. The compiler makes his points with a strong sense of a territorial entity, 'this Western land', *terra ista occidentale*, with its patriarchal seat in Rome, and the only alternative he can discern to following the customs of the patriarchal see is to adopt practices that are essentially *peregrinas*, 'wandering' or 'foreign', for without Roman authority there is no real reason to do one thing rather than another. For all the compiler's energy and vituperation, there is little in *Ordo Romanus XIX* to suggest that he was located anywhere near the centre of affairs, and his approach seems markedly out of sympathy with Charlemagne's claim that it was *not* injurious for the Franks to have used a non-Roman liturgy before Pippin because liturgical discrepancies, however extensive and systemic, were not in themselves against faith. Yet there are surely echoes of real complaints, both from secular and temporal magnates in the time of Pippin and beyond, when the compiler evokes those who name Saint Martin and other great saints of the Gallican calendar in defence of their conservatism. This sounds like the voice of those with monasteries or other churches whose liturgies and cults were part of their kindred's history, of their landed identity, and of their autonomy in appointing abbots or priests to them. Perhaps one can also hear the voice of bishops and abbots not inclined to admit so many saintly immigrants from Rome into their liturgical calendars. For the kind of dangerous talk one might have heard in the circle of a certain Wulfoaldus, perhaps summoning Franks opposed to Pippin's Lombard campaign to his *castellum* near Verdun, and crushed for it in 755, there is no better source than *Ordo Romanus XIX*. The value of that text lies precisely in the way it engages with a traditionalist resistance to Romanizing change that was probably much more common than the pro-Carolingian sources suggest.

Methods: The Importance of Blood and Fidelity

Hence the importance of blood and proven ties of loyalty to the success of the liturgical project that Pippin and his advisers began. A network of connections, based upon blood, comes into view with two letters from Pope Paul I to Pippin.

One of these reveals that a member of the Roman *schola cantorum* had been teaching Frankish singers at Rouen. The second inventories a consignment of books sent to Pippin from Rome, including an *antiphonale* and a *responsale* (see Ch. 15). In addition to what it has often been said to reveal about the first glimmerings of a 'Carolingian Renaissance', this letter offers a more concealed testimony to the familial dimension of Pippin's liturgical work. The pope who sent these books, Paul I, was the brother of Stephen II with whom Pippin had begun treaties of peace in 754. The prelate to whom Paul sent a Roman singer so that he might teach the singers of Rouen, Bishop Remedius, was Pippin's half-brother. The two contemporary documents that definitively reveal Pippin's involvement in liturgical initiatives therefore show two powerful kindred performing services for one another through a pair of brothers.

Among the men of distant or no blood relation to the king, the most important of the early reformers among the *fideles* were assuredly Bishop Chrodegang of Metz, a tireless advocate of the Romanizing reform who may have had some blood connection with the Carolingians, and Fulrad, the abbot at St-Denis where Pope Stephen had wintered in 754 after the Ponthion council. These men had broad connections in the core territories of the kingdom, notably Chrodegang, who was also abbot of Sint Truiden in deep Carolingian heartland and the founder of Gorze that became the parent house for Gengenbach and Lorsch, the latter a prize given to Chrodegang and eventually placed under Charlemagne's royal protection. Among the great secular *fideles*, Pippin could presumably look to Autchar; he can be traced in Pippin's circle from almost the beginning of latter's kingship in 751 and was perhaps related to the king through his mother-in-law, who bore the name of Pippin's second wife, Bertrada.[28]

Beyond such men as these, there were many other possibilities for gradually disseminating anything achieved, at Rouen or elsewhere, by such sustained exposure to Roman chanting as it was possible for Frankish singers to maintain. Pippin had inherited a de facto power from his ancestors to appoint abbots with as much or as little consultation as he chose to offer the community; he also had a regalian authority to influence the choice of candidates for bishoprics. In other words, he possessed the power to create an entourage of territorial magnates, effectively his clients, which united around him, attended him when they could and then witnessed his documents. Of the many examples that might be chosen, Pippin's diploma for the royal abbey of Prüm that he refounded with Bertrada in 762 is one of the most important, since it is unlikely Pippin would have consented to an abbot of this house who did not share his commitment to liturgical change. Founded on fiscal land, and built close to the remains of the old Roman road through the Ardennes from Maastricht to Trier, this monastery was very much a family affair. Established in the 720s by ancestors of Bertrada, it was 'constructed anew' by Pippin and his queen, according to the text of the king's diploma, so an exalted company was required to sign the document in which the king granted the abbey certain privileges. In addition to Pippin and Bertrada, the signatories included their sons Charles (Charlemagne) and Carloman, twelve counts and these nine bishops:[29]

GENEBAUDUS	Laon
GAUZLENUS	Le Mans
FULCHARICUS	Tongres (through an advocate)
ADALFREDUS	Noyon
WULFRAMNUS	Meaux
MEGINGAUDUS	Würzburg
BERETHELMUS	Cologne
BASINUS	Speyer
WEOMADUS	Trier

There is a map of the eastern heartlands here. The signatories show a single western reach beyond the core territory to Le Mans, a see of considerable importance for Carolingian influence in the Breton March. Frankish-Roman chant will not be definitively implanted here until the second quarter of the ninth century when there is definite evidence of it arriving with a *consanguineus* of Charlemagne (see below, pp. 348–9). There is a single eastern extension to Würzburg, the see only recently founded by Boniface but with Carolingian and papal support. Otherwise Tongres, Cologne, Speyer, Trier, Noyon, Laon and Meaux are all cities in the easterly sectors of the Seine–Rhine core. As for the bishops themselves, the ravages of time have been cruel to most of them. Gauzlenus of Le Mans is perhaps the only one who is much more than a name, and he owes his prominence to the day he obtained the bishopric by allegedly having the resident prelate blinded during a banquet. Pippin commanded that Gauzlenus should be blinded in his turn for this offence, at least according to the tradition remembered in the cathedral close of Le Mans. As one might expect, these bishops were among the more diligent royal servants; three of them attended the council of Compiègne in 757, and five were at the council of Attigny in 762. When they otherwise emerge from obscurity, they sometimes cut an impressive figure. Weomad of Trier, venerated as a saint in his diocese until the end of the nineteenth century, was active in the foundation of the abbey of Lorsch, north of Mannheim. Here and there, one can trace other lines of association between some of them. Megingaudus of Würzburg and Basinus of Speyer, for example, were ordained on the same day by Boniface; Basinus was a predecessor of Weomad's at Trier. These were the kinds of links that mattered, and which the king could draw to himself.[30]

Pippin could also rely upon a group of loyal abbots that he constantly enlarged by grants of immunity. It had long been the royal practice to influence the appointment of bishops to their sees; the power of appointing abbots, however, was by no means a Merovingian royal prerogative. Pippin's ancestors had forcefully appointed or ejected abbots using de facto powers as Mayors of the Palace, and those powers passed to Pippin when he became Mayor and then rapidly became all but indistinguishable from his royal prerogatives once he became a king. By championing the Benedictine Rule, with its insistence upon the moral and spiritual excellence of any man fit to become an abbot, Pippin and his advisers strove to create a meritocracy of election to abbacies in which the king's promotion of his candidate, with or without consulting the monks, began to appear (as in some respects it was) an act in the public good, since the choice was the king's and not that of a founder who would perhaps be inclined to promote his own kindred who might not meet the strictest standards for election. By these means, not without their own vulnerability to corrupt practice, royal scribes or notaries found their way to abbacies. Fulrad of St-Denis, the abbot who looked after Pope Stephen during the winter he spent in Francia and perhaps the first Frankish churchman to preside over a Romanizing reform of the rite in his house, was the most distinguished of these, but there were others. The notary Widmar became abbot of St-Riquier in Picardy, while the notary Baddilo probably became abbot of Marmoutier in the Touraine. When Pippin looked for support in the early years of the reform, he surely found some support among the *fideles* here, to say nothing of other half-brothers at Tours and Murbach.[31]

—⁓⁓—

The work done at Pippin's behest has a curiously sharp foreground with an immense panorama behind. In the centre of the scene is the cathedral of Rouen – even perhaps one specific chamber in the *domus ecclesiae* – where Frankish singers are having their first (and conceivably their last) sustained contact with a Roman teacher. Beyond lies the immense scope of a chant reform that was designed to embrace the churches ruled by the king's blood-relatives and *fideles*, then the major churches and monasteries of the largest kingdom the medieval West had ever known. The realm was so large by 800, indeed, that Charlemagne's poets were not guilty of gross affectation when they called it *Europa*. Roman poets, like their Greek forebears, adored sonorous geographical names, and *Europa* had long been a term to conjure with in imperial or consular panegyrics. This does not mean the expression was an empty one. As an evocation of a transalpine entity, it had antecedents in the time of Pippin. We shall see that the concept of a Frankish–Roman *imperium* is already found in sacramentaries of the 760s when Frankish priests were praying for its protection. If Europe exists when the temperate grasslands and forests of the North European Plain are in contact with the Mediterranean through transalpine links, then the concept of a Frankish–Roman *imperium* expressed an idea of Europe more fluently than it conveyed any political or juridical reality to eighth-century minds. So once the foreground at Rouen has been made as sharp as possible, there will be every reason to move on to the wider background: in effect, to the rise of European Music.

15

PIPPIN AND HIS SINGERS, II:
MUSIC FOR A FRANKISH-ROMAN *IMPERIUM*

Franks and Romans Face to Face

At some time in the 760s, a singer sent from Rome by Pope Paul I was introduced to a group of Frankish clergy serving the cathedral of Rouen. This visiting professor of plainchant came on high authority, for he was the second in command of the Roman *schola cantorum*, and in accordance with the ancient traditions of the Roman schools he was eligible for promotion to first position in the event of his superior's death. The choice of Rouen for his work as a teacher in Francia was by no means a fortuitous one. As mentioned above, Bishop Remedius of Rouen was Pippin's brother, or more correctly his half-brother as the son of Charles Martel by a different mother, and his involvement in plainchant reform at this early date establishes the link between the Carolingians' liturgical work and their cousins (in the old sense of the word) at the very beginning of the enterprise. These lines of blood or wider kindred will soon appear again with Pippin's queen, Bertrada, perhaps with Bishop Chrodegang of Metz and certainly with some of the imperial chaplains who served in the palaces of the Empire during the ninth century. For his part, Bishop Remedius of Rouen was raised in the royal palace among the *nutriti*, installed and schooled wherever his father Charles Martel chose to station that part of the royal entourage as the needs of peace, council or conflict took him around the realm. Remedius therefore passed his boyhood years closer to the centre of political events than Pippin, who was raised at the abbey of St-Denis, near Paris. Remedius was probably intended for the church from the beginning, to judge by his Latin name which not only recalls the Gallo-Roman bishop who baptized Clovis but also stands well outside the range of Pippinid and Merovingian names used by the Carolingians until their eclipse. Pippin, by appointing Remedius to the see of Rouen in 755, placed his brother in a region of considerable importance to the growth of Pippinid influence in the Seine basin, still vital for maintaining a Carolingian presence on the river marking the western limits of the royal heartlands. The lower Seine was one of the kingdom's fluvial gateways, and Rouen

> fmem militauit. Tvnc frs eidē
> cenobii auctore karlomanno confisi
> romā ueniunt ꝫ apud scissimū pa
> pam zacharā lacrimabilē querimon
> iam deponunt ꝑ corpe sct scissimi pa
> tris a solo ꝓ ad gallias translato. Qui
> continuo eundē karlomannū ac socios
> ei in franciā dirigit. scribens auctori
> tate apltica pippino regi francoꝝ ut cor
> pus egregii patris auino restituat
> loco. Qui ubi ad regem puenert : por

61   Part of the sixth lesson for the feast of Saint Remedius of Rouen. The passage describes the efforts of Pippin's brother Karloman, once he had entered the monastery of Montecassino, to obtain the relics of Saint Benedict from Fleury, using Remedius as an intermediary. The effort failed, for Remedius was temporarily struck blind and cured only after he prostrated himself and promised to leave Benedict in Francia, where, it seems, that great saint was most content. Rouen, Médiathèque, MS 1411 (U. 64), fol. 64ᵛ.

guarded the key point where barge-traffic from the interior could finally be transferred to sea-going vessels. To these natural advantages Remedius added the benefits of good governance. He continued to enjoy the king's esteem, and in 760 we find him in Rome, as one of Pippin's envoys or *missi*, negotiating with Pope Paul and the Lombard king Desiderius for the return of lands to Saint Peter. The house-chronicle of Rouen praises him for the benefices he brought to the church and for the contribution he made from his own wealth; he is one of the few eighth-century Frankish prelates who achieved sainthood and was subsequently commemorated in a Life, the *Vita Sancti Remigii*, composed before 1090 (Pl. 61).[1]

What were the Franks trying to achieve by inviting a Roman singer to Rouen? Frankish dealings with Roman chant were essentially empirical. One might suppose that the sounds of the Roman music were held before Frankish ears, so to speak, to produce a human archive that was liable to be undermined by forgetfulness, caprice and mortality. The material in this archive was not only evanescent, it was also unverifiable in specifically musical terms save when the singers themselves had a chance to check their repertory against Roman originals when they were available, which may not have been very often. Whether this be an accurate reconstruction of the process or not, the extensive legislation issued by the Carolingian bishops gives no sign that prelates expected to scrutinize the

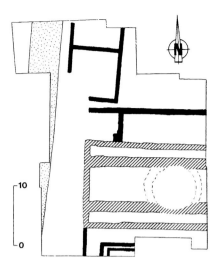

Fig. 3   Part of the North Church of St Stephen and the cathedral group at Rouen in the middle to later years of the 8th c. From Le Maho, 'Les Fouilles de la cathédrale de Rouen 1985 à 1993'.

music of the services sung by priests, for example, in the larger churches of their diocese, although they might wish to verify that presbyters were following the Roman order of service with the necessary ritual items. This suggests that the Franks at Rouen would not have perceived the singing of their Roman teacher(s) as a musical counterpart to the 'norm of correctness', the 'rules of the early fathers' or indeed the *Romae disciplina* that they were seeking to reinstate in their canonical legislation. What the Franks heard at Rouen was probably viewed as Roman usage rather than anything conveyed by the term *norma rectitudinis* meaning canonical practice. In short, the singers at Rouen were not engaged in anything Remedius or Pippin would have understood by the terms *recuperare* or *restaurare*, and therefore the work of those singers does not quite belong with the other initiatives conventionally associated with Carolingian reform.[2]

To better understand where the work of the singers does belong, we should begin with the room at Rouen where a Roman cantor taught his Frankish pupils and work outwards in ever-widening circles of interpretation that eventually encompass what it meant in the eighth century to have a chant both Frankish and Roman. This may seem a quixotic project, since everything that can be *known* about the lessons given at Rouen has already been said in the first paragraph of this chapter. Whatever one attempts to add must be essentially speculative, but the challenge here is not to avoid speculation. Instead, it is to explore every possible source, and every line of argument, with the potential to make any reconstruction of what took place at this seminal moment in the history of Frankish–Roman chant more plausible and better informed. Consider, for example, the room itself where the Roman cantor and his pupils met, as one might say, voice to voice. Here, where it may seem everything must be lost, it is possible that something can be saved. Figure 3 shows part of the North Church of St Stephen and the cathedral group at Rouen in the middle to late years of the eighth century according to the evidence of relatively recent excavations. At the time represented by the levels exposed, the cathedral did not possess the separate buildings for the canons it was soon to acquire, marking a reform of their common life. Anglo-Frisian silver deniers found on the site reveal the small construction shown here to the north was relatively new in the 760s; there was a wooden gallery supported by posts, and together with the various modifications it represents the only building campaign approximately dateable to the episcopate of Remedius. Did the Roman songmaster and his Frankish pupils work here, in a Frankish imitation of the small buildings or *habitacula* associated with similar work in Rome? This space might just be the mysterious atelier where the Rouen phase of work on Frankish–Roman chant began.

The music heard there, or indeed perhaps devised within those walls, is lost. With the exception of antique letter systems transmitted in the *De Institutione musica* of Boethius, known to relatively few in the 760s, no Western source shows any form of musical notation known to have been in use when Remedius was bishop of Rouen. If there is any historical link between the first Western notations that appear around 820–40 and earlier systems of markings in papyrus sources from the eastern Mediterranean, which may or may not be forms of notation, the continuity has so far proved impossible to trace. (There may be room for a breakthrough here, but none seems imminent.) There are no decipherable remains of Roman chant in Roman manuscripts until the 1070s and there can be no dependable basis for assuming that the music in those sources bears a close relation to what the singers of Rouen heard in the 760s. Strictly speaking, there are no readily decipherable traces of what the Franks called their 'Roman' chant until approximately the same period, although the sources with staff notation that appear towards the end of the eleventh century can be collated with versions in older notational states to yield a reconstruction of the music in a tenth-century or sometimes a ninth-century condition. By then, the Roman cantor and his Franks at Rouen had been dead for many generations. The two musical repertories, Roman and Frankish–Roman, contain many chants that plainly have a historical relation to one another, but it remains unknown what that relation might be. For the most part, the Roman repertory of the 1070s is perhaps Gregorian chant fed back to Rome by German imperial ascendancy in Italy and then filtered through a robust and independent dialect of liturgical monody in eleventh-century Rome whose antiquity and ancestry are unclear.[3]

The Franks of Rouen would have expected relatively stabilized melodies to figure prominently among the materials they learned from the Roman cantor. The *Passio* of Saint Praiectus suggests that the Merovingian Franks of the seventh century used genres of stabilized chant at Mass, such as the *Sonus*, which could be quite elaborate if modern attempts to isolate them amidst the remains of Gregorian, Ambrosian and Old Spanish music can be judged successful. Whatever the scope for variation or elaboration in performance, a late Merovingian singer on this understanding of his art had either studied a chant so that he could give a competent account of it or he had not, and the story of Praiectus suggests that divine intervention was necessary to remedy the deficiency if his education in plainsong had not yet reached that particular chant. Many of the Gregorian melodies finally recorded in Frankish manuscripts from *c*.900 onwards convey the same impression of an art in which a singer could have a precisely measurable competence. Nonetheless, the notion of a 'stabilized' melody passed from a teacher to pupil, from a Roman cantor to the Franks, has certain limitations.

Consider a comparison with recent work in the field of New Testament studies, where much attention has been given to the question of what patterns of agreement between written sources can reveal about the workings of an antecedent oral tradition. Attempts have been made to restore the essential structure or 'aphoristic core' of the sayings attributed to Jesus from the various versions of them in the four canonical gospels and in the *Gospel of Thomas*. By methodically comparing all attestations, and by separating details attested in a number of sources from those represented in only a few, or even in only one, the aim of this research has often been to lift something from its various subsequent engagements in tradition and to recover 'the core of the complex': the heart of the saying. In a sense, the square-note editions of the modern *Graduale Triplex* attempt to do something similar, distilling a core musical utterance from the static of notational variation in the earliest musical sources. Among historians of the New Testament, attention has often been drawn to the fluctuating nature of speech-acts: to the statement and restatement that occurs to clarify meaning, convey emphasis and counter the sheer volatility of attention:

> speech, in distinction from writing, is not traceable to external verification. Speech surrenders itself in the act of speaking . . . the quest for the historical Jesus is heavily based on the premise of the retrievability of the single, literal saying. It is widely assumed to be an inescapably logical fact of linguistic life. But what characterises orality is plurality of speech acts rather than the original saying. It is an incontestable fact of oral life that speakers tend to restate words and retell stories in order to assure connection with hearers.[4]

Much of this is easy to shape into questions about 'the intractably difficult issue' of song in the Rouen context. Did the Franks there have a concept corresponding to the 'retrievability of the single, literal' singing? What would a literal singing have been? In what sense were the performances of Simeon 'traceable to external verification'? Did his singing of Roman music 'surrender itself' in the act of singing leading irresistibly to 'a plurality' of song acts? To some extent, the answer to the last of these questions must surely be a positive one: the range of materials that support the modern musician's concept of a stabilised musical entity lifted above the contingences of time, human weakness and caprice simply did not exist in the 760s. The Rouen singers were presumably trying to learn a corpus of Roman ways to sing particular texts so that they could reproduce what their teacher did in a way he (and they) judged to be satisfactory, or at least to be adequate for present purposes. In matters of melodic detail, the Romans and Franks at Rouen could verify nothing in writing, as far as we can discern, and therefore the music existed as a sensation in the ear and in the throat, perhaps with the occasional visual consolidation of a written text as a mnemonic resource. Yet that visual dimension is precisely what might encourage one to suppose that there was indeed a musical equivalent to an 'aphoristic core' and something 'literal' in much of the musical material Simeon sought to impart: something that was too elaborate to be learned as a simple intonation formula and which found its way, no doubt somewhat transformed, into the musical sources. The earliest Frankish tonaries and discussions of plainsong mode (the latter are already fluent by the 840s) show that Frankish singers, possibly under Roman tutelage, rapidly developed the sense of an 'aphoristic core' at the suprasegmental level of tune-classes defined by compass, centre of melodic gravity and scalar pattern. At the segmental level of the specific chant and its individual syllables, it was vital that the texts formed a written tradition. Here, in short, was a form of musical notation: a 'literal' dimension in the strict sense of the word. Simeon's first task was presumably to teach the Franks an appointed Roman text, quite possibly with reference to such copies, imparting it as a structure of grammar and sense with pauses to be articulated by music supplying various degrees of closure; if there is anything sufficiently marked in the corpus of Frankish-Roman chant that it probably derives from a formative stage in the repertory, it is this. By repeatedly singing the Latin syllables, Simeon could gradually focus his pupils' memory of the chant as a set of relationships between grammatical sense, melodic ductus and a succession of colours created by the vowels of the syllables, each one tinting a melodic detail not just with the musical pitches but with the pattern of harmonics imposed by the vowel being sung.

The degree to which a Roman core could pass unscathed through the filter of spoken communications between a Roman cantor and the Franks is another matter. Singing and speaking must have been constantly alternating with one another at Rouen, producing a complex interplay of demonstration, imitation, correction and further explanation. This is where the teacher, Simeon, becomes the centre of attention himself. His name is a form of Simon, of Semitic origin, rarely found in the West during the first millennium and then mostly in sources emanating from Italy eastwards. Although the name is virtually unknown amongst the Western bishops before 800, it often appears in episcopal lists for the eastern churches, be they Byzantine, Coptic, Syrian-Jacobite or Nestorian, with cases appearing as early as 325 (Amida in Mesopotamia), then reaching to the end of the first millennium and beyond. Examples in the four or five generations before the events at Rouen include instances from Karrhai (Haran, 620), Edessa (629), and closer to the period of importance here Apollonias (Bithynia,

691), Alexandria (the Coptic Church, 693) and Dara in Mesopotamia (725). Save for the cases in Alexandria and Apollonias (where the church was Byzantine), these were all Syrian-Jacobite foundations. Of some twenty saints named Simeon in sources both Eastern and Western before the thirteenth century, virtually all are either known to have been of eastern origin or were subsequently associated with a tradition assigning them to a home in Syria, Arabia, Armenia or the Levant. It remains unknown how widely speakers of Greek (not necessarily as a first language) were recruited into the *schola cantorum*, although as late as the twelfth century a Roman writer can still give mangled transliterations into the Latin alphabet of songs performed in Greek during the Easter revels when the leader of the *schola cantorum* wore horns and rode on an ass (see above, p. 253). The point should not be laboured, for onomastic evidence is fragile at the best of times. Nonetheless, there is some reason to suppose that Simeon the 'Roman' teacher of chant belonged to the considerable population of Byzantine immigrants from the eastern Mediterranean living in eighth-century Rome.[5]

If this is so, then the common Latin speech that Simeon needed to communicate with the Franks was perhaps at best a second language, after his native Greek, and perhaps even a third language after Greek and some other. His pupils, in contrast, spoke a Latin from the other extreme of what had once been the Western Roman Empire. If Simeon was indeed a Greek or a Syrian for whom Latin was a second or third language, it is exceedingly unlikely he could add a fourth in the form of Frankish to accommodate any speakers of that tongue in the Seine basin. (He could perhaps barely pronounce a Frankish word with a clutch of consonants like *thuruhskluog*, 'he smote through'). Simeon and the Franks would therefore have communicated as speakers in such form of the common Latin speech, perhaps already better called proto-Romance, as Simeon could muster, overcoming as best he could the differences between the speech of the lower Seine and the speech of Rome. To suggest that Simeon and the Franks found their best means of communication not in language but rather in the scalar patterns of the music with which their minds were saturated would no doubt be going too far; the Franks and their teacher could probably understand one another tolerably well for the most part if modern linguists are correct in supposing the inhabitants of all *Romania* were mutually intelligible to one another, albeit perhaps with some difficulty, at this date. Nonetheless, comparison of French *fait* with Italian *fatto*, both < FACTU(M), or French *amour* with Italian *amore*, both < AMORE(M), suggests how the loss of final syllables in the common Latin speech of Gaul may have made Simeon's speech sound somewhat quaint and archaic to his Frankish pupils. Their speech may have sounded barbarous to him: a deeply provincial version of the language that still had no other name than *lingua Latina* or *lingua Romana* and one that Simeon had heard spoken in its historical capital among the highest princes of the Western and Latin Church. Differences in the articulation of consonants, and in the colour of vowels, especially those prolonged in melismas, may often have prompted Simeon to rethink what he should impart just as it may have caused the Franks to ponder what they should retain.[6]

This means there were at least four varieties of speech in use as work proceeded. There was liturgical Latin as sung in Rome, liturgical Latin as sung in Rouen, the common Latin speech of Rome (perhaps with a Greek or Syrian inflection) and the common Latin speech of the lower Seine basin (perhaps with a Frankish colouring). It would be a mistake to underestimate the difficulties of communication that such layers could produce. The Anglo-Saxon missionary Wynfreð of Crediton, otherwise known as Boniface, seems to have had no trouble making his common Latin speech intelligible at Pippin's court among the Franks, but when he was requested by Pope Gregory III in Rome to prove the orthodoxy of his faith he asked to submit an account of his beliefs *in writing*. He may have wished to ponder and revise the content of such an important statement, the foundation of the missionary work the pope entrusted him to perform, but it is also possible that Wynfreð when in Rome could not do as Romans did. Perhaps he feared entrusting his reputation for doctrinal orthodoxy to his mastery of Latin as it was spoken amongst the most senior clerics in the Eternal City, and perhaps because his pronunciation, probably based upon a sound-per-letter approach, the manner that came naturally to Anglo-Saxons who learned their Latin from grammar and had never spoken it as a native tongue. One would give much to know the bearing of any such difficulties upon the moments when Simeon made the code-switch from his variety of the common Latin speech of Rome into his variety of liturgical Latin and expected the Franks to shift into theirs or follow his. The switch may well have exerted a considerable influence upon what the Franks heard, since it is possible that Simeon sounded final syllables in singing so that melody flowed into them: at times, perhaps, with results that the Franks found unfamiliar.[7]

Almost nothing is known of the musical vocabulary and articulacy of the singers who met at Rouen. There are few traces of literate musical reflection in the Occident between the immensely influential but incomplete treatise *De Institutione musica* of Boethius (d. 524) and the recovery of that book among the Franks, perhaps through Irish intermediaries, in the ninth century. Any lights in the intervening period probably burned low as the members of the senatorial and land-owning classes, who could develop a taste for such learning, gradually vanished. Sidonius Apollinaris in the fifth century already gives clear signs that those who spoke Latin as a native tongue were discouraged by the necessity to use sesquipedalian musical terms of Greek origin (see above, p. 188). There is no Merovingian or Roman music theory from this period, and it is therefore impossible to reconstruct the musical articulacy, the framing concepts and terms, or the analytical powers that singers at Rouen employed to conceptualize what they heard from Simeon, to separate surface from depth, to distinguish substance from ornament.

Something can perhaps be learned from the inventory of books that Pope Paul I sent to Pippin, evidently at the king's request, some time between 758 and 763 (see the Appendix to this chapter). The consignment included an unidentified 'art of grammar by Aristotle', a manual of orthography, a book of geometry and another textbook of grammar in addition to two books, an *antiphonale* and a *responsale*, which probably contained the texts of Roman office chants. Saving future discoveries, it will never be possible to ascertain whether the books Pippin received corresponded at all closely to the request he sent to Rome, but the mention of chant-books together with treatises on grammar and orthography is very much what the future development of Frankish music theory would lead one to expect. Grammar offered a means for training the ear by classifying vowels and consonants into subclasses, distinguishing vowels into long and short, and explaining the doctrine of the acute, grave and circumflex accents, each representing a module of pitch that rose (acute accent), fell (grave accent) or rose and then fell (circumflex accent). The concept of a pitch-movement or *accentus* was a versatile one that could be extended from the level of the syllable to analytical thinking about substantial musical phrases in chants or indeed to an entire chant (Ch. 17). It is tempting to suppose that the *antiphonale*, the *responsale* and two books on grammar were placed on the same shelf, together with the material on Latin spelling. Pope Paul had sent a small reference library for the task of conceptualizing the elements of plainsong. Perhaps it was Simeon himself who placed the order for these books through the king; that might explain why some of them are described as being 'in the Greek language' in one textual layer of the letter. If it was indeed Simeon, then it begins to seem that the *schola cantorum* had become a germinating cell of the 'Carolingian renaissance' in its very beginnings under Pippin. The books were perhaps designed to bring Franks who were still essentially late Merovingians up to the level of an education in the Roman *schola* that could seemingly encompass letters (meaning grammar and metrics), basic arithmetic for the computation of Easter, the rudiments of astronomy, and the cycle of liturgical days and feasts, to look no further (see below, pp. 327–8).[8]

Simeon and his Frankish pupils had been bred in different ecological and dietary zones: the Franks on the temperate plains and forest lands if they were predominantly local men, as seems likely, and Simeon perhaps somewhere in the eastern Mediterranean and then in Rome, still connected to Constantinople and more broadly to the Arabo-Byzantine Mediterranean. Nobody who has read the famous jibe at the expense of Frankish singers by John the Deacon, an impeccably Roman author of the 880s, will be inclined to underestimate the importance of dietary differences between northern and southern Europe to ways of singing. John blames the 'bibulous throats' of the Franks for what he judges to be their musical ineptitude when faced with the more subtle aspects of Roman chant, and the taunt spans almost a millennium of Latin writing when he expands it to encompass their 'Alpine bodies'. John knew his Classics. In the *Aeneid*, Virgil describes the 'Alpine pikes' of the invading Gauls shown in the prophetic shield given to Aeneas, founder of Rome's destiny (viii. 653–70), while Ovid speaks of the same Celts as the 'Alpine enemy' or *Alpina hostis* (*Fasti*, vi. 358). This is the tradition evoked when John declares that the Alpine bodies of Gauls and Germans are incapable, by their very nature, of accommodating themselves to the refinements of the Roman music. For all the depth of literary allusion in John's taunt, however, it would be mistake to minimize the importance of the subtle forms of estrangement and difficulty when Franks who derived their fats from milk and butter rather than olive oil, and who favoured cereal-based drinks such as beer as much or more than wine, tried to sing like a Roman. In John the Deacon's eyes, the Frankish singers are alien beings more to be feared than trust-ed and ultimately more to be scorned than feared, especially for the voracious drinking that does indeed mark several pages of Chrodegang's Rule for the canons of Metz, to say nothing of the spectacular calorific intake to which Frankish singers in the time of John the Deacon became accustomed on major feast-days of the liturgical year (see below, p. 342). Such was the view of a Roman cleric in the 880s, long after Pippin, but the materials for a Frankish–Roman estrangement, indeed antagonism, were ancient and certainly accessible in the room at Rouen. There were probably some subjects best avoided there.[9]

Kenneth Levy has proposed that the Franks developed an antipathy to the Roman musical style they heard at Rouen, and perhaps elsewhere, partly because of 'national resentments' between the Roman and Frankish singers. Despite the necessary reservations about the use of the term 'national' in an eighth-century context, Levy may well be right. The lessons brought together pupils and a teacher who not only came from different ecological backgrounds and dietary regimes but also from different political systems. They constructed their histories accordingly. The singers of Rouen were subjects of a king, but Simeon was locat-ed somewhere between the old *de jure* order that made him an imperial subject within the Byzantine duchy of Rome and the new *de facto* polity in which Pippin was the temporal protector of the Roman Church in Italy. The Franks were proud of ancient victories that the Romans remembered as barbarian incursions, and they were contemptuous of what had once been the murderous policy of the Romans towards Christians, in comparison with the Franks' dutiful veneration of the martyrs.[10]

The document that cries out to be heard in this context is the revised edition of the *Lex Salica*, originally the body of law issued in the time of Clovis and a foundational document of Frankish identity. This corpus of laws, constantly evolving, was issued in three versions during the Merovingian period, to which Pippin added a fourth, the so-called '100-Title text'. This has a new prologue dated in various early sources to the thirteenth year of Pippin's reign, and there-fore to 763–4. The author was probably the royal notary Baddilo, whose name appears in a string of documents running from 757 to 766 and who is perhaps to be identified with the 'Baidilus clericus palatinus' mentioned in a source of the early ninth century as abbot of Marmoutier, near Tours. If this is correct, then the new preface to the Salic Law was drafted by one of Pippin's palace chaplains ideally positioned by virtue of time, place and occupation to reveal the attitudes of the early 760s around the king and his closest *fideles*, including his servants the chaplains and the royal singers. The preface opens with these battlesome lines, beginning with a stretch of rhythmic prose, which vaunt the Franks at the expense of the Roman name:

> Gens francorum inclita,
> auctorem deo condita,
> fortis in arma,
> firma pace fetera,
> profunda in consilio,
> corporea nobilis,
> incolumna candore,
> forma egregia,
> audax, uelox et aspera,
> ad catholicam fidem conuersa
> emunis ab heresa;
> dum adhuc [ritu] tenerentur barbaro,
> inspirante deo,
> inquerens scienciae clauem,
> iuxta morem suorum qualitatem
> desiderans iusticiam,
> costodiens pietatem. . . .

haec est enim gens, que fortis dum esset robore ualida romanorum iugum durissimum de suis ceruicibus excusserunt pugnando, atque post agnicionem baptismi sanctorum martyrum corpora, quem romani igne cremauerunt uel ferro truncauerunt uel besteis lacerando proiecerunt, franci [reperta] super eos aurum et lapides preciosos ornauerunt.

Renowned people of the Franks, founded by God, strong in arms, faithful in every treaty of peace, wise in counsel, noble of body, with unimpaired radiance, excelling in form, bold, quick and hard, converted to the Catholic faith, protected against heresy; when the pagan rite still survived, inspired by God, seeking the key of wisdom, they desired justice and maintained their dutifulness as is their nature. . . . this is the people who, moreover, when they were strong in might, beat the oppressive Roman yoke from their necks in battle, and who, after their baptism, took the bodies of the saints whom the Romans burned in fire, cut to pieces with swords or threw to wild beasts so that they might be torn to shreds. The Franks raised shrines of gold and precious stones upon them.[11]

Like the denizens of some other Western kingdoms, the Franks interpreted their distant past as a formative period of victories over Roman armies. A new narrative has replaced the memory of a Roman Empire oppressed by foreign invaders and harried to death in the West, for the Franks believed Rome once oppressed *them* with a heavy yoke of servitude and that they threw it off by force of arms. Although it is anybody's guess what bearing this construction of history had upon the work where Franks were supposed to relinquish (one might even say surrender) their own liturgy and replace it with a Roman rite, one can say that this was a meeting of different cultures with the potential to become a confrontation. The only narrative account of Frankish and Roman singers meeting, in John the Deacon's Life of Gregory, shows just such a confrontation happening and imagined as taking place in the time of Charlemagne. The force of this passage is much weakened in the poor translation (actually a loose paraphrase in places) that has gained currency in recent years, for there John's term *procacitas* to describe the Franks is rendered 'precocity'. It means 'impudence'.[12]

The work at Rouen began in favourable circumstances. The Franks obtained the services of the second-in-command from the Roman *schola cantorum*; the king was involved, and the work was done under the supervision of his brother in a wealthy church; books were ordered from Rome, probably in connection with this work, perhaps by Simeon himself, and they duly arrived. Within the room at Rouen, however, matters may have seemed somewhat less auspicious. At this time of Frankish ascendancy, with a new and quasi-imperial tutelage of Rome recently established, one may imagine that neither side was necessarily inclined to minimize the differences of culture that separated Mediterranean Romans from Franks, nor quickly disposed to yield when competing constructions of history or contemporary politics emerged. As mentioned above, it was at precisely this time that one of Pippin's chaplains compiled a new preface to the Salic Law, evidently with royal approval, which presents the creation of Christian civilization as the work of a Frankish takeover and provides superb material for a Frankish repost to any Roman taunt. A generation later, Charlemagne's biographer Einhard will think nothing of dining with a high official of the Roman Church and airily referring to the many '*neglected* sepulchres of the martyrs' (emphasis mine) at Rome. The further one proceeds in the ninth century with writers such as Notker Balbulus on the Frankish side, and John the Deacon on the Roman, the deeper the impression of Frankish–Roman antipathy and rivalry becomes. This was not a context liable to favour exact imitation of contour and nuance in the musical surface of a chant performed by a teacher, nor was it one where pupils would be ready in every case to abandon what previous generations of Franks had deemed good in favour of what a single Roman visitor, and perhaps a 'Syrian', deemed better.[13]

What did it all come to? Neither the house-chronicle of the Rouen cathedral nor the *Life of Remedius* mentions any liturgical initiative in connection with Bishop Remedius, while any influence exerted beyond the cathedral close seems at first to have been slight. The chronicle of St-Wandrille, a great abbey in the diocese of Rouen, records that Abbot Witlaic was bound in friendship or *amici-*

tia to Bishop Remedius but it gives no sign of any liturgical work during Witlaic's tenure. The only chant-book he gave to his house is listed in the chronicle as an antiphoner of the use of Tours, probably acquired during his earlier years as *camerarius* of St-Martin in that city. What is more, Witlaic's successor seems to have inherited very little in the way of a song-school, for when Gervoldus became abbot of St-Wandrille in 787 he had to found a school himself, possibly on the basis of his experiences in the queen's household (of which more below). Only during *his* abbacy did the monastery receive the first *antiphonarium romanum* listed in the chronicle, a gift from the bibliophile priest Harduin. The broader picture presents a similar aspect. Under Charlemagne, the centre of gravity for Frankish–Roman chant seems to have shifted eastwards from Rouen and the Lower Seine to Aachen and Metz.[14]

Yet to be eclipsed is not the same as to be without influence; it can be a sign of a very positive influence, as when a pupil is inspired to eclipse his master. There are traces that the Rouen achievement was long remembered. These appear in the second edition of the chronicle by Sigebert, monk of Gembloux (d. 1112). In this revised and expanded edition of the book, undertaken by Sigebert himself, the entry for the year 751 introduces a reference to Remedius of Rouen immediately adjacent to a notice of Pippin's liturgical reforms:

> [751] . . . Remedius brother of the same king Pippin, archbishop of Rouen, flourishes in Gallia. Pippin the King improved the churches of Gallia with chants of Roman authority by his labours. [Pl. 62]

In one matter of precise detail, this entry is incorrect, for Remedius was appointed to his see in 755, not in 751. Broadly speaking, however, the information is accurate: there was a Romanizing liturgical initiative at Rouen during the episcopate of Remedius and he was indeed Pippin's brother. Where did Sigebert find this information, so long after the event? He cannot have found it in the *Life of Remedius*, for that text has nothing to say on the matter of plainsong reform, and the Codex Carolinus (which is our principal source for the Rouen episode) is not known to have circulated very widely. Sigebert cannot have drawn upon any extant Carolingian annals, for they are all silent on the subject of Pippin's liturgical initiatives. By some unknown line of transmission, therefore, Sigebert encountered material at some time after the completion of the first version of his chronicle and before the completion of the second, expanded text. It would seem to have been an annal, otherwise unknown, that remembers the liturgical work at Rouen and elsewhere.[15]

As a result of this supplement to the second edition of the chronicle, Rouen eclipses Metz in Sigebert's book. Not surprisingly, he repeats the stories, found in the pages of John the Deacon and Notker Balbulus, about the Roman singers supposedly in contact with Metz; nonetheless, Sigebert makes no mention of any Messine reform of chant under either Pippin or Charlemagne. He principally remembers Chrodegang of Metz, the prelate who dominates most modern

Athalongus prbr̄ p̄ illatam sibi cecitate ammonituf querere corpa ciliani socior̄ q̄: ei. inuenif sec̄m corporib; uisu recpit. ea q̄: re sc̄s Bonefatiuf moguntie epc ab athalongo ad se relata castrum wirzburch ad honore ciliani mr̄t qui ad p̄: dicandum ibi a papa Conone epc ordinatuf fuerat. ibiq; morus & quietis locū a d̄o accepat. epalis sedis pniuilegio insigniri decreuit. p̄niminq; ibi ep̄m sc̄m Bunghardum inuenit. M̄ aruan p̄ncipatur sarracenis annis xi. R̄ arolomann̄ fr̄ pippini regis rome azacharia papa in monachū attonsuf. p̄mo m̄serapti mon te in cenobio quod ipse fundatur. deinde apud castrum cassinū laudabili uita entuuir.

Pippinuf Griphone fr̄em suū contra se rebellantem. in saxoniam p̄sequitur. S̄ arracent intestino bello colliduntur.

Pippinus Grifone insaxonia & eiuf complices Taffilonem. Landfridū & sucoi ger̄ bello uictos captr̄. & Taffilonem quidē Baioarie duci facit. Griphoni uero in Neustria xii. comitatus concedit. qd illi n̄ sufficit: s; ad warfar iū in aq̄ tania fugit. In Calabria & sicilia fit pestilentia & mortalitas homm̄ nimia. In uestib; homm̄ & inueftis ecclaz̄ apparent cruciule quasi oleo designate.

Rachis langobardor̄ rex dum rupto federe romam inquietare nititur. a zacha ria papa non solum a malo reprimitur. sed etiam eius instinctu cū uxore & filiis romam ueniens. monachuf efficitur. cui haistulfus frater eius substitu tuf regnat annif. vii.

Oldricuf rex francor̄ in monachū consoratur: pippinuf uero princeps auctori tate aplica & francor̄ electione a sc̄o Bonefacio moguntie archiepo in regem ungitur & consecratur. & regnat annis. xviii. post annos currer̄. lxxxviii. p̄ quā maiores dom̄ cepunt principari sup reges francorum.

Pippinuf rex contra saxones pugnat. Gripho frater pippini p̄mitur. & Re migi eiusdē pippini regis fr̄ rodomensis archiepc in gallia claret. Pippin̄ rex galliarum ecclias cantib; romane auctoritatis studio meliorauit.

Stephanus. lxxxvii. romane ecc̄ie p̄sidet. M̄ arua amira pempto. m̄hamad p̄ncipatur. sarracenif annis. v. H̄ aistulpho langobardor̄ rege contra roma nos adeo grandescente ut tributum exigere ab unuuf cuisq; capite. steph̄s papa ad erpetend̄u pippini regif auxiliū cogitur in franciam uenire. Cui inueniendo

---

62   The revised edition of Sigebert's chronicle showing the entry mentioning Remedius of Rouen and Pippin's Romanizing reform of chant. The full text of the entry, second from bottom, runs: *Pippinus rex contra Saxones pugnat. Gripho frater Pippini perimitur et Remigius eiusdem Pipini regis frater Rodomensis archiepiscopus in Gallia claret. Pippinus rex Galliarum ecclesias cantibus romane auctoritatis studio meliorauit* ('King Pippin fights against the Saxons. Gripho brother of Pippin is slain and Remedius brother of the same King Pippin, archbishop of Rouen, flourishes in Gallia. King Pippin improved the churches of Gallia with chants of Roman authority by his labours'). Cambridge, Corpus Christi College, MS 51 (Christ Church, Canterbury, ultimately from a St-Bertin exemplar), p. 185. Reproduced by permission. The next entry mentions Pope Stephen's visit to Francia.

accounts of eighth-century work, for his successful efforts to bring the relics of Roman saints to his Messine cathedral. As far as chant reform under Pippin is concerned, Sigebert remembers only Remedius and Rouen.

If Sigebert has preserved the content of the material he found with some fidelity, then it offered a coherent view of the Romanizing reform as a royal undertaking. In that respect it recalls the *Vita Beregisi* of the 930s, and it may be no coincidence that this is another text from within the dense circuit of churches and abbeys in what is today Belgium (see above, Pl. 60). In both of these texts, there is also an explicit reference to chants, to Rome and to Pippin of a kind that is entirely lacking in the extant annals and chronicles of the eighth and ninth centuries. This region of central Belgium is where Sigebert passed his life and therefore where he is most likely to have found the material about Remedius. This strengthens the case for Rouen's influence, for there is a sense in which Sigebert, for all his skills as a historian, was not well placed to find material with such a westerly emphasis, unless it had travelled far on waves of interest and respect. Gembloux is some considerable distance from Rouen; the great churches arrayed around it included Metz, Sint Truiden, Tongres, St-Amand, Liège and Nivelles, defining another district altogether from the lower Seine where Rouen lies.

Bertrada

In most modern histories of Gregorian chant and its beginnings, Pippin's queen, Bertrada (d. 783) is almost entirely forgotten. Yet as a matter of course, her household had its *nutriti* or young men in training, and it says much for the importance of her hall that one of the *scolares* there in the 760s was a youth from Septimania bearing the Visigothic name Witiza, better known to posterity as Benedict of Aniane. He was destined to become an outstanding reformer of Frankish monastic life during the reign of her son Charlemagne. Bertrada saw her husband's reign to the end and lived on for another fifteen years, including a period in which she was a major player in Frankish–Lombard politics.[16]

One of the earliest traces of the liturgical work Bertrada and Pippin sponsored can perhaps be detected in several sources that come together curiously well. The first is the Frankish-Gelasian Sacramentary, a principal monument of Frankish interest in the Roman liturgy and widely supposed to be a compilation from the period of Pippin's reign. The extant copies of this book for the celebrant at Mass, none of which is earlier than the last decades of the eighth century, derive from a model sometimes called the 'Roman sacramentary of King Pippin', and while that may seem a somewhat enthusiastic title (it is rarely used today) the book reveals unmistakable signs of closeness to the royal court, not least in the abundance of material it provides for Masses in time of war or for days when the Frankish army rides out, all presenting the Franks as the true champions of the

Catholic and Apostolic Church. A case has been made for supposing that this sacramentary emerged from an atelier associated with Pippin and Bertrada. It has long been known that the only indigenous Frankish saint commemorated in the book is Praiectus, the seventh-century bishop of Clermont whose relics were translated to the abbey of Flavigny during Pippin's 761 offensive in Aquitaine. A connection less often made concerns the Life of this same saint, for we have already seen that the *Passio* of Praiectus is unique among the surviving Merovingian Lives for the way it lifts a veil on the workings of a choir school. Praiectus is described there as more talented than his contemporaries 'in *Soni* and antiphons', where the *Sonus* may be the Offertory chant of the Gallican rite, seemingly a demanding and elaborate chant that apparently bequeathed some of its music to the corpus of Frankish–Roman Offertories. One episode in the text, discussed above, shows Praiectus studying in the household of Genesius, archdeacon of Clermont, and finding himself guided by the Holy Spirit to sing the melody of a *Sonus* that jealous classmates had challenged him to perform, even though he had never studied it. Thus a saint whose relics were translated by Pippin is the *only* indigenous saint in the Frankish-Gelasian Sacramentary that Pippin and Bertrada may have sponsored and the *only* Merovingian saint whose Life, among the surviving texts, so closely concerns the study and performance of chant. Perhaps Pippin and Bertrada had found a patron for their reform.[17]

Some time before 783, Bertrada's chapel acquired a chaplain named Gervoldus who later became abbot of St-Wandrille, the monastery near Rouen that produced an important and early collection of biographies for its abbots that is the principal source for his life. Gervoldus may have been a member of the Agilolfing kindred that had long provided Bavaria with its ducal line and an independent tradition of liturgical reform on a Roman model. He may be descended from the Gairebaldus who was *referendarius* to Pippin's father Charles Martel in 727 and his father Walcherius is possibly the Uualcherius who is listed as one of Pippin's *fideles* in a document of 748. When he became a cleric, Gervoldus was taken to the royal palace and assigned to Bertrada's chapel; she eventually secured his preferment to the bishopric of Évreux, but Gervoldus renounced it and became instead the abbot of the royal monastery of St-Wandrille, a position he assumed in 789. Once installed there, he continued to be an important royal servant with responsibilities along the northern stretches of coast, which included a journey to Anglo-Saxon England as Charlemagne's envoy to King Offa of Mercia. Despite his eminence and his royal patron, however, Gervoldus does not receive unqualified praise in the house-chronicle of St-Wandrille; the monks resented the way Charles Martel and Pippin had nominated some abbots of mediocre quality, and the biographer of Gervoldus reports he was 'not greatly skilled in letters'. His skills as a singer and music teacher, however, attract unqualified praise:

> Gervoldus . . . born to noble parents, became a cleric; brought to the palace, he was made a chaplain to queen Bertrada. Thanks to her, he was granted

the see of Évreux by Charlemagne . . . but at his own request Gervoldus renounced the episcopate and obtained both from God and from the invincible king Charles this monastery of St-Wandrille. . . . He established a school in the monastery, for he found virtually everyone there ignorant of letters, and he intensively gathered Christ's flock from different places and taught them with the best melodies of chant, as far as the monastic routine allowed. For the aforesaid Gervoldus, although not greatly skilled in the other concerns of letters, was, however, gifted in the art of chanting and not lacking in excellence and sweetness of voice.[18]

These 'best melodies of chant', *optimi cantilenae soni*, presumably contained elements of the emerging Frankish–Roman plainsong, for a gifted singer in the chapel of Pippin's queen would surely have been involved in the work associated with the king and *consanguinei* such as Remedius of Rouen. Bertrada was present at Ponthion when Stephen II arrived in 754 and again at St-Denis when the pope anointed the royal family there. Her private chapel seems just the place where early results to create a Frankish version of Roman chant would receive a welcome. Gervoldus was certainly an advocate of Roman plainsong by the time he left her chapel and took up the abbacy of St-Wandrille, for it was during his tenure the monks received the Roman antiphoner given to them by the priest Harduin, mentioned above. The tradition in the abbey remained strong. One of Gervoldus's pupils in the school at St-Wandrille was his relative Ansegisus, the next abbot of the monastery (823–33), who commissioned a magnificent antiphoner for the house with silver letters on purple parchment, enclosed in ivory plaques and seemingly akin to the famous Monza cantatorium, at least in its appearance (Pl. 63). The letters were apparently uncials, for the chronicler remarks that Ansegisus had the antiphoner copied 'in a similar manner' to the gospels he commissioned, and they were written in a golden *littera romana* on purple parchment.[19]

Can it be entirely coincidental that this work was done in a major abbey of the diocese of Rouen? Why did Gervoldus, a fine singer but seemingly no great scholar, forsake the prospect of a bishopric, so enticing to many, to become the abbot of a monastery not far from the cathedral where a Roman song-master had taught Frankish pupils under Bishop Remedius some twenty years before, and where his predecessor in office, Witlaic, had formed bonds of *amicitia* with Remedius? Simeon's labours at Rouen were interrupted when he was summoned back to Rome upon the death of his superior in the *schola cantorum*, and arrangements were made for the singers of Rouen cathedral to follow him in order to continue their studies. Given these difficult circumstances, it is possible that the work of consolidating a Frankish–Roman repertory at Rouen for the liturgical year extended from the 760s into the 780s, when Gervoldus chose to become abbot of a major and royal house in the Rouen diocese.

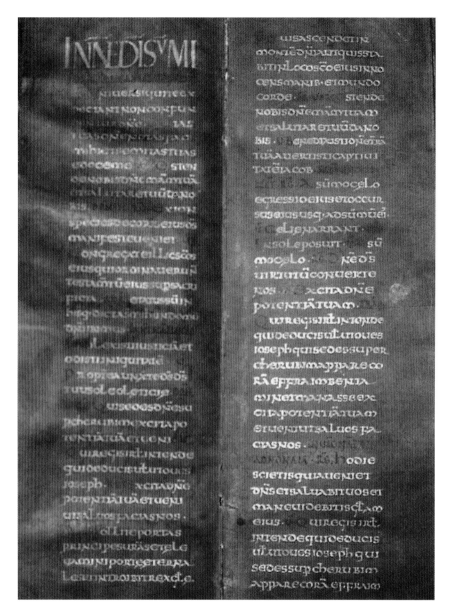

63 The Monza cantatorium, fols. 2ᵛ–3ʳ. Monza, Museo del Tesoro del Duomo, Inv. No. 88. This luxurious manuscript has an excellent claim to represent many important aspects of the St-Wandrille antiphoner commissioned by Abbot Ansegisus. One of the principal early sources for the Frankish–Roman gradual, the Monza book gives the texts of cantor's chants, namely the gradual, Tract and Alleluia, in uncial script of silver and gold on purple parchment, set within plaques of ivory. Apart from the use of gold, and perhaps the elongated format (for nothing is known of the St-Wandrille manuscript in that regard) it plainly has much in common with the description of the St-Wandrille volume and might even be genetically related to it, since the number of Frankish centres capable of producing work of such luxurious quality cannot have been very high. The Monza cantatorium has no musical notation (if that is the right way to describe a book that records only the verbal texts of chants) and the St-Wandrille house-chronicle does not say whether their antiphoner was noted.

Frankish–Roman Chant for a New Imperium

The traces of liturgical work which date from Pippin's reign are few but vivid: a consignment of books from Rome and the arrival of a Roman singer from the *schola cantorum*, all perhaps ultimately inspired by a meeting between the king and Pope Stephen II by the stripling River Saulx as it winds through the immense flatlands of Champagne, the plains whose fertility was the basis for Frankish strength (Pl. 64). These welcome but scattered details make one suspicious of any larger historical context, whether it be of the Occident 'turning medieval', as Kantorowicz supposed, or some other. The reticence of the contemporary chronicles also seems to counsel caution. Nonetheless, there are some documents from the very heart of the liturgical work attempted under Pippin and then continued, perhaps after a hiatus, by Charlemagne, which may provide a route back to an eighth-century understanding of an expansive historical and political context for learning the chant of Rome.

These are the Frankish-Gelasian sacramentaries mentioned above, books for the celebrant at Mass deriving from a lost exemplar generally dated to the 760s, and therefore within the reign of Pippin and contemporary with the work at Rouen. Some earlier sacramentaries contain prayers for the safety of 'the dominion of the Romans', *Romanorum imperium*, which can mean only the Roman

64   The River Saulx at Ponthion. The Carolingian *villa* lay in the field on the left bank.

Empire as it survived principally in Asia Minor. That is exactly what one would expect, for Byzantium was not some decaying autocracy making absurd claims for ancient rights long since foregone, but the last chapter of a salvation history that would not be complete until the Last Judgement. In Pippin's lifetime, and long after, an emperor still ruled in Constantinople as the temporal head *de jure* of a universal religion 'with millions of adherents guided by an educated clergy who daily led prayers for the perpetuation of his rule'. Some copies of the Frankish-Gelasian sacramentary, however, show a striking addition to those prayers: the 'dominion of the Romans' becomes the 'dominion of the Romans and the Franks', *Romanorum Francorumque imperium*. The Byzantine emperors, at least in their own view, did not share their right to an imperial title with any-one, and in that sense the 'dominion of the Romans and the Franks' is an expres-sion with no juridical basis. The question then arises whether the sense of *Romani* has been narrowed, in the wake of the Frankish-papal alliance in 754, to mean the pope, his clergy and the military class of Rome in the patriarchal see of the Latin West. Construed in this way, the 'dominion of the Romans and the Franks' might be intended to express the notion of the Roman bishop's spiritual authority in the West and the Franks' duty to protect him as the supreme tem-poral power within his patriarchate, initiated at Ponthion in 754.[20]

This is the interpretation suggested by one of the most intriguing sources for the concept of such a Frankish–Roman *imperium*. It is the earliest surviving medieval map devoted to Europe alone, prepared in the years before 1120 by Lambert, a canon of St-Omer for his *Liber Floridus*. This is a substantial ency-clopedia of salvation and universal history in Lambert's own hand (see Frontispiece). The chart is headed EUROPA MUNDI PARS QUARTA, 'Europe the fourth part of the world', and shows Europe with the East at the top, as in many medieval world maps. Italy appears at the summit, separated from the rest of the European landmass by mountains traversed by the *Mons Jovis*, the Great Saint Bernard Pass. Spain appears at the foot of the page. In accordance with the doctrine that Europe comprises a fourth of the world rather than a third (the more common understanding, but already questioned by Herodotus) Lambert's map shows *Europa* occupying a quarter-segment of a circle. This is all highly unusual for a twelfth-century chart, or indeed for any known map in the Western cartographic tradition before the sixteenth century, but Lambert's diagram has another claim to distinction. It appears to be a *political* map, and perhaps the earliest Occidental example in existence, for Lambert has drawn a red line, from approximately the Elbe to the Adriatic, enclosing what the accompanying legend calls 'the dominion of the Romans and the Franks', the *Romanorum Francorumque imperium*.

The line crosses the Danube and bears no relation to the course of the Rhine, also marked in red. This frontier therefore corresponds to no natural boundary but shows instead an *imperium* conceived in the Roman manner as a dominion over different peoples and polities. Towards the east, and beyond the borders of this *imperium*, lie some highly emblematic names: *Gothi, Wandali, Huni* and *Sclaui*. With the exception of the Slavs, all of these peoples had disappeared long before Lambert of St-Omer compiled his map; their names come from writers like Augustine, Jerome, Orosius and Jordanes: men who lived to hear that Rome had been sacked by Goths, that Carthage and the grain fleet had fallen to the Vandals, or that Attila and his Hunnic archers were encamped beyond the walls of Nîmes. This part of the map is a chart of perennial fears of intrusion and pillage, focused by the experience of the western Roman Empire in the turbulent events of the fifth century.[21]

Since the *Romani* in Lambert's map share their *imperium* with the Franks they cannot be the Romans of Antiquity, which also explains why the line does not encompass Spain, eventually conquered by the Romans from coast to coast. Lambert's red line also bypasses Britain, marked only by its name in the blue waters at the bottom of the chart. Nor can the Romans at issue be subjects of the Holy Roman Empire of the German Nation, established in 962, for that polity never included the entirety of modern France (Gallia), which lies here firmly within Lambert's Frankish–Roman entity. If the line encloses Roman Catholic Europe as it was towards 1120, when Lambert drew the map, together with the many kingdoms ruled by men and women of Frankish descent, then there are some surprising omissions. Here it becomes especially significant that none of Spain is included, even though the Christians had pressed as far south as Toledo in the generation before Lambert. The Hungarian kingdom is also omitted, although its history as a Catholic kingdom dates from 1000, and the Slavs are placed firmly outside in a way that ignores the early history of the Catholic Church in western Slavic lands.

The most plausible conclusion is therefore that Lambert's map shows the Frankish Empire that came into existence with Charlemagne's acclamation as Emperor of the [Western] Romans in 800; at least, that is how one would be tempted to describe it at first attempt. The territorial correspondence with the Carolingian Empire is close, and there may even be scope for the proposal that Lambert's map has Carolingian models. The accompanying legend is written in the present tense ('these lands pertain to the *imperium* of the Romans and the Franks'), and almost exactly the same language is used in a letter of Pope Sergius II (844–7) concerning Drogo, son of Charlemagne and bishop of Metz, where Charlemagne is said to have made the *Romanorum Francorumque imperium* into 'one body'. The vital point here is that such language was already in use in the time of Pippin, as some of the sacramentaries reveal, and as one would expect if the imperial title conferred upon Charlemagne in 800 was in part 'a bold attempt by the Papacy . . . to define the peculiar relationship that had evolved between the Papacy and the Frankish rulers over the preceding century'.[22]

Lambert of St-Omer's map shows *Europa*, which seems a big word to use in connection with an eighth-century king like Pippin, but many historians agree it is at home in the reign of Charlemagne, occasionally praised by his apologists for being the 'father of Europe', and more besides. Contrary to the impression often given, however, this was nothing new. By the end of the seventh century, the progenitors of the Carolingians had already attracted flattery from writers who knew *Europa* was a poetic word in the high style like many other geographical names abundantly employed in antique verse praising consuls and emperors. The founder of Carolingian fortunes, Pippin I of Landen, was remembered in the 690s as a magnate from a distinguished house, 'known to all that dwell in *Europa*'. There was similar praise for Pippin II of Herstal, 'a prince over many regions and cities in *Europa*'. Frankish writers did not have to wait for Charlemagne, or for his acceptance of the Roman imperial title, to speak of *Europa*; perhaps there is even a sense in which King Pippin and his advisers trusted they were not presiding over a *reform*, a recuperation, but instead over the creation of a new rite of liturgical music for the Latin West that was by now largely coterminous with their own kingdom, empire and sphere of influence. It was to be a *Romanorum Francorumque cantus*.[23]

APPENDIX TO CHAPTER 15

POPE PAUL'S GIFT OF BOOKS TO PIPPIN

The unique source of Pope Paul's letter to Pippin, inventorying a gift of various books, is Vienna, Nationalbibliothek, Cod. 449, fol. 36^r. There is a facsimile in *Codex Epistolaris Carolinus*, ed. Unterkitcher, and an edition in MGH EMKA, 527–9. This collection is an album of letters from popes to the Franks beginning in the time of Pippin's father Charles Martel and commissioned by Charlemagne in 791. The Frankish replies, or the Frankish letters to which the Roman letters are replies, are not included. The volume offers a selection and edition from the originals that were presumably on papyrus and sometimes in such a poor state that it was necessary to renew (*renovare*) and rewrite (*rescribere*) parts of them from memory onto parchment. Only one copy of this edition survives and it is relatively late, produced for Archbishop Willibert of Cologne between 870 and 879. What is more, a reviser of the ninth century or even of the tenth has worked over many of the letters, correcting obvious faults and bringing the text up to the level of late Carolingian Latinity. On what authority did he do this? Did he have access to the originals (surely even more decayed than they were in 791) and is he making fresh guesses about the readings of faded passages? Is he sometimes simply correcting Willibert's copy against a good manuscript of Charlemagne's original transcription and edition? These questions have no answer, and it remains uncertain how much genuine eighth-century material survives in the letter quoted above.[1]

The list of books sent by Pope Paul to Pippin looks curiously plausible. The letter Paul sent with them inventories a small working library for harder studies than many a Frankish cleric or scribe had undertaken for a long time. In addition to a pair of liturgical books, called *antiphonale* and *responsale* and presumably containing office antiphons and responsories in separate books, as was the Roman custom, the list includes an unidentified grammar attributed to Aristotle, together with manuals of geometry, orthography and again grammar. There was also an *horologium nocturnum*, perhaps a water-clock to measure the intervals between the Hours of the night for communities observing a dawn office. For the section where Paul names the books he has sent, the scribe of the main hand produced the text shown here in italics; the later corrector added the corrections shown in bold and in their proper position:

etiam   **ae**
Direximus itaque excellentissime precellentiae uestrae et libros
quantos reperire potuimus id est antiphonale et responsale
            A   te   D   A   **libros**
insimul artem gramaticam aristolis dionysii ariopagitis
geometricam orthografiam gramaticam omnes greco eloquio
        ores   **lo**
scriptas necnon et horogium nocturnum.

Apart from one point of style (*etiam* for *itaque*, and the easing of the sense with *libros*), the reviser had corrected what is obviously meaningless (hence *aristolis* becomes *Aristotelis*, *horogium* becomes *horologium*). Names of authors are given a *littera notabilior*. Orthography is made consistent (*excellentissime* becomes *excellentissimae*). The reviser was also perturbed by *libros . . . omnes greco eloquio scriptas* with its rudimentary mistake (*scriptas*, construed as an adjective, does not agree with *libros*). The reviser may also have been puzzled by this report that a pope had sent a Frankish king various books in Greek, and one may well share that sense of surprise today. Greek books were probably not rare in Rome at this date, for a long series of Greek popes had just come to an end. Pippin was presumably bilingual in Frankish and the common Latin speech but he was surely no more of a Greek scholar than most of his clergy. There may be some truth in Paul's claim to have sent everything he could find that was spare, for despite the signs that Paul's predecessor Zacharias had laboured to enhance the stock of books in papal Rome it is possible to overestimate the surplus of resources that were available to the pontiffs of the eighth century. One would give much to know whether any of this passed through the reviser's mind, or what sources of information he had. He corrected the text so that it reads *greco eloquio scriptores*: 'writers in the Greek tongue'. The difference appears slight, but may actually be cardinal. 'Books in the Greek tongue' is obviously a statement about books; they are necessarily in Greek. 'Writers in the Greek tongue' is just as obviously a statement about writers, and could indicate authors that originally wrote in Greek but could also be read in a Latin version. So it is possible that this letter does indeed provide evidence for the transmission of Latin liturgical materials from Rome to the royal court as early as the 760s.[2]

Notes

1   **The letter:** MGH EMKA, 527–9. For the *Codex Epistolaris Carolinus*, there is a model discussion in McKitterick, *Charlemagne*, 66–8. Further discussion in *Codex Carolinus*, ed. Hack.
2   **Greek popes:** Ekonomou, *Byzantine Rome and the Greek Popes*. **Zacharias and Roman books:** Osborne, 'Papal Court Culture'.

16

SINGERS OF THE NINTH CENTURY:
METZ AND THE PALATINE CHAPEL

The ninth century brings the names of Frankish singers and chaplains in relative abundance. The palace chapels of the emperors around 840 rang with the voices of Drogo, Guntarius and Ruetaldus among many other chaplains, most of them with resolutely Germanic names like these. At Metz, whose cantors in cathedral and monastery occupied a special place in the plainsong economy of the Franks, Gregorian chant rose on the voices of Theotgerus, Crimleicus, Gausthelmus and Arnidus, together with an indefinite number of other Messine clergy seemingly listed as *cantores* in the necrology of Reichenau (see below, Pl. 68). Of the men named here so far, only Crimleicus of Metz has left enough trace for a profile of him to be drawn, and even then the sketch must necessarily be tentative, leaving much to the imagination. Yet despite the obscurity that surrounds these and many other individuals, there is enough light to reveal that an age of unparalleled opportunity had begun for men in Francia with good voices and an aptitude for study. So it was, at least, for those who were able by virtue of talent and birth, or by virtue of talent and good luck, to serve in the palaces and principal churches of the Frankish Empire. The value that Charlemagne and his advisers placed upon Latin grammar, punctilious spelling and hard study of the Bible or the Fathers created a situation in which those who had laboured to acquire skill in singing, in reading or in both were able to show on a daily basis, by their participation in the choral liturgy, that they belonged to an educated elite and a nursery of future governors at the *culmen regiminis*, the peak of government. In other words, the emperors who saw and heard these cantors and chaplains in choir every day were constantly reminded what their options were the next time a bishopric fell vacant.

To be sure, able men known to be good singers had achieved advancement before. We have already encountered a sixth-century example in Gallus of Clermont and an eighth-century case in Aidulfus *ex cantore episcopus* at Auxerre. This is a thin record, however, and while the case of Gallus has all the marks of a royal patronage system already in place, in northern Gaul, within a few decades of the last Western Roman emperor, the example of Aidulfus was not one the clerics of Auxerre would wish to repeat since he leapt from the grade of cantor to bishop without passing through the intermediary clerical orders. This leaves Gallus of Clermont, plucked from a monastery by a bishop who was serving (in effect) as a talent-scout for the cathedral, as a more or less isolated instance in some three centuries of post-Roman ecclesiastical history in the Western lands. After 800, the line of progress from chapel, cathedral or monastic choir to an episcopal throne is much more visible in the biographies of chaplains or cantors that can be teased from chronicles, charters, necrologies and literary works such as the *Actus Pontificum* of Le Mans. This does not mean that all the workings of the process are clear, and indeed they probably never were straightforward since this was not a *system* of patronage but a way of capitalizing upon opportunities as they arose when talented men passed in and out of the palaces, cathedrals and monasteries. Indeed, much remains uncertain about the professional identity and scope of those who were charged to sing something, whatever it might be, in the Frankish–Roman rite of the imperial palaces and chapels under the ninth-century Carolingians, and who might be sent to other churches such as Metz or Lyon (to name two of which we have record). How much musical responsibility was actually entrusted to those who held the position of imperial *capellanus* or chaplain? Was there an underclass of singing men in the Carolingian palaces, principally responsible for the chants of Mass and Office while the imperial chaplains, valued royal servants, came and went in the Empire according to the business they had been charged to perform? Who are the *palatini* or palace singers whose custom of classifying the antiphon *O Sapientia* as mode 1 rather than mode 2 (as in the earliest tonaries) was known to the music theorist Aurelian around 840? Broadening the scope of these questions, did the palaces, monasteries or great cathedrals house anyone who anticipated the figure of the cantor-author, one of the most remarkable and yet least-explored figures of the eleventh century onwards? Many different kinds of source must be gathered to frame even the rudiments of an answer to questions such as these: an entry in a necrology, a treatise on the ascetic life, some stories about the comportment of an emperor, the dedication of a music treatise, the biography of a bishop. Yet no matter how widely the materials range, the thread of the royal and imperial bloodline will continue to count. More than one of the cantors and chaplains who will surface was a *consanguineus* of Charlemagne.

   In this seminal century for the transmission of Frankish–Roman chant through the Empire, questions about the identity of singers inevitably raise issues about the dissemination of the music: who was doing the work, with what support and by what means. So the best place to begin is a simplified map of plainsong in Charlemagne's realm, charting the principal zones of political and liturgical territory whence singers of Frankish–Roman chant might travel in a wide variety of contexts that do not always reveal a systematic campaign of dissemination from 'the centre'; they show instead the many different ways in which singers found cause to move, and to make contact with others, as a great many political actors across the Carolingian dominion cooperated in the great Frankish project of acquiring lands, wealth and influence to strengthen yet further their place in the most powerful polity of the Christian West.

Plainsong Maps 750–850: A Rapid Conspectus

In some respects, the scope of Charlemagne's activity resembled his father's. All the core cities and lands of the 750s and 760s retained their importance into the ninth century. During the early decades of his reign, Charlemagne was still fighting major campaigns in Aquitaine, Saxony, Bavaria and the Lombard kingdom, as Pippin had done. In all these regions, however, Charlemagne built upon his father's work to achieve political solutions that were more decisive, often because they were more ruthless, enlarging his sphere of influence. His evangelism at the point of a sword in Saxony eventually secured a victory beyond his father's ambitions. In Aquitaine and Italy he redrew the political map; whereas Charles Martel had been unable to give any lands in Aquitaine to his sons, and certainly none in Lombardy (an autonomous and friendly kingdom), Charlemagne saw one of his sons anointed king of Aquitaine by a pope and another made king of Lombardy. Thus the autonomy of Aquitaine was dissolved in holy oil and the crown of Lombardy was set to pass down the Carolingian bloodline. (The deposed king of the Lombard dynasty fled to Constantinople; if he hoped for imperial intervention on his behalf, it was forlorn indeed.) In the south, the Carolingians were no more respectful of ducal autonomy in the duchies of Benevento and Spoleto than they had been in the north.

The map of plainsong in Francia around 800 was an array of local topographies and micro-regions. For the Carolingians, the best hope of extending the liturgy of their own palatine chapel, or of its congeners at Metz and St-Denis, lay in the regions where everything, not just a reform of chant, remained to be done. In Saxony, where the Franks were busy creating a diocesan organization in a formerly pagan territory, singers could be transplanted from established centres to the nodal points of Christian organization, notably the new see of Paderborn with its royal palace (Pl. 65). To judge by the experience of Lyon (of which more below), no more than single carrier was necessary. There was a good chance here that the services of rank-and-file clergy drafted into the new churches could be brought into some kind of accord with the usage of the palace chaplains or the Messine clergy. In this context, the work of teaching the Frankish–Roman rite was but one departmental operation in the much larger task of moving an entire concern eastwards by building churches, installing monks or clerics and importing relics from Rome. In many other areas, Frankish–Roman chant must have arrived like a royal barge on the river by a great city; it was imposing, and it came with great authority, but the process of disembarking everything necessary and

65   Reconstruction of the palace complex at Paderborn in its 9th-c. state. (Model by Roese Design, Darmstadt, 1999.) Paderborn, Westfälisches Museum für Archaeologie, Museum in der Kaiserpfalz.

then of negotiating with the local notables to achieve durable results in the face of strong regional opinion, or of customs long entrenched, was generally slow. What is more, the lines of transmission could be thin. The rite of Aachen was brought to Lyon with a single singer from Metz, which means that Charlemagne's liturgy came to the gateway of southern Gaul, so rich in ecclesiastical and liturgical history, with just one man who arrived, dismounted and began his work. In this case, the passage of the new rite was considerably eased by the compliance of a devoted royal *fidelis*, Bishop Leidradus of Lyon, who had explicitly asked Charlemagne to send a singer to his cathedral. In other regions, however, the grain of local politics, or of liturgical tradition, may have been considerably more resistant to any kind of liturgical innovation. In Aquitaine, a region that rarely appears in the principal chronicles except as the target of Carolingian indignation, Pippin wrought terrible destruction throughout his years as Mayor and then as king, raiding rural forts, burning and looting. As late as 820, Louis the Pious can still be found forfeiting the lands of garrisons in these fortresses determined to continue their resistance. In Bavaria, which had known periods of anti-Carolingian alliance with Aquitaine in the 740s, there was a strong, indigenous tradition of liturgical reform associated with the work of the Agilolfing dukes and based, like the Carolingian effort, on Roman models (see above, pp. 276–9). If the saints a man chose to honour, and the liturgy he expected to attend, were ever used as a form of political dissent at the level of castle chapel and regional church, then it was surely here in these outlying dukedoms.

In Italy, the chart of liturgies was as complex as the fractured geopolitics of the peninsula. The Ambrosian rite, protected from extinction by the mystique of the great saint with whose name it has so long been associated, was still celebrated, as it continued to be throughout the Middle Ages, but there were also many other liturgical districts. Churches in the duchy of Rome, together with many others in the patrimony of Saint Peter elsewhere, presumably continued to use the Roman music that Simeon of the Roman *schola cantorum* taught at Rouen, or various dialects of that repertory. At Naples there were liturgies in both Greek and Latin, but by 800 the Byzantines' hold on this western outpost had been weakened by the separatist policies of the dukes including Stephen, both duke and bishop, who sent singers to study at the Roman *schola cantorum* in the late 760s. Benevento, formerly the political core of the most southerly of the two Lombard duchies, continued to use its distinctive repertory of chant into the eleventh and twelfth centuries, when substantial notational records of the music were produced, albeit showing many signs of pressure from its Frankish–Roman counterpart. Official steps to eradicate this music accompanied a much later German involvement in Italy when the Salian emperors sought to place reliable compatriots on the throne of Saint Peter. In 1057 Pope Stephen IX, a Lotharingian, ruled that Beneventan chant should henceforth be replaced by Frankish-Roman plainsong at the great abbey of Montecassino.[1]

There were so many ways for Frankish–Roman chant to cross the Alps into Italy that any attempt to envisage lines of transmission soon becomes a conspectus of Frankish consolidation in the northern and central reaches of the peninsula after Charlemagne's conquest of Lombardy in 774. As the new *regnum Italiae* was secured, Frankish magnates received benefices there to create the royal following that Pippin, Charlemagne's son and king in Italy, calls 'our Frankish *fideles* who are with us in Italy, or who remain'. Many other Franks who moved south became counts, replacing the Lombard dukes of the old political order. Some of these men were members of great kindreds, such as the Unruochinger, that soon appear as holders of substantial lands on both sides of the Alps. The prime example in that lineage is Eberhard of Friuli, son-in-law of the emperor Louis the Pious and holder of an immense territory in Lombardy, Alemannia and Francia. Frankish magnates also received Italian churches and their lands as benefices, such as the Graf Liutfrid II, who possessed the *curtis* of the cathedral of Saint John the Baptist in Monza. Churches and monasteries of Francia also became landholders in Italy, as did the Franks who became prelates. Within the first two generations of the Lombard conquest in 774, Franks can be traced as bishops at Spoleto, Verona, Vicenza, Vercelli and Milan, among other cities, and some were concurrently abbots of Frankish monasteries. (Bishop Sigoald of Spoleto, for example, was also abbot of Echternach.) To inflect these lines of contact still further, some Frankish bishops held the governance of monasteries in Italy, as in the case of Ebbo of Reims, who controlled the abbeys of Bobbio and Stavelot, creating an especially potent nexus of houses.[2]

These transalpine networks have to be teased from many different sources, but especially from the *Libri memoriales*, the books in which churches kept a record of those with whom they had formed a prayer association. Musicologists have barely opened these volumes, even though they are especially rich for Reichenau, Brescia, Sankt Gallen, and other houses in exactly the transalpine zone where the information is most needed. A clutch of names in the *Liber memorialis* kept at the great abbey of Reichenau, for example, shows this famous monastery on Lake Constance making contact with the (by now) Frankish royal abbey of Nonantola in the time of its abbot Peter (804–24/5). He can be traced at Aachen in 814, close to the time when bishop Leidradus obtained its rite for the cathedral of Lyon through the intermediary of a singer from Metz. We shall soon find a Messine cantor at Reichenau, recorded as a benefactor (for his teaching of Frankish-Roman chant?) in the *Liber memorialis*. The relationships can be set out in a diagram as follows:

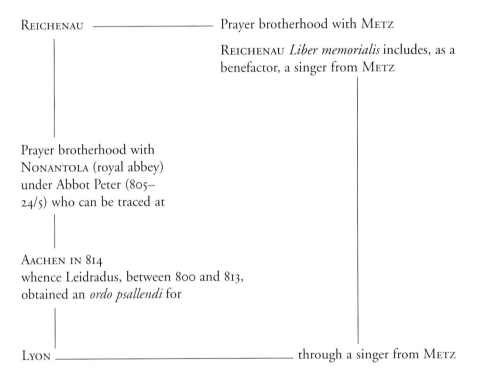

REICHENAU ──────────────── Prayer brotherhood with METZ

REICHENAU *Liber memorialis* includes, as a benefactor, a singer from METZ

Prayer brotherhood with NONANTOLA (royal abbey) under Abbot Peter (805–24/5) who can be traced at

AACHEN IN 814 whence Leidradus, between 800 and 813, obtained an *ordo psallendi* for

LYON ──────────────────────── through a singer from METZ

The kinds of pattern that can appear as different streams of information like this converge rarely permit precise conclusions, but they suggest the kinds of connection that could arise.[3]

The outstanding ninth-century monument to the adoption of the Frankish–Roman repertory in Italy is the famous cantatorium now in the cathedral treasury of Monza. This is a cantor's book containing graduals, alleluias and tracts, and although there is no musical notation the contents are nonetheless introduced as 'a book of musical art' in a contemporary note that fancifully connects it with Gregory I and the Roman *schola cantorum*. The description of a book without notation as a volume of 'musical art' is puzzling only if one forgets how well the *texts* of chants served as a form of musical notation by recording the syllables through which the melody sounded, and by revealing a grammatical structure that was itself a kind of musical mnemonic since the musical phrases responded to it with varying degrees of closure. The manuscript is written in uncials of silver and gold on purple parchment, but the silver has mostly oxidized. The effect is one of the most lavish and grave *romanitas*, looking back to the kind of volume that Wilfrid of Hexham contemplated with longing on a Roman altar and to the luxurious manuscripts produced in Theoderic's Italy. Since the Monza cantatorium assigns 29 August to both Saint John the Baptist, which is a Gallican feast, and Saint Sabina, it is almost certainly a Frankish production made for the cathedral where it still resides, dedicated to John the Baptist. (Such books could certainly be produced in ninth-century Francia; see above, p. 321.) The Monza cantatorium is widely agreed to be a ninth-century book; if it was indeed brought to Italy by a Frankish magnate then good candidates can be sought among the members of the Etichonid kindred. Hugo of Tours and his wife Ava were both buried in Monza cathedral, and Hugo is remembered in the cathedral's necrology for having given the church all his possessions. Their son Liutfredus is listed in 846 or 847 among those 'who have benefices in Italy' and is also remembered in the necrology. His sister, Irmingard, married Lothar I, son of the Louis the Pious. There is also a Liutfredus II, plainly a relative, who held the *curtis* of Monza cathedral as a benefice in the next generation. This was an exalted Frankish clan who could well afford to commission a book like this scintillating cantatorium.[4]

Saxony in the same period has left no liturgical books, but the chronicles provide material to reconstruct a set of circumstances in which the Roman faith and its rite almost certainly came to a particular centre, namely Herisburg, now Obermarsberg in North-Rhine Westphalia. The compiler of the *Annales Mettenses priores* calls this settlement a *castrum*, the term he also applies to the episcopal city of Clermont, for Herisburg was close to a Saxon cult-complex of major importance. The sacred tree called Irminsul stood on a hill nearby. The name means 'great/universal pillar', suggesting this fane was venerated as a world-support, somewhat like the Old Norse Yggdrasil or world-tree. When Charlemagne captured Herisburg in his Saxon campaign of 772 he destroyed the Irminsul and installed a Frankish garrison in the *castrum*. A miraculous fountain of water immediately rewarded this pious work, ending a drought threatening to curtail Charlemagne's demolition of the shrine complex (which was extensive enough to involve his men in three days of work). In 776, when the Saxons brought up many siege engines to retake Herisburg and their ruined holy site, there was already a church in the *castrum* that the compiler of the *Annales Mettenses priores* calls a *basilica*. During the Saxons' attempt to take the site, two fiery shields appeared in the air above the basilica to protect it, providing a second testimony to the divine force Charlemagne had released by obliterating the pagan shrine. The Franks prevailed in the ensuing struggle, and many Saxon families who no longer wished to be part of their king's resistance to Frankish power accepted baptism there. By 785, at the latest, Herisburg was a place where Charlemagne could choose to spend Easter with his entire family. On that occasion the clerical forces of the basilica, installed as part of the Frankish garrison or *custodia* put in place by Charlemagne, were no doubt enhanced by the palatine chaplains who followed him on his travels, and he would surely have wished to implant the psalmody of the Frankish–Roman rite, in its current state of evolution, in a basilica so close to former pagan site of major importance, and in a baptismal church with a vital role to play in the conversion of the Saxons.[5]

The Heartlands

When the sites that Charlemagne chose for his councils, or where he passed the seasons of Christmas and Easter, are plotted on a map, they reveal a triangular zone of political activity, the deep Carolingian heartland, whose defining points all correspond to concentrations of merchants along principal waterways:

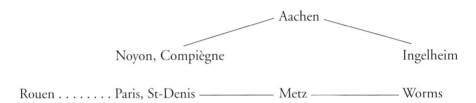

At the western angle lie Paris and St-Denis, fed by the Seine moving downriver to Rouen. The fair at St-Denis, originally convened for the saint's day (9 October) in the Merovingian period, was extended to as much as four weeks under Charlemagne, a clear indication that traders were coming from further afield and therefore wishing to stay longer. At the eastern angle of the triangle lie the Rhineland sites of Worms and Ingelheim. A line from Paris to Worms creates the base line of the triangle and it runs very close to the city of Metz, on the Moselle. Charlemagne built three palaces within a day's ride of major permanent markets, or emporia, providing the large number of Franks and their servants who gathered for his assemblies with a great many goods, just as the assemblies provided the merchants with an unparalleled density of wealthy customers. A Carolingian council under Charlemagne was a fair occasion in more senses than one.[6]

  The activities of Frankish singers and makers of liturgical books can readily be mapped upon this territory. If there was some overlap between the chaplains and the royal notaries, as has often been suspected, then it is possible that chaplains trained in Frankish–Roman chant were stationed, so to speak, in any number of palaces whence they were sent to do the king's business in the surrounding region, very often without his presence. To consider specific centres (for Metz, see below), the importance of Aachen as a Carolingian palace has probably been exaggerated in the past, but it is well known that the site acquired a palace and chapel under Charlemagne that was already associated with a prestigious and palatine form of Frankish–Roman chant by the 840s and perhaps well before, since the *ordo psallendi* of Aachen was transmitted to the cathedral church of Lyon, and to certain nearby monasteries of the archdiocese, before Charlemagne's death in 816. The chaplains who sang here are probably to be identified with the *palatini* mentioned in the 840s by the music theorist Aurelian and a mobile group, required to follow the emperor to any palace where he chose to reside. They must often have been present at Worms and especially at Ingelheim, whose chapel figures in Ermoldus's luxurious account of ceremonies to mark the baptism of the Danish king in 826 (see below, pp. 356–7). Rouen, across to the west, was the scene of the earliest traceable encounters between Frankish and Roman singers. Among the handful of earliest Frankish–Roman liturgical books without notation, several probably derive from this western zone around the Seine basin, namely Senlis/St-Denis (the SILVANACTENSIS), Corbie (the CORBIENSIS) and perhaps Soissons (the COMPENDIENSIS), showing how much activity was concentrated in the regions once strongly favoured by the Merovingians. (Of the twenty-five fiscal possessions in this Parisian region, Charlemagne created twenty-one; the Carolingians were an Austrasian family, but it is easy to forget the importance of their links with the Paris district.) In contrast, the centres documented as *receiving* Frankish–Roman chant in the literary sources for the same period are Lyon, Reichenau and Le Mans, all beyond the territory mapped above.[7]

The reign of Charlemagne shows clear signs that the work of editing and disseminating Frankish–Roman chant was becoming more consistently consolidated in the eastern zone. His father Pippin is most often recorded at the palaces of Attigny, Quierzy, Verberie and Compiègne, showing a somewhat westerly core of activity and a clear attempt to retain contact with Merovingian centres between the Seine and the Meuse. Pippin invited Pope Stephen II to winter at St-Denis, near Paris, and made provision for a Roman singer to continue teaching Frankish pupils from the cathedral of Rouen, all choices which show the same westerly emphasis. This is unlikely to be an illusion created by the surviving documents, for Pippin was raised at St-Denis and the territories allotted to him by Charles Martel lay in Neustria, Burgundy and the south (it was Pippin's brother Karloman who received the lands lying eastwards in Austrasia, Alemannia and Thuringia). With Charlemagne, however, there is a definite swing to the east. Although he made appearances at the palaces so often used by his father, he is more often found at Thionville, Mainz, Worms, Ingelheim, Herstal and Aachen, a marked shift towards (and across) the Rhine. The Seine basin remained vital, as some of the earliest Frankish–Roman graduals without musical notation suggest, but more was entrusted now to the palatine singers further east and to the canons of Metz.

Perhaps from the territory of modern Austria comes one of the most remarkable documents for the dissemination of Frankish–Roman chant by internal networks operating in accordance with the royal will but on the participants' own initiative as part of the habitual epistolary communication between the heads of religious houses asking favours from their colleagues. It is already well known that such traditions of correspondence could lead to the creation and dissemination of new chants; the letter from Helisachar, chancellor of the Frankish Empire, to Nebridius of Narbonne provides a famous example from the period 814–22. But the letter now to be introduced seems to be the only one known in which the head of one religious house asks another specifically for the loan of a cantor so that the repertory of Frankish–Roman chant can be consolidated (or indeed introduced for the first time) in his church. This is a letter preserved in Section II of a formulary entitled the *Liber Traditionum*, a collection assembled in Salzburg. The manuscript is now lost and is perhaps destroyed, but a near-complete transcription survives in the papers of the eighteenth-century antiquary and abbot of St Emmeram, Froben Forster. As it stands, the Latinity of the letter is poor and by no means what a reader accustomed to the best productions of the Carolingian period would expect. Nonetheless, the vital passage is clear enough, and proves to be a request from a bishop or abbot that his correspondent should send a cantor equipped to teach Roman chant:

> To the most noble and gracious man, filled with the spirit of wisdom, and to that friend; he that is indeed your trusted ally, however undeserving and unworthy, intends by these letters expressive of his lowliness the eternal salvation of your crown of blessedness. We have sent this letter, explaining our need, to the scrutiny of your wisdom and presence, because trustworthy envoys are rarely to be found that truthfully and candidly speak the truth to friends. On that account we have sent this silent and mute little page as if it were an envoy, that you may take it in your honest hands, read it with clear eyes and interpret it in the best manner with a holy mouth, and with a fervent petition we beseech you that you graciously give assent to our request. *Deign to grant the single cantor we are asking for, so that, a son to ours and yours, he may apply himself to reinforce loyal pupils in chanting according to the authority of the Roman Church, to the praise of Almighty God, to the honour of his Church, and to your own eternal reward* (emphasis added).[8]

Since the 'chanting according to the authority of the Roman Church' mentioned here almost certainly refers to Frankish–Roman chant rather than music brought fresh from Rome, this letter is a uniquely explicit example of the Gregorian music spreading along lines of friendship, and perhaps of prayer-confraternity. The language of friendship and good will here is fulsome, but the terms can be paralleled in other letters of the collection where, for example, a churchman asks another to send him a skilled painter. Viewed in this light, cantors trained in Frankish–Roman chant join the scribes, masons, glaziers, painters and other skilled men that monks and clergy of the eighth and ninth century can be found sending to one another as a favour in response to a specific request. In the usual manner of formularies, the *Liber Traditionum* does not include the name of either the sender of this letter nor the recipient. Nonetheless, all is not lost. Many of the other letters that appear in this Section II of the *Liber Traditionum* are found elsewhere in other collections, but this one has so far been found nowhere else. It may be a Salzburg document.

Metz

In the second half of the eighth century, the cathedral of Metz housed the first cell of singers outside Rome known to have been configured into *a schola cantorum* on the Roman model and under that title. In the 780s, an English pupil of Alcuin named Sigulf went to Rome to study liturgical rites (*ecclesiasticum ordinem*) but chose Metz for *cantus*. By the late ninth century, the eminence of the Messine *schola cantorum* had long since declared itself even to those who had reason to adopt a mixed view of the Franks. In the 870s, the Lombard chronicler Andreas of Bergamo called Metz the fountainhead of the chant 'that resounds throughout all Francia and Italia to this day as an adornment to many cities and churches', although he tellingly regarded the original impetus there as more papal than royal. (He had not forgotten the depredations of the Franks in Charlemagne's Lombard campaign.) Andreas's Roman contemporary John the Deacon sneered at Frankish attempts to learn Roman chant save in the sanctuary at Metz. According to John, Charlemagne discovered while in Rome that the chant of his singers did not accord with the Roman, so he left two 'industrious clerics' behind to be trained in the authentic Roman music. Eventually he recalled them to Metz and from there, or so John claims, the chant of the Frankish kingdom was corrected anew after the Messine example. When those who had received this Roman training were no more, John continues, Charlemagne discovered that the chant of many churches in his kingdom was out of accord with the Messine practice, whereupon Pope Hadrian sent two Roman teachers who established that the Metz tradition was the best, albeit corrupted by a certain 'natural wildness' in the Franks which they presumably could not cure. From this point on, John declares, all Frankish churches owed to Metz the deference in matters of chant that Metz owed to Rome. It says much for the Messine *schola* that this determined Frankophobe, steeped in a much older Roman contempt for drunken barbarians but also conscious of their vast appetites in his own day, speaks so highly of the cathedral and its community.

His contemporary in Swabia, Notker Balbulus, was even prepared to put aside his pride in the traditions of his abbey of Sankt Gallen and admit that 'in our time all church singing is called Metz chant'.[9]

There was a long history to this deference to Metz. In the late 500s, Venantius Fortunatus praised the region of Metz and the Moselle, describing a northern Arcadia where the river

> Lambit odoriferas vernanti gramine ripas
> Et lavat herbarum leniter unda comas.

bathes the sweet-smelling banks with their verdant grass, while the wave gently washes the crests of the green stalks.[10]

Such poetry reveals little about the appearance of Merovingian Metz or its landscape, but says much about its geopolitical position. Nearby lay the city of Trier, further down the Moselle, the site of the Roman imperial court for a period in the fourth century and the headquarters of the Praetorian Prefecture. Metz was part of the well-equipped and militarized infrastructure of the late Roman Empire that passed up the Moselle, joining the Rhine at Koblenz and went on to Cologne. After the major disturbances of the fifth century in this region, Metz passed into Merovingian hands in the early sixth, together with Trier and Reims. The kings found there the remains of a Roman monumentality; there were two amphitheatres, the greater housing a church believed to be the oldest of the city (a sure sign of fifth-century contraction and the formation of a micro-urban community within the much narrowed circuit of walls provided by the arena). There was an aqueduct originally built to bring water from the nearby village of Gorze, and an imposing Maison Quarrée, used as a royal palace (see above, Pl. 48), that may once have borne comparison with its namesake at Nîmes. These monuments were perhaps less apparent to the kings as 'Roman' than as especially large and useful structures of durable material, patched and layered with the encrusted repairs and rebuilding of centuries, but still regarded as fitting expressions of an ambition to rule in the manner of Roman provincial governors writ large by their freedom from imperial oversight.

Once the Merovingian kings came to Metz, many new churches appeared – perhaps a dozen in the sixth century alone – as Austrasian aristocrats drawn to the royal court looked to the profit of their souls and of their kindred. By the eighth century there were at least forty-three ecclesiastical foundations in the city, including the cathedral of St Stephen with four churches on its southern flank by 800 and grouped near a large cloister. After Saint Stephen, the principal heavenly protector was Saint Arnulph, a Carolingian forebear and powerful magnate of Austrasia who became bishop of Metz in 614. Around 640 his remains were placed in the monastery of the Holy Apostles in Metz, thereafter St Arnulph. With the shift of emphasis eastwards that marks the passage of royal power from Pippin to Charlemagne, Metz became the Carolingians' city, not in the sense of a royal urban capital, for the Carolingians never had one, but rather because the abbey of St Arnulph was their dynastic basilica. Bishop Chrodegang of Metz was a long-standing servant of the family and a trusted ally of Pippin when Carolingian kingship began in 751.[11]

An Austrasian from the high nobility of the Franks, Chrodegang came from Hesbaye in what is now eastern Belgium, and may have had some blood connection with the Carolingian house. His long period of loyal service began in youth when his parents placed him in the household of Pippin's father, Charles Martel, to be raised as a *nutritus*. Chrodegang rose to become *referendarius*, the keeper of the seal who recognized documents issued by the king or the Mayors. This was one of the reasons, in addition to Chrodegang's aristocratic origin in deep Carolingian heartland, why Pippin placed such trust in him and why he was one of the two royal *missi* appointed to conduct Pope Stephen II across the Alps to Francia. A generation later, Paul the Deacon captured the fundamental simplicity of the matter when he wrote that Chrodegang was chosen because in all things he was trustworthy: *in omnibus locuples*. Chrodegang was also first-rate material for a bishop, later an archbishop, in Pippin's service: literate, capable and determined. He did not need the stimulus of events of 753, with its papal visit, to contemplate a reform of his cathedral community in the light of Benedict's *Rule* with its humane model for a common life; it sufficed to be a loyal supporter of Pippin and Karloman far back in 745 when the Council of Soissons could already commend 'the holy rule', without specifying the Rule at issue because it was tacitly understood to be Benedict's.[12]

Long before his visit to Rome in 753, Chrodegang was probably pondering how the life of clergy in a great urban church could be founded upon the common life of the apostles but in a way not injurious to the supply of aristocratic recruits necessary for the dignity of a metropolitan church, not always men of a dependably ascetic temper. In the Rule he devised for his canons, a document probably begun long before the Roman visit of 753, Chrodegang anticipates that many who join the cathedral community will wish to retain the profit of their inheritance and yet still be inclined to adopt a more regulated form of clerical life than most Frankish cathedrals had known for many years. He summons his canons to consider the common life of the apostles, and to 'draw their souls towards a kind of copy of that [apostolic] fellowship' (xxxi), but he also reassures them his Rule is a guide for those who say 'we cannot relinquish everything' (xxxi). Whereas Benedict had regarded the ownership of goods or land as a vice to be eradicated from the monastery, Chrodegang's canons were not to be bound by a vow of poverty, nor were they necessarily called to a life of strict enclosure. Many of them lived together in the houses or *mansiones* forming part of the cloister, but others were resident further away in the city, or its broader territory, with their servants. It is revealing that Chrodegang does not present his manual as a Rule, with all the constriction of liberty the term implies, but rather as a 'little statute', which seems decidedly more accommodating.[13]

To peruse these statutes is to recognize how radically Chrodegang's regulations undermine the modern notion of Gregorian chant as an essentially disembodied music of calm and spiritual tranquillity. Whatever the Franks had adopted from Roman singers, they had absorbed it into their own dietary world of beer, meat and fats taken as butter or lard. John the Deacon's Roman jibe about the 'bibulous throats' of the Franks, which in his view prevented them from reproducing the subtleties of Roman chant, does not seem so gratuitous when one reads Chapter 30 of the Rule, 'On the feast-days of the saints'. After a fairly cursory passage concerning liturgical matters, Chrodegang gets to the core of the issue, which is to ensure there is adequate meat and drink. The Rule is replete (the word seems justified) with provisions for meals, with beer and wine, at different times of the liturgical year, notably the major feasts such as Epiphany, *Laetare* Sunday, Ascension, Pentecost, Christmas and Easter. (It is no great surprise that Saint Arnulph of Metz is the patron saint of brewers.) The more festive the liturgy that the Messine canons sang the more abundantly they ate. The calorific intake of Frankish monks and clergy on certain commemorative days of the year in the ninth century has been estimated at a staggering 9,000 calories, which is just under four times the daily recommended quantity today for a healthy and moderately active male. Far from being disembodied, Gregorian chant at Messine festivals was performed by some of the most carnal singers the world has ever known.[14]

Chrodegang's second step is to explain what he expects in return for such concessions, and many of his requirements are directed towards the liturgical life of the community. The frame of reference is Roman from the outset, with many words, phrases or even entire passages borrowed from the Rule of Saint Benedict (although Chrodegang's reference to 'the consolations of beer', when wine is not available, is resolutely Frankish). The debt to Benedict includes much that Chrodegang has to say about the Divine Office. The canons are to sing Matins 'when digestion is completed', followed by a period of study. For Benedict, this time 'left after Matins' is 'for those with an incomplete knowledge of the psalter or the readings', and so it is for Chrodegang, although his requirements are more elaborate. The canons of Metz are required to sing forty or fifty psalms during this period at the discretion of the bishop, while those who have no psalter, or no lesson to study for the next day's Mass, are to meditate (VIII). Those who cannot do so must sing or read in the church, so that 'nobody should presume in this period to sleep' (V).

Other details suggest a process of revision after Chrodegang's experiences at Rome in the autumn of 753. He had met the high officials of the Roman Church with their impressive and quasi-palatine titles, and now he requires the canons to address their fellows by prefacing a man's name with his title of office, according to the Roman custom (II). Thus every time the canons meet, they are reminded of due hierarchy 'according to the legitimate institution of the Roman Church'. Except in cases of illness, they are not to bear their staffs into the choir-stalls, 'according to the Roman tenet' (VII). All canons who live in the city are to come to the chapter meeting on Sundays in their 'vestments of office, as is the Roman custom' (VIII). Chrodegang's administration for his cathedral also owes much to the sense of order and decorum manifest in Roman liturgical ceremonial as he probably knew it from *Ordo Romanus I* and as he had certainly seen it with his own eyes. He strove to adopt Roman customs in his ministry, taking care to consecrate bishops, priests, deacons and other orders on Ember Saturdays in March, June, September and December, 'as is the custom of the Roman Church' (so says Paul the Deacon). He may well have taken part in this ceremony during his Roman sojourn of 753.

Chrodegang's third step is to seek heavenly protectors from Rome. Saints who had long guarded the papal city were now invited to add the region of Metz to their charge as some of their relics were transported to their new area of responsibility. Chrodegang asked Pope Paul I for relics of the martyrs Gorgonius, Naboris and Nazarius, which he placed in his own monastic foundation of Gorze, in the monastery of St-Hilaire and at Lorsch. (It is perhaps no coincidence that Chrodegang received relics of Nazarius; Pope Stephen II anointed Pippin king of the Franks on the feast-day of Saints Nazarius and Celsus, 28 July in the Roman calendar.) Chrodegang may well have acquired these relics in the spirit of the revised Salic Law, issued during his lifetime with a triumphalist preface proclaiming how well the Franks served the earthly remains of the martyrs whom the Romans had slain (see above, pp. 314–16). Frankish deference to the Eternal City had its limits.

After his experiences in Rome, Chrodegang came to regard the Roman liturgy as part of the alchemy that could turn the common metal of an urban church into the gold of a virtuous common life. The earliest biographical record of Chrodegang, written at the behest of his successor Angilram by Paul the Deacon, draws all the above themes together in a succinct notice: the importance of the experience in 753–4 when Chrodegang brought a pope across the Alps, his concern to organize the common life of his clergy, the importance of Roman relics, and finally the implantation of Roman chant amongst the singers of his cathedral:

> Since Chrodegang was trustworthy in all things, he was chosen by Pippin, and by all the assembly of the Franks, and sent to Rome. There he called the venerable Pope Stephen to *Gallia*, as was the fervent desire of all. Chrodegang gathered clergy, and caused them to live a common life, as if in a monastery, within the enclosure of the cloister. He gave them a Rule showing how they should live the Christian life. He endowed them with a sufficiency of supplies and means of livelihood, so that, having no need to take time off for duties leading away from eternal life, they needed only to be vigilant for divine service. These clergy being abundantly imbued with divine law and with Roman chant, he commanded that the custom and *ordo* of the Roman Church be kept, which had not been the case hitherto in the Church of Metz.[15]

Paul duly emphasizes Chrodegang's labours to enhance the endowments of his cathedral, providing 'a sufficiency of supplies (*annonas*) and means of livelihood' so that the canons could attend to their liturgical tasks, needing 'only to be vigilant for divine service'. The word *anonna*, once the term for the tax in corn or oil levied for Rome, should probably be translated 'grain' in this passage and its meaning duly sensed in the weight of sacks and the dust of the millstone; no early medieval bishop, and certainly not Chrodegang, was liable to forget the importance of sheer *produce* to the success of the common life. The 'means of livelihood' probably refers to the farms, estate-centres, mills, woods and fishponds which formed the core of a church's disposable wealth in *immobilia* and might be exploited to pay for the manufacture of liturgical books (see Pl. 66). Chrodegang's canons were free to concentrate upon devotions and liturgical duties, including the task of becoming 'abundantly imbued with divine law and with Roman chant', where [Frankish-]Roman plainsong and divine law together are presented as the two influences, both acquired by arduous study and apt disposition of the spirit, which suffuse or 'imbue' the clergy with holiness of life. There is a strong sense here that the Roman liturgy brings discipline and wholesomeness to the spiritual constitution of all who use it, so profoundly has it been shaped by Rome's freedom from heresy and by an ancient claim to authority expressed in the papal custom of calling the canonical tradition of the Church simply *Romae disciplina*.

Nothing could be closer to the heart of this common life at Metz, supported by resources leaving the canons free for devotions and for the edifying effects of *cantus romanus*, than the core of trained singers in the *schola cantorum*. In Rome, Metz or anywhere else, such a body of specialized singers was impossible to establish without endowments and focused material support, for, as one modern scholar has said, it is

> no small thing to set up a group like the schola cantorum; it requires a goodly measure of economic prosperity, spiritual commitment and common psychological well-being to release valuable clergy from their other duties, and to provide a residence for them and support them generously while they devote themselves exclusively to the development of ecclesiastical music.[16]

Metz in the 750s certainly met the criterion of economic prosperity, and Chrodegang's lavish provision of food and drink on certain days of the liturgical year has already revealed one contemporary way to understand what 'psychological well-being' could mean. The Messine *schola cantorum* first definitively appears in the time of Bishop Angilram (768–91), when it possessed a fourfold hierarchy on the Roman model, but the school was undoubtedly founded under Chrodegang, for there is no other way he could have ensured 'that the custom and *ordo* of the Roman Church should be kept', in the words of Paul the Deacon, than by applying to the task his well-established principle of supporting abundant time for study with lavish material provision. There was also a system of

66 The cost of making an antiphoner in late October 973, as shown in the late 17th-c. copy of the Cartulary of the Cathedral Chapter of Agde (Hérault). Salomon, bishop of Agde, and the chapter of Agde, enter into a contract with Lusinus, presbyter, who is to prepare an antiphoner in return for the usufruct of two manses with *curtes* and a garden; two manses and five fields at Aviaz; a manse in the villa 'Saturianus' with all grounds pertaining to it; three portions of land and two vines and a tenement at Prades. He must not sell the lands or properties on, and at his death they will revert to the chapter. Montpellier, Médiathèque Emile Zola, MS 33, p. 220.

reward, indeed payment. By the time of Bishop Angilram, there was a schedule of statutory emoluments for the cantors who sang specified graduals, tracts and Alleluias on certain feast-days of the liturgical year. These ritual items are cited by incipit in the scale of payments, and they all prove to be Frankish–Roman or Gregorian texts placed in the liturgical positions to which the later graduals, with or without notation, or the later Frankish ordinals, will assign them.[17]

During Easter week, for example, the singers were deputed to perform the Tracts *Deus, deus meus* on Palm Sunday and *Qui habitat* on Good Friday. One might choose to suppose the melodies used in Metz in the time of Angilram were not the ones that appear in the musical sources of 900 and beyond, nor even their ancestors, but rather melodies or forms of intonation eventually replaced by work done under Charlemagne or indeed his son Louis the Pious. Yet the simplest hypothesis is surely that the Messine *schola cantorum*, organized on the basis of its Roman model, was already by the 770s performing a repertory with some consolidated Frankish–Roman chants, including important items for soloists like the Tract, within a generation of Pippin at the most. Indeed, the citation of Frankish–Roman texts in these payments suggests that it is by no means beyond the bounds of possibility that 'a landmark first edition of the eighth-century Gregorian mass antiphoner . . . circulated under Pippin'.[18]

In the absence of notation, of which there is as yet no trace until the 840s, melodies of these chants could be transmitted from Metz to other churches only in exactly the same way as at Rouen when Franks sat down with a Roman master. Singers who knew the material by heart had to spend long hours teaching singers who did not by performing the music repeatedly, by breaking it down into such musical elements as were considered helpful to the process of memorization, by using whatever technical terminology and concepts as were then in existence to clarify matters, and by tabling whatever written copies of the verbal texts were deemed necessary for success until the music was judged to be lodged in the memories of their pupils in a satisfactory way. Viewed in retrospect, this may seem an extraordinary labour requiring exceptional commitment and organization, yet it is unlikely any churchman of the eighth century would have viewed the task in quite those terms. Many Frankish monasteries began as colonies from other houses, the abbot dispatching a small company of his monks to a new site where they might find only a few buildings (if that) and some of the founder's kin with everything to learn, not just their plainsong. In the eyes of contemporaries, the dissemination of the Roman rite and its Frankish–Roman chant may have seemed nothing very new in the life of a Frankish Church which had always expanded by a process of cooperative filiation.

Most of the work to disseminate Gregorian chant in this way is hidden from view, the singers from the Messine *schola cantorum*, or elsewhere, departing and returning unseen, sometimes perhaps only one or two at a time. The letter to Charlemagne from Leidradus of Lyon, however, briefly discussed above, momentarily lifts the veil on the process. Leidradus was a Bavarian, one of the numerous Germanic bishops Charlemagne had appointed to sees of central and southern Francia; he served as one of the emperor's two *missi* to the Narbonnaise where attempts were made to bribe him with Islamic gold coins, carpets from Arabia, leather from Cordova, ivories from the Ganges, perfumes from Syria and even a vase with scenes of an orgiastic bacchanalia. Such things were not impossible to find in southern Gaul around 800, but Gregorian chant was still a distinctly northern commodity, and Leidradus brought it to his see from Aachen via the cathedral of Metz. According to his own account (see Pl. 67), Leidradus petitioned Charlemagne for a cleric from Metz to be sent; as a result of this sojourn by a single man in Lyon, Leidradus was able to institute the order of psalmody according to the palatine rite of Aachen. He makes no distinction between the rite of the palace and of Metz cathedral; today, it is impossible to say how well they agreed, but it is revealing that Leidradus thought the same liturgy and chant had been installed in two heartland centres. He believed that such a thing was

67   A page from the 15th-c. copy of the letter of Leidradus of Lyon. Lyon, Bibliothèque municipale, MS 1488, fol. 201. The reference to the 'scolas cantorum' appears at the top of the page.

possible within the contemporary criteria for success in such an undertaking, or
at least he was happy to endorse imperial claims to that effect.[19]

Two copies of Charlemagne's capitulary of Thionville (805), near Metz, shed
further light on the work of the Messine *schola cantorum*. At one point, most
manuscripts have the heading *De cantu*, 'concerning chant', with no further
details, but two sources have the note *ut discatur et ut cantores de Mettis revertan-
tur*, 'that it be learned and that the cantors should return from Metz'. Might this
preserve oral instructions given to the *missi* charged to explain the provisions of
the capitulary in the area assigned to them? As it stands it is ambiguous, since it
could mean that singers from other churches must leave Metz when their period
of study is over, or (interpreting the construction with *de* in a more Romance
manner) that singers 'of Metz' should return home from the churches where they
have been teaching. Both would describe documented situations, as revealed by
Sigulf's journey from York to the Messine *schola cantorum* in the early 760s and
the cantor from Metz who taught at the cathedral of Lyon. One can well imagine why clerics and monks who went to study in the *schola cantorum* at Metz did
not always return promptly to their own foundations, not least because there was

a great deal of music to learn and much else to imbibe (in every sense of the word) in that wealthy metropolitan church.[20]

The vast majority of singers who passed through the Messine *schola cantorum* will remain obscure forever. There is one cantor, however, who became the bishop of a cathedral with assiduous chroniclers, and as a result the broad outlines of his life can be traced. This is Aldricus, who eventually became bishop of Le Mans. Cantors had become bishops before (we have already encountered examples from Merovingian Clermont and Auxerre) but the biography of Aldricus shows something quite different. The Carolingian sponsorship of Frankish-Roman chant had turned those who were expert in its performance into a reservoir of literate talent, paternalistically nurtured in the royal chapels, or in the stalls of Metz, so that they might one day become an instrument of royal government by serving as the emperor's men in a strategic see as bishop.

Aldricus was presented to the emperor and his son Louis in 812 when he joined the circle of young men being raised in the imperial household, the *nutriti*. After nearly a decade at Aachen and elsewhere, Aldricus conceived a desire to live the common life of cathedral canons following a quasi-monastic rule. Louis, who now reigned as emperor, assigned prebends in the cathedral of Metz to Aldricus and to the pair of clerics he kept with him, but the emperor also tried to discourage him from leaving. Perhaps he wished to make him an imperial chaplain and keep him by for the many services he could render at court. This was not to be. Aldricus took up his Messine prebend and for the next eleven years he studied 'Roman chant, grammar and Holy Scripture'. His ascent during these years was swift, for he became senior cantor and was such a fine teacher of chant and grammar that he assumed the title of *primicerius scholae*. In 832, he achieved a conspicuous honour when Louis chose him to be his confessor, and in the same year he was consecrated bishop of Le Mans. This was a see of considerable importance to the Carolingians, who always needed to be vigilant lest dissident members of the local nobility in Mayenne should form alliances with the Bretons, never more than nominal subjects of the Frankish kings. The Carolingians had no deep roots in the Armorican peninsula, no royal palaces or family monasteries in the extreme west of the kingdom, and local families such as the Robertians, eventually to produce a king of the Western Franks, could eclipse them in regional politics. This was a place where the Carolingians needed a friend.

Aldricus wished to impose a duty of common life upon his clergy at Le Mans, just as Chrodegang had done some two generations earlier. He constructed an aqueduct and a cloister, 'where the canons could live according to Rule and in a canonical fashion'. The Rule was presumably the expanded version of Chrodegang's 'little statute' approved at the council of Aachen in 816 for use throughout the kingdom. The Le Mans chronicle sounds no note of resentment as it describes how canons who had hitherto gone 'wandering in the city, in various houses, to the detriment of the divine office' were thus constrained. Aldricus went on to build upper rooms (*solarios*, presumably for study) and cellars for storage. 'Still this was not enough', say his biographers. He built a further series of houses, gave the cloister 'a new and double roof' and set up more dwellings for the use of the brothers. Soon there was a new church within the cloister, dedicated to the patron of Metz cathedral, Saint Stephen, and supplied with six altars. Two hospitals followed them. As a former cantor of Metz and relative of the emperor, Aldricus would surely have wished these reforms of the community at Le Mans to include implantation of the Frankish–Roman chant he learned at Metz. As it came to the cathedral, the new chant could have passed from the mother-church to the priests and monks of the diocese in various ways, not least through Aldricus's own work in founding new monastic houses. He also established six days when the canons, monks and priests of Le Mans were to gather and celebrate certain anniversaries of his episcopate. These commemorations included the anniversary of his enthronement and of the day he consecrated a new apse in the cathedral. All of the visiting clergy were to take part in Matins, then the Mass, before adjourning to the canons' refectory for an occasion whose conviviality is unashamedly emphasized in the canons' account.[21]

A second cantor from Metz can be rescued from oblivion, this time from the abbey of St Arnulph. He is named, with other cantors, in a spectacular *Liber memorialis* begun *c*.820 at the abbey of Reichenau and probably compiled by the scribe, teacher and librarian Reginbert. This abbey, set on an island in Lake Constance, lay where speakers of Proto Romance, Alemans, Franks and Raetians converged. The connections of this house were excellent, as those of a monastery near a major land-route from Francia into Italy were bound to be, and the *Liber memorialis* reveals in detail the extensive affiliations of the monastery to about fifty houses north of the Seine and east of the Rhine. The pages often have a somewhat distressing appearance, for the close-packed writing readily suggests a throng of the dead organized into columns for the day's dole of intercessory prayers, sometimes jostled by anxious new arrivals where there is space for them (Pls 68a and b). Among the many religious communities commemorated in this volume are the brothers of a Messine abbey, which must be the house of St Arnulph since Gorze has an entry elsewhere in the book. Their entry is written in one of the hands dateable to the late 820s or 830s, which accords with the pride of place given there to Bishop Drogo (826–55), a son of Charlemagne and abbot by right of St Arnulph.

In a manner that reveals the importance of the abbey's cantors, the scribe identifies several by their title of office, a gesture without parallel anywhere else in the volume. This entry is clearly visible in Plates 68a and b. Most of these individuals are no more than mere names, but one of them appears elsewhere in the book, this time among the benefactors to Reichenau. His name is Crimleicus and once again he is styled there as *cantor*. Since these are the only appearances of this name among the many thousands of entries in the Reichenau *Liber memorialis* it seems very likely the same individual is concerned in each case. Here therefore is a cantor of Metz, who is also listed as a benefactor to Reichenau in an entry giv-

68a A Metz (St Arnulph) page from the *Liber memorialis* of the abbey of Reichenau, begun *c*.820.

68b A Metz page from the *Liber memorialis* of the abbey of Reichenau. Detail of the section where one of the scribes has signalled that the names coming next (how many of them?) are *Cantores*. It is highly probable that at least the first three names after the heading are singers, for the last on the line, Crimleicus, appears again in the book as a cantor. Zürich, Zentralbibliothek, MS Rh. hist 27, p. 87.

ing him his title of office. In what sense had he been a benefactor to the abbey? The coming of Gregorian chant to Reichenau was surely more complicated than the arrival of one singer, but that is how it worked at Lyon, to judge by the letter of Leidradus, and in a related case at Rouen, where lessons were given by a single Roman singer to Frankish pupils. Hence it is possible than Crimleicus did indeed do something significant to carry Frankish–Roman chant between two churches, here remembered as a form of benefaction, which indeed it was. If so, this is an example of dissemination from Metz taking place as the religious houses of the kingdom pursued what was now understood to be their business, and on their own initiative, by forming confraternities of prayer.[22]

There is more to be said about Crimleicus, for he may be one of the very early medieval cantors who was also an author in the manner of some notable figures of the eleventh century onwards. An extensive manual for the conduct of the religious life, widely agreed to be of ninth-century date, bears a preface in which the author addresses 'his most beloved father in Christ and namesake, Grimlaicus'. Curious though it may seem, both the author of this manual and its dedicatee bear the relatively rare name of Grimlaicus. Entitled *Regula Solitariorum*, the treatise is an extensive Rule in sixty-nine chapters for those who wish to live in individual cells as part of a monastic community with small garden, with cells nearby for their pupils and a tub for washing once every forty days. They are to pass their lives in prayer, self-scrutiny and psalmody, inviting paupers to their table, schooling pupils entrusted to them, conversing with the other solitaries in cells nearby and communicating with the main body of the ecclesiastical community by means of a window which allows them to participate in the liturgies of Mass and Office, albeit at a distance. Grimlaicus strongly discourages potential solitaries from settling in rural oratories or in *villa* estate-churches where they are likely to be poorly sustained; he writes with major monasteries in mind. He had certainly chosen this life himself, for he admits that when he first made the decision to become a solitary he was shamefully anxious about his bodily comforts: 'I was not slack in inquiring where I would get clothing and lights, where

I would get wood and vegetables, and things like that . . . Alas, how subtly does that worker of evil, the devil, deceive us, and with what total blindness does he cover the eyes of our mind!'[23]

Might Grimlaicus the author of this *Regula Solitariorum* and Crimleicus the singer from St Arnulph of Metz be the same man? The names are etymologically identical and the compiler of the *Regula* clearly had connections with Metz and more particularly perhaps with the cult of Saint Arnulph. He knows a story about a miraculous event in the life of Arnulph that is not recorded in the surviving Life of that prelate and may represent a tradition of the abbey. He also regards Arnulph of Metz as the supreme model for all solitaries:

> Saint Arnulph the bishop, in accordance with divine command, sold all he had and distributed the proceeds to the poor. Not only did he abandon his temporal possessions but also his bishopric . . . and afterwards sought seclusion in a cell, and there he spent many days in divine worship . . . I have therefore placed the example of such a man here, so that solitaries may learn to despise all vain things and long for heavenly ones with all their might.[24]

This strongly suggests that the presbyter named Grimlaicus who composed the *Regula Solitarorum* was active in the archdiocese of Metz, perhaps in Metz itself, and more specifically in the abbey of St Arnulph. He was also a firm believer in the spiritual value of the cantor's art, and content to place himself in the long tradition of praise for the spiritual benefits of singing psalms to induce tears and dissolve hardness of heart:

> Puerile games and laughter do not delight us but holy readings and the spiritual music of melody instead. However hard-hearted we are, and unable to produce tears, our hearts are turned to compunction when we hear the sweetness of psalms. There are many who are moved by the sweetness of chant to bewail their sins, and readily brought to tears, by the sweet sounds of a singer.[25]

Thus the name of the author, the ninth-century date and the Messine context bring Grimlaicus the writer and Crimleicus the cantor closer together. If they are the same, then the *Regula Solitariorum* offers some insight into the spirituality and erudition a ninth-century cantor might possess, or at least one whose position as a singer in no way hindered his spirituality from maturing into that of an ardent ascetic. The text of the *Regula* cites Benedict, Gregory, Augustine, Jerome, the *Vitas patrum* and a wealth of Scripture, and even if these references are mostly taken from florilegia, they show how mistaken it would be to envisage the ninth-century Frankish cantor as 'a mere singer'. To be sure, Grimlaicus the author does not display Aurelian's concern for an urbane Latin style (there is not much call for that in manuals addressed to ascetics) but the *Regula* is nonetheless an erudite production in the best traditions of its genre. It also provides an important reminder of how prismatic a great Frankish church or abbey could be as pilgrims, exiles, itinerant priests and others came in, perhaps to remain for a protracted period, before passing out again in diffused rays, some to illuminate other centres with what they had learned during their residence. Grimlaicus gathers passages from the Scriptures, and from the Rule of Benedict, which call for charity to guests. He adds, perhaps on his own account, that 'if someone of the Catholic faith comes to us and says: "I wish to stay for some time among you to derive profit thereby" then he should be received, for as the Lord says: *I will cast out nobody who comes to me*'. The spread of Frankish–Roman chant in its Messine form may owe something to this tradition of monastic hospitality. This would be another illustration of the way Frankish–Roman music spread by the customary and largely autonomous workings of churches in their dealings with one another.[26]

The Palatine Chapel

The earliest Frankish compilation of music theory from the ninth century, associated with the name of a certain Aurelian and entitled *Musica Disciplina*, remarks on the way the *palatini* assign the antiphon *O Sapientia* to mode 1 rather than mode 2, 'on account of its higher tessitura'. These *palatini* are by definition the singers who served the emperor in the chapel of any palace to which he took them, as part of his household, when he came into residence there for one of the great liturgical feasts of the year, especially Christmas or Easter. Aurelian's passing reference to their teaching, though brief, is nonetheless enough to reveal a group addressing a shared repertory of Gregorian plainsong with a common body of theoretical thinking, which was evidently particular to them in certain respects. (*O Sapientia* is widely classified as mode 2, contrary to the teachings of the *palatini*, in the tonaries.) Although it is a common mistake to suppose that the Carolingian court was itinerant during much of the year, in the manner of its descendant in the Holy Roman Empire, these palatine singers can nonetheless be described as a mobile group whose internal organization, periods of concerted movement or dispersion through the palaces of the kingdom are hard to bring into focus. When the emperor celebrated the highest feasts of the liturgical year they presumably journeyed with him, or to find him, in some numbers, although we have no idea how many might travel at one time. (Only two, perhaps, would have been needed for a performance of *O Sapientia* to the satisfaction of an emperor who came into residence at the appropriate time in the Advent season; services glittering with the 'diverse orders of a radiant clergy', like the one described by the poet Ermoldus Nigellus, must have been rare events.) Other journeys, including military campaigns, may have involved a skeleton staff, perhaps only a single chaplain who also served as a confessor or as a notary.[27]

Aurelian, whoever he was, plainly had some exposure to these *palatini* and to their musical art, although it is not immediately clear how he acquired it. He calls himself one who was formerly a *vernaculus* or servant of the monastery of Moutier-St-Jean, also called Réôme, north of Autun. Although now thoroughly downcast, *abiectus*, he writes his treatise at the request of the 'brothers', presumably those who were formerly his fellow monks. There are many stories in early medieval sources of monks falling foul of their abbot, or their entire community, so there is nothing implausible in this self-portrait (nor indeed in the luxuriantly Roman name of Aurelian, well attested in southern Gaul, parts of modern Switzerland and northern Italy; he was probably a southerner and it is no great surprise to find him south of the Frankish heartlands between Auxerre and Autun). In this somewhat reduced state, perhaps of exile, Aurelian dedicates his treatise to Bernardus, described by Aurelian as an arch-cantor whose recent ancestors include Charlemagne himself. This was the Bernardus whom Charles the Bald wished to make bishop of Autun at some time between late January 841 and early July 843, when Archbishop Wenilo of Sens sent a letter expressing the royal wish that Bernardus should be appointed to the vacant see. The letter reveals that Berno (the name is simply the short form of Bernardus) was an imperial chaplain and confirms Aurelian's statement that he was a relative of Charles, adding that he was 'tenderly reared' by Charles's father, Louis the Pious, and subsequently advanced to high honour. This Bernard was Charlemagne's son by an unknown mother. For some unknown reason, he was never appointed to the see of Autun, though Aurelian writes in expectation of the appointment; the vital document in an otherwise confused and fragmentary dossier shows Bernard as one of the signatories to the proceedings of Charles the Bald's council of Germigny, held in early October 843, where he uses the formal version of his name, subscribing as 'Bernardus abbas sancti Iohannis', that is to say as Bernard the abbot of the same Moutier-St-Jean where Aurelian had once been a monk, which forms yet another thread in the mysterious weave of the relationship between these two men. The house lay near the eastern frontier of Charles's kingdom, as agreed at Verdun in 843, and well towards the south of core Carolingian territory.[28]

The word *archicantor* is a rare one and predominantly Roman; in Aurelian's usage it may not be a genuine term of office but rather an expression of praise; if so, then Bernard was not an arch-chanter by title but rather 'the chief cantor, in my opinion, of all Holy Church'. Since Bernard was an imperial chaplain, and Aurelian addresses him with a warm reference to 'the pious affection of your mind towards me . . . whom you have purely loved, advised, taught and nourished', it is possible that Aurelian himself had at some time been associated with the palatine chapel. A senior *palatinus* like Bernard, of the royal blood, would have had many servants or members of the imperial court to perform a variety of tasks for him. Hincmar of Reims refers to these attendants in his treatise on the governance of the palace, *De Ordine Palatii*, as the second order of servants, comprising young men attached to a senior palatine official who holds an important charge in the palace. Hincmar casts their relationship as one of *magister* to *discipulus*, each honouring the other and the pupil 'receiving support by seeing his master and speaking with him'. Was Aurelian at one time a palatine servant and *discipulus* of Bernard? He certainly refers to the quality of Bernard's affection and encouragement, but there is also a passage that might be read as a reminiscence of the unusually lenient governance that Bernard exercised over a group of dependents who were technically his servants. 'We used to regret (*dolebamus*) that you were too patient, but now I see that you held back from the blow so that you might strike more forcibly.' The first-person plural in *dolebamus* is not the royal 'we', for that is decidedly not Aurelian's style in this prostrate and dedicatory letter. Aurelian also refers to himself in the letter, and most emphatically, as Bernard's man in a manner that can perhaps be taken as another reference to what was once a benign master–servant relationship in the palace: 'Downcast, I am still yours, and whether the world wishes it or not, I am yours: yours, I say, yours.'[29]

If this is a correct interpretation, then the teaching of the *Musica Disciplina* offers some guide to the training of the *palatini*, and to the wellsprings of their professional self-esteem, always bearing in mind that it is the work of a monk who mentions the *palatini* explicitly only to register a matter in which they seem to stand outside common practice. When reading it so, one is reminded on almost every page that the study of plainsong was virtually the only intellectual discipline known to the ninth-century Occident in which a substantial body of material wholly unknown to Classical authors had to be brought to order and theorized. In grammar, metrics, astronomy and geometry most of the material required for proficiency was already available in venerable manuals that had only to be hunted out, copied and studied. In order to theorize Frankish–Roman plainchant, however, it was necessary to adapt terms and concepts from existing studies, especially grammar, sometimes by subtly changing the meaning of key terms or by using them metaphorically (as when terms for rhetorical effects were applied to particular turns of melody) to create a new apparatus.

The fundamental task of Aurelian's book is to provide a kind of discursive tonary in which chants are discussed under the appropriate modal headings, sometimes to clarify general principles by isolating musical details deemed anomalous in chants of their class in that mode, and sometimes simply to illustrate what is representative. The eight modes of Carolingian theory were essentially patterns of tones and semitones in a diatonic series; a modal category was also a bundle of related ways to begin, continue and end a melody in relation to a centre of gravity and a zone of preponderant musical activity relative to that centre. Modal teaching therefore provided the basis for a sophisticated art of analytical listening and memorization, but it may have come to maturity somewhat later than a good deal of the music it purports to rationalize. In other words, much of the Frankish–Roman plainsong that Aurelian discusses was probably developed before the great effort of modal theorizing began in earnest. The book constantly deals with the consequences of this slippage, turning the cantor's art into a vast mosaic of specific cases to be weighed and pondered. Thus Aurelian notes departures from modal custom in the chants he discusses ('there is a variant here') and gives reassurances to keep a sense of proportion amidst the welter of examples that do not always yield to generalizations ('it does not seem incongruous that . . .'). With so much to debate, Aurelian's tone is inevitably somewhat polemical at times, suggesting lively discussion among trained cantors for whom Frankish–Roman chant represented a quickening of intellectual as well as musical life. Aurelian insists upon points that 'some deny', disputes the arguments of others who say 'therefore, it seems that . . .' and ventures to offer resolutions. One remembers that the *palatini* enter Aurelian's account only because they had something to argue about with other singers.

Aurelian is especially interested in chants where the cantor must lead a psalm verse back into a reprise of part of the antiphon, the Gallican practice. This had to be accomplished with a smooth transition from verse to antiphon but also in a manner that secured good grammatical and theological sense. Hence it would be a grave error to suppose that the *palatini* or any other Carolingian cantors 'were musicians, not textual scholars'; taking the term 'scholar' in an appropriately relaxed sense, one can say that they had to be both as they adjusted the demands of words and music, giving priority to the former in cases of conflict. The cantor was therefore required to possess a good understanding of grammar; Aurelian cites Priscian as a matter of course and his language is saturated with the terminology of grammar and metrics. He insists that the cantor must be wise, prudent, and so studious that he uses the term *litteratura* for the text of a chant, following a usage probably derived from the Irish grammarians. This exalted notion of the cantor's skill does much to explain the determinedly scholarly décor of the *Musica Disciplina*. When Aurelian begins to explain why there are eight modes of Gregorian plainsong, for example, he pours forth a stream of zodiacal and computistical material, suggesting how deeply the cantor's expertise had begun to acquire the aura of exacting liberal study. Singers had not possessed this kind of pride in their craft since the days of Visigothic Spain.[30]

Once trained, the palatine singers provided the sumptuous liturgy that had become an important part of Carolingian dealings with kings and magnates. The outstanding witness to such an occasion is the exiled poet Ermoldus Nigellus, describing the ceremonies at Ingelheim in 826 when Louis the Pious received King Harald of Denmark, his family and a large entourage for their baptism. Writing in the hope of restoring himself to favour (and in this respect rather like Aurelian), Ermoldus probably gives 'a wonderfully distorted impression' of what took place on this occasion, but his poem nonetheless reveals the condition to which the most exalted services of the Carolingian churches and abbeys undoubtedly aspired. He celebrates the grandeur of the architectural setting, the richness of the liturgy and the profligate feasting after the Danish king's baptism, all an expression of Louis's magnificence and the client status of the Danish king. In the 'immense palace, resting upon a hundred columns', adorned with many paintings that Ermoldus painstakingly describes, the Danish king and his family were baptized with Louis standing godparent to Harald, the empress Judith to the Danish king's wife and Prince Lothar to the king's son. The status of the precentor on this occasion was so high that Ermoldus names him twice as Theuto, who 'disposed the choir of clergy due to sing with due observance'. Nothing further is known about this man, but he may be identical with a later abbot with that name at Marmoutier, for an abbacy was certainly one kind of preferment Carolingian chaplains could receive in the ninth century when a more determined effort was being made to appoint better men to abbacies and to fill vacant sees. Other cases include Hucbert, at one time the *precentor palatii* (the position held later by Theuto) who became bishop of Meaux from 823. In the reigns of Charlemagne and Louis the Pious, the path from the chapel to a bishop's throne or an abbot's stall became such an important highway that some resented the way chaplains were considered to be a special group of servants amongst the palatine attendants. Walafrid Strabo denounces them for their ambition, while in 836 Paschasius Radbertus of Corbie condemns them for belonging to neither the monastic nor the canonical order. These men 'in the palace, which are commonly called *capellanos*', he declares, 'hope and labour for authority over churches. They strive, for the sake of money, to satisfy their worldly aims.' The *palatini* must have been doing well to attract this kind of scorn.[31]

Some of these men were certainly palace chaplains, and they lived a pampered existence. A *petitio* addressed to Louis the Pious in 829 by various bishops complained of palatine priests and chaplains who were 'unadvisedly well maintained'. Yet it was obviously impossible for such an important instrument of imperial patronage as the palace chapel to be entirely reserved for those whom Nature had endowed with a fine or even a passable singing voice. As a waiting room for preferment to episcopal or other office, the chapel necessarily encompassed men who had been admitted because they were literate and well-bred men of the royal kindred, sure of advancement and well able to read a lesson but not necessarily to sing a gradual. This means that there must also have been a staff of men in clerical orders who ranked as *palatini* in the sense that they were palace ministers, but who were not necessarily chaplains in line for the highest preferment save when Fortune favoured them (as it sometimes did, according to Notker Balbulus, of whom more below). In a sustained comparison between palatine servants and secular government, Walafrid Strabo compares the most senior chaplains or *summi capellani* to counts and the minor chaplains or *capellani minores* to *vassi dominici*: the royal benefice holders. These two groups are clearly the ones who have been prominent in our account so far. Singers or *cantores*, however, come near the bottom of the list with the minor clerical orders, in accordance with a long-standing (and evidently unchanged) tradition. Strabo equates cantors with *commentarienses* or registrars, but psalmists, seemingly a different group, are matched with *carminum pompaticos relatores* or ceremonial reciters of verse. These might be clerical poets declaiming euologistic verse in Latin metre or, at the other end of the scale, professional secular entertainers perhaps singing in Frankish. Whatever the precise allusion at issue (and it does sound precise), this distinction between the figure of the cantor/registrar and the psalmist/ declaimer of verse suggests a division between those who bore the title of cantor but were primarily required to serve in some capacity where literate skills were required, and those who only sang. All ranked well below the senior and lesser chaplains.[32]

The author who has most to reveal about chapel singers is the one whom we may feel least inclined to trust. This is Notker Balbulus, Monk of Sankt Gallen, whose account of Charlemagne's life, the *Gesta Karoli Magni* (the title is not contemporary), with its many layers of anecdote and its political vision of a new universal Empire, is in part a mirror for princes. The patron of the book, Charlemagne's great-great grandson, is presented with the image of an exemplary ruler and therefore with a flattering (but in places characterful) portrait of his most distinguished ancestor. The *Gesta* is also a repository of amusing stories, including some for those who know the liturgy and its plainchant extremely well. (Few readers of the book today know why it is funny that a poorly educated cleric, standing in for a better man at a palatine service, should choose the Lord's Prayer as a psalm verse for the responsory *Domine, si adhuc populo tuo sum necessarius*; it is because the respond ends *fiat voluntas tua*, 'thy will be done'). The *Gesta* raises many questions about a monk's sifting of traditions, both written and oral, pertaining to events four generations before his own time. A surprisingly large number of Notker's stories concern singers, and while few of them can be relied upon as accounts of specific events (they are deliberately imprecise in the use of personal names) they frequently ring true as a general record of what could occur in terms of recruitment and promotion. To be sure, these anecdotes almost certainly reveal more about the *palatini* of the 880s than of the 780s, but it should cause no surprise if they seem generally convincing, for there was nothing remote about the abbey of Sankt Gallen. The monastery's *Liber Vitae* of 813–14 reveals that it was bound in ties of prayer-confraternity to 'a host of houses in Alemannian and Bavarian regions, though Tours, Langres, Prüm and Weissenburg are represented as well'. The names of the bishops included cover the sees of Constance, Chur, Mainz, Worms, Châlons, Milan, Strasburg and Cremona. Where cross-checking is possible, Notker's understanding of how the palatine chapels worked seems consistent with other indications. Thus when he relates how Charlemagne once praised a relative of his who had sung the *Alleluia* very well during Mass in a palatine service – and few chants in the Gregorian repertory make a greater impression when sung in an accomplished manner – the story recalls the career of Aldricus, a *consanguineus* of Charlemagne nurtured at Aachen, who eventually rose to become the Primicerius of the singers at Metz (see above, pp. 348–9).[33]

Notker's anecdotes suggest that it would be quite wrong to draw a firm distinction between chaplains destined for high office and much humbler singing men who bore the brunt of the work, often without such prospects. He tells how Charlemagne once filled a vacant bishopric with a cleric drawn from the ranks of those to whom the *magister scholae* assigned the Matins Responsories each day, one per singer. His choice fell on a man who was 'not a little adorned with nobility and learning', and yet who was foolish enough to spend the night of his appointment in feasting and drinking; he did not appear that night for the service on the Eve of Saint Martin, which left the responsory assigned to him, *Domine, si adhuc populo tuo sum necessarius* mentioned above, entirely unaccounted for. It was taken by an unskilled singer, to the detriment of the service. Yet if this story suggests a relatively closed circle of singers with excellent prospects, often of noble birth and yet with substantial musical duties to perform, there are times when Notker often seems to be evoking a porous palatine chapel with a broad base of recruitment and a shifting staff of personnel coming and going. He tells how certain young *pauperes* and nobles were set to learn the scribal arts and the elements of the notary's craft with Clement, a historical figure who was master of the palace school under Charlemagne and remained so under Louis the Pious. One of the poor boys succeeded so well in his studies (much better than the nobles in the same group) that he was promoted into the chapel. Here he would have passed under the authority of the master of the singers. He proved 'especially good at reading and singing', and was eventually given a bishopric.[34]

The poorly instructed man who deputized for his colleague and sang *Domine, si adhuc populo tuo sum necessarius* is airily described by Notker as 'a certain cleric in the king's retinue'. Elsewhere, Notker insists that 'No external person (*alienus*) not even if he were famous, dared to join the emperor's choir (*chorum*) unless he could read and chant', which clearly allows for the participation of outsiders or strangers. One cannot say that 'the young man who was a relation of the king and sang the *Alleluia* most beautifully' is precisely placed. Is he one of the household *nutriti*, a student in the 'palace school'? No better defined is the 'incomparable cleric' in the royal household, otherwise undefined, save that he is a demon (!), who managed to be a fine singer, a scholar, a master of chant and a poet. However elitist it may have been at the centre, the imperial chapel was a porous body around the edges, with singers recruited in as many different ways as there were means for the king to encounter a talented man.[35]

69 Neumes, widely given the overdetermined name 'palaeofrankish' today, in Valenciennes, Bibliothèque municipale 148, fol. 71ᵛ (Aurelian, *Musica Disciplina*). Copied in darker ink (compare the much lighter marks of contraction that float in the same interlinear field towards the bottom of the image), these were probably not inserted in the primary campaign of copying, but represent a second layer whereby effects that Aurelian took pride in *describing* with a terminology adapted from grammar are distilled with new graphic, not linguistic, techniques.

17

SINGERS, SOUNDS AND SYMBOLS

The oldest examples of musical notation found in a Western and post-Classical source probably date from some time between 820 and 840. Within this period of twenty years, Bishop Agobard of Lyon expressed his displeasure that some singers 'studied from earliest youth until the hoariness of old age', because in doing so they neglected their 'spiritual studies, readings and the study of divine eloquence'. Agobard was attempting to prune an antiphoner compiled by his rival Amalarius, so he had reasons of his own to emphasize that the work of the song-school at Lyon was burdensome. Nonetheless, it is striking that such an explicit complaint, the first of its kind, should so closely coincide with the first recoverable traces of a practical musical notation after many centuries when it seems that Occidental musicians had no use for one. The song-school known to Agobard was the *schola cantorum* that Bishop Leidradus had organized soon after 800, teaching the liturgy of the imperial chaplains. Even in a major see like Lyon, it was not a simple matter to keep a palatine rite in good order so far from its major centres in the north, and wherever Carolingian bishops or abbots under-stood that old standards of provision for the performance of the liturgy would no longer do, the work of a choir school was necessarily intensive. Yet lessons in plainsong competed for time in the monastic and clerical day with classes on grammar, also held after Matins and Prime, together with the long periods of observance required for Mass and Office. In a context such as this, it is easy to envisage how some means of tracing melodies in writing would have been useful to cantors in training. A notation could give the novice a visible trace of what a teacher had sung earlier in the day, charging the written signs with musical sound, so to speak, as the pupil simultaneously listened and studied them. A notational record might be even more useful for priests and deacons: the non-specialists with materials to intone and inflect, with careful attention to the posi-tion of word accent, at the appropriate place. In all cases, notation somewhat eased the necessity for personal contact between with teacher and pupil by allow-ing the shadow of someone absent to fall.[1]

   The reasons for the apparent emergence of musical notation amongst the ninth-century Franks might therefore appear relatively straightforward. There was a need for some means to channel musical sound onto parchment through the narrow conduit of a quill, and various means were found: neumes, tonaries, lettered diagrams of lyre-strings. Yet there can be no simple assessment of how a need for notation arose amongst Carolingian singers. Any system of writing or drawing reveals a certain amount and no more, defined by the shortfalls that users believe can be adequately supplied by personal contact, immediate or deferred. All medieval notations of clerical or monastic origin reflect a human situation where expenditure of time, maintenance of good will and the performance of assigned duties were held in equilibrium. These notations were the deposit of a form of life. Those who live differently, as we do, are poorly placed to determine the advantages and shortcomings of medieval notations as their users experienced them. This is not to say, however, that the first impressions of a modern musician confronted with ninth-century notation will necessarily be false. Like virtually all forms of non-alphabetic notation before the invention of the stave, soon after 1000, the earliest Frankish neumes on record do not measure the intervals between the constituent notes of the melody (Pl. 69). The singer knows that a step must be made, but he does not know how large it should be. This looks like a major drawback now, and it is reassuring to know that a ninth-century specialist like Hucbald of St-Amand, deep in the Carolingian heartlands, regarded it in much the same way. He knew far better than we do what these notations *could* convey, and he has some interesting things to say on that count; nonetheless, he did not believe the virtues of the neumes absolved the serious musician from pondering ways to circumvent their imprecision in the matter of pitch and to guide singers better.[2]

The idea of a *need* for notation nonetheless simplifies the complex and wide-ranging sources of Frankish interest in articulate and critical thought about musical sound. In the layered dossier of music theory associated with the name Aurelian, details of plainchant melody, or complete chants, are perceived through the medium of a sophisticated and urbane Latin rather than through the neumes that were apparently added to the most famous manuscript of the text after the main campaign of copying (Pl. 69). If the neumes were germane to Aurelian's original text of the 840s, they were seemingly designed to clarify a specific point made in the surrounding prose, not to record a complete chant. Perhaps the neumes, in the judgement of the scribe who added them, reproduced the change that occurred in the spoken instruction for which the treatise is in some measure a substitute. In effect, the neumes replicate in visual terms the shift of communicative means when a teacher decided to sing his point rather than simply to explain it. Yet it is probably more important to recognize that Aurelian's material emerged from a culture inspired by the example of Classical poets, and of their Christian descendants in late antiquity, to value the art of description, whether it be of a battle, a palace, a season of the year or anything else that a churchman might choose or a novice might be compelled to undertake in class. The Aurelian dossier reveals an interest in the art of evoking details of vocal melody with the technical terminology that a reformed Carolingian Latin could now readily accommodate, just as it could welcome learned references and a leisurely tone. The abundance of language about musical detail in the Aurelian dossier, combined with the restricted use of dedicated means to show it, makes the treatise a sustained act of description in a broad sense of the term. The text reaches after something beyond itself with some luxuriance, not always appreciated by modern readers, and the gap created by the impossibility of language actually becoming the thing described is essential to the art of the process. With terms such as *accentus acutus, concentus, causa euphoniae* and *sonoritatis euphonia*, aided by the technique of referring to melodic details syllable by syllable in rigorously segmented texts, Aurelian stimulates the reader to sift his memory for the musical passage he wishes to discuss.[3]

A significant proportion of the surviving ninth-century notations, though certainly designed for singers in the sense of those deputed to sing in a liturgical service, do not record the repertory of trained cantors. Instead, they show lessons, prayers and Mass Ordinary intonations: material for priests and deacons. These men, often with no special training as singers, needed to know how to apportion musical formulae that they already knew in general terms to the syllables of any Latin text assigned to them. The predetermined undulations of the formula – the departures from a monotone – had to be accommodated to the length of the text, to its grammatical structure and to the disposition of accented syllables, where the inflections were chiefly to be made. To be accomplished successfully, this task required careful preparation and a level of Latinity that cannot have been common among the general run of Carolingian priests, especially in rural churches. The notations that addressed these problems were certainly meeting a need, but not one that had arisen among those who would otherwise have been required to spend hours memorizing chant. Nor was it the need that many modern musicians in the Occident will intuitively suppose musical notation is principally designed to address: to store musical entities that are too long or elaborate for memorization. The best way to understand how notation rose among the Franks is accordingly to balance any reconstruction of problems and solutions in choir school or priest's house with a sense of the broad interests and concerns that made the prospect of music-writing seem intellectually exciting perhaps even before it was found to be useful. The various systems of notation that singers used in ninth-century Francia arose from intellectual speculation combined with practical resourcefulness, and from the deep respect for antique authority, balanced by ingenuous adaptation, which characterizes the intellectual life of the Carolingian Franks.[4]

Their roots lay in Latin grammar. The Classical and late antique manuals of grammar known to the Franks were principally directed to the segmental elements of language, namely the individual phonemes as expressed by single letters, or in some cases by groups of letters, formed into connected syllables. The grammars build knowledge upwards from the materials of the alphabet and the sounds they control on a single-sound-per-symbol basis. Among the materials the Franks inherited for notating vocal pitch at the level of the syllable were the three accent marks of grave, acute and circumflex that the Roman grammarians used, following the practice of their Greek predecessors, to distinguish the relative pitch that was ostensibly required to mark the accented syllable of a Latin word. The ancient grammarians consistently imply that these accents are rudimentary, but to the Franks they appeared both advanced and enigmatic for the simple reason that they did not speak Latin as a tone language in the manner the accents were designed to notate. It is possible that nobody had ever done so. This discrepancy does much to explain why the teaching of *accentus* made such a strong appeal to the intellect of Frankish scholars, and why a passage like this from Isidore's *Etymologies* might give them pause:

> The name *accentus* arose because it is adjacent to music . . . the acute accent is so called because it raises and sharpens a syllable [´]. The grave accent is so called because it lowers it and pulls a syllable down [`]. Thus it is the reverse of the acute. The circumflex consists of high and low; beginning in the acute position it descends to the grave position and thus as it both ascends and descends the circumflex accent results [∧].[5]

Reading an account like this, it was easy for ninth-century scholars to sense that the accents were the key to a lost exactitude of hearing that might somehow be recovered or redirected. That is one of the reasons why *accentus* teaching finds a place in most of the new grammars compiled in the ninth century. It is there in the grammar of Murethach, an Irishman who began to teach at Auxerre towards 840, and also in the manual by Sedulius Scottus, dating from the 840s. Both use terms borrowed from Isidore, or from some intermediary, to describe how the acute accent 'raises' the pitch of a syllable and 'points' it, while the grave accent 'lowers' the pitch or 'pushes it down'. Discussions of the accents by late antique grammarians such as Victorinus, and many other aspects of *lectio*, the art of reading, now begin to appear repeatedly in Frankish grammatical compendia. In the ninth century, Lupus of Ferrières probably had good reason to remark that many Frankish churchmen were more concerned to improve their Latin than to better their conduct.[6]

   All this teaching was resolutely based upon the individual letter and the syllable. Neither the antique nor the Carolingian grammars deal systematically with the larger patterns of intonation that supervene in actual speech and reading. Yet the concern for clear and expressive *lectio* necessarily raised the minds of the Carolingian Franks from the level where their grammatical studies dwelled to patterns of intonation on the higher plane of breath-group and sentence. Modern linguists have repeatedly confirmed what competent speakers of a language intuitively know, namely that patterns of intonation play a vital role in the creation of meaning. For those in the ninth century with a renewed commitment to clear and even affective reading, this meant thinking in terms of the larger structures of pitch that such delivery required. Supervening elements of speech such as intonation, however, are much harder to broach in a systematic fashion than individual letters or their phonetic referents, and Frankish treatises on grammar, like their antique models, deal with them very intermittently. Nonetheless, Carolingian scholars could learn from an ancient grammarian like the much-anthologized Victorinus that good reading requires *modulatio*, which sounds like a considered intonation, especially when read in the light of ninth-century attempts to define the term. '*Modulatio*', says Remigius of Auxerre, 'is the expression of a complex and varied sonority, not achieved with one pitch but with many diverse pitches, that is to say with low and high.' That is surely how many readers understood Victorinus when he describes *modulatio* as 'an artful flexion of the voice, during continuous discourse, into a more pleasing style of declamation, producing a delightful manner of listening for the sake of avoiding harshness'. This seems to confront the difficulty of representing a pleasing intonation in writing by describing it with an opulent sentence (Pl. 70).[7]

The task facing a Carolingian singer, as a theorist of chant in even the most relaxed sense, was closely related to the one that preoccupied a reader seeking a better technique of *modulatio*, and yet it was also fundamentally different. When a cantor wished to teach or discuss precise details of any Gregorian plainsong he needed to think downwards from the level of the complete melody to its constituent modules at the syllabic level, not least because the syllables provided a convenient means to isolate the melodic detail he wished to discuss. Readers seeking to teach or cultivate an intelligent practice of spoken intonation, however, had to proceed in the opposite direction, working upwards from tone as it was actually taught in terms of the accents, at the level of the syllable, to much larger

70 Part of the *Ars* of Victorinus concerning the art of reading or *lectio*. The section concerning intonation, *modolatio*, begins in the sixth line. Sankt Gallen, Stiftsbibliothek, Cod. 877, p. 5, 9th c.

structures of breath-group and sentence. These comparable but reverse developments attest to rather more than the 'intellectual and artistic ferment' that has
quite rightly been evoked in the past as a quality of ninth-century Frankish culture important for the rise of notation; they show a process of intelligent
manoeuvre between segmental and suprasegmental levels in music and language,
each one with the potential to enhance and inspire speculation in the other.
Precise forms of indebtedness are difficult to trace here between one form of
enquiry and the other, and it may be unwise to seek them. What matters is not
how the Franks reasoned from one proposition to the next, but how the materials they inherited encouraged them to listen in many different contexts with
more acuity so that they might extend the range of phenomena brought within
the scope of writing and articulate thought.[8]

Spelling it out for Singers: Hucbald of St-Amand

Alphabetic writing is the most ancient tradition of sound-to-symbol thinking in
the Occident. The characters of an alphabet isolate nodal points in a stream of
spoken sound and label each node with a single sign, rarely with two. No matter
how sophisticated it became, the music theory of the ninth-century Franks
neither forgot the foundational position of the letters in elementary schooling
nor neglected them as a means to conceive how individual sonorities could be
isolated for study and then reassembled into a stream of vocal sound:

> just as letters are the elements of articulate vocal sound and make the individ-
> ual parts of syllables, so syllables in turn form words and names to make a
> complete text. In the same way, the *pthongi* that are called 'sounds' in Latin are
> the sources of sung vocal sound, and the content of all music lies in their
> resolution.[9]

So begins the famous Frankish treatise known as the *Musica Enchiriadis*. This
passage seems so clear, and so securely located within the Occidental tradition of
alphabetic thinking, one may be forgiven for forgetting that in some respects it
is *new*. Frankish scribes charged to write Latin documents during the pre-
Carolingian centuries did not require the stringent correspondence between
sound and symbol that their Carolingian descendants sought to achieve. The
diplomas and charters of the Merovingian period, especially those of a more
provincial character compiled far from the royal court, contain many incorrect
(that is to say non-Classical) spellings, mistaken inflections and proto-Romance
constructions such as the periphrastic genitive with *de*. Vowels in inflectional
syllables are often treated with some indifference so that a notary may write
omnebus not *omnibus*, *nicessitatem* not *necessitatem* and *tamin* not *tamen*; he may
write *talis epistulas*, effacing the correct grammatical inflection in the first word

because it is unstressed and may not have existed in the common Latin speech evolving towards Old French *tels*. He could write *tradere racionͤ*, eroding the inflectional syllable *-em* in the second word because it was unstressed and perhaps weakly sounded in speech or not sounded at all. (Final *-m* had been silent in spoken Latin for many centuries by now, but scribes in other parts of Europe continued to spell it.) The sounds the Merovingian scribes used in voicing their texts probably varied considerably according to the education of the reader and the section of the document involved; the *aurenga*, or sonorous initial statement of pious principle at the beginning of the charter, for example, was a different matter from the 'business' section further inside, where binding undertakings were given and where the language is often simpler and shows more Romance developments. Some readings were presumably given in something close to the common Latin speech with such conscious elevations of register as lay within the reader's power and were considered necessary. In short, a Merovingian notary did not think very closely from sound to symbol and back again.[10]

This means that there were letters, and even some syllables, in the Merovingian scribe's spellings that were not necessarily present when he read the text aloud. The same might be said for many languages, not least Modern English, where most speakers write the word *knight* without noticing that three of the five consonants are no longer sounded. Yet there is such a marked difference between the spellings used in Frankish documents of the 850s as opposed to those of the 750s that the Franks had plainly given much fresh thought in the interim to the way their alphabetic writing functioned. The later sources are much more consistently Classical, or if that is too strong a word (since their Classical appearance owes something to the policies of nineteenth-century editors) they seem more carefully modelled on the usage of Irish and Anglo-Saxon scholars who had never spoken Latin as a native tongue and who therefore approached it as a second language to be learned with some scrupulosity in the matter of spelling and in the pronunciation the spelling implied. Pippin was already receiving manuals of grammar and spelling from Rome in the 760s, but it was in the ninth century that scholars in the Frankish kingdom began to compose new treatises concerning aspects of Latin grammar, including orthography. Some were Irishmen like Murethach, others Anglo-Saxons like Alcuin. By the ninth century, sets of alphabetic letters and symbols that work by alphabetic means begin to appear in manuscript anthologies of texts, stimulating the imagination and the sheer intellectual reverie of ninth-century Frankish minds. This was the great age of the cipher: the single pen-trace fraught with meaning that was known or (more intriguing still) was partially known or simply mysterious (Pls 71 and 72).[11]

The Franks' concern with a reformed Latin spelling in the ninth century reveals the true character, and indeed the true dignity, of a Carolingian renaissance that was never too proud to devote its energy to the humblest concerns. Many of the 'bad Merovingian spellings' disappear in the Carolingian period following a reform that owes much to the formative presence of Italians, Irishmen,

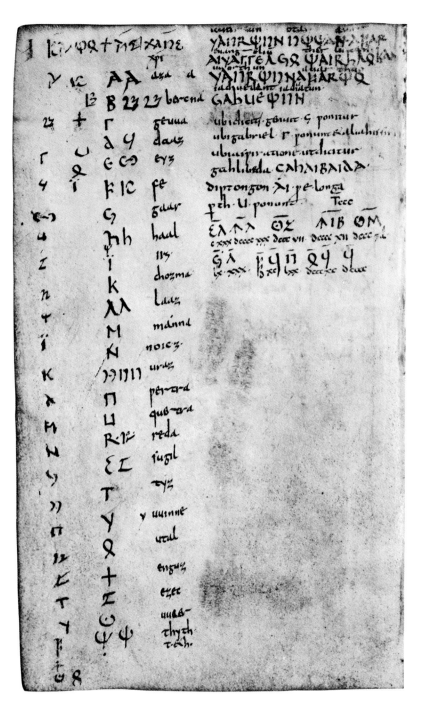

71 Sign repertories (i). A page of alphabets, from Salzburg, probably compiled in 799 during the episcopate of Bishop Arno. The top right-hand corner of the page shows the letters that Wulfilas used for his translation of the Bible into Gothic. Vienna, Österreichische Nationalbibliothek, CPV 795, fol. 90. Such inventories of signs filled 9th-c. readers with an antiquarian curiosity, a quixotic desire to experiment and a mission to teach all at once. They reveal a deep fascination with the task of controlling an inventory of vocal sounds with a set of pen-traces.

Visigoths and Anglo-Saxons at Charlemagne's court. In Alcuin's treatise *De Orthographia*, a deceptively pedestrian treatise on spelling 'probably . . . designed to assist scribes in the scriptoria when copying Latin texts from defective exemplars', the Latin alphabet is treated letter by letter with notice given of troublesome words that scribes are liable to misspell. Sometimes this is because they may be inclined to pronounce them in an evolved way; thus Alcuin counsels scribes to write *taberna*, using the traditional Latin spelling, and not *taverna*. There is clearly an implication that the Franks must also say the word as *taberna* because it is written with a *b*. Alcuin also reminds scribes that *aer* has two syllables, contrary to its development in the common Latin speech. He requires that the spelling 'uu' in a word like *vacuus* should be pronounced with two syllables. The treatise also considers some words in pairs, carefully chosen to anticipate the confusion of readers who fail to assign a distinctive sound value to each letter so that *beneficius* and *veneficius*, for example, are indistinguishable when read aloud.[12]

The effect of such reforms was to make the High Latin of the liturgy (or what had passed for a High Latin in Merovingian Francia) higher still. It was only a matter of time before the discrepancies between a reformed ecclesiastical Latin and the common Latin speech became so great that it was necessary to invent a new spelling system for the common tongue. Some of the most revealing ninth-century results appear in a manuscript from the Frankish abbey of St-Amand. They form a set of notes for a homily on the Book of Jonah where spellings notating the common Latin speech and those from standard Latin jostle in an astonishing and macaronic argot:

> JONAS PROPHETA HABEBAT *mult laboret e mult penet (a cel populum co* DICIT) FACIEBAT *grant jholt et eret molt las.*[13]

> Jonah the prophet had laboured much and much exerted himself (he says to the people) it was very hot and he was very tired.

Some of this is spelled as conventional Latin (JONAS PROPHETA HABEBAT, for example) although what the scribe would have *said* when he read those spellings aloud is another question. The remaining words are distinctly rustic in spelling, such as the remarkable alphabetization of common Latin speech in *jholt* (<CALIDUS) on its journey towards Modern French *chaud*.

This curious document provides a context for the musical notation that was invented, perhaps at the very same abbey, by the Frankish scholar Hucbald and presented in his treatise *De harmonica Institutione* of *c*.880. On most pages of this manual the importance of alphabetic thinking is plain. 'The sounds and differences of words are recognized by letters in writing', Hucbald declares, 'and in such a way that the reader is not led into doubt. In the same way, musical signs were once devised [in ancient Greece] so that every melody notated by their means, once these signs have been learned, can be sung even without a teacher.' By Hucbald's time, various families of neumatic notation were established in

72 Sign repertories (ii). Greek lyre-notation characters with the accompanying string-names, from the *De harmonica Institutione* (*c.*900) by Hucbald of St-Amand. Cambridge, University Library, MS Gg.v.35, fol. 271, 11th c. Both the layout and the appearance of the table reveal a parity with the rack of alphabets shown in Plate 71 above.

Francia, as he observes, and they were essential for indicating 'the slowness or speed of the melody, or where the sound demands a tremulous voice', together with other nuances of performance. Much of the art of the Carolingian singer was concentrated here. However, because the neumes did not measure the exact distance between the notes of a melody they could not be used without a teacher, 'although they are of some help as an aid to one's memory'. Hucbald's solution is to supplement the neumes with an alphabetic spelling of the pitches, creating a bilingual notation. Turning to the treatise 'of that most sagacious man Boethius', he adapts a series of characters from the letter notations of the ancient Greeks that he found there (Pl. 72). Borrowing the closest Latin alphabet shape, he uses the characters *f*, *c*, *p* and *m* to spell the four finals of the plainchant modes, DEFG, and similarly for the other characters. This is perhaps the kind of solution to be expected from Hucbald, the author of a Latin poem, *Carolus calvus*, in which every word begins with the same letter; there could scarcely be a clearer way of showing an interest in the way symbols identify nodes of sound by alphabetic means. But Hucbald does not intend the alphabetic characters of his new notation to be employed alone; as mentioned above, the characters are to be written above the conventional neumes, or near them, because the neumes remain vital to show various aspects of performance that 'the letters cannot reveal'.[14]

This sense of what musical notation can and cannot do is supported by a sophisticated understanding of what actually happens in a sound-per-symbol method of spelling, as one might expect from an author who lived at a time when the earliest known sustained experiments in Romance writing were being made, and in the region (perhaps the very place) where some of the earliest surviving examples were copied. To devise a system of spelling is to listen to the fluid motion of the voice and then identify a series of nodal points that letters can express, always with a realistic sense that much in the stream of sound will escape notation. In the same way, Hucbald seeks to spell a motion of musical pitch that could be very fluid in performance, to judge by his brief account of what the neumes alone can convey. Hucbald's method can never have involved a simple process of 'writing down the notes' heard in performance, one by one, a letter per note. Imagine a supple rendition of a chant with moments of what Hucbald calls 'tremulous' voice, including the mysterious 'notes that cantors call *vinola*', according to his contemporary Remigius of Auxerre, and that Aurelian describes as a kind of *tremula vox*. Add special uses of the voice when certain letters closed off a syllable, notably the nasal consonants *m* and *n*, and the possibility of ornaments, glissandi and other effects of which little can be said for certain. This begins to suggest the kind of analytical listening required from anyone who wished to spell out a chant melody into constituent pitches in the ninth century, as from anyone required to explore a new spelling system or to invent one. Only those who have invented a spelling themselves, perhaps, can appreciate the kind of critical listening that is necessary to resolve the nuances of speech sounds into a new form of alphabetic deposit. As a much later observer, Robert Robinson, commented in his treatise *The Art of Pronunciation*, from 1617, there is always a danger that an inventor or user may be guilty of

> taking one simple sound of mans voice to be two, at other times taking two, three or four simple sounds to be but one, and according to that mistaken order fitting letters for them, whereby writing is thereby in some part made defective, besides by many other errors used therein, as by misplacing of letters, contrary to the order wherein they are pronounced, inserting of superfluous letters, where there is no need, nor any sound at all expressed for them, making one letter serve for two different sounds . . .[15]

For Hucbald of St-Amand, the subtlety of ear that the process of experimenting with a new Romance spelling required, and the sound-to-symbol acuity necessary to use (or indeed to invent) a bilingual form of musical notation to guide singers, were perhaps essentially one form of discernment.

Singing out Syllables

The emergence of texts spelled as the common Latin speech has implications for the art of singers and for musical notations that survive before 900. One might approach them through another example of the common West Frankish tongue in writing, this time in a litany that was probably sung at Pippin's council of Soissons in 744. Like some other litanies, this one contains various confusions, garbled spellings, bogus saints whose names are no more than the detritus of scribal error and even a few demons who have been admitted, needless to say, by mistake. One detail, however, is unique to this litany. In several places, the communal response to the invocation is not presented in the form that will become familiar in later litanies, *Tu illum adjuva*, 'You [Saint X], give him aid', but as *Tu lo juva*. This looks like an attempt to spell *Tu illum adjuva* as those words were pronounced in the common Latin speech. The scribe has presumably transcribed a response in which the voices of laity and clergy were joined in chant – by now a rare occurrence outside the Kyrie acclamations in Greek – and therefore requiring the common speech to be used. As the conclusions of Chapter 9 above imply, the admission of the lay voice here necessarily introduces a Low form of Latin that is acceptable in this context only because the High Latin of the liturgy can be momentarily suspended to allow people and clergy together to call upon the saints.[16]

It is possible to imagine how the liturgical Latin of singers had long been resistant to such changes in the common speech as the degradation or loss of final syllables. The evolution of their Latin was probably arrested in late antiquity by the innately conservative character of liturgical celebration and especially by the ear's readiness to accept archaic and redundant morphology when the syllables at issue have music flowing into them, following its own musical logic. Speakers of Modern English sing a familiar Christmas carol with the line 'Let steeple bells be *swung-en*' without the archaic form of the strong past participle causing any difficulty, just as French ears accept final *-e* in song when it represents an inflection no longer voiced in standard Francien, as in *chanté-e*. The singers of Francia and elsewhere between 550 and 750 may therefore have used a Latin that was relatively scrupulous in preserving syllables weakened or lost in the common speech. What is more, some Frankish singers from the 760s had begun to learn the chant of Rome, or were at least exposed to the practice of Roman singers, both in Rouen and in the Eternal City (Chs. 14–15). Despite the uncertainty that surrounds these studies and what they actually entailed in terms of musical results, the work presumably involved the Frankish cantors in periods of intense and protracted listening to Romans whose Latin was quite conservative in its treatment of final syllables. The evidence of Modern Italian provides many signs of this conservatism, notably in words that have retained their Latin syllabic structure, or something very close to it, such as VITA > *vita* (but French *vie*), CABALLUS > *cavallo* (but French *cheval*) and MEDIUS > *mezzo* (but French *mi*).

If Frankish singers used a relatively conservative Latin in the matter of final syllables lost in the common speech of Gaul, where such losses had been extensive, then the experience of listening to Romans would have confirmed their practice and perhaps have extended it. This is may be one of the more important and lasting reforms hidden under the surface of Carolingian rhetoric about Roman chant in Francia.

With priests and deacons who had not received a cantor's training, however, it might be a very different matter. It was plainly no disadvantage that presbyters should teach their congregations in the common Latin speech or in Frankish, the more 'rustic' the better in some cases. A famous canon issued by the Council of Tours in 813 actually requires clergy in West Francia to deliver their homilies in the common tongue or *rustica romana lingua*, seemingly regarded as a kind of patois. The ideal Carolingian priest could therefore range from *tu lo juva* when delivering a homily to something better represented by *tu illum adjuva* in his prayers and chanted readings. From the reign of Charlemagne onwards, the quality of the priesthood, especially in a rural context, became the subject of a new and intense concern that is reflected in the capitularies issued by Frankish bishops. They insist that priests should be irreproachable in their conduct, scrupulous in their performance of their liturgical duties and solicitous for the salvation of those whom they must teach at least the Creed and the *Pater Noster*. The bishops also require that the priests should possess a library of books, including an antiphonale, missale, lectionary and manual of computus, for many of the presbyters addressed in this legislation were men of reasonable substance, free landowners with a residence, with servants to work the estate and with an income from tithes.[17]

The capitularies make no explicit reference to books with musical notation, and yet it has already been mentioned above that a high proportion of the extant ninth-century notations show lessons, prayers and Mass Ordinary intonations: material for priests and deacons. This illustrates the prevailing character of musical notation in the ninth century: it is a single fibre-optic thread, so to speak, in the thick cable of techniques for securing a spiritual and competent celebration of the liturgy by the presbyters, and not in itself especially conspicuous. What the capitularies do say is that priests should be more conscientious, and better schooled, in their performance of psalmody. A presbyter must learn to sing the psalms correctly (*recte*) and, as Hincmar of Reims declares,

> psalmorum etiam verba et distinctiones regulariter ex corde cum canticis consuetudinariis pronuntiare sciat.

> he [the priest] should also know how to utter (*pronuntiare*) the words of the psalms and the sense units in the correct manner by heart, and with the customary chants.[18]

There is no need to press the meaning of the Latin word *pronuntiare* here towards its modern English equivalent 'to pronounce'; these capitularies can no more be expected to isolate matters of Latin elocution for discussion than to distinguish books with musical notation from those without. A concern for correct elocution may nonetheless be embraced here as in some other stern but laconic pronouncements about 'regular' and 'distinct' performance of the chant. It is certainly possible to imagine how the less-educated clergy might profit from some means to show how this should be achieved when music entrusted to them in a liturgical celebration had to be accommodated to the syllabic structure of the texts assigned. Any deacon or presbyter who saw the word *sperantibus* neumed as

spe-ran-ti-bus

in a responsorial tone, for example, was reminded that liturgical Latin had been reformed to incorporate a new grammatical expertise and that he had better be diligent. The notation here uses a special kind of neume, a liquescent, to signal

73   Part of a bifolium from an 8th-c. copy of the Psalms. Rome, Vatican City, Biblioteca Apostolica Vaticana, Pal. Lat 187. *CLA* 80a. Probably West Frankish. The text begins BEATUS UIR QUI NON HABIIT IN CONSILIO IMPIORUM ET IN UIA PECCATORUM NON ESTETIT . . . Scribes of the 8th c., writing text alone, sometimes record the prosthetic *e* that developed before initial s+consonant, whence the spelling *estetit* for *stetit* in the fourth line of this fragment from an inexpertly written Psalter.

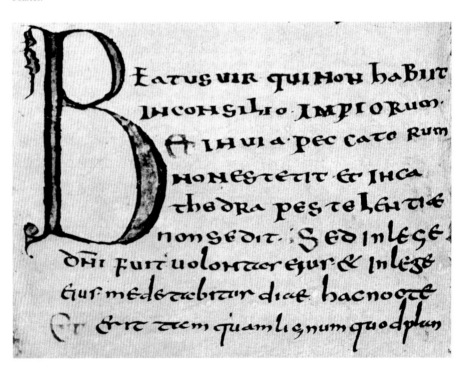

the presence of the nasal consonant (*n*) that closes the second syllable of the word, perhaps to show that the voice is to flow into that consonant during the second pitch. A minute pondering of text and music together, in the light of intensified grammatical study and the use of treatises such as Alcuin's *De Orthographia*, had evidently encouraged the Franks to sift the conjunction of verbal and musical sound with great care. The notation also shows the singer that every syllable of the word *as written in correct spelling* must be sounded, and that any syllable customarily sounded *but not written in correct spelling* must be suppressed to reduce interference from the common Latin speech. Thus the prosthetic *e* which developed very early in Latin before initial s+consonant is definitively excluded by the neumes in this example: the presbyter is not to sing **e-spe-ran-ti-bus* (Pl. 73).[19]

What Signs to Use? A Matter of Accent

At first, it seems that the voices of a ninth-century schoolroom can be distinctly heard in this exchange between a master and a pupil, discussing the accentuation of Latin words:

Q   How should one accent the word *Donātŭs*?
A   With a circumflex.
Q   Why so?
A   Because in words of three syllables, four syllables or beyond, if the last syllable is short, and the penultimate is long by nature, the penultimate is to be circumflexed.
Q   How?
A   *Donâtus.*
Q   How should one accent the word *făx*?
A   With an acute.
Q   Why so?
A   Because a monosyllable with a short vowel is to be pronounced with an acute accent.
Q   How?
A   *Fáx.*
Q   How should one accent the word *rēs*?
A   With a circumflex.
Q   Why so?
A   Because a monosyllable that has a long vowel is to be pronounced with a circumflex accent.
Q   How?
A   *Rês.*[20]

This attempt to transcribe an inhumanly systematic lesson in progress comes from the *Cunabula Grammaticae Artis Donati*, a short treatise circulating in the ninth century and cast in dialogue form throughout. The compiler is concerned here with the fundamental question faced by Carolingian monks and clergy who not only wished to write a more correct and Roman Latin but also to speak one. How were the prescriptions of the ancient grammarians concerning the accentuation of Latin to be followed? This was in large measure a musical question. As we have seen, many of the Roman grammarians known to the Franks defined Latin as a tone language: the accented syllable of a word was to be spoken at a relatively higher pitch than others (the acute accent), or with a rising and falling pitch (the circumflex accent) according to the length of the vowel, the reasons for treating it as long and the quantity of the vowel in the syllable immediately following. All other syllables were voiced at the mean pitch, the grave accent. Even this rudimentary account is enough to convey something of the Franks' sense that these matters were getting them into deep water. The pupil in the extract quoted, who already knows as much as his master, deftly plants questions using specimen words that will allow the teacher to illustrate different criteria for assigning the accent, all selected from existing grammars reaching back to late antiquity (*Donātus*, *făx* and *rēs*). Yet while this exchange bears no relation to an actual lesson – it is a classroom play for two voices, in effect, to be used as a pedagogical exercise – the dialogue strongly suggests that practical demonstration did take place with pupils imitating the sound they heard. This dialogue would have no pedagogical value unless the master using the text in class spoke the word *somehow* in a relevant way, as the text requires him to do.

Although the accents are discussed in treatises such as the *Cunabula* with methodical care, and laid out with evident concern for improving Latin elocution, there were many reasons why the Franks could not use them in the recommended way and were bound to be frustrated in their attempts to capture the Roman voice. In contrast to Classical Greek, Latin may never have been spoken with a pitch accent at any time for which there is historical record, and was certainly not enunciated that way as a matter of course in the time of Charlemagne. The Franks therefore found themselves reading manuals commending a practice that may never have been practised but reflected instead the long tradition of basing Latin grammars on Greek models. Yet it would be too simple to say that the Franks regarded the issue of tone in Latin enunciation as closed, or that the three accents confronted them with a demand there was no possible way to meet. The relation between their theory and their practice was more complex than that. As grammarians, the Franks wished to appropriate, and if possible to use, all the grammatical materials that they had inherited or rediscovered. The greater the difficulty they encountered in trying to make ancient tools work, the more intense their pondering of sound-to-symbol relationships might become.[21]

No Frank who studied the tools offered by *accentus* could mistake the fact that they are designed to guide the declamation of metrical poetry and in that sense belong in the domain of measured and calibrated sound. The grammars, in their explanation of the accents, often distinguish between vowels that are long by nature and those made long by position, as when a vowel appears in a closed syllable before two consonants or a complex consonant such as *x*. These guides to *accentus* therefore envisage an idealized and quasi-musical declamation of Latin metrical verse where correct composition required precisely this discernment between naturally long and naturally short but contextually lengthened vowels. (It is the difference between *Dōnātus* and *făx* scanned in metrical verse as *fāx* because of the *x*.) The belief that Latin should have a pitch accent, like Greek, was dear to the Classical Latin poets who regarded tone 'as an artefact of the literary language' and not as a prosaic matter in any sense of the term. A Frankish churchman could sense this easily enough from the materials he had.[22]

This already suggests that there was more to Frankish transactions with the accents than an unbridgeable gap between a system of markings prescribing pitch at the level of the syllable and a Carolingian Latin that was not a tone language. A chasm like that would have left the Franks with an inert apprehension of the meaning of the accents in musical terms, but that was not the case. Most Frankish scholars knew their Virgil, many their Ovid and Horace; the verses of those poets are shot with allusions to musical uses of the voice (*Arma virumque cano* . . .) that cumulatively seem to evoke some lost form of musical or semi-musical delivery: some high sublimity of poetry on the voice that makes prose and normal speech seem lowly and earthbound. Viewed in this light, musical notation with neumes seems designed to satisfy an intellectual desire as much as a practical need. Some Frank(s) saw how the accents could be rescued from obsolescence, and could capitalize upon their deeply intriguing poetic and musical aura, if they were adapted to denote modules of precisely calibrated pitch, syllable by syllable, in plainsong. The first *need* to be satisfied by notation with neumes may therefore have been an intellectual one (if that is quite the right word) arising from a deeper level of sound-to-symbol thinking than the Merovingians had known and an aural appetite sharpened by a fascination with all kinds of alphabetism leaving its trace upon Carolingian charters, upon Hucbald's bilingual notation and upon the St-Amand sermon. The desire to provide priests or anyone else with a written record of what they sang came next.[23]

More than a thousand years after Charlemagne and Alcuin, the Benedictines of Solesmes in northern France began an attempt to restore Roman plainsong for use in the Catholic Church. Modern historians of music have often noticed the parallel with the Carolingians' great project to bring 'Roman' chant to Francia. One of the founding fathers at Solesmes, Dom Joseph Pothier, insisted that French singers should strive henceforth to remove the sounds of their vernacular when they sang. Choirs were enjoined to sound the letter 'n' in *constantia*, for

example, and not to leave it silent as in French *constance*. They were to pronounce a word like *intende* with the same vowels as *in terra*, and not with the
nasalized 'e' of French *temps*. When in doubt, Pothier urged French choirs to
follow 'the usage of countries that have conserved traditions [of pronunciation]
better', primarily Italy, and to follow the spelling. 'Each vowel must have its
proper sound', he wrote, and 'each consonant should have the articulation which
distinguishes it.' The words are Pothier's, but in general terms they could just as
well be Alcuin's. Without really knowing it, Pothier was a Carolingian musician.
So in a sense are we all.[24]

PART III

TOWARDS THE FIRST EUROPEAN REVOLUTION

D URING THE ELEVENTH CENTURY, many obscure saints decided that it was time to make a bid for fame. Just after 1000, at Lembeek in Brabant, Saint Veronus appeared repeatedly to a priest – who clearly did not believe his eyes the first time – and insisted that the site of his tomb should be made known to the populace. Veronus believed he had lain in obscurity long enough. Not far away, in the town of Sint Truiden, the patron saint of the abbey there began to produce miraculous cures after some years of quiescence, and persisted in doing so until the pilgrims became so numerous that their tents came up to the abbey's gate and the local market began to thrive. The monks who reported these events should no doubt be allowed to tell their story in their own way, but from a modern point of view there is not much doubt what was happening. The story of Saint Veronus is recorded because the Comital family of Hainaut translated his relics to Mons, their seat, in the hope of building up his cult and their rents together; the turn of the first millennium is precisely the time when one would expect a powerful family like these counts to be consolidating their patrimony around a *castellum* and the cult of any saints honoured in their own castle chapel. At Sint Truiden, the case was slightly different. There were weavers in that town, 'commonly regarded as more arrogant than any other traders', according to the house-chronicle of the abbey. To judge by the confidence and importance of these artisans, the industrial revolution of the northern textile-workers was already under way, and the principal actors were making their own way in the world by dint of hard work. They were respectable men. Why should they be in thrall forever to the monks?

The reawakening of Veronus, Truiden and many other saints between 900 and 1100 provided a means for monks and clergy with no conception of abstract economic forces to explain what was beginning to happen in many towns, especially those located between the Somme and the Meuse–Rhine delta. Miracles attracted pilgrims, who brought money, merchants and markets in their wake. A slow economic revival was beginning, impelled by a significant increase in the area of land given over to cereal crops as lords like the counts of Hainaut saw the advantages of making clearances and bringing new lands under the plough. Many monks and clergy could see no reason to look further for an explanation for what was happening about them than the work of their holy patrons, even if the result was often a mixed blessing. In a sense they were right, but they had things in the wrong order. It was the economic quickening that stirred the saints into fresh activity, not the other way round.

In many different abbeys and cathedrals of the Latin West, men capable of writing new chants for singers to perform in the liturgy of the Sanctorale, and often good singers themselves, responded to what was taking place. When this music can be deciphered today it is because the scribes notated it using various types of musical stave. These eleventh- and twelfth-century staves are plainly the ancestors of the mainstream forms which are still in use and have exerted such a formative influence over the development of the Western musical tradition. Effectively a form of graph, and perhaps related to contemporary developments in the use of the counting board or abacus, the stave was devised around 1025 from an existing repertory of graphic techniques and notational devices by a monk named Guido 'of Arezzo'. This familiar form of Guido's name conceals the fact that he did much of his formative work at Pomposa, in the Po Valley, where he came to the attention of a kindred that had greatly enhanced its position by making clearances in marshy areas and by creating new walled settlements: the Canossa. Guido's invention, to which every Occidental musician is indebted, has an economic context in one of the most dynamic areas of the eleventh century outside Flanders and Brabant.

Yet there is more to the inventor of the stave than this. Even before the end of Carolingian imperial power in 987, many began to recognize that the collapse of the Carolingian order, and the rise of competing principalities like the County of Hainaut, had created a climate of violence and disorder that could be remedied only by a restoration of the peace of Christ. An unlikely – and unprecedented – alliance of monks, lower clergy and the artisans of the cities began the work. The members of this alliance knew that it could be accomplished only if the Church had men who were pure in their bodies (because they were celibate and therefore free from the corruption of sex), just as they were pure in their motives (because they were free from any taint of having acquired their clerical office by paying for it: the heresy of simony). One of the earliest voices to be heard in this cause belonged to a certain Wido, already identified by the 1070s as Guido of Arezzo on the basis of information provided by his pupils. The desire to cleanse pollution in the life of the Church was Guido's most forceful impulse, as much when he intervened at an early stage in the conflict that was to shape medieval civilization into two separate domains of spiritual and temporal power, as when he offered the Universal Church a notational device for singers of the liturgy that was destined to shape the course of Western music.

One would give much to know how Guido's new notation came to the many monasteries and cathedrals where, by 1150, it was used. Did individual carriers, who had learned it elsewhere, bring the system to each new house? How was the work of transferring the music from older books – or indeed form the memories of the elderly – actually accomplished? There is perhaps only one case history that can be illuminated in any detail from a literary as opposed to a musical source and it takes us back to the monastery of Sint Truiden, now in Belgium, where a young man named Rudolph was teaching Guido's system in the remains of a burned and ruinous abbey soon after the year 1100, struggling to integrate what he heard from the older monks with what he saw in the oldest graduals of the house, just as in later life he struggled with the weavers of the town who, more prophetic than they knew, were becoming conscious of their growing strength.

74 The earliest copy of the charter or *testamentum* establishing the right of Bishop Stephen of Liège to be regarded as the composer of the Office in honour of the Holy Trinity sung at the cathedral. In the normal charter manner, the text begins with an address to all who might encounter it, now or in the future, leading to the name and title of the person issuing the document (*Omnibus sanctam Trinitatem confitentibus ... Richarius Tungrensis ecclesie episcopus*), and ends with a dating clause, clearly visible where a later hand has rendered the date in words, in darker ink, above the Roman numerals (*Actum est hoc Leodii sub die xvi Kalendas Decembris anno Domini dccccxxii inditione vᵃ regnante Heinrico rege gloriosissimo anno xi*); Anselmus, *Gesta Episcoporum Leodiensium*, xx. Wolfenbüttel, Herzog August Bibliothek, Cod. Guelf. 76.14 Aug 2°, fol. 56ᵛ.

18

COMPOSING FOR SINGERS 900–1100, I:
SCHOLARS IN THE SERVICE OF SAINTS

A Find at Liège

Some time before 1055 the clergy of Liège discovered a curious document in the archives of their cathedral (Pl. 74). Their house-chronicler Anselm calls it a *testamentum*, the standard term for a charter attested by witnesses. Dated 16 November 932, and subscribed by Bishop Richarius of Tongres and Liège, the parchment concerned what would now be called a matter of rights over a composer's intellectual property. Hitherto, the clergy of Liège had always supposed a certain Hubald was responsible for an impressive series of Office antiphons and responsories they sang on the Feast of the Holy Trinity. According to the new charter, however, Bishop Richarius wished it to be known these chants of 'sweetest music' were the work of 'that venerable man Bishop Stephen [903–20], our predecessor'. The bishop also announced he was founding an *oratorium* in the cathedral where Stephen was buried, with an altar dedicated to the Trinity. In the part of the document Anselm decides to paraphrase rather than quote, Richarius specified the sources for the income to provide the oratory with lights and other things necessary for the liturgy.[1]

This charter, seemingly unique among the records of medieval music, may be a genuine document of 932 or a later forgery; either way, the bishop's determination to claim these chants for his predecessor in such a document says much about the prestige plainsongs could confer upon a church in the tenth century if they were well disseminated and securely attributed. There is some astute musical criticism in the *testamentum*, and the canons of Liège knew it. Stephen's Office for the Holy Trinity is one of several he composed using the technique of moving, chant by chant, through the eight plainsong modes in numerical order, producing a terrace of tessituras with the last chant placed considerably higher in the voice than the first. This device also appears, and at a similarly early date, in Hucbald of St-Amand's Office *In plateis* for Saint Peter, which may have encouraged some to suppose the Office for the Trinity was also the work of this famous hagiographer, music theorist and composer whom Anselm disingenuously calls 'a

Hubald who is not known to me'. Later in the tenth century, and into the eleventh, the device of proceeding through the modes became widespread in West Frankish Offices, and the charter therefore does more than settle a matter of attribution: it identifies Bishop Stephen as a figure of seminal importance in the musical innovations of recent generations with special reference to Office plainsong; from a vantage point in 932, the ostensible date of the *testamentum*, a devoted son of the Church of Liège could perhaps already discern the potential importance of Stephen's contribution. By 1000, the significance of his work would be clearer still. Like many medieval charters, the one found at Liège only gains in significance by being counted a late forgery.

The *testamentum* is also a seminal document in the history of the composer's right to be remembered by name for his work. A charter was the form of document usually compiled as the memorandum of an occasion when rights to a property, or to a privilege, were acknowledged before witnesses; the use of that form here implies that Stephen *owned* his chants in perpetuity, as a monastery might own a mill, a bridge or a pond, and that his right of ownership might be challenged. In the words of the charter, *stabilire curavit*: 'he took pains to found' or 'to stabilize' the melodies. They were musical entities.[2]

Although Stephen of Liège is the only maker of chant whose rights of ownership are enshrined in such a *testamentum*, there are many other documents from the period 900–1100 which give the names of composers and reveal some of the circumstances in which they created their music, usually for feasts of the Sanctorale. All of the individuals involved were male members of monastic or clerical communities who composed for singers and would have been singers themselves, if not necessarily cantors. In some of these documents, especially the prologues to Lives of saints, it is the composers who speak; in others, those who knew them, or had reason to cherish their memory, offer a brief memoir, sometimes with revealing details of a kind unavailable elsewhere. As a result, the number of composers named in chronicles, Lives of saints, biographies of bishops, lists of abbots and catalogues 'of illustrious men', among other sources, is remarkably high for the period 900–1100, and far in excess of anything any earlier period in the Christian West can show. The following list of composers (mostly omitting persons extensively discussed elsewhere, such as Ademar of Chabannes, Hermannus Contractus, Notker Balbulus, Tuotilo, Wulfstan of Winchester and Hucbald of St-Amand) has been assembled from a substantial selection of these texts, listed in the Appendix to Chapter 19. In virtually all cases, the individual is said to have 'put forth' (*edidit*), 'made' (*fecit*) or 'composed' (*composuit*) something called *cantilena, cantica, cantus, responsoria, antiphonas* or *hymnos*. The ambiguity of terms like *canticum* and *carmen* (which might mean simply 'poem') is sometimes relieved by expressions which leave no doubt about the presence of music, such as *versificandi et modulandi . . . cantusque suaves edendi . . . cantus dulciori composuit melodia . . . in mellica dulcedine . . . musice artis dictaverat pneumatibus*. References to creations in words, music or both identifiable as sequences or tropes are rare (see below). With the exception of Sigo (50), who created music for texts written by another, and of Guido, bishop of Auxerre (24) who wrote new texts for existing chants in order to create an association between the saint from whom the melodies were borrowed and the one to whom they were given, the sources either explicitly say that the individual concerned composed music anew or they can be read that way without strain.

1. Abbo, monk of Fleury (d. 1004)
2. Adso, abbot of Montier-en-Der (d. 985)
3. Ainard, first abbot of St-Pierre-sur-Dives (1046–*c.*1078)
4. Alberic, monk of Montecassino (*fl.* 1089)
5. Alfanus, monk of Montecassino, archbishop of Salerno (1058–85)
6. Angelrann, abbot of St-Riquier (d. 1045)
7. Arnold of Vohburg, prior of St Emmeram (d. before 1050)
9. Arnulf, precentor of Chartres (11th c.)
10. Balther of Säckingen, monk of St Fridolin (*fl. c.*1000)
11. Bruno of Toul, Pope Leo IX (1049–54)
12. Constantine of Fleury, abbot of St-Mesmin-de-Micy, then abbot of Nouaillé (d. 1014)
13. Desiderius, abbot of Montecassino, Pope Victor II (1055–7)
14. Drogon of Bergues (*c.*1030–84)
15. Durand, abbot of Troarn (1059–88)
16. ?Eberwin, abbot of St Martin Trier (*fl. c.*1000). See below, Pl. 75.
17. Folcard de St-Bertin (*fl.* 1068–84)
18. Gerard of Corbie, first abbot of La Sauve-Majeure (d. 1095)
19. Gerard, bishop of Toul (963–94)
20. Gerbert, abbot of St-Wandrille (1062–89)
21. German, abbot of Bergues-St-Winnoc (1027–41)
22. Goscelin of St-Bertin (d. after 1114)
23. Gottschalk of Limburg, imperial chaplain (by 1099)
24. Guido, bishop of Auxerre (d. 961)
25. Guitmund, monk of St-Évroul (*fl. c.*1066)
26. Magister Henricus (*fl. c.*1080)
27. Heribert, bishop of Eichstätt (1022–42)
28. Heriger, abbot of Lobbes (990–1007)
29. ?Isembert, first abbot of Ste-Catherine-du-Mont (1033–54)
30. John, abbot of St-Arnulph, Metz (d. *c.*977)
31. John, *scholasticus* and monk of St Matthias, Trier (d. 1047)
32. Lambert, second abbot of St Lawrence, Liège (d. 1070)
33. Leo of Ostia, monk of Montecassino (end of 11th c.)
34. Letald, abbot of St-Mesmin-de-Micy (*fl. c.*1000)
35. Odo, first abbot of Cluny (879–942)
36. Odo, monk of St-Maur-des-Fossés (11th c.)

37. ?Odorann of Sens, monk of St-Pierre-le-Vif (d. *c*.1046)
38. Olbert, abbot of Gembloux (d. 1048)
39. Osbern, monk of St Augustine's, Canterbury (d. ?1094)
40. Otloh, monk of St Emmeram (d. *c*.1070)
41. Paulus Judeus, monk of Fulda (11th c.)
42. Peter Damian, monk of Fonte Avellana, later cardinal (d. 1072)
43. Radbod, bishop of Utrecht (901–18)
44. Reginald Calvus, monk of St-Évroul (*fl. c*.1066)
45. Reginold, bishop of Eichstätt (966–91)
46. Remi, abbot of Mettlach (10th c.)
47. Roger, monk of Chabannes (*fl. c*.1050)
48. Roger of le Sap, abbot of St-Évroul (1091–1123)
49. Sigebert, monk, then abbot of Gembloux (d. 1112)
50. Sigo, schoolmaster at Chartres (fl. *c*.1040)
51. Sigo II, precentor of Chartres (11th c.)
52. Stephen, abbot of St James, Liège (d. 1112)
53. Stephen, bishop of Liège (903–20)
54. Waiferius, monk of Montecassino (*fl*. late 11th c.)

The most reliable of the documents used for this list are probably those in which a composer speaks of his own work, usually referring to an Office project involving both a prose Life of the saint to serve as lessons and chants. (See Appendix to Ch. 19, names numbered here as 7, 10, 34, 39, 40 and 49.) These stand within the sober tradition that allowed a writer to inventory the writings he had contributed to the life of the Universal Church without the suspicion of immodesty. Gregory of Tours and Bede come to mind as distinguished examples. The potted biographies 'of illustrious men', usually writers of homilies, letters or treatises on theology, form a closely related genre, since they are essentially expanded lists of works (nos 4, 5, 11, 13, 30, 35 38, 49, 51 and 54). In many cases, the report is given by someone who knew the composer personally or by a monk or cleric in the same house writing not very long after the event, as in the case of Peter the Deacon for the musicians of Montecassino (nos 4, 5, 13, 33 and 54) or the house-chronicles of the cathedrals at Eichstätt (nos 27 and 45) and Auxerre (no. 24). Such material should always be treated with care, needless to say, for the *testamentum* concerning Bishop Stephen of Liège suggests how quickly a clerical community could forget even the circumstances surrounding the creation of music by one of its own prelates; this could happen within less than a generation, if the date of 932 is trustworthy for that document. Much of the information in these house-chronicles dates from a period when such sources were well under way and often attracted sequences of continuators who might be contemporaries of the events described. In the matter of plainsong composition, signs of inflated claims, either in the interest of an individual or a particular house, are surprisingly rare; the sequence *Sancti spiritus adsit nobis gratia*, a chant that a com-

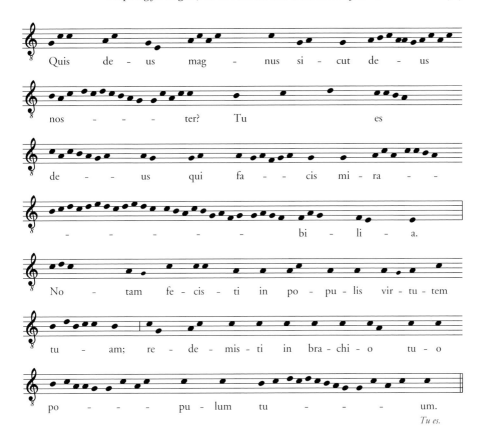

Ex. 1   *Quis deus magnus,* responsory from the Office of the Holy Trinity by Bishop Stephen of Liège. Klosterneuburg, Augustiner Chorherrenstift-Bibliothek, 1012, fol. 122ᵛ. Noted antiphoner from Klosterneuburg, 12th c.

poser could hardly avoid having attached to his name if a later admirer wished to plume up his reputation, since it is attributed to various musicians, appears only once on the list (no. 21), and there is only one sign of a compiler simply repeating verbatim the terms of praise used elsewhere (nos 2 and 19).

When the music of these composers can be traced, there are often signs of the most carefully deliberated compositional projects. Let two brief examples suffice. Example 1 shows part of a responsory from Bishop Stephen's Office of the Holy Trinity as it appears in a twelfth-century noted antiphoner from Klosterneuburg, one of the earliest and clearest of the staff-notation sources. A glance is enough to show emphatically that it plays with a single musical idea for the opening words *Quis deus magnus sicut Deus noster?* This is the oscillation of a minor third between *c* and *a,* inherent in the chant's characteristic mode 3 beginning for the opening word *Quis,* all wonderfully poised somewhere between a sense of motivic extemporization and planned intricacy of design in the way characteristic of so much Gregorian and later plainsong. Yet this melody could surely accommodate a certain number of minor changes from the form shown in the example without the fundamental musical idea being effaced. Much would depend upon where the change was made; a significant departure from the form shown here would be considerably more consequential at the beginning, for example, where the chant registers mode 3 in the singer's mind, than at any other point. As the years passed, most medieval singers could no doubt acquire empirical experience of this kind of variation, whether deliberate or inadvertent, as the gravitational pull of some other chant, or of a similar motif deployed in a comparable context elsewhere (perhaps because it was typical of the mode in question), drew a few notes or a chant, or perhaps a complete phrase, to somewhere else in the voice. The sources of *Quis deus magnus* provide ample evidence of that. Other changes were perhaps of an inexplicable kind, belonging to 'noise' in the transmission: 'a cumulation of random changes that reflect no relationships – indeed no causes of any kind except for the inevitable tendency of people to reproduce a text in a form slightly different from the one in which they received it'. The Liège charter nonetheless shows that this scope for variation no more diminished the sense among contemporaries of signal and stabilized achievement in composition than a dense intertextual web of allusions and quotations in a literary work, liable to be changed or misunderstood by scribes in many details, diminished the sense of consolidated achievement in authorship.[3]

Example 2 shows a more elaborate case, a responsory from the Office for Gregory the Great composed by Bruno of Toul, later Pope Leo IX (d. 1054). Bruno was eventually buried near the tomb of Saint Gregory in Rome, at Saint Peter's basilica, according to his own wishes. The source chosen gives the striking end of the chant in a notably clear and elaborate form. After five lines controlled by the non-Gregorian disciplines of strict syllable count, end-rhyme and a translucent modality, so that all the musical phrases end on either d or g, there is a calculated effect of musical climax here, already achieved in some houses of the late eleventh century, and for other chants, by polyphonic elaborations. (In at least one case these elaborations are attributed to a named individual and called *adinventiones*; see above, no. 36.) Bruno prefers to establish the sense of culmination with a virtuosic use of monophonic melody. The example shows an ecstatic series of descending stepwise figures on the word *gloria*, raised high in the tessitura of the Office, sounding like a tower of bells, constantly seeking the peal of sound that alone seems able to release the musical and devotional energy (they are of course indistinguishable) built up by this point. (Needless to say, the sources do not give a consistent picture of this remarkable section, some abbreviating it to a single statement in a way that the scribe of our chosen source was not prepared to do.) Although composed in praise of Gregory I, the music is wilfully and even exuberantly non-Gregorian, and begins to suggest what Bruno's contemporary biographer means when he praises his hero for 'not only equalling the ancients but also surpassing some of them in the sweetness of his melody'. This is in every

Ex. 2 *Sanctus papa Gregorius*, responsory from the Office of Saint Gregory the Great composed by Bruno of Toul (Leo IX). Fribourg, Bibliothèque cantonale et universitaire ms. L 322, fol. 274$^{r–v}$. Noted breviary of the diocèse of Lausanne (? Domdidier), *c.* 1300.

way the pointedly modern work of a *modernus*. The music is reminiscent of a similarly ecstatic passage, composed over a century later by another strikingly original voice, Hildegard of Bingen, whose material survives in one copy almost certainly prepared under her direction (Ex. 3). Hildegard weights her line with text, as Bruno does not, but in both cases, the sense of rapture and profligate invention is created by a carefully crafted and deliberated compositional project.

In some respects, and notably with Bishop Stephen and Leo IX (=Bruno of Toul), the list of composers above reveals a surprisingly western emphasis on the lands between the Loire and the Meuse. An inventory of music theorists active in the period 900–1100 would have considerably more to say about places now in Germany, Switzerland and Austria than centres in France, and a survey of

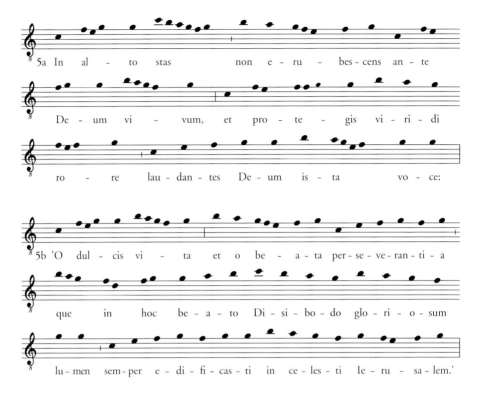

5a In al - to stas non e - ru - bes - cens an - te

De - um vi - vum, et pro - te - gis vi - ri - di

ro - re lau - dan - tes De - um is - ta vo - ce:

5b 'O dul - cis vi - ta et o be - a - ta per - se - ve - ran - ti - a

que in hoc be - a - to Di - si - bo - do glo - ri - o - sum

lu - men sem - per e - di - fi - cas - ti in ce - les - ti Ie - ru - sa - lem.'

Ex. 3   A passage from Hildegard of Bingen's sequence *O presul*, in honour of Saint Disibod. Wiesbaden, Hessische Landesbibliothek, MS 2 (Rupertsberg, *c*.1180–90), fol. 72ʳ⁻ᵛ. From *Abbess Hildegard of Bingen: Sequences and Hymns*, ed. Page

composition for the same two centuries would be much concerned with work done east of the Rhine. The showing of East Frankish musicians on the list is by no means negligible, and it could be improved by adding a few well-known figures who have been much discussed elsewhere, such as Notker, but the tally of composers that can be assembled from biographical notices of bishops and abbots, from Lives of saints and from other literary documents is nonetheless dominated by churchmen from West Francia. Like so many aspects of early medieval music, this is as much a matter of long-term geopolitics as of differing approaches to musical art.

With the death of Charlemagne's grandson Charles the Bald in 877, the Carolingian house endured a series of accidents and misfortunes. Charles's son Louis died within sixteen months of his coronation. A legitimate and in some ways a very able successor, Boso, was opposed by his Carolingian cousins and died in obscurity in 887. There were two more Carolingians, Louis and Carloman, still in their teens and showing signs of promise, but the former died in a riding accident and the latter was killed while hunting. The West Frankish nobles turned to the emperor, Charles the Fat, thereby superficially reuniting the West Frankish and East Frankish kingdoms under a single ruler (this was the moment when Notker Balbulus of Sankt Gallen completed his *Gesta Karoli Magni*, with its nostalgic evocation of Charlemagne as an idealized patron of chant, to Charles). This was a desperate choice, however, for Charles had not been successful as a defender of either Italy or Rome; he was forced to abdicate in 887. The next year, the West Frankish nobles chose Odo, count of Paris, a powerful nobleman of proven martial ability, but he was a Robertian and not a Carolingian. The precedent for a West Frankish ruler from another kindred than Charlemagne's had now been set, and in 911 the East Frankish kingdom acquired its first non-Carolingian ruler in Conrad, a Franconian. When, in 987, the magnates of West Francia met and decided to offer the crown to Hugh Capet, and not to Charles of Lotharingia, a direct descendant of Charlemagne, the reign of the Carolingian royal house came to an end.

The mythology of the Capetians as the 'makers of France' has left its mark on the narrative sources used for the above list. The chronicles and saints' Lives written in northern France have long been treated as documents from the core region where West Franks became Frenchmen during the Capetian ascendancy after 987. Materials from the region between the royal city of Orléans up to Paris and beyond were therefore regarded as especially worthy of scholarly care and attention. This is one of the reasons why the list is weighted towards lands lying to the north of the Loire, where the early Capetians made themselves most visible by doing justice, by wearing their crowns at the Christmas or Easter courts, and by moving from one monastery or church to another in search of the hospitality that enabled them to live on the meagre revenues of a vastly reduced royal domain. King Robert the Pious (996–1031), for example, is known to have entered Aquitaine only once, and there were no particular forces drawing him further south to Occitania. It may be no coincidence that Aquitaine is barely represented on the list of composers (Adhemar has been well discusssed elsewhere), and Occitania is not represented at all. In contrast, a small but notable group of musicians can be placed near Orléans at the abbeys of Fleury and St-Mesmin-de-Micy. The plainsongs composed by Constantine of Fleury and Letald, together with the broad intellectual interests of Abbo, testify to the geopolitical importance that Orléans and its district retained until the mid-eleventh century, when the centre of Capetian royal power moved northwards to Paris.

If a map of these composers would seem, in some measure, to be a chart of Hugh Capet's France, it would look much more like a map of Charlemagne's Empire west of the Rhine. Metz, Toul, Trier, Liège, Lobbes and Gembloux trace a territory that makes a Carolingian *haut lieu de mémoire*. Built upon deep and remarkably self-sufficient traditions of acquiring relics, and of venerating the sainted founders of monasteries and churches, the plainsong traditions in this region, as revealed by the works of composers listed above, show no trace of absorbing any influences from further south than Brioude in the Auvergne (nos 24, 34). This indifference to the saints below the olive-line marks, as vividly as any single corpus of material could, the transition of power in late antiquity across the Alps from Rome to the North European Plain where men and women from Ireland, Anglo-Saxon England, the Frankish heartland and Aquitaine had slowly created a landscape of converted settlements with churches, shrines and reliquaries.

Until recently, it was the custom chiefly to trace the development of composition during the period 900–1100 in terms of the ways existing liturgies were elaborated with new music, with new text, or with new music and text together. The manifestations of this compositional activity included especially the extensive repertory of sequences and (to use an old word in a very broad sense for a moment) of tropes, revealing an impressive range of techniques for making an existing liturgy more festive and for endowing it with more materials to edify and inspire contemplation. A monk or cleric could intervene in the chants appointed for a service by composing passages of melismatic music to enhance the grandeur of an existing plainsong; he might write some text for an existing melisma, creating what is commonly called a *prosula*; many of the earliest sequences seem to have arisen in this way. He might also create new lines of text, often written in metre for a lapidary effect, supplied with new music so that they could be interpolated into an existing item of the Proper or Ordinary. Even this summary account of some common procedures can begin to suggest the scope and variety of the musical and textual means that were developed to extend, elaborate and interpret the liturgy from the ninth century onwards. By the eleventh, they were being used on a pan-European scale, but Aquitaine and certain regions east of the Rhine have long been zones of special interest for the relatively abundant material that survives from both. Yet these are precisely the regions which are either barely represented on the list of composers (as in the case of Aquitaine, though the addition of Ademar of Chabannes, extensively studied elsewhere, would add a major figure from the Limousin) or which appear less often than one might expect (namely the regions east of the Rhine, though the addition of Notker Balbulus and Tuotilo, both of Sankt Gallen and widely discussed elsewhere, would improve the eastern showing).

There are some traces on the list of musicians who were known for sequences and proses, but they are surprisingly few. In the far north of Western Francia, German, abbot of Bergues-St-Winnoc, is credited with the prose *Sancti spiritus adsit nobis gratia*, but this chant was also attributed to others, even to King Robert the Pious. The imperial chaplain Gottschalk of Limburg (or 'of Aachen') is associated with several sequences and proses, although he shares the credit for at least one of them, the prose *Dixit Dominus: Ex Basan convertam* for Saint Paul, with Paulus Judeus, a monk of Fulda. Work of the more interpolative kind long associated with troping appears with Bishop Reginold of Eichstätt, prelate of a cathedral whose house-chronicle is unusually forthcoming about the musical initiatives of the clergy. The chronicle praises him for various compositions in

honour of Saint Nicholas and Saint Willibald, then mentions, as a separate enterprise, his creation of melismata (*notulas*) to place at the end of certain 'very long
responsories', adding text to them 'in the manner of sequences'. Guitmund, of
the Norman abbey of St-Évroul, 'put forth many sweet-sounding chants in the
troper and antiphonary' according to the chronicler Orderic Vitalis, who must
often have sung them since he was a monk of St-Évroul himself. Something comparable is suggested by the memoir of Adso of Montier-en-Der, credited with
'certain chants of hymns elucidating Ambrosian hymns with glosses' (*glossulis*).
This implies some kind of addition regarded as interpretative, although it was
work of an unusual kind if the reference to Ambrosian hymns is to be taken in
the strict sense. Curiously enough, the whole passage appears verbatim in a memoir of Adso's contemporary Gerard, bishop of Toul.[4]

Even when these few case histories are gathered in, it still seems that a great
deal of musical material in the surviving chant manuscripts is not alluded to in
the texts assembled for the Appendix to Chapter 19. Many tropes survive for the
Gloria, for example, extending from the Seine–Rhine productions found as early
as the ninth century to later productions from Aquitaine and East Francia.
Where are the references to churchmen praised for creating these, or indeed
tropes for the Introit? For the most part, the compilers of the literary sources are
interested only in antiphons and responsories for the feasts of the Sanctorale, or
they believe those to be the only productions whose scope and importance will
do lasting credit to someone (often a superior or venerable predecessor) whom
they have cause to remember. The process of producing tropes, regarded until
very recently as 'the most distinctive, most important artistic phenomenon of the
Middle Ages' in music, seems to count for relatively little among these writers;
the same might be said for the complex layers of formulaic activity that went into
the making of Office antiphons and responsories, or the equally complex forms
of change and redaction that might accompany their transmission. None of these
things dulled the impression amongst writers of 900–1100 that a man could be
credited with the composition of chants as readily as he could be credited with
the authorship of books. Indeed, a significant proportion of the composers are
known only because medieval cataloguers of 'illustrious men' placed new compositions side by side with tracts on theology, sermons or letters without any
sense that the chants were distinctively volatile or indeterminate.[5]

The Monastic Orpheus

Some time before 1123, Peter the abbot of Cava in Campania found that the local
seigneur was sporadically emerging from his *castrum* of San Severino and harass-
ing the workers on the rural estates of the monastery. He even drove them from
one of the fields as they were in the midst of sowing. The lord's motives are
unlikely to have been very complex; the archives of the abbey of Cava are exten-

sive and they leave no doubt that the monastery owned a considerable amount of land. Lord Roger of San Severino had every reason to enlarge the scope of his tenantry by threatening its rural serfs as a prelude to appropriating its good arable land, and it would not have taken much for his group of armed and mounted men, the garrison of the *castellum*, to see off the abbey's peasants in the field. Instead of raising a militia or appealing to his diocesan, however, Abbot Peter decided to defend the furrows with plainsong. He went out to the field with the serfs and a few monks and 'instantly began to sing chant'. Lord Roger appeared with his men, but at the sound of the plainsong his mood was softened to the point where he became penitent, even lacrimose, and prostrated himself at the abbot's feet. 'Thus', says Peter's biographer, 'we know that psalmody softens the ferocity of evil spirits and puts them to flight.'[6]

To find David with his music and Saul with his demon so vividly evoked in a scene of conflict between the proprietor of a fortified settlement and an abbot provides a keen reminder of what monks and clergy actually possessed in their repertory of liturgical plainsong, considered in relation to the pressures and opportunities of the eleventh and twelfth century that were especially likely to come from their dealings with lords in an expansionist frame of mind. Like the music of David's harp, plainsong was a means of healing to which thousands of men and women all over Latin Europe had daily access; it was also, as the miraculous appearance of saints during worship occasionally revealed, a form of conjuration. Taken out of its familiar setting, as it was in the fields near the abbey of Cava, or on the relic processions that preceded the Peace of God councils, plainsong could seem even more potent than in church since its power to transform and sanctify incongruous surroundings was made especially apparent.

The majority of the composers recorded in the literary sources were monks, twenty of whom eventually became (or were already at the time they did their composing) the abbots of their houses. This reflects not only the spirituality and sheer ability of many men with compositional skills but also the relative abundance of literary sources from monastic houses. The extended chronicle was still an essentially monastic genre at this date; there is no cathedral counterpart to Orderic Vitalis, for example, whose *Ecclesiastical History* is such a well-informed source of references to the chant-makers in the second half of the eleventh century between Rouen and Bayeux (nos 3, 15, 25, 29 and 48). The monks were also especially active as compilers of saints' Lives; their contemplative engagement with a particular *terroir* and its saints, enhanced during generations of prayer and landed benefactions, inspired them to revise or rewrite the Lives of saints with especial dedication, sometimes adding antiphons and responsories as a freestanding act of piety or to serve as Office chants to accompany a Life they had revised or written, often in response to a commission that could come from a count as readily from an abbot (for an instance of the former, see below). This offered a large canvas for displaying the skills of hagiographer, the prose-stylist, the poet and the musician, resulting in a *work* (the term seems appropriate) that must often have taken a considerable amount of time to unfold in performance. There could also be political motives for enhancing feasts of the Sanctorale in this way. When the members of a cathedral chapter were in contention with their bishop it was an internal matter, unlikely to generate new hagiographical works or chants in honour of saints whose relics lay in the cathedral altars; for monks, however, it was quite otherwise, for the saints of a monastery and their liturgies defined a monastery's grounds for resisting the imposition of bishops, or for challenging the intrusions of counts, quite as much as any document recording their rights or jurisdictions in a cartulary.

Many monastic composers accordingly worked 'in house' to elaborate the liturgy of their own foundation. They range from relatively minor figures up to immensely distinguished men like Desiderius, abbot of Montecassino and later Pope Victor II (1055–7). The case of Desiderius shows how easily one might underestimate the scope of these men. Sometimes, to be sure, these musicians seem provincial, but they are occasionally inward-looking in ways that anticipate the age of Saint Anselm (d. 1109) with its introspective devotion and even perhaps its 'discovery of the individual'. The study of churchmen who composed music for singers between 900 and 1100 is often enhanced by their willingness to study themselves. The signs are already present around 1080 with Otloh of St Emmeram, author of *A Book Concerning the Temptations of a Certain Monk* which records how he compiled a Life of Saint Alto 'together with certain chants' in a context of penitential self-examination. Yet the high proportion of monks among these composers, with twenty abbots as opposed to eight bishops, should not suggest a cloistered art in a pejorative sense of the term. Osbern of Canterbury studied with Saint Anselm across the Channel at Bec, and Arnold of Vohburg composed chants for Saint Emmeram while on the eastern edge of Latin Christendom at Esztergom. Balther of Säckingen made his plainsongs for Saint Fridolin on his return from Spain during a formative period in Christian contacts with Islamic science through southern bridgeheads like Catalonia. Adso of Montier-en-Der provided unspecified *psalmodia* of which 'the Church of Troyes speaks warmly'. Despite the emphasis the *Rule* of Saint Benedict gives to stability, even a monk who was not driven into exile by contention in his house, or by the instincts of a wandering scholar, was liable to travel in the course of his life. After spending some years in a monastic school, a young monk might eventually move on to another community, often because a mentor took him to another monastic house when he assumed a charge there. Monks who became accomplished teachers themselves were especially liable to be moved, for their skills were highly valued and they might find themselves seconded to teach for extended periods in another monastery or indeed in a cathedral school. Adso of Montier-en-Der was for a time a pupil in the school of the monastery at Luxeuil then master of the cathedral school at Toul, an establishment with a distinguished place in the system of promoting imperial chaplains to major bishoprics of the Reich. Adso maintained this position while residing at the nearby monastery of St-Évre, where he also taught. When Alberic, the abbot of St-Évre, became abbot of Montier-en-Der, he took Adso with him to be the master in the school, and Adso eventually followed him as abbot in due course. These were the kinds of movement and connection, paralleled in many a composer's history, which ensured musical composition was far from being a solitary pursuit. It brought a monk or cleric to the notice of his superiors and could place him within a wide network of friends and correspondents.

The Notation Question

The literary sources never suggest that new compositions achieved written form as a matter of course. They imply that all plainsongs, new or old, principally existed in the memories of those who knew them by heart, and that composition was an essentially empirical process of compounding and modifying what one had so often heard. Until the twelfth century, no technologies of notation were widely known that allowed a master in a monastic or cathedral school to set an exercise in composition and then collect the results for correction as he might ask his students to write a description of spring in a Latin grammar class. If such musical exercises were ever set, the student had to sing his effort since all that the master would see on the pupil's slate or wax tablet would be neumes incapable of revealing the melody to his gaze. Alphabetic notation would reveal the pitches but give a somewhat impoverished sense of how the words and music accorded together. Not until the twelfth century, when staff-notation had become widely available, is there an explicit reference to a monastic superior picking up the work of a pupil as he drafts a composition on a wax tablet, singing what he sees and then making corrections by scraping the wax with his fingernail. Before such things were possible, the transmission or simple communication of a chant demanded face-to-face meetings and refused the deferral or even cancellation of the personal contact that alphabetic writing made possible in a letter. The literary sources suggest that this was the prevailing practice throughout the tenth and eleventh centuries. New chants were probably transmitted from the composer to the schoolmaster or *scholasticus*, who then taught the new melodies to his class; Arnold of Vohburg refers to this process when his chants for Saint Emmeram were introduced into the liturgy at Estzergom, replacing old ones. Notated versions, when made, existed primarily for cantors to prove their version of a chant was the correct one, or for singers to consult when some forgetfulness, or some discrepancy, sent them back to the mute but canonical model kept in writing.[7]

    References to liturgical books in connection with these composers are accordingly very rare, and the two clearest examples are both found in the writings of one author, Orderic Vitalis, whose abbey of St-Évroul was refounded in 1050 after some fifty years in which the site of the abbey had lain unoccupied. This naturally encouraged Orderic to mention the monastery's written records wherever he could, since virtually nothing remained from the five-hundred-year period between the foundation of the house in the late 600s and Orderic's own time (he could find only one charter, dated 900, for that entire period). Here the sense of an eleventh-century surge in literacy, as a means to take matters in hand after a long and unhappy interim, is very marked. Orderic refers to seven antiphons by Reginald Calvus, a monk of his house, 'which you can find written in the antiphonaries of St-Évroul'. He also praises Guitmund, another monk of the house, for compositions recorded in liturgical books, namely 'the troper and the antiphoner'. Yet when it comes to the dissemination of a newly composed chant, Orderic has only a case of oral transmission to report. He tells how Arnulf, Precentor of the cathedral of Chartres, composed chants in response to a request from the abbot of St-Évroul, but according to the secular use; when the time came for those commissioned plainsongs to be delivered from the cathedral of Chartres to the abbey where they were to be used, the monastery sent two singers, Hubert and Ralph, to learn them, no doubt by listening to the composer himself. No matter what was deposited in notation, the work that really counted in the late eleventh century was still being done face to face.[8]

The period covered by these composers nonetheless spans two of the most important centuries in the history of Western techniques for making written records of musical sound, and with very varied results. As we have already seen, the first relatively systematic and consolidated documents of Frankish-Roman chant in musical notation appear by *c.*900, using neumes that sketch the general contour of melodies without precisely calibrating the size of intervals. The experienced eye of the tenth and eleventh centuries could no doubt discern familiar melodic turns here and there in the neumes, especially perhaps at the beginning of musical phrases, where formalized gestures often occur. A skilled eye still can. Yet these notations could not reveal a melody to anyone entirely ignorant of it and they are indecipherable today unless the music they contain was later renotated on a stave (Pl. 75). Guido of Arezzo developed that device in the 1020s, adapting existing graphic conventions to create a system of lines with meaningful *spaces* between them, making it possible to notate plainsong so the melody could be read at sight from the script alone (see Ch. 20). Nonetheless, the various forms of Guido's system did not spread rapidly. Hence it is no surprise that many of the plainsongs by our composers have not yet been discovered in staff-notation. Some of them may never be. What is more, many East Frankish musicians did not welcome Guido's new invention, which could indeed play havoc with the traditional appearance of liturgical books where it was employed, quite apart from its interference with the established equilibrium of skills and the arrangements for imparting them in each house. In some centres, these musicians kept the traditional appearance of their books, using a notation without staves, well into the fifteenth century, bequeathing a silence unbreakable now the networks of schooling and friendship that gave their music a voice are no more.

relis lacessite. & filios hominu iuste iudicare
implorate matri ecclesie ut iniuste ablata
restituant. ne innouissimo ante tribunal
xpi consentientes cu raptorib; rei de taciturni-
tate iudicentur. EPL.

IN FESTIVITATE SCI MAGHERICI ARCHI

GLORIOSE xpi pontifex MAGHERICE hac
quam meruisti die celos penetrare noi tui flagi-
tamus famuli ut te implorante post decursum
huius uite superne patrie nitea iuua gaudia percipere. AD CANTICA R

A Insapientia domini semp moratus est presul mag-
nericus ideo memoria eius inbenedictio ne erit
& elemosinas illius enarrabit omnis ecclesia seorum.

VENERANDE DE PRESVL RES.

an tistes magneri ce qui decede terre
imo necio meruisti pontifica le de cui
subi re tu apostasti du a rogitu mut succur-
rer mereamur adpasto-
rem animarum te ducente pueni re. Tu nobis
Dote sane tuis de i presul sui duit se omnib;
talem

75 Office chants for Saint Magneric. In the late 10th c. Abbot Eberwin of St Martin's abbey, Trier, composed
or revised a life of Saint Magneric. The text appears in this manuscript, raising the possibility that Eberwin, like
many monastic hagiographers, may have composed these chants as part of a more comprehensive project that
involved writing or revising the Life of a saint to produce a complete Matins *opus*, so to speak, in text (often in
verse) and music. Trier, Stadtbibliothek/Stadtarchiv, MS 1379/143, fol. 12ʳ.

The labour of renotating a composer's work on a stave was perhaps rarely a straightforward matter, for the principal virtue that made Guido's system a musical blessing was precisely what made it a political liability. Staff-notation refused all ambiguity about the size of an interval. Two notes either stand a major third apart in Guido's notation or they do not; there is no way of leaving open the possibility the interval might be a minor third or a fourth instead. This was the prime virtue of the system and the reason Guido invented it, yet when compositions were transferred to the stave this precision could enforce controversial choices favouring one informant's version of the oral tradition over another. In many cases, there was perhaps little reason to undertake the arduous and contentious labour of renotating the chants of recent composers save when the plainsongs were especially valued, like Bruno of Toul's chants for his predecessor Saint Gregory, or when plainsongs in honour of a patronal saint were revered in churches with an especially rich musical culture, whence perhaps the lavish copies of chants for Saint Emmeram by Arnold of Vohburg.[9]

The corpus of decipherable music associated with these composers is nonetheless appreciable, with an impressive core of highly crafted Offices by Arnold of Vohburg, Letald of St-Mesmin-de Micy and Bruno of Toul, among others. There is certainly more material to be found, but the rate of survival for the texts seems at present to be considerably higher than for the melodies. Whatever this owes to the predominantly oral tradition in which many chants were carried, it also reveals the materials early modern antiquarians valued and printed from manuscript sources which cannot always be identified today and in some cases are lost. In the 1600s, and in a context of quickening scientific enquiry and incipient archaeology, Jesuit and Benedictine scholars began to trace the history of religious orders and the cults of saints with manuscripts, inscriptions, tombs, seals and indeed anything an international network of correspondents could bring to their notice, but they could not find much of value in plainsong. As they laboured to separate what was authentic and trustworthy from what was false and mendacious, a set of antiphons or responsories in praise of a saint could shed light on the history of a cult or of the churches where it was promoted, but the music, paradoxically for an art of sound, seemed mute. Impossible to reproduce in a printed work without great difficulty or expense, and expressed in notations which were only partially understood, its language had passed into oblivion in a way the Latin tongue could not.

Fortunately, the literary sources have much to disclose even when no decipherable trace of the music they mention has been found. They weave the art of composition into a texture of patrons, commissions, projects and contacts. Arnold of Vohburg stayed six weeks at Esztergom and composed some antiphons with responsories in honour of Emmeram, 'not so much aflame with ideas as with a soul given over to praise of the Martyr'; the bishop had them taught to his monks and clergy so that they might sing them publicly. Balther of Säckingen composed chants for Saint Fridolin when he found a Life of that saint in an abbey on the Moselle; he put his work into a letter and sent it to his master Notker, probably Notker Labeo of Sankt Gallen, for a candid opinion. Bruno of Toul returned to his native lands after his consecration as Pope Leo IX and composed chants for the Roman martyr Gorgonius, whose relics lay at Gorze, at the request of the abbot of the house; he did the work while residing at Metz, the Carolingians' old capital of Gregorian chant. Taken together, materials like these represent the largest deposit of anecdotal material about musical composition to be found anywhere between 900 and 1100.

Plainsong and Patrimony: Composers and the Importance of Place

A new chant in honour of a saint was often a hymn to a landowner from his tenants. Down to the finest detail of village and hamlet, the modern road maps of Europe bear traces of the devotion that brought settlements, roads and wells into the protection but more precisely into the *ownership* of saints during the Middle Ages. Today, names such as San Gimignano, St-Denis or Santiago no longer carry any sense of territorial lordship by a saint, although that is what they once implied; the fact that the highest party in any transfer or gift of land was a transcendental being rather than an earthly count or bishop made no difference to the nature of the contracts involved, or to their juridical status, save that the penalties for defaulting on agreements, or for breaking down fences, were likely to be especially severe and long-lasting, indeed eternal. Only perhaps in holy wells, like Saint Frideswide's spring near Oxford, does the sense of saintly property, with the possibility of blessing, but also the threat of penalties for trespass, still linger to provide some sense of what saintly ownership meant in the period 900–1100. Yet when a medieval devotee made a donation to a church or monastery it was a personal gift to the patron through his or her earthly representatives, not a bequest to an institution; a benefaction *ad sanctum Dionysium*, for example, was intended for the martyr himself. Nonetheless, no territory could be the exclusive property of the saints, for while their interventions in human affairs were often spectacular and mostly beneficent, their rights were invariably exercised through abbots or bishops. Those rights were also championed, and just as often challenged, by temporal lords, notably the counts who had a measure of jurisdiction in the cities and often served as the representatives, or *advocati*, of the abbeys.

Composers occasionally created their chant to honour the most exalted landowners in the company of saints. Ainard of St-Pierre-sur-Dives, praised for his fine voice, composed 'melodious chants . . . for the King of Kings . . . for the pure Virgin Mary who bore the Saviour of the world, for angels and apostles and martyrs and confessors and virgins'. Stephen, abbot of St James in Liège from 1095, made chants for Saint Benedict, Saint James the brother of the Lord and

John the Evangelist. Yet in marked contrast to the Frankish-Roman chants developed under the Carolingians, filling a Sanctorale densely populated by saints of the Roman Church, the new music of 900–1100 more often marks the age of the saintly subaltern. Some of the saints honoured with new chant had founded the monasteries where those same plainsongs were made; these saints were often drawn from local nobility, like Guibert, the founder of the abbey of Gembloux (no. 49). Some had been abbots or bishops in the relatively recent past; others were evangelists active in the Seine–Rhine lands or even east of the Rhine, like Emmeram (no. 7) and Fridolin (no. 10). A few were saints whose relics had recently been translated from one site to another, not always legitimately, while others had formerly lain in unknown tombs whose location was fortuitously 'discovered' (no. 32) or was revealed to a devotee in a dream by the saints themselves (no. 37).

No matter how they were made, these discoveries of relics and the ensuing plainsong for the new cult often reveal a cell of jurisdiction, such as an abbacy or a lordship, extending the scope of its influence and revenue by enhancing the cult of a saint. The modern appetite, seemingly insatiable, for uncovering vested interests and conflicts in original sources that appear to minimize them has often led historians to emphasize the importance of saintly cults as a monastic weapon, in effect, to be used against intrusive bishops or secular lords. A saintly patron always outranked a spiritual or temporal lord. Yet the composition of new plainsongs often reveals harmonious relationships between monks, clergy and nobility in the consolidation of territories and communities. In 1094, relics of Saint Mennas were found at Monte Taburno and translated to the Italian city of Caiazzo, where the local count and his son had recently rebuilt the cathedral. Through the abbot of Montecassino, Count Rainulf of Caiazzo commissioned a Life of Saint Mennas from the monk Leo of Ostia, whose record of these events appears in the Prologue to the *Vita Sancti Mennatis* he wrote in response. In addition to the Life, Leo says he also wrote 'certain chants, moreover, and melodies of sweet praises', *laudum suavium melodias*. The count had a clear idea what he wanted when he placed his commission, for he required that both the Life and the plainsongs should 'minister instruction to the simple folk of the region'. This seems commonplace enough, but it reveals an Italy where the populations in many cities and towns had long been demanding higher standards of ministry and continence from their clergy. This *populus* of city dwellers and rural workers from the agricultural hinterlands was a major constituency, indeed an audience, for a composer to address in the impacted context of an early medieval community like Caiazzo (Pl. 76). Texts written and enunciated in the liturgical Latin of Montecassino were probably still intelligible to laity in the Caiazzo region without substantial phonetic or grammatical modification, for this is too early to draw a trenchant distinction between Latin and vernacular(s) in Italy. A composer of plainsong could still hope to 'minister instruction to the simple folk of

76   View of Caiazzo. The impacted appearance of this small city around its cathedral, whose tower is visible in the centre of the image, suggests how conspicuous and formative an intervention Count Rainulf made into the urban life of Caiazzo by commissioning chants for a new liturgy of Saint Mennas once the relics had come to the basilica.

the region', under the tutelage of an abbot and a territorial magnate, for the texts of his compositions were cast in a heightened and archaizing form of the common speech.[10]

The creation of new chants for a saint could contribute to the consolidation of lordships in a much less developed context than Caiazzo. Around 1000 the settlement of Mons, today in western Belgium, comprised little more than the *castellum* built by the counts of Hainaut on *La butte montoise* and the Merovingian church of Ste-Waudru. The comital family, seeking to consolidate but also to extend its patrimony, began to covet lands in neighbouring Brabant, and in 1004 they found an unexpected ally among the saints. In that year, Saint Veronus appeared to a presbyter at Lembeek, in the *pagus* of Brabant, and indicated the place where his bones lay. When the tomb was finally recognized, many miracles followed and brought devotees from the area of Nivelles, Namur and Hesbaye. This is not a large catchment area, but it was enough to interest Count Raginerus IV of Hainaut (d. 1013). Lembeek lay in a separate county, but Raginerus nonetheless went there barefoot, in the depths of winter, to move the relics of

Veronus to Ste-Waudru. According to Olbert, abbot of Gembloux from 1012 to 1048 and the monk from whom the count commissioned an inventory of Veronus's miracles, this was done to protect the saint's relics at a time of war among the magnates of Lotharingia, and Lembeek was indeed unfortified. As so often, the cult of a saint was enhanced in this instance to promote the peace of Christ at a time when there was no effective central power to suppress conflict, but also to strengthen one party's chance of emerging victorious. Count Raginerus was the *advocatus* or protector of the abbey of Gembloux, and he commissioned Abbot Olbert to write a Life of Saint Veronus and compose chants for his Office. Olbert also produced antiphons and responsories at a later date for Saint Waudru of Mons. The count and his wife rewarded the abbey for this work by transferring their landed holdings in Dion-le-Val to the monastery of Gembloux (unfortunately, the act does not survive, so it is impossible to assess what a good plainsong office was worth in terms of rents, mills and farms). The comital family of Hainaut had long been expanding its territory at the expense of Brabant, and the translation of Veronus's relics from Lembeek to Mons appears to be a case of *furtum sacrum*, or holy theft, by the count of Hainaut at the expense of his Brabantine neighbour. Olbert's plainsongs therefore celebrated the success of a covert raid by an aristocratic house. There could scarcely be a clearer instance of a powerful kindred building up its lordship by consolidating the territory around a garrisoned castle, moving outwards from that stronghold and finding a use for the singer's art.[11]

New compositions were sometimes used to make a fresh start in the life of a monastic house that could also be a new beginning in the politics of a region, given the depth to which abbots, bishops and counts were involved in the conflicts of county and diocese over land, incomes and rights. To speak of such departures as 'political' is to translate the language of the original documents into modern terms at the cost of coarsening the motives of those involved. Monastic writers of the period 900–1100 principally expressed such new beginnings as the work of invisible participants, the saints, newly prepared to collaborate in human affairs. No doubt that is how they often perceived them. In the early 1040s, for example, a new wave of miraculous cures began to draw large crowds on Sundays to the abbey of St-Florent near Saumur. Abbot Frederick of St-Florent saw this was the moment to reorganize the liturgy of the abbey's patron, so he commissioned an account of the saint's recent miracles from Raignaldus, master of the cathedral school of Angers and a pupil of the renowned Fulbert, bishop of Chartres. The old responsories dating from the 990s now seemed unacceptable, so Raignaldus produced new texts set to music by Sigo, master of the cathedral school of Chartres and another pupil of Fulbert. Sigo also composed music for two hymns Raignaldus had written, *Canat chorus fidelium* and *Sancte confessor*. He may be identical with the Sigo who became the next abbot of St-Florent, a monk remembered for his skills in grammar, dialectic, rhetoric, arithmetic and music, for his knowledge of Greek and Hebrew, and for his meticulous work in correcting and emending books including a psalter, a Mass antiphoner, a copy of the Pauline Epistles and a text of the Acts of the Apostles.[12]

Viewed in terms of St-Florent's recent history, this collaboration between the abbot of the house, the schoolmaster of Angers cathedral and his opposite number at Chartres, both of them pupils of Fulbert, seems somewhat surprising. Many lines of tension had been resolved for this musical collaboration to occur. For well over a generation by now the abbots of St-Florent had been players in the embittered politics of two comital houses, Angers and Blois–Tours–Chartres, vying for influence in the middle Loire. In the 990s, Abbot Robert of St-Florent had been an opponent of Fulk Nerra, count of Anjou, and the abbey retained its decidedly Blésois sympathies into the early eleventh century. So did Fulbert of Chartres. In 1026, Fulk Nerra captured Saumur and burned the abbey of St-Florent, driving out the monks and installing canons. Whatever its Blésois leanings, the abbey was now decisively in the hands of Fulk as count of Anjou and of his trusted ally, Bishop Hubert of Angers. Only in 1041 did the monks succeed in building a new abbey. In the light of these events, the creation of the new chants at St-Florent, and the collaboration between schoolmasters of Chartres and Angers in their composition, becomes luminous. The crowds who came to the abbey on Sundays were worshipping in a new abbey after some twenty years in which there had been no monks, only canons; no wonder the saintly patron of the house responded to this restoration of his honour by rousing himself to produce a new wave of miraculous cures. Behind the scenes, the chants used for his cult, dating from the time of Abbot Robert, the 'sometime opponent' of Anjou, were discreetly abandoned. New chants emerged from a symbolic collaboration between the schoolmasters of Angers and of Chartres, working together for the liturgy of a monastery which was now so far reconciled to its old enemy Anjou that Fulk's son, Geoffrey Martel, attended the dedication ceremony. Anjou and Chartres were in harmony in more senses than one. This is the singer's art serving high diplomacy.[13]

Further to the north and west, facing the bleak Channel ports, Abbot Angelrann of St-Riquier composed chants for cult-centres in a string of coastal settlements as he drifted in and out of sympathy with the ambitions of the local comital family of Ponthieu (see Pl. 77). The Carolingian world produced few grander abbeys than St-Riquier, lying between the rivers of the Somme and the Authie, for the buildings comprised three different monastic churches, each with a community of monks to ensure a perpetual liturgy or *laus perennis*. Yet despite its prestige, some of the abbey's attempts to extend the settlements whence it could draw rents and tolls met with mixed success. St-Riquier is neither on a major fluvial route nor on a Roman highway; aerial photographs reveal traces of roads between the abbey and the Somme that were never paved and constantly shifting their course because they were liable to be washed away. Angelrann joined this community around 1000, during a phase of consolidation after the long period the house-chronicler Hariulf calls, perhaps with pardonable exagger-

77   Count Guido of Ponthieu. Bayeux Tapestry. English, 11th c. Musée de la Tapisserie de Bayeux (Calvados).

ation, 'the time of desolation'. The reigning abbot soon noticed the young Angelrann's promise and allowed him to study with Fulbert of Chartres. When he was fully instructed in grammar, music and dialectic, Angelrann returned to St-Riquier and eventually became abbot there at the instigation of King Robert the Pious.[14]

Among the monuments of Angelrann's wisdom or *sapientia*, including a substantial amount of hagiographical material in verse, were chants for the saints Riquier (with a 'sweeter melody' than the old ones), Valéry and Wulfram. These were all saints who stood guard by the Lower Somme. Valéry was the first abbot

78   The high Gothic form of the collegiate Church of St-Vulfran in Abbeville. Anonymous and undated 19th-c. print, collection of the author.

of the monastery dedicated to him near the Channel port that is still called St-Valery-sur-Somme after him, while Wulfram was the saintly patron of the church founded by Enguerrand I, count of Ponthieu, in a fortified place or *castrum* on the Somme; a little after the time of Angelrann, the Bayeux tapestry reveals the exalted state of this family, well able to foster a church that eventually matured into the collegiate foundation of St-Vulfran in an expanding settlement that is today the town of Abbeville (Pl. 78). As for Saint Riquier, the patron of Angelrann's abbey, his lands were always at risk. The lands of the count were less extensive than those of the abbey, and in many places poorer; much of the shoreline was undrained marsh, and there was considerable woodland cover not yet cleared. The count, the *advocatus* or abbey's representative and protector in its temporal affairs, was eager to sequester lands from the abbey. By long custom, the 'knights' (*militia*) of the county would come to the abbey of St-Riquier on the patronal festival to commemorate 'the apostle of Ponthieu'; Angelrann used these occasions to draw Count Enguerrand's attention to these incursions, or so the house-chronicler Hariulf claims, and he would surely have strengthened his position by providing chants and readings to enrich the liturgy on that day, exalting the true owner of the territory.[15]

The Composer as Reader and Scholar

A composer was liable to inspire jealousy in those less able. Abbo of Fleury (d. 1004) studied music 'in secret, on account of the envious', while Gerard of La Sauve-Majeure (d. 1095) composed chants 'attracting the jealousy of others'. The composition of plainsong was usually a bid, by versatile men of marked ability, for the kind of fame within the reach of monks or clerics who were often the second or third sons of parents whose first sons were members of the warrior class. The motive, in addition to honouring a saint, was to be remembered in the prayers of the community and of all who sang the chants. 'He has made his name eternal by writing the lives of saints and composing chants in their honour', says Sigebert of Gembloux of his predecessor Olbert (d. 1048), and as a result, 'his praiseworthy memory still lives'. No first-born son in arms, during this dawn of Western knighthood, could have asked for more.

At the very least, a successful composer had to be proficient in the twin arts of versifying and composing music, called the *gemina scientia* or 'twinned skill' in the reports of Ainard of Dive as if it were one art with two facets. Composition rested on an assured knowledge of Latin grammar, with all the aural sensitivity to vocal nuance that study was designed to impart, for the creation of new chants was essentially a form of applied Latinity. Advanced proficiency in *grammatica* is repeatedly mentioned in relation to composers such as Desiderius of Montecassino, who wove his musical art into the 'web of grammar', or Sigebert of Gembloux, inspired to compose new chants by grammatical solecisms in the materials he replaced. Guitmund of St-Évroul was 'most accomplished in the grammatical art' and Sigo II of Chartres was *grammatica imbutus*. Constantine of Fleury was simply called a 'grammarian' by his friend Gerbert of Aurillac, though it seems to a modern eye that his range of talents was much wider. The recorded cases of collaboration (which are very few) seem to have arisen either because it pleased the members of a monastic or clerical circle to express an *amicitia* in this way, or because an author could not fashion music: not because a composer could not fashion words. (See Appendix to Ch. 19, under 'Sigo I, Schoolmaster at Chartres'.) A good many composers, it seems, took authorship in their stride. Olbert of Gembloux distinguished himself 'writing the lives of saints and composing music in their honour', and John, abbot of St-Arnulph in Metz, 'wrote responsories of Lucia the blessed virgin and martyr . . . and a Life of Glodesindis with a night office'. Such men had no need of a librettist.

There may never have been a period when a greater number of influential and scholarly individuals have regarded music as an art of importance to both their influence and their scholarship than 900–1100. Many were duly praised for their skills 'in liberal studies', and while such references are sometimes too vague to reveal very much, the letters between Constantine of Fleury and Gerbert of Aurillac, later Pope Sylvester II (999–1003), provide a detailed picture of what a composer's interest in the liberal arts could encompass at what contemporaries judged to be a high level. Constantine was for some time a schoolmaster or *scholasticus* at Fleury, and during these years he composed chants for the Translation of Saint Benedict's relics. While at Fleury, his interests were broad. One of the letters he received from Gerbert gives rules for the abacus, including multiplication and division, but it is unlikely Constantine needed this advice to supervise the abbey's accounts; towards 1000 the abacus was a piece of scientific apparatus like the musician's monochord, more for experiments and for giving demonstrations than making reckonings. The art of putting figured counters in columns, using the rules governing numbers to base 10, was still the preserve of the specialized *abacista* and was only just beginning to be discussed in short treatises like the one Gerbert addressed to Constantine. As applied to the advanced study of music, this numerate interest emerges in the letter where Gerbert explains a passage from the musical treatise of Boethius dealing with superparticular proportions for Constantine's benefit; this was by no means a new study, but the letter nonetheless shows two learned men in correspondence about a matter of music theory, whereas their predecessors in the ninth century, at least in their correspondence, were generally more concerned to communicate about niceties of Latin grammar or metrics, albeit with the occasional flight into the movements of the stars or methods for the calculation of the date of Easter. Another letter from Gerbert to Constantine concerns a passage in Boethius's companion book on arithmetic. These churchmen knew that the monastic mind, by long tradition, was essentially literary in tone, and they wished to build upon the Carolingian legacy to do something about it.[16]

As the tenth century passes to the eleventh, the nascent cathedral schools unmistakably begin to make their presence felt in the surviving accounts of composers. Abbo, monk of Fleury (d. 1004), was able to study astronomy in Paris, where he benefited from a very early stage in the confluence of masters that eventually became the juridical core of the University. Returning to Orléans, he paid for lessons in music from a master who is perhaps the first professional teacher of the musical art to be mentioned in any medieval source. In the words of Aimon, Abbo's friend and biographer, Abbo 'purchased the sweetness of the art of music . . . from a certain cleric for no mean sum'. These lessons took place *after* Abbo's time as a teacher of reading and chant in the Fleury school, so some higher flights of musical learning must be involved, some of which can perhaps be glimpsed in Abbo's surviving cosmographical and scientific works. These details suggest there may be some substance in the very late evidence concerning Abbo's activities as a composer. In addition to his other travels, Abbo spent two years at Ramsey abbey, in the English fenlands, with the result that he was remembered in England as 'a very learned monk' or *swiðe gelæred munuc*. Amidst other poetry he is known to have composed in England, it is perhaps just possible he left behind the sequence and responsories in honour of Saint Stephen that the English antiquary Bale reports having seen in the sixteenth century, but which may otherwise have left no trace.[17]

Even more than the lives of Abbo and Constantine, the career of Balther from Säckingen shows traces of the new interests and materials beginning to stimulate scholars in the monasteries and cathedral schools after the turn of the millennium. In approximately 1000, Balther decided it was time to journey far afield for the sake of new learning. His monastery lay to the south of the Black Forest, not far from Sankt Gallen, where he had studied with a famous master and musician named Notker who is probably Notker Labeo (d. 1022); he believed it was now time to consult 'the masters of Western Gaul' across the Rhine. Balther's travels eventually brought him to Hispania, probably the Spanish March (in effect, the future Catalonia), for it seems Balther was following Gerbert of Aurillac's path. Gerbert spent three years in the March, one of the bridgeheads where Latin Europe was by now making contact with the learning of Islamic scholars. There, in libraries at Vic and Ripoll, Gerbert drew upon the synthesis of Greek, Arabic, Jewish and Latin learning just beginning; by 970, Bishop Atto of Vic was already teaching a profound knowledge of mathematics, according to the Frankish chronicler Richer, and the monastery of Ripoll possessed a substantial library of works devoted to mathematics and what passed for science. At about the same time, archdeacon Llobet of Barcelona translated a treatise on the astrolabe from the Arabic. There is good reason to suppose Balther reached the valley of the Aude to join a great Carolingian extension of a Roman highway, the *strata francisca*, running through the Pyrenees, across the Cerdagna to Ripoll and Gerona. He remained in Hispania, lost from view, for some four years (a year longer than Gerbert), when he decided he wished to return 'and see the familiar sights of my homeland'.[18]

Balther's journey back brought him to a monastery on the Moselle. He revealed to the abbot that he revered Saint Fridolin, the Irish founder of the monastery he had had left five years before. The abbot was pleased to hear this, and produced a Life of that saint. 'At this', Balther writes, 'I was greatly delighted, for I remembered the monastery of Säckingen lacked a Life of Fridolin; the book containing it was carried away when the monastery was laid waste by [Hungarian] pagans.' Balther asked the abbot if he could borrow the book, but permission was refused, and no parchment was available for making a copy. 'So I sat down and recited it, and retained what I read in my memory. Sometimes I memorized the words with the sense, sometimes the sense alone without the construction of the precise words, so that I might be able to record what I read there for the memory of others.' Next, he composed a series of responsories for Fridolin and put the entire dossier in a letter to his old master, seemingly Notker Labeo of Sankt Gallen:

> Therefore, most devout father and teacher, commending myself to your invincible faith, I beseech you to determine whether this present booklet, with the responsories I have composed according to the art of music, should be sung on the Feast of Saint Fridolin or destroyed in the flames . . .

Balther speaks to Notker as one monk to another, albeit as pupil to master, with no trace of contrition as he describes his years as a 'wanderer' or *gyrovagus*, the term Saint Benedict uses in his *Rule* for any monk who cannot sustain the stillness which is the first step towards mastering himself. Like many scholars of the period 1000–1200, when the commercial life of Europe began to quicken, Balther regarded learning as a commodity to be sought from the places renowned as the best sources of supply. If that meant travelling far, as a merchant would seek the best cloth in Rome or the finest leather in Córdoba, then the journey must be made. Travelling for the sake of study seems to need neither justification nor apology, even from a monastic musician.

19

COMPOSING FOR SINGERS 900–1100, II:
COURTLINESS AND OTHER MODES

The Most Ingenious Bee

At the beginning of the twelfth century, Abbot Sigebert of Gembloux looked back upon the achievements of his life to draft an entry for himself as the last in a catalogue of illustrious men. This was not the moment to be unduly modest, and Sigebert duly recalled how he had improved the *Life of Maclovius* by 'filing and scraping' the original. He had also composed antiphons and responsories for Maclovius and Saint Guibert, founder of Gembloux, by 'honeying' them (*mellificavi*). Sigebert seems confident he has reached the same high levels of achievement in both the words and the music, but there is an arresting contrast between the imagery he uses for the creation of text as opposed to the composition of melody. His literary work is like the exacting craftsmanship of the metalworker, painstakingly filing the surface of an intractable material to make fine adjustments. Using a different but associated image, Sigebert says he revised the text of Maclovius's Life by rubbing, *fricando*, probably meaning the process of correcting text on parchment with the blade of a knife; like Geoffrey Chaucer's scribe nearly three centuries later, Sigebert's task in revising the *Life of Maclovius* was to rub and scrape. Once again, the text is presented as something durable, an entity deposited in writing by minute and sharply visualized effort, this time on the surface of the parchment.[1]

For music, however, Sigebert shifts the ground of appreciation from exacting craftsmanship with durable results, and from the labours of penmanship, to the production of honey: a perishable and liquid substance that refuses all intricacy and ingenuity because it cannot be worked, and which offers the sensations most likely to please an undemanding palate. No doubt the contrast between Sigebert's vocabulary for describing his work with text and music could be exaggerated, for in both cases the terms he uses have a long history. Nonetheless, his association of text, but not melody, with the durable medium of writing, reflects perceptions traceable from his own time, when melodies were principally carried in an oral tradition in the day-to-day business of singing, through to the scholars of the seventeenth century, who regarded the Latin texts of chants as valuable documents of ecclesiastical history or hagiography but treated the melodies with relative indifference. There is a long-term perception of the early medieval composer's activity here that is substantially correct. Plainsong composition between 900 and 1100 was a largely empirical matter pursued as the ancillary to a *literary* art dominated by self-conscious stylists such as Sigebert, namely hagiography.

New chants between 900 and 1100 were often inspired by dissatisfaction with the literary and grammatical standard of a hagiographical text encountered by chance, or laid on the composer's desk by a superior who commissioned a replacement. Sigebert's decision to compose chants for Saint Maclovius as he cleared away the barbarisms of an antiquated *Vita sancti Maclovii* can be paralleled again and again. Bishop Stephen of Liège made plainsongs for Saint Lambert when he took a Life of that saint 'fashioned in a rudimentary manner a long time ago' and 'polished it with the charms of urbane language'. Abbot Angelrann composed chants for Saint Riquier when he revised the Life and replaced it with one in verse, candidly described by the chronicler Hariulf as 'more pleasing' (*jocundiorem*). Even the writings of the most illustrious Carolingian stylists were not immune from a rewrite by now; Gerard of La Sauve-Majeure made plainsongs for Saint Adelhard when he read the Life of that saint by Paschasius Radbertus, a former luminary of Corbie. Gerard found Paschasius's work 'so full of prolix lamentation, so lovesick with the language of the Song of Songs, it seemed more like an epithalamium than the text of a liturgical Office'.[2]

The imagery of 'filing' an old text implied specific operations: restoring Classical usage in the cases of the nouns after prepositions, for example, or ensuring deponent verbs retained their passive form but active sense. Texts such as the prose *Life of Saint Lambert* by Stephen of Liège reveal what the more subtle task of introducing 'urbanity' into an older text might require: an accumulation of phrases ending with similar or identical grammatical forms, a scatter of hexameters here and there, some allusions to Virgil or another Classical poet. The question of how contemporary singers perceived superior craftsmanship in *musical* terms, however, cannot be approached in quite the same way. The new chants have survived much less well than the Lives they once accompanied, or have been less diligently sought, so it is not often possible to compare new music with the older chant it was designed to replace in the few recorded cases where that seems to have happened. Yet enough music survives to form some idea of what accomplished craftsmanship meant to musicians of the tenth or eleventh centuries, and some aspects of musical style or procedure can be illuminated with the rich tradition of music theory: a remarkable body of work which shows monks and clergy striving to codify a vast body of material unknown to Classical civilization, an effort in which they alone, among students of the liberal arts, were then engaged.

Whatever Sigebert of Gembloux means to imply about his musical crafts-manship by saying he 'honeyed' his chants, he certainly suggests that he made diligent and eclectic use of materials in a flourishing state. To 'honey' anything was to behave like the most admired of all beings in Creation under humanity, and one that commended itself to both the clerical and the monastic mind, namely the resourceful bee or *apis ingeniosus*. No image is more common in the writings of 900–1100, and none was more consistently saved from the wearing effects of usage by the daily reminder of what it meant through the example of diligent scholars and teachers. As the bee gathered nectar from far and wide, bringing its gains to the hive, so Sigebert had ranged widely to find the elements, often slight in themselves, which he would compound by his dedicated industry into a new substance that was a blessing to his own community and to others.[3]

The comparison seems well chosen, for the question of how a musician such as Sigebert would have understood superior craftsmanship in melody can per-haps be answered best in terms of a sensitivity to precise details that seemed well or poorly selected, both for their passing quality as felicities or blemishes and for their effect, be it constructive or deleterious, upon the integrity of the larger melodic structures in which they occurred. There are many signs that details occurring very few times in a single plainsong, and perhaps only once, might be regarded as diagnostic of success or failure in the composer's control of the mate-rials, just as they could mark the charlatan or, towards the end of the period, reveal the courtier (see below). To some extent, this sounds like the criteria of musical judgement in many later periods where precise details of counterpoint or dissonance treatment could be marks of failure. The musicians of the tenth and eleventh centuries had no monopoly on sensitivity to detail. Yet amongst these musicians, a language for being articulate about good and bad practice in com-position emerges for the first time in the Western tradition and it is by no means emancipated from grammar and metrics where expertise meant freedom from the precise but egregious errors that betrayed a writer's want of schooling. (The death of metrical conventions in twentieth-century poetry challenges the mod-ern listener to develop a sense of what this kind of scrupulosity means; today, nobody gasps to find Paul Verlaine placing the caesura in an Alexandrine some-where *other* than between the sixth syllable and the seventh; Rimbaud did.) Like a false quantity in a dactylic hexameter or the incorrect case of a noun following a preposition, the incorrectly placed semitone in a chant could be heard as a viti-ating barbarism or solecism. In a similar way, musical effects could be considered as if they were words with an inherent registration: some poetic and high style, some more informal, some vulgar and badly out of place if not used with care. We shall return to that. What mattered in each case was a schooled decorum that a single inappropriate gesture might destroy (always the way with good manners) and where 'schooled' very often meant the concerns of the classroom. As in the literary arts, judgements about what was correct and civil in a musical composition were framed in relation to a grammar of procedure, the eight plainsong modes. Composers in the tenth and eleventh centuries were closely and even obsessively concerned with these modes, and their art is unintelligible without some sense of what they meant.[4]

The Modal Question

There were essentially two grounds for critical thought about the behaviour of melody in the tenth and eleventh centuries. The first was an implicit comparison with Gregorian or Frankish-Roman chant; together with Ambrosian and other hymnody, this was the work of the 'ancient authors', the *antiqui auctores*, that Bruno of Toul was believed by some to have surpassed, just as it was the *vetus cantus* whose manner Letald of St-Mesmin-de-Micy says he did not wish entirely to abandon. The second ground for judging a melody was the body of music theory, deposited in a great many treatises from the ninth century onwards and much concerned with the classification of plainsong melodies into eight modes. These modes were arranged in four pairs and closely associated in the ninth century with the 'Greeks' (presumably Byzantines wherever they were to be found, including Italy) and with genuine or spurious Greek terminology. The modal system, in its mature form, offered eight subsets of musical grammar. In effect, each mode commended various ways in which a melody in that mode might begin, continue and end; it also offered an understanding of how much (and how often) a melody should rise or fall below its home pitch and set a scalar pattern of tones and semitones for it. There is almost no way of describing this system – medieval authors never found one – so that its true nature as a sophisticated tool of memorization, analytical listening and critical appreciation emerges unscathed from the abstraction and pedantry bedevilling all expositions of grammar, musical or textual.[5]

In its Western form, the modal system was principally used in relation to Gregorian chant, but the question of how the modes relate to these melodies is more complex than some other vexed negotiations between theory and practice in Western music. In this case, the range of possible answers extends from theory viewed as a work of codification after the event to theory considered as a means of guiding the generation of the music in the first place. (This assumes that the Franks knew some form of modality when they evolved Frankish-Roman chant in the time of Pippin and Charlemagne, which is by no means certain.) Two fundamental facts make the matter yet more involved. The practice of distinguishing eight categories of modes, divided into four pairs and associated with Greek precedent, is by no means distinctively Frankish, for it also appears in the traditions of Byzantine, Slavonic, Georgian and Armenian chant, to look no further. What is more, relatively systematic and notated sources of the Gregorian music do not appear before *c.*900, by which time the repertory they contain has probably undergone successive layers of independent redaction, in many points of detail, to make the chants accord better with modal doctrines that were the gateway to systematic classification, listening and memorization. This further obscures the relation between theory and practice at the formative stage of the repertory.

Although the Gregorian music was no doubt sometimes recast, on its way to the earliest manuscripts, to make it conform more closely to the kinds of melodic behaviour that modal theory was describing with increasing articulacy and prescriptive authority, there is no reason to suppose the repertory as a whole was systematically redrafted. Once the labour of evolving Frankish-Roman melodies was under way, or even substantially completed, no useful purpose would have been served by tampering with them in a radical way as a second layer of activity, bound to proceed unevenly and piecemeal as the music passed to different centres. This would have compromised the ideal of uniformity from the start, or very near it. The Frankish modes were a guide to the pervading wisdom and civility of Gregorian plainsong, and modal teaching was perhaps more often a means to distinguish core practices from peripheral ones than to serve as a Procrustean bed for systematic refashioning of the music.

This is a necessarily simplified view of a complex situation, but if it is broadly correct then Gregorian chant as it appears in the earliest comprehensive records has not been profoundly remade to accord with modal theory but represents instead a body of coherent musical thinking and empirical practice which is older than the manuscripts and presumably dates from the time of Pippin and Charlemagne, when the music is widely assumed to have come into being. Gregorian chant does indeed reveal an impressive consensus about the range of notes a plainsong should generally use, how often the music should pause for breath, how a scale of tones and semitones can be given a musical grammar so that certain melodic gestures are more readily heard as full or partial closes than others. The singers involved in generating the Gregorian music also seem to have perceived (and remembered) their melodies in groups according to a 'home' pitch within a scalar pattern, according to the disposition of the melody to move and linger above or below that pitch. The only plausible source for these forms of coherence is the shared and sophisticated enterprise of structural listening and melodic invention whence Gregorian plainsong began to emerge, presumably somewhere between the Seine and the Rhine, during and after the time of Pippin (d. 768).

The art of composition between 900 and 1100 was widely regarded in its day as a means to distil the potential within the Gregorian repertory for what can be described, without undue exaggeration, as a more ordered universe of hearing regulated above all by the modes. Years of experience singing Gregorian chant had given many singers fastidious ears; they discovered that Gregorian music did not fully satisfy the taste by which it was enjoyed. To create music that would do so, it was necessary to start again, so to speak, and to improve upon the

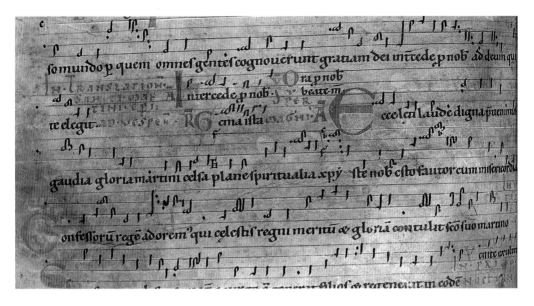

79   Antiphoner, 11th c., Bibliotheek der Rijksuniversiteit, Utrecht, MS 406 (3.J.7), fol. 133ᵛ, detail, showing Radbod's Magnificat antiphon, *Ecce leti.*

Gregorian heritage, the music of the ancients, in a way contemporaries believed was certainly possible because they were moderns. That is why Bruno of Toul could be praised for 'not only equalling the ancient authors, but excelling some of them in honeyed sweetness', while Angelrann of St-Riquier composed new chants for his patron 'even though there were plenty of old ones; his had a sweeter melody' (see Appendix).

Some of the earliest layers of work in this vein include the chants of Bishop Radbod of Utrecht, a late Carolingian who had studied at the palace school of Aachen and must often have heard the Frankish-Roman music sung to a high standard. In 918, lying on his deathbed in Utrecht, Radbod repeatedly sang a chant of his own composition in honour of Martin, the greatest saint of Gaul and a crucial supernatural ally in such a liminal place at such a time. Singing in alternation with psalms, Radbod chose his Mode II antiphon *Ecce leti* (see Pl. 79 and Ex. 4).

Neither the general ductus and compass of this melody, with its adjacent falling fourths at *gloria Martini*, nor the way the tessitura allows the singer to seat the melody securely in the voice and negotiate from there, would cause any real surprise in a Gregorian plainsong. The moment of luxuriance at *Christe* magnifies the prayer for Christ's intercession in a manner quite at home in the familiar means of Gregorian expression. Yet in other ways Radbod has already moved some distance from the Gregorian repertory. His lines of numbered syllables and regular accents establish a harmony of verbal sound that is by no means native to

Ex. 4   *Ecce leti*, Magnificat antiphon by Radbod, bishop of Utrecht (901–18). Antiphoner from St Mary's Church, Utrecht, 12th c. with some additions up to the 15th, Bibliotheek der Rijks-universiteit, Utrecht, MS 406 (3.J.7), fol. 133ᵛ. See Pl. 79.

the older chant, for Frankish-Roman texts often recall the best periods of Roman legal prose. Yet it is the emphatic and almost pedantic modality of the melody that most clearly marks this as an example of a modern at work, for although it is clearly the composition of a singer whose hearing is saturated with Gregorian chant, the melody extends along the trellis of its mode in a highly controlled manner, mostly articulating the ends of poetic lines by pausing on either the final of the mode (*D*) or on the fifth degree above (*a*). This is presumably one kind of style – widespread in the tenth and eleventh centuries – that composers regarded as a musical equivalent of what they accomplished when, often as part of the same project, they took the existing Life of a saint and made it 'more schooled', *cultius*, and 'more urbane' *urbanius*. In musical terms, this sharpness of modal focus was perhaps what warranted the judgement that a new chant was 'sweeter' (*dulciori*) than those of an older layer, or composed 'in an elegant manner' (*eleganter*). The degree of control shows an increasingly clear notion of what compositional endeavour should encompass, and therefore perhaps of the composer.

   In such a context as this, it becomes easier to understand why the only stylistic manifesto to survive from the composers of 900–1100 is intimately concerned with modality. Letald, a monk of St-Mesmin-de-Micy, composed a Life of Saint

Julianus and dispatched it to Avesgaud, bishop of Le Mans (1000–36), with a set of responsories and antiphons, as Avesgaud had requested. In the accompanying letter, Letald writes that he has made a special effort to avoid causing distaste, *fastidium*, by working through the plainchant modes in sequence, as Bishop Stephen of Liège had done several generations before. Singers will therefore hear and feel the chants ascending through the entire acknowledged range of melodic and tonal grammar during the course of a service:

> I have indeed (*sane*) divided the sequence of responsories and antiphons as you asked, in which, for the sake of avoiding prolixity, I have made the substance of each one from a single mode, nor in general (*omnino*) did I wish to distance myself from the guise of the old chant, lest I should produce barbarous or inexpert melody. The newfangled work of some musicians does not please me for they so abandon that guise they seem to be entirely contemptuous of following the old *auctores*. Those who are free to make marriages wish to produce children that resemble human beings, rather than to produce the likeness of some previously unseen monster.[6]

Letald wishes to avoid *fastidium*, a term often used in medieval Latin for the weariness and distaste a reader may feel when a writer is unduly prolix or enters into an excessive degree of detail. The meaning of the passage seems to be that the technique of using more than one mode in any given chant is akin to tiresome prolixity, not a form of musical variation to give pleasure. Letald admires the economy of the older music and does not distance himself from it 'in general' (or perhaps 'in every respect', depending upon the force of *omnino*) lest he should commit the musical equivalent of a grammatical barbarism. The notion of a musical fault as akin to a grammatical or metrical solecism is very strong here, and Letald still accepts that the music of the old makers or *veteres auctores* exemplifies and teaches a received musical language against which innovations are to be judged. The task of judging what is innovative, or even just up to date, in Letald's music does indeed prove to be a delicate one, for his is an essentially classical art of plainsong where every new effort is in some measure a negotiation with the agreed excellences of a received corpus of work, and if a composer refuses that commerce then his music will seem both incorrect and uncivil. Such heedlessness produces the kind of gratuitous novelty, or *novitas*, which Letald cannot tolerate and assesses in terms of details that are diagnostic of a composer's success or failure in handling modality.

His comparison between chants marred by novelty and marriages issuing in a monstrous birth, *monstri effigiem*, alludes to the 'snake-tressed monstrous phantom', the *anguicomam monstri effigiem* of Statius's *Thebaid* (vi. 495). It is probably a criticism of plainsongs beginning in one mode and ending in another (perhaps via the intermediary of a third mode), producing the musical equivalent to a monster or chimera. Letald is presumably thinking of chants such as the antiphon *Urbs fortitudinis*, mentioned in several treatises of *c.*900 onwards for its

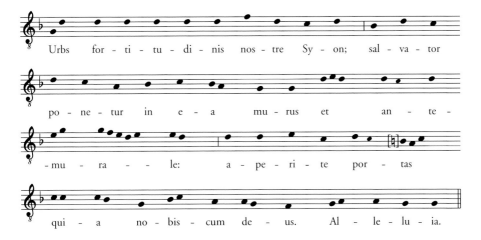

Ex. 5   *Urbs fortitudinis,* antiphon for the Third Sunday in Advent (but often assigned in other sources to the second). Worcester Cathedral Library, MS F. 160, p. 12. Monastic antiphoner from Worcester, 13th c. The 'troublesome' b natural discussed by some theorists is by no means consistently signed in the sources of this antiphon, and is sometimes emended away, as here.

hybrid modal character established by the single *b*natural at *por-TAS*, shifting the melody from a transposed mode 1 to mode 8 (see Ex. 5). This inflection may be a late development, for the classification of this chant seems to cause no difficulty in the list of chants by mode attributed to Regino, monk of Pippin's foundation at Prüm (d. 915). If so, then *Urbs fortitudinis* provides a yet more suggestive illustration of what Letald has in mind: the vogue for a form of *novitas* created by introducing semitone steps, perhaps only once in the course of an entire chant, thus expanding the musical language at the cost of modal clarity, in defiance of mainstream Gregorian precedent, and in further defiance of a pervasive tendency in the period 900–1100 towards a more emphatic modality, illustrated above in the work of Radbod. For some composers, it seems, as for their descendants in the fourteenth century, the semitone was 'the condiment of all music' and it was time, in the judgement of some, to add more spice.[7]

Others took a much more disparaging view of such experiments. Around 1100, John of Affligem blames careless musicians for jumbling different modal signals together in a single melody, cultivating what he calls a *pruritus aurium*. This is translated in the standard English version of John's treatise as an attempt to 'tickle the ears', but that is not the way John perceives such details as the moment of modal dislocation in melodies such as *Urbs fortitudinis*. The term *pruritus*, 'an itch', has a long history in Christian Latin to mean the urging of disordered bodily appetite. The root is the verb *prurio*, having the literal senses 'to itch' and by transference 'to long for a thing, to be wanton'. Hence *pruriginosus*, 'having an itch' in the most physical sense of an encrusted wound that drives the sufferer to distraction, but also in the figurative senses 'lecherous, lascivious'. John's reference to composers in the new fashion who mix modes to satisfy the 'the itch of the ears', the *pruritus aurium*, is probably alluding to the dire prophecy in 2 Timothy 4: 3–4: 'For the time will come when they will not endure sound doctrine, but after their own lusts shall they heap to themselves teachers, having itching ears (*prurientes auribus*), and they shall turn away their ears from the truth and shall be turned unto fables.' John, like Paul, fears the influence of new doctrines, and of new teachers. At best, they gratify the appetite for novelty. At worst, they disturb the equilibrium of body and spirit with uncontrolled desires. No pious Christian of the twelfth century would be tickled by the prospect of that.[8]

To judge by chants such as Radbod's *Ecce leti*, these composers often wish to establish emphatically modal music that distils the modality of Gregorian chant from its many varied and diffuse manifestations in that repertory, and yet they use this often stringently rationalized version of the Gregorian musical language to stage moments which do not distil anything from the Gregorian heritage but dissent from it instead and are very conspicuous as a result, almost avant-garde. Example 6 shows the Magnificat antiphon *Gaudeat tota* from First Vespers of the Office of Saint Wolfgang, composed by Hermannus, monk of Reichenau, probably not long before 1052. In the way they close, as subdivided here, the melodic phrases assert the final of the mode (*D*), the fifth degree above (*a*) or the octave (*d*) to such a degree that the effect of precise details like those boxed in the example at *doctrina* is marked in performance. The deliberate refusal at *docTRINA* to provide the sound so assiduously offered hitherto, namely a phrase ending on either *D* or *a*, is all the more striking for the delaying effect of the repeated pitches that prepare it. One could scarcely hope to follow more intimately than this the traces of an eleventh-century mind at work to create strategic musical effects, whether they be in the mind of Hermannus or of his scribe. The adjacent skips downward on *ET CORPO-re* in stave 7, spanning a major third and then a fourth, are an avant-garde touch, not entirely unknown to Gregorian style but plainly being staged here as a one-off surprise, wilfully out of keeping with the prevailing melodic idiom of the piece and offering a challenge to the voice which is not at all reduced by tradition (unlike the falling fourth at the beginning of stave 8, which would be second nature to any singer raised on Gregorian plainsong). This device appears nowhere else in this chant, much like the striking fall of a sixth in stave 11 at *suf-FRA-gi-um*.

Why did such a modally focused style arise? The desire to do better than one's masters, the natural wish of all gifted pupils, probably explains some of what occurred. Ears trained in the Gregorian music were increasingly able to discern how its procedures could be improved upon (at least if one supposes, as musicians between 900 and 1100 generally did, that successive rationalizations of musical procedure are likely to be improvements). Viewed in this light, the progressive styles of the tenth and eleventh century show much the same prevailing concerns as the music theory of the same period, overwhelmingly concerned to

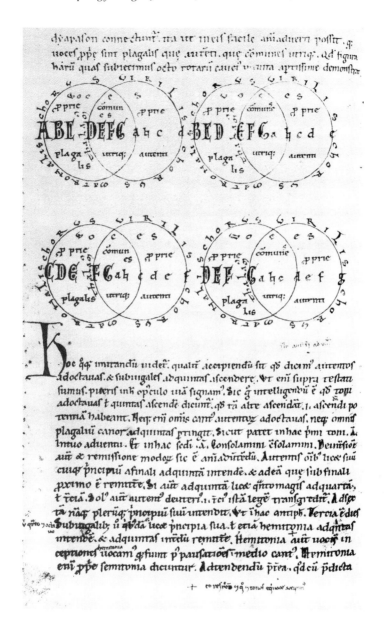

80 Charts of modal structures from the treatise of John of Affligem. Leipzig, University Library 79, fol. 103ᵛ, early 12th c.

interrogate, systematize and tidy the Gregorian heritage. This is what one might expect from men so confident they could improve on Merovingian and even Carolingian Latin, and in some respects so interested in the minor scientific enlightenment around 1000 (Pl. 80).

Yet it is tempting to suppose the new compositional styles were also influenced by changes in the duties of singers, specifically by a manner of performance consolidated at about the time when signs of the new styles arise with composers such as Stephen of Liège. Simply speaking, the change involves the replacement of solo psalmody by choral. As late as the first half of the ninth century, Aurelian and Amalarius still know a tradition of solo psalmody, but by approximately 900 the choral form seems to have been the prevailing type. Large numbers of singers who had not participated hitherto in certain forms of psalmody, or not in such an extensive manner, were now required to sing. Without forsaking artistic ambition, the new styles provided rank-and-file singers with chants of a sharp modal focus, an aid to both memorization and performance. Modal coherence of this high degree also means the final of the chant and the fifth above appear so insistently that the notes of the melody begin to be filtered as if by a drone – somewhere within the inner ear, perhaps, *there is a drone* – giving every note in the chant a new explicitness of meaning, relative to a few emphatic points of reference. This happens as the final and fifth above seem to dissolve into the drone as consonances, while other notes, notably those which lie a tone below the final or a tone below the upper fifth, acquire meaning as quasi-appoggiaturas. Hermannus of Reichenau has spelled such a moment out in Example 6 at *WolfGANgi* in stave 2, marking the saint's name with a doubling (and therefore a prolongation) of the *g* before it 'resolves' upwards into what we are calling the implied *D–a* drone. When such chants were produced in sets for Matins that worked through the modes in order, rank-and-file singers received a complete practical education in the contemporary structures of musical thought.[9]

Composers and a Courtly Style

The antiphons and responsories of a composer like Hermannus may seem very distant from anything that might be called an art of courtly lyric, a term so often associated today with secular households, poetry in a vernacular language and the casuistries of refined love. Yet the first medieval author to identify a quality of *curialitas* or 'courtliness' in music, writing around 1100, sees no reason to give the novice composer any other models of excellence than liturgical plainsong, and he locates the essence of a courtly manner in details of melodic behaviour perceived and assessed in modal terms. In short, everything needed for a courtly musical style in Latin song was already available in the eleventh century. What was needed for a courtly style to emerge was a new kind of individual.

A search for the rise of the courtly composer might well begin with one of the best-documented musicians of all, namely Bruno of Toul, later Pope Leo IX (1049–54):

> There was in Bruno such an astonishing and such a noble elegance of character that, together with his amazing physical beauty, each of his actions pleased

Ex. 6 *Gaudeat tota*, Magnificat antiphon from First Vespers of the Office of Saint Wolfgang, composed by Hermannus, monk of Reichenau, probably not long before 1052. Bayerische Staatsbibliothek, clm 14872. From Hiley, 'Style and Structure', p. 158.

the hearts of all . . . He was a brilliant exponent of divine and human sciences, and above all he had an agreeable talent for musical art; not only did he equal the achievements of some of the ancient masters, but he excelled them for his knowledge of a sweet accord. He composed responsories for the veneration of Saint Cyriacus, Saint Hildulfus, archbishop of Trier, for the blessed virgin Odila, and for the venerable Gregory, doctor and Apostle of the English. He enlarged the divine service with admirable musical adornments.

These are the works of a devout churchman and an able administrator, yet there is something more, for Bruno emerges from his biography as an accomplished courtier. The son of noble parents from Lotharingia, he received an education 'in letters and in all the virtues fitting for young nobles' in the cathedral school at Toul. Eventually, his parents obtained a place for him in the household of the Holy Roman Emperor Conrad, with a view to having him enter the imperial chapel. His words pleased the hearts of all and there was a wondrous and noble elegance in his manners; he was graced with 'amazing physical beauty'.[10]

Bruno is not the only important ecclesiastical figure of the eleventh-century Empire praised for the 'elegance of his manners', *morum elegantia*. The expression becomes increasingly common in the period 950 to 1100 together with formulations as such as *gratia morum*, 'grace of manners'. Notker, a chaplain of Otto III, was 'very distinguished for the elegance of his manners', while Otto, bishop of Bamberg, so impressed the Poles on his missionary journeys to the east that 'they marvelled at the elegance of his manners'. Bernward of Hildesheim 'was sought after by several lords who admired his *morum gratia*', while Meinwerk of Paderborn 'was judged worthy of service at the royal court because of his *morum elegantia*'. From approximately 950 onwards, the cathedral schools that trained these men begin to appear in profusion. Hildesheim was a reputed centre by 954 and Trier by 956; within a few years Worms, Liège, Mainz, Speyer, Bamberg and Regensburg 'come to life', together with Würzburg and Cologne. In these schools 'the goal was not knowledge for its own sake or knowledge for the glory and worship of God, but rather knowledge to be applied in the practical duties of running the empire . . . it was instruction that turned gifted young men into trained administrators and loyal supporters of the emperor . . . [and it] originated at court, in the chapel'.[11]

This context accords remarkably well with the earliest-known manual for the aspiring composer of Latin song, which forms chapter 18 in a wide-ranging treatise on music by an author who gives his name as John. Little else can be said of him save that he probably wrote around 1100 and dedicated his book to an Abbot or Bishop Fulgentius (see further below, p. 468). Yet for all these uncertainties, John's treatise reveals for the first time what 'courtliness' or *curialitas* entailed among composers eager to please (for that is the first duty of courtly behaviour) and just as determined to be praised. If John's treatise does indeed date from *c*.1100, as commonly supposed, then he is very up to date indeed when he speaks of *curialitas* or courtliness. The term *curialitas* in a context implying the sense 'courtliness' cannot be found before 1080, when a chronicle of the church at Hildesheim refers with marked disapproval to the *ambitiosa curialitas* or 'ambitious courtliness' of clerics in the diocese. This is fragile evidence, but it agrees remarkably well with the proposed date of John's treatise. What is more, there is widespread agreement that whoever John was, he came from Germany, perhaps from somewhere between Bamberg and the Alpine monastery of Sankt Gallen (John expects his readers to know the proper Office of Saint Gall by heart). The imperial milieu evoked by the Lives of the German bishops who were praised for their courtliness and for their *elegantia morum* would suit John very well, and might one day lead to a plausible identification of him.[12]

Although John's manual is addressed 'to boys and those not yet mature', his horizon for the ambitions of these young readers, as singers and composers, extends to an audience for new music that he never defines closely, although it includes the young and the old (ch. 18) and it forms a company with whom a composer can expect to have sustained and convivial relations. John anticipates that the members of this audience may sometimes request a composer to make a new composition for their enjoyment, and insofar as the tastes of that audience can be reconstructed from the material John encourages composers to provide in response, they are lofty. John begins his chapter on composition with an allusion to Horace's *Ars poetica*, recalling the interest in Classical poetry and prose that emerges in the details pertaining to several composers. Adso of Montier-en-Der supplied Adalbero, archbishop of Rheims, with a copy of an *istoriam Julii Caesaris*, perhaps the *Gallic War*, and Gerbert of Aurillac asked Constantine of Fleury, maker of chants for Saint Benedict, whether he had copies of the works of Cicero. Gerbert of Aurillac wrote to Remi of Mettlach asking for a copy of the *Achilleidos* of Statius. The tastes of the audience envisaged by John would certainly have encompassed settings of poetry by Statius, for John recommends composers to set 'the lamenting verses of the poets' (ch. 17) and this is an excellent description of material sometimes excerpted from Statius and set in sources of the eleventh and twelfth centuries. Lines from the lament of Hypsipyle in Statius's *Thebaid, Huc adtollite gentes* (xii. 322 ff.), form a cento excerpted as a free-standing lyric in the famous Cambridge Songs, a collection whose model was apparently compiled around 1050 in the lower Rhineland, and which may therefore be well placed to represent important elements of the song culture John knew. Two earlier manuscripts contain material from the same passage with neumes. John regards such plangent material as especially worthy of the composer's art, but he also anticipates festive contexts requiring music appropriate to pleasure or *lasciviae*. Once again, the Cambridge Songs collection may provide appropriate examples of Latin lyrics, some perhaps intended for chaplains or even precocious choirboys to make an impression with their performance of a lyric or narrative poem that is humorous (*ridiculum*) or tells a far-fetched story (*mendax*).[13]

When John alludes to the audience for song, he is presumably looking out-wards from the choir school to an abbot's lodgings, to an episcopal house, to the courts of temporal magnates and even perhaps to the imperial palace. It is sure-ly no coincidence that John shows himself exceptionally well aware, among the medieval music theorists, that untrained secular entertainers can achieve impres-sive results that are greatly appreciated, including minstrels (*joculatores, histriones*) and the leaders of dances performed to lyrics, the *chorearum praecentores*. There is a sense of court music here, and in all its varieties. Nonetheless, all the techni-cal information John provides, including the models for emulation, derives from the repertory of sacred chant that he knew, and he has no difficulty using the musical grammar of liturgical plainsong to help composers delight their hearers and win their praise in a courtly context. He readily accepts that a composer, a *compositor* or *modulator*, will be 'eager for praise'. To accomplish this, John advis-es the novice to fashion his material in a strategic way according to the tastes of the audience. Everything, in other words, is calculated for effect, as the elements of courtly arts usually are. So it is not surprising John has a large vocabulary for describing the gratifying effects of different modes. Listeners can be 'pleased' by their music, 'taken' with it, 'delighted', 'attracted', 'stirred' or 'melted' by melody. It is a delicate matter, John maintains, to please, for one can never please all. In an intriguing reference to his own performances, he says he once sang melodies to a group of people, 'and what one praised highly, another disliked profoundly' (ch. 16).[14]

Chapter 16 brings up courtliness by name. John evokes the various effects of the eight plainchant modes including the *curiales vagationes* or 'courtly wander-ings' of the first. Courtliness returns in chapter 18, where John briefly mentions some of the contexts a composer should anticipate for the performance of his melodies so he can choose modal material for them in the appropriate manner. Some modes, John remarks, are suitable when the prevailing mood is sad, and some for when it is joyous; other modes are apt for *curialitas*. What does John mean by this quality of courtliness or by the 'courtly wanderings' of mode 1? An answer is suggested by another and later treatise, heavily dependent upon John, namely the *Summa Musicae*. In one chapter, the author explains how certain mode 1 chants descend to their final 'in a courtly and gradual fashion', *curialiter et paulatim*. He gives the incipits of several chants illustrating the point, and in an ideal world one would be able to cite versions of these plainsongs in a manu-script from his own foundation, wherever that may be. For the time being, and perhaps forever, we have only the relevant plainsongs as they appear in an impor-tant scatter of noted service-books. The chants in these versions endorse the pro-posal that a mode 1 chant moves 'in a courtly and gradual fashion' because it descends to its final in a stepwise manner, never falling through any distance greater than a tone. The ends of a selection of these chants are shown in Example 7. Is this melodic motion 'courtly' because courtliness was assumed to require an appearance of calm restraint, and the concealment of abrupt or impatient

Ex. 7   Musical incipits of chants that descend to their final 'in a courtly and gradual fashion', *curialiter et paulatim,* according to the *Summa Musicae.* The chants are (a) *Circumdantes circumdederunt me,* (b) *Nisi ego abiero,* (c) *Reges Tharsis* and (d) *Volo pater,* all mode 1. From Page, *The Summa Musicae,* 29 (AS = *Antiphonale Sarisburiense,* ed. Frere; WA = *Antiphonaire monastique . . . de Worcester,* LA = *Antiphonaire monastique . . . de Lucques,* LU = *Liber Usualis*).

impulse? The courtly songs of the twelfth and thirteenth centuries are beginning to appear over the horizon, and many of the loftiest examples will show a keen appreciation of what John and the *Summa Musicae* identify as courtly style. Example 8 shows a relevant *grand chant* from the heart of the high-style trouvère tradition, by Gautier de Dargies.[15]

———〰———

In some respects, the men who made chant for singers between 900 and 1100 do not accord with most received ideas of 'the composer' since the seminal period in the late fifteenth century when the cult of the Master began. All were churchmen in the broad sense, being either monks or clerics living some form of collegiate life; they generally dwelled amongst the members of their audience, so to speak, and did not often have to seek them out or entice them (although John hints at a much broader horizon). All were regarded as men whose musical talent was but one star in a large constellation of other aptitudes, perhaps for learning of a decidedly scientific cast, by the standards of the age, and certainly including the ability to write accomplished metrical poetry and prose. The composer of this period was not a musical journeyman working for an ecclesiastical institution and forming part of a musical establishment the higher clergy might feel they had cause to mistrust, nor was he a 'catch' some particular centre had made an effort to attract for musical services alone. He was, however, a polymath, and often a politician.

Ex. 8   Gautier de Dargies, *Cant li tans pert sa choulour* (with *G* 'final'). From the Chansonnier d'Arras (Arras, Bibliothèque municipale, MS 657), fol. 156. Northern French, 13th c.

APPENDIX TO CHAPTER 19

CONSPECTUS OF NARRATIVE LITERARY SOURCES CONCERNING SOME LESSER-KNOWN COMPOSERS OF 900–1100

This list was prepared independently of Kelly's inventory in *Musica e storia*, 14 (2006), 95–125 and differs substantially from it. The list given here is based in the great majority of cases upon editions of primary sources (which are quoted in the entries), for it was principally compiled by searching the electronic databases of PL, MGH and *AS* for key terms such as 'edidit' or locutions such as 'cantum fecit'. To these results were added extra material accumulated over the years in other, less systematic, ways. The present list, covering just two centuries, has a narrower chronological range than Kelly's, which extends to the beginning of the sixteenth century.

For the period under consideration, this list adds twenty-four names to Kelly's inventory. They are Adso, abbot of Montier-en-Der; Alberic, monk of Montecassino (questionable case); Balther of Säckingen; Constantine of Fleury; Drogon of Bergues; Eberwin, abbot of St Martin Trier (a questionable case); Gerard of Corbie; Gerard, bishop of Toul; German, abbot of Bergues; Guido, bishop of Auxerre; Guitmund, monk of St-Évroul; Heribert, bishop of Eichstätt; John, abbot of St-Arnulph, Metz; Leo of Ostia; Odo, monk of St-Maur-des-Fossés; Osbern, monk of St Augustine's, Canterbury; Otloh, monk of St Emmeram; Paulus Judeus, monk of Fulda; Reginald Calvus, monk of St-Évroul; Roger of le Sap, abbot of St-Évroul; Sigo II, precentor of Chartres (questionable case); Stephen, abbot of St James, Liège; and Waiferius, monk of Montecassino.

For the most part this list omits composers who have been extensively studied elsewhere, such as Hucbald, Hermannus Contractus, Tuotilo and Notker, all of whom are represented in Kelly's list. If such composers figure appreciably in this book, however, they are included. There are as yet very few editions of the chants of these composers in those instances where they have been traced in a decipherable notation. Where such editions exist, they are listed.

Abbo, monk of Fleury (d. 1004)

'De sancto Stephano sequentiam unam ac responsoria': *Index Britanniae Scriptorum: John Bale's Index of British and Other Writers*, ed. Poole and Bateson, 1. See also Aimon of Fleury, *Vita Abbonis*, 390.

Adso, abbot of Montier-en-Der (d. after 985)

'Opuscula praeterea plura versifice composuit, hymnorum etiam aliquanta cantica, Ambrosianos hymnos elucidans glossulis . . .': *Miracula S. Bercharii* (*BHL* 1179); *AS* Octobris VII, 1022.

See also Adso, *De Ortu et Tempore Antichristi*, ed. Verhelst (with Adso's own catalogue of his books before his departure on a pilgrimage to Jerusalem) and Gerbert d'Aurillac, *Correspondance*, ed. Riché and Callu, Letters 8 (983) and 81 (986). For possible links between Adso, the cantor-chronicler Richer, and Abbo of Fleury, see Glenn, *Politics and History in the Tenth Century*, 274–5.

Ainard, first abbot of St-Pierre-sur-Dives (1046–c.1078)

'Hic fuit natione Teutonicus, geminaque scientia pleniter imbutus, uersificandi et modulandi cantusque suaues edendi peritissimus. Hoc euidenter probari potest in historiis Kiliani Guirciburgensis episcopi, et Katerinae uirginis aliisque plurimis cantibus quos elganter idem edidit in laudem Creatoris': Orderic Vitalis, *The Ecclesiastical History*, ed. and trans. Chibnall, ii. 352–5.

Orderic Vitalis (iv. 296–9) lists Ainard with two other abbots (Gerbert of St-Wandrille and Durand of Troarn) who 'stood out among the most skilled singers trained in the art of music for their ability to sing (?compose) sweetly' ('Inter praecipuos cantores scientia musicae artis ad modulandum suauiter potiti sunt, et dulcisonos cantus antiphonarum atque responsoriorum ediderunt. De summo Rege quem laudant cherubin et seraphim et omnis militia coelorum, de intacta uirgine Maria quae nobis peperit saluatorem saeculorum, de angelis et apostolis ac martiribus, de confessoribus ac uirginibus, mellifluas laudes ex dulcissimo corde manantes prompsuerunt, et Aecclesiae pueris ad concinendum Domino cum Asaph et Eman, et Aethan et Idithun et filiis Chore fideliter tradiderunt.'

Alberic, monk of Montecassino (fl. 1089)

Peter the Deacon, *Liber de viris illustribus Cassinensibus*, 1033, reports that Albericus composed 'in musica Dialogum' and 'hymnos in sancti Nicolai', among others. See also Alberic, *De Rithmis*, ed. Davis.

Rome, Biblioteca Apostolica Vaticana, lat. 3797 ('V' in Damian scholarship) is the richest and most complete of the eleventh-century manuscripts of the works of Peter Damian. The most recent inventory, although cursory, is in *Sermones*, ed. Lucchesi, pp. xiii–xvii; see also Lucchesi, 'Sull'antica tradizione manoscritta di S. Pier Damiani', placing V in 'la tradizione avellanese'. The poetry begins on fol. 359 and extends to fol. 361ᵛ, mostly the epigrammatic verse for which Damian was well known, and the longer pieces in hexameters and elegaic couplets. A second series occupies fols. 361ᵛ–366ᵛ, mostly *hymni* and *rithmi*. These have no music, but at fol. 372 the first verses of a great number of these poems appear. Many are in the same order as the full version (along with some poems not represented in the previous folios), with neumes that are – I suspect – on dry-point lines with F- and c-clefs. There is an inventory of the hymns in Blum,

'Alberic of Monte Cassino and the Hymns and Rhythms Attributed to Saint Peter Damian', where it is argued that an important number of these hymns are the work of Alberic of Montecassino. Lucchesi, in his edition of the *Sermones*, p. xvii, apparently regards all the hymns, and their musical settings, as Damian's, since he does not place the beginning of the 'scripta non damianaea' until fol. 375ᵛ. For additional works on syllabic quantity and other matters of grammar in the widest sense, recently attributed to Alberic, see Gibson and Newton, 'Pandulf of Capua's *De Calculatione*'. See also Boynton, 'Orality, Literacy and the Early Notation of the Office Hymns', 122–4.

Alfanus, physician and monk of Montecassino, later archbishop of Salerno (1058–85)

Peter the Deacon, *Liber de viris illustribus Cassinensibus*, 1030, credits Alfanus with a 'cantus S. Sabinae' in addition to numerous hymns. This is a full Office, edited Lentini and Avagliano in *I carmi di Alfano I, Arcivescovo di Salerno*. *AH* 22: 188–9 prints a poem of his from Cod. Cass. 280 noting the neumes, of which there is a facsimile in Lentini and Avagliano. The notation, unheighted neumes, appears to have been added later and not originally envisaged.

Angelrann, abbot of St-Riquier (d. 1045)

'Angelrannus venerabilis inter suae magnae sapientiae monumenta in sancti Richarii honore, quamvis antiqui abundaret, quosdam cantus dulciori composuit melodia necnon sanctorum Gualarici abbatis, et Wlfranni archiepiscopi honori proprios cantus coaptavit; beati quoque Vincentii martyris passionem metrice composuit, sanctaeque virginis Austrebertae vitam metro subegit': Hariulf: *Chronique de l'abbaye de Saint-Riquier*, ed. Lot, Bk IV, xi.

Arnold of Vohburg, prior of St Emmeram (d. before 1050)

Prefatory letter to the *Vita Sancti Emmerami* (*BHL* 2541). The Office, with context and details of sources, is edited in *Historia Sancti Emmerammi Arnoldi Vohburgensis circa 1030*, ed. Hiley.

Arnulf, precentor of Chartres (11th c.)

Reported as a pupil of Fulbert and as the composer of an Office for Saint Évroul, according to the secular cursus, at the request of Abbot Robert of St-Évroul. Two monks from the abbey were sent to Chartres to learn it. Guitmund, monk of St-Évroul (q.v.) composed the extra material necessary for the monastic cursus. Orderic Vitalis, *The Ecclesiastical History*, ed. Chibnall, ii. 108–9.

Balther of Säckingen, monk of St Fridolin (fl. c.1000)

'iste presens libellus una cum cantilena responsoriorum que per musicam artem in festivitate sancti Fridolini canenda composui . . .': prefatory letter to Notker, in his *Vita Fridolini*, 354–5. Koch, *Sankt Fridolin und sein Biograph Balther*, contains a new edition of the prefatory material at 28–31 using a fragmentary source not known to the MGH editor.

Bruno of Toul, afterwards Pope Leo IX (d. 1054)

'Sapientia divinarum humanarumque artium in eo refulgebat amplissima maximeque delectabilis musicae artis peritia, qua antiquis auctoribus non modo aequiperari poterat, imo in mellica dulcedine nonnullos eorum praecellebat. Nam componens responsoria in veneratione gloriosi Cyriaci martiris sanctique Hildulphi Trevirorum archipraesulis, nec-non beatae Odilae virginis atque venerandi Anglorum apostoli Gregorii doctoris divini laudes servitii mirifico decore ampliavit': *Vita Leonis* (*BHL* 4818), in *La Vie du pape Léon IX*, ed. Parisse and Goullet, 54.

    See also Sigebert of Gembloux, *Catalogus . . . De Viris illustribus*, ed. Witte, 93–5; id., *Chronica cum Continuationibus*, 359; Helinand of Froidmont, *Chronicon* (PL 212: 941), following Sigebert, *Catalogus verbatim*; Anonymous of Melk, ed. Ettlinger, no. LXXXV; Richer, *Gesta Senoniensis Ecclesiae*, 280. His epitaph is in Bernard, 'Les Offices versifiés attribués a Léon IX (1002–1054)', 91. See also Kartsovnik, 'The Eleventh-Century Office for St. Gregory the Great', and Hiley, 'The English Benedictine Version of the *Historia Sancti Gregorii*'.

Constantine of Fleury, abbot of St-Mesmin-de-Micy, then abbot of Nouaillé (d. 1014)

'His etenim diebus, historia patris Benedicti adventus, quam Constantinus, illius loci nutritus, atque abbatie Miciacensis honore ab Arnulfo, Aurelianensium presule donatus, musice artis dictaverat pneumatibus, suasu Helgaudi precentoris permissuque Gauzlini abbatis, Floriacensi loco primo insonuit': Andreas of Fleury, *Vita Gauzlini*, ed. Bautier and Labory, 38.

    See also Gerbert d'Aurillac, *Correspondance*, ed. Riché and Callu, Letters 86 (986), 92 (987), 139 (988), 143 (988), 191 (994), and also the 'scientific letters' in Annexe 5: 1–6. For an anonymous poem in praise of Constantine, see Dümmler, 'Gedichte aus Frankrich'.

Desiderius, abbot of Montecassino, later Pope Victor II (d. 1057)

'Cantum etiam B. Mauri composuit, in quibus qui vult artis grammaticae tramitem, et monochordi sonori Magade reperiet notas': Peter the Deacon, *Liber de Viris illustribus Cassinensibus*, 1028–9.

Drogon of Bergues (c.1030–84)

Goudesenne, *Les Offices historiques*, 102, 247–9.

Durand, abbot of Troarn (1059–88)

Orderic Vitalis, *The Ecclesiastical History*, ed. Chibnall, ii. 296–9: see above under Ainard.

?Eberwin, abbot of St Martin, Trier (fl. c.1000)

See caption to Pl. 75. Eberwin, *Life of St Magneric*, AS Julii VI, 183–92, PL 154: 1243–4.

Folcard de St-Bertin (fl. 1068–84)

'et sancti Oswaldi Guigornensis episcopi aliorumque sanctorum quorum propage de Albione processit, delectabiles ad canendum historias suauiter composuit': Orderic Vitalis, *The Ecclesiastical History*, ed. Chibnall, vi. 150.

Gerard of Corbie, founder and abbot of La Sauve-Majeure (d. 1095)

'Exaltando etiam taliter, magnificavit vitam ipsius, [Adelhardus] apostrophis elegiacis et superfluitate sui offendentem animos legentium. Extirpari [enim] fecit ex ipsa sentes superfluitatum et plane reductam ad florem historiae mysticae, hexametro decoravit festivitatis. Parum quid fiebat memoriae; sed compositis Antiphonis et Responsoriis, alta et digna fecit venerari celebritate; nec absque plurimorum invidia . . .': *Vita Geraldi*, 417.

Gerard, bishop of Toul (963–94)

'Opuscula praeterea plura versifice composuit, hymnorum etiam aliquanta cantica, Ambrosianos hymnos elucidans glossulis': Widricus, *Vita S. Gerardi Episcopi*, 488, where the information is verbatim the same as reported of Adso.

Gerbert, abbot of St-Wandrille (1062–89)

Orderic Vitalis, *The Ecclesiastical History*, ed. Chibnall, ii. 296–9: see above under Ainard.

German, abbot of Bergues-St-Winnoc (1027–41)

'Hic est qui composuit multas sequentias sive responsoria, quibus Romana utitur ecclesia, nimirum prosam de Spiritu sancto *Adsit nobis gratia*, responsoria de Nativitate

Domini *Judea et Jerusalem*: de Sancto Petro, *Cornelius Centurio*; de sanctis martyribus, *Concede nobis* et *O constantia martyrum*': *Chronique et cartulaire de l'abbaye de Bergues-St-Winnoc*, ed. Pruvost, i. 36–7.

Goscelin of St-Bertin

For narrative and musical sources see Sharpe, 'Words and Music by Goscelin of Canterbury'.

Gottschalk of Limburg, imperial chaplain (by 1099)

Dreves, *Godescalcus Lintpurgensis: Gottschalk, mönch vom Limburg*, 25–43. McGrade, 'Gottschalk of Aachen, the Investiture Controversy, and Music for the Feast of the *Divisio Apostolorum*'.

Guido, bishop of Auxerre (d. 961)

'Nam inter cetera honestatis opera, dictatu proprie manus edidit responsoria cum antiphonis, canenda in sollempnitate sancti martyris Iuliani, instar tamen armonie habentia melodiam Germani gloriosi, ob hoc precipue quod isdem pontifex sanctissimus, sicut in gestis ipsius inuenitur, predicti martyris sollempnis natalicii diem uniuersis incognitum, Domino sibi reuelante, ostenderit celebrandum . . .': *De Gestis Episcoporum Autissiodorum*, ed. Bonnerue et al., 231.

Guitmund, monk of St-Évroul (fl. c.1066)

'grammaticae artis et musicae peritissimus erat; quod nobis adhuc testantur antiphonae et responsoria quae ipse condiderat. Plures enim dulcisonas cantus in trophario et antiphonario edidit. Hic hystoriam sancti patris Ebrulfi additis ix antiphonis et tribus responsoriis perfecit. Nam ad uesperas super psalmos quatuor antiphonas condidit, et in secundo nocturno tres ultimas adiecit; quartum etiam responsorium et octauum et duodecimum et antiphonam ad cantica et ad secundas uesperas ad canticum de Euangelio pulcherrimum antiphonam edidit. Ipsam nimirum hystoriam Arnulfus cantor Carnotensis Fulberti episcopi discipulus secundum usum clericorum rogatu Rodberti abbatis iam ediderat, et duobus iuuenibus monachis Huberto et Rodulfo a praedicto patre Carnotum missis primitus cantauerat': Orderic Vitalis, *The Ecclesiastical History*, ed. Chibnall, ii. 108–9.

Magister Henricus (fl. c.1080)

Teacher of Gottschalk of Limburg, and mentioned by him as composer of the respond *Omnis lapis pretiosus*: Dreves, *Godescalcus Lintpurgensis*.

Heribert, bishop of Eichstätt (1022–42)

'His tam cito sublatis, denuo nobilitati cessit cura pastoralis. Heribertus namque, nobilis genere, nobilior moribus, vir eleganter literatus, sancti illius Heriberti Coloniensis archiepiscopi cognatus et aequivocus, divina favente gratia factus est episcopus. Hic Herbipoli nutritus, edoctus, egregia dictandi dulcedine in tantum enituit, ut tunc temporis hac in arte nulli secundus fuerit. Hic Spiritu sancto efflatus, sex ymnos pulcherrimos composuit, unum de sancta cruce: *Salve crux sancta*; alterum de sancto Willibaldo: *Mare, fons, hostium*; tertium de sancta Walpurga: *Ave flos virginum*; quartum de sancti Stephani inventione: *Deus deorum Domine*; quintum de sancto Laurentio: *Conscendat usque sydera*; sextum de omnibus sanctis: *Omnes superni ordines*. De sancta Maria vero fecit quinque intimas orationes, quarum omnium commune initium est: *Ave Maria gratia plena*. Fecit etiam duas has initiatas [?]modulationes: *Advertite, omnes populi* et *Peccatores, peccatrices quandam*': *Anonymus Haserensis de Episcopis Eichstetensibus*, 261.

See also Boynton, 'Orality, Literacy and the Early Notation of the Office Hymns', 121.

Heriger, abbot of Lobbes (990–1007)

'In honore etiam eius duas antiphonas scilicet *O Thome Didime* et *O Thome apostole* composuisse dicitur, et hymnum de sancta Maria virgine: *Ave per quam*, et quaedam alia': *Gesta Abbatum Lobbiensium*, 309.

?Isembert, first abbot of Ste-Catherine-du-Mont (1033–54)

Orderic Vitalis, *The Ecclesiastical History*, ed. Chibnall, ii. 298 n. 1; see above under Ainard.

John, abbot of St-Arnulph, Metz (d. c.977)

'Hic denique piae memoriae Johannes inter perplura quae intra gymnasium Sophiae peregit exercitia, responsoria beatae virginis et martyris Luciae authentica modulatione composuit, nec non et beatae Glodesindis vitam cum officio nocturnali': *De Fundatione sancti Arnulphi Metensis*, 196.

John, monk and scholasticus of St Matthias, Trier (d. 1047)

'Erat autem in omni genere scientiarum doctissimus, sed in Musica praecipua eruditione singularis, qui ad honorem Omnipotentis Dei et Sanctorum ejus multos Cantus et prosas composuit, ac regulari melodia dulciter ornavit': Johannes Trithemius, *Annalium Hirsaugensium*, 184.

For the proposal that this John mentioned by Trithemius (d. 1516) may be Johannes 'of Affligem', see Malcolm, 'Epistola Johannis ad Fulgentium Episcopum'. The argument is unconvincing since it requires one to assume this John knew of Guido's notation almost as soon as it was invented, which is not impossible, but unlikely.

Lambert, second abbot of St Lawrence, Liège (d. 1070)

'Quin etiam musice quaedam de ipso [Herbertus] composuit, in versibus quoque faciendis claro fretus ingenio': Reiner of St Lawrence, *De claris Scriptoribus Monasterii sui*, 17. Rupertus, *Chronicon Sancti Laurentii Leodiensis*, 275, is textually virtually identical. Herbertus is Saint Heribert of Cologne.

Leo of Ostia, monk of Montecassino (end of 11th c.)

'Ut autem fideles quique populi, ad eius convenientes sollemnia, haberent unde se eadem die in eius laudibus festivius exercerent, non illa tantum que luculentissimo tanti presulis stilo digesta fuerant, congestis undecumque sententiis competentibus ampliari et spatiari poposcerat, sed et cantus insuper aliquot et laudum suavium melodias rogaverat valde devotus inde componi': Leo of Ostia, 'Vita Sancti Mennatis', ed. Orlandi.

Letald, monk of Fleury, abbot of St-Mesmin-de-Micy (fl. c.1000)

'Sane responsoriorum et antiphonarum, ut petistis, digessimus ordinem; in quibus pro vitando fastidio de unoquoque modo singula compegimus corpora: neque omnino alienari volumus a similitudine veteris cantus, ne barbaram aut inexpertam, uti perhibetur, melodiam fingeremus. Non enim mihi placet quorumdam musicorum novitas, qui tanta dissimilitudine utuntur, ut veteres sequi omnino dedignentur auctores: nam hi qui conjugiis vacant, malunt liberos hominibus similes gignere, quam alicujus invisi monstri effigiem procreare': Letald, *Vita Sancti Juliani*, 784.

 See also Hiley, 'The Historia of Julian of Le Mans by Létald of Micy'; Head, 'Letaldus of Micy and the Hagiographic Traditions of Selles-sur-Cher'.

Odo, first abbot of Cluny (879–942)

'maxime componendis in honore sanctorum cantibus elegans ingenium habuit.': Sigebert of Gembloux, *Catalogus . . . De Viris illustribus*, ed. Witte, 86.

'Tres vero hymnos in ejus laude [sc. Saint Martin] composuit, e quibus unius tantum exemplar inserere huic operi adjudicavi. *Rex Christe, Martini decus; / Hic laus tua tu illius; / Tu nos in hunc te colere / Quin ipsum in te tribue*. Similiter duodecim antiphonas ternas per singulas habentes differentias, quarum verba et vocum consonantia adeo sibi invicem concordant, ut nihil in sensum plusminusve, nihil in symphoniae modulationibus reperiri dulcius posse videatur. Retinentur hactenus Beneventi': *Vita Sancti Odonis*, 48.

 Dom P. Thomas, 'Saint Odon de Cluny et son oeuvre musicale'.

Odo, monk of St-Maur-des-Fossés (11th c.)

During Matins for Saint Babolenus, after the twelfth lesson, four brothers are singing the responsory *Sanctus Domini Confessor* 'in jubilo vocis cum organo'. The precentor

Hilduard leaps into their midst and begins the responsory *Ecce vera Israelita*, but cannot prevail; he admits defeat, declaring that he will never have the *adinventiones* of Odo sung in the church again, for Odo was 'auctor huius operis'. This is one of only two references to polyphony (see Sigo II) unless one counts Gerbert's reference to Constantine's skill in 'his quae fiunt ex organis'. *Miracula Sancti Baboleni Abbatis Fossatensis*, 183. See Huglo, 'Du répons de l'Office avec prosule au répons organisé'.

?Odorann of Sens, monk of St-Pierre-le-Vif (d. c.1046)

Various works in his autograph manuscript, Biblioteca Apostolica Vaticana, Reg. lat. 577; see *Odorannus de Sens: Opera omnia*, ed. Bautier et al. (Paris, 1972), including two copies which derive from it. For items of music theory in the manuscript, including chants in letter notations, see the inventory on pp. 30–1 and pl. II–IV. An Office for Saint Savinianus appears on fols. 91^v–94^r, with staves, but added later, probably s. xii. (NB: there are works apparently by Odorann in the MS which are not in his hand; see Bautier, 258–63.) The Office is edited in Villetard, *Office de Saint Savinien et de Saint Potentien*. Odorann was a skilled metalworker and made a reliquary for Saint Savinianus. It is possible that these chants are a later transcription on a stave of compositions by him.

Olbert, abbot of Gembloux (d. 1048)

'Olbertus, ex monacho Lobiensi abbas Gemblacensis, humane et ecclesiastice scientie studio et religionis fervore insignis, nomen suum eternavit vitas sanctorum scribendo, cantus in honore sanctorum componendo . . .': Sigebert of Gembloux, *Catalogus . . . De Viris illustribus*, ed. Witte, 92.

'Sed et in hoc in aecclesiis Dei ejus laudabilis memoria adhuc vivit, quod vitas aliquorum sanctorum aliquibus in locis liquide et polite composuit, et de gestis eorum in laude Dei secundum regulam musicae disciplinae, in qua multum valebat, dulcissime cantus modificavit. Inter quae quia Raginero comite vitam sancti Veronis confessoris composuit, cantum etiam de eo melificavit, antiphonas quoque super matutinales laudes in transitu Sanctae Waldetrudis, ipse comes Raginerus et Hathuidis conjunx ejus quicquid praedii habebant in Dion aecclesiae nostrae tradidit': Sigebert of Gembloux, *Gesta abbatum Gemblacensium*, 625–6.

Osbern, monk of St Augustine's, Canterbury (d. ?1094)

'Illius itaque freti auxilio, cujus gratuita bonitate sumus quidquid bene sumus; cujus largiflua miseratione sapimus quidquid bene sapimus; tangamus psalterium, tangamus & citharam: ut in altero sempiternam Martyris gloriam exultando prædicemus, in altero corporales ejus passiones imitando veneremur. Ac quemadmodum præcipiente invictissimo totius latinitatis magistro a Lanfranco Archiepiscopo, musica virum modulatione dudum extulimus: sic cogentibus his quas diximus rationum causis, oratoria eumdem narratione extollamus': Osbern, *Life of Ælfheah*, 631.

'Quod ipse [Lanfrancus] postmodum devote exsecutus est, quin et historiam Vitae ac passionis ejus [Aelfegi] diligenti studio fieri praecepit. Quam quidem historiam non solum plano dictamine ad legendum verum etiam musico modulamine ad canendum a jocundae memoriae Osberno Cantuariensis ecclesiae monacho ad praeceptum illius nobiliter editam, ipse sua prudentia pro amore martyris celsius insignivit, insignitam autorizavit, auctorizatam in ecclesia Dei legi cantarique instituit, nomenque martyris hac in parte non parum glorificavit': Eadmer, *De Vita et Conversatione Anselmi Archiepiscopi Cantuariensis*, in *Eadmeri Historia Novorum in Anglia*, ed. Rule, 352–3.

'Cantuariae cantor Osbernus, qui eius uitam [sc. Dunstani] Romana elegantia composuit, nulli nostro tempore stilo secundus, musica certe omnium sine controuersia primus': William of Malmesbury, *Gesta Regum Anglorum*, ed. and trans. Mynors, Thomson and Winterbottom, i. 240.

On the evidence that Osbern was a theorist, and for an edition of a treatise that may be by him, see *Osbern(?): De Musica*, ed. Smits van Waesberghe, 59–65 *et passim*.

Otloh, monk of St Emmeram (d. c.1070)

Vita of Saint Alto 'una cum quibusdam carminibus ad eundem sanctum pertinentibus': *Liber de temptatione cuiusdam monachi*, 336. 'He may be the author of a Kyrie trope' according to Hiley, *Western Plainchant*, 471.

Otloh is the partner in the dialogue in William of Hirsau's *Musica*, ed. Harbison. He also appears as the partner of William of Hirsau in another dialogue, a treatise on astronomy. He also compiled a *Vita* of St Magnus of Füssen (*BHL* 5163) 'compulsus fratrum duorum precibus intimis et assiduis', one of whom was William of Hirsau.

Otloh was an indefatigable scribe (*Liber de temptatione*, 354–61) who copied 'uno minus xx libros missales' plus other books, and his hand appears in two books of music theory: Munich clm 14523 (which includes all Guido's writings) and 18937; see Huglo and Meyer, *Manuscripts from the Carolingian Era up to c.1500*, 113–16 and 139–41, and Meyer, *Manuscripts from the Carolingian Era . . . Addenda, Corrigenda*, 335–6 and 345.

Paulus Judeus, monk of Fulda (11th c.)

'Paulus Iudaeus, Fuldensis monachus, Vitam sancti Herhardi Ratisponnensis episcopi, sed et de conversione sancti Pauli apostoli composuit prosam, cuius hoc est exordium: Dixit Dominus: Ex Basan convertam': Anonymous of Melk, ed. Ettlinger, 77.

Peter Damian, monk of Fonte Avellana, later cardinal (d. 1072)

See Alberic of Montecassino.

Radbod, bishop of Utrecht (901–18)

For his antiphon *Ecce leti*, see Pl. 79.

'habes in his ad integrum a se compositis quae diei noctisque sufficiunt officiis sanct-issimi confessoris Martini, qui gemma sacerdotum est, in solemnitate translationis cele-brandis. Quem etiam sibi prae ceteris specialem elegit patronum . . .': *Vita Radboti*, 14. Edition of Office for the translation of St Martin in MGH, *Poetae Latinii Aevi Carolini*, iv:1, 163–5b.

Lochner, 'Un Évêque musicien au Xᵉ siècle: Radbod d'Utrecht', transcribes chants from Utrecht, Bibliotheek der Rijksuniversiteit MS 406 (3.J.7), Antiphoner, s. xii, a com-posite manuscript. Facsimile edition in *Utrecht, Bibliotheek der Rijksuniversiteit MS 406 (3.J.7)*.

Reginald Calvus, monk of St-Évroul (fl. c.1066)

'Porro Rainaldus Caluus responsorium ad laudem Domini quod ad uesperas canitur, et vii antiphonas edidit quae in Vticensibus antiphonariis scriptae reperiuntur': Orderic Vitalis, *The Ecclesiastical History*, ed. Chibnall, ii. 108–9 (following on directly from the passage quoted above under 'Guitmund').

Reginold, bishop of Eichstätt (966–91)

'Post hoc venerabiles patres Reginoldus episcopus factus est, carnali quidem nobilis prosapia, sed nobilior scientia; litteris non solum Latinis et Grecis, sed etiam Hebreis imbutus, et quod unicum et singulare in eo fuit, optimus huius temporis musicus. Hic inprimis historiam sancti Nicolai fecit, et per hoc episcopalem dignitatem promeruit. Accepto autem episcopatu, summo studio summaque devotione historia de sancto Willibaldo carmina conposuit, totamque scientiae suae vim in his decorandis atque mirabiliter variandis excitavit. Hinc est enim, quod quibusdam responsoriis longissimis in fine notulas apposuit, eisdemque notulis versiculis instar sequentiarum subiunxit': *Anonymus Haserensis de episcopis Eichstetensibus*, 257.

See also Jones, *The Saint Nicholas Liturgy and its Literary Relationships*.

Remi, abbot of Mettlach (10th c.)

'Jubente Trevirorum Archiepiscopo Eckberto, cantum de sancti Eucharia, Valerio et Materno, primis Trevirorum episcopis, dulci et regulari modulatione composuit. Duobus etiam monachis ex Gandavo coenobii Blandiniensis ordinis nostri discipulis suis rogan-tibus, cum ex Mediolacu ad sua jam essent reversuri, de sancto Bavone cantum compo-suit nocturnalem . . . Litanias et cantilenas que in rogationibus frequentatur ipse com-posuit': Trithemius, *Annalium Hirsaugensium*, i. 122.

See also Gerbert d'Aurillac, *Correspondance*, ed. Riché and Callu, Letters 134 (988), 48 (988 or beginning of 989), 152 (989), 162 (989) and 169.

Roger of le Sap, abbot of St-Évroul (1091–1123)

'Hymnos quoque plures de eodem patre [sc. Saint Évroul] Rogerius de Sappo aliique studiosi fratres ex deuotione pia dictauerunt, suisque posteris in bibliotheca Vticensi commendauerunt': Orderic Vitalis, *The Ecclesiastical History*, ed. Chibnall, ii. 109 (following on directly from the passage quoted above under 'Reginald Calvus').

Sigebert, monk, then abbot of Gembloux (d. 1112)

'Arte autem musica antiphonas et responsoria de sanctis Maclovo et Guiberto melificavi': Sigebert of Gembloux, *Catalogus . . . De Viris illustribus*, ed. Witte, 104. See also his *Vita Guicberti*.

Sigo I, schoolmaster at Chartres (fl. c.1040)

'Hoc in loco multa magna fiebant antiquitus miracula: ideoque sabbatorum diebus maximus illic infirmorum agebatur concursus, ex quibus Raignaldus vir singularis exempli et Andevagensium scholarum magister, Fulberti episcopi doctrina eruditus, Frederici abbatis monitu, S. Florentii miracula cum praefatiuncula, scilicet ab 'Ardente puero in metallica' regione usque ad 'sauciatum spina in Arvernica patria' descripsit. Illa quoque responsoria temporibus domni Roberti abbatis, quia non is grata erant, idem Raignaldus nova, quae nunc utimur verborum series composuit. Sigo vero Carnotensis ecclesiae decanus, ipsiusque Fulberti cum ceteris a puero doctor, cantum fecit. Duos quoque hymnos ipse Raignaldus dictavit: *Canat chorus fidelium* et *Sancte confessor*': *Historia Sancti Florentii Salmurensis*, in *Chroniques des églises d'Anjou*, ed. Marchegay and Mabille, 287. See also Fanning, *A Bishop and his World before the Gregorian Reform*, docs. 36 and 37.

Sigo II, precentor of Chartres (11th c.)

> Charitate Sigo noster plenus atque gratia,
> Multa praebens ore, manu advenis solatia,
> Singularis organali regnabat in musica.

Adelman of Brescia, *De Viris illustribus sui Temporis*, second redaction, towards 1048, PL 143: 1296. This is one of the few instances where there may be a reference to polyphony.

Stephen, abbot of St James, Liège (d. 1112)

'. . . succedat Stephanus . . . qui cantum beati Benedicti et sancti Iacobi apostoli fratris beati Iohannis euangeliste aliqua preclara mirifice composuit': *Lamberti parvi Annales*, 647.

Stephen, bishop of Liège (903–20)

For his authorship of the Office in honour of the Holy Trinity see Pl. 74. Edition of chants from the Office, after the neumes of the Hartker antiphoner, in *Nocturnale Romanum*, Proprium de Tempore, 504–20.

'Stephanum qui, eo quod Metensis aecclesiae fuerit canonicus et protomartiris alumnus, de inventione ipsius quae cantantur responsoria edidisse dicitur ... Vitam sancti Lamberti simpliciter antiquitus dictatam urbani sermonis expolivit facetiis, et responsoria quae in sollempnitate ejus cantamus, composuit': Anselmus, *Gesta Episcoporum Leodiensium*, 1083–4. See Pl. 74.

'Stephanus, ex clerico Mettensi episcopus Leodiensis, vitam et passionem sancti Lamberti scriptam incultius a Godescalco clerico scripsit urbanius ad Herimannum Colonie archiepiscopum et cantum nocturnum in honorem eiusdem martyris. Canticum etiam de sancta trinitate et canticum de inventione Stephani prothomartyris autentica et dulci modulatione conmposuit': Sigebert of Gembloux, *Catalogus ... De Viris illustribus*, ed. Witte, 87.

'Domino Patri Herimanno archipraesuli Stephanus humilis Tungrorum episcopus ... Nam a quibusdam nobiscum agentibus festum sancti Lantberti, qui litteraria videbantur sibimet scientia praediti, non minimum sumus despectuosis risuum injuriis lacessiti, quando quidem priscorum haud quaquam cato eloquio edita legebatur apud nos praefati Patris vita et passio, atque nulla propria officiorum cantabatur modulatio. Abhinc sane frequenti fratrum nostrorum precamine rogatus, saepissimis vicibus exstiti coactus, ea omnia suscipere innovanda proprii impensione sensus, notamque hujusmodi infamiae a nobis propellendam omnibus ... Enimvero neque fastu superbiae tumens, neque quemquam Patrum contemptu habens, quinimo praelibatae utilitati parere libens, stylo praepollentioris ingenii eamdem acceleravi comens. Exinde musicae artis ratione authentica subnectuntur cum antiphonis responsoria nova, in quibus ordini lectionum series respondet tonorum; quatenus sibi aequando extendi quitur numerus horum. Adhuc etiam animi visu exstat delectabile in tanti patroni immorari laude': *Vita Lamberti* (*BHL* 4683), *AS* Septembris V, 581–2.

  See also Auda, *L'École musicale liègeoise au Xe siècle: Étienne de Liège*, and Björkvall and Haug, 'Text und Musik im Trinitätsoffizium Stephans von Lüttich'.

Waiferius, monk of Montecassino (fl. late 11th c.)

'Benedictus qui et Guaiferius, Salernitanus, sanctitate et religione conspicuus, suavis eloquio, ingenio magnus, sermone facundus. Scripsit ad Trojanum episcopum Vitam sancti Secundini et cantum ejus . . . Hymnos de eodem . . .': Peter the Deacon, *Liber de Viris illustribus Cassinensibus*, 1037.

l pfos deteftanf. dicebat mente modefta
m ille libraf certe pro papatu dare uellem
u t qd ego glifco fimoniacof maledictof
e iicerem cunctof per totum deniq; mundu
m usica feu cantuf iftum laudare tedaldu
n oncessant seper. renouantur co faciente
m icrologu libru sibi dictat Guido peritus
m uficus. et monachus. ncen heremita beandus
Q uod innulti marchionef longobardie
ftudier feparatei Chonradu a Bonefacio.
et qd Bonefaciuf duxe uxore comitiffa
Richilda. et de magnobello qd tota fere
longobardia fee cu Bonefacio et chon
rado incuuilio lo. qeppe regina urbe
OLAICOS ERS REDEATSTil uf. hic co plane
llloru fuma canoffe cura redundat
V tgenitor uel auuf. fic illam feper amart
P acif amatoref. for tef funt utq; leones
H i pace ueram cu profperitate tenebant

23

20

'IN OUR TIME, OF ALL MEN, SINGERS ARE THE MOST FOOLISH': GUIDO OF AREZZO AND THE INVENTION OF THE STAVE

The Unknown Guido

In the eleventh century, and indeed long after, a plainsong melody principally existed as a feeling in the throat, a sensation in the ear and a penumbra of associations created by years of repetition, by the lengthening and shortening of days or by the arrival and disappearance of seasonal fruits at the common table. Many singers could add associations that reached to the deepest layers of their childhood memory when joys and injustices were felt with an especial keenness: memories of teachers and the praise or blame that they apportioned, reminiscences of the rooms where they passed their boyhood learning the chants, day after day, occasionally receiving the expected beatings when they were negligent. In relation to this dense complex of memory and association, the visual appearance of chants in notation may have counted for little in the minds of many singers. There is no sign that the composers active between 900 and 1100, for example, were anxious to have their new plainsongs recorded in musical notation, and even the clergy of a great church like Notre-Dame de Paris expected their plainsong to be performed from memory in the central Middle Ages. The emergence of practical notations in the ninth century (to judge by what survives) began the slow process of creating visual analogues of vocal sound, providing a means to detach the music, however gradually, from particular modes of existence that could be sustained only by the kinds of collegiality that kept individuals together for long periods. Nonetheless, the question of what made musical notation 'useful' to any particular individual in the tenth century remains a question about different ways of living some form of common life and balancing its demands. A singer's need for notation (if he had one) might vary considerably according to the office he held, the books it was his business to consult, the general scrupulosity of the church in which he served, the time that accomplished singers could

spare to train him, and much else besides. Any form of musical notation therefore implicitly set out a scheme for using the gift of time to better advantage and
profit of the spirit.

   In the ninth century, when the repertory of Gregorian chant for the Mass was
being consolidated but much still remained to be done for the music of the
Office, churchmen began to register how much time was spent in becoming proficient in both repertories. In 838, Agobard of Lyons insisted that 'too many
singers study from earliest youth until the hoariness of old age' to learn their
chants, so that they can be numbered among the cantors; as a result they neglect
their 'spiritual studies, that is to say readings and the study of divine eloquence'.
Agobard's contemporary Aurelian would have looked down upon any cantor
who was guilty of such neglect, but the passage nonetheless suggests an impoverishment of studies, and even of the spiritual life, that Aurelian would surely
have recognized though it was no part of his literary purpose to say so. To be sure,
Agobard's writings relate to a particular phase in the evolution of Frankish-
Roman chant when several influential bishops were seeking to make changes to
the Office antiphoners of their churches, and the changes he contemplated concerned the verbal not the musical texts; he also implicitly concedes the status that
the cantor had acquired in the wake of the Carolingian reforms of liturgy, for
some clearly judged the rewards of the cantor's office to be worth the long years
of study 'from earliest youth until the hoariness of old age'. But even though
much of Agobard's work must be understood in a polemical and Lyonnais context, his complaint that many singers were compelled to neglect other studies can
be heard in a thin but important scatter of later sources. Much the same observation appears in a treatise possibly compiled in the region of Milan around
1000, the *Dialogus de Musica*, which claims that some singers 'devote fifty years
of their lives in vain to the practice and study of singing'. The compiler of another brief *De Musica*, long attributed to Odo of Cluny but also probably Italian,
insists upon the use of the monochord letters in teaching chant, for without
them

> we lose as much time in learning the antiphoner as we would need to spend
> getting to know divine authority and grammar; and what is worse, no amount
> of time is enough to reach such a perfection of study that we can learn even
> the smallest antiphon without the labour of a master, and if we happen to for-
> get it, there is no way in which we can recover our memory of it.

These are some of the reasons why the most famous of all medieval music theorists, Guido of Arezzo, thought singers to be the most foolish (*fatui*) of men, or
rather to be those whose greatest labours were likely to produce the smallest
results.[1]

   The four authentic treatises by Guido, often called Guido of Arezzo, have
probably been more intensively read during the last thousand years than any
other writings composed by a musician. They have almost invariably been stud-

ied as a musician's work, but that approach imposes some unexpected limitations and has even made some seminal aspects of Guido's writing invisible. Consider a brief passage in an authoritative English translation of his *Epistola ad Michahelem*, a letter written to a fellow monk at the abbey of Pomposa in the Po Valley. Among other things, Guido uses this letter to explain the system of notation he has invented, essentially the direct ancestor of the staff-notation that is still in use today and the device that has in many ways defined the course of Western music. He also describes how it received papal approval from Pope John XIX (1024–32). Guido insists in the letter that his new system will help novices to learn their plainsong more quickly, contracting a lifetime's work into just two years. So far so good; this is the Guido one expects to meet from nearly a thousand years of the reception of his works. Yet Guido is not content to say only that his new method will allow a lifetime of study to be accomplished in twenty-four months, although that is already saying a great deal; he also maintains that monks and clergy will now have more time for prayer, for the recitation of psalms, for nocturnal vigils and for the other works of devotion. Referring to the nocturnal vigils that represent one of the more ascetic devotions he has in mind, Guido envisages that monks and clergy will now be able to keep them *cum puritate*, 'with purity'.[2]

That simple expression, which distils so much of the political and ecclesiastical history of the eleventh century, is missing from the one standard English translation of the *Epistola at Michahelem*, thus effacing Guido's meaning at precisely the point where his conceptions need the most careful attention because they cannot readily be mapped onto those of today. The purity of monks and especially of clergy, meaning freedom from the contagion of money or sexual contact, among other things, was a matter of intense concern in the eleventh-century West, and it is traceable from the early decades of the new millennium when town-dwellers in the castellated communities of northern Italy and elsewhere began to demand higher standards of ritual purity from their clergy, through to the late years of the century when the dispute concerning the proper domains of temporal and spiritual power became painfully acute. There is therefore a wealth of material at hand to interpret what Guido means by expecting monks and clergy to attend their vigils *cum puritate* now that they will be able to complete their training in plainsong more quickly. His new notation will give them more time to enhance and deepen the quality of their spiritual life; they will have the means, if they are prepared to make the effort, to be cleansed from any temptation to simony and have more time fervently to pray for freedom from the troubling dreams and *phantasmata* that sully the body in the hours of nocturnal prayer and have effects that are worse still in sleep. Guido, long remembered by his patrons as an ascetic (Pl. 81), has restored to monks and clergy the time they need to live Christian lives to a high standard of observance and rectitude.[3]

A measure of insensitity to the ascetic temper of Guido's life and work has sometimes gone further in recent years than simply overlooking a seminal expression in one of his books. In many cases, the neglect has extended to the point of ignoring *a complete treatise* that he left to posterity. Guido is commonly regarded today as the author of four works, all of them musical tracts, whereas his legacy almost certainly runs to five treatises, the last being devoted to a sharply different matter, or so modern habits of thought make it seem. To be fair, the abundant transmission of Guido's musical works gives no clue to the existence of this extra item, which is a trenchant letter on the subject of simony (the sale or purchase of ecclesiastical offices) addressed to one of the most exalted ecclesiastics in Italy, Archbishop Heribert of Milan (1018–45). What is more, this letter, now commonly known as the *Epistola Widonis*, was widely attributed in the late eleventh century and beyond to a Pope Paschal. A pope will trump a choirmaster any day, so it is hardly surprising that Guido has principally been regarded as a somewhat lowly choirmaster who, in his determination to do his daily work more efficiently, evolved a means of recording the pitches of a melody so dependable that no other system has ever commanded widespread acceptance in a Western musical tradition. That is enough to remember anybody by. Why look further? The answer is that Guido's motives for devising his notation reach far beyond the demands of the choir school to his concerns about the state of the contemporary Church. Something similar might be said of all the medieval writers who laboured in the vineyard of music theory; each one knew that the accord of well-trained singers gave unique expression to fraternal *caritas* and to the Church as the company of the faithful. Yet Guido's body of work, taken as a whole with the fifth item, the *Epistola Widonis* on the subject of simony, is exceptional for both the depth and the virulence of its engagement with developments, both political and ecclesiastical, which gave the Latin West its consolidated medieval form.[4]

Simony, invariably construed as a heresy and broadly defined as trafficking in the Holy Spirit, takes its name from the primordial moment in the nascent Church's campaign to free the workings of the Spirit from any contact with the fees and bribes associated with the offices and rites of the pagan temples. (Acts of the Apostles 8: 18, 'And when Simon [Magus] saw that through the laying on of the apostles' hands the Holy Ghost was given, he offered money'.) The great movement of conscience that marked the eleventh century made simony a matter of renewed concern. It introduced many different forms of impure or rapacious motive into the life of the Church, set a temporal value on spiritual offices and turned bishops and abbots into political figures. The Peace Council of Poitiers (1000/14) forbade clergy to seek offerings for any sacraments, including penance, while the Council of Bourges (1031) insisted that clergy should not receive any gift for ordinations. The Council of Gerona (1068) condemned 'the detestable heresy of simony', showing how the language of condemnation became more virulent as the eleventh century progressed. In the *Epistola Widonis* it is already a language of sexually transmitted disease and violation of the female body, for simony 'pollutes the chastity of Holy Church with a disgusting contagion'. Barely has the letter begun before the author speaks with the righteous anger of Ezekiel: 'I say unto the wicked, thou shalt surely die' (3: 18). The author has heard that Archbishop Heribert of Milan confers holy orders in return for gifts or other payments, whence 'the Holy Spirit thunders through Gregory' and cries: 'Whoever is not greatly inflamed against the heresy of Simony will have the same share as Simon Magus who first committed this disgraceful act, that must be atoned for.' Augustine (actually Fulgentius of Ruspe) comes next in this fiery circle of authorities. 'Do not doubt that every heretic and schismatic, however much he may give alms or shed his blood for Christ, is to be given over to the devil and his angels for burning in eternal fire.' Thus it was that Christ ejected the money changers from the Temple, Dathan and Abiron were swallowed up by the ground for soliciting the governance of the priesthood, and Saint Peter placed Simon Magus under perpetual anathema. The *Epistola Widonis* continues:

> It is excessively shameful that the Church should now, in its fullest vigour, succumb to a such a bestial enemy that it had the power to conquer in its infancy with such strength . . . who cannot see that the Masses and prayers of such prelates or priests [guilty of simony] will bring the wrath of God upon the people and not placate him in the way we believe such observances can do? For it is written: 'Whatsoever is not of faith is sin' [Romans 14: 23] . . . When, therefore, do we shun such bishops, abbots, clerics and others if we hear the Masses of those, and pray with those, with whom we take excommunication upon ourselves? Just to believe such men to be priests is to go entirely astray, as Peter said to Simon Magus: 'Thy money perish with thee, because thou has thought that the gift of God may be purchased with money' [Acts 8: 20].[5]

By the 1070s, some well-informed commentators believed that the author of this letter was a certain Wido or Guido (the spelling variant is trivial) and identified him with the musician Guido of Arezzo. The testimony comes from the canonists around Lake Constance between approximately 1076 and 1088. During the last decades of the eleventh century, the see of Constance had a strong tradition of reform, represented among others by the canonist Bernold of Constance (*c*.1054–1100), who was sufficiently impressed by Guido of Arezzo to borrow the title *Micrologus*, the name of Guido's most famous treatise on music, for one of his own works. (No doubt Guido would have made the loan willingly had he lived long enough to know of it, for Bernold's *Micrologus* is a commendation of the Roman liturgy.) When Bernold compiled another of his writings, a collaborative letter entitled *De Damnatione Schismaticorum*, probably in 1076, he had cause to refer to the *Epistola Widonis* and there he attributed it, as some manuscripts do, to Pope Paschal. This attribution makes no sense, not least because the *Epistola*, despite the rebuke it offers, clearly looks up to its addressee, the archbishop of Milan. Eventually, Bernold acquired better information. In a manuscript of the letter now at Stuttgart, a near-contemporary annotator who is almost certainly Bernold himself has added a marginal note that reveals the result of fresh research into the authorship of the *Epistola Widonis*. 'This letter is not by Pope Paschal', the note declares, 'but by a Guido who also wrote a treatise on music; that is what certain men most dedicated to the monastic life assert, who have most diligently investigated this matter with his pupils.'[6]

One would give much to know the identity of the pupils who provided information about Guido, or indeed the identity of the 'men most dedicated to the monastic life' that had received the tradition from them. If Guido lived until the 1050s, which is certainly possible, then the traditions gathered about his authorship of the *Epistola*, first reported in the late 1070s, might have been received from his pupils in the strict sense of that word. If so, then the information came up from the south. Another possibility is that the news descended from the north, perhaps from Regensburg, where the composer Otloh was already copying the complete musical works of Guido in the lifetime of Bernold (see Appendix to Chapter 19, under of 'Otloh of St Emmeram'). Nothing certain can be said on either count, but it is at least clear from this note that the tradition about Guido and the *Epistola Widonis* was transmitted by those dedicated to a strict form of the monastic life (*religiosissimi*; that would fit the abbey of St Emmeram at Regensburg), which says something about the reputation Guido left behind. Bernold refers twice more to the *Epistola Widonis*, and is careful to call it 'the writing of Guido the musician' and 'the writing of Guido the musician about simoniacs'.[7]

For some indication of Guido's place in a groundswell of dissatisfaction among many laymen, monks and clergy during the first half of the eleventh century, one need only survey a few key events. In 1049, the Lotharingian pope and composer Leo IX used the Council of Rheims to make all the assembled prelates swear that they had not paid for their offices, and that they were therefore free from any taint of simony. The bishop of Langres fled the Council and was deposed; others were in evident difficulty. On 10 May 1057, the clergy of Milan assembled for the translation of the relics of Saint Nazzaro and suddenly faced an uprising of the laity. The ringleaders of the new movement compelled the clergy to swear that they would observe chastity in future. The leader of the Milanese townsmen, Ariald, soon widened the scope of his attack to encompass simony. His followers, given the insulting name *Patarini* or 'rag-pickers', subsequently dominated the city of Milan for twenty years without actually controlling it, defying the archbishop and placing their own priests in many of the urban churches. It says much about the nature of eleventh-century reform that these two confrontations were impelled by a pope in one case and by a disaffected citizenry on the other, albeit with some clerical and monastic support, just as it reveals much about Guido's conviction and prescience that he made a prelate of Milan the target of his *Epistola Widonis* some years before the *Patarini* took the ecclesiastical affairs of that city in hand. Guido wrote that letter as a lowly churchman addressing an exalted one, and in doing so he gives one of the earliest examples of a development that was fundamental to the rise of the *Patarini* and for other movements towards reform of the Church in the eleventh century: the right of the lowly to hold their pastors to account and then to rebuke them for their shortcomings, especially in the matter of chastity and simony.

In this, as in many things, the *Epistola Widonis* permits a deeper reading of Guido the choirmaster and inventor of the first Western notation that was both practical and unambiguously prescriptive in the matter of pitch. Guido's *Epistola ad Michahelem* shows the same concern with simony as the *Epistola Widonis* when he explains his decision not to remain in Rome where John XIX had asked him to teach the papal clergy; Guido returned to his old abbey of Pomposa instead 'since now nearly all the bishops have been convicted of the heresy of simony'. The condemnation is lofty and sweeping. Also reminiscent of the *Epistola Widonis* is the self-possessed and even self-righteous tone detectable in Guido's troubled relationship with his spiritual father and namesake, the abbot of Pomposa, not least in the somewhat vengeful episode when Guido sought him out to get an apology once the pope had approved the new system of teaching and notation; it seems that the abbot had not encouraged Guido in either. Above all, it is Guido the impassioned corrector of falsity that we meet in both the *Epistola Widonis* and the musical works: a man who believes he has the right to correct anyone, however exalted, and to remind them what the consequences of negligence will be in the next life. In personal terms, there are signs that this cost Guido dear, and led at least once to exile. If he was prepared for that, it is because he knew that in spiritual terms the stakes were high. When Guido evokes the dissent that can arise among singers who have learned different versions of a chant, or who have remembered the details of a chant differently, he is not inclined to use moderate or reassuring language, still less to be conciliatory. This strife is a 'grave mistake', a *gravis error*, which produces a 'perilous discord' or *periculosa discordia*, where the meaning of *periculosa* can only be that it endangers the immortal soul.[8]

There may be another way to place Guido in the wider current of eleventh-century reform, in addition to the *Epistola Widonis*. His life and writings sometimes intersect with the career of his contemporary Peter Damian, eventually cardinal-bishop of Ostia (1007–72). Damian was one of the most powerful controversialists of the eleventh century, 'a notorious and contradictory character' whose many writings and letters argue for the unique position of the Roman Church and for a purification of the religious life. Especially in his earlier years, Damian regarded this great task as a collaborative project, of immense moment, for the emperors and the popes together. A lifelong opponent of simony and a lurid advocate of clerical continence (his polemic against sodomy, the *Liber Gomorrhianus*, was an embarrassment to many), he was also one of the first to call for a systematic revision of the collections that monks and clergy used to study the past decisions of the Church in council, the material that was soon to become, duly revised and systematized, the body of Canon Law. Damian was also a champion of Rome's claim to be the ultimate arbiter in all matters concerning the authenticity and orthodoxy of any given chapters in conciliar proceedings. By 1034, he had entered the monastery at Fonte Avellana (about fourteen miles from Gubbio in the Apennines), whose name hovers above the biography of Guido of Arezzo without ever definitively coming to rest. One of the manuscripts traceable to Fonte Avellana may be the major anthology of Damian's works, now in the Biblioteca Apostolica Vaticana, where a number of Latin hymns attributed to him are notated, in a Guidonian manner, on dry-point (or very lightly inked) staves with the lines bearing the F-clef and c-clef in colour. In 1040–1, Damian was at Guido's former monastery of Pomposa, where he compiled the Life of Saint Romuald. Together with Lives of John Gualbert and Dominic of Sora, among others, the Life of Romuald is an outstanding text for recovering what it may have meant for Guido, in the context of monastic renewal in early eleventh-century Italy, to desire (in his own words) a 'modicum of solitary life'. Damian's account returns repeatedly to Romuald's desire for solitude, the *heremi desiderium* or longing for the hermitage that Guido may indeed have eventually found, to judge by the memory he left behind as an *heremita beandus*, a blessed hermit (see above, Pl. 81).[9]

Latinity may provide another link between Peter Damian and Guido. A wide-ranging analysis of *cursus*, the rhythmic patterns employed at the close of phrases or complete periods in Latin prose, reveals Guido to be the first author of the Middle Ages who prefers the *cursus velox*, as in *álea cònstitútum*. This rhythm is indeed very common in Guido's writing, and adorns the last words of his famous aphorism: 'In our time, of all men, singers are the most foolish' (*fátui sùnt cantóres*), which appears in the title of this chapter. The same pattern is common in the prose of Peter Damian and has been taken to suggest that Guido 'was educated in the same tradition' as Peter Damian, in the schools of the Po Valley. The dedicatory letter of the *Micrologus* suggests another, comparable link between the two men. Addressing Bishop Theodaldus with an elegant ellipsis, Guido wishes his master *quicquid servus et filius*, 'whatever a servant and son [would wish]'. There seem to be very few instances of this mode of address before the period of Guido and Peter Damian. The latter uses it three times in letters of the period 1048–65, and also employs the shorter form *quicuid servus*, which is rare before him. There is probably much more to Guido of Arezzo than will ever meet the eye, and certainly more than the choir school.[10]

Armed with a notation that left no doubt about the melodic contour of a chant, Guido set out to purify the Latin plainsong of the Roman Church according to his own judgement. His task was to free monks and clerics for the daily devotions, with an ascetic character, that would distinguish them sharply and forever from those touched by the impurities of sex and venality. More deeply still, Guido is concerned with the issue of pollution: with the 'simony and clerical unchastity [that] represented sources of contagious pollution which infected the body of Christ, stained the church, and hence threatened the *corpus chris-tianorum*, the Church'. Guido's notion of an error in plainsong is much more than simply empirical or pragmatic; he is concerned with defilement, and when the first champions of his notation north of the Alps begin to appear they will mostly be advocates of the papal cause in the struggle between *regnum* and *sacerdotium*: between Emperor and Pope. That is a matter for the next chapter. For the moment, there is more to say about Guido in the context of the eleventh century: his patrons, the affiliations of his new notational system to contemporary science, and the journey to Rome that gave his new system a papal imprimatur and may even have impelled him to the northern verge of Christendom.[11]

Clefs and Clearances: Guido and the Canossa

Some time in the first decades of the eleventh century, Guido became a monk of Pomposa, near Ferrara. Situated in the eastern marshes of the Po valley, this monastery in the diocese of Ravenna lay close to the routes taken by the Holy Roman Emperors Conrad II and Henry III into Italy. Their recorded journeys led down from cities on the imperial *iter* like Regensburg, through Brixen to the principal bridgeheads of imperial advance into Italy, Ravenna and Verona. Guido's master at Pomposa, and the man whom he calls his 'spiritual father', was his namesake Abbot Guido, famous for his asceticism and repeatedly drawn to a life of sylvan solitude: to the discipline of uncooked food taken from the bush and the rigours of a roofless bedchamber. During his abbacy, the monastic church at Pomposa was enlarged and the markedly Roman porch created, probably in 1026, with a panel by the architect whose inscription is visible to this day. It is a fitting monument to an abbot of considerable stature. After his death, his body was taken by the emperor Henry III and interred in the cathedral at Speyer, the mausoleum of the Salian house. (There are some signs that Abbot Guido was not only a spiritual adviser to Henry but also a relative.) The eminence of this abbot, and the importance of the community that he governed at Pomposa, were both of great account to Guido the musician, who describes his abbot as 'a man most esteemed by God' and as the head of an abbey that he had made 'the first in Italy'. For all his own asceticism, Guido did not wish to be associated with a backwater, and was never to be so.[12]

While at Pomposa, Guido passed into the orbit of the most powerful kindred on the Po Plain, the Canossa. Here it is possible to appreciate the singularity of what might be called the Guido moment. In his lifetime, the Canossa had only recently risen to a position of eminence, deriving their wealth from clearances in the Po marshes. One could scarcely wish for a clearer case of an aristocratic house in the eleventh century prospering by clearing land, creating settlements and establishing tenantries. The Canossa combined drainage of the marshlands with a policy of slash and burn to clear woodlands, much of it accomplished by peasants who were rewarded, if that is the right word, by having their communities walled (we are in the early years of the *incastellamento*) and then subjected to tax and rule by the Canossa. Their male line was rapidly drawing to a close in Guido's time and finally failed in 1055, although the female line was destined to last until 1115 with immense distinction in the person of Matilda of Tuscany (Pls 81 and 82). Guido would have seen the greatest secular magnate of the house, Boniface of Canossa, in the abbey church at Pomposa; many years later, Boniface was remembered for the annual visits to the abbey where, it was said, he would lament his sins and be washed clean by the prayers of the brothers. It is even claimed that Boniface, recalled by one modern historian as 'monstrous and violent', once stripped himself naked and submitted to a public whipping by the abbot of Pomposa as penance. Another story, from the same source, shows him admiring the demeanour of the choirboys in the monastery, who continually sang with their eyes cast down. Boniface arranged for a servant to climb to a high place in the abbey and then cast golden coins onto the stone flags of the presbytery. They landed there with a resounding din, but not one of the choirboys raised his eyes.[13]

Guido of Arezzo may have been standing among the singers when the coins hit the floor. If so, this was only one of his many contacts with the Canossa. After his time at the abbey of Pomposa, which seems to have ended badly or at least in some kind of conflict with the abbot, Guido appears in the entourage of the bishop of Arezzo, although not among the inner and privileged circle of the canons. There is nothing coincidental about Guido's new home, for the bishop whom he served was Theodaldus of Canossa (1023–36), the brother of Boniface whom Guido must have seen at Pomposa, whether the musician was present for the famous shower of coins or not. The family was clearly not prepared to let Guido go. Bishop Theodaldus and Boniface are both shown in a luxurious twelfth-century copy of the *Vita Mathildis* (Pl. 82). Guido's precise reasons for leaving the abbey of Pomposa remain impossible to establish, but that may not matter very much since his change of community under a cloud can be paralleled in the lives of many eleventh-century monks; sharing a confined space with the same individuals, day after day, could create many kinds of tension that could be released only by exile. What seems certain, however, is that Guido's move from Pomposa to Arezzo owed something to the continuing interest of a family that still remembered him as a gifted musician, and as a valued servant of Bishop Theodaldus, into the first decade of the twelfth century.

Now, for the second time, Guido found an able man to serve. Bishop Theodaldus of Arezzo ensured that good archives were kept, with the result that many of his charters survive, and he often appears elsewhere as a benefactor, notably in the charters of the new eremetical foundation of Camaldoli. Unlike some of his fellow prelates, Theodaldus noticed the forms of solitary Christian life that implicitly challenged the well-appointed existence of the bishops in their urban palaces; the charters show that he wished to further the cause of the

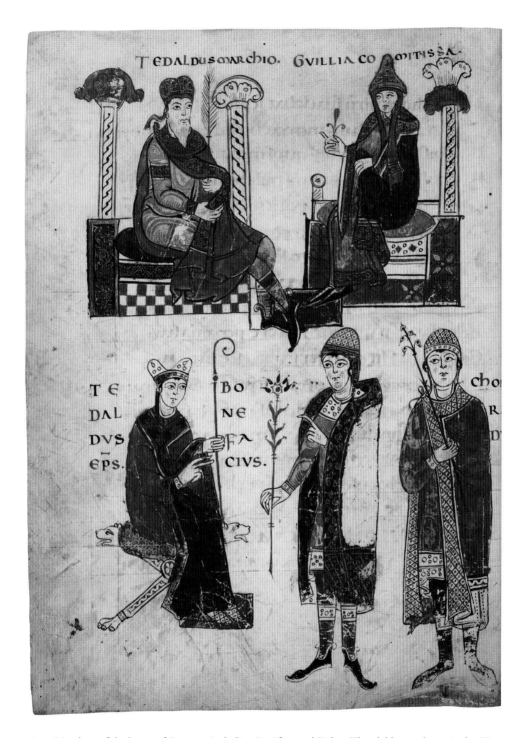

82　Members of the house of Canossa, including Boniface and Bishop Theodaldus, as shown in the *Vita Mathildis*. Rome, Biblioteca Apostolica Vaticana, Lat. 4922, fol. 21ᵛ, 12th c.

reformed monastic life practised at Camaldoli, with an emphasis upon solitary prayer. Theodaldus was also an impressive preacher, for one of his sermons left a mark on Peter Damian, a severe critic; he was also a builder, completing the collegiate church of Saint Donatus that his predecessor had been unable to finish, ruling that the canons should celebrate the liturgy there from the feast of the consecration until Maundy Thursday, when they should join him in the episcopal Church of Saint Stephen. Guido of Arezzo, who must often have passed the building site, praises the result in his *Micrologus* for its 'exceedingly marvellous plan', and shows once again his satisfaction at being part of a distinguished community. He describes the canons as 'outstandingly spiritual men, most plentifully fortified by the practice of the virtues and most abundantly distinguished by their pursuit of wisdom'. Since Guido is writing an open letter to Theodaldus here, we might expect him to praise the canons in this way, and it must be said that the surviving traces of learning and authorship from the circle around Theodaldus of Arezzo are somewhat thin apart from Guido's own work. But in his *Epistola ad Michahelem* Guido praises Peter the Provost of the canons – perhaps with a certain reserve – for being 'a most learned man by the standards of our time' (Pl. 83). After the debacle at Pomposa, whatever it may have been, Guido clearly thought that he had fallen on his feet. It is very characteristic of this period, at least in the more dynamic areas of western Europe like the Po valley, that Guido's experiments with methods of teaching and notating music should owe something to the clearance of lands, and the drainage of marshes, whence his masters derived much of their wealth and influence.[14]

Among the five authentic works of Guido, two of his musical treatises describe a notational system that he emphatically presents as his own new solution to an old objective: to find a means of reducing a melody to a written record that singers can use to perform an unknown chant at sight, without the aid of a teacher. Viewing Guido's system (or rather systems) today, and looking back through nearly a thousand years of the history of the stave, it is easy to forget that singers of the eleventh and twelfth centuries saw it as a bilingual method that integrated neumes and alphabetic letters, using the lines merely as a visual convenience to prolong the meaning of a letter across the page. The lines and spaces of Guido's systems, and of all subsequent staves in mainstream practice, cor-

83   The signature of Peter the Provost, who accompanied Guido on his visit to Rome to meet John XIX, as it appears on this document witnessing a privilege of Bishop Theodaldus, dated 4 March 1028. The entry reads + *ego petrus presbyter et prepositus consensi et subscripsi* ('I Peter, priest and provost, have agreed and subscribed'). Arezzo, Archivio Capitolare Canonica, 88.

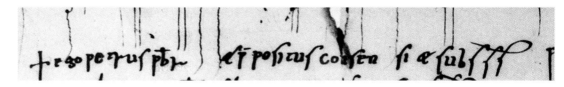

respond to a musical scale whose degrees are assigned a letter of the alphabet, residually present in the various clefs that are still in use today, but much more actively present in many forms of Guido's method. His point of departure was therefore an alphabetic method of recording pitch. In manuals of plainsong, and to some extent in systematic copies of chants, he and his pupils would sometimes have seen melodies written with letters used to indicate pitches in this way; such notations were known and used in Guido's Italy, principally as a pedagogical tool, and he regarded them as infantile in the strict sense because they failed to communicate any nuances of phrasing or performance and demanded very little in the way of aural-to-visual sophistication. What musicians really needed to aid the process of learning, studying and emending their chants was a system that employed neumes to convey nuances of performance supported by letters that alphabetized the pitches and could therefore spell the melody in an unambiguous fashion. Guido accordingly placed a rack of letters on the left-hand side of the page, where writing began, so that each letter needed only to be written once and remained in force, prolonged across the page in its own 'rank' or *ordo*. The next step was to mark these ranks or *ordines* to the eye with a line that could be traced in ink but did not have to be, for it might be ruled only in dry-point (with results that do not yield very well to photography). The great innovation of the system is that both the lines *and the spaces between them* mark a rank; this is what makes the new method fundamentally and crucially different from the string-notations found in earlier Carolingian treatises, where lines represent the chords of a musical instrument and the spaces between have no meaning. (Some of those who saw staff-notation for the first time may well have objected that it occupied too much space, and that it required excessive expenditure of money, in materials, and of time, in planning and executing the page.) Since one of the principal tasks facing any singer confronted with a new chant was to know where the semitone steps lay, Guido recommended that the two lines with a semitone step beneath them, for *F* and *c*, be ruled in red and yellow ink respectively. Now all that remained was for a scribe to place the neumes he already knew, in their standard or somewhat adapted form, in the appropriate ranks. In practice, therefore, the Guidonian stave was a bundle of graphic techniques that was continually being untied and reorganized as scribes experimented with them. Colourful enough it may sound from Guido's own account, but later scribes were sometimes inclined to go further in guiding the eye, hence the use of green in many manuscripts to mark the lines without a clef (Pl. 84).[15]

Guido's own account of his system is most suggestive precisely where it may now seem most opaque. As he lays out the principles of his notation, our own familiarity of the musical stave recedes and it becomes dimly possible to appreciate the character of the intellectual challenge it presented to its first users:

> The notes are so arranged that each sound, however many times it may be repeated in the chant, is always to be found in its own, single rank (*ordo*); and so that you may better perceive these ranks, there are close-packed lines, and

some ranks are assigned to these same lines and some to the space between the lines. Therefore, however many sounds there are on one line, or in one space, they all sound in the same way . . .[16]

If this seems curiously laboured, it is partly because Guido is clarifying these matters for novices, some of them only boys; but it is also because he is explaining his system to readers that had hitherto known musical notation, if they had known it at all, as a form of *script*. With his new method, notation had become a *chart* in the specialized sense of a graphic layout where symbols have place-value on the page. To read this chart, the viewer must interpret a relatively complex visual array that integrates verbal text, lines, spaces, alphabetic clef-letters, neumes and contrasting colours with an eye that needs to be guided at all times by a trained ear and an increasingly sophisticated symbol-to-sound perception.

Although Guido intended his notation for singers and not for philosophers, one should not miss the element of eleventh-century science that was involved in its making. In his lifetime, the Mediterranean symposium was just beginning that had recently seen some great men like Gerbert of Aurillac, and some lesser ones like Balther of Säckingen, travel to the libraries of Spain or southern Italy in search of texts on such matters as astronomy or medicine, many of them translated from Arabic and in their turn translated from the Greek. Peter Damian looked askance upon a certain Gualterus who had 'so pursued learning around the borders of the Occident for nearly thirty years that he had entered not only the cities of the Germans and French but also those of the Spaniards and the Saracens'; he also cites the case of a certain Hugh of Parma, a man 'of such ambition for learning in the arts' that he 'provided himself with an astrolabe of brilliant silver' and became a chaplain of the emperor Conrad while he 'panted after a bishopric'. By mid-century, and so perhaps at the time when Guido was in his last years, it becomes possible to pick up the traces of such careers with men like Alfanus, a gifted musician who was fluent in Greek, a renowned physician and a churchman of sufficient reputation and gravity to become archbishop of Salerno. (See Appendix to Chapter 19, under 'Alfanus, archbishop of Salerno'.) Guido, for his part, claims to have met some 'very acute philosophers' whose search for musical learning had taken them to French masters, while others had studied with Germans. Some had even been to the Greeks. Reports of consultations with 'Greeks' form something of a topos in medieval music theory between the ninth century and the twelfth, but there is good reason to suppose that Guido's remarks have substance to them. In 1005, the Byzantine recovery of Dyrrachium renewed an important line of communication between Italy and Byzantine Asia, while Arab conquests in the south drove many refugees from the Greek theme of Kalabria into central and northern Italy. Both in Pomposa and Arezzo, Guido's range of contacts may have been broad, but his writings do not suggest that he was often troubled by the opposition, of considerable moment to Peter Damian, between the holy simplicity required of a monk and a sinful pride in learning.

84 Part of the *Proprium de tempore* from a Cistercian gradual, prepared using one of the most visually emphatic forms that Guidonian notation ever assumed. This is a relatively late example (of the 13th or early 14th c.) showing German neumes placed upon a five-line stave with the *c*-line ruled in yellow, the *F*-line in red, according to Guido's instructions, but with the remaining lines ruled in green save the top line when there is a *c*-clef, which is ruled with dry-point. The lines at the top right of the page show how the entire page was first ruled with dry-point. The red lines through the stave, which appear to be part of the original campaign of copying, variously divide the chant according to the sense of the text (although it seems unlikely that some of the phrases thus created were sung in one breath). In at least one case (at *Surge*) the lines clarify the structure of the music, in this case, setting off a melodic repetition. Universitätsbibliothek Erlangen-Nürnberg, MS 113, fol. 16ᵛ, 13th or early 14th c.

His time at Arezzo, where he dwelled as a monk among the canons serving a bishop, accords with many signs that studious but ascetic men in the eleventh century, with a commitment to the arts of measurement, were quite ready to serve a prelate. Their focus of interest might be the astrolabe, the abacus or the leading instrument of exact science, the musician's monochord.[17]

The passage where Guido laboriously explains the workings of the stave has its closest parallels in contemporary treatises on the counting board or abacus, a relatively new subject for technical manuals in Guido's lifetime. Indeed, the background to Guido's work as the 'inventor' of the musical stave does not just lie with the work of the choir school; it also touches the intellectual interests represented, at their highest level, by Gerbert of Aurillac (*c.*950–1003) and by many other lesser figures who studied the abacus, monochord or astrolabe and wrote treatises upon them with *parvuli* or 'small boys' in mind, as Guido did. With the aid of these instruments the study of the numerical subjects among the seven liberal arts might open outwards to experiments, the *experimenta* mentioned in this context by Bernold of Constance during the last decade of the eleventh century. The treatises on the abacus are especially suggestive for they show the same scrupulous attention to place-value as the stave. Just as Guido emphasizes the virtue of 'a perfect placing of the neumes', so the abacus manuals identify the true skill of the *abacista* as a mastery of 'placements, that is to say locations': the art of putting figured counters in the right columns using the rules governing numbers to base 10. They also show the same commitment to lay matters out as clearly as possible, to *ducere oculum* or 'lead the eye', which is the heart of Guido's system with its colour-coded lines creating what is in effect a graph with pitch on the *x*-axis and the sequence of time on the *y*-axis. Above all, the abacus manuals also provide a context for Guido's use of significant spaces in his notation. The concept of a meaningful space, essential to the workings of Guido's stave, has one of its closest parallels in the columns of the abacus and in what one of Guido's Italian contemporaries, Laurence of Amalfi, calls their *lineale spatium vacuum*, their 'extended empty space'. So perhaps it should be no surprise that the closest parallel to an imperious eleventh-century drawing of Guido seated at his monochord may be a sketch of his younger contemporary, Pandulf of Capua, with his board abacus and its counters marked with early Occidental forms of Hindu-Arabic numerals. Both images show Italians who had mastered two of the eleventh century's principle instruments for rigorous enquiry and formal demonstration.[18]

The Roman Journey

It is very characteristic of the Guido story that his invention was approved by an exalted churchman, Pope John XIX, whom Guido would probably have wished to reproach, had it not been so obviously in his interests to remain silent. The account of this meeting appears in his *Epistola ad Michahelem*, the letter to a monk of Pomposa that mentions Guido's long struggle to champion his methods of notating and reforming the melodies of plainsong. The letter also reveals how Guido eventually triumphed over his opponents when Pope John XIX invited him to Rome, having heard the renown (or so Guido claims) of the song-school at Arezzo. During the meeting that eventually took place, presumably somewhere in the papal apartments in the Lateran palace, the pope inspected Guido's antiphoner with his own hands:[19]

> John, of the highest apostolic seat, who now governs the Roman church, hearing the fame of our school and greatly marvelling how, by means of our antiphoner, boys might learn chants they had never heard, invited me with three emissaries. I therefore went to Rome with Grimaldus, the most reverend Abbot, and Peter, Provost of the canons of the Church of Arezzo, the most learned man of our times. The pope, very delighted by my arrival, speaking of many things and asking much, frequently turning the pages of our antiphoner as if it were a marvel and studying the prefatory rules, did not leave that place or move from where he sat until he had learned one versicle he had never heard, fulfilling his wish, so that he might as soon as possible discover in himself what he scarcely believed in others.

This encounter filled Guido with a quite justifiable pride, for how often did a messenger bring a document to the papal court and find himself rewarded with the sight of the pope handling the material himself? Once John XIX had studied the 'prefatory rules' he was even able to sing a versicle from Guido's antiphoner, relying entirely upon the resources of the notation he found there because it was one he had never heard. (These rules survive as a separate treatise by Guido, the *Prologus in Antiphonarium*.) As a result of this interview, Pope John formed such a high estimation of both Guido and his methods – again according to Guido – that he invited him to remain in Rome and teach the Roman clergy. If this story is true, and there is no real reason to doubt the essentials, then it is a tale of persistence rewarded. Nonetheless, Guido sounds a pessimistic note here and there in the letter. The workings of the Divine Will are obscure, he declares, which explains (for evidently nothing else can) his struggle to prevail. For many years, the truth he wished to impart had been 'trampled by deceit', the charity that he should have received 'crushed by spite'. He has at last emerged from this battle with his detractors and enemies, but only as a weary and embittered campaigner who has learned that the life of monks is almost always characterized by envy or *invidia*. Hence the *Epistola ad Michahelem* is neither a dedicatory epistle marked by flattery nor a piece of theological polemic, even though Guido knew how to write letters of both kinds. It mostly praises Guido himself. Hence Pope John is 'very delighted' by Guido's arrival and regards the new antiphoner as a 'marvel'. The abbot of Pomposa, formerly one of his detractors, is also named in the *Epistola*, but only because Guido sought him out, well aware that the approval he had received from Pope John left his venerable opponent in a weak position. In effect, Guido went to demand an apology from the abbot, or at least an expression of regret, and he received it. Not many choirmasters of the eleventh century had the chance to wring such an admission from the spiritual counsellor to a Holy Roman Emperor.

Pope John XIX came from the Roman family of the Tusculani, and if the Holy Roman emperors had one clear priority in their reforms of the church in Guido's later years, and beyond, it was to extricate the papacy from that clan and from its rivals. Guido's deference may have been somewhat forced during his interview with Pope John, for the pontiff had inherited the papal throne from his brother, laying him open to a form of the charge that Guido levelled against Heribert of Milan in the *Epistola Widonis*, namely that John XIX had obtained the office through simony. Guido is unlikely to have exonerated John from this condemnation, and indeed he left Rome soon after the interview, having declined or postponed the pontiff's offer to teach the singers of the papal chapel because 'nearly all' the bishops could be charged with the heresy of simony. Yet in retrospect, the summons to Rome that Guido received does John credit, for it looks like one of the first green shoots of eleventh-century reform to have emerged from Rome itself, and it grew within the circle of a pope who has long been disparaged. The encouragement John XIX offered to Guido is one of the most positive things recorded of that prelate and an important element in the reassessment of his pontificate.[20]

Guido claims that he was summoned to Rome by the pope, but the truth may be somewhat more complex in a way that opens a curious chapter in Guido's story. It may place him at the opposite end of Latin Europe, training singers in the diocese of Hamburg-Bremen. The eleventh-century chronicler of that see, Adam of Bremen, reports that Archbishop Hermannus (1032–5) 'brought to Bremen the music-master Guido, at whose instance he corrected the chant and the life of the cloister'. Of all the archbishop's efforts, 'this was the only one that was successful'. This evokes the practice, well attested in the Carolingian Church and revived in the eleventh century, of associating a reform of chant very closely with a reorganization of the common life of monks or canons concerned, and especially with a life that required continence, regular attendance at night offices and continual residence in a common cloister. Indeed, the association between 'corrected' chant and a reformed manner of life could scarcely be closer than it is in Adam of Bremen's remark that Hermannus 'corrected the chant and the life of the cloister'. Many have been inclined to deny that the Guido in question here is Guido of Arezzo, or that a sojourn in distant Bremen may lie behind Guido's reference to his 'exile in a distant land' in the *Epistola ad Michahelem*, but the dates present little difficulty. The *Epistola* is commonly assigned to 1030–2, which coincides with the reign of the archbishop who invited a music master named Guido to Hamburg-Bremen (1032–5), and accords with the proposal that the archbishop summoned Guido at the beginning of his episcopate in 1032, and that Guido wrote to Michael soon afterwards, mentioning his 'exile'.[21]

There is also a possible link between Guido and Bremen in the person of Knút (popularly known as Canute), the king of Demark, Norway and England (d. 1035), and his queen, Emma. Knút and Emma were of great interest to Adam of Bremen because the queen was a notable benefactress of the church there; Adam praises her warmly as 'the most devout Emma, who loved the Church at Bremen exceedingly'. The importance of this connection is that Knút can be placed in the milieu of Pope John XIX, who so famously approved Guido's antiphoner. Knút was an especially honoured guest at Rome in 1027 when the emperor Conrad received the imperial title of Augustus from John XIX, an event that also brought Guido's master Theodaldus and some members of the Arezzo chapter to Rome. This is revealed by a charter dated 31 March 1027, wherein Conrad renews some of the canon's possessions and privileges. Peter the Provost of Arezzo, one of the men whom Guido says accompanied him to meet John XIX, is named in this charter, as one would expect. Hence there may be some merit in reviving the old proposal that this was the time, 1027, during the months of the imperial consecration in Rome, when Guido journeyed to that city and had his interview with John XIX. (It may not count for much that Guido says nothing of the imperial consecration, nor of the great confluence of clergy that accompanied it, in his account of his Roman visit; Guido is everywhere the hero of his own story.) The great synod of bishops and abbots which followed the acclamation of the emperor was certainly attended by Guido's namesake and former master, Guido of Pomposa, and our musician's presence in Rome at this time would explain how he was able to be in the Eternal City to meet John XIX and then appear in the residence of abbot Guido 'after only a few days', which does not sound like an interval sufficient for the journey from Rome to distant Pomposa in the Po valley. The experience of conversing with a great many visiting bishops, or at least of conversing *about* them, may lie behind Guido's otherwise unaccountably broad generalization that 'nearly all the bishops are infected with the heresy of Simony'. It is at least possible that Pope John spoke of Guido's innovations to his honoured guest Knút, or to his advisers, when they were in Rome for the ceremonies of 1027, and that this is why a choirmaster named Guido appears a few years later, so far from home, in the temporary service of a church at Bremen with which Knút and his queen, Emma, had a close connection.[22]

Guido's Collected Edition

At some stage in his life, perhaps relatively late, Guido may have issued his musical writings as a set. They present a field of musical study but also form a narrative (if that is not too strong a word) recounting a monk's labour to create something of moment to the singers of the Universal Church. To be sure, Guido cannot be compared in this regard with his contemporary Otloh of St Emmeram (d. *c.*1070), whose account of his own writings, and indeed of his spiritual drama, come as close to an autobiography in the modern sense as one has any right to expect from an eleventh-century author, but by the standards of any age Guido was a writer much concerned with his name, his reputation and the circumstances in which they had been variously abased or exalted. By general agreement, his four authentic musical treatises are the *Micrologus*, the *Regulae rhythmicae*, the *Prologus in antiphonarium* and the *Epistola ad Michahelem*. They are preserved, whole or in part, in at least seventy manuscripts ranging from the eleventh century to the sixteenth and beyond, an impressive total that spans much of Latin Christendom, though most of the sources derive from the kingdom of France or Imperial territory (essentially Germany and northern or central Italy) with a respectable showing from England. In the majority of the manuscripts, from all periods, the scribes copied all four of Guido's musical works, and in many sources the four treatises are placed back to back, thus strengthening the impression of a set. What is more, the four books very often appear in the same order, which is *Micrologus, Regulae, Prologus* and *Epistola*, or abbreviated MRPE. Even in the earliest layer of manuscripts, cautiously dated to the eleventh or twelfth century today, the MRPE order can be discerned, complete or in modules, amidst a scattering of other materials.

Time and time again, scribes seem to have received Guido's four books in this canonical order. Very occasionally, the scribes register that sense in explicit terms, at least in some of the later sources. A London manuscript of the fourteenth century (Lo4, from France) prefaces the *Regule* with the words 'Here begins the second book of the same Guido'. One source of the thirteenth century (V4, from south Germany or Austria) says considerably more, showing that the scribe had pondered the order of Guido's works and discerned some significance in it. The *Micrologus* and *Regule* pass by with plain or explanatory rubrics of the usual kind, but the *Prologus* is announced as '[Guido's] third book' and the *Epistola*, the letter to Michael of Pomposa, is called 'An epistolary recapitulation of all the work of the same Guido, [addressed] to a monk'.[23]

It will never be known whether this represents Guido's own understanding of the *Epistola*, but since the MRPE order is so deeply rooted in the manuscript tradition of his works there is a chance that the order is Guido's own. It may result from a conscious process of editing his musical works, composed at different times, at some later stage when they were all complete. The order may be chronological (none of Guido's works can be precisely dated) and for what it may be worth, the MRPE order is not so very distant from the sequence MPRE, widely accepted as the one in which Guido wrote them. But might the order be more potent than chronology, as the note in the Vienna manuscript suggests, referring to the 'epistolary recapitulation' of the last book in the set? There does seem to be a persistent concern when the treatises are read in this sequence, and it is essentially a graded course in staff-notation and a vindication of the method. The set begins with the *Micrologus*, or more precisely with the acrostic at the beginning of that work, which reveals Guido's name, followed by the prefatory letter that places him as the valued servant of Bishop Theodaldus of Arezzo. This was the book that some medieval commentators were disposed to treat as a free-standing text for detailed commentary, for the chapters of the *Micrologus* form a remarkably comprehensive manual, given the overall size of the book, and one that is well able to stand on its own. Guido does not appear to have used his staff-notation in this treatise, presumably because that notation is a bilingual system that relies upon a novice's acquaintance with the monochord letters and with basic musical structures, which it is the purpose of the *Micrologus*, among many other things, to teach. Guido alludes to this in the next treatise of the sequence, the *Regule*, by saying 'we have proved notation by letters to be the best' then proceeding to introduce the reader to staff-notation. At the end of the *Regule*, Guido alludes to an antiphoner he has made, which we are clearly to understand was copied in some form of his staff-notation throughout. This prepares the reader for the third treatise of the set, which is the prologue to that antiphoner, and for the fourth, the *Epistola*, which describes how John XIX read that prologue when he examined the antiphoner in Rome and commended it, together with its new notational system. Hence the last of the four books gives a circumstantial account of Guido's vindication, and Guido is ready to close the set of treatises by referring the reader back to all his works, as he does at the end of the last of the four, the *Epistola* (380–8). He is also ready to borrow valedictory words from the Apostle: I have fought the good fight, I have finished the race, I have kept the faith. As for the rest, a crown of justice awaits me.'[24]

No matter how colourful it may appear with its lines of red and yellow, Guido's stave was the work of an essentially ascetic mind. As mentioned above, the Canossa clan remembered him as *heremita beandus*, 'the blessed hermit'. The description suggests that Guido ended his days in monastic seclusion; he says himself that he had always desired a measure of *vita solitaria*. His notation is designed to secure uniformity in liturgical performance: the conformity of the individual to the common rule. In that regard he did more than provide some important resources for a reorganization of the common life, symbolized by the unanimity of voices in choir. He also promoted the commitment to peace through uniformity of cultic observance that is one of the most ancient streams of Catholic thought about the conduct of the common life. There is a kind of associative thinking here, quite alien to modern categories such as 'the Church', or 'politics', making it ultimately impossible to draw any clear distinction between what we might be inclined to call (using phrases from the *Epistola Widonis*) 'physical corruption', 'the corruption of heresy' and the 'disorder' that can occur in monasteries, cathedral churches and the wider world of king and nobles. It was one part of Guido's work to bring the materials at the heart of choral worship into a sharper focus and impose an order upon them. His notation presents every chant in such a way that there is no longer a need for contention or an excuse for caprice, and he emphasizes that his system will allow the true Roman chant of Pope Gregory the Great to be recorded and transmitted in an accurate and canonical form. From now on, singers will know that they have the true tradition, the musical counterpart of the doctrinal tradition at the heart of Catholicism, because they are singing from the antiphoner of Gregory, not the book of some 'Leo or Albert'. (He was not troubled by the fact that his antiphoner was the work 'some Guido', although that is very likely to have been one of the criticisms levelled at him in Pomposa.) No reader of Guido can mistake his dogmatic and combative tone, evident in all his five writings, or long remain in doubt that there is an implicit association in his work between the lines of his stave and several senses of the potent notion of a rule, Latin *regula*, whose meanings included 'a ruler for drawing lines', 'a norm for behaviour' and 'a form of the common life for monks or canons'. Perhaps the association goes deeper still, associating the monks and clergy who attend vigils 'with purity', unpolluted by simony or sexual contact, with the purity of corrected chant recorded in a new notation that Guido disingenuously compares to glass: pure and transparent to its object.[25]

21

BRINGING SINGERS TO BOOK:
RUDOLF OF SINT TRUIDEN AND
GUIDO'S INVENTION

An Imperial Horizon

In the late 1070s, it was still possible for Bernold of Constance to encounter persons in contact with singers and others who had been Guido of Arezzo's pupils. Guido's writings had begun to cross the Alps by now, and perhaps long since, catching powerful currents flowing north to south and back again. The long sequence of toll-stations along the Rhine, out of Lake Constance, suggests a considerable volume of movement on that major fluvial route in the eleventh century. A large proportion of the longer journeys, such as might take a company from Italy to the upper Rhine, were probably still being made, as they were in Carolingian times, by dealers in luxuries en route to assured points of sale. A merchant from Constance mentioned in a Latin lyric of the eleventh century carried 'treasure' in his ship, while the traders from Italy noticed by the chronicler Ekkehard IV, writing in Sankt Gallen to the south of Constance, probably dealt in the spices, glasswork and textiles that the Venetians and others brought from their contacts in Byzantium: commodities whose high value made long-distance travel worthwhile. Books rarely moved in the Middle Ages as a special delivery or consignment; instead, they were displaced when their carriers had some other reason to travel: when there was an opportunity to join the safety of a company, or to take a ship, that arose in relation to other purposes. No monk or cleric with books by Guido in his bag needed to wait very long, it seems, to find either a berth or a mounted company going north out of Italy in the eleventh century.[1]

These north–south connections also traced imperial routes. The emperor Conrad II (1027–39) appears in some eleventh-century chronicles taking a boat along the river to Constance. Observers on the banks would have seen the emperor, his courtiers and other attendants passing in a flotilla such as north European commerce in the first decades of the new millennium did not produce. So whatever the dissemination of Guido's works and reputation may owe to opportunities created by the movement of luxury commodities, it probably owes as much or more to the transalpine journeys of the emperors and their servants. The earliest manuscripts of Guido's four treatises include three of *c*.1100 traceable to monastic houses in Bamberg, Regensburg and Augsburg, all cities appearing repeatedly on the itineraries of the emperors Henry III (1039–56) and Henry IV (1056–1106). These rulers spent much of the year travelling through the Empire to do justice, issue diplomas and maintain contacts with the great princes, both lay and ecclesiastical, and their transalpine visits can be traced through the documents issued by their chanceries at points of rest. The diplomas of Henry III, for example, trace an itinerary from Regensburg through Ebersberg, Brixen and Trento to Verona, using the Brenner Pass; another journey took the imperial retinue from Augsburg to Florence via Lucca. A map of Henry IV's itineraries shows Augsburg and Bamberg in the category of cities with between six and twenty recorded visits, while the same emperor visited Regensburg more than twenty times. On these journeys the imperial court relied heavily upon the resources of the greater abbeys and bishoprics. If there were any places north of the Alps where the returning tide of imperial clergy, soldiers, notaries and other staff was especially likely to leave some deposit of what it had picked up on the way, they were Bamberg, Regensburg and Augsburg, precisely the cities where Guido's writings were being studied by the last quarter of the eleventh century.[2]

At Regensburg, in the abbey of St Emmeram, a monk named William was reading Guido's books with his teacher Otloh, an indefatigable scribe whose hand appears in two volumes of music theory, one of which includes all Guido's works (see Appendix to Chapter 19, under 'Otloh of St Emmeram'). This could have been at any time from the earlier 1060s. At Freising, lying between Augsburg and Regensburg, and so in favoured territory for the route south towards the Brenner, Bishop Ellenhard (d. 1078) received the dedication of a music treatise by a certain Aribo that mentions 'domnus Guido' repeatedly and admiringly. It is not difficult to envisage how such men could have obtained their Guidonian material from imperial servants on the move. If William of St Emmeram needed new copies of Guido's works when he became abbot of Hirsau, for example, he could have done worse than approach his new diocesan, Bishop John of Speyer, who was liable to be drawn into transalpine travel at any time, like any other bishop of the Reich close to the emperor. John appears as one of the 'interveners' in an imperial diploma of Henry IV given at Verona. John was also the episcopal guardian of the tomb in Speyer cathedral that housed the relics of Guido's spiritual father and namesake, the abbot of Pomposa, at one time a famed ascetic and valued spiritual counsellor of the emperor. One would give much to know if Bishop John was aware of the association between his cathedral (the mausoleum of the Salian Emperors) and a seminal figure in the Guido story.[3]

John of Affligem: An Early Admirer

The Guido celebrated in the music treatise by William of St Emmeram, eventually abbot of Hirsau, is principally the pragmatic theorist of the plainchant modes and the master of the monochord. There was considerably more to Guido's legacy and reputation than the device of notating on a staff. There is quite a different emphasis, however, in the musical treatise by the theorist, known only as John, who compiled a *De Musica* probably at some time during the decades on either side of 1100. This John maintains that when neumes are used without a Guidonian apparatus they are 'without rule', *irregulares*, and therefore they 'promote error rather than knowledge' among singers. By showing all the intervals plainly, the new method allows a novice singer 'to learn the entire antiphoner or *graduale* without a master'. True to these principles, John employs forms of Guido's staff-notation in his Tonary, and with the enthusiasm of a recent convert he devotes chapter 22 to 'the usefulness of the neumes that Guido invented'. Without them there can only be folly and ignorance.

There is perhaps no music theorist of the Middle Ages whom one can more confidently describe as a singer than John. He refers to performances that he gave himself, offering his audience *cantiones* that are perhaps settings of Latin lyric verse and discovering in the process that it is impossible to please all of the people all of the time. 'What one listener praised to the heights, another disliked profoundly.' John also provides an exceptionally vivid glimpse of three singers around 1100 comparing their own versions of chants and standing up for their teachers:

> One says, 'Master Trudo taught me this way'. Another rejoins: 'But I learned it like this from master Albinus'; and to this a third remarks, 'Master Salomon certainly sings differently' . . . rarely, therefore, do three men agree about one chant. Since each man prefers his own teacher, there arise as many variations in chanting as there are teachers in the world.[4]

John is probably envisaging three men from different houses, brought together in one place by the various kinds of circumstance that could compel the pupils of different chant teachers to sing together. When a new monastic foundation was stocked with monks from an older house, when a monk left an abbey to become a teacher in another, or when monastic houses were forcibly closed and the monks sent into exile, situations like the one described by John could no doubt easily arise. John is thoroughly Guidonian in his conviction that the use of staff-notation can put an end to such disputes, and that it allows a master to address his teaching to the entire Latin Church, not simply to a *circle*. It is not rare to find a particular abbot or bishop of this period remembered as an assiduous corrector of chants (William of St Emmeram comes to mind) but with the older neumes the work could only be done face to face, or rather voice to voice. The corrector could pass on his edited versions to a certain circle of singers with whom he was in regular contact, and perhaps through intermediaries he might transmit them to any dependent churches where he had authority. The teacher who wielded staff-notation, however, and who used it to prescribe correct practice in one chant after another, could address a much wider audience, subject only to the limitations imposed by the reprehensible slowness of others to master the new methods or their folly in rejecting them. John, by isolating what he judged to be errors in the chants he heard, gathers to himself an authority that cannot be perceived purely in musical terms alone because no medieval editors of plainsong made their appeal for better practice to a free-standing form of purely *musical* discernment. They made it instead to conscience: to the regulator of each individual's spiritual life. The only way to issue that appeal was to adopt the voice of the teaching Church. John even styles himself *servus servorum dei*, 'servant of the servants of God', a title by no means unknown among bishops and abbots but so widely used by the bishops of Rome that some medieval readers believed that John was to be identified with a pope of that name.[5]

John's use of that style is one of several mysteries surrounding the identity and milieu of this, the first northerner to advocate Guido's new notation in a surviving treatise and to make it a major pedagogical issue. The book is dedicated to a certain Fulgentius, named in some sources of the text as 'bishop of the English' but also as *antistes*, indicating a bishop or abbot (the term means literally a leader or 'one who stands in front'). The various headings to the treatise, devised by scribes or taken over from their exemplars, call Fulgentius a bishop or even an archbishop. The puzzle here, as has long been known, is that no Fulgentius has ever been found among the clergy or monks of Norman England and it is perhaps unlikely that any will emerge in the future. The only plausible candidate seems to be the Fulgentius from Brabant, not from England, who became the abbot of Affligem, now in Belgium, in the year 1084. This man was well known between the Meuse and the Rhine, where the conflicting allegiances of different sides in the strife between papacy and Empire had made monastic and clerical communities eager for news about positions and personalities. Fulgentius's name appears in many of the Affligem charters, again in its official history, and again in the chronicle of at least one other important abbey, the house at Sint Truiden, between Leuven and Aachen. This suggests that something went badly wrong at a very early stage in the transmission of John's text for Fulgentius to be presented in all witnesses as a bishop or abbot 'of the English'. The only escape from complete quandary may be to assume, with Smits van Waesberghe, that *anglorum* is a corruption of *angelorum* ('of the angels'), perhaps because it was abbreviated *angłorum* in an early exemplar of the text. In purely scribal terms, this is an easy mistake to make, especially perhaps in an area of Low-German Latin where the words *anglorum* and *angelorum* were all but indistinguishable when spoken. That very near homophony explains why it was often considered legitimate to express the sense 'of the angels', requiring *angelorum*, by the form *anglorum* ('of the English') in hexameters, for metrical reasons, as in some lines by the eleventh-century poet Egbert of Liège:

> Illa Salem mater, cui nomen uisio pacis,
> Anglorum numero constabit tota hominumque.

> She, mother Jerusalem, whose name means 'vision of peace', will be entirely comprised of angels and mankind.[6]

What does John mean by calling Fulgentius 'leader of the angels'? It certainly implies no special link to Affligem or to any other house of monks or clergy, despite what has often been assumed. The answer seems to be much simpler. A standard point of canon law taught that '*angelus* is a Greek word meaning *messenger* and therefore priests, canons and monks, who proclaim the commandments of God, are called angels'. John's expression 'leader of angels' may therefore mean nothing more or less than 'abbot' or 'bishop': one who heads a community of monks or clergy as an archangel leads an angelic host. There are several close parallels to this usage in eleventh-century writings. Fulbert of Chartres calls Abbot Odilo of Cluny 'archangel of monks', and Peter Damian gives the same title to Abbot Hugh of Cluny. Damian also calls Abbot Desiderius of Montecassino *archangelus monachorum*, 'archangel of monks'.[7]

Placing John at Affligem, as one may with some confidence, explains a number of things about his use of Guido's new notation. John writes with particular zeal, but not only because he believes (rightly) that Guido's system is as yet unknown to many; he also knows that his abbey of Affligem is almost as new as the musical staff. According to the house chronicle, compiled in various layers during the first half of the twelfth century, the abbey of Affligem arose from the situation of lawlessness along the road between Ghent and Brussels. In the region of Aalst a group of six knights had long been preying upon pilgrims and merchants using the public road, but their behaviour changed completely in 1083. Some time before Easter in that year, they heard a sermon by an itinerant monk named Wedericus from St Peter's abbey in Ghent, one of many licensed or unlicensed preachers at large around 1100 and sent forth as emissaries of the imperial or papal cause. Such men could have an effect beyond all modern expectation. Driven to repentance by his words, or so the house-chronicle of Affligem claims, the robber knights spent three months in religious poverty with Wedericus and then confessed their crimes at Cologne before the archbishop.[8]

If there is an element of sustained fiction here, as there so often is in accounts of monastic origins, it is probably to be sought above all in the use of familiar literary topos: the implantation of a monastic house on land notorious hitherto for being the haunt of devils and thieves. One could scarcely ask for an account that shapes specific events and actors more determinedly than this one into the conventional drama of cleansing by monastic foundation. Yet the element of pious fiction does not necessarily extend to Wedericus, the itinerant preacher, for he is known from elsewhere, and there is a strong likelihood that the report of the knights' penitential journey to Cologne is also based upon actual events. The supporting evidence lies with the Truce of God council convened at Cologne on the twentieth of April in the very year the knights are supposed to have had their change of heart; indeed, it was called soon after Easter, by which time the house-chronicle says the knights had made up their minds to change their manner of life. The Truce of God councils were concerned with peace in the sense of Christian charity within a reformed and well-governed Church, but they also reached outwards to the depredations of thieves and robbers, the violence of sieges, the days of the liturgical year (especially the fasting days) when it was forbidden to bear arms, and the penalties, carefully graded according to rank, for murder or mutilation. The Truce of God council at Cologne, whose highly abbreviated proceedings survive, would have provided penitent knights with an entirely appropriate context for making a public confession and for receiving their penance. They made a *humilis confessio* at Cologne, according the house-chronicle, and perhaps as part of this very council; in response, Archbishop Sigewin commanded them to found a monastic house near the road where they had disturbed the peace.[9]

When John's treatise is contextualized in its Affligem setting, the device of staff-notation once more finds its place in the current of what is often known today by the unduly simplified name of the Gregorian Reform, named after Gregory VII (1073–85). However it is to be regarded, it is certain that new waves of reform gave an especially intense form to disputes and conflicting notions of the spiritual and temporal domains reaching back to the *Epistola Widonis*. The itinerant preacher Wedericus who was ultimately responsible for the abbey of Affligem, at least according to the house-chronicle, received his authorization from Pope Gregory VII, and the sins he addressed in his sermons will certainly have included the malfeasance of clergy, monks and laymen in Flanders or Brabant who supported Gregory's rival, the antipope Clement III. Whatever Wedericus said that changed the lives of the robber-knights (if that is indeed how things occurred), he was remembered as a determined reformer who preached at a time when sterner spirits like his own believed the scandals of simony and clerical marriage were so oppressing the Church that 'there was scarcely any distinction between the life of the clergy and the life of the laity', as the chronicle of Affligem puts it. As for Fulgentius, he was available to lead the community at Affligem only because he had fled his own abbey of St-Vanne, together with many of his fellow monks, rather than take an oath before the bishop of Verdun that he disavowed Gregory VII and recognized the Holy Roman Emperor's antipope Clement III. John's *De Musica*, with its spirited advocacy of Guidonian notation, was written for a house with a deep involvement in the conflict between spiritual and temporal powers and for an abbot whose sympathies had been shown to be decidedly papal. Guido would have approved.[10]

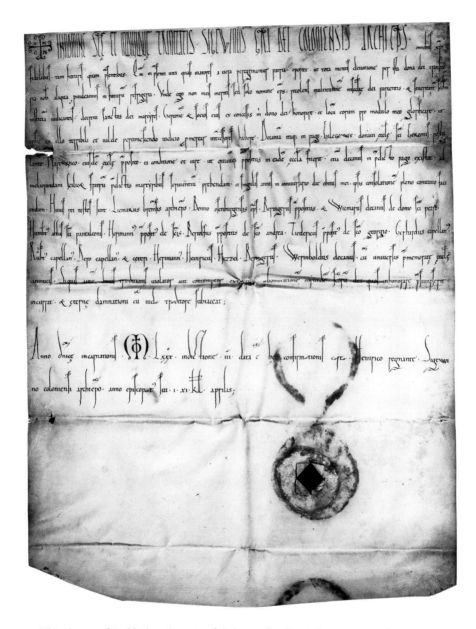

85 This charter of Archbishop Sigewin of Cologne, dated at Cologne, 22 March 1080, conveys some impression of the powerful clerical and monastic community that would have assembled for the Truce of God synod held at Cologne in 1083 when the abbey of Affligem was probably created. Sigewin summoned all the clergy of his archdiocese. The witnesses to this document, issued in favour of the Church of St Gereon in Cologne, include Liemar, archbishop of Bremen, Benno bishop of Osnabruck, Abbot Humbert of St Pantaleon, Hermannus the provost of Xanten (a future archbishop of Cologne) and others, including several chaplains. Cologne, Erzbischofliche Diözesan und Dombibliothek, St Gereon A 1 c. 1. Photograph provided by the Lichtbildarchiv älterer Originalurkunden, Marburg/Lahn (number 14642).

The monastery of Affligem, which still exists but in new buildings on the original site, deserves an eminent position in the early reception of Guido's invention by singers north of the Alps. Nonetheless, there is much that John's book for Fulgentius of Affligem does not reveal. There is no suggestion how one might deal with the objection that the staves, by allowing the student to work alone, deprive the novice of the spiritual nourishment and *caritas* of studying face to face with a superior. Nor does John offer advice to scribes using staff-notation for the first time, perhaps having to adapt the neumes they had been trained to write and planning a page whose visual rhetoric was unlike anything they had previously known. When staves were ruled, the neumes ceased to look like a form of diacritic placed above the text, almost an extension of the grammarian's art (which is probably what the first neumes were); instead, the neumes receded into a mesh of coloured lines, perhaps as scandalous to some conservative spirits as the polychrome pipes and vents of the Centre Pompidou in Paris today, and for much the same reason: they offended the eye and put too much on show. In one sense, that was precisely the point: by making radical changes to the visual decorum of liturgical books, Guido probably hoped his new techniques would radicalize the user's conscience, instilling a measure of fresh scrupulosity in chanting that could be extended to other aspects of the clerical or religious life. John would surely have followed him in this, and the polemical edge of his treatise in some places suggests he was well aware of the need to drive an important message home in the face of both laxity and principled resistance. Many, however, did not get the point, and in parts of what are now Germany and Austria, scribes were still not using Guidonian notations as late as the fifteenth century, to judge by their continuing attachment to staffless neumes.

The process whereby such resistance was gradually overcome elsewhere is usually concealed from view, primarily because chronicles, letters and other literary sources rarely provide the kind of anecdotal evidence necessary to disclose it. In the same way, one can rarely look over the shoulder of a scribe as he decides what to correct while transferring the chant repertory of his house into Guidonian notation. It was this act of transference, perhaps, that was likely to cause the greatest conflict, for it was inevitably a process of editing, as most acts of writing are, however unconsciously the editing is done. When the music was transferred to staff notation from someone's memory – which means from someone's identity as defined by his history and his affiliations to a particular place – then trouble was surely to be expected. As soon as John introduces the new notation in his *De Musica* he condemns those who stand by the old staffless neumes as 'lovers of error and falsehood'. He can now enlighten them all. The task of filtering the repertory of a particular house, for the first time, through the demands of a notation giving a specific indication of pitch was unlikely to remain a tranquil business for long, and some scribes may have regretted the days when the older notations did not compel them to record the melodies in a manner so legible and therefore so vulnerable to a challenge. 'If, as sometimes happens, a musician takes singers to task about a chant which they perform either inaccurately or crudely', says John, 'they become angry and make a shameless uproar and are unwilling to admit the truth, but defend their error with the greatest effort.' Behind almost every paragraph of John's remarks about Guido's new notation there lurks the danger of recrimination and dissent.[11]

For the most part, this contention takes place behind the façades of the liturgical books that survive, so it is fortunate that one monastic chronicle does provide an insight into the reception of Guidonian notation. By a curious coincidence, it relates the activities of a man who, in later years, stayed at Affligem during the time of Fulgentius (he may have known John) and whose abbey owned lands nearby, at Aalst. The account in question describes how a young man named Rudolf, formerly a student at Liège, brought the Guidonian arts to a monastery in the town of Sint Truiden, today in eastern Belgium. It explains why he decided to record the abbey's chant in a new *graduale,* collating the oral witness of the older monks with the books in the monastery's chest; there is also an account of how he accomplished the work. No doubt the process of making a new *graduale* was often more complex than it is made to appear in the source we shall be following, where it seems to be the accomplishment of one man working single-handed; nonetheless, it is plausible that a single carrier introduced Guidonian learning to some centres, and Rudolf of Sint Truiden was seemingly one of them. What emerges from this account is the vital importance of making a new *graduale* at a time when a major fire – the source of so much renewed effort in the Middle Ages – had stripped the abbey down to a few rooms, and when the conflicts of the reform movement had taken their toll on the Sint Truiden monks. Rudolf made the new liturgical book as part of a sustained attempt to recreate and reorganize a community whose collective life was sustained by remembrance: by a recollection of their common past and of the rights they had accrued, by prayers for the dead, and by the respect paid to the older monks of the house. Working with old books and with the oral tradition guarded by the elderly monks, he did not set out to make the abbey's chant conform to the usages of the diocese, even though he recognized that the chant dialect of his abbey was in some measure anomalous, and that the dioceses in question were ones of great prestige (the bishops of Liège had the spiritual jurisdiction over the abbey of Sint Truiden, the bishops of Metz the temporal). Instead, Rudolf wished to investigate what has been called, in a different context, 'a community of memory with more or less reach and endurance' by ascertaining how far back he could reach and by gauging how much had endured.[12]

The Abbey of Sint Truiden and the Need to Start Again

Today, Sint Truiden can stand for many towns in Belgium or northern France that were once in the deep heartlands of Frankish and Carolingian power but are now quiet and provincial (Pl. 86). All around, in the mostly flat or gently undulating landscape, there are towns whose names resonate through the history of the Franks. Aachen is nearby; Liège and Nivelles are not far away. The tower of the medieval abbey, begun during the abbacy of Gontran (1034–55), still rises above the town square, the site of the market whence the abbey drew tolls and rents. During the abbacy of Adelard II (1055–82) Sint Truiden acquired its first circuit of defensive walls and two new churches within them, presumably to accommodate a demographic increase within the *oppidum* and its hinterlands (the descendant of one of these churches can be seen on the right in the illustration). Adelard also began to rebuild various parts of the monastery left broken and ruinous since the depredations of the Vikings towards 880–1. The abbey's

86   The market square at Sint Truiden. The tower of the abbey, to the left of the picture, begun during the abbacy of Gontran (1034–55), is an abiding presence in the *Gesta*, rising 'like a high citadel in the midst of the town' (iii. 6). At various times in the decades around 1100 it was used as a prison, as a fort and as a garrison building. These violent and coercive purposes for the tower reflect the troubled history of the abbey in those years. On the right stands the Church of the Blessed Virgin, rebuilt in a Gothic style but originally one of the churches founded during the abbacy of Adelard II (d. 1082) using wealth brought to the monastery by a revival in the cult of Saint Truiden. It was presumably built in response to a demographic increase within the *oppidum*, which acquired its first set of defensive walls in this same period.

house in Liège was repaired for the use of monks or abbots who wished to consult with the bishop, their spiritual overlord.

These details are recorded in the house-chronicle of the abbey, the *Gesta Abbatum Trudonensium* or 'Deeds of the Abbots of Sint Truiden'. Beginning with a dedicatory letter to Nicholas, provost of the abbey of St-Denis near Paris, this substantial work begins with seven books composed by Rudolf himself, followed by various continuations spanning the next three hundred years. Books I–VII are Rudolf's account of the trials his monastery endured in the second half of the eleventh century, often using eyewitness reports and composed towards the end of the year 1114 or 1115. With Book VIII, probably from *c.*1136, the First Continuator takes up the narrative at Rudolf's request and describes (among many other things) how Rudolf introduced Guidonian arts to the abbey around 1100. Book IX, from 1136–7, is a memoir Rudolf composed and addressed to Stephen, bishop of Metz, concerning the events of his abbacy from 1108 to 1136. Taken as a whole, the *Gesta* therefore appears to be the very essence of a good monastic chronicle: the record of one community throughout the generations, slowly and carefully assembled in layers, and rarely looking so far back that all contact with reliable oral tradition is lost. It is a deeply partisan account of one abbey's labour to re-establish itself as a viable liturgical community while struggling, at the same time, to align itself safely, under various abbots, with one or other party in the conflict between *regnum* and *sacerdotium*. The book also shows a sharp distrust of the townspeople. The narrative shows considerable literary gifts; the description of a passage through the snow and ice of the Great Saint-Bernard pass (XII, 6–7), or the account of a journey with a military retinue (where Rudolf watches, in astonishment, as the soldiers pitch camp each night and raid the local settlements for supplies and fodder) are especially striking (VII, 3).[13]

In the middle years of the eleventh century, the marketplace at Sint Truiden gradually developed into what the First Continuator of the *Gesta* calls a place of *nundina* or fairs (VIII, 12). There were weavers, maltsters, bakers and brewers in the town, and it is telling that the weavers are the only ones whom the abbey's documents associate with an arrogant bearing. It would seem that the textile-based industrial revolution of northern Europe was already under way, and the market at Sint Truiden was beginning to see the results in the form of fair-days and confident weavers. The monks of the house did not see that the palfreys, oxen, cows, sheep and cheese brought to them as offerings in ever-increasing quantities were connected with the quickening economic life of the town (I, 8–10). Instead, they saw that the saintly patron of their abbey had decided to heal the sick with renewed vigour, bringing a stream of pilgrims along the roads to the monastery and creating a shanty-town of tents on the major feast-days (perhaps also fair-days) of the liturgical year. The *Gesta* reports such a crowd of pavilions with accompanying fires at night, and such an abundance of merchants with horses and wagons, that the monks spoke as if their monastery were under siege. The throng attracted a 'crowd of merchants' with a 'clamour of men buying and selling' in the market square beneath the abbey's tower when the pilgrims gathered, a long-term problem (I, 10; VII, 10). The noise of these vendors and others, sounding far into the night, made it difficult for the monks to meet even the basic demands of the *Rule*, and the younger monks (according to the singularly staid sentiments of the *Gesta*) were only too pleased to have the round of silence and choral praise broken. To make matters worse, Abbot Adelard fell ill and was taken to Liège, where he lay raving before the shrine of Saint Wolbodon. He died in 1082. The bishops of Metz and Liège acted swiftly together in consort with the emperor, and imposed their own candidate, a certain Lanzo. In this, they overruled the monks' own choice of abbot, with bitter consequences. Many of the monks fled or went into exile into other monasteries, some of them travelling as far as England (II, *passim*).

On 9 March 1086, the event occurred which was to shape the life of Rudolf when he came to Sint Truiden a decade or so later. A fire broke out in the town and rapidly spread to one of the monastery towers when a stork's nest burst into flames. From that moment on, little could be saved. 'At length therefore it fell, the monastery fell' wrote Rudolf in later years, with passionate emphasis as he looked back upon the disaster (II, 13). The monks were henceforth confined to a small building, the upper floor serving as their dormitory and refectory, the lower as the school and infirmary. There were no sources of light or heat, even where the sick lay in their beds, and the brothers were afraid to absent themselves from Matins, even for reasons of Nature, so fearful were they of the dark and of falling in the slippery mud (VI, 4). Several more years of strife intervened, with not a little violence and bloodshed that scarred the relationship between the monks and the townspeople.

The Arrival of Rudolf

This is the context for the arrival of Rudolf, who enters the narrative of the *Gesta* at the beginning of Book VIII, the work of the First Continuator. An excellent Latinist, a fine teacher and a gifted musician (but a less than wonderful singer, to judge by a passing remark at XI, 16) he was born in Moutier-sur-Sambre, near Namur. He had already spent an undisclosed period of time at the abbeys of Burtscheid and Gladbach when he came to Sint Truiden, but it is the years he passed in the schools of Liège which provide the most illuminating context for his skills as a musician. At Liège, where he remained until the age of 18, Rudolf was engaged in the study of Latin grammar and prose composition, together with the craft of writing metrical or quantitative poetry (VIII, 2). These were studies that contributed to the highly valued quality of *religiosa urbanitas*: a piety given breadth and refinement by a cultivated literary taste. The composition of metrical verse was necessarily confined to those who had shown great promise in their early schooling, for it required a sound knowledge of Latin quantity laid down in childhood when the memory is best able to absorb tables and mnemonics, together with a keen ear for patterns of lightness and heaviness in syllables, refined during a lifetime of experience as taste gradually matured. The diocese of Liège fostered an especially impressive series of musicians and composers who had been educated in this way. Stephen, bishop of Liège 903–20, is one of the earliest on record, and many others followed him, including Heriger, who became abbot of Lobbes in 990, and Olbert of Gembloux (d. 1048). Lambert, who was the abbot of St Lawrence in Liège in the next generation, composed chants for St Heribert of Cologne, founder of the abbey of Deutz; Stephen, abbot of St James in Liège from 1095, honoured the universal saints Benedict, James the Apostle and John the Evangelist with plainsongs composed 'in a wondrous fashion'. Younger men among the Liège composers, not included in the Appendix to Chapter 19 on grounds of chronology, included Wazelin, Nizo, Giselbert and Johannes, all active in the last years of Rudolf's abbacy, and Reiner, monk of St Lawrence in Liège, the chronicler who provides much of this information. In Dr Johnson's phrase, the lands between the Meuse and the Moselle were 'a nest of singing birds'.[14]

With a background in the schools of Liège, a young man of 18 at the end of the eleventh century might harbour ambitions to become a canon in the chapter of some wealthy cathedral. This may have been Rudolf's intention at some stage, but when he first came to the abbey of Sint Truiden just before 1100 he was already in search of a monastery where the *Rule* of Saint Benedict was observed with a scrupulosity to match the demands of his conscience. During his first night as a guest in the house, Abbot Theuderic asked him the purpose of his journey. As Rudolf gave his reply, Theuderic began to appreciate that here was a becoming young man, with excellent Latinity, who would be an asset to a monastic community still living in 'a naked, broken and horrible vastness of a temple' after their great fire. At this time the community contained only ten monks and four pupils in the makeshift school, all of whom are named as the rhetoric of the *Gesta* steers towards one of the favourite topoi of monastic history: the impoverished and depleted community, whose members scarcely reach double figures, on the verge of a transformation at the hands of one man destined to become abbot. With the needs of these boys (and much else) in mind, Abbot Theuderic resolved to keep Rudolf in and direct his talents to the school.

Once there, Rudolf began to compile valuable documents, including teaching aids for the boys and materials for the use of the abbot:

> Theuderic, asking him who he was and whence he came, and also with what intention had set out, learned that his intention was good and noticed that he was a young man beautifully educated in Latin letters. He began wisely to ponder how he might keep him at Sint Truiden, believing that he would be of much use, first in instructing the boys in learning and doctrine for him, and

afterwards, if it should so happen, to promote him to some ecclesiastical position either within the monastery or without. When he had persuaded him to stay by his gracious speech, he first set him to teach the boys and to make certain most useful compilations, full of many divine sayings worthy to be written, and many canons of councils. In the first year, Rudolf also wrote for Theuderic that most useful volume containing much from Scripture, and he also taught boys, mere beginners who could scarcely decline *musa*, not only the art of letter-writing but also how to compose metrical Latin poetry (VIII, 4).[15]

There were many drawbacks to being a teacher, or indeed a pupil, amidst the ashes of this abbey shortly after 1100, not least because Rudolf spoke only the common Latin speech now recognized as a separate language and called Walloon (the adverb *gualonice*, '[spoken] in a Walloon manner', is used in the *Gesta*) together with an educated Latin speech, close to the form used in the liturgy that was nobody's native tongue. Nonetheless, the four boys in this school enjoyed one distinct advantage: their master was an expert in 'the art of music according to Guido':

> Rudolf bore a great labour in teaching them, since he did not know how to speak to them in a Germanic tongue, and some of the boys knew so little as yet that they could not understand him in their native Low German, nor in Latin, nor, if I may say so, in a Walloon manner. . . . He instructed them in the art of music according to Guido, and was the first to introduce that art into our cloister. To the amazement of the senior monks he made them sing straight away, only by looking, with art and yet with a silent master, what they had never learned by hearing (VIII, 4).[16]

The last sentence of this would have gladdened Guido's heart, for it describes exactly what he set out to achieve and bequeath to the Universal Church. Yet the question of what is meant by 'the art of music according to Guido' can have no simple answer. It must have included the fundamental technique of solmization and the system of hexachords using the syllables *ut, re, mi, fa, sol, la*. The *ars musica secundum Guidonem* will also have included the techniques for dividing up a monochord and perhaps the method of composing new settings of Latin texts by mechanically correlating the vowels of each word with a table of pitches (a technique of which both Guido and John have a curiously high opinion). Nonetheless, only two aspects of Rudolf's musical work are mentioned in the *Gesta* that are directly relevant to his advocacy of Guidonian methods: his ability to notate music 'by art' (*per artem*) and his ability to train the boys so that they could sing a chant at sight (VIII, 4). Taken together, these activities leave no doubt: Rudolf had learned to use a form of Guidonian staff-notation at Liège for which solmization and monochord studies were the necessary preparation.[17]

Some sense of the material that Rudolf encountered there can probably be gained from a manuscript of music theory now at Darmstadt. This is a compilation of Guidonian material once in the possession of the monastery of St James in Liège and possibly copied there. Dating from the beginning of the twelfth century, it reaches back to within a few decades or so of Rudolf's studies in that city and the years when he was a frequent visitor to St James after it had successfully modelled its monastic life upon the usages of Cluny, inspiring Rudolf (amidst much controversy) to introduce the same customs at Sint Truiden (VIII, 16–17). This section of the manuscript contains all Guido's musical treatises in the MRPE order: the *Micrologus*, the *Regule rhythmice*, the *Prologus in Antiphonarium* and the *Epistola ad Michahelem*: a complete set for anyone seeking to acquire the 'art of music according to Guido'. If the materials known to Rudolf at Liège resembled these, which seems highly likely, then the extraordinary variety of the Guidonian art becomes apparent once again. At this date, it is still impossible to speak of 'Guidonian staff-notation' as if it were a stable entity rather than a bundle of graphic tools, for there are many different forms of staff notation in the Darmstadt manuscript and at least *sixteen* different techniques for representing pitch in this one section of the manuscript alone. Many do not use staves at all, for in numerous musical examples of his *Micrologus*, Guido does not; in those that do, the lines may be ruled with a dry-point; some of them may be inked or all of them may be; one or more clef letters, not always placed upon the left-hand side (they are sometimes on the right) may appear and vanish. Sometimes pitch letters are placed upon the dry-point lines rather than neumes, connected or not connected by lines as the scribes may choose and according to the models before them. There is even an intermediary stage between a stave-line that is inked, and one ruled with a dry-point: it is a kind of comb that marks each rank with a few millimetres of ink then ceases, leaving the rest of the 'line' dry. The notations most familiar to Rudolf in liturgical books could have taken any or all of these forms.[18]

By an exceptional piece of good fortune, the evidence for Rudolf's use of the stave can be enhanced with some of his own compositions that may offer a guide to his practice. These survive in Université de Liège, Bibliothèque générale, MS 12, from the first half of the twelfth century and perhaps a Sint Truiden book, for a note records it was there in the seventeenth. Rudolf's chants for the translation of Truiden and Eucharius are notated here with Messine neumes on dry-point lines. These melodies were probably composed while Rudolf was either the schoolmaster of the abbey or the *decanus*, for the texts are by his predecessor as abbot, Theuderic. One antiphon also survives from his chants for Saint Quentin (Pl. 87).[19]

Rudolf of Sint Truiden was an exceptional man, but many things are familiar in the portrait of him that emerges from Book VIII of the *Gesta*. Like some other monks, bishops and abbots who are praised for their musical skills in chronicles

87 Chants by Rudolf of Sint Truiden in honour of the monastery's patron. Université de Liège, Bibliothèque générale de Philosophie et Lettres, MS 12, fol. 99ᵛ, 12th c. The *F*-line is ruled in red, the others are indistinguishable from the dry-point lines used for the text, so the 'staves' are formed when lines of Latin text frame the standard dry-point ruling for a full page of text into groups (generally) of four. There are five different clef combinations adjusted according to the tessitura of the melody *dfac, bdf, fgabcde* (creating the phenomenon, rare in modern staff-notation, of a cleffed space), *face[f]* (creating adjacent staff lines a semitone apart, again a practice that is no longer widely employed) and *bdfa*.

and narrative sources, Rudolf was a *scholasticus*. Neither the translation 'scholar' (implying too much specialization) nor 'schoolmaster' (which is too lowly) will quite suffice to translate this medieval term. A composite picture of the *scholasticus* emerges from many literary sources of the eleventh and twelfth centuries, suggesting a valued teacher with a superior ability to write elegant Latin and especially to compose metrical verse; he is interested in bookish matters traversing the post-medieval boundary between science and art (and therefore embracing matters such as the mathematics and proportions of the monochord). Very often, and this was certainly true of Rudolf, the abilities of the *scholasticus* were sharpened during an adolescence spent on the move; indeed, there was sometimes a lingering sense of worldliness about such men, a breath of the open road which they might one day choose again, and which was often an important part of their reputation. Abbot Theuderic of Sint Truiden knew he had such a man at his table when Rudolf came to his monastery during the course of his wanderings. One therefore became a *scholasticus* by settling somewhere, at least for a time, and by being valued as a teacher with much to impart and a gift for doing so. Such men included Constantine (*fl. c.*1000), who composed the office for the translation of Saint Benedict used at Fleury and is called a *nobilis scholasticus* by Gerbert of Aurillac (coming from such a quarter, this was high praise indeed), and John, monk of St Lawrence in Liège around 1140, a *scholasticus* who composed chants for Saint Christopher and Saint Mary of Egypt. With these teachers and musicians, a fundamental figure in the history of medieval and Renaissance music is already present: the master of grammar and chant attached to a monastery, or a cathedral church, whose expertise as a teacher, as a singer, as a composer, or as all three together, could be of a high order.

   Not long after his arrival at Sint Truiden, Rudolf decided to renotate the Mass chants of his abbey. This committed him to an immense amount of manual labour since he prepared the parchment himself from its raw state, or so the *Gesta* maintains, and was solely responsible for the copying. The project also involved him in the arduous work of comparing the oral tradition of his house with the testimony of the existing graduals, surely in some form of staffless notation, and of editing the result. Just after 1100 the manufacture of a new *graduale* could not be – if it had ever been – a simple matter of parchment, ink and long hours of work. For a monastic house like Sint Truiden, the choice of what to notate, down to matters of the finest melodic detail, was also a decision about whose version of the oral tradition should be given precedence in a community markedly inclined to rivalry, faction and dissent (as collegiate communities often are). Should the chant known to a bright young man like Rudolf, not long since emerged from the schools of Liège, be given precedence over the versions sung by 80-year-olds whose tradition was in some respects demonstrably idiosyncratic or ungrammatical because it could not be notated on a stave? Beyond that, the choice of what to notate, and the arrangement of the calendar, represented a particular relationship between the entrenched localism of most medieval liturgical communities and their wider connections with the authority of a bishop, perhaps of a metropolitan, that they might wish to affirm or contest by following or not following the usage of the cathedral or metropolitan church.

Why did Rudolf choose to undertake such an exacting and delicate task? The simplest answer is that the community and resources of his abbey had been so depleted by the fire of 1086 that it was necessary to recreate the monastic life of the house around its choral liturgy. As far as it goes, that is a convincing explanation, but it probably does not go far enough, for by the standards of the monks who sheltered beneath the tower of Sint Truiden's abbey Rudolf, although a young man, had seen something of the world and its political and ecclesiastical affairs. He had been a student at Liège, where nobody could escape the consequences of the continuing struggle between *regnum* and *sacerdotium*, the temporal and spiritual powers with Emperor and Pope at their summit, just as no abbot could hope to rule his monastery without becoming involved, at various times, in factions on one side or the other. The *Gesta* shows that Rudolf certainly did not avoid such potentially dangerous choices, and Books I–IX provide every encouragement to view his work with the chant of his house in terms of the protracted struggle that began well before he was born.[20]

'Gregorian Reform' and Gregorian Chant: Why Make a New Graduale?

In 1049, the Lotharingian nobleman and composer Bruno of Toul became pope, taking the name Leo IX. This was a clear sign that the emperor Henry III and his advisers were determined to reform the papacy by giving the see to trusted imperial chaplains, wresting the throne of Saint Peter from Italian families, who were widely condemned for regarding it as a private property, indeed a *cosa nostra*. Had not Guido's bishop, John XIX, inherited the see from his brother? With the accession of Gregory VII (1073–85), however, the attempt to reform the papacy begun by Henry III assumed a virulent life of its own, as it was bound to do since its ingredients were so diverse and had been simmering since the time of the *Epistola Widonis* some fifty years before. The conflict between Gregory VII and the emperor Henry III, then his son Henry IV, was essentially a clash between two powers that both drew deeply upon the same Roman legacy of imperial triumph and dominion. One of these powers, the Roman Church, was a spiritual entity, but with immense temporal possessions, that anticipated the kingdom of heaven by working for the kingdom of Christ on earth; the other, the Holy Roman Empire, was a temporal entity, but with immense obligations to the spiritual life of the Empire, that would eventually be swept away among the chaos of the last things. Nonetheless, the legacy of Constantine as a Roman-Christian Emperor, and the continuing example of Byzantium, provided ample stimulus for conceiving the Holy Roman Emperor as God's appointed ruler, just as the history of apostolic mission gave the Roman Church a potent but ill-defined form of territorial authority which conferred on popes the right to remind kings that their kingdoms lay in a Roman obedience. Gregory VII insistently claimed that he was adding nothing to the tradition of the Catholic Church in making claims for papal power and he could cite such famous documents as the letter where Innocent I (401–17) reminds Bishop Decentius of Gubbio that all the churches in 'Italy, the Gauls, the Spains, Africa, Sicily and the intervening islands' had begun with priests consecrated by the 'venerable apostle Peter or his successors'. The whole of the Latin-Christian West, in other words, was ultimately the creation of the Roman Church. All Christians dwelling there had incurred obligations to Rome, and from the Roman point of view they were conveniently difficult to delimit.[21]

During Gregory's papacy the issue of clerical purity became urgent and contentious. The papal circle insisted that the higher clergy should form sanctified orders of persons set apart, purified by their repeated denial of the body's appetites for food, sleep and sexual congress, purified further by a want of bribery and corruption in their appointment and free from any taint of bloodshed. A religion that owed so much to the Jewish rules of purity and impurity here came into conflict with a more pragmatic and essentially Roman-imperial tradition of governance that did not readily envisage the possibility of conflict between the demands of religion and state. With bitter determination, Gregory and his supporters opposed one practice of governance that had been a principal instrument of Christian rulers since the time of Clovis: the prerogative of a king or emperor, though he be a layman, to approve candidates to bishoprics, indeed to nominate them, and to have them enthroned. The Holy Roman Emperors appointed trusted men from the ranks of the imperial chaplains to serve as bishops in the strategic sees of the Empire, and invested them with ring and staff; recent history had shown that they could also nominate a pope and have the election carried through. Gregory, however, insisted that lay magnates could not henceforth appoint bishops and invest them with their insignia, just as they were not to appropriate lands over which the Church had a temporal claim (an issue that always hovered somewhere between the terrestrial and the transcendent, somewhat to Rome's advantage). These forms of lay influence, even lay dominance, were regarded by many churchmen as potential sources of impurity that the reformers described, and no doubt perceived, in terms of disease and physical corruption.[22]

During the two generations before Rudolf came to Sint Truiden, the popes and their circle increasingly associated the liturgy of Rome with full membership of the Roman obedience. Leo IX (d. 1054) was famous as a musician who not only composed a widely known Office in honour of Gregory the Great but also stipulated that he should be buried near Gregory's tomb in Saint Peter's basilica. In 1058, a cleric from Leo's inner circle, his countryman Frederick of Lorraine, became pope as Stephen IX (1057–8) and almost immediately ruled that the repertory of 'Ambrosian' (that is to say Beneventan) chant at the abbey of

Montecassino, where he had until recently been abbot, should be replaced by [Frankish-]Roman plainsong. Beneventan chant was indeed ousted, but very slowly, in Italy during a process that took some four centuries. With Beneventan chant at least nominally suppressed, Gregory VII could turn his attention from 1073 to the Mozarabic plainsong of Spain. Gregory knew that King Alfonso VI of Castile and León was striving to expand and repopulate the territories of his kingdom as he made fresh conquests against the forces of Islam. Alfonso listened as Gregory VII exhorted him to adopt the Roman liturgy, for the pope presented him with a vision of Spain's Christian history from apostolic times, a profound expression of Gregory's own convictions but also well calculated to accord with the long-term aspirations of the king, whatever the frustrations and setbacks he encountered on the battlefield or in the council chamber. In 1074, the second year of Gregory's pontificate, Alfonso received a mighty letter from Gregory calling Spain back to the Roman fold after its many centuries of pollution by heresy (a reference to Priscillianism and Arianism) and by the depredations of invading Goths and Saracens. The apostles and their delegates had evangelized Spain, Gregory insisted, leaning heavily on Romans 15: 14 and 28, among other sources, to make the point. King Alfonso and his advisers should recognize the Roman Church as their mother and adopt the Roman order of service, 'not the Toledan or any other'. They should take their proper place in Latin Christendom, in the world that looked back to the apostles and to the Roman Empire, ending their isolation by adopting the same rite as 'other kingdoms of the west and north'. This was a tempting vision for a king who surely believed that the history of Spain had taken a grievous turn with the Moorish invasion, and one that seemed anomalous when viewed in terms of the other old western Roman provinces. At a council in Burgos, convened in 1080, Alfonso decreed that the *Romanum officium* should be celebrated henceforth 'in all parts of Spain under my dominion'. That included a great deal of northern Spain, and after 1085 it included Toledo, the ancient royal capital of the Visigothic kings; even there the indigenous Mozarabic liturgy and chant of Spain was eventually pushed aside – but not entirely replaced.[23]

Rudolf of Sint Truiden was an ally of the papal cause. Looking back upon the days before his arrival, when an emperor had imposed his choice of abbot upon the monks through the bishops of Metz and Liège, Rudolf became incensed because 'it is not canonical to place the illicit power of the emperor in such a matter before apostolic authority' (III, 2). That is Gregorian language. There is a note of discreet satisfaction when he records that an emperor had invested his predecessor with the abbacy of Sint Truiden '*because it was the custom at that time*' (III, 7). Rudolf was evidently determined it should be the custom no more. Recording that a former abbot of the house had obtained the position by a form of bribery, he unhesitatingly calls it, with the intemperate language used by all parties in the dispute, the 'madness of raving simoniacs' (I, 2 and 4). There is something of the nascent canon lawyer here, and there are other traces of it. The

Gesta records that while Rudolf was teaching the 'art of music according to Guido' his abbot asked him to assemble 'many canons of councils' (VIII, 4). Much later in life, Rudolf compiled a forthright letter on the question of canonical elections addressed to Bishop Alexander of Liège, the imperial nominee for that see, which will have done nothing to ingratiate him with the emperor's supporters in the city (XI, 6). This aspect of Rudolf's learning breaks through the early books of the *Gesta* in several places, notably in his account of the episode mentioned above when the emperor imposed Abbot Lanzo upon the house. This was precisely the kind of offence in the matter of an election, arising from lay interference, that new compilations of canon law like the *Collectio Canonum* (*c.*1086) of Anselm of Lucca, or Rudolf's own collection, were designed to address (II, 9–11). Although Rudolf compiled his account of Lanzo's appointment some twenty years later, and is describing events in which he did not participate, the issue still seems to burn the parchment as he lays out the 'authorities of the Holy See' that forbid such a move.[24]

In his contacts with laymen, a vital issue for the Gregorian reformers, Rudolf was implacable. The desire to disentangle the abbey from the townsmen, whose labour and offerings did so much to sustain it, runs through the *Gesta* from Rudolf's campaign against the horse contests the monks enjoyed with townspeople during the Rogation days of September (III, 3; VIII, 10) to the work of sealing the cloister so that local laymen and clergy could not exercise their customary right to pass through the inner parts of the abbey (VIII, 14). The materials Rudolf wrote for the *Gesta* show a deep distrust of the townspeople: the weavers, maltsters, bakers and brewers mentioned in one of his own charters. He regards them as 'seditious people' and a threat to both the abbey's security and its treasury (III, 2). He would certainly have understood the Gregorians' insistence that churches had to be freed from the control of laymen, for the *Gesta* bears constant witness to a church battered by local feuds and (in the eyes of the monks) by rapacious counts. Late in his abbacy, Rudolf looked back upon years in which the monastery's lay advocate, supposedly the guardian of its legal rights, and several local bishops all commanding their own private militias, had contended together with much violence or robbed the farms and stores of the monastery's *villae*. This painful history was written upon the face of the monastic site, a 'vast space of a broken monastery in need of repair' (II, 4). Local nobles had seized lands belonging to the monastery, and the altar of the monastic church had not so long ago been stained with blood in a riot, a gross impurity (III, 3).

For Rudolf, as for Guido, staff-notation was a means to fix an edited and corrected version of chant as part of a far-reaching attempt to raise standards in the religious and clerical life. For Guido, it was a method to teach a corrected Roman chant as part of a comprehensive reform only intermittently associated, as yet, with the papacy; it is more closely linked to grass-roots movements in northern Italian cities such as Milan, and with men of minor importance like Guido himself. For Rudolf, writing two generations later when some popes of extraordinary mettle had occupied the throne of Saint Peter, staff-notation was a pedagogical device now closely associated – at least in his mind – with a papal allegiance in the conflict between *regnum* and *sacerdotium*. One can recognize some of Guido's deepest wellsprings here, notably the sense that a corrected repertory of chant, fixed by staff-notation, is vital for the purified life of monk and cleric, uncorrupted by the taint of money, sexual pollution and contact with those who are neither monks nor clerics. What makes Rudolf's work so intriguing, however, is the sober empiricism of his methods. Working around 1100, he had even more reason than Guido to associate a purified chant with a duly edited *Roman* chant, and yet Rome strikes no figure in the account of what he accomplished. Rudolf took stock of the situation in his abbey, settled on a realistic aim, and pursued it.

Rudolf Begins Work

These events at Sint Truiden, and those on the wider stage of the eleventh-century Church, suggest that Rudolf will surely emerge from the *Gesta* as a stern and unbending corrector of chant. The Gregorian reforms had left no scope for a diligent corrector of plainsong to work independently of currents in the wider life of the Church, to say nothing of his own diocese where, as mentioned above, bishops and abbots were often forced by events to take a stand in the conflict between *regnum* and *sacerdotium.* Yet while the *Gesta* undoubtedly does show Rudolf using Guido's notation as a means to comb out what he finds to be irregular in the chant of the house, the chronicle definitely does not show another John of Affligem searing his way through the 'ignorance of fools that corrupts the chant'. The account of Rudolf's labours in the *Gesta* is all the more convincing for the emphasis it gives to a determined reformer's recognition that judicious compromise might be necessary in a local context despite the universalism of his own reforming instincts and those of the popes whose cause he championed. His depth of conviction, his legalism, and even his willingness to be forthright in a contentious situation were not translated into a self-defeating authoritarianism when he made his *graduale*, and he did not lose the ability to be conciliatory (which was surely one of Guido's failings) when he began it.

The first continuator of the *Gesta* (VIII) places the work of making the *graduale* in Rudolf's first years at the monastery, soon after 1099, and traces it to his discovery that he could not sing 'according to the use of the cloister' when he arrived. The monks' manner of singing 'did not accord, we do not know how this came about, with that of any other house in our Province' (VIII, 5). As a result, Rudolf often found himself unable to participate. This is all somewhat curious, to say the least. The abbey of Sint Truiden lay within the temporal jurisdiction of the bishop of Metz, a church of outstanding importance for the development and dissemination of Gregorian chant whose name has often figured in this book. Until the eleventh century, the bishops of Metz usually held the abbacy of Sint Truiden, which explains why Chrodegang, a principal architect of Frankish-Roman chant under Pippin, was at one time the abbot. (A tenth-century Life even records that Chrodegang received his education in the abbey; the Life is unreliable in many points of detail, but this is not impossible, since Chrodegang's family came from the nobility of the Hesbaye region.) Perhaps the abbey had evolved its own chant dialect from the usages brought to the monastery when a few of the monks returned after the enforced diaspora a generation before Rudolf (II, 12); monastic chronicles of the period 1050–1150 reveal many flights of this kind, with monasteries emptied then refilled, and with stragglers left wandering from house to house. Nonetheless, the abbey of Sint Truiden not only had connections with Metz, it also lay close to Aachen and Charle-magne's imperial chapel. One may well understand why the First Continuator of the *Gesta* abandoned any attempt to explain why his abbey followed an idiosyncratic *usus cantandi*.[25]

The chronicle shows how a gradual process of theorization overtook the plain-song performance of the abbey after approximately 1100, some of its dialectal ele-ments being gradually replaced with common elements of musical language as taught by pedagogues such as John of Affligem. The work of theorization began with Rudolf, or so the *Gesta* maintains, and continued into the generation of his pupils, singers who paid their teacher the supreme compliment of surpassing him in their exactitude of musical judgement. They recognized that Rudolf's work of bringing the abbey's chant to book had not gone far enough, that his *graduale* was incorrect in some places or ill-judged in others, and that he had been unduly deferential to the abbey's dialect of Frankish-Roman plainsong. Those are the opinions of the 1130s and 1140s, when Rudolf's pupils were in the ascendancy among the singers. The *Gesta* is probably unique among the narra-tive sources of the twelfth century for the way it maps different stages of inter-action between plainchant theory and plainchant practice at a time when so many writers were keen to open fresh negotiations between the two, John of Affligem and William, abbot of Hirsau among them. The chronicle distinguish-es three phases. In the first, the singing of the house followed its own traditions insofar as they had survived fire and dispersal. The second phase was marked by the arrival of Rudolf with his Guidonian learning, leading to the creation of a new antiphoner in staff-notation; this was the first attempt to filter the abbey's chant through the Guidonian stave. In the third and final stage, in the 1130s and 1140s, his pupils moved forwards from the point their master had reached and sought a more extensive correction of their practice according to modal and other plainsong grammar. The *Gesta* reports that they treated Rudolf's *graduale* with affection and indulgence, and that Rudolf, by the early 1130s an old man and now the abbot of the house, saw both the characteristic strengths and fail-ings of youth on every page (VIII, 5).

The reference to the abbey's musical dialect in the first and earliest of these three phases is by no means the only allusion in texts of the eleventh and twelfth centuries to lack of unanimity in the choir, or to chants badly in need of correction; that is the problem a great deal of contemporary music theory was written to address, and it provides some insight into what may be involved here. The sense of a chant proceeding like a well-crafted line of Latin metrical verse, without solecism or barbarism, focused trained ears especially upon the placement of semitone steps in relation to a chant's modal identity. Today, when the necessary erudition and ear-training in both fields of endeavour is weakened or obliterated, it is a challenge to recover the experience of trained musicians in the eleventh century who heard a semitone step below the final of the Dorian authentic mode (in modern terms and concepts, a *c* sharp) in much the same way as they perceived the false quantity in *cŏgere* (for *cōgere*) when improperly used in a hexameter. Nonetheless, one misplaced semitone could mar a melodic line in plainsong as surely as a false quantity could spoil a hexameter. Some of the problems troubling Rudolf probably arose from a custom in the abbey of placing semitone steps where staff notation could not record them without making illicit extensions of the system such as *E* flat, requiring the notator to indicate that *E* had a semitone step *below* it as well as above. Did Rudolf always succeed in persuading his fellow monks that they should sing the notated result rather than the form they were accustomed to use? Almost certainly not, and thus a measure of obsolescence, or of undue deference to usage, was built into his antiphoner from the beginning, and his pupils knew it. In cases where Rudolf decided such things had to be notated, he could do so without solecism only by transposing the passage down a fourth, or up a fifth, so that the ungrammatical *E* flat became the grammatical *b* flat. Other problems no doubt included the various faults that theorists like John of Affligem address so extensively: chants performed in the wrong mode, or in a mixture of modes like a musical chimera, leading to blatant disagreements between Rudolf and other singers, including some in the crucial final phrases of each chant. That might easily have led to reciting tones for psalm verses in responsorial chants Rudolf was not expecting, to say nothing of melodic 'variants' he had never encountered.

There are many accounts of remarkable men in the eleventh and twelfth centuries, often bishops or abbots, who found ways to restock their churches with books and other liturgical treasures after a lean period presented by their apologists as a time of impoverishment and desertion, but it is not so very common to find, as here, that the seminal figure manufactures the necessary materials with his own hands. For Rudolf, it was literally a headache, achieved with *grauissima capitis sui infirmitate*, 'a serious malady of the head'. The *Gesta* reports that the *graduale* was made 'with his own hand; he cleaned the parchment, pricked it, ruled dry-point lines (literally *sulcavit*, 'he ploughed it'), wrote the text, illuminated it and supplied it with musical notation' (see Pl. 88, which reproduces this section of the text). Equally unusual is the emphasis the *Gesta* places upon the

88   Rudolf of Sint Truiden discovers that the chant of the abbey does not accord with that of other churches in the ecclesiastical province and begins to make a *graduale* of his own. The passage has been marked in the left-hand margin by a later reader. Mechelen, Pastoraal Centrum, Grootseminarie MS 4, fol. 42ʳ.

need to conduct any reform of the house's plainsong with as much tact as the reformer could muster. The monastic family at Sint Truiden had its elders, as most long-established monasteries and cathedral chapters did, and with all the acrimony of those whose bodily pains were increasing at the same rate as their influence was declining, these seniors were inclined to regard the younger members of the house as both impulsive and presumptuous. The *Gesta* contains some trenchant passages revealing their censorious attitude; even when Rudolf was elected *decanus* he still had to broach any reform of the monastery's customs, whatever they might be, with 'a kind artfulness' and to proceed with 'a soft and gradual tread', for he was a relatively young man himself, and a newcomer (VIII, 5). Contemplating a reform in the manner of wearing the hood and habit, for example, he respectfully questioned an old monk named Stepelinus, from a distinguished local family, whose memory of life and customs in the abbey reached back nearly eighty years; better than that, he remembered how, as a young boy, he had observed the customs of monks in the house who were some eighty years of age themselves. Rudolf therefore regarded Stepelinus as a precious witness to the usages 'that our holy and ancient fathers observed' (VIII, 8). 'Holy fathers' is always a potent phrase in medieval Latin; here it seems to mean the past generations of Sint Truiden monks whose customs in chanting could be recovered only by unspooling a twine of memory that lead Rudolf back, through the elders of the house like Stepelinus, to the years beyond the fire.[26]

Rudolf seems to have approached the compilation of his new *graduale* in much the same spirit as his reforms of monastic dress or his compilation of the *Gesta*. He used 'what I have learned from many, and what I might most faithfully learn from questioning the brothers who were members of our community at the time, and who spoke to me thereafter of these things face to face' (IV, II). It is noticeable that Rudolf makes no attempt (or at least none is recorded) to correct the usage of his abbey in accordance with the chant of other churches in the province, or of the metropolitan church. Nor did he try to bring the melodies into line with his own conception of what Gregorian chant should be (in this sense he was no pupil of Guido). Rudolf's project in notating a new *graduale* was part of a comprehensive but pragmatic attempt, pursued on several fronts, to remodel the monastic life of the house using as many of its older traditions as he could still recover. In the Preface to the *Gesta* he candidly admits that he has abandoned any attempt to trace the history of the abbey before the time of abbot Adelardus I (d. 1034) on the grounds that he has no reliable information about any earlier abbot. That is equivalent to saying he was not prepared to go back to any period lying beyond the memory of Stepelinus, spanning some eighty years, and already mentioned above as one of his valued informants. Searching through the monastic library, Rudolf had found a Carolingian inventory of the abbey's treasures, dated 870; there was also a small book containing a Life of Saint Sylvester, a text on the translation of Saint Benedict and a sermon on the assumption of the Virgin with a list of abbots and some other sparse information. It made a thin dossier. Otherwise, Rudolf found nothing in writing to draw upon for his historical and musical work apart from the various Lives of Saint Truiden and some liturgical books of the abbey that included a few 'old graduals'.

Rudolf began his work with what was to hand, collating the oral traditions of the house, as represented by the older monks, with the testimony of the old chant-books:

> he made a *graduale* with his own hands . . . and notated it with music, syllable by syllable, if I may so put it, first debating the usage of the old *graduales* with the seniors. But when, on account of a bad abuse and corruption of the chant, he could in no wise conform it to correct practice in many places, and could not notate it according to art (except what accorded with regular and

true-sounding principle), and when he did not readily wish to lose accord with the usage of the church, then, as I have said, he only troubled himself with a wondrous and indescribable effort in vain, because a true principle cannot accommodate a false usage, but he proceeded in this way, not allowing himself to pass by anything in the use of that church which could be sung in some part of the monochord (VIII, 5).[27]

Rudolf's choice of informants was both wise and politic, for there was probably no possibility of choosing younger monks as helpers, even had he wished to do so. The elders would not have allowed it, if the remarks attributed to them at various points in the *Gesta* can be taken at face value. No doubt a large measure of oral testimony was necessary from these venerable informants because the old graduals Rudolf consulted were surely in heighted or indeed unheighted neumes, revealing much but not enough, and not necessarily endowed with greater authority in the judgement of Rudolf than the versions of the melodies that elders like Stepelinus carried in their memories. Indeed, the *Gesta* is silent on the matter of whether Rudolf gave precedence to the written or the oral tradition when he discovered discrepancies between the two; presumably he proceeded with the work of collating the oral testimony with the notation of the old books only because he continually found the relationship between the two was close enough to make sustained comparison viable and worthwhile, but there must have been many discrepancies of detail, indeed of substance. The *Gesta* summarizes the whole process of consultation and editing which Rudolf undertook as a matter of 'debating' (*discutiens*) the usage of the house, and the Romance derivatives of this word, among them French *discuter*, Italian *discutere* and Spanish *discutir*, all suggest a process of discussion and perhaps even lively debate as Rudolf negotiated his way between visual signs, musical sounds, his own better judgement and his duty of deference to the elders. Gathering this information, he renotated the chants 'syllable by syllable', *syllabatim*, breaking them down into syllable–melody modules (VIII, 5).[28]

The author of this passage, the First Continuator of the *Gesta* and almost certainly a monk of Sint Truiden who had seen this *graduale* and studied with Rudolf, believed his master had shown excessive respect for the *usus* or the customary melodies used in the abbey. The passage quoted above makes this clear. Despite the emphasis in the *Gesta* on the dilapidated and reduced state of the post-fire monastery that Rudolf found, it is very apparent that the elder monks whom he consulted had a strong sense of a local, Sint Truiden tradition and were not prepared to see it compromised. The assurance in the passage quoted above that Rudolf 'did not readily wish to lose accord with the usage of the church' probably says less about his respect for what he heard the elderly monks sing than about the power of elders to overrule him or at least to make difficulties. (Anyone who has been part of a long-standing collegiate community today will know what that means.) There is no reference anywhere here to 'Gregorian chant' or

'Roman chant', and the Carolingians seem to have been entirely forgotten. Rudolf's task as the elders saw it, and as he (perhaps reluctantly) came to see it himself, was to record the venerable plainsong of the house. There could not be a clearer testimony to the continuing power of local tradition.

In a year the book was finished, 'containing all the small and great things that pertain to the *graduale* with the Rogationtide antiphons and the blessing of the Easter Candle'. At once the boys and the young men, presumably those studying in the monastic school, began to participate in a new tradition of learning and notating chant, following the 'exemplar of Rudolf's book'. At length, these pupils absorbed the master's learning to the point where they could improve upon it, notating in a more correct and accurate manner. When the generation of elders like Stepelinus had passed away, and Rudolf was on the way to becoming a *senior* himself, the effectiveness of his reforms and teaching during a generation is apparent in the way one of his pupils, the First Continuator, acknowledges the pressures that compelled his master to work hastily and make many compromises that seemed unwise in retrospect. He had sometimes used the wrong register, even the wrong octave, in his haste to complete his exacting project, in large measure perhaps an intricate exercise in a kind of musical dictation with constant (and potentially confusing) cross-reference to a different notational system. He sometimes erred by 'notating with acute or superacute letters what should have been notated with lower ones'. Acknowledging this, Rudolf sought to have his book withdrawn, but for love of their master the pupils were not ready to see the volume abandoned. Rudolf nonetheless placed a note in the volume, 'between two marks', calling it 'a *graduale* not so much according to rule as use, and finally according to neither use nor rule' (VIII, 5).[29]

———

Initially conceived as a means to allow one monk, a relatively new arrival, to accord with his fellows, or at least presented that way in retrospect, Rudolf's *graduale* developed into the means for a continuing reform of chant in the abbey. Staff-notation seems to be acting as a correcting filter; because the lines and spaces of the staff corresponded to monochord letters it imposed a default sequence of tone and semitone steps. The staff could not prevent a notator from making mistakes, as Rudolf's work proved, but it resisted falsities in chant because 'a true principle cannot accommodate a false usage' and be written down *secundum artem*, 'according to art'. Guido's stave was not simply a notation that emerged from a comprehensive desire for reform; it was a comprehensively reforming notation.

22

SINGERS IN THE MAKING OF EUROPE

Silencing Singers with Theft and Murder

By the twelfth century, the Latin West could be imagined as a soundscape of Latin chant with enough shared material for it to be sensed as a *place* of common worship and given a name: *Latinitas*. The Frankish-Roman repertory of chants for the Mass figured prominently in this body of ritual song, and was spread by many different methods of colonization and conquest, both internally by the foundation of new houses in abandoned or waste areas, and externally by crusade in Spain, eastern Europe and Livonia. The singers of the Latin churches were therefore masters of an art that belongs with the use of the Latin tongue, with the currency of the charter as a juridical instrument and with the crusade as an armed, penitential pilgrimage; these were the elements that helped to impel what Robert Bartlett has called 'the making of Europe' by conquest, colonization and cultural convergence. This chapter, which makes a point of ranging widely, is placed last because there is a sense in which it marks the destination to which everything has led: the creation of a ministry of music, the foundation of a uniquely influential chant repertory in Gregorian plainsong and the development of staff-notation, which allowed chants in a stabilized form to be carried to the ends of the Christian world.

A robbery on the edge of London, carried out some time before 1143, provides an insight into the meaning that books of Latin ritual music had by now acquired. Thieves broke into a church in Smithfield, an ill-favoured place of public executions and abattoirs in the twelfth century, as it was long to remain. Nonetheless, the robbers were not so very rapacious on this occasion. The only item they took from the unfortunate church, the Priory of St Bartholomew the Great, was an antiphoner, essential for the maintenance of the choral liturgy. As the house-chronicle of the priory records in its Middle English version, the book 'was necessarie to them that schulde synge ynne the chirche'. Once the loss was reported, the Prior and the canons searched without success, but that same night the patron of the house, Saint Bartholomew, visited the Prior in his chamber and gave him the information he needed to recover it. The Prior was to saddle his horse early next morning and go into the city of London, then he should make his way to the Jewish quarter and loose the reins, leaving the horse to the governance of the saint. The Prior followed these commands, and in the morning he found the book that he sought in the house of a Jew, located in the street that is still called Old Jewry.[1]

If the library of St Bartholomew's Priory owned a collection of Marian miracle stories, as many foundations in the twelfth century did, then the canons would perhaps have known a more famous story involving the Jews and the materials of Latin Christian plainsong. This tells of a Christian child, of tender years, who is learning at school to sing an antiphon in honour of Mary. In the various versions of the story, this antiphon is sometimes a chant from the post-Gregorian layer of plainsong, such as *Salve regina*; in Geoffrey Chaucer's version it is *Alma redemptoris mater*. Occasionally the chant comes from a much older layer, such as the responsory *Gaude Maria Virgo* with its lofty arch of melody in the Verse (Ex. 9). The story tells how the child rehearses the antiphon as he passes through the Jewish quarter on his way home. The Jews are infuriated by this irruption of Christian plainsong into their district, especially since the chant is Marian and is therefore an offensive celebration of the Israelite God taking human form. They capture the child as he passes and murder him, only to find that he continues to sing, revealing his whereabouts to the Christians, with predictable consequences.[2]

These two stories are told in very different ways. One is about a book stolen from a well-known priory in London and recovered in a principal thoroughfare of the capital. The other, in all versions, is much less precise. The story of the murdered chorister might be called a medieval urban myth, taking the term 'myth' in more than the colloquial sense of 'something that did not actually occur'. A myth gives symbolic form to aspects of the culture shared by those who recount it, and to achieve this potency a mythical story will often dehistoricize its contents, shedding the contingent details that hold the telling down to a particular understanding of what it means to say that the story is *true*. Chaucer places his version of the murdered-schoolboy story in 'a great city of Asia', an imprecision which is certainly calculated, for medieval England produced several instances of alleged child-murder by Jews and one of the most famous, the case of Saint Hugh of Lincoln, was well known to Chaucer. Like the tale of the antiphoner stolen from Smithfield, but in a different way that is closer to the heart of myth, the story of the murdered child gives symbolic form to a certain conception of Christendom. It is a place where the Latin chant of singers rises in a constant reverberation of sound that continues when the markets are closed and the city gates shut after curfew. In the two stories, the consensus of monasteries, churches and schools working to this end is so closely identified with the proper social order that only crime can silence the singing and worshipping voice. Even then, the consequences of theft and murder are only momentary. The voice breaks out again for that is what the saints desire, and the chants to be sung are international plainsongs known by Chaucer's time, with various melodies,

Ex. 9 The responsory *Gaude Maria Virgo: Gabrielem archangelum*. From *Antiphonale Saris-buriense*, ed. Frere, pl. 402–3.

from Cadiz in Spain to Esztergom in Hungary. What is more, there is nothing in the identity of the criminals to stir fresh fears, only to confirm old hatreds. The culprits are the Jews: the ancient enemy safely contained, for the most part, within a designated quarter of the city and by the legislation that curtails their freedom. Both of the two stories reassuringly ignore the possibility of disharmony arising within the Christian community itself.[3]

In some respects, the reality of liturgy in the medieval West was considerably less serene and concerted than these two stories suggest. Spain, with its unique history of Islamic conquest and internal crusade on a massive scale, provides a pertinent example. In the 1080s Alfonso VI, conqueror of Toledo, began the work of suppressing the Mozarabic liturgy of Spain in favour of the Frankish-Roman, together with its Gregorian chant imported from beyond the Pyrenees. Yet this liturgy did not come in a sealed pipeline. The stream was a broad one, and it bore along narrative material known to us now because it was deposited in texts such as the *Song of Roland* or the Latin *Historia Turpini*. Both relate how Charlemagne, the chief sponsor of Gregorian chant, conducted wars in Spain and (according to the *Historia Turpini*) uncovered the hidden relics of Saint James in Galicia. The most luxurious copy of that narrative is still in the cathedral library at Santiago, for which it was probably made (Pl. 89). To another anonymous writer of the twelfth century, however, these stories of Charlemagne were dangerous nonsense: a distraction from Spain's true models of virtue and piety at a time when it was suffering the attacks of what would now be called Islamic fundamentalists, the Almoravids. This is the author of the *Historia Silense*, probably writing in León, who regarded the stories of Charlemagne's wars in Spain as Frankish lies; the truth, he maintains, is that the king reached Saragossa and accepted a bribe offered in gold, 'after the manner of the Franks', and simply went home. This chronicler does not search beyond the Pyrenees for ways to consolidate a Spanish identity both Latin and Catholic; instead, he looks back to King Reccared and the Visigothic kingdom after 589. Writing a generation after the suppression of the Old Spanish liturgy began in approximately 1080, he has not forgotten the specific chants that were sung 'in the manner of Toledo' at Christmas Matins, for he can quote their texts from the Old Spanish rite. The Romano-barbarian history of Spain still counts for a great deal to him, perhaps more than Spain's membership of a twelfth-century European Union prefigured as an association of Latin-Christian kingdoms whose singers used Gregorian chant.[4]

A century later, Rodrigo Jiménez de Rada, consecrated bishop of Toledo in 1207/8, also writes of the Spanish Visigoths with admiration, praising their learning but especially dwelling upon the late antique victories over Rome that were often so important to the way the ruling elites of medieval kingdoms constructed their remote and formative history. He relates how Alfonso VI introduced the Frankish-Roman rite and suppressed the Old Spanish, but he does not conceal the resistance the king encountered from *clerus*, *milicia* and *populus*,

89 The Frankish infantry and heavy cavalry leave Aachen to locate the tomb of Saint James. One of two prefatory pictures to the *Historia Turpini* in the Codex Calixtinus. Santiago de Compostela, Cathedral Library, no shelfmark, fol. 162ᵛ.

terms that imply virtually every subject of the kingdom. Rodericus also recounts the well-known story of the judicial duel that pitted King Alfonso's knight, fighting for the Frankish-Roman liturgy, against another warrior, described by Rodericus as the champion of the people or *populus*, who fought for the Old Spanish or Toledan liturgy. When the people's knight won the combat, Alfonso nonetheless rejected the result; when books of both rites were placed in a fire and the volume of Old Spanish liturgy sprang from the flames of its own accord, the king rejected that too. In the end, he could prevail only by adapting an imperial dictum for royal use: *Quo volunt reges uadunt leges*: Laws go in the direction kings wish. Under the influence of an alliance between Cluny and Gregory VII, even a monarch like Alfonso could not see the importance of the indigenous Spanish rite, but his people could. So could the clergy and chivalry, at least according to Rodrigo Jiménez de Rada.[5]

In Italy, the chronicle written by Landulf Senior of Milan (d. *c.* 1075) offers material for an alternative history of Latin plainsong during the early Middle Ages, one in which the Franks appear less as the central beam of a great liturgical barn and more as a rock creating violent eddies in what should have been the even flow of late imperial history. Like the compiler of the *Historia Silense*, Landulf regards Charlemagne as a marauder, avid for gold and tribute, but he goes further: the Frankish emperor now appears as a brutal destroyer, violently opposed to the liturgy of Milan, once a great Church in an imperial capital. On the Lombard campaign, as described by Landulf, Charlemagne burns any books of the Ambrosian rite that he can find or dispatches them across the Alps, 'sending them into exile'. In a manner curiously reminiscent of the Spanish duel between two knights, a Frankish-Roman book and a volume of the Ambrosian rite are left closed, and clasped, upon an altar, so that God may decide which liturgy should prevail by opening the one he endorses. After three days of fasting and prayer, the clergy find that both books have remained unopened, but with a terrible clamour the finger of God suddenly opens them both in their presence. By no means abashed for resisting the divine will in this way, Charlemagne returns to Francia, killing Milanese clergy and destroying Ambrosian books as he goes. Only one missal remains.[6]

For Landulf, the flourishing state of the Milanese rite implies a political perspective in which the distant figures of Charlemagne and Pope Gregory VII (1073–85) are both diminished in stature. Landulf's references to the health and independence of Ambrosian chant gather around the person of Archdeacon Wibert, a man so extensively praised by Landulf for his day-to-day involvement with the chant of Milan cathedral that one may readily forget who he is. Wibert became the antipope Clement III in 1084, in opposition to Gregory VII. As Landulf evokes Wibert's achievements at Milan he describes a golden age, now either lost or disappearing, when the Holy Roman Emperors and the popes were not in sharp conflict over the limits of temporal rights in spiritual matters, and when the popes had not begun Gregory VII's uncompromising and absolutist reform to create a clergy purified for ritual tasks by perpetual celibacy. According to Landulf, there was a strong musical tradition at Milan in Wibert's time there as archdeacon. Deeply learned in Ambrosian plainsong, he was present every day in the choir with a staff, 'ruling or emending the ecclesiastical Offices', and he oversaw the two schools of singers convened in the atrium of the cathedral. He required that the clergy of Milan should be 'adorned with chant, reading and good morals', and he took the lenient, decidedly non-Gregorian view that married priests unable to remain continent were not sinful men but wanted only the measure of divine mercy that made it possible to control the weakness of the flesh.[7]

Wibert was in no sense lax in matters of clerical discipline. As an ally of the emperor Henry IV, he was more opposed to the methods of the 'Gregorian' reformers than to their aims, and he eventually legislated against clerical marriage at the Roman synod of 1089. He stood for the traditional powers of the Western and German emperors, whose line began with Charlemagne, to appoint bishops, but in Landulf's portrayal Wibert does not condone the universal imposition of Charlemagne's Frankish-Roman liturgy and its plainsong. He maintains instead the independence of a liturgy that Charlemagne was believed to have damaged with great brutality. The tangle of Roman and imperial politics in the late 1070s therefore came close to producing, in Wibert, a legitimate pope who might well have *opposed* the suppression of Mozarabic chant in Spain after 1080 had he been on the throne of Saint Peter, in contrast to Gregory VII, who strove for it. Wibert saw the need for reforms, but not necessarily (at least in his Milanese days) for a higher clergy committed to celibacy. He shows a route that the Latin West could have taken, and might have done with profit, but could not. The path was blocked by circumstances distilled in the fact that Wibert as Clement III is remembered as the antipope of these years.

The Church of Milan has never forgotten its history, and a neo-Mozarabic liturgy is still celebrated in several side chapels of the cathedral at Toledo. Yet by 1200 the especially fraught circumstances in which the anonymous Spanish monk composed his *Historia Silense*, with Almoravids threatening Toledo, were long passed, and the conflict between *regnum* and *sacerdotium* had been won by the Gregorian party with the creation of a recognizably medieval clergy. The *idea* of a universal plainsong repertory increasingly shaped the way in which those clerics after 1200 envisaged the world in which they lived, despite the large number of minor (and not so minor) discrepancies between the usages of different churches, and despite the fractures, sometimes painful, caused by individual histories at Milan and elsewhere. It is not the measure of demonstrable unity in rites and melodies achieved that matters here, but rather the willingness of Latin Christians to believe that they worshipped in essentially the same way, and chanted essentially the same melodies, in a place increasingly called 'the Latin world' or *Latinitas* after 1100. To authors of late antiquity like Jerome, Cassiodorus and Isidore, *latinitas* meant the Latin language and the resources of vocabulary and grammar in Latin that variously allowed, impeded or prohibited exact translations to be made of Scriptures and commentaries written in Greek. The word carries a very different but related sense when Lanfranc of Bec (d. 1089) refers to the fame of a particular churchman and declares that 'all *Latinitas* knows this'. *Latinitas* is now a place, and it had its own repertory of chant. When, in the next generation, Saint Malachy (d. 1148) first studied the core of Latin chant for the Mass and Office, his biographer, Bernard of Clairvaux, judged that he was learning to sing 'according to the manner of the entire world', which meant singing 'after the usage of the Holy Roman Church'. Malachy was moving away from the localism (and primitivism) of his Irish background, or so Bernard believed, and that was by no means a purely Cistercian perspective. In relation to that sense of universalism, the question of whether an Alleluia was appended to a particular chant on a particular day, or whether the Introit *Deus in loco* was sung in the Lydian or Mixoloydian mode (the example is from John of Affligem), did not always have to weigh very heavily in the general mind, however much it mattered to the specialists whom we call the 'music theorists'.[8]

Chants, Colonies and Conquests

The Carolingians gave much of western Europe a liturgy that could be regarded as Frankish by those to whom it was relatively new (like the singers of Spain in the 1200s, for whom it was *ell offiçio de França*), but which was also believed to be Roman. Any reader of the papal biographies in the *Liber pontificalis* could learn that this liturgy supposedly embodied the successive contributions of many popes, reaching back to somewhere near the consolidation of a secure papacy under Constantine and indeed further to Saint Peter. To spread that liturgy was therefore to accept Christ's charge to his apostles and go out into the whole world. In the words of Rodrigo Jiménez de Rada, the task of all able magnates, indeed of all Christians, was to 'expand the bounds of the faith', whether by founding a hospital or monastery in a place where there had been none before, or by an adventurism that might require a penitential shedding of blood. The spiritual rewards were clear and the temporal rewards might include a new lordship when a magnate was able to 'expand the bounds of his sword'. For Rodericus, a writer with an exceptionally well-informed knowledge of the languages and regions of western Europe, the Latin idiom *dilatare terminos* ('to expand the bounds') was as apt for the dissemination of the Catholic faith into pagan territory as it was for the spread of an accompanying feudal jurisdiction kept in place with armed knights. Such lords expected a church or monastery to be 'a busy, efficient, orderly community, maintaining an elaborate sequence of church services, which called for a high degree of skill and expert knowledge', and that was also the kind of community they hoped to transplant.[9]

Yet the underlying metaphors of thought in this context were not so much martial as agricultural. Without liturgy, there was no *cultus* in any sense of the word: no cult at the altar and no systematic cultivation of grain. The association between the two was profound. As Otto of Bamberg, the apostle of Pomerania, pressed forward through what is now eastern Germany, one of his biographers saw him as a celestial gardener pulling up evil by the roots and planting good where the power of devils had once sprouted forth, like weeds. One of the most important chant treatises of the Middle Ages, by John of Affligem, emerges from a context very like this, since Affligem abbey was founded in a remote spot, infested with thieves, as a penitential gesture, or so the chronicle of the house would have us believe. Where the seeds of the gospel and choral liturgy had not yet fallen on fertile ground, Nature was barren of harvest, void and even corrupt, producing monstrosities like the dog-headed men whom Adam of Bremen reported in the Russian slave-markets, yapping a form of human speech. In Livonia, where the work of conquest and conversion is well documented, a Christian headquarters existed in the stockade settlement of Riga whence merchants, knights and Cistercian monks set out to explore the surrounding countryside and 'sow the seed of the gospel'. Going 'where no apostle had ever been', they left Riga to baptize and lay out parishes while the merchants sought out the trading stations for furs, amber and slaves. Henry of Livonia's chronicle shows some of the accompanying monks and clergy bravely singing the sequence at Mass while hostile horsemen galloped around their church, or chanting the responses 'but half alive' when supplies were short in winters so severe that the extremities of the body froze. In an especially vivid passage, the *Livonian Rhymed Chronicle* describes a party of merchants striking out along the River Dvina, taking care to have with them 'a wise man to read and chant the service'. If a single image can express the work of the Latins in this and other frontier territories, this one of a clerical or monastic singer taking a boat with knights and merchants into a northern heart of darkness will serve very well.[10]

The Cistercian monks were among those especially active in Livonia, and no religious order before the coming of the friars in the thirteenth century did more to disseminate the musical literacy of the stave in a context of colonization. With their roots in the asceticism of the eleventh century that impelled the first Carthusians into the mountainous wilderness near Grenoble, the nascent order of Cistercians made an initial attempt in 1109 to import the chant of Metz, the old capital of Frankish-Roman chant. The monks were much displeased with what they found there, and could not discover that any of the churches, even those of metropolitan status or those within the same province, possessed the same manner of chanting. (Rudolf of Sint Truiden encountered the same problem and in precisely the same years.) Much had been changed, or so the Cistercians believed, through the ignorance of singers or, which was worse, through their determination to have music that seemed to them more beautiful.

This is rhetoric of a very familiar kind, and probably reveals more about the zeal of these reformed Benedictines than about the state of chant in their day; it does not mean they denied the existence of a common chant repertory in the Latin West any more than the ignorance of many scribes prompted them to reject that the Occidental churches had a common language in Latin. What mattered was to achieve the most authentic and rationalized edition of 'the chant promulgated by the blessed pope Gregory'. In the 1140s, the Cistercians entrusted a second reform of their chant to their most able teacher and advocate, Saint Bernard of Clairvaux, a clear sign of how profoundly the White Monks identified a purified version of Gregory's chant with the reformed monastic discipline – with the *truth* – of their enterprise.[11]

From the very beginning of their Order, staff-notation was essential for the establishment of that truth. The notations of the Messine books enabled the Cistercians to make copies of the Metz chant in a pitch-definitive form and carry it away for study, just as it allowed them to issue a new edition and send it far afield. One of the most curious and characteristic aspects of their reform, namely that no chant should exceed a range of ten notes, owes something to what the Cistercian Abbot Gui's treatise on plainsong calls *notandi necessitas*: the requirements of notation. The five-line stave, the largest then in common use, accommodates only eleven notes without leger lines. During the course of the twelfth century, the Cistercians carried staff-notation to many parts of the Latin West, often establishing houses in remote places that were nonetheless (like the mother house of Cîteaux) near major arterial routes. Far-flung expansion was by no means an essential part of their original vision – Bernard of Clairvaux was puzzled why anyone should wish to found a monastic house in so distant a place as Spain – and there were parts of the Latin West where their implantation by 1200 was thin, notably in Hungary. Yet with their communities of lay brothers to create farms, build barns and byres or dig canals and ditches, the Cistercians became a major force in twelfth-century agriculture and animal husbandry, often near frontier zones. From the conquest of Lisbon in 1147, their houses were often associated with the defence and repopulation of conquered territories in what is now Portugal, while in parts of the east a magnate like the margrave Leopold of Babenberg could recognize the importance of implanting the Cistercians near a frontier. In 1133 he donated land for the abbey of Heiligenkreuz, simultaneously a prayer factory on his eastern march and an important source of the eiderdown effect whereby farms and settlements serve to slow or detain an invader who, of necessity, would swiftly traverse barren land. In similar and potentially hostile circumstances, Cistercians can be found in Livonia. Staff-notation seems to have travelled with them wherever they went, as surely as their store of chalices, hoes and spades. To this day, a fine twelfth-century antiphoner in staff-notation lies on the library shelves at Heiligenkreuz to prove it.[12]

To evangelists in the field, like Otto of Bamberg in the early years of the twelfth century, the plainchant of singers in a clerical party was a useful source of impressive opulence, together with incense and vestments made of expensive dyed or embroidered textiles. As early as the sixth century, a Frankish king could be seduced away from his paganism (or so a Christian queen had supposed) by a display of rich hangings, and according to the *Russian Primary Chronicle* it was the luxurious textiles, incense and chant of the Byzantine Church that drew Vladimir, prince of Kiev, towards the Greeks and away from the Latins. The German missionaries discovered that choral plainsong could be useful in other ways. Otto of Bamberg once entered a dangerous district accompanied by wagons of vestments, missals and other things 'which it is hard to find in a pagan country'. On one occasion his party was encircled, as night fell, by a band of local men who came upon them in a forest. He escaped death because the leader of the group was a Christian, but on another occasion, when he and his clergy were not so lucky in whom they met, they owed their lives to their plainsong. Threatened with imminent martyrdom, the clerics in Otto's entourage began to sing psalms and chants that the pagans, who paused to listen, construed as an impressive display of insouciance in the face of death. Amazed, their hearts were softened and they relented.[13]

In eleventh-century Spain, where frontiers could be shifting but sharply drawn, at least in the short term, the testament of Ramiro I de Aragón, dated 1061, speaks of frontier monasteries in the same breath as new bridges or *castellos de fronteras de mauros*, 'castles on the frontiers with the Moors'. In eleventh-century Aragón, implanting a monastery with its singers was work that consolidated the Christian presence near a disputed margin, just like building a *castellum*. At this date, the monks of the monasteries Ramiro had in mind were singing Old Spanish chant, but were less than a generation away from the decision by Alfonso VI, the conqueror of Toledo (1085), to replace the Spanish plainsong with the Frankish-Roman. In effect, Alfonso abolished a long-standing liturgical frontier with the other Latin kingdoms in the north so that he could rebuild his liturgical rampart against Islam as the outpost of *Latinitas* in the south. Far to the east, in the Levant, there were isolated attempts to establish a liturgical frontier well before the First Crusade that did the work – but to no lasting effect – in the Holy Land after 1099. When Abbot Richard of St-Vanne (d. 1046) journeyed to Antioch, he pressed on into one or both of the neighbouring emirates, celebrating Masses outside the walls of the cities he encountered and singing, amidst a hail of stones, while a group of clerics sang the choral responses at a safe distance. Manning the walls of those cities, the Muslims and others had good reason to be alarmed, for they were seeing the extreme periphery of an encroaching Latin civilization manifest as a priest and a group of singers.[14]

Staff-notation, like some other characteristic resources of Latin Christendom, including the charter and the use of plate-armour, was on the move from the end of the eleventh century onwards as knights from many parts of Latin Christendom, eventually content to be known simply as *Franks*, went east. The Council of Clermont, convened by Urban II in 1095 to conduct business that included the proclamation of an armed and penitential pilgrimage to Jerusalem, was ultimately responsible for the creation of Latin bishoprics in the Holy Land and for the slow process of staffing churches in conquered territories with Western clergy that followed the unexpected success, in 1099, of what is now called the First Crusade. The musical stave travelled with the sacramentaries of priests and with the antiphoners of chaplains and monks.[15]

The thirteenth-century continuation of the chronicle by William of Tyre mentions the installation of canons in the principal mosque (the *mestre Mahommerie*) in Damietta, a process that required the diversion of funds and rents to this mosque (and to others, including former churches) so that they could obtain the necessary resources, including their liturgical books or *livrez*. By the first decades of the twelfth century, and so more or less from the beginning of the crusading movement, priests who celebrated Mass in the Church of the Holy Sepulchre in the Latin kingdom of Jerusalem were using a sacramentary with delicate forms of northern French staff-notation, copied in Jerusalem but using exemplars shipped out from the West. Would it have been possible to mount a sung service in the new Frankish churches of the Holy Land if the singers, priests and chaplains who served them, not always men of the highest ability, had been required to learn all their chants by heart from the beginning? At a much later date, one influential advocate of a new crusade emphasized the need to train singers in the most expeditious way. The *Opusculum tripartitum* by Humbert of Romans, written around 1274 in response to a papal request for advice concerning the feasibility of a new crusade, envisages that any projected expedition must rest upon a thorough reform of the Church. In giving his advice, Humbert surveys many abuses that are sorely in need of reform:[16]

> it is the custom that the singers do not sing by art (*per artem*), which can be learned in about a year, but rather by practice alone (*per usum*), which can scarcely be learned in six years. And therefore there are many unlettered clergy in these places, because they are compelled to spend time learning this musical practice that could be occupied in the study of letters. And therefore it would seem to be very much better for all to sing 'by art'.[17]

The context leaves little doubt that singing 'by practice alone', *per usum*, means the long process of learning chant by heart, a custom well attested throughout the Middle Ages even (or perhaps one should say especially) in some of the greatest churches such as Notre-Dame of Paris. Learning to sing *per artem* must therefore mean singing from staff-notation, with the necessary training in matters such as the modes and solmization. The passage about the relative efficiency of learning 'by art' as opposed to 'practice' is reminiscent of Guido's own remark in the *Epistola ad Michahelem* that his teaching and notation allow a singer to learn chant in two years (Humbert thinks it can be done in one) whereas without it the process cannot be accomplished in only ten years (Humbert thinks it can scarcely be done in six). When attempts to hold Jerusalem for the Latins had failed, the Franciscan Galvano de Levanto lamented that 'there is only the abominable melody of Saracens' in the Holy Land 'where there should be the worship of Jesus Christ and chant (*psalmodia*)'. The silencing of Latin-Christian singers is the most vivid means he can find to express the loss of the Christian East. With the fall of Acre in 1291, the last major bastion of the Christian presence in Outremer, the muezzin and minaret definitively silenced the cantor and the bell-tower. In the same year another Italian friar, Ricoldo of Monte Croce, travelled through much of what is now Iraq and found a missal on sale in Al-Mawsil, north of Baghdad, probably looted from one of the churches in Acre. The attempt to extend the chant of Latin singers had failed in Palestine and Syria; now its dismembered materials were adrift in the bazaars of the Orient.[18]

The Hospital Chapel: Singers and the Boundaries of Christendom

In addition to what was achieved in conquest beyond frontiers, there was also internal colonization to be done, directed to barren places or sites that had not hitherto been used for a liturgical or charitable purpose. This is revealed with particular clarity by the great many hospitals, often with attendant chapels or small chantries, founded during the period 1000–1300. (The antiphoner stolen from St Bartholomew's Priory in Smithfield was made for a church founded jointly with a hospital that is still functioning.) This development is especially telling in the east, notably in Brandenburg, Livonia and Silesia, for there it occurred at one advancing edge of Latin-Christian conquest. The favoured dedication for the new hospitals in these regions invoked the Holy Spirit, a suitably universal choice for houses regarded as outposts of the Universal Church, even though the foundations were located in new settlements and were therefore embedded in a sharply local and sometimes perhaps a transitory context. It says much about conceptions of the hospital that dedications almost always alluded to 'international' saints such as Nicholas, Mary Magdalene, Thomas, Bartholomew and Lazarus; medieval travellers and patients lodged under the sign of a saint whose name evoked the open road because it was known everywhere.

Many charters survive to illustrate the creation of hospitals and chaplaincies down the Oder River from Lübeck via Rostock down to Stettin, Lebus and Breslau. The work was done by the bishops of the new episcopal sees founded there, or by incoming magnates who saw very clearly that the work of carving out a new lordship in formerly pagan territory was not enough to ensure their salvation; their charitable duties remained pressing and indeed probably intensified as the new settlements attracted more settlers than they could house or feed. Brandenburg had a hospital by 1220, seemingly founded by one of the bishop's feudatories; even the cathedral there had received its charter only in 1161, a church built in a region 'that up to our own time has been possessed by pagans and infested with the cult of idols'. In Spandau, a Holy Spirit hospital with a daily *divinum officium* had appeared by 1261. Lübeck acquired its Holy Spirit hospital by the late thirteenth century and Riga by 1220, the work of Bishop Albert, whose other initiatives included the foundation of a chivalric order, the Sword-Brothers, as a standing army of occupation. These charitable foundations were closely related to the juridical but also to the social consolidation of these new settlements; they often attracted the attention of new confraternities that gathered for Masses of the dead and other services, just as they were the object of internal pilgrimages on certain feast-days when indulgences were granted to all who came for prayer. At Colbergh, today the Polish Kołobrzeg, a confraternity of citizens 'seeking the bonds of brotherhood' agreed to gather each year, on a day of their own choosing, at the Holy Spirit hospital for Mass, prayers and almsgiving. The witness lists of the many charters which reveal these initiatives gradually show indigenous names like Zulizlaus, Jarozlaus, Priznoborus and Mozkot, although never entirely vanquished, nonetheless ceding ground to Jacobus, Johannes, Paulus, Willemus, Heinricus, Bartholomaeus and Stephanus, biblical and Frankish names that came with the Western colonizers. The making of Europe has left few more intimate traces.[19]

Inventories of the goods contained in hospitals and leprosaria suggest that few were so small or dilapidated that they might not possess a service book of some kind to enable at least the basic elements of a sung service to be held. While it is only to be expected that an important foundation like the hospital of St-Raymond at Toulouse should possess a missal, an epistolarium, a breviary and a psalter among its chapel goods, or that the chaplains of the Great Hospital at Norwich should receive a 'book of chant and a missal' as a bequest from the city's bishop, it is another matter to discover that a run-down leprosarium at Montgeron, near Corbeil, had a liturgical book. Even though the grange of this hospital was empty and roofless for the most part, with the chambers deserted and ruinous, the episcopal visitors in 1351 found a small volume which they inventoried as 'a kind of missal'. This may not have been a noted service book, but there are many cases among these inventories where there is no such uncertainty. The leprosaria and other hospitals in the diocese of Paris, inventoried in 1351–69, encompassed seventy-two houses; their holdings included a total of 202 service books, eighty-two of them described as volumes with musical notation. The fourteenth century is relatively rich in such documents, many of them no doubt listing significantly older materials. In England, an inventory of God's House in Southampton, from 1362, records a missal, a psalter, an antiphoner, two graduals and a 'Sunday troper'. An inventory of the Ospedale di S. Maria di Colle from 1342, now in the archives of the Comune di Perugia, reveals a missal, an *antiphonarium nocturnum*, a lectionary, a psalter and a booklet containing material for the feast of Corpus Christi. The associated leprosarium had two antiphoners, a missal and a lectionary, among other books. In 1313, the auditors of a leposarium in Estella (Navarre), on the pilgrim road to Santiago, found *un missel . . . et un officieiri nou et bon.* This may or may not have been supplied with

90   The decayed chapel of a French leper-house or *maladrerie*. The Romanesque detailing on the main door marks it as a 12th-c. structure, although a number of the windows have been Gothicized at a later date. Anonymous and undated print, collection of the author.

musical notation, but there is no doubt about the 'book of chant on parchment with a white cover' inventoried at one of Girona's hospitals in 1362. Such references are a reminder that the chapel of the royal hospital in Burgos is perhaps as likely a destination for the celebrated Las Huelgas manuscript of Latin sacred song and polyphony as the adjacent convent of Cistercian nuns with which it has often been associated.[20]

The statutes of hospitals are sometimes explicit about their musical provision. The clerics serving the Hôtel-Dieu in Pontoise from 1265 were to sing Matins *à notte* and *touttes les heures canoniales et la messe . . . à notte*, while at Tours in 1263 the singers were commanded to read and sing according to the custom of the Church of St Stephen. Foundation charters are usually more reticent, but there are occasional references to the provision that the founders or governors expected. At Cammin, in Pomerania, one hospital was staffed by a priest and a *scolaris* who were required to sing Mass but allowed to say the Hours and vigils *sine nota*. Many centuries later, Charles Dickens wrote of a nineteenth-century hospital in London where 'the dim light which burnt in the room increased rather than diminished the ghastly appearance of the hapless creatures in their beds, which were ranged in long rows on either side'. The scene was perhaps not so different in many a larger medieval hospital as the sound of chant arose from the altar, the principal therapy available once urine had been tested, poultices applied and simples given out.[21]

The inmates of some hospitals, especially the leprosaria, formed semi-monastic communities living under a form of the Rule of Saint Augustine and waiting for release into a new life of eternal *salus*. When the thirteenth-century trouvère Baude Fastoul contracted leprosy and took leave of his friends in Arras, bound for the hospital of Grand Val, he spoke of himself as a pilgrim and even as a monastic solitary venturing *en un desert*. Such meanings may seem strange today, not least because they imply a duty of penance and self-examination at a time of sickness rather than the absolute right to care and indulgence that is taken for granted in the modern developed world; nonetheless, pilgrimage and monastic withdrawal, in a context of daily liturgy, provided medieval sufferers with two of their most potent metaphors for giving meaning to the grave changes in their lives that sickness might enforce. Hospitals, indeed, were rich in metaphor and association. Not for reasons of hygiene alone were so many hospitals and the accompanying chapels built close to rivers; lepers are associated in a wide range of medieval narratives with cures produced by a miraculously cleansing bath in a river's course. The bridges over these waters, places that can so readily draw the mind to unexpected depths of contemplation, were often chosen as the site of hospitals and their chapels. Examples can be found throughout Latin Europe. In 1185 Pamplona had a hospital of St-Julien *de ponte superiori*, while a hospital chapel of St Nicholas stood *super pontem* at Salisbury in the thirteenth century. In Modena, the Templars maintained a hospital by the Ponte S. Ambrogio, while a direct descendant of the medieval Hôtel-Dieu in Paris stood by one of the bridges across the Seine. The water flowing beyond the door could also be a reminder of baptism: the only bath that was truly cleansing, especially for the lepers. (Hospital dedications to John the Baptist are very common and far outnumber others in medieval England, for which there are especially good figures.) The water might also turn the mind to prayers or vows, not least because a medieval bridge was often a fragile structure liable to break or be carried away by flood; it is no accident that England has a city named Pontefract, or that one of the major ecclesiastical buildings of medieval York celebrated the new-found solidity of a bridge that had once given way beneath an archbishop (Pl. 91). Saint Arnulf, a distinguished forebear of the Carolingians, is reported to have become so alarmed when he crossed a bridge over the Moselle in spate that he cast his ring into the current with a vow that he would think himself loosed from the bonds of sin the day he saw that ring again. (Needless to say, he did see it again.) The tokens and rings that the heroes and heroines of medieval romance throw into rivers with vows and declarations find their counterpart in the medieval pilgrim badges, recovered in substantial numbers from the rivers where they were seemingly thrown from bank or bridge as votive offerings.[22]

Although many hospitals were built in cities and towns, the imagery of claiming barren territory for the gospel, or of colonizing lands infested with thieves and devils, was often associated with these institutions, not least because they were sometimes built for travellers in places far from any other source of protec-

91   The 12th-c. bridge chapel of St William, York, demolished in the 19th c. Prepared for J. Britton's *Picturesque Antiquities of the English Cities* (London, 1830). The chapel was built to commemorate a miracle that occurred in 1154. In that year, a wooden bridge over the Ouse River collapsed while Saint William of York was making his way to the Minster to be consecrated archbishop with a throng of citizens. Through divine intercession, no lives were lost. Engravings of architectural details not visible in this print, but apparent in some others of the same subject, show that the core of the chapel was not Gothic, as it appears here, but Romanesque. This building has long since disappeared.

tion and support. In parts of Spain, where the issue of populating empty territories with Christians could be especially pressing, the charters of hospitals and other documents repeatedly emphasize (and no doubt sometimes exaggerate) the remoteness of the location chosen for a new foundation. A reading for the Office of Saint Dominic of Calzada (d. 1109) celebrates the hospital he founded in a place 'once overgrown with forest and frequented by robbers, very dangerous to travellers . . . [but] now fertile and pleasant'. In 1103, King Alfonso VI granted funds to the bishop and clergy of Oviedo to build a hospital in Copián (Mieres) on a mountainous site; using terms borrowed from Deuteronomy 32: 10, and with strong overtones of monastic withdrawal, the foundation charter describes the site as a region of 'vast solitude' that would now be populated with pilgrims and other wayfarers. They could expect to find board, lodging and a hospital chapel that Alfonso, the champion of Frankish-Roman chant in Spain, would surely have expected to be staffed with priests and chaplains able to use Gregorian plainsong.[23]

The Time of the Proper

The creation of a Europe-wide repertory of plainsong changed the means of communication between heaven and earth. In all his many chapters about the life of monks and clergy in sixth-century Gaul, Gregory of Tours never suggests that plainsong might be something earthly singers share with those of heaven. At no point does any pious man or woman in Gregory's book have a vision (or audition) of a saint singing a text and associated melody from the rites used on earth. By the tenth century, however, reports begin to appear that heavenly singers had woken up to the existence of a widely disseminated set of chants for Mass and Office that they should learn themselves. Soon after 900, a female recluse named Wiborada, dwelling near the abbey of Sankt Gallen, received a vision of the abbey's patron singing the Gregorian Introit *Ne timeas Zacharia* for the Nativity of John the Baptist 'with a company of radiant souls'. This is one of the earliest visitations of its kind on record. On another occasion, and with divine help, she was able to perform the massive Lenten Tract *Qui habitat*, notated at Sankt Gallen during her lifetime in the earliest surviving cantatorium (Pl. 92). Wiborada's biographer, Ekkehard I of Sankt Gallen, merely calls it the 'Tract for the First Sunday in Lent', confident that readers will know the chant in question and will appreciate that it was a remarkable undertaking for a woman to perform such a plainsong without specialist training.[24]

Such visions and dreams were not the prerogative of solitary women leading lives of contemplation made all the more intense by being on the edge of the liturgy. The chronicler Thietmar of Merseburg (d. 1018) reports a dream in which he saw two boys coming out of the old treasury at Magdeburg singing the responsory *Martinus Abrahe sinu*. At this time a female solitary named Susu had just died, and Thietmar construed the words of this chant about a saint 'received into the bosom of Abraham' as an assurance from heaven that Susu was saved. 'You should know, for certain', he told his brethren, 'that a soul dear to God has just departed from this light.' Considerably more spectacular was the vision granted to Gerard of Sauve-Majeure (d. 1095) as he lay prostrate near the door of his abbey church, alone in prayer. Gerard saw Christ with angels and archangels enter the monastery to prepare for the celebration of Mass; as Christ approached the altar the question was duly asked whether everyone required for the service was present. Christ himself replied that one person was missing: the individual who was at this very moment occupied in prayer by the door. Gerard was brought forward and placed in the choir, whereupon the heavenly company began to sing the Introit *Gaudeamus omnes in Domino*. A later abbot of the same house, while still a novice, collapsed as he sang Matins in the infirmary chapel and had a vision of another celestial liturgy; as his fellow monks gathered anxiously around him, the future abbot followed the course of the heavenly rites with occasional exclamations that allowed the community to follow it in fragments: 'How beautifully Our Lady sings the *Ave maris stella* . . . How beautifully

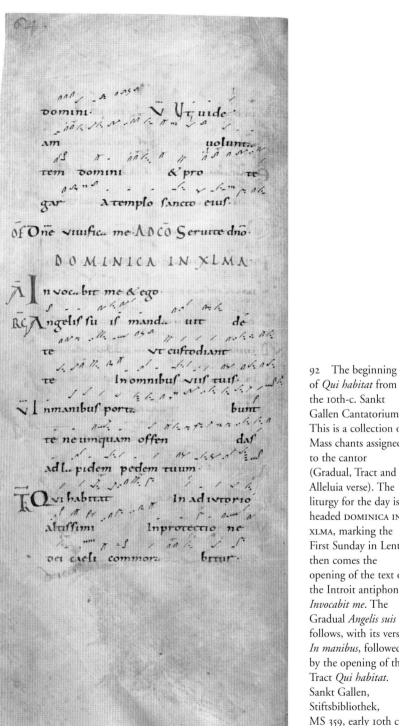

domini. V Vt uide

am uolunt

tem domini & pro te

gar A templo sancto eius.

OF One uiuifica me AD CO Serutte dno.

DOMINICA IN XLMA

A In vocabit me & ego.

RC Angelis su if manda uit de

te ut custodiant

te In omnibus uiis tuis.

V In manibus porta bunt

te ne umquam offen das

ad lapidem pedem tuum.

TO Qui habitat In adiutorio

Altissimi In protectio ne

dei caeli commora bitur.

92 The beginning of *Qui habitat* from the 10th-c. Sankt Gallen Cantatorium. This is a collection of Mass chants assigned to the cantor (Gradual, Tract and Alleluia verse). The liturgy for the day is headed DOMINICA IN XLMA, marking the First Sunday in Lent; then comes the opening of the text of the Introit antiphon, *Invocabit me*. The Gradual *Angelis suis* follows, with its verse *In manibus*, followed by the opening of the Tract *Qui habitat*. Sankt Gallen, Stiftsbibliothek, MS 359, early 10th c., fol. 64.

two men are now singing the Alleluia.' The art of liturgical singers was truly universal if it traversed the boundary between this life and the next.[25]

From the tenth century onwards, Lives of Saints, chronicles and other writings begin to include accounts of miraculous cures that took place during the liturgy at a moment defined by the point the singers had reached in the order of Mass or Office. The instances involving Office chants are often the least precise and rarely give the textual incipit of the plainsong in question. This is presumably because any important church or monastery was liable to have feasts in its Sanctorale that were regional rather than universal, and yet it is precisely these stories of cures or visions during Office chants that reveal most about the social and political importance of the saints and the music that served them. The liturgical cures are most often found in sources from West Francia, where the central political authority was comparatively weak; there, the proliferating cults of saints marked the increasing regionalism of the post-Carolingian political order, but those same cults could also create bonds of *amicitia* between donors, founders, monks, clergy and *populus* that kept levels of open conflict down. In the early twelfth century, Ralph Tortarius of Fleury tells of a peasant named Durandus whose lower limbs were so twisted that he could barely walk and who was compelled to beg from door to door; he was eventually brought by his relatives to the abbey of Patriciacus on the feast-day of the translation of Saint Benedict. When he asked to be taken into the church for the night office, the monks agreed; during the fourth responsory, he lay by a relic of Saint Benedict and was immediately healed. The chants at issue were presumably those composed for precisely this feast by Constantine of Fleury (see above, p. 432). At the abbey of Figeac, in the Limousin, when the monks were singing the Vespers antiphon in honour of Saint Vivian *Homo iste fecit mirabilia in vita sua* ('this man did wondrous works during his lifetime'), a cripple in the congregation suddenly began to cry aloud and to extend his contorted limbs, 'and thus he who came on four legs departed on two' (Pl. 93). This chant seems to have been a distinctively southern antiphon whose musical sources known at present reach from Aquitaine to Sankt Gallen and down to the Beneventan region, and its text is such an obvious cue for a saint to rouse himself to a work of healing that the compiler of the story cannot resist identifying it. There were even occasions when chant acted as a conjuration so

93   The plainsong cue for Saint Vivian to cure a cripple in the abbey of Figeac. Hartker Antiphoner, Sankt Gallen, Stiftsbibliothek, MS 391, p. 187.

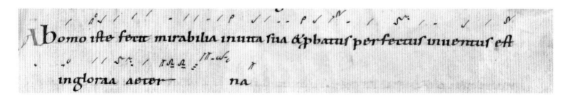

Ex. 10   Music to conjure Saint Augustine. *Verbum dei usque,* the twelfth responsory from the prose Office of St Augustine. From *Antiphonale Sarisburiense,* ed. Frere, pl. 509–10.

that the saint being honoured duly appeared. On one occasion in the 1130s, when the monks of the Cistercian house of Aumône (diocese of Blois) had reached the last responsory at Matins for the feast of Saint Augustine, the saint himself appeared to a monk named Christianus, 'in the most splendid raiment, with a smiling face, and with eyes that shone like two stars' (Ex. 10).[26]

In stories involving Mass chants it is much more common for an author to be specific about the chant at issue because the material was liable to be less regional. Some of these narratives, mostly to be found in collections of *miracula*, involve ritual items that had been in use for a very long time, but which begin to appear in stories of healing as the stream of material widens after 1000. In 1034, at the abbey of Corbie in Picardy, a paralysed man who had spent years trailing himself 'around the borders of the townspeople' on crutches was cured, after a night spent in prayer, just as the monks reached the end of Matins and were singing the versicle 'Per singulos dies benedicimus te' of the *Te Deum*. At the abbey of Figeac, in southern France, Saint Vivian healed a cripple as the principal Mass of the day reached the *Hymnus trium puerorum*, beginning *Benedicite omnia opera Domini Domino*; the cripple shivered, stretched out his limbs and was entirely cured. A lame man named Rambertus, crippled since birth, suddenly found the use of his legs at Figeac while the deacon was intoning the *Benedicamus Domino* and an appended Alleluia 'with sweet harmony' after Mass on Easter Saturday.[27]

These plainsongs serve as a kind of coordinate, identifying the liturgical moment when the cure occurred in a manner the writers assume will be widely understood. In a similar way, a reference to a specific plainsong could be used to fix the day when something occurred or was planned to take place. The chants at issue are almost invariably Introit antiphons and therefore the first Proper chant of the service. One of the earliest examples shows Saint Anselm referring to his consecration as archbishop of Canterbury (1093) 'on the Sunday when the Introit *Populus Syon* is sung'. After 1100, however, it becomes increasingly common for chroniclers and others to place an event 'on the Sunday of *Laetare Jerusalem*' (the Fourth Sunday in Lent) or in relation to other Introits that include *Oculi mei* (Third Sunday in Lent), *Dum sanctificatus* (Pentecost Sunday), *Esto mihi* (Sixth Sunday after Pentecost) and *Dicit Dominus: Ego cogito* (Thirty-Third Sunday after Pentecost). In Spain, the Introit *Iustus es, Domine* (Twenty-Third Sunday after Pentecost) was used to locate an event in the house-chronicle of Compostela at a time when the liturgy of the Church of Santiago was still being comprehensively reformed on Frankish-Roman (here meaning Cluniac) lines. In 1131, the Introit *Laetare Jerusalem* identifies an appointed day in a letter of Innocent II, showing that this method to define the day of some past or imminent event was already so universally understood that it could be used in a document issued by the patriarch of the Latin West. The repertory of liturgical singers had by now joined the movement of celestial bodies as a cycle that defined the passage of time.[28]

By sharing a large body of Proper chants for the liturgy, the monks and clergy of the Latin West also shared a means to record contingent events so that they would be perceived, wherever the account was read, not just in terms of time measured by the hourglass or water-clock, but also *sub specie aeternitatis*. For those entrusted to relate the major events in the life of a pious magnate or churchman, the implications of the common liturgical culture for the art of giving depth to a narrative could be considerable. In 1202, Abbot William of Eskill in Zeeland died on the eve of Easter, and one of his disciples traced his last hours through the liturgical services in which the saint barely had the strength to engage. On the Thursday William tried to perform the *Mandatum* ceremony but was too weak to wash the brothers' feet. Led to his chamber, he eventually asked for his bed to be carried into the choir so that he could take part in the Easter Day liturgy. At Matins, the choir had just begun the third responsory, *Dum transisset sabbatum*, when a sign was given that Abbot William was now at the point of death. His life began to pass away as the Sabbath passed. Dawn broke, and after singing the responsory *Ut venientes ungerent Jesum*, describing the anointing of Christ's body, the Prior and some of the brothers left the choir to anoint William with holy oil. William was then dressed in penitential clothes and laid on a bed of cinders. He died soon afterward, rising to a new life on the day of the Resurrection as the choir tearfully but triumphantly sang the appointed chant to end the service before the beginning of Lauds, *Te Deum laudamus*. William passed the last years of his life in one of the most remote abbeys of Latin Christendom; yet by the time of his death in 1202 there were many hundreds of churches and monasteries where this account would have been understood, in its fullest and most moving spiritual depth, because the Office antiphoners and ordinals in those houses prescribed essentially the same sequence of chants for these same hours. The compiler perceives the meaning of what happened, and the *facts* of what happened, in terms of the appointed readings and chants.[29]

The success of the Cistercians, mentioned above, helped to generate many reports of how Marian antiphons such as the *Salve regina* could ward off the assaults of the devil, cause a storm to abate or even summon the presence of the Holy Mother so that she stood in the very place where the monks were singing. The foundation of the Franciscan and Dominican orders multiplied stories of this kind and carried them far afield. Jordanus, second Master of the Dominicans in 1222, is reported to have required all the members of his Order to sing the *Salve regina* every night, after Compline, to beseech the aid of the Virgin against the attacks of demons. This Marian antiphon could summon the Holy Mother as surely as it could banish devils, and it was therefore considered especially appropriate for the last service of the day before facing 'the perils and dangers of this night'. A certain noblewoman who was accustomed to attend Compline in a Dominican church saw the Blessed Virgin, in the midst of the choir, serving as a precentor, inciting the brothers to sing the *Salve regina* more loudly and in a slower manner (*alcius et morosius*). When the chant was over, the same woman saw the Virgin bow her head to the Master of the Order and subsequently do the same to all the other friars in the choir. Stories of such plainsong visions are quite common. The monks in an unspecified house, perhaps a Cistercian foundation, were singing the *Salve regina* after Compline when one of the most venerable among them saw the Virgin in prostration before Christ, beseeching him to protect their Order; they had just reached the words 'Eya, ergo, advocata nostra'. This same chant had a talismanic power to quell the diabolic forces that the monks and friars believed to be active all around them in the forces of nature. While a great storm was raging with thunder and lightening, the members of a Cistercian community made their way quickly to their conventual church where they immediately began to sing the *Salve regina*. When they reached the words 'Eya, ergo, advocata nostra, illos tuos misericordes oculos ad nos converte' (Eya! therefore, our advocate, turn those merciful eyes of yours towards us') there was a massive clap of thunder and all the glass in the church shattered. Terrified, the monks knelt and sang the words 'et Jesum benedictum fructum ventris tui nobis per hoc exilium ostende' ('and show us, in this exile, Jesus, the blessed fruit of thy womb'). Now the words of both chants became literally true: the cross that was hanging between the choir of the monks and the choir of the lay brothers turned to face the monastic choir ('illos oculos ad nos converte', 'turn those eyes towards us') and Christ was made visible in the image that came to life ('Jesum . . . ostende', 'show . . . Jesus'). The image of Christ opened its eyes, 'contrary to the nature of a wooden object', and the storm abated. The breath of singers was enough to set the thin curtain hanging between this world and the next into motion.[30]

Charlemagne, the Latin Heartlands and the Stave

Although there have been several references to Frankish-Roman or Gregorian chant in this chapter, it may seem that the Carolingians who fostered that music have been drifting below the horizon. To some extent, this eclipse of the Carolingians is justified. By the tenth century, only those with special loyalties remembered the liturgical work of Pippin, and even at a monastery of old Carolingian heartlands like Sint Truiden, not far from Aachen, the memory of Charlemagne could count for remarkably little when it was time to make a new *graduale* soon after 1100. Yet in those parts of Latin Europe where it was most important to remember and to idealize Charlemagne as the maker of a Christian Europe – often in territories where that Europe was still being made by conquest and consolidation – the Frankish Emperor was not only commemorated as a great conqueror, he was also associated with the art of music and in particular, despite the glaring anachronism involved, with the technique of notating music on a stave. It seems that the device which had done so much to enable singers to be trained more expeditiously, and which allowed chants to be transported for hundreds of miles in writing and then accurately retrieved, could not long remain independent of the Charlemagne mythos.

This is revealed with particular clarity by a seminal document for the social and political history of staff-notation, namely the twelfth-century source of music, both monophonic and polyphonic, which is generally known today as the Codex Calixtinus. Probably copied in central France around 1160, this is a composite volume containing a wealth of material pertaining to the cult of Saint James at Compostela in Galicia; it ranks as a document of prime importance for understanding the protracted attempt of some Spanish kings and bishops to reconnect the expanding Latin-Christian civilization of Spain to lands north of the Pyrenees and to Rome. The traces of that enterprise are especially apparent in the numerous chants the book contains in honour of Saint James. These are not necessarily liturgical pieces in the strict sense of being ritual items appointed for specific order of service; some may have been designed for refectory entertainment of the kind much easier to imagine than to document in chronicles and other sources. Fortunately, there are some striking exceptions, as in *The Book of the Foundation of Walden Monastery* (Essex), which describes a feast in the bishop's hall of St Paul's, in London, during the time of Bishop Richard (1152–62):

> After the meal the tables were removed and singers (*cantores*) entered advancing in slow procession over the floor of the bishop's hall. They sang with alternating voices, praising God in words of jubilation, delighting the bishop as much as the abbot and all who were assembled there with the sweetness of their singing.[31]

The reference to 'alternating voices' would certainly accommodate the refectory performance of pieces in the Codex Calixtinus such as the responsories, if performed in the customary liturgical manner with alternation between soloists and chorus.

All the items in the Codex are notated on rubricated staves with bold yet delicate neumes. Vertical lines through the pairs of staves show the separation of words and phrases or clarify the co-ordination of voices where the texture is especially complex (Pl. 94). These marks would certainly have been useful to singers who were trying to put the pieces together (to 'compose' them in one medieval sense of the term) by finding ways to synchronize the melodic material in each voice, by experimenting with the duration of pitches, which the notation does not specify, and by feeling for structural points of consonance around which to consolidate the results of their experiments. These compositions represent the art of the trained singer in the most cultivated form it had achieved by 1150.[32]

A later hand has added attributions in red ink to many of the pieces in the manuscript, both the polyphonic items and the chants. This makes the Codex Calixtinus virtually the only musical source before the fourteenth century where

nof ergo intereffe polo abfq; termi no.

Ut menf noftra regi regum benedicat domi mino;

magifter anard° vieiliacenfis

nnua gaudia iaco be de bita funt tibi dan da.

Organa dulcia conueniencia funt re fo nan da.

Et iuf relica facta phennia funt referinda · Organa ʒ̃ Hec quoq; fplen
dida secla p omnia funt memoranda · Organa ʒ̃ Tam pia tam bona
tanta dogmata funt ʒ mitanda · Organa ʒ̃ Hec facra comoda flori
da fulgida funt adamanda · Organa d.

arriquf efs goneuentinuf

acobe fancte tuum repetito tempo re feftum · fac pre

polyphonic pieces appear with the name of their composer or redactor. Some of the attributions are probably or definitely false; it is no surprise to find the famous Fulbert of Chartres mentioned six times, for example, for his name was indeed *un nom qui chante* and would come easily to any scribe seeking to dispel the anonymity of a Latin plainsong. Some of the other names, however, are perhaps too vague to have been worth inventing and may be genuine ('a certain Galician scholar'). Nonetheless, whether these attributions really are a major source for the musical skills of Capetian churchmen or not, they involve considerably more than an attempt to rescue a collection of pieces from anonymity. Minor figures and a few unknowns aside, the annotator has worked through the musical items adding the names of clerics who moved in the most exalted circles of the northern French Capetian heartlands. Some of them were eventually bishops (Alberic of Bourges was an archbishop), and some were involved in the main intellectual and theological disputes of the earlier twelfth century. Their names, or their episcopal sees, variously associate them with Bourges, Chartres, Châteaurenard (perhaps the small town of that name to the east of Orléans), Parthenay, Picardy, Soissons, Troyes (in two cases), Vézelay and perhaps in one instance with Laon. Only with Benevento, Malines and a vague reference to Galicia do the attributions reach beyond the Capetian core lands.[33]

With its nascent corporation of masters, Paris figures prominently in the careers of at least two Calixtine composers: Alberic of Bourges and Jocelin of Soissons. The latter's career provides one example, among several offered by the book, of just how high the scribe who added the attributions in the Codex Calixtinus was aiming when he chose his names (or, if some of the pieces really are the work of these men, how ambitious the original collector had been in gathering material). Jocelin, bishop of Soissons from 1126 to 1152, was a major figure in the intellectual and ecclesiastical life of the French kingdom during the first half of the twelfth century. He approved a rule for the Templars at Troyes in 1128 together with Bishop Hatto of Troyes, credited with seven two-part compositions in the Codex Calixtinus. Jocelin was known to John of Salisbury, who mentions him in his *Metalogicon,* and to Abbot Suger of St-Denis, who addresses him in the Prologue to his Life of Louis VI. These were illustrious friends indeed. One

---

94 (*facing page*) Conclusion of the two-voice composition *Ad superni regis decus* (top four staves) attributed on the previous folio to *magister alberic[us] archiep[iscopu]s bituricensis* (= Alberic, archdeacon of Reims 1131–6 and archbishop of Bourges, 1136–41), followed by the two-voice *Annua gaudia* attributed to *magister airardus vieiliacensis* (for ? *viceliacensis*) and the beginning of the two-voice *Iacobe sancte* attributed to an *antiquus episcopus boneuentinvs*. In *Ad superni* , the last section of the intricacy of the Calixtine staff-notation, and the scribe's close attention to the sounding potential of the notation, is plain. The scribe here has clearly anticipated difficulties of co-ordination in this predominantly note-against-note melismatic section, and he provides some very closely spaced 'fences' through the stave to clarify what sounds against what in performance. There are numerous erasures. Santiago de Compostela, cathedral library, without shelfmark, Codex Calixtinus, fol. 215ᵛ.

chronicler praises Jocelin (and Alberic of Bourges, another Calixtine musician) for being among 'the most illustrious men for learning and piety'. Like Alberic, Jocelin was a severe critic of Peter Abelard, ridiculing him as 'more of a minstrel than a learned man'. He was also one of three bishops who wrote to Innocent II condemning Abelard after the council of Sens in 1140, and with Abelard's principal adversary, Bernard of Clairvaux, he founded the Cistercian abbey of Longpont, where he was eventually buried.[34]

How did a page of music by such composers look to the archbishop of Santiago and the canons for whom the Codex Calixtinus was prepared? The question could be answered in several ways, one of which would be to broaden it and propose that the whole collection looks distinctly hostile to Abelard, giving a great deal of space to men who opposed him but none to a controversial figure who was a celebrated maker of songs himself (hence, perhaps, the jibe about him being more of a minstrel than a scholar). Yet perhaps the most persuasive answer would be that a page of this notation would certainly have looked like something deeply implicated in the long-term formation of a Latin West from a Frankish and Carolingian core. The style of the painting that opens the text, showing Charlemagne's infantry and cavalry riding out from Aachen to uncover the shrine of St James (see above Pl. 89), is not related to the brilliant colour panels and primitivism of indigenous Mozarabic art, just as the musical notation on staves is French and not closely akin to the kinds used for Mozarabic chant. All this is obvious at a glance today, as it probably was in the twelfth century, for the Codex Calixtinus was designed for a cathedral whose prelate, Diego Galmirez, persistently cultivated the abbot of Cluny as an intermediary between himself and the papacy in his long struggle to have his church placed in a trans-Pyrenean corridor and raised to metropolitan rank.[35]

Yet to some twelfth-century eyes there was also something emphatically *Carolingian* about the appearance of this musical notation, although one must look well beyond the parts of the volume usually colonized by historians of music to find it. One section of this composite codex contains the *Historia Turpini*, or History of Turpin, one of the most familiar figures of the Old French verse narratives, the *chansons de geste*. He is the archbishop of Reims who meets his death at Roncesvalles, with Roland and Oliver. As the *Song of Roland* has it in an account of *c*. 1100:

> Turpins de Reins tut sun escut percet,
> Quasset sun elme, si l'unt nasfret el chef,
> E sun osberc rumput e desmailet,
> Parmi le cors nasfret de .iiii. espies,
> Dedesuz lui ocient sun destrer.
> Or est grant doel quant l'arcevesque chiet. AOI.

[the Saracens] have entirely pierced Turpin's shield, broken his helm, thus they have wounded him in the head, broken and damaged the mail of his hauberk, and wounded him in the midst of the body with four spears. They kill his horse under him; there is great lamentation when the archbishop falls. AOI.

The chronicle of Turpin in the Codex Calixtinus is a forgery (if that term is appropriate in a medieval context), but every medieval reader whose opinion can be determined regarded it as a genuine narrative of Charlemagne's conquests in Spain. In 1272–4 the Dominican Master General, Humbert of Romans, pressed the need for a crusade upon Gregory X by citing the chronicle's prefatory letter. 'As we read in Turpin's epistle about the deeds of Charlemagne in Hispania', says Humbert, 'Saint James appeared to Charlemagne and commanded him to free Compostela from the Saracens. Thus we see how it pleases God and the saints when lands are cleansed by Christian force.' Humbert could scarcely have made the work of pseudo-Turpin carry more weight. At the end of the fifteenth century, Trithemius still regarded the *Historia Turpini* as an authentic work by the historical Turpin, archbishop of Reims.[36]

The scribes of the Codex Calixtinus also treated this chronicle with grave respect, for they began it with luxurious illumination and ornament that is without parallel elsewhere in the book (Plate 89 illustrates one of the two images they provided; the other shows Turpin himself). Yet if the *Historia Turpini* begins with fine pictures, it ends with a description of paintings that seem to be finer still. Before the colophon in which 'Turpin' beseeches his readers for their prayers, he describes a series of images that Charlemagne commissioned for his palace at Aachen upon his return from the Spanish campaign. In addition to scenes of Charlemagne's Spanish wars, there are paintings of the seven liberal arts. As the chronicler describes the portrait of music he insists upon the cardinal importance of notation upon a four-line stave. Without it, there is no art of music at all:

> Music was depicted there, which is the art of singing well and correctly. The offices of Holy Church are celebrated and adorned with music, whence it is held more dear. With the aid of this art, singers in church sing and make polyphony [*organum*] . . . And it should be known that there is no music according to this art unless it is written out with four lines.[37]

The *Historia Turpini* therefore associates the four-line stave with Charlemagne and his imperial palace. If the chronicler had any concept that this was an anachronism, he does not show it. He regards it as much more important to associate the device with the emperor whose conquests were long associated with the making of a Latin-Christian Europe, and with a political heartland re-envisaged in the attributions of the musical pieces as the Capetian core with its great cathedrals and monasteries at Paris, Troyes, Chartres, Bourges and possibly Laon.

The musical stave was a Latin-Christian invention and was confined, for many centuries, to the Occidental lands where Latin was the exclusive language of liturgical singing. It provided the means for an aggressively expansionist civilization to train singers relatively quickly so that the flag of the Latin liturgy could be planted in Spain, in Livonia, in the Holy Land, and in a great many of the larger hospitals and chapels, often in rural or indeed wild locations. There is something to lament there, but also something to laud. The world has the Passions of J. S. Bach, and the late quartets of Beethoven, because monks, clergy and knights of the central Middle Ages sought a form of life with a rigour to match their consciences, then drained marshes, took boats along uncharted rivers or attempted to reclaim, at huge cost to themselves and to others, new lands for Christendom.

CONCLUSION

THE TASK OF TRYING TO FORM AN IMPRESSION of Christians and their singers in their first three centuries is like assessing the position of Muslims today using only the websites of Islamic extremists and official pronouncements about the War on Terror. Neither the triumphant proclamation by Origen that Christians should regard the imperial government as corrupt nor the violent reprisals of Nero against the Christians of Rome illuminates the daily lives of Christians among their polytheistic neighbours. When Pliny and Trajan considered complaints against the believers of Pontus soon after 100 they had to make decisions on the spot; since there was no body of legislation in existence for them to apply it would seem that no significant trials of Christians had so far been held. Hence it is probably correct to say that devotees of Jesus in the first century, and long after, generally lived peaceably with their neighbours under the eyes of the polytheistic Roman state. They espoused a great many different doctrines, notably in their Christology, but there are early signs of a mainstream in the making that would have commended itself to non-Christians since it was based upon households. There the biological family, the dependents, free artisans and slaves might all be converts. Such households brought together under one roof the entire constituency addressed by a proto-Catholic wing of the Christian movement that was dedicated, at least in theory, to a universal and egalitarian ministry under the guidance of patrons and elders, and which was widely associated with the doctrines of a fully human and yet divine Christ born of a woman without knowledge of a man. The Pastoral Epistles of the New Testament already show Christians being advised to follow models of conduct that any Roman censor would have approved as the signs of an upright and public morality based upon the household and the authority of a paterfamilias. Those Epistles are brief and by no means consistent in the instructions they give for respectable Christian families; no doubt too much could be made of them; yet to return to the analogy with Islam, we may say that Christianity survived because it had its equivalents to the Muslim families running shops and local businesses in modern European cities, not because it had teachers who preached the destruction of the existing social order.

The hymnody of Christian gatherings was part of the general clamour rising heavenwards from cultic assemblies in the eastern Mediterranean and probably had much in common with the ritual singing of other religions. The earliest synod of bishops to identify a Christian minister of ritual song, convened at Laodicea at some time in the fourth century, has nothing to say about the character of the singers' music or its manner of performance. Either there was a long-standing and consolidated difference between the music of a Christian *psaltes*, a Jewish *psalmologos* and a pagan hymnodist, or the prelates did not regard the sonorities and musical procedures of the mainstream Church as a particular domain of musical style and sonority within the musical culture of respectable cults. One should be careful here not to make too much of the excited polemics of a Jerome against 'theatrical' manners of singing. The principal purpose of Christian singing was to laud a divine power and to intensify the bonds of community, and those were aims that any Jew or polytheist could recognize.

The materials of Mediterranean song, in their great abundance, nonetheless gave some Christian groups certain musical forms and styles that they regarded as expressions of the beliefs that distinguished them from competing communities. For those who hoped to rise in the flesh for the Millennium and then the general judgement, ritual singing was a way to celebrate the continuity of bodily existence on both sides of the grave. The voice was one of the higher faculties of the body that Tertullian and others believed would survive in the blessed state where the lower would no longer be required. This view of hymnody was founded upon a belief in the bodily resurrection of Christ as the divine exemplar of all resurrections and a commitment to accept the flesh as potentially corrupting but not itself corrupt. It was therefore an orthodox view opposed to most forms of Gnosticism, where the soul's enclosure within a muddy garb of flesh was apt to be regarded as a disastrous accident. Other forms of Christian belief had different rites and conceptions. In the second-century *Acts of John* a ring-dance performed to a song with choral refrain is associated with a Christology so profoundly unorthodox that one can well imagine other Christian communities, with different commitments, repudiating such dances as indissolubly associated with heretical beliefs. Here the diversity of early Christian music comes into view, impossible to describe in terms of a single trajectory. The *Acts of John* was never destined to enter the scriptural canon, and in the first millennium dancing never found a secure place in mainstream Christian liturgy; nonetheless, public dancing on certain Israelite festivals was possibly one of the earliest forms of worship amongst Jesus-believing Jews and their Gentile adherents. There are also other traces in the earliest Christian worship of something akin to the cultic dances of polytheism. Any attempt to dismiss the ring-dance of virgins in the third-century *Banquet* by Methodius as allegory pure and simple, for example, runs the risk of allowing a certain Puritanism to close down the possibility that some groups celebrated a Christianized version of a Bacchic dance. One might add that there is no such thing as allegory pure and simple; allegory, like irony, requires that some elements in the matters being brought into relation should be *true*.

The Christian ministry of ritual song therefore has no single source or clear line of development. In the same way, the figure of 'the Christian singer' proves very nebulous for some considerable time. The earliest singer known by name is 'Gaios', praised for his hymnody in a Greek epitaph of the third or fourth century, but he was not a minister of music in the sense of bearing a relevant title of office. He was a presbyter. Some churches were perhaps accustomed to press any member of the clergy, regardless of his order, or any male member of the community, into service as a singer if he possessed the necessary talents, which can never have been in abundant supply. In Rome and Gaul, for example, deacons appear as psalmists (sometimes very good ones) in texts and inscriptions of the fifth and sixth centuries. There is one strand in early Christian musicianship, however, that remains visible in the longer term. Some of the earliest known singers in Christian rites were called 'readers', *lectores*, holding a minor order that can be traced in Carthage as early as *c*.200. There were Occidental churches where this usage persisted into the late 500s, and in Gallican sacramentaries there are fossilized traces of it as late as the 700s, notably in the ordination rituals for lectors that exhort them to voice *moduli*, perhaps a vestige of a reference to music. The extension of the title *lector* to those whose duties were partly musical, or even exclusively so, lends support to no particular theory about the techniques of late antique psalmody, least of all to the claim that early strata of lector chant can be discerned in plainsong sources notated many hundreds of years later. The tradition of using the term *lector* to mean 'one who reads and sings' or even 'one who only sings' principally reflects the late antique practice of regarding the pre-Eucharistic psalm(s) as a form of reading.

By the first half of the third century there are clear signs in Carthage that *lectores* were often boys or adolescents. Material scattered through the West, but especially strong for Africa, confirms that these young readers were sometimes singers, perhaps often so. At Augustine's church in Hippo Regius there appears to have been nobody to chant the Fore-Mass psalm save the young *lector*, while in Ambrose's church at Milan the work was done by a *puerulus*, though perhaps not exclusively so. There is probably a direct historical link between the custom of appointing males to the lectorate in boyhood or adolescence and the domestic worship of mainstream Christian communities in the house-churches of the second and third centuries. Among the wealthier Christians of an urban quarter, whence a community might derive its ministers and the hosts for its assemblies, it would have been fully in accord with the traditions of Roman education for a young male offspring to be given the task of declaiming letters and other texts eventually received as Scripture, whether they were to be said or sung. This might have been done before or during the communal meals that can rarely be firmly distinguished as either love feast or Eucharist much before the third century, if then. Some recent historians of early Christianity have suspected that Christians valued a child's voice as especially appropriate to gospels that Caesarius of Arles in the early 500s calls 'the most unadorned of narratives'. If so, this can probably be extended to the singing voice of many a *lectur ennocens*, to quote the undated epitaph of one who died at the age of 13.

There are signs in Jerome's translation of the Bible that ministers of ritual song called *cantor* existed in parts of the West by *c*.400. The date easily accommodates the proposal that separate departments of reading and singing in the wealthier churches arose in parallel with developments in the fourth-century imperial administration, civil and military, towards a proliferation of titles, insignia and departmental empires. (Clergy and bureaucrats were often recruited from much the same social strata.) Yet this was by no means universal. The deacons, standing at the threshold where the ministries of the altar gave way to the minor orders, had also assumed a charge of reading and singing in some major churches by 400. Long associated with the tasks of carrying and reading letters or other documents, the deacons were a natural choice for the delivery of lessons and indeed of psalmody, if they were capable of doing so. By the late fourth century, the Christian epigraphy of Rome begins to register a few of these deacon psalmodists, who can perhaps stand for many more, both in Rome and elsewhere. The deacons were never to be entirely silenced in the liturgies of the West, as many medieval ordinals reveal (to say nothing of the *Exultet*), but the situation whereby bishops would expect these trusted messengers and confidants to take turns performing the responsorial psalm was not destined to last. Soon after 500, the term *cantor* as a title of office definitively appears in the documents and inscriptions of some major churches around the Mediterranean littoral, creating a map with a distinctly late Roman and maritime appearance suggesting deep roots. They include Ravenna, Marseille, Naples, Trento and Mértola. By 500, Naples already possessed something like a college of singers ruled by a *primicerius* as if it were a palatine ministry, and Lusitania yields what may be another example with Andreas the *princeps cantorum*, who died at Mértola in 525. Shortly before 532, Ravenna was able to spare four *cantores* for an embassy to Rome, suggesting that a substantial college of singers had been established in the cathedral there. The Roman body of singers, the *schola cantorum*, may have existed long before the first evidence of it in *Ordo Romanus I* (*c*.700). The degree of organization in the churches of Carthage, Naples, Ravenna and perhaps of Mértola at a much earlier date suggests that may be so.

The earliest sources where *cantor* appears as a title of office all adhere to the seat of Roman power: the Mediterranean littoral that conquest had turned into a vast fiscal district. The work of supervising musical provision within the churches remained the work of Romans in the sixth century – meaning bishops who were indigenous men and Latin-speakers for the most part. The Germanic speakers who had arrived in the fifth as invaders or as generals in Rome's service, and who then metamorphosed into competing warlords and finally emerged holding the Romano–barbarian office called kingship, had only to let these prelates, wielding an authority so deeply rooted in the imperial achievement, continue with their task. It was nonetheless one in which the kings had a profound interest themselves. In the new political order of the Western realms, kings were apt to regard conversion to Christianity (but not necessarily to Catholicism) as part of the process whereby they assumed the powers and duties conferred by being Rome's heirs. A *romanitas* survived, notably in the use of the Latin language for official documents and a literate administration, often in an attenuated form. In the sixth century, there were prelates who still spoke in terms of Roman provincial boundaries, who composed Latin verse and who compiled annals; especially in the domain of festive liturgy, they were a link with the world that the ancestors of the kings had known in the higher levels of Roman military service, learning to value its costly cloaks, furnishings, banners, insignia and titles. A Frankish queen of the early sixth century believed that the sight of luxurious hangings and textiles might convert her husband. All the while, Rome and Byzantium offered a continuing example of opulence expressed with expensive textiles, precious metals and sonorous titles that proclaimed supreme honour and eternal victory through liturgy. To maintain rich services, at least in major churches of the kingdom, with a staff of good singers was one of the ways in which a king came into his inheritance as surely as moving into the old governor's palace.

The traces of recruitment to royal chapels and cathedrals in the sixth century, though very sparse, are revealing. In the Vandal state, Carthage supported a song-school with at least twelve boys in a class (if this biblical number can be trusted). These boys served the Catholic Church of the city, but the royal chapels of the Arian Vandals will not have been allowed to slip behind; indeed, the lector who had once taught these young singers had converted to Arianism, perhaps to prosper better in royal service. In the sixth century, thanks to the writings of Gregory of Tours and other documents, the Frankish kingdoms are the best documented of all the Western realms, and they already show that curious combination of increasing martial strength and a need to depend upon southerners for elements of the Roman legacy that will one day take Frankish singers to Italy for *cantus romanus*. A psalmist at Metz in the mid-century was probably a Visigoth from Languedoc or Spain. Another may have been a Greek. Not long after 500, a bishop of Clermont can be found removing from his monastery in the Auvergne a gifted singer who eventually entered the service of the Frankish king at Cologne, Reims or Trier. This psalmist from Clermont became a royal favourite. For a Frankish king like Theuderic, who was only a second-generation Christian, a good liturgical singer from the Auvergne was like purple silk or best pepper: a highly desirable import from the south. Insofar as it enriched his clerical establishment and the liturgy of his churches, it made him a miniature Constantine as surely as the Roman recipes, with pepper and spices, written down for his cooks by Anthimus.

Singers and the Rise of Western European Music

Whatever else it may imply, the term 'Western Europe' is a way of referring to certain patterns of communication between the grassland–deciduous forest environment of the North and the lands of the summer drought, the Mediterranean. Unless there is contact between the plains and the Romans' Great Sea, then as far as the expenditure of human energy is concerned there is no west European peninsula, only the micro-context of separate and more or less land-locked or coastal communities. The Roman imperial administration, at its height, had been able to maintain excellent transalpine contacts. Networks of civil and military communication brought supplies of oil for lamps and military rations, incense for the imperial and other cults, silk for hangings and cloaks, and pepper (among many other spices) to the North European Plain. Those plains, however, produced few of the commodities traditionally regarded as the more exquisite luxuries in the ancient world, commanding a price that made them worth transporting far afield. To be sure, economic history is usually made of simpler things than luxuries: leather, basic tools and ceramics matter more to the development of economic life than silk, glass and spices. Luxuries, however, are essential for tracing patterns of long-distance communication because goods of high value, with assured elite markets, are almost always worth the cost of transporting the commodity far. There is therefore a sense in which the patterns of transalpine communication associated above with a west European space have often been energized by the transit of luxuries when there was no transalpine state moving bulk goods for its armies or tax grain for its capital. Until the advent of the Frankish Empire, the only transalpine state of the first millennium was Roman.

By the seventh century, the Roman world-system was in disarray on a Eurasian scale. The incursions of Byzantium's Persian and Muslim competitors interrupted routes and reduced the base of the surviving empire's taxable land. Archaeology reveals traces of private dwellings, often of inferior quality, being built over the spaces and streets of many classical cities in both the eastern and the western empires. There are abundant traces of stone from classical buildings plundered for use in defensive walls, and of open, unfortified sites contracting to a walled nucleus or *kastron*. In East and West alike, most of the old classical cities generally shrank within their relatively impoverished hinterlands, protecting small enclosures of liturgical opulence within their cores where incense, oil, vessels of precious metals and expensive textiles for vestments were used (and in the case of incense, expended) with relative profligacy.

In the West, Gregory of Tours (d. 594) knows of herbs and papyrus brought into Gaul from Egypt, but he finds no reason to mention the Mediterranean ports of Arles, Fos or Narbonne. He names only Marseille, suggesting that the long-distance contacts of the other ports were much diminished. By the 720s, the Mediterranean shoreline of Africa had fallen to Islam, finally closing down the old Roman space where the three continents of the old world hinged together in a superb set of maritime opportunities. The coastline that produced Tertullian, Augustine and the earliest known traces of the psalm later known (in Roman usage) as the gradual, now passed out of the Latin-Christian system. Spain, conquered, became the western extreme of an Islamic maritime system that looked across to Persia. The Visigothic realm that might have become the axial culture of the early medieval West in place of the Frankish, had it survived, and a kingdom where liturgical singers had a high notion of their calling, retreated to the north with its back against the mountains.

The ascendancy of the Pippinids in the late 600s therefore coincides with certain indications that a long-term decline of Mediterranean maritime commerce was now approaching its lowest point. The decline of Marseille by 700, suggested by the archaeology of the shallow-draft harbour area, is especially suggestive for the state of commerce out of the Mediterranean into the Frankish heartlands, for this port was the Franks' principal gateway to the Great Sea. By the time of Pippin, the gate appears to have been rotting on its hinges. Excavation has so far revealed few traces of good-quality buildings erected far into the eighth century at Marseille, while signs of the port's integration into trans-Mediterranean networks become virtually illegible at the same time. A Merovingian royal diploma of 692 (in its surviving form) tellingly licenses the agents of the abbey of St-Denis to purchase oil 'according to what is available on the quay' at Marseille, which does not suggest a great abundance of supply. Traces of Frankish connections with other ports of the southern French littoral such as Arles, Fos or Narbonne (rapidly silting up by now) are thin. The decline of these ports, or at least their gradual loss of contact with their northern markets, must have significantly reduced the supply of luxuries available to the Franks, notably spices (including incense), silks and linen. Pollen evidence from the region of St-Denis suggests that the Franks were making renewed efforts to produce linen by the ninth century, probably for vestments, among other garments. The Carolingians, with their homeland on the northern reaches of the European plains, were liable to be early losers in the parting of the ways between Latin Europe and the Arabo-Byzantine Mediterranean. Liturgy, however, crossed the boundary and was a form of Roman, aulic opulence. The only Roman teacher of chant who can be proven to have crossed the Alps at their request was perhaps a Syrian; at the very least, he represented the powerful Byzantine influence upon eighth-century Roman liturgy and art (Pl. 95).[1]

This is not to say that the Carolingian elites were impoverished. Few regions of the early medieval West show a more healthy level of economic contact between micro-regions than Francia. What is more, a new arc of trade, with only faint Roman precedents, was now reaching down from the Frisian Islands and the Baltic to the lands of the Abbasid Caliphate. Nonetheless, the image of Rome as the 'omnipotent commander of the world's resources' remained, for it is deeply inscribed in the luscious décor of poetry by Sidonius Apollinaris or Venantius

95   Wall-painting of Madonna and Child from the lower basilica of San Clemente, Rome. 8th c.

Fortunatus. It lingered in titles of office such as *referendarius*, in papal letters claiming command of the world's churches and in Byzantine gifts. Italy lay all the while on the southern horizon, and beyond that Byzantium, both representing what remained of Roman imperial pageantry, lavish expenditure and luxurious consumption, in Old Rome now concentrated in the sumptuous theatre of liturgical celebration. No matter how impoverished Italy's inhabitants had become by the eighth century relative to Augustan levels, the peninsula was still well placed (in the literal sense of the expression) to receive spices, herbs, medicines and textiles brought from Africa and Asia. 'Perfumes are things with a fragrant smell that parts of Arabia send us, or Italy', writes the ninth-century Frankish liturgist Amalarius of Metz, inserting a reference to Italy into the text he is quoting, which originally had none (*Etymologies*, xvii. 8). For Amalarius, a festive liturgy with singers performing Frankish-Roman chant, and with incense, silks and linen, brought the odours of an Italian market to the Moselle.[2]

During the early 750s a geopolitical situation rapidly arose that drew the Franks much more closely to Italy and established close (but perhaps only temporary) contact between Frankish singers and the Roman *schola cantorum*. Responding to Lombard incursions, an imperial subject, Pope Stephen, turned to a barbarian king, Pippin, to make good a shortfall of imperial strength in a particular theatre of war, Italy. This sounds like a late antique situation, and indeed an appeal to the Franks was one of the oldest weapons in the arsenal of late antique imperial policy. Whence it is perhaps better understood in terms of a continuing imperial context in the West rather than too emphatically in terms of a process of Roman-papal separatism from the Byzantines. Nonetheless, this was undoubtedly the period when the popes chose to position themselves at the eastern extreme of the Latin Occident and not at the western extreme of the Greek Orient as represented by Byzantium. Conscious of a new entity, a *romanorum francorumque imperium*, for which his priests said prayers, Pippin and his advisers resolved to introduce the liturgy of Rome into at least the royal chapels and the churches governed by members of the royal family (Rouen) or the most trusted *fideles* (St-Denis and Metz), creating what was in effect a *romanorum francorumque cantus*. The pope had come to Ponthion in 754 with singers of the Roman *schola cantorum* – later sources leave little doubt of that – whose presence in the papal retinue has left a diffuse but unmistakable background noise in a number of ninth-century sources. As a result of the alliance between Pippin and Pope Stephen founded that year, and regarded as binding upon their descendants, a Roman singer came northwards to Rouen and it seems likely that the Franks followed him home. These were early moves in a slow enhancement of transalpine communications as retinues, messengers and armies began to

96 Silk textile, probably Persian, 8th or 9th c., from the Abbey of Faremoutiers (Seine-et-Marne). Abbaye Bénédictine de Notre-Dame et de Saint-Pierre, Faremoutiers.

move between Rome and its Frankish protectors. In short, a transalpine western Europe began to revive, albeit very slowly, and no activity marked this broader horizon more potently, or more often, than the daily celebration of an emerging Frankish–Roman liturgy by priests, deacons and singers.

The wide dissemination of this Frankish–Roman music from the ninth century onwards was not exactly the work of a 'central power', although it certainly represented an example of early medieval government working, in the usual manner, through lines of blood and *fidelitas*, together with the necessary (and healthy) awareness among the Frankish magnates, both spiritual and temporal, that they were part of a great co-operative enterprise in pursuit of salvation and public order under the king. Singers passed from church to church when prelates asked for them to be sent as a favour, as at Lyon and perhaps Salzburg, as much as by royal command. A comprehensive map of connections, if only we could draw one, would probably be as much a chart of friendship and alliance between cathedrals and abbeys as a map of direct intervention by the emperors. To judge by the course of Christian conversion in the royal house of Denmark during the reign of Louis the Pious, or in Iceland and Hungary soon after 1000, there was an emerging sense of a Latin and Western core, essentially Frankish, to which newly converted polities were drawn in a way that helps to explain why their kings sought baptism in the first place. In these core lands there was a shared liturgy and a common repertory of plainsong, or what was believed to be so in the face of widespread variation. The highly visible initiatives of the eleventh century, including the suppression of Beneventan chant at Montecassino and of Mozarabic chant in Spain, both on papal authority, are in part late manifestations of a long-standing drift towards coalescence around shared liturgical and musical experience. Soon after 1100, a pope could write to almost anywhere in Latin Christendom convoking magnates or bishops to a meeting on the Sunday when the Frankish-Roman introit *Laetare Jerusalem* was sung, and expect to be understood.

In the liturgy of the Hours, however, and especially in the feasts of the Sanctorale, it is the proliferating localism of the tenth and eleventh centuries that emerges most strongly. Between 900 and 1100, many new plainchants were composed for singers to perform in honour of saints whose relics had recently been discovered, sometimes in circumstances suspiciously favourable to the territorial interests of a particular magnate, as at Mons or Caiazzo, or the needs of an abbey. Some of the saints honoured with new music were very new themselves, for they might be the bishops or abbots of a recent generation whose families had landed interests in the abbeys or cathedrals they had lately ruled. With the erosion and final disappearance of the Carolingian Empire, the collapse of power into the smaller cells of bishopric, abbacy, county and dukedom was most advanced in western Francia. Hence it may be no coincidence that the number of composers known from that region between 900 and 1100, many of then eventually bishops

or abbots who produced music in honour of more or less local saints, is so substantial. (There has probably never been a time in the history of Western music
when the art of the singer has been of deeper moment to so many men of learning than in the tenth and eleventh centuries.) The cult of the saints, furthered
with new Lives and chants, was a means to defend the interests of a house and
to secure peace in cases of dispute. By making gifts of land to the saints in
person, and only secondarily to the monks, nuns or clergy who served their
churches, powerful families entered into a contractual relationship with a heavenly being who became their neighbour in the fullest juridical and personal sense
if the land they gave away bordered other territory that was their own. They also
wove themselves into networks of friendship and cooperation that connected
them to monks and clergy (whose bishops and abbots were often drawn from the
same local families) and to other kindred that had made similar gifts. Land was
the hard currency of social relations, given and received back in a continuing
process of exchange to ease conflicts or confirm local alliances, and at the heart
of each transaction was a celestial landowner who, like any lord or lady, reacted
well to a new song in his or her praise.

The interplay between the universal and the particular emerges clearly in the
person of Guido of Arezzo. The context for his work is closely defined, for he
seems to have been protected during the documented phases of his life by one
kindred: the Canossa from the Po Valley in a distinctly expansionist frame of
mind. Having invented a form of musical stave, Guido took his new system to
the pope in Rome. The roots of the invention he displayed there are ultimately
Carolingian, not only because the stave is indebted to the tradition of graphic
inventiveness that began with the charts devised by ninth-century scribes as they
compiled materials about the Liberal Arts, but also because Guido's notation
emerged from his attempt to edit and teach a correct version of Roman chant for
the Universal Church, a thoroughly Carolingian ideal. Guido's system is also
Carolingian in a more troubled sense. The 'forgotten' fifth treatise among his
writings addressed to singers and teachers is a polemical letter to a Milanese
prelate on the heresy of simony, understood in the broadest sense to mean any
kind of trafficking in the Holy Spirit; the letter reveals how tightly Guido's
motives as a reformer of notation, and as a teacher of singers, were intertwined
with the eleventh-century move to realize the Carolingian ideal of a reformed
and conscientious church, guided by the wisdom of the Scriptures and canon
law. In the eleventh century this concern was believed to require a much
sharper distinction between the purified ministers of the altar and the laity, whatever their rank, than anything the holders of a German imperial office that
descended from Charlemagne could condone. Guido's fifth treatise is one of the
earliest documents in the large and fraught dossier that the conflict between
spiritual and temporal power, *regnum* and *sacerdotium*, produced. The stave was
created for singers, whom Guido regarded as 'the most foolish of men' for their

unproductive labours, but in a broader sense it also emerged from the process whereby the mechanisms of early medieval government were finally and painfully overhauled, especially those whereby kings and emperors had long nominated men they could trust to episcopal sees, invested them with ring and staff and then counted on their loyalty.

———

An appeal to the idea of a transcendent Rome accounts for much of what may seem most European about the history of singers traced in this book. By long custom, dwellers in Europe and countries with a strong European imprint are drawn to Roman symbols of power and coercion such as the purple (still worn by bishops), the legionary eagle (an emblem of the United States' government) and the *fasces*, whence the term 'fascist'. At the end of the Second World War, when fascism was defeated and the Roman-imperial eagle commandeered by Nazism was thrown down, the political classes in some European states began the project of European reconstruction by evoking the Roman foundations of European civilization. In Britain, Winston Churchill hoped that the members of the various nation states would eventually say 'I am a European' when asked for their nationality, just as a Roman citizen once said *civis romanus sum* in any part of the Empire. By the choice of location, a certain *romanitas* was written into the Treaty of Rome that initiated the European Community in March 1957, but more by the fulfilment of Churchill's dream that citizenship of the Union be granted to every person holding the nationality of a member state (*Treaty of Rome*, II, Article 8: 1–3). The first trans-European currency since the Roman Empire has now been established (but not in Britain), showing idealized examples of Roman and Romanesque architecture, among other images, carefully abstracted from the particularities of any one building to suggest trans-European archetypes. The euro banknotes might just as well be marked with a chant from the repertory of a Frankish singer around 900, or with the staff-notation of Guido d'Arezzo. Perhaps one day they will be. That would be a fitting tribute to the contribution made by singers of the Christian West to the formation of a European identity.

NOTES

Introduction

1 **The Central-Asian origins of the bow:** Bachmann, *The Origins of Bowing*.

2 **The songs at Poitiers:** MGH RMSS, ii. 375–6 (*Vita Sanctae Radegundis*).

3 **A wide, blurred borderland:** S. Wood, *The Proprietary Church*, 109. Individuals called 'monks' will occur often in this book; in one place they have a section to themselves (Ch. 6) and their work as composers of new chants, especially for the Office, dominates Chs. 18 and 19, but the information about monastic singers in Rules and Customaries, together with the context required to understand what they can reveal, is work for another chronicler.

4 **The case of the Easter Vigil:** Compare Bernard, *Du chant romain*, 107–9, who gives the appealing account of these chants alluded to here. For attempts to reconstruct the melodic history of chants in much later (7th- and 8th-c.) phases, the master in this domain is Levy; see *Gregorian Chant and the Carolingians, passim*.

1 A Prospect of the Sea

1 **'The Transformation of the Roman World':** See below, n. 11. For an excellent summary, see Hen, *Roman Barbarians*, 1–26. For consumption, see now Bang, *The Roman Bazaar*. Recent major surveys include Heather, *Empires and Barbarians*; idem, *The Fall of the Roman Empire*; Wickham, *Framing the Early Middle Ages*; and idem, *The Inheritance of Rome*.

2 **The Frankish queen and the hangings:** Gregory of Tours, *LHD*, ii. 29.

3 **Res gestae:** 'Augustus', *Res gestae divi Augusti*, ed. Cooley, §§31 (Cadiz to the Elbe, p. 90) and 8 (the enrolments, p. 66). Augustus intended that the text should be placed near his mausoleum in the Campus Martius, and set up in other cities of the Empire. On the map of Agrippa that accompanied the *Res gestae* at Rome, see Nicolet, *Space, Geography and Politics*, 95–112. **Roman communications and early Christianity:** The sociological emphasis in studies of the early Church during the last thirty years has often brought out this theme. For a conspectus, see Schnabel, *Early Christian Mission*, i. 444–79.

4 **Roman maritime trade:** See Du Plat Taylor and Cleere, *Roman Shipping and Trade* (on Britain and the Rhine provinces), and Haley, *Baetica felix* (on one of the principal oil-exporting regions of the Empire). **Maritime movement along the Red Sea and the Gulf:** the outstanding primary source for the early imperial period is the *Periplus Maris Erythraei*, edited with full and illuminating commentary by Casson, with bibliography. See also Desanges, *Recherches sur l'activité des Méditerranéens* and Rougé, *Recherches*. For Roman trade and the East see Ball, *Rome in the East*, esp. 74–5 (with map) and 131 (summary of the Indian commodities); Greene, *The Archaeology of the Roman Economy*, esp. 17–44; Young, *Rome's Eastern Trade*, esp. 27–135. **Commodities:** Begley and De Puma, *Rome and India*; Miller, *The Spice Trade of the Roman Empire*. The subject broadens to the debate about the Roman 'economy'. See Bang, *The Roman Bazaar*; W. V. Harris, 'Between Archaic and Modern'; Hopkins, 'Taxes and Trade' (seminal, but now contested); Jacques and Scheid, *Rome*, 291–4 (a useful overview); Liebeschuetz, *The Decline and Fall of the Roman City*, 408–9 (on the term 'economy' in a Roman context); and Mattingly, 'Oil for Export' (with overview at 33 n.).

5 **Rome's duty of care:** For a Roman 'minister of external affairs', see Lampe, *From Paul to Valentinus*, 397–408, with the data for the 'popes' at 402 (derived from Eusebius, *EH*, iv. 22–3; v. 4 and 244). **Trastevere:** Lampe, op. cit., 49–54 and (on Rome more broadly, as revealed by Paul's Epistle to the Romans) 153–83. See

also Richardson, 'Augustan Era Synagogues in Rome'; Snyder, 'The Interraction of Jews with Non-Jews in Rome'; Brändle and Stegemann, 'The Formation of the First "Christian Congregations" in Rome'. **Marcion's donation:** Lampe, op. cit., 245–6. See also Marjanen and Luomanen, *A Companion to Second-Century Christian 'Heretics'*, 100–24.

6   **Conditions along the land route:** Diodorus Siculus (xx. 42) relates that a large army set out from Cyrene with the aim of conquering Carthage in 308 BC, but was severely tried by thirst and hunger during the long march along the sandbanks, 'a waterless land filled with savage creatures' and poisonous snakes. For conditions along the coast road in Tripolitania see Mattingly, *Tripolitania*, 1–16 and 61 (the taverns 'best avoided'). **Cyrenaica:** Horden and Purcell, *The Corrupting Sea*, 65–74, which reveals the ecological and climatic diversity of the 'region' of Cyrenaica.

7   **Elvira:** *Concilios Visigóticos*, ed. and trans. Vives, 5 (Canon XVIII, *De clericis negotia et nundinas sectantibus*). On maritime contacts between this region of Spain and the wider Mediterranean, see Villela Masana, 'Les Voyages'. **Anteros:** PG 10: 167–74 (to the province of Baetica and the ecclesiastical province of Toledo). For Anteros/Anterus see Lampe, *From Paul to Valentinus*, 25 and 371.

8   **The buying power of the legionary encampments:** see e.g. Fentress, *Numidia*, 175. **The British forts:** *Tabulae Vindolandenses* II, ed. Bowman and Thomas, 136 ('piper') and Pl. XII; for context see Bowman, *Life and Letters*. On imported comestibles in Roman Britain, see now Cool, *Eating and Drinking in Roman Britain*. **Julianos Euteknios:** for edition, discussion of interpretations and translation see Horsley, *New Documents*, i. 68–9. **Cologne:** for Bishop Maternus, see Eusebius, *EH*, x. 5; the Frankish and apparently Christian commander is mentioned by Ammianus Marcellinus in *Res gestae*, xv. 5. For evidence of trade and supply along this route in the early 1st c. AD, see Desbat and Martin-Kilcher, 'Les Amphores sur l'axe Rhône-Rhin'.

9   **Acts of Peter:** *Acta Apostolorum Apocrypha*, ed. Lipsius and Bonnet, i. 50–3. Translation in *New Testament Apocrypha*, ed. Schneemelcher, ii. 285–321.

10   **Thomas:** *Acts of Thomas*, ed. Klijn. **Contacts with India:** See further Schnabel, *Early Christian Mission*, i. 479–99. **Malabar coast:** P. Brown: *The Body and Society*, 122–3. **Eusebius:** *EH*, ii. 14. **Frumentius:** Rufinus, *Historia ecclesiastica*, i. 9 (PL 21: 478–80). For context see Desanges, *Recherches sur l'ac-tivité des Mediterranéens*, 348–53 *et passim*. For early Christians privileging one another in financial dealings see Hippolytus, *Refutatio omnium Haeresium*, ix. 7.

11   **The 'Fall' of Rome:** It is possible to mention only some outstanding works (see also n. 1 above). *LRE*, 1025–68 remains fundamental. For the historiography until the early 1980s see Demandt, *Der Fall Roms*. Heather, 'The Huns and the End of the Roman Empire in Western Europe' is now cardinal, a powerful reformulation and refinement of external explanations for the fall of the Empire. For a broader presentation of the argument see id., *The Fall of the Roman Empire*. Halsall, *Barbarian Migrations and the Roman West, 376–568*, is a recent survey, while Hen, *Roman Barbarians*, is especially good on the theme of a transformed *Romanitas* at the royal courts. Ward-Perkins, *The Fall of Rome*, is a succinct and polemical attempt to restore a 'collapse of civilization' narrative (Heather's theme is comparable). MacMullen, *Corruption and the Decline of Rome* emphasizes the importance of internal forces. For the movements of barbarians, the volumes in the series *The Peoples of Europe* give valuable surveys (see entries under Christie, Heather, James and Thompson in the bibliography). Outstanding surveys include studies of social, political and archaeological history by Delogu (on medieval Rome), Fontaine and Hillgarth (on the seventh century), Goffart, Innes, James, Mathisen, Moorhead, Rouche (notably the essays edited in *Clovis*) and I. Wood are listed in the bibliography. Hendy, 'From Public to Private', is a compact but wide-ranging survey of the numismatic evidence. Important monographs appear regularly, including Christie, *From Constantine to Charlemagne* (an archaeology of Italy); Handley, *Death, Society and Culture* (on the evidence of epigraphy in Gaul and Spain, 300–750) and J. M. H. Smith, *Europe after Rome*. See also McCormick, *Origins of the European Economy*, and Wickham, *Framing the Early Middle Ages* (both fundamental). There is much essential material in the volumes of the series The Transformation of the Roman World (see Bibliography under Hansen/Wickham, Hodges/Bowden, Pohl, Pohl/Reimitz and Pohl/Wood/Reimitz). For the long tradition of writing the 'barbarian invasions' of Late Antiquity in terms of floods and waves, see Goffart, *Rome's Fall and After*, 9–10, and 119. For the concept of 'late antiquity', which has played an important part in the revisionist process since it has proved so elastic, see espe-

cially Treadgold, 'Taking Sources on their Own Terms'. **Questions of ethnicity:** See Pohl, 'Telling the Difference', which includes, *inter alia*, the question of whether there were ethnically distinctive armaments, such as the 'Frankish' axe the francisca, and the difficulty of distinguishing between 'Byzantine', 'Germanic' and 'nomadic' material in the archaeological record. For ethnic identity among the early Franks, see James, *The Franks*. For recent work on the important issue of ethnicity and peoples in the Late Roman Empire, see Amory, *People and Identity* (sharply sceptical); Curta, *The Making of the Slavs*; Pohl (ed.), *Kingdoms of the Empire*. See also Pohl and Reimitz, *Strategies of Distinction*, and Randsborg, *The First Millennium*, 137, referring to 'the romantic notion that barbarian peoples organised themselves around internal identities which persisted essentially unchanged over the centuries'. On the association of that view with forms of European nationalism and modern political extremism, see Geary, *The Myth of Nations*. The **'half-Vandal generalissimo':** Matthews, *Western Aristocracies*, 234 and 268; cf. 289.

12 **'not only the foes of the Romans':** Thompson, *The Huns*, 40. **The Huns:** Ammianus Marcellinus, *Res gestae*, xxxi. 2; Priscus (in *The Fragmentary Classicising Historians*, trans. Blockley, 255–377); Claudian, *In Rufinum*, i. 323–31; Jordanes, *Getica*, xxiv–xliii; Zosimus, *New History*, v. 20. For the literary and archaeological record of the Huns, see Bona, *Les Huns*; Maenchen-Helfen, *The World of the Huns* (including a substantial, but inconclusive, discussion of whether the Huns were a Turkic people); Sinor, 'The Hun Period' and Thompson, op. cit. For the movement of the Huns as a precipitate of intrusion into the Western Empire, see Heather, 'The Huns and the End of the Roman Empire in Western Europe'. For a striking example of memories of the Hunnic invasion in later centuries assuming symbolic shapes, see Goffart, 'Paul the Deacon's *Gesta Episcoporum Mettensium*'.

13 **The impacting crises:** Heather, 'The Huns'. **African losses:** *LRE*, 816–17. **Vandal sea power:** Reddé, *Mare Nostrum*, 647–52. **Vandal continuities:** Courtois, *Les Vandales et l'Afrique* (including, Appendix II, Latin inscriptions of presumed Vandal date; on which see now *Les Inscriptions funéraires*, ed. Ennabli, i and ii). Revealing studies of precise issues include Freed, 'The Late Series of Tunisian Cylindrical Amphoras at Carthage' (showing how much weight of interpretation might hang on very fragmentary archae-

ological evidence) and Humphrey, 'Vandal and Byzantine Carthage'; Wickham, *Framing the Early Middle Ages*, 17–22; 87–93, *et passim*. **Volume of shipping in the Western sea:** for assessments of the aftereffects of Vandal conquest see the essays in *La navigazione mediterranea nell'alto Medioevo*; Durliat, 'Les Conditions du commerce au VIe siècle'; Lewis, 'Le Commerce et la navigation' (for the impact on Gaul); McCormick, 'Bateaux de vie'. **The shippers at Arles:** Sirks, *Food for Rome*, 119. **Blockading the African ports:** Zosimus, vi. 3. **Claudian:** *De bello Gildonico*, i. 17–27.

14 **'Hungry barbarians':** Ammianus Marcellinus, *Res gestae*, xiv–xvi, *passim*; xxxi, *passim*; Procopius, *Gothic War*, iii. 3; vi. 3–6; 25. Marius of Avenches, s.a. 569; Hydatius, *The Chronicle*, ed. and trans. Burgess, s.a. 410, 422 and 452–3. Olympiodorus, *Frammenti storici*, 38.

15 **Pirenne:** On the views of Pirenne, see most recently Delogu, 'Reading Pirenne Again'; Hodges, 'Henri Pirenne'; Hodges and Whitehouse, *Mohammed*; Loseby, 'Marseille and the Pirenne Thesis I and II'; McCormick, *Origins of the European Economy*, 115–19 (an important summary of a complex discussion); 442 (connections between the Frankish world and the Eastern Mediterranean at their lowest ever by 750, but destined for an upturn in the time of Charlemagne without ever reaching the levels that obtained before 750), *et passim*; Purcell and Horden, *The Corrupting Sea*, 153–72. **The importance of 'cheaper' goods:** Carandini, 'Italian Wine and African Oil', 16: 'What matters from an economic point of view is not so much earning a great deal from a few choice items as earning a lot – or even a little – from large quantities of goods.' **The substantial cut-back in Mediterranean-wide exchange:** Wickham, 'Production, Distribution and Demand', 371. For material of cardinal importance in this debate, see once more the volumes of the series *The Transformation of the Roman World* listed in the bibliography under Chrysos and Wood, Hodges and Bowden; Pohl and Wood; Pohl, Reimitz and Wood; Hansen and Wickham. **The 'early medieval depression' in political and cultural histories:** see especially the outstanding survey in Moorhead, *The Roman Empire Divided*, 248–70; the essays in Mango, ed., *Byzantine Trade* (especially Kingsley, 'Mapping Trade by Shipwrecks') and the essays in Bowman and Wilson, eds, *Quantifying the Roman Economy* (especially Wilson, 'Approaches').

2   The God of the Household and his Music

1   **'The earliest traditions':** Hurtado, 'The Origin and Development of Christ-Devotion', 72. See also Hill, *The Johannine Corpus*, 3–10. Among recent historical and textual studies which trace central elements of New Testament teaching and interpretation to Christ himself, Stuhlmacher, 'Isaiah 53 in the Gospels and *Acts*', is pertinent; see also Hofius, 'The Fourth Servant's Song', and Markschies, 'Jesus Christ as a Man before God'. For attempts to explain the spread of Christianity in all its forms, see McKechnie, *The First Christian Centuries*; Praet, 'Explaining the Christianization of the Roman Empire' and Stark, *The Rise of Christianity*. Mullen, *The Expansion of Christianity*, is a gazetteer listing a vast amount of early textual and archaeological material. More studies will be mentioned in the following notes. Orthodoxy and heresy in the early Church has attracted much recent attention in recent years, especially the notion of an originary orthodoxy only ever taking heretical directions by pressure from without. See Elm et al., *Orthodoxie*; Le Boulluec, *La Notion d'hérésie* and Marjanen and Luomanen, *A Companion to Second-Century Christian 'Heretics'*.

2   **Patroklos:** G. J. Riley, as quoted in Crossan, *The Historical Jesus*, 29.

3   **The Acts of John:** for text, French translation and lavish commentary see *Acta Iohannis*, ed. Junod and Kaestli; for the hymn see i. 198–207 (text and translation), ii. 632–42 discussion with bibliography and context. The material quoted here, which begins at chapter 95 and has often been regarded as part of the oldest layer of the hymn, is quoted from the editors' reconstruction at p. 200. English translation in *New Testament Apocrypha*, ed. Schneemelcher, ii. 181–4, also in *The Apocryphal New Testament*, trans. Elliott, 318–19. See also Hill, *The Johannine Corpus*, 258–63, which (at 258) is the source of the quote ('a lengthy, romantic . . .') cited here. See also *The Acts of John*, ed. Lalleman, 26, *et passim*; Bowe, 'Dancing into the Divine'; R. H. Miller, 'Liturgical Materials in the *Acts of John*' and Schneider, 'The *Acts of John*'. On the complex textual history of the book see, in addition to the edition by Junod and Kaestli, the same authors' *L'Histoire des actes apocryphes*. For patristic attitudes to dance, see Andresen, 'Die Kritik der alten Kirche am Tanz'.

4   **'sacrifice, communal meals . . .':** Harland, *Associations*, 45. **Methodius:** Methodius, *The Banquet*, ed. Musurillo and Debidor, 308–21.

5   **Celsus and the aulos:** Origen, *Contra Celsum*, iii. 16. Appendix to Chapter 3, no. 8.

6   **'Scythian and despotic':** *Contra Celsum*, i. 1.

7   ***Ekklesia*:** for a conspectus of the term in Christian sources see Moulton, et al., *Concordance to the Greek New Testament*, 330–1; Bauer–Danker, s.v. ἐκκλησία; *DACL* s.v. *Église*; Hainz, *Ekklesia*; Linton, 'Ekklesia' in *Reallexikon für Antike und Christentum*, iv. 905–20, and Tena-Garriga, *La Palabra 'Ekklesia'*. For the foundations of ecclesiology in Canon Law see the *Dictionnaire de droit canonique*, s.v. *Église* and *Églises*, and Gaudemet, *Église et cité*.

8   **Families and the dissemination of cults:** Barclay, 'The Family as Bearer of Religion', and MacDonald, *Early Christian Women*, 198–200 *et passim* on the evangelizing potential of household relations. **Didache:** Slee, *The Church in Antioch*, 55–7, argues that the *Didache* is of Antiochene provenance and that it dates from the middle of the 1st c. In *La Doctrine des douze apôtres*, Rordorf and Tuilier, 98, dismiss the theory of Antiochene origin, while Zetterholm, *The Formation of Christianity in Antioch*, does not raise the issue. For **The Shepherd of Hermas** see Pernveden, *The Concept of the Church in the Shepherd of Hermas*. **Origen and the councillors:** *Contra Celsum*, viii. 75. **Ignatius** reminds the communities he addresses that their Church must have an *episkopos* or bishop at its head, served by a group of elders or presbyters, and below them a group of deacons, 'servants of the church of God'. For Ignatius, this is the only valid form of Christian organization, and it is achieved when the Christians of each city join in loving subjection to their *episkopos*. See *To the Ephesians*, 1. 3; 2. 2; 4. 1–2; 5. 3; 6. 1; 20. 2; *To the Magnesians*, 2; 3; 6; 7; 13; *To the Trallians*, 2; 3; 7. 2; 12. 2; 13. 2; *To the Philadelphians*, Prologue; 1; 3 and *To the Smyrneans*, 8; 12. 2 (all in *The Apostolic Fathers*, ed. and trans. Ehrman). For the development of ministries and orders see also Bobertz, 'The Development of Episcopal Order'; Faivre, 'La Question des ministères à l'époque paléochrétienne', and id., *Naissance d'une hiérarchie*; Gibaut, *The Cursus Honorum*, 14 (the presbyterate and the Sanhedrin); Harland, *Associations*, 182 *et passim* and Jay, 'From Presbyter-Bishops to Bishops and Presbyters'. For Rome, see Brent, *Hippolytus*; Lampe, *From Paul to Valentinus*; and Pernveden, op.

cit. The essays in Delage, *Les Pères de l'Église et les ministères*, form an especially important collection on the early Christian ministries.

9 **Great men of the generation:** Levine, *The Ancient Synagogue*, 421. See Bobertz, 'The Role of Patron'. **Acts of Peter:** *Acta Apostolorum Apocrypha*, ed. Lipsius and Bonnet, i. 66–7. Compare Slee, *The Church in Antioch*, 110–11, who identifies the bishops and deacons of the *Didache* as Gentile householder patrons and hosts of the *Didache* community. It is difficult to enforce a distinction between such patrons and what might be called clerical offices in the making. Some of the earliest layers of information about the election and ordination of Christian ministers seem to be speaking of both at once. In the complex dossier of liturgical and other regulations now generally called the *Apostolic Tradition*, commonly assigned to the early years of the 3rd c. but intermittently recording customs that may be considerably more archaic, the provisions for ordination are marked by the innate prestige and social status of the ordinands. The 'elders' or presbyters are envisaged as governors of the local Christian community, not as liturgical functionaries, giving their counsel 'to help and govern' the people (Bradshaw et al., *Apostolic Tradition*, ch. 7, §2 in Latin, Ethiopic and *Testamentum Domini*).

10 **Palestinian housing:** Hirschfeld, *The Palestinian Dwelling*. **Claudius Ephebus and Valerius Biton:** *I Clement*, 63. 3 and 65. 1; Lampe, *From Paul to Valentinus*, 184–6.

11 **Severus Alexander:** All sources used for this paragraph are cited and illuminatingly discussed in Bodel, 'An Outline'. **Workers in wool and leather:** *Contra Celsum*, iii. 55.

12 **Paul and worship in Corinth:** In addition to the valuable commentaries of Thiselton, *The First Epistle to the Corinthians*, see MacDonald, *The Pauline Churches*, 61–71, and Meeks, *The First Urban Christians*. For context see especially Holmberg, *Paul and Power*, and Murphy-O'Connor, *Saint Paul's Corinth*. For the context of pagan festive dining, see Harland, *Associations*.

13 **'An accepted conventional procedure':** Rappaport, *Ritual and Religion*, 124, quoting J. L. Austin. See also Bell, *Ritual: Perspectives and Dimensions*, and id., *Ritual Theory, Ritual Practice*; Habinek, *The World of Roman Song*, 34–57. **'Not very profound':** Rappaport, op. cit., 120.

14 **'People sing to make sure . . .':** Zuckerhandl: *Man the Musician*, 42. Many further reflections of interest and value in Begbie, *Theology, Music and Time*.

15 **Isidore of Seville:** *De ecclesiasticis Officiis*, i. 5.

16 **Ignatius on hymnody:** *To the Ephesians* 4. **Plutarch and Philo:** Parallel passages are usefully cited in Schoedel, *Ignatius of Antioch*, 51–3, with illuminating commentary. In common with many authorities, Schoedel accepts the middle of the three recensions of the letters of Ignatius, giving the Greek text followed here as an authentic work

17 **Sibling commitments:** This emphasis marks many of the essays in Katz, *The Cambridge History of Judaism*, iv, notably Schwartz, 'Political, Social and Economic Life', 26 (evidence for Jews living under Roman not Jewish Law in Arabia, evidence that can perhaps be extrapolated further), and Rutgers and Bradbury, 'The Diaspora'. Compare Boyarin, *Border Lines*; Dunn, *The Parting of the Ways*, and Mimouni, *Le Judéo-christianisme ancien*. **Synagogue Psalmody:** McKinnon, *The Temple*, Essay VIII, 'On the Question of Psalmody in the Ancient Synagogue'. Compare J. A. Smith, The Ancient Synagogue and its Music'; id., 'First-Century Christian Singing' (notably open to the use of apocryphal texts), and id., 'The Ancient Synagogue, the Early Church and Singing'. There is an important counter voice in Karp, 'Interpreting Silence'. See also Haas, 'Zur Psalmodie der christlichen Frühzeit', Hamman, 'L'Utilisation des psaumes', and D. S. Katz, 'Biblische Kantillation'. **The Mishnah:** English translation by Neusner. Recent syntheses include Kraemer, 'The Mishnah' (interpreting the text as '[p]erhaps . . . the early rabbinic vision of a restored, Torah-perfected, "messianic" world'), and Neusner, *Rabbinic Judaism*. **The synagogue:** There has been much debate here, often focusing on the question of how early, and how widely, purpose-built buildings were created for Jewish gatherings. See K. Atkinson, 'On Further Defining the First-Century CE Synagogue', with bibliography; Binder, *Into the Temple Courts*; Burtchaell, *From Synagogue to Church*; Levine, *The Ancient Synagogue*; id., 'The Development of Synagogue Liturgy'; id., 'The Nature and Origin of the Palestinian Synagogue Reconsidered', and White, *Building God's House*, ch. 4. Harland, *Associations*, is now essential for understanding the synagogue, both as 'building' and as 'assembly', in a broad historical context. **Early Christian music, including the influence of the synagogue:** in addition to older strata of

work, comprehensively inventoried in the bibliography accompanying *MECL*, see McKinnon, 'Early Christian Music'; id., *The Temple*; see also Bastiaensen, '*Psalmi, Hymni* and *Cantica*'; Bradshaw, *The Search for the Origins of Christian Worship*; id., 'Ten Principles'; Bradshaw and Hoffman, *The Making of Jewish and Christian Worship*; Foley, *Foundations of Christian Music*; Quasten, *Musik und Gesang;* Saxer, 'Culte et liturgie'; all studies by J. Smith in the Bibliography; Sparksman, *The Minister of Music*; and Talley, *The Origins of the Liturgical Year*.

18   **Aphrodisias:** Reynolds and Tannenbaum, *Jews and God-Fearers at Aphrodisias*, 5 (text) and 46 (discussion). There has been much discussion as to the date of this inscription. Trebilco ('The Jews in Asia Minor'), 80 n., gives full bibliography and dates the inscription to the late 2nd or early 3rd c. **Rome:** Horsley, 'Epitaph for a Jewish Psalm-Singer'.

19   **Philo and the *Therapeutai*:** *De Vita contemplativa*, ed. Daumas, trans. Miquel, 2. 11; 3. 24; 11. 90. Philo stresses that they are philosophers. Among recent discussions, see Deming, *Paul and Celibacy*, 9–11 and 90–1. **Eusebius:** *EH*, ii. 17. Compare Melito of Sardis on Jewish psalmody and dancing at Passover (*Sur la Pâque*, ed. and trans. Perler, 104–7). Compare Van Unnik, 'A Note on the Dance of Jesus'. Junod and Kaestli, *Acta Iohannis*, 625 n., regard the possibility of a connection with Jewish dancing as 'très douteuse', but do not give their reasons.

20   **'Interested outsiders':** Fredriksen and Irshai, 'Christian Anti-Judaism', 986. **John Chrysostom:** *Adversus Judaeos*, i. 2. **Augustine:** *Sermones de Vetero Testamento*, 110; *In Iohannis Evangelium Tractatus*, iii. 19; *Enarrationes in Psalmos*, 1280. **Licinianus of Cartagena:** *Epistolae*, in *Liciniano*, ed. Madoz, 128: 'ballare, saltare, et membra a deo bene condita saltando male torquere, et ad excitandum libidinem nugatoribus cancionibus proclamare'. In this general context, see also T. H. Connolly's admirable study, 'Traces of a Jewish-Christian Community'.

21   **Lucian:** *The Dance*, 15–16.

22   **Music at the Roman sacrifices and in cults:** Quasten, *Musik und Gesang* remains essential, although Wille, *Musica Romana*, 26–74, is the definitive survey of the literary evidence for Roman pagan practice. For a useful selection from the iconographic record see Fleischhauer, *Etrurien und Rom*, and for instrumental music at the meals of the *collegia* and the colleges of young singers, Harland, *Associations*, 57–9, 123–5 *et passim*. More general surveys in Klauck, *The Religious Context of Early Christianity*, 16 *et passim*, and Sendrey, *Music in the Social and Religious Life of Antiquity*, esp. 369–496. See also Habinek, *The World of Roman Song*.

23   *Letter to Diognetus* 2 and 5.

24   **The epitaph:** Text in *MAMA*, viii. 23–5. The editors hope Tēlphidēn is a mistake for Tēlphidōn, 'Mammeis of the Telephidai'. Destephen, *Prosopographie*, s.v. Gaios 2.

25   **An 'end-time new creation . . . has irrupted':** Beale, *The Book of Revelation*, 175, from whom I also borrow the phrase 'an-already-and-not-yet' view of the end-time glory of God (ibid. 732).

26   **Christian dissent from the doctrine of bodily resurrection:** Irenaeus, *Against Heresies*, v. 31. 1, on heretics 'despising the handiwork of God and not admitting the salvation of the flesh'.

27   **Apostolic Fathers and bodily resurrection:** *I Clement*, 26. 3; Ignatius, *To the Trallians*, 9. 2; (pseudo-) Clement, *II Clement*, 9. 1–5. See Foster, 'Polymorphic Christology'.

28   **Tertullian:** text and translation in *Tertullian's Treatise*, ed. and trans. Evans, vii, xlviii, lx and lxi. **Celsus and the body:** Origen, *Contra Celsum*, v. 14 and vii. 34–6 (attacking Christians who believe they will be in paradise with their physical senses).

29   **'You have been given a mouth':** *Tertullian's Treatise*, ed. and trans. Evans, lxi.

30   **Apostolic Tradition:** The most recent and authoritative (parallel) translation of the versions, with full textual and contextual commentary together with bibliography of previous reconstructions and editions of the separate versions, is Bradshaw et al., *Apostolic Tradition*. The principal earlier reconstructions are by Botte and Dix (revised Chadwick). See also Bradshaw, *Eucharistic Origins*, 48 ff. On Hippolytus, see Brent, *Hippolytus and the Roman Church*.

31   **Testamentum:** quoted from Bradshaw et al., *Apostolic Tradition*, 157. For commentary see *The Testamentum Domini*, ed. Sperry-White (proposing a date before 381). The older translation is by Cooper and Maclean. On the singing of children see Quasten, *Musik und Gesang*, 133–41, and Bakke, *When Children Became People*, 251–7.

32   **The hosts:** Bradshaw et al., *Apostolic Tradition*, chs. 27. 2 (Latin, Sahidic, Arabic and Ethiopic) and 28. 1, 'he that invites you' (all witnesses to the text).

3   *Echoes of Christian Music*

1   **The fig episode:** compare Luke 13: 6–9. **Jesus as the dinner sage:** W. Braun, *Feasting and Social Rhetoric*, 1 *et passim*; for the food-making miracles, see Luke 5: 1–10 and 9: 13–17; Matthew 14: 16–21 and 16: 9–11; Mark 6: 35–44 and 8: 19–20; John 2: 6–10. For the imagery of the Messianic Feast, see Matthew 8: 11; 22: 1–4; Luke 12: 37 and 22: 30. Compare Braun, op. cit., *passim*, and Crossan, *The Essential Jesus*, 10. **The beatitude:** It is revealing that the corresponding beatitude in Luke's gospel is sharply literal, replacing the longing for righteousness with a dull ache in the belly: 'Blessed are ye that hunger now, for ye shall be filled' (6: 21).

2   **The Antioch context:** Slee, *The Church in Antioch,* which presses the *Didache* into service as a crucial document for the Antioch church in the mid-1st c., is especially thought-provoking. Compare Zetterholm, *The Formation of Christianity in Antioch.*

3   **Ignatius:** *To the Ephesians*, 20. 2. Compare Bahr, 'The Seder of Passover and the Eucharistic Words', 181–2: 'An important point to note about the Jewish festive meal of the Tannaitic period is that it paralleled the contemporary Graeco-Roman festive meal, except for the specifically religious elements, e.g., prayers were said at the same points in both meals, but the content of the prayers was different . . . I shall treat the paschal meal as one among many Jewish festive meals, and set the Jewish festive meals in the larger context of other festive meals in that period of history.'

4   **Paul and the words of institution:** Maccoby, *Paul and Hellenism*, takes the radical (but not unprecedented) position that the Eucharist and the words of institution are largely a Pauline creation. See also Klauck, 'Die Sakramente und der historische Jesus', and Økland, *Women in their Place, passim.*

5   **McGowan:** 'Naming the Feast'. Compare Bradshaw et al., *Apostolic Tradition*, 151 (referring to the terms *eucharistia* and *agape* as used by Ignatius in *To the Smyrneans*, 8): 'Although scholars have often taken *eucharistia* ('thanksgiving') and *agape* ('love feast') as describing different events, there is no clear evidence that either the terms or the events themselves were so distinguished at this early period.' See also Bradshaw, *Eucharistic Origins*, 29–30. Some liturgists, such as Gregory Dix, have placed the separation towards the end of the 2nd c.; among musicologists, McKinnon was prepared to see the earliest stirrings of a separation between Eucharist and *agape* in the 1st c. ('The Fourth-Century Origin of the Gradual', as reprinted in id., *The Temple*, Essay IX, 93). See also *DACL*, s.v. *Agape*; Alcock, 'The *Agapè*'; Keating, *The Agapé and the Eucharist*. For the term, see Bauer and Danker, *A Greek–English Lexicon of the New Testament*, s.v. ἀγάπη. The New Testament sources of the word are Jude 12 and some manuscripts of 2 Peter 2: 13. In the Latin sources, the outstanding document is Tertullian, *Apologeticum*, 39, in *Opera*, i. 150–3. **The Eucharist:** For the Jewish matrix, see Bahr, 'The Seder of Passover'; Bradshaw et al., *Apostolic Tradition*, ch. 26 (segregation of the faithful from catechumens, a chapter with Jewish parallels). Among many fundamental historical and theological surveys are Betz, *Eucharistie in der Schrift und Patristik*; Bradshaw, *Eucharistic Origins*; Keller, *Eucharistie und Parusie*; Klawans, 'Interpreting the Last Supper'; Lietzmann, *Mass and Lord's Supper*. Jastrzębowska, 'Les Scènes de banquet', catalogues the pictorial material showing early Christian meals. See also id., *Untersuchungen zum christlichen Totenmahl*. Compare Smith, *From Symposium to Eucharist.*

6   **The *Acts of Paul*:** See Appendix to this chapter, item 5. ***Acts of Peter*:** *Acta Apostolorum Apocrypha*, ed. Lipsius and Bonnet, i. 51. See also Thomas, 'The "Prehistory" of the *Acts of Peter*'. **Prayers that do not explicitly cite the words of institution:** Vogel, 'Anaphores eucharistiques préconstantiniennes'.

7   Goguel, *The Primitive Church*, 59.

8   ***Acts of Paul*:** Text in *Acta Pauli*, ed. Schubart and Schmidt, 50; translation in *New Testament Apocrypha*, ed. Schneemelcher and trans. Wilson, ii. 237–70 (and 214–15 for the use of the text by Tertullian, Hippolytus and Origen). For the sources of the text, see Van Haelst, *Catalogue*, 605–11. See also the essays in Bremmer, *The Apocryphal Acts of Paul and Thecla*, notably Hilhorst, 'Tertullian on the *Acts of Paul*', 161–3 (proposing that the text might be as old as AD 68–98); Broughton, 'From Pious Legend to Feminist Fantasy'. **The compiler's knowledge of the Pauline corpus:** S. J. Davis, 'A "Pauline" Defense of Women's Right to Baptize'?

9   **Justin:** Recent critical editions of the text are by Barnard, Marcovich, and Munier. The older critical text is by Wartelle with facing French translation. For the *Apologies*, see *MECL* 24 (where it is said that Justin 'fails' to mention psalmody) and 25. On Justin himself, see Lampe, *From Paul to Valentinus*, 257–84, and for his descriptions of Christian assemblies Bradshaw,

Eucharistic Origins, 61–77, and specifically on the issue of psalmody, McKinnon, *The Temple*, essays VIII, 190–1 and IX, 95. On the text see Parvis, 'The Textual Tradition of Justin's Apologies'. **Christian intellectuals:** Pouderon, 'Réflexions sur la formation d'une élite intellectuelle'.

10 **'A blend of the familiar and the novel':** MacDonald, *The Pauline Churches*, 64.

11 **The words of prayer:** Gelston, 'ΔΙ ΕΥΧΗΣ ΛΟΓΟΥ'.

12 **Letter to Diognetus:** xi. 6 (*Apostolic Fathers*, ed. and trans. Ehrman, ii. 156–7). On the question of the authenticity of chs. 11 and 12, see ibid. 124 (source of the summary quoted here). Marrou, in *A Diognète*, 219–40 *et passim*, makes a case for their authenticity (as also for a date in the region of 200 and an Alexandrian provenance). Rizzi, *La questione dell'unità*, also accepts them as genuine and at 78–9 discusses 'the fear of the law is sung'.

13 **De anima 9. 4:** Tertullian, *Opera*, ii. 792. Translation adapted from *MECL*, 82. **The woman as healer:** Barrett-Lennard, 'The *Canons of Hippolytus* and Christian Concern with Illness, Health and Healing', and Bradshaw et al., *Apostolic Tradition*, ch. 14.

14 **Canere and legere:** For these verbs throughout the corpus of Tertullian's writings see Claesson, *Index Tertullianus*, s.v. *cano* and *lego*.

15 **Tertullian as a Montanist heretic:** McKinnon: *The Temple*, Essay IX, 96. **Heretical hymns:** *New Grove Online*, s.v. 'Christian Church, Music of the Early', §1, 3v ('probably a service of the enthusiastic Montanist heresy. The "psalms", moreover, may very well have been heretical hymns . . .'). For studies of this aspect of Tertullian, see the following note. The fundamental works of general orientation are Barnes, *Tertullian*, and Fredouille, *Tertullien*.

16 **Tertullian and the *Acts of Paul*:** Hilhorst, 'Tertullian on the *Acts of Paul*'. **The 'New Prophecy':** for examples of the term see *Contra Marcionem* 3. 24; 4. 22 and 5. 16 in Tertullian, *Opera*, i. 542, 601 and 711. **Montanism:** For a succinct but well-documented account of Montanism, with good bibliography, see Trevett, 'Montanism', in Esler, *The Early Christian World*, 929–51, together with the studies listed below.

17 **Passion of Perpetua:** Text and translation in *The Passion of SS. Perpetua and Felicity*, ed. and trans. Shewring. I am much indebted to Leofranc Holford-Strevens in this paragraph.

18 **Montanism and Tertullian:** Braun, 'Tertullien et le Montanisme'; Munier, 'L'Autorité de l'Église'; Osborn, *Tertullian*, 209–19; Tabbernee: *Montanist Inscriptions and Testimonia*, 54–7. **'The Montanist Catholic':** Trevett, *Montanism*, 69 (but note that Trevett accepts the existence of a Montanist group in Carthage).

4   *Psaltes* and *Lector*

1 **Canons of Laodicea:** For the proceedings, with Latin and French translation, see *Discipline générale antique*, ed. Joannou, at 130–55. For the sees of Pacatian Phrygia, see Destephen, *Prosopographie*, 989–90. **Laodicea:** On the early Christian history of this city, including its economic aspects, see Mullen, *The Expansion of Christianity*, 98–9 (pre-320 material). For the archaeology of the city, the outstanding sources are now the essays in Traversari, *Laodicea di Frigia*, and for the basilicas Sperti, 'Ricognizione archeologica a Laodicea'. Unfortunately, the question of the date when the synod was held cannot be finally resolved. Canon VII mentions the followers of Photinos of Sirmium, condemned in the years around 350, but that might be an interpolation and the chapters give clear signs of layering that invalidate any attempt to tie the proceedings to a single period. They form two groups according to the opening formula they employ (1–19 and 20–59), which suggests they represent two chronological layers of material from different councils. Alternatively, they may represent the proceedings of one council that chose to restate a large body of earlier canons (or chapter headings) verbatim. There are references to singers in both layers. The best one can say is that there is information here that a synod of 4th-c. bishops judged relevant to conditions in Asia Minor.

2 **The *psaltes* at Laodicea:** The reference to a *psaltes* in the proceedings has often been discussed in the literature on the cantor. Among the principal materials are Dyer, 'Cantor'; *MGG, Sachteil*, s.v. *Kirchenmusiker*, 1; Faivre, *Naissance d'une hiérarchie*, 189–90; Foley, 'The Cantor', 210–11; *DACL*, s.v. *chantre*; R. E. Reynolds, *Clerical Orders*, Essays III, IV, 99 (n.) and VI, 246–7; id., *Clerics in the Early Middle Ages*, Essay I, 7–8; Sparksman, *The Minister of Music*, *passim*.

3 **The meaning of 'canonical':** *A Patristic Greek Lexicon*, ed. Lampe, s.v. κανονικός, sense 3 (citing the Laodicea proceedings), 'regularly or properly

appointed', but perhaps also 'orthodox'. Later ordination rituals: see below, n. 17.

4 **The Rhodus notary:** Destephen, *Prosopographie*, s.v. Épaphroditos. **Codices:** see Gamble, *Books and Readers in the Early Church*; Grafton and Williams, *Christianity and the Transformation of the Book* and Roberts, *Manuscript, Society and Belief*, 10 (on texts marked up with 'reading' aids (accents, breathings, punctuation and other critical signs)). **Marking up a text:** It remains unknown when the singers of the Christian West first began to use forms of musical notation. Markings in papyri of the 4th to 8th c. AD suggest that some form of notation may have been used in Egypt and parts of the eastern Mediterranean to teach the cantillation of Psalms and other texts, but the meaning of the markings remains uncertain. For the papyrus notations see Jourdain-Hemmerdinger, 'Fonction du chant dans les discours et lectures publiques'; Papathanasiou and Boukas, 'Early Diastematic Notation'. The arguments in Floros, *Universale Neumenkunde* (now available in English as *Introduction to Early Medieval Notation*), are still being assessed.

5 **Cyprian and the 'auditions' for readers:** *Epistola* 29 ('cum presbyteris doctoribus lectores diligenter probaremus . . .').

6 **Laodicea and the canon:** *Discipline générale antique*, ed. Joannou, at 130–55, canon LIX (only materials from the canonical Scriptures to be sung; 'homemade' psalms therefore banned). For the list of canonical books see Metzger, *The Canon of the New Testament*, 15 and 210. **African bishops consulting overseas:** *Concilia Africae*, ed. Munier, 43 ('ita ut de confirmando isto canone transmarina ecclesia consulatur').

7 **Marcionite hymns:** Hahneman, *The Muratorian Fragment*, 157 and 173–4.

8 **The opinions of Faustus:** Augustine, *Contra Faustum*, PL 42: 370–1: 'sacrificia vero eorum vertistis in agapes, idola in martyres, quos votis similibus colitis: defunctorum umbras vino placatis et dapibus; solemnes Gentium dies cum ipsis celebratis, ut calendas, et solstitia: de vita certe mutastis nihil; estis sane schisma, a matrice sua diversum nihil habens nisi conventum. Necnon et priores vestri Judaei, segregati etiam ipsi a Gentibus sculpturas solum dimiserunt: templa vero, et immolationes, et aras, et sacerdotia, atque omne sacrorum ministerium eodem ritu exercuerunt, ac multo superstitiosius quam Gentes. De opinione vero monarchiae in nullo etiam ipsi dis-

sentiunt a Paganis: quare constat vos atque Judaeos schismata esse Gentilitatis; cujus fidem tenentes et ritus, modice quamvis immutatos, de sola conventuum divisione putatis vos esse sectas.'

9 **Slightness of the differences between Christians and Romans:** R. A. Markus, *The End of Ancient Christianity*, 27–8 *et passim*.

10 **Psalmody no longer a form of reading:** For the abundant evidence that psalmody in the pre-Eucharistic service was considered a form of reading until the late 4th c. (and in many places until the 5th c.) see Jeffery, 'The Introduction of Psalmody', 465 (observing that, as late as Augustine, 'It is as if reading and psalmody were not clearly distinct activities'); McKinnon, *The Temple*, Essays VIII, 185 (with literature there cited), IX, 104 and X, 221; Nowacki, 'Antiphonal Psalmody', 296–7, with citation of patristic authorities. For *legere* see now Habinek, *The World of Roman Song*, esp. 59–74; Newman, 'De verbis canere et dicere'.

11 ***Apostolic Constitutions:*** Text, facing French translation and commentary material in *Les Constitutions apostoliques*, ed. Metzger, offering (i. 48–9) the interpretation that the text is designed to fill the lacuna of legislation from the early Church. For the Antiochene provenance, see i. 55–7 (but not from the same Antiochene church as John Chrysostom) and for the date (c.380), 59 (the relatively late appearance of the term *psaltes* for a Christian ministry of ritual song being part of the evidence cited). Further on this text and Antioch see Maxwell, *Christianization and Communication*, 75–80. Unsurprisingly, all the references to singers use words formed with the Greek stem *psall-* 'to pluck'. See ii. 57. 5 (the singer performs hymns after readings while the people respond); ii. 58. 4 (mentioning the psalmist); v. 17. 2 (the singer may marry after ordination); viii. 10. 10 (the bidding prayer for the faithful includes readers and psalmists); viii. 12. 43 (appearing to imply that the office of singer was there 'from the beginning'); viii. 13. 14 (psalmists partaking of the Eucharist after lectors, subdeacons and deacons); viii. 13. 16 and viii. 14. 1 (Psalm 22 as a communion hymn, using the term *legesthō* for the manner of performance though the performer is a psalmist); viii. 28. 7–8 (two references); viii. 31. 2 (psalmists receiving their share of the remaining oblations); viii. 46. 13 (the reader an apostolic institution; the compiler remains silent about the singer) and viii. 47, 26 (again allowing readers and psalmists to marry after ordination).

12 **The Diocese of Asia:** Destephen, *Prosopographie*. **Psaltes elsewhere:** for a late example from Alexandria, see *Recueil des inscriptions grecques-chrétiennes d'Égypte*, ed. Lefebvre, Alexandria, 2. For the Jews of Corycus, see M. H. Williams, 'The Jewish Community of Corycus' and id., 'The Jews of Corycus'.

13 **Mosaic pavements:** For a 4th-c. liturgical reader who dedicated mosaics at Antioch with a lay colleague see Destephen, *Prospographie*, s.v. Eidoméneus, and for a later example, Hèraklios[5]. **Artisan inscriptions:** *Early-Christian Epitaphs*, ed. Johnson. **Tabeis:** Destephen, s.v. Tabeis. **Stipends:** id., 'L'Apport de la prosopographie', 290.

14 **Porphyrios singer of antiphons:** Destephen, *Prosopographie*, s.v. Porphyrios[1]. **'does not exclude refrains . . .':** Nowacki, 'Antiphonal Psalmody', 304. I reluctantly reject Destephen's Nonnos[4], *psaltou*, since the key term is created by a conjectural emendation.

15 **The bishops:** See below, Ch. 8. **The Asian cities:** Liebeschuetz, *The Decline and Fall of the Roman City*, 29–103 provides an admirable and Empire-wide survey; see also S. Campbell, 'Signs of Prosperity' (on Aphrodisias); Foss, *Ephesus after Antiquity*; Harrison, 'Churches and Chapels of Central Lycia'; and Mitchell, *Anatolia*, ii.

16 **Saint Jerome and the singers:** *Commentariorum in Epistolam ad Ephesios Libri Tres*, PL 26: 528: 'Audiant haec adolescentuli: audiant hi quibus psallendi in ecclesia officium est, Deo non voce, sed corde cantandum: nec in tragoedorum modum guttur et fauces dulci medicamine colliniendas, ut in ecclesia theatrales moduli audiantur et cantica, sed in timore, in opere, in scientia Scripturarum.' Translation in McKinnon, *MECL*, item 333. **Psaltes as a minor order:** Jerome, *Sancti Eusebii Hieronymi Epistulae*, ed. Hilberg, lii. 13.

17 **Augustine's lectors:** McKinnon, 'Liturgical Psalmody', 15 and n., gathers the evidence. **Victor of Vita:** *Historia Persecutionis Wandalicae*, 10–11. Further on Victor, see below, Ch. 10. The singer's *melos* may simply be a Fore-Mass psalm, but chosen from one of the Alleluia psalms in the Psalter, any psalm to which an Alleluia refrain has been added or something else again. The people are both 'listening and singing' (*audiente et canente populo dei*). If all or part of a psalm is involved, then the reader's use of a book suggests responsorial psalmody with the lector singing the entire psalm and never at risk of losing his place when the choral refrain of the congregation 'interrupts' the text between each verse. For the link between responsorial psalmody and the use of books, see Nowacki, 'Antiphonal Psalmody'. **Gennadius:** In Cushing, 'Hieronymus . . . Gennadius', lxxx. (The lectionary was compiled by Musaeus, 'Massiliensis ecclesiae presbyter, vir in Divinis Scripturis doctus et in earum sensibus subtilissima exercitatione limatus, lingua quoque scholasticus, hortatu Sancti Venerii episcopi, excerpsit de Sanctis Scripturis lectiones totius anni festivis aptas diebus; responsoria etiam Psalmorum capitula tempori et lectionibus congruentia. Quod opus tam necessarium a lectoribus in Ecclesia conprobatur . . .'). Commentary in Gamber, 'Das Lektionar und Sakramentar des Musäus'. For possible traces of Musaeus's lectionary see *Das älteste Liturgiebuch*, ed. Dold, pp. xciv–xcviii (on the responsorial psalms). **Ambrose's oration:** *Sant'Ambrogio: Le orazioni funebri*, ed. Banterle, 62. An adult lector-singer, from the time of Ambrose, was Martyrius, a Greek from Cappadocia, sent by the bishop of Trent in a party of missionaries to the Tyrolese Alps, where he 'first intoned the song (*canticum*) of divine praise to the ears of a deaf region'. The use of *canticum* may be more than a figure of speech. In the first half of the 5th c., the Palestinian historian Sozomen mentions a certain 'Marcianus who was a singer (*psaltes*) and reader (*anagnōstes*) of holy writings' at Constantinople, where he was one of the bishop's notaries up to 352, when he was slain. This is perhaps the clearest instance on record of one individual meriting both *titles* of office, which here emerge into the light as a distinct pair, perhaps for the first time if *psaltes* was indeed the title that Marcianus bore in the 350s, and not simply the one that Sozomen gives him many generations later. For Martyrius see Vigilius of Trento, *Epistolae*, PL 13: 551, and Pietri and Pietri, *Prosopographie*, Vigilius[1] and Martyrius[2].

18 **Braga II:** *Concilios Visigóticos*, ed. and trans. Vives, 98 (Canon XLV). ***De officiis vii graduum:*** Reynolds, *Clerical Orders*, Essay II. **Missale Francorum:** *Missale Francorum*, ed. Mohlberg, 4; discussion in Smyth, *La Liturgie oubliée*, 104–7, and on the ordination documents, 137. **Gellone:** *Liber Sacramentorum Gellonensis*, ed. Dumas, 2506–9. **Angoulême:** *Liber Sacramentorum Engolismensis*, ed. Saint-Roch, 2062–4. **Moduli:** *Novum Glossarium Mediae Latinitatis*, s.v. *modulus*, senses 10, *chant (a) en general, (b) chant ecclesiastique*, 11, *mode (musical)* and 12, *musique instrumentale*; *OLD*, s.v. *modulus*.

19 **The emergence of a ministry of reading:**

Davies, 'Deacons, Deaconesses and the Minor Orders in the Patristic Period'; Faivre, *Naissance d'une hiérarchie*; Foley, *Foundations of Christian Music*; Quacquarelli, 'Alle origini del "lector"'; Sparksmann, *The Minister of Music*. See also Bradshaw, *Eucharistic Origins*, 61–77. **Acts of Peter and the Transfiguration reading:** *Acta Apostolorum Apocrypha*, ed. Lipsius and Bonnet, i. 66–7.

20 **Oral and written traditions:** Halverson, 'Oral and Written Gospel'; 'Hengel, 'Eye-Witness Memory', 74; Reed, 'ΕΥΑΓΓΕΛΙΟΝ' (on Irenaeus); C. M. Thomas, 'The Prehistory of the *Acts of Peter*' is an admirably clear presentation of one case with a broader relevance; see also the essays in Bockmuehl and Hagner, *The Written Gospel*. For the proposal that there was a written 'Cross gospel' in existence before the synoptics, and used by them, see Crossan, *The Cross that Spoke*.

21 **Christian reading and readers (including the history of the codex):** Cribiore, *Writing, Teachers and Students* (based on papyri); Gamble, *Books and Readers*; Haines-Eitzen, *Guardians of Letters*; McCormick, 'Birth of the Codex'; Roberts, *Manuscript, Society and Belief*; Roberts and Skeat, *The Birth of the Codex*. **Justin and the Scriptures:** Osborn, *Justin Martyr*, 120–38; Pryor, 'Justin Martyr and the Fourth Gospel'.

22 **Tertullian:** *De Praescriptione Haereticorum*, xli. For Tertullian's Latin usages see Janssen, *Kultur und Sprache*, *passim*, and for *lector*, 101–3. For the proposal that a certain 'native hostility to institutions' weakened the chances of survival of various Gnostic sects see Scott, 'Churches of Books?' The importance of Africa in the emergence of the Old Latin translation of the holy books of the synagogue and the materials of the New Testament has long been acknowledged. Burton, *The Old Latin Gospels*, 14–19; Soden, *Das lateinische Neue Testament in Afrika*.

23 **Christian architecture:** The outstanding guide in English is the two-volume study by White, *The Social Origins of Christian Architecture*. The textbook site is the Christian building at Dura Europos. See Gutmann, *The Dura-Europos Synagogue*; Kraeling, *Dura Final Report (Synagogue)* and id., *Dura Final Report (Christian Building)*; White, *The Social Origins of Christian Architecture*, i. 7–8, 15, 21–2 *et passim*. Weitzmann and Kessler, *Frescoes of Dura Europos Synagogue*. For an example of a recent find, see Bisconti, 'La scoperta di una piccola basilica'. Saxer, '*Domus ecclesiae*', surveys of use of this term in early

Christian texts. On the vexed question of the Roman titular churches and their presumed connections to pre-existing private houses, there is a recent review of the question, with bibliography, in Hillner, 'Families, Patronage and the Titular Churches of Rome'. **Acts of Paul:** The warehouse or grange is mentioned in ch. 10, and was supposedly hired by Luke and Titus when Paul arrived in Rome, for all three apostles to preach. **Baths:** *Martyrdom of Justin*, 2, and on the impossibility of identifying 'Myrtinus's baths' see Lampe, *From Paul to Valentinus*, 259 and n.; on the textual problems of the passage, compare White, op. cit., i. 110 and Belardini, 'Il Titolo di S. Ciriaco *in Thermis*'; Cerrito, 'Oratori ed edifici'; Stasolla, '*Balnea* ed edifici di culto'. **Pudenziana:** Brenk, *Die Christianisierung*, 50. **The Church at Nicomedia:** the eyewitness report of its destruction is given by Lactantius in *De Mortibus Persecutorum*, 186.

24 **Cyprian:** *Epistolae* 183–5 and 186–92.

25 ***Adolescens* in epitaphs:** Handley, *Death, Society and Culture*, 66. **Appas:** Destephen, *Prosopographie*, s.v. Appas[1]. **Commodian:** *Carmina*, ed. Martin, 60–1 (and pp. x–xiii for Commodian's milieu, accepted as being Rome, and a discussion of his dates, lightly urging the case for the 4th c.). For the difficulties of dating Commodian, and the proposal that he may have been writing as early as 220–40, see Daniélou, *The Origins of Latin Christianity*, 99–100. *Filiolus* regularly renders *tekna* in the Vulgate version of the New Testament (as for example in Mark 10: 24; John 13: 33; Galatians 4: 19; 1 John 2: 1, 12, 18, *et passim*). Souter (*A Glossary of Later Latin*, s.v. *filiolus*) gives 'children (*of ordinary Christians in pupilage*)' but cites no source.

26 **The purchasing agent:** Sidonius Apollinaris, Ep. 6. 8, on Amantius, the agent, working out of Marseille and entered on the register of readers (*lectorum . . . albus*). I am grateful to Ralph Mathisen for drawing my attention to this reference.

27 **Childhood in the late Roman period both pagan and Christian:** The literature is very rich, reflecting recent interest in the Roman and early Christian family. Bakke, *When Children Became People*, gives a review of the principal recent literature at pp. 1–14, the matter of cultic participation at p. 49 and on differentiation from adults and affective feeling, pp. 46–7; Bunge, *The Child in Christian Thought*; Carter, *Households and Discipleship* (especially ch. 4, 'Children, Household Structures and Discipleship'); Clark, 'The Fathers and the Children'; Currie,

'Childhood and Christianity' (a useful conspectus and discussion); Huskinson, *Roman Children's Sarcophagi* (important material abundantly illustrated); Leyerle, 'Appealing to Children'; Rawson, *Children and Childhood in Roman Italy*; Steenberg, 'Children in Paradise' (on the theme of Adam and Eve as 'children' in Irenaeus); Strange, *Children in the Early Church*; D. Wood (ed.), *The Church and Childhood.* **The inscriptions praising learning and studiousness:** *docti egregi iuvenes* (*CIL* vi. 1619), *ingenio clarus . . . dicendi peritus* (*CIL* viii. 12159.1.5–7) and *praeclarus studiis . . . ultra annos sapiens* (*CIL* ix. 5012). **Declamation and the child in pagan and Christian tradition:** Quasten, *Musik und Gesang*, esp. 133–41 ('Die Entwicklung des Knabensanges') remains fundamental. See also Osiek and Balch, *Families in the New Testament World*, 64–8 and 156–73; Di Berardino, 'Maestri cristiani del III Secolo', making the valid point that 'La partecipazione ai riti liturgici era una paideia in atto: la preghiera commune, le letture sacre, il sermone, la carità vissuta dei credenti educavano ad un genere di vita nuova'; Marrou, *Mousikos aner*, discusses pictorial material (much of which is now authoritatively catalogued in Huskinson, *Roman Children's Sarcophagi*); see also Uzzi, *Children*, and Kaster, *Guardians of Language*, on the education offered by grammarians; Quacquarelli, 'Alle origini del "Lector"', 384 ('Quando I cristiani divennero più numerosi, si cercò di calcare l'esempio dei giovani declamanti nelle scuola di retorica . . .'); id., *Scuola e Cultura*, 20–7 *et passim.* For the Greek custom of having the children of the community sing at state festivals, see Rawson, *Children and Childhood*, 311–35 and Wiedemann, *Adults and Children in the Roman Empire*, 182–7.

28 **Trebius Iustus:** Casalone, 'Note sulle pittura dell'ipogèo di Trebio Giusto a Roma'; Wilpert, 'Die Malereien der Grabkammer des Trebius Justus'. **Roman-Christian attitudes to wealth:** Cooper, 'Poverty, Obligation and Inheritance'.

29 **The innocence of the child's voice:** for the African conciliar material, see *Conciliae Africae*, ed. Munier, 33, 38 and 122; Currie, *Childhood and Christianity*, 199; Lane-Fox, 'Literacy and Power', 144.

30 **The theme of being as a child:** An outstanding text is the *Pedagogue* of Clement of Alexandria; see *Le Pédagogue*, ed. and trans. Marrou et al., i. 23–9 (commentary), and i. 4. 10. 3 (sanctity of marriage); i. 5. 12 ff. (scriptural testimonies for the faithful as children; a child's simplicity of spirit and innocence); i. 6.

25. 1 (Gnostic contempt for the Great Church's practice of calling the faithful 'children'). Compare Eyben, 'Young Priests in Early Christianity'.

31 **Clement and *nēpiotēs*:** see previous note. Compare Brown, *The Body and Society*, 127–8. **The Western Fathers on the theme of boyish innocence:** See especially Ambrose, *De virginitate* (PL 16: 273). **Liberius:** *ILCV*, 967. **Brown:** op. cit., 71.

32 **Apostolic Fathers:** see especially *I Clement*, 1. 3 and *Didache*, 4. 9. For epitaphs and the 'nuclear' family see Carletti, 'Un mondo nuovo'; Saller and Shaw, 'Tombstones'; and Shaw, 'Latin Funerary Epigraphy'. Se also now Kampen, *Family Fictions in Roman Art*. For the marriage debate Brown, *The Body and Society*, is fundamental; see also Elm, *Virgins of God*; Grubbs, 'Pagan and Christian Marriage'; Hunter, 'Resistance to the Virginal Ideal'; and Uro, 'Asceticism and Anti-familial Language'.

33 **Abitina:** Text in *Passio SS. Dativi*, ed. De' Cavalieri. Mullen, *Expansion of Christianity*, 300, s.v. Abitina(e), gathers the bibliography.

34 **Augustine:** McKinnon, 'Liturgical Psalmody', 15 and n. **Ambrose:** *Le orazioni funebri*, ed. Banterle, 62. **Jerome:** *Commentariorum in Epistolam ad Ephesios*, PL 26: 528 (dated 388). **The 'Expositio':** *Expositio antiquae Liturgiae Gallicanae*, ed. Ratcliff, 6, and for commentary upon this precious but enigmatic text, see Bernard, 'La "Liturgie de la victoire"' and Smyth, *La Liturgie oubliée, passim.*

5 Lectors in Rome and Elsewhere

1 **The catacomb:** Ferrua, *The Unknown Catacomb.*

2 **Liturgy in late antique Rome:** De Blaauw, *Cultus et Decor* is now fundamental. See also Carmassi, 'La liturgia romana'; Chavasse, *La Liturgie de la ville de Rome*; Dyer, 'Prolegomena to a History of Music and Liturgy at Rome'; Jeffery, 'The Introduction of Psalmody'; id., 'Monastic Reading and the Emerging Roman Chant Repertory'; id., 'Rome and Jerusalem' (esp. 214–19). McKinnon, *The Advent Project*, dates the emergence of the greater part of the Roman Mass Proper to the late 7th c.

3 **Liber pontificalis:** Much recent scholarship follows Duchesne's chronology of the layers of the compilation in *LP* I, but nonetheless sounds a note of caution, as for example Carmassi, 'La prima redazione', 236, and Geertman, 'Documenti'. See also

the essays in Cooper and Hillner, *Religion, Dynasty and Patron-age*, especially Blair-Dixon, 'Memory and Authority'. Among many other studies that use the *Liber pontificalis* for liturgical or architectural history, see Chavasse, 'Les Grands Cadres', which seems disinclined to question the testimony given there, and Reekmans, 'Les Constructions des papes', which finds no solid basis for the information concerning pre-Constantinian buildings.

4   **The early 'popes' and their reforms:** *LP* I, 127–9. For these personages, see Lampe, *From Paul to Valentinus*, 510–12.

5   **The account of Celestine:** Text and layout adapted from Geertman, 'Le biografie', s.v. Celestine.

6   **Jungmann:** *The Mass of the Roman Rite*, I, 322. **Celestine and the Christological controversy:** J. N. D. Kelly, *Early Christian Doctrines*, 280–343, esp. 324.

7   **Jeffery:** 'The Introduction of Psalmody', 159. See also id., 'Rome and Jerusalem', 212, with its judicious note of caution about the date at which responsorial psalmody was introduced at Rome: 'Responsorial psalmody may have entered the Roman Mass only in the 420s . . .'.

8   **Roman books and the Jerusalem lectionary:** Jeffery, 'Rome and Jerusalem', 209–12, source of the quotations here.

9   **Titulus of Pudentiana:** Krautheimer et al., *Corpus Basilicarum*, iii. 277–302.

10   **Fasciola:** Krautheimer et al., *Corpus Basilicarum*, iii. 148; Lampe, *From Paul to Valentinus*, 23 n. *et passim*. **Pallacina:** Huelsen, *Chiese di Roma*, 189–90; Pietri, *Roma Christiana*, 21–2. **Fullonices:** for the tanners in the Trastevere district, see Lampe, op. cit., 50. Compare Castagnoli et al., *Topografia e urbanistica di Roma*, 245–6. **On the titular churches:** Hillner, 'Families, Patronage and the Titular Churches'; see also Brenk, *Die Christianisierung*, 49–157 and De Blaauw, *Cultus et Décor*.

11   **Christian Onomastics:** *ILCV* is the most convenient single repository of trans-imperial scope; *ICUR* NS for Rome, supplemented by the Christian prosopography of Italy by Pietri and Pietri, of Africa by Mandouze, and of the diocese of Asia by Destephen. The names of the lectors are discussed in Pietri, *Roma Christiana*, 149–50. See also, id., 'Remarques sur l'onomastique chrétienne de Rome'. Christians rarely objected to ostentatiously pagan names, as they may now appear, such as Saturninus.

12   Αρτουριαε ιν πακε idus Iunias: *ILCV*, 2558. **Questions of identity and the inscriptions:** Adams, *Bilingualism*, 23, 37, 91, 365–402.

13   **Greek and Latin liturgy in Rome:** The most recent survey is Lafferty, 'Translating from Greek to Latin', arguing for the seminal importance of a 'tenacious pagan presence' in Rome and placing the substance of the change in the 3rd c.; Lampe, *From Paul to Valentinus*, 143–6; Pietri, *Roma Christiana*, 103–4.

14   **'Papal legends':** for the texts see Mombritius, *Sanctuarium*, ed. Mombritius, i. 44 and 172, and for a study, Sessa, 'Domestic Conversions', also on private churches. For those, see also Bowes, *Private Worship*; Brenk, *Die Christianisierung*, 49–157; Cerrito, 'Oratori ed edifici di culto minori', and Hillner, 'Families, Patronage and the Titular Churches', with bibliography.

6   The Psalmody of Urban House-Ascetics

1   **Bishoprics at Córdoba and Cologne:** the documents up to 325 are summarized in Mullen, *The Expansion of Christianity*, 223–4 and 254. See Van Dam, *The Roman Revolution of Constantine* for a recent survey. **Western synods:** the earliest layers of surviving proceedings are probably those of the Council of Elvira (Granada), convened *c.*300, but including some later layers of material that have been interpolated (*Concilios Visigóticos*, ed. Vives, 1–15 for the text, with facing Spanish translation). **Athanasius:** The bibliography on Athanasius and Antony is immense; among the more stimulating of recent studies, much concerned with Athanasius' 'construction' of Antony and more broadly with the beginnings of desert monasticism, see Chitty, *The Desert a City*; Desprez, *Le Monachisme primitif*; Goehring, *Ascetics, Society and the Desert*, and id., 'Withdrawing from the Desert'.

2   **Epitaphs:** Material of assuredly pre-Constantinian date is very rare, although some materials (notable the epitaph of a lector reproduced in Ch. 4 as Pl. 18) were given 3rd-c. or even earlier datings when first discovered. For Rome, much of the material is absorbed into Pietri, *Roma Christiana*. **The Fathers:** The outstanding guide is *MECL*, with a bibliography that lists most of the relevant literature before the mid-1980s. More recent studies include Bocciolini Palagi, 'Girolamo e le insidie del canto'; E. Ferguson, 'Toward a Patristic Theology of Music'; and Wylie, 'Musical Aesthetics and Biblical Interpretation'.

3   **The 'psalmodic movement':** The seminal essay is McKinnon, *The Temple*, Essay XI, 'Desert Monasticism and the Later-Fourth Century Psalmodic

Movement, to which should be added id., 'The Book of Psalms, Monasticism and the Western Liturgy' and id., 'The Origins of the Western Office'. McKinnon's conclusions in his 'Desert Monasticism' article are explored, developed and refined in Dyer, 'The Desert, the City and Psalmody' and to some extent in Jeffery, 'Monastic Reading'. See also Dyer, 'The Psalms in Monastic Prayer', and id., 'Observations on the Divine Office in the Rule of the Master'.

4 **Meditation:** The Hebrew is *hāgāh*, rendered *meletēsei* in the Septuagint; for the word used for the growling of a lion see Isaiah 31: 4; for the cooing of a dove, Isaiah 38: 14. For further bibliography and illuminating discussion, see Dyer, 'The Desert, the City and Psalmody', 17–21 (at 21, the source of the quotation here).

5 **'Monasticism was born':** McKinnon, 'Desert Monasticism', reprinted in id., *The Temple*, Essay XI, 505. Much depends upon what one means by 'institution'. Compare Clark, *Reading Renunciation*, 31, on the need to abandon the 'big bang' theory of monastic origins; Frend, 'Monks and the End of Greco-Roman Paganism in Syria and Egypt'; Goehring, 'Withdrawing from the Desert'. On the economic and ecological aspects, which constantly undermine the rhetorical distinction of the Fathers between *eremōs* and *oikumenē*, 'desert' and 'world', see Bagnall, *Later Roman Egypt*; Goehring, *Ascetics, Society and the Desert*; and id., 'The World Engaged'. **The first 'monk':** Judge, 'The Earliest Use of *Monachos*'.

6 **The Psalms as a collection for private reading:** Much of the relevant bibliography and discussion is assembled in Whybray, 'The Wisdom Psalms'; see also Kugel, 'Topics in the History of the Spirituality of the Psalms'. **Justin and Psalm 22:** *Dialogue with Trypho*, xcviii–cvi.

7 **Tertullian and domestic psalmody:** For the Latin text and (French) translation of the *De Exhortatione Castitatis*, see Moreschini and Fredouille, *Exhortation à la chasteté*.

8 **Tertullian and the horarium:** Text and translation in Evans, *Tertullian's Tract on the Prayer*, xxv and xxvii. For a summary of opinion on Tertullian's horarium, see Bradshaw et al., *Apostolic Tradition*, 213–15; see also ibid. 156–60 for the 2nd- or 3rd-c. evidence of the *Apostolic Tradition* concerning the use of Alleluia responses. For valuable context see also McKinnon, *The Temple*, Essay XII ('Preface to the Study of the Alleluia'). Further bibliography is usefully gathered in Jeffery, *Rome and Jerusalem*, 211 n. 10.

9 **The psalms in the papyrus schoolbooks:** Roberts, *Manuscript, Society and Belief*, 53 (source of the quotation here) *et passim*; Cribiore, 'Literary School Exercises'.

10 **Babylas:** Kaster, *Guardians of Language*, 387.

11 **Athanasius and the learned virgin:** The story is told in Athanasius's Encyclical Letter (PG 25: 230–1). On the date of the letter see Kannengiesser, *Arius and Athanasius*, Essay V, 92. For *philologousan* see Bauer–Danker, *A Greek–English Lexicon of the New Testament*, s.v. Φιλόλογος (with a note that the term is often used in inscriptions, especially of slaves and freedmen, to mean 'fond of words', 'scholar'), and *A Patristic Greek Lexicon*, ed. Lampe, s.v. Φιλολογευς, 'scholar'.

12 **Macrina:** Text and French translation in Gregory of Nyssa, *Vie de sainte Macrine*, ed. Maraval, 149–51. **Paula:** Jerome, *Epistulae*, in *Sancti Eusebii Hieronymi Epistulae*, ed. Hilberg, Ep. cvii.

13 **'Simply continuing to do . . .':** Bradshaw, 'Ten Principles', 6.

14 **Jerome's classification of Egyptian monasticism:** *Sancti Eusebii Hieronymi Epistulae*, ed. Hilberg, Ep. xxii. 34.

15 **'Withdrawal from certain social patterns':** Goehring, *Ascetics*, 17.

16 **Apotaktikos:** for discussion of this term, see Judge, 'The Earliest Use of *Monachos*', and Goehring, *Ascetics*, esp. 53–72.

17 **Agathon:** Judge, 'The Earliest Use of *Monachos*', 82.

18 **The *Epistolae de Virginitate* of pseudo-Clement:** The standard edition is still Beelen, *Epistolae binae de Virginitate*, with Latin translation. What remains of the Greek is printed in *Patres Apostolici*, ed. Funk, ii. 61–8. The ancient citations are Jerome, *Adversus Jovinianum* (PL 23: 228) and Epiphanius, *Panarion*, 30. 15 (*Epiphanius*, ed. Holl, i. 352). The most recent study, endorsing a third-century date and a Syrian provenance, is Caner, *Wandering, Begging Monks*, 69–77. For the letters in the context of the large pseudo-Clementine literature see *Dictionnaire de théologie catholique*, iii. 219–222, and Duensing, 'Die dem Klemens von Rom zugeschriebenen Briefe'. For the dating see *Patres Apostolici*, ed. Funk, ii. i–vii, proposing the 3rd c. at the earliest, and perhaps the 4th, since the letters are not mentioned by Eusebius; Harnack, 'Die pseudoclementischen Briefe *de virginitate*', argues for the region of 200, since exorcism is not yet a clerical preserve and because it shows

as yet no signs of a clerical hierarchy. The entry in the *Dictionnaire de théologie catholique* also argues that the letters are ancient 'car elles supposent qu'il n'existe pas encore de monastère proprement dit, les vierges et les personnes consacrées à Dieu continuant d'habiter leurs propres demeures'.

19 **Augustine:** Sermo clxviii, *In Pascha* (PL 39: 2071): 'phylacteria vel characteres diabolicos . . . suspendant'. **Chrysostom:** cited in Lightstone, *The Commerce of the Sacred*, 36 and 88. **Jerome**: *Epistulae*, ed. Hilberg, Ep. lii, 13. **Psalm amulets:** Kayser, 'Gebrauch von Psalmen zur Zauberei', and for studies of specific examples Préaux, 'Une Amulette chrétienne'; Daniel and Maltomini, 'From the African Psalter and Liturgy'; Warga, 'A Christian Amulet on Wood'; Van Haelst, *Catalogue des papyrus littéraires juifs et chrétiens*, items 84–240. **Rabbis and magic:** Swartz, 'Jewish Magic in Late Antiquity', 700–9, with excellent bibliography, 709 n. There is valuable context in Roberts, *Manuscript, Society and Belief*.

20 **The Armenian translation:** *Le Codex arménien Jérusalem 121*, ed. Renoux, 215–19. '**In the oldest manuscript lectionaries**': Jeffery, 'Rome and Jerusalem', 209. **The Byzantine rite:** *Das Byzantinische Prokeimena-Repertoire*, ed. Hintze, Transcription I, 3. **The Frankish-Roman:** *AMS*, 9a. **The Psalter of St-Germain:** For a catalogue of the verses marked *R* in this manuscript, and a review of psalms with no such marking that probably did not require it, even though they were performed in a responsorial manner, see Huglo, 'Le Répons-graduel'.

21 **The amulet:** Discussion in Nicole, *Textes grecs inédits*, 43–9. For a critical edition of the Septuagint text, see *Vetus Testamentum Graece iuxta LXX Interpretes*, ed. Rahlfs, 240, and for the Vulgate, *Biblia Sacra . . . [Liber psalmorum]*, 206–8. For the Frankish-Roman evidence, the first layers of which are purely textual, see *AMS*, 40ᵃ, which shows that only the Monza and Compiègne sources give more than an incipit, and they concur that the chant comprises verses 1–7 then 11–16. For musical sources, see *Graduale Triplex*, 73–6, collating Sankt Gallen 359 and the Laon antiphoner.

22 **Chrysostom:** Lightstone, *The Commerce of the Sacred*, 12, 36 and 88.

7 Deacons as Readers and Psalmists

1 **Didache XV:** Illuminating discussion in Faivre, 'La Question des ministères', 17–18. **Deacons:** For the order of deacons in the first four centuries see *Catholicisme*, ed. Jacquemet, s.v. 'diacre'; *DACL*, s.v. 'diacre'; *Dictionnaire de droit canonique*, s.v. 'diacre'. Cabié, 'Quand les "Sept" deviennent des diacres'; Davies, 'Deacons, Deaconesses and the Minor Orders' (compare Martimort, *Deaconesses*); Gryson, 'Les Degrès du clergé'; Schöllgen, *Die Anfänge der Professionalisierung des Klerus*. See also now the essays in Delage, *Les Pères de l'église et les ministères*, especially Faivre, op. cit.; Hamman, 'La Formation du clergé'; Roques, 'Prêtres et diacres', and, for the later period, Vannier, 'Les Diacres d'après Saint Augustin'.

2 **Duties of deacons:** Bradshaw et al., *Apostolic Tradition*, 60–3, including the evidence of the various derivatives and redactions, among them the *Testamentum Domini* and the *Canons of Hippolytus*; *Apostolic Constitutions*, ed. Metzer, ii. 50–3 (editor's detailed conspectus). **Egeria:** *Journal de Voyage*, ed. Maraval, 234–319. Much of the relevant material is translated in *MECL*, items 242–54. For context, see especially Augé, 'Una liturgia del peregrinaje'; Hunt, *Holy Land Pilgrimage in the Later Roman Empire*, 50–82.

3 **Deacons:** Pietri and Pietri, *Prosopographie*, s.v. Heraclius³; Hilarius¹. See also Syrus¹, Hilarius², Homobonus², Leo¹ and ⁷ Paulus¹⁰ and ¹², Quiracius¹, Commilito, Anastasius³, Hilarus², Hormisda¹, Johannes¹¹⁶ and ¹¹⁷ Mandouze, *Prosopographie (Afrique)*, s.v. Bessula¹; Paulus⁹; Quintus². See also Catullinus; Charus¹, Deuterus¹, Lazarus, Marcellinus⁵, Marcellus³, Novellus², Paulus⁹, Peregrinus⁵ and Quintus². **Deacons as letter-carriers:** This was recognized long ago by Gorce in *Les Voyages, l'hospitalité et le port des lettres*, 211. See now Gillett, *Envoys and Political Communication*; Graham, *News and Frontier Consciousness*, 119–20, and Sotinel, 'How were Bishops Informed?' **Augustine and Paulus:** Mandouze, *Prosopographie*, s.v. Paulus⁹.

4 **Basil:** Letters CCXLV (PG 32: 926) and XCII (ibid. 477–80). See also Pietri and Pietri, *Prosopographie*, s.v. Sabinus².

5 **Anastasius:** Pietri and Pietri, *Prosopographie (Italie)*, s.v. Anastasius³. *Epistolae Romanorum Pontificum*, ed. Thiel, 260. **Hormisda:** Pietri and Pietri, op. cit., s.v. Hormisda¹. Thiel, op. cit., 685. **Lazarus:** Augustine, *Sermones Selecti*, ed. Lambot,

132–43. Pietri and Pietri, *Prosopographie (Italie)*, s.v. Lazarus.

6 **The site (and historical importance) of Toledo:** Martin, *Géographie du pouvoir*, 205–74. **The Proceedings of Toledo I:** *Concilios Visgóticos*, ed. Vives, 19–33. **The Canons of Toledo I:** ibid. 20, Canon II ('Item placuit, ut de poenitente non admittatur ad clerum, nisi tantum necessitas aut usus exegerit inter ostiarios deputetur vel inter lectores, ita ut evangelium et Apostolum non legant'), and 20–1, Canon IV ('Subdiaconus autem defuncta uxore si aliam duxerit, et ab officio in quo ordinatus fuerit removeatur, et habeatur inter ostiarios vel inter lectores').

7 **Apostolic Constitutions:** *Constitutions apostoliques*, ed. Metzger, ii. 57, 5. **Clerical obligations:** This composite portrait, based upon Western sources, in which Gallican traditions (and Gallican compilations) loom large, has been assembled from the following conciliar material: Council of Elvira (?300) in *Concilios Visigóticos*, ed. Vives, 1–15; First Council of Toledo (400), ibid. 19–33; Second Council of Carthage (390) in *Concilia Africae*, ed. Munier, 12–19; Second Council of Arles (442–506) in *Concilia Galliae*, ed. Munier, 114–30; *Statuta Ecclesiae antiqua*, ed. Munier, *passim* (probably compiled in Gaul *c.*475); Council of Agde (506) in Caesarius of Arles, *Opera omnia*, ed. Morin (1937–42), ii. 36–59; the *Breviatio Canonum* of Ferrandus (523–46) in *Concilia Africae*, ed. Munier, 287–306. **Clerical celibacy:** The literature is immense. Major works include Abbott, *A History of Celibacy*; Cholij, *Clerical Celibacy in East and West*; Cochini, *Origines apostoliques du célibat sacerdotal*; Deming, *Paul on Marriage and Celibacy*; and Frazee, 'The Origins of Clerical Celibacy in the Western Church'. Heid, *Celibacy*, makes a convincing case that Christian communities, even in apostolic times, looked to their leaders for the kind of dedication, and the kind of spirituality, that could best be expressed either by living a celibate life (i.e. life without a partner), or a continent life (i.e. cohabitation without sexual relations once childbearing was done). **Elvira:** *Concilios Visigóticos*, ed. Vives, 1–15.

8 **African sources:** *Concilia Africae*, ed. Munier, 38, Breviarium Hipponense ('Vt lectores usque ad annos pubertatis legant'), 39 (decisively giving the name of *clericus* to readers, seemingly in the face of contrary opinion) and 122, 'Canones in causa Apiarii'. **Testamentum Domini:** Bradshaw et al., *Apostolic Tradition*, ch. 11. **Canons of Hippolytus:** Bradshaw, ch. 11.

9 **Fortress Empire:** S. Williams, *Diocletian*, 141. **Late Roman administration:** on the question of office and insignia as forms of social distinction, see Kelly, *Ruling the Later Roman Empire*. See also Banaji, *Agrarian Change*, 50–1; T. S. Brown, *Gentlemen and Officers* (on later proto-Byzantine and Byzantine developments); *LRE*, 52–60, 613–14, and *passim*; Richardot, *La Fin de l'armée romaine*, 49–62 (on military command and the 'goût du particularisme propre au Bas-Empire'). **Dress and insignia:** Callu, 'L'Habitat et l'ordre social'.

10 **The deacon and the purple:** Ammianus Marcellinus, *Res gestae*, xiv. 9, 7. For the sumptuary legislation concerning the right to wear the purple see Suetonius, *Twelve Caesars*, ed. Page, Julius, 43 (Julius Caesar forbids the wearing of scarlet robes or pearls by those beneath a certain rank); Caligula, 35 (King Ptolemy of Egypt enters the amphitheatre in a purple cloak that excited 'universal admiration', much to Caligula's 'disgust'); Nero, 32 (Nero forbids the use of the Tyrian purple dye and sends sellers of it into the markets so that he can arrest the tradesmen who bought it). A general grabbing purple textile from a standard: Ammianus Marcellinus, *Res gestae*, xv. 5, 1–2.

11 **Deacons as psalmodists:** I regretfully leave out of account here the extensive list of a deacon's psalmodic duties at the community supper in the Ethiopian derivative (and only there) of the *Apostolic Tradition*, material which has no close parallel in any other witness to the Greek original. See Bradshaw et al., *Apostolic Tradition*, 156–7, who cautiously remarks in the commentary (at 159) that the information seems 'a little too precise and detailed for a second- or third-century text'.

12 **Heikhalot:** Elior, 'Early Forms of Jewish Mysticism', 761–83.

13 *Diaconus* or *diaconatus* in verse: *ILCV*, 1212 (Pietri and Pietri, *Prosopographie*, s.v. Sinodus; *ILCV*, 1217 (6th c., Viennensis); *ILCV*, 1218 (Clermont); *ICUR* NS 4, 10228 (?4th c.). *Levita* in Roman prose: The famous polemic against the pride and presumption of Roman deacons by Ambrosiaster (fl. 366–84) also uses *levita* in addition to *diaconus* (*Quaestiones Veteris et Novi Testamenti*, ed. Souter, 193–8). For the author himself, Pietri and Pietri, *Prosopographie*, s.v. Ambrosiaster is definitive. See also Lunn-Rockliffe, *Ambrosiaster's Political Theology*. For further on the deacons, see Bligh, 'Deacons in the Latin West'; Gibaut, *The Cursus Honorum*; Moule, 'Deacons in the New Testament'; and Symonds, 'Deacons in the Early Church'.

14 **Ambrosiaster:** *Quaestiones Veteris et Novi Testamenti*, ed. Souter, 193–8. For earlier signs of contention about the position of deacons, see Bradshaw et al., *Apostolic Tradition*, 64–6, observing (at 64) that the section on deacons in the *AT* seems 'rather defensive in tone, as though stemming from a situation of controversy over the role of the deacon and over the bishop alone laying his hand on the candidate'. Compare Prat, 'Les Prétensions des diacres romains'. **Deacons in conciliar legislation:** *Statuta Ecclesiae antiqua*, ed. Munier, canons 58 (deacons may give out the Eucharistic elements in time of necessity), 59 (deacons to sit where presbyters instruct them), 60 and 96 (a deacon is endowed at ordination with a *ministerium* not a *sacerdotium*); *Concilia Galliae*, ed. Munier, 117, Second Council of Arles (442–506), canon 15 (deacons not to sit among presbyters nor to presume to give out the Eucharist if a presbyter is present); *Concilia Africae*, ed. Munier, 12–13, Second Council of Carthage (390), Section 2 (deacons to be continent, like presbyters and bishops). **Braulio:** Reply to Eugenius of Toledo, who had discovered the abuse (PL 80: 683). Braulio allowed that the abuse might also arise from the deacons' ignorance of the duties that they could canonically perform.

15 **The Exultet:** The foundational study is T. F. Kelly, *The Exultet*. See further id., 'Structure and Ornament in Chant'. In the earliest Gallican sacramentaries, beginning *c.*700, the *Exultet* is consistently attributed to Augustine 'when he was a deacon'. See *Missale Gothicum*, ed. Rose, 225; *The Bobbio Missal*, ed. Lowe, 69 and *Missale Gallicanum Vetus*, ed. Mohlberg, 35. The use of *levita* in the sense 'deacon' seems to have been primarily an Italian and more specifically a Roman usage before 400, as witness the want of relevant material in (1) Mandouze et al., *Prosopographie* (*Afrique*); (2) the 'Christiana' sections of *CIL*, principally v (*Gallia Cisalpina*), VIII (*Africa*) and Supplement (*Africa Proconsularis, Numidia* and *Mauretania*), x (*Campania, Sicilia, Sardinia*, save 1195 (= Diehl 1235), Atripaldae), XII (*Gallia Narbonensis*) and XIII (*Trium Galliarum et Germaniarum*); (3) the indexes to all volumes of *Année epigraphique* reveal no material of relevant date; and (4) *Inscriptiones Hispaniae Christianae*, ed. Hübner, which has two examples, 283 and 383, both very late.

16 **Virgil:** *Aeneid*, v. 724; vi. 608 and 661. **Model books:** For the use of model books for epitaphs see Handley, *Death, Society and Culture*, 23–34.

17 **Gregory's synod:** Gregory the Great, *Registrum Epistolarum*, ed. Ewald and Hartmann, 362–7.

8   A New Political Order

1 **Boethius:** *De Institutione musica*, i. 34 (pp. 223–5 Friedlein). The language of slavery is insistent: 'quasi serviens famulatur . . . servitio . . . servitioque . . . famulantur . . .'. Translation in *Fundamentals of Music*, trans. Bower, 50–1.

2 ***Humanitas*:** *De Institutione musica*, i. 1 (p. 179 Friedlein).

3 **Royal building:** for Thrasamund, see *Anthologia Latina*, ed. Shackleton Bailey, poems 201–5; for Theoderic, Moorhead, *Theoderic in Italy*, 42–3, and for Liutprand, Gauthier, 'From the Ancient City', 55–6.

4 **Urban history:** There are numerous major collections of essays, including Brogiolo and Ward-Perkins, *The Idea and Ideal of the Town*; Brogiolo et al., *Towns and their Territories*; Christie and Loseby (eds), *Towns in Transition*, and Lepelley, *La Fin de la cité antique*. See also Christie, *From Constantine to Charlemagne* (an archaeology of Italy; compare the valuable synthesis in Wickham, *Early Medieval Italy*, 80–114); Gauthier, 'From the Ancient City', and Liebeschuetz, *The Decline and Fall of the Roman City*. For Britannia, see Arnold, *Roman Britain to Saxon England*, 21–47. For Gaul, the volumes of Gauthier and Picard, *Topographie chrétienne des cités de la Gaule* are essential. See also, for some major northern centres, Pycke, '*Urbs fuerat quondam*' (on Tournai); Halsall, *Settlement and Social Organisation* (on Metz; compare Bachrach, 'Fifth-Century Metz'). For southern Gaul see also Klingshirn, *Caesarius of Arles*; Loseby, 'Marseille and the Pirenne Thesis, I and II' (compare Delogu, 'Reading Pirenne Again'); and Rouche, *L'Aquitaine*, 271–7. For Spain see Kulikowski, *Late Roman Spain and its Cities* and Martin, *La Géographie du pouvoir*, especially 205–74 on Toledo.

5 **The private churches and the issue of episcopal influence:** The seminal study is now Bowes, *Private Worship* (at 3, source of the quotation).

6 **The bishop:** Bowes, *Private Worship*; Breukelaar, *Historiography and Episcopal Authority*; Heinzelmann, *Bischofsherrschaft in Gallien*; Klingshirn, *Caesarius of Arles* (a major study of a seminal figure; compare Heinzelmann, *Gregory of Tours*); Liebeschuetz, *The Decline and Fall of the Roman City*, 137–68; id., *Barbarians and Bishops*; Lizzi Testa, *Vescovi e strutture ecclesiastiche nella città tardoantica*; Loseby, 'Bishops and Cathedrals' (on 5th-c. Gaul); Martin, *La géographie du pouvoir*, 113–33 (on Visigothic Spain); Mathisen, 'Barbarian Bishops'; Pettiau, *Aspects of*

Episcopacy (wide ranging, on the 7th c.); Rapp, *Holy Bishops* (a comprehensive survey from the Pastoral Letters of the New Testament to the 6th c.); Scheibelreiter, *Der Bischof*; Sotinel and Rebillard, *L'Évêque dans la cité du IVe au Ve siècle*; Stocking, *Bishops, Councils and Concensus*; **The Brescia forum:** Wickham, *Early Medieval Italy*, 83.

7 **Geneva:** Bonnet, 'Les Salles de réception'; id., 'Éléments de la topographie chrétienne'; Picard, 'La Fonction des salles'. For the early cathedrals, Guyon, 'Émergence at affirmation d'une topographie chrétienne', dealing with southern Gaul, is a model. See also next n.

8 **Vienne:** Reynaud and Jannet-Vallat, 'Les Inhumations privilégiées à Lyon et à Vienne' (on the more recent archaeology); Jannet-Vallat et al., *Vienne aux premiers temps chrétiens*; Pelletier, *Vienne gallo-romaine au Bas-Empire*. For trading links, more up-to-date information appears in the 'dossier' *Le Rhône romain* published in *Gallia*, 56 (1999). See also McCormick, *Origins of the European Economy*, 77–82. **The Claudianus dossier:** Sidonius, *Epp.*, iv. 2 (Claudianus writes to Sidonius); 3 (Sidonius replies); 11 (Sidonius's letter to Petreius with the encomium of C and his epitaph); v. 2 (Sidonius asks Nymphidius to return his copy of C's treatise *De Statu Animae*); Claudianus Mamertus, *Opera*, ed. Engelbrecht, comprising the *De Statu Animae* and, at 203–6, C's letter to Sapaudus. Brittain, 'No Place for a Platonist Soul', gathers bibliography.

9 **'The humblest ecclesiastic':** Sidonius, *Epp.*, vii. 12. 4. For aspects of the clerical *cursus*, see Mathisen, *Roman Aristocrats*, 89–104, and the essays in Delage (ed.), *Les Pères de l'église et les ministères*.

10 **Sidonius:** *Epp.*, iv. 11. 2.

11 **Claudianus as phonascus:** *Epp.*, iv. 11. 13–17.

12 **The epitaph:** *Epp.*, iv. 11. 6. For the proposal that the preface to Claudianus's lectionary survives, see Morin, 'Notes liturgiques'. **The Jerusalem lectionary:** Jeffery, 'Rome and Jerusalem', is the outstanding guide in English. **The lectionary at Marseille:** R.E. Cushing, 'Hieronymus. *Liber de viris inlustribus* – Gennadius. *Liber de viris inlustribus*', entry LXXX in the catalogue of Gennadius. Commentary in Gamber, 'Das Lektionar und Sakramentar des Musäus von Massilia'. For possible traces of Musaeus's lectionary see *Das älteste Liturgiebuch der lateinischen Kirche*, ed. Dold.

13 **'before the altar':** see e.g. Ambrose, *De Sacramentis* (PL 16: 419); Pseudo-Isidore, *Epistola ad Leudefredum* (PL 83: 895). **Niceta of Remesiana:**

Turner, 'Niceta of Remesiana II', 235. **Pseudo-Augustine:** *Quaestiones ex Veteri et Novo Testamentum* (PL 35: 2247). **Aldhelm:** *Opera*, ed. Ehwald, 16, line 46 ('Classibus et geminis psalmorum concrepat oda').

14 ***Phonascus:*** Quintilian, *Institutio oratoria*, ii. 8. 15 and xi. 3. 19; Suetonius, *Twelve Caesars*, Augustus 84 and Nero 25.

15 **Claudianus as scholar:** For the argument that Claudianus probably read all his Greek material in Latin translation, see Brittain, 'No Place for a Platonist Soul'.

16 **Claudianus and Greek**; For the Letter to Sapaudus see Engelbrecht, Claudianus Mamertus, *Opera*, 203–6, and for 'Greece the teacher' ibid. 203.

17 **Sidonius to Polemius:** Carmina, xiv [introductory letter] 1–2.

18 **Childeric:** Brulet, 'La Tombe de Childéric'. I am not convinced by the arguments of Halsall, 'Childeric's Grave', who wishes to leave the question of whether Childeric was a pagan open. **Conversion of the kings:** Excellent surveys are available, especially Cusack, *The Rise of Christianity in Northern Europe*; Dumézil, *Les Racines chrétiennes de l'Europe*; and R. A. Fletcher, *The Conversion of Europe*. More concentrated surveys include E. James, *The Franks*, 121–61; Heather, *The Goths*, 131–78; Christie, *The Lombards*, 182–203. On the Sueves, whose history is particularly complex, see García Moreno, 'La Conversion des Suèves'. The material on the Visigoths includes Mathisen and Sivan, 'Forging a New Identity' (on Visigothic Aquitaine); Martin, *La Géographie du pouvoir*; and Thompson, 'The Conversion of the Visigoths'. For the conversion of Clovis (with some inevitable wrangling about the date of his baptism) see Fauvarque, 'Le Baptême de Clovis'; Moorhead, 'Clovis' Motives for Becoming a Catholic'; and Shanzer, 'Dating the Baptism of Clovis'.

19 **Attacks on Trier:** Salvian, *De Gubernatione Dei*, in *Libri que supersunt*, vi. 39, 75 and 82, referring to what may be four separate attacks by Franks.

20 **Anthimus:** *Anthimi De Observatione Ciborum*, ed. Liechtenhan. There is a translation (and a classicizing text) in *Anthimus: On the Observance of Foods*, trans. Grant.

21 **Theuderic and Gallus:** Gregory of Tours, *Liber Vitae Patrum*, MGH SSRM, i. 679–86. The key passage is at 681: 'Tunc abba ista, nuntiis referentibus, discens, puerum clericum fecit. Erat autem egregiae castitatis et tamquam senior nihil perversae appetens, a iocis se etiam iuvenilibus cohibebat, habens mirae dulcedinis vocem cum modulatione suavi, lectioni

incumbens assiduae, delectans ieiuniis et abstenens se multum a cibis. Quem cum beatus Quintianus episcopus ad eundem monasterium veniens cantantem audisset, non eum permisit ultra illuc reteneri, sed secum ad civitatem adduxit et ut caelestis pater in dulcedine spiritali nutrivit. Cumque, defuncto patre, vox eius magis ac magis, die adveniente, conponeret, atque idem in populis maximum haberet amorem, nuntiaverunt haec Theoderico regi; quem dicto citius arcessitum tanta dilectione excoluit, ut eum proprio filio plus amaret; a regina autem eius simili amore dilegebatur non solum pro honestate vocis, sed etiam pro castimonia corporis. Nam tunc Theodericus rex ex civibus Arvernis clericos multos adduxit, quos Trevericae eclesiae ad reddendum famulatum Domino iussit adsistere; beatum vero Gallum a se nequaquam passus est separari. Unde factum est, ut, eunte rege in Agripinam urbem, et ipse abiret simul.' Translation in *Life of the Fathers*, trans. James, 33–42.

22 **Vannes:** *Concilia Galliae*, ed. Munier, 155, Canon xv. **Gerona:** *Concilios Visigóticos*, ed. Vives, 39, Canon i. **Braga I:** Vives, op. cit., 71 (Canon i, imposing the same *ordo psallendi* in morning and evening offices, and Canon ii, calling for a uniform lectionary); 72 (Canon iv, the *ordo missae* to follow the written example from Rome); 73 (Canon xii, only canonical texts to be read or sung). **Toledo IV:** Vives, op. cit., 188.

23 **Caesarius:** Caesarius of Arles, *Opera*, ed. Morin, i. 314–16. **Tours:** *Concilia Galliae*, ed. De Clercq, 182–3, Canon xix (xviii).

24 **Antiphons:** Nowacki, 'Antiphonal Psalmody', is a comprehensive review of the literary sources.

9 Schooling to Silence the Layman's Voice

1 **Augustine's church:** McKinnon, 'Liturgical Psalmody', catalogues Augustine's material. For the reference to the congregational singing, see below. **Ambrose:** *Enarratio in Psalmos*, 8: 'Quantum laboratur in ecclesia, ut fiat silentium, cum lectiones leguntur. Si unus loquatur, obstrepunt universi; cum psalmus legitur, ipse sibi est effector silentii; omnes locuntur, et nullus obstrepit.' For the Victor of Vita passage see above, p. 100. **Alleluia response:** Compare the sermon by Chromatius of Aquileia using both *respondere* and *responsio* in the context of the Alleluia response (*Sermons*, ed. Lemarié, trans. Tardif, ii. 176 and 178). **Responsorial psalmody:** the best conspectus of Eastern and Western sources is still *MECL*, nos

78 (seemingly domestic), 102, 139, 178, 184, 208, 221, 276, 289, 364, 374 and 398, to which one should add especially Jeffery, 'The Introduction of Psalmody' and Nowacki, 'Antiphonal Psalmody' for comment.

2 **Niceta of Remesiana:** *De Psalmodiae Bono*, sections ii, vi and xiii, in Turner, 'Niceta of Remesiana, II'. **Detractors of psalmody:** ibid., ii. **Isidore:** *De ecclesiasticis Officiis*, 6: 'Primitiva autem Ecclesia ita psallebat, ut modico flexu vocis faceret resonare psallentem, ita ut pronuntianti vicinior esset quam canenti. Propter carnales autem in Ecclesia, non propter spiritales, consuetudo cantandi est instituta, ut qui verbis non conpunguntur, suavitate modulaminis moveantur.'

3 **Liturgical Latin:** The study of liturgical Latin is in many respects a wasteland viewed through the distorting optic of Roman texts. For trenchant discussion, see Bernard, 'Les Latins de la liturgie' and Rose, 'Liturgical Latin'.

4 **Ambrose:** De *Officiis Ministrorum*, PL 16: 55. The adjective *subrusticus*, 'clownish, rustic' (together with *agrestis*, 'crude', 'barbarous', which Ambrose also employs) alludes to Cicero (*Brutus* 259 and *Orator* 161). **The grammars:** discussion in Banniard, *Viva Voce*, 242–3; see also Herman, 'Spoken and Written Latin', 36. **Consentius:** *Grammatici Latini*, ed. Keil, v. 391–2. For syncope, see Joly, *Fiches de phonétique*, passim. For the Latin of the Old Latin and Vulgate Bibles, Mohrmann, *Études sur le latin des chrétiens*, is fundamental, if by no means recent, so too id., *Liturgical Latin*; both should be read in the light of Rose, *Liturgical Latin* (offering a good overview). For the early Middle Ages, the entirety of Banniard, op. cit., is germane, so too Bernard, 'Les Latins de la liturgie'. See in addition, Amsler, 'History of Linguistics' (for the relationship between language change and schooling, or want of it) and Haverling, 'On Linguistic Development' (for the situation c.400).

5 **Athalaric and the grammarians:** Cassiodorus, *Variae*, 286–7. **The Gothic Faction:** Procopius, *Gothic War*, v. 2–3; Amory, *People and Identity*, 68–74, 152–61 and 449, s.v. *Athalaricus. **Networks in Italy:** Kaster, *Guardians of Language*, 267–9, s.v. Deuterius, and 378, Anonymous 11 (a Christian *[m]agister ludi litterarii*).

6 **Pedigree of a bishop:** Heinzelmann, *Gregory of Tours*, 7–35.

7 **Agroecius:** *Grammatici Latini*, ed. Keil, vii. 113; Kaster, *Guardians of Language*, 381–2. '**A rustic and filthy speech**': *LHD*, ix. 6.

8 **Remigius of Reims and Clovis:** MGH E iii MKA, i. 112–13. See Chauvot, 'Images positives', and

Flobert, 'Le Latin à la cour de Clovis'. Scheibelreiter, 'Clovis', 351–2, supposes that writing to a barbarian king in this way was a sign of Gallo-Roman complacency, even arrogance. On Merovingian Latin, and especially on the relationship between speech and writing, the works of Banniard, notably *Viva Voce*, are seminal, to which should now be added Van Acker, 'Dans les méandres' and id., *Ut quique rustici*. See also items by Wright and Van Uytfanghe in the bibliography.

9   **O and U:** Cassiodorus, *Institutiones*, ed. Mynors, 46. For examples see *CLA passim*, where Lowe usually comments (censoriously) on egregious cases in the commentaries to the plates. Further context in Biville, 'Normes "orthographiques" et oralité'.

10   **V and B:** *Institutiones*, ed. Mynors, 46.

11   **Cassiodorus, *De Orthographia*:** *Grammatici Latini*, ed. Keil, vii. 143–210.

12   ***Latinum* and *vulgi more*:** Augustine, *De Doctrina Christiana*, iv. 10. Banniard, *Viva Voce*, 65–104, offers a sustained discussion of Augustine from this and related points of view. **Augustine:** these examples are drawn from *De Doctrina Christiana*, ii. 13 (the error in psalmody and *inter homines/ hominibus* on which see Banniard, *Viva Voce*, 103) and *Enarrationes in Psalmos*, xxxvi. 3. 6 (*fenerat*; on which see Herman, 'Spoken and Written Latin').

13   **Definition of diglossia:** this is the basis for discussion laid out in the seminal article of Ferguson, 'Diglossia', 325. For a conspectus of the literature to 2000, see Hudson, 'Outline of a Theory of Diglossia'. Schiffman, 'Diglossia as a Sociolinguistic Situation', is a good introduction. Latinists and Romanists have often discussed issues raised by the concept of diglossia in the context of early medieval Latin, although they have not always employed the term. See Banniard, *Viva Voce*; Dahmen et al. (eds), *Latein und Romanisch*; Dardel, 'Niveaux de la langue'; id., 'Remarques sur la simplification morphologique'; Herman, 'Spoken and Written Latin'; Janson, 'Language Change'; Van Uytfanghe, 'Le Latin des hagiographes mérovingiens'; Varvaro, 'Latin and Romance'.

14   **The 'oral usage of the people':** Herman, 'Spoken and Written Latin', 32. **Schooled Latin still intelligible in eighth-century Gaul:** Banniard, *Viva Voce*, 254 ff.

15   ***Justus ut palma florebit*:** PM, 2 and 3. *****konseljo:** Joly, *Fiches de phonétique*, 74–6.

10   *Ministers of Music in the Sixth-Century Kingdoms*

1   **Luxorius:** I use the text of *Anthologia Latina*, ed. Shackleton Bailey, 298, but without accepting his (tempting) emendation of the second *pulpita* in line 3 to *pulpam* so as to remove a tautology and create wordplay. For a slightly different text (but not in any respect that bears directly upon the matters at issue here) see Rosenblum, *Luxorius*, 120–3. **The title:** 'In diaconum festinantem ad prandium cauponis'. Context in Hen, *Roman Barbarians*, 82–3, and Miles, 'The *Anthologia Latina*'.

2   **The 'Romanness' of southern Gaul:** Among many recent discussions see Esders, *Römische Rechtstradition*, 268–316 on the traditions of Roman law in Burgundy; Handley, *Death, Society and Culture*, 46–7; Hen, *Culture and Religion*, passim (appropriately sceptical); Lauranson-Rosaz, *L'Auvergne et ses marges*, 161–223 (on the 8th c. and later); Rouche, *L'Aquitaine*, 387–444. **Gregory's lineage:** Heinzelmann, *Gregory of Tours*, 7–35. **Law:** For episcopal concern with Roman law as the foundation of the Church, see the collection of documents in Joannou, *La Législation impériale*; Gaudemet, *Église et cité*, and Hoeflich, 'Gelasius I and Roman Law'. For the Theodosian Code, see Esders, *Römische Rechtstradition* (notably on Burgundy, at 268–86); Harries and Wood, *The Theodosian Code*; I. Wood, 'Roman Law'; and Wormald, 'Lex scripta'. **Bonitus of Clermont:** MGH SSRM, vi, 110–39, especially 120 ('Postea vero cum natus adolevisset et esset praefata cum parentibus in urbe constitutus, grammaticorum inbutus iniciis necnon Theodosii edoctus decretis . . .'). For another southern legist see the *Vita* of Desiderius of Cahors (d. 655) in MGH SSRM, iv, 563–4, and Wormald, 'Lex scripta', on Leo of Narbonne. **Gregory on the senators of Clermont:** *Gloria Confessorum*, 751.

3   **The deacon of Gallus:** Gregory of Tours, *Liber Vitae Patrum*, 683–4. **Orléans V:** Proceedings and subscriptions in *Concilia Galliae*, ed. De Clercq, 147–6. On the identification of this as the council at issue in Gregory's Life of Gallus, see *Life of the Fathers*, trans. James, 38 n. In the same book of Lives, Gregory describes an occasion when Nicetius, bishop of Lyon (d. 552) rose for the dawn office of his cathedral. 'After observing two antiphons' he took his seat and heard a deacon begin to sing the *psalmus responsurius* in the sanctuary (*Liber Vitae Patrum*, 694).

4   **Gregory of Tours:** LHD, viii, 1-4. For commentary upon these episodes see Heinzelmann,

Gregory of Tours, 61–2; McKinnon, *The Temple*, Essay xiv, 206–7 (drawing conclusions, in my view unwarranted, about the 'lector' chant of Merovingian Gaul); and Taft, *Liturgy of the Hours*, 150. This episode is redolent of the passage in 2 Chronicles 29: 30 where king Hezekiah cleanses the Temple after a time of wickedness, commanding 'the Levites to sing praise unto the Lord with the words of David and of Asaph the Seer'. For the Hezekiah typology in Gregory's account of Guntram, see Heinzelmann, op. cit., 51–60.

5   **Mass of Saint Martin:** For the possibility that two Masses for Martin in the Aquitanian MS Paris, BNF lat. 776 may be Merovingian, or at least that the version of the Mass *O beatum virum* there 'may be the closest to the early form of [that] Mass', see Planchart, 'The Geography of Martinmas', 129, which gathers (and supersedes) earlier literature.

6   ***Statuta Ecclesiae antiqua:*** *Concilia Galliae*, ed. Munier, 183–4; *Les* Statuta Ecclesiae Antiqua, ed. Munier, 99. The clerical hierarchy of the text is *episcopus, presbyter, diaconus, subdiaconus, acolitus, exorcista, lector, ostiarius, psalmista, sanctimonialis virgo, viduae vel sanctimoniales, sponsus et sponsa*. The superiority of the reader over the singer is apparent in their respective rites of initiation, the reader being installed by the bishop and the singer by the presbyter, who need not consult the bishop to have his choice confirmed. For the *Statuta Ecclesiae antiqua* and the liturgy, see the introductory material and notes in *Les* Statuta Ecclesiae Antiqua, ed. Munier, which are still indispensable. For further context see Coquin, 'Le Sort des *Statuta Ecclesiae Antiqua*' and Smyth, *La Liturgie oubliée*. Loseby, 'Bishops and Cathedrals', offers a succinct but valuable conspectus of bishops and the urban network in late antique Gaul. Compare Klingshirn, *Caesarius of Arles*, 75, 79–80 on the *Statuta*.

7   **Gennadius and the psalmist as 'lector':** R. E. Cushing, 'Hieronymus. *Liber de viris inlustribus*', 88–9. **Cantor:** I eliminate from consideration here *ILCV* 1195: '+ hic leuitarum primus in ordine uiuens / dauitici cantor carminis iste fuit', quoted above, p. 170, where it does not appear that the term *cantor* is the title of a ministry.

8   **Andreas:** Andreas is mentioned by Pfisterer, *Cantilena Romana*, 233.

9   **Status at Mértola:** Handley, *Death, Society and Culture*, 58–9.

10   **Siting of cathedrals:** Loseby, 'Bishops and Cathedrals' provides an admirable conspectus for southern Gaul, with broader relevance. On the creation of episcopal complexes within (often contracting) old Roman centres, there is only space here for general surveys. See especially Ward-Perkins, *From Classical Antiquity to the Middle Ages*; M. Miller, *The Bishop's Palace*, 16–53. Rapp, *Holy Bishops*, passim, gathers much useful material. **'An official of a second Empire-wide administration':** Liebeschuetz, *The Decline and Fall of the Roman City*, 139. **Naples:** See Desmulliez, 'Le Dossier'. **Marseille:** Hitchner, 'Meridional Gaul'; Loseby, 'Marseille and the Pirenne Thesis, i and ii'; Horden and Purcell, *The Corrupting Sea*, 142, 163–6; Bonifay et al., *Fouilles à Marseille*. **Classe and marble:** Harper, 'The Provisioning of Marble'; Rougé, 'Portes et escales dans l'Empire tardif'. **Mértola:** Jorge, 'Church and Culture in Lusitania', 109. **Pliny**, *NH*, iv. 22. 116. Mértola's contacts with Ravenna were continuous, partly as a result of its proximity to Mérida (recorded as receiving Greek traders in their ships from the east in the 6th c.) but also because of Mértola's own communities of Greeks, Syrians and Jews.

II   *Schooling Singers in the Cathedrals*

1   **Isidore of Seville:** *De ecclesiasticis Officiis*, i. 5 and ii. 12. For details of the ordinations and induction rituals, see Ch. 4 n. 18.

2   **Schola:** *OLD*, s.v. *schola*; *MLLM*, s.v. *schola*; Souter, *Glossary of Late Latin*, s.v. *schola*; Patristic Greek Lexicon, ed. Lampe, s.v. σχολή; *DACL*, s.v. *schola*. On the 'militarisation of social imagery' in Byzantine Italy see Wickham, *Early Medieval Italy*, 77–8.

3   **The Vandals:** Courtois, *Les Vandales et l'Afrique*, though outdated, is still valuable; Francovich Onesti, *I Vandali*, is a good recent synthesis. The essays in Berndt and Steinacher, *Das Reich der Vandalen*, are essential. Also important among works in English are Hen, *Roman Barbarians*, 59–93, and Wickham, *Framing the Early Middle Ages*, 87–93 *et passim*. Other studies are cited below. **Arianism:** For Arius, the key text in English is still R. Williams, *Arius*. See also Gregg, *Arianism*; Wiles, *Archetypal Heresy*; and Williams, *Ambrose of Milan and the End of the Nicene–Arian Conflicts*. Like all Arians, the Vandal Arians regarded their doctrine as scrupulously in accord with Scripture. For the debate in a 5th-c. African and Vandal context (but seen through

Catholic eyes), see the *Altercatio Sancti Augustini cum Pascentio Arriano*, PL 33: 1156–62. Arianism was condemned at the council of Nicaea in 325, but it returned as the accepted doctrine of the imperial church for a brief period under Constantius II (337–61), its creed was restated at Constantinople in 360, and as late as the emperor Valens (364–78) its teachings were regarded with some favour.

4   **The murdered lector:** Victor of Vita, *Historia Persecutionis Wandalicae*, 10. The passage is cited in Huglo, 'The Cantatorium', 96–7, where the singer (the text is translated from a French original) is called 'cantor', yet it is important to retain the Latin term used by Victor, which is *lector*. For Victor of Vita, see Lancel, 'Victor de Vita' and the annotated translation by Moorhead, *History of the Vandal Persecution*. For a bishop Victor of Regia, see Mandouze et al., *Prosopographie*, s.v. Victor[79]. The history of Alleluia chants and refrains is complex: see McKinnon, *The Temple*, Essay XII ('Preface to the Study of the Alleluia'); Pfisterer, 'Italian and Gallican Alleluia psalmody'; and Jeffery, 'Rome and Jerusalem', 211 n. 10, which gathers relevant bibliography. For the Jerusalem tradition in the 5th c. see *Le Codex arménien*, ed. Renoux, 176–8.

5   **The twelve boys saved:** Victor of Vita, *Historia Persecutionis Wandalicae*, 50 'vocales strenuous atque aptos modulis cantilenae'. **Theucarius:** Mandouze et al., *Prosopographie*, TEVCHARIUS[1]. **Orphanotropheion:** see below, p. 222.

6   **'Imperial models':** Wickham, *Framing the Early Middle Ages*, 89.

7   **Martin of Braga:** *Opera omnia*, ed. Barlow, 258 ('Numquid quia Ariani Psalmum, Apostolum, Evangelia, et alia multa ita ut Catholici celebrant . . .'). **Altercatio Sancti Augustini cum Pascentio Arriano:** PL 33: 1160 ('Nam sciendum est, Amen et alleluia, quod nec Latino nec Barbaro licet in suam linguam transferre, hebraeo cunctas gentes vocabulo decantare') and 1162 ('non solum Barbaris lingua sua, sed etiam Romanis, *Sihora armen*, quod interpretatur, *Domine, miserere*'). For this text, see Heil, 'Augustin-Rezeption'. On Gothic and Vandalic liturgy, see Ebbinghaus, 'Gotica XI: The Gothic Calendar'; Francovich Onesti, *I Vandali*; *Gotische Literaturdenkmäler*, ed. Stutz; Gros, 'Les Wisigoths et les liturgies occidentales', and Tiefenbach, 'Das wandalische *Domine Miserere*'.

8   **Boethius:** *De Institutione musica*, i. 1 (p. 181 Friedlein).

9   **Roman and Vandal Identity:** See Clover, 'The Symbiosis of Romans and Vandals'; Kleeman, 'Quelques réflexions'; Modéran, 'Une Guerre de religion' (including material on the similarity of Catholic and Arian rites); Rummel, '*Habitus Vandalorum?*' on the issue of distinctive dress. For tenuous but important evidence for what may be the celebration of the liturgy in Vandalic, see the passages from Pseudo-Augustine, *Altercatio Sancti Augustini cum Pascentio Arriano*, cited n. 7. I am grateful to Professor Jonathan Conant for this reference. On the issue of Arianism and non-Roman identity, see Rouche, 'Introduction', xii (Shäferdiek, 'L'Arianisme germanique', 189, in the same volume, is more cautious); compare Mathisen and Sivan, 'Forging a New Identity', 38, and Díaz y Díaz, 'El Latin de España', 35, simplifying Visigothic society into Arian Goths and Hispano-Romans 'en su práctica totalidad católicos', who used their Catholicism as a 'bandera' to distinguish themselves from Gothic Arians. There is much further bibliography and discussion in Amory, *People and Identity*.

10   **The Rhône:** Material from literary and archaeological sources appears throughout McCormick, *Origins of the European Economy*; Reynolds, *Trade in the Western Mediterranean*; and Wickham, *Framing the Early Middle Ages*. For a fine description of the hazards of navigating this river, see *Vita Apollinaris episcopi Valentinensis*: MGH SSRM, iii. 200–1. **Vienne:** for the inscriptions, see *RICG*, xv. 11, 35, 39, *et passim*.

11   *Passio Praiecti*: MGH SSRM, v. 228. *Modulum* is the reading of one source and gives good sense but the case of *meditum* is different. This is the reading of the MGH edition, but it is unsatisfactory. The word has been emended here (assuming a scribal error of the simplest kind) to *ineditum*, which gives better sense. Context for this work and complete translation (not followed here) in Fouracre and Gerberding, *Late Merovingian France*, 254–300. **Council of Vaison:** Caesarius of Arles, *Opera*, ed. Morin, ii. 86 (placing the requirement upon priests, and referring specifically to *iuniores lectores* who are not (or not yet) married). For the education of Merovingian saints see Heinzelmann, '*Studia sanctorum*'.

12   **Modulus:** There is probably little to be gained by putting pressure on this term, the meanings being so varied that virtually any theory about the meaning of this passage could find support. See *Novum Glossarium Mediae Latinitatis*, s.v. *modulus*, senses 10, *chant* (a) *en general*, (b) *chant ecclesiastique*; 11, *mode*

(musical) and 12, *musique instrumentale*; *OLD*, s.v. *modulus*. **Merovingian chant:** for a discussion of the evidence of Gregory of Tours and the interpretation that it concerns lector chant, see McKinnon, *The Temple*, Essay XIV, 206–8.

13   **Gogon's letter:** *Epistulae Austrasicae*, ed. Gundlach, 440–2; compare 431–2, 434–5 and 469–70. **Fortunatus on Gogon:** MGH AA, iv/1, poems VII, 1–4.

14   **Theodosius:** The name was borne by bishops of Auxerre (from c.508), Vaison (554) and Rodez (until 583). **Sinths:** Köbler, *Gotisches Wörterbuch*, s.v. *sinths*. **Sinderith and others:** *PLRE*, IIIb, s.v. Sinderith, and Pietri and Pietri, *Prosopographie*, s.v. Sindila[1].

15   **Gogon and Spain:** See Fortunatus's poem to Gogon in MGH AA iv/1, poem VII: 1, 41–2.

16   **Metz:** For the city within the walls as largely deserted in the 400s, see Halsall, *Settlement and Social Organisation*, 228–31. Revisions in Bachrach, 'Fifth-Century Metz'. See also Piva, 'Metz: Un gruppo episcopale'.

17   **The Offertory chants:** Levy, 'Old Hispanic Chant', and *Gregorian Chant*, 31–81.

18   **Ravenna:** *LRE*, 895 and 911.

19   **Leovigild's council:** John of Biclar, *Chronicon*, ed. Collins, 71. John disdains the king's 'new error'. **The rebellion of Hermengild:** Again, John of Biclar is stern (ibid.). **The conversion:** The principal narrative sources are Isidore, *Historia Gothorum* and *De Origine Gothorum*, ed. Rodriguez Alonso, and John of Biclar. Collins, *Early Medieval Spain*, 32–143, gives a narrative and analytical account; Martin, *La Géographie du pouvoir* is more thematic, but essential; Thompson, *The Goths in Spain*, is now somewhat dated, but still useful; so too the same author's 'The Conversion of the Visigoths to Catholicism'. For further context, see Collins, '¿Dónde estaban los arrianos'; Orlandis, 'El Arrianismo Visigodo Tardío'; and Saitta, 'La conversione de Reccaredo'.

20   **Toledo III:** Proceedings in *Concilios Visigóticos*, ed. Vives, 107–45. Core primary sources listed in previous note. Useful secondary literature includes the essays in *Concilio III de Toledo*. See also García Moreno, 'El Concilio III de Toledo'; id., 'Gothic Survivals in the Visigothic Kingdoms of Toulouse and Toledo'; and Ramos-Lisson, 'Grégoire le Grand, Léandre et Reccarède'. **Arian books and liturgy:** *Concilios Visigóticos*, ed. Vives, 117. **The Creed and the Lord's Prayer:** ibid. 124–5 and 186–225, for the proceedings of Toledo IV. For the enlargement of the

Visigothic Liturgy in the 7th c. see Díaz y Díaz, 'Literary Aspects'; Levy, *Gregorian Chant*, 67–9.

21   **One order of chanting at Toledo IV:** *Concilios Visigóticos*, ed. Vives, 188, Canon II. **Gerona, Braga I and Narbonne:** *Concilios Visigóticos*, ed. Vives, 39 (Gerona, Canon I), 71 (Braga I, Canon I) and 146–7 (Narbonne, Canon II). Compare Vannes and Tours: *Concilia Galliae*, ed. Munier, 155 and *Concilia Galliae*, ed. De Clercq, 182–3.

22   **Clustering in Toledo:** Wickham, *Framing the Early Middle Ages*, 96.

23   **The 'De viris illustribus' of Ildefonsus of Toledo:** Hildefonsus, El 'De viris illustribus', ed. Merino, 122 (John of Saragossa), 'In ecclesiasticis officiis quaedam eleganter et sono et oratione composuit'; 130 (Conantius of Palentia), 'ecclesiasticorum officiorum ordinibus intentus et prouidus: nam melodias soni multas nobiliter edidit'; 130 (Braulio of Saragossa), 'Clarus et iste habitus canoribus . . .'; 134 (Eugenius of Toledo), 'Cantus passiuis usibus uitiatos, melodiae cognitione correxit, officiorum omissos ordines curamque discreuit'. For Bishop Leander of Seville, see the comment by his brother Isidore of Seville: 'in sacrificiis quoque, laudibus atque psalmis multa dulci sono composuit' (Isidore, El 'De viris illustribus', ed. Merino, 150). These sources have often been mentioned in passing, as for example by Díaz y Díaz, 'Literary Aspects of the Visigothic Liturgy', 73, also citing evidence for the composition of Mass formularies, and Levy, *Gregorian Chant*, 67–8. **The qualities of the bishops:** Hildefonsus, El 'De viris illustribus', 122–3 ('Iohannes . . . largus et hilaris') and 130–11 ('Conantius . . . communi eloquio facundus et gratus').

24   **The poem in the antiphoner of León:** Edition of this poem and the other three prologues in Brou and Vives, *Antifonario*, 3–7. A better edition of the second prologue, following but adapting and supplementing an earlier edition by Meyer, can be found in Wright, *Late Latin*, 183–4, with useful comments on the prosody. I am most grateful to Michel Huglo for allowing me to see his study of the Prologues, with an accompanying edition, prior to publication.

25   **The date of the Prologues:** In 1928, Dom Luciano Serrano placed Prologue I in the 7th c. (*Antiphonarium mozarabicum de la Catedral de León*, ed. Serrano, p. xviii), II perhaps in the 8th, and III and IV in the 8th or 9th (ibid., pp. xviii–xix). In 1954, Díaz y Díaz ('Los Prólogos del Antiphonale Visigothicum') placed Prologues II, III and IV, which he regarded as

the work of the same author, in the context of the late 11th-c. move, after the reconquest of Toledo, to replace the Mozarabic rite with the Roman. In 1955, these datings were strongly contested by Vives ('En torno a la Datación'), who drily remarked that Díaz y Díaz might have reached other conclusions had he actually seen the manuscript. Díaz y Díaz replied ('Contribuciones al Estudio de la Pervivencia de Eugenio de Toledo', 117); not accepting all of Vives's arguments, he made the valuable observation that one Prologue incorporates material from verse by Eugenius of Toledo; implications of this discovery for dating remain unknown, but would be consistent with a 7th-c. origin. On the Wamba note, see *Antiphonarium Mozarabicum*, ed. Serrano, p. xviii, and Anglès, *La Música a Catalunya*, 10. Dom Serrano attributed the Prologues to the 8th or 9th c. **Leander's homily:** text, commentary and translation in Fontaine, 'La Homilía de San Leandro', 249–69 at 265.

12   *Schooling Singers in Rome*

1   ***Liber diurnus*:** *Liber diurnus*, ed. Foerster, 182–3. Background in Santifaller, *Liber diurnus* (although Santifaller used the edition of Sickel, who did not know the Clarmontanus manuscript).

2   **The abbots:** *Ordines Romani*, ed. Andrieu, ii. 224.

3   **Rome and its ecclesiastical organization:** The bibliography is extensive. Of special value are De Blaauw, *Cultus et Decor*; Brenk, *Die Christianisierung*; Dyer, 'Prolegomena'. More broadly, see the essays in Cooper and Hillner (eds), *Religion, Dynasty and Patronage*, the essays in Guidobaldi and Guidobaldi (eds), *Ecclesiae Urbis*; Pietri, *Roma Christiana*; and Willis, *Essays*, and id., *Further Essays*. **Lest the order of cantors should be imperilled:** *Liber diurnus*, ed. Foerster, 262–3.

4   ***Ordo Romanus I*:** *Ordines Romani*, ed. Andrieu, ii. 67–108.

5   **'I am here':** *Ordines Romani*, ed. Andrieu, ii. 79. On the various *scholae* see Noble, 'Literacy and the Papal Government'; id., *The Republic of Saint Peter*, 184–255; and id., 'Rome in the Seventh Century'.

6   **The Advent Project:** The theory is propounded in McKinnon, *The Advent Project*, 62–5 *et passim*. In speaking briskly of 'extemporization' as I do here, I remain mindful of excellent work done to refine the notion (as for example in Crocker, 'Thoughts on Responsories'), or in many studies by Levy and Treitler.

7   **Advent in the liturgical books:** Joseph Dyer, personal communication to the author. Compare McKinnon's own remarks, *The Advent Project*, 10–11.

8   **Education by the *Prior cantorum*:** *LP* I, 371. Compare Jeffery, 'Rome and Jerusalem', 229–30. I am grateful to Professor Thomas F. X. Noble for advice on some of these points. For historians who seem to have little difficulty believing that the *schola cantorum* existed as early as the time of Gregory the Great, see Hubert, 'Les Résidences des étrangers à Rome', 180; Llewellyn, *Rome in the Dark Ages*, 123–4; Noble, *The Republic of Saint Peter*, 230; and Riché, *Education et culture*, 340.

9   **The *schola cantorum*:** Dyer, 'The *Schola Cantorum*' (fundamental, and with bibliography of earlier material) and now id., 'Boy Singers'. For a different view, especially on the matter of a pre-7th-c. origin, see Bernard, 'La *Schola cantorum* romaine', and Pfisterer, *Cantilena Romana*, 232–4. See also Hucke, 'Die Entstehung'; id., 'Zu einigen Problemen' (considering a possible link between the rise of the *schola* and the liturgies of the stational churches); McKinnon, *The Advent Project*; Smits van Waesberghe, 'Neues über die Schola Cantorum'; Tomasello, 'Ritual, Tradition and Polyphony'; Van Dijk, 'Gregory the Great; and id., 'Papal Schola'. The 'Prior cantorum' is mentioned in *Ordo Romanus I*. It seems to have been Helmut Hucke who first associated the reference to the 'prior' of the singers in the biography of Sergius I with the existence of the *schola cantorum* ('Zu einigen Problemen', 400). **Gregory's letters:** R. A. Markus, *Gregory the Great*, 14–15 and 206, proposing 'a few thousand' as a plausible number and rejecting the figure of 20,000 proposed by Pitz, *Papstreskripte im frühen Mittelalter*, 252.

10   **Caesarius:** *Opera*, ed. Morin, ii. 150.

11   **Hospitals in Byzantium:** Angeletti and Cavarra, 'Influenze Bizantine'; P. Brown, *Poverty and Leadership*; Constantelos, *Byzantine Philanthropy and Social Welfare*; Horden, 'The Earliest Hospitals'; T. S. Miller, *The Birth of the Hospital in the Byzantine Empire*; id., *The Orphans of Byzantium*; Patlagean, *Pauvreté économique*; J. P. Thomas, *Private Religious Foundations*. For Rome, see especially Hubert, 'Les Résidences des étrangers à Rome'. For Merovingian Gaul there is Sternberg, *Orientalium More Secutus*.

12   **Symmachus:** *LP* I, 263. **Celestine's letter:** Cooper, 'Poverty, Obligation and Inheritance', 169.

Vigilius, ibid. 296. **Pelagius**, ibid. 309. **Characteristic new foundations:** Ward-Perkins, *From Classical Antiquity to the Middle Ages*, 56–7.

13   **Deacons and hospitals:** Pietri and Pietri et al., *Prosopographie*, ANTONIVS[11], FLORENTIVS[18] and CRESC-ITVRVS.

14   **The orphan boy and the solidi:** Gregory the Great, *Registrum*, ed. Norberg, iii. 35. **Boys going spare in the *Liber diurnus*:** *Liber diurnus*, ed. Foerster, 96–7 (a church receives a *puer*), 98 (*Praeceptum de donando puero*), *et passim*. **Gregory's orphan:** *Dialogues*, ed. and trans. de Vogüé, iii. 140.

15   ***Cena Cypriani* and the Cornomania:** MGH PAK, IV, 870–1, including the lines 'Hac ludat papa Romanus in albis pascalibus, / Quando venit corona-tus scolae prior cornibus, / Ut Silenus cum asello derisus cantantibus, / Quo sacerdotalis lusus designet misterium.' **The twelfth-century account:** Fabre, in Benoît, *La Polyptyque*, 1–36, introduces and edits the text. This description, in the *Liber politicus* by a canon of Saint Peter's named Benedict, states that the cere-mony was abandoned during the pontificate of Gregory VII (1073–85). See also T.S. Miller, *The Orphans of Byzantium*, 217–18.

16   **The school of notaries from at least 565:** Noble, *The Republic of Saint Peter*, 219 n. 37. **The palatine ministries:** *LRE*, 572–86.

17   **Agnellus:** MGH SSRL 322. **Ursicinus:** Pietri and Pietri et al., *Prosopographie*, VRSICINVS. For the Greek context see Burgarella, 'Presenze greche'; Ekonomou, *Byzantine Rome*; and Sansterre, *Les Moines grecs*.

18   **John the Deacon:** *Vita Sancti Gregorii Magni*, PL 75: 90–2. For discussion and assessment, see R. A. Markus, *Gregory the Great*, 2 and Berschin, *Biographie und Epochenstil*, iii. 372–87.

19   **John's account:** PL 75: 90.

20   **Gregory's *hospitale*:** LP I, 506; see *The Lives of the Eighth-Century Popes*, trans. Davis, 156 n., who observes that 'both deaconry and hostel were in front of the great staircase of Saint Peter's on the present site of the obelisk'. **S. Gregorio de Cortina:** Huelsen, *Le chiese di Roma*, 257, and for this important identifica-tion: Dyer, 'The *Schola Cantorum*', 25. **Alfarano:** Cerrati, in Alfarano, *De Basilicae Vaticanae antiquissi-ma et nova Structura*, 23, identifying a *xenodochium* near the stairs, founded by Gregory for the *schola can-torum*, and a church of Saint Gregory. (Alfarano's engraving of 1589–90 transfers a drawing of 1571, and is therefore second-hand.) For Mallius, *De Basilica*

S. Petri Apostoli Antiqua in Vaticano, see *AS* Junii, vii. 42–3.

21   **Gregory's bed:** Dyer, 'The *Schola cantorum*', interprets John the Deacon to mean that the couch was housed near the Lateran. ***Notitia Ecclesiarum Urbis Romae*:** text in *Itineraria*, ed. Geyer, 311: 'ascende ad Gregorii lectum patris sancti . . . et ibi habes altaria xi'. On the proposed date in (or shortly after) the pontificate of Honorius I (625–38), see Valentini and Zucchetti, *Codice*, ii. 69–70. Noble, 'Rome in the Seventh Century', 68–9; Thacker, 'Memorializing Gregory the Great', 72. **Life of Pope Stephen V:** *LP* II, 196: 'in oratorium beati Gregorii ubi eius lectus habetur'. It is not difficult to explain why a building that John calls a 'dwelling' should be called 'oratory' by a fellow Roman in the same years. The *habitaculum* described by John may have included a small chapel, especially if the building were perceived as essentially a charitable foundation or a hospital of some kind.

22   **Beatus vir:** Full study in Hornby, 'Exploring the Transmission History of *Beatus Vir*'.

23   **Gregory of Girgenti:** Greek text and (German) translation in Berger, *Leontios Presbyteros von Rom*, 144–5 and 274–5; commentary in Guillou, *Culture et société*, Essay VI, 295–6.

13   Steering in Distant Waters

1   **Innocent's letter of 411 on the foundation of churches:** Text, translation and commentary in Connell, *Church and Worship*. There is a more recent edition in *La Lettre du pape Innocent Iᵉʳ à Décentius de Gubbio*, ed. Cabié. *Regesta Pontificum*, ed. Jaffé et al., 311.

2   **Church of Clermont:** *LHD*, x. 31.

3   **Innocent's letter to Victricius:** PL 20: 469–81 (*Regesta*, ed. Jaffé et al., 286). **Victricius:** Griffe, *La Gaule chrétienne*, i. 305–10, and Matthews, *Western Aristocracies and Imperial Court*, 154–5. **The trans-alpine letters of fifth- and sixth-century popes:** The material is most conveniently available, albeit some-times in poor or misattributed texts, in PL 20 and suc-ceeding volumes. Generally on the themes discussed here, see Curran, *Pagan City and Christian Capital*; Gaudemet, *Église et cité*; and McShane, *La Romanitas et le Pape Léon le Grand*. **On envoys and letters:** in general, see Gillett, *Envoys and Political Communica-tion*; Letourneur, 'La Circulation des messagers';

Sotinel, 'How were Bishops Informed?'; and the essays in Andreau and Virlouvet, *L'Information et la mer dans le monde antique*.

4   **The storehouses:** Coccia, 'Il Portus Romae'. **Early medieval Rome:** There is a massive literature on the buildings, papal administration, economy and symbolism of early medieval Rome. A selective list would include: Brown, *Gentlemen and Officers* (on the governing class in Byzantine Rome); Cooper and Hillner (eds), *Religion, Dynasty and Patronage* (collected essays); Curran, *Pagan City and Christian Capital*; De Blaauw, *Cultus et Decor*; Delogu and Paroli, *La storia economica di Roma*; Ekonomou, *Byzantine Rome*; Geertman (ed.), *Atti del colloquio internazionale Il Liber Pontificalis*; Guidobaldi and Guidobaldi (eds), *Ecclesiae Urbis* (collected essays); Huelsen, *Le chiese di Roma*; Krautheimer, *Rome*; Krautheimer, Frazer and Corbett, *Corpus Basilicarum Christianarum Romae*; Llewellyn, *Rome in the Dark Ages*; Noble, *The Republic of Saint Peter*; id., 'Literacy and the Papal Government'; id., 'Rome in the Seventh Century'; Pietri, *Roma christiana*; J. M. H. Smith (ed.), *Early Medieval Rome* (collected essays); Ward-Perkins, *From Classical Antiquity* (on buildings and new foundations). Other materials are cited below.

5   **Archaeological discoveries in Rome:** Delogu and Paroli, *La storia economica di Roma*; Rovelli, 'La circolazione monetaria', including the Crypta Balbi finds; McCormick, *Origins of the European Economy*, 614–38. **Pope Gregory's works of restoration and adornment:** *LP* I, 396–414; translation in *Lives of the Eighth-Century Popes*, trans. Davis, 3–16.

6   *Ordo Romanus I:* For the ranks and legal rights see *Ordines Romani*, ed. Andrieu, ii. 68. **The 'senate':** ibid. 91.

7   **Life of Wilfrid:** Text and translation in Eddius Stephanus, *The Life of Wilfrid*, ed. and trans. Colgrave, 12, 34–6, 44–6, 66 and 120. **Roman contacts and textile markets:** Delogu, 'L'importazione di tessuti preziosi'; McCormick, *Origins of the European Economy*, 618–30.

8   **The vestments:** *Life of Brigid* (*Vita II*, by Cogitosus: PL 72: 786) and for details, Sharpe, *Medieval Irish Saints' Lives*, 13. The glosses are printed in *Thesaurus Palaeohibernicus*, ed. Stokes and Strachan, ii. 329 and 347. **Bede and the 'spiritual commodities':** Bede, *Historia Abbatum*, ed. Plummer, 369.

9   **Braga I:** Martin of Braga, *Opera omnia*, ed. Barlow, 105–15. For context see Collins, *Early Medieval Spain*, 19–24. **Vigilius' letter:** PL 69: 15–19.

10   **Leander:** Ramos-Lisson, 'Grégoire le Grand, Léandre et Reccarède'. **Isidore:** PL 83: 903; translation from *The Letters of Isidore of Seville*, trans. Ford, 31. **Ibiza:** *Liciniano de Cartagena*, ed. Madoz, 125–9. **Taio of Saragossa:** *Epistola ad Eugenium Toletanum Episcopum*: PL 80: 725.

11   **Brigid Vita I:** *AS* Februarii, i. 131. Translation in Connolly, '*Vita Prima*'. For dating, see McCone, 'Brigit in the Seventh Century' (dating Vita I to *c*.750) and Howlett, 'Vita I' (proposing a 7th-c. date).

12   **Benedict Biscop:** Bede, *Historia Ecclesiastica*, iv. 18 and v. 19, together with *Historia Abbatum*, 364–87. For context see Dumville, 'The Importation of Mediterranean Manuscripts'; Wormald, 'Bede and Benedict Biscop'. **Picts:** Bede, *Historia Ecclesiastica*, v. 21; **Frisians, etc.:** ibid., v, 9.

13   **John:** Bede, *Historia Ecclesiastica*, iv. 18. **Ordo Romanus XIX:** *Ordines Romani*, ed. Andrieu, iii. 224.

14   **The Lucca manuscript:** see Duchesne's brief account in *LP* I, pp. clxiv–clxvi. The codex is a collection of manuscripts of approximately the same date, but originally independent. A date of *c*.800 would perhaps be safest, but McKinnon (*The Advent Project*, 96–7) favours a slightly earlier date. For discussion and texts see Hiley, *Western Plainchant*, 510–11; McKinnon, '*Gregorius presul*'. There is much uncertainty about the date of the Monza cantatorium (*AMS*, no. 1, with description) for it has been placed in the late 8th c. (as by Hesbert) and in the mid-9th. For a succinct digest of opinion and bibliography see Levy, *Gregorian Chant*, 84–5.

15   **Aldhelm's poem:** For the full text see Aldhelm, *Opera*, ed. Ehwald, 14–18. For details of Aldhelm's poem with discussion and translation, see *The Poetic Works of Aldhelm*, 1–45 and 47–9, ed. and trans. Lapidge and Rosier. Broader context in Orchard, *The Poetic Art of Aldhelm* (useful but pedestrian). The debt of *Gregorius presul* to Aldhelm did not escape the sharp eyes of Strecker (MGH PAK, iii, 1069–72). **Poetic style:** I am grateful to Dr Neil Wright for advice on this matter. Compare the (prose) *Life of Saint Guthlac* by Felix. This can be dated to approximately 730–40; much of the text shows a considerable debt to Aldhelmian vocabulary, but there is a drift towards a more Bedan lexis, especially in the later chapters. See Felix, *Life of Saint Guthlac*, ed. and trans. Colgrave, 17–19.

16   *Clofesho:* *Councils*, ed. Haddan and Stubbs, iii. 362–76. See also Keynes, *The Councils of Clofesho*, and for the disaster which virtually destroyed the only

copy of the proceedings (London, British Library, MS Cotton Otho A. I) see also id., 'The Reconstruction of a Burnt Cottonian manuscript'. In a musicological context, the most recent discussion of the proceedings is McKinnon, *The Advent Project*, 94–6.

17　**Gertrude:** *Vita Sanctae Gertrudis*, MGH SSRM, ii. 457. Translation in Fouracre and Gerberding, *Late Merovingian France*, 319–26.

18　**Regensburg and its stones** ('sectis constructa lapidibus'): *Vita Emmerami* by Arbeo, bishop of Freising (Sepp, 'Vita S. Emmerami', 223 and 226; 'lapidibus quadris edificata'). BHL 2538. Dietz and Fischer, *Die Römer in Regensburg*. **Rupert's clearances:** *Gesta Hrodberti*, MGH SSRM, vi. 159–60.

19　**Theoto's decretals:** MGH L, iii. 451–4. The key passage, at 451, instructs the pope's representatives to introduce the rite of 'sacrificandi et ministrandi sive etiam psallendi ex figura atque traditione sancta apostolica ac Romanae sedis ecclesiae . . .' to all clergy that have been canonically elected. For Theoto's visit to Rome, see *LP* I, 398 (*Lives of the Eighth-Century Popes*, trans. Davis, 5–6), and for the context Jahn, *Ducatus Baiuvariorum*, 25–75 (esp. 33–5 and 73–5); id., 'Hausemeier und Herzöge', 331–5, on rivalry with the Pippinid-Carolingians, and Koller, 'Die bairisiche Kirchenorganisation'.

20　**Stephen of Naples:** John the Deacon, *Gesta Episcoporum Neapolitanorum*, 425–6; *Monumenta*, ed. Capasso, i. 262–3, *et passim*. **Stephen's oath on the life of the pope:** ibid. (Eufrosina, abbess of SS Marcellinus and Peter, gives Stephen 'consul' a house with a garden in Naples). **The epitaph of Stephen's son Caesarius:** ibid. ii/2, 218–19, with commentary in Brown, *Gentlemen and Officers*, 161–2. The authenticity of this epitaph has been questioned.

14　*Pippin and his Singers, I*

1　**Aidulfus:** *Les Gestes des évêques d'Auxerre*, ed. Bonnerue et al., 134–7. There is a problem with the chronology of Aidulf, for the explicit reference to Charles Martel and Pippin in his biographical notice does not accord with the dates that have been assigned to his episcopate. They include 751–66 and 756–71 (summary in Bonnerue, pp. lvi–lvii and 134 n.).

2　**St-Julien:** Lesne, *Histoire de la propriété ecclésiastique*, ii. 78. **St Goar:** Wandalbert of Prüm, *Vita et Miracula Sancti Goaris*, 41.

3　**Pippin's questions:** MGH EKA, i. 479–87.

Context in Noble, *The Republic of Saint Peter*, 63 and S. Wood, *The Proprietary Church*, 521. Zacharias saw that the reference to *missarum solemnia* in the second line of Pippin's question leaves no room for doubt; the lessons mentioned in the same line must be the readings of the Gallican Mass while the Response is all or part of the *responsorium*, in ritual terms the Gallican equivalent of the Roman Gradual. (The import of the reference to *Alleluia* is less certain; it may imply a brief response or antiphon affixed to a psalm in a practice long associated with the Easter season, whence the importance of Holy Saturday in Pippin's question.) See McKinnon, *The Temple*, Essay XII. Further bibliography in Jeffery, 'Rome and Jerusalem', 211 n. 10. **Zacharias's reply:** MGH EKA, i. 482, citing part of the Gelasian decretal given in Dionysius (PL 67: 309–10). Facsimile of the unique source in *Codex Epistolaris Carolinus*, ed. Unterkircher, fol. 8ᵛ. The citation that Zacharias actually gave may have been more extensive. **'Public marriages':** MGH L, ii. C, i. 36 (Pippin's Synod of Ver, 755). **'Public baptisteries':** ibid. 34. For the adverb *publice*, see *Lexicon Latinitatis Nederlandicae Medii Aevi*, s.v. *publice*, 'sense 2' (citing Alcuin) 'cunctis audientibus'.

4　**Pippin:** For Charlemagne's key document about his father's work, see *Opus Caroli Regis*, ed. Freeman and Meyvaert, 135–6. The dossier of literary evidence has been assembled many times; most recently, and with illuminating comment (but without Andreas of Bergamo or the *Vita Beregisi*) in Levy, 'A New Look at Old Roman Chant' (11). For allusions, often brief, to the events of this chapter in works of musicology and liturgical history, see Apel, *Gregorian Chant*, 79; Hornby, *Gregorian and Old Roman*, 1–3; Hucke, 'Die Einführung des gregorianischen Gesangs'; id., 'Toward a New Historical View', 464–7 (seminal); id., 'Zu einigen Problemen'; 412; Karp, *Aspects of Orality*, 32 and 406; Levy, *Gregorian Chant and the Carolingians*, 31; id., 'Gregorian Chant and the Romans'; Robertson, *Service-Books*, 25–33; Vogel, 'La Reforme culturelle' and 'Les Motifs'. In the matter of the reform as an aspect of Pippin's politics, or the concern for unity, among the most judicious are Claussen, *The Reform of the Frankish Church*, 287–8 (on Chrodegang); Hiley, *Western Plainchant*, 514–18 (at 516, duly suspicious of arguments about liturgical reform as 'a means of buttressing the political unity imposed in many regions by force of Frankish arms'), Jeffery, 'Rome and Jerusalem', 235–6 (on the question of the results), and P.F. Williams, *The Organ*, 63.

Pfisterer, *Cantilena Romana*, is a distinguished addition. **The musical expertise available in the time of Pippin:** McKinnon, *The Advent Project*, 396. Very little is known about the Merovingian office of cantor, if indeed it bore that name at all widely in pre-Carolingian times. **The supposed decadence of the Merovingian Church:** For the much-debated report by Wynfreth of Crediton ('Boniface') see Boniface, *Die Briefe*, ed. Tangl, 50; important discussions in Nelson, 'The Merovingian Church in Carolingian Perspective' and I. Wood, *The Merovingian Kingdoms*, 250–52. For Charles Martel see Fouracre, *The Age of Charles Martel*, 133–4, which discusses Charles's reputation as a despoiler of church property. See also S. Wood, *Proprietary Church*, 74–89. Cyrille Vogel favoured the view that the liturgical materials of the late Merovingian Church had sunk into the doldrums (see *Medieval Liturgy*, 149, and id., 'Les Motifs de la romanisation', 18), perpetuating a long-established view that the 750s mark a break in Frankish ecclesiastical history. Uncompromisingly damning judgements of the late Merovingian Church are still ventured from time to time, as in Noble, *Republic of Saint Peter*, 63.

5   **Turning medieval:** Kantorowicz, *Laudes Regiae*, 54.

6   **'Enemies in the circuit . . .':** *Annales Mettenses priores*, ed. Simson, 30. **Rebellions:** For one expression of the staunchly pro-Carolingian view, see *Annales Mettenses priores* for 742–44 and on through the reign of Pippin. The situation in Francia during the 740s is well evoked in McKitterick, *The Frankish Kingdoms*, 33–40, and in Noble, *The Republic of Saint Peter*, 65–71. Patlagean, 'Variations impériales', offers an important (if unduly dismissive) counter view to Noble's general contentions about papal separatism from the eastern Roman Empire in the 8th c., as presented in *The Republic of Saint Peter*.

7   **'with the consent . . .':** MGH CRF, i. 29. Compare Althoff, *Family, Friends and Followers*, 114–15. **Synods of the early 740s:** Text in MGH C: L, ii. CRF, i. 24–30. **Concepts of Reform:** Claussen, *The Reform of the Frankish Church*, 1–7; Fleckenstein, *Die Bildungsreform Karls des Grossen*. **Kings and synods:** Nelson, 'National Synods'. See also De Jong, *'Ecclesia'*, and Hannig, *Consensus fidelium*.

8   **Pippin and his brothers:** for Charles Martel's division of his lands see *Annales Mettenses Priores*, ed. Simson, 32. **Crushing the castellans:** A charter of Pippin from 29 July 755, granting to Saint Denis 'a certain place in the *pagus* of Verdun called "The Mount

of the Archangel Saint Michael" . . . with its *castellum*, its dependents and the clerics that served it'. A certain Wulfoaldus had sought to use this 'for the receiving of our enemies', *ad nostros inemicos recipiendu[m]*. At the time this charter was witnessed, Pippin's first Lombard campaign had just ended. Wulfoaldus was perhaps using his *castellum* as a rallying point for Frankish clans opposed to Pippin's Lombard campaign. ChLA, 599.

9   **Imperial subjects:** I incline to the position of Patlagean, 'Variations impériales', on the continuing importance of the imperial context. See also von Finckenstein, 'Rom zwischen Byzanz und den Franken'. **The Lombards:** Wickham, *Framing the Early Middle Ages*, 115–23, 206–19 *et passim*; Noble, *Republic of Saint Peter*; Christie, *The Lombards*, esp. 102–8.

10   **Fourth Life of Boniface:** *Vita Sancti Bonifatii*, ed. Levison, 99. **Stephen's prostration:** *Annales Mettenses priores*, ed. Simson, 45. For conciliar prostration, see *Die Konzilsordines*, ed. Schneider, 176 ff. (*Ordo I*).

11   **Stephen evokes the fires of hell:** MGH EKA, i. 496.

12   **Saint Peter's letter:** MGH EKA, i. 501–3.

13   **Pippin's undertakings at Ponthion** (a small selection from a large literature): Affeldt, 'Untersuchungen zur Königserhebung Pippins'; Angenendt, 'Das geistliche Bündnis'; Noble, *Republic of St. Peter*, 71–98; Patlagean, 'Variations impériales'; and Scholz, *Politik*, 46–77. Caspar, *Pippin und die römiche Kirche*, although outdated, remains fundamental.

14   **Singers in the papal party:** Robertson, *Service-Books*, 29. **The List:** Liutprand, *Opera omnia*, ed. Chiesa, 173–4.

15   **Andreas of Bergamo:** *Chronicon*, MGH SSRL, 224 ('His temporibus aecclesiae Romane Leo papa regebat et oppressiones a Langubardis multa patiebat; ex sede propria exiens Francia, repetavit cum multis sapientissimis ars litterarum, maxime cantores . . . [They are installed at Metz] . . . Qui ibidem per annos tres resedentes, tanta quidem dignitatem cantores ibi fecerunt, ut per totam Franciam Italiamque pene multe civitates ornamentum aecclesiae usque hodie consonant').

16   **Notker:** *Gesta Karoli Magni*, ed. Haefele, 12–15. Rankin, 'Ways of Telling Stories'. Further on Notker, see Ch. 16 n. 33.

17   **Strabo:** Strabo, *Libellus*, ed. Harting-Corrêa. **The chants for the day:** AMS 18.

18   ***Admonitio generalis***: MGH CRF, i. 60. **'Lost'**

legislation: Porter, *The Gallican Rite*, 17 n. and 54, also supposes that the *Admonitio generalis* is here re-enacting 'a general order to the French [*sic*] clergy', issued by Pippin. For evidence that Charlemagne could extract at least one document, promulgated twenty years before, from the 'archive' of his father's administration, see the king's memorandum for the *missi* in Aquitaine of 789 (MGH CRF, no. 24).

19 **Augustine:** *Ennarationes in Psalmos*, 1503. **Liturgy in the councils:** *Concilia Galliae*, ed. Munier, 155. **Liturgical provisions of Agde and Vaison:** Caesarius of Arles, *Opera omnia*, ed. Morin, ii. 48 (Agde Canon xxx) and 86–7 (Vaison, unnumbered), the Kyrie and threefold Sanctus as an anti-heretical, presumably anti-Arian, move. **Epaone:** *Concilia Galliae*, ed. De Clercq, 30. **Gerona and Valencia:** *Concilios Visigóticos*, ed. Vives, 39 (Gerona Canon I, using the term *ordo . . . psallendi*), and 61 (Valencia Canon I, the position of the gospel reading). **Braga I:** Vives, op. cit., 71 (Canon I, same *ordo psallendi* in morning and evening offices, and Canon II, calling for a uniform lectionary); 72 (Canon IV, *ordo missae* to follow written example from Rome); 73 (Canon XII, only canonical texts to be read or sung; compare 102, Braga II, Canon 67). **The language of peace:** Noble, *The Republic of Saint Peter*, 265–6, gathers the many different expressions of peace and *amicitia* from papal letters to the Franks.

20 ***Opus Caroli Regis contra Synodum:*** ed. Freeman and Meybaert, 135–6.

21 **Vogel:** Les Échanges', 58 (*une césure très nette*). Compare Klauser, 'Die liturgischen Austausch-beziehungen', esp. 169 (the division of the successive phases of Romanization of the liturgy north of the Alps into in 'zwei scharf geschiedenen Perioden'. *Antecessores nostri:* see Goffart, 'The Name "Mero-vingian" and the Dating of Beowulf', 98: 'Far from excising the past, the Carolingians were at pains to affirm the continuity between themselves and their predecessors.'

22 **Pippin's speech:** *Annales Mettenses priores*, ed. Simson, 34–5. Brief discussion in Noble*, Republic of Saint Peter*, 65.

23 **The case of Eucharius:** Fouracre, *The Age of Charles Martel*, 122–6, and Althoff, *Family, Friends and Followers*, 32. **Eligius:** I. Wood, 'The Work of Audoenus of Rouen', 82. **The Frankish noble who hated 'Romans':** Wandalbert of Prüm, *Vita et Miracula Sancti Goaris*, 50.

24 ***Opus Caroli Regis Contra Synodum:*** ed.

Freeman and Meyvaert, 135–6. Freeman has long championed the Visigothic refugee Theodulf as the principal compiler of this book. For broad reviews of scholarship on the question of Roman and Gregorian chant in the last fifty years see Bernard, 'Sur un aspect controversé'; Hucke, 'Toward a New Historical View'; and Hughes, 'Evidence for the Traditional View'. **The Gallican rites:** the entry '*Gallicane (liturgie)*', by Leclercq, in *DACL* is still an outstanding guide to issues and sources, including comparisons with the Roman rite. For consideration of musical issues, see Huglo et al., 'Gallican Chant', *New Grove Online*; Levy, 'Latin Chant outside the Roman Tradition', 93–101. More broadly on the liturgy, see Smyth, *La Liturgie oubliée*.

25 **'Perhaps Charlemagne and his followers':** Robertson, *Service-Books*, 27. **Saint Germanus's relics:** MGH SS xv/1, 6.

26 **The magnates' reply:** S. Wood, *The Proprietary Church*, 790.

27 ***Ordo Romanus XIX:*** text in CCM, i. 53–63. For an inventory of the manuscript, a succinct consideration of the question of dating, and another edition, see *Ordines Romani*, ed. Andrieu, i. 330–3 (inventory) and iii. 211–27 (introduction and edition). There is a valuable discussion of this text, including the non-Roman elements, in Jeffery, 'Eastern and Western', 128–9.

28 **Chrodegang's relation to the Carolingians:** Claussen, *The Reform of the Frankish Church*, 21–2.

29 **The Prüm charter:** MGH DK, i. 21–5.

30 **The bishops:** For Gauzlenus of Le Mans see *Actus Pontificum*, ed. Busson and Ledru, 244. Weomad of Trier is listed as a saint by Gams, *Series Episcoporum*, 318, but almost every sign of his cult seems to have vanished.

31 **Baddilo and others:** For these appointments see Semmler, 'Pippin III und die fränkischen Klöster', 90.

15 *Pippin and his Singers, II*

1 **The letter from Paul:** MGH EKA, ii. 553–4. This well-known and much-discussed letter shows that the *Secundus* in the Roman *schola cantorum* had already spent an undisclosed period of time in Rouen teaching Frankish singers, but the pope had to recall him before his work was done. In due course, arrangements were made for the Franks to follow him south.

It is unknown whether they actually went. **Remedius:** *Acta Archiepiscoporum Rotomagensium* (PL 147: 276). **Rouen:** For the strategic importance of the city to the Pippinids see Claussen, *The Reform of the Frankish Church*, 32–3, and on the granting of a *pallium* to Rouen, Boniface, *Die Briefe des heiligen Bonifatius*, ed. Tangl, Letter 57 (744). **Remedius in Rome:** *Codex Carolinus*, 519–20.

2   **'Recuperation':** On balance, I am not persuaded by the argument of Claussen (*The Reform of the Frankish Church*, 287) that the Franks believed the Roman rite had been the original rite of Metz and that they were seeking to recuperate it.

3   **Roman and Frankish chant:** An example is provided by the argument (in many ways a good one) that Roman chant *c.*675 was already to some degree a closed repertory of melodies. As far as music is concerned, this can be based only upon information provided by manuscripts copied long after the period in question. See Jeffery, 'Rome and Jerusalem', 214–24, and more contentiously, McKinnon, *The Advent Project*. For these issues, and on the markedly non-Gregorian style of much 11th-c. Roman chant, see Connolly, 'Introits and Archetypes'; Crocker, 'Thoughts on Responsories'; Dyer, '*Tropis semper variantibus*' (fundamental on the Offertories)'; Hornby, *Gregorian and Old Roman*, and ead., 'The Transmission of Western Chant'; Hucke, 'Die Einführung'; Karp, *Aspects of Orality*, especially Essay VII; Kelly, *The Beneventan Chant*, 161–81; Levy, 'A New Look at Old Roman Chant', I and II; Levy, *Gregorian Chant and the Carolingians*, 31–81 and id., 'Gregorian Chant and the Romans'; McKinnon, *The Advent Project*, 375–403; Van Deusen, 'An Historical and Stylistic Comparison' (on the graduals). **Notation:** For the papyrus notations, see Ch. 4 n. 4. Survey and catalogue of the earliest post-classical Western notations by Hiley in *New Grove Online*, Notation, §III, 1, 'History of Western Notation, Plainchant'. There is astute thinking on the purpose of the earliest notations in Treitler, *With Voice and Pen*, and throughout Levy, *Gregorian Chant*. The date when neumes came into use in the Frankish West is a controversial issue. Levy, op. cit., 82–108, argues that there was a neumed archetype of Gregorian chant by *c.*800; Bernard, *Du chant romain*, 717–24, favours the view that neumes were invented around 800. Grier, 'Adémar de Chabannes', cautiously discusses very late evidence that may point in the same direction. Compare the remarks of Busse Berger, *Medieval Music*, 84. Levy's

position, still not widely accepted, is contested in Hornby, 'The Transmission of Western Chant'. Compare Floros, *Universale Neumenkunde.*

4   **Kelber**, 'The Quest for the Historical Jesus', 107–8. **The sayings of Jesus:** See especially Crossan, *In Fragments* and *The Historical Jesus.* For textual criticism applied to the issue, see Robinson et al. (eds), *The Critical Edition of Q.*

5   **The name Simeon in the eastern sees:** *Hierarchia ecclesiastica Orientalis*, ed. Fedalto, *passim*; examples here from i. 97; ii. 587, 805, 811 and 842. For context and further bibliography, see Ekonomou, *Byzantine Rome.* In the late 5th c. Sidonius Apollinaris remarked, no doubt somewhat facetiously, that the clergy of Ravenna were moneylenders while the psalmists were 'Syrians', though his meaning is doubtful (Sidonius, *Epp.* i. 8, 2).

6   **Evolution of Romance:** Much of the bibliography is surveyed above in the notes to Ch. 9; outstanding surveys relevant here are Wright, *A Sociophilological Study of Late Latin*, and Banniard, *Viva Voce.*

7   **Wynfreð:** Wright, *A Sociophilological Study of Late Latin*, 95–109.

8   **The letter:** MGH EKA, ii. 528–9.

9   **John the Deacon:** *Vita Gregorii Magni* (PL 75: 90–2)

10   **'National resentments':** Levy, 'A New Look at Old Roman Chant, II', 196.

11   **Lex Salica:** *Lex Salica*, ed. Eckhardt, ii. 2–9. **Baddilo:** *Acta Translationis sancti Savini* (PL 126: 1502–3).

12   **John the Deacon's Life of Gregory:** PL 75: 90–2. Van Dijk renders *procacitas* as 'precocity' ('Papal Schola versus Charlemagne', 24) and has been widely followed. The best English translation currently available is in Strunk, *Source Readings*, rev. McKinnon, 179–90.

13   **Einhard:** *Translatio SS. Marcellini et Petri*, AS Junii I, 182. On Einhard's church at Michelstadt and the settlement of the Odenwald, see Wickham, 'European Forests', 520–1. Important clearances of forest land may already have begun at the abbey of Lorsch to the west (ibid. 519–20).

14   **House-chronicle of Rouen:** PL 147: 276 (for Remedius). **Witlaic:** *Chronique des abbés de Fontenelle*, ed. and trans. Pradié, 128–133. **Harduin:** ibid. 140–3. See I. Wood, 'Saint-Wandrille and its Hagiography'.

15   **Sigebert:** *Chronica cum Continuationibus*, ed. Bethmann, 332. Bethmann's reconstruction of the tex-

tual history of the chronicle is incorrect, because he wrongly believed that his Manuscript 1, now Brussels 18239, was an autograph copy. I am grateful to Professor Tino Licht, of the University of Heidelberg, for the information that this manuscript was actually copied around 1120 in an unknown centre in the region of Gembloux.

16 **Benedict of Aniane:** *Vita Benedicti Anianensis*, MGH SS xv/i, 201, on the provisions that Benedict's father made for his education: 'Hic pueriles gerentem annos prefatum filium suum in aula gloriosi Pipini regis reginae tradidit inter scolares nutriendum . . .'.

17 **The ateliers:** McKitterick: 'Royal Patronage of Culture', 99–100. **Frankish-Gelasian Sacramentary:** *Liber Sacramentorum Gellonensis*, ed. Dumas, i, pp. xx–xxiii, including links with the court. For the Praiectus material see items 186–9, and for Masses in time of war or for the host, 654–5 and 2744–9, 2750–7. *Le Sacramentaire gélasien*, ed. Chavasse, 5–27. **Music of the *Soni* in Frankish-Roman Offertories:** Levy, *Gregorian Chant and the Carolingians*, 31–81.

18 **Gervoldus in the *Gesta abbatum* of St-Wandrille:** Text of these extracts in *Chronique*, ed. Pradié, 134 and 140, with discussion of date at pp. xxv–xxviii, suggesting 823–33 for the section including Gervoldus. See also I. Wood, *The Merovingian Kingdoms*, 277–8. On the possibility that Gervoldus was an Agilolfing, see Werner, 'Noble Families', 163–4. On the question of chaplains at this date, one must reluctantly put aside a spurious charter of Pippin (762) in the Gorze cartulary, destroyed in 1944, which bears the attestation of 'Johannis capellani prefati regis'. For the text, see *Cartulaire de l'Abbaye de Gorze*, ed. Herbomez, 22–3.

19 **Monza cantatorium:** Texts in *AMS* I, description and plate at pp. ix–xi; Huglo, 'The Cantatorium'. See also Stiegemann and Wemhoff, *Kunst und Kultur*, ii. 831–3, and for sister materials, 834–6. **Ansegisus:** *Chronique*, ed. Pradié, 162–3. On Ansegisus and his canonical collection, see the introduction and edition in *Die Kapitulariensammlung*, ed. Schmitz, *passim*.

20 **'Millions of adherents':** Goffart, *Rome's Fall and After*, 23. **The Frankish-Gelasian sacramentary:** *Liber Sacramentorum Gellonensis*, ed. Dumas, 653 (*Feria VI in Passione Domini*). This manuscript is the earliest witness to the lost exemplar. For the phrase *francorum et romanorum imperium*, in various forms, in Frankish-Roman sacramentaries, see Tellenbach, 'Römischer und christlicher Reichsgedanke'. **The Christian Roman Empire:** Cameron, *Christianity*

and the Rhetoric of Empire; Gaudemet, *Église et cité*; McShane, *La Romanitas*.

21 **Lambert of St-Omer:** Derolez, 'Lambert van Sint-Omaars als kartograaf'; Lecoq, 'La Mappemonde du *Liber Floridus*', and more broadly, Brincken, 'Europa in der Kartographie des Mittelalters'.

22 **The terminology of *Romanorum Francorumque imperium*:** The letter of 844 from Pope Sergius II praising Charlemagne for having made the Roman and Frankish *imperium* into one body, addressed 'ad episcopos transalpinos', is in PL 106: 913 (*Regesta*, ed. Jaffé, 2586). The expression *romanorum francorumque imperium*, in various forms, is not uncommon in the 9th c. It was not generally used to form an imperial title in Ottonian diplomas. **Carolingian maps:** For surviving 8th- and 9th-c. materials see *Itineraria et alia Geographica*, ed. Geyer. **'A bold attempt':** McKitterick, *The Frankish Kingdoms*, 72.

23 **The term *Europa* in the late antique panegyrics:** Sidonius Apollinaris, *Panegyric on Maiorianus* (458), line 8 ('undis / exsultans Europa sophos') and 207 ('istum iam Gallia laudat / quodque per Europam est'), and Claudian, *Panegyric on the Sixth Consulship of the Emperor Honorius* (404), 104 'Europae Libyaeque hostes'. **The term *Europa* and the Pippinids:** For Pippin of Landen see MGH SSRM, ii. 454(A) ('Quisnam in Euruppa habitans, huius progenie altitudinem, nomina ignorat et loca?'), and for Pippin of Herstal the *Vita prima Sancti Lamberti* in MGH SSRM, vi. 361.

16 Singers of the Ninth Century

1 **Beneventan chant:** T. F. Kelly, *The Beneventan Chant*, is the standard survey; see pp. 39–40 on the suppression at Montecassino.

2 **The Franks in Italy:** The major works are Hlawitschka, *Franken, Alemannen, Bayern und Burgunder in Oberitalien* (still the standard treatment) and Ludwig, *Transalpine Beziehungen*, a study of the Frankish presence in Italy based upon *Libri memoriales*.

3 **Peter of Nonantola:** Ludwig, *Transalpine Beziehungen*, 132.

4 **Monza cantatorium:** see Ch. 15 n. 19. **The Monza Necrology:** Frisi, *Memorie*, iii. 136 (for Hugo) and 120 (for Liutfredus). For Liutfredus I and II, see Hlawitschka, *Franken*, 221–6.

5 **Herisburg:** *Annales Mettenses priores*, ed. Simson, 58, 65 (the basilica), 72–3 (Charlemagne's residence there).

6 **The vigour of interregional trade in Francia:** Wickham, *Framing the Early Middle Ages*, 799–803. An outstanding narrative source is Wandalbert of Prüm, *Vita et Miracula Sancti Goaris,* abounding in references to riverine trade in northern Francia in the time of Charlemagne.

7 **Overlap between notaries and chaplains:** discussion in McKitterick, *Charlemagne*, 137–213, esp. 211. **Ermoldus and Ingelheim:** see below. **The early graduales:** Text in *AMS*. See also Jeffery, 'Oldest Sources'. Surveys in Hiley, *Western Plainchant*, 299–303, and Levy, *Gregorian Chant*, 86.

8 **The letter of Helisachar:** see Levy, *Gregorian Chant*, 178–86, discussion with Latin text and translation. Succinct overview and essential bibliography in Bernard, *Du Chant romain*, 739–5, with Latin text and French translation. **The letter in the Salzburg formulary:** text in *Salzburger Formelbücher*, ed. Bischoff, 38. The key passage runs: 'Nos etiam rogantes cantorem unum pollicere dignati estis, ut secundum Romanae ecclesiae auctoritatem cantileno *filius nostris vestrisque* fideles discipulos confirmare studium haberet . . .'. The words in italics are impossible as a syntagm, and *cantileno* is a gross error. I am grateful to Dr Alice Rio for an enlightening discussion about the *Liber Traditionum*, and to Dr Leofranc Holford-Strevens for advice about the text.

9 **Andreas of Bergamo:** see above, p. 289. **John the Deacon:** PL 75: 90–2. **Notker:** *Gesta Karoli Magni*, ed. Haefele, 15. Compare Rankin, 'Ways of Telling Stories'. For the liturgical importance of Metz and its *schola*, *Der karolingische Tonar von Metz*, ed. Lipphardt, esp. 1–6, remains seminal. For the pictorial evidence of the ivory cover of the Drogo Sacramentary, see R. E. Reynolds, 'A Visual Epitome . . . *Drogo Sacramentary*' and Unterkircher, *Zur Ikonographie*.

10 **Metz:** for the city within the walls as largely deserted in the 400s, see Halsall, *Settlement and Social Organisation*, 228–31; a very different view in Bachrach, 'Fifth-Century Metz'. See also Piva, 'Metz: Un gruppo episcopale'. Metz has been well served by historians and archaeologists. For some of the principal contributions see Gauthier, *Province ecclésiastique de Trèves*, 33–52, with rich bibliography and maps; Halsall, op. cit., with maps of the city in various phases of its reconstructed Roman, Merovingian and early

Carolingian history. **The Poem:** *Die Moselgedichte*, ed. Hosius, 102. On the cathedral of St Stephen, see the cited works by Gauthier, Halsall and Piva.

11 **Arnulph:** On the Pippinids' claim to blood relationship to Arnulph see Fouracre, *The Age of Charles Martel*, 33–4; Halsall, *Settlement and Social Organisation*, 15–16; Oexle, 'Die Karolinger und die Stadt des heiligen Arnulf'.

12 **Chrodegang:** For all matters touching his life and work, see now Chrodegang, *The Chrodegang Rules*, ed. Bertram, and Claussen, *The Reform of the Frankish Church*. Succinct overview and essential bibliography in Bernard, *Du Chant romain*, 725–9.

13 **Chrodegang's Rule:** The text exists in essentially two versions, a shorter one of thirty-four chapters which represents the original compilation and a longer of eighty-six chapters interpolated with much material from the Aachen reforming councils of 816. Workable texts of both, from 17th-c. editions, are conveniently available for comparison in PL 89: 1057–96 (longer) and 1097–1120 (shorter). Note that the PL text of the shorter version contains some interpolations from the time of Chrodegang's successor Angilram, one of which explicitly names him (1107–8). The longer version includes a section *De cantoribus* (1079) which is derived from the 816 Aachen council (MGH L, iii. C, i/i. CAK, i/i, 414). For the textual history of the Rule, see Claussen, *The Reform of the Frankish Church*.

14 **Chrodegang and food:** Claussen, *Reform*, 80–92. **The calories:** Rouche, *Le Choc des cultures*, 109–37.

15 **Paul the Deacon:** MGH SS, ii. 267–8.

16 **The needs of a *schola*:** McKinnon, *The Advent Project*, 359–60.

17 **The payments:** Text in Andrieu, 'Règlement d'Angilramne de Metz'.

18 **A landmark first edition:** Levy, 'Gregorian Chant and the Romans', 8 (I have resolved Levy's abbreviation GREG 8). For the so-called 'Tonary of Charlemagne', dated by Huglo, along with the rest of the book, to 'a few years before the feast of Easter in 800', see Huglo, 'The Cantatorium', 90. For the mnemonic function of the tonaries – essentially a form of musical notation – see Busse Berger, *Medieval Music and the Art of Memory*, 47–84.

19 **Leidradus:** Müller, 'Die Kirche von Lyon im Karolingerreich'. Succinct overview and essential bibliography in Bernard, *Du Chant romain*, 736–9. There is some instability in the textual tradition of his letter,

and a separate branch, represented by a text published in 1573, does not mention Metz; in this version Charlemagne sends 'one who was of the Church of Lyon a long time ago'. It is not difficult to understand how, in later centuries, a reviser might have wished to suppress the debt of the church of Lyon to the church of Metz by erasing its name and presenting the singer who brought the rite as an old alumnus of Lyon. The principal source for Leidradus's service as a *missus*, conducted with Theodulf of Orléans, is Theodulf's poem *Contra Iudices* in MGH PAK, i. 493–517. See also Ewig, 'Descriptio Franciae', 290.'

20   **The manuscripts:** Biblioteca Apostolica Vaticana, Pal. Lat. 582, fols 19ᵛ–20ʳ (?Reims) and Paris, BNF MS latin 9654, fol. 23ᵛ (Lotharingia; Metz?). See Mordek, *Bibliotheca Capitularium*, 786 and 567. For the texts, the only available edition is still MGH CRF, i. 120–2.

21   **Aldricus:** The circumstances of Aldricus's life are recorded in a biography compiled by the canons of his cathedral at Le Mans. I use the text in MGH SS, xv/i. 304–27, which presents the material as a free-standing *Gesta Aldrici*. For the complete chronicle of the Le Mans bishops, see *Actus Pontificum*, ed. Busson and Ledru. The authenticity and importance of the *Actus* are discussed in Le Maître, 'L'Œuvre d'Aldric du Mans'. On Aldricus, see also Ewig, 'Descriptio Franciae', 292–3, and Smith, *Province and Empire*, 80, 92.

22   **The *Liber memorialis* of Reichenau:** *Das Verbrüderungsbuch der Abtei Reichenau*, ed. Autenrieth, Geuenich and Schmid, is a facsimile and edition. For context see McKitterick, *History and Memory*, 165.

23   **The *Regula Solitariorum*:** the text is printed in PL 103: 573–664, after the Holste-Brockie text of 1759. The oldest source is Berlin, Staatsbibliothek zu Berlin, Preußisches Kulturbesitz, MS Phillipps 1876, dating from the 10th or 11th c. For Grimlaicus, see K. S. Frank, 'Grimlaicus'.

24   **Grimlaicus and Arnulph:** PL 103: 654 (the story about Arnulph) and 579 (the passage translated here).

25   **Grimlaicus on chant and compunction:** PL 103: 619 ('Quapropter non nos oblectet pueriles jocus ac risus, sed lectiones sacrae et spiritualis melodiae cantus. Quamvis enim dura sint corda nostra ad lacrymas producendas, mox tamen ut psalmorum dulcedo insonuerit, ad compunctionem cordis animum nostrum inflectit. Multi enim reperiuntur qui cantus suavitate commoti sua crimina plangunt, atque ex ea parte magis flectuntur ad lacrymas, ex qua psallentis insonuerit dulcedo suavitatis'). See further 624–5.

26   **Later cantor-authors:** Fassler, 'The Office of Cantor'. **Sources:** For Grimlaicus's sources, biblical and patristic, nothing yet rivals the annotated translation by Andrew Thornton, OSB (in press). **'I wish to stay for some time':** PL 103: 598.

27   **Aurelian on the *palatini*:** Aurelian of Réôme, *Musica Disciplina*, ed. Gushee, 92. **O Sapientia in the earliest layer of tonaries:** Huglo, *Les Tonaires*, 36. **Chaplains:** The outstanding guide to the origin and formation of the chapel is Fleckenstein, *Die Hofkappelle*. Volume 1 deals with the Carolingian period. For terminology, see pp. 14–43. More broadly see Bullough, '*Aula renovata*' and Bullough and Corrêa, 'Texts, Chant and the Chapel of Louis the Pious'. For the palaces and their use, see now McKitterick, *Charlemagne*, 137–213. **Aurelian as a composite:** As the treatise stands in the earliest manuscript, now at Valenciennes and dating from around 900 (Pl. 69) the *Musica Disciplina* is clearly composite to the point where the convention of referring to Aurelian as the author is only a serviceable fiction (that will be maintained here). For a minute discussion of a seminal chapter, see Huglo, *Les Tonaires*, 49–58.

28   **Charles's chapel:** Nelson, *Charles the Bald*, 96. **Berno/Bernard:** See McKitterick, *Charlemagne*, 92. **Wenilo's letter:** For the text see Lupus of Ferrières, *Epistulae*, ed. Marshall, 79–81. The date of the letter has been disputed, as the prefatory note in Marshall's edition makes clear. My *terminus a quo* is set by the consecration of the recipient, Amulus of Lyon (13 Jan. 841), and the *terminus ad quem* by a charter of Altheus, bishop of Autun, which is dated 5 July 843, by which time the issue of who should become bishop of Autun had clearly been settled and Wenilo's letter on Berno's behalf would have been unnecessary. The list of abbots of Moutier-St-Jean, printed by Roverius (*Reomaus*, 437–9), of unknown date and supplied with what Roverius calls 'antiquis notis chronicis', contained a note that Abbot Bernardus did indeed became bishop of Autun. This note was probably added to the list – perhaps many centuries after these events – by one who knew Wenilo's letter that seeks the see of Autun on Berno's behalf. There is no trace of a Bishop Berno or Bernardus in the cartulary of Autun, even though there are charters for all three of the bishops who occupy the chronological range in which Berno would have to be fitted. See *Cartulaire de l'église d'Autun*, ed.

Charmasse, nos 31 (Modoinus 815, still bishop in 838), 46 (Bishop Altheus, 843), and 7 (Bishop Jonas, 850). **The council of Germigny:** MGH C, iii. 7.

29 **Archicantor:** the most famous example (though it is not exactly the same term) is John the Roman *archicantator* mentioned by Bede (*Ecclesiastical History*, iv. 18 (16)). **Hincmar:** *De Ordine Palatii*, ed. Prou, 68. **Aurelian:** *Musica Disciplina*, ed. Gushee, 53–5.

30 **'Not textual scholars':** Bullough and Corrêa, 'Texts, Chant and the Chapel of Louis the Pious', 493. **Aurelian's requirements of the best cantors:** Aurelian, *Musica Disciplina*, ed. Gushee, 118 (*prudens . . . cantor . . . studiosus cantor*), 122 (*sagax cantor*), 127 (*prudens*). **Litteratura:** Law, *Grammar and Grammarians*, 251.

31 **'Wonderfully distorted':** R. A. Fletcher, *The Conversion of Europe*, 224. **Theuto:** Ermoldus Nigellus, ed. Faral, 2286 and 2316. Bullough and Corrêa ('Texts, Chant and the Chapel of Louis the Pious', 491–2) make a curiously misguided attempt to argue that Theuto is blowing a horn or trumpet of some kind, whereas he is surely intoning the beginning of the Introit in a stentorian voice. Louis's archchancellor Helisachar, author of an important letter concerning Frankish-Roman chants of the Office, based upon his experiences during a visit to Aachen, was present at Ingelheim on this occasion and is named at 2294. **Hucbert:** Fleckenstein, *Die Hofkapelle*, i. 232–3; compare the case of Anstrannus, 'cantor', cited there. **Strabo:** *Visio Wettini*, ed. and trans. Knittel; discussion in Airlie, 'Bonds of Power', 193–4. **Paschasius:** Dümmler, 'Radberts *Epitaphium Arsenii*', 66. This curious work, in dialogue form, is a Life of Paschasius's colleague Wala, given the pseudonym Arsenius.

32 **The *petitio*:** MGH, L CRF, II/II, 39. **Strabo's comparisons:** Strabo, *Libellus*, ed. Harting-Corrêa, 192–3.

33 **Contacts of Sankt Gallen:** McKitterick, *History and Memory*, 164. **Notker:** Ganz, 'Humour as History'; Innes, 'Memory, Orality and Literacy' and (especially) MacLean, *Kingship and Politics*, 199–229. **The Alleluia:** *Gesta Karoli Magni*, ed. Haefele, 25 ('quidam iuvenis, cognatus Regis, optime in quadam festivitate caneret alleluia . . .').

34 **The *pauper* and the bishopric:** *Gesta Karoli Magni*, ed. Haefele, 4–5.

35 **The 'incomparable cleric':** *Gesta Karoli Magni*, ed. Haefele, 5: 'habuit incomparabilis Karolus incomparabilem clericum in omnibus, de quo illud ferebatur, quod de nullo unquam mortalium: quia videlicet et scientia litterarum secularium atque divinarum cantileneque ecclesiastice vel iocularis novaque carminum compositione sive modulatione, insuper et vocis dulcissima plenitudine inestimabilie delectatione cunctos praecelleret.'

17 Singers, Sounds and Symbols

1 **Earliest notations:** see Ch. 15 n. 3. **Agobard:** *Opera omnia*, ed. van Acker, 337–51, esp. 350. **Training of singers:** Regulations for the conduct of the monastic day (mostly post-Carolingian) reveal that the periods after Matins and Prime were often favoured for lessons, but they disclose nothing about the way masters conducted their classes. Boynton, 'The Liturgical Role of Children', and ead., 'Training for the Liturgy'; Fassler, 'The Office of the Cantor'.

2 **Hucbald and the neumes:** Chartier, *L'Œuvre musicale d'Hucbald de Saint-Amand*, 194. For related theoretical reflections on writing, see especially Harris, *The Origins of Writing* and *Rethinking Writing*.

3 **Aurelian:** *Musica Disciplina*, ed. Gushee. On textual matters see Bernhard, 'Textkritisches'. See also Atkinson, *The Critical Nexus*, *passim*. On the palaeofrankish neumes see Arlt, 'Anschaulichkeit und analytischer Charakter'; Levy, *Gregorian Chant and the Carolingians*, is essential reading here.

4 **The destination of the extant ninth-century notations:** Treitler, *With Voice and Pen*, 365–428.

5 **Segmental and suprasegmental aspects of language:** the outstanding discussion and manual is now Fox, *Prosodic Features and Prosodic Structure* (see especially initial definitions 1–5, and 179–268 on tone). **Isidore and the accents:** *Etymologies*, i. xviii–xix. As Isidore explains, the term *accentus* is essentially musical, for his comment that accent is 'adjacent to music' simply translates the Greek term usually Latinized as *prosodia*, incorporating the term *ōidē* 'song'. *Accentus* is supposedly derived from AD CANTUM, itself a calque of *prosodia*. For the accents as a tool of the Greek grammarians, see Allen, *Vox Graeca*, 106–22. For the Latins, the core ancient and early medieval authorities include Donatus, *Ars maior* (ed. Holtz), 609–11; Victorinus, *Ars* (*Grammatici Latini*, ed. Keil, vi. 185–215); Pseudo-Priscian, *De accentibus* (ed. Keil, op. cit., ii. 519–28); 'Sergius', *In Donatum* (ed. Keil, op. cit., vi. 482–4); 'Servius', *Commentarius in Donatum* (ed. Keil, op. cit.,

iv. 426–7); Pompeius, *Commentum* (ed. Keil, op. cit., v. 125–33); Martianus Capella, *De Nuptiis*, iii. 268; Isidore, *Etymologies*, i. xviii and xix. For discussions of *accentus* in new grammars of the 7th–9th centuries, see *Ars Laureshamensis*, ed. Löfstedt, 177–8; Sedulius Scottus, *In Donati Artem maiorem*, ed. Löfstedt, 40–50; and Murethach, *In Donati Artem maiorem Murethach*, ed. Holtz, 37–43. For the accent-theory of the origin of neumes, see Atkinson, '*De accentibus toni oritur nota que dicitur neuma*'; id., 'Glosses on Music' (incorporating important material from commentaries on Martianus); and id., *The Critical Nexus*, with abundant survey of earlier literature. It fell to Atkinson to show, to my mind with success, that the 'accent' theory had long been formulated without due regard to the testimony of late antique and medieval grammarians.

6 **Lupus:** PL 119: 502: 'Sic linguae vitia reformidamus et purgare contendimus; vitae vero delicta parvipendimus et augemus.'

7 **Victorinus:** for the text, see Pl. 70. **Remigius:** *Commentum in Martianum Capellam*, ed. Lutz, ii. 350. For discussion see Bielitz, *Musik und Grammatik*; Wille, *Musica Romana*, 452–3, and *HMT*, s.v. *Modulatio/Modulation*.

8 **Frankish concerns with intonation in reading:** see especially Hildemar, *Epistola ad Ursum Beneventanum episcopum de recta legendi ratione* (PL 106: 395–8). This letter should be read in tandem with Hildemar's extensive discussion of reading in his *Expositio Regulae Sancti Benedicti*, 426–31. On Hildemar, see now also De Jong, 'Growing up in a Carolingian Monastery'. **'Intellectual and artistic ferment':** Atkinson, 'Glosses on Music', 199.

9 *Musica Enchiriadis*: see *Musica et Scolica Enchiriadis*, ed. Schmid, 3.

10 **Merovingian Latin:** See Banniard, *Viva Voce*; Herman, 'Spoken and Written Latin'; Janson, 'Language Change'; Rio, *Legal Practice and the Written Word*, esp. 9–26; Van Acker, 'Dans les méandres'; and id., *Ut quique rustici*; Van Uytfanghe, 'Le Latin des hagiographes mérovingiens'.

11 **Latin in Anglo-Saxon England:** See A. Campbell, *Old English Grammar*, §§545–64 for the telling evidence of loan words, and Wollmann, 'Early Latin Loan Words in Old English'. A seminal if polemical discussion is Wright, *Late Latin*, weighed and discussed in the essays in id. (ed.), *Latin and the Romance Languages*. See also Irvine, 'Bede the Gramarian'; Parkes, '*Raedan*'; id., 'The Contribution of Insular Scribes' and the seminal studies by Law in the bibliography.

12 **Assisting scribes:** McKitterick, 'Latin and Romance', 132. **Alcuin:** The text of the *De Orthographia* is in PL 101: 901–20 and *Alcuini Orthographia*, ed. Bruni. In Alcuin's *Dialogue concerning Rhetoric and the Virtues*, where the English scholar's partner is none other than Charlemagne, Alcuin gives the emperor the plain advice that 'each letter must have its proper sound'. Text and translation in *The Rhetoric of Alcuin and Charlemagne*, ed. and trans. Howell, 138–9.

13 **The notes for the sermon on Jonah:** Dion (ed.), *La Cantilène de sainte Eulalie*, 65–7.

14 **'Without a teacher':** Chartier, *L'Œuvre musicale d'Hucbald de Saint-Amand*, 194. **Carolus calvus:** The poem is discussed in Wright, *Late Latin*, 133–5. **Things letters cannot reveal:** Chartier, *L'Œuvre musicale*, 196.

15 **Robert Robinson:** *The Phonetic Writings of Robert Robinson*, ed. Dobson, 5.

16 **Litany of Soissons:** Coens, 'Anciennes Litanies', 132–43. For the historical context see Ewig, 'Beobachtungen', 75–7. *Anglo-Saxon Litanies of the Saints*, ed. Lapidge, is indispensable. The text of the Soissons statutes is in MGH CRF, i. 28–30.

17 **Carolingian priests:** There is a useful survey of the capitulary legislation, and of the social status of priests, in Van Rhijn, 'Priests and the Carolingian Reforms'. For the original texts see the editions in *Capitula Episcoporum*, ed. Brommer, Pokorny and Stratmann.

18 **Hincmar and the psalms:** ibid., ii. 34–5.

19 **Syllables:** Compare Van Uytfanghe, 'Latin mérovingien', 83, referring to northern Gaul from the late 8th c. onwards: 'In effect, the Carolingian renaissance certainly seems to have accelerated the sense of linguistic self-consciousness, at least in northern Gaul. In this region, the reform of the pronunciation, and more particularly the obligation to pronounce – in the liturgy, for example – all the letters and syllables, which was not done before, accentuated the contrast between the language of texts and the spoken language' (my translation).

20 **The dialogue:** *Cunabula Grammaticae Artis Donati*, PL 90: 613–32. See Law, *The Insular Latin Grammarians*, 103 n. 2. I am grateful to the late Dr Law for her advice about this work.

21 **Latin accent:** for a French view, see Joly, *Fiches de phonétique*, which assumes throughout that 'l'accent de hauteur devient accent d'intensité' in the first three centuries AD. General discussion in Posner, *The Romance Languages*, 99. In Isidore's discussion, the

language of volume breaks through the language of pitch, as for example in *Etymologies*, i. xviii ('ibi sonus crescit et desinit . . . [gravis] minus enim sonat quam acutus et cicumflexus . . .').

22   **Tone as 'an artefact of the literary language':** Posner, *The Romance Languages*, 99.

23   **Song and Roman Classical verse:** For the issue of singing and saying in various kinds of Roman public, private, and professional recitation of prose and verse, see Allen, 'Ovid's *Cantare*', and Habinek, *The World of Roman Song*.

24   **Solesmes:** Dom Joseph Pothier, *Les Mélodies grégoriennes*, 105–32, and PM, 2: 42 ff., and 7: 128–66; Bergeron, *Decadent Enchantments*.

18   *Composing for Singers 900–1100, I*

1   **Stephen of Liège:** Anselmus, *Gesta Episcoporum Leodiensium*, MGH SS, vii. 200 (PL 139: 1083–5). *Index Scriptorum Operumque Latino-Belgicorum Medii Aevi*, ed. Genicot and Tombeur, ii. 35. Editions of music by Stephen in Auda, *L'École musicale liègeoise au Xe siècle*. There is an edition of material from the Trinity Office in the *Nocturnale Romanum*. See also Björkvall and Haug, 'Text und Musik im Trinitäts-offizium Stephans von Lüttich'. Details of the literary sources used for most of the composers mentioned in what follows are given in the Appendix to Ch. 19. To avoid duplication, footnotes in this chapter have been kept to a minimum.

2   **In plateis:** Chartier, *L'Œuvre musicale d'Hucbald de Saint-Amand*, gives a barely legible transcription, 392–9. See also Goudesenne, 'A Typology', 31. For the progressive musical styles of 900–1100, see especially the bibliographical excursus in *Antiphonen*, ed. Dobszay and Szendrei, 1, 22*–34*; Hiley, '*Cantate Domino*', 127–33; id., 'The Music of Prose Offices'; id., 'Style and Structure'; id. 'The *Historia* of St. Julien of Le Mans'. See also Reaney in Jones, *The Saint Nicholas Liturgy*; Steiner, *Studies in Gregorian Chant, passim*; and Szendrei, 'Zur Stilistik der Melodien des Emmeram-Offiziums'.

3   **'Noise' in the transmission:** Hughes, 'From the Advent Project to the Late Middle Ages', 188.

4   **Sequences and tropes:** The bibliography is so extensive, any selection is bound to seem idiosyncratic. Crocker, *The Early Medieval Sequence*, is foundational on basic problems for the earliest layers of the repertory; id., *Studies in Medieval Music Theory and the Early Sequence* (virtually all pertinent here); id., 'The Troping Hypothesis'; Fassler, *Gothic Song* (Victorine material, especially sequences, in a dense historical context); Hiley, *Western Plainchant*, 172–286 (tropes and sequences); Iversen, 'Compositional Planning and Tropes'; Van Deusen, 'Sequence Repertories: A Reappraisal'. There have been many regional studies in the last twenty years, including Bower, 'The Sequence Repertoire of the Diocese of Utrecht'; Hiley, 'The Repertory of Sequences at Winchester'; Jensen, *Tropes and Sequences in the Liturgy of the Church in Piacenza*, among others. The sequence has also attracted studies emphasizing intellectual and political history.

5   **Layers of composition and transmission:** for Office chants, see especially Goudesenne, *Les Offices historiques*.

6   **The Cava episode:** *Vita Sancti Petri abbatis Cavensis*, AS Martii, i. 332.

7   **The wax tablet:** Rosenfeld, 'Technologies for Musical Drafts', esp. 60–2, editing the key passage.

8   **The literacy issue:** for the 11th c., Boynton, 'Orality' and Fassler 'The Cantor' present useful data. **St-Évroul:** Chibnall, 'The Merovingian Monastery of St. Évroul'. Guido, bishop of Auxerre (d. 961), is praised for putting forth chants 'with his own hand', and since these plainsongs were contrafacta (words written to pre-existing melodies) this might imply that Guido copied his material in notation; yet the expression may simply mean that the bishop did the work of creating the new texts himself, without delegating it to one of his clergy. A curiously elaborate reference to the bridges of the monochord by Peter the Deacon may imply that chants composed by Desiderius of Montecassino existed in some form of notation (*monochordi sonori magade reperiet notas*), but this might equally be an ostentatious way to record that Desiderius supplied his own chant texts with a musical setting. For a useful survey, see Turco, 'Neumennotation und Komposition'.

9   **Arnold of Vohburg:** *Historia Sancti Emmerammi*, ed. Hiley, provides discussion, facsimiles and transcriptions.

10   **Caiazzo:** for context, see Cowdrey, *The Age of Abbot Desiderius*, 39–41, and Howe, *Church Reform and Social Change*. **Latin and vernacular in Italy:** The topic emerges throughout the essays in Wright, (ed.), *Latin and the Romance Languages*, but see especially Danesi, 'Latin vs Romance'.

11   **Olbert:** Genicot and Tombeur, *Index Scrip-*

torum Operumque Latino-Belgicorum Medii Aevi, ii. 233. For the urban and political context see Nicholas, 'The Role of Feudal Relationships'; Zylbergeld, 'Les Villes en Hainaut au moyen âge'. For the broader social, economic and theological context of such events as the translation of Veronus, and the cult of saints, the bibliography is very extensive. Works of special value considering the social and political background to the cult of saints between 900 and 1100 include Barthélemy, *L'An mil*; Fanning, *A Bishop and his World* (on Hubert of Angers); Geary, *Furta Sacra* (on relic theft); Head, *Hagiography and the Cult of Saints*; id. and Landes (ed.), *The Peace of God*; Moore, *The First European Revolution*; Rosenwein, *To be the Neighbour of Saint Peter*.

12 **Saint Florent:** *Historia Sancti Florentii Salmurensis*, in *Chroniques des églises d'Anjou*, ed. Marchegay and Mabille, 287. For Sigo as *magister scholarum* at Chartres, see Fanning, *A Bishop and his World*, docs. 36 (inauthentic, but an authentic witness list) and 37 (same).

13 **Blois and Anjou:** Fanning, *A Bishop and his World*, 44–63, provides valuable historical context.

14 **St-Riquier:** Agache, *La Somme pré-romaine*, 205; Fossier, *La Terre et les hommes*, 191–4.

15 **Wulframnus:** the necrology of St-Wulfran in Paris, BNF lat. 10113, fol. 34, names Count Enguerrand I as 'the builder of this place' (cited in *Recueil des actes des comtes de Pontieu*, ed. Brunel, 11). For a genealogy of the comital line see the table in *Carmen de Hastingae Proelio*, ed. Morton and Muntz, 130.

16 **Gerbert:** For the primary sources for Gerbert's interests, see Gerbert d'Aurillac, *Correspondance*, ed. Riché and Callu, Annexe 5:1 (Gerbert explains rules for the abacus to Constantine of Fleury; rules for multiplication and division); 5:2 (Gerbert defends the study of numbers); 5:3 (Gerbert explains the planisphere); 5:4 (Gerbert explains a passage from the *De Musica* of Boethius on superparticular proportions); 5:5 (more of the same); 5:6 (a related matter from the *De Arithmetica*). See also Glenn, *Politics and History*, esp. 54–69, and the essays in Ollich I Castanyer (ed.), *Actes del Congrés Internacional Gerbert d'Orlhac i el seu temps*, especially Cassinet, 'Gerbert et l'introduction de la numération decimale arabo-indienne en occident chrétien', 715–26. For context on the 11th-c. Trivium and Quadrivium, see Beaujouan, *Par raison de nombres*. **Abacus:** Evans, 'Duc Oculum', and id., 'Difficillima et Ardua'.

17 **Abbo:** Aimon of Fleury, *Vita Abbonis*, 390.

Riché, *Abbon de Fleury*, is the most recent biography. See also Glenn, *Politics and History*, passim. On the Fleury group that includes Constantine, see Head, *Hagiography and the Cult of Saints. Abbo of Fleury and Ramsey*, ed. Peden, pp. xi–xv, gives a conspectus of Abbo's life and works, and an edition of a scientific work (with traces, perhaps, of Abbo's advanced musical studies at 73–4 and 79).

18 **Catalonia:** for Richer's account, see Richer, *Historia Francorum*, in *Richer*, ed. Latouche, ii. 50. Context and further details in Bonnassie, *La Catalogne*, 254–6. For broader context, Beaujouan, *Par raison des nombres*.

19   Composing for Singers 900–1100, II

1 **Sigebert:** For the sources pertaining to Sigebert, and all other composers mentioned, see the Appendix to this chapter.

2 **Paschasius:** the Life is edited in PL 120: 1507–56. See Ganz, *Corbie*, 103–20.

3 **The most resourceful bee:** for examples, chosen at random, from an immense harvest, see PL 89: 614 (Willibald); 137: 87 (Wulfstan of Winchester) and 139: 394 (Aimon of Fleury).

4 **Good and bad practice in composition:** much of the material from the theorists is quoted and illuminatingly discussed in Traub, 'Zur Kompositionslehre'. For a survey of terminology, mostly from technical writings, see Bandur, 'Compositio/Komponisten'.

5 **The modes:** Jeffery's magisterial essay, 'The Earliest Oktōēchoi', gathers up much significant literature on the modes and makes a conspectus here unnecessary. Hiley, *Western Plainchant*, 454–77; Falconer, 'The Modes before the Modes'. See also Traub, 'Zur Kompositionslehre'.

6 **Letald's manifesto:** Appendix, s.v. Letald. Discussion in Hiley, 'The *Historia* of St. Julian of Le Mans'.

7 **What is up to date in Letald:** Hiley, 'The *Historia*', offers a useful discussion. ***Urbs fortitudinis:*** Falconer, 'The Modes before the Modes', 133–4, with citations of discussions in medieval theorists.

8 **Pruritus:** John of Affligem, *De Musica*, ed. Smits van Waesberghe, 96. I allude to the translation in *Hucbald, Guido and John*, trans. Babb, 125. Further on John see below, pp. 467–73.

9 **Solo psalmody:** The key text is Dyer,

'Monastic Psalmody'. See also Nowacki, 'Antiphonal Psalmody', 288–9 and Falconer, 'The Modes before the Modes', 139–40.

10   **Bruno of Toul as courtier:** *Vita Leonis*, in *La Vie du Pape Léon IX*, ed. Parisse and Goullet, 52–3.

11   **'Morum elegantia':** The sources are cited by Jaeger, in *Scholars and Courtiers*, Essay x, 'The Courtier Bishop in *Vitae* from the Tenth to the Twelfth Century', 301–7. **The imperial court:** Jaeger, *The Origins of Courtliness*, is fundamental, so too the essays in idem, *Scholars and Courtiers*, notably Essay 1 ('Cathedral Schools and Humanist Learning, 950–1150') and Essay x cited above. See also Fleckenstein, *Die Hofkapelle der deutschen Könige*.

12   **John:** John of Affligem, *De Musica*, ed. Smits van Waesberghe, remains the standard edition. The thorny issues surrounding the date, location and identity of John are fully discussed by Palisca in his introduction to *Hucbald, Guido and John*, trans. Babb, ed. Palisca, 87–100; a slightly expanded version of that essay appears in Palisca, 'An Introduction'. See also the revised version of Palisca's entry 'Johannes Cotto (Johannes Affligemensis)' in *New Grove Online*. (Contrary to the claims of that article, however, there is no decisive evidence that John was a monk, and Fulgentius was not English; he was from Brabant.) Important studies include Huglo, 'L'Auteur du traité', and Malcolm, 'Epistola Johannis ad Fulgentium Episcopum'. For further bibliography see D. R. Williams and Balensuela, *Music Theory from Boethius to Zarlino*, 120–2. **Curialitas:** See *Mittellateinisches Wörterbuch*, ii, s.v. *curia, curialiter, curialitas*, and for the Hildesheim example, Jaeger, *The Origins of Courtliness*, 155–61.

13   **The lyrics:** *Die Cambridger Lieder*, ed. Strecker, nos 29 and 32 (two versions of *Huc adtollite*), 7 (lament for Heribert, archbishop of Cologne), 9, 17 and 27 (laments for the emperor Henry II), 33 (lament for the emperor Conrad), 35 ('quibus ludus est animo et iocularis cantus hoc advertant ridiculum') and 15 ('Mendosam quam cantilenam ago / Puerilis commendatam dabo, / Quo modulos per mendaces risum / Auditoribus ingentem ferant'). There has been much recent work of high quality on the earliest Latin lyric repertories. See Barrett, 'Notated Verse'; Wälli, *Melodien aus Mittelalterlichen Horaz-Handschriften*, and Ziolkowski, *Nota bene*.

14   **John and the minstrels, etc:** John of Affligem, *De Musica*, ed. Smits van Waesberghe, 51 and 77. **John**

and the musical pleasures: ibid. 117: 'Itaque si iuvenum rogatu cantum componere volueris, iuvenilis sit ille et lascivus, sin vero senum, morosus sit et severitatem exprimens', and 109. John's teaching here is indebted to classical rhetorical teaching, notably its affective purpose and relation to public office.

15   **Summa Musicae:** The Summa Musicae, ed. Page, 29. Bernhard, 'La *Summa musice* du Ps.-Jean de Murs' makes the case for dating this text in the early 14th c.

20   *Guido of Arezzo*

1   **Agobard:** *Opera omnia*, ed. van Acker, 350. Context in Huglo, 'Les Remaniements de l'antiphonaire grégorien'. **The *Dialogus*:** GS, i. 251. Huglo, 'Der Prolog'; id., 'Un nouveau manuscrit du *Dialogue*'. **Pseudo-Odo:** *De Musica* (GS, i. 265), referring to the use of the monochord letters. For a facsimile of this treatise in a manuscript of the 11th and 12th cc. see *Firenze, Biblioteca Nazionale Centrale, Conventi Soppressi, F. III. 565*, ed. Santosuosso, fols 44^v–58.

2   **'With purity':** *Guido d'Arezzo's Regule Rithmice*, ed. Pesce, 410–11. A few sources read *pietate*. One source (C1) omits.

3   **Guido and the observances:** The words *cum puritate* are not rendered in the original edition of *Source Readings*, ed. Strunk, and its single-volume derivatives, nor in the revised edition, ii. 102. *Guido d'Arezzo*, ed. Pesce, 410–11, does respond to Guido's text in the facing translation.

4   **Heribert of Milan:** Taviani, 'Un Archevêque de Milan'.

5   **The *Epistola Widonis*:** Translated here from the text in Gilchrist, 'Die *Epistola Widonis*', 595–6. See also id., 'The *Epistola Widonis*'. **The language of corruption and sexuality:** For the Councils cited here and other material, Remensnyder, 'Pollution, Purity and Peace', is outstanding, together with the other essays in Head and Landes, *The Peace of God*. See also the essays in Frassetto, *Medieval Purity and Piety*, and Moore, 'Heresy and Disease'.

6   **Bernold's *Micrologus*:** The most readily accessible edition is in PL 151: 979–1022. For sources and discussion see Taylor, 'A New Inventory'. **The attribution to Guido:** The note is quoted from the Stuttgart manuscript by *Libelli de Lite*, ed. Thaner, i.

2: 'Hanc epistolam ad Mediolanensem ecclesiam non Pascalis fecit sed quidam Wido, qui et musicam composuit; sic enim viri religiosissimi asserunt, qui hoc ex discipulis eiusdem diligentissime exploraverunt.' See also ii. 41 (*De Damnatione Schismaticorum*). **Epistola Widonis:** For the various recensions see *Libelli de Lite*, ed. Thaner, i. 1–7, and Gilchrist, 'Die *Epistola Widonis*' (edition of the longer recension) and id., 'The *Epistola Widonis*'.

7   **The Constance circle:** For Gebhard III, Bernold and the Constance circle see Autenrieth, *Die Domschule*; Blumenthal, 'The Papacy and Canon Law'; Robinson, 'Bernold von Konstanz'; id., 'Zur Arbeitsweise Bernolds von Konstanz'. For the background to the work of Bernold, in a liturgical context, see R. E. Reynolds, 'Liturgical Scholarship', 114–15.

8   **Periculosa discordia, etc.:** Guido, *Prologus in Antiphonarium*, in *Tres Tractatuli*, ed. Smits van Waesberghe, 62; *Guido d'Arezzo*, ed. Pesce, 410–11. Compare Bruno of Würzburg (PL 142: 505): 'periculosa est adulatio, quae excludere potest hominem a regno dei'.

9   **Peter Damian:** His career has often been surveyed; see e.g. Cowdrey, *Pope Gregory VII*, 39–43, on a decade of close association between Damian and the papacy; id., *The Age of Abbot Desiderius*, *passim*; and K. G. Cushing, *Papacy and Law*. **Peter Damian's hymns:** See the Appendix to Ch. 19, under 'Alberic, monk of Montecassino'. **Romuald:** Peter Damian, *Vita Beati Romualdi*, ed. Tabacco, and Balboni, 'San Pier Damiano'. The Romuald material is well employed in several essays in Rusconi, *Guido d'Arezzo*, notably Cantarella, 'La *Vita Beati Romualdi*'. For John Gualbert see MGH SS, xxx/2, 1076–1110. For Dominic of Sora see Howe, *Church Reform and Social Change*.

10   ***Cursus* in Guido:** Janson, *Prose Rhythm in Medieval Latin*, 41–3. Peter Damian, *Epistolae*, in *Die Briefe des Petrus Damiani*, ed. Reindel, i. 248–78, 282–4, 334–6, and iii. 472–6, all instances of *quicquid servus et filius*. See also Lanham, *Salutation Formulas in Latin Letters to 1200*, 10, which traces no formula of the 'quicquid' type before Gerbert of Aurillac (d. 1003).

11   **'Simony and clerical unchastity':** Remensnyder, 'Pollution, Purity and Peace', 297.

12   **Imperial journeys:** for the routes of Conrad II, see *Die Urkunden der Deutschen Könige und Kaiser*, ed. Bresslau, iv. 54–148 (1026–7) and 315–89 (1036–7). **Abbot Guido of Pomposa:** The *Vita prima Sancti Guidonis Abbatis* (*BHL* 8876) relates the ascetic,

indeed the eremitical, deprivations to which Abbot Guido submitted himself, his miracles, and the circumstances of his burial at Speyer. See now also Samaritani, 'Contributi alla Biografia di Guido a Pomposa e Arezzo', and id., with Di Francesco, *Pomposa: Storia, arte, architettura*; Novarra, 'La chiesa pomposiana nelle trasformazioni medievali'. **Guido's assessment of abbot Guido and Pomposa:** *Guido d'Arezzo*, ed. Pesce, 452–5.

13   **The Canossa:** the outstanding primary sources include the anonymous *Cronica Sancti Genesii Episcopi*, ed. Affò, 45–56, which describes the *ruricolae* making clearances in the Po marshes and the progenitor of the house, Adalbert-Atto, moving in to incastellate and secure lordship, and the *Vita Mathildis*, now available in a lavish facsimile edition with edited text in *Vita der Mathilde von Canossa*, ed. Pernoud et al. For the materials used here see lines 1078–82 and 1103–37. The principal secondary sources include Fumagalli, *Le origini di una grande dinastia feudale*; Golinelli, *I poteri dei Canossa*; and Rinaldi, 'Da Alberto Atto a Bonifacio'.

14   **Theodaldus's charters:** *Documenti per la storia della città di Arezzo*, ed. Pasqui, i. 168–277. **Camaldoli:** *Regesta Chartarum Italiae*, ed. Schiaparelli and Baldasseroni, ii: *Regesta di Camaldoli*. **The building work:** *Historia Custodum Aretinorum*, 1477, and *Documenti*, ed. Pasqui, i. 176–8 (Theodaldus confirms and extends the privileges of the architect, Maginardus). **References in Guido's writings:** Guido, *Micrologus*, ed. Smits van Waesberghe, 81–4 and *Guido d'Arezzo*, ed. Pesce, 450–1.

15   **Guido's accounts of his notation:** *Guido d'Arezzo*, ed. Pesce, *passim*. This edition places the text of three of Guido's works on a proper text-critical basis, but there is still much to be gained from Guido, *Tres Tractatuli*, ed. Smits van Waesberghe, and Guido, '*Regulae Rhythmicae*', ed. Smits van Waesberghe and Vetter. For context, the essays in Rusconi, ed., *Guido d'Arezzo* are essential. Still of value, for its outstanding breadth of reference, is Smits van Waesberghe, *De Musico-Paedagogico*, which may be supplemented, with caution, by Oesch, *Guido von Arezzo*. For Guido outside a musicological context, see especially Delumeau, *Arezzo*. **Surveys of Guidonian notation and its dissemination:** Smits van Waesberghe, *De Musico-Paedagogico*, 47–135, and *New Grove Online*, Notation, §III, 1 (v) (b). See also Flotzinger, 'Zur Ubernahm der Liniennotation' (on the influence of the Benedictines in Germany). For Spain, there is now

Zapke, 'Sistemas de Notación', which sets new standards for the provision of colour digital images in this context. For eastern Europe see Szendrei, 'The Introduction of Staff Notation'; idem, 'Choralnotation in Mitteleuropa'; and idem, 'Staff Notation of Gregorian Chant in Polish Sources'. For Britain, see Sharpe, 'Words and Music by Goscelin of Canterbury', and Hartzell, *Catalogue*. **An infantile system:** *Guido d'Arezzo*, ed. Pesce, 460–1. **Lines as 'strings':** For this tradition in pre-Guidonian theory see Chartier, *L'Œuvre musicale d'Hucbald de Saint-Amand*, 160; Huglo, 'Les Instruments de musique chez Hucbald'; and *Musica et Scolica Enchiriadis*, ed. Schmid, 14 and 16. **Neumes transferred from a staffless to a staffed state:** survey in Smits van Waesberghe, *De Musico-Paedagogico*, 47–85. Schlager, 'Neumenschrift und Liniensystem', examines an interesting case, so also Hiley in *Arnoldus Vohburgensis, Historia Sancti Emmerammi*.

16   **'The notes are so arranged':** *Guido d'Arezzo*, ed. Pesce, 418–19. Translation mine.

17   **Guido, Damian and science:** *Guido d'Arezzo*, ed. Pesce, 460–1 (on consulting Greeks); Peter Damian: *De sancta Simplicitate Scientiae Inflanti anteponenda*, 699–700. See Cantin, *Les Sciences séculières et la foi*.

18   **'Experimenta':** Bernold of Constance, *Chronicon*, 451–2, *sub anno* 1091, on William of Hirsau. **Gerbert:** *Correspondance*, ed. Riché and Callu, Annexe 5:1 *et passim*. See also Cassinet, 'Gerbert et l'introduction de la numération decimale arabo-indienne en occident chrétien'; Huglo, 'Gerbert, théoricien de la musique, vu de l'an 2000'; more broadly Beaujouan, *Par raison de nombres*, and Bergmann, *Innovationen im Quadrivium des 10. und 11. Jahrhunderts*. **Visualization and diagrams:** For two compact but useful surveys see Law, *Grammar and Grammarians*, 250–9, and Eastwood, 'Innovation and Reform in Latin Planetary Astronomy'. **The abacus:** Evans, '*Duc Oculum*' and id., '*Difficillima et Ardua*'. **Laurence of Amalfi:** *Opera*, ed. Newton, 78; Gibson and Newton, 'Pandulf of Capua's *De Calculatione*'. Perhaps there is something in the suggestion that the medieval abacus, whose columns ran down the page in the 11th c. but evolved into a form with lines across the page, was influenced by the example of the musical stave. See Menninger, *Number Words and Number Symbols*, 340–1. A number of the Guido manuscripts reveal broader interest in quadrivial science; see *Guido d'Arezzo*, ed Pesce, inventories of

K, Lo4, Lo6, M4, O2, RV, V4 and W2. **The graph principle in the earlier Middle Ages:** Lattin, 'The Eleventh Century MS Munich 14436'; Eastwood, 'Plinian Astronomical Diagrams in the Early Middle Ages'; North, 'Coordinates and Categories'; and Gray Funkhouser, 'A Note on a Tenth-Century Graph'. For some of the fundamental spatial metaphors involved in the perception of pitch in Western music, of considerable importance to the development of the stave, see Duchez, 'La Répresentation spatio-verticale', some of whose concerns are brought closer to those of this chapter in id., 'Des neumes à la portée'. **The images:** Guido of Arezzo with a monochord in Florence, Biblioteca Nazionale Centrale, Conventi Soppressi, F. III. 565, fol. 58, from the end of the 11th c. (facsimile in *Firenze, Biblioteca Nazionale Centrale*, ed. Santosuosso); Pandulf of Capua with his abacus marked with Hindu-Arabic numerals in Vatican City, Biblioteca Apostolica Vaticana, Ottob. Lat. 1354, fol. 55ᵛ.

19   **Epistola ad Michahelem:** for the text followed in these paragraphs see *Guido d'Arezzo*, ed. Pesce, 448 and 450.

20   **John XIX:** In recent decades a rather more positive view of John XIX has emerged, especially in relation to his dealings with Cluny. See especially Herrmann, *Das Tuskulanerpapsttum*; other bibliography is gathered in Howe, *Church Reform and Social Change*, 21; and Cowdrey, *The Cluniacs*, 36–43. Essential primary sources are calendared in Santifaller, 'Chronologisches Verzeichnis'.

21   **Denying it was Guido:** Smits van Waesberghe, *De Musico-Paedagogico*, 27–8, and Oesch, *Guido von Arezzo*, 17. For the reference to exile, see *Guido d'Arezzo*, ed. Pesce, 440, 'Inde est quod me vides prolixis finibus exulatum . . .'. **Adam of Bremen:** *Gesta Hammaburgensis*, ed. Trillmich and Buchner, 310. **Dating the letter to Michael:** Smits van Waesberghe, *De Musico-Paedagogico*, 24.

22   **Emma:** *Quellen*, ed. Trillmich and Buchner, 282 (Adam of Bremen); **Knút in Rome:** ibid. 570 (Wipo, *Gesta Chuonradi II*). The charter is printed in *Documenti*, ed. Pasqui, i. 178–80. Compare Oesch, *Guido von Arezzo*, 17.

23   **V4 inventory:** *Guido d'Arezzo*, ed. Pesce, 204 (the *Prologus* headed 'Tertius eius de musica', and the *Epistola* as 'Epistolaris recapitulatio totius operis eiusdem Guidonis ad monachum').

24   **Commentaries upon the *Micrologus*:** *Expositiones in Micrologum Guidonis Aretini*, ed. Smits van Waesberghe.

25 **'Blessed hermit':** The passage is discussed in Smits van Waesberghe, *De Musico-Paedagogico*, 35–6. **Vita solitaria:** ibid. 81. **Gregorian authority:** For references to Gregory and his authority in the musical writings of Guido see *Guido d'Arezzo*, ed. Pesce, 348–9, 370–1, 412–13 and 516–17; Guido, *Micrologus*, ed. Smits van Waesberghe, 207. For references in the *Epistola Widonis*, see Gilchrist, 'Die *Epistola Widonis*'. But see also Hiley, '*Cantate Domino Canticum Novum*'. The number of unsignalled allusions to Gregory's writings in Guido's texts has yet to be assessed. Among those that might be tentatively advanced at this stage are *sacri verbi studium* in the prefatory letter to the *Micrologus* (ed. Smits van Waesberghe, 81); compare Gregory, *Homilia in Evangelia* (PL 76: 1076). **Regula:** *MLLM*, s.v. *regula*. **Silver and glass:** Guido, *Micrologus*, ed. Smits van Waesberghe, 76, and *Guido d'Arezzo*, ed. Pesce, 442. For exegesis of glass, commonly emphasizing transparency and especially purity, see Johannes de Deo, *Penitentiale* (PL 99: 1091); Haymo of Halberstadt, *Expositio in Apocalypsin* (PL 117: 1008); Rhabanus Maurus, *De Universo* (PL 111: 474).

21 *Bringing Singers to Book*

1 **Sankt Gallen and the routes:** Maurer, *Konstanz in Mittelalter*, i: *Von den Anfängen zum Konzil*, *passim*, and for the Rhineland tolls, Pfeiffer, *Rheinische Transitzölle im Mittelalter*. For the Constance trader in the Latin lyric (from the [older] Cambridge Songs) see *Die Cambridger Lieder*, ed. Strecker, 41–4. The bibliography on early Venice and her northern trade is naturally very large; a lucid survey is available in Von Falkenhausen, 'Between Two Empires'. In an entry for the year 1017, Thietmar of Merseburg mentions 'four large Venetian ships, filled with different kinds of spices', that were lost (Thietmar of Merseburg, *Die Chronik*, ed. Holtzmann, vii. 76). A valuable insight into 11th-c. Venetian trading cargoes arriving in Pavia, some of them presumably for transit northwards across the Alps, is provided by a royal Lombard document known as the *Instituta Honorancie Civitatis Papie* (MGH SS, xxx/2, 1450–9), requiring Venetians to pay a toll, mentioning pepper, cinnamon, galingale, ginger, ivory combs, mirrors and apparel.

2 **Conrad's journey:** Ekkehard IV, *Casus Sancti Galli*, 84. **The abbeys and the Guido sources:** inventories in *Guido d'Arezzo*, ed. Pesce, 96–100 (K), 133–5

(M5) and 209–15 (W2). On the abbeys of St Emmeram and SS. Ulrich and Afra, see Hemmerle, *Die Benediktinerkloster in Bayern*, ii. 45–50 and 238–47. **Imperial stays:** Map of imperial journeys in Mackay and Ditchburn (eds), *Atlas of Medieval Europe*, 54. On the imperial *iter* and the custom whereby the court lived at the expense of the bishops in the great sees, see Robinson, *Henry IV*, 10–11.

3 **The eleventh-century Regensburg source of Guido's musical writings:** Munich Clm 14523, part III (Huglo and Meyer, *Manuscripts . . . in the Federal Republic of Germany*, 113–16 and 139–41). Inventory and references in *Guido d'Arezzo*, ed. Pesce, 133–5. Smits van Waesberghe, *Musikerziehung*, 112, dates this manuscript to approximately 1040, which seems early. **William of Hirsau and Otloh:** William's music treatise is edited in *Musica Willehelmi Hirsaugensis*, ed. Harbinson. For the references to Guido see pp. 15, 41, 47–9, 51 (two references) 52, 54 and 70–3. For William's scientific interests, the outstanding source is the appreciative and contemporary obituary by Bernold of Constance in his *Chronicon*, 451–2, *sub anno* 1091. This is the source of the parallel material in William's *Vita* (MGH SS, xii. 209–25). There is valuable context in Resnick, 'Scientia Liberalis, Dialectics and Otloh of Saint Emmeram', and Evans, '*Studium Discendi*'. **John of Speyer in Verona:** MGH DRIG Henry IV, Pars I, 569–70. See Gawlik, *Intervenienten und Zeugen*, 133.

4 **John's singing:** *De Musica*, ed. Smits van Waesberghe, 110. **The dispute among singers:** ibid. 134. I find no support for the suggestion in Malcolm, 'Epistola Johannis Cottonis', that the *cotta* was the vestment of a cantor.

5 **John as pope:** *De Musica*, ed. Smits van Waesberghe, 25 n. 28.

6 **John's identity and milieu:** for the essential bibliography, see Ch. 19 n. 12. **Antistes:** for the senses, including 'priest', 'rector', 'bishop' and 'abbot', see *Mittellateinisches Wörterbuch*, s.v. *antistes*. **The 'angels' emendation:** discussed by Smits van Waesberghe in *De Musica*, 22–5, but in an unsatisfactory way, for there is no question of the 'angels' usage being peculiarly or even especially used of the monks of Affligem, as he maintains. One of the supporting pieces of evidence he cites (25 n. 23) appears to be doubly incorrect; the correct reference is seemingly PL 204: 933 and the text is actually referring to the flight of monks from St-Vanne at Verdun. For the position in Canon Law see e.g. Rupert of Deutz, *De*

Sancta Trinitate, ed. Haacke, viii. 8: 'Angelus enim graece, latine nuntius dicitur; sacerdotes igitur, canonici atque monachi, qui Dei praecepta annuntiant, angeli vocantur.' This text was often assumed to be part of a decree by Boniface IV (PL 80: 105). Compare Peter Damian, *Opuscula varia* (PL 145: 516) and Ivo of Chartres, *Decreta* (PL 161: 550). The importance of the Canon Law evidence in this context is briefly picked up by Malcolm, 'Epistola Johannis', 161, via an entry in Du Cange, but is not traced to any medieval source and is therefore left undeveloped. **Egbert of Liège:** *Fecunda Ratis*, ed. Voigt, 211 (two examples).

7   **Fulbert of Chartres on Abbot Odilo:** PL 141: 251. **Peter Damian on Hugh of Cluny:** PL 144: 374. **Peter Damian on Abbot Desiderius:** Cowdrey, *The Age of Abbot Desiderius*, 35.

8   **Foundation of Affligem:** *Exordium Affligemensis*, in MGH SS, ix (as *Chronicon Affligemense*), 407–8; also Coosemans and Coppens, 'De eerste kroniek van Affligem'. For this text see Genicot and Tombeur, *Index Scriptorum*, iii/2, 17–18. There has been much debate over the value and date of this text. See especially Dereine, 'La Critique de l'*Exordium Affligemense*'; id., 'Le Problème de la date de la fondation d'Affligem'; and id., 'La Spiritualité "apostolique" des premiers fondateurs d'Affligem (1083–1100)'; Verleyen, 'L'*Exordium Affligemense*'. I am not persuaded that it is mistaken to connect the *iter publicus* mentioned in this text with commercial movement between the North Sea coast and Cologne (Bonenfant, 'L'Origine des villes brabançonnes et la "route" de Bruges à Cologne').

9   **Holiness brought to a place of robbers:** Sigebert of Gembloux, *Chronographiae Auctarium Affligemense*, ed. Gorissen, 116, and then repeatedly in the charters assembled in *Cartulaire d'Afflighem*, ed. Marneffe. **The Truce of God council at Cologne:** MGH L iv, Con i, 602–3. For general context, see the essays in Head and Landes (eds), *The Peace of God*. The *Exordium Affligemensis* reports that the six knights did their penance before the archbishop of Cologne, but names Anno [ii], who died in 1075, which creates an insoluble chronological difficulty. I join Dereine in assuming that Sigewin (d. 1089) is the archbishop meant ('La Spiritualité apostolique', 48 n., and id., 'Le Problème de la date de la fondation d'Affligem'). The mistake is not difficult to account for, since Anno was one of the most prominent and controversial figures of the 11th-c. imperial episcopate. A condensed version of the foundation narrative appears in the Affligem ver-

sion of the chronicle of Sigebert of Gembloux, the *Auctarium Affligemense*, ed. Gorissen, 16–17 *et passim*.

10   **The Gregorian Reform:** see especially Gilchrist, 'Was there a Gregorian Reform Movement in the Eleventh Century?'. **Wedericus:** *Exordium Affligemensis*, 407: 'Wedericus sacerdos et monachus Sancti Petri Gandensis coenobii . . . qui apostolicae auctoritatis licentia roboratus Flandriam et Brabantiam provincias circuibat . . .'. **'Scarcely any distinction':** ibid. 407. **Fulgentius's flight:** Dauphin, 'L'Abbaye de Saint-Vanne de Verdun', 247 proposing that Fulgentius's abbey, prior to his arrival at Affligem, was St-Vanne, and not St-Airy.

11   **'Lovers of error':** *De Musica*, ed. Smits van Waesberghe, 139. **'They become angry':** ibid. 66 ('irati impudenter obstrepunt').

12   **A community of memory:** Blustein, *The Moral Demands of Memory*, 183.

13   **Gesta Abbatum Trudonensium:** The *Gesta* has often been printed, but rarely with renewed reference to the principal witness that was for some time untraced but is now MS 4 of the Grootseminarie in the Pastoraal Centrum at Mechelen in Belgium (hereafter Mechelen 4). The principal editions are by Köpke, in MGH SS, x. 213–448 (reprinted in PL 173: 11–434) and *Chronique de l'abbaye de Saint-Trond*, ed. De Borman. Both have their limitations, as pointed out by Tombeur, 'Notes sur le texte de Raoul de Saint-Trond'. I cite the Köpke edition, which is much more widely available (in either MGH or PL) than De Borman's, but for the material of direct relevance to the musical activities of Rudolf I cite the Mechelen manuscript. This is the manuscript that Tombeur ('Notes sur le text', 96) declares the oldest and best, compiled 'guère postérieur à la redaction de l'oeuvre'. For this manuscript see De Clercq, *Catalogue des manuscripts du Grand Séminaire de Malines*, Codex 4. For an inventory of the works of Rudolf of Sint Truiden, in both prose and verse, see Genicot and Tombeur, *Index Scriptorum*, iii/2, 222–33. The *Gesta* is highly regarded and has stimulated so much interest in the abbey that only a selection of material can be presented here. See Simenon, 'Les Chroniqueurs de l'abbaye de Saint-Trond', and Tombeur, 'Un Nouveau Nom'. For the abbey, its estates and its ties with the local nobility and townsmen, see Boes, *L'Abbaye de Saint-Trond*; Charles, *La Ville de Saint-Trond*; and Linck, *Sozialer Wandel in klösterlichen Grundherrschaften*, 116–246. For a summary of musicologists' transactions with Rudolf see *New Grove Online*, s.v. 'Rodolfus of

Sint Truiden', and for another brief reference, but in a context close to the one being developed here, see Flotzinger, 'Zur Ubernahm der Liniennotation'. For a musical treatise attributed on no very strong grounds to Rudolf, see *Die Quaestiones in Musica*, ed. Steglich.

14 **Rudolf's attainments:** Mechelen 4, fol. 40ᵛ: 'Sub scolari disciplina et studio litterarum Leodii positus usque ad xviiiᵒ annos etatis sue ibi mansit; ubi quantum metro et prosa profecerit ex scriptis eius et opusculis que postea fecit plane intelligi poterit.' **Wazelin [II]:** Reiner of St Lawrence (late 12th c.), *De claris Scriptoribus Monasterii sui* (PL 204: 24). **Nizo:** ibid. 26. **Giselbert:** ibid. 25. **John:** ibid. 26.

15 '**Theuderic, asking him who he was**': Mechelen 4, fol. 41ᵛ: 'Qui interrogans eum quis et unde esset, quoque qualique mente proficisceretur, cum bonum eius propositum intellexisset, formosumque et pulchre litteratum iuuenem illum attenderet, cepit sagacissime satagere, quomodo eum sibi retineret, utilem sibi eum fore credens, primum ad instruendos sibi disciplina et doctrina pueros suos, deinde ad promouendum in aliquod, si ita forte accideret, ut accidit, ecclesiasticum intus aut foris ministerium. Cui cum persuasisset demorandi secum uoluntatem gratiosi oris facundia, primum ei scolares pueros scolaribus disciplinis instruendos commisit, quasdamque utilissimas compilationes, plenas plurimarum diuinarum sententiarum scribendas et multorum decreta conciliorum. Scripsit igitur ei eodem primo anno uolumen illud utilissimum multum continens scripturę et pueros uix "musa" declinare sciolos non tam dictamen quam metrum quoque componere docuit' (=PL 173: 115).

16 '**Rudolf bore a great labour**': Mechelen 4, fol. 41ᵛ: 'Grauissimum autem sustinuit laborem ad introducendos eos, cum ipse loqui eis theutonicam nesciret, et quidam puerorum paruitate adhuc scientię et natiua illis lingua theutonica neque latine neque, ut ita dicam, gualonice possent eum intelligere. Uicit tamen labor improbus omnia uincens, et eodem anno fecit eos litterate facillime intelligere quicquid uolebat eis legere. Instruxit etiam eos arte musica secundum Guidonem, et primus illam in claustrum nostrum introduxit, stupentibusque senioribus faciebat illos solo uisu subito cantare tacita arte magistra, quod numquam auditu didicerant' (=PL 173: 115).

17 **Rudolf using the stave:** A later reference in the *Gesta* to Rudolf notating music with monochord letters (=PL 173: 116–17) does not invalidate this claim, since Guidonian notation is essentially a bilingual system where the neumes are accompanied by an abbreviated method for 'spelling' the pitch with letters. **The chronology of Rudolf's early life:** Rudolf arrived at Sint Truiden during the abbacy of Theuderic, and therefore in or after 1099, the momentous year which saw the fall of Jerusalem in the First Crusade. When he arrived he was a *juvenis*, according to the First Continuator of the *Gesta*, but this is a notoriously flexible term. Rudolf was certainly at the abbey by 1103 when he took the place of Boso as *decanus*. Before this relatively narrow window of time between 1099 and 1103 he had studied in Liège and had been at the monastery of Burtscheid, long enough to reach the rank of major provost there. The *Gesta* contains a reference to his presence at Burtscheid before the death of Abbot Azelinus in 1091. Rudolf had also spent some time at Gladbach. Taking all this into account, he was probably born around 1070, placing the period of his studies at Liège, including the *ars musica secundum Guidonem*, between approximately 1080 and 1088. The Burtscheid years would therefore fall between *c.* 1088 and *c.* 1099. In 1099 Rudolf would have been around 30 years of age, and in his late sixties at his death in 1138.

18 **The Darmstadt source:** See Huglo and Meyer, *Manuscripts from the Carolingian Era*, 39–41, and Meyer, *Manuscripts . . . Addenda*, 278–9. Inventory also in *Guido d'Arezzo*, ed. Pesce, 60–3. The Guidonian material lies in the second section of the manuscript, fols 68–146, commonly dated to the beginning of the 12th c. **The Liège context:** Auda, *L'École musicale liègeoise au Xᵉ siècle*; Smits van Waesberghe, *Muziekgeschiedenis der Middeleeuwen*; id., 'Some Music Treatises and their Interrelation'. The claims of this article have not worn well over the years.

19 **Rudolf's Office:** There is an inventory of the texts in this manuscript in *Analecta Bollandiana*, 5 (1886), 314–17, and an edition of the texts at 365–72. Folios 96ᵛ–101ᵛ contain the office for Saint Truiden, followed by the office for the Translation of Truiden and Eucharius on fols 100ᵛ–101ʳ. All are noted. Edition of music in Auda, *L'École musicale liègeoise . . . l'Office de S. Trudon*'. The compositions are referred to in the *Gesta* (MGH edn. 332; PL 173: 220): 'Iste abbas fuit vir magnae litteraturae suo predecessori Theoderico non impar, prout ejus epistolae diversae, dictamina, prosae et metra apud nos conscripta testantur. Qui inter caetera fecit antiphonas et responsoria et cantum de sancto Quintino et de sancto Trudone ad laudes, ymnum Ad laudem regis glorie cum antiphona de

sancto Stephano *O Caritatis*.' The chants for Truiden are returned to later in the *Gesta*, just before the beginning of the *Continuatio Tertia*, Pars ii (MGH edn 387; PL 173: 322), explaining how Abbot Theuderic composed a Life of Saint Truiden and a sermon for the translation of Eucharius and Truiden together with the responsory *O viri misericordie* and the antiphon *Urbis eterne*, plus 'antiphons, responsories and versicles' sung for the Feast of the Deposition of Saint Truiden. These were set to music by Rudolf, 'vir litteratissimus, in musica Guidonis Aretini expertus'. The sermon, and the office whose texts are derived from it, appear in Université de Liège, Bibliothèque générale, MS 12, fols 93ᵛ–96ʳ and 100–101ʳ. At fol. 101ᵛ, there is a hymn for Saint Quentin, presumably one of the chants in honour of this saint composed by Rudolf, and noted.

20   **The conflict of *regnum* and *sacerdotium*:** Among the best historical surveys either written in English or translated are Cowdrey, *Pope Gregory VII*; Morris, *The Papal Monarchy*; Robinson, *The Papacy*; Tellenbach, *The Church in Western Europe*. Cowdrey, *The Register of Pope Gregory VII*, makes key documents readily accessible. See also R. E. Reynolds, 'Liturgical Scholarship at the Time of the Investiture Controversy'. In the present context, it is vital also to have the late 10th-c. perspective. See the essays in Frassetto, *Medieval Purity and Piety*, and Remensnyder, 'Pollution, Purity and Peace'. For more sharply focused work of relevance here see Verleyen, 'La Querelle des investitures et l'introduction de la règle de saint Benoît à Affligem'.

21   **Innocent's letter:** Text, translation and discussion in Connell, *Church and Worship*. More recent edition in Innocent I, *La Lettre du pape Innocent Iᵉʳ à Décentius de Gubbio*, ed. Cabié.

22   **The language of corruption:** Moore, 'Heresy and Disease'.

23   **The Beneventan episode**; T. F. Kelly, *The Beneventan Chant*, 39 *et passim*. **Gregory's letter to Alfonso:** Cowdrey, *Register*, 67–9. See also id., 'Pope Gregory VII (1073–85) and the Liturgy'. For context see Minguez, *Alfonso VI*, esp. 223–8, and Gambra, *Alfonso VI*, esp. the king's letter of July 1077 (ii, doc. 47) and ibid., doc. 67. **The Burgos council:** Don Pelayo, *Crónica del Obispo Don Pelayo*, ed. Sánchez Alonso, 80: 'Tunc Adefonsus rex uelociter Romam nuncios misit ad Papam Aldebrandum cognomento Gregorius; ideo hoc fecit, quia romanam misterium habere uoluit in omne regno suo. Memoratus itaque

Papa Cardinalem suum Ricardum, Abbatem Marsiliensem, in Ispania transmisit. Qui apud Burgensem urbem Concilium celebrauit confirmauitque rom-anum misterium in omni regno Regis Adefonsi Era mcxiiii.' For the other chronicle sources of the reign see Valdeavellano, *Historia de España*, 44–8, and García Moreno, 'Las Primeras Crónicas de la Reconquista', 562–623. Context in Lomax, *The Reconquest of Spain*, 31–61, and McKay, *Spain in the Middle Ages*. There is much valuable context in Walker, *Views of Transition: Liturgy and Illumination in Medieval Spain*. For the 'received' history of the adoption of the Roman rite see *Primera Crónica General de España*, ed. Menéndez Pidal, ii. 542–3, which includes the stories of the duel to determine which rite should be accepted and of the two books, one of the Roman rite and one of the Mozarabic, placed together in the fire to see which would best survive the ordeal.

24   **The Reform and canon law:** Cushing, *Papacy and Law in the Gregorian Revolution* and Blumenthal, 'The Papacy and Canon Law'.

25   **The chant out of accord with other churches of the province:** Mechelen 4, fol. 42ʳ: 'usus enim noster cantandi, nescimus unde hoc acciderit, nulli comprouintialium nostrorum conuenit . . .' (PL 173: 116). **Chrodegang:** See John of Gorze, *Vita Chrodegangi Episcopi Mettensis*, 556 (a late source): 'commendavit eum monasterio Sancti Trudonis educandum et nutriendum'.

26   **Censoriousness towards the young monks:** Mechelen 4, 'iuuenum indisciplinatione et insolentia (fol. 43ʳ) . . . nouam stultorum et indisciplinatorum iuuenum presumptionem (fol. 43ʳ) . . . insolentia nichilominus dissolutorum iuuenum' (fol. 44ʳ).

27   **Making the *graduale*:** Mechelen 4, fol. 42ʳ: 'graduale unum propria manu formauit, purgauit, punxit, sulcauit, scripsit, illuminauit, musiceque notauit, syllabatim, ut ita dicam, totum usum prius a senioribus secundum antiqua illorum gradualia discutiens. Sed cum usum eorum per quamplurima loca, propter uitiosam abusionem et corruptionem cantus, nullomodo ad rectam regulam posset trahere, et secundum artem non posset notare, nisi quod regulari et uerisona constaret ratione, ipse autem ab usu ęcclesię non facile uellet dissonare, miro, ut dixi, inedicibilique labore in hoc tantum se frustra afflixit, quod ex toto usum mendacem regula uera tenere non potuit, sed in hoc profecit quod quicquid alicubi in monocordo cantari potuit, de usu ęcclesię non preter-

misit se preterire' (=PL 173: 116–17). **B flat:** see Blackburn, 'The Lascivious Career of B-Flat.'

28 **Discutiens:** See the important note in Lewis and Short, *A Latin Dictionary*, s.v. *discŭtĭo*; Souter, *A Glossary of Later Latin*, s.v. *discutio*; *Mittellateinisches Wörterbuch*, s.v. I *discutio*, senses 1 and 2.

29 **Faults in notating too quickly:** Mechelen 4, fol. 42^r: 'Multa tamen, propter negligentiorem suam perficiendi operis uelocitatem, que per grauiores litteras notari debuerunt, per acutas siue per superacutas notauit, et quę per acutas siue per superacutas per grauiores; quod incorrectum reliquit alia sollicitudine intercurrente. Consummauit [42^v] autem uno anno opus illud propria, ut dixi, manu, de omnibus paruis et magnis qu   pertinere uidentur ad gradualem cum antyphonis rogationum et benedictione cerei in pascha' (=PL 173: 117).

22 *Singers in the Making of Europe*

1 **The *Foundation Book* of St Bartholomew:** *The Book of the Foundation of St. Bartholomew's Church*, ed. Moore, 19–20.

2 **The murdered chorister:** For bibliography on this story and its many versions, see Page, 'Marian Texts and Themes', 34–44.

3 **Myth:** Blustein, *The Moral Demands of Memory*, 176–239, to which I am indebted in this section. As much more recent cases of the blood-libel show, including some from the 20th c., it stirs a sediment lying deep in the Catholic imagination of Europe that is ready to rise – as the elements of ethnic hatred often are – when conflicts that may have little or nothing to do with ethnicity and religion in the first instance create the necessary disturbance. In the Polish town of Kielce, a rumour that Jews had abducted a Christian child arose as recently as 1946. See the British daily *The Guardian* for 1 Aug. 1997 ('Polish film-makers revive suspicion that pogrom was engineered'). I owe this reference to Professor Anne Dunan-Page.

4 ***Historia Silense:*** 129–30 (on the Franks' false claims) and 207–9 (the chants that were sung 'in the manner of Toledo').

5 **Roderigo Jiménez de Rada:** *Historia de Rebus Hispaniae sive Historia Gothica*, ed. Valverde, 207–9.

6 **Charlemagne as destroyer and the story of the books:** Landulphus Senior, *Historiae Libri Quatuor*, ed. Cutolo, 37–9.

7 **Wibert in Landulf's chronicle:** ibid. 74–8.

8 **Latinitas:** For Isidore, see *Etymologiae*, 1. 4. 15 and 7. 4. 12. **Lanfranc:** *De Corpore et Sanguine Domini adversus Berengarium Turonensem Liber*, PL 150: 410. See further, *Novum Glossarium Mediae Latinitatis*, s.v. *latinitas*, 3) (documenting the sense 'Roman church' as early as Anastasius Bibliothecarius in a text of 871–4) and 4). ***Vita Sancti Malachiae:*** Bernard of Clairvaux, *Opera*, iii, 316.

9 **'An orderly community':** R. W. Southern, quoted in Geary, *Furta Sacra*, 68. **The frontier:** There has been much interest in the concept of the frontier in recent years. For late antiquity and the early Middle Ages, see the essays in Pohl, Wood and Reimitz (eds), *The Transformation of Frontiers*, especially Reimitz, 'Conversion and Control: The Establishment of Liturgical Frontiers in Carolingian Pannonia', and Wood, 'Missionaries and the Christian Frontier'. Id., 'The Frontiers of Western Europe' is a valuable survey. For the proposal that Gregorian chant and the Frankish-Roman liturgy were used by the Carolingians in Italy, in a monastic context, as frontier-markers with Beneventan territory, see Hodges, 'In the Shadow of Pirenne'.

10 **Otto of Bamberg:** AS Julii I, 404. **Riga:** For the apostolic context of the settlement there, see *The Livonian Rhymed Chronicle*, trans. Smith and Urban, 1–3.

11 **The Cistercian reform:** Maître, *La Réforme cistercienne du plain-chant*, is the best introduction with an edition and translation of the treatise by Gui d'Eu. See also *Cantum quem Cisterciensis Ordinis Ecclesiae Cantare*, ed. Guentner, for other crucial documents. For the dissemination of the order, see the essays in *Unanimité et diversité cisterciennes*, which includes detailed studies of foundation patterns in Spain, Hungary and Eastern Europe.

12 **Cistercians in Portugal:** Rucquoi, 'Les cisterciens dans la péninsule ibérique', 498. **In the east:** Kłoczowski, 'Les Cisterciens en Europe du centre-est' and Pilat, 'Les réseau des cisterciens en Europe du centre-est'.

13 **The Frankish queen:** Gregory of Tours, *LHD*, ii. 29. **Vladimir:** *The Russian Primary Chronicle*, ed. and trans. Cross and Sherbowitz-Wetzor, 110–11. **Otto of Bamberg:** *Vita Ottonis Episcopi Bambergensis*, AS Julii I, 404.

14 **Testament of Ramiro I:** *Cartulario de San Juan de la Peña*, ed. Arteta, 201.

15 **Expansion of the Latin West:** The outstanding study in English is still Bartlett, *The Making of*

Europe. See also Christiansen, *The Northern Crusades*; Hamilton, *The Latin Church in the Crusader States*; Riley-Smith, 'The Latin Clergy'. For the crusades as an example of medieval colonialism, see Prawer, 'The Roots of Medieval Colonialism'. Later medieval language for speaking of such 'colonialism' is usefully discussed in Flori, '*Pur eshalcier sainte crestiënté*'. **Crusaders as 'Franks':** Bull, 'Overlapping and Competing Identities'.

16   **Continuation of William of Tyre:** *Recueil des historiens des croisades: Historiens occidentaux*, ii. 594. **Manuscripts in the Church of the Holy Sepulchre:** For context see Folda, *The Art of the Crusaders in the Holy Land*, and Beddie, 'Some Notices of Books in the East in the Period of the Crusades'. **The council of 1274:** Schein, *Fideles Crucis*, 36–44.

17   **Humbert of Romans:** *Opusculum Tripartitum*, ed. Brown, ii. 223.

18   **Galvano de Levanto:** Kohler, 'Traité du recouvrement de la Terre Sainte', 367–8: 'ubi cultus Jhesu Christi deberet et psalmodia, ibi fit a Saracenis abominabilis melodia'. **The looted missal:** Schein, *Fideles Crucis*, 125.

19   **Hospitals in the east:** For the Brandenburg hospital, see *Codex diplomaticus Brandenburgensis*, ed. Riedel, viii. 104 (the Dom) and 137–8 (hospital), and ibid. 300–1, for Spandau. For Riga see *Riga's ältere Geschichte*, ed. Napiersky, pp. cxxxix–cxl. For Lübeck, see *Codex diplomaticus Lubecensis*, i. 480 ff., and for Colbergh *Pommersches Urkundenbuch*, ii. 188–9.

20   **St-Raymond:** *Documents sur l'ancienne province de Languedoc*, ed. Douais, 27. **The Great Hospital:** Norfolk County Record Office, Case 24, Shelf B, 1–2. On this hospital see Rawcliffe, *Medicine for the Soul*. **The leprosaria:** Touati, *Maladie et société* is an outstanding study of the houses in the diocese of Sens, whence the figures given here are derived. **Southampton:** *The Cartulary of God's House*, ed. Kaye, Appendix IX. The **Ospedale di S. Maria di Colle:** Perugia, Archivo Storico, Serie inventari, 15, fols 3ᵛ–4ᵛ. **Estella:** de Parga et al., *Las Peregrinaciones*, iii. 75. **Girona:** Batlle i Prats, 'Inventari', 73.

21   **Pontoise and Tours:** *Statuts d'Hôtels-Dieu*, ed. Le Grand, 130–1 and 109. **Cammin:** *Pommersches Urkundenbuch*, ii. 393. **Dickens:** 'The Hospital Patient' (*Sketches by Boz*).

22   **Baude Fastoul:** *Les Congés d'Arras*, ed. Ruelle, Fastoul, 23–4, and 160. For psalmody on bridges, see Cambridge, Sidney Sussex College, MS 95, fol. 10 (Miracles of the Virgin). On this occasion the psalm

was not enough; the man fell from the bridge and the Virgin placed him back upon it, complete with his horse. For bridges see Boyer, *Medieval French Bridges*, 54; P. Murray et al., *Living Bridges*, and (especially) Dinzelbacher, 'Il ponte come luogo sacro'. **Saint Arnulph on the bridge:** Paul the Deacon, *Libellus de Ordine Episcoporum Mettensium*, PL 95: 704.

23   **Dominic of Calzada:** *AS* Maii III, 168, Lectio v. **Copián:** De Parga et al., *Las Peregrinaciones*, iii. 62–3.

24   *Ne timeas Zacharia:* Ekkehard I, *Vitae Sanctae Wiboradae*, ed. Berschin, 56. *Qui habitat:* ibid. 42.

25   **Thietmar of Merseburg:** *Die Chronik*, ed. Holtzmann, viii. 9. **Gerard:** *AS* Aprilis I, 418 (Vita I, Gerard *standing* at door) and 425 (Vita II, Gerard in prostration). *BHL* 3417 and 3418–19.

26   **The account by Ralph Tortarius:** *Les Miracles de saint Benoît*, ed. Certain, 340–1 (*BHL* 1129). **The Vivian miracle:** *Translatio Sancti Viviani Episcopi*, 263. For the sources of the antiphon *Homo iste*, the CANTUS index gives Paris, BNF MS lat 1085, fol. 295ʳ (Aquitanian, most chants abbreviated) and the Hartker antiphoner from Sankt Gallen, to which may be added Benevento, Biblioteca Capitolare 21, fol. 295ʳ (facsimile in PM 22). **The appearance of Augustine:** *Vita Christiani de Eleemosyna*, 45–6 (*BHL* 1735ab), in Leclercq, 'Le Text complet'. For the Office, see Szendrei, 'On the Prose *Historia* of St. Augustine'.

27   **The cure at Corbie:** *Miracula Sancti Autberti*, 201–3 (*BHL* 863–71). **The first Vivian miracles:** *Translatio Sancti Viviani Episcopi*, 267–8.

28   **Anselm:** *Epistolae*, PL 159: 37. *Historia Compostellana*, i, p. lxvi. **Innocent II:** *Epistolae*, PL 179: 111.

29   **The death of Abbot William:** *Vita Willelmi Abbatis*, in *Vitae Sanctorum Danorum*, ed. Gertz, 339–40 (*BHL* 8908).

30   **The *Salve regina* stories:** These examples are all taken from the rich collection of such tales in Cambridge, Sidney Sussex College MS 95, fols 80ᵛ–81ʳ [II: 68], 81ʳ⁻ᵛ [II: 69], 81ᵛ–82ʳ [II: 71] and 82ʳ⁻ᵛ [II: 72], an early 15th-c. MS from Thorney Abbey in the English Fenlands. Much of the material is from significantly older collections, some from the 12th and 13th cc. (including Caesarius of Heisterbach). Inventory of all stories in M.R. James, *Descriptive Catalogue*, 76–109.

31   **Walden monastery:** text and translation (adapted here) in *The Book of the Foundation of Walden Monastery*, ed. Greenway and Watkiss, 100–1.

32 **Codex Calixtinus:** The manuscript is now available in a superb facsimile. The complete textual contents are edited in *Liber Sancti Jacobi*, ed. Whitehill et al. For contrasted editions of the music, see Van der Werf, *The Oldest Extant Part-Music*, and Karp, *The Polyphony of Saint Martial and Santiago de Compostela*. On some of the attributions see Huglo, 'The Origin of the Monodic Chants'.

33 **Spain and the Capetian lands:** see especially Herbers et al., *España y "Sacro Imperio"*.

34 **Jocelin:** For the rule for the Templars at Troyes, 1128, see *Sacrorum Conciliorum nova et amplissima Collectio*, ed. Mansi, xxi. 359. **Praise for Jocelin:** *Recueil des historiens des Gaules et de la France*, xiii. 328 and 330: 'viros per religione ac sapientia illustres' (the other being Alberic of Bourges) and 'scientia litterarum atque consilii prudentia clarissimum'. **Jocelin ridicules Abelard:** *Recueil des historiens*, xiv. 442 (context in Clanchy, *Abelard*, 91). **Jocelin's letter to Innocent II:** *Recueil des historiens*, xiii. 656. **Foundation of Longpont:** foundation charter in *Gallia Christiana*, x. 111–12.

35 **Mozarabic and Romanesque styles of painting in Spain:** See Walker, *Views of Transition*, 23.

36 **Song of Roland:** *La Chanson de Roland*, ed. and trans. Brault, 2077–82. Translation mine. **Humbert of Romans:** *Opusculum tripartitum*, 200 and 206. On this crusading memoir, see Schein,

Fideles Crucis, 28–36. **Trithemius:** *De Scriptoribus ecclesiasticis*, 120–1. In the 17th c. the Bollandists declared the chronicle a fabrication and expressed their amazement that Trithemius had been deceived (*AS* Januarii ii, 875).

37 **'Music was depicted there':** Pseudo-Turpin, *Karolellus*, ed. Schmidt, 180–2.

Conclusion

1 **Linen pollen:** for specimens from 9th–10th-c. layers of the *villa* of Villers-le-Sec, in the domain of the abbey of St-Denis, see Cuisenier and Guadagnin, *Un Village*, Figure 60. **Parting of the ways:** McCormick, *Origins of the European Economy*, 34, and for spices in Francia, 710–14.

2 **'Omnipotent commander of the world's resources':** Bang, *The Roman Bazaar*, 291. **Amalarius:** *Opera liturgica*, ed. Hanssens, iii, 1:1. Several recent major surveys have greatly illuminated this economic and commercial context: Christie, *From Constantine to Charlemagne* (an archaeology of Italy); Horden and Purcell, *The Corrupting Sea*, 163–6; McCormick, *Origins of the European Economy*; Moorhead, *The Roman Empire Divided*, 248–70; and Wickham, *Framing the Early Middle Ages*, esp. 693–824.

BIBLIOGRAPHY

Primary Sources

Manuscripts

ARRAS
Bibliothèque municipale, MS 657 (Chansonnier d'Arras).

AREZZO
Arezzo, Archivio Capitolare Canonica, MS 88. Archives of bishop Theodaldus and chapter of Arezzo.

BERLIN
Staatsbibliothek Preußischer Kulturbesitz, cod. theol. lat. 276.

CAMBRIDGE
Corpus Christi College, MS 51. Revised edition of Sigebert of Gembloux's chronicle.
Fitzwilliam Museum, MS 86–1972. Fragment of the *Notitia dignitatum*.
Sidney Sussex College, MS 95. Miracles of the Virgin.
Trinity College, MS 368. Isidore of Seville, *Etymologiae*.
University Library, MS Gg.V. 35. Hucbald, *De Institutione musica*.
University Library, MS Kk.5.16. The Moore Bede.

COLOGNE
Erzbischöfliche Diözesan und Dombibliothek, St. Gereon MS A 1 c. 1. Charter of archbishop Sigewin of Cologne.

COLOGNY-GENÈVE
Fondation Martin Bodmer, MS C 74. The *Graduale* of Santa Cecilia in Trastevere.

DARMSTADT
Hessische Landes-und Hochschulbibliothek, MS 1988. Compilation of music theory.

EGMOND-BINNEN
Abdij van Egmond, without shelfmark. Clarmontanus source of *Liber diurnus*.

FLORENCE
Biblioteca Nazionale Centrale, Conventi Soppressi, F. III. 565. Compilation of music theory.

FRIBOURG
Bibliothèque cantonale et universitaire, MS L 322. Noted breviary of the diocèse of Lausanne.

GHENT

Bibliotheek van de Universiteit, MS 92. Autograph manuscript of the *Liber Floridus* of Lambert of Saint Omer.

KLOSTERNEUBURG

Augustiner Chorherrenstift-Bibliothek, MS 1012. Noted antiphoner from Klosterneuburg.

LE MANS

Bibliothèque municipale, 99 (*Gesta Aldrici*).
——224 (*Actus pontificum Cenomannis in urbe degentium*).

LEÓN

Archivo Capitular, Codex 8. Antiphoner.

LIÈGE

Université, MS 12. Saints' Lives and chants for Truiden.

LYON

Bibliothèque municipale, MS 1488 (1464), fols. 198–204, letter of Leidradus of Lyon to Charlemagne.
Archives départementales du Rhône, fonds de Saint-Pierre, 27 H 2, letter of Leidradus of Lyon to Charlemagne.

MECHELEN

Pastoraal Centrum, Grootseminarie MS 4. *Gesta abbatum Trudonensium.*

MONTPELLIER

Archives de l'Hérault, Registre G.20, 219. (Cartulary of the Chapter of Saint Stephen, Agde).
Bibliothèque de la Faculté de Médecine H 136, Salic Law.
——H 149, Dijon Tonary.
——Cod. 412 *Ordo Romanus I.*

MONZA

Museo del Tesoro del Duomo, Inv. No. 88. The Monza cantatorium.

MUNICH

Bayerische Staatsbibliothek, clm 14872. Office of Saint Wolfgang by Hermannus, monk of Reichenau.

NAMUR

Bibliothèque de la Société Archéologique de Namur, Musée des Arts Anciens du Namurois, MS 15, fols. 20^v–25^r. *Vita Beregisi.*

NORWICH

Norfolk County Record Office, Case 24, Shelf B, 1–2. Will of Bishop William de Spufford.

OXFORD

Magdalen College, P [64]. Fragment from a papyrus codex showing part of Matthew 26.

PARIS

Archives nationales, K 4, 6.[1] Charter of Pippin as Mayor of the Palace.

ROUEN

Bibliothèque municipale, MS 141. Lessons for the feast of Saint Remedius of Rouen.
——MS 1411 (U. 64), fols. 63–65ʳ (*Life of Remedius of Rouen*).

SANKT GALLEN

Stiftsbibliothek, MS 359. Cantatorium.
——390–1. Hartker Antiphoner.

SANTIAGO DE COMPOSTELA

Cathedral Library, no shelf mark. Codex Calixtinus.

TRIER

Stadtbibliothek/Stadtarchiv, MS 1379/143. Chants for St. Maigneric.

UTRECHT

Bibliotheek der Rijksuniversiteit, MS 406 (3.J.7). Antiphoner.

VALENCIENNES

Bibliothèque municipale 148 (Aurelian, *Musica Disciplina*).

VATICAN CITY

Biblioteca Apostolica Vaticana, Lat. 4922. *Vita Mathildis.*
——Ottob. Lat. 1354, fol. 55ᵛ (image of Pandulf of Capua).
——Pal. Lat. 187. Bifolium from an eighth-century (? Frankish) copy of the psalms.
——Regin. Lat 886. Theodosian Code.

VIENNA

Österreichische Nationalbibliothek, Cod. 449 (*Codex Carolinus*).
——CPV 795, fol. 90. Alphabets.

WIESBADEN

Hessische Landesbibliothek, MS 2 (Rupertsberg, *c.*1180–90). Hymns and Sequences of
    Hildegard of Bingen.

WOLFENBÜTTEL

Herzog August Bibliothek, Cod. Guelf. 76.14 Aug 2°. Anselmus, *Gesta Episcoporum
    Leodiensium.*

WORCESTER

Cathedral Library, MS F. 160. Monastic antiphoner from Worcester.

ZÜRICH

Zentralbibliothek Rh. Hist. 27 (Reichenau, *Liber memorialis*).

Papyri

(Numbers after Van Haelst, *Catalogue des papyrus littéraires juifs et chrétiens*.)
84, 85, 88, 93, 94, 105, 121–2, 124, 129, 132, 152, 160, 169, 183–202, 220–2, 225, 227–8, 232.

Epigraphy

ILCV
    1265a–b, 1266, 1268–70, 1273–4A, 1277A, 1279, 1281, 1283, 1285, 1286A, 3869.

ICUR

 NS i. 284, 3200, 6098.

 NS iii. 8143, 8165, 8719.

 NS iv. 11746.

CIL

 v. 4847; viii. 453; x. 1193; x. 7252; xi. 1704; xi. 1709; xiii. 2799.

RICG

 i. 19, 90, 106, 134–5, 170, 192–5, 197, 214, 234, 258.

 viii. 16, 23.

 xv. 11, 35, 39, 50, 71–2, 81–2, 87, 92, 95, 97.

Early-Christian Epitaphs from Anatolia, ed. G. J. Johnson (Atlanta, Ga., 1995).

Inscripciones Cristianas de la España Romana y Visigoda, ed. J. Vives (Barcelona, 1942).

Inscriptiones Hispaniae Christianae, ed. A. Hübner (Berlin, 1900).

Les Inscriptions funéraires chrétiennes de Carthage, ed. L. Ennabli, 3 vols (Paris, 1975, 1982 and 1991).

Inscriptions latines de Tunisie, ed. A. Merlin (Paris, 1944).

Recherches archéologiques à Haïdra, ed. N. Duval, 2 vols (Paris, 1975 and 1981).

Recueil des inscriptions grecques-chrétiennes d'Égypte, ed. G. Lefebvre (Cairo, 1907).

Editions of Primary Sources

Abbo of Fleury and Ramsey: Commentary on the Calculus of Victorius of Aquitaine, ed. A. M. Peden (Oxford, 2003).

Acta Apostolorum Apocrypha, ed. R. A. Lipsius and M. Bonnet, 3 vols (Leipzig, 1891–1903).

Acta Archiepiscoporum Rotomagensium, in PL 147: 273–80.

Acta Iohannis, ed. E. Junod and J.-D. Kaestli, 2 vols (CCSA 1–2; Turnhout, 1983).

Acta Pauli, ed. W. Schubart and C. Schmidt (Hamburg, 1936).

Acta Sanctorum Ordinis Sancti Benedicti, ed. J. Mabillon, vols 1–5 in 7 (Paris, 1668–85) and vol. 6 in 2 (Paris, 1701).

The Acts of John, ed. P. J. Lalleman (Leuven, 1998).

The Acts of Thomas, ed. A. F. J. Klijn (Leiden, 2003).

Actus Pontificum, in G. Busson and A. Ledru, 'Actus Pontificum cenomannis in urbe degentium', *Archives historiques du Maine*, 2 (1901).

Adalbert of Bamberg, *Vita Henrici II Imperatoris*, in MGH SS, iv. 792–811.

Adam of Bremen, *Gesta Hammaburgensis Ecclesiae Pontificum*, in *Quellen des 9. und 11. Jahrhunderts*, ed. Trillmich and Buchner.

Adelman of Brescia, *De Viris illustribus sui Temporis*, in PL 143: 1295–8.

Adso of Montier-en-Der, *Miracula S. Bercharii*, AS Octobris VII, 956–1031.

—— *De Ortu et Tempore Antichristi*, ed. D. Verhelst (CCCM 45; Turnhout, 1976).

Agobard of Lyon, *Opera omnia*, ed. I. van Acker (CCCM 52; Turnhout, 1981).

Aimon of Fleury, *Vita Abbonis*, in PL 139: 387–414.

Alberic of Montecassino, *De Rithmis*, in H. H. Davis, 'The "De Rithmis" of Alberic of Monte Cassino: A Critical Edition', *Mediaeval Studies*, 28 (1966), 198–227.

Alcuin, *De Orthographia*, ed. S. Bruni (Florence, 1997).

—— *The Rhetoric of Alcuin and Charlemagne*, trans. W. S. Howell (Princeton, 1941), with a reprint of the Latin text of Halm.

Aldhelm, *Opera*, ed. R. Ehwald (MGH AA xv; Berlin, 1919).

—— *The Poetic Works of Aldhelm*, ed. and trans. M. Lapidge and J. L. Rosier (Cambridge, 1985).

Alfanus, *Carmina*, ed. in A. Lentini and F. Avagliano, *I carmi di Alfano I, Arcivescovo di Salerno*, Miscellanea Cassinese, 38 (Montecassino, 1974).

Alfarano, *De Basilicae Vaticanae antiquissima et nova Structura*, in D. M. Cerrati, 'Tiberii Alpharani de Basilicae Vaticanae Antiquissima et Nova Structura', *Studi e Testi*, 26 (Rome, 1914).

Das älteste Liturgiebuch der lateinischen Kirche, ed. A. Dold ([Beuron in] Hohenzollern, 1936).

Amalarius of Metz, *Opera liturgica*, ed. M. Hanssens, 3 vols (Studi e testi, 138–40; Rome, Biblioteca Apostolica Vaticana, 1948–50).

Ambrose, *De Officiis Ministrorum*, in PL 16: 23–184.

—— *De Virginitate*, in PL 16: 265–302.

—— *Enarratio in Psalmos*, ed. M. Petschenig, as *Sancti Ambrosi Opera*, vi. *Explanatio Psalmorum*, CSEL 64 (Vienna, 1999).

—— *Funeral Orations*, in *Sant'Ambrogio: Le orazioni funebri*, ed. G. Banterle (Milan, 1985).

Ambrosiaster, *Quaestiones Veteris et Novi Testamenti*, ed. A. Souter (Vienna, 1908).

Ammianus Marcellinus, *Res gestae*, in *Ammianus Marcellinus*, ed. J. C. Rolfe, 3 vols (Loeb Classical Library; Cambridge, Mass., 1934–5).

Les Anciennes Versions latines du deuxième livre des Paralipomènes, ed. R. Weber (Vatican City, 1945).

Andreas of Bergamo, *Chronicon*, in MGH SSRL, 220–30.

Andreas of Fleury, *Vie de Gauzlin, abbé de Fleury*, ed. R.-H. Bautier and G. Labory (Paris, 1969).

Anglo-Saxon Litanies of the Saints, ed. M. Lapidge (London, 1991).

Annales Mettenses priores, ed. B. de Simson (Hannover and Lepizig, 1905).

The Annals of St-Bertin, trans. J. Nelson (Manchester, 1991).

Anonymous of Melk, ed. E. Ettlinger in *Der Sog. Anonymus Mellicensis De Scriptoribus ecclesiasticis* (Karlsruhe, 1896).

Anonymus Haserensis de Episcopis Eichstetensibus, in MGH SS, vii. 253–66.

Anselmus, *Gesta Episcoporum Leodiensium*, in PL 139: 1067–1102.

Anthimus, *De Observatione Ciborum ad Theodericum Regem Francorum Epistula*, ed. E. Liechtenhan (Berlin, 1928).

—— *Anthimus: On the Observance of Foods*, trans. M. Grant (Totnes, 1996).

Anthologia Latina, i: *Carmina in Codicibus scripta*, ed. D. R. Shackleton Bailey (Stuttgart, 1982).

Antifonario Visigótico Mozárabe de la Catedral de León, ed. L. Brou and J. Vives, 2 vols (Barcelona and Madrid, 1953–9).

Antiphonaire monastique: XIIe siècle: Codex 601 de la Bibliothèque capitulaire de Lucques (PM 9; Solesmes, 1906).

Antiphonaire monastique: XIIIe siècle: Codex F. 160 de la Bibliothèque de la cathédrale de Worcester (PM 12; Tournai, 1922).

Antiphonale Sarisburiense: A Reproduction in Facsimile of a Manuscript of the

Thirteenth Century, ed. W. H. Frere, 4 vols (London, 1901–15). Reprinted in 6 vols (Farnborough, 1966).

Antiphonarium Mozarabicum de la Catedral de León, Editado por los PP Benedictinos de Silos, ed. P. D. Luciano Serrano (León, 1928).

Antiphonen, ed. L. Dobszay and J. Szendrei, 3 vols (Monumenta Monodica Medii Aevi, 5; Basle, 1999).

The Apocryphal Acts of the Apostles, trans. F. Bovon, A. R. Brock, and C. R. Matthews (Cambridge, Mass., 1999).

The Apocryphal New Testament, trans. J. K. Elliott (Oxford, 1993). Revised edition of following item, with new translations.

The Apocryphal New Testament, trans. M. R. James (Oxford, 1924).

Apostolic Constitutions, in *Les Constitutions apostoliques*, ed. M. Metzger (SC 320, 329 and 336; Paris, 1985–).

—— *Didascalia et Constitutiones Apostolorum*, ed. F. X. Funk (Paderborn, 1905).

The Apostolic Fathers, ed. and trans. B. D. Ehrman, 2 vols (Loeb Classical Library; Cambridge, Mass. and London, 2003).

Arbeo of Freising, *Vita Sancti Emmerami*, in B. Sepp, 'Vita Sancti Emmerami', *Analecta Bollandiana*, 8 (1889), 22–55.

Arnoldus Vohburgensis, *Historia Sancti Emmerammi*, ed. D. Hiley (Institute of Mediaeval Music; Ottawa, Ont., 1996).

Ars Laureshamensis, ed. B. Löfstedt (CCCM 40A; Turnhout, 1977).

Athenagoras, *Legatio pro Christianis*, ed. M. Marcovich (Berlin and New York, 1990).

Augustine, *Confessiones*, in *S. Aureli Augustini Confessionum Libri XIII*, ed. M. Skutella (Stuttgart, 1981).

—— *De Doctrina Christiana*, in *La Doctrine chrétienne [de saint Augustin]. Texte critique du CCSL revu et corrigé*, ed. M. Moreau et al. (Paris, 1997).

—— *De Musica*, ed. G. Marzi (Florence, 1969).

—— *De Quantitate Animae*, in PL 32: 1035–80.

—— *Enarrationes in Psalmos*, ed. E. Dekkers and I. Fraipont (CCSL 38–40; Turnhout, 1956).

—— *Epistolae ex duobus Codicibus nuper in Lucem prolatae*, ed. J. Divjak (CSEL 88; Vienna, 1981).

—— *In Johannis Evangelium Tractatus CXXIV*, ed. R. Willems (CCSL 36; Turnhout, 1954).

—— *Sermones de Vetero Testamento*, ed. C. Lambot (CCSL 41; Turnhout, 1961).

—— *Sermones selecti*, ed. C. Lambot (Brussels, 1950).

'Augustus', *Res gestae divi Augusti: Text, Translation and Commentary*, ed. A. E. Cooley (Cambridge, 2009).

Aurelian of Réôme, *Musica Disciplina*, ed. L. Gushee (CSM 21; Rome, 1975).

Ausgewählte Märtyrerakten. Neubearbeitung der Knopfischen Ausgabe von G. Krüger; vierte Auflage, mit einem Nachtrag von Gerhard Ruhbach, ed. R. Knopf (Tübingen, 1965).

Balther of Säckingen, *Vita Fridolini*, in MGH RMSS, iii. 354–69.

Bede, *Epistola ad Ecgberctum*, in *Venerabilis Baedae*, ed. Plummer, i. 404–23.

—— *Historia Abbatum*, in *Venerabilis Baedae*, ed. Plummer, i. 364–404.

—— *Historia Ecclesiastica*, in *Bede's Ecclesiastical History of the English People*, ed. and trans. B. Colgrave and R. Mynors (Oxford, 1969).

—— *Opera didascalica*, ed. C. W. Jones et al. (Bedae Venerabilis Opera, Pars vi:1–3, CCSL 123; Turnhout, 1975).

—— *Opera exegetica*, ed. D. Hurst and J. E. Hudson (CCSL 119; Turnhout, 1969 and 1983).

—— *Venerabilis Baedae Historiam Ecclesiasticam Gentis Anglorum, Historiam Abbatum, Epistolam ad Ecgberctum una cum Historia Abbatum Auctore anonymo*, ed. C. Plummer, 2 vols (Oxford, 1876).

Benedict of Aniane, *Concordia Regularum*, ed. P. Bonnerue, 2 vols (CCCM 168; Turnhout, 1999).

Benedict of Nursia, *La Règle de saint Benoît*, ed. A. de Vogüé (SC 181–6; Paris, 1971–2).

Benoît, *La Polyptyque du chanoine Benoît*, ed. P. Fabre (Lille, 1889).

Bernard of Clairvaux, *Vita Sancti Malachiæ*, in *Opera*, ed. J. Leclercq et al., 8 vols (Rome, 1957–77), iii, 307–78.

Bernold of Constance, *Chronicon*, in MGH SS, v. 385–467.

—— *Micrologus*, in PL 151: 979–1022.

Beroldus, *Kalendarium et Ordines*, in *Beroldus, sive, Ecclesiae Ambrosianae Mediolanensis Kalendarium et Ordines, Saec. XII ex Codice Ambrosiano*, ed. M. Magistretti (Milan, 1984).

Biblia Sacra iuxta Latinam Vulgatam Versionem, ed. B. Fischer, et al., 2 vols (Stuttgart, 1983).

The Bobbio Missal, ed. E. A. Lowe, 2 vols (Henry Bradshaw Society, 58 (1920) and 61 (1924); repr. in one vol., Woodbridge, 1991).

Boethius, *De Institutione musica*, in *Anicii Manlii Torquati Severini Boetii De Institutione arithmetica Libri Duo, De Institutione musica Libri Quinque*, ed. G. Friedlein (Leipzig, 1867).

—— *Fundamentals of Music*, trans. C. Bower, ed. C. V. Palisca (New Haven and London, 1989).

Boniface, *Ars grammatica*, in *Bonifatii (Vynfreth) Ars grammatica [accedit Ars metrica]*, ed. G. J. Gebauer and B. Löfstedt (CCSL 133b; Turnhout, 1980).

—— *Epistolae*, in *Die Briefe des heiligen Bonifatius*, ed. M. Tangl (Leipzig, 1912).

The Book of the Foundation of St. Bartholomew's Church in London, ed. N. Moore (Early English Text Society, OS 163; Oxford, 1923).

The Book of the Foundation of Walden Monastery, ed. D. Greenway and L. Watkiss (Oxford, 1999).

Das Byzantinische Prokeimena-Repertoire, ed. G. Hintze (Hamburg, 1973).

Caesarius of Arles, *Opera*, ed. D. G. Morin, 2 vols (Maredsous, 1937–42).

—— *Opera*, ed. D. G. Morin, 2 vols (CCSL 103 and 104; Turnhout, 1963).

Die Cambridger Lieder, ed. K. Strecker (Berlin, 1926).

Cantum quem Cisterciensis Ordinis Ecclesiae Cantare . . . ed. F. J. Guentner (CSM 24; Rome, 1974).

Capitula Episcoporum, ed. P. Brommer, R. Pokorny and M. Stratmann, 4 vols (Hannover, 1984–2005).

Carmen de Hastingae Proelio, ed. and trans. C. Morton and H. Muntz (Oxford, 1972).

Cartulaire d'Afflighem, ed. E. De Marneffe (Louvain, 1894).

Cartulaire de l'Abbaye de Gorze: MS. 826 de la Bibliothèque de Metz, ed. A. d'Herbomez (Paris, 1898).

Cartulaire de l'église d'Autun, ed. A. de Charmasse, 2 vols (Paris and Autun, 1865).

Cartulario de San Juan de la Peña, ed. A. U. M. Arteta (Valencia, 1962).

The Cartulary of Flavigny, 717–1113, ed. C. C. Bouchard (Cambridge, Mass., 1991).

The Cartulary of God's House, Southampton, ed. J. M. Kaye (Southampton, 1976).

Cassiodorus, *Institutiones*, ed. R. A. B. Mynors (Oxford, 1937).

—— *Variae*, ed. Th. Mommsen (MGH AA xii; Berlin, 1894).

La Chanson de Roland, ed. and trans. G. J. Brault (University Park and London, 1984).

Chrodegang of Metz, *The Chrodegang Rules: The Rules for the Common Life of the Secular Clergy from the Eighth and Ninth Centuries: Critical Texts with Translations and Commentary*, ed. J. Bertram (Aldershot, 2005).

—— *Regula Canonicorum*, ed. W. Schmitz (Hannover, 1989).

Chromatius of Aquileia, *Sermons*, ed. J. Lemarié, trans. H. Tardif (SC 154 and 164; Paris, 1969 and 1971).

The Chronicle of Hydatius and the Consularia Constantinopolitana, ed. and trans. R. W. Burgess (Oxford, 1993).

Chronique de l'Abbaye de Saint-Trond, ed. C. De Borman, 2 vols (Liège, 1877).

Chronique des abbés de Fontenelle, ed. and trans. P. Pradié (Paris, 1999).

Chronique et cartulaire de l'abbaye de Bergues-St-Winnoc, ed. R. P. A. Pruvost, 2 vols (Bruges, 1875–78).

Claudian, *Claudian*, ed. M. Platnauer, 2 vols (Loeb Classical Library; Cambridge, Mass., 1963).

Claudianus Mamertus, *Opera*, ed. A. Engelbrecht (CSEL XI; Vienna, 1885).

Clement I, First Letter (*I Clement*), in *Apostolic Fathers*, ed. and trans. Ehrman, i. 34–151.

Clement (pseudo-), *II Clement*, in *Apostolic Fathers*, ed. and trans. Ehrman, i. 164–99.

—— *Epistolae binae de Virginitate*, ed. and trans. J. T. Beelen (Louvain, 1856).

Clement of Alexandria, *Le Pédagogue*, ed. and H.-I. Marrou, trans. M. Harl, C. Mondésert and C. Matray (SC 70, 108, 158; Paris, 1960–70).

—— *Opera*, ed. O. Stählin, 4 vols (Leipzig, 1905–60).

Le Codex arménien Jérusalem 121, ed. A. Renoux, 2 vols (Patrologia Orientalis, 35–6; Turnhout, 1969–71).

Codex Carolinus, ed. W. Gundlach (MGH EMKA, i; Berlin, 1892), 469–657.

—— *Codex Epistolaris Carolinus*, ed. F. Unterkircher (Graz, 1962).

Codex Carolinus: Päpstliche Epistolographie im 8. Jahrhundert, ed. A. T. Hack (Päpste und Papsttum, 35; Stuttgart, 2006–7).

Codex diplomaticus Brandenburgensis, ed. A. F. Riedel (Berlin, 1836–69).

Codex diplomaticus Lubecensis, 3 vols (Lübeck, 1843–1908).

Commodian, *Carmina*, ed. J. Martin (CCSL 128; Turnhout, 1960).

Concilia Africae a. 345–a. 525, ed. C. Munier (CCSL 149; Turnhout, 1974).

Concilia Galliae a. 314–a. 506, ed. C. Munier (CCSL 148; Turnhout, 1963).

Concilia Galliae a. 511–a. 695, ed. C. De Clercq (CCSL 148A; Turnhout, 1963).

Concilios Visigóticos y Hispano-Romanos, ed. and trans. J. Vives (Barcelona and Madrid, 1963).

Les Congés d'Arras, ed. P. Ruelle (Paris, 1995).

Councils and Ecclesiastical Documents Relating to Great Britain and Ireland, ed. A. W. Haddan and W. Stubbs, 3 vols (Oxford, 1869–78).

The Critical Edition of Q, ed. J. M. Robinson et al. (Leuven, 2000).

Cronica Sancti Genesii Episcopi, in I. Affò, *Illustrazione di un antico piombo del Museo borgiano di Velletri* (Parma, 1790), 45–56.

Cummian, *Cummian's Letter De Controversia Paschali*, ed. M. Walsh and D. Ó Cróinín (Toronto, 1988).

Cyprian of Carthage, *Epistolae*, in *Sancti Cypriani episcopi Epistularium*, ed. G. F. Diercks (CCSL 3, Turnhout, 1976–99).

Damasus, *see* Ferrua, *The Unknown Catacomb*.

'De Cultu sancti Martini', *Analecta Bollandiana*, 3 (1884), 245–6.

De Fundatione sancti Arnulphi Metensis, in PL 138: 189–96.

De Gestis Episcoporum Autissiodorum, ed. P. Bonnerue et al., in *Les Gestes des évêques d'Auxerre*, i (Paris, 2002).

Didache, in *Apostolic Fathers*, trans. Ehrman, i. 416–43. Also in *La Doctrine des douze apôtres*, ed. and trans. Rordorf and Tuilier.

Discipline générale antique (IVᵉ–IXᵉ s.), i, pt. 2: *Les Canons des synodes particuliers*, ed. P.-P. Joannou (Grottaferrata, 1962).

La Doctrine des douze apôtres, ed. and trans. W. Rordorf and A. Tuilier (SC 248; Paris, 1978).

Documenti per la storia della città di Arezzo, ed. U. Pasqui, 3 vols (Florence, 1899–1937).

Documents sur l'ancienne province de Languedoc, ed. C. Douais, 3 vols (Toulouse, 1901–6).

Donatus, *Ars maior*, ed. in L. Holtz, *Donat et la tradition de l'enseignement grammatical: Étude sur l'Ars Donati et sa diffusion (IVᵉ–IXᵉ siècle), et édition critique* (Paris, 1981).

Eadmer, *De Vita et Conversatione Anselmi Archiepiscopi Cantuariensis*, in *Eadmeri Historia Novorum in Anglia*, ed. M. Rule (Rolls Series; London, 1884), 352–3.

Eberwinus of Trier, *Vita Sancti Magnerici*, AS Julii VI, 183–92.

Eddius Stephanus, *The Life of Wilfrid*, ed. and trans. B. Colgrave (Cambridge, 1927).

Egbert of Liège, *Fecunda Ratis*, ed. E. Voigt (Halle, 1889).

Egeria, *Journal de voyage*, ed. P. Maraval (SC 296; Paris, 1982).

Einhard, *Vita et Gesta Karoli Magni*, ed. and trans. L. Halphen (Paris, 1923).

Ekkehard I, *Vitae Sanctae Wiboradae*, ed. and trans. W. Berschin (Sankt Gallen, 1983).

Ekkehard IV, *Casus Sancti Galli [continuatio]*, in MGH SS, ii. 75–147.

Epiphanius, *Ancoratus* and *Panarion*, ed. K. Holl in *Epiphanius*, 2nd edn, ed. J. Dummer (Berlin 1980).

Epistle of Barnabas, in *The Apostolic Fathers*, ed. and trans. Ehrman, ii. 12–21.

Epistola Widonis, in J. T. Gilchrist, 'Die *Epistola Widonis* oder Pseudo-Paschalis: Der erweiterte Text', *Deutsches Archiv für Erforschung des Mittelalters*, 37 (1981), 576–604.

Epistolae Romanorum Pontificum genuinae et quae ad eos scriptae sunt, ed. A. Thiel, 2 vols (Braunsberg, 1867–68 ; repr. Hildesheim and New York, 1974).

Epistulae Austrasicae, ed. W. Gundlach (CCSL 117; Turnhout, 1957).

Ermoldus Nigellus, *Poem on Louis the Pious*, in *Poème sur Louis le Pieux*, ed. and trans. E. Faral (Paris, 1932).

Eugippius, *Vita Sancti Severini*, in MGH AA i/ii. 1–30.

Eusebius of Caesarea, *The Ecclesiastical History*, trans. K. Lake, J. E. L. Oulton and H. J. Lawlor, 2 vols (Loeb Classical Library; London, 1926 and 1932).

Exordium Affligemensis, in MGH SS, ix. 407–17 (as *Chronicon Affligemense*).

Expositio antiquae Liturgiae Gallicanae, ed. E. C. Ratcliff (Henry Bradshaw Society, 98; London, 1971).

Expositio totius Mundi et Gentium, ed. and trans. J. Rougé (Paris, 1966).

Expositiones in Micrologum Guidonis Aretini, ed. J. Smits van Waesberghe (Amsterdam, 1957).

Felix, *Life of Saint Guthlac*, ed. and trans. B. Colgrave (Cambridge, 1956).

Firenze, Biblioteca Nazionale Centrale, Conventi Soppressi, F. III. 565, ed. A. Santosuosso (Publications of Mediaeval Musical Manuscripts, 19; Ottawa, Ont., 1994).

Fredegar, *The Fourth Book of the Chronicle of Fredegar*, ed. and trans. J.M. Wallace-Hadrill (London, 1960).

—— *Fredegarii et aliorum Chronica*, ed. B. Krusch (MGH SSRM, ii; Hannover, 1888).

Frisi, A.F., *Memorie storiche della città di Monza, compilate sull'opera del Anton-Francesco Frisi e continuate dal Giuseppe Marimonti* (Monza, 1841).

Gallia Christiana in provincias ecclesiasticas distributa, 16 vols (Paris, 1715–1865).

Galvano de Levanto, *Liber de Recuperatione Terrae sanctae*, in C. Kohler, 'Traité du recouvrement de la Terre Sainte adressé, vers l'an 1295, à Philippe le Bel par Galvano de Levanto, médecin génois', *Revue de l'Orient Latin*, 6 (1898), 343–69.

Gennadius, *Liber de Viris inlustribus*, in R.E. Cushing, 'Hieronymus. *Liber de viris inlustribus* – Gennadius. *Liber de viris inlustribus*', *Texte und Untersuchungen zur Geschichte der altchristlichen Literatur*, 14 (1896), 1–112.

Gerbert d'Aurillac, *Correspondance*, ed. P. Riché and J.P. Callu, 2 vols (Paris, 1993).

Gesta Abbatum Lobbiensium, in MGH, SS xxi. 307–33.

Gesta Abbatum Trudonensium, in MGH, SS x. 213–448, reprinted in PL 173: 11–434.

Gesta Aldrici, in MGH SS, xv. 304–27.

Gesta Hrodberti, in MGH SSRM, vi. 140–62.

Les Gestes des évêques d'Auxerre, ed. P. Bonnerue et al., i (Paris, 2002).

The Gnostic Scriptures: A New Translation, trans. B. Layton (New York and London, 1995).

Gothische Literaturdenkmäler, ed. E. Stutz (Stuttgart, 1966).

Graduale Triplex (Abbaye de Saint-Pierre de Solesmes, 1979).

Grammatici Latini, ed. H. Keil, 8 vols (Leipzig, 1844–93).

Greek Musical Writings, trans. A. Barker, 2 vols (Cambridge, 1984 and 1989).

Gregory the Great, *Dialogues*, ed. and trans. A. de Vogüé (SC 251, 260 and 265; Paris, 1978–80).

—— *Registrum Epistolarum*, ed. P. Ewald and L.M. Hartmann (MGH E, 102; Berlin, 1891–9).

—— *Registrum Epistularum*, ed. D. Norberg, 2 vols (CCSL 140; Turnhout, 1982).

Gregory of Nyssa, *Vie de sainte Macrine*, ed. P. Maraval (SC 178; Paris, 1971).

Gregory of Tours, *De Virtutibus Sancti Martini Episcopi*, in MGH SSRM, i. 585–661.

—— *Gloria Confessorum*, in MGH SSRM, i/ii. 744–820.

—— *Liber Vitae Patrum*, in MGH SSRM, i/ii. 661–744.

—— *Life of the Fathers*, trans. E. James (Liverpool, 1985).

—— *Opera*, ed. W. Arndt and B. Krusch (MGH SSRM, i; Hannover, 1885).

Grimaldi, G., *Descrizione della Basilica Antica di S. Pietro in Vaticano: Codice Barberini Latino 2733*, ed. R. Niggl (Vatican City, 1972).

Grimlaicus, *Regula Solitariorum*, in PL 103: 573–664.

Grotans, Anna A, *Reading in Medieval St. Gall* (Cambridge, 2006)

Guido of Arezzo, *Epistola Widonis*, in *Libelli de Lite Imperatorum*, ed. Thaner, i. 1–17.

—— *Micrologus*, ed. J. Smits van Waesberghe (CSM 4; Rome, 1955).

——*Opera* [*sc. de Musica*], in *Guido d'Arezzo's* Regule Rithmice, Prologus in Antiphonarium *and* Epistola ad Michahelem: *A Critical Text and Translation*, ed. and trans. D. Pesce (The Institute of Mediaeval Music, Musicological Studies, 73; Ottawa, 1999).

——*'Regulae Rhythmicae'*, ed. J. Smits van Waesberghe and E. Vetter (DMA A IV; Buren, 1985).

——*Tres Tractatuli Guidonis Aretini: Guidonis 'Prologus in Antiphonarium'*, ed. J. Smits van Waesberghe (DMA A. III; Buren, 1975).

Hariulf, *Chronique de l'Abbaye de Saint-Riquier*, ed. F. Lot (Paris, 1894).

Helinand of Froidmont, *Chronicon*, in PL 212: 771–1082.

Helmhold, *Chronica Sclavorum*, in MGH SS, xxi. 1–99.

Henry of Livonia, *The Chronicle of Henry of Livonia*, trans. J. A. Brundage (Madison, 1961).

Hermannus Contractus, *Historia Sancti Wolfgangi Episcopi Ratisbonensis*, ed. D. Hiley (Institute of Mediaeval Music; Ottawa, Ont., 2002).

Hermas, *The Shepherd*, in C. Osiek, *Shepherd of Hermas* (Minneapolis, 1999).

Hierarchia ecclesiastica Orientalis: Series Episcoporum Ecclesiarum Christianarum Orientalium, ed. G. Fedalto, 2 vols (Padua, 1988).

Hildefonsus of Toledo, *El 'De viris illustribus' de Ildefonso de Toledo*, ed. C. C. Merino (Acta Salmanticensia, Filosofía y letras, 65; Salamanca, 1972).

Hildegard of Bingen, *Abbess Hildegard of Bingen (1098–1179): Sequences and Hymns*, ed. C. Page (Newton Abbot, 1982).

Hildemar, *Epistola ad Ursum Beneventanum Episcopum de recta legendi Ratione*, in PL 106: 395–8.

——*Expositio Regulae Sancti Benedicti*, in *Vita et Regula SS. P. Benedicti una cum Expositione Regulæ a Hildemaro tradita*, ed. R. Mittermüller (Regensburg, 1880).

Hincmar, *De Ordine Palatii*, ed. and trans. M. Prou (Paris, 1885).

'Hippolytus', *Apostolic Tradition*, in *La Tradition apostolique de saint Hippolyte: Essai de reconstitution*, ed. B. Botte (Münster, 1963).

——*The Canons of Hippolytus, with a Translation by Carol Bebawi*, ed. P. F. Bradshaw (Bramcote, 1987).

——*Refutatio omnium Haeresium*, ed. M. Marcovich (Berlin, 1986).

——*The Treatise on the Apostolic Tradition of St. Hippolytus of Rome*, ed. G. Dix, reissued with corrections, preface and a bibliography by Henry Chadwick (London, 1991).

Historia Abbatum, in Bede, *Venerabilis Baedae*, ed. Plummer, 388–404.

Historia Augusta, in *Histoire Auguste*, trans. A. Chastagnol (Paris 1994) (includes Latin text).

Historia Compostellana, ed. E. F. Rey (CCCM 70; Turnhout, 1988).

Historia Custodum Aretinorum, in MGH SS, xxx/ii. 1468–82.

Historia Sancti Florentii Salmurensis, in *Chroniques des églises d'Anjou*, ed. P. Marchegay and E. Mabille (Paris, 1869), 181–328.

Historia Silense, ed. J. Pérez de Urbel and A. G. Ruiz-Zorrilla (Madrid, 1959).

The History of the Franks, trans. L. Thorpe (Harmondsworth, 1977).

Holtz, L., *Donat et la tradition de l'enseignement grammatical: Étude sur l'Ars Donati et sa diffusion (IVᵉ–IXᵉ siècle), et édition critique* (Paris, 1981).

Honorat de Marseille, *La Vie d'Hilaire d'Arles*, ed. and trans. P.-A. Jacob (SC 404; Paris, 1995).

Hucbald of Saint-Amand, *Opera*, in *L'Œuvre musicale d'Hucbald de Saint-Amand*, ed. Y. Chartier ([Montréal], 1995).

Hucbald, Guido and John on Music, trans. W. Babb, ed. C. V. Palisca (New Haven and London, 1978).

Humbert of Romans, *Opusculum tripartitum*, in *Fasciculus Rerum expetendarum et fugiendarum*, ed. E. Brown (London, 1690).

Ignatius, St, *Letters*, in *The Apostolic Fathers*, ed. and trans. Ehrman, i. 202–321.

Index Britanniae Scriptorum: John Bale's Index of British and Other Writers, ed. R. L. Poole and M. Bateson, reissue with new introduction (Cambridge, 1990).

Innocent I, *Letter to Decentius of Gubbio*, in M. F. Connell, *Church and Worship in Fifth-Century Rome: The Letter of Innocent I to Decentius of Gubbio* (Cambridge, 2002).

—— *La Lettre du pape Innocent Ier à Décentius de Gubbio (19 mars 416): Texte critique, traduction et commentaire*, ed. R. Cabié (Bibliothèque de le Revue d'Histoire Ecclésiastique, 58; Louvain, 1973).

Instituta Honorancie Civitatis Papie, in MGH SS, xxxi/ii. 1444–60.

Irenaeus, *Against Heresies*, in *Irénée de Lyon: Contre les Hérésies*, ed. A. Rousseau and L. Doutreleau (SC 263–4; Paris, 1979–82).

Isidore of Seville, *De ecclesiasticis Officiis*, ed. M. C. Lawson (CCSL 113; Turnhout, 1989).

—— *De Fide catholica ex Veteri et Novo Testamento contra Judeos*, in PL 83: 449–538.

—— *El 'De viris illustribus' de Isidoro de Sevilla*, ed. C. C. Merino (Salamanca, 1964).

—— *Epistolae*, in *The Letters of Isidore of Seville*, trans. G. B. Ford (Amsterdam, 1970).

—— *Etymologiae*, in *Isidori Hispalensis Episcopi Etymologiarum sive Originum*, ed. W. J. Lindsay, 2 vols (Oxford, 1911).

—— *Historia Gothorum* and *De Origine Gothorum*, in *Las Historias de los Godos, Vandalos y Suevos de Isidoro de Sevilla*, ed. C. Rodriguez Alonso (León, 1975).

Itineraria et alia geographica, ed. P. Geyer, 2 vols (CCSL 175–6; Turnhout, 1965).

Jerome, *Commentariorum in Epistolam ad Ephesios Libri Tres*, in PL 26: 439–554.

—— *Epistulae*, in *Sancti Eusebii Hieronymi Epistulae*, ed. I. Hilberg (CSEL 54–6; Vienna, 1910–18); new enlarged edn with indexes (Vienna, 1996).

—— *Liber de Viris inlustribus*, in R. E. Cushing, 'Hieronymus. *Liber de viris inlustribus* – Gennadius. *Liber de viris inlustribus*', *Texte und Untersuchungen zur Geschichte der altchristlichen Literatur*, 14 (1896), 1–112.

Jiménez de Rada, Rodrigo, *Historia de Rebus Hispaniae sive Historia Gothica*, ed. J. F. Valverde (CCCM 72; Turnhout, 1987).

John of Affligem, *De Musica cum Tonario*, ed. J. Smits van Waesberghe (CSM 1; Rome, 1950).

John of Biclar, *Chronicon*, in *Victoris Tunnunensis Chronicon cum Reliquiis ex Consularibus Caesaraugustanis et Iohannis Biclarensis Chronicon*, ed. C. Cardelle de Hartmann; *Commentaria historica ad Consularia Caesaraugustana et ad Iohannis Biclarensis Chronicon*, ed. R. Collins (CCSL 173A; Turnhout, 2001).

John of Gorze, *Vita Chrodegangi Episcopi Mettensis*, in MGH SS, x. 552–72.

John Chrysostom, *Adversus Judaeos*, in PG 48: 839–942.

John the Deacon (Naples), *Gesta Episcoporum Neapolitanorum*, in MGH SSRL, 424–36.
John the Deacon (Rome), *Vita Sancti Gregorii Magni*, in PL 75: 59–242.

Jordanes, *Getica*, in *Jordanis Romana et Getica*, ed. Th. Mommsen (MGH AA v/i; Berlin 1882).

Justin Martyr, *Apologiae pro Christianis*, ed. M. Marcovich (New York, 1994).

——*Apologie pour les Chrétiens*, ed. and trans. C. Munier (Fribourg, 1995).

——*Apologies*, ed. and trans. A. Wartelle (Paris, 1987).

——*Dialogue avec Tryphon*, ed. and trans. P. Bobichon (Fribourg, 2003).

—— *The First and Second Apologies*, ed. L. W. Barnard (New York, 1997).

Die Kapitulariensammlung des Ansegis, ed. G. Schmitz (Hannover, 1996).

Der karolingische Tonar von Metz, ed. W. Lipphardt (Münster, 1965).

Karolus Magnus et Leo Papa: Ein Paderborner epos vom Jahre 799, ed. H. Baumann et al. (Paderborn, 1966).

Die Konzilsordines des Früh- und Hochmittelalters, ed. H. Schneider (MGH OCC; Hannover, 1996).

Kyrillos von Skythopolis, ed. E. Schwartz (Leipzig, 1939).

Lactantius, *De Mortibus Persecutorum*, in *L. Caeli Firmiani Lactanti Opera Omnia*, ii/i (CSEL 27, Prague, etc., 1893), 171–238.

Lambert, *Lamberti parvi Annales*, in MGH SS, xvi. 645–50.

Landulphus Senior, *Historiae Libri Quatuor*, ed. A. Cutolo, in L. A. Muratori, *Rerum Italicarum Scriptores*, iv, rev. and corr. edn (Bologna, 1942).

Laurence of Amalfi, *Opera*, ed. F. Newton (MGH, Die Deutschen Geschichtsquellen des Mittelalters: Quellen zur Geistesgeschichte des Mittelalters, 7; Weimar, 1973).

Leges Visigothorum, ed. K. Zeumer (MGH LNG, i; Hannover, 1902).

Leo of Ostia, *Life of Saint Mennas*, in 'Vita Sancti Mennatis', ed. G. Orlandi, *Istituto Lombardo, Accademia di scienze e lettere: Rendiconti, Classe di lettere e scienze morali e storiche*, 97 (1963), 467–90.

Létald of Saint-Mesmin-de-Micy, *Vita Sancti Juliani*, in PL 137: 781–96.

Letter to Diognetus, in *A Diognète*, ed. H.-I. Marrou (SC 33; Paris, 1951).

Leontios, *Life of Gregory of Girgenti*, in *Leontios Presbyteros von Rom: Das Leben des heiligen Gregorios von Agrigent*, ed. A. Berger (Berlin, 1995).

Lex Salica, ed. K. A. Eckhardt (MGH LNG; Hannover, 1969).

Libelli de Lite Imperatorum et Pontificum Saeculis XI et XII conscripti, ed. F. Thaner, 3 vols (Hannover, 1891–7).

Liber diurnus Romanorum Pontificum, ed. H. Foerster (Bern, 1958).

Liber Sacramentorum Engolismensis, ed. P. Saint-Roch (CCSL 159; Turnhout, 1987).

Liber Sacramentorum Gellonensis, ed. A. Dumas, 2 vols (CCSL 159; Turnhout, 1981).

Liber Sancti Jacobi: Codex Calixtinus, ed. W. M. Whitehill, J. Carro García, and G. Prado (Santiago de Compostela, 1944).

Licinianus of Cartagena, *Epistolae*, in *Liciniano de Cartagena y sus Cartas*, ed. J. Madoz (Madrid, 1948).

Life of Benedict of Aniane, trans. A. Cabaniss, in *Soldiers of Christ*, ed. T. Noble and T. Head (London, 1995), 213–54.

Liutprand of Cremona, *Opera omnia*, ed. P. Chiesa (CCCM 156; Turnhout, 1998).

The Lives of the Eighth-Century Popes, trans. R. Davis (Liverpool, 1992).

The Livonian Rhymed Chronicle, trans. J. C. Smith and W. L. Urban (Bloomington, Ind., 1977).

Lupus of Ferrières, *Epistulae*, ed. P. K. Marshall (Leipzig, 1984).

Mallius, Petrus, *Basilicae veteris Vaticanae Descriptio*, AS Junii VII, 37–56.

Marius d'Avenches, *La Chronique de Marius d'Avenches*, ed. J. Favrod (Lausanne, 1991).

Martianus Capella, *De Nuptiis Philologiae et Mercurii*, ed. C. E. Lutz (Leiden, 1962–5).

Martin of Braga, *Opera omnia*, ed. C. W. Barlow (New Haven, 1950).

Melito of Sardis, *Sur la Pâque*, ed. and trans. D. Perler (SC 123; Paris, 1966).

Methodius of Olympus, *The Banquet*, in *Méthode d'Olympe: Le Banquet*, ed. and trans. H. Musurillo and V.-H. Debidour (SC 95; Paris, 1963).

—— *L'inno del Simposio di S. Metodio Martire*, ed. M. Pellegrino (Turin, 1958).

Miracula Sancti Autberti, in *Analecta Bollandiana*, 19 (1900), 198–212.

Miracula Sancti Baboleni Abbatis Fossatensis, *AS* Junii V, 181–3.

The Mishnah: A New Translation, trans. J. Neusner (New Haven, 1988).

Missale Francorum, ed. L. C. Mohlberg (Rome, 1957).

Missale Gallicanum Vetus, ed. L. C. Mohlberg (Rome, 1958).

Missale Gothicum, ed. L. C. Mohlberg (Rome, 1961).

Missale Gothicum, ed. E. Rose (CCSL 159D; Turnhout, 2005).

Monumenta ad Neapolitani Ducatus Historiam pertinentia quae partim nunc primum, partim iterum Typis vulgantur, ed. B. Capasso, 2 vols (Naples, 1881–92).

Die Moselgedichte des Decimus Magnus Ausonius und des Venantius Fortunatus, ed. C. Hosius (Marburg, 1926).

Murethach, *In Donati Artem maiorem Murethach*, ed. L. Holtz (CCCM 40; Turnhout, 1977).

Musica et Scolica Enchiriadis una cum aliquibus Tractatulis adiunctis, ed. H. Schmid (Munich, 1981).

New Testament Apocrypha, ed. W. Schneemelcher, trans. R. M. Wilson, 2 vols (London, 1963–5).

Niceta of Remesiana, *De Psalmodiae Bono*, in C. H. Turner, 'Niceta of Remesiana II', *Journal of Theological Studies*, 24 (1923), 225–52.

Nocturnale Romanum: Antiphonale sacrosanctæ Romanæ Ecclesiæ pro nocturnis Horis (Rome, 1997–2002).

Notker Balbulus, *Gesta Karoli Magni*, ed. H. F. Haefele (Berlin, 1962).

Odorannus of Sens, *Opera omnia*, ed. R.-H. Bautier et al. (Paris, 1972).

Olbert of Gembloux, *Miracula Veroni*, in MGH SS, xv/ii. 749–53.

Olympiodorus, *Frammenti storici: Olimpiodoro Tebano. Introduzione, traduzione e note con in appendice il testo greco*, ed. R. Maisano (Naples, 1979).

Opus Caroli Regis contra Synodum (Libri Carolini), ed. A. Freeman and P. Meyvaert (MGH Co II, Supplementum I; Hannover, 1998).

Oracional Visigótico, ed. J. Vives (Barcelona, 1946).

Orderic Vitalis, *The Ecclesiastical History*, ed. and trans. M. Chibnall, 6 vols (Oxford, 1969–80). Cited by edition volume number.

Les Ordines Romani du haut moyen âge, ed. M. Andrieu (Spicilegium Sacrum Lovaniense, 11, 23–4, 28; Louvain, 1931–56).

Origen, *Contra Celsum*, in *Origène: Contre Celse*, ed. M. Borret (SC 132, 136, 147, 150 and 227; Paris, 1967–76).

—— *Contra Celsum*, ed. and trans. H. Chadwick (Cambridge, 1980).

(?)Osbern, *De Musica*, in *Codex Oxoniensis Bibl. Bodl. Rawl. C 270*, ed. J. Smits van Waesberghe (Buren, 1979).

—— *Life of Ælfheah*, *AS* Aprilis II, 631–41.

Otloh of St. Emmeram, *Liber de temptatione cuiusdam monachi*, ed. and trans. S. Gäbe (Bern, etc., 1999).

Passio Perpetuae, in *The Passion of SS. Perpetua and Felicity MM: A New Edition and Translation . . . together with the Sermons of S. Augustine upon these Saints*, ed. and trans. W. H. Shewring (London, 1931).

Passio Praiecti, in MGH SSRM, v. 219–48.

Passio SS. Dativi, in P. F. De' Cavalieri, 'Passio SS. Dativi . . .', *Studi e Testi*, 65 (Vatican City, 1935), 47–71.

Patres Apostolici, ed. F. X. Funk, 2nd enlarged edn (Tübingen, 1901).

Paul the Deacon, *Libellus de Ordine Episcoporum Mettensium*, in PL 95: 699–710.

Pelayo, Don, *Crónica del Obispo Don Pelayo*, ed. B. Sánchez Alonso (Madrid, 1924).

The Periplus Maris Erythraei, ed. L. Casson (Princeton, 1989).

Peter Damian, *De sancta Simplicitate Scientiae Inflanti anteponenda*, PL 145: 695–704.

—— *Epistolae*, in *Die Briefe des Petrus Damiani*, ed. K. Reindel (MGH BdK, 4; Munich, 1983–93).

—— *Sermones*, ed. G. Lucchesi (CCCM, 57; Turnhout, 1983).

—— *Vita Beati Romualdi*, ed. G. Tabacco (Rome, 1957).

Peter the Deacon, *Liber de Viris illustribus Cassinensibus*, in PL 173: 1009–62.

Philip of Clairvaux, *Miracula [Bernardi] in Itinere Germanico patrata*, in PL 185: 369–86.

Philo of Alexandria, *De Vita contemplativa*, ed. F. Daumas, trans. P. Miquel (Paris, 1963).

Pliny, *Letters and Panegyrics*, ed. B. Radice, 2 vols (Loeb Classical Library; Cambridge, Mass., 1969).

Pommersches Urkundenbuch (Stettin, 1868–).

Primera Crónica General de España que Mandó Componer Alfonso el Sabio y se Continuaba bajo Sancho IV en 1289, ed. R. Menéndez Pidal, 2 vols (Madrid, 1955).

Priscus, in *The Fragmentary Classicising Historians of the Later Roman Empire: Eunapius, Olympiodorus, Priscus and Malchus*, trans. R. C. Blockley, 2 vols (Liverpool, 1981–3).

Procopius, *Gothic War*, in *Procopius*, ed. and trans. H. B. Dewing and G. Downey, 7 vols (Loeb Classical Library; Cambridge, Mass., and London, 1940, repr. 1961).

Pseudo-Augustine, *Altercatio Sancti Augustini cum Pascentio Arriano*, in PL 33: 1156–62.

—— *Quaestiones Veteris et Novi Testamenti CXXVII*, ed. A. Souter (CSEL 50; Vienna, 1908).

Pseudo-Turpin, *Karolellus atque Pseudo-Turpini Historia Karoli*, ed. P. G. Schmidt (Stuttgart, 1996).

Die Quaestiones in Musica, ed. R. Steglich (Leipzig, 1911).

Quellen des 9. und 11. Jahrhunderts zur Geschichte der Hamburgischen Kirche und des Reiches, ed. W. Trillmich and R. Buchner (Darmstadt, 1961).

Radbert, *Epitaphium Arsenii*, in E. Dummler, 'Radbert's *Epitaphium Arsenii*', *Abhandlungen der Königlichen Akademie der Wissenschaften zu Berlin*, 1899–1900 (1900), 3–98.

Recueil des actes des comtes de Pontieu (1026–1279), ed. C. Brunel (Paris, 1930).

Recueil des historiens des croisades, 14 vols (Paris, 1841–1881; repr. Farnborough, 1967).

Recueil des historiens des Gaules et de la France, 24 vols (Paris, 1840–1904; repr. Farnborough, 1967–78).

Regesta Chartarum Italiae, ii: *Regesta di Camaldoli*, ed. L. Schiaparelli and E. F. Baldasseroni (Rome, 1907).

Reiner of St Lawrence, *De claris Scriptoribus Monasterii sui*, in PL 204: 15–40.

Remigius of Auxerre, *Commentum in Martianum Capellam*, ed. C. E. Lutz, 2 vols (Leiden, 1962–5).

Rhetores Latini Minores, ed. C. Halm (Leipzig, 1863).

Richer, *Gesta Senoniensis Ecclesiae*, in MGH SS, xxv. 249–345.

Richer, *Historia Francorum*, in *Richer: Histoire de France*, ed. and trans. R. Latouche, 2 vols (Paris, 1930 and 1937).

Riga's ältere Geschichte in Übersicht, Urkunden und alten Aufzeichnungen, ed. K. E. Napiersky (Monumenta Livoniae Antiquae, 4; Riga, 1844).

Robinson, Robert, *The Phonetic Writings of Robert Robinson*, ed. E. J. Dobson (Early English Text Society, Original Series, 238; Oxford, 1957).

Rodericus Ximeniez de Rada, *Historia de rebus Hispaniae sive Historia Gothica*, ed. J. F. Valverde, CCCM 72 (Turnhout, 1987).

Rudolf of Sint Truiden et al., *Gesta Abbatum Trudonensium*, in *Chronique de l'Abbaye de Saint-Trond*, ed. De Borman.

Rufinus, *Historia ecclesiastica*, in PL 21: 461–540.

Rupert of Deutz, *De Sancta Trinitate et Operibus eius*, ed. H. Haacke (CCCM 24; Turnhout, 1972).

Rupertus, *Chronicon Sancti Laurentii Leodiensis*, in MGH SS, viii. 261–79.

The Russian Primary Chronicle, ed. and trans. S. H. Cross and O. P. Sherbowitz-Wetzor (Cambridge, Mass., 1953).

Le Sacramentaire gélasien (Vaticanus Reginensis 316): Sacramentaire presbytéral en usage dans les titres romains au VIIe siècle, ed. A. Chavasse (Tournai, 1958).

Sacrorum Conciliorum nova et amplissima Collectio, ed. G. D. Mansi, 56 vols (Paris, 1759–98).

Salvian of Marseilles, *Libri que supersunt*, ed. C. Halm (MGH AA i/i; Berlin, 1887).

Salzburger Formelbücher und Briefe aus Tassilonischer und Karolinischer Zeit, ed. B. Bischoff (Munich 1973).

Sanctuarium seu Vitae Sanctorum, ed. B. Mombritius, 2 vols (*c.*1480; repr. Paris, 1910, repr. again, New York, 1978).

Sedulius Scottus, *In Donati Artem maiorem*, ed. B. Löfstedt (CCCM 40B; Turnhout, 1977).

Septuaginta: id est Vetus Testamentum Graece iuxta LXX Interpretes, ed. A. Rahlfs, 2 vols (Stuttgart, 1935).

Series Abbatum Flaviniacensium, in MGH SS, viii. 502–3.

Sidonius Apollinaris, *Epistolae*, in Poems *and Letters*, ed. and trans. W. B. Anderson, 2 vols (Loeb Classical Library; Cambridge, Mass., 1963–5).

Sigebert of Gembloux, *Catalogus Sigeberti Gemblacensis Monachi De Viris illustribus*, ed. R. Witte (Bern, 1974).

—— *Chronica cum Continuationibus*, ed. D. K. C. Bethmann (MGH SS, vi; Hannover, 1844).

—— *Chronographiae Auctarium Affligemense*, ed. P. Gorissen (Brussels, 1952).

—— *Gesta Abbatum Gemblacensium*, in PL 160: 591–622.

—— *Vita Guicberti*, in PL 160: 661–76.

Source Readings in Music History, trans. O. Strunk (New York, 1950); relevant material revised by J. McKinnon as *Source Readings in Music History*, ii: *The Early Christian Period and the Latin Middle Ages* (New York and London, 1998).

Sozomen, *Historia ecclesiastica*, in *Sozomène: Histoire ecclésiastique*, ed. J. Bidez et al. (SC 396 and 418; Paris, 1983 and 1996).

Les Statuta Ecclesiae antiqua, ed. C. Munier (Paris, 1960).

Statuts d'Hôtels-Dieu et de léproseries, ed. L. Le Grand (Paris, 1901).

Strabo, Walafrid, *Libellus de Exordiis et Incrementis quarundam in Observationibus ecclesiasticis Rerum*, in *Walahfrid Strabo's* Libellus de Exordiis et Incrementis Quarundam in Observationibus Ecclesiasticis Rerum: *A Translation and Liturgical Commentary*, ed. and trans. A. L. Harting-Corrêa (Leiden, 1996).

Suetonius, *Suetonius*, ed. T. E. Page, trans. J. C. Rolfe (London, 1912).

The Summa Musicae: *A Thirteenth-Century Manual for Singers*, ed. C. Page (Cambridge, 1991).

Tabulae Vindolandenses II, ed. A. K. Bowman, J. D. Thomas, and J. Adams (London, 1994).

Tatwin, *Opera omnia*, ed. M. de Marco and F. Glorie (CCSL 133 and 133A; Turnhout, 1968).

Tertullian, *Adversus Marcionem*, trans. and ed. E. Evans (Oxford, 1972).

—— *De Anima*, ed. J. H. Waszink (Amsterdam, 1947).

—— *De Oratione*, in *Tertullian's Tract on the Prayer*, ed. and trans. Evans.

—— *De Praescriptione Haereticorum, Ad Martyras, Ad Scapulam*, ed. T. H. Bindley (Oxford, 1893).

—— *De Resurrectione Carnis*, in *Tertullian's Treatise on the Resurrection*, ed. and trans. Evans.

—— *Exhortation à la chasteté*, ed. C. Moreschini and J.-C. Fredouille (SC 319; Paris, 1985).

—— *Opera*, 2 vols (CCSL 1; Turnhout, 1954).

—— *Tertullian's Tract on the Prayer*, ed. and trans. E. Evans (London, 1953).

—— *Tertullian's Treatise on the Resurrection*, ed. and trans. E. Evans (London, 1960).

The Testament of Our Lord, trans. J. Cooper and A. J. Maclean (Edinburgh, 1902).

The Testamentum Domini: *A Text for Students*, trans. G. Sperry-White (Bramcote, 1991).

Textes grecs inédits de la collection papyrologique de Genève, ed. J. Nicole (Geneva, 1909).

Thesaurus Palaeohibernicus: A Collection of Old-Irish Glosses, Scholia, Prose, and Verse, ed. W. Stokes and J. Strachan (Cambridge, 1901–3).

Thietmar of Merseburg, *Die Chronik des Bischofs Thietmar von Merseburg und ihre Korveier Überarbeitung*, ed. R. Holtzmann (MGH SRG NS 9; Berlin, 1955).

Tortarius, Ralph, *Miracula Sancti Benedicti*, in *Les Miracles de saint Benoît*, ed. E. de Certain (Paris, 1858).

Translatio Sancti Viviani Episcopi, in *Analecta Bollandiana*, 8 (1889), 256–77.

Trithemius, J., *Annalium Hirsaugensium complectans Historiam Franciae et Germaniae* (Sankt Gallen, 1690).

—— *De Scriptoribus ecclesiasticis* (Paris, 1512).

Die Urkunden der Deutschen Könige und Kaiser, iv: Die Urkunden Konrads II, ed. H. Bresslau (MGH DRIG, iv; Hannover and Leipzig, 1909).

Die Urkunden der Merowinger, ed. T. Kölzer et al. (MGH DRF [*e stirpe Merowingica*]; Hannover, 2001).

Utrecht, Bibliotheek der Rijksuniversiteit MS 406 (3.J.7), ed. I. de Loos, C. Downey and R. Steiner (Institute of Mediaeval Music, Publications of Musical Manuscripts, 21; Ottawa, Ont., 1997).

Venantius Fortunatus, *Opera*, MGH AA, iv/1. Edition of verse, with French translation and commentary, in *Venance Fortunat: Poèmes*, ed. M. Reydellet, 2 vols (Paris, 1994).

Das Verbrüderungsbuch der Abtei Reichenau, ed. J. Autenrieth, D. Geuenich and

K. Schmid (MGH LMN, NS 1; Hannover, 1979).

Vetus Testamentum Graece iuxta LXX Interpretes, ed. A. Rahlfs (Stuttgart, 1935).

Victor of Vita, *Historia Persecutionis Wandalicae*, in MGH AA, iii/i, 1–58.

—— *History of the Vandal Persecution*, trans. J. Moorhead (Liverpool, 1992).

Vigilius of Trent, *Epistolae*, in PL 13: 549–58.

Visio Wettini, ed. and trans. H. Knittel (Heidelberg, 2004).

Vita Apollinaris Episcopi Valentinensis, in MGH SSRM, iii. 194–203.

Vita Benedicti Anianensis, in MGH SS, xv/i, 198–220.

Vita Boniti, in MGH SSRM, vi. 110–39.

Vita Christiani de Eleemosyna, in J. Leclercq, 'Le Texte complet de la Vie de Christian de l'Aumône', *Analecta Bollandiana*, 71 (1953), 21–52.

Vita Desiderii, in MGH SSRM, iv. 547–602.

Vita Gerardi, AS Aprilis 1, 414–23.

Vita Leonis (= Bruno of Toul), in *La Vie du Pape Léon IX (Brunon évêque de Toul)*, ed. M. Parisse and M. Goullet (Paris, 1997).

Vita Mathildis, in *Vita der Mathilde von Canossa: Codex Vaticanus Latinus 4922*, ed. R. Pernoud et al., 2 vols (Zürich, 1984).

Vita Ottonis Episcopi Bambergensis, AS Julii 1, 379–425.

Vita Prima Sancti Guidonis Abbatis, in *Acta Sanctorum Ordinis Sancti Benedicti*, ed. Mabillon, vi/1. 508–15.

Vita Radboti, in *Analecta Bollandiana*, 6 (1887) 5–15.

Vita Sanctae Gertrudis, in MGH SSRM, ii. 447–74.

Vita Sancti Bonifatii Archiepiscopi Moguntini, ed. W. Levison (Hannover and Leipizig, 1905).

Vita Sancti Dominici Sorani Abbatis et Miracula, in *Analecta Bollandiana*, 1 (1882), 279–322.

Vita Sancti Odonis, in PL 133: 43–86.

Vita Sancti Petri Episcopi Oxomensis, in F. B. Plaine, 'Vita S. Petri, Oxomensis episcopi in Hispania, ab anonymo suppari conscripta', *Analecta Bollandiana*, 4 (1885), 10–20.

Vita Sancti Remedii, AS Januarii II, 235–6.

Vitas Sanctorum Patrum Emeretensium, ed. A. Maya-Sánchez (CCSL 116; Turnhout, 1992).

Vita Wilhelmi Hirsaugensis, in MGH SS, xii. 209–25.

Vita Willelmi Abbatis, in *Vitae Sanctorum Danorum*, ed. M.C. Gertz, 2 vols (Copenhagen, 1908–10), i. 287–386.

Wandalbert of Prüm, *Vita et Miracula Sancti Goaris*, ed. A. Önnerfors (Frankfurt, 1981).

Widricus, *Vita S. Gerardi Episcopi*, in MGH SS, iv. 485–509.

William of Hirsau, *Musica Willehelmi Hirsaugensis*, ed. D. Harbinson (CSM 23; Rome, 1975).

William of Malmesbury, *Gesta Regum Anglorum*, ed. and trans. R.A.B. Mynors, R.M. Thomson and M. Winterbottom; general introd. and commentary by R.M. Thomson, 2 vols (Oxford Medieval Texts; Oxford, 1998–9).

Wipo, *Gesta Chuonradi II*, in *Quellen des 9. und 11. Jahrhunderts*, ed. Trillmich and Buchner.

The World of El Cid: Chronicles of the Spanish Reconquest, trans. S. Barton and R. Fletcher (Manchester, 1988).

Zosimus, *Histoire nouvelle*, ed. and trans. F. Paschoud, 3 vols (Paris, 1971–89).

Secondary Sources

Abbott, E., *A History of Celibacy* (Cambridge, 2001).

Adamik, T., 'The Language and Style of *The Acts of Peter*', in B. García-Hernandez (ed.), *Estudios de Lingüística Latina. Actas del IX Coloquio Internacional de Lingüística Latina*, 2 vols (Madrid, 1988), 1063–72.

Adams, C., and R. Laurence, *Travel and Geography in the Roman Empire* (London, 2001).

Adams, J., *Bilingualism and the Latin Language* (Cambridge, 2003).

Affeldt, W., 'Untersuchungen zur Königserhebung Pippins: Das Papsttum und die Begründung des karolingischen Konigtums im Jahre 751', *Frühmittelalterliche Studien*, 14 (1980), 95–187.

Agache, R., *La Somme pré-romaine et romaine d'après les prospections aériennes à basse altitude* (Amiens, 1978).

Airlie, S., 'Bonds of Power and Bonds of Association in the Court Circle of Louis the Pious', in P. Godman and R. Collins (eds), *Charlemagne's Heir* (Oxford, 1990), 191–204.

—— , W. Pohl and H. Reimitz, eds, *Staat im frühen Mittelalter*, Forschungen zur Geschichte des Mittelalters, xi (Vienna, 2006).

——'*Semper Fideles*? Loyauté envers les Carolingiens comme constituant de l'identité aristocratique', in R. Le Jan (ed.), *La Royauté et les élites dans l'Europe carolingienne* (Lille, 1998), 129–57.

Alcock, A., 'The *Agapè*', *Vigiliae Christianae*, 54 (2000), 208–9.

Allen, W., Jr., 'Ovid's *Cantare* and Cicero's *Cantores Euphorionis*', *Transactions and Proceedings of the American Philological Association*, 103 (1972), 1–14.

Allen, W. S., *Vox Graeca* (Cambridge, 1987).

Althoff, G., *Family, Friends and Followers: Political and Social Bonds in Medieval Europe*, trans. C. Carroll (Cambridge, 2004).

Amory, P., *People and Identity in Ostrogothic Italy 489–554* (Cambridge, 1997).

Amsler, M., 'History of Linguistics, "Standard Latin" and Pedagogy', in V. Law (ed.), *History of Linguistic Thought in the Early Middle Ages* (Amsterdam, 1993), 49–66.

Andreau, J., and C. Virlouvet (eds), *L'Information et la mer dans le monde antique* (Rome, 2002).

Andresen, C., 'Die Kritik der alten Kirche am Tanz der Spätantike', in F. Heyer (ed.), *Der Tanz in der modernen Gesellschaft* (Hamburg, 1958), 139–68.

Andrieu, M., 'Règlement d'Angilramne de Metz (768–791) fixant les honoraires de quelques fonctions liturgiques', *Revue des sciences religieuses*, 10 (1930), 348–69.

Angeletti, L. R., and B. Cavarra, 'Influenze bizantine nelle strutture sanitarie dei secoli V–X in Roma', *Medicina nei secoli*, 5 (1993), 279–97.

Angenendt, A., 'Das geistliche Bündnis der Päpste mit den Karolingern (754–796)', *Historisches Jahrbuch*, 100 (1980), 1–94.

Anglès, H., *La Música a Catalunya fins al Segle XIII* (Barcelona, 1935).

Apel, W., *Gregorian Chant* (London, 1958).

Archiepiscopatus Coloniensis, ed. S. Weinfurter et al. (SEECO, Series V: *Germania*, i; Stuttgart, 1982).

Ariès, P., *L'Enfant et la vie familiale sous l'Ancien Régime* (Paris, 1960).

Arlt, W., 'Anschaulichkeit und analytischer Charakter: Kriterien der Beschreibung und Analyse früher Neumenschriften', in Huglo (ed.), *Musicologie médiévale*, 29–55.

Arnold, C. J., *Roman Britain to Saxon England: An Archaeological Study* (London, 1984).

Atkinson, C. M., *The Critical Nexus: Tone-System, Mode and Notation in Early Medieval Music* (New York, 2008).

——'*De accentibus toni oritur nota que dicitur neuma*: Prosodic Accents, the Accent Theory and the Paleofrankish Script', in Boone (ed.), *Essays*, 17–42.

——'Glosses on Music and Grammar and the Advent of Music-Writing in the West', in Gallagher et al. (eds), *Western Plainchant in the First Millennium*, 199–215.

Atkinson, K., 'On Further Defining the First-Century CE Synagogue: Fact or Fiction?', *New Testament Studies*, 43 (1987), 491–502.

Auda, A., *L'École musicale liègeoise au Xe siècle: Étienne de Liége* (Brussels, 1923).

——*L'École liégeoise au XIIe siècle: L'office de Saint Trudon* (Paris, 1911).

Augé, M., 'Una liturgia del peregrinaje', *Ecclesia Orans*, 2 (1985), 113–25.

Aune, D. E. (ed.), *Greco-Roman Literature and the New Testament: Selected Forms and Genres* (Atlanta, Ga., 1988).

Autenrieth, J., *Die Domschule von Konstanz zur Zeit des Investiturstreits* (Stuttgart, 1956).

Ayres-Bennet, W., *A History of the French Language through Texts* (London, 1996).

Bachmann, W., *The Origins of Bowing*, trans. N. Deane (Oxford, 1969).

Bachrach, B., 'Fifth-Century Metz: Late-Roman Christian *Urbs* or Ghost-Town?', *Antiquité Tardive*, 10 (2002), 363–81.

Bagnall, R. S., *Later Roman Egypt: Society, Religion, Economy and Administration* (Aldershot, 2003).

Bahr, G. J., 'The Seder of Passover and the Eucharistic Words', *Novum Testamentum*, 12 (1970), 181–202.

Bakke, O. M., *When Children Became People: The Birth of Childhood in Early Christianity* (Minneapolis, 2005).

Balboni, D., 'San Pier Damiano maestro e discepolo in Pomposa', *Benedictina*, 22 (1975), 74–89.

Balch, D. L., 'Household Codes', in Aune (ed.), *Greco-Roman Literature*, 25–50.

——*Let Wives Be Submissive: The Domestic Code in I Peter* (Ann Arbor, 1981).

——and Osiek, C. (eds), *Christian Families in Context: An Interdisciplinary Dialogue* (Grand Rapids, Mich. and Cambridge, 2003).

Ball, W., *Rome in the East: The Transformation of an Empire* (London and New York, 2000).

Bambeck, M., 'Fischer und Bauern gegen Philosophen und sonstige Großkopfeten – ein christlicher "Topos" in Antike und Mittelalter', *Mittellateinisches Jahrbuch*, 18 (1983), 29–50.

Banaji, J., *Agrarian Change in Late Antiquity: Gold, Labour and Aristocratic Dominance* (Oxford, 2001).

Bandur, M., 'Compositio/Komponisten', *HMT*. Reprinted in Eggebrecht, *Terminologie*, 15–48.

Bang, P. F., *The Roman Bazaar* (Cambridge, 2008).

Banniard, M., 'La Rouille et la lime: Sidoine Apollinaire et la langue classique en Gaule au Ve siècle', in L. Holtz (ed.), *Mélanges J. Fontaine* (Paris, 1992), 413–27.

——*Viva Voce: Communication écrite et communication orale du IVe au IXe siècle en Occident latin* (Paris, 1992).

Barclay, J. M. G., 'The Family as Bearer of Religion in Judaism and Early Christianity,' in Moxnes (ed.), *Constructing Early Christian Families*, 66–80.

Barnes, T. D., *Tertullian: A Historical and Literary Study* (Oxford, 1971).

Barrett, S. J., 'Music and Writing: On the Compilation of Paris, Bibliothèque Nationale lat. 1154', *Early Music History*, 16 (1997), 55–96.

——'Notated Verse in Ninth- and Tenth-Century Poetic Collections' (Ph.D. thesis, University of Cambridge, 2000).

Barrett-Lennard, R., 'The *Canons of Hippolytus* and Christian Concern with Illness, Health and Healing', *JECS* 13 (2005), 137–64.

Barthélemy, D., *L'An mil et la paix de Dieu: La France chrétienne et féodale, 980–1060* (Paris, 1999).

Bartlett, R., *The Making of Europe: Conquest, Colonization and Cultural Change 950–1350* (London, 1993).

Bastiaensen, A. R., '*Psalmi, Hymni* and *Cantica* in Early Jewish-Christian Tradition', *Studia Patristica*, 21 (1989), 15–26.

Batlle i Prats, Ll., 'Inventari dels béns de l'hospital de la seu de Girona (10 gener 1362)', *Estudis Universitaris Catalans*, 19 (1934), 58–80.

Beale, G. K., *The Book of Revelation: A Commentary on the Greek Text* (Grand Rapids, Mich. and Carlisle, 1999).

Beaujouan, G., *Par raison de nombres* (Aldershot, 1991).

Beddie, J. S., 'Some Notices of Books in the East in the Period of the Crusades', *Speculum*, 8 (1933), 240–2.

Begbie, J. S., *Theology, Music and Time* (Cambridge, 2000).

Begley, V., and R. D. De Puma, *Rome and India: The Ancient Sea Trade* (Madison, Wis., 1991).

Belardini, B, 'Il Titolo di S. Ciriaco *in Thermis*: Localizzazione e nuovi documenti', *Rivista di archeologia cristiana*, 74 (1998), 373–400.

Bell, C., *Ritual: Perspectives and Dimensions* (Oxford, 1987).

——*Ritual Theory, Ritual Practice* (Oxford, 1992).

Bergeron, K., *Decadent Enchantments: The Revival of Gregorian Chant at Solesmes* (Berkeley, 1998).

Bergmann, W., *Innovationen im Quadrivium des 10. und 11. Jahrhunderts: Studien zur Einführung von Astrolab und Abacus im lateinischen Mittelalter*, Sudhoff's Archiv, Beihefte 26 (1985).

Bernard, M., 'Les Offices versifiés attribués à Léon IX (1002–1054)', *Études grégoriennes*, 19 (1980), 89–164.

Bernard, P., 'A-t-on connu la psalmodie alternée à deux chœurs, en Gaule, avant l'époque carolingienne? *Revue bénédictine*, 114 (2004), 291–325, and 115 (2005), 33–60.

——'Les Chants liturgiques chrétiens en Occident, source nouvelle pour la connaissance de l'Antiquité tardive: une archéologie musicale au service de l'histoire', *Antiquité tardive*, 3 (1995), 147–57.

——*Du chant romain au chant grégorien IVe–XIIIe siècle* (Paris, 1996).

——'Les Latins de la liturgie (Antiquité tardive et Moyen-Âge): Vingt-cinq années de recherches (1978–2002)', *Bulletin Du Cange: Archivum Latinitatis Medii Aevi*, 60 (2002), 77–170.

——'La "Liturgie de la victoire": Mise en scène du pouvoir, Ordo Missae et psalmodie responsoriale dans l'antiquité tardive et le haut Moyen Âge. Réflexions à partir de l'Expositio du Pseudo-Germain de Paris', *Ecclesia Orans*, 13 (1996), 349–406.

—— 'La *Schola cantorum* romaine et les échanges liturgiques avec la Gaule au vi⁰ siècle', *Études grégoriennes* 27 (1999), 61–120.

—— 'Sur un aspect controversé de la réforme carolingienne: "Vieux romain" et "grégorien"', *Ecclesia orans*, 7 (1990), 163–88.

Berndt, G.B., and R. Steinacher (eds), *Das Reich der Vandalen und seine (Vor-) Geschichten*, Forschungen zur Geschichte des Mittelalters, xiii (Vienna, 2008).

Bernhard, M., 'La *Summa musice* du Ps.-Jean de Murs: Son auteur et sa datation', *Revue de musicologie*, 84 (1998), 19–25.

—— 'Textkritisches zu Aurelianus Reomensis', *Musica Disciplina*, 40 (1986), 49–61.

Berschin, W., *Biographie und Epochenstil im Lateinischen Mittelalter*, 3 vols (Stuttgart, 1986–1992).

——, J. Felixberger and H. Goebl, *Französische Sprachgeschichte: Lateinische Basis, interne und externe Geschichte, sprachliche Gliederung Frankreichs mit einer Einführung in die historische Sprachwissenschaft* (Munich, 1978).

—— and D. Hiley (eds), *Die Offizien des Mittelalters: Dichtung und Musik* (Tutzing, 1999).

Betz, J., *Eucharistie in der Schrift und Patristik* (Freiburg, 1979).

Bielitz, M., *Musik und Grammatik: Studien zur mittelalterlichen Musiktheorie* (Munich, 1977).

Binder, D.D., *Into the Temple Courts: The Place of the Synagogue in the Second Temple Period* (Atlanta, Ga., 1999).

Bisconti, F., 'La scoperta di una piccola basilica paleocristiana presso le catacombe di Villa S. Faustino a Massa Martana (Todi)', *Rivista di archeologia cristiana*, 74 (1998), 27–55.

Das Bistum Würzburg, ed. A. Wendehorst (SEECO: *Germania Sacra*, NF I; Berlin, 1962).

Biville, F., 'Normes "orthographiques" et oralité dans la latinité tardive: Le latin du *De orthographia* de Cassiodore', in Wright (ed.), *Latin vulgaire, latin tardif*, 381–91.

Björkvall, G., and A. Haug, 'Text und Musik im Trinitätsoffizium Stephans von Lüttich: Beobachtungen und Überlegungen aus mittellateinischer und musikhistorischer Sicht', in Berschin and Hiley, *Die Offizien des Mittelalters*, 1–24.

Blackburn, Bonnie J., 'The Lascivious Career of B-Flat', in *Eros and Euterpe: Essays on Music and Eroticism from the Middle Ages to the Baroque*, ed. Massimo Ossi (forthcoming).

Blair-Dixon, K., 'Memory and Authority in Sixth-Century Rome: The *Liber Pontificalis* and the *Collectio Avellana*', in Cooper and Hillner (eds), *Religion, Dynasty, and Patronage*, 59–76.

Blaut, J.M., *Eight Eurocentric Historians* (New York and London, 2000).

Bligh, J., 'Deacons in the Latin West since the Fourth Century', *Theology*, 58 (1955), 421–9.

Blum, O.J., 'Alberic of Monte Cassino and the Hymns and Rhythms Attributed to Saint Peter Damian', *Traditio*, 12 (1956), 87–148.

Blumenthal, U.-R., 'The Papacy and Canon Law in the Eleventh-Century Reform', *Catholic Historical Review*, 84 (1998), 201–8.

Blustein, J., *The Moral Demands of Memory* (Cambridge, 2008).

Bobertz, C.A., 'The Development of Episcopal Order', in H.W. Attridge and G. Hata (eds), *Eusebius, Christianity and Judaism* (Detroit, 1992), 183–211.

—— 'The Role of Patron in the *Cena Dominica* of Hippolytus' *Apostolic Tradition*', *Journal of Theological Studies*, NS 44 (1993), 170–84.

Bocciolini Palagi, L., 'Girolama e le insidie del canto', in *Paideia Cristiana: Studi in onore di Mario Naldini* (Rome, 1994), 467–76.

Bockmuehl, M., and D. A. Hagner, (eds), *The Written Gospel* (Cambridge, 2005).

Bodel, J., 'An Outline of Roman Domestic Religion', in Bodel and Olyan (eds), *Household and Religion in Antiquity*, 248–75.

——and S. M. Olyan (eds), *Household and Religion in Antiquity* (Oxford, 2008).

Boes, G., *L'Abbaye de Saint-Trond, des origines jusqu'en 1155* (Saint-Trond, 1970).

Böhner, K., 'Urban and Rural Settlement in the Frankish Kingdom', in M. W. Barley (ed.), *European Towns: Their Architecture and Early History* (London, 1977), 178–202.

Bokser, B. M., *The Origins of the Seder: The Passover Rite and Early Rabbinic Judaism* (Berkeley and London, 1984).

Bona, I., *Les Huns* (Paris, 2002).

Bonenfant, P., 'L'Origine des villes brabançonnes et la 'route' de Bruges à Cologne', *Revue belge de philologie et d'histoire*, 31 (1953), 399–447.

Bonifay, M., M.-B. Carré, and Y. Rigoir (eds), *Fouilles à Marseille: Les mobiliers (Ier–VIIe siècles ap. J.-C.)* (Paris, 1998).

Bonnassie, P., *La Catalogne au tournant de l'an mil* (Paris, 1990).

Bonnet, Ch., 'Éléments de la topographie chrétienne à Genève (Suisse)', *Gallia*, 63 (2006), 111–15.

——'Les Salles de réception dans le groupe épiscopal de Genève', *Rivista di archeologia cristiana*, 65 (1989), 71–86.

Boone, G. M. (ed.), *Essays on Medieval Music in Honor of David G. Hughes* (Cambridge, Mass., 1995).

Born, G., and D. Hesmondhalgh (eds), *Western Music and its Others: Difference, Representation and Appropriation in Music* (Berkeley, 2000).

Bowe, B. E., 'Dancing into the Divine: The Hymn of the Dance in *The Acts of John*', *JECS* 7 (1999), 83–104.

Bower, C. M., 'The Grammatical Model of Musical Understanding in the Middle Ages', in J. Gallacher and H. Damico (eds), *Hermeneutics and Medieval Culture* (Albany, NY, 1989), 133–45.

——'The Sequence Repertoire of the Diocese of Utrecht', *Tijdschrift van de Koninklijke Vereniging voor Nederlandse Muziekgeschiedenis*, 53 (2003), 49–104.

Bowes, K., *Private Worship, Public Values, and Religious Change in Late Antiquity* (Cambridge, 2008).

Bowman, A. K., *Life and Letters on the Roman Frontier: Vindolanda and its People*, 3rd edn (London, 2003).

—— and A. Wilson (eds), *Quantifying the Roman Economy* (Oxford, 2009).

Boyarin, D., *Border Lines: The Partition of Judaeo-Christianity* (Philadelphia, 2004).

Boyer, M. N., *Medieval French Bridges: A History* (Cambridge, Mass., 1976).

Boynton, S., 'The Liturgical Role of Children in Monastic Customaries from the Central Middle Ages', *Studia liturgica*, 28 (1998), 194–209.

——'Orality, Literacy and the Early Notation of the Office Hymns', *JAMS* 56 (2003), 99–168.

——'Training for the Liturgy as a Form of Monastic Education', in G. Ferzoco and C. Muessig (eds), *Medieval Monastic Education* (London, 2000), 7–20.

Bradshaw, P., *Eucharistic Origins* (London, 2004).

—— *The Search for the Origins of Christian Worship: Sources and Methods for the Study of Early Liturgy* (London, 2002).

—— 'Ten Principles for Interpreting Early-Christian Liturgical Evidence', in id. and L. A. Hoffman (eds), *The Making of Jewish and Christian Worship* (Notre Dame, Ind., and London, 1991).

—— and L.A. Hoffman (eds), *The Making of Jewish and Christian Worship* (Notre Dame, Ind., 1991).

—— Johnson, M.E., and L.E. Phillips, *The Apostolic Tradition: A Commentary*, ed. H. W. Attridge (Minneapolis, 2002).

Brändle, R., and E.W. Stegemann, 'The Formation of the First "Christian Congregations" in Rome in the Context of Jewish Congregations', in Donfried and Richardson (eds), *Judaism and Christianity in First-Century Rome*, 117–27.

Braudel, F., *La Méditerranée et le monde méditerranéen à l'époque de Philippe II*, 2nd edn (Paris, 1966); trans. S. Reynolds as *The Mediterranean and the Mediterranean World in the Age of Philippe II*, 2 vols (London, 1975).

Braun, R., 'Tertullien et le Montanisme: Église institutionelle et église spirituelle', *Rivista di storia e letteratura religiosa*, 21 (1985), 245–7.

Braun, W., *Feasting and Social Rhetoric in Luke 14* (Cambridge, 1995).

Braunfels, W., et al. (eds), *Karl der Grosse*, 5 vols (Düsseldorf, 1965).

Bremmer, J.N. (ed.), *The Apocryphal Acts of Paul and Thecla* (Kampen, 1996).

Brenk, B., *Die Christianisierung der spätrömischen Welt: Stadt, Land, Hause, Kirche und Klöster in frühchristlicher Zeit* (Wiesbaden, 2003).

Brent, A., *Hippolytus and the Roman Church in the Third Century: Communities in Tension before the Emergence of a Monarch Bishop* (Leiden, 1995).

Breukelaar, A.H.B., *Historiography and Episcopal Authority in Sixth-Century Gaul: The Histories of Gregory of Tours Interpreted in their Historical Context* (Göttingen, 1994).

Briand-Ponsart, C., and C. Hugoniot, *L'Afrique romaine de l'Atlantique à la Tripolitaine* (Paris, 2005).

Brincken, A.D. von den, 'Europa in der Kartographie des Mittelalters', *Archiv für Kulturgeschichte*, 55 (1973), 289–304.

Brittain, C., 'No Place for a Platonist Soul in Fifth-Century Gaul? The Case of Mamertus Claudianus', in Shanzer and Mathisen, *Society and Culture*, 239–62.

Brogiolo, G.P., 'Lettura archeologica di un territorio pievano: L'esempio Gardesano', in *Cristianizzazione ed organizzazione ecclesiastica delle campagne nell'alto Medioevo*, 281–300.

—— and B. Ward-Perkins (eds), *The Idea and Ideal of the Town between Late Antiquity and the Early Middle Ages* (Leiden, 1999).

—— N. Gauthier, and N. Christie (eds), *Towns and their Territories between Late Antiquity and the Early Middle Ages* (Leiden, 2000).

Broughton, L.C., 'From Pious Legend to Feminist Fantasy: Distinguishing Hagiographical License from Apostolic Practice in the *Acts of Paul/Acts of Thecla*', *Journal of Religion*, 71 (1991), 362–83.

Brown, P., *The Body and Society: Men, Women and Sexual Renunciation in Early Christianity* (London, 1990).

—— 'Christianity and Local Culture in Late-Roman Africa', *Journal of Roman Studies*, 58 (1968), 85–95.

——*Poverty and Leadership in the Later Roman Empire* (Hanover, NH and London, 2002).

Brown, T. S., *Gentlemen and Officers: Imperial Administration and Aristocratic Power in Byzantine Italy A.D. 554–800* (Rome, 1984).

Brulet, R., 'La Tombe de Childéric et la topographie funéraire de Tournai à la fin du vᵉ siècle', in Rouche, *Clovis*, 59–78.

Brun, J.-Pierre, *Le vin et l'huile dans la Méditerranée antique: Viticulture, oléiculture et procédés de transformation* (Paris, 2003).

Brundage, J. A., *Medieval Canon Law* (London, 1995).

Brunhölzl, F., 'Der Bildungsauftrag der Hofschule', in Braunfels et al., *Karl der Grosse*, ii., 28–41.

Bull, M., 'Overlapping and Competing Identities in the Frankish First Crusade', in *Le Concile de Clermont de 1095 et l'appel à la croisade* (Rome, 1997), 195–211.

Bullough, D. A., '*Aula renovata*: The Carolingian Court before the Aachen Palace', *Proceedings of the British Academy*, 71 for 1985 (1986), 267–301.

——and A. L. H. Correâ, 'Texts, Chant and the Chapel of Louis the Pious', in Godman and Collins (eds), *Charlemagne's Heir*, 489–508.

Bunge, M. J. (ed.), *The Child in Christian Thought* (Grand Rapids, Mich., 2001).

Burgarella, P., 'Presenze greche a Roma: Aspetti culturali e religiosi', in *Roma fra Oriente e Occidente*, 943–88.

Burtchaell, J. T., *From Synagogue to Church: Public Services and Offices in the Earliest Christian Communities* (Cambridge, 1992).

Burton, P., *The Old Latin Gospels: A Study of their Texts and Language* (Oxford, 2000).

Busse Berger, A. M., *Medieval Music and the Art of Memory* (Berkeley, 2005).

Cabié, R., 'Quand les "Sept" deviennent des diacres', *Bulletin de littérature ecclésiastique*, 97 (1996), 219–26.

Callu, J.-P., 'L'Habitat et l'ordre social: Le témoignage de l'*Histoire Auguste*', *Antiquité tardive*, 12 (2004), 187–94.

Cameron, A., *Christianity and the Rhetoric of Empire: The Development of Christian Discourse* (Berkeley, 1991).

Campbell, A., *Old English Grammar* (corrected edn, Oxford, 1962).

Campbell, S., 'Signs of Prosperity in the Decoration of Some 4th–5th Century Buildings at Aphrodisias', in C. M. Roueché and R. R. R. Smith (eds), *Aphrodisias Papers*, 3 (Ann Arbor, 1996), 187–99.

Caner, D., *Wandering, Begging Monks: Spiritual Authority and the Promotion of Monasticism in Late Antiquity* (Berkeley, 2002).

Cantarella, G. C., 'La *Vita Beati Romualdi*: Specchio del monachesimo nell'età di Guido d'Arezzo', in Rusconi (ed.), *Guido d'Arezzo*, 3–20.

Cantin, P., *Les Sciences séculières et la foi: Les deux voies de la science au jugement de S. Pierre Damian 1007–1072* (Spoleto, 1975).

Carandini, A., 'Italian Wine and African Oil: Commerce in a World Empire', in K. Randsborg (ed.), *The Birth of Europe: Archaeological and Social Development in the First Millennium A.D.* (Rome, 1989), 16–24.

Carletti, C., 'Un mondo nuovo: Epigrafia funeraria dei Cristiani a Roma in età postcon-stantiana', *Vetera Christianorum*, 35 (1998), 39–67.

Carley, J. P., and A. Dooley, 'An Early Irish Fragment of Isidore of Seville's *Etymologiae*', in L. Abrams and J. Carley (eds), *The Archaeology and History of Glastonbury Abbey: Essays in Honour of the Ninetieth Birthday of C. A. Ralegh Radford* (Woodbridge, 1991), 135–61.

Carmassi, P., 'La liturgia romana tra il V e il IX secolo', in M. S. Arena et al. (eds), *Roma dall'antichità al medioevo* (Rome, 2001), 144–53.

—— 'La prima redazione del *Liber Pontificalis* nel quadro delle fonti contemporanee: Osservazioni in margine alla vita di Simmaco', in Geertman (ed.), *Atti*, 235–66.

Carr, K., 'Les Francs, les Wisigoths et "la longue durée" ', in Rouche (ed.), *Clovis*, 421–33.

Carter, W., *Households and Discipleship: A Study of Matthew 19–20* (Sheffield, 1994).

Casalone, C., 'Note sulle pittura dell'ipogèo di Trebio Giusto a Roma', *Cahiers archéologiques*, 12 (1962), 53–64.

Caspar, E. L. E., *Pippin und die römische Kirche: Kritische Untersuchungen zum fränkisch-päpstlichen Bunde im VIII. Jahrhundert* (Berlin, 1914).

Cassinet, J., 'Gerbert et l'introduction de la numération décimale arabo-indienne en Occident chrétien: Le *Liber abaci*', in Ollich i Castanyer, 725–6.

Castagnoli, F., et al., *Topografia e urbanistica di Roma* (Bologna, 1958).

Catholicisme, ed. G. Jacquemet (Paris, 1956–).

Cerrito, A., 'Oratori ed edifici di culto minori di Roma tra il IV secolo ed i primi decenni del V', in Guidobaldi and Guidobaldi (eds), *Ecclesiae Urbis*, 397–418.

Charles, J., *La Ville de Saint-Trond au moyen-âge* (Bibliothèque de la Faculté de Philosophie et Lettres de l'Université de Liège, fasc. 173; Paris, 1965).

Chartier, Y., *L'Œuvre musicale d'Hucbald de Saint-Amand* ([Montréal], 1995).

Chauvot, A., 'Images positives, images négatives des Barbares dans les sources latines à la fin du Ve siècle et au début du VIe siècle après J.-C', in Rouche (ed.), *Clovis*, 3–14.

Chavasse, A., 'Les Grands Cadres de la célébration à Rome *in urbe* et *extra muros* jusqu'au VIIIe siècle', *Revue bénédictine*, 96 (1986), 7–26.

—— *La Liturgie de la ville de Rome du Ve au VIIIe siècle: Une liturgie conditionnée par l'organisation de la vie in urbe et extra muros* (Rome, 1993).

Chibnall, M., 'The Merovingian Monastery of St. Evroul', in C. J. Cuming and D. Baker (eds), *Popular Belief and Practice* (Cambridge, 1972), 31–40.

Chitty, D., *The Desert a City: An Introduction to the Study of Egyptian and Palestinian Monasticism under the Christian Empire* (Oxford, 1966).

Cholij, R., *Clerical Celibacy in East and West*, 2nd edn (Leominster, 1989).

Christiansen, E., *The Northern Crusades* (London, 1997).

Christie, N., *From Constantine to Charlemagne: An Archeology of Italy* AD *300–800* (Aldershot, 2006).

—— *The Lombards* (Oxford, 1998).

—— and Loseby, S. (eds), *Towns in Transition: Urban Evolution in Late Antiquity and the Early Middle Ages* (Aldershot, 1996).

Chrysos, E., and Wood, I. (eds), *East and West: Modes of Communication* (Transformation of the Roman World, 5; Leiden, 1999).

Claesson, G., *Index Tertullianus* (Paris, 1974–5).

Clanchy, M. T., *Abelard: A Medieval Life* (Oxford, 1999).

Clark, E. A., 'The Fathers and the Children', in E. Ferguson (ed.), *Christianity and Society: The Social World of Early Christianity* (New York, 1999), 237–63.

—— *Reading Renunciation: Asceticism and Scripture in Early Christianity* (Princeton, 1999).

Claussen, M. A., *The Reform of the Frankish Church: Chrodegang of Metz and the* Regula Canonicorum *in the Eighth Century* (Cambridge, 2004).

Clover, F. M., 'The Symbiosis of Romans and Vandals in Africa', in E. K. Chrysos and A. Schwarcz (eds), *Das Reich und die Barbaren* (Vienna and Cologne, 1989), 57–73.

Coates-Stephens, R., 'Dark Age Architecture in Rome', *Papers of the British School at Rome*, 65 (1997), 177–232.

Coccia, S., 'Il Portus Romae alla fine dell'antichità nel quadro del sistema di approvvigionamento della città di Rome', in A. G. Zevi and A. Claridge (eds), *Papers in Memory of Russel Meiggs* (London, 1996), 293–307.

Cochini, C., *Origines apostoliques du célibat sacerdotal* (Namur, 1981).

Coens, M., 'Anciennes Litanies des saints', *Analecta Bollandiana*, 54 (1936), 5–37; 55 (1937), 49–69; 59 (1941), 272–98 and 62 (1944), 126–68.

Coleman, R., 'Vulgar Latin and the Diversity of Christian Latin', in Herman (ed.), *Latin vulgaire–latin tardif*, 37–52.

—— 'Vulgar Latin and Proto-Romance: Minding the Gap', *Prudentia*, 25 (1993), 1–14.

Collins, R., '¿Dónde estaban los arrianos en el año 589?', in *Concilio III de Toledo*, 222–36.

—— *Early Medieval Spain: Unity in Diversity 400–1000*, 2nd edn (London, 1995).

Concilio III de Toledo XIV Centenario 589–1189 (Toledo, 1989).

Connell, M. F., *Church and Worship in Fifth-Century Rome: The Letter of Innocent I to Decentius of Gubbio* (Cambridge, 2002).

Connolly, S., '*Vita Prima Sanctae Brigitae*: Background and Social Value', *Journal of the Royal Society of Antiquaries of Ireland*, 119 for 1989 (1990), 5–49.

Connolly, T. H., 'Introits and Archetypes: Some Archaisms of the Old Roman Chant', *JAMS* 25 (1972), 157–74.

—— 'Traces of a Jewish-Christian Community at S. Cecilia in Trastevere', *PMM* 7 (1998), 1–19.

Constantelos, D., *Byzantine Philanthropy and Social Welfare* (New Brunswick, NJ, 1968).

Cool, H. E. M., *Eating and Drinking in Roman Britain* (Cambridge, 2006).

Cooper, K., 'Poverty, Obligation and Inheritance', in Cooper and Hillner (eds), *Religion, Dynasty, and Patronage*, 165–89.

—— and J. Hillner (eds), *Religion, Dynasty, and Patronage in Early Christian Rome, 300–900* (Cambridge, 2007).

Coosemans, V., and C. Coppens, 'De eerste kroniek van Affligem', *Affligemensia: Bijdragen tot de geschiedenis van den abdij van Affligem*, 4 (1947), 1–41.

Coquin M., 'Le Sort des *Statuta Ecclesiae Antiqua* dans les collections canoniques jusqu'à la Concordia de Gratien', *Recherches de théologie ancienne et médiévale*, 28 (1961), 193–224.

Countryman, L. W., *The Rich Christian in the Church of the Early Empire: Contradictions and Accommodations* (New York and Toronto, 1980).

Courtois, C., *Les Vandales et l'Afrique* (Paris, 1955).

Cowdrey, H. E. J., *The Age of Abbot Desiderius: Montecassino, the Papacy and the Normans in the Eleventh and Early Twelfth Centuries* (Oxford, 1983).

—— *The Cluniacs and the Gregorian Reform* (Oxford, 1970).

—— *Pope Gregory VII (1073–1085)* (Oxford, 1998).

—— 'Pope Gregory VII (1073–85) and the Liturgy', *Journal of Theological Studies*, NS 55 (2004), 55–83.

—— *The Register of Pope Gregory VII (1073–1085): An English Translation* (Oxford, 2002).

Cribiore, R., 'Literary School Exercises', *Zeitschrift für Papyrologie und Epigraphik*, 116 (1997), 53–60.

—— *Writing, Teachers and Students in Graeco-Roman Egypt* (Atlanta, Ga., 1996).

Cristianizzazione ed organizzazione ecclesiastica delle campagne nell'alto Medioevo: espansione e resistenze (SSCISAM 28; Spoleto, 1980).

Crocker, R. L., *The Early Medieval Sequence* (Berkeley, 1977).

—— *An Introduction to Gregorian Chant* (New Haven and London, 2000).

—— *Studies in Medieval Music Theory and the Early Sequence* (Aldershot, 1997).

—— 'Thoughts on Responsories', in Boone (ed.), *Essays*, 77–85.

—— 'The Troping Hypothesis', in id., *Studies*, Essay XIII.

Crossan, J. D., *The Cross that Spoke: The Origins of the Passion Narrative* (San Francisco, 1988).

—— *The Essential Jesus: What Jesus Really Taught* (San Francisco, 1995).

—— *In Fragments: The Aphorisms of Jesus* (San Francisco, 1983).

—— *The Historical Jesus: The Life of a Mediterranean Jewish Peasant* (Edinburgh, 1991).

Cubitt, C., *Anglo-Saxon Church Councils c650–c850* (London and New York, 1995).

Cuisenier, J., and R. Guadagnin, *Un Village au temps de Charlemagne: Moines et paysans de l'Abbaye de Saint-Denis, du VIIe siècle à l'an mil* (Paris, 1988).

Culto cristiano: Politica imperiale Carolingia. Convegni del Centro di Studi sulla Spiritualità Medievale, Università degli Studi di Perugia, 18 (Todi, 1979).

Curran, J. R., *Pagan City and Christian Capital: Rome in the Fourth Century* (Oxford, 2002).

Currie, S., 'Childhood and Christianity from Paul to the Council of Chalcedon' (Ph.D. diss., University of Cambridge, 1993).

Curta, F., *The Making of the Slavs: History and Archaeology of the Lower Danube Region c. 500–700* (Cambridge, 2001).

Cusack, C. M., *The Rise of Christianity in Northern Europe, 300–1000* (London, 1999).

Cushing, K. G., *Papacy and Law in the Gregorian Revolution: The Canonistic Work of Anselm of Lucca* (Oxford, 1998).

Cushing, R. E., 'Hieronymus. *Liber de viris inlustribus* – Gennadius. *Liber de viris inlustribus*', *Texte und Untersuchungen zur Geschichte der altchristlichen Literatur*, 14 (1896), 1–112.

Dahmen, W., et al. (eds), *Latein und Romanisch* (Tübingen, 1987).

Danesi, M., 'Latin vs Romance in the Middle Ages: Dante's *De vulgari eloquentia* Revisited', in R. Wright (ed.), *Latin and the Romance Languages*, 248–57.

Daniel, R. W., and F. Maltomini 'From the African Psalter and Liturgy', *Zeitschrift für Papyrologie und Epigraphik*, 74 (1988), 253–85.

Daniélou, J., *The Origins of Latin Christianity* (London, 1977).

Danker, F. W. (ed.), *A Greek–English Lexicon of the New Testament and other Early Christian Literature*, 3rd edn (Chicago and London, 2000).

Dardel, R. de, 'Niveaux de la langue intermédiaires entre le latin classique et le protoroman', in M. Iliescu and M. Marxgut (eds), *Latin vulgaire–latin tardif: Actes du IIIe colloque international sur le latin vulgaire et tardif* (Tübingen, 1992), 83–91.

—— 'Remarques sur la simplification morphologique en latin oral', in G. Calboli (ed.), *Latin vulgaire–latin tardif: Actes du IIe colloque international sur le latin vulgaire et tardif* (Tübingen, 1990), 89–100.

Dauphin, H., 'L'Abbaye de Saint-Vanne de Verdun et la querelle des investitures', *Studi Gregoriani*, 1 (1947), 237–61.

Davids, P. H., *The Epistle of James: A Commentary on the Greek Text* (Exeter, 1982).

Davies, J. G., 'Deacons, Deaconesses and the Minor Orders in the Patristic Period', *Journal of Ecclesiastical History*, 14 (1963), 1–15.

Davis, S. J., 'A "Pauline" Defense of Women's Right to Baptize? Intertextuality and Apostolic Authority in the Acts of Paul', *JECS* 8 (2000), 453–60.

Dearn, A. 'The Abitinian Martyrs and the Outbreak of the Donatist Schism', *Journal of Ecclesiastical History*, 55 (2004), 1–18.

De Blaauw, S., *Cultus et Decor: Liturgia e architettura nella Roma tardoantica e medievale* (Vatican City, 1994).

De Clercq, C., *Catalogue des manuscrits du Grand Séminaire de Malines* (Gembloux and Paris, 1937).

De Jong, M., '*Ecclesia* and the Early Medieval Polity', in Airlie, Pohl and Reimitz, *Staat*, 113–32.

—— 'Growing up in a Carolingian Monastery: Magister Hildemar and his Oblates', *Journal of Medieval History*, 9 (1983), 98–128.

Delage, P.-G. (ed.), *Les Pères de l'Église et les ministères* (La Rochelle, 2008).

Delogu, P., 'L'importazione di tessuti preziosi e il sistema economico romano nel IX secolo', in id. (ed.), *Roma medievale*, 123–41.

—— 'Reading Pirenne Again', in Hodges and Bowden (eds), *The Sixth Century*, 15–40.

—— (ed.), *Roma medievale* (Florence, 1998).

—— and Paroli, L. (eds), *La storia economica di Roma nell'alto Medioevo alla luce dei recenti scavi archeologici: Atti del seminario, Roma 2–3 aprile 1992* (Florence, 1993).

Delumeau, J. M., *Arezzo: Espace et société 715–1230*, 2 vols (Rome, 1996).

Demandt, A., *Der Fall Roms: Die Auflösung des römischen Reiches im Urteil der Nachwelt* (Munich, 1984).

Deming, W., *Paul on Marriage and Celibacy: The Hellenistic Background of I Corinthians 7*, 2nd edn (Grand Rapids, Mich. and Cambridge, 2004).

Dereine, Ch., 'La Critique de l'"Exordium Affligemense" et les origines de l'Abbaye d'Affligem', *Cahiers bruxellois*, 14 (1969), 5–24.

—— 'Le Problème de la date de la fondation d'Affligem', *Cahiers bruxellois*, 3 (1957), 179–63.

—— 'La Spiritualité "apostolique" des premiers fondateurs d'Affligem (1083–1100)', *Revue d'histoire ecclésiastique*, 54 (1959), 41–65.

Derolez, A., 'Lambert van Sint-Omaars als kartograaf', *Franse Nederlanden*, 1 (1976), 14–30.

De Rossi, G. B., *La Roma sotterranea cristiana* (Rome, 1864–77).

Desanges, J., *Recherches sur l'activité des Méditerranéens aux confins de l'Afrique* (Paris, 1978).

Desbat, A., and S. Martin-Kilcher, 'Les Amphores sur l'axe Rhône-Rhin', in *Amphores romaines et histoire économique: Dix ans de recherche* (Rome and Paris, 1989), 339–65.

Desmulliez, J., 'Le Dossier du groupe épiscopal de Naples: État actuel des recherches', *Antiquité tardive*, 6 (1998), 345–54.

De Souza, P., *Piracy in the Graeco-Roman World* (Cambridge, 1999).

Desprez, V., *Le Monachisme primitif* (Béyrolles-en-Mauge, 1998).

Destephen, S., 'L'Apport de la prosopographie à la connaissance des clercs: L'exemple du diocèse d'Asie', in Delage (ed.), *Les Pères*, 279–94.

—— *Prosopographie chrétienne du Bas-Empire*, iii: *Diocèse d'Asie (325–641)* (Paris, 2008).

Díaz y Díaz, M.C., 'Anecdota Wisigothica', *Acta Salmanticensia. Filosofía y Letras*, 12 (1958), 9–134.

—— *El Códice Calixtino de la Catedral de Santiago: Estudio Codicológico y de Contenido* (Santiago, 1988).

—— 'Contribuciones al Estudio de la Pervivencia de Eugenio de Toledo', in id., 'Anecdota', 117–22.

—— 'El Latín de España en el siglo VII: Lengua y escritura según los textos documentales', in Fontaine and Hillgarth (eds), *Le Septième Siècle*, 25–40.

—— 'Literary Aspects of the Visigothic Liturgy', in James (ed.), *Visigothic Spain*, 61–76.

—— 'Los Prólogos del Antiphonale Visigothicum', *Archivos Leoneses*, 8 (1954), 227–57.

Di Berardino, A., 'Maestri cristiani del III secolo nell'insegnamento classico', *August-inianum*, 12 (1972), 549–56.

Di Francesco, C., and A. Samaritani (eds), *Pomposa* (Ferrara, 1999).

Dictionnaire de droit canonique, ed. R. Naz, 7 vols (Paris, 1935–65).

Dictionnaire de théologie catholique, ed. A. Vacant et al., 18 vols (Paris, 1915–51).

Dietz, K., and T. Fischer, *Die Römer in Regensburg* (Regensburg, 1996).

Dinzelbacher, P., 'Il ponte come luogo sacro nella realtà e nell'immaginario', in S.B. Gajano and L. Scaraffia (eds), *Luoghi sacri e spazie della santità* (Turin, 1990), 51–60.

Dion, M.-P. (ed.), *La Cantilène de sainte Eulalie: Actes du colloque de Valenciennes, 21 mars 1989* (Valenciennes, 1990).

Dix, G., *The Shape of the Liturgy*, with additional notes by P.V. Marshall (New York, 1982).

Donfried, K.P., and P. Richardson (eds), *Judaism and Christianity in First-Century Rome* (Grand Rapids, Mich., 1998).

Dreves, G.M., *Godescalcus Lintpurgensis: Gottschalk, Mönch von Limburg an der Hardt* (Leipzig 1987).

Drinkwater, J., and H. Elton (eds), *Fifth-Century Gaul: A Crisis of Identity?* (Cambridge, 1992).

Duchesne, L., *L'Église au VIe siècle* (Paris, 1925).

Duchez, M.-E., 'La Représentation spatio-verticale du caractère musical grave-aigu et l'élaboration de la notion de hauteur de son dans la conscience musicale occidentale', *Acta Musicologica*, 51 (1979), 54–73.

—— 'Des neumes à la portée', in Huglo (ed.), *Musicologie médiévale*, 57–60.

Duensing, H., 'Die dem Klemens von Rom zugeschriebenen Briefe über die Jungfräulichkeit', *Zeitschrift für Kirchgengeschichte*, 63 (1950–1), 166–88.

Dumézil, B., *Les Racines chrétiennes de l'Europe: Conversion et liberté dans les royaumes barbares V^e–VIIIe siècle* (Paris, 2005).

Dümmler, E., 'Gedichte aus Frankreich', *Neues Archiv*, 2 (1877), 24–7.

—— 'Radberts *Epitaphium Arsenii*', *Abhandlunden der königlichen Akademie der Wissenschaften zu Berlin, philosophisch-historische Klasse 2* (Berlin, 1900), 1–98.

Dumville, D.N., 'The Importation of Mediterranean Manuscripts into Theodore's England', in Lapidge (ed.), *Archbishop Theodore*, 96–119.

Duncan, J.S., et al. (eds), *A Companion to Cultural Geography* (Oxford, 2004).

Dungan, D.L., *Constantine's Bible* (London, 2006)

Dunn, J.D.G., *The Parting of the Ways: Between Christianity and Judaism and their Significance for the Character of Christianity*, 2nd edn (London, 2006).

Du Plat Taylor, J., and H. Cleere (eds), *Roman Shipping and Trade: Britain and the Rhine Provinces* (London, 1978).

Durliat, J., 'Les Conditions du commerce au vɪᵉ siècle', in Hodges and Bowden (eds), *The Sixth Century*, 89–117.

Duval, Y., *Chrétiens d'Afrique à l'aube de la paix constantinienne: Les premiers échos de la grande persécution* (Paris, 2000).

——and J. Ch. Picard (eds), *Inhumation privilégiée du IVᵉ au VIIIᵉ s. en Occident: Actes du colloque tenu à Créteil les 16–18 mars 1984* (Paris, 1986).

Dyer, J., 'Boy Singers of the Roman *Schola Cantorum*', in S. Boynton and E. Rice (eds), *Young Choristers 650–1700* (Woodbridge, 2008), 19–36.

——'Cantor', in *New Grove Online*.

——'The Desert, the City and Psalmody in the Late Fourth Century', in Gallagher et al. (eds), *Western Plainchant in the First Millennium*, 11–43.

——'Monastic Psalmody of the Middle Ages', *Revue bénédictine*, 99 (1989), 41–74.

——'Observations on the Divine Office in the Rule of the Master', in Fassler and Baltzer (eds), *The Divine Office in the Latin Middle Ages*, 74–98.

——'Prolegomena to a History of Music and Liturgy at Rome in the Middle Ages', in Boone (ed.), *Essays*, 87–107.

——'The Psalms in Monastic Prayer' in Van Deusen (ed.), *The Place of the Psalms*, 59–89.

——'The *Schola Cantorum* and its Roman Milieu in the Early Middle Ages', in H. Cahn and A.-K. Heimer (eds), *De Musica et Cantu: Studien zur Geschichte der Kirchenmusik und der Oper. Helmut Hucke zum 60. Geburtstag* (Hildesheim, 1993), 19–40.

——'The Singing of Psalms in the Early Medieval Office', *Speculum*, 65 (1989), 535–78.

——'*Tropis semper variantibus*: Compositional Strategies in the Offertories of Old Roman Chant', *Early Music History*, 17 (1998), 1–60.

Eastwood, B. S., 'Innovation and Reform in Latin Planetary Astronomy', in M. W. Herren et al. (eds), *Latin Culture in the Eleventh Century*, 2 vols (Turnhout, 2002), i. 264–97.

——'Plinian Astronomical Diagrams in the Early Middle Ages', in E. Grant and J. E. Murdoch (eds), *Mathematics and its Applications to Science and Natural Philosophy in the Middle Ages* (Cambridge, 1987), 141–72.

Ebbinghaus, A., 'Gotica XI: The Gothic Calendar', *General Linguistics*, 15/1 (1975), 36–9.

Eggebrecht, H. H. (ed.), *Terminologie der musikalischen Komponisten* (Stuttgart, 1996).

Ekenberg, A., *Cur cantatur? Die Funktionen des liturgischen Gesanges nach den Autoren der Karolingerzeit* (Stockholm, 1987).

Ekonomou, A., *Byzantine Rome and the Greek Popes: Eastern Influences on Rome and the Papacy from Gregory the Great to Zacharias AD 590–752* (Plymouth, 2007).

Elior, R., 'Early Forms of Jewish Mysticism', in Katz (ed.), *The Cambridge History of Judaism*, iv. 749–91.

Ellis, E. P., *The Making of the New Testament Documents* (Leiden, 1999).

Ellmers, D., 'Shipping on the Rhine during the Roman Period: The Pictorial Evidence', in Du Plat Taylor and Cleere (eds), *Roman Shipping and Trade*, 1–14.

Elm, S., et al. (eds), *Orthodoxie, christianisme, histoire* (Rome, 2000).

—— *Virgins of God: The Making of Asceticism in Late Antiquity* (Oxford, 1996).

Elsner, J., *Imperial Rome and Christian Triumph: The Art of the Roman Empire AD 100–450* (Oxford, 1998).

Ennabli, L., *La Basilique de Carthagenna et le locus des sept moines de Gafsa: Nouveaux édifices chrétiens de Carthage* (Paris, 2000).

Esders, S., *Römische Rechtstradition und merowingisches Königtum: Zum Rechtscharakter politischer Herrschaft in Burgund im 6. und 7. Jahrhundert* (Göttingen, 1997).

Esler, P. F. (ed.), *The Early Christian World*, 2 vols (London and New York, 2000).

Etter, B. K., *From Classicism to Modernism: Western Musical Culture and the Metaphysics of Order* (Aldershot, 2001).

Evans, G., '*Difficillima et Ardua*: Theory and Practice in Treatises on the Abacus 950–1150', *Journal of Medieval History*, 3 (1977), 21–38.

——'*Duc Oculum*: Aids to Understanding in some Medieval Treatises on the Abacus', *Centaurus*, 19 (1975), 252–63.

——'*Studium Discendi*: Otloh of Saint Emmeram and the Seven Liberal Arts', *Recherches de théologie ancienne et médiévale*, 44 (1977), 29–54.

Ewig, E., 'Beobachtungen zur Entwicklung der fränkischen Reichskirche unter Chrodegang von Metz', *Frühmittelalterliche Studien*, 2 (1968), 67–77.

——'Descriptio Franciae', in Braunfels (ed.), *Karl der Grosse*, i. 143–77.

——'Saint Chrodegang et la réforme de l'Église franque', in *Saint Chrodegang*, 25–53.

Eyben, E., 'Young Priests in Early Christianity', in M. Wacht (ed.), *Panchaia: Festschrift für Klaus Thraede* (Münster, 1995), 102–20.

Faivre, A., *Naissance d'une hiérarchie: Les premières étapes du cursus clérical* (Paris, 1977).

——'La Question des ministères à l'époque paléochrétienne: Problématiques et enjeux d'une périodisation', in Delage (ed.), *Les Pères*, 3–38.

Falconer, K., 'The Modes before the Modes: Antiphon and Differentia in Western Chant', in Jeffery (ed.), *The Study of Medieval Chant*, 130–45.

Fanning, S., *A Bishop and his World before the Gregorian Reform: Hubert of Angers (1006–1047)*, Transactions of the American Philosophical Society, 78 (1988).

Fassler, M., *Gothic Song: Victorine Sequences and Augustinian Reform in Twelfth-Century Paris* (Cambridge, 1993).

——'The Office of the Cantor in Early Western Monastic Rules and Customaries: A Preliminary Investigation', *Early Music History*, 5 (1985), 29–51.

——and Baltzer, R. (eds), *The Divine Office in the Latin Middle Ages* (New York, 2000).

Fauvarque, B., 'Le Baptême de Clovis, ouverture du millénaire des saints', in Rouche (ed.), *Clovis*, 271–86.

Fentress, E. W. B., *Numidia and the Roman Army: Social, Military and Economic Aspects of the Frontier Zone* (Oxford, 1979).

Ferguson, C., 'Diglossia', *Word*, 15 (1959), 325–40.

Ferguson, E., 'Toward a Patristic Theology of Music', *Studia Patristica*, 24 (1993), 266–83.

Ferreiro, A. (ed.), *The Visigoths* (Leiden, 1999).

Ferrua, A., *The Unknown Catacomb* (Florence, 1991).

Finckenstein, A. G. F. von, 'Rom zwischen Byzanz und Franken in der ertsen Hälfte des 8. Jahrhunderts', in K. R. Schmith and R. Pauler (eds), *Festschrift für E. Hlawitschka* (Munich, 1993), 230–6.

Finley, M., *The Ancient Economy*, rev. edn (Berkeley and London, 1999).

Fischer, B., *Lateinische Bibelhandschriften im frühen Mittelalter* (Freiburg, 1945).

Fleckenstein, J., *Die Bildungsreform Karls des Grossen als Verwirklichung der* Norma Rectitudinis (Bigge, 1953).

—— *Die Hofkapelle der deutschen Könige*, 2 vols (Suttgart, 1959–66).

Fleischhauer, G., *Etrurien und Rom* (Musikgeschichte in Bildern, II/5; Leipzig, 1964).

Fletcher, P., *Education and Music* (Oxford, 1987).

Fletcher, R. A., *The Conversion of Europe: From Paganism to Christianity, 371–1386* (London, 1997).

Flobert, P., 'Le Latin à la cour de Clovis selon Anthime', in H. Petersman and R. Kettemann (eds), *Latin vulgaire–latin tardif: Actes du Ve Colloque international sur le latin vulgaire et tardif* (Tübingen, 1992), 19–29.

Flori, J., '*Pur eshalcier sainte crestiënté*: Croisade, guerre sainte et guerre juste dans les anciennes chansons de geste françaises', *Le Moyen Âge*, 97 (1991), 171–87.

Floros, C., *Universale Neumenkunde*, 3 vols (Kassel, 1970); English edn: *Introduction to Early Medieval Notation*, rev., trans. and with an illustrated chapter on cheironomy by N. K. Moran (Warren, Mich., 2005).

Flotzinger, R., 'Zur Ubernahm der Liniennotation durch die Benediktiner im deutschen Sprachraum', in G. Fleischhauer et al. (eds), *Die Klöster als Pflegestätten von Musik und Kunst: 850 Jahre Kloster Michaelstein* (Michaelstein, 1997), 75–86.

Folda, J., *The Art of the Crusaders in the Holy Land, 1098–1187* (Cambridge, 1995).

Foley, E., 'The Cantor in Historical Perspective', *Worship*, 56 (1982), 194–213.

—— *Foundations of Christian Music: The Music of Pre-Constantinian Christianity* (Nottingham, 1992).

Fontaine, J., 'De la pluralité à l'unité dans le "latin carolingien"', in *Nascità dell'Europa de Europa carolingia: Un 'equazione' da verificare* (SSCISAM 27; Spoleto, 1981), 765–805.

—— 'Fins et moyens d'enseignement ecclésiastique dans l'Espagne wisigothique', in *La scuola nell'occidente latino dell'alto medioevo* (SSCISAM 19; Spoleto, 1972), 145–202.

—— 'La Homilía de San Leandro ante el Concilio III de Toledo: Témática y Forma', in *Concilio III de Toledo*, 262–9.

—— and J. N. Hillgarth (eds), *Le Septième Siècle: Changements et continuités* (Studies of the Warburg Institute, 42; London, 1992).

—— and Pellistrandi, C. (eds), *L'Europe héritière de l'Espagne wisigothique* (Madrid, 1992).

Foss, C., *Ephesus after Antiquity: A Late Antique, Byzantine and Turkish City* (Cambridge, 1979).

Fossier, R., *La Terre et les hommes en Picardie jusqu'à la fin du XIIIe siècle*, 2 vols (Paris, 1968).

Foster, P., 'Polymorphic Christology: Its Origins and Development in Early Christianity', *Journal of Theological Studies*, NS 58 (2007), 66–99.

Fouracre, P., *The Age of Charles Martel* (Harlow, 2000).

—— 'Eternal Light and Earthly Needs: Practical Aspects of the Development of Frankish Immunities', in W. Daies and P. Fouracre (eds), *Property and Power in the Early Middle Ages* (Cambridge, 1995), 53–81.

—— and Gerberding, R. A., *Late Merovingian France: History and Hagiography, 640–720* (Manchester, 1996).

Fox, A., *Prosodic Features and Prosodic Structure: The Phonology of Suprasegmentals* (Oxford, 2002).

Francis, J. A., *Subversive Virtue: Asceticism and Authority in the Second-Century Pagan World* (University Park, Pa., 1995).

François, J., and N. Tabouillot, *Histoire générale de Metz*, 8 parts in 6 vols (Metz, 1787–90).

Francovich Onesti, N., *I Vandali: Lingua e storia* (Rome, 2002).

Frank, A. G., 'East and West', in P. Herrmann and A. Tausch (eds), *Dar al Islam: The Mediterranean, the World System and the Wider Europe: The 'Cultural Enlargement' of the EU and Europe's Identity* (New York, 2004), 183–229.

Frank, K. S., 'Grimlaicus, *Regula solitariorum*', in F. J. Felten and N. Jaspert (eds), *Vita religiosa im Mittelalter: Festschrift für Kaspar Elm zum 70. Geburtstag* (Berlin, 1999), 21–35.

Frassetto, M. (ed.), *Medieval Purity and Piety: Essays on Medieval Clerical Celibacy and Religious Reform* (New York and London, 1998).

Frazee, C. A., 'The Origins of Clerical Celibacy in the Western Church', *Church History*, 41 (1972), 149–67.

Fredouille, J.-C., *Tertullien et la conversion de la culture antique* (Paris, 1972).

Fredriksen, P., and O. Irshai, 'Christian Anti-Judaism: Polemics and Policies', in Katz (ed.), *The Cambridge History of Judaism*, iv. 977–1034.

Freed, J., 'The Late Series of Tunisian Cylindrical Amphoras at Carthage', *Journal of Roman Archaeology*, 8 (1995), 155–91.

Frend, W. H. C., 'Monks and the End of Greco-Roman Paganism in Syria and Egypt', *Cristianesimo nella storia*, 11 (1990), 469–84.

Fumagalli, V., *Le origini di una grande dinastia feudale: Adalberto-Atto di Canossa* (Tübingen, 1971).

Gaeng, P. A., 'Variétés régionales du latin parlé: Le témoignage des inscriptions', in Herman (ed.), *Latin vulgaire–latin tardif*, 77–86.

Gallagher, S., J. Haar, J. Nádas and T. Striplin (eds), *Western Plainchant in the First Millennium: Studies in the Medieval Liturgy and its Music* (Aldershot, 2003).

Gamber, Kl., 'Das Lektionar und Sakramentar des Musäus von Massilia', *Revue bénédictine*, 69 (1959), 198–215.

Gamble, H. G., *Books and Readers in the Early Church: A History of Early Christian Texts* (New Haven and London, 1995).

Gambra, A., *Alfonso VI: Cancillería, Curia e Imperio*, 2 vols (León, 1997–8).

Gams, P. B., *Series Episcoporum Ecclesiae Catholicae: Quotquot innotuerunt a Beato Petro Apostolo* (Regensburg, 1873).

Ganz, D., *Corbie in the Carolingian Renaissance* (Sigmaringen, 1990).

——'Humour as History in Notker's *Gesta Karoli Magni*', in E. B. King, J. T. Schaefer and W. B. Wadley (eds), *Monks, Nuns and Friars in Medieval Society* (Sewanee, Tenn., 1989), 171–83.

García Moreno, L. A., 'El Concilio III de Toledo y la Historia de España Altomedieval', in A. H. Ballina (ed.), *Memoria Ecclesiae: Las Raíces Visigóticas de la Iglesia en España: En Torno al Concilio III de Toledo; Santoral Hispano-Mozárabe en España. Actas del Congreso Celebrado en Toledo (21 y 22 de Septiembre de 1989)* (Oviedo, 1991), 9–20.

——'La Conversion des Suèves au catholicisme et à l'arianisme', in Rouche (ed.), *Clovis*, 199–216.

—— 'Gothic Survivals in the Visigothic Kingdoms of Toulouse and Toledo', *Francia*, 21 (1994), 11–15.

—— 'Las Primeras Crónicas de la Reconquista', *Boletín de la Academia de la Historia*, 100 (1932), 562–623.

Gaudemet, J., *Église et cité: Histoire du droit canonique* (Paris, 1994).

—— *Les Sources du droit de l'Église en Occident du II⁰ au VII⁰ siècle* (Paris, 1985).

Gauthier, N., 'From the Ancient City to the Medieval Town: Continuity and Change in the Early Middle Ages', in Mitchell and Wood (eds), *The World of Gregory of Tours*, 47–66.

—— *Province ecclésiastique de Trèves (Belgica Prima): Topographie chrétienne des cités de la Gaule des origines au milieu du VIII⁰ siècle*, i (Paris, 1986).

—— and Picard, J.-Ch., *Topographie chrétienne des cités de la Gaule: Des origines au milieu du VIII⁰ siècle* (Paris, 1986–).

Gawlik, A., *Intervenienten und Zeugen in den Diplomen Kaiser Heinrichs IV (1056–1105)* (Kallmünz, 1970).

Geary, P. J., *Furta Sacra: Thefts of Relics in the Central Middle Ages* (Princeton, 1978).

—— *The Myth of Nations: The Medieval Origins of Europe* (Princeton, 2002).

Geertman, H. (ed.), *Atti del colloquio internazionale Il Liber Pontificalis e la storia materiale. Roma, 21–22 febbraio 2002 = Mededelingen van het Nederlands Instituut te Rome: Antiquity*, 60–1 (2001–2).

—— 'Le biografie del *Liber Pontificalis* dal 311 al 535: Testo e commentario', in Geertman (ed.), *Atti*, 285–355.

—— 'Documenti, redattori e la formazione del testo del *Liber Pontificalis*', in Geertman (ed.), *Atti*, 267–84.

—— *More Veterum: Il* Liber Pontificalis *e gli edifici ecclesiastici di Roma nella tarda antichità e nell'alto medioevo* (Groningen, 1975).

Gelston, A., 'ΔΙ ΕΥΧΗΣ ΛΟΓΟΥ', *Journal of Theological Studies*, NS 33 (1982), 172–5.

Georgi, D., 'The Early Church: Internal Jewish Migration or New Religion?', *Harvard Theological Review*, 88 (1995), 35–68.

Gibaut, J. St. H., *The Cursus Honorum: A Study of the Origins of Sequential Ordination* (New York, 2000).

Gibson, C. A., and F. Newton, 'Pandulf of Capua's *De Calculatione*: An Illustrated Abacus Treatise and Some Evidence for the Use of Hindu-Arabic Numerals in Eleventh-Century South Italy', *Mediaeval Studies*, 57 (1995), 293–335.

Gibson, M. (ed.), *Boethius: His Life, Thought and Influence* (Oxford, 1981).

Gilchrist, J., 'The *Epistola Widonis*, Ecclesiastical Reform and Canonistic Enterprise 1049–1141', in id., *Canon Law in the Age of Reform, 11th–12th Centuries* (Aldershot, 1993), Essay X.

—— 'Was there a Gregorian Reform Movement in the Eleventh Century?', in id., *Canon Law in the Age of Reform*, Essay VII.

Gillett, A., *Envoys and Political Communication in the Late Antique West 411–533* (Cambridge, 2003).

Glenn, J., *Politics and History in the Tenth Century: The Work and World of Richer of Reims* (Cambridge, 2004).

Godman, P., and R. Collins (eds), *Charlemagne's Heir: New Perspectives on the Reign of Louis the Pious* (Oxford, 1990).

Goehring, J.E., *Ascetics, Society and the Desert: Studies in Early Egyptian Monasticism* (Harrisburg, 1999).

—— 'Withdrawing from the Desert: Pachomius and the Development of Village Monasticism in Upper Egypt', *Harvard Theological Review*, 89 (1996), 267–85.

—— 'The World Engaged: The Social and Economic World of Early Egyptian Monasticism', in id. (ed.), *Gnosticism and the Early Christian World: In Honor of James M. Robinson* (Sonoma, Calif., 1990), 134–44.

Goffart, W., 'The Name "Merovingian" and the Dating of *Beowulf*', *Anglo-Saxon England*, 36 (2007), 93–101.

—— 'Paul the Deacon's *Gesta Episcoporum Mettensium* and the Early Design of Charlemagne's Succession', *Traditio*, 42 (1986), 59–93.

—— *Rome's Fall and After* (London, 1989).

Goguel, M., *The Primitive Church*, trans. H.C. Snape (London, 1964).

Golinelli, P. (ed.), *I poteri dei Canossa* (Bologna, 1994).

González-Salinero, R., 'Catholic Anti-Judaism in Visigothic Spain', in Ferreiro (ed.), *The Visigoths*, 123–50.

Gorce, D., *Les Voyages, l'hospitalité et le port des lettres dans le monde chrétien des IVe et Ve siècles* (Paris, 1925).

Goudesenne, J.-F., *Les Offices historiques ou* historiae *composées pour les fêtes des saints dans la province ecclésiastique de Reims 775–1030* (Turnhout, 2002).

—— 'A Typology of *Historiae* in West Francia (8–10c)', *PMM* 13 (2004), 1–31.

Grafton, A., and M. Williams, *Christianity and the Transformation of the Book: Origen, Eusebius and the Library of Caesarea* (Cambridge, Mass., and London, 2006).

Graham, M.W., *News and Frontier Consciousness in the Late Roman Empire* (Ann Arbor, 2006).

Gray Funkhouser, H., 'A Note on a Tenth-Century Graph', in G. Sarton et al. (eds), *Osiris* (Bruges, 1936), 259–62.

Greene, K., *The Archaeology of the Roman Economy* (London, 1986).

Greenfeld, L., *The Spirit of Capitalism: Nationalism and Economic Growth* (Cambridge, Mass. and London, 2001).

Gregg, R. (ed.), *Arianism: Historical and Theological Reassessments* (Philadelphia, 1985).

Grier, J., 'Adémar de Chabannes, Carolingian Musical Practices, and *Nota Romana*', *JAMS* 56 (2003), 434–98.

—— *The Musical World of a Medieval Monk: Adémar de Chabannes in Eleventh-Century Aquitaine* (Cambridge, 2006).

Griffe, É., *La Gaule chrétienne à l'époque romaine*, 3 vols (Paris, 1965).

Groom, N., *Frankincense and Myrrh: A Study of the Arabian Incense Trade* (London, 1981).

Gros, M., 'Les Wisigoths et les liturgies occidentales', in Fontaine and Pellistrandi (eds), *L'Europe héritière*, 125–35.

Grubbs, J., 'Pagan and Christian Marriage: The State of the Question', *JECS* 2 (1994), 361–412.

Gryson, R., 'Les Degrés du clergé et leurs dénominations chez saint Ambroise de Milan', *Revue bénédictine*, 76 (1966), 119–27.

—— *Les Origines du célibat ecclésiastique du premier au septième siècle* (Gembloux, 1970).

Guidobaldi, F., and A.G. Guidobaldi (eds), *Ecclesiae Urbis: Atti del Congresso internazionale di Studi sulle chiese di Roma (IV–X secolo)*, 3 vols (Vatican City, 2002).

Guillou, A., *Culture et société en Italie byzantine (VI⁶–XI⁶ s.)* (London, 1978).

——'Rome, centre des produits de luxe d'Orient au haut moyen âge', *Zographe*, 10 (1979), 17–21.

Gutmann, J. (ed.), *The Dura Europos Synagogue: A Re-evaluation* ([Chambersburg, Pa., 1973).

Guyon, J., 'Émergence et affirmation d'une topographie chrétienne dans les villes de la Gaule méridionale', *Gallia*, 63 (2006), 85–110.

Haarhoff, T. J., *Schools of Gaul: A Study of Pagan and Christian Education in the Last Century of the Western Empire* (Oxford, 1920).

Haas, M., 'Zur Psalmodie der christlichen Frühzeit', *Schweizer Jahrbuch für Musikwissenschaft*, NS 2 (1982), 29–51.

Habinek, T., *The World of Roman Song: From Ritualized Speech to Social Order* (Baltimore, 2005).

Hahneman, G. M., *The Muratorian Fragment and the Development of the Canon* (Oxford, 1992).

Haines-Eitzen, K., *Guardians of Letters: Literacy, Power and the Transmitters of Early Christian Literature* (Oxford, 2000).

Hainz, J., *Ekklesia: Strukturen paulinischer Gemeinde-Theologie und Gemeinde-Ordnung* (Regensburg, 1971).

Haley, E. W., *Baetica felix: People and Prosperity in Southern Spain from Caesar to Septimius Severus* (Austin, Tex., 2003).

Halsall, G., *Barbarian Migrations and the Roman West, 376–568* (Cambridge, 2007).

——'Childeric's Grave, Clovis' Succession, and the Origins of the Merovingian Kingdom', in Shanzer and Mathisen (eds), *Culture and Society*, 116–33.

——*Settlement and Social Organisation: The Merovingian Region of Metz* (Cambridge, 1995).

Halverson, J., 'Oral and Written Gospel: A Critique of Werner Kelber', *New Testament Studies*, 40 (1994), 180–95.

Hamilton, B., *The Latin Church in the Crusader States: The Secular Church* (Aldershot, 1980).

Hamman, A. G., 'La Formation du clergé latin dans les quatre premiers siècles', *Studia Patristica XX: Papers Presented to the Tenth International Conference on Patristic Studies Held in Oxford* 1987 (Leuven, 1989), 238–49.

——'L'Utilisation des psaumes dans les deux premiers siècles chrétiens', *Studia patristica*, 18 (1989), 363–74.

Hammer, C. I., Jr., 'Country Churches, Clerical Inventories and the Carolingian Renaissance in Bavaria', *Church History*, 49 (1980), 5–17.

Handley, M. A., *Death, Society and Culture: Inscriptions and Epitaphs in Gaul and Spain, AD 300–750* (British Archaeological Reports, International Series, 1135; Oxford, 2003).

Hannig, J., *Consensus Fidelium: Frühfeudale Interpretationen des Verhältnisses von Königtum und Adel am Beispiel des Frankenreiches* (Stuttgart, 1982).

Hansen, I. L., and C. Wickham (eds), *The Long Eighth Century* (The Transformation of the Roman World, 11; Leiden, 2000).

Harland, P., *Associations, Synagogues and Congregations: Claiming a Place in Ancient Mediterranean Society* (Minneapolis, 2003).

Harnack, A. von, 'Die pseudoclementischen Briefe *de virginitate* und die Entstehung des

Mönchthums', *Sitzungsberichte der Königlich Preussischen Akademie der Wissenschaft zur Berlin*, 28 (1891), 361–85.

Harper, J. G., 'The Provisioning of Marble for the Sixth-Century Churches of Ravenna: A Reconstructive Analysis', in R. L. Colella et al. (eds), *Pratum Romanum: Richard Krautheimer zum 100. Geburtstag* (Wiesbaden, 1997), 131–48.

Harries, J., and I. Wood (eds), *The Theodosian Code* (London, 1993).

Harris, R., *The Origin of Writing* (London, 1986).

—— *Rethinking Writing* (London, 2000).

Harris, W. V., 'Between Archaic and Modern: Some Current Problems in the History of the Roman Economy', in id. (ed.), *The Inscribed Economy* (Ann Arbor, 1993), 11–29.

Harrison, R. M., 'Churches and Chapels of Central Lycia', *Anatolian Studies*, 13 (1963), 117–51.

Hartzell, K. D., *Catalogue of Manuscripts Written or Owned in England up to 1200 Containing Music* (Woodbridge, 2006).

Haverling, G. V. M., 'On Linguistic Development and School Tradition: Direct and Indirect Evidence of the Development of Late Latin', *Classica et Medievalia*, 55 (2004), 323–48.

Head, T., *Hagiography and the Cult of Saints: The Diocese of Orléans, 800–1200* (Cambridge, 1990).

—— 'Letaldus of Micy and the Hagiographic Traditions of Selles-sur-Cher', *Analecta Bollandiana*, 107 (1989), 393–414.

—— and R. Landes (eds), *The Peace of God: Social Violence and Religious Unrest in France around the Year 1000* (Ithaca and London, 1992), 280–307.

Heather, P. J., *The Fall of the Roman Empire: A New History* (London, 2005).

—— *The Goths* (Oxford, 1998).

—— 'The Huns and the End of the Roman Empire in Western Europe', *English Historical Review*, 110 (1995), 4–41.

—— *Empires and Barbarians: Migration, Development and the Birth of Europe* (Basingstoke and Oxford, 2009).

Heid, S., *Celibacy in the Early Church: The Beginnings of a Discipline of Obligatory Continence for Clerics in East and West* (San Francisco, 2000).

Heil, U., 'Augustin-Rezeption im Reich der Vandalen: *Die Altercatio sancti Augustini cum Pascentio Arriano*', *Zeitschrift für Antikes Christentum*, 11 (2007), 6–29.

Heinzelmann, M., *Bischofsherrschaft in Gallien: Zur Kontinuität römischer Führungsschichten vom 4. bis zum 7. Jahrhundert: soziale, prosopographische und bildungsgeschichtliche Aspekte* (Munich, 1976).

—— *Gregory of Tours: History and Society in the Sixth Century*, trans. C. Carroll (Cambridge, 2001).

—— '*Studia sanctorum*: Éducation, milieu d'instruction et valeurs éducatives dans l'hagiographie en Gaule jusqu'à la fin de l'époque mérovingienne', in M. Sot (ed.), *Haut moyen-âge: Culture, éducation et société. Études offertes à P. Riché* (Nanterre, 1990), 105–38.

Heisterbergk, B., *Name und Begriff des Jus Italicum* (Tübingen, 1885).

Helleman, W. E. (ed.), *Hellenization Revisited: Shaping a Christian Response within the Greco-Roman World* (London, 1994).

Hellerman, J. H., *The Ancient Church as a Family* (Minneapolis, 2001).

Hemmerle, J., *Die Benediktinerkloster in Bayern* (Germania Benedictina, 2; Augsburg, 1970).

Hen, Y., *Culture and Religion in Merovingian Gaul, A.D. 481–751* (Leiden, 1995).

——'Liturgische hervormingen onder Pepijn de Korte en Karl de Grote: De illusie van romanisierung', *Millennium* 15 (2001), 97–113.

—— *Roman Barbarians: The Royal Court and Culture in the Early Medieval West* (New York, 2007).

—— *The Royal Patronage of Liturgy in Frankish Gaul to the Death of Charles the Bald* (Henry Bradshaw Society, Subsidia 3; London, 2001).

——and R. Meens (eds), *The Bobbio Missal: Liturgy and Religious Culture in Merovingian Gaul* (Cambridge, 2004).

Hendy, M. F., 'From Public to Private: The Western Barbarian Coinages as a Mirror of the Disintegration of Late-Roman State Structures', *Viator*, 19 (1988), 29–78.

Hengel, M., 'Eye-Witness Memory and the Writing of the Gospels', in Bockmuehl and Hagner (eds), *The Written Gospel*, 70–96.

Herbers, K., Valdeón Baruque, J., and Rudolf, K. (eds), *España y 'Sacro Imperio': Procesos de Cambiòs, Influencias y Acciones Recíprocas en la Época de la Europeización (Siglos XI–XIII)* (Valladolid, 2002).

Herman, J., *Du Latin aux langues romanes* (Tübingen, 1990).

——'Spoken and Written Latin in the Last Centuries of the Roman Empire: A Contribution to the Linguistic History of the Western Provinces', in Wright (ed.), *Latin and the Romance Languages*, 29–43.

——(ed.), *Latin vulgaire–latin tardif. Actes du Ier colloque international sur le latin vulgaire et tardif* (Tübingen, 1987).

Herrmann, K.-J., *Das Tuskulanerpapsttum (1012–1046): Benedikt VIII, Johannes XIX, Benedikt IX* (Päpste und Papstum, 4; Stuttgart, 1973).

Herrmann, P., *Itinéraires des voies romaines* (Paris, 2006).

Hiley, D., '*Cantate Domino Canticum Novum*: Old and New in Medieval Chant and the Status of St. Gregory', *Musica e storia*, 14 (2006), 127–41.

——'The English Benedictine Version of the *Historia Sancti Gregorii* and the Date of the Winchester Troper', *Cantus Planus: Papers Read at the Seventh Meeting* (Budapest, 1998), 287–303.

——'The *Historia* of St. Julian of Le Mans by Létald of Micy: Some Comments and Questions about a North French Office of the Early Eleventh Century', in Fassler and Baltzer (eds), *The Divine Office in the Latin Middle Ages*, 444–62.

——'The Music of Prose Offices in Honour of English Saints', *PMM* 10 (2001), 23–37.

——'The Repertory of Sequences at Winchester', in Boone (ed.), *Essays*, 153–93.

——'Style and Structure in Early Offices of the Sanctorale', in Gallagher et al. (eds), *Western Plainchant in the First Millennium*, 157–79.

—— *Western Plainchant: A Handbook* (Oxford, 1995).

Hilhorst, A., 'Tertullian on the *Acts of Paul*', in Bremmer (ed.), *The Apocryphal Acts*, 150–63.

Hill, C. H., *The Johannine Corpus in the Early Church* (Oxford, 2004).

Hillner, J., 'Families, Patronage and the Titular Churches of Rome, *c*300–*c*600', in Cooper and Hillner (eds), *Religion, Dynasty, and Patronage*, 225–61.

Hirschfeld, Y., *The Palestinian Dwelling in the Roman-Byzantine Period* (Jerusalem, 1995).

Hitchner, R. B., 'Meridional Gaul, Trade and the Mediterranean Economy in Late Antiquity', in Drinkwater and Elton (eds), *Fifth-Century Gaul*, 122–31.

Hlawitschka, E., *Franken, Alemannen, Bayern und Burgunder in Oberitalien (774–962)* (Freiburg, 1960).

Hodges, R., 'Henri Pirenne and the Question of Demand', in Hodges and Bowden (eds), *The Sixth Century*, 3–14.

—— 'In the Shadow of Pirenne: San Vincenzo al Volturno and the Revival of Mediterranean Commerce', in R. Francovich and G. Noyé (eds), *Storia dell'Altomedioevo italiano (VI–X secolo) alla luce dell'archeologia: Atti del Convegno internazionale* (Siena, 1992), 109–27.

—— and W. Bowden (eds), *The Sixth Century: Production, Distribution and Demand* (The Transformation of the Roman World, 3; Leiden, 1998), 15–40.

—— and D. Whitehouse, *Mohammed, Charlemagne and the Origins of Europe* (London, 1983).

Hoeflich, M. H., 'Gelasius I and Roman Law', *Journal of Theological Studies*, NS 26 (1975), 114–19.

Hofius, O., 'The Fourth Servant's Song in the New Testament Letters', in Janowski and Stuhlmacher (eds), *The Suffering Servant*, 163–88.

Holmberg, B., *Paul and Power: The Structure of Authority in the Primitive Church as reflected in the Pauline Epistles* (Lund, 1978).

Hopkins, K., 'Christian Number and its Implications', *JECS* 6 (1998), 185–226.

—— 'Taxes and Trade in the Roman Empire (200 B.C.–A.D. 400)', *Journal of Roman Studies*, 70 (1980), 101–25.

Horden, P., 'The Earliest Hospitals in Byzantium, Western Europe and Islam', *Journal of Interdisciplinary History*, 35 (2005), 361–89.

—— and N. Purcell, *The Corrupting Sea: A Study of Mediterranean History* (Oxford, 2000).

Hornby, E., 'Exploring the Transmission History of *Beatus uir*, the Mass Proper Chant for St Gregory', *PMM* 12 (2003), 97–127.

—— *Gregorian and Old Roman Eighth-Mode Tracts* (Aldershot, 2002).

—— 'The Transmission of Western Chant in the 8th and 9th Centuries: Evaluating Kenneth Levy's Reading of the Evidence', *Journal of Musicology*, 21 (2004), 418–57.

Horsley, G. H. R., 'Epitaph for a Jewish Psalm-Singer', in id., *New Documents*, i. 115–17.

—— *New Documents Illustrating Early Christianity*, 5 vols (North Ryde, Aus., 1981–9).

—— 'Speak no Evil', in id., *New Documents*, ii. 42–6.

Howe, J., *Church Reform and Social Change in Eleventh-Century Italy: Dominic of Sora and his Patrons* (Philadelphia, 1997).

Howlett, D., 'Vita I Sanctae Brigitae', *Peritia*, 12 (1998), 1–23.3

Hubert, É., 'Les Résidences des étrangers à Rome', in *Roma fra Oriente e Occidente*, 163–204.

Hucke, H., 'Die Einführung des gregorianischen Gesangs im Frankenreich', *Römische Quartalschrift*, 49 (1954), 172–87.

—— 'Die Entstehung der Überlieferung von einer musikalischen Tätigkeit Gregors des Großen', *Musikforschung*, 8 (1955), 259–64.

—— 'Gregorianischer Gesang in altrömischer und fränkischer Überlieferung', *Archiv für Musikwissenschaft*, 12 (1955), 74–87.

—— 'Toward a New Historical View of Gregorian Chant', *JAMS* 33 (1980), 437–67.

—— 'Zu einigen Problemen der Choralforschung', *Musikforschung*, 11 (1958), 385–414.

Hudson, A., 'Outline of a Theory of Diglossia', *International Journal of the Sociology of Language*, 157 (2002), 1–48.

Huelsen, C., *Le chiese di Roma nel Medio Evo* (Florence, 1927).

Hughes, D., 'Evidence for the Traditional View of the Transmission of Gregorian Chant', *JAMS* 40 (1987), 377–404.

—— 'From the Advent Project to the Late Middle Ages: Some Issues of Transmission', in Gallagher et al. (eds), *Western Plainchant in the First Millennium*, 181–98.

Huglo, M., 'L'Auteur du traité de musique dédié à Fulgence d'Affligem', *Revue belge de musicologie*, 31 (1977), 5–19.

—— 'The Cantatorium: From Charlemagne to the Fourteenth Century', in Jeffery (ed.), *The Study of Medieval Chant*, 89–101.

—— 'Du répons de l'Office avec prosule au répons organisé', in B. Edelman and M. H. Schmid (eds), *Altes im Neuen* (Tutzing, 1995), 25–36.

—— 'Gerbert, théoricien de la musique, vu de l'an 2000', *Cahiers de civilisation médiévale*, 43 (2000), 143–60.

—— 'Les Instruments de musique chez Hucbald', in G. Cambier (ed.), *Hommages à André Boutemy* (Brussels, 1976).

—— 'Un Nouveau Manuscrit du *Dialogue* sur la Musique du Pseudo-Odon (Troyes, Bibliothèque Municipale 2142)', *Revue d'histoire des textes*, 9 (1979), 299–314.

—— 'The Origin of the Monodic Chants in the Codex Calixtinus', in Boone (ed.), *Essays*, 195–205.

—— 'Der Prolog des Odo zugeschriebenen *Dialogus de Musica*', *Archiv für Musikwissenschaft*, 28 (1971), 134–46.

—— 'Les Prologues de l'antiphonaire de Léon' (forthcoming).

—— 'Les Remaniements de l'antiphonaire grégorien au ixe siècle: Hélisachar, Agobard, Amalaire', in *Culto cristiano*, 102–13.

—— 'Le Répons-graduel de la Messe: Évolution de la forme, permanence de la fonction', *Schweizer Jahrbuch für Musikwissenschaft*, NS 2 (1982), 53–73.

—— *Les Tonaires: Inventaire, analyse, comparaison* (Paris, 1971).

—— and Meyer, Christian, *Manuscripts from the Carolingian Era up to c. 1500 in the Federal Republic of Germany* (The Theory of Music, iii; Munich, 1986).

—— (ed.), *Musicologie médiévale: Notations et séquences* (Paris, 1987).

—— Bellingham, J., and M. Zijlstra, 'Gallican Chant', *New Grove Online*.

Hummer, H. J., *Politics and Power in Early Medieval Europe: Alsace and the Frankish Realm, 600–1000* (Cambridge, 2005).

Humphrey, J. H., 'Vandal and Byzantine Carthage: Some New Archaeological Evidence', in Pedley (ed.), *New Light on Ancient Carthage*, 85–120.

Hunt, E. D., *Holy Land Pilgrimage in the Later Roman Empire AD 312–460* (Oxford, 1982).

Hunter, D. G., 'Resistance to the Virginal Ideal in Late Fourth-Century Rome: The Case of Jovinian', *Theological Studies*, 48 (1987), 45–64.

Hurtado, L., 'The Origin and Development of Christ-Devotion: Forces and Factors', in K. J. O'Mahony (ed.), *Christian Origins: Worship, Belief and Society* (Sheffield, 2003), 52–82.

Huskinson, J., *Roman Children's Sarcophagi: Their Decoration and its Social Significance* (Oxford, 1996).

Index Scriptorum Operumque Latino-Belgicorum Medii Aevi, ed. L. Genicot and P. Tombeur (Brussels, 1973–).

Innes, M., 'Memory, Orality and Literacy in an Early Medieval Society', *Past and Present*, 158 (1998), 3–36.

——*State and Society in the Early Middle Ages: The Middle Rhine Valley 400–1000* (Cambridge, 2000).

Irvine, M., 'Bede the Grammarian and the Scope of Grammatical Studies in Eighth-Century Northumbria', *Anglo-Saxon England*, 15 (1986), 15–44.

Iversen, G., 'Compositional Planning and Tropes', *Studia Musicologia: Academiae Scientiarum Hungaricae*, 39 (1998), 201–14.

Jacquemet, G., et al. (eds), *Catholicisme*, 12 vols (Paris, 1948–90).

Jacques, F., and J. Scheid, *Rome et l'intégration de l'Empire* (Paris 1990).

Jaeger, C. S., *The Origins of Courtliness: Civilizing Trends and the Formation of Courtly Ideals 939–1210* (Philadelphia, 1985).

——*Scholars and Courtiers: Intellectuals and Society in the Medieval West* (Aldershot, 2002).

Jahn, J., *Ducatus Baiuvariorum: Das Bairische Herzogtum der Agilolfinger* (Stuttgart, 1991).

——'Hausmeier und Herzöge: Bemerkungen zur agilolfischen-karolingischen Rivalität bis zum Tode Karl Martells', in J. Jarnut et al. (eds), *Karl Martell in seiner Zeit* (Sigmaringen, 1994), 317–44.

James, E., *The Franks* (Oxford, 1988).

——(ed.), *Visigothic Spain* (Oxford, 1980).

James, M. R., *A Descriptive Catalogue of the Manuscripts in the Library of Sidney Sussex College* (Cambridge, 1895).

Jannet-Vallat, M., et al., *Vienne aux premiers temps chrétiens* (Paris, 1986).

Janowski, B., and Stuhlmacher, P. (eds), *The Suffering Servant: Isaiah 53 in Jewish and Christian Sources*, trans. D. P. Bailey (Grand Rapids, Mich., 2004).

Janson, T., 'Language Change and Metalinguistic Change: Latin to Romance and Other Cases', in Wright (ed.), *Latin and the Romance Languages*, 19–28.

——*Prose Rhythm in Medieval Latin* (Lund, 1975).

Janssen, H., *Kultur und Sprache: Zur Geschichte der alten Kirche im Spiegel der Sprachentwicklung von Tertullian bis Cyprian* (Nijmegen, 1938).

Jastrzębowska, E., 'Les Scènes de banquet dans les peintures et sculptures chrétiennes des IIIᵉ et IVᵉ siècles', *Recherches augustiniennes*, 19 (1979), 3–90.

——*Untersuchungen zum christlichen Totenmahl aufgrund der Monumente des 3. und 4. Jarhhunderts unter der Basilika des Hl. Sebastian in Rom* (Europäische Hochschulschriften, Archäologie, 38; Frankfurt am Main, 1981).

Jay, E. G., 'From Presbyter-Bishops to Bishops and Presbyters: Christian Ministry in the Second Century. A Survey', *Second Century*, 1 (1981), 125–62.

Jeffers, J. S., *Conflict at Rome: Social Order and Hierarchy in Early Christianity* (Minneapolis, 1991).

Jeffery, P., 'The Earliest Oktōēchoi: The Role of Jerusalem and Palestine in the Beginnings of Modal Ordering', in id. (ed.), *The Study of Medieval Chant*, 147–209.

—— 'Eastern and Western Elements in the Irish Monastic Prayer of the Hours', in Fassler and Baltzer (eds), *The Divine Office in the Latin Middle Ages*, 99–143.

—— 'The Introduction of Psalmody into the Roman Mass by Pope Celestine I (422–432): Reinterpreting a Passage in the *Liber Pontificalis*', *Archiv für Liturgiewissenschaft*, 26 (1984), 147–65.

—— 'Monastic Reading and the Emerging Roman Chant Repertory', in Gallagher et al. (eds), *Western Plainchant in the First Millennium*, 45–103.

—— 'The Oldest Sources of the *Graduale*: A Checklist of Manuscripts Copied before about 900 AD', *Journal of Musicology*, 2 (1983), 316–21.

—— *Re-Envisioning Past Musical Cultures: Ethnomusicology in the Study of Gregorian Chant* (Chicago, 1992).

—— 'Rome and Jerusalem: From Oral Tradition to Written Repertory in two Ancient Liturgical Centres', in Boone (ed.), *Essays*, 207–48.

—— (ed.), *The Study of Medieval Chant: Paths and Bridges, East and West. In Honour of Kenneth Levy* (Cambridge, 2001).

Jehle, F., and A. Enderle-Jehle, *Die Geschichte des Stiftes Säckingen* (Aarau, 1993).

Jensen, B. M., *Tropes and Sequences in the Liturgy of the Church in Piacenza* (Lewiston, NY, 2002).

Joannou, P.-P., *La Législation impériale et la christianisation de l'Empire romain* (Rome, 1972).

Johnson, M. E., and L. E. Phillips, *The Apostolic Tradition: A Commentary* (Minneapolis, 2002).

Joly, G., *Fiches de phonétique* (Paris, 1999).

Jones, C. W., *The Saint Nicholas Liturgy and its Literary Relationships, Ninth to Twelfth Centuries* (Berkeley, 1963).

Jorge, A. M., 'Church and Culture in Lusitania in the v–viii Centuries: A Late-Roman Province at the Crossroads', in Ferreiro (ed.), *The Visigoths*, 99–121.

Jourdain-Hemmerdinger, D., 'Fonction du chant dans les discours et lectures publiques', in C. Meyer (ed.), *Aspects de la musique liturgique au Moyen Âge* (Paris, 1991), 15–41.

Judge, E. A., 'The Earliest Use of *Monachos* for "Monk" (P. Coll. Youtie 77) and the Origins of Monasticism', *Jahrbuch für Antike und Christentum*, 20 (1977), 47–71.

—— 'Jews, Proselytes and God-Fearers Club Together', *New Documents Illustrating Early Christianity*, 9 (1986–70), 73–80.

Jungmann, J. A., *The Mass of the Roman Rite: Its Origins and Development (Missarum sollemnia)*, trans. F. A. Brunner (Westminster, NJ, 1986).

Junod, E., and J.-D. Kaestli (eds), *L'Histoire des actes apocryphes des Âpotres du III au IX⁰ siècle: Le cas des Actes de Jean* (Geneva, 1982).

Kampen, N. B., *Family Fictions in Roman Art* (Cambridge, 2009).

Kannengiesser, C., *Arius and Athanasius: Two Alexandrian Theologians* (Aldershot, 1991).

Kantorowicz, E. H., *Laudes Regiae: A Study in Liturgical Acclamations and Mediaeval Ruler Worship* (Berkeley and Los Angeles, 1958).

Karp, T., *Aspects of Orality and Formularity in Gregorian Chant* (Evanston, Ill., 998).

—— 'Interpreting Silence: Liturgy, Singing and Psalmody in the Early Synagogue', *Rivista internazionale di musica sacra*, 20 (1999), 47–109.

—— *The Polyphony of Saint Martial and Santiago de Compostela*, 2 vols (Oxford, 1992).

Kartsovnik, V., 'The Eleventh-Century Office for St. Gregory the Great in the

Manuscript Tradition', *Cantus Planus, Papers Read at the Sixth Meeting* (Budapest, 1995), ii. 615–27.

Kaster, R.A., *Guardians of Language: The Grammarian and Society in Late Antiquity* (Berkeley, 1988).

Katz, D.S., 'Biblische Kantillation und Musik der Synagoge: Ein Rückblick auf die ältesten Quellen', *Musiktheorie*, 15 (2000), 57–78.

Katz, S.T. (ed.), *The Cambridge History of Judaism*, iv: *The Late Roman-Rabbinic Period* (Cambridge, 2006).

Kayser, C., 'Gebrauch von Psalmen zur Zauberei', *Zeitschrift für deutschen morgenländischen Gesellschaft*, 42 (1988), 456–62.

Keating, J.F., *The Agapé and the Eucharist in the Early Church* (London, 1901).

Kelber, W.H., 'The Quest for the Historical Jesus from the Perspectives of Medieval, Modern and Post-Enlightenment Readings, and in View of Ancient Oral Aesthetics', in J.D. Crossan, L.T. Johnson and W.H. Kelber (eds), *The Jesus Controversy: Perspectives in Conflict* (Harrisburg, Pa., 1999), 75–115.

Keller, E., *Eucharistie und Parusie* (Freiburg, 1989).

Kelly, C., *Ruling the Later Roman Empire* (Cambridge, Mass., 2004).

Kelly, J.N.D., *Early Christian Doctrines* (London, 1965).

Kelly, T.F., *The Beneventan Chant* (Cambridge, 1989).

—— *The Exultet in Southern Italy* (Oxford, 1996).

—— 'Medieval Composers of Liturgical Chant', *Musica e storia*, 14 (2006), 95–125.

—— 'Structure and Ornament in Chant: The Case of the Beneventan *Exultet*', in Boone (ed.), *Essays*, 249–76.

Keynes, S., *The Councils of Clofesho* (Brixworth Lecture 1993; Leicester, 1994).

—— 'The Reconstruction of a Burnt Cottonian Manuscript: The Case of Cotton Otho A. I', *British Library Journal*, 22 (1996), 113–60.

King, K.L., *What is Gnosticism?* (Cambridge, Mass., 2003).

Kingsley, S., 'Mapping Trade by Shipwrecks', in Mango (ed.), *Byzantine Trade*, 31–6.

Klauck, H.J., *The Religious Context of Early Christianity: A Guide to Graeco-Roman Religions*, trans. Brian McNeil (Edinburgh, 2000).

—— 'Die Sakramente und der historische Jesus', in id. (ed.), *Gemeinde, Amt, Sakrament: Neutestamentliche Perspektiven* (Würzburg, 1989).

Klauser, Th., 'Die liturgischen Austauschbeziehungen zwischen der römischen und der fränkisch-deutschen Kirche vom achten bis zum elften Jahrhundert', *Historisches Jahbuch*, 53 (1933), 169–89.

Klawans, J., 'Interpreting the Last Supper: Sacrifice, Spiritualization and Anti-Sacrifice', *New Testament Studies*, 48 (2002), 1–17.

Kleeman, J., 'Quelques réflexions sur l'interprétation ethnique des sépultures habillées considérées comme vandales', in *L'Afrique vandale*, i. 123–9.

Klingshirn, W.E., *Caesarius of Arles: The Making of a Christian Community in Late Antique Gaul* (Cambridge, 1994).

Kłoczowski, J., 'Les Cisterciens en Europe du centre-est au moyen âge', in *Unanimité et diversité cisterciennes*, 421–39.

Köbler, G., *Gotisches Wörterbuch* (Leiden, 1989).

Koch, M., *Sankt Fridolin und sein Biograph Balther: Irische Heilige in der literarischen Darstellung des Mittelalters* (Zürich, 1959).

Kohler, C., 'Traité du recouvrement de la Terre Sainte, addressé, vers l'an 1295, à Philippe le Bel par Galvano de Levanto, médecin génois', *Revue de l'orient latin*, 6 (1898), 343–69.

Koller, H., 'Die bairische Kirchenorganisation des 8. Jahrhunderts: Ansätze, Konzepte, Verwirklichung' in E. Boshof and H. Wolff (eds), *Das Christentum im bairischen Raum: Von den Anfängen bis ins 11. Jahrhundert* (Cologne, 1994), 273–89.

Kraeling, C., *Dura Final Report VIII, Part I: The Synagogue* (New Haven, 1956).

—— *Dura Final Report VIII, Part II: The Christian Building* (New Haven, 1956).

Kraemer, D. 'The Mishnah', in S. T. Katz (ed.), *The Cambridge History of Judaism*, IV, 299–315.

Kraus, T. J., ' "Uneducated", "Ignorant", or even "Illiterate"? Aspects and Background for an Understanding of *agrammatoi* (and *idiotai*) in Acts 4.13.', *New Testament Studies*, 45 (1999), 434–9.

Krautheimer, R., *Rome: Profile of a City 312–1308* (Princeton, 1980).

—— Frazer, A. K., and S. Corbett, *Corpus Basilicarum Christianarum Romae*, 5 vols (Vatican City, 1977).

Kugel, J. L., 'Topics in the History of the Spirituality of the Psalms', in A. Green (ed.), *Jewish Spirituality: From the Bible through the Middle Ages* (London, 1986).

Kulikowski, M. E., *Late Roman Spain and its Cities* (Baltimore, 2004).

Lädstatter, S., *Die Materielle Kultur der Spätantike in den Ostalpen* (Vienna, 2000).

Lafferty, M. K., *L'Afrique vandale et byzantine, Antiquité Tardive*, 10–11 (2002–3).

—— 'Translating from Greek to Latin: *Romanitas* and *Christianitas* in Late-Fourth Century Rome and Milan', *JECS* 11 (2003), 21–62.

Lampe, P., *From Paul to Valentinus: Christians at Rome in the First Two Centuries* (Minneapolis, 2003).

Lancel, M. S., 'Victor de Vita, témoin et chroniqueur des années noires de l'Afrique romaine au vᵉ siècle', *Academies des inscriptions et belles-lettres: Comptes rendus des séances de l'année 2000*, iii (Paris, 2000), 1199–219.

Lane-Fox, R., 'Literacy and Power in Early Christianity', in A. K. Bowman and G. Woolf (eds), *Literacy and Power in the Ancient World* (Cambridge, 1994), 126–48.

Lanham, C. D., *Salutation Formulas in Latin Letters to 1200: Syntax, Style and Theory* (Munich, 1975).

Lapidge, M. (ed.), *Archbishop Theodore: Commemorative Studies on his Life and Influence* (Cambridge 1995).

Lattin, H. P., 'The Eleventh-Century MS Munich 14436: Its Contribution to the History of Coordinates, of Logic and of German Studies in France', *Isis*, 38 (1947–8), 205–25.

Lauranson-Rosaz, C., *L'Auvergne et ses marges (Velay, Gévaudan) du VIIIᵉ au XIᵉ siècle: La fin du monde antique?* (Le Puy-en-Velay, 1987).

Laurence, R., and A. Wallace-Hadrill (eds), *Domestic Space in the Roman World: Pompeii and Beyond, Journal of Roman Archeology*, Supplementary Series, 22 (1997).

Law, V., *Grammar and Grammarians in the Early Middle Ages* (London and New York, 1997).

—— *The Insular Latin Grammarians* (Woodbridge, 1982).

—— 'The Study of Grammar in Eighth-Century Southumbria', *Anglo-Saxon England*, 12 (1983), 43–71.

Le Boulluec, A., *La Notion d'hérésie dans la litterature grecque, IIᵉ–IIIᵉ siècles* (Paris, 1985).

Lecoq, D., 'La Mappemonde du *Liber Floridus* ou la vision du monde de Lambert de Saint-Omer', *Imago Mundi*, 39 (1987), 9–49.

Leeb, H., *Die Psalmodie bei Ambrosius* (Vienna, 1967).

Le Maho, J., 'Les Fouilles de la cathédrale de Rouen 1985 à 1993: Esquisse d'un premier bilan', *Archéologie médiévale*, 24 (1994), 1–49.

Le Maître, P., 'L'Œuvre d'Aldric du Mans et sa signification (832–857)', *Francia*, 8 (1980), 43–64.

Lepelley, C. (ed.), *La Fin de la cité antique et le début de la cité médiévale de la fin du IIIe siècle à l'avènement de Charlemagne* (Bari, 1996).

Leppert, R., and McClary, S. (eds), *Music and Society: The Politics of Composition, Performance and Reception* (Cambridge, 1987).

Lesne, E., *Histoire de la propriété ecclésiastique en France*, 6 vols (Lille, 1910–43).

Letourneur, M.-J., 'La Circulation des messagers chez Jérôme', in M. Garrido-Hory (ed.), *Routes et marchés d'esclaves* ([Besançon], 2002), 127–37.

Levine, L. I., *The Ancient Synagogue*, 2nd edn (New Haven and London, 2005).

—— 'The Development of Synagogue Liturgy in Late Antiquity', in E. M. Meyers (ed.), *Galilee through the Centuries: Confluence of Cultures* (Winona Lake, Ind., 1993), 123–44.

—— 'The Nature and Origin of the Palestinian Synagogue Reconsidered', *Journal of Biblical Literature*, 115 (1996), 425–8.

—— and Weiss, Z. (eds), *From Dura to Sepphoris: Studies in Jewish Art and Society in Late Antiquity* (Portsmouth, RI, 2000).

Levinskaya, I., *The Book of Acts in its Diaspora Setting* (Grand Rapids, Mich., 1996).

Levy, K., *Gregorian Chant and the Carolingians* (Princeton, 1998).

—— 'Gregorian Chant and the Romans', *JAMS* 56 (2003), 5–42.

—— 'Latin Chant outside the Roman Tradition', in R. Crocker and D. Hiley (eds), *The Early Middle Ages to 1300* (New Oxford History of Music, 2; Oxford, 1990), 69–110.

—— 'A New Look at Old Roman Chant', *Early Music History*, 19 (2000), 81–104, and 20 (2001), 173–97.

—— 'Old Hispanic Chant in its European Context', in E. C. Rodicio et al. (eds), *Actas del Congreso Internacional 'España en la Música de Occidente'* (Madrid, 1987), i. 3–14.

Lewis, A. A., 'Le Commerce et la navigation sur les côtes atlantiques de la Gaule du ve au viiie siècle', *Le Moyen Âge*, 5 (1953), 249–98.

Lewis, C. T., and C. Short, *A Latin Dictionary* (Oxford, 1969).

Lexicon Latinitatis Nederlandicae Medii Aevi, ed. J. W. Fuchs and Olga Weijers, 9 vols (Leiden, 1977–2005).

Leyerle, B., 'Appealing to Children', *JECS* 5 (1997), 243–70.

Liebeschuetz, J. H. W. G., *Barbarians and Bishops: Army, Church and State in the Age of Arcadius and Chrysostom* (Oxford, 1992).

—— *The Decline and Fall of the Roman City* (Oxford, 2001).

Lietzmann, H., *Mass and Lord's Supper: A Study in the History of the Liturgy* (Leiden, 1979).

Lightstone, J. N., *The Commerce of the Sacred: Mediation of the Divine among Jews in the Graeco-Roman Diaspora* (Chico, Calif., 1984).

Linck, E., *Sozialer Wandel in klösterlichen Grundherrschaften des 11. bis 13. Jahrhunderts: Studien zu den Familiae von Gembloux, Stablo-Malmedy und St. Trond* (Göttingen, 1979).

Little, L. K. (ed.), *Plague and the End of Antiquity* (Cambridge, 2007).

Lizzi Testa, R., *Vescovi e strutture ecclesiastiche nella città tardoantica: L'Italia Annonaria nel IV–V secolo d. C.* (Como, 1989).

Llewellyn, P., 'The Roman Church in the Seventh Century: The Legacy of Gregory I', *Journal of Ecclesiastical History*, 25 (1974), 363–80.

—— *Rome in the Dark Ages* (London, 1971).

Lloyd, G. E. R., 'Greek Democracy, Philosophy and Science', in J. Dunn (ed.), *Democracy: The Unfinished Journey 508 BC–AD 1993* (Oxford, 1992), 41–56.

Lochner, F., 'Un Évêque musicien au xᵉ siècle: Radbod d'Utrecht (+917)', *Tijdschrift van der Vereniging voor Nederlandse Muziekgeschiednis*, 38 (1988), 3–35.

Lohse, E., 'Entstehung des Bischofsamtes in der frühen Christenheit', *Zeitschift für die Neutestamentliche Wissenschaft und die Kunde der älteren kirche*, 71 (1980), 58–73.

Lomax, D. W., *The Reconquest of Spain* (London, 1986).

Loseby, S. T., 'Bishops and Cathedrals: Order and Diversity in the Fifth-Century Urban Landscape of Southern Gaul', in Drinkwater and Elton (eds), *Fifth-Century Gaul*, 144–55.

—— 'Marseille and the Pirenne Thesis I: Gregory of Tours, the Merovingian Kings and '"un grand port"', in Hodges and Bowden (ed.), *The Sixth Century*, 203–29.

—— 'Marseille and the Pirenne Thesis II: "Ville morte"', in Hansen and Wickham (eds), *The Long Eighth Century*, 167–93.

Lucchesi, G., 'Sull'antica tradizione manoscritta di S. Pier Damiani', *Benedictina*, 24 (1977), 209–25.

Ludwig, U., *Transalpine Beziehungen der Karolingerzeit in Spiegel der Memorialüberlieferung* (Hannover, 1999).

Lunn-Rockliffe, S., *Ambrosiaster's Political Theology* (Oxford, 2007).

Maccoby, H., *Paul and Hellenism* (London, 1991).

McCone, K. R., 'Brigit in the Seventh Century: A Saint with Three Lives?' *Peritia*, 1 (1982), 107–45.

McCormick, M., 'Bateaux de vie, bateaux de mort: Maladie, commerce, transports annonaires et le passage économique du Bas-Empire au Moyen Âge', in *Morfologie sociali e culturali in Europa fra tarda antiquità e alto medioevo* (SSCISAM 45; Spoleto, 1998), 35–122.

—— 'The Birth of the Codex and the Apostolic Life-Style', *Scriptorium*, 39 (1985), 150–8.

—— *Origins of the European Economy: Communications and Commerce AD 300–900* (Cambridge, 2001).

McDonald, L. M., *The Formation of the Christian Biblical Canon* (Peabody, Mass., 1995).

MacDonald, M. Y., *Early Christian Women and Pagan Opinion: The Power of the Hysterical Woman* (Cambridge, 1996).

—— *The Pauline Churches: A Socio-Historical Study of Institutionalization in the Pauline and Deutero-Pauline Writings* (Cambridge, 1988).

McGee, T. J., *The Sound of Medieval Song: Ornamentation and Vocal Style according to the Treatises* (Oxford, 1998).

McGowan, A. B., *Ascetic Eucharists: Food and Drink in Early Christian Ritual Meals* (Oxford, 1999).

—— 'The Inordinate Cup: Issues of Order in Early Eucharistic Dining', *Studia Patristica*, 35 (2001), 283–91.

—— 'Naming the Feast: The *Agape* and the Diversity of Early Christian Ritual Meals', *Studia Patristica*, 30 (1997), 314–18.

McGrade, M., 'Gottschalk of Aachen, the Investiture Controversy, and Music for the Feast of the *Divisio Apostolorum*', *JAMS*, 49 (1996), 351–408.

McKay, A., *Spain in the Middle Ages: From Frontier to Empire 1000–1500* (London, 1977).

Mackay, A., and F. Ditchburn (eds), *Atlas of Medieval Europe* (London and New York, 1997).

McKechnie, P., *The First Christian Centuries: Perspectives in the Early Church* (London, 2001).

McKinnon, J., *The Advent Project: The Later Seventh-Century Creation of the Roman Mass Proper* (Berkeley, 2000).

—— 'The Book of Psalms, Monasticism and the Western Liturgy', in Van Deusen (ed.), *The Place of the Psalms*, 43–58.

—— 'Desert Monasticism and the Later Fourth-Century Psalmodic Movement', *Music & Letters*, 75 (1994), 505–19; repr. in id., *The Temple*, Essay XI.

—— 'Early Christian Music', *New Grove Online*.

—— 'The Fourth-Century Origin of the Gradual', *Early Music History*, 7 (1987), 91–106; repr; in id., *The Temple*, Essay IX.

—— '*Gregorius presul composuit hunc libellum musicae artis*', in T. J. Heffernan and E. A. Matter (eds), *The Liturgy of the Medieval Church* (Kalamazoo, 2001), 673–94.

—— 'Liturgical Psalmody in the Sermons of Saint Augustine', in Jeffery (ed.), *The Study of Medieval Chant*, 7–24.

—— 'The Origins of the Western Office', in Fassler and Baltzer (eds), *The Divine Office in the Latin Middle Ages*, 63–73.

—— *The Temple, the Church Fathers and Early Western Chant* (Aldershot, 1998*)*.

McKitterick, R. (ed.), *Carolingian Culture: Emulation and Innovation* (Cambridge, 1994).

—— *Charlemagne: The Formation of a European Identity* (Cambridge, 2008).

—— *The Frankish Church and the Carolingian Reforms 789–895* (London, 1977).

—— *The Frankish Kingdoms under the Carolingians 751–987* (London and New York, 1983).

—— *History and Memory in the Carolingian World* (Cambridge, 2004).

—— 'The Illusion of Power in the Carolingian Annals', *English Historical Review*, 115 (2000), 1–20.

—— 'Latin and Romance: An Historian's Perspective', in Wright (ed.), *Latin and the Romance Languages*, 130–45.

—— Review of Kenneth Levy, *Gregorian Chant and the Carolingians*, in *Early Music History*, 19 (2000), 279–91.

—— 'Royal Patronage of Culture in the Frankish Kingdoms under the Carolingians', in *Committenti e produzione artistico-letteraria nell'alto medioevo Occidentale* (SSCISAM 39; Spoleto, 1992), 93–129.

—— (ed.), *The Uses of Literacy in Early Mediaeval Europe* (Cambridge, 1990).

MacLean, S., *Kingship and Politics in the Late Ninth Century: Charles the Fat and the End of the Carolingian Empire* (Cambridge, 2003).

MacMullen, R., *Corruption and the Decline of Rome* (New Haven and London, 1988).

Maconie, R., *The Concept of Music* (Oxford, 1993).

McShane, P. A., *La Romanitas et le Pape Léon le Grand: L'apport culturel des institutions impériales à la formation des structures ecclésiastiques* (Montréal, 1979).

Madoz, J. (ed.), *Liciniano de Cartagena y sus cartas* (Madrid, 1948).

Maenchen-Helfen, O., *The World of the Huns: Studies in their History and Culture* (Berkeley, 1973).

Magnou-Nortier, E., 'Capitulaire "De villis et curtis imperialibus" (vers 810–13): Texte, traduction et commentaire', *Revue historique*, 67 (1998), 643–89.

Maître, C., *La Réforme cistercienne du plain-chant: Étude d'un traité théorique* (Brecht, 1995).

Malcolm, J., 'Epistola Johannis Cottonis ad Fulgentium Episcopum', *Musica Disciplina*, 47 (1993), 159–69.

Mandouze, A., et al., *Prosopographie chrétienne du Bas-Empire*, i: *Prosopographie de l'Afrique chrétienne (305–533)* (Paris, 1982).

Mango, M. M. (ed.), *Byzantine Trade 4th–12th Centuries* (Farnham, 2009).

Marjanen, A., and Luomanen, P., *A Companion to Second-Century Christian 'Heretics'* (Leiden, 2005).

Markschies, C., 'Jesus Christ as a Man before God: Two Interpretive Models for Isaiah 53 in the Patristic Literature and their Development', in Janowski and Stuhlmacher (eds), *The Suffering Servant*, 223–320.

Markus, D. D., 'Performing the Book: The Recital of Epic in First-Century C.E. Rome', *Classical Antiquity*, 19 (2000), 138–79.

Markus, R. A., *The End of Ancient Christianity* (Cambridge, 1990).

—— *Gregory the Great and his World* (Cambridge, 1997).

Marrou, H.-I., *Mousikos aner: Études sur les scènes de la vie intellectuelle figurant sur les monuments funéraires romains* (Grenoble, 1937).

Martimort, A. G., *Deaconesses: An Historical Study* (San Francisco, 1986).

Martin, C., *La Géographie du pouvoir dans l'Espagne visigothique* (Lille, 2003).

Mathisen, R. W., 'Barbarian Bishops and the Churches *in barbaricis gentibus* during Late Antiquity', *Speculum*, 72 (1997), 664–97.

—— 'Bishops, Barbarians and the "Dark Ages": The Fate of Late-Roman Educational Institutions in Late-Antique Gaul', in R. B. Begley and J. W. Koterski (eds), *Medieval Education* (New York, 2005), 3–19.

—— *Ecclesiastical Factionalism and Religious Controversy in Fifth-Century Gaul* (Washington, DC, 1989).

—— *Roman Aristocrats in Barbarian Gaul: Strategies of Survival in an Age of Transition* (Austin, 1993).

—— and H. S. Sivan, 'Forging a New Identity: The Kingdom of Toulouse and the Frontiers of Visigothic Aquitania', in Ferreiro (ed.), *The Visigoths*, 1–62.

Matson, D. L., *Household Conversion-Narratives in Acts* (Sheffield, 1996).

Matthews, J. F., 'Anicius Manlius Severinus Boethius' in Gibson (ed.), *Boethius*, 15–43.

—— *Western Aristocracies and Imperial Court A.D. 364–425* (Oxford, 1975).

Mattingly, D. J., 'Oil for Export? A Comparison of Libyan, Spanish and Tunisian Olive Oil Production in the Roman Empire, *Journal of Roman Archaeology*, 1 (1988), 33–56.

—— *Tripolitania* (London, 1995).

Maurer, H., *Konstanz in Mittelalter*, i: *Von den Anfängen zum Konzil* (Constance, 1989).

Maxwell, J. LaRae, *Christianization and Communication in Late Antiquity : John Chrysostom and his Congregation in Antioch* (Cambridge, 2006).

Meeks, W.A., *The First Urban Christians: The Social World of the Apostle Paul* (New Haven, 1983).

Menninger, K., *Number Words and Number Symbols: A Cultural History of Numbers*, trans. P. Broneer (New York, 1992).

Metzger, B.M., *The Canon of the New Testament: Its Origin, Development and Significance* (Oxford, 1997).

Meyer, Christian, *Manuscripts from the Carolingian Era . . . Addenda, Corrigenda* (The Theory of Music, 6; Munich, 2003).

Miles, R., 'The *Anthologia Latina* and the Creation of Secular Space in Vandal Carthage', *Antiquité tardive*, 13 (2005), 305–20.

Millar F., *A Greek Roman Empire: Power and Belief under Theodosius II (408/450)* (Berkeley and London, 2006).

—— 'Local Cultures in the Roman Empire: Libyan, Punic and Latin in Roman Africa', *Journal of Roman Studies*, 58 (1968), 126–34.

Miller J.I., *The Spice Trade of the Roman Empire, 29 B.C. to A.D. 641* (Oxford, 1969).

Miller, M., *The Bishop's Palace: Architecture and Authority in Medieval Italy* (Ithaca, 2000).

Miller, R.H., 'Liturgical Materials in the *Acts of John*', *Studia Patristica*, 13 (1975), 375–81.

Miller, T.S., *The Birth of the Hospital in the Byzantine Empire* (Baltimore, 1985).

—— *The Orphans of Byzantium: Child Welfare in the Christian Empire* (Washington, DC, 2003).

Mimouni, S.C., *Le Judéo-christianisme ancien: Essais historiques* (Paris, 1998).

Minguez, J. Ma., *Alfonso VI: Poder, Expansión y Reorganización Interior* (Handarribia, 2000).

Mitchell, K., and I. Wood (eds), *The World of Gregory of Tours* (Leiden, 2002).

Mitchell, S., *Anatolia: Land, Men and Gods in Asia Minor*, 2 vols (Oxford, 1995).

—— 'The Cult of Theos Hypsistos', in P. Athanassiadi and M. Frede (eds), *Pagan Monotheism in Late Antiquity* (Oxford, 1999), 81–148.

Mittellateinisches Wörterbuch (Berlin, 1959–).

Modéran, Y., 'Une Guerre de religion: Les deux Églises d'Afrique à l'époque vandale', *Antiquité tardive*, 11 (2003), 21–44.

Mohrmann, C., *Études sur le latin des chrétiens*, 4 vols (Rome, 1975).

—— *Liturgical Latin, its Origins and Character* (London, 1957).

Moore, R.I., *The First European Revolution, c.970–1215* (Oxford, 2000).

—— 'Heresy and Disease', in W. Lourdeaux and D. Verhelst (eds), *The Concept of Heresy in the Middle Ages* (Louvain and The Hague, 1976), 1–11.

Moorhead, J., 'Boethius and Romans in Ostrogothic Service', *Historia*, 27 (1978), 604–12.

—— 'Clovis' Motives for Becoming a Catholic Christian', *Journal of Religious History*, 13 (1985), 329–39.

—— *The Roman Empire Divided 400–700* (London, 2001).

—— *Theoderic in Italy* (Oxford, 1992).

Mordek, H., *Bibliotheca Capitularium Regum Francorum Manuscripta* (Munich, 1995).

Moreau, M. (ed.), *La Doctrine chrétienne* (Paris, 1997).

Morin, Dom G., 'Notes liturgiques', *Revue bénédictine*, 30 (1913), 226–34.

Morris, C., *The Papal Monarchy: The Western Church from 1050 to 1250* (Oxford, 1989).

Moule, C. F. D., 'Deacons in the New Testament', *Theology*, 58 (1955), 405–7.

Moulton, W. F., A. S. Geden, and I. H. Marshall, *Concordance to the Greek New Testament* (London, 2002).

Moxnes, H. (ed.), *Constructing Early Christian Families: Family as Social Reality and Metaphor* (London, 1997).

Mullen, R. L., The *Expansion of Christianity: A Gazetteer of its First Three Centuries* (Leiden, 2004).

Müller, H., 'Die Kirche von Lyon im Karolingerreich', *Historische Jahrbuch*, 107 (1987), 224–53.

Munier, Ch., 'L'Autorité de l'Église et l'autorité de l'Esprit d'après Tertullien', *Revue des sciences religieuses*, 58 (1984), 77–90.

Murphy-O'Connor, J., *Saint Paul's Corinth: Texts and Archaeology* (Wilmington, Del., 1983).

Murray, A. C. (ed.), *After Rome's Fall: Narrators and Sources of Early Medieval History* (Toronto, 1998).

Murray, P., et al., *Living Bridges: The Inhabited Bridge, Past, Present and Future* (London, 1996).

La navigazione mediterranea nell'Alto Medioevo (SSCISAM 25; Spoleto, 1975).

Nelson, J., *Charles the Bald* (London, 1992).

——'The Merovingian Church in Carolingian Perspective', in Mitchell and Wood (eds), *The World of Gregory of Tours*, 241–59.

——'National Synods, Kingship as Office and Royal Anointing: An Early Medieval Syndrome', in G. J. Cuming and D. Baker (eds), *Councils and Assemblies* (Studies in Church History, 7; Cambridge, 1971), 41–59.

——and Gibson, M. T. (eds), *Charles the Bald: Court and Kingdom*, 2nd rev. edn (Aldershot, 1990).

Neusner, J., *Rabbinic Judaism: Disputes and Debates* (Atlanta, Ga., 1994).

Newman, I. C., 'De verbis canere et dicere eorumque apud Poetas Latinos ab Ennio usque ad aetatem Augusti usu', *Latinitas*, 13 (1965), 86–106.

Nicholas, K. S., 'The Role of Feudal Relationships in the Consolidation of Power in the Principalities of the Low Countries, 1000–1300', in S. Bachrach and D. Nicholas (eds), *Law, Custom and the Social Fabric in Medieval Europe* (Kalamazoo, 1990), 113–30.

Nicolet, C., *Space, Geography and Politics in the Early Roman Empire* (Ann Arbor, 1991).

Noble, T. F. X., 'Literacy and the Papal Government in Late Antiquity and the Early Middle Ages', in McKitterick (ed.), *The Uses of Literacy*, 82–133.

—— *The Republic of Saint Peter* (Philadelphia, 1984).

——'Rome in the Seventh Century', in Lapidge (ed.), *Archbishop Theodore*, 68–87.

Noll, R., *Römische Siedlungen und Strassen im Limesgebiet zwischen Inn und Enns, Oberösterreich* (Der römische Limes in Österreich, 21; Vienna, 1958).

North, D., 'Coordinates and Categories: The Graphical Representation of Functions in Medieval Astronomy', in E. Grant and J. E. Murdoch (eds), *Mathematics and its Applications to Science and Natural Philosophy in the Middle Ages* (Cambridge, 1987), 173–88.

Novarra, P., 'La chiesa pomposiana nelle trasformazioni medievali', in Di Francesco and Samaritani (eds), *Pomposa*, 153–75.

Novum Glossarium Mediae Latinitatis (Copenhagen, 1957–).

Nowacki, E., 'Antiphonal Psalmody in Christian Antiquity and the Early Middle Ages', in Boone (ed.), *Essays*, 287–315.

Oesch, H., *Guido von Arezzo* (Bern, 1954).

Oexle, O.G., 'Die Karolinger und die Stadt des heiligen Arnulf', *Frühmittelalterliche Studien*, 1 (1967), 250–364.

Økland, J., *Women in their Place: Paul and the Corinthian Discourse of Gender and Sanctuary Space* (London, 2004).

Ollich i Castanyer, I. (ed.), *Actes del Congrés Internacional Gerbert d'Orlhac i el seu temps* (Vic, 1999).

Orchard, A., *The Poetic Art of Aldhelm* (Cambridge, 1994).

Orlandis, J., 'El Arrianismo Visigodo Tardio', *Cuadernos de Historia de España*, 65–6 (1981), 5–20.

Osborn, E., *Justin Martyr* (Tübingen, 1973).

—— *Tertullian: First Theologian of the West* (Cambridge, 1995).

Osborne, J., 'Papal Court Culture during the Pontificate of Zacharias (AD 741–52)', in C. Cubitt (ed.), *Court Culture in the Early Middle Ages: The Proceedings of the First Alcuin Conference* (Turnhout, 2003), 223–34.

Osiek, C., and Balch, D. L., *Families in the New Testament World: Households and House Churches* (Louisville, Ky., 1997).

Page, C., 'Marian Texts and Themes in an English Manuscript: A Miscellany in Two Parts', *PMM* 5 (1996), 23–44.

Palisca, C., 'An Introduction to the *Musica* of Johannes dictus Cotto vel Affligemensis', in B. Gillingham and P. Merkley (eds), *Beyond the Moon: Festschrift Luther Dittmer* (Musicological Studies, 53; Ottawa, Ont., 1990), 144–62.

Papathanasiou, I. and Boukas, N., 'Early Diastematic Notation in Greek Hymnographic Texts of Coptic Origin: A Reconsideration of the Source Material', in G. Wolfram (ed.), *Paleobyzantine Notations* (Leuven, 1995), 1–25.

Parga, L. V. de, Lacarra, J. Ma., and Uría Ríu, J. (eds), *Las Peregrinaciones a Santiago de Compostela*, 3 vols (Madrid, 1948–9).

Parker, A. J., *Ancient Shipwrecks of the Mediterranean and the Roman Provinces* (Oxford, 1992).

Parkes, M. M., 'The Contribution of Insular Scribes of the Seventh and Eighth Centuries to the "Grammar of Legibility"', in A. Maierù (ed.), *Grafia e interpunzione del latino nel medioevo* (Castello, 1987), 15–30.

—— '*Raedan areccan, smeagan*: How the Anglo-Saxons Read', *Anglo-Saxon England*, 26 (1987), 1–22.

Parvis, P., 'The Textual Tradition of Justin's Apologies: A Modest Proposal', *Studia Patristica*, 36 (2001), 54–60.

Paschke, B. A., 'The *cura morum* of the Roman Censors as Historical Background for the Bishop and Deacon Lists of the Pastoral Epistles', *Zeitschrift für die Neutestamentliche Wissenschaft*, 98 (2007), 105–119.

Patlagean, E., *Pauvreté économique et pauvreté sociale à Byzance, IVᵉ–VIIᵉ siècles* (Paris, 1977).

—— 'Variations impériales sur le thème romain', in *Roma fra Oriente e Occidente*, 2–47.

A Patristic Greek Lexicon, ed. G. H. W. Lampe (Oxford, 1961–8).

Patzia, A.G., *The Emergence of the Church: Context, Growth, Leadership and Worship* (Downers Grove, Ill., 2001).

Peacock, D.P.S., 'The Rhine and the Problem of Gaulish Wine in Roman Britain', in Du Plat Taylor and Cleere (eds), *Roman Shipping and Trade*, 49–51.

Pedley, J.G. (ed.), *New Light on Ancient Carthage* (Michigan, 1980).

Pelletier, A., *Vienne gallo-romaine au Bas-Empire, 275–468 après J.-C.* (Lyon, 1974).

Pernveden, L., *The Concept of the Church in the Shepherd of Hermas* (Lund, 1966).

Perret, L., *Catacombes de Rome: Architecture, peintures murales . . . inscriptions, figures et symboles gravés sur pierre*, 6 vols (Paris, 1851–5).

Perrot, C., 'The Reading of the Bible in the Ancient Synagogue', in M.J. Mulder (ed.), *Mikra: Text, Translation, Reading and Interpretation of the Hebrew Bible in Ancient Judaism and Early Christianity* (Philadelphia, 1988), 137–59.

Pettiau, H.P.C., 'Aspects of Episcopacy in Seventh-Century Western Europe' (Ph.D. diss., University of Cambridge, 2002).

Pfeiffer, F., *Rheinische Transitzölle im Mittelalter* (Berlin, 1997).

Pfisterer, A., *Cantilena Romana: Untersuchungen zur Überlieferung des gregorianischen Chorals* (Paderborn, 2002).

—— 'Italian and Gallican Alleluia psalmody', *PMM* 17 (2008), 55–68.

Pflaum, H.-G., and N. Duval (eds), *L'Onomastique latine* (Paris, 1977).

Phillips, N., 'The Dasia Notation and its Manuscript Tradition', in Huglo (ed.), *Musicologie médiévale*, 157–73.

Picard, J.-C., 'La Fonction des salles de réception dans le groupe épiscopal de Genève', *Rivista di archeologia cristiana*, 65 (1989), 87–104.

Pietri, Ch., 'Remarques sur l'onomastique chrétienne de Rome', in Pflaum and Duval (eds), *Onomastique latine*, 437–45.

—— *Roma Christiana: Recherches sur l'Église de Rome, son organisation, sa politique, son idéologie de Militiade à Sixte III (311–440)*, 2 vols (Rome, 1976).

—— and L. Pietri et al., *Prosopographie chrétienne du Bas-Empire*, ii: *Prosopographie de l'Italie chrétienne (313–604)* (Paris, 2000).

Pietri, L., 'Les Prêtres de *parochiae* et leur ministère: L'exemple de la Gaule de l'Antiquité tardive', in Delage (ed.), *Les Pères*, 341–64.

Pilat, Z., 'Les Réseaux des Cisterciens en Europe du centre-est du XIIe au XVe siècle', in *Unanimité et diversité cisterciennes*, 441–51.2

Pirson, F., 'Rented Accommodation at Pompeii: The Evidence of the *Insula Arriana Polliana VI, 6*', in Laurence and Wallace-Hadrill (eds), *Domestic Space*, 165–81.

Pitz, E., *Papstreskripte im frühen Mittelalter: Diplomatische und rechtsgeschichtliche Studien zum Brief-Corpus Gregors des Grossen* (Sigmaringen: Thorbecke, 1990).

Piva, P., 'Metz: Un gruppo episcopale alla svolta dei tempi (secoli IV–IX)', *Antiquité tardive*, 8 (2000), 237–64.

Planchart, A.E., 'The Geography of Martinmas', in Gallagher et al. (eds), *Western Plainchant in the First Millennium*, 119–56.

Pohl, W., 'Telling the Difference: Signs of Ethnic Identity', in Pohl and Reimitz (eds), *Strategies of Distinction*, 17–69.

—— (ed.), *Kingdoms of the Empire: The Integration of Barbarians in Late Antiquity* (The Transformation of the Roman World, 1; Leiden, 1997).

—— and Reimitz, H., *Strategies of Distinction: The Construction of Ethnic Communities 300–800* (The Transformation of the Roman World, 2; Leiden, 1998).

——Wood, I., and Reimitz, H. (eds), *The Transformation of Frontiers: From Late Antiquity to the Carolingians* (The Transformation of the Roman World, 10; Leiden, 2001).

Porter, W. S., *The Gallican Rite* (London, 1958).

Posner, R., *The Romance Languages* (Cambridge, 1996).

Pothier, J., *Les Mélodies grégoriennes d'après la tradition* (Tournai, 1881).

Pouderon, B., 'Réflexions sur la formation d'une élite intellectuelle chrétienne au IIe siècle', in id. and J. Doré (eds), *Les Apologistes chrétiens et la culture grecque* (Paris, 1998), 237–69.

Praet, D., 'Explaining the Christianization of the Roman Empire', *Sacris Erudiri*, 33 (1992–3), 5–119.

Prat, F., 'Les Prétensions des diacres romains au quatrième siècle', *Recherches de science religieuse*, 3 (1912), 463–75.

Prawer, J., 'The Roots of Medieval Colonialism', in V. P. Goss and C. V. Bornstein (eds), *The Meeting of Two Worlds: Cultural Exchanges between East and West during the Period of the Crusades* (Kalamazoo, 1986), 23–38.

Préaux, C., 'Une Amulette chrétienne aux Musées Royaux d'Art et d'Histoire de Bruxelles', *Chronique d'Egypte*, 20 (1935), 361–70.

Prosopographie (Italy). See Pietri and Pietri.

Pryor, J. W., 'Justin Martyr and the Fourth Gospel', *Second Century*, 9 (1992), 153–69.

Pycke, J., '*Urbs fuerat quondam, quod adhuc vestigia monstrant*: Réflexions sur l'histoire de Tournai pendant le haut moyen âge (v^e–xe siècle)', in *La Genèse et les premiers siècles des villes médiévales dans les Pays-Bas méridionaux* (n.p., 1990), 211–31.

Quacquarelli, A., 'Alle origini del "lector"', in *Convivium Dominicum: Studi sull'eucarestia nei Padri della Chiesa antica e Miscellanea patristica* (Catania, 1959), 381–406.

——*Scuola e cultura dei primi secoli cristiani* (Brescia, 1974).

Quasten, J., *Music und Gesang in den Kulten der heidnischen Antike und christlichen Frühzeit* (Münster, 1930), trans. B. Ramsey as *Music and Worship in Pagan and Christian Antiquity* (Washington, DC, 1983).

Ramos-Lisson, D., 'Grégoire le Grand, Léandre et Reccarède', in *Gregorio Magno e il suo tempo*, i: *XIX Incontro di Studiosi dell'antichità cristiana in collaborazione con l'École française de Rome, Roma, 9–12 maggio 1990* (Rome, 1991), 187–98.

Randsborg, K., *The First Millennium in Europe and the Mediterranean: An Archaeological Essay* (Cambridge, 1991).

Rankin, S., 'Ways of Telling Stories', in Boone (ed.), *Essays*, 371–94.

Rapp, C., *Holy Bishops in Late Antiquity: The Nature of Christian Leadership in an Age of Transition* (Berkeley and Los Angeles, 2005).

Rappaport, R. A., *Ritual and Religion in the Making of Humanity* (Cambridge, 1999).

Rawcliffe, C., *Medicine for the Soul: The Life, Death and Resurrection of an English Medieval Hospital. St Giles's, Norwich, c. 1249–1550* (Sutton, 1999).

Rawson, B., *Children and Childhood in Roman Italy* (Oxford, 2003).

Rawson, E., *Intellectual Life in the Late Roman Republic* (London, 1985).

Reddé, M., *Mare Nostrum: Les infrastructures, le dispositif et l'histoire de la marine militaire sous l'Empire romain* (Paris, 1986).

Reed, A. Y., 'ΕΥΑΓΓ ELION: Orality, Textuality and the Christian Truth in Irenaeus' *Adversus Haereses*', *Vigiliae Christianae*, 56 (2002), 11–46.

Reekmans, L., 'Les Constructions des papes avant la période carolingienne répertoriées dans le *Liber Pontificalis*', in M. Van Uytfanghe and R. Demeulenaere (eds), *Aevum inter utrumque: Mélanges offerts à Gabriel Sanders* (Steenbrugge , 1991), 355–66.

Regesta Pontificum Romanorum ab Condita Ecclesia ad Annum post Christum natum MCXCVIII, ed. P. Jaffé, rev. G. Wattenbach, S. Loewenfeld, F. Kaltenbrunner and P. Ewald, 2 vols (Leipzig, 1881–8).

Reif, S. C. 'The Early Liturgy of the Synagogue', in W. Horbury, et al. (eds), *The Cambridge History of Judaism*, iii: *The Early Roman Period* (Cambridge, 1999), 326–57.

Remensnyder, A. G., 'Pollution, Purity and Peace: An Aspect of Social Reform between the Late Tenth Century and 1076', in Head and Landes (eds), *The Peace of God*, 280–307.

Resnick, I. M., 'Scientia Liberalis, Dialectics and Otloh of Saint Emmeram', *Revue bénédictine*, 97 (1987), 241–52.

Reynaud, J. F., and M. Jannet-Vallat, 'Les Inhumations privilégiées à Lyon et à Vienne (Isère)', in Duval and Picard (eds), *Inhumation privilégiée*, 97–107.

Reynolds, J., and R. Tannenbaum, *Jews and God-Fearers at Aphrodisias* (Cambridge, 1987).

Reynolds, P., *Trade in the Western Mediterranean: The Ceramic Evidence* (British Archaeological Reports, International Series, 604; Oxford, 1995).

Reynolds, R. E., *Clerical Orders in the Early Middle Ages: Duties and Ordination* (Aldershot, 1999).

—— *Clerics in the Early Middle Ages: Hierarchy and Image* (Aldershot, 1999).

—— 'Liturgical Scholarship at the Time of the Investiture Controversy: Past Research and Future Opportunities', *Harvard Theological Review*, 71 (1978), 109–24.

—— 'A Visual Epitome of the Eucharistic *Ordo* from the Era of Charles the Bald: The Ivory Mass Cover of the *Drogo Sacramentary*', in Gibson and Nelson (eds), 241–60.

Richardot, P., *La Fin de l'armée romaine (284–476)* (Paris, 2001).

Richardson, P., 'Augustan Era Synagogues in Rome', in Donfried and Richardson (eds), *Judaism and Christianity*, 17–29.

Riché, P., *Abbon de Fleury: Un moine savant et combatif (vers 950–1004)* (Turnhout, 2004).

—— *Éducation et culture dans l'Occident barbare, VIᵉ–VIIIᵉ siècle*, 4th edn (Paris, 1995).

Rieth, E. (ed.), *Méditerranée antique: Pêche, navigation, commerce* (Paris, 1998).

Riley-Smith, J., 'The Latin Clergy and the Settlement in Palestine and Syria, 1098–1100', *Catholic Historical Review*, 74 (1988), 539–57.

Rinaldi, R., 'Da Adalberto Atto a Bonifacio: Note e riflessioni per l'edizione di un codice diplomatico canossano prematildico', *Bullettino dell'Istituto italiano per il Medio Evo*, 101 for 1997–8 (1999), 13–91.

Rio, A., *Legal Practice and the Written Word in the Early Middle Ages: Frankish Formulae, c. 500–1000* (Cambridge, 2009).

Rives, J. B., *Religion and Authority in Roman Carthage from Augustus to Constantine* (Oxford, 1995).

Rizzi, M., *La questione dell'unità dell''Ad Diognetum'* (Milan, 1989).

Robbins, P., 'Cultural Ecology', in Duncan et al. (eds), *A Companion to Cultural Geography*, 180–93.

Roberts, C. H., *Manuscript, Society and Belief in Early Christian Egypt* (London, 1979).

—— and T. C. Skeat, *The Birth of the Codex* (London, 1983).

Robertson, A. W., *The Service-Books of the Royal Abbey of Saint-Denis: Images of Ritual and Music in the Middle Ages* (Oxford, 1991).

Robinson, I. S., 'Bernold von Konstanz und der gregorianische Reformkreis um Bischof Gebhard III', *Freiburger Diözesan-Archiv*, 109 (1989), 155–88.

—— *Henry IV of Germany: 1056–1106* (Cambridge, 1999).

—— *The Papacy 1073–1198: Continuity and Innovation* (Cambridge, 1990).

—— 'Zur Arbeitsweise Bernolds von Konstanz und seines Kreises: Untersuchungen zum Schlettstädter Codex 13 (formerly 99)', *Deutsches Archiv für Erförschung des Mittelalters*, 34 (1978), 51–122.

Robinson, J. A T., *Redating the New Testament* (London, 1976).

Roma fra Oriente e Occidente (SSCISAM 49; Spoleto, 2002).

Roques, D., 'Prêtres et diacres dans la Cyrénaïque tardive (iiie–vi^e siècle)', in Delage (ed.), *Les Pères*, 323–40.

Rose, E., 'Liturgical Latin in the Missale Gothicum (Vat. Reg. lat. 317)', *Sacris Erudiri*, 42 (2003), 97–121.

Rosenblum, M., *Luxorius: A Roman Poet among the Vandals* (New York and London, 1961).

Rosenfeld, R. A., 'Technologies for Musical Drafts, Twelfth Century and Later', *PMM* 11 (2002), 45–72.

Rosenwein, B. H., *To be the Neighbor of Saint Peter: The Social Meaning of Cluny's Property, 909–1049* (Ithaca and London, 1989).

Rostovtzeff, M. I., *The Social and Economic History of the Roman Empire* (Oxford, 1926).

Rouche, M., *L'Aquitaine des Wisigoths aux Arabes 418–781: Naissance d'une région* (Paris, 1979).

—— *Le Choc des cultures: Romanité, germanité, chrétienté durant le haut moyen âge* (Villeneuve d'Ascq, 2003).

—— 'Introducton', in id. (ed.), *Clovis*.

—— (ed.), *Clovis: Histoire et mémoire*, 2 vols (Paris, 1997).

Rougé, J., 'Ports et escales dans l'Empire tardif', in *La navigazione mediterranea nell'Alto Medioevo* (SSCISAM 25; Spoleto, 1975), i. 67–128.

—— *Recherches sur l'organisation du commerce maritime en Méditerranée sous l'Empire romain* (Paris, 1966).

Rousselle, A., *Porneia: De la maîtrise du corps à la privation sensorielle, IIe–IVe siècles de l'ère chrétiennne* (Paris, 1983).

Rovelli, A., 'La circolazione monetaria a Rome nei secoli VII e VIII: Nuovi dati per la storia economica di Roma nell'alto medioevo, in Delogu (ed.), *Roma medievale*, 79–91.

Roverius, P., *Reomaus, seu historia monasterii S. Ioannis Reomaensis in Tractu lingoensis: primariae inter Gallica Coenobia antiquitatis, ab anno Christi CCCXXV* (Paris, 1637).

Rucquoi, A., 'Les Cisterciens dans la péninsule ibérique', in *Unanimité et diversité cisterciennes*, 487–523.

Rummel, P. von, '*Habitus Vandalorum*? Zur Frage nach einer gruppen-spezifischen Kleidung der Vandalen in Nordafrika', in *L'Afrique Vandale*, i. 131–41.

Rusconi, A. (ed.), *Guido d'Arezzo monaco pomposiano* (Florence, 2000).

Rutgers, L. V., and Bradbury, S., 'The Diaspora: *c.* 235–638', in Katz (ed.), *The Cambridge History of Judaism*, iv. 492–518.

Sabatini, F., 'Dalla scripta latina rustica alle scriptae romanze', *Studi medievali*, 9 (1968), 320–58.

Saint Chrodegang: Communications présentées au colloque tenu à Metz à l'occasion du douz-ième centenaire de sa mort (Metz, 1967).

Saitta, B., 'La conversione de Reccaredo: Necessità politica o convizione personale', in *Concilio III de Toledo*, 375–84.

Saller, R. P., and Shaw, B. D., 'Tombstones and Roman Family Relations in the Principate: Civilians, Soldiers and Slaves', *Journal of Roman Studies*, 74 (1984), 124–56.

Salzmann, J., 'Pliny and Liturgy—A Reconsideration', *Studia Patristica*, 10 (1989), 389–95.

Samaritani, A., 'Contributi alla biografia di Guido a Pomposa e Arezzo', in Rusconi (ed.), *Guido d'Arezzo*, 111–29.

Sanders, E. P. (ed.), *Jewish and Christian Self-Definition*, i: *The Shaping of Christianity in the Second and Third Centuries* (Philadelphia, 1980).

——with Baumgarten, A. I., and Mendelson, A., *Jewish and Christian Self-Definition*, ii: *Aspects of Judaism in the Graeco-Roman Period* (London, 1981).

——with Meyer, B. F., *Jewish and Christian Self-Definition*, iii: *Self-Definition in the Greek and Roman World* (London, 1982).

Sanders, J. T., *The New Testament Christological Hymns: Their Historical and Religious Background* (Cambridge, 1971).

Sansterre, J. M., *Les Moines grecs et orientaux à Rome aux époques byzantine et carolingien-ne* (Brussels, 1983).

Santifaller, L., 'Chronologisches Verzeichnis der Urkunden Papst Johanns XIX 1024 Juni bis 1032 August', *Römische historische Mitteilungen*, 1 (1956–7), 35–7.

—— *Liber diurnus: Studien und Forschungen* (Stuttgart, 1976).

Sarath, E., 'A New Look at Improvisation', *Journal of Music Theory*, 40 (1996), 1–38.

Sawyer, P. H., and I. N. Wood (eds), *Early Medieval Kingship* (Leeds, 1977).

Saxer, V., 'Culte et liturgie', in Mayeur, J.-M., et al. (eds), *Histoire du Christianisme (des origines à 250)* (Paris, 2000), 437–89.

——'*Domus ecclesiae* . . . in den frühchristlichen Literarischen Texten', *Römische Quartalschrift für Christliche Altertumskunde und Kirchengeschichte*, 83 (1988), 167–79.

Scheibelreiter, G., 'Clovis, le païen, Clotilde, la pieuse: À propos de la mentalité barbare', in Rouche (ed.), *Clovis*, 349–67.

—— *Der Bischof in Merowingischer Zeit* (Vienna, 1983).

Schein, S., *Fideles Crucis: The Papacy, the West and the Recovery of the Holy Land 1274–1314* (Oxford, 1991).

Schieffer, R., *Die Entstehung von Domkapiteln in Deutschland* (Bonn, 1976).

Schiffman, H. F., 'Diglossia as a Sociolinguistic Situation', in F. Coulmas (ed.), *The Handbook of Sociolinguistics* (Oxford, 1997), 205–16.

Schlager, K., 'Neumenschrift und Liniensystem: Zum Notationswechsel in der Munchener Handschrift CLM 23037', *Musik in Bayern*, 29 (1984), 31–41.

Schnabel, E. J., *Urchristliche Mission* (Wuppertal, 2002), author's translation published as *Early Christian Mission* (Leicester, 2004).

Schneider, P. G., 'The *Acts of John*: The Gnostic Transformation of a Christian Community', in Helleman (ed.), *Hellenization Revisited*, 241–69.

Schoedel, W. R., *Ignatius of Antioch: A Commentary upon the Letters* (Philadelphia, 1985).

Schöllgen, G., *Die Anfänge der Professionalisierung des Klerus und das kirchliche Amt in der syrischen Didaskalie* (Münster, 1998).

Scholz, S., *Politik — Selbstverständnis — Selbstdarstellung: Die Päpste in karolingischer und ottonischer Zeit* (Stuttgart, 2006).

Schwartz, S., 'Political, Social and Economic Life in the Land of Israel, 66–c.235', in S. T. Katz (ed.), *The Cambridge History of Judaism*, iv. 23–52.

Scott, A. B., 'Churches of Books? Sethian Social Organisation', *JECS* 3 (1995), 109–22.

Semmler, J., 'Pippin III und die fränkischen Klöster', *Francia*, 3 (1975), 88–146.

Sénac, P., *Les Carolingiens et al-Andalus* (Paris, 2002).

Sendrey, A., *Music in the Social and Religious Life of Antiquity* (Rutherford, 1974).

Sessa, 'Domestic Conversions: Households and Bishops in the Late-Antique "Papal Legends"', in Cooper and Hillner (eds), 79–114.

Shäferdiek, K., 'L'Arianisme germanique et ses conséquences', in Rouche (ed.), *Clovis*, i: 185–97.

Shanzer, D., 'Dating the Baptism of Clovis: The Bishop of Vienne versus the Bishop of Tours', *Early Medieval Europe*, 7 (1998), 29–57.

——*A Philosophical and Literary Commentary on Martianus Capella's* De nuptiis Philologiae et Mercurii, *Book I* (Berkeley, 1986).

——and Mathisen, R. (eds), *Society and Culture in Late Antique Gaul: Revisiting the Sources* (Aldershot, 2001).

Sharpe, R., *Medieval Irish Saints' Lives: An Introduction to Vitae Sanctorum Hiberniae* (Oxford, 1991).

——'Words and Music by Goscelin of Canterbury', *Early Music*, 19 (1991), 94–7.

Shaw, B. D., *At the Edge of the Corrupting Sea* (Oxford, 2006).

——'Latin Funerary Epigraphy and Family Life in the Later Roman Empire', *Historia*, 33 (1984), 457–97.

Sherwin-White, A. N., *The Letters of Pliny: A Historical and Social Commentary* (Oxford, 1966).

Simenon, G., 'Les Chroniqueurs de l'Abbaye de Saint-Trond', in *Mélanges Godefroid Kurth*, 2 vols (Liège and Paris, 1908), i. 61–71.

Sinor, D., 'The Hun Period', in id. (ed.), *The Cambridge History of Early Inner Asia* (Cambridge, 1990), 177–205.

Sirks, A. J. B., *Food for Rome: The Legal Structure of the Transportation and Processing of Supplies for the Imperial Distributions in Rome and Constantinople* (Amsterdam, 1991).

Sitwell, N. H. H., *Roman Roads of Europe* (London, 1981)

Slee, M., *The Church in Antioch in the First Century CE* (Sheffield, 2003).

Smith, D. E., *From Symposium to Eucharist: The Banquet in the Early Christian World* (Minneapolis, 2002).

Smith, J. A., 'The Ancient Synagogue and its Music: A Reconsideration in the Light of Ideas Presented by Theodore Karp', *Rivista internazionale di musica sacra*, 24 (2003), 17–38.

——'The Ancient Synagogue, the Early Church and Singing', *Music & Letters*, 65 (1984), 1–16.

——'First-Century Christian Singing and its Relationship to Contemporary Jewish Religious Song', *Music & Letters*, 75 (1994), 1–15.

——'Three Anglican Church Historians on Liturgy and Psalmody in the Ancient Synagogue and the Early Church' (forthcoming).

——'Which Psalms were Sung in the Temple?', *Music & Letters*, 71 (1990), 167–86.

Smith, J. M. H. (ed.), *Early Medieval Rome and the Christian West* (Leiden, 2000).

—— *Europe after Rome: A New Cultural History 500–1000* (Oxford, 2005).

—— *Province and Empire: Brittany and the Carolingians* (Cambridge, 1992).

Smits van Waesberghe, J. M., *De Musico-Paedagogico et Theoretico Guidone Aretino eiusque Vita et Moribus* (Florence, 1953).

—— *Musikerziehung: Lehre und Theorie der Musik im Mittelalter* (Musikgeschichte in Bildern, 3/iii (Leipzig, 1969).

—— *Muziekgeschiedenis der Middeleeuwen*, 2 vols (Tilburg, 1939–42).

—— 'Neues über die Schola Cantorum zu Rom', *Musices Aptatio*, 1 (1984–5), 338–46.

—— 'Some Music Treatises and their Interrelation: A School of Liège (c. 1050–1200)?' *Musica Disciplina*, 3 (1949), 95–118.

Smyth, M., *La Liturgie oubliée: La prière eucharistique en Gaule antique et dans l'Occident non romain* (Paris, 2003).

Snyder, G. F., 'The Interraction of Jews with Non-Jews in Rome', in Donfried and Richardson (eds), *Judaism and Christianity*, 69–90.

Soden, H. von, *Das lateinische Neue Testament in Afrika zur zeit Cyprians nach Bibelhandschriften und Väterzeugnissen* (Leipzig, 1909).

Sotinel, C., 'How were Bishops Informed? Information Transmission across the Adriatic Sea in Late Antiquity', in L. Ellis and F. L. Kidner (eds), *Travel, Communication and Geography in Late Antiquity: Sacred and Profane* (Aldershot, 2004), 63–72.

—— and E. Rebilard (eds), *L'Évêque dans la cité du IVe au Ve siècle: Image et autorité* (Rome, 1998).

Sotomayor, M., 'Penetración de la Iglesia en los Medios Rurales de la España Tardoromana y Visigoda', in *Cristianizzazione ed organizzazione ecclesiastica delle campagne nell'alto Medioevo*, 639–70.

Souter, A., *A Glossary of Later Latin to 600 AD*, rev. edn (Oxford, 1996).

Sparksman, B. J., 'The Minister of Music in the Western Church: A Canonical-Historical Study' (Ph.D. diss., Catholic University of America, 1980).

Sperti, L., 'Ricognizione archeologica a Laodicea di Frigia: 1993–1998', in Traversari (ed.), *Laodicea di Frigia*, 29–103.

Stanton, G. N., 'The Fourfold Gospel', *New Testament Studies*, 43 (1997), 317–46.

Stark, R., *The Rise of Christianity: A Sociologist Reconsiders History* (Princeton, 1996).

Stasolla, F. R., '*Balnea* ed edifici di culto', in Guidobaldi and Guidobaldi (eds), *Ecclesiae Urbis*, i: 143–51.

Steenberg, M. C., ' "Children in Paradise": Adam and Eve as "Infants" ' in Irenaeus of Lyons', *JECS* 12 (2004), 1–22.

Stegner, W. R., 'The Ancient Jewish Synagogue Homily', in Aune (ed.), *Greco-Roman Literature*, 51–69.

Steiner, R., *Studies in Gregorian Chant* (Aldershot, 1999).

Sternberg, T., *Orientalium More Secutus: Räume und Institutionen der Caritas des 5. bis 7. Jahrhunderts in Gallien* (Münster, 1991).

Stiegemann, C., and Wemhoff, M., *Kunst und Kultur der Karolingerzeit: Karl der Grosse und Papst Leo III in Paderborn. Katalog der Ausstellung, Paderborn 1999*, 3 vols (Mainz, 1999).

Stocking, R. L., *Bishops, Councils and Consensus in the Visigothic Kingdom 589–633* (Michigan, 2000).

Stowers, S. K., 'Theorizing the Religion of Ancient Households and Families', in J. Bodel and S. M. Olyan (eds), *Household and Religion in Antiquity* (Oxford, 2008), 5–19.

Strange, W. A., *Children in the Early Church* (Carlisle, 1996).

Stroumsa, G. A. G., *Another Seed: Studies in Gnostic Mythology* (Leiden, 1984).

—— *La Fin du sacrifice: Les mutations religieuses de l'Antiquité tardive* (Paris, 2005).

—— 'The Scriptural Movement of Late Antiquity and Christian Monasticism', *JECS* 16 (2008), 61–77.

Stuhlmacher, P., 'Isaiah 53 in the Gospels and *Acts*', in Janowski and Stuhlmacher (eds), *The Suffering Servant*, 147–62.

Swartz, M. D., 'Jewish Magic in Late Antiquity', in Katz (ed.), *The Cambridge History of Judaism*, iv. 699–720.

Symonds, P., 'Deacons in the Early Church', *Theology*, 58 (1955), 408–14.

Szendrei, J., 'Choralnotation in Mitteleuropa', *Studia Musicologica Academiae Scientiarum Hungaricae*, 30 (1988), 437–46.

—— 'The Introduction of Staff Notation into Middle Europe', *Studia Musicologica Academiae Scientiarum Hungaricae*, 23 (1986), 303–19.

—— 'On the Prose *Historia* of Saint Augustine', in Fassler and Baltzer (eds), *The Divine Office in the Latin Middle Ages*, 430–43.

—— 'Staff Notation of Gregorian Chant in Polish Sources from the Twelfth to the Sixteenth Century', in *Notae Musicae Artis: Notacja muzyczna wródłach polskich XI–XVI wieku* (Kraków and Warsaw, 1999), 187–281.

—— 'Zur Stilistik der Melodien des Emmeram-Offiziums', in Berschin and Hiley (eds), *Die Offizien des Mittelalters*, 87–107.

Tabbernee, W., *Montanist Inscriptions and Testimonia: Epigraphic Sources Illustrating the History of Montanism* (Macon, Ga., 1997).

Taft, R., *The Liturgy of the Hours in East and West* (Collegeville, Minn., 1986).

Talley, T. J., *The Origins of the Liturgical Year* (Collegeville, Minn., 1991).

Taviani, H., 'Un Archevêque de Milan dans l'historiographie de sa ville', *Provence historique*, 25 (1975), 325–35.

Taylor, D. S., 'A New Inventory of Manuscripts of the *Micrologus de ecclesiasticis observationibus* of Bernold of Constance', *Scriptorium*, 52 (1998), 162–91.

Tellenbach, G., *The Church in Western Europe from the Tenth to the Early Twelfth Century*, trans. T. Reuter (Cambridge, 1993).

—— 'Römischer und christlicher Reichsgedanke in der Liturgie des frühen Mittelalters', *Sitzungsberichte der Heidelberger Akademie der Wissenschaften, Philosophisch-Historische Klasse*, 25 (1934), 3–65.

Tena-Garriga, P., *La Palabra 'Ekklesia': Estudio Histórico-Teológico* (Barcelona, 1958).

Thacker, A. T., 'Memorializing Gregory the Great: The Origin and Transmission of a Papal Cult in the Seventh and Early Eighth Centuries', *Early Medieval Europe*, 7 (1998), 59–84.

Thiselton, A. C., *The First Epistle to the Corinthians: A Commentary upon the Greek Text* (Grand Rapids, Mich., 2000).

Thomas, C. M., 'The "Prehistory" of the *Acts of Peter*', in F. Bovan (ed.), *The Apocryphal Acts of the Apostles* (Cambridge, Mass., 1990), 39–62.

Thomas, J. P., *Private Religious Foundations in the Byzantine Empire* (Washington, DC, 1987).

Thomas, Dom P., 'Saint Odon de Cluny et son oeuvre musicale', in *A Cluny: Congrès scientifique. Fêtes et cérémonies liturgiques en l'honneur des saints Abbés Odon et Odilon, 9–11 juillet 1949* (Dijon, 1950), 171–80.

Thompson, E. A., The Conversion of the Visigoths to Catholicism', *Nottingham Medieval Studies*, 4 (1960), 4–35.

—— *The Goths in Spain* (Oxford, 1969).

—— *The Huns*, rev. and with an afterword by P. Heather (Oxford, 1996).

Thornton, Andrew, 'An Invitation to the Rule for Solitaries by Grimlaicus', *American Benedictine Review*, 59 (2008), 198–212.

Thrift, N., 'Performance and Performativity: A Geography of Unknown Lands', in Duncan et al. (eds), *A Companion to Cultural Geography*, 121–36.

Tiefenbach, H., 'Das wandalische *Domine Miserere*', *Historische Sprachforschung*, 104 (1991), 251–68.

Tomasello, A., 'Ritual, Tradition and Polyphony at the Court of Rome', *Journal of Musicology*, 4 (1985), 447–71.

Tombeur, P., 'Notes sur le texte de Raoul de Saint-Trond', *Bulletin du Cange: Archivum Latinitatis Medii Aevi*, 32 (1962), 95–115.

—— 'Un Nouveau Nom de la littérature médiolatine: Gislebert de Saint-Trond', *Cahiers de civilisation médiévale*, 10 (1967), 435–46.

Touati, F.-O., *Maladie et société au Moyen Âge: La lèpre, les lépreux et les léproseries dans la province ecclésiastique de Sens jusqu'au milieu du XIVᵉ siècle* (Brussels, 1998).

Traub, A., 'Zur Kompositionslehre in Mittelalter', *Beiträge zur Gregorianik*, 17 (1994), 57–90.

Traversari, G. (ed.), *Laodicea di Frigia* (Roma, 2000).

Treadgold, W., 'Taking Sources on their Own Terms and on Ours: Peter Brown's Late Antiquity', *Antiquité tardive*, 2 (1994), 153–9.

Trebilco, P., 'The Jews in Asia Minor, 66–c. 235 CE', in Katz (ed.), *The Cambridge History of Judaism*, iv. 75–82.

Treitler, L., *With Voice and Pen: Coming to Know Medieval Song and How it was Made* (Oxford, 2003).

Trevett, C., 'Montanism', in Esler (ed.), *The Early Christian World*, 929–51.

—— *Montanism: Gender, Authority and the New Prophecy* (Cambridge, 1996).

Trümper, M., 'Material and Social Environment of Greco-Roman Households in the East: The Case of Delos', in Balch and Osiek (eds), *Families in the New Testament World*, 19–43.

Turcan, R., *The Cults of the Roman Empire*, trans. A. Nevill (Oxford, 1996).

Turco, A., 'Neumennotation und Komposition', *Beiträge zur Gregorianik*, 37 (2004), 39–54.

Turner, C. H., 'Niceta of Remesiana II', *Journal of Theological Studies*, 24 (1923), 225–52.

Unanimité et diversité cisterciennes: Filiations – réseaux – relectures du XIIᵉ au XVIIᵉ siècle (Saint-Etienne, 2000).

Unterkircher, F., *Zur Ikonographie und Liturgie des Drogo-Sakramentars (Paris, Bibliothèque nationale, Ms. Lat. 9428)* (Graz, 1977).

Uro, R., 'Asceticism and Anti-familial Language in the *Gospel of Thomas*', in Moxnes (ed.), *Constructing Early Christian Families*, 216–34.

Uzzi, J. D., *Children in the Visual Arts of Imperial Rome* (Cambridge, 2005).

Valdeavellano, Luis G. de, *Historia de España de los Origenes a la Baja Edad Media* (Madrid, 1980).

Valentini, R., and Zucchetti, G., *Codice topografico della città di Roma* (Turin, 1960).

Van Acker, M., 'Dans les méandres de la communication verticale mérovingienne: Connaissances passives et pertes d'informations', in Wright (ed.), *Latin vulgaire, latin tardif VIII*, 463–71.

—— *Ut quique rustici et inlitterati hec audierint et intellegant: Hagiographie et communication verticale au temps des Merovingiens (VII*^e*–VIII*^e *siècles)* (Leuven, 2007).

Van Dam, R., *Leadership and Community in Late Antique Gaul* (Berkeley, 1985).

—— *The Roman Revolution of Constantine* (Cambridge, 2007).

Van der Werf, H., *The Oldest Extant Part-Music and the Origins of Western Polyphony*, 2 vols (Rochester, NY, 1993).

Van Deusen, N., 'An Historical and Stylistic Comparison of the Graduals of Gregorian and Old Roman Chant' (Ph.D. diss., Indiana University, 1972).

—— 'Sequence Repertories: A Reappraisal', *Musica Disciplina*, 48 for 1994 (1998), 99–112.

—— (ed.), *The Place of the Psalms in the Intellectual Culture of the Middle Ages* (Albany, NY, 1999).

Van Dijk, S.J.P., 'Gregory the Great Founder of the Urban "Schola Cantorum"', *Ephemerides Liturgicae*, 77 (1963), 335–56.

—— 'Papal Schola "versus" Charlemagne', in P. Fischer (ed.), *Organicae Voces: Festschrift J. Smits Van Waseberghe* (Amsterdam, 1963), 21–30.

Van Haelst, J., *Catalogue des papyrus littéraires juifs et chrétiens* (Paris, 1976).

Vannier, M.-A., 'Les Diacres d'après saint Augustin', in Delage (ed.), *Les Pères*, 121–9.

Van Rhijn, C., 'Priests and the Carolingian Reforms: The Bottlenecks of Local *Correctio*', in R. Corradini, R. Meens, C. Pössel and P. Shaw, P. (eds), *Texts and Identities in the Early Middle Ages* (Vienna, 2006), 219–37.

Van Unnik, W.C., 'A Note on the Dance of Jesus in the *Acts of John*', *Vigiliae Christianae*, 18 (1964), 1–5.

Van Uytfanghe, M., 'Latin mérovingien, latin carolingien et rustica romana lingua: Continuité ou discontinuité?', *Revue de l'Université de Bruxelles*, 1 (1977), 65–88.

—— 'Le Latin des hagiographes mérovingiens et la protohistoire du français: État de la question', *Romanica Gandensia*, 16 (1976), 5–90.

Varvaro, A., 'Latin and Romance: Fragmentation or Restructuring?' in Wright (ed.), *Latin and the Romance Languages*, 44–51.

Verleyen, W., '*L'Exordium Affligemense*: Légende ou réalité?', *Revue d'histoire ecclésiastique*, 90 (1995), 471–83.

—— 'La Querelle des investitures et l'introduction de la règle de saint Benoît à Affligem (1083–1086)', *Revue bénédictine*, 112 (2002), 139–47.

Verner, D.C., *The Household of God: The Social World of the Pastoral Epistles* (Chico, Calif., 1981).

Villela Masana, J., 'Les Voyages et les correspondances à caractère religieux entre l'Hispanie et l'extérieur selon la prosopographie chrétienne (300–589)', in E. Dassmann and J. Engemann (eds), *Akten des XII. Internationalen Kongresses für christliche Archäologie* (Münster, 1995), 1255–61.

Villetard, H., *Office de Saint Savinien et de Saint Potentien, premiers évêques de Sens: Texte et chants, étude hagiographique, liturgique et musical publiés d'après le manuscrit d'Odoranne*, Bibliothèque musicologique, 5 (Paris, 1956).

Vives, J., 'En torno a la Datación del Antifonario Legionense', *Hispania Sacra*, 8 (1955), 117–24.

Vogel, C., 'Anaphores eucharistiques préconstantiniennes: Formes non traditionelles', *Augustinianum*, 20 (1980), 401–10.

——'Les Échanges liturgiques entre Rome et les pays francs jusqu'à l'époque de Charlemagne', in *Le chiese nei regni dell'Europa occidentale* (SSCISAM 7; Spoleto, 1960), 185–296.

——*Medieval Liturgy: An Introduction to the Sources*, trans. and rev. W. Storey and N. Rasmussen (Washington, DC, 1986).

——'Les Motifs de la romanisation du culte sous Pépin le Bref (751–68) et Charlemagne (774–814)', in *Culto cristiano*, 15–41.

——'La Réforme culturelle sous Pépin le Bref et sous Charlemagne', in *Die Karolingische Renaissance* (Graz, 1965), 173–242.

——'Saint Chrodegang et les débuts de la romanisation du culte en pays franc', in *Saint Chrodegang*, 91–109.

Von Falkenhausen, V., 'Between Two Empires: Byzantine Italy in the Reign of Basil II', in P. Magdalino (ed.), *Byzantium in the Year 1000* (Leiden and Boston, 2003), 135–59.

Von Görtz-Wrisberg, I., 'A Sabbath Service in Ostia: What Do We Know about the Ancient Synagiogal Service?', in B. Olsson et al. (eds), *The Synagogue of Ancient Ostia and the Jews of Rome* (Stockholm, 2001), 167–202.

Vössing, K., *Schule und Bildung im Nordafrika der römischen Kaiserzeit* (Brussels, 1997).

Walker, R., *Views of Transition: Liturgy and Illumination in Medieval Spain* (London, 1998).

Wallace-Hadrill, A., '*Domus* and *Insulae* in Rome: Families and Housefuls', in Balch and Osiek (eds), *Families in the New Testament World*, 3–18.

——'Greek Knowledge, Roman Power', *Classical Philology*, 73 (1988), 224–33.

Wälli, S., *Melodien aus mittelalterlichen Horaz-Handschriften: Edition und Interpretation der Quellen* (Monumenta Monodica Medii Aevi, Subsidia 3; Kassel, 2002).

Ward-Perkins, B., *From Classical Antiquity to the Middle Ages: Urban Public Building in Northern and Central Italy* AD *300–850* (Oxford, 1984).

—— *The Fall of Rome and the End of Civilization* (Oxford, 2005).

Warga, R.G., 'A Christian Amulet on Wood', *Bulletin of the American Society of Papyrologists*, 25 (1988), 149–52.

Weber, M., *The Rational and Social Foundations of Music*, trans. and ed. D. Martindale, J. Riedel and G. Neuwirth (Carbondale, Ill., 1958).

Weitzmann, K., and Kessler, H., *The Frescoes of Dura Europos Synagogue and Christian Art* (Dumbarton Oaks, 1990).

Werner, K.-F., 'Noble Families in Charlemagne's Kingdom', in T. Reuter (ed. and trans.), *The Medieval Nobility: Studies on the Ruling Classes of France and Germany from the Sixth to the Twelfth Century* (Amsterdam, 1979), 137–202.

White, L.M., *The Social Origins of Christian Architecture*, i: *Building God's House in the Roman World: Architectural Adaptation among Pagans, Jews, and Christians*; ii: *Texts and Monuments for the Christian* Domus ecclesiae *in its Environment* (Harvard Theological Studies, 42; (Cambridge, Mass., 1990).

Whittaker, C. R., 'Amphorae and Trade', in Desbat and Kilcher (eds), *Amphores romaines*, 537–9.

Whybray, R. N., 'The Wisdom Psalms', in J. Day, R. P. Gordon and H. G. M. Williamson, (eds), *Wisdom in Ancient Israel* (Cambridge, 1995), 152–60.

Wickham, C., *Early Medieval Italy: Central Power and Local Society 400–1000* (Ann Arbor, 1989).

—— 'European Forests in the Early Middle Ages: Landscape and Land Clearance', in *L'Ambiente vegetale nell'alto medioevo* (SSCISAM 30; Spoleto, 1990), 479–548.

—— *Framing the Early Middle Ages: Europe and the Mediterranean, 400–800* (Oxford, 2005).

—— *The Inheritance of Rome: A History of Europe from 400–1000* (London, 2009).

—— 'The Other Transition: from the Ancient World to Feudalism', *Past and Present*, 103 (1984), 3–32.

—— 'Production, Distribution and Demand, II', in Hansen and Wickham (eds), *The Long Eighth Century*, 345–77.

Wiedemann, T. E. J., *Adults and Children in the Roman Empire* (London, 1989).

Wiles, M., *Archetypal Heresy: Arianism through the Centuries* (Oxford, 1996).

Wille, G,. *Musica Romana: Die Bedeutung der Musik im Leben der Römer* (Amsterdam, 1967).

Williams, D. H., *Ambrose of Milan and the End of the Arian–Nicene Conflicts* (Oxford, 1995).

Williams, D. R., and Balensuela, C. M., *Music Theory from Boethius to Zarlino: A Bibliography and Guide* (Hillsdale, NY, 2007).

Williams, M. A., *Rethinking 'Gnosticism': An Argument for Dismantling a Dubious Category* (Princeton, 1996).

Williams, M. H., 'The Jewish Community of Corycus: Two More Inscriptions', *Zeitschrift für Papyrologie und Epigraphik*, 92 (1992), 248–52.

—— 'The Jews of Corycus: A Neglected Diasporan Community from Roman Times', *Journal for the Study of Judaism*, 25 (1994), 274–86.

Williams, P. F., *The Organ in Western Culture, 750–1250* (Cambridge, 1993).

Williams, R., *Arius* (London, 1987).

Williams, S., *Diocletian and the Roman Recovery* (London, 1996).

Willis, G. G., *Essays in Early Roman Liturgy* (London, 1964).

—— *Further Essays in Early Roman Liturgy* (London, 1968).

Wilpert, J., 'Die Malereien der Grabkammer des Trebius Justus aus dem Ende der konstantinischen Zeit', in F. Dölger (ed.), *Konstantin der Grosse und seine Zeit* (Freiburg, 1913), 276–96.

—— *Roma sotterranea: Le pitture delle catacombe romane*, 2 vols (Rome, 1903).

Wilson, A., 'Approaches to Quantifying Roman Trade', in Bowman and Wilson, *Quantifying the Roman Economy*, 213–58.

Wollmann, A., 'Early Latin Loan Words in Old English', *Anglo-Saxon England*, 22 (1993), 1–26.

Wood, D. (ed.), *The Church and Childhood* (Oxford, 1994).

Wood, I., 'The Frontiers of Western Europe', in Hodges and Bowden (eds), *The Sixth Century*, 231–53.

—— *The Merovingian Kingdoms (450–751)* (Harlow, 1994).

——'Roman Law in the Barbarian Kingdoms', in A. Ellegård and G. Åkerström-Hougen (eds), *Rome and the North* (Jonsered, 1991), 5–14.

——'Saint-Wandrille and its Hagiography', in I. Wood and G. A. Loud (eds), *Church and Chronicle in the Middle Ages: Essays Presented to John Taylor* (London, 1991), 1–14.

——'The Work of Audoenus of Rouen and Eligius of Noyon in Extending Episcopal Influence from the Town to the Country in Seventh-Century Neustria', *Studies in Church History*, 16 (1979), 77–91.

Wood, S., *The Proprietary Church in the Medieval West* (Oxford, 2006).

Wooding, J. M., *Communication and Commerce along the Western Sea-Lanes AD 400–800* (Oxford, 1996).

Woolf, G., *Becoming Roman: The Origins of Provincial Civilisation in Gaul* (Cambridge, 1998).

Wormald, P., 'Bede and Benedict Biscop', in Gerald Bonner (ed.), *Famulus Christi: Essays in Commemoration of the Thirteenth Centenary of the Birth of the Venerable Bede* (London, 1976), 141–69.

——'*Lex scripta* and *Verbum Regis*: Legislation and Germanic Kingship from Euric to Cnut', in Sawyer and Wood (eds), 105–38.

Wright, R., *Actes du VIIIe colloque international sur le latin vulgaire et tardif, Oxford, 6–9 septembre 2006* (Hildesheim, 2008).

——*A Sociophilological Study of Late Latin* (Turnhout, 2002).

——(ed.), *Late Latin and Early Romance in Spain and Carolingian France* (Liverpool, 1982).

——(ed.), *Latin and the Romance Languages in the Early Middle Ages* (London and New York, 1991).

——(ed.), *Latin vulgaire, latin tardif: A* Pseudo-Turpin, *Karolellus atque Pseudo-Turpini Historia Karoli*, ed. P. G. Schmidt (Stuttgart, 1996).

Wylie, A. B., 'Musical Aesthetics and Biblical Interpretation in John Chrysostom', *Studia Patristica*, 32 (1997), 386–92.

Young, G. K., *Rome's Eastern Trade: International Commerce and Imperial Policy 31 BC–AD 305* (London, 2001).

Zapke, S. (ed.), *Hispania Vetus: Manuscritos Litúrgico-Musicales de los Orígenes Visigóticos a la Transición Francorromana (Siglos IX–XII)* (Bilbao, 2007).

——'Sistemas de Notación en la Península Ibérica: De las Notaciones Hispanas a la Notación Aquitana (Siglos IX–XII)', in Zapke, *Hispania Vetus*, 189–243.

Zetterholm, M., *The Formation of Christianity in Antioch: A Social-Scientific Approach to the Separation between Judaism and Christianity* (London, 2003).

Zijlstra, A. M. G., *Zangers en schrijvers: De overlevering van het gregoriaans van ca 700 – ca. 1150* (Utrecht, 1997)

Ziolkowski, J. M., *Nota bene: Reading Classics and Writing Melodies in the Early Middle Ages* (Turnhout, 2007).

Zuckerhandl, V., *Man the Musician* (Princeton, 1973).

Zylbergeld, L., 'Les Villes en Hainaut au moyen âge: Origines et premiers développements (XIe–XIIIe siècles)', in J.-M. Cauchies and J.-M. Duvosquel (eds), *Recueil d'études d'histoire Hainuyère*, 2 vols (Mons, 1983), 141–86.

INDEX OF PRINCIPAL MANUSCRIPTS CONSULTED

INDEX OF SELECTED TEXTS

Classical (and non-Christian) authors and texts are listed first, followed by the foundational documents of Christian tradition: canonical scriptures, apocryphal texts, pseudepigrapha, Jewish writings (texts by non-Christian Israelites), selected works of the patristic period, and Councils of the Church. Thereafter the entries are alphabetical.

Old French Verse

Theology (post-patristic)

Treatises on the Clerical Cursus

GENERAL INDEX

SUMMARY PROSOPOGRAPHY OF READERS AND SINGERS

This list makes no claim to be a comprehensive record, though it does attempt to give an inventory of the readers and singers who figure in the chapters of this book (together with a few others who came to light after the main text of the book had gone to press and for whom there are, therefore, no page references). Readers have been included on the grounds that some may have been readers and singers, or, indeed, singers only. The singers mentioned by John the Deacon, Notker Balbulus and Ekkehard IV in their inter-related and semi-legendary accounts of Frankish and Roman singers striving to establish (or subvert) Roman chant in Francia have not been included

Eastern Mediterranean: Christian Psalmists

'GAIOS' (3rd/4th c.), PRESBYTER AND HYMNODIST 45, 87, 90, 97, 525

Mentioned in an epitaph at Dinek Serai, southern-central Turkey, commemorating a deacon named Nestor. The inscription, in Greek verse, reveals that Gaios was a presbyter and 'far the best in hymns . . . beautiful hymns for even posterity to learn'. MAMA, viii. 23–5. Destephen *Prosopographie*, GAIOS 2

MARCIANUS (fl. 5th c.), LECTOR AND SINGER 544n

Sozomen mentions a certain 'Marcianus who was a singer and reader of holy writings' at Constantinople, where he was one of the bishop's notaries up to 352, when he was slain

MARTYRIUS (fl. 4th c.), LECTOR AND SINGER 544n

A Greek from Cappadocia, sent by the bishop of Trento in a party of missionaries to the Tyrolese Alps,

where he 'first intoned the song (*canticum*) of divine praise to the ears of a deaf region'. The use of *canticum* may be more than a figure of speech. Vigilius of Trento, *Epistolæ*, PL 13:551

PORPHYRIOS (365/419), SINGER OF ANTIPHONS 98, 544n

Named in an inscription re-employed for the mosque at Bayad, listing seventy members of guild dedicating a church to Saint George. Two municipal magistrates, men of considerable status, head the list, but in first place after them comes 'Porphyrios the singer of antiphons'. Destephen, *Prosopographie*, PORPHYRIOS 1

PHILOXENOS (3rd c./4th c.), PSALTES

Named in a papyrus from Oxyrhynchus (PGM LXVI), a divisive charm in which an unidentified writer tries to sever the relationship between Philoxenos, *psaltes*, and two other males, his 'friend' Gennadios and the presbyter Pelagios. The text is accompanied by a drawing of two naked men. For the interpretation that Philoxenos is a Christian *psaltes*, and that the charm does not (and yet it surely does!) have a homoerotic element, see R. W. Daniel, 'Intrigue in the Cloister: PGM LXVI', *Zeitschrift für Papyrologie und Epigraphik*, 89 (1991), 119–120

Eastern Mediterranean: Jewish Psalmists

BENJAMIN (?before 212) 42–3, 44, 84–5

Listed in an inscription from Aphrodisias, in what is now western Turkey about 140 km east of Ephesus, which may date from before the universal grant of

Roman citizenship in 212 AD. Reynolds and Tannenbaum, *Jews and God-Fearers at Aphrodisias*, 5 and 46

GAIANOS (4th c.)   43, 44

Epitaph in the Jewish catacomb of the Via Nomentana, Rome. Horsley, 'Epitaph for a Jewish Psalm-Singer'

Western Psalmists

AIDULFUS (fl. ?720–40), CANTOR OF THE CATHEDRAL OF AUXERRE   281–2, 329, 330

Eventually became bishop of the See. Bonnerue *et al.*, *Les Gestes des évêques d'Auxerre*, 134–7

ALDRICUS (d. 856), *PRIMICERIUS CANTORUM* OF THE CATHEDRAL OF METZ   348–9, 358, 567n

Presented to Louis the Pious; a *nutritus* at Aachen; assigned a prebend at Metz; begins studies of Frankish-Roman chant there; becomes *primicerius* of the Messine *schola*; becomes bishop at Le Mans. MGH SS, 15: 304–27, *Gesta Aldrici*. Busson and Ledru, *Actus Pontificum*

ANDREAS (d. 525), *PRINCEPS CANTORUM* OF THE CHURCH OF MÉRTOLA   216, 234, 249, 297, 526

Epitaph from Mértola: *Andreas famulu[s] dei princeps cantorum sacrosancte aeclisiae mertilliane. . . .* Vives, *Inscripciones Cristianas de la España Romana y Visigoda*, number 93

ANONYMI: FRANKISH EPISCOPAL (9th c., first quarter)

The bishop of an unspecified see in Francia holds a lavish banquet in the time of Charlemagne with noble guests; the meal closes with an undisclosed number of 'most skilled masters of the art of singing…with every kind of musical instrument'. Possibly singers from the cathedral. Haefele, *Gesta Karoli Magni*, 24

ANONYMI: PAPAL OF 754   288–91

According to Walafrid Strabo's *Libellus de exordiis*, composed in 842–4, 'the more perfect knowledge of chanting, which now virtually all Francia loves, was brought by Pope Stephen, at Pippin's request, through his clergy (*per suos clericos*) when he came to

Francia in the first place to Pippin, the father of Charlemagne, to seek justice for Saint Peter against the Lombards, whence the use of it has grown strong far and wide'

ANONYMOUS: PALATINE 1 (9th c., first quarter)   358

A young relative of Charlemagne (*iuvenis . . . cognatus Regis*) who sings the Alleluia so well during Mass in a palatine service that he is singled out for praise by the emperor. Haefele, *Gesta Karoli Magni*, 25

ANONYMOUS: PALATINE 2 (9th c., first quarter)   359, 568n

An 'incomparable cleric' in the royal household who managed to be a fine singer, a scholar, a master of chant, secular song and a poet. Seemingly a devil, since he vanishes from Charlemagne's side leaving only a smouldering coal. Haefele, *Gesta Karoli Magni*, 45–6

ANONYMOUS: PALATINE 3 (9th c., first quarter)   358, 359

'A certain cleric in the king's retinue', poorly educated and much disliked, but pitied by Charlemagne; standing in for a better man at a palatine service of Saint Martin, he mistakenly chooses the Lord's Prayer as a psalm verse for the Responsory *Domine, si adhuc populo tuo sum necessarius* because it ends *fiat voluntas tua*. Haefele, *Gesta Karoli Magni*, 7–9. *See also* ANONYMOUS: PALATINE 4

ANONYMOUS: PALATINE 4 (9th c., first quarter)   359

Assigned a vacant bishopric, since he was 'not a little adorned with nobility and learning', he spent the night of his appointment in feasting and drinking. He therefore did not appear for the service on the Eve of Saint Martin, which left the Responsory assigned to him, *Domine, si adhuc populo tuo sum necessarius*, unaccounted for. He forfeits the bishopric. Haefele, *Gesta Karoli Magni*, 7–9. *See also* ANONYMOUS: PALATINE 3

ANONYMOUS: PALATINE 5 (9th c., first quarter)   359

One of certain young *pauperes* and nobles who set to learn the scribal arts and the elements of the notary's craft with Clement, a historical figure who was master of the palace school under Charlemagne and remained so under Louis the Pious. One of the poor boys succeeded so well in his studies (much better than the nobles in the same group) that he was promoted into the chapel. He proved 'especially good at reading and singing', and was eventually given a bishopric. Haefele, *Gesta Karoli Magni*, 4–5

ANSTRANNUS (9th c., first half), CANTOR

Bishop of Verdun from 800. Fleckenstein, *Die Hofkapelle*, I, 232–3

ANTONIUS (fl. *c* 525), CANTOR OF THE CATHEDRAL OF RAVENNA   216

Agnellus of Ravenna, *Liber Pontificalis Ecclesiae Ravennatis*. MGH SSRL, 318–22. *See also* HONORIUS; MELITUS; TRANQUILLUS

ARMENTARIUS (6th c.), CLERIC OF CLERMONT

A cleric serving bishop Gregory of Tours, who, according to Gregory, had a deep knowledge of the scriptures and could memorise a chant so easily it seemed he were inscribing in his mind rather than pondering what he had to learn: 'tam facile erat sonorum modulationes apprehendere, ut eum non putares hoc meditari, sed scribere . . .'. *De miraculis sancti Martini episcopi*, Chapter 33. MGH SSRM, i

BERNARDUS/BERNO (d. 849), *ARCHICANTOR*   354–5, 567–8n

Son of Charlemagne; abbot of Moutier-Saint-Jean, also called Réôme, north of Autun. Signatory to the proceedings of Charles the Bald's council of Germigny, October 843. MGH C, III, 7. Dedicatee of Aurelian's *Musica Disciplina*, who calls him 'the chief cantor, in my opinion, of all Holy Church'

CATALENUS (fl. 8th c., first half), ABBOT OF ST MARTIN'S, ROME   272

One of three abbots of St Martin's recorded by the compiler of *Ordo Romanus XIX* around 750 as men skilled 'in the chant for the course of the year', the *cantus anni circuli*. Andrieu, *Ordines Romani*, iii. 224. *See also* JOHN *ARCHICANTATOR*; MAURIANUS; VIRBONUS

CLAUDIANUS (d. 470–1), PRESBYTER AND *PHONASCUS* AT THE CATHEDRAL OF VIENNE   183–8, 189, 227, 552n

Brother of the bishop of Vienne; choir-trainer, compiler of a lectionary. Epitaph in Sidonius, Epp. IV, 11. 13–17. Correspondence in Sidonius, Epp. IV, 2. 3. 11; V, 2. Engelbrecht, *Claudiani Mamerti Opera*, gives a text of his treatise *De Statu Animae* and, at 203–6, Claudianus's letter to Sapaudus

CRIMLEICUS, CANTOR OF THE ABBEY OF ST ARNULPH, METZ (9th c.)   329, 349–53, *350*, *351*, 552n, 567nn

Has two entries in the Reichenau *Liber memorialis*. Autenrieth, Geuenich and Schmid, *Das Verbrüderungsbuch der Abtei Reichenau*, 87. One entry lists him among the benefactors of Reichenau abbey. Probably to be identified with the Grimlaicus author (or dedicatee) of a *Regula solitariorum*. Text in PL 103, 573–664

DEUSDEDIT (5th c.), ARCHDEACON AND PSALMIST OF ROME   170

Interred at some time during the fifth century in an uncertain region of the cemetery of Callixtus: 'The first among the order of levites (= archdeacon) he was a singer of Davidic song'. ILCV 1195; ICUR NS, 4, 12601. Pietri and Pietri, *Prosopographie*, DEVSDEDIT 1

DONATUS OF CARTHAGE (fl. 3rd c., first half), FRIEND OF CYPRIAN OF CARTHAGE   62

Possibly a lawyer. His singing voice for Christian hymnody is enthusiastically praised in Cyprian's *Ad Donatum* XVI. Molager, *Cyprien de Carthage: A Donat et La Vertu de Patience*, 114–17

GALLUS (d. 551), PSALMIST AT COURNON, CLERMONT, TRIER AND COLOGNE   189–93, 213–14, 219, 297, 329, 330

From the 'senatorial order' of Clermont and the uncle of Gregory of Tours. Entered the monastery of Cournon; taken from there by bishop Quintianus of Clermont into the *domus ecclesiae* for the excellence of his singing voice. Taken to royal court by king Theuderic. Last years spent as Bishop of Clermont. Gregory of Tours, *Liber Vitae Patrum*. MGH SSRM, I. 679–86

GEORGIUS (d. ?765), PRIOR OF THE ROMAN *SCHOLA CANTORUM*

The death of Georgius compelled Pope Paul I to recall Simeon (q.v.) from Rouen. MGH EKA 553–4. Nothing further is known of him

GERVOLDUS (d. ?807), SINGER AND FRANKISH ROYAL CHAPLAIN   317, 320–1, 565n

Possibly an Agilolfing by descent. Chaplain of Pippin's queen Bertrada. A gifted singer, he became abbot of St-Wandrille, where he schooled his pupils in chant. Charlemagne's envoy to England. Pradié, *Chronique*, 134 and 140, with discussion of date at pp. xxv–xxviii, suggesting 823–33 for the compilation of the section including Gervoldus

HONORIUS (fl. *c*.525), CANTOR OF THE CATHEDRAL OF RAVENNA   216

Agnellus of Ravenna, *Liber Pontificalis Ecclesiae Ravennatis* (MGH SSRL, 318–22). Pietri and Pietri, *Prosopographie*, HONORIVS 5. *See also* ANTONIUS; MELITUS; TRANQUILLUS

HUBERTUS (fl. *c*.1066), MONK OF ST-ÉVROUL   397, 431, 434 (*see also* General Index: Guitmund, monk of St-Évroul)

One of the two young monks sent from the abbey St-Évroul to learn chants composed in honour of the abbey's patron saint composed by Arnulf, precentor of Chartres. Orderic Vitalis, *The Ecclesiastical History*, ed. Chibnall, iii, 108–9

HUCBERT (9th c., first half), IMPERIAL PRAECENTOR 357, 568n

Precentor palatii, he became bishop of Meaux from 823. Fleckenstein, *Die Hofkapelle*, i. 232–3

'IDITHUN' (fl. *c*.800), IMPERIAL PRAECENTOR

Mentioned in Alcuin's poem on education at the court of Charlemagne as a singer and teacher of the boys ('Instituit pueros Idithun modulamine sacro/Utque sonos dulces decantent, voce sonora'). MGH PAK, I, 245–6

JOHN OF AFFLIGEM (fl. *c*.1100), MUSIC THEORIST 467–73

Uses the title *servus servorum dei*. His treatise was written for Fulgentius, abbot of Affligem. Giving unusually full and revealing material about composition and intended audiences for song, this determined advocate of Guido's staff-notation refers to his own performances of *cantiones*, with the result that songs pleasing to some were displeasing to others. Smits van Waesberghe, *Johannis Affligemensis De Musica cum Tonario*, 110

JOHN (late 7th c.), ROMAN *ARCHICANTATOR* AND MONK OF ST MARTIN'S   270, *271*, 272

Brought by Benedict Biscop to his monastery of Wearmouth-Jarrow to teach the monks the 'yearly cursus of chanting' together with 'its ordo of rite, chanting and reading aloud'. So that he might 'teach the monks . . . the mode of chanting throughout the year', John 'committed to writing all things necessary for the celebration of festal days'. Bede, *Historia Ecclesiastica*, iv. 18

LAURENTIUS (fl. *c*.530), CANTOR OF THE CATHEDRAL OF TRENTO   216

Paid for a stretch of mosaic pavement dated 530–5. CIL *Supplementa Italica*, 6, 173–5. Pietri and Pietri, *Prosopographie*, LAURENTIVS 61

LEO (5th c.), DEACON, PSALMIST AND BISHOP   168, 170, 171

Bishop of a (?)suburbicarian church in Rome. Epitaph, probably referring to his time as a deacon, claims 'I wished to chant among the people, the prophet's music going forth'. ILCV 997; ICUR NS 7, 19004. Pietri and Pietri, *Prosopographie*, LEO 4

MARINUS (fl. *c*.500), *PRIMICERIUS CANTORUM* IN THE CATHEDRAL OF NAPLES   215, 234, 249

Mentioned by Eugippius, *Vita Sancti Severini*. He experiences a miraculous cure. MGH AA, I, ii. 30. Pietri and Pietri, *Prosopographie*, MARINVS 2

MARTINUS (fl. *c*.650), SINGER AT THE CATHEDRAL OF CLERMONT   229, 557n

Mentioned in the *Passio Praiecti*. MGH SSRM, V, 228

MAURIANUS (fl. 8th c., first half), ABBOT OF
ST MARTIN'S, ROME   272

One of three abbots of St Martin's recorded by the
compiler of *Ordo Romanus XIX* around 750 as men
skilled 'in the chant for the course of the year', the
cantus anni circuli. Andrieu, *Ordines Romani*, iii,.224.
See also JOHN *ARCHICANTATOR*; CATALENUS;
VIRBONUS

MELITUS (fl. *c*.525), CANTOR OF THE CATHEDRAL OF
RAVENNA   216

Agnellus of Ravenna, *Liber Pontificalis Ecclesiae
Ravennatis* (MGH SSRL, 318–22). Pietri and Pietri,
Prosopographie, MELITVS. *See also* ANTONIUS;
HONORIUS; TRANQUILLUS

MODERATU[S] (fl. *c*.510), CANTOR OF 'IOVACUS' IN
BATAVIA   215

Mentioned in Eugippius, *Vita Sancti Severini*. MGH
AA, I, ii. 26

PRAIECTUS (d. 676), BISHOP OF CLERMONT   229,
557n

While being schooled in the house of Genesius,
archdeacon of Clermont, Praiectus is challenged by
Martinus (q.v.) to sing a *sonus* (?Gallican offertory
chant) that he has not yet studied. With divine help,
he is able to do so. Episode in the *Passio Praiecti*.
MGH SSRM, V, 228

REDEMPTUS, DEACON OF ROME AND PSALMIST
168–9, *169*, 170, 171, 196

Interred in the fourth or fifth century in the
cemetery of Callistus. Redemptus performed well as
a musician, 'with a nectared singing' that certainly
included psalms since he celebrated the 'ancient
prophet with serene music'. ICUR NS 4, 10129.
Fragments of the original epitaph survive. Pietri and
Pietri, *Prosopographie*, REDEMPTVS 1

RODULFUS (fl. *c*.1066), MONK OF ST-ÉVROUL   397,
431, 434 (*see also* General Index: Guitmund, monk of
St-Évroul)

One of the two young monks sent from the abbey
St-Évroul to learn chants composed in honour of the
abbey's patron saint composed by Arnulf, precentor
of Chartres. Orderic Vitalis, *The Ecclesiastical History*,
ed. Chibnall, iii, 108–9

SABINUS (5th c.), ARCHDEACON OF ROME AND
PSALMIST   165, 169–70, 171, 196, 197

Interred at some time during the fifth century
beneath the porch of the basilica of S. Lorenzo fuori
le mura. His epitaph claims VOCE . . . MODVLATVS
. . . CECINI . . . [DIVE]RSIS SONIS. ILCV 1194; ICUR
NS, 7, 18017. Pietri and Pietri, *Prosopographie*,
SABINVS 5

SIMEON (fl *c*.760), SECUNDUS THEN PRIOR OF ROMAN
SCHOLA CANTORUM   Ch. 15 *passim*, 310–12, 333, 564n

On the (admittedly slender) basis of onomastic
evidence, probably a Byzantine or a 'Syrian'. Sent to
the cathedral of Rouen in the 760s, at the request of
Pippin's half brother, Bishop Remedius, to teach
Roman *psalmodii modulatio* to the Franks. As
secundus in the *schola*, he was recalled to Rome when
the Prior died. Arrangements were made for his
Frankish pupils to follow him

SINDERIC (fl. *c*.560), (?VISIGOTHIC) PSALMIST OF THE
CATHEDRAL OF METZ   192, 230–3, 297

Mentioned in a letter of the Merovingian magnate
Gogon. Gundlach, *Epistulae Austrasicae*, 440–2.
See also THEODOSIUS

THEUTO (fl. *c*.826), IMPERIAL PRAECENTOR   357,
568n

Mentioned twice by Ermoldus Nigellus, with praise
for his trumpet like voice, in a versified account of
the ceremonies at Ingelheim in 826 when Louis the
Pious received King Harald of Denmark, his family
and a large entourage for their baptism. May be
identical with a later abbot with that name at
Marmoutier. Faral, *Poème sur Louis le Pieux*, 2286
and 2316

THEODOSIUS (fl. *c*.560), (?GREEK) PSALMIST OF THE
CATHEDRAL OF METZ   231

Mentioned in a letter of the Merovingian magnate
Gogon. Gundlach, *Epistulae Austrasicae*, 440–2. *See
also* SINDERIC

TRANQUILLUS (fl. *c*.525), CANTOR OF THE CATHEDRAL
OF RAVENNA   216

Agnellus of Ravenna *Liber Pontificalis Ecclesiae
Ravennatis*. MGH SSRL, 318–22. *See also* ANTONIUS;
HONORIUS; MELITUS

VALENTINIANUS (6th c.), DEACON AND CANTOR   216

Mentioned by Gregory of Tours, *Liber vitae patrum.* MGH SSRM, I, 683, 686

VIRBONUS (fl. 8th c., first half), ABBOT OF ST MARTIN'S, ROME   272

One of three abbots of St Martin's recorded by the compiler of *Ordo Romanus XIX* around 750 as men skilled 'in the chant for the course of the year', the *cantus anni circuli.* Andrieu, *Ordines Romani,* iii. 224. *See also* JOHN ARCHICANTATOR; CATALENUS; MAURIANUS

Western Readers (omitting very fragmentary inscriptions)

ALEXIUS (4th c.), LECTOR OF ROME   123, 124

Lector de Fullonices. Inscription from the Catacomb of Marcus and Marcellianus. He was married for fifteen years. Pietri and Pietri, *Prosopographie,* ALEXIVS

ANONYMI 1–12 (484), OF VANDAL CARTHAGE   222–4

Twelve boys, all Catholics and accomplished singers, saved from exile by their former teacher Theucarius, *lector,* a convert to Arianism. They subsequently lived some form of common life. Victor of Vita, *Historia Persecutionis Wandalicae.* MGH AA IV/I, 50. *See also* THEUCARIUS

ANONYMOUS 13 (late 5th c.), OF VANDAL CARTHAGE   100, 195, 196, 221–2

At an Easter Sunday service in Regia, perhaps modern Arbal in Algeria, an unnamed lector mounts the pulpit to sing the *alleluiaticum melos,* only to be slain by the arrow of an Arian soldier. He is killed in the very act of singing, so that the book falls from his hands. Victor of Vita, *Historia Persecutionis Wandalicae.* MGH AA IV/I, 10

APPAS (4th c.), READER   106

Epitaph From Laodicea in Pisidia, describing him as 'young and of fine appearance'. Destephen, *Prosopographie,* APPAS 1

ATTIUS PROCULUS (4th c.), LECTOR   126

Epitaph from Brescia. Died age 18. Pietri and Pietri, *Prosopographie,* Attius PROCVLVS 1

AURELIUS (3rd c., first half), LECTOR OF CARTHAGE   106

Mentioned in a letter of recommendation from Cyprian of Carthage. Appointed to read the *Evangelica lectio, Evangelium domini, Evangelium Christi.* Described as an *adolescens* and *annis adhuc novellis.* Cyprian, *Epistolae,* 183–5. *See also* CELERINUS

CASTALINUS, LECTOR OF AFRICA PROCONSULARIS   127

Inscription from Haidra. Died age 6. Byzantine period. Duval, *Recherches,* 108

CELERINUS (3rd c., first half), LECTOR OF CARTHAGE   105

Mentioned in a letter of recommendation from Cyprian of Carthage. A Carthaginian who had recently suffered during the Decian persecution in Rome, Celerinus was appointed while a young man. Cyprian, *Epistolae,* 186–92. *See also* AURELIUS

CINNAMIUS OPAS (331–77), LECTOR OF ROME   122, 122, 124

Lector tituli Fasciole . . . amicus pauperum. Died age 46. Interred at S. Paolo fuori le mura. *See above,* Pl. 24. Pietri and Pietri, *Prosopographie,* Cinnamius OPAS

CLAUDIUS ATTICIANUS (318–38), LECTOR OF ROME   118, 124

Epitaph from Maius Catacomb. Married to Claudia Felicissima. Pietri and Pietri, *Prosopographie,* Claudius ATTICIANVS

CRESCONIUS, LECTOR OF CARTHAGE   127

Lector regionis primae. Died aged 11. Byzantine period. Merlin, *Inscriptions Latines de Tunisie,* 1122

EQ[UITIUS] HERACLIUS (318–38), LECTOR OF ROME   124, 126

Lector r[egionis] sec[undae]. Inscription from the Domitilla catacomb. Died age 19. Pietri and Pietri, *Prosopographie,* Eq[uitius] HERACLIVS 1

EUSEBIUS (d. 370), LECTOR OF ROME   125

Lector urbis romanae . . . natione Sardus, bishop of Vercelli from *c.*340. Jerome, *De Viris illustribus* (PL 23, 679)

FAVOR (fl. ?*c* 300), LECTOR OF ROME   *106*, 124

Epitaph from the Catacomb of S. Agnese. Pietri and Pietri, *Prosopographie*, FAVOR .

FELIX (fl. b. 304), AFRICAN LECTOR   114–15

Part of the Christian community gathered for the Sunday Eucharist in the house of Octavius Felix at Abitina, possibly modern Chahoud el-Batin, in Africa Proconsularis, in February 304. Son of the presbyter Saturninus. *See also* SATURNINUS JUNIOR

FUNDANIU[S] [I]OVIANUS (4th/5th c.), LECTOR OF FLORENCE   126

Lec[to]r. Died at age 17. Pietri and Pietri, *Prosopographie*, FUNDANIU[S] [I]OVIANVS

GEMMULUS (6th/7th c.), LECTOR OF ROME   126

Lictor t[i]t[uli] s[an]c[t]ae marturis Caecil[i]ae in Trastevere. Died age 16. Pietri and Pietri, *Prosopographie*, GEMMVLVS

IOHANNES, LECTOR   127

Inscription from Haidra, Byzantine period. Died age 6. Duval, *Recherches*, 63

LEOPARDUS (360–84), LECTOR OF ROME   122–3, 124, 126

Lector de Pudentiana . . . mirae innocentiae. Died age 24. Pietri and Pietri, *Prosopographie*, LEOPARDVS 1

MEGALUS (4th c.), LECTOR OF ROME   124

Pietri and Pietri, *Prosopographie*, MEGALVS

NAVIGIUS (4th/5th c.), LECTOR   124

Known from the epitaph of his granddaughter. Son of Cresimus (?bishop of Subaugusta) and father of Primigenius, *lector* (q.v.). Pietri and Pietri, *Prosopographie*, NAVIGIVS

PASCENTIUS (d. 422), LECTOR OF ROME   125, 126

Lector de Fasc[iola]. Inscription from catacomb of Domitilla. Pietri and Pietri, *Prosopographie*, PASCENTIVS

PASSIBUS (4th/5th c.), LECTOR OF AFRICA PROCONSULARIS   127

Inscription from Cape Bon (Tunisia). Died age 14. Mandouze, *Prosopographie*, PASSIBVS

POMPEIUS LUPICINUS (5th or 6th c.), LECTOR OF FLORENCE   126

Died age 5. Pietri and Pietri, *Prosopographie*, Pompeius LVPICINVS 2

PRIMIGENIUS (4th/5th c.), LECTOR   125

From a Cypriot family and clerical dynasty. Known from the epitaph of his daughter. Son of Navigius (q.v.) and married to Asella. Interred in the cemetery *ad aquas Bullicantes*, two miles from Rome. Pietri and Pietri, *Prosopographie*, PRIMIGENIVS

PROFICIUS (4th c.), LECTOR AND EXORCIST OF ROME   124

Lec[tor] et exorc[ista]. Named in the epitaph of his wife Istercoria from the Ad Decimum catacomb. Pietri and Pietri, *Prosopographie*, PROFICIVS

QUINTUS (6th c.), LECTOR OF AFRICA PROCONSULARIS   127

Named in a mosaic epitaph from the basilica of Uppenna (Henchir-Chigarnia, Tunisia). Died age 22. ICLV 1286A; CIL VIII 23045. Mandouze, *Prosopographie*, QVINTVS 5

RUFINUS (371–402), LECTOR OF ROME   124

Inscription from the basilica of S. Hermes. Died age 31. ICUR I, 507. Pietri and Pietri, *Prosopographie*, RVFINVS 2

SATURNINUS JUNIOR (fl. 304), AFRICAN LECTOR   114–15, 87

Part of the Christian community gathered for the Sunday Eucharist in the house of Octavius Felix at Abitina, possibly modern Chahoud el-Batin, in Africa Proconsularis, in February 304. Son of the presbyter Saturninus. *See also* FELIX

SEVERUS, LECTOR   127

Lectur ennocens, Viennensis. Died age 13

[SI]MPLICIUS (?4th c.), LECTOR OF ROME   123, 124

Inscription from catacomb of Marcus and
Marcellianus. Pietri and Pietri, *Prosopographie*,
[SI]MPLICIVS 2

THEUCARIUS (fl. *c*.484), CATHOLIC TURNED ARIAN
LECTOR IN VANDAL CARTHAGE   222–3

Rescued twelve boys, all Catholics, accomplished
singers and his former pupils, from exile. Victor of
Vita, *Historia Persecutionis Wandalicae*. MGH AA
IV/I, 50. Mandouze, *Prosopographie*, TEUCARIVS 1.
See also ANONYMI 1–12

TIGRIDIUS, LECTOR OF AUTUN   127

[L]ector . . . castus puer. ICLV 1281; CIL XIII 2799

TYBERIUS (d. 566), LECTOR OF MÉRTOLA   127

[L]ictor. Died age 14. ICLV 1283. Huebner,
Inscriptiones, Supplementum, 314

VICTOR (4th c.), LECTOR OF ROME   123, 124, 126

Inscription from catacomb of Callixtus. Died age 24.
Pietri and Pietri, *Prosopographie*, VICTOR 4

VITALIS, LECTOR OF AFRICA PROCONSULARIS   127

Inscription from Haidra, probably of Byzantine date.
Died age 5. ICLV 1285; CIL VIII 453. Duval,
Recherches, 404

Ut mens nostra regi regum

magister anardus vierliacensis

nnua gaudia ia

Organa dulcia conuenie

Et tua celica facta phennia fu

dida secla p omnia sunt men